Do It Yourself And Save Money!

Do It Yourself And Save Money!

By The Editors of Consumer Guide®

HARPER & ROW, PUBLISHERS

NEW YORK

Cambridge
Hagerstown
Philadelphia
San Francisco

London
Mexico City
Sào Paulo
Sydney

1817

Published by
Harper & Row, Publishers
10 East 53rd Street
New York, New York 10022

Library of Congress Catalog Card Number: 80-81338
ISBN: 0-06-010861-4

Illustrations: Clarence A. Moberg

Table of Contents

CONTENTS

FLOORS AND STAIRS 134

CONTENTS

CEILINGS 159

WINDOWS 169

DOORS 190

ELECTRICITY   210

PLUMBING   220

FINISHING TOUCHES   233

CONTENTS

ENERGY-SAVERS 262

STRUCTURAL WORK 274

CONTENTS

YARD AND PATIO   361

WALKS, DRIVES, WALLS, AND FENCES   393

CAR   415

CONTENTS

CONTENTS

FOOD AND DRINK   490

CONTENTS

CONTENTS

CLOTHES   541

CRAFTS AND HOBBIES 571

CONTENTS

PLAYTHINGS   604

SPORTS   619

PROFESSIONAL SERVICES   646

USEFUL INFORMATION   662

INDEX   682

Introduction

Easy come, easy go—more often it's only easy go. Where does it go? If you're like most people, your money goes for day-to-day living, for essentials that can't wait, for an occasional catastrophe. And saving is hard when there's nothing left to save.

The answer is simple: instead of paying for professional services, expensive ready-mades, and low-quality consumer goods, hang on to your money and do the job—or make the item—yourself. *Do It Yourself and Save Money!* will equip you to take care of your home, your yard, and your car; to keep yourself and your family healthy, well-groomed, and well-dressed; to put up your own food, perform your own professional services, make your own clothes, furniture, and toys—everything, in fact, that you can do yourself instead of paying someone else to do for you.

But I'm Just Not Handy!
You've seen plenty of do-it-yourself books that seem to be written for the professional handyman—that rare breed born with a hammer in one hand and a wrench in the other; or with an instinctive and comprehensive knowledge of carpentry, sewing, or mechanics. *Do It Yourself and Save Money!* is not for them; it's for you. The more than 500 projects included here are chosen and presented to be really practical and workable, no matter how little experience you have. Each project is clear, complete, and illustrated. Everything you need to know is right there, from what you'll need to how long it will take.

Hard to believe? But it's true. If a project is too risky or too complicated or too hard to work on from a book, you won't find it here; if it's better to call a professional, *Do It Yourself* tells you so. But for the vast range of products and services you spend money on every day, *Do It Yourself and Save Money!* presents a real alternative—a balance of self-sufficiency and enjoyment, living well and economically. And all it takes is a little initiative.

The Projects: 500-Plus, and Counting
Just what is *Do It Yourself and Save Money!?* Most do-it-yourself books are filled with plumbing and painting and carpentry, electrical work and maintenance procedures. You'll find those here, and more besides—projects that tell you how to build furniture, how to decorate with style, how to save energy, how to make your own home care products. You'll find instructions

for every imaginable task associated with furniture, appliances, electricity, walls and floors, doors and windows, structural work, yard care, and car maintenance. But there's more to *Do It Yourself* than that.

All of these are projects you'd expect to find here; they belong in a do-it-yourself book. But, as you'll discover, there's far more to it than that — and *Do It Yourself and Save Money!* proves it.

There's a whole world of projects here that will surprise and delight you — and, even better, will start you thinking in your own do-it-yourself direction. For example, you'll discover how to give haircuts, represent yourself in small claims court, groom your pets, regrip a golf club, hook a rug, patch a boat hull, build a ski rack, make a jigsaw puzzle, build a rocking horse, make a terrarium, rebind a book, mount slides, resole shoes, recycle clothes, and dozens of other projects, both ordinary and not so ordinary. The possibilities are endless, and the scope of *Do It Yourself and Save Money!* is amazingly wide.

High grocery bills? Read how you can make your own yogurt, peanut butter, granola, bread, and liqueurs; how you can freeze, can, and preserve bountiful summer crops; how to make jellies and preserves, dry your own fruit, smoke your own meat. If you've ever been appalled at the price or the quality of grocery-store food, now you can discover how much cheaper it is — and how much better it tastes — to grow, put up, and put together your own edibles.

Is your economic downfall clothes, or toys, gadgets or elegant home accessories? You'll find them here, in equally elegant do-it-yourself form. Does your money go for toothpaste and deodorant, shampoo and after-shave, lotions and creams? Try making your own — the instructions are all here. Whatever you're spending your money on now, *Do It Yourself and Save Money!* can show you how to spend less — and how to enjoy it more.

Don't Wait!
With inflation gobbling your paycheck faster than you can earn it, you can't afford to just sit back and hope things get better. *Do It Yourself and Save Money!* shows you how to spend less for everyday goods and services, with more than 500 ways to stop paying other people for things you can do and make yourself. Take action today to beat the cost-of-living spiral — you can't afford not to.

Furniture

Make Your Own Furniture Polish

To preserve your wood furniture, polish it periodically. This preparation is a simple one, but its quality is strictly professional. **Equipment:** measuring spoons, double boiler, mixing spoon, pint jar with cover. **Ingredients:** carnauba wax, mineral oil, lemon oil. Buy carnauba wax at a paint or hobby store. **Yield:** about 1 pint.

Melt 1 tablespoon of carnauba wax in the top of a double boiler. Add 1 pint of mineral oil to the melted wax and stir until completely blended. If you want the polish to smell like lemon, add a few drops of lemon oil and stir well. Pour into a clean jar and cover tightly.

Apply to finished wood with a clean soft cloth and buff to a fine shine.

Clean Upholstered Furniture

Fast action can usually remove even the worst stains; regular cleaning is easy with aerosol upholstery cleaners. **Tools:** vacuum cleaner with brush or fabric attachment, soft clean cloths, clean sponges, mixing cup and spoons. **Materials:** furniture polish, aerosol spray upholstery cleaner, white vinegar, liquid detergent, commercial stain remover, aerosol spot lifter, ammonia, hydrogen peroxide, laundry starch, lemon juice, mineral spirits, rubbing alcohol or alcohol-based stain remover, salt. **Time:** 10 minutes to ½ hour.

Cleaning. Keep upholstery clean by vacuuming it regularly, using the brush or fabric attachment of the vacuum. Clean and condition wood frame parts with furniture polish, following the manufacturer's instructions. Soiled upholstery should be washed or professionally dry-cleaned, as its care label directs. If the upholstery is old or there is no care label, test the cleaner on an inconspicuous part of the upholstery before you clean the entire piece of furniture. Remove stains completely.

Aerosol foam upholstery cleaners are safe for most types of upholstery; read the label for specific recommendations. Do not use aerosol cleaners on velvet or silk. To apply an aerosol cleaner, shake the can thoroughly and spray the fabric evenly and lightly. Don't spray foam on the wood of the frame; if you do accidentally get foam on the wood, wipe it off immediately.

Rub the foam in gently with a clean damp sponge, rinsing the sponge and squeezing it out as soon as it starts to look dirty. Let the upholstery dry completely, as directed by the cleaner's manufacturer; then vacuum thoroughly and polish wood frame parts.

Food, drink, and animal stains. These stains can usually be removed with water-based cleaners; stubborn stains require commercial stain removers. Whatever cleaner you use, treat the upholstery gently—if sponging or light rubbing doesn't remove a spot, don't try to scrub it out. Call a professional cleaner.

To remove stains from *alcoholic drinks,* blot with a clean cloth and then sponge with cold water. Sponge the fabric with a mixture of 1 part white vinegar and 4 parts water, and let dry completely.

To remove *coffee, tea, fruit juice,* or *soft drinks,* blot and then sponge with a mild, lukewarm solution of liquid detergent and water. Squeeze the sponge out well to avoid overwetting the fabric. Sponge with clean water and let dry. If the stain persists, sponge it with a mixture of 1 part white vinegar and 4 parts water; let dry. If the stain still persists, apply a commercial stain remover, following the manufacturer's instructions. Use an aerosol spot lifter as directed to remove bad stains, but test for colorfastness before applying. Remove residue as directed, or, if necessary, clean the entire piece of furniture.

Treat *chocolate* stains in the same way—blotting, sponging with liquid detergent, and rinsing. If the stain persists, sponge the stained area carefully with a mixture of 1 tablespoon of ammonia and 1 cup of water, being careful not to overwet the fabric. Let dry completely. If necessary, apply commercial stain remover or spot lifter as above.

Blot *milk* or *ice cream* and sponge with cold water; sponge again with a cool, strong solution of liquid detergent and water. Rinse and blot dry. If the stain persists, sponge with a mixture of 1 tablespoon of ammonia and 1 cup of cold water; then sponge again with a mixture of 1 part white vinegar and 2 parts cold water. If a yellow stain remains, sponge a few drops of hydrogen peroxide into the fabric. Let the fabric dry completely.

To remove stains from *blood* or *egg,* blot and sponge immediately with cold water, letting the sponge soak up as much of the stain as possible. Keep blotting as long as the stain keeps dissolving; then sponge with a cool, strong solution of liquid detergent and water, rinse, and blot dry. If the stain persists, sponge the stained area with a mixture of 1 tablespoon of ammonia and 1 cup of cold water; then sponge again with a mixture of 1 part white vinegar and 2 parts cold water. Be careful not to overwet the fabric. For stubborn spots, sponge a few drops of hydrogen peroxide into the fabric; or mix laundry starch to a paste with a little cold water and apply to the fabric. Let dry completely and then vacuum. If the stain still persists, use an aerosol spot lifter as

directed, but test for colorfastness before applying.

Household stains. Most product stains can be removed with solvent cleaners; mildew and similar discolorations can be bleached out with lemon juice. If necessary, clean the entire piece of furniture with an aerosol cleaner after removing the stains. Before applying any type of solvent cleaner, test the fabric for colorfastness in an inconspicuous area; if the cleaner bleaches the fabric, have the piece of furniture professionally cleaned. Apply the cleaner lightly and rub gently to avoid damaging the fabric.

Use a commercial stain remover, as directed, to remove *grease* or *oil.* Apply the fluid with a clean cloth, turning the cloth as you work so that a clean part of it is always against the stain. If the stain persists, use mineral spirits. Clean the fabric as above to remove any residue.

Remove *ballpoint ink* with rubbing alcohol, or with an alcohol-based commercial stain remover. Blot *liquid ink* quickly and sponge the fabric with a mild solution of liquid detergent and lukewarm water, rinsing the sponge frequently, as long as the stain keeps dissolving. For upholstery made of natural fabrics, sponge the stained area with lemon juice and sprinkle it with salt; let it dry completely and vacuum clean. If ink stains persist, or for stains in synthetics, have the piece of furniture professionally cleaned.

Paint must often be removed by professional cleaners. Remove paint with the solvent it's made with—water for latex or poster paint, mineral spirits for oil-base paint. Let dry completely. Don't try to remove nail polish or lacquer; the solvent could damage the fabric. Call a professional.

Sponge *glue* with hot water to dissolve and lift the stain; if the stain persists, sponge it with a mixture of 1 part white vinegar and 4 parts water and let dry. Clean the entire piece of furniture as above. If glue stains are extensive, call a professional cleaner.

Mildew stains can be removed with lemon juice. Sponge the stained fabric with lemon juice and set the piece of furniture in the sun; let dry completely. For stains in synthetics, sponge the fabric with lemon juice and sprinkle it with salt; let dry as above and vacuum clean.

Clean and Condition Leather Upholstery

Properly taken care of, leather upholstery mellows as it ages; treat it gently and it will last forever. **Tools:** clean soft cloths, sponge, small mixing dish and spoon, double boiler. **Materials:** saddle soap, dry cleaning fluid or white vinegar, lanolin or castor oil, white petroleum jelly. **Time:** about 1½ hours to clean a chair.

Dust leather frequently with a soft cloth to prevent dirt buildup. To clean evenly dirty furniture, use a clean sponge to lather saddle soap; apply the foam to the leather and rub it in gently. Rinse the sponge, squeeze it out and wipe the leather clean. Be careful not to soak the leather; use only the foam of the saddle soap, and squeeze the sponge almost dry. Let the leather dry completely, at least 12 hours, and then buff with a clean soft cloth.

Remove stains from leather upholstery as quickly as possible. Blot dry with a soft cloth. Test color-fastness in an inconspicuous place before removing spots. Remove oily stains carefully with commercial dry cleaning fluid, dabbed on with a clean cloth; remove non-oily stains with a mixture of half white vinegar and half warm water. Saddle-soap the entire piece of furniture, let dry, and buff.

Restore cracking leather and condition drying leather with lanolin or castor oil. Warm the lanolin or oil carefully in the top of a double boiler; don't let it get hot. Wipe the oil onto the damaged leather with a soft cloth, applying an even coat to all surfaces. Let dry 24 hours and buff with a clean soft cloth; reapply, let dry, and buff again. For light-colored leather, condition with white petroleum jelly instead of lanolin or oil; apply, let dry, and buff as above.

Strip Finished Wood

It's actually easier to refinish an entire piece of furniture than to try to refinish one badly damaged section. Either way, you'll have to remove the old finish first. Start with a small project, like a kitchen chair, before you tackle a big job. **Tools:** screwdriver, plastic bucket, rubber gloves, medium-size paintbrush, putty knife, paint scraper, fine-toothed file, nutpick, scissors, safety goggles, tongs, toothbrush. **Materials:** plastic dropcloths or newspaper; paste-type, waxless, nonflammable paint and varnish remover; burlap, grade 1/0 steel wool, denatured alcohol, clean lint-free cloth, solvent for paint remover, clean rags. **Time:** varies depending on piece of furniture, but process can be very slow.

Before starting to work, prepare a well-ventilated work space—in good weather, work outside. Spread plastic dropcloths or newspaper to protect the floor or grass. If the piece of furniture has hardware, make a sketch of it; sketch all handles, knobs, and hinges and key the sketches to the diagram of the whole piece. Key hardware, doors, and drawers this way so you'll be able to put them back on the right way.

Remove all handles, knobs, and hinges to be cleaned separately. If possible, remove all doors and drawers to be stripped separately. Don't force any part of the piece; if you can't get a part off or out easily, let it alone. If hardware has been painted over, set it in a plastic bucket.

Before starting to work, read the instructions on the container of paint remover. Pour paint remover over the hardware in the plastic bucket to cover it completely; set the bucket aside.

Wearing rubber gloves, apply paint remover carefully to the piece of furniture with a paintbrush, blobbing it on rather than brushing. Coat the surface of the wood thickly and evenly, being careful not to leave any gaps. Cover only as much wood as you can scrape within a short time; work on large pieces of furniture section by section.

Let the paint remover work for 15 to 20 minutes. While you wait, round the sharp corners of a putty knife with a fine-toothed file. Smooth the edges of the knife carefully. If you'll be working on large flat surfaces, round the corners of a paint scraper the same way.

After 15 to 20 minutes, test the treated wood; the paint remover on its surface should look thick and mushy. Scrape the treated surface firmly along the grain with the putty knife or paint scraper. If the wood is ready to be scraped, both paint remover and old finish will come off completely, exposing clean, bare wood.

If your test scrape doesn't get down to bare wood, reapply paint remover to the scraped spot, wait 10 minutes, and try again. If you still can't scrape down to bare wood, apply a second thick coat of paint remover, right over the first coat. Wait 15 to 20 minutes and test again. If the test scrape still doesn't get down to bare wood, apply a third thick coat of paint remover and wait 15 to 20 minutes; then try again. Three coats of paint remover should work on even stubborn finishes.

Remove the old finish as soon as the paint remover has softened it completely; don't let it dry. Scrape flat surfaces clean with the round-cornered putty knife or paint scraper, working with the grain and being careful not to gouge the wood. Clean narrow grooves carefully with a nutpick. To remove the finish from a curved or round piece of wood, cut narrow strips of burlap about a foot long. Wrap a burlap strip around the piece of wood and pull both ends to rub the wood clean. Replace the strip with a clean piece of burlap as soon as it becomes clogged with paint remover and old finish. Repeat the procedure on

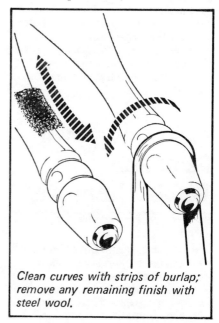

Clean curves with strips of burlap;
remove any remaining finish with
steel wool.

each area of the piece of furniture.

When all paint remover has been scraped or rubbed off, examine the stripped piece of furniture. If the old finish still adheres in some areas, apply paint remover and scrape these areas again; or if the remaining finish is confined to a small area, sand the stubborn spot clean with grade 1/0 steel wool. Use steel wool to remove the last traces of old finish from narrow crevices and grooves.

Finally, wipe down the entire piece of furniture with burlap to remove dirt and any remaining paint remover. Apply denatured alcohol to the newly stripped wood with a clean, lint-free cloth, rubbing lightly along the grain of the wood. Let stand 24 hours before refinishing.

To clean painted-over hardware, remove it from the bucket of paint remover, using tongs and being careful not to splatter the remover. Wearing safety goggles and rubber gloves, set each treated handle, knob, or hinge on a plastic dropcloth and brush it carefully clean with a toothbrush. Remove thick spots of paint with a nutpick. Wipe each piece with a clean rag, or rinse carefully in the solvent for the paint remover and then wipe. If further cleaning is necessary, rinse with plain water before applying cleaning compounds.

Before reassembling, finish each part of the piece of furniture separately. Replace all hardware after the finishing is completed.

Make Your Own Paint and Varnish Remover

To strip the finish from old furniture, there's no need to buy any special remover. You can easily make your own with a few ingredients. **Equipment:** measuring cup, funnel, gallon container with cap. **Ingredients:** acetone, benzene, wood alcohol. Buy these ingredients at a paint store. **Yield:** about 1 gallon.

Caution: These ingredients are extremely volatile and flammable; the fumes are also toxic . Work in a well-ventilated place.

Measure 5⅓ cups of acetone, 5⅓ cups of benzene, and 5⅓ cups of wood alcohol into a gallon container. Cap the container tightly and shake the contents to mix them thoroughly.

To use, apply the solution to the surface to be treated with an old paintbrush. Allow it to stand for about ½ hour, and then scrape it off.

Stain Wood Furniture

Stain furniture to add color or change the color of the wood—use a dark stain to change the wood's character; use a light stain to accent the grain and deepen the color. **Tools:** small paintbrush, screwdriver, sanding block, vacuum cleaner, stir sticks, rubber gloves, new small or medium natural-bristle paintbrush. **Materials:** varnish, newspaper; coarse-, medium-, and fine-grit sandpaper; clean lint-free cloths, tack cloth, petroleum jelly, oil-base wiping stain, felt floor-buffing pads. **Time:** about 2 to 5 hours, depending on the piece of furniture; in addition, about ½ hour 24 hours after staining.

Before you stain a piece of furniture, test it with whatever varnish you'll use to finish it, to make sure it should be stained. Brush varnish carefully onto a small, inconspicuous area of the wood to see what it looks like without staining; if you want a darker finish, go ahead.

Remove drawers and doors before staining; work on them separately. If possible, remove all hardware—handles, knobs, and hinges. Make a sketch so you'll be able to replace all the pieces correctly. Don't force any part; if you can't remove a piece easily, leave it in place.

Sand the piece of furniture thoroughly before staining it—spread newspaper to protect the floor. If the wood is very smooth, sand it lightly with fine-grit sandpaper. If the surface is rough, sand it carefully with coarse-, medium-, and then fine-grit sandpaper to smooth it. Use a sanding block where possible, and always sand with the grain of the wood. Sand off all burns, water marks, and scratches; imperfections will be made more obvious by the stain.

When the entire piece of furniture has been thoroughly sanded, vacuum up all loose sawdust. Go over the piece with a clean, lint-free cloth and then with a tack cloth to remove all dust. Coat any hardware not removed before sanding with a thin coat of petroleum jelly, being careful not to get any on the wood.

Stir the stain thoroughly before applying it to distribute the pigment evenly; stir it frequently as you work. If you're mixing stains to get a specific color, mix enough stain to cover the entire piece of furniture.

Wearing rubber gloves, apply the stain to the wood with a clean, lint-free cloth, wiping it along the grain of the wood and then against the grain. Let the stain stand on the wood for a few minutes, but don't let it dry; wipe off the excess with a clean cloth. Work across the piece of furniture, wiping stain on and removing the excess; apply the stain evenly to avoid blotches of deeper or lighter color. Use a small paintbrush to stain hard-to-reach areas.

If you want a darker finish, let the stain dry according to the manufacturer's instructions; then apply and wipe off a second coat of stain. Let the piece of furniture dry for 24 hours.

When the stain is completely dry, rub the piece of furniture thoroughly with a clean felt floor-buffing pad. If you plan to finish the piece of furniture with polyurethane varnish, it needs no further preparation. If you'll be using the traditional furniture varnish, apply a coat of shellac to seal the stain before you finish the piece of furniture. Finish the piece of furniture before replacing drawers, doors, and hardware.

Finish
Wood Furniture

Finishing furniture isn't hard, but it does take care and patience. The results are worth the trouble. **Tools:** screwdriver, sanding block, vacuum cleaner, stir sticks, new small or medium natural-bristle paintbrushes, artists' paintbrush. **Materials:** newspaper; coarse-, medium-, and fine-grit sandpaper; clean lint-free cloths, tack cloth, petroleum jelly, grade 0000 steel wool, rags. *For a traditional furniture varnish finish*—new white shellac, denatured alcohol, felt floor-buffing pads, furniture varnish, mineral spirits; *for a polyurethane finish* (on hard-wear surfaces)—gloss or satin-finish polyurethane varnish, mineral spirits. **Time:** 6 to 8 hours for bare wood, less for prepared surfaces.

Before finishing a piece of furniture, remove drawers and doors; work on them separately. If possible, remove all hardware—handles, knobs, and hinges. Make a sketch so you'll be able to replace all the pieces correctly. Don't force any part; if you can't remove a piece easily, leave it in place.

If the piece of furniture has not been stained and prepared, sand it thoroughly before applying the finish— spread newspaper to protect the floor. If the wood is very smooth, sand it lightly with fine-grit sandpaper. If the surface is rough, smooth it carefully with coarse-, medium-, and then fine-grit sandpaper. Use a sanding block on flat surfaces, and always sand with the grain of the wood. Sand off any stains, scratches, and burns; the finish will make them more obvious.

When the piece of furniture has been thoroughly sanded, vacuum up all loose sawdust. Dust the piece with a clean, lint-free cloth and then go over it carefully with a tack cloth to remove all dust. If you couldn't remove all the hardware, coat any remaining handles, knobs, or hinges lightly with petroleum jelly, being careful not to get any on the wood.

Furniture varnish. If you're using polyurethane varnish, the wood needs no further preparation. If you're using regular furniture varnish, seal the sanded piece of furniture with a coat of shellac.

Thin new white shellac with denatured alcohol according to the manufacturer's instructions. Apply the shellac with a new natural-bristle paintbrush, dampened with denatured alcohol; do not use an old brush. Brush the shellac on evenly along the grain of the wood, working quickly. Let dry completely, about 1 hour, and rub firmly along the grain with a felt floor-buffing pad. Remove any remaining imperfections by rubbing lightly along the grain with grade 0000 steel wool.

Before applying the varnish, close the windows in the room; vacuum thoroughly. If possible, maintain the temperature above 70° F. Spread clean newspaper to protect the floor, and work in bright light.

Go over the piece of furniture with a tack cloth to remove all dust. Apply furniture varnish over the shellac coat, using a good-quality new natural-bristle

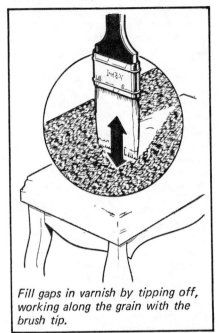

Fill gaps in varnish by tipping off, working along the grain with the brush tip.

brush; do *not* use the same brush you applied the shellac with. Don't shake or stir the varnish. Brush the varnish on with long, even strokes along the grain of the wood; hold the brush lightly but firmly at an angle so that the bristles don't bend. Cover one entire surface at a time.

As you cover each surface, go back over it to remove specks of dirt or fuzz from the varnish. Use the tip of an artists' brush to lightly touch each speck; lift the brush carefully and wipe each speck off the brush with a clean cloth before removing the next one.

Brush back across the grain of the wood to cover the surface evenly, using additional varnish if necessary to avoid drag. Remove specks again with the artists' brush. Finally, fill in any gaps in the varnish by tipping off in the direction of the grain. To do this, set the tip of the brush lightly on the wet varnish, at right angles to the grain of the wood. Lift the brush, touch the varnish again with the tips of the bristles, and lift again. Repeat from side to side on the surface, always following the grain of the wood. Remove specks with the artists' brush as

you finish tipping off each surface.

Let the newly varnished piece of furniture dry completely, at least 48 hours and preferably 1 week. Remove specks carefully with the artists' brush as they appear. Clean up with mineral spirits.

Polyurethane varnish. Polyurethane varnish should not be applied over shellac. When the piece of furniture has been thoroughly sanded and any remaining hardware has been coated with petroleum jelly, apply the varnish directly. Use a good-quality brush; do not shake or stir the varnish.

Go over the piece of furniture with a tack cloth to remove all dust. Brush the varnish carefully along the grain of the wood, using slow, even strokes. Hold the brush lightly but firmly at an angle so that the bristles don't bend. Cover one entire surface at a time. Unless the manufacturer's directions specify otherwise, apply the varnish as above, brushing along the grain, removing specks, and tipping off. Let dry about 12 hours, or as specified by the manufacturer, and apply a second coat of varnish; let dry at least 48 hours and preferably 1 week. Clean up with mineral spirits.

Finish a Bar

Alcoholic drinks can stain a wood bar badly. To resist alcohol, soda, and water, finish a new wood bar with this protective coating. **Equipment:** quart jar with cover, measuring cup, measuring spoons, mixing spoon. **Ingredients:** kerosene, white vinegar. **Yield:** about 3 cups.

Measure 3 cups of kerosene into a quart jar and add 1 tablespoon of white vinegar; mix well. Cover tightly.

To apply the finish, wipe it onto the wood with a soft cloth and rub it in well with the grain until the wood is completely saturated. Wipe off the excess and then polish dry with a terry-cloth towel. Let dry for 24 hours. Repeat the application several times, waiting 24 hours between applications.

Antique-Finish Wood Furniture

If you don't want to refinish a piece of furniture completely, you can perk it up in a weekend by antiquing it. **Tools:** screwdriver, sanding block, two small paintbrushes, artists' brush; coarse brush, sponge, or steel wool. **Materials:** newspaper, fine-grit sandpaper, tack cloth, petroleum jelly, satin-finish antiquing enamel or clear gloss varnish undercoat, antiquing glaze overcoat, cheesecloth, clean rags, mineral spirits. **Time:** 2 days, about 2 to 3 hours each day; if more than one undercoat is needed, 3 days.

The antiquing process consists of applying a glaze over an enamel or clear varnish undercoat and then partially removing the glaze to produce an uneven or "antique" texture. To completely hide the old finish, use a satin-finish enamel undercoat; to mellow a brand-new piece, use clear gloss varnish. Use a light glaze over a light undercoat, a dark glaze over a dark undercoat. Complete antiquing kits are available.

Work in a clean, dry area, with the temperature about 60° F. Spread newspaper under the piece of furniture to protect the floor. Remove all hardware—knobs, handles, and hinges—and make a sketch of the piece of furniture so you'll be able to replace the hardware correctly. Don't force anything; if you can't remove a piece easily, leave it in place. Remove doors and drawers, and work on them separately.

Prepare the piece of furniture by sanding it carefully along the grain with fine-grit sandpaper; do *not* use paint or varnish remover. Go over the sanded piece with a tack cloth to remove all dust. Coat any hardware left on the piece of furniture with petroleum jelly, being careful not to get any on the wood.

To cover the old finish completely, apply satin-finish enamel, brushing it carefully along the grain of the wood with a small paintbrush. Let dry completely—24 hours or as the manufacturer specifies. A second coat of enamel is rarely necessary, but if you can still see traces of the old finish, apply enamel again and let it dry completely.

If you want to mellow a brand-new piece of furniture instead of covering the finish completely, sand the piece lightly with fine-grit sandpaper; then apply two coats of clear gloss furniture varnish, sanding lightly between coats. Let the varnish dry completely.

Apply antiquing glaze over the enamel or varnish undercoat. Brush the glaze on with a clean paintbrush, working evenly in the direction of the grain to cover the surface with an even glaze tone. Let the glaze stand for a few minutes, according to the manufacturer's instructions, but don't let the glaze dry.

Wipe the glaze to produce the desired antiqued effect. For a subtle darkening, use a folded pad of cheesecloth. Starting at the center of the main surface, wipe the wet glaze off with a circular motion; a film of glaze will remain. Work toward the edges of the surface with less and less pressure, so that more glaze is left on the surface at the edges. Do not wipe glaze from grooves or carvings. Blend the glaze as you work so that no obvious wiping pattern or edge is left.

Let the glaze dry about 24 hours, or as directed by the manufacturer. If grooves or carvings aren't dark enough, apply more glaze sparingly with an artists' brush; do not repeat the wiping. Let dry completely.

To produce a more dramatic finish, use a coarse brush, a sponge, or steel wool to texture the glaze, wiping as desired to produce a grained, stippled, or swirled pattern. Apply more glaze as desired to darken grooves and corners.

When the glaze is completely dry, go over the piece of furniture with a clean tack cloth. If you don't like the glaze, it can be removed with a clean rag and mineral spirits; reapply, texture the glaze, and let dry. Finally, replace doors, drawers, and hardware.

If the piece of furniture will be subjected to heavy wear and you don't mind spending extra time, protect it with two finish coats of furniture varnish, sanding lightly between coats. Let dry completely before using.

Repair Burn Spots in Upholstery

Cigarette burns in upholstery look awful, but they aren't catastrophic— reweaving a burn is as easy as darning a sock. **Tools:** sharp scissors, embroidery hoop; long sewing needle or darning needle, or curved upholstery needle; pressing cloth or clean handkerchief, electric iron. **Materials:** thread or yarn to match upholstery. **Time:** about 1 hour for a small hole.

If the damaged upholstery has a zipper or can be easily removed from the piece of furniture, remove it; don't try to remove tacked-on upholstery. If you can remove the upholstery, stretch it in an embroidery hoop while you work.

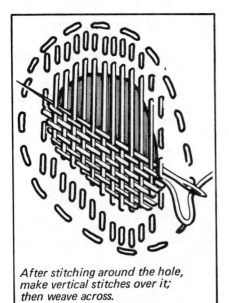

After stitching around the hole, make vertical stitches over it; then weave across.

Choose your mending thread carefully. Use thread or yarn that matches the color of the upholstery fabric and is the same thickness as the woven threads or smaller; the closer you come to an exact match, the less visible the repair will be. Use a long sharp sewing needle or, for thick threads or yarn, a sharp darning needle. If working directly on the furniture, you may want to use a curved upholstery needle.

Supporting the burned area with your hand, carefully cut out all damaged threads; trim back to undamaged material all around the burn, but keep the hole as small as possible. Be careful not to cut into the padding under the upholstery fabric.

Cut a length of thread long enough to reweave the entire damaged area. Thread your needle and stitch around the damaged area with a running stitch to mark the outline of the repair and keep the raw edge of the hole from stretching. Cut the thread.

Without tying a knot in the thread, weave the needle in and out just inside of the stitched outline to make a vertical row of running stitches from top to bottom of the outline. At the top of this row of stitches, leave a tiny loop of thread and stitch down, parallel to the first row and one thread closer to the hole. Repeat, making close vertical rows of stitches across the damaged area. When you reach the hole, weave the thread up to the opening and then straight across the hole; weave it in again at the other side. Be careful not to pull the thread too tight or the repair will pucker.

Work across the damaged area until the hole is entirely covered with a vertical latticework, firmly woven in on all sides. Then turn the stretched upholstery 90 degrees, or move so that you can work at right angles to the rows of stitching. Starting at the corner where you finished the last vertical row, stitch straight across the vertical lattice stitches. Weave the thread carefully in and out over the vertical stitches, working over and under each individual thread to weave a firm patch over the hole.

Continue this weaving process, being careful not to pull the thread too tight, until the entire damaged area has been rewoven. Secure the thread by running it through the fabric next to the rewoven patch several times, making cross stitches until the thread is firmly held. Cut the thread carefully at the surface of the fabric.

To complete the repair, wet a pressing cloth or a large clean handkerchief and wring it out. Fold it double and set it over the rewoven patch. Using a hot iron, press lightly, lifting toward the edges, to blend the texture of the patch into the upholstery. Smooth with your fingers as necessary.

Repair or Replace Furniture Buttons

A loose or missing furniture button doesn't have to mean costly upholstery bills; you can do the job as well yourself. **Tools:** sewing scissors, staple or tack remover, straight upholstery needle, sewing needle, staple gun or tack hammer. **Materials:** heavy-duty buttonhole thread, cover-it-yourself buttons, matching or complementary fabric, thread, staples or tacks. **Time:** 1 to 2 hours.

Repairing a loose button. Turn the piece of furniture on its side—or, if it's large, on its face. The bottom of a couch or chair is often lined with a sheet of muslin or other lightweight fabric; removing this lining gives you access to the interior of the chair. Detach the lining only as much as necessary to reach into the chair or couch; work as close to the loose button as possible. If the lining is sewn to the upholstery around the frame, clip a stitch or two and gently pull the fabric back from the upholstery, undoing the stitches a few at a time. If the lining is stapled or tacked, remove the fasteners a few at a time to release the lining; be careful not to tear the fabric.

With the lining detached as necessary, reach through the opening into the piece of furniture and locate the position of the loose button. Carefully cut the threads that hold the button in place—make sure you don't cut into the upholstery fabric. Remove the button.

Thread a straight upholstery needle with at least two long strands of buttonhole thread. Reach into the piece of furniture with the threaded needle and push the needle through the upholstery where the button should be, from the inside to the outside. Leave at least a foot of thread loose at the beginning for tying. Thread the button onto the needle on the outside of the piece of furniture and return the threaded needle through the same hole to secure the button.

Pushing the button as far into the cushion as desired, make a few firm overhand stitches into the cushion on the underside to be sure the button is tightly secured. Cut the needle loose, and tie the loose ends of the thread tightly together, using several square knots.

Finally, with the piece of furniture still on its side, blindstitch the underlining back into place with a sewing needle. Or, if the lining is stapled or tacked, fasten it to the frame as necessary to match the original fasteners.

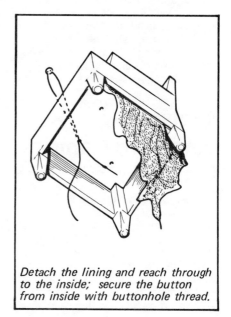

Detach the lining and reach through to the inside; secure the button from inside with buttonhole thread.

Replacing a missing button. If you have the button, reattach it as above. If the button is lost, buy a cover-it-yourself button the same size as the other buttons on the furniture; if you can't get a good match, consider replacing all the buttons. Many manufacturers include a swatch of fabric with the furniture so incidental repairs can be made; use this fabric to cover the new button. Make sure any pattern in the fabric is placed correctly on the button. Follow the manufacturer's instructions to cover the button, and attach it as above.

If you don't have any matching fabric, check underneath the couch or chair for extra fabric at the seams, or where any gathers are made. Another source for extra material is the cushions. Turn the cushion covers inside out and see if there's enough fabric in the seam allowance to cover the button. Use this excess fabric to cover the new button, following the manufacturer's instructions; attach the button as above.

If no extra fabric is available, recover all the buttons in a complementary fabric; buy the fabric at a dry goods store or use a compatible upholstery fabric. Replace missing buttons, recover all old buttons, and reattach them as above.

Finally, with the piece of furniture still on its side, blindstitch the underlining back into place with a sewing needle. Or, if the lining is stapled or tacked, fasten it to the frame as necessary to match the original fasteners.

Replace Damaged Caning

Unless the original cane was hand-woven, it's easy to replace damaged cane chair seats, chair backs, or table-tops. Take a good look at the edge of the old cane. If there is a groove all around the frame, you can do the re-caning yourself. If there are individual holes through the wood, the cane must be rewoven by hand; in this case, take the chair to a professional. **Tools:** tape measure, bucket, sharp chisel, wood wedges the same thickness at the narrow edge as the groove around the frame, hammer, utility knife. **Materials:** prewoven cane, spline, large towel, masking tape, white glue. Buy splining when you get the sheet of cane. **Time:** about 1 hour.

Measure the opening where the new cane will go, from inside edge to inside edge. Add at least 2½ inches to both the length and the width. Carefully measure the width of the groove around the opening; the width of the groove determines the width of the spline. Buy a sheet of prewoven cane large enough to cover the opening, plus 2½ inches in both directions, and spline of the proper width. To make the new cane and the spline pliable, soak them in a bucket of hot water for 15 minutes before using them.

Remove the old cane, using a chisel to pry up the spline. Clean the groove carefully with the chisel. Remove the new cane from the water and blot it dry with a towel. Tape the sheet of cane in place over the open frame, covering the groove and extending over the outside edge of the frame.

Starting at the center of the front edge or of one short side, wedge the cane into the groove around the opening, using a hammer and a narrow wood wedge to drive it firmly into place. Work along the groove with the wedges and hammer and set the cane all along the front; it must be firmly driven in and flattened squarely along the bottom of the groove or it will come loose as soon as the wedge is moved to the next section. Leave the wedges in place in the groove, if necessary, to hold the cane. When the entire front or side of the caning has been wedged into the groove, stretch the sheet of cane firmly across the open frame and, again starting at the center, wedge the opposite side into place; then wedge the remaining sides. Remove the tape. Be careful to keep the sheet of cane stretched evenly and firmly over the frame.

When the cane has been evenly

Recover Insert Chair Seats

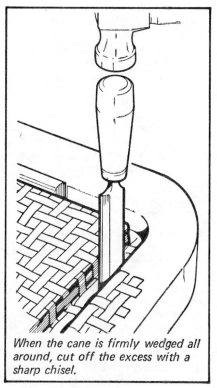

When the cane is firmly wedged all around, cut off the excess with a sharp chisel.

Many wood or metal chairs, especially for dining room or kitchen use, are built with removable insert seats. It's easy to replace shabby or worn seat covers. **Tools:** screwdriver, tack hammer or staple remover and staple gun, sharp scissors, straight pins. **Materials:** ½-inch- to 1½-inch-thick sheet foam (the same thickness as the old padding), fabric or plastic for new seat covers, masking tape, flat-headed upholstery tacks or heavy-duty staples. **Time:** about ½ to 1 hour per chair.

Complete each chair before starting on the next one. Turn the chair upside down and locate the screws that hold the chair seat in place. Remove the screws. Set the chair right side up, holding the seat so it doesn't fall out; then lift the seat off the frame of the chair.

Turn the chair seat upside down. Many insert chair seats are simply plywood, covered with padding and then with fabric; some chairs have webbed seats. The procedure is the same in either case.

Remove the old fabric covering the seat, using a tack hammer or a staple remover carefully to pry out the old fastenings. Be careful not to damage the wood. Set the old cover aside to use as a pattern.

In old chairs, the padding under the seat cover may have to be replaced. If the padding is badly deteriorated, remove it from the seat, being careful not to tear it. Using the old padding as a pattern, cut a new padding insert from sheet foam; the thickness of the foam should match the thickness of the original chair seat. If the padding has compacted but is not badly deteriorated, cut a layer of thin sheet foam and set it directly over the old padding.

To cut the new seat cover, spread out the fabric or plastic for the new covers. Lay the old cover flat over the new fab-

driven into the groove all around the frame, remove the excess cane. Slant the blade of a sharp chisel against the cane at the bottom of the groove, setting it squarely in the outside corner of the groove. Tap the chisel sharply with a hammer to cut the cane. Repeat around the groove until all excess cane has been trimmed away, removing wedges as you go.

Remove the spline from the hot water and blot it dry with a towel. Lay a bead of white glue along the groove over the newly trimmed cane, all around the frame. Lay the spline into the groove, pulling it tight and working around the chair; drive it firmly into place with the hammer and the wooden wedge. Bend the spline carefully around corners, being careful not to crack it. Cut the spline to make a tight joint where its two ends meet.

Let the glue dry thoroughly as directed by the manufacturer, at least 8 hours.

ric, wrong side to right side, and pin it firmly to the fabric. Cut the new fabric exactly around the pinned-down pattern. Unpin the old seat cover and discard it.

Lay the newly cut seat cover flat, wrong side up. Set the chair seat upside down on the fabric, centered in the correct position, to form a sandwich of fabric, foam, and seat. Fold the edges of the fabric over the bottom of the seat, stretching the new cover firmly into place. Tape the fabric edges to the bottom of the chair seat with masking tape to hold them firmly in place until they're attached.

Working on one side of the chair seat at a time, fold the cut edge of the fabric over and tack or staple it to the chair seat. Stapling is easier, but if the new covers are heavy fabric or plastic, flat-headed upholstery tacks may hold better. Staple or tack every 1 to 1½ inches around the seat. Adjust the fabric as necessary to remove wrinkles and keep the cover tightly and evenly in place as you work; remove masking tape as you go.

Attach one side of the chair completely, then the opposite side. Fold the corners in neatly to attach the third and fourth sides of the cover, mitering the

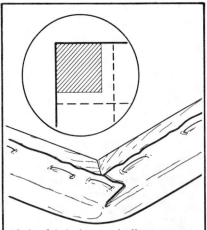

If the fabric is very bulky, cut out the shaded area to fold each corner neatly.

fabric smoothly. If the cover is very bulky fabric or plastic, cut out the square of material formed by the folds at each corner, being careful not to cut into the top of the cover.

Finally, when the entire cover is firmly and evenly attached, turn the chair seat over. Locate the screw holes where the seat is attached to the chair and punch through the fabric into these holes with an awl. Set the newly covered seat into place, align the screw holes, and replace the screws tightly.

Repair Damage to Finished Wood

Gouges, burns, stains, and cracks all look bad, but in most cases it's easy to repair the damage. **Tools:** small dishes and stir sticks, electric iron, artists' paintbrush, rubber gloves, plastic credit card, putty knife, sanding block, small sharp knife. **Materials:** furniture polish, clean soft cloths, cigarette ashes, salad oil, linseed oil, grade 0000 steel wool, salt, rottenstone, furniture paste wax, talcum powder, white tissue paper, fine-grit sandpaper, hydrogen peroxide, oxalic acid, wax wood touchup sticks, plastic wood or wood putty. **Time:** 10 minutes to 2 hours, depending on damage; for extensive repairs, several days, 10 minutes to 2 hours a day.

A thorough cleaning and polishing hides many minor flaws, so try this before you take more drastic steps. Use an oil-based furniture polish. If this doesn't work, or if the damage is more severe, use the specific methods that follow.

White spots and rings. Water stains and heat marks can be removed with abrasives; start with a mild abrasive and work up to stronger measures if necessary. Clean the stained surface thoroughly with a soft damp cloth. Mix cigarette ashes with salad oil in a small dish, using enough ashes to form a paste. Rub gently over the stain with a dry cloth, working with the grain of the wood. If the stain is still visible, spread more oil and ashes on the wood and let the oil soak in for a day or so; rub again. Remove the paste with a damp cloth and polish the surface.

If a stain isn't removed by oil and ashes, pour a little salad oil or linseed oil onto the spot; rub lightly along the grain of the wood with grade 0000 steel wool. For deeper stains, add 5 or 6 shakes of table salt to the oil and rub again. Clean and polish the surface.

If 10 minutes' work with steel wool doesn't remove a stain, use rottenstone, a fine powdered-stone wood abrasive. Pour a little rottenstone into a small dish. Moisten a clean, soft cloth with linseed oil and dip it into the rottenstone; rub the stained area gently along the wood grain. Wipe the stained area clean every 10 to 15 seconds as you work to check your progress; stop rubbing as soon as the stain disappears. Clean and polish the surface; use a high-gloss furniture paste wax to restore the shine in the cleaned area. If the spot is still noticeably dull, and you don't mind a satin finish instead of a high gloss, dull the entire surface to match with rottenstone and linseed oil.

Dark stains. To remove soaked-in *grease*, sprinkle a thick coating of talcum powder on the spot and cover it with several sheets of white tissue paper. Press slowly and carefully with a medium-hot dry iron to draw the grease out of the wood. Move the paper to place clean paper over the spot; repeat as necessary. Be careful not to touch the finished wood directly with the iron.

To remove other stains, rub with rottenstone and linseed oil. Don't use sandpaper until rottenstone fails; then try these remedies. To remove stains from *wine, fruit, or blood,* sand the damaged surface lightly. Apply hydrogen peroxide to the stain with an artists' brush and let it work a few minutes; then clean and polish the surface. Remove *ink* stains with oxalic acid diluted with warm water, applied with a brush to the stained area only. *Caution: Wear rubber gloves; oxalic acid is poisonous.* Clean with a damp cloth, and polish the surface. If you can't remove

dark stains, take the piece of furniture to a professional

Dents. If the wood fibers aren't broken, you can probably repair a dent. For a shallow dent, pour a little hot water into the depression; wait 5 minutes and wipe with a clean cloth. To repair a deep or large dent, wet a clean cloth and wring it out. Spread the cloth over the dent, cover it with a dry cloth, and press carefully with a medium-hot dry iron. Be careful not to touch the finished wood directly with the iron. Let the entire surface dry completely; then polish it.

Scratches, cracks, and gouges. To fill minor scratches, use wax wood touchup sticks, available in hardware stores. They're made in colors to match most furniture. Run the tip of the touchup stick down the scratch or gouge, applying enough pressure to fill the opening with wax. Remove excess wax with the edge of a plastic credit card and polish the surface.

To fill deep scratches, cracks, or gouges, clean the damaged area thoroughly and sand it carefully with fine-grit sandpaper to smooth any rough or splintered edges. Use plastic wood or wood putty to fill the hole; buy the plastic wood or putty in a stain color to match the finish of the undamaged wood. Apply the plastic wood or putty with a putty knife; smooth the surface, rounding it very slightly above the surrounding wood, and let dry overnight.

When the filled-in area is dry, smooth it carefully with grade 0000 steel wool or fine-grit sandpaper; use a sanding block if possible to prevent gouging the wood, but be careful not to damage the finished wood around the patched area.

If the patched area isn't conspicuously different from the finished wood, wax the piece of furniture with a high-gloss furniture paste wax; apply more wax to the patched area as necessary and polish the entire surface. If the patched area is still noticeably dull and you don't mind a satin finish, dull the entire surface to match with rottenstone and linseed oil, as above.

Burns. Remove all charred wood, shaving it out carefully with a small sharp knife. Sand the damaged area smooth with fine-grit sandpaper, being careful not to damage the finished wood around it. For minor burns, use a wax stick to cover the damage; remove excess wax with a credit card. For deep burns, fill the area with plastic wood or wood putty in a stain color to match the finish of the undamaged wood. Let the plastic wood or putty dry overnight, smooth it with grade 0000 steel wool or sandpaper, and wax and polish the piece of furniture.

Repair Damaged Wood Veneer

The veneer on old wood furniture sometimes blisters or curls at the edges. It looks hopeless, but the repair is a simple one. **Tools:** electric iron, weights, sharp craft knife or single-edge razor blade, artists' brush, putty knife or paint scraper, small paintbrush, C-clamps, scrap wood, small sharp chisel, heavy book, toothpicks. **Materials:** smooth cardboard, clean soft cloths, furniture polish, carpenters' glue, matching wood veneer, masking tape, contact cement, medium- and fine-grit sandpaper, white glue, tack cloth, non-penetrating oil stain, finish to match, paste furniture wax. **Time:** 10 minutes to 3 hours, depending on the extent of the damage.

Blisters. If a veneered surface shows only small blisters, it can usually be flattened with heat. Set a sheet of smooth cardboard over the blistered area. Press firmly with a medium-hot dry iron, moving the iron slowly and evenly back and forth, until the blisters soften and flatten. Be careful not to touch the wood directly with the iron. Weight the smoothed-out area, leaving the cardboard in place, for 24 hours; then polish the surface.

To repair a large blister in veneer, cover the damaged surface with a clean dry cloth. Spread a wet cloth over this one and then cover with another dry cloth. Press carefully with a medium-hot iron, being careful not to touch bare wood or crack the blistered wood, until the bubbled veneer softens. Remove the cloths.

Working quickly, use a sharp craft knife or a single-edge razor blade to cut the blister open down the middle, along the grain of the wood. Be careful not to cut into the wood under the veneer. Remove any loose dirt or crumbled glue from the slit with an artists' brush. Press down on the sides of the blister to make the cut edge gap open; squeeze a little carpenters' glue into each side of the opening. Smooth the loose veneer into place over the glue and wipe off any excess. Weight the repaired area for 24 hours; then remove the weights and polish the surface.

Loose veneer. Veneer that has come loose from the base wood of a large flat surface can usually be reglued. Cover the loose veneer with dry and wet cloths and press firmly but carefully to dampen and soften it. Working quickly but carefully, lift the softened veneer back from the furniture surface and remove the old glue underneath it with a putty knife or a paint scraper. Scrape the bottom of the veneer very gently and wipe off any melted glue with a clean cloth; scrape the base wood surface and wipe it clean. Use an artists' brush to clean the edge where the veneer begins to lift.

Apply carpenters' glue to the cleaned base wood with a small brush, working in the direction of the veneer grain. Then, starting at the solidly glued veneer and working out toward the loose edge, smooth the veneer gently but firmly into place. Press out from the center to the edges to force out any excess glue; wipe off the excess with a clean cloth.

Weight or clamp the entire glued area for 24 hours, using an even weight all across the surface or a flat piece of scrap wood to distribute the pressure of one or more clamps. Protect the furniture surface with clean cloths or blocks of scrap wood. When the newly glued veneer is dry, remove the weights or clamps and polish the entire surface thoroughly.

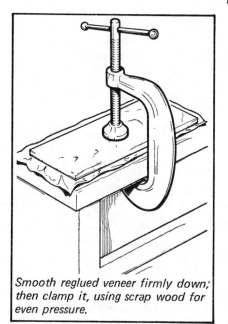

Smooth reglued veneer firmly down; then clamp it, using scrap wood for even pressure.

Burns and scratches. Because veneer is thin—often less than ⅛ inch—deep burns and scratches can be hard to repair. If surface treatments don't work because the whole thickness of the veneer layer is damaged, use a matching piece of veneer to patch the damaged area. Choose a veneer of the same wood as the damaged surface, with a similar grain pattern and color.

Remove all wax and dirt from the damaged area. Set a piece of matching veneer over the spot to be patched, with the grains matching, and secure it firmly with masking tape; make sure the new veneer is tight against the surface to be patched. Holding the taped-down veneer steady, cut an oblong patch with a sharp craft knife, through the new veneer and into the damaged surface; cut firmly and evenly through the entire thickness of the damaged veneer layer. Make the patch just large enough to cover the damaged area; point the ends with the grain of the wood and curve the sides smoothly in a shield shape. Be careful not to let the taped-down veneer slip.

When the patch and the damaged surface beneath it are completely cut

through, remove the sheet of new veneer and carefully pop out the patch; set it aside. With the tip of the knife, very carefully work the blade under the cutout old veneer to separate it from the base wood; if necessary, score the veneer with a small sharp chisel to break up the damaged area. Remove only the top layer of damaged veneer, and be careful not to damage the outline of the patch. Do *not* cut out more than one layer of wood.

When the old veneer is completely cut out, test the patch of new veneer for fit in the cutout patch; it should fit perfectly. If necessary, trim the edges of the old veneer slightly with a craft knife; do not trim the edges of the patch.

To apply the patch, lightly coat the back of the patch and the cutout area in the old veneer with contact cement. Let the cement cure, as directed by the manufacturer; then carefully press the patch into place. Weight the patch with a heavy book for at least 1 hour.

If the veneer patch doesn't fit the cutout area exactly, make a filler with a piece of scrap veneer. Rub the scrap veneer with a piece of medium-grit sandpaper to produce a small amount of sanding residue; mix this sanding residue with 2 or 3 drops of white glue to yield a mixture the same color as the veneer. Remove the weight from the patch and carefully fill the joints with the sawdust-glue mixture, using a toothpick to apply the filler. Remove any excess and let the patch dry for about 48 hours.

When the patch is completely dry, sand it very lightly with fine-grit sandpaper until the patch is exactly flush with the surrounding wood and the edges of the cut veneer blend in with the surrounding wood. Wipe the surface clean with a tack cloth and then carefully apply a nonpenetrating oil stain as necessary to the sanded area, blending it into the undamaged veneer. Let the stain dry completely, as directed by the manufacturer; sand the area lightly, wipe it clean, and finish the damaged area to match and blend with the original finish. To complete the repair, polish the refinished surface with paste furniture wax.

Repair Wobbly Furniture

Unsteady chairs and tables are easily dealt with. **Tools:** screwdriver, adjustable wrench or pliers, utility knife, stool or small stepladder, miter box, backsaw, pencil, drill, putty knife. **Materials:** hollow fiber plugs or wood toothpicks, carpenters' glue, scrap pieces of 1 × 2 pine or hardwood, flathead wood screws, steel corner braces or tabletop fasteners, plastic wood or wood putty, wax paper. **Time:** about 10 minutes to 1 hour, plus additional drying time, depending on the problem.

First identify the wobbly leg or legs—turn a chair or light table upside down to do this; you'll need an assistant to lift each end of a heavy table while you check the legs at that end. If the frame is simply screwed together at the corners, tighten the screws. If there is a metal bracket braced across the corner, tighten the bolt that holds the bracket in place.

If the bolt in a corner bracket is tight but the leg still wobbles, remove the bolt. If you're working on a table that's too heavy to turn over, have your assistant support the weight of the table while you work on it. The support bracket is sometimes set into slots on each side of the table frame; if it has slipped out of these slots, reseat the bracket and tighten the bolt.

If the screws in a simple frame or the bolt in a reinforced corner can't be tightened, remove them. Coat a standard hollow fiber plug with carpenters' glue and insert it into the enlarged screw or bolt hole; trim it flush at the surface of the hole. Let the glue dry about 8 hours and then replace the screw or bolt. Or wedge the loose screw or bolt with wood toothpicks to tighten it. Dip toothpicks into carpenters' glue and set them around the perimeter of the hole; snap them off at the surface of the hole. Let the glue set partially, according to the manufacturer's instructions;

then coat the screw or bolt with glue and screw it firmly into place. Let dry 24 hours before placing weight on the repaired leg—support the end of a heavy table on a stool or small stepladder.

If a chair or table doesn't have corner braces, make braces to fit with pieces of pine or hardwood 1 × 2 set diagonally across the corners and screwed into place. The length of each brace depends on how far from the corner you set it—keep it inconspicuous.

Miter one end of a piece of 1 × 2, using a miter box and a backsaw and cutting at a 45-degree angle. Hold the mitered piece into the corner to be braced and mark the length necessary; then miter the other end of the brace as marked.

Drill one hole at each end of the brace's long side, aiming the holes so that the screws that hold the brace are aimed straight into the corner frame. Drill holes slightly smaller than the wood screws you're using. Hold the brace in place and mark the screw holes on the frame of the chair or table; drill the holes carefully. Apply a coat of carpenters' glue to the faces of the brace that touch the table, set the brace into the corner, and screw it tightly into position. Let dry 24 hours before placing weight on it.

Where extra strength is needed, reinforce weak or wobbly legs with steel

To tighten a corner bracket, remove the bolt; reseat the bracket and replace the bolt.

Fix Loose Chair Rungs

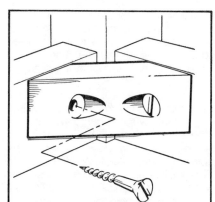

Make 1 x 2 braces to reinforce weak corners; miter to fit, glue, and screw the brace in.

For extra strength, use steel corner braces to support a weak chair or table leg.

Fix wobbly chair rungs before they get worse—the repair is a simple one. **Tools:** screwdriver, pocketknife, sponge, glue injector (available at hardware stores) or toothpicks, adjustable clamp or 5-foot length of sturdy cord and 8- to 10-inch sturdy dowel, clean rags. **Materials:** steel wool, household carpenters' glue, silk thread. **Time:** ½ to 1 hour.

Make sure first of all that the wobble isn't caused by loose screws. Turn the chair upside down and locate the screws holding the chair together. Make sure they're tight.

If the screws are all tight, the glue cementing the rungs to the chair legs has probably weakened. Identify the loose rung or rungs by pressing on the various parts of the chair. A rung that moves even slightly should be reglued.

If possible, completely remove the end of the rung from its hole in the chair leg. Rungs very loose at both ends should come out completely, although you may have to unscrew the legs from the chair—remember how to put the chair back together again. Don't force the rungs out of the chair.

Strip all old glue from the prong at the end of the loose rung, using steel wool wrapped around the prong. Clean the hole in the chair leg the same way, or use a pocketknife to get at the glue. Be careful not to scratch the finish; if you use a knife, be careful not to cut into the wood—a tight fit is essential to a good repair.

Apply a thin coat of carpenters' glue to both the rung prong and the hole in the chair leg. Insert the end of the rung into the hole, wiggling it to evenly distribute the glue. Remove excess glue with a damp sponge. If you had to disassemble the chair to get the rung out of the hole, reassemble it at this point.

If you can't remove the end of the rung from the chair leg, turn the chair on

corner braces or tabletop fasteners. Set the braces into position so that they support the chair seat or tabletop, mark the screw holes, drill, and screw the braces into place.

If all its legs are tight and a table or chair still wobbles, chances are the floor is uneven. If you can't repair the floor and don't want to move the chair or table, build up the rocking leg with plastic wood or wood putty to meet the low spot in the floor. Set a piece of wax paper under the leg and let the extender dry thoroughly, as directed by the wood putty manufacturer. If you move the table or chair to a level spot, remove the extender with a putty knife or a knife.

Clamp the glued rung with a cord around the chair legs, twisted and propped to maintain pressure.

Many times the problem is not in the glue but in the wood itself. A wobble of long standing may result in a cracked prong at the end of the rung. In this case, you must reinforce the prong to make the repair.

Take the rung out of the hole in the chair leg and remove the old glue. Apply a thin coat of carpenters' glue to the damaged prong. Wrap the glued prong tightly with a layer of silk thread. Measure the thickness of the prong against the hole in the chair leg. If the prong is still not thick enough to make a tight fit in the hole, apply another thin coat of glue and then wind another layer of silk thread onto the prong. Finally, apply glue to both prong and hole, insert the end of the rung into the hole in the chair leg, clamp or tie, and let dry 8 to 12 hours.

its side so you can get at the loose joint. Force glue into the hole around the loose rung, using a glue injector or simply squeezing glue around the rung and pushing it into the hole with the end of a toothpick. Set the chair upright again.

You must apply prolonged pressure to the glued joint. An adjustable clamp large enough to stretch across the chair legs connected by the rung is ideal—if you own one, by all means use it. Set the clamp in place, using clean rags to protect the chair legs, and tighten it firmly. Let the glued joint dry for 8 to 12 hours before unclamping it.

If you don't have a clamp, you'll need a 5-foot length of sturdy cord and an 8- to 10-inch sturdy dowel. Wrap the cord around the chair legs that hold the rung, placing the cord slightly below the rung. Use clean rags under the cord to protect the chair legs. Knot the cord, letting it hang loosely. Insert the dowel in the loop of the knotted cord and turn it to twist the cord, pulling the chair legs firmly and steadily together. Hold the dowel firmly as you tighten the cord.

When the cord is tight, prop the end of the dowel at the seat or rung to hold the cord tightly twisted. Leave the cord on the chair for 8 to 12 hours while the glue hardens.

Mend Broken Furniture

Most broken furniture parts are easy to repair. **Tools:** sturdy cord, C-clamps or pipe clamps, 8- to 10-inch sturdy dowel, pliers, wire cutters, pencil, drill, small handsaw, screwdriver, sharp chisel, putty knife. **Materials:** carpenters' glue or hide glue, clean dry cloths, wax paper, brads, 1/8-inch to 3/8-inch doweling, medium- and fine-grit sandpaper, steel mending plates, flathead wood screws, plastic wood or wood putty. **Time:** about 1 to 3 hours.

Breaks in nonstructural rungs or spindles can simply be glued. Use carpenters' glue or, if there are chips missing along the broken edges, hide glue. Pull the broken ends of the rung or spindle apart and coat the raw side of each end with glue. Join the glued pieces exactly, pressing them firmly together. Wipe off any excess glue with a damp cloth.

Wrap a sheet of wax paper around the glued break to protect the wood; then twist a length of sturdy cord around the mended break, wrapping it firmly over the entire area. Clamp the piece of furniture with C-clamps or pipe clamps, using cloths to protect the wood under the clamps. Or tie another length of cord tightly around the piece of furniture to press the mended ends together; insert an 8- to 10-inch dowel into the loop of this cord and twist it to brace the mended piece firmly. Prop the end of the dowel under a firm part of the piece of furniture to keep the cord twisted tightly.

Let dry 24 hours and remove the ropes. Fill any chips along the break with hide glue or plastic wood and let dry.

Breaks in structural parts—the arm or leg of a chair, for instance—must be reinforced. Pull the ends of the broken piece apart. Using the side of a pair of pliers, pound a small brad partway into one broken end, in the center of the piece of wood and at right angles to the break; leave the head of the brad sticking out. Cut the head off with wire cutters, leaving the sharp end of the brad.

Put the two broken ends carefully together, exactly as they should be joined. Push firmly so that the brad left in the one end leaves a mark on the other. This is where the reinforcement, a piece of wood doweling, should be inserted. Pull the pieces apart and pull out the brad with the pliers.

Use ⅛-inch to ⅜-inch doweling, depending on the thickness of the part to be reinforced. Doweling, sold by the foot, is available either plain or spirally scored. If you can get it, buy the spirally scored kind; it holds glue better.

Drill holes in the raw ends of the broken part to match the diameter of the dowel you're using. Following the marks left by the brad, drill about 1 inch into each broken end. Hold the drill aimed at right angles to the break, and make sure the two holes are exactly aligned. Drill for a shorter dowel where necessary, for a longer dowel when the broken part is heavy.

Cut a piece of doweling to approximately the right size and insert it dry into the drilled holes to check its length. Trim it to fit exactly; the dowel should fit

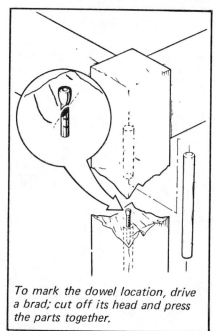

To mark the dowel location, drive a brad; cut off its head and press the parts together.

firmly into the drilled holes. Sand the ends of the dowel to round the cut edges slightly before gluing it into place.

Attach the dowel by squeezing a little glue into one drilled hole; twist the dowel into place in that end of the broken piece. Coat the raw face of this doweled end with glue and squeeze a little glue into the drilled hole in the other end. Carefully join the two broken ends, sliding the dowel into its hole and pressing firmly to match the broken ends exactly. Wipe off excess glue with a damp cloth.

Wrap a sheet of wax paper around the mended part, wrap it with sturdy cord, and tie or clamp the piece of furniture to press the glued ends together. Let dry 24 hours, unclamp, and fill in any chips.

Structural parts that must take heavy use, or that can't be doweled unless the piece of furniture is completely taken apart, should be reinforced with steel mending plates. Clean, glue, and clamp or tie the broken part—a split chair seat, for example—and let it dry completely; unclamp it. Turn the piece of furniture upside down and set one or

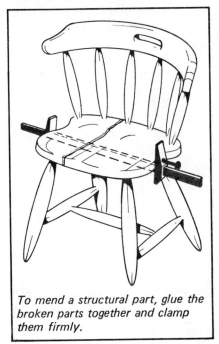

To mend a structural part, glue the broken parts together and clamp them firmly.

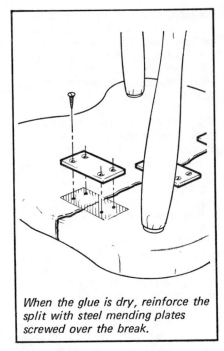

When the glue is dry, reinforce the split with steel mending plates screwed over the break.

more mending plates parallel over the mended split, spacing them evenly about one plate's length apart so that each bridges the split. Use four large mending plates, about 4 inches long, for a chair seat; use fewer and smaller plates for smaller breaks. Mark the position of each plate and of all screw holes with a pencil.

Drill a starter hole at each marked screw hole, align each mending plate over its predrilled holes, and fasten the plates securely with flathead wood screws, tightening them as much as possible. Make sure the screws aren't longer than the wood is thick, or the points will go completely through the mended part.

For a neater job, when small mending plates are used, mortise the plates into the wood. Before screwing each plate into place, trace its outline onto the piece of wood. Chisel out the marked area evenly with a sharp wood chisel, to sink the plate about ⅛ inch below the mended surface. Screw in the plate and cover it with plastic wood or wood putty, smoothing it in with a putty knife.

Mend Broken Marble

Most marble repairs are surprisingly simple with a two-part epoxy glue especially made for the purpose. Very large, heavy pieces of marble, such as mantelpieces, should be handled by a professional stonemason. **Tools:** small mixing sticks, putty knife, spray bottle, artists' small paintbrush, sanding block. **Materials:** small mixing dish; two-part marble epoxy glue (resin and hardener), marble pigment, and painters' whiting, all available at hardware stores; fine-grit wet-type sandpaper, marble polish, masking tape. **Time:** 1 hour.

Before starting to work, mix a small amount of glue in a shallow dish, combining resin and hardener as directed by the manufacturer. Add pigment, experimenting until the epoxy-pigment mixture matches the marble. Let this test batch harden, timing it so you have an idea how much glue to mix at once and how quickly you'll have to work. Make a note of the pigment you used and the epoxy's hardening time, and save the test batch as a visual reference.

A perfectly flat work surface is essential. Start the repair by laying out the pieces of the marble slab, jigsaw-puzzle style, on your work surface. Note any chipped areas that must be filled. Slide the pieces apart, still in order but with about 2 inches between pieces.

Mix epoxy resin and hardener and add pigment; be sure to mix only as much glue as can be applied within the epoxy's hardening time. If you must glue together several pieces of marble, you may have to work in stages, mixing enough glue for the first joins and then remixing for the rest of them.

Coat the broken edges of the pieces to be joined with the epoxy-pigment mixture and quickly slide them together, keeping the pieces flat on the work surface and being careful to match them exactly. Scrape off any excess glue with a putty knife.

Add epoxy-pigment mixture to fill small chips in the surface or along the join, using enough glue to leave a slight mound on the marble surface. Let the joined and mended marble dry thoroughly, at least 8 hours.

When the epoxy is completely dry, smooth the filled-in chips with fine-grit wet-type sandpaper, misting the marble thoroughly with water before you sand. Repeat until the marble surface is smooth and even, and polish the slab with marble polish.

To repair large chips in the edges of a marble slab or restore a damaged corner, add painters' whiting to thicken the epoxy-pigment mixture. Experiment with a test batch to mix a smooth, thick paste, and note hardening time and pigment and whiting proportions.

Set the damaged marble slab on a flat work surface. Use masking tape to outline the desired contour along the edge to be restored: lay tape straight across a gap in an edge; extend tape in a frame around a broken-off corner,

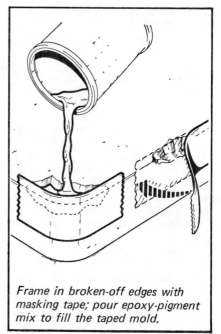

Frame in broken-off edges with masking tape; pour epoxy-pigment mix to fill the taped mold.

being careful to match the shape of any undamaged corners. The top edge of the tape should stick up slightly above the surface of the marble.

Mix epoxy resin and hardener and add pigment and whiting. Pour the epoxy-whiting paste carefully into the masking-tape frame, using enough epoxy to match the level of the marble surface but not enough to spill over onto the undamaged marble. At this point, you can match colored streaks in marble by applying a little dry pigment with a small watercolor brush, brushing it in very lightly so you don't leave brush marks. Let the restored edge or corner dry at least 8 hours.

When the newly molded edge is completely dry, remove the tape and sand the repaired area with fine-grit wet-type sandpaper, first misting the surface of the slab thoroughly. Repeat until the filled-in area is completely smooth and the marble-epoxy joint is not conspicuous. Be careful to sand large areas absolutely flat—use a sanding block to keep from gouging or rippling the epoxy. Polish the restored slab with marble polish.

Build a Bookcase

There's no need to have books and magazines scattered all over when you can quickly build a simple freestanding bookcase for them. **Tools:** measuring rule, pencil, square, straightedge, power saw, hammer, miter box, handsaw, nail set. **Materials:** ¾-inch grade A-B interior plywood, carpenters' glue, 6-penny finishing nails, ⅛-inch tempered hardboard, ⅝-inch brads, 1-inch brads, shelf-edge molding, wood filler, sandpaper, stain or paint. **Time:** about 2 to 4 hours, plus finishing time.

The overall outside dimensions of this bookcase are 30 inches wide, 12½ inches deep, and 54¾ inches high. The bottom shelf is 15 inches high; the other two shelves are 12 inches high.

Cut two 12 × 54-inch pieces of ¾-inch plywood for the bookcase sides. Cut a 12 × 30-inch piece of ¾-inch plywood for the top. Cut a 12 × 28½-inch piece of ¾-inch plywood for the bottom. Cut all pieces so that the face grain of the plywood runs lengthwise.

Set the four cut pieces on edge on a flat working surface in the form of a rectangle, with the bottom piece between the sides and the top piece on top of the sides. Apply a bead of carpenters' glue along all butt joints and align the joints carefully so that all faces are flush. Drive three 6-penny finishing nails into each joint.

Cut a 30 × 54¾-inch piece of ⅛-inch tempered hardboard for the back; make sure that the piece is perfectly square. Set the back on the bookcase frame, and adjust it until the frame is square and flush with all edges of the back piece. Apply a bead of glue all along the edge of the bookcase frame and set the back piece into place with its smooth side facing the inside of the bookcase. Secure the back with ⅝-inch brads, about 12 inches apart and ⅜ inch in from the edges.

Set the bookcase up on its side, and measure off 15 inches along that side from the face of the bottom piece. With

a square and a pencil, make a light line across the side from front to back to mark the edge of the shelf. From that line, measure out ¾ inch and draw another light line. Measure up another 12 inches and draw a line, then up another ¾ inch and draw another line. Measure up another 12 inches and ¾ inch, and draw lines marking the top shelf. Turn the bookcase over onto its other side and repeat to mark the shelves on that side. These guidelines mark the levels where the shelves will be set.

Cut three 11½ × 28½-inch pieces of ¾-inch plywood for shelves; make sure that the face grain runs lengthwise. Apply a bead of glue to each end and the back edge of each shelf. Slip each shelf into position, carefully aligned on the guidelines. Nail it in place by driving

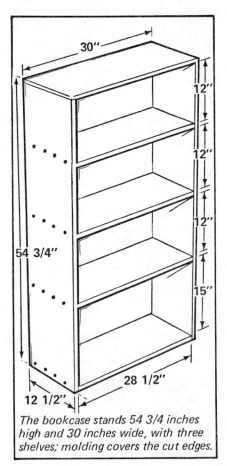

The bookcase stands 54 3/4 inches high and 30 inches wide, with three shelves; molding covers the cut edges.

four 6-penny finishing nails through the bookcase sides from the outside and into the shelf ends at each joint.

Lay the bookcase face down. Measure up from the bottom at each side a distance of 16⅛ inches, and make a mark at each point. Line the marks up with a straightedge, and draw a pencil line between them. Similarly, measure up 12 inches from that line and draw another line, then measure up another 12 inches and make another line. Nail the back piece to the rear shelf edges along these guidelines, using 1-inch brads spaced every 6 inches.

Lay the bookcase face up. Cut two 54¾-inch lengths of shelf-edge molding. Miter each end to a 45-degree angle. Apply a bead of glue to the edges of the sides. Set the moldings in place, and align them carefully. Secure the molding with 1-inch brads spaced every 10 to 12 inches.

Cut two 30-inch lengths of molding. Miter each end to a 45-degree angle. Apply a bead of glue along the edges of the top and bottom pieces. Set the molding into place and align the pieces carefully. Secure the molding with 1-inch brads spaced every 10 to 12 inches.

Cut three 28½-inch lengths of molding. Apply glue to the leading edges of the shelves. Set the molding in place, and secure the strips with 1-inch brads.

With a nail set and hammer, sink all of the nailheads—except those on the back panel—slightly below the surface of the wood. Fill the nailhead holes with wood filler. Sand the bookcase smooth.

Finally, stain or paint as desired.

Make a Record Cabinet

Stereo records should be stored vertically in a closed, dust-free cabinet placed in a relatively cool location. Such a cabinet is not difficult to construct, and can be made in modular form so that other units can be added whenever

collections grow larger. **Tools:** measuring rule, pencil, square, straightedge, power saw, hammer, nail set, handsaw, electric drill with bit, paintbrushes. **Materials:** ¾-inch grade A-B interior plywood, carpenters' glue, 6-penny finishing nails, wood filler, sliding door track, ¼-inch tempered hardboard, two finger grips, sandpaper, primer, paint. **Time:** about 2 hours, plus painting time.

The inside dimensions of the record cabinet are 14 inches high and 14 inches deep. Overall dimensions are 24 inches wide, 14¾ inches deep, and 17½ inches high (including base). For additional units to be stacked on top of the first, the base can be omitted.

Cut the pieces for the cabinet's base from ¾-inch grade A-B interior plywood: front, 2 × 20 inches; back, 2 × 18½ inches; sides, 2 × 11 inches. Stand these pieces up on edge in a rectangular shape on a flat working surface, arranged with the back piece between the side pieces, and the front piece overlapping the ends of the side pieces. Apply carpenters' glue to the joint faces, align the butt joints carefully, and nail the pieces together with two 6-penny finishing nails at each joint. Check with a square to make sure that all corners are right-angle corners.

Cut a 14¾ × 22½-inch plywood panel for the cabinet bottom, with the plywood face grain running in the long dimension. Run a bead of glue all around the top edge of the base, and set the bottom on the base with the back edge of the bottom flush with the back of the base and centered so that there's a 2-inch overhang at each side. Nail the bottom to the base with a 6-penny finishing nail spaced about 2 inches in from each corner, with another centered between the corner nails, along all four of the base pieces.

Cut the top, back, and side pieces for the cabinet from ¾-inch plywood; cut a 14¾ × 24-inch piece for the top, two 14 × 14¾-inch pieces for the sides, and a 14 × 22½-inch piece for the back. Run a bead of glue along the edge of one side of the bottom, and align a side piece so that its bottom

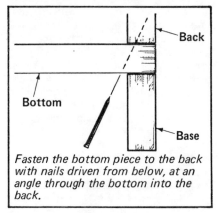

Fasten the bottom piece to the back with nails driven from below, at an angle through the bottom into the back.

Turn the assembly upside down, and drive three more 6-penny finishing nails at a slight angle through the bottom and into the bottom edge of the back; start the nails at the joint formed by the back piece of the base and the bottom of the cabinet.

Turn the assembly right side up again, and run a bead of glue along the top edge. Set the top piece in place, align it so that the edges are flush, and nail it in place using the same method used for nailing the bottom to the base.

With a nail set and hammer, sink all nails slightly below the surface of the wood. Fill all nailhead holes, as well as any imperfections in the wood or joints, with wood filler. Sand the entire cabinet smooth, paying special attention to all exposed plywood edges.

Cut the two lengths of sliding door track to fit exactly between the sides of the cabinet. Secure the deeper of the two tracks to the underside of the cabinet top, with its outer face flush with the cabinet edge. Install the shallower bottom track in the same way. Use glue, small screws, or brads to hold the tracks in place, depending on the type of track used.

Cut two door panels to size from ¼-inch hardboard. Each door panel is

edge is flush with the bottom surface of the bottom piece and the front and back edges are flush with the front and back edges of the bottom. Nail the side piece with three 6-penny finishing nails; repeat with the opposite side piece.

Run a bead of glue along the bottom edge and both side edges of the back piece. Position it at the rear of the cabinet, between the sides and resting on the bottom, with the rear surface flush with all rear edges. Nail it in place by driving three 6-penny finishing nails through each side, into the edges of the back.

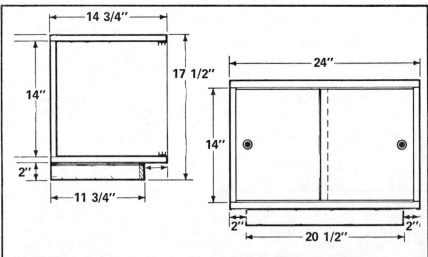

The cabinet is 24 inches wide, sized to hold LP records. Make additional units without the base and stack them.

11½ inches in width, but their heights (approximately 13¹⁄₄ inches) will vary slightly depending on the type of track used. Instructions for determining door height will be provided with the track.

Sand the door panels smooth, and round all top and bottom edges and corners slightly. Drill a hole near the leading edge of each door—about midway down—for a finger-grip, a small metal cup. Set the doors in the tracks, and test them for smooth operation.

Apply a coat of primer to the entire cabinet, inside and outside, but leave the track grooves and the bottom edges of the doors unpainted. Apply two coats of semigloss interior latex paint. The inside of the doors need not be painted.

Finally, force-fit and glue the finger grips into the doors.

Build a Desk

A desk can be a big help in taking care of household paperwork, and it need not be elaborate to do a good job. This model is easy to build and can be used even where space is limited. **Tools:** measuring rule, pencil, square, straightedge, power saw, hammer, miter box, handsaw, nail set, paintbrushes. **Materials:** 1 × 4 and 2 × 4 stock, carpenters' glue, 6-penny finishing nails, ¾-inch grade A-B plywood, 8-penny finishing nails, shelf-edge molding, ¾-inch brads, wood filler, sandpaper, primer, paint, two-drawer file cabinet. **Time:** about 3 to 4 hours, plus time for painting.

This desk is designed to accommodate a standard two-drawer file cabinet measuring 29 inches high, 15¼ inches wide, and 22 inches deep, set at one end as one of the desk's supports. If the file cabinet used is a different size, you'll have to alter the following desk dimensions accordingly. The overall dimensions of the desk in this project are 48 inches in length, 24 inches in depth, and 29¾ inches in height. It can be used with a chair of standard height, including a stenographer's chair.

Cut two pieces of 1 × 4 to 30¾ inches long, one piece of 1 × 4 to 20½ inches long, and one piece of 2 × 4 to 20½ inches long.

Set the 1 × 4 and 2 × 4 pieces on edge on a flat working surface, in the form of a rectangle. Position the 2 × 4 side piece with its outside face back exactly ¾ inch from the ends of the front and back 1 × 4's. Apply carpenters' glue to the joints, and after aligning them carefully, nail them together with two 6-penny finishing nails each.

Cut a 20½ × 29-inch piece of ¾-inch plywood for the desk's end panel. Position the panel against the 2 × 4 side piece on the outside face, between the front and back pieces, with the top edge flush with the top of the desk frame. Apply glue to the butt joints, and a generous coating of glue to one face of the end-panel/side-piece joint. Secure the panel by driving a pair of 8-penny finishing nails through the faces of the front and back pieces of the framework and into the edges of the plywood panel. Also drive six 6-penny finishing nails—staggered and spaced— through the face of the end panel and into the 2 × 4 side piece.

Cut a 24 × 48-inch piece of ¾-inch plywood for the top of the desk, with the plywood face grain running lengthwise. Apply glue to the top edge of the desk-frame/end-panel assembly, and position the top so that it overhangs at the rear by ¾ inch, at the front by 1¼ inches, and at the right side by 1 inch. Nail the desk top to the framework with 6-penny finishing nails, driven through the top and into the edges of the frame members and end panel; nail at each corner, spaced about 2 inches from the corners in each direction, and space the remaining nails about 11 to 12 inches apart. Drive three more 8-penny finishing nails down into the 2 × 4 side member.

Cut strips of shelf-edge molding to fit along the front and side edges of the desk top, and to cover the front edge of the end panel; fit each piece of molding individually.

If you use square-edge molding, butt joints can be employed, but rounded-

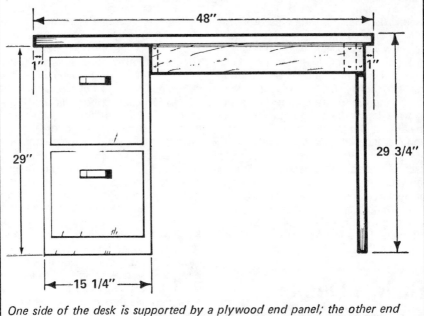

One side of the desk is supported by a plywood end panel; the other end of the desk top rests on a standard two-drawer file cabinet.

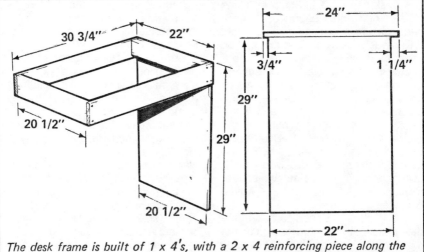

The desk frame is built of 1 x 4's, with a 2 x 4 reinforcing piece along the plywood end panel. The desk top overhangs the frame; shelf-edge molding finishes the edges.

edge molding is best mitered to 45 degrees to form perfect right-angle corners on the top piece.

Apply glue to the molding and position the strips. Secure the strips with ¾-inch brads.

With a hammer and nail set, sink all nailheads slightly below the surface of the wood. Fill the nailhead holes, as well as any imperfections in the wood surface or joints, with wood filler. Sand the entire desk to a smooth finish.

Apply a coat of primer, followed by two coats of semigloss interior latex (or other) paint. Let the paint dry completely; then set the desk into position over a two-drawer file cabinet.

Make a PVC Pipe Chair and Ottoman

PVC (polyvinyl chloride) plumbing pipe works fine for plumbing, but it also makes attractive, easy-to-assemble indoor or outdoor furniture. Spice up the drab color of the pipe with bright vinyl paint. **Tools:** measuring rule, pencil, miter box and backsaw, handsaw, utility knife, scissors, sewing machine, hammer or grommet setter. **Materials:** 1½-inch PVC plastic pipe, assorted fittings (T-fittings and 45- and 90-degree elbows), solvent cement with applicator, vinyl paint, canvas (or other suitable fabric), metal grommets, leather lacing. **Time:** about 4 to 6 hours, plus painting time.

With a miter box and backsaw, cut the following lengths of 1½-inch-diameter PVC pipe: two 17½-inch pieces, twelve 16½-inch pieces, two 15½-inch pieces, two 6½-inch pieces, eight 5½-inch pieces, twelve 1½-inch pieces. Cut the last twelve pieces slightly shorter than specified; they are used for reinforcement when two fitting joints and elbows butt against each other.

Assemble the chair *without* using solvent cement, as diagrammed in the accompanying illustration; use a utility knife to smooth any burrs. Once you're satisfied that the pieces fit properly, disassemble them.

Work in a well-ventilated area and follow product directions for solvent-cementing. To join a section of PVC pipe to a fitting, spread a generous amount of solvent on the last ½ inch of the pipe and within the collar of the fitting. With another length of pipe, pound

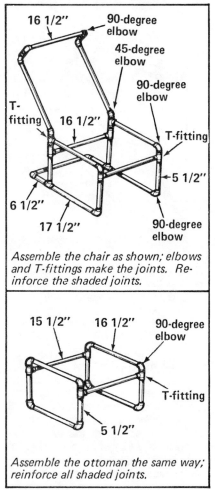

Assemble the chair as shown; elbows and T-fittings make the joints. Reinforce the shaded joints.

Assemble the ottoman the same way; reinforce all shaded joints.

the pipe into the collar as far as it will go. Twist the pipe in the fitting about ¼ inch to spread the solvent evenly and to ensure a solid weld.

Right-angle joints must be squared. To achieve accurate three-dimensional alignment, adjust the angle of the fittings on a flat surface, as illustrated, before the joints solidify. Or assemble entire rectangular sections quickly enough to make any necessary joint adjustments.

Repeat the procedure to assemble the ottoman.

If you want a brighter color, spray the furniture frames with a bright-colored vinyl paint. Let the paint dry thoroughly.

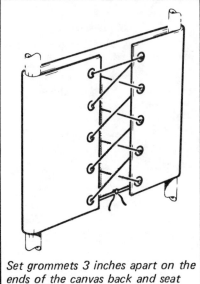

Set grommets 3 inches apart on the ends of the canvas back and seat pieces; tie them together with leather lacing.

To complete the chair and the ottoman, cut three pieces of canvas (or other suitable fabric), 17 inches wide and long enough to wrap around the parallel support pipes, with a gap of 3 inches for lacing the canvas together on the back or bottom of the furniture—approximately 42 inches. Sew a 1-inch seam all around.

Set grommets at 3-inch intervals, 1 inch from the edges of the canvas to be laced together; cross-cut two small ⅛-inch slits in the canvas for each grommet.

With a 4-foot piece of leather lacing, tie the canvas as illustrated, to the chair seat and back and to the ottoman seat.

Build a Telephone Stand

If you want a special spot for your desk-style telephone, this easy-to-build stand/cabinet keeps phone, note pad and pencil, and telephone directories in one convenient place. **Tools:** measuring rule, pencil, square, straightedge, power saw, hammer, miter box, handsaw, coping saw, screwdriver, nail set, paintbrushes. **Materials:** ¾-inch grade A-B plywood, carpenters' glue, 6-penny finishing nails, shelf-edge molding, 1-inch brads, 1 × 2 clear pine stock, two 7 × 23-inch stock louvered doors, two cabinet knobs, four decorative surface-mount hinges, two cabinet door roller-catch assemblies, wood putty, sandpaper, primer, latex paint. **Time:** about 3 to 4 hours, plus finishing time.

Cut the six main pieces of the telephone stand from ¾-inch plywood: bottom, 14 × 14³⁄₁₆ inches; sides, 14 × 23⅞ inches; top, 15 × 17 inches; back, 14³⁄₁₆ × 23⅛ inches. Cut all pieces with the plywood face grain running parallel to the long dimension.

Lay the back piece on a flat working surface and apply a bead of carpenters' glue along one of its long edges. Stand the bottom piece up against the glued edge, with the corners of the pieces flush. Nail the bottom to the back with four 6-penny finishing nails.

Lay the glued and nailed assembly on its side and run a bead of glue along

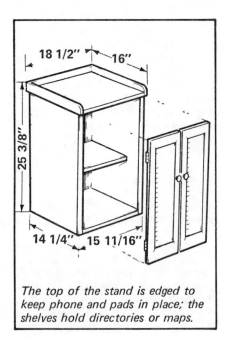

The top of the stand is edged to keep phone and pads in place; the shelves hold directories or maps.

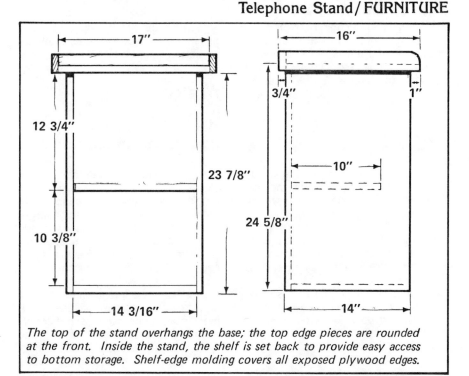

The top of the stand overhangs the base; the top edge pieces are rounded at the front. Inside the stand, the shelf is set back to provide easy access to bottom storage. Shelf-edge molding covers all exposed plywood edges.

the uppermost edge. Set a side piece into place so that the top corners meet, the bottom edge of the side is flush with the bottom surface of the bottom piece, and one side edge is flush with the outside surface of the back. Nail the side into place with three 6-penny finishing nails spaced and driven into the edge of the bottom; drive five more nails into the edge of the back. Turn the assembly over, and repeat to attach the other side piece.

Set the assembly upright, and run a bead of glue along the top edges of the back and side pieces. Set the top piece into place so that the rear edge is flush with the back surface of the cabinet; leave a 1-inch lip at the front, and center the top so that there's a lip of about ¾ inch at each side. Secure the top with three 6-penny finishing nails along each side and four more across the back, driven down into the edges; space the nailing line along the sides 1³/₃₂ inch in from the edge of the top piece.

Cut a 10 × 14³/₁₆-inch piece of plywood for the shelf, and check it for a snug fit between the sides of the stand. With a measuring rule, square, and pencil, locate and mark a guideline across the inside face of each side piece, 10⅜ inches up from the inside face of the bottom piece. Apply glue to the back and side edges of the shelf and slip it into place, aligned on the guidelines.

Draw light pencil guidelines on the sides and back of the cabinet to mark the edges of the shelf. Secure the shelf with three 6-penny finishing nails, driven through the sides and into each end of the shelf. Drive four more nails through the back of the cabinet into the edge of the shelf.

Lay the stand on its back. Cut strips of shelf-edge molding to fit all of the front edges of plywood—top, bottom, sides, and shelf. Fit the molding exactly, using either butt or mitered joints. Apply glue to the edges, and secure the strips with 1-inch brads set about 6 inches apart.

Cut two lengths of 1 × 2 pine stock to 15¾ inches, plus the thickness of the shelf edging—the edging will probably be ⅜ inch thick, but this can vary slightly. Round the top of one end of each edging piece to a radius of about ¾ inch or to a gentle curve, so that the two pieces are identical and well-rounded.

Apply a bead of glue along the side edges of the top piece of the cabinet. Secure each pine strip with three 6-penny finishing nails, rounded end forward and flush at front and back, with the bottom edge aligned with the bottom surface of the top piece. Drive the nails into the edges of the top piece.

Cut a 17-inch-long piece of 1 × 2 pine stock. Apply glue to the rear edge of the top piece and to the ends of the pine strip. Position the strip between the first two pine strips, with the top edges flush, and secure it with four spaced 6-penny finishing nails. Align the top corners, and drive two more 6-penny nails through the side strips into the ends of the back strip.

Mount a cabinet knob on each door, on the longitudinal centerline of the door and 6 inches down from the top. Mount hinges on each door, on opposite sides, with the top of the top hinges 4 inches down from the top of each door and the bottom of the bottom hinges 4 inches up from the bottom of the door.

Set each door into place, and adjust it so that there is a ¹/₁₆-inch clearance at top, bottom, and side. Secure the hinges to the stand's edges; center each screw exactly in the hinge mounting hole and drive it perfectly straight to align the door properly.

Mount the roller catches to latch the doors, following the instructions provided by the manufacturer. Set a catch on each side of the top piece, on the inside, with each catch centered on the longitudinal centerline—in line with the knob—of the inside door frame.

Remove the doors and take the hardware off. With a hammer and nail set, sink all visible nailheads slightly below the surface of the wood. Fill the nailhead holes and any imperfections in the joints or wood surfaces with wood putty, and sand both the cabinet and the doors smooth.

To finish the stand, apply a coat of primer, followed by two coats of interior semigloss latex (or other) paint.

Make a Plant Stand

To give a favorite plant some extra elevation, make a plant stand for it. This simple stand works well on a table or on the floor—for more height or larger plants, change the dimensions to suit yourself. **Tools:** measuring rule, pencil, carpenters' square, handsaw or saber saw; drill with ¾-inch, ⁹/₆₄-inch or #28, and ¹/₁₆-inch or #52 bits; straightedge, chisel, hammer, fine-toothed flat file, miter box and backsaw, nail set, sanding block, countersink, screwdriver, paintbrush. **Materials:** ¾-inch grade A-A or furniture-grade plywood, half-round molding, hide glue, 3-penny finishing nails, medium- and fine-grit

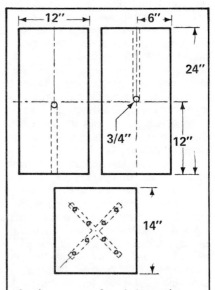

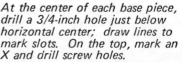

At the center of each base piece, drill a 3/4-inch hole just below horizontal center; draw lines to mark slots. On the top, mark an X and drill screw holes.

sandpaper, rag, 2-inch #6 flathead wood screws, plastic wood. paint or stain. **Time:** about 3 hours, plus drying and finishing time.

For a finished and professional-looking stand, use ¾-inch grade A-A or furniture-grade plywood; buy half-round molding to cover the cut edges. Measure and mark two plywood base pieces 12 inches wide and 24 inches long, with the grain of the plywood running the long way; use a carpenters' square to keep the corners accurate. Cut the base pieces with a handsaw or a saber saw.

Measure and mark the horizontal and vertical centerline of each piece. On the vertical centerline of each piece, mark a point ⅜ inch below the horizontal centerline. Drill a ¾-inch hole at this point. To avoid splintering, drill through the marked point just until the bit starts to protrude from the other side; then turn the piece of plywood over and drill through the other side to complete the hole.

With a straightedge, draw lines from the sides of the hole down to the bottom of each base piece, outlining a ¾-inch-wide slot on each piece. Carefully cut out the marked slots with a handsaw or a saber saw; cut along the inside of the lines, so that the slots are an even ¾ inch wide. Square the rounded tops of the slots with a saber saw or a chisel and hammer. If you use a chisel, be careful not to splinter the wood; make many small cuts instead of one or two large ones. Smooth the raw edges of the slots carefully with a fine-toothed flat file; test the slots as you work with a scrap piece of ¾-inch plywood, and file only until the slots are wide enough to accept the scrap. Smooth the slots carefully and accurately; the cut sides must be flat and square, and the edges must not splinter or become rounded.

To make the top of the stand, mark and measure a 14-inch-square piece of plywood, using a carpenters' square to keep the corners straight. Using a miter box and a backsaw, cut four 14-inch pieces of half-round molding, mitering the ends at a 45-degree angle. Attach the strips of molding to the edges of the

plywood top; apply hide glue to the back of each strip and then nail it into place with 3-penny finishing nails; sink the nailheads with a nail set. Allow the glue to dry completely, as directed by the manufacturer.

To finish the cut edges of the base pieces, cut four 24-inch pieces of half-round molding with squared ends. Apply hide glue to the back of each molding strip and nail the strips onto the outside long edges of the base pieces with 3-penny finishing nails; sink the nailheads with a nail set. Let the glue dry as directed.

When the glue is completely dry, sand the base pieces and the top as necessary; use a sanding block and medium- and fine-grit sandpaper. Smooth the edges where the molding meets the edge of the plywood, but do *not* sand the inside surfaces of the slots in the base pieces.

To assemble the stand, apply hide glue to the inside edges of the slots in the base pieces. Put the two pieces together at right angles, with the glued

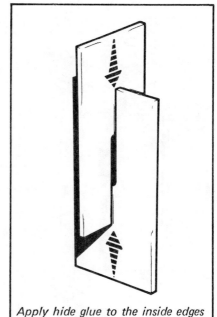

Apply hide glue to the inside edges of the slots; lock the slotted pieces firmly together to form the base.

slots interlocking firmly and the top and bottom edges of the base pieces flush. Set the base on a flat surface and adjust it so that the pieces are perfectly in line and square with one another; then carefully wipe away any excess glue that has leaked from the joints. Let the glue dry completely, as directed by the manufacturer.

When the glue is completely dry, put the stand together. Draw an X on the bottom side of the top piece, from corner to corner; draw a light X on the other side. Set the top piece on the assembled base and align it so that the penciled X on the bottom is hidden by the edges of the base X. The top piece is attached to the base with screws; mark points for two screws along each arm of the lightly drawn X on the top. Then remove the top from the base.

At each marked point, drill a hole completely through the top piece; use a $^9/_{64}$-inch or #28 bit. Countersink each hole so that the head of each assembly screw will lie slightly below the surface of the wood. Replace the top on the base, align it, and mark the screw holes

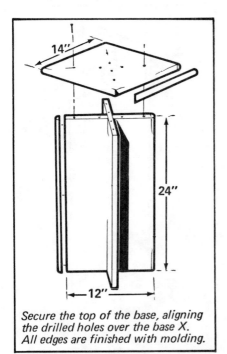

Secure the top of the base, aligning the drilled holes over the base X. All edges are finished with molding.

on the edges of the base X. With a $^1/_{16}$-inch or #52 bit, drill pilot holes 1 inch deep at the marked points on the edges of the base. Apply a coating of hide glue to the edges of the base X, set the top into place, and secure the top to the base with 2-inch #6 flathead wood screws through the holes in the top and into the predrilled holes in the base. Quickly turn the stand over and wipe off any excess glue.

Fill screw and nail holes, and any visible cracks at the edges of the half-round molding, with plastic wood; lightly sand the top of the stand to remove the penciled X. Sand all visible wood surfaces as necessary. Paint or stain as desired.

Make a Woodbox

To contain the mess of the fireplace woodpile, make this combination woodbox and fireside seat. It holds two stacks of 18-inch logs, as well as fireplace matches and magazines; the top is padded for comfortable sitting. **Tools:** measuring rule, pencil, square, straightedge, handsaw or power saw, hammer, electric drill, hole saw attachment for drill, miter box and backsaw; if desired, wood chisel; electric carving knife, scissors, tack hammer, nail set, paintbrush. **Materials:** ¾-inch grade A-B plywood, carpenters' glue, 6-penny and 3-penny finishing nails, ½-inch wood dowel, shelf-edge molding, ¾-inch brads; 3-foot, ¾-inch-wide piano hinge with installation screws; 2- or 3-inch foam padding, silicone adhesive, upholstery material, decorative upholstery tacks, wood filler, sandpaper; primer or stain, or finish desired. **Time:** 5 to 6 hours, plus finishing time.

Use ¾-inch grade A-B plywood to make the woodbox. Measure and cut two 15¼ × 39-inch pieces for the front and back, two 15¼ × 28½-inch side pieces, and one 20 × 47¾-inch piece for the bottom. On a flat work surface, stand the sides, front, and back on edge in the form of a rectangle, with the sides

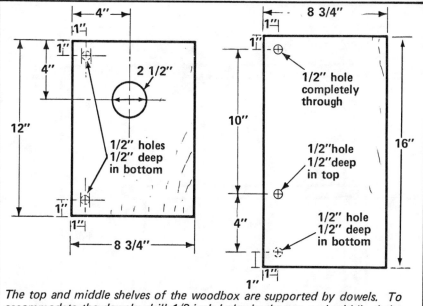

The top and middle shelves of the woodbox are supported by dowels. To accommodate the dowels, drill 1/2-inch holes in the top and middle shelves, as shown. In the top shelf, bore a 2 1/2-inch opening to hold a box of matches.

butted between the front and back pieces; make sure the best plywood surfaces face outside. Apply a bead of carpenters' glue to the edges, align the butt joints, and drive six 6-penny finishing nails to secure each joint.

Apply a bead of glue to the upper edge of the assembly, and set the bottom piece on the assembly, best face down, with the right side edge flush with the right outside surface, facing the box in upright position. Align the front and back edges with an 8¾-inch lip at the left-hand side.

To make the shelves for the woodbox, cut one 8¾ × 16-inch piece of ¾-inch plywood for the middle shelf, and one 8¾ × 12-inch piece for the top shelf. Drill two ½-inch holes ½ inch deep into the underside of the top shelf, centered on its length, 1 inch from the outside edge; place one hole back 1 inch from the rear edge, the other 1 inch from the front edge. Do *not* let the drill bit point break through the upper surface of the top shelf.

Drill two ½-inch holes at corre-

sponding locations in the middle shelf; the rear hole should go through the shelf, and the forward hole should be only ½ inch deep, in the top of the shelf. Then drill a third hole into the underside of the middle shelf, ½ inch deep and centered 1 inch from the side edge and 1 inch back from the front edge.

Drill two ½ inch holes ½ inch deep in the upper surface of the bottom lip. Center one hole 1 inch from the rear and side edges, and center the other hole 1 inch from the side edge and 15 inches from the rear edge.

Using an electric drill with a hole saw attachment, bore a 2½-inch hole through the top shelf, centered 4 inches in from the rear edge and 4 inches from the outside edge. A standard fireplace match container about 12 inches high and 2¼ inches in diameter will fit in this hole, with its base resting on the middle shelf.

Measure 6⅞ inches up from the upper surface of the bottom lip, and make a light pencil line across the side of the box from front to back. Make a

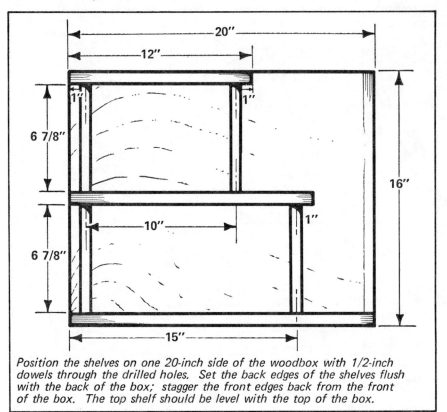

Position the shelves on one 20-inch side of the woodbox with 1/2-inch dowels through the drilled holes. Set the back edges of the shelves flush with the back of the box; stagger the front edges back from the front of the box. The top shelf should be level with the top of the box.

second line ¾ inch above the first line. These guidelines mark the position of the middle shelf.

Cut two 7⅞-inch pieces and one 15½-inch piece of ½-inch wood dowel. Apply carpenters' glue to both ends of one short dowel, and stand it in the forward hole of the bottom lip. Apply glue to the edge of the middle shelf, and set it into place on the guidelines drawn on the side of the box. Drive four 6-penny finishing nails into the shelf edge from inside the box.

Apply a few drops of glue to the rear hole in the bottom lip, and slide the long dowel through the rear hole in the middle shelf into the hole in the bottom lip. Apply glue to the top end of the long dowel, and to both ends of the remaining short dowel. Stand the short dowel in the forward hole of the middle shelf, and insert the tops of both dowels into the holes in the underside of the top

shelf. Align the top shelf flush with the top edge and back of the box, and apply glue to this edge of the shelf. Drive three 6-penny finishing nails into the top shelf from inside the box.

Carefully drill a $1/16$-inch hole into the edge of the shelf and through the dowels at each dowel insertion point. These holes should be horizontal, centered on the vertical centerline of the dowel, and spaced ¼ inch down from the upper shelf surfaces or ¼ inch up from the lower surfaces. Drive a 3-penny finishing nail into each hole to pin the dowels into place.

With a miter box and backsaw, cut and fit strips of shelf-edge molding to cover the side and forward edges of the two upper shelves, and the side edge of the bottom lip. Apply a bead of glue to the back of the molding, and secure the molding with ¾-inch brads.

Measure and cut a 21 × 39-inch

piece of ¾-inch plywood for the wood-box cover. Position one leaf of a 3-foot piano hinge, centered lengthwise, along the rear edge of the cover on the underside, with the hinge barrel to the outside. Use the hinge as a template to mark hole locations for the hinge screws. Drill pilot holes for the screws, and secure the hinge with the screws provided.

Stand the cover up on the rear top edge of the box, align the cover and the second hinge leaf, and mark the locations for screws. Drill pilot holes, and secure the hinge by driving the screws down into the edge of the woodbox. If desired, the hinge can be mortised into the box. Cut a narrow strip out of the upper edge of the back of the box, equal to the length of the hinge and the thickness of both leaves in folded position. This will allow the cover to lie perfectly flat.

With the cover down, trim and fit a piece of foam padding to the cover, to make the seat cushion; use an electric carving knife or a large scissors. Apply dabs of silicone adhesive at random over the cover of the box, and press the foam into place. Let the adhesive dry for about 4 hours.

When the adhesive is dry, cut a piece of upholstery material to fit over the foam pad, compressing it slightly and rounding the squared upper edges of the foam, to cover all exposed edges of the cover with an extra ¾ inch on all sides. Starting at the front edge of the cover, fold the material under ¾ inch; align and stretch the material taut, and secure it to the front edge of the cover with decorative upholstery nails. Then stretch the material taut across the foam pad to the rear edge of the cover, again folding under a ¾-inch strip of material, and secure it to the rear edge. Finally, stretch the material down taut on each side, folding the corners to

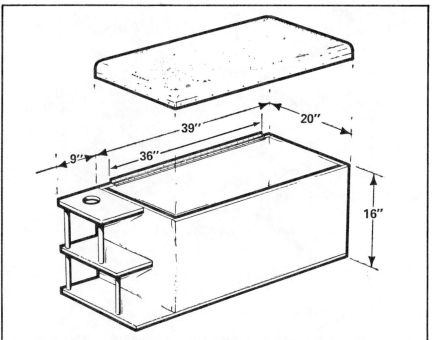

Attach the top of the woodbox with a 3-foot piano hinge; if desired, mortise the hinge into the box. Fit a piece of foam padding to the cover to make a seat cushion, and cover the padding with upholstery material, secured with decorative upholstery nails.

miter them neatly and folding the edges under; secure it with tacks.

To finish the woodbox, remove the cover from the box. With a nail set and hammer, drive all visible nailheads slightly below the surface of the wood. Fill all nail holes, and any imperfections in the joints or wood, with wood filler; sand the woodbox smooth. Finish the interior of the woodbox with one coat of primer or stain; it need not be fully finished. Finish the outside of the woodbox as desired.

Make an Open-Box Room Divider

Open boxes stacked to create a wall make an inexpensive and very versatile room divider. Once the divider is built, you can rearrange, add, or subtract

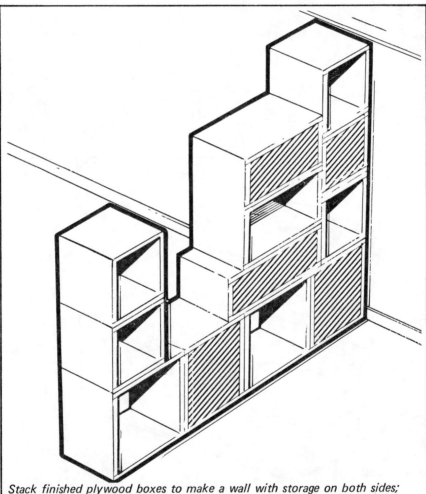

Stack finished plywood boxes to make a wall with storage on both sides; use larger boxes at the bottom, smaller ones near the top. For heavy loads, add a back panel to each box. Small walls don't need reinforcement; screw the boxes together in large walls.

boxes to adjust the storage space or fit a different room. **Tools:** measuring rule, pencil, straightedge, carpenters' square, handsaw or power saw, hammer, nail set, putty knife, sanding block or belt sander, paintbrush, drill, screwdriver. **Materials:** graph paper, ¾-inch grade A-B interior plywood, carpenters' glue, 8-penny finishing nails, plastic wood, spackling compound; coarse-, medium-, and fine-grit sandpaper or sanding belts; paint or stain, 1¼-inch #8 flathead wood screws. **Time:** ½ to 1 hour per box.

Plan your divider wall carefully. Measure the area the wall will cover and draw the wall to scale on graph paper, calculating box sizes exactly. For increased stability, use fairly large and long boxes along the bottom of the divider; use smaller boxes, if you want them, at the top. Don't make the difference in depth between boxes so great that it makes stacking difficult or diminishes the usefulness of the boxes. As you plan, remember that the depth of the shortest box will be the minimum thickness of the wall. All box sides don't have to be butted up against other box sides; you can plan spaces between boxes too.

Make the boxes of ¾-inch grade A-B interior plywood; calculate how many 4 × 8-foot sheets of plywood you'll need, and plan your cutting to make the best use of the wood. Start building with the bottom row of boxes and work up the divider row by row. Set the boxes into place as you complete them; measure them and adjust your plan as necessary. Because slight size differences can add up to a significant difference overall, you may have to custom-fit the top row of boxes at the ceiling.

To make each box, measure and mark a square or rectangle for each side of the box; use a straightedge and a carpenters' square to make sure the sides are even. Be sure to allow for the width of the saw blade; cut the sides for one box and assemble the box before cutting the sides for the next box. Use a handsaw or a power saw to cut the sides.

Join the sides of the box with simple butt joints, with the edge of one side butted firmly against the face of the other. Apply a bead of carpenters' glue to the butted end and press the two pieces firmly together; hold them in place and secure the joints with 8-penny finishing nails set about every 2 inches.

If you don't plan to use the divider for heavy things, you can leave the boxes completely open. If you plan to store books, records, or anything similar in the divider, add a back panel to each box. Measure and cut a piece of plywood to the inside size of the open box; apply a bead of carpenters' glue to the edges of the back and set it into the open frame, flush with the back edge. Nail it into place with 8-penny finishing nails. Let the glue dry as directed by the manufacturer.

To finish the box, sink the nailheads with a nail set and cover them with

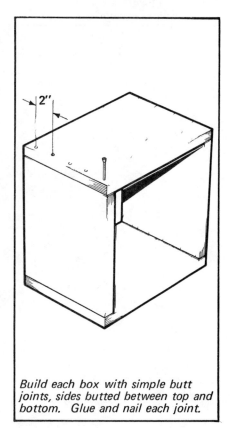

Build each box with simple butt joints, sides butted between top and bottom. Glue and nail each joint.

FURNITURE/Room Divider

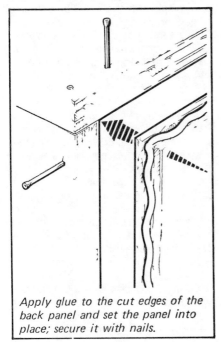

Apply glue to the cut edges of the back panel and set the panel into place; secure it with nails.

plastic wood. Sand the raw edges of the box with coarse-, medium-, and then fine-grit sandpaper, using a sanding block or a belt sander. If the boxes will be painted, an easier alternative is to smooth the cut edges with spackling compound; let the compound dry completely, as directed, and sand the edges smooth. Don't paint or stain the box until the entire wall is completed.

Fit the boxes together as you work until the wall is completely assembled. When you're satisfied with the fit of the wall, take the boxes down, and sand or paint as desired. Let the boxes dry completely, as directed, and then reassemble the wall. For extra stability, fasten the boxes together with 1¼-inch #8 flathead wood screws; drill screw holes near each corner of the side of one box and then screw the box firmly to the side of the next box. This fastening isn't necessary with small divider walls, but it's a good idea to screw large walls together.

Kitchen

Laminate a Countertop

Covering a kitchen counter or a vanity with plastic laminate is painstaking, but not really demanding. With care and patience, you can lay a plastic laminate sheet on any clean, well-supported ¾-inch plywood or particle board base. **Tools:** measuring rule, hammer, nail set, putty knife, belt sander, pencil, straightedge, carpenters' square, safety goggles; saber, circular, or table saw with fine-toothed carbide-tipped blade; nylon paintbrush or notched spreader, roller or rolling pin, router with edge-trimming bit for plastic laminates, fine-toothed flat file. **Materials:** plastic wood or wood putty; medium- and medium-fine-grit sanding belts, rags, tack cloth, precut plastic laminate edge strips, sheet plastic laminate, nonflammable contact cement, brown paper or wax paper, solvent for cement. **Time:** about 4 to 6 hours for a plain countertop.

Buy a sheet of plastic laminate big enough to cover the countertop completely, with a slight overhang on all sides; buy precut laminate edge strips to finish the sides of the countertop. Choose a nonflammable, water-solvent contact cement, or use the adhesive recommended by the laminate manufacturer. Rent a router with an edge-trimming bit for plastic laminates; if you don't have one, rent a saber or circular saw with a fine-toothed carbide-tipped blade. At least 48 hours ahead of time, set the plastic laminate in the room where it will be used to bring it to the correct temperature and humidity.

Prepare the counter surface carefully. Sink any protruding nails with a hammer and a nail set; fill cracks and cover nailheads with plastic wood or wood putty. Sand the surface with a belt sander and a medium-grit sanding belt to smooth and level it thoroughly. If you're covering an old countertop, remove the old finish completely; sand down to clean, bare wood to provide a good base for the laminate. Wipe off all dust and sanding debris and then go over the entire counter surface with a tack cloth.

Carefully measure and mark the sheet of plastic laminate to the approximate size of the countertop; it should be large enough to overhang the counter ⅛ to ¼ inch on all sides. Use a carpenters' square and a straightedge to make sure the marks are accurate. Plastic laminates are very brittle; wear safety goggles to trim the laminate sheet. Support the laminate sheet firmly as close to the cutting line as possible; hold it down firmly to prevent shattering and chipping. Carefully and slowly cut the sheet as marked with a saber saw, a circular saw, or a table saw with a fine-toothed carbide-tipped blade. Cut the laminate face down with a saber saw or circular saw, face up with a table saw.

Before laying the top sheet, cover the edges of the countertop with precut laminate edge strips, carefully butted together at the corners. Measure and cut the front and side edge strips to the correct length. Apply contact cement to the back of each edge strip and to the edges of the countertop as directed by the manufacturer, using a nylon paintbrush or a notched spreader. Let the adhesive cure and test for bonding readiness as directed.

Carefully press each edge strip into place over the cemented counter edge, first side strips and then front. The bottom of the strip should be flush with the bottom of the edge; let the top of the edge strip stick up above the coun-

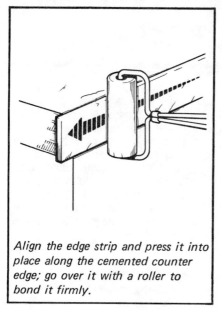

Align the edge strip and press it into place along the cemented counter edge; go over it with a roller to bond it firmly.

cemented surface is covered. The paper will not stick to the cemented surface.

Set the laminate sheet carefully into place on the countertop; make sure you don't disarrange the paper. Align the laminate sheet exactly on the countertop, butted firmly against the wall behind the counter, if any, and overhanging the counter slightly on all open sides. Keeping the laminate exactly in position, carefully slide out the brown paper or wax paper strips along the counter, pressing the laminate to bond it in place as you go; be careful not to let air bubbles form between the laminate and the countertop. If the countertop is a long one, you'll need an assistant to hold the laminate in place as you remove the paper.

To bond the sheet of laminate firmly and evenly in place, go over the entire counter surface with a roller or a rolling pin. Be sure to press out any air bubbles left between the laminate and the countertop.

To complete the countertop, carefully

tertop. You must align the edge strip perfectly as you press it down; once it makes contact with the cemented edge, it can't be moved. Butt the strips firmly together at the corners of the counter, front strip over sides. After applying each strip, go over it firmly with a roller or a rolling pin to bond it firmly to the counter edge.

Wearing safety goggles, trim the protruding upper edges of the edge strips with a router and an edge-trimming bit for plastic laminates. With a belt sander and a medium-fine-grit sanding belt, sand the cut edges carefully to bring them exactly flush with the counter surface. If the edge strip sticks up only a little, router trimming is unnecessary; use the belt sander to bring the edges flush. Use a fine-toothed flat file to smooth the edge in tight spots.

Wipe the countertop clean and go over it with a tack cloth. Following the manufacturer's instructions, apply contact cement to the entire counter surface and to the entire back of the laminate sheet; let the adhesive cure as directed. When the cement is dry, cover the entire countertop surface with brown paper or sheets of wax paper, laid back to front; make sure all the

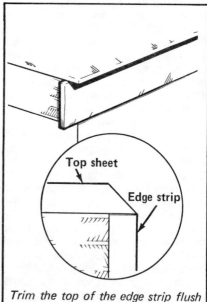

Trim the top of the edge strip flush with the countertop; then lay the top sheet. File the cut top edge to a bevel.

trim off the overhanging laminate edges with a router and an edge-trimming bit for plastic laminates; wear safety goggles as you work. Use a fine-toothed flat file to trim tight spots. Trim the edge of the top laminate sheet exactly flush with the outside face of the edge strip. Finally, bevel the cut edge of the top sheet slightly with a fine-toothed flat file.

Remove excess cement from the completed counter with water or the cement solvent; use water or solvent sparingly so it doesn't seep into the joints of the countertop. Scrape off large blobs of cement with a scrap of laminate; do *not* use a metal scraper. Clean the countertop according to the manufacturer's instructions.

Build a Pantry Behind a Door

Kitchen storage space is always at a premium, but there is potential storage behind every closed door—build this simple behind-the-door pantry to take advantage of it. **Tools:** measuring rule, pencil, carpenters' square, handsaw or power saw, drill, countersink, screwdriver, hammer, sanding block, paintbrush. **Materials:** 1 × 4 and 1 × 2 pine stock, 1-inch flathead wood screws, carpenters' glue, 7-penny finishing nails, medium- and fine-grit sandpaper, paint, 2-inch angle irons. **Time:** 4 to 6 hours, plus finishing time.

The dimensions used here are for a pantry unit 21½ inches wide and 60 inches high, with four inside shelves. You can adjust these figures for a unit to fit a wide or narrow door, for any height desired. Keep the outside width of the unit at least 7 inches narrower than the door, to allow for the doorknob and provide the necessary clearance when the door is opened and closed.

Build the frame for the pantry of 1 × 4 pine stock. Measure and mark two pieces of 1 × 4 60 inches long and six pieces 20 inches long; use a carpenters' square to keep the ends even. Cut the pieces of 1 × 4 with a handsaw or a power saw.

Put together a rectangular box from the two 60-inch pieces and two of the 20-inch pieces, with the long sides butted over the ends of the short sides at the corners. At each corner, drill two holes for 1-inch flathead wood screws through the face of the long side piece; countersink the screw holes so that the screw heads will lie flush with the surface of the wood. Set the side piece into position over the edge of the cross piece, mark the screw holes, and drill holes into the edge of the cross piece. Apply a bead of carpenters' glue to the cut edge of the cross piece and to the end of the side piece, join the pieces, and secure the corner with two 1-inch flathead wood screws driven through the drilled holes.

Cut retaining strips and shelf supports from 1 × 2 pine stock. Measure, mark, and cut six pieces of 1 × 2 21½ inches long to hold stored goods on the shelves; measure and cut eight pieces of 1 × 2 3½ inches long for shelf supports. Plan the spacing for the pantry shelves, with tall things on the bottom and four shelves spaced as desired inside the frame. Measure the things you plan to store in the unit to determine the desired shelf spacing—a good spacing might allow 10 inches between the top of the frame and the first shelf, 10 inches from first to second and second to third, 12 inches from third to fourth, and 18 inches from the fourth shelf to the bottom of the frame. Or, if you don't need such widely spaced shelves, add a shelf to this basic unit.

To make the shelves, measure down from the top of the frame along each side piece and mark the shelf positions—make sure you measure exactly the same on each side. The marked shelf positions do not allow for the thickness of the wood; measure ⅜ inch down from each marked line to mark the tops of the shelf support pieces. Set a 3½-inch 1 × 2 shelf support piece at each marked shelf point, on each 1 × 4 side piece. To secure the shelf supports, use 7-penny finishing nails and carpenters' glue. Apply a

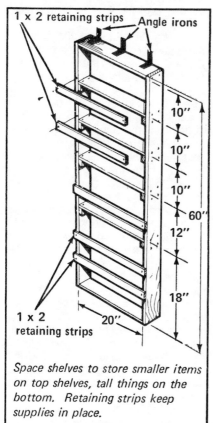

1 x 2 retaining strips — *Angle irons*

10"

10"

10"

60"

12"

18"

1 x 2 retaining strips — 20"

Space shelves to store smaller items on top shelves, tall things on the bottom. Retaining strips keep supplies in place.

into the support and two nails from the outside of the frame into the shelf edge. Stagger the nails so they don't hit against each other.

To complete the shelf unit, nail 1 × 2 retaining strips across the front of the unit, one strip 2 inches above each shelf. Secure the retaining strips with two 7-penny finishing nails driven through each end. To keep tall things in place on the bottom of the unit, nail two retaining strips across the open area, placed as desired.

To complete the pantry, sand all rough spots and edges with medium- and then fine-grit sandpaper. Paint as desired.

Finally, hang the pantry unit on the door, centered on the door's width and set conveniently on its height. Use three 2-inch angle irons across the top of the unit and three across the bottom; mark the screw holes, and drill, and countersink. Fasten the irons to the door with 1-inch flathead wood screws. If the door is a hollow-core type, be careful to attach the unit to the solid blocking inside the door—tap on the door to locate the blocking. Hollow-core doors are blocked around the edges, and sometimes also have other blocking. Mark and drill the mounting holes on the top and bottom pieces of the pantry unit, set the unit into place, and secure it with screws driven into the drilled holes.

Build a Roll-Out Storage Shelf

For more convenient access to pans or small appliances, build this handy roll-out shelf unit into a base cabinet. **Tools:** measuring rule, pencil, carpenters' square, straightedge, handsaw or power saw, hammer, screwdriver, nail set, paintbrush. **Materials:** ¾-inch grade A-B interior plywood, 1 × 2 and 1 × 3 pine stock, carpenters' glue, 4-penny finishing nails, two standard 22-inch-long drawer slide assemblies with installation screws, wood filler,

bead of carpenters' glue to the face of each shelf support and to the face of the side frame piece, as marked. Set the support flat against the frame, with its top edge exactly flush with the marked support line, and nail through the outside face of the side piece into the face of the 1 × 2 support bracket. Drive two 7-penny finishing nails into each shelf support.

Use the remaining pieces of 20-inch 1 × 4 to make the pantry's four shelves. For each shelf, apply a bead of carpenters' glue to the bottom edges of the board's cut ends, and to the top edge of the two shelf brackets that will support it. Set the shelf into place across the two brackets, and make sure it's straight and flush against the supports. Secure each end with two 7-penny finishing nails from the top of the shelf sandpaper, primer and semigloss interior latex paint, or finish desired. **Time:** about 4 to 6 hours, plus finishing time.

To fit a standard 18 × 24-inch base cabinet, measure and cut a 13¼ × 21¼-inch piece of ¾-inch grade A-B interior plywood for the roll-out shelf. Cut a 13¼-inch piece of 1 × 2 pine stock. Apply a bead of carpenters' glue to one 13¼-inch edge of the shelf, and set the 2-inch face of the 1 × 2 strip against the edge, flush at the bottom and at each end. Secure the strip with four 4-penny finishing nails.

Cut two 22-inch pieces of 1 × 2. Apply glue to the side edges of the shelf. Set the two strips against the edges, flush at the bottom and at each end, and secure each strip with six 4-penny finishing nails.

Cut a 14¾-inch piece of 1 × 3 pine stock. Turn the shelf assembly upside down, and apply glue to the remaining 13¼-inch edge of the shelf. Set the 1 × 3 strip against the edge so that the ends are flush, the top edges are flush, and the bottom edge protrudes 1 inch

below the bottom surface of the shelf.

With the shelf still upside down, draw two lines across the bottom surface from front to back, each 1¼ inches in from the side. Center the upper half of a standard 22-inch-long drawer slide assembly on each guideline, and attach the slides with the screws provided. Installation instructions for drawer slides vary from brand to brand; follow the manufacturer's specific installation instructions.

Determine and mark the front-to-back centerline of the cabinet's existing shelf, by measuring the *exact* distance between the sides of the door opening and marking the midway point. Measure 6⅛ inches to both right and left of the centerline mark, along the front edge of the shelf. With a carpenters' square and a pencil, draw front-to-back lines at right angles to the shelf edge at each of these points. Center the bottom half of one drawer slide assembly on each of these guidelines, and attach the slides with the screws provided.

Mesh the slides and roll the new shelf into place in the cabinet, checking for

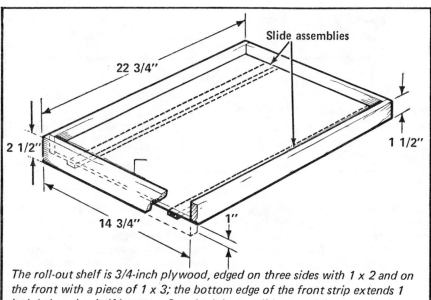

The roll-out shelf is 3/4-inch plywood, edged on three sides with 1 x 2 and on the front with a piece of 1 x 3; the bottom edge of the front strip extends 1 inch below the shelf bottom. Standard drawer slide assemblies are used to move the shelf.

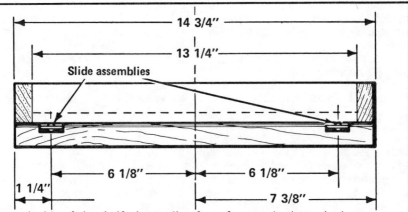

On each side of the shelf, draw a line from front to back on the bottom surface, 1 1/4 inches in from the side. Center the upper half of a 22-inch drawer slide assembly over each guideline, and attach the slides securely.

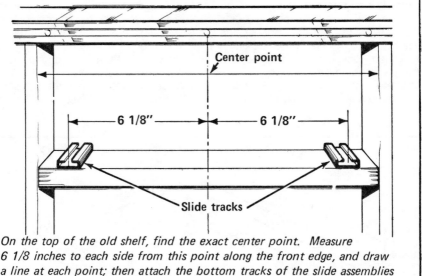

On the top of the old shelf, find the exact center point. Measure 6 1/8 inches to each side from this point along the front edge, and draw a line at each point; then attach the bottom tracks of the slide assemblies over the guidelines.

ease of operation; there should be ⅛ inch clearance between the side of the door opening and the shelf side, at each side. The cabinet door must be able to open far enough so that it leaves the cabinet opening completely clear and does not obstruct the passage of the new shelf. Make any slide adjustments necessary for smooth operation.

Remove the roll-out shelf and remove the slide halves. With a nail set and hammer, sink the nailheads slightly below the surface of the wood. Fill the nail holes and any surface or joint imperfections with wood filler, and sand the shelf smooth.

To finish the shelf, apply a coat of primer and then two coats of semigloss interior latex paint, or whatever finish you like. Let the finish dry completely between coats. Apply at least one coat of finish to the bottom of the shelf to seal the wood.

When the finish is completely dry, replace the slide halves and install the shelf in the cabinet.

Build a Soffit Cabinet

A lot of good storage space may be going to waste over the tops of the wall cabinets in your kitchen. It's easy to enclose this space with soffit cabinets. **Tools:** hammer, crosscut saw, hacksaw, measuring rule, square, level, screwdriver, plumb, brace and ¼-inch bit, caulking gun, block plane, paintbrush. **Materials:** ¼-inch tempered hardboard and/or ¼-inch hardwood-faced plywood, 1 × 4 clear pine stock, self-tapping machine screws, aluminum sliding door tracks, 10-penny and 16-penny finishing nails, toggle bolts, construction adhesive, track screws, cedar shingle shims, medium-grit sandpaper, door hardware; paint, stain, or varnish; dropcloths, cloths. **Time:** about 2 days.

The tops of the kitchen cabinets form the base for the soffit cabinets; the ceiling forms the top and the wall forms the back of the cabinet. Building a soffit cabinet is simply installing a series of sliding doors along the fronts of the wall cabinets to form the soffit storage space.

Measure, cut, and nail a length of ¼-inch tempered hardboard to the tops of the kitchen wall cabinets. Drill pilot holes in the hardboard for the nails, which are driven into the front and back rails of the kitchen cabinets. Tack the hardboard into place; there's no need to spike it for strength. If the cabinets below are steel, use self-tapping machine screws instead of nails. The hardboard forms the base of the soffit cabinet.

Measure, cut, and nail a 1 × 4 clear

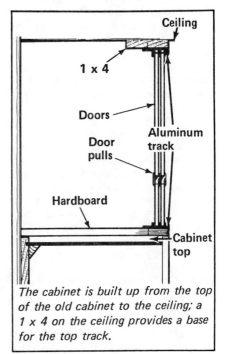

The cabinet is built up from the top of the old cabinet to the ceiling; a 1 x 4 on the ceiling provides a base for the top track.

pine board (grade B or better) to the ceiling, directly above the front edge of the cabinets. Use a square and level to make sure the board is in alignment and parallel to the cabinet fronts. Nail the board to the ceiling joists through the ceiling wall covering, if possible. Otherwise, fasten the board to the ceiling with toggle bolts, countersinking the bolt heads below the surface of the wood. Shim the board slightly with cedar shingles to fill any low spots.

Measure, cut, and install the aluminum sliding door track to the hardboard along the front edges of the wall cabinets. Use construction adhesive to fasten the track to the hardboard. The sliding door track—as well as the hardboard—must be flush with the front of the cabinet. Now measure, cut, and install the aluminum track on the ceiling 1 × 4, directly above the bottom track. Before securing the top track, make sure the tracks are in alignment. To get perfect alignment, insert a scrap piece of hardboard in the tracks. Then plumb (vertically level) the hardboard, moving the top track as necessary. When the hardboard is plumb, mark the position of the upper track. Screw and glue the track to the 1 × 4.

The doors of the soffit cabinet are constructed of either ¼-inch tempered hardboard or hardwood-faced plywood with a C-grade back. Use plywood if you want to stain the wood; use hardboard if the wood will be painted.

To determine the height of the sliding doors, measure the distance between the slots of the bottom track and the slots of the top track; subtract ¼ inch from this measurement. To determine the length of the doors, measure the distance between the sides of the cabinet and divide by the number of doors to be used; add 1 inch to each door measurement for overlapping purposes. Cut the doors according to these measurements.

To determine the dimensions of the cabinet's sides, measure the height and width of the opening on the side—if an adjacent wall won't form the side—and cut plywood to this measurement.

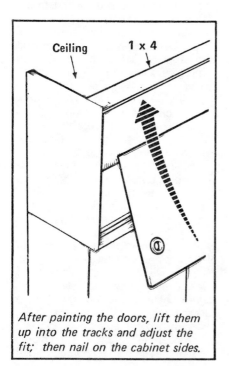

After painting the doors, lift them up into the tracks and adjust the fit; then nail on the cabinet sides.

Paint or stain the doors and sides and let them dry completely. When painting, seal both ends and edges of the doors and sides with paint to keep moisture out and prevent warping.

Complete the job by adding the door opening/closing hardware. Use either recessed door pulls or mounted hardware that complements the hardware on the cabinets below. To install recessed door pulls, locate and drill a hole the diameter of the pull in the doors and insert the pulls. The pulls are friction-fit; push them in. To install flush-mounted hardware, locate and drill holes for the screws and attach the hardware to the doors from the back of the doors.

Place the doors into the slots and check them for fit. If they're too large, plane them to size, using a block plane, plane carefully, removing only a little wood. Install the doors and nail on cabinet sides, if necessary.

Custom-Make a Spice Rack

Even if you search long and hard, you may never be able to find a spice rack to suit you. This rack is both easy to make and inexpensive. **Tools:** measuring rule, pencil, straightedge, carpenters' square, handsaw or saber saw, drill with ¼-inch bit, hammer, nail set, screwdriver, paintbrush. **Materials:** ⅜-inch grade A-B or furniture-grade plywood, piece of ¼-inch dowel, hide glue, 1-inch brads, small brass hangers, plastic wood, medium- and fine-grit sandpaper, stain or paint. **Time:** 1 to 1½ hours, plus finishing time.

Plan the spice rack to fit your containers—standard spice cans are 2½ inches deep, and an 18-inch rack holds 12 standard cans. Line up the tins or bottles you want to display and measure them for the length, height, and depth the rack should be. Use ⅜-inch grade A-B or furniture-grade plywood for a professional finish.

To make the rack, use your measured dimensions. Measure and mark the bottom panel on a piece of plywood, with the grain running the length of the shelf; use a carpenters' square and a straightedge to keep your marks even. Cut the panel out carefully with a handsaw or a saber saw. Measure and mark the two side pieces of the rack, exactly as wide as the bottom piece and high enough to accommodate the spice containers, either square or rectangular. Cut the side pieces carefully, making sure that their corners are square and that the two pieces are exactly alike.

Drill a ¼-inch hole at one corner of one of the side pieces, evenly spaced from the two sides of the corner. Set this piece on top of the other side piece and use it as a template to mark a matching hole. Carefully drill a ¼-inch hole through the second side piece so that it exactly matches the first one. The corners with the drilled holes are the top front corners of the side pieces.

Measure and mark a plywood back panel ¼ inch longer than the bottom piece and 3 to 5 inches higher than the side pieces; cut it out carefully. With the back panel laid flat, butt the back edge of one side piece against one side of the back panel, with the bottom edge of the side piece flush with the bottom edge of the back. Carefully outline the back edge of the side piece on the back panel; this outlined area will be cut out so that the side piece fits smoothly into the side of the back piece. Repeat this procedure to outline the other side piece on the back. Then, being careful to cut within the traced outlines, cut out the marked corners of the back piece. Finally, measure and cut a piece of ¼-inch dowel to the exact length of the untrimmed top of the back piece.

To assemble the spice rack, apply hide glue to the cutout edges, on one notched side of the back panel. Fit a side piece into the notch, with the drilled hole at the opposite top corner and the edges of the side piece flush with the back face and bottom edge of the back panel. Secure the side piece with sev-

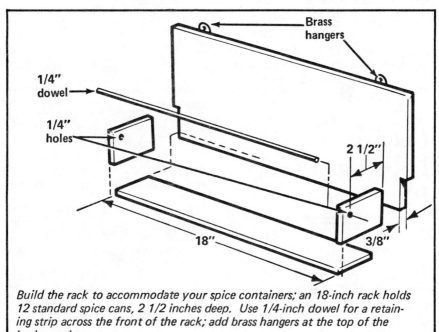

Build the rack to accommodate your spice containers; an 18-inch rack holds 12 standard spice cans, 2 1/2 inches deep. Use 1/4-inch dowel for a retaining strip across the front of the rack; add brass hangers at the top of the back panel.

eral 1-inch brads driven through the side and into the edge of the back panel; use a nail set to sink the heads of the brads below the surface of the wood.

Apply a drop or two of hide glue around one end of the dowel, on the turned surface and not on the cut end. Insert the glued end of the dowel into the hole in the side piece, pushing it from the inside out, so that the end of the dowel is flush with the outside face of the side piece. Apply a drop or two of hide glue to the other end of the dowel and insert it into the drilled hole in the unattached side piece, from the inside face out. Then, holding the dowel in place, quickly glue and nail the second side piece into place. Sink the nailheads with a nail set.

Apply hide glue sparingly to three cut edges of the bottom panel and slide it into place, butted firmly between the side pieces and against the back of the rack. Nail the bottom piece firmly into place with brads driven through the back into the edges of the side pieces and through the side pieces into the ends of the bottom piece.

To complete the rack, attach small brass hangers to the upper rear edge of the back with the screws provided. Fill nail holes and imperfections with plastic wood, and sand the rack as necessary with medium- and fine-grit sandpaper. Stain or paint the rack as desired.

Build a Food Processor Blade Rack

Food processor blades are sharp and unhandy to store, but building a rack for them is easy. Mount this blade rack on a convenient wall to hold the blades within your reach and out of the kids'. **Tools:** measuring rule, pencil, carpenters' square, handsaw, saber saw or coping saw, fine-toothed file, drill,

screwdriver, paintbrush, hammer. **Materials:** 1 × 3 pine stock, sandpaper, carpenters' glue, 2-inch #8 flathead wood screws, wood filler, stain or primer and finish as desired, picture hangers. **Time:** about 1 hour, plus finishing time.

This rack accommodates four food processor blades, but it can easily be adapted to hold fewer or more blades. Build it to suit your own blade storage requirements.

Measure and cut two 24-inch pieces of 1 × 3 pine stock for the front and back of the rack. Cut two 1-inch pieces of 1 × 3 for the sides.

Measure your food processor blades for the exact diameters of the blade shafts, so you can customize the rack slots to fit your blades. This rack holds two blades with shaft diameters slightly less than 1¾ inches, and two blades with diameters slightly less than 1 inch.

On one 24-inch 1 × 3, pencil the outlines for four 2-inch slots with their centerlines 3½, 9¼, 15, and 18½ inches from one end; make the two outer slots 1¾ inches wide, the two inner slots 1 inch wide. Or adjust the width of the slots to fit your processor's blades.

With a saber saw or a coping saw, cut out each slot. Round the ends of each slot with a fine-toothed file. Sand the slots smooth.

Butt the end of the back piece against one edge of a side piece, with the top and bottom edges even. Drill two $5/64$-inch pilot holes for screws completely through the back and side pieces, ½ inch from the top and bottom edges. Drill two more holes at the other end of the back piece and the other side piece.

Lay all four pieces on edge—the front piece with its slots facing up—with the side pieces butted between the front and back. Apply a bead of carpenters' glue along all joints. At each screw hole location, drive a 2-inch #8 flathead wood screw through the back, through the sides, and into the front piece.

Apply wood filler to any imperfections in the surface of the wood and the joints. After the filler dries, sand the

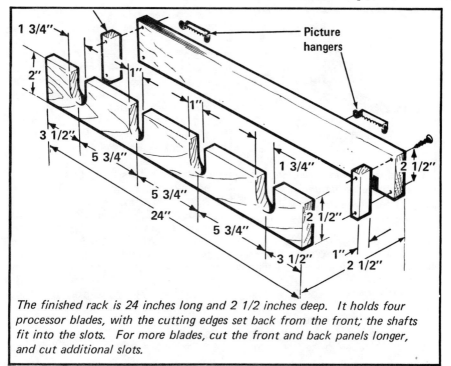

1 3/4"

2"

1"

Picture hangers

3 1/2"

5 3/4"

1"

1 3/4"

5 3/4"

24"

5 3/4"

2 1/2"

2 1/2"

3 1/2"

1"

2 1/2"

The finished rack is 24 inches long and 2 1/2 inches deep. It holds four processor blades, with the cutting edges set back from the front; the shafts fit into the slots. For more blades, cut the front and back panels longer, and cut additional slots.

entire rack smooth. Stain the blade rack or apply a coat of primer, as desired, followed by two coats of semigloss latex enamel. Let each finish coat dry thoroughly, as directed by the manufacturer.

To hang the rack, attach a picture hanger near each end of the back of the rack.

Tile a Countertop

With ceramic tile, you can turn any countertop or bar top into an elegant, heatproof, durable work surface. **Tools:** measuring rule, pencil, tile cutter, tile nippers, safety goggles, notched trowel, wood straightedge, carpenters' square, hammer, scrap plywood, thick towel, miter box and backsaw, nail set, mixing pan and stir stick, sponges; if desired, paintbrush. **Materials:** ceramic tiles, ceramic tile adhesive; if desired, wood molding, 3- or 4-penny finishing nails, wood filler, and sandpaper; tile grout, clean cloths; if desired, primer and interior latex paint; tile-and-grout sealer. **Time:** about 8 hours for a 2 × 10-foot countertop, plus curing and painting time.

Lay ceramic tile on any well-supported, ¾-inch-thick countertop; choose glazed tiles or mosaic tiles, or splurge on hand-painted ones. Buy extra tile to allow for breakage, and rent a tile cutter for trimming. You'll also need tile nippers. Buy tile grout as recommended by the tile manufacturer.

Before starting to work, arrange the tiles on the countertop to see how the tile pattern will work out. The starting point for laying tiles is up to you. Everything must line up square and even—the tiles should align with one another, with the back wall, and with the counter edges. If the tiles must be trimmed, cut them with a tile cutter; wear safety goggles to protect your eyes.

Clean the countertop and dry it thor-

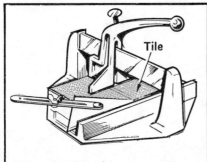

Tile

Trim edge tiles with a rented tile cutter; cut large tiles individually, small ones in full or partial sheets.

the countertop. A square is helpful in keeping the tiles on course. If necessary, use tile nippers to final-trim the tiles.

After all the tiles have been set, wrap a piece of scrap plywood, big enough to cover several tiles at once, in a thick towel. Place it on the tiles and tap gently with a hammer to bed the tiles in the adhesive, with their surfaces level with one another. Be careful not to crack the tiles.

After the tiles have been set and bedded, install wood molding, if desired, around the counter edges. Cut strips of molding to fit with a miter box and backsaw. Place the top edge of the molding flush with the surface of the tiles, and secure the molding to the countertop edges with 3- or 4-penny finishing nails. Sink the nailheads slightly below the surface of the molding with a nail set and hammer, and fill the holes with wood filler. Sand the molding smooth.

Remove excess adhesive from the

oughly. Apply ceramic tile adhesive to the entire counter surface with a notched trowel.

Set the trimmed tiles on the adhesive, working from your layout. If there's a straight wall in back of the counter, you can use it as a guide. Otherwise, tack a wood straightedge to the front edge of

After applying tile adhesive to the entire counter surface, set rows of tiles in place according to the planned layout. Work from the wall out; on corner areas, work out from the corner along both walls.

tile surfaces and joints. Let the adhesive cure for at least 24 hours, as recommended by the manufacturer.

When the adhesive is completely cured, mix grout according to the manufacturer's instructions. With a wet sponge, spread the grout onto the tile surface and work it into the tile joints. Wipe away excess grout with a damp sponge.

Let the grout dry until a whitish film appears on the tile; then carefully clean the tile with a clean, soft cloth. Smooth the grouted joints firmly with your finger to make them uniform. Then let the grout dry completely, as directed by the manufacturer.

To finish the countertop, apply a coat of primer and then two coats of interior latex paint to the wood molding. Let the paint dry and the grout cure fully, as directed by the manufacturer, before using the countertop. After about 2 weeks, treat the countertop with a silicone-based tile and grout sealer.

Install a Tile Backsplash

A ceramic tile backsplash, besides protecting the walls behind kitchen sinks, stoves, or countertops, or bathroom vanities, makes a beautiful accent to the room. Choose any tiles you like, plain or fancy. **Tools:** measuring rule, bucket and sponge, tile nippers, safety goggles, pencil, straightedge, level, notched trowel, mixing pan and stir stick, sponges, caulking gun. **Materials:** household detergent; if required, sealer; ceramic tiles, edging or cap tiles, ceramic tile adhesive, clean cloths, tile grout, silicone caulk. **Time:** about 4 to 5 hours.

Decide on the area the backsplash will cover, and plan the backsplash in full tiles. Buy glazed square tiles—a few handpainted ones can really spark the wall. For the top row of tiles, use full-size bullnose or edging tiles with rounded edges; or cap the top row of regular tiles with special quarter-round cap or stripe pieces. Buy a few extras to allow for breakage. Buy tile grout as recommended by the tile manufacturer.

Before starting to work, prepare the wall surface. Remove any wallpaper. Clean the wall with household detergent and remove any loose or flaking paint; roughen glossy surfaces with sandpaper, and fill any substantial cracks or holes. If the tile manufacturer recommends that a sealer be applied to the wall, apply the sealer as specified, and let it dry as directed by the manufacturer.

When the wall is prepared, measure and lay out the backsplash area. Measure the length and height of the area to be covered with tile; begin your height measurement 1/8 inch above the surface of the countertop. On a flat surface, make a test layout; lay vertical and horizontal rows of tiles, spaced correctly.

Plan the backsplash with full-size tiles only. If you must fit tiles around fixtures, use tile nippers to slowly cut the desired shapes; wear safety goggles to protect your eyes.

Double-check all measurements to be sure they're accurate, and transfer the exact layout to the wall with a pencil and straightedge. Work from the sink, stove, or counter edge up; use a level to keep your layout straight.

Apply ceramic tile adhesive to the lower area of the wall, using a notched trowel. Starting at one bottom corner, set the first horizontal row of tiles; space them correctly, following your penciled guidelines. Press each tile firmly to ensure a good bond. Apply more adhesive and set successive rows of tiles, adjusting and aligning them as you work and checking the spacing carefully. As you lay the tiles, clean off excess adhesive before it has a chance to cure. Finally, set the cap tiles into place.

When the entire backsplash area has been tiled, allow the adhesive to cure completely for at least 24 hours, as directed by the manufacturer. Make sure you don't let the tile get wet.

When the adhesive is completely cured, mix tile grout as directed by the manufacturer. With a wet sponge,

Starting at the bottom of the wall, set rows of tiles to build up the back-splash row by row. Spread adhesive for each row in turn; make sure each tile is properly aligned and firmly bonded. Place painted tiles as desired.

spread the grout onto the tile surface and work it into the tile joints. Wipe away excess grout with a damp sponge.

Let the grout dry until a whitish film appears on the tile; then carefully clean the tile with a clean, soft cloth. Smooth the grouted joints firmly with your finger to make them uniform. Then let the grout dry completely, as directed by the manufacturer.

When the grout has cured and the tile is thoroughly clean, seal the backsplash with a bead of silicone caulk along the joint between the countertop and the bottom row of tiles. Let the caulk dry completely before using the countertop.

Fix a
Sink Spray Hose

A kitchen sink spray hose assembly is no more complicated than a garden hose; repair or replacement is easy. **Tools:** awl or nail, basin wrench, adjustable wrench, pliers, sharp knife. **Materials:** depending on the problem; new sprayer assembly, spray head, packing washer, pipe thread tape. **Time:** about 1 hour.

Caution: Before you start working, turn off the water to the sink, either at the shutoff fixtures below the sink or at the main water shutoff for the house.

If the spray head isn't working, and the hose doesn't appear to be damaged, remove the spray head—usually by twisting it—and check for mineral deposits; sometimes these deposits block the flow of water through the sprayer nozzle. Remove the deposits with an awl or the end of a nail. Replace the spray head and flush it clean with fresh water.

If the old spray head leaks, remove the head and replace the packing washer. This washer is located between the end of the head and the coupling that connects the hose to the head.

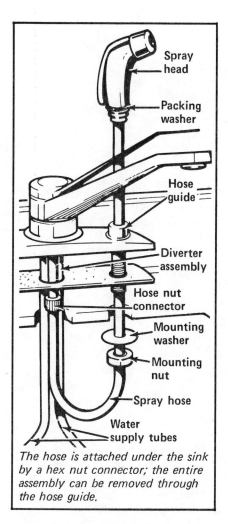

Spray head

Packing washer

Hose guide

Diverter assembly

Hose nut connector

Mounting washer

Mounting nut

Spray hose

Water supply tubes

The hose is attached under the sink by a hex nut connector; the entire assembly can be removed through the hose guide.

To install the replacement hose assembly, first remove the hose coupling from the diverter assembly under the faucet. The diverter, a simple pipe nipple that screws into the bottom of the faucet, is located between the supply lines under the sink. The sink hose is connected to the opposite end of the nipple.

With a sharp knife, cut the sink hose in half near the faucet connection. Remove the hose from the sink, pulling it up through the hose guide in the sink top. Then remove the hex nut connector from the pipe nipple below the diverter assembly of the faucet. Use a basin wrench to remove the hose connection on the diverter.

To install the new hose, remove the spray head from the new hose assembly. Thread the nozzle end of the hose up through the hose guide in the sink and replace the spray head. Under the sink, connect the hex nut to the diverter pipe and tighten it with a basin wrench. Turn on the water and test for leaks. If you find a leak in the hex nut connection, tighten the nut, but don't tighten it too much. The pipe is usually brass, and the threads won't take a lot of twisting pressure. If this doesn't stop the leak, remove the nut and wrap a layer or two of plastic pipe sealer tape around the threads of the diverter pipe. Then replace the nut and reconnect the hose.

If the head still doesn't work properly, replace it. Remove the old head, take it to a store that sells plumbing supplies, and buy a new head that matches the old one. The design isn't important, but make sure the threads of the new head match the threads of the old unit. Attach the new head to the hose with a wire snap (usually) and a coupling; make sure that the wire snap matches the groove in the end of the hose coupling and that the packing washer is in its proper position.

If the hose still doesn't work or if the hose under the sink is noticeably damaged, replace the entire assembly with a new one of the same type.

Replace a Kitchen Faucet

Replacing an obsolete or damaged kitchen faucet sounds complicated, but it isn't. **Tools:** measuring rule, two adjustable wrenches, basin wrench, putty knife, fine-toothed hacksaw. **Materials:** clean cloth; replacement faucet with spray hose, special adapters or transition fittings, and accessory copper tubing as required; plumbers' putty. **Time:** about 2 to 3 hours.

Before buying a new faucet, measure

KITCHEN/Replace a Faucet

the old one from handle center to handle center. If you're replacing a two-handle faucet with the single-lever type, you must buy a faucet with a base wide enough to completely cover the two holes of the old handles. Under the sink, examine the copper supply lines from the faucet to the water pipes, and the pipes themselves. When you buy the new faucet, tell the dealer exactly how the old one is connected, and buy any adapters, transition fittings, escutcheon plates, or extra copper tubing you'll need to connect the new one. The supply tubing may be attached to the new faucet or not; if not, it will probably be included with the faucet. Buy a faucet with a spray hose only if your sink has a hose opening.

Before starting work, turn off the water supply to the sink; close the shutoff valves under the sink or turn off the main water supply for the house. Turn the faucets on to drain the pipes and to make sure the water is off.

To remove the old faucet, disconnect the copper supply lines from the hot and cold faucet openings. Loosen the nuts and unscrew the fittings that connect them, using an adjustable wrench or a basin wrench. If the faucet is made so it is directly attached to the tubing, with no connecting nut and fitting, loosen the nut and unscrew the fitting at the bottom of the tubing, where it connects to the shutoff valve or to the water pipe. Pull the disconnected tubing free.

Next, loosen the nuts that hold the faucet to the sink, directly under the hot- and cold-water handles. Use a basin wrench to remove the nuts.

If the old faucet has a spray hose, remove the mounting nut that connects the hose to the faucet under the sink; if a separate nut holds the spray head base, remove this nut. Then hold the hose by the spray head and pull it out through its mounting hole.

Carefully remove the old faucet assembly. Clean the sink thoroughly where the new faucet will be mounted, and dry it with a clean cloth.

If the new faucet has a special base gasket that seals it to the top of the sink, place the gasket on the sink so that the

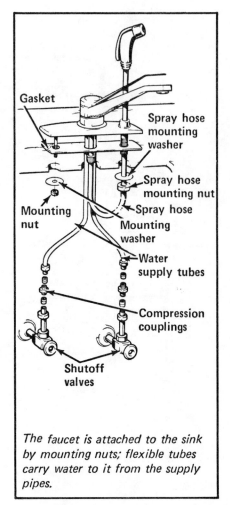

The faucet is attached to the sink by mounting nuts; flexible tubes carry water to it from the supply pipes.

holes line up with the openings. If your new faucet doesn't have a gasket, apply plumbers' putty to its base with a putty knife. Insert the new faucet assembly carefully and position it exactly on the sink.

If the new faucet has a spray hose, install the hose before you connect the faucet to the sink. If the hose includes a mounting rim for the hose opening in the sink, pry off the old cap and clean and dry the sink under it. Set the chrome mounting rim into the opening, slide the mounting washer onto the stud under the sink, and tighten the mounting nut to hold it in place. If the sink has a spray hose opening but the new faucet doesn't have a hose, cap the opening with a chrome escutcheon plate, held under the sink with a mounting nut.

Insert the connection end of the spray hose through its opening and connect it to the faucet under the sink, using an adjustable wrench to tighten the coupling nut. Then attach the faucet to the sink. On each side of the faucet under the sink, slide the mounting washer and nut into place on the faucet mounting stud. Hand-tighten the nuts and make sure the faucet and the gasket are correctly placed; then tighten the nuts with a basin wrench.

Finally, connect the water supply lines. If you're attaching the new faucet's supply tubing to the old faucet's copper tubing, line up the ends of the corresponding tubes and connect them with compression couplings; you'll probably be able to use the old couplings. Use one adjustable wrench to hold the fitting tight and another wrench to tighten the compression nut. If the old and new supply tubes together are too long, cut off the excess length from the old tubing before you connect the faucet; use a fine-toothed hacksaw to cut the tubing.

If the old faucet didn't have detachable supply lines, or if the new lines are long enough to reach the shutoff valves or (if there are no valves) the water pipes, connect the new tubing directly to the shutoff valves or pipes, using two wrenches to tighten the compression fittings. Remove old supply lines before attaching direct new lines; use adapters or transition fittings as necessary to connect the lines. If the new lines aren't long enough and there is no old tubing to connect to, add accessory copper tubing as necessary, with compression fittings.

To complete the job, turn on the water supply to the sink, full force. Check both tubing and faucet carefully for leaks. If there's any sign of a leak, turn off the water and inspect all connections to be sure they're tight and properly made, with special adapters as required. Correct any problems and turn the water on.

Sharpen Knives and Scissors

Even the best steel dulls eventually, and inexpensive knives and scissors are usually not too sharp to start with. Keep fine steels sharp and salvage dulled blades with periodic honing. **Tools:** whetstone, deep pan, fine-grit silicon carbide slipstone, sharpening steel, screwdriver or hammer. **Materials:** household or light machine oil, soft cloths, mineral spirits, box with lid or sealable plastic bag. **Time:** about 15 minutes to ½ hour.

Buy a whetstone with one coarse and one fine side. To prepare the stone for use, put it in a deep pan and cover it with household or light machine oil; let it soak overnight. Remove any dirt or loose particles with a soft cloth soaked in mineral spirits. Between uses, store the prepared whetstone in a box with a lid or a sealable plastic bag.

Knives. To sharpen a very dull knife, use first the coarse and then the fine side of the whetstone; to sharpen a blade in better shape, use only the fine side. Have badly chipped or serrated knives professionally sharpened.

Oil the surface of the whetstone lightly. If you can see the cutting bevel on the knife blade, keep the knife at this bevel as you work; otherwise, hold the knife with the blade at a 30-degree angle to the stone.

Holding the knife blade firmly at the bevel angle, push the full length of the blade gently but firmly away from you, at a diagonal across the stone. Lift the knife blade at the end of the stroke, turn the knife over, and repeat, stroking the blade away from yourself across the stone. Repeat, using alternating strokes on the two sides of the blade, for the same number of strokes on each side. These alternating strokes remove any tiny burrs caused by the sharpening. For very dull blades, follow this sharpening procedure on first the coarse side and then the fine side of the stone. Re-

Holding the knife at the angle of the cutting bevel, stroke it firmly across the stone. Sharpen both edges.

Sharpen carving knives with a fine-grit slipstone, making circular strokes along the edge at the cutting bevel.

move debris from the knife blade with a soft cloth.

To sharpen carving knives and other fine stainless steel blades, use a fine-grit silicon carbide slipstone instead of the whetstone. Holding the slipstone at the proper bevel angle to the knife blade, whet the cutting edge of the knife with tight circular passes of the stone. Whet both sides of the blade alternately to keep the cutting edge even.

To touch up the cutting edge of a carving knife, use a sharpening steel. With the blade of the knife away from you, pull the edge of the knife blade lightly down the length of the steel, stroking the entire length of the blade from handle to tip. Repeat on the other side of the knife blade. Stroke the sides of the blade alternately along the steel to produce the desired cutting edge; about six strokes per side is usually adequate.

Scissors. Sharpen scissors on a lightly oiled whetstone, maintaining the existing bevel on the outside edge of each blade. Unless a scissors is very dull, use only the fine side of the whetstone. Don't try to sharpen pinking shears; have them taken care of professionally.

Open the scissors wide, and set the

outside beveled face of one blade flat on the whetstone. Angle the blade back at a slight diagonal. Holding the scissors firmly, stroke the blade firmly but gently away from you, at a diagonal

With the scissors opened wide, firmly stroke the outside beveled face of each blade along the whetstone.

across the stone; stroke from handle to tip of the blade. Lift the scissors at the end of the stroke, and repeat, working only on the beveled side of the blade, to produce an even cutting edge. Wipe the blade clean with a soft cloth; then sharpen the other blade of the scissors the same way.

When both blades of the scissors have been sharpened, open and close the scissors once or twice. The blades of the scissors should touch lightly all along their cutting edges. If the blades are too tight against each other, slightly loosen the pivot screw that holds them together. If the blades are too loose, tighten the pivot screw. If the blades of the scissors are held together by a rivet instead of a pivot screw, tap the rivet lightly with a hammer to tighten the blades.

Mend China, Porcelain, and Glass

Careful assembly and clamping are the key to mending delicate objects. With patience and the right glue, you can repair even the most fragile china, porcelain, and glass. **Tools:** small mixing dish and stick; clamping supports—masking tape, pan filled with sand, clothespins, modeling clay, rubber bands, scrap wood and nails, or paraffin. **Materials:** clear epoxy glue, toothpicks, cotton swabs, acetone (nail polish remover). **Time:** 5 minutes or more, depending on damage.

Because you'll need time to fit broken pieces exactly together, quick-bonding glue should not be used for mending delicate pieces. Buy clear epoxy glue, sold in two parts, resin and hardener; mix only as much glue as you need. Epoxy dries completely waterproof.

Clamping. Before mixing the glue, prepare a clamp to hold the object together while the epoxy cures. Choose an appropriate method, as detailed

below, to achieve a secure set. Don't apply glue to the broken pieces until the clamp is prepared.

To hold a glued cup handle or the stem of a glass, gently wrap strips of masking tape around the cup or glass. Use at least two vertical strips to encircle a glass with a mended stem; keep the pressure on the strips even so the mended joint doesn't slip.

To hold a cracked or pieced plate or similar object, fill a pan with sand. Embed the uncracked portion of the plate in the sand, with the broken edges straight up so that the glued pieces will be held in place by gravity. If necessary, use clothespins to clamp large pieces in place. For a mended teapot, cup, or pitcher, nestle it into the sand as necessary to hold the glued pieces in place.

Modeling clay is an excellent clamping material. Mold lumps of clay to support mended cups, glasses, or other objects with the broken part up. The mended pieces will be held in place by their own weight. Or set a mended plate on edge in a drawer, and support its bottom edge with a base of modeling clay.

Use strips of masking tape to hold a mended wine glass; keep the pressure on the strips even so the stem doesn't slip.

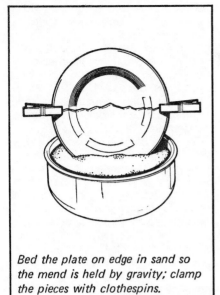

Bed the plate on edge in sand so the mend is held by gravity; clamp the pieces with clothespins.

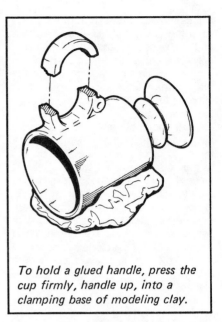

To hold a glued handle, press the cup firmly, handle up, into a clamping base of modeling clay.

Stretch rubber bands around a mended glass or cup; they should be tight enough to hold the pieces securely but not tight enough to stress the pieces. Or, to hold a flat or shallow object, use a piece of scrap board for a base. Set the mended object onto the board; at appropriate spots around it, mark points on the board. Remove the object and drive nails partway into the board at the marked points. Replace the object and stretch rubber bands from nail to nail over it to hold it in place.

Gluing. To mend the broken object,

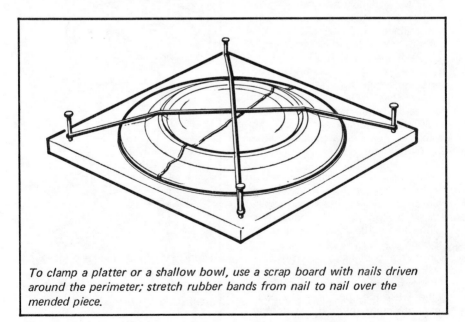

To clamp a platter or a shallow bowl, use a scrap board with nails driven around the perimeter; stretch rubber bands from nail to nail over the mended piece.

clean the pieces thoroughly and let them dry completely. Before mixing the glue, fit the broken pieces carefully together so you'll be able to reassemble them correctly. Lay the pieces out in order on your work surface.

In a small mixing dish, mix only as much glue as you'll need to reassemble the object; stir together equal parts of resin and hardener, as directed by the manufacturer. With a toothpick, apply a very thin coat of glue to the raw edges of one broken piece; carefully join it to the main piece. Press the pieces gently but firmly together. Remove excess glue with a cotton swab moistened with acetone (nail polish remover).

Repeat to glue all broken pieces to the main piece, applying glue and removing the excess piece by piece. If the object is broken into many pieces, work from the inside pieces out to reassemble the object. Be sure you're confident of the assembly procedure before you start gluing.

Finally, clamp and support the mended object securely, as detailed above. Let the epoxy cure as directed by the manufacturer; curing usually takes about 1 week for maximum strength. Don't unclamp the object until the full curing period has passed.

Rebuilding. If a plate, saucer, or platter is badly shattered, and you have another one like it, use the unbroken object to make a mold. In the top of a double boiler, carefully heat paraffin until it's soft or barely melted. Lightly oil the bottom of the unbroken object and pack softened paraffin over it, or set the object bottom up in a small deep pan and pour melted paraffin over it to cover the bottom completely. Let the paraffin set completely and remove the unbroken object.

To reassemble the broken object, apply glue as above and fit the broken pieces together inside the mold. If possible, work from the center of the object out and up. The wax mold will hold the pieces at the proper angle as you reassemble them. If desired, reassemble the object in several stages. Let the epoxy cure completely before removing the mended object.

Make Brass, Silver, and Copper Cleaner

Brass cleaner, silver cleaner, and copper cleaner—this inexpensive mixture does the job for all of them. **Equipment:** measuring cup, measuring spoons, mixing spoon, mixing bowl, small saucepan, small jar with lid. **Ingredients:** water, salt, oxalic acid, powdered pumice, turpentine, lard, tincture of green soap. Buy tincture of green soap at a pharmacy; buy oxalic acid at a hardware store. **Yield:** ¾ to 1 cup.

To ½ cup of hot tap water, add 1 teaspoon of salt and ½ tablespoon of oxalic acid. Stir to dissolve and pour the solution into a mixing bowl. *Caution: Oxalic acid is poisonous. Handle it carefully, and wash measuring and mixing containers thoroughly before using them again.*

Add 1 cup of powdered pumice to the solution and stir until smooth; add ½ teaspoon of turpentine and stir again. Melt 2 tablespoons of lard in a small saucepan and add it to the mixture with 2 tablespoons tincture of green soap. Beat briskly by hand to mix the oils into the paste completely. Spoon the cream into a small jar.

To use the cleaner, apply it with a clean cloth or sponge and rub gently; rinse with hot water and polish dry.

Make a Kitchen Apron

Cover-up aprons are cheerful, practical, and fun to wear; they're also great gifts. For a real bargain, make your own —this pattern fits most sizes. **Tools:** tape measure, scissors, tailors' chalk or pencil, straightedge, straight pins,

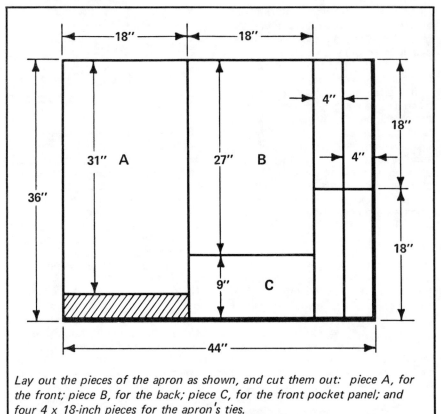

Lay out the pieces of the apron as shown, and cut them out: piece A, for the front; piece B, for the back; piece C, for the front pocket panel; and four 4 x 18-inch pieces for the apron's ties.

sewing machine, steam iron and ironing board. **Materials:** washable fabric, thread, double-fold bias tape. **Time:** 1 to 2 hours.

Fabric. To make an average-size apron, buy 1 yard of 44- or 45-inch-wide fabric; make sure it's washable. If you're making the apron for a larger-than-average person, buy 1½ yards of fabric. You'll also need 6 yards of double-fold bias tape, in a matching or contrasting color.

Assembly. Open the fabric and smooth it out. Measure it to lay out three main pieces and four small pieces, as illustrated, with the length of piece A along one selvage edge. For a smaller apron, make pieces A and B narrower. For a larger apron, make pieces A and B wider, as required; cut the four small pieces from the extra ½ yard of fabric. Mark the fabric carefully with tailors'

chalk or a pencil and a straightedge, and cut the pieces out.

Along one long side of piece C, make a line of machine stitching ⅛ inch from the raw edge. Cover the raw edge with double-fold bias tape, being careful not to stretch it; pin the tape into place and then machine-stitch it. If your sewing machine has a zigzag stitch, use it to stitch the tape on.

Lay piece C across one end of piece A, with the right side of piece C against the wrong side of piece A, to match the unfinished 18-inch ends. Pin the pieces together, and stitch them together ½ inch from the raw matched edges. Fold piece C over to the right side of piece A to form a long pocket at the bottom of piece A. Press the seam flat.

Pin the sides of piece C to piece A; match them carefully. Stitch piece C down to piece A on each side, ¼ inch

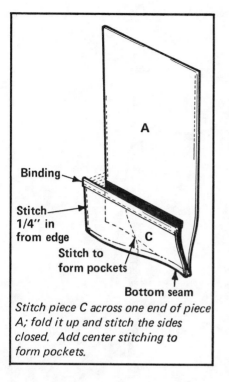

Stitch piece C across one end of piece A; fold it up and stitch the sides closed. Add center stitching to form pockets.

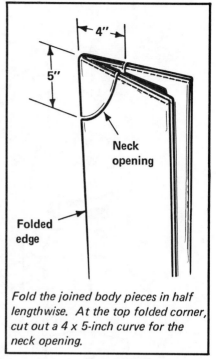

Fold the joined body pieces in half lengthwise. At the top folded corner, cut out a 4 x 5-inch curve for the neck opening.

from the matched edges. Make a line of stitching across the center of piece C to attach it to piece A in the middle of the pocket strip, forming two pockets; backstitch at the beginning and the end of each line of stitching. If desired, you can stitch piece C to form more than two pockets, or to make pockets of different sizes.

Lay pieces A and B together, right sides together, to match the top edges. Pin the top edges together and then stitch them together ½ inch from the raw edges; backstitch at the beginning and the end of the seam.

Leaving the joined pieces face to face, fold them in half lengthwise. In the corner formed by the folded edge and the stitched-together top edge, mark a curve for the apron's neck opening, 4 inches along the top from the fold and 5 inches along the fold from the top. Carefully cut out the marked-off curve; make sure you keep the layers of fabric even as you cut.

Open the apron and press the shoulder seams open. To finish the neck opening, make a line of machine stitching all around the opening, ⅛ inch from the raw edge. Cover the raw edge with double-fold bias tape, being careful not to stretch it; ease the tape carefully around the curves. Pin the tape into place and then stitch it down. If your sewing machine has a zigzag stitch, use it.

To finish the back of the apron, turn the bottom edge of piece B under 2 inches; press it and turn it under again 2 inches; press again and pin the hem into place. Machine-stitch the hem near the top edge. Finish the long sides of the apron, from the back all the way around to the front, with double-fold bias tape; no preliminary stitching is necessary.

To make ties for the apron, use the four small 4 × 18-inch pieces of fabric. For each tie, fold a strip of fabric in half lengthwise, right sides together, and stitch the long edge and one end together ½ inch from the edge; backstitch at each end of each seam. Clip the corners and turn the ties right side out.

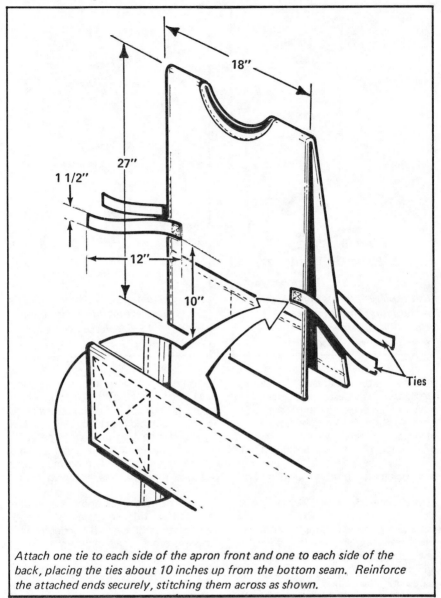

Attach one tie to each side of the apron front and one to each side of the back, placing the ties about 10 inches up from the bottom seam. Reinforce the attached ends securely, stitching them across as shown.

Press the seam edges flat. On the unfinished end of each tie, fold the raw edges under ½ inch and press them.

Pin the unfinished ends of the ties to the apron, one on each side of the front and one on each side of the back, about 10 inches up from the bottom edge of the apron. Overlap the ties about 2¼ inches onto the apron. Stitch each tie into place on the apron with a square of stitching ¼ inch from the edges; stitch across the open end, along the sides of the tie, and across the tie just inside the apron edge. Stitch an X across each open square. Backstitch to reinforce the tie stitching securely.

If desired, add trim, appliqué, or other decorations.

Make Pot Holders from Old Towels

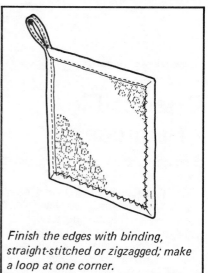

Finish the edges with binding, straight-stitched or zigzagged; make a loop at one corner.

To get the last mile of use from old towels and washcloths, turn them into pot holders. Your salvage will stand up better than most store-boughts. **Tools:** tape measure, straightedge, pencil, scissors, sewing machine, 8-inch plate, straight pins. **Materials:** worn towels or washcloths, scraps of cotton fabric, thread, prefolded bias tape. **Time:** ½ to 1 hour per pot holder.

Measure and cut squares from the good parts of worn towels—8 inches is a good size, but make them larger if you prefer. Use at least two squares for each pot holder; if the towels are very thin, use three or more squares. Use worn washcloths as is. For strictly utilitarian pot holders, leave the towel layers uncovered; for fancier ones, cut cover squares the same size from scraps or new pieces of cotton fabric.

For each pot holder, stack two or more towel squares together; set a square of cotton fabric on the top and one on the bottom, right sides out. Quilt the stacked layers together on a sewing machine, making parallel rows of straight stitching about 1 inch apart, all across the square. Turn the stitched-together square 90 degrees and quilt again at right angles to the first lines of stitching, forming an all-over quilted square pattern. Or, if desired, stitch diagonally to make quilted diamond shapes, or use any free-form pattern.

When the square is completely

Stack towel squares between squares of fabric; machine-quilt the layers together.

quilted, trim the edges as necessary; use a straightedge and a pencil to get them square. Or, if you want a round pot holder, center an 8-inch plate on the quilted square and trace around it; carefully cut off the marked corners.

Finish the edges of the pot holder with prefolded bias tape. Starting at a corner, place the slightly wider side of the bias tape along the bottom edge of the pot holder, and bring the narrower side up over the raw edges of the fabric. Carefully miter the tape at the corners of the pot holder or ease it around curves; make sure you don't stretch the tape around corners or curves. Pin or baste the tape into place as you go. At the end of the pot holder, leave 2½ inches of extra tape.

Beginning at the starting corner of the bias tape, stitch carefully over the folded-down bias tape, as close to the inside edge as possible. If your sewing machine has a zigzag stitch, use it. At the end of the pot holder, use the extra 2½ inches of bias tape to make a loop for hanging the holder. Continue your stitching with a straight stitch all along the extra tape; then double the tape back and stitch its end to the edge of the pot holder with back-and-forth stitches. The loop should lie at the corner of the pot holder.

Bath

Ceramic-Tile a Bathroom

For a beautiful, durable, and easy-to-maintain bathroom, ceramic tile is unsurpassed. Setting the tile is both painstaking and time-consuming, but it doesn't demand great skill. With care, you can do a professional-caliber job—at far less than the professional cost. **Tools:** measuring rule, putty knife or scraper, sanding block, long straight-edge, pencil, paintbrush; if required, hammer and power saw or handsaw; 3- or 4-foot-long piece of scrap wood, level, notched trowel, utility knife, tile cutter, tile nippers, safety goggles, whetstone, sponge, sponge trowel, scrap plywood, caulking gun, plastic dishpan, and stir stick; cloths, coarse towels. **Materials:** graph paper, spackling compound, coarse- and medium-grit sandpaper, wall primer; if required, 1/4-inch hardboard and 4- or 6-penny annular-ring nails; ceramic tile adhesive, ceramic tile and trim tiles, grout, silicone caulk, sheet plastic film, masking tape, rugs. **Time:** major project; after preparation, at least 10 to 12 hours for a bathtub area, or 8 to 10 hours for a floor; additional drying time required between steps.

Materials. Ceramic tile is available in two main types, for use on walls and on floors. Wall tiles are usually bigger; the most common size is 4 1/4 inches square. Floor tiles, called mosaic tiles, are thicker and smaller. Choose tile carefully to get the effect you want; you can use mosaic tile on walls, but you can't use wall tile on a floor. Tile the floor, the area around the tub, or the whole bathroom—the techniques are the same for a small area or the whole room.

Tile is sold in several forms: in individual units, in 1 × 1-foot or 1 × 2-foot sheets of ungrouted tile held together by paper or by plastic spacers, and in sheets of pregrouted tile. If it's available in the tile size and color you want, pre-grouted tile is the easiest type to install; it requires sealing only where sheets of tile meet. You'll also need special trim tiles, usually sold in 6-inch or 1-foot lengths, to finish the edges of the tiled surfaces—to cap wall tile where it stops partway up a wall; to edge wall bases; to trim corners; and, if you're using mosaic tile on all surfaces, to join wall and floor surfaces.

Choose the type and size of tile you want to use. Before you buy the tile, make a scale drawing on graph paper of the wall and floor surfaces to be tiled. For each wall, count the number of tiles needed each way, or calculate the number of tiles per square foot and multiply by the wall area to be covered; add 10 to 15 tiles to allow for breakage. For the floor, calculate the square footage to be covered and compute the number of sheets of tile needed; add one sheet of tiles to allow for breakage. Calculate the number of trim tiles you'll need—cap, base, inside or outside corner, wall-floor corner—along every edge of every surface; add a few tiles of each type to allow for breakage. The ceramic tile dealer can help you estimate, or can provide precise estimating instructions from the tile manufacturer.

To apply the tile, buy ceramic tile adhesive, as recommended by the tile manufacturer. Buy grout as recommended to finish the tile. Figure quantities for tile adhesive and grout from the manufacturer's instructions.

Preparation. Carefully prepare all surfaces to be tiled. If you're working over already ceramic-tiled walls, the tile must be sound and undamaged; if it's cracked or bulging, the tile must be removed and the wall prepared or rebuilt. If the walls are papered or covered with stick-on tiles, the paper or tiles must be removed and the wall surface thoroughly cleaned. If the walls are painted, the paint must be removed or abraded to provide a firm base for the tile.

To prepare the walls, remove old wall coverings and clean the walls as required. Scrape off loose paint with a putty knife or scraper. Fill all cracks and holes with spackling compound, and let the compound dry completely. If the walls are painted, sand them lightly with coarse-grit sandpaper to scratch the paint thoroughly.

The surface of the wall must be level, or the tile won't bond properly to it. To test each wall, hold a straightedge on edge and draw it along the wall. Mark low spots and high spots. Fill low spots sparingly with spackling compound. Sand high spots smooth with medium-

grit sandpaper. Then recheck the level and adjust as necessary. Finally, paint all newly patched areas with wall primer.

To prepare the floor, make sure it's level and smooth. If possible, remove the legs of the sink. If you're tiling over ceramic tile, the tile must be sound and unbroken. If the floor is wood, or resilient sheet or tile, it must be solid and smooth, with no open cracks and no loose edges. To prepare a warped or badly damaged floor, cover it completely with ¼-inch hardboard. Butt sheets of hardboard together, leaving $^1/_{32}$ inch between sheets, and nail them into place with 4- or 6-penny annular-ring nails. Stagger hardboard joints; set nails every 4 inches around each sheet.

Application. When both wall and floor surfaces are thoroughly prepared, you're ready to set the tile. To cut wall tiles to size as required, rent a tile cutter from the ceramic tile dealer. To cut mosaic tiles and to fit tiles around fix-

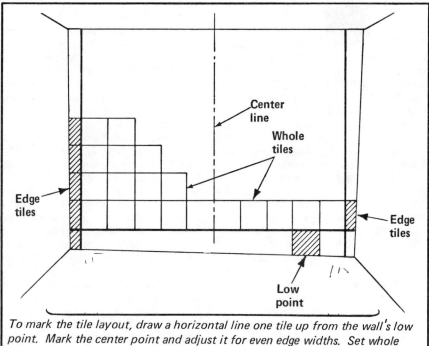

To mark the tile layout, draw a horizontal line one tile up from the wall's low point. Mark the center point and adjust it for even edge widths. Set whole tiles first, row by row, then edge tiles.

tures, buy tile nippers. You'll also need a notched trowel and a sponge trowel.

Tile the walls first. To make trimming easier, start working at the bathtub wall. Using a level, locate the low point of the top tub edge along the wall; mark this point. Measure up the height of one tile from the marked point. At this point, draw a line all across the wall. Measure along this line to find the center of the wall. At the center point, draw a vertical line on the wall; use the level to make sure it's at right angles to the horizontal.

Mark a 3- or 4-foot-long piece of scrap wood to use in laying out the tile. Lay out a row of tiles and mark the piece of wood at each tile joint, so you have a tile-width measuring stick. Hold the stick up to the wall on the horizontal line, with one end at or near one end of the wall, and one tile mark lined up on the center point. The distance from the end of the stick to the corner of the wall is the width of the end tile. Repeat this procedure from the center point to the other wall corner.

For most wall tiles, the tiles at each end of the wall should be the same width, as indicated on the measuring stick. If you get different widths at the two ends of the wall, move the vertical center point as necessary so that the end tiles will be the same width. If you're using mosaic tiles, plan the tile layout so that a curved corner tile fits into the corner and the first whole tile butts directly into the corner piece. Cut tiles to fit along only one side of the wall.

When the horizontal tile layout has been adjusted, draw a vertical line from the horizontal at each end of the wall to mark the outside edge of the last full tile on that side. The horizontal line above the tub and the vertical lines at the ends of the wall mark the area to be tiled with whole tiles. Tile this area first; then cut edge tiles as necessary and install cap and base tiles. If you're using mosaic tiles, place a strip of curved corner tiles off the horizontal first; then tile along the horizontal from the corner strip. At the other end of the wall, set corner tiles before cutting the edge tiles.

To set the whole tiles, work in 3-foot-square areas across and up the wall.

Starting at one marked corner, place tiles lined up along the horizontal line to the center of the wall; then go back and start another course from the vertical. Work up the first half of the wall in horizontal courses. Then complete the wall, starting at the last tiles on the first half to fill in course by course up the wall.

For each section of the wall, apply ceramic tile adhesive with a notched trowel. Spread the adhesive in an even layer, holding the trowel at an angle to force the adhesive into ridges as deep as the trowel's notches. Make sure the ridges of adhesive are even, with no gaps and no low spots.

Set each wall tile individually, pressing the tile into the adhesive to make sure the entire tile is firmly bonded. If you're using sheets of tile, treat the sheets as individual tiles; set them carefully into place, smoothing the rows of tiles firmly on the adhesive. If necessary, cut the paper backing or plastic spacers on the end sheets to trim them to the required whole-tile width; use a utility knife, and be careful not to chip the tile.

As you finish setting each row of tile, check its alignment with a level. Reset tile as you work, if necessary, to keep the rows of tile level. Tile up to the desired level on the wall, so that all whole tiles have been installed. At the bottom of the wall, and around the sides of the tub, stop with the last whole tile above the floor or next to the tub.

When all whole tiles are in place, cut the edge tiles to fit and install the trim tiles. For each edge tile, use a tile cutter to cut the tile to the required size; wear safety goggles while you cut. If the cut edge of the tile is rough, smooth it with a whetstone. Fit edge tiles carefully into place, up from the horizontal starting line on each side of the wall, across the wall under the horizontal line, and then, if necessary, down the side of the tub.

Use tile nippers to fit tiles around pipes or other obstacles, and to fit them around curved tub edges. Wearing safety goggles, use the nippers to crumble the tile to the required shape, bit by bit. If a pipe or other obstacle falls near the center of a tile, cut the tile in

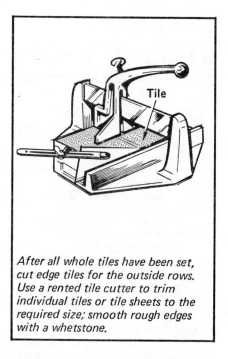

After all whole tiles have been set, cut edge tiles for the outside rows. Use a rented tile cutter to trim individual tiles or tile sheets to the required size; smooth rough edges with a whetstone.

working across the wall in courses of sheets; press each sheet firmly into place. As you work, carefully pound the sheets of tile down with a sponge trowel to force the adhesive up into the tile joints. Near the edges of the floor, cut sheets of tile apart as necessary to trim them to the required whole-tile width. Work around fixtures and other obstacles to the closest whole tile; cut out sections of the tile sheets as required.

When the main floor area is covered, cut edge tiles and fit tiles around obstructions, as above. Use a tile cutter and tile nippers to cut or crumble the tiles. For the edges of the floor, leave the tiles in sheets to trim them evenly; to fit tiles around fixtures, cut individual tiles with the tile nippers. If you used mosaic tile with curved wall-floor corners, match the floor edge tiles carefully to the curved corner tiles.

Finally, if you're using sheets of tile backed with paper, remove the paper backing. Carefully soak the paper with warm water and a sponge; use enough water to wet the paper thoroughly, but not enough to drip into the tile joints. Peel the softened paper off the tile and wipe up excess water.

When all the tile is installed, let it

half and then crumble it from both sides with the nippers.

Finally, install cap tiles and, if necessary, trim tiles. Finish all rows of edge tiles with the appropriate cap or base tiles, to make a rounded edge wherever the tile meets the wall or floor. If you're using wall tiles, install base tiles along the base of the wall, aligned with the wall tiles. If you're using mosaic tiles with a curved wall-floor joint, install strips of curved corner pieces along the base of the wall. Turn corners with special inside or outside corner tiles, as required. Cut trim tiles as required with the tile cutter and the nippers.

Repeat to tile all walls of the room. When all walls are tiled, install the floor tile. Start working at the most conspicuous edge of the floor, usually along the bathtub. Lay out the tile as above, working from the last whole tile along the tub and out along the walls abutting the tub wall.

Starting at one corner of the floor along the whole-tile line, apply ceramic tile adhesive to the prepared floor, section by section. Set each sheet of mosaic tile into place along the line,

To fit tile around a pipe, cut the tile in half; then cut the required shape in each half with tile nippers.

stand ungrouted for 24 hours to let the adhesive cure. If you must walk in the room, protect the floor with a piece of scrap plywood; remove the plywood when you leave the room. Do *not* let the newly applied tile get wet.

When the adhesive has fully cured, as directed by the manufacturer, grout the tile. If you're using pregrouted tile, all that's necessary is to seal the joints between sheets of tile. Carefully apply silicone caulk to each joint, as directed by the manufacturer. Let the caulk dry completely, as directed; in a tub area, let it cure for at least 12 hours before getting the walls wet.

In most cases, the tile must be finished with cement grout. Mix grout with water in a plastic dishpan, as directed by the manufacturer. Start grouting at the far wall of the room, and grout all walls completely before you do the floor.

Apply the grout with a sponge trowel. Moisten the tile with a sponge and then spread grout evenly over the dampened tile, pressing the sponge trowel to force grout into the tile joints. Be careful not to leave any gaps; in tight corners, apply grout with a sponge. The tile joints should be smoothly filled, with no gaps and no blobs.

Let the grout dry for about ½ hour; then carefully wipe off excess grout with a damp cloth. Wipe the tiles firmly, but don't gouge the grout out of the tile joints. A thin film of grout will probably still be left on the tile.

Let the grout dry completely, as directed by the manufacturer. When the grout is dry, rinse the wall. Remove the remaining excess grout with a coarse towel.

Let the grout cure completely, as specified by the manufacturer, before you let the tile get wet. Curing time can be as long as 2 weeks. If you must use the newly tiled bathroom during the curing period, cover the walls around the tub with sheet plastic film, securely taped to seal out all moisture. Protect the floor with rugs, and wipe up any spills immediately. After the curing period is over, fill any wide gaps around fixtures with silicone caulk.

Recaulk a Bathtub or Sink

Missing caulking, probably the commonest of household ills, is also one of the easiest to cure. **Tools:** putty knife, utility knife or single-edge razor blade, sponge, toothbrush, hair dryer, caulking gun. **Materials:** concentrated all-purpose cleaner, liquid bleach, clean rags, silicone caulk or bathtub caulk. Bathtub caulk is available in white or colors. **Time:** ½ to 1 hour.

Scrape out all old caulk around the tub or sink with a putty knife. To remove stubborn patches, slice through the old caulk to form a clean corner; scrape with the putty knife. Remove soap residue with concentrated household cleaner; if the joint is mildewed, scrub it with a toothbrush dipped in a strong bleach solution. Flush thoroughly with clean water.

Dry the joint with a clean rag, rubbing firmly to remove any grit or bits of caulk. Wrap the blade of the putty knife with a clean rag and draw it along the open joint, and if the joint is deep or very

After cleaning and drying the tub edge, apply caulk in a smooth bead to fill the open joint completely.

open, use a hair dryer to dry the area thoroughly.

Cut the nozzle of the caulking tube at an angle to make an opening slightly larger than the smallest open joint; you will need to recut the nozzle to work on larger joints. Apply caulk evenly all around the open edge of the tub or sink. If you're using a tube of bathtub caulk, squeeze the tube carefully by hand to apply a firm, even bead of caulk all around the edge.

Immediately after applying the caulk, smooth it into place along the joint. The easiest way to finish the caulked joint is to draw your finger or thumb quickly along the bead of caulk, pressing it into place and smoothing its surface as you go. Remove caulk from your hands with a dry, clean rag, and wash them as soon as you finish the job.

Let the caulk dry for several hours before allowing it to get wet. Don't touch it until it has cured completely, as specified by the manufacturer.

Make a Shower Curtain

Refresh your bathroom fast with this easy, inexpensive shower curtain. Use any fabric you like—a sheet works fine. **Tools:** measuring tape, scissors, straight pins, sewing machine, steam iron and ironing board, straightedge, pencil, grommet setter. **Materials:** ready-made clear plastic shower curtain, fabric, thread, heavy nonwoven interfacing, grommets, shower curtain hooks. **Time:** about 1 to 2 hours.

Buy a ready-made clear plastic shower curtain the right size for your tub or shower, and as many grommets and shower curtain hooks as the plastic curtain has holes. You'll need 4½ yards of 44- or 45-inch fabric for a curtain 6 feet wide, or 2¼ yards of fabric for a curtain 3 feet wide; or use a sheet large enough to cover the tub or shower opening completely. Buy ½ yard of heavy nonwoven interfacing.

Measure the plastic shower curtain to determine its exact dimensions. For a curtain 3 feet wide, cut a piece of fabric 3 inches wider and 6 inches longer than the plastic curtain—for a standard curtain, 39 × 78 inches. For a curtain 6 feet wide, cut two lengths of fabric from the 4½ yards of fabric, each piece 6 inches longer than the plastic curtain. Or, if you're using a sheet, trim the sheet to measure 6 inches longer and 3 inches wider than the plastic curtain.

For a 6-foot curtain, place the two pieces of fabric, right sides together, on a flat surface, and pin them down one long side. Leaving a ½-inch seam allowance, sew the two pieces of fabric together by machine along the pinned edge; remove the pins. Open the sewn-together pieces to form one large panel, and press the seam open.

Measure and trim the width of the panel to match the width of the plastic shower curtain, plus 3 inches. If you don't have to trim much, cut the entire amount from one long edge. If the panel must be trimmed more than an inch or two, cut half of the required amount from each long edge of the double panel, to keep the seam centered on the finished curtain.

Turn the long side edges of the panel under ½ inch and press them with a steam iron. Turn each edge under again 1 inch and pin it in place. Stitch along the turned edge on each side to make a 1-inch hem; backstitch at the beginning and the end of each hem. Remove the pins.

Turn the bottom edge of the panel under ½ inch and press it. Turn the creased edge under again 2½ inches; pin it in place. Stitch along the turned edge to make a 2½-inch hem across the bottom of the panel; backstitch at the beginning and the end of the hem. Remove the pins.

To reinforce the top edge of the shower curtain, use heavy nonwoven interfacing. With a straightedge, mark the piece of interfacing into 2-inch-wide crosswise strips. Cut the strips apart. Overlap strips end to end and sew the lapped edges together to form one long strip at least as wide as the fabric panel.

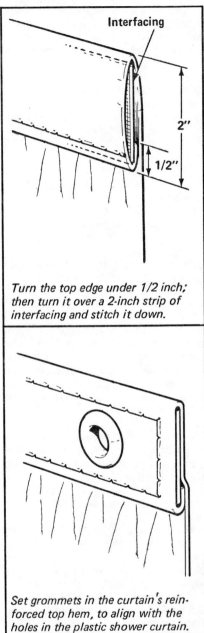

Turn the top edge under 1/2 inch; then turn it over a 2-inch strip of interfacing and stitch it down.

Set grommets in the curtain's reinforced top hem, to align with the holes in the plastic shower curtain.

Measure and trim the long strip to match the panel width exactly.

Turn the top edge of the fabric panel under ½ inch and press it in place. Slip the long strip of interfacing under the turned edge across the wrong side of the panel. Turn the fabric and the interfacing under again to form a 2-inch hem with the interfacing inside. Topstitch along the edge of the hem, along the top edge of the panel, and across both open ends of the hem; backstitch at the beginning and the end of each seam.

To complete the curtain, spread the fabric panel out, wrong side up, and lay the plastic curtain on it. Align the top and sides of the two panels. On the top hem of the fabric panel, mark the locations of the holes in the plastic curtain. With a grommet setter, install a grommet at each marked point.

Set a shower curtain hook through each hole in the plastic curtain and through the corresponding grommet on the fabric curtain. Hang the two curtains together, with the plastic curtain inside the tub or shower and the cloth curtain facing into the bathroom. For a finishing touch, make window curtains to match the shower curtain.

Install Bathroom Carpeting

Carpeting a bathroom is easy with cushion-back carpeting. Choose your carpeting carefully for the best results. **Tools:** measuring rule, bucket and sponge, putty knife or paint scraper, pencil, long sharp scissors, single-edge razor blade. **Materials:** water-resistant, washable cushion-back carpeting; household cleaner, spackling compound, brown wrapping paper, masking tape, double-faced carpet tape. **Time:** about 3 hours.

Before buying carpeting, measure your bathroom carefully. Draw a floor plan of the room and mark the sink, toilet, and tub or shower enclosure on it. Take this plan with you to the carpet dealer. You may be able to buy a precut carpet kit to fit your bathroom. If you can't buy a carpet kit, try to get carpeting as wide as the bathroom, to eliminate seams. Buy water-resistant carpeting that can be easily laundered; it should weigh at least 36 ounces per square yard.

Before installing the carpeting, make sure the bathroom floor is in good shape. Wash the floor thoroughly and rinse it well; let it dry completely. Fill any cracks or gouges with spackling compound. If the door opens into the bathroom, remove it from the frame, if possible.

Make a pattern of brown wrapping paper to cut the carpet from. Spread strips of brown paper on the floor and tape the strips with masking tape. Cut the paper to fit it exactly around fixtures—toilet, vanity or sink, tub or shower enclosure. The paper pattern should cover the floor exactly as you want the carpeting to. Mark the top side of the paper pattern plainly.

Cut the carpet in another room. Spread the carpet on the floor, face down. Lay the paper pattern over the back of the carpet, top side down. Tape the pattern to the carpet back with short strips of masking tape along all open

Cut the carpeting from the paper pattern; then roll it into place, smoothing it down around fixtures.

edges, securing it around the cutout fixture openings as well as along wall edges. Cut the carpeting to the pattern with a long, sharp scissors, working in the direction of the pile wherever possible. Be sure to cut all slits for fixtures. Remove the cut masking tape. If the carpeting must be pieced together with more than one piece, butt the pieces firmly together and tape them on the back with masking tape.

When the carpeting has been cut exactly to the paper pattern, roll or fold it and set it in place in the bathroom. Unfold the carpeting into place and smooth it down around the fixtures. Use a single-edge razor blade to trim any excess at the walls or around the fixtures. Finally, rehang the door.

Because bathroom carpeting must be washed periodically, it's best not to attach it to the floor. Cushion-back carpeting is stable, and doesn't need to be anchored in a small room. If the carpeting moves or curls at the doorway or other heavy-traffic areas, anchor it with strips of double-faced carpet tape.

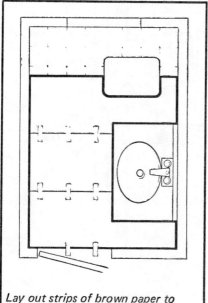

Lay out strips of brown paper to make a pattern; tape the strips together and cut around fixtures.

Replace a Lavatory

An old wall-mounted lavatory that's supported by a bracket screwed to the wall is easy to replace with a modern wall-mounted fixture. **Tools:** adjustable wrench, smooth-jawed wrench, basin wrench, screwdriver. **Materials:** new lavatory, bucket, cloth tape, padding, plumbers' putty. **Time:** 2 to 4 hours.

If the new and old lavatories are the same style, you may be able to use the original bracket. If so, there's no need to remove the old bracket. Check with the dealer when you buy the new fixture to see if a new bracket is required.

Before you start to work, turn off the water lines—hot and cold water supply—to the lavatory. If there are no fixture shutoff valves, turn off the main water shutoff valve for the whole house.

Put a bucket under the lavatory's drain trap. If the trap is equipped with a clean-out plug, use an adjustable wrench to unscrew the plug to drain the water from the trap. Otherwise, you'll have to drain the water after you remove the trap itself.

Wrap cloth tape around the slip nuts that connect the trap to the tailpiece and to the drain extension, to protect them.

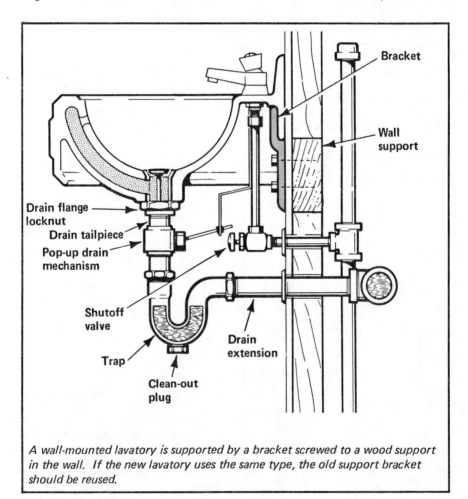

A wall-mounted lavatory is supported by a bracket screwed to a wood support in the wall. If the new lavatory uses the same type, the old support bracket should be reused.

Loosen each slip nut with a smooth-jawed wrench. Carefully pull the trap down to free it from the tailpiece and the extension. If you haven't drained the trap, keep it upright; then pour the water in the trap into the bucket.

With a basin wrench, loosen the coupling nut on the water supply line under each faucet. Then, with the adjustable wrench, loosen the supply line coupling nuts at the fixture's shutoff valves. Remove the two supply lines.

Disconnect the pop-up drain linkage—if present—under the lavatory. Then grasp the lavatory firmly and lift it straight up off the wall bracket. Set it aside.

If you're using a new faucet, there's no need to remove the old one from the lavatory. If you're reusing the old faucets, use a wrench to remove the retaining nuts and washers that secure the assembly. Remove the pop-up drain mechanism—if present—and loosen the drain flange locknut holding the flange and tailpiece. Remove the flange and tailpiece.

If a new wall bracket is required, remove the old one from the wall, using a screwdriver or a wrench to remove its fasteners. Center the new wall bracket and secure it in place with the fasteners provided.

If your old lavatory was not equipped with shutoff valves for the water supply lines, install them before installing the new lavatory. Then proceed as below.

Carefully place the new lavatory on its side on a folded blanket or other padding, to protect it from damage. Apply plumbers' putty around the base of the faucet assembly and put it into place, or use the assembly's gasket if one is supplied with the new unit. From under the lavatory, screw the retaining nuts onto the faucet shanks and tighten them with the basin wrench. Set the drain flange and tailpiece into the drain opening and tighten the flange locknut with a wrench.

Install the pop-up drain linkage mechanism—if present—to the tailpiece, following the manufacturer's instructions. Screw the coupling nuts of the water supply lines to the faucet

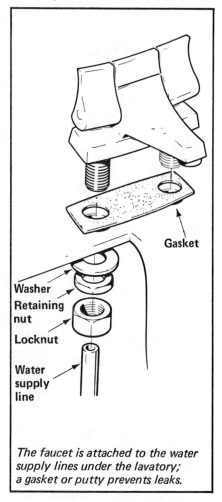

Gasket

Washer

Retaining nut

Locknut

Water supply line

The faucet is attached to the water supply lines under the lavatory; a gasket or putty prevents leaks.

shanks, and tighten each nut with a basin wrench.

Carefully lift the lavatory and position it over and onto the wall bracket. Screw the coupling nut for each supply line to its shutoff valve, and tighten it with the adjustable wrench.

Install the trap by screwing one slip nut to the drain tailpiece and the other to the drain extension. Tighten the nuts with the smooth-jawed wrench. If you removed a clean-out plug from the trap, replace it.

Finally, turn on the water supply, or turn on the water supply at each shutoff valve. Turn on both faucets full force and check all connections for leaks. If there are any leaks, turn off the faucets and tighten, or reseat and tighten, the leaking connection; then remove the tape from the trap's slip nuts.

Install a Recessed Bathroom Cabinet

A fast, easy, and inexpensive way to make storage space in a small bathroom is with a between-the-studs cabinet. Choose any style you like; add as many cabinets as you need. **Tools:** magnetic stud finder, brace and bit, wire coat hanger, utility knife, pencil, keyhole saw or saber saw, putty knife, hammer, measuring rule, level, screwdriver, paintbrush. **Materials:** cabinet designed for 16-inch studding, cedar shims, 16-penny finishing nails, 1-inch panhead (pointed) screws, sandpaper, paint, spackling compound, scrap piece of 2 × 4. **Time:** about 2 hours.

Choose a location on the bathroom wall for the cabinet. Locate two studs in the wall with a magnetic stud finder. The studs are usually spaced 16 inches apart on center; the cabinet will fit between these studs.

Drill a small hole into the wall, between studs, where you want to install the cabinet. Straighten out a wire coat hanger and insert it into the hole. Probe up and down in the stud space to locate any wires or pipes that might be in the cabinet's way. If you find wires or pipe, patch the hole with spackling compound and choose another spot without obstructions.

Draw vertical lines marking the location of the two studs. Measure the height of the cabinet, and draw horizontal lines between the stud lines to mark the top and bottom of the cabinet. These guidelines mark the dimensions of the cabinet.

Drill holes at opposite corners of the guidelines with a brace and a ¼-inch bit, keeping the drill *inside* the lines. Then insert a keyhole saw or saber saw into the starter holes and cut along the

lines. Remove the piece of wallboard and trim rough edges along the wall opening with a utility knife.

Cut two 2 × 4's to fit horizontally between the studs. Then toenail one 2 × 4 to the studs at the cabinet's bottom location. Although the cabinet actually hangs on the studs, these 2 × 4 headers help strengthen the wall and position the cabinet in the opening.

Set the cabinet into the opening on the bottom 2 × 4 and level the cabinet; prop cedar shims under the cabinet to obtain the proper level. Mark the location of the top of the cabinet on the studs and remove the cabinet. Position the top 2 × 4 header at this location and then toenail it into place.

Set the cabinet back into the opening and level it. Fasten it first to the studs. There will be predrilled holes in the sides of the cabinet to guide the screws; screws may or may not be included with the cabinet. Use the screws provided, or use 1-inch pan screws, to fasten the cabinet to the studs and, if screw holes

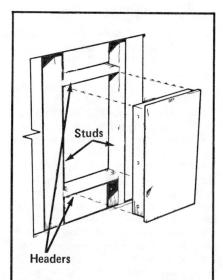

Studs

Headers

The cabinet is set in between the wall studs, with the door flush with the wall surface. To strengthen the wall and hold the cabinet firmly, nail 2 x 4 headers to frame it in at top and bottom.

are predrilled in the metal, to the top and bottom headers. If there are no screw holes there, the screws along the sides will be adequate.

The mirror or door on the cabinet is usually framed to hide any imperfections in the wall covering. If necessary, fill any nicks or miscuts with spackling compound, and let the compound dry. Then lightly sand the surface and touch up or paint the wall.

Replace a Towel Rack

A broken ceramic towel rack doesn't have to be ignored or covered up— replace it with a new ceramic rack to match the room. **Tools:** electric drill with ⅛-inch masonry bit, cold chisel, hammer, putty knife, mixing pan and stir stick, screwdriver, grease pencil. **Materials:** replacement ceramic towel rack, ceramic tile adhesive, plaster of paris, tile grout, contact cement, metal ceramic tile fixture clips; plastic, fiber, or lead screw anchors; flathead metal screws, masking tape. **Time:** about 2 hours.

Sometimes metal clips are used to support ceramic towel racks. Before you start the repair, remove any setscrew on the rack's bottom and lightly tap upward on the bottom of the fixture with a hammer. If the towel rack comes loose, remove it. Reset a new fixture on the mounting bracket.

If the broken towel fixture is recessed in the tile wall, break it out with a cold chisel and hammer. *Caution: Wear safety goggles to protect your eyes.* Be careful not to chip or crack the surrounding tiles. When the fixture is out, carefully clean the mastic and grout from the wall surface.

If the recess in the wall is deep, mix plaster of paris to a fairly stiff consistency. Trowel this mixture into the recess with a putty knife and then press in the new fixture; install the towel bar before mounting the fixture. Let the

plaster of paris ooze out around the joints of the fixture until the fixture is flush with the surrounding tiles. Then remove the excess plaster of paris with the tip of the putty knife and smooth the joints with your finger.

If the recess in the wall is flush with the backs of the tiles, set the new fixture with ceramic tile adhesive; use a fairly thick coating of adhesive on the back of the fixture, and press firmly to bond the fixture to the wall surface. Install the towel bar before mounting the fixture. Secure the fixture with masking tape until the adhesive is thoroughly dry, about 1 week. Then fill the joints around the fixture with tile grout.

Mix tile grout with water to the consistency of thick whipped cream. Press the grout into the joints around the fixture with a putty knife. Then smooth the joints with your finger to give the joints a concave configuration.

A loose towel rack can be glued to the tile. If the rack is still in good condition, reglue it to the tile with a contact cement made for this purpose. Fasten the rack firmly to the wall with several strips of masking tape. Let the adhesive dry for 1 to 2 days.

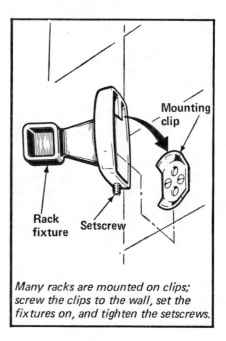

Many racks are mounted on clips; screw the clips to the wall, set the fixtures on, and tighten the setscrews.

Adhesive doesn't have the gripping power of metal clips, which are fairly easy to flush-mount to the tiles. First, position the new rack on the tile and mark the tile with a grease pencil where the rack will be mounted. Also mark the screw hole locations.

With an electric drill and a ⅛-inch masonry bit, drill holes for the metal clips that hold the fixtures; most clips require two holes spaced about ¾ inch apart. Operate the drill slowly to prevent tile breakage. Drill completely through the tile and into the wall. Then insert plastic, fiber, or lead screw anchors into the holes. Fasten the clips to the tiles with screws through the clips and into the anchors. Slip the new towel rack over the clips and fasten it with a setscrew at or near the bottom of the rack.

Replace a Ceramic Tile

Ceramic tile is tough stuff, but loose tiles, or broken ones, can be a problem. If you can match the damaged tile, replacing it is easy. **Tools:** putty knife, notched mastic spreader, small mixing dish and stick, sponges, clean towel, scissors; safety goggles, power drill with carbide bit, glass cutter, cold chisel, hammer. **Materials:** medium-grit sandpaper, tile mastic, masking tape or wood toothpicks, tile grout mix, plastic bag, adhesive tape; spackling compound, replacement tile. **Time:** about 1 hour, plus drying time between steps.

Remove loose tiles completely, being careful not to damage them. Scrape out loose grout around the tile with the sharp edge of the putty knife and pry the tile gently out from the wall. Scrape the exposed wall where the tile was to remove all old mastic and grout; if necessary, sand it carefully to remove bumps. Clean the back of the tile the same way.

Spread mastic onto the exposed wall, using a notched spreader. Set the tile carefully over the mastic and press it firmly into place, sliding it slightly up and down to work it into the mastic. Press hard enough to bring the surface of the tile flush with the other tiles.

To keep a wall tile from sliding, break wood toothpicks in half and wedge pieces of toothpick in around the newly set tile, being careful not to pull it away from the wall. Tape the tile in place with strips of masking tape in both directions. Tape floor tiles without wedging them.

Let the mastic cure completely, according to the manufacturer's instructions; then remove tape and toothpicks and grout the tile edges. Mix tile grout as directed on the package. Apply the grout with a damp sponge, smearing it over the tile to force it into the joints. Let dry for about 15 minutes. Wipe the wall surface carefully with a damp sponge to remove most of the excess grout.

Let the grout dry completely, at least 12 hours. Remove any remaining excess and polish the tiles with a clean, dry towel. If the wall or floor will get wet during either mastic curing or grout dry-

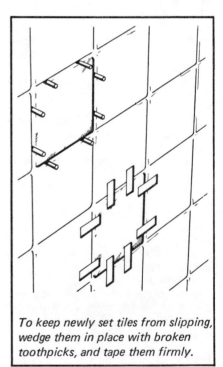

To keep newly set tiles from slipping, wedge them in place with broken toothpicks, and tape them firmly.

ing time, cover the newly set tile with a patch cut from a plastic bag, sealed firmly all around with adhesive tape.

To replace a cracked or broken ceramic tile, you must break the tile up without damaging the surrounding tiles. Stick a piece of masking tape across the center of the tile. Then, wearing safety goggles, drill a hole through the center of the tile all the way to the wall beneath it, using a power drill with a carbide bit. The tape on the surface of the tile will keep the bit from slipping.

Score an X across the tile over the drilled hole. Wearing safety goggles, break up and remove the tile with a cold chisel and hammer. Be careful not to hit the surrounding tiles.

Scrape or chisel the wall surface under the tile to remove old mastic and grout; if necessary, sand it carefully to smooth and level the tile area. If the old tile pulled plaster away from the wall, fill in the holes with spackling compound, applied just to the level of the wall surface. Let the patched area dry completely.

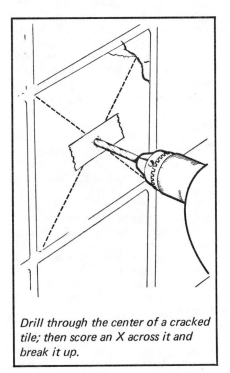

Drill through the center of a cracked tile; then score an X across it and break it up.

Install the replacement tile as above —spread mastic, set the tile into place, and grout the joints. Protect the tile with plastic until it is completely cured; remove excess grout.

Regrout Ceramic Tile

Crumbling grout is a common ailment in ceramic tile walls and floors, and it can cause more serious damage. Regrout as soon as possible to keep the problem from spreading. **Tools:** stiff scrub brush, bucket, sponges, toothbrush, putty knife or nut pick, vacuum cleaner, mixing pan and stir stick, rubber gloves, clean towel. **Materials:** household floor and wall cleaner, liquid bleach, tile grout mix, silicone tile grout spray. **Time:** ½ to 1 day.

Scrub the wall or floor thoroughly with household cleaner, using a stiff scrub brush; remove mildew with a stiff toothbrush dipped into a strong bleach solution. Rinse the area thoroughly with clean water. Remove all loose grout from the tile joints with the sharp edge of a putty knife or the point of a nut pick. Sweep up the debris and vacuum carefully to remove all dust and grout particles.

Mix tile grout as directed by the manufacturer, stirring it to a thin, smooth paste. Wearing rubber gloves, apply the grout to the wall or floor with a damp sponge, smearing it across the tiles to force grout into the joints. Apply grout over the entire area, wipe off the excess with a clean damp sponge, and apply more grout, repeating as necessary until there are no gaps in the newly grouted joints. Remove excess grout carefully with a damp sponge.

Let the grout dry for at least 12 hours; do *not* let the wall or floor get wet. When it is completely dry, remove any remaining excess grout and polish the tiles with a clean dry towel. Let the grout cure completely, as directed by the manufacturer; keep the wall or floor dry during this period. Finally, apply a silicone tile grout spray as directed to seal the newly grouted joints.

Replace a Ceramic Soap Dish

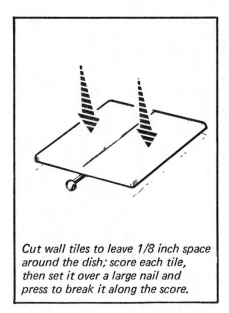

Cut wall tiles to leave 1/8 inch space around the dish; score each tile, then set it over a large nail and press to break it along the score.

An old ceramic-tile bathroom is often marred by a loose or broken wall soap dish. It's easy to restore the room's elegance with a new ceramic dish. **Tools:** hammer, cold chisel, safety goggles, stiff-bladed putty knife, glass cutter, straightedge, utility knife, carpenters' square, 20-penny nail, grease pencil, whetstone, notched spreader, mixing pan and stir stick. **Materials:** new soap dish, if needed; coarse-grit sandpaper, ceramic tile adhesive, masking tape, tile grout, ceramic tile sealer. **Time:** about 1 hour.

If the soap dish is loose, pry it out of the wall with a putty knife. If the dish is tight, but broken, remove the grout in the joints around the dish with a utility knife and the point of a 20-penny nail. Use the tip of the putty knife to pry the dish off the wall. If that fails, break the dish with a hammer and cold chisel. *Caution: Wear safety goggles to protect your eyes.* Then remove the pieces of the dish.

With a putty knife, remove all old plaster, adhesive, and tile grout from the wall and the edges of the surrounding ceramic tiles. Check the new soap dish for fit in the tile field. If possible, use a new soap dish the same size as the old one. If the new dish is too large, you'll have to trim the surrounding tiles.

To do this, reposition the dish on the tiles and trace around it with a grease pencil. Clean the grout out of the tile joints and then pry off the necessary tiles with a putty knife. Clean off the adhesive on the wall and the backs of the tiles with coarse-grit sandpaper. Measure and mark the trim lines on the tile with a carpenters' square.

The tile should be cut to allow a ⅛-inch space between tile and dish; make the final cutting mark ⅛ inch back

from the grease pencil mark on each tile. Use the point of a nail to scratch cutting marks on the tiles.

Score the face of each tile along the scribed trim line, using a glass cutter and a straightedge. Press the glass cutter down hard on the tile. Place the scored tile on a solid surface with the 20-penny nail under the scored line, and press the tile firmly along the line to break it. If the broken edge is very rough, smooth it with a whetstone. Grout will hide the rough broken edge—up to a point.

Using a notched spreader, apply ceramic tile adhesive to the wall around the soap dish opening. Then set the tile around the edges, spacing the tiles ⅛ inch apart. Let the tiles set for 2 days.

When the tile around the dish is thoroughly dry, spread adhesive liberally in the opening for the soap dish; be careful not to leave any gaps. Press the dish firmly into the adhesive, leaving ⅛-inch joints between the tile and the dish. If there's extra space, leave the extra at the bottom of the dish, where the joint won't show.

When the dish is in position, wipe off excess adhesive. Fasten the dish firmly to the wall with several strips of masking tape. Let the adhesive dry for about

Make Your Own Tile Cleaners

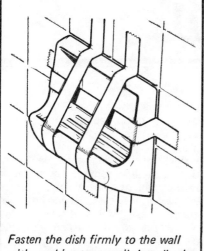

Fasten the dish firmly to the wall with masking tape until the adhesive is completely set.

1 week; make sure the wall doesn't get wet.

When the adhesive is completely set, remove the masking tape from the dish. Mix ceramic tile grout with water to the consistency of thick whipped cream; make sure you use a grout recommended by the soap dish manufacturer. Press the grout into the tile joints with your finger. When the grout is fairly dry, smooth the joints with your finger; then let the grout dry completely, as recommended by the manufacturer. After 1 week, coat the joints and the tile with ceramic tile sealer.

To cut grease and remove dirt, soap, and discoloration from ceramic tile and grout, use these inexpensive and effective mixtures.

TILE CLEANER. **Equipment:** measuring cup, bucket, stir stick. **Ingredients:** baking soda, white vinegar, ammonia, water. **Yield:** about 1 gallon.

Measure ¼ cup of baking soda, ½ cup of white vinegar, and 1 cup of ammonia into a bucket; add 1 gallon of warm water and stir to dissolve the baking soda.

Apply the tile cleaner with a sponge; wear rubber gloves to protect your hands. Rinse with clear water.

GROUT CLEANERS. **Equipment:** measuring cup, bucket, stir stick. **Ingredients:** liquid chlorine bleach or baking soda, water. **Yield:** about 1 quart of bleaching liquid, or paste cleaner as desired.

To clean darkened grout, add ¼ cup of liquid chlorine bleach to 1 quart of warm water; scrub into grout with a toothbrush, and rinse with clear water. To remove heavy dirt, mix 3 parts baking soda and 1 part water to a paste. Scrub the paste into the grout with a damp cloth; rinse with clear water.

Walls

Paint a Room

Because you care more about the finished room, this is one job you can do better than the professionals. **Tools:** bucket and large sponge, utility knife, screwdriver, trouble light, hammer, putty knife, vacuum cleaner, wide paint scraper, sanding block, wall-cleaning sponge (available in paint and hardware stores), dust mop, medium-size paintbrush, paint roller, roller cover, roller extension handle or mop handle, roller pan. **Materials:** clean sheets, dropcloths, household detergent or TSP (trisodium phosphate) for washing walls, spackling compound, masking tape, plastic bags, newspapers, fine-grit sandpaper, paint stir sticks, latex interior paint; if desired, interior latex semigloss enamel paint for trim. Read the paint cans to determine the amount of paint you need. **Time:** from 1 day to a week, depending on patching.

Thorough preparation is the key to a good paint job, and containing the mess is the way to keep the rest of your house or apartment livable during the process. Paint one room completely before beginning work on another, and keep a clean pair of shoes at the door so you don't track paint all over the house.

First clear the room. Remove all drapes, area rugs, light fixture covers, and pictures. If you plan to put the pictures back in the same places, leave the nails or fasteners in the walls; otherwise, remove them. Pack loose items and move as much furniture as possible out of the room. Push large pieces together in the middle of the room and cover them with clean sheets. Cover the entire floor surface, including the furniture in the middle of the room,

with dropcloths—to keep the edges of the floor clean, spread newspapers along the baseboards and tape them in place.

Walls and ceiling must be clean. Scrape them to remove any loose or flaking paint, being careful not to gouge the plaster. Remove dust and cobwebs from the ceiling with a dust mop. If the old paint is very dirty, wash walls and ceiling with household detergent or a TSP solution, using a large sponge. Let dry completely before proceeding.

Apply masking tape to protect edges that won't be painted along woodwork and trim. Drive in any loose nails. Remove switch cover plates and outlet covers, first cutting carefully around the edges to keep the break clean. If you want the covers to match the walls, set them aside to be painted separately. Loosen all light fixtures, again first cutting around the edges, and let them hang clear of the ceiling. Cover the dangling fixtures with plastic bags. You should work by daylight, if possible; use a hanging trouble light if you need more light.

Interior walls should be as smooth as possible. After loose paint has been removed, most small flaws can be patched with spackling compound. Apply the compound with a putty knife, using quick, firm, even strokes to fill dents and small holes. To keep the patched surface even in areas where patching is extensive, use a wide paint scraper.

Long cracks need more work. Scrape along cracks with the sharp edge of the putty knife to break out any loose plaster and paint chips. Vacuum the crack to remove loose material and press spackling compound into the crack with your finger, following the line of the crack. Apply more compound sparingly, using the wide scraper to

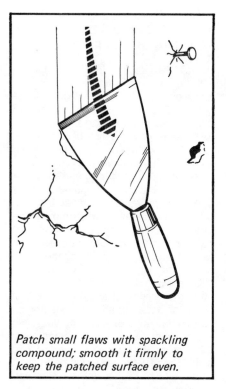

Patch small flaws with spackling compound; smooth it firmly to keep the patched surface even.

With ceiling and wall surfaces clean and smooth, you're ready to paint. Stir the paint thoroughly, following the directions on the can. Paint all corners and edges that adjoin masked trim by hand; use the tip of the brush to produce a clean edge along a surface that won't be painted. Paint ceiling edges first, then wall edges and door and window frame edges. Set the brush aside, but don't clean it yet; you may need it for touchups.

Now pour some paint into the roller pan, filling only the deep part of the tray; clean the edge of the paint can with the stir stick as you stop pouring. Dip the roller into the paint and roll it up and down the slope of the pan to load it evenly.

Paint the ceiling first. If you have strong arms, you can use a roller extension handle or a wooden mop handle to let you reach the ceiling without a ladder, but this requires firm control. If you're doubtful, use the roller without an extension. Set up a scaffold with two stepladders and a plank to give you a solid footing.

You must paint the entire ceiling without stopping or it will streak. Starting at one edge, apply paint to a two- or three-foot-wide area of ceiling, using even zigzag strokes. Fill in with cross-strokes, keeping the strokes close together. Keep the roller well loaded with paint but not dripping. Repeat this procedure across the entire ceiling, covering one area at a time and using cross-strokes to blend each area into the ones painted previously.

Use the same technique to paint the walls, working in vertical strips from left to right (if you're left-handed, you may want to work from right to left). Use cross-strokes to smooth and blend vertical strokes, and don't stop in the middle of a wall. Turn the roller, if possible, to paint the horizontal strips above doors and windows.

If you want switch plates and outlet cover plates to match the new paint, lay them out on a sheet of newspaper. Roll paint on and let dry. Let all new paint dry completely, and replace fixtures, switch plates, and cover plates.

cover and smooth the compound all along the crack. Fill nail holes in painted wood trim the same way, applying spackling compound with your finger and smoothing it with a putty knife.

Let the patches dry completely, preferably overnight. The compound will be bright white when it dries. Using fine-grit sandpaper and a sanding block, smooth the patched areas carefully to match the surrounding wall area. Spackling compound shrinks as it dries, so you will probably have to repatch large nail holes and deep cracks at least once. Follow the same procedure, sanding the new patches smooth when they are dry.

To complete your preparations, go over wall and ceiling surfaces with a special dry wall-cleaning sponge to remove all loose plaster dust. Vacuum the room to eliminate as much dust as possible. Finally, prime all patched areas with a light coat of paint, applied with a medium-size brush. Let dry several hours or overnight.

Woodwork can be painted with either regular flat interior paint or semigloss enamel trim paint. The semigloss is more durable and easier to keep clean, and gives a more formal effect.

Remove all masking tape from baseboards and other trim, being careful not to mar the new paint. Stir the paint thoroughly. Paint the trim with a medium-size brush, brushing along the grain. Hold a sheet of light cardboard butted against the trim to protect the newly painted wall, painting with one hand and moving the cardboard mask with the other to keep the mask in place as you work along the trim.

Finally, paint windows, door frames, and doors. Mask window glass and open the windows three or four inches; move the sash after you paint to keep it from sticking. Mask doorknobs and lock plates before painting, and let the paint dry before removing the tape.

Clean brush, roller, paint pan, and other tools with cool, soapy water. Rinse thoroughly. Fold dropcloths paint side in.

Install Wallboard

Finishing a framed-in space—attic, basement, wherever—doesn't have to cost a fortune; wallboard, also known as gypsum board and drywall, is easy to install. You'll need a helper for this job. **Tools:** screwdriver, measuring rule, two 2 × 4's an inch or so longer than the room is high, two 3-foot pieces of scrap board, hammer, stepladder, pencil, sharp utility knife and extra blades, steel straightedge, two 4-foot or one 8-foot 2 × 4 for snapping wallboard, drill, keyhole saw, broad-bladed drywall knife, sanding block; paint pan, brush, roller, and roller cover. **Materials:** common nails, ½-inch-thick tapered-edge wallboard sheets—the standard size is 4 feet by 8 feet—5-penny coated drywall nails, premixed joint compound, joint tape, metal corner bead for each outside corner in room, medium- and fine-grit sandpaper, vacuum cleaner; if

desired, baseboard and quarter-round molding; interior latex paint or primer. **Time:** about 4 days per room; 1 day more for painting.

Wallboard comes in 4 × 8 sheets, with tapered edges to make taping the joints easier. The trick is to install the board with as few joints as possible, so plan the wall and ceiling layouts carefully before you buy. It's usually better to install the board horizontally along the walls, if you have a strong helper, than vertically; you'll end up with fewer joints. Buy wallboard at a lumberyard or building supply outlet, and ask a knowledgeable salesman to compute the quantities of joint compound, tape, and nails you'll need. Have corner beads cut to measure. Don't try to bring the board home yourself; have it delivered.

Begin with the ceiling. Before you start, make two T-braces. Nail a 3-foot piece of scrap board at right angles across the end of each of your two room-height 2 × 4's. Use common nails; make sure the braces are good and solid. These T-braces will support most of the weight of the wallboard as you work on the ceiling.

Raise the first sheet of wallboard into position and wedge the braces upright beneath it. Try to span the width of the ceiling, if possible, to eliminate unnecessary joints. Use a pencil and straightedge to draw a line on the wallboard from each exposed beam on the ceiling across the panel. This step isn't essential; it's just to make the beams easier to see as you nail. Starting at the center of the panel, drive wallboard nails through the board and into the wood beams above it. Each panel must be nailed all along each ceiling beam it touches, always working from the center out, with nails at 7-inch intervals along the beams. Draw lines on each panel as you work to make the nailing easier.

As you work, set the nails below the surface of the wallboard. When each nail is driven flush with the wallboard, give it a final quick, sharp tap to depress the surface of the board around the nail head. Be careful not to hit the board too hard or it will crack.

Install panels over the rest of the ceiling the same way. Measure and mark edge boards carefully to fit. Draw the cut lines on the paper facing of the boards. Score along the lines with a steel straightedge and a sharp utility knife, cutting only through the paper. Slide a 2 × 4 under the board along the scored edge and snap the scored-off edge sharply down over the edge of the 2 × 4 to break the core of the wallboard; use 2 × 4's along the full length of the score, and make sure the knife blade is sharp. Cut carefully through the paper backing to release the snapped-off piece of wallboard.

When the ceiling is complete, follow the same procedure to cover the walls —an easier process, because you can work in a more natural position. Start at a corner and work around the room, driving nails every 7 inches along the wall studs, beginning 7 inches below the ceiling.

If you and your helper can handle the weight, install the top layer of wallboard first, butting the edges straight up against the ceiling. Then install the bottom layer, with sheets placed exactly below those in the top row. As on the ceiling, pound each nail to drive it slightly below the surface of the wallboard without breaking the paper, forming regular rows of dimpled nails.

Make cutouts in the wallboard to accommodate switch cover plates, outlets, and fixtures. Measure carefully and draw the entire outline on the board. Drill a hole in the center of the area to be cut out and use a keyhole saw to cut around the edges. Score the corners with a sharp utility knife so you don't tear the paper.

In a plain box-shaped room, you won't need metal corner beads. If the room is irregularly shaped, however, any corners jutting into the room must be finished with metal corner beads. Cover each outside corner with a bead, hold it firmly in place, and drive drywall nails through the holes in both sides of the corner to hold the edge in place.

When the drywall has been completely installed, every joint must be

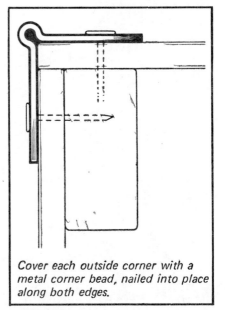

Cover each outside corner with a metal corner bead, nailed into place along both edges.

filled and taped, and every dimpled nail head must be covered, on both the ceiling and the walls. With a broad-bladed drywall knife, spread joint compound for several feet along the joint where the tapered edges of two sheets of drywall meet. Smooth the surface of the filled joint level with the wall surface.

Now lay wallboard joint tape directly onto the joint, centering it along the layer of joint compound. Smooth the paper into the joint with the drywall knife. Drywall tape is perforated, and some joint compound will squeeze out onto the surface of the tape as you work; smooth it along with the drywall knife, feathering it lightly out at the sides. Work on several feet of joint at a time, moving steadily ahead to keep joint compound, tape, and smoothed-over tape even all along the joint.

Tape corner joints along their entire length at once. Cut a piece of joint tape to fit and fold it in half the long way, creasing it carefully to give it a sharp inside edge. Fill the tapered corner with joint compound and press the tape into place down the joint; then smooth the tape, feathering the compound out at least 1½ inches on each side. Apply joint compound in a wedge shape to

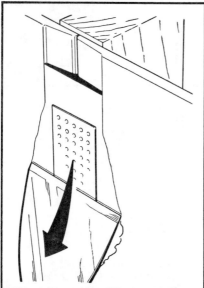

Fill each wallboard joint with joint compound; then smooth joint tape over the compound.

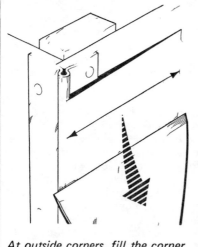

At outside corners, fill the corner bead with joint compound, feathered back to the wall.

corner beads, feathering from the rounded corner back to the flat wall. Finally, fill all nail dimples with joint compound, smoothing the patches flat with the drywall knife. Keep the joints as smooth as possible to minimize sanding later.

Let the joint compound dry for 24 hours. When it is completely dry, apply a second layer of joint compound to all joints, corners, and nail dimples. Feather the compound farther out this time from inside and outside corners. Let dry for 24 hours and repeat a third time, this time filling corner beads completely and feathering back about 8 inches from both inside and outside corners. Let dry for 24 hours.

When the three coats of joint compound have completely dried, sand all joints, corners, and dimples smooth with medium-grit and then fine-grit sandpaper. Sand corners carefully so you don't leave gouges. Vacuum thoroughly to remove all loose plaster dust.

Wait several days to let the joint compound harden. Finally, prime walls and ceiling with interior latex paint or primer; install baseboard and quarter-round molding, if desired.

Repair Drywall Nail Pops

When the wood framing behind drywall shrinks and loosens a nail, the nail can pop out. Nail pops come back no matter how many times you patch them, but they're easy to fix permanently. **Tools:** hammer, nail set, putty knife, small paintbrush. **Materials:** drywall nails, spackling compound, fine-grit sandpaper, paint to touch up repair. **Time:** 10 minutes for the repair; about 2 days for patch and touchup drying.

First, drive the old drywall nail deep into the wall, using a nail set placed straight against the problem stud. Pound another drywall nail into the wallboard about 2 inches from the old nail, either above or below it. This will hold the board tightly against the framing. Set the head of this nail just below the surface of the wallboard, driving it in with a final light hammer blow to dimple the surface after you've driven the nail flush with the wall surface.

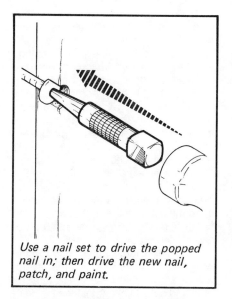

Use a nail set to drive the popped nail in; then drive the new nail, patch, and paint.

Fill the old nail depression and cover the new nailhead with spackling compound, sparingly applied with a putty knife. Let the patches dry thoroughly and sand them smooth. Patch, let dry, and sand again; patch a third time if necessary. Touch up the wall carefully, applying paint with the side of a small brush; don't stroke the paint on or the touchup will show.

Patch Holes in Wallboard

Even large holes in wallboard are easy to repair, and the finished patch is almost invisible. **Tools:** measuring rule, hammer and large nail, pencil, keyhole saw, sponge, paint scraper or spackling knife, utility knife, sanding block, screwdriver; paint pan, brush, roller, and roller cover. **Materials:** clean tin can lid, string, scrap wood, plaster of paris, mixing dish, small mixing stick, fine-grit sandpaper, scrap wallboard, contact cement or flathead screws, spackling compound, paint. **Time:** 1 to 2 hours for patching and sanding; additional time for drying and painting.

Holes less than 3 inches in diameter can be backed and filled. Remove any crumbling plaster or paper from the edges of the hole and measure it across. To make a backing, use a clean (washed in hot, soapy water) tin can lid at least 1½ inches bigger than the hole. Punch two holes at the center of the lid with a hammer and a large nail, and thread a foot-long piece of string through the holes.

Hold the lid over the hole and mark its edges on the wall with a pencil. With a keyhole saw, cut a narrow slit centered on the hole in the wall, a little longer than the diameter of the tin can lid.

Choose a stick of scrap wood at least 4 inches longer than the diameter of the hole, and set it aside to use as a brace. Wet the edges of the hole and the slit with a sponge. Mix plaster of paris according to the manufacturer's directions and set it at hand.

Holding both ends of the string threaded through it, slide the lid carefully through the slit in the wall. Pull the ends of the string to bring the lid flat against the back of the wall. Still holding the ends of the string with one hand, fill the hole and the slit with plaster of paris, smoothing plaster carefully against the tin can lid. Leave the surface of the patch indented slightly below the wall surface.

Still holding the ends of the string sticking out from the plaster, set the bracing stick over the hole, at right angles to the filled-in slit and directly between the two strings. Tie the two ends of the string firmly over the stick, pulling the knot tight so that the tin can lid inside the wall and the stick on the outside are both securely held. Let the patch dry for 24 hours.

When the plaster is completely dry, cut the string and remove the stick. Pull gently on an end of the string; if it comes loose, pull the string carefully out of the wall. If the string doesn't pull loose, cut the ends flush with the new plaster. Don't try to force the string or you'll break the patch.

Finish the job by applying another coat of plaster of paris to level the patch. Let it dry completely and sand it

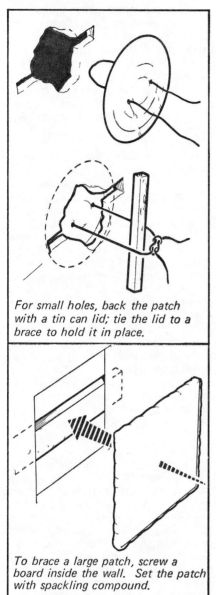

For small holes, back the patch with a tin can lid; tie the lid to a brace to hold it in place.

To brace a large patch, screw a board inside the wall. Set the patch with spackling compound.

with a pencil. Set the patch aside and cut out the traced area; use a utility knife to score the paper before cutting away the damaged wallboard. Remove the sawed-out piece from the wall.

Measure the hole across the long way. To back a small patch, use a piece of thin scrap wood about 4 inches longer than the hole's longer dimension. Apply contact cement to the ends of the piece of wood and to the back of the wall where the brace will bridge the hole. Let the cement dry. Insert the brace sideways into the hole, position it so that the cemented areas match, and set the brace firmly into place, flat against the inside of the wall.

To brace a large patch, use a lightweight board about 6 inches longer than the hole. Slide the board into the hole and hold it flat against the inside of the wall. To hold it in place, drive countersunk screws through the wall and into the ends of the board. Tighten the screws until the heads are below the surface of the wall.

Spread spackling compound over the exposed side of the secured brace, and cover the edges of the plasterboard patch with compound. Set the patch carefully into place, making sure it is flush with the wall surface. Hold it in place for a few minutes while the spackling compound hardens.

Complete the job by spackling over the outlines of the patch and the exposed screw heads. Let dry completely and sand the area smooth; repeat if necessary. Prime the patched area, let dry for several hours, and repaint the entire wall.

Patch Cracks in Plaster

Small cracks in plaster can be fixed with routine pre-painting work, but big ones demand more drastic measures. **Tools:** beer can opener, vacuum cleaner, mixing dish and stir stick,

smooth with fine-grit sandpaper; repeat if necessary. Prime the patched spot, let it dry for several hours, and then repaint the entire wall.

To patch a large hole or badly damaged area, cut a square or rectangular piece of wallboard a little larger than the hole. Set this patch flat on the wall over the hole and trace carefully around it bucket, medium-size paintbrush, putty knife, broad paint scraper, sanding block, small trowel. **Materials:** plaster of paris, fine-grit sandpaper, interior latex paint for primer. **Time:** ½ to 1 hour per crack, plus drying time between steps.

Large cracks must be scraped and cleaned. With the pointed end of a beer can opener, remove loose plaster from the crack. Turn the point of the opener sideways each way to widen the opening and undercut it slightly. Vacuum the crack to remove loose plaster and dust.

Mix plaster of paris with water to a thick paste, being careful to remove all lumps. It hardens quickly, so mix only enough to fill the crack you're working on. Spackling compound isn't suitable for large repairs.

Paint the crack thoroughly with water, using firm brush strokes along the crack to wet the plaster inside to its full depth. Apply plaster to the crack with a putty knife or broad paint scraper, forcing plaster in to the full depth of the crack. Smooth the surface of the crack to remove excess plaster.

Let the new plaster dry completely, preferably overnight; it will turn bright white as it dries. Sand the patched area with fine-grit sandpaper to smooth and level it, then repeat the wetting and filling procedure, if necessary. Let the plaster dry again and sand it smooth. Before painting the wall, prime the patch with a light coat of paint.

Before patching a large crack in an outside wall, look for the cause of the damage. If there is a structural problem —a cracked foundation wall, for instance—it must be corrected before you make inside repairs.

Fill wide openings as above. Break out any loose chunks of plaster, undercut the crack with a beer can opener, and vacuum to remove all dust. Wet the opening thoroughly on both sides, as far in as you can reach with the paintbrush. Mix enough plaster of paris to fill the opening completely.

Using a putty knife or a small trowel, fill the opening with plaster, pressing plaster all the way into the crack to fill it from the inside out. Smooth the surface

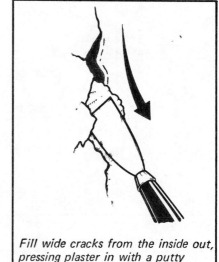

Fill wide cracks from the inside out, pressing plaster in with a putty knife or a trowel.

with a broad paint scraper. Let the plaster dry at least 24 hours, moisten it with a wet paintbrush, and fill the crack again to level the surface. Let dry for 24 hours and sand smooth. Before painting the wall, prime the patch with a light coat of paint.

Stucco Walls and Ceilings

Road-map walls and ceilings can be impossible to repair, but they're very easy to disguise. Hide the cracks and give the room a new look with stucco paint. **Tools:** bucket and sponge, putty knife or paint scraper, paint roller with loop-textured roller cover; trowel; stiff brush, metal comb, sponge, or sturdy cord for texturing; utility knife, 3-inch paint roller, stepladder. **Materials:** plastic dropcloths, masking tape, strong household detergent, spackling compound, textured or stucco paint, piece of scrap plywood or hardboard, liquid detergent. **Time:** about 4 hours for a small room, plus additional preparation time as necessary.

With a stiff brush or a metal comb, work stucco to the desired texture.

Choose textured or stucco paint, depending on how badly cracked the walls and ceiling are. Lightly textured paints are mixed with sand and other small aggregates; they hide minor flaws but not major ones. Heavy stucco paints can be applied with a trowel or a roller; choose this type to cover really bad walls. Read the paint label carefully and buy generously; the worse the wall, the more paint you'll need. Sometimes stucco paint covers only about 25 square feet per gallon can.

Before starting to work, prepare the surfaces to be stuccoed. If you're stuccoing clean walls, with no large open cracks, leave the furniture in the room; if you're stuccoing the ceiling or the surfaces require preparation, move it out. Remove drapes, pictures, and rugs. Move any remaining furniture together in the middle of the room and cover it with plastic dropcloths; cover the floor with dropcloths and fasten them to the baseboards with masking tape. Protect light fixtures, woodwork, and faceplates with masking tape.

If the room is very dirty or greasy, clean the surfaces to be stuccoed with a solution of strong household detergent and hot water; rinse and let dry completely. Small cracks will be filled in by the paint. Fill large cracks and deep gouges with spackling compound,

pressing it in firmly and smoothing it with a putty knife or paint scraper. Let the patched areas dry completely, at least 8 hours. If the spackling compound has shrunk or cracked, apply more compound to smooth the patched areas; let dry completely. No sanding is necessary.

Spread lightly textured paint with a roller, using the type of roller cover recommended by the manufacturer. Spread thick stucco paint with a roller and a special loop-textured roller cover, or with a trowel. Before starting to paint, experiment with the paint on a piece of scrap plywood or hardboard until you know how to get the effect you want. Try using a roller for a uniform stippled effect, a trowel for a random texture, a stiff brush for a rough look.

The paint will start to set up as you work, depending on the humidity; in a heated room, this can take as little as 15 minutes. As you finish applying an area of paint, go back and texture it further to produce different effects. You can brush it into waves or curves with a stiff brush, or make random cross-hatching with a metal comb, or blob it with a sponge; for a bark texture, wind sturdy cord around a roller and roll up and down the already applied paint. In general, the thicker the paint you use, the coarser the texture you can produce and the worse damage you can cover.

When you've decided on a texture and perfected your technique, apply paint to the surfaces to be stuccoed. Paint the ceiling first, again spreading paint in small areas and texturing it as you go; paint corners and edges first and then fill in the main area. To reach tight spots, cut a loop-textured roller cover in half and work with a 3-inch roller; or, if you're troweling the paint on, use a putty knife. Use the same technique to paint the walls, starting at a corner and working around the room, spreading and then texturing as you go.

Let the paint dry at least 8 hours, according to the manufacturer's instructions. Pick up the dropcloths and remove the masking tape after the stucco is dry. Clean up with water and liquid detergent.

Cover Walls with Fabric

Fabric is one wall covering that demands little in the way of patching; any reasonably smooth wall surface will do. **Tools:** stepladder, measuring rule, pencil, chalked plumb bob, long table, sharp scissors, staple gun, hammer. **Materials:** fabric, paper, straight pins, heavy-duty staples, household glue, lightweight stiff cardboard; cloth ribbon, braid, or narrow molding strips; small finishing nails or brads. **Time:** about 1 day.

Choose fabric as wide as possible. Figure the number of wall-height strips you'll need to cover the walls, and calculate yardage accordingly. If the fabric has a repeating pattern, it must be matched on adjacent panels, like wallpaper; add at least 2 yards to your total. If you want to edge the wall with ribbon at floor and ceiling, calculate footage and add at least 2 yards. Buy ribbon and fabric together.

Start in the least prominent corner of the room—behind the door, for example. Measure out along the ceiling from the corner a distance equal to the width of the material, less about ¼ inch. Set the plumb bob at this point and snap a chalk line to mark the edge for the first panel of fabric. Measure the height of the room from floor to ceiling.

Roll out the fabric on a long table, face up. Cut the first panel of fabric as long as the height of the room, plus 2 inches. Unroll and cut the fabric to be used all around the room, matching it carefully to the pattern in the first panel.

To determine the exact length of each panel, measure the height of the wall where the panel will go and add 2 inches. Measure above and below windows and doors and cut fabric accordingly, being careful to match patterns on both short strips. Pin a numbered tag to each panel as you work to keep the panels in order around the room.

Lift the first panel of fabric up into

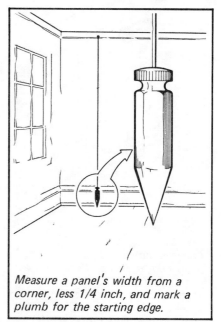

Measure a panel's width from a corner, less 1/4 inch, and mark a plumb for the starting edge.

place against the wall at the marked corner. Turn the top end of the panel under 1 inch, holding it in place at both sides with your fingers. Stretch the panel of fabric smoothly along the top edge of the wall and adjust it so that the outside edge of the panel lies exactly along the chalk line on the wall.

Holding the fabric carefully to keep it lined up exactly with the chalk line, staple the turned-under top of the fabric to the wall. Space the staples about 1 inch apart, as close to the ceiling and as even as possible. If the fabric is very heavy or sags badly, apply household glue sparingly along the turned-under end; press into place until the glue sets.

Working from the top of the wall down, staple the corner side of the fabric to the wall, about ¼ inch from the edge. Space the staples evenly, about 1 inch apart, and keep them straight up and down. Smooth the fabric carefully as you work to keep it lined up with the chalk line. Repeat to staple the other side of the fabric, setting staples ¼ inch from the edge. At the bottom of the panel, fold the excess fabric under and staple it firmly and smoothly along the baseboard.

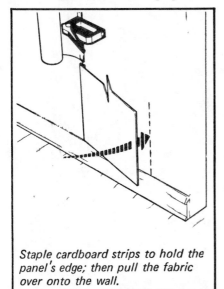

Staple cardboard strips to hold the panel's edge; then pull the fabric over onto the wall.

Before hanging more fabric, cut sheets of stiff lightweight cardboard into ½-inch-wide strips. You'll need enough cardboard to make a solid floor-to-ceiling strip at each seam in the wall. Cut the strips as uniformly as possible; their outlines will be noticeable under the completed fabric paneling.

To hang the second length of fabric, hold it against the first panel, face to face, with the wrong side of the fabric out. Leave 1 inch of fabric extra at the top of the panel. Line the edges of the panels up carefully. Set a few staples in the second panel, through the first panel and to the wall, about ½ inch in from the matched edges of the panels. These staples are just to tack the fabric into place; they are not a final seam.

Staple ½-inch-wide strips of cardboard over the matched edges of the panels, lined up exactly with the edges. Attach the strips evenly to form a smooth, level edge, with no gaps and no overlaps; place the staples close together.

When the cardboard seam is securely stapled, pull the second length of fabric back over the cardboard strips to form a blind seam. Stretch the fabric smoothly out from the joint and staple it into place on the wall, working from the center of the panel up and down and placing staples about ¼ inch in from the edge. At the top and bottom of the panel, turn the excess fabric under and staple the panel neatly at ceiling and baseboard. Use glue if necessary to keep the fabric from sagging.

Repeat the cardboard-strip technique to apply each new panel of fabric, stapling the cardboard to the wrong side of the panel and then folding the fabric around and into place. To work around windows and doors, cut the fabric with about 1 inch excess on all sides of the obstruction. Turn the excess fabric under and crease it into place with your fingers, smoothing it as you go. Use staples only at the stress points— around windows and doors, at corners or seams—if possible, attach the fabric with glue.

When the last panel has been stapled into place, turn the edge of the first panel under the edge of the last and crease the seam with your fingers. Don't use staples on the final seam; glue the folded fabric down, holding it smoothly in place until the glue sets.

To cover the staples in the fabric along the ceiling and the baseboard, glue a long piece of cloth ribbon or braid over the edge of the fabric, all around the room. Turn the ends under carefully so they don't ravel. Instead of ribbon, you can also tack narrow molding strips over the stapled fabric along the baseboard.

Remove Old Wallpaper

Removing wallpaper is always messy, but it isn't difficult. Rent a steamer—available at paint stores—to remove more than one layer of paper; or, for small jobs, use a garden sprayer and wallpaper remover. **Tools:** rented wallpaper steamer (burner, boiler, and large and small steam plates) or garden sprayer, screwdriver, broad paint scraper, ladder (if the ceiling must be scraped, two ladders and a sturdy plank), safety goggles, rubber gloves, bucket, large sponge. Get operating instructions for the steamer when you rent it. **Materials:** lightweight plastic dropcloths, masking tape, strong household detergent; if you're using a garden sprayer, wallpaper remover and coarse sandpaper. **Time:** about 1 day for an average-size room.

Before starting work, move all furniture out of the room and remove drapes, pictures, and rugs. Remove switch cover plates. Cover the entire floor with lightweight plastic dropcloths, using masking tape to secure the edges. If you're using a garden sprayer, tape the dropcloths along the top of the baseboard molding, pressing firmly to make a watertight seal; cover electric switches and outlets with plastic and seal these edges too.

Set up the electric boiler assembly of the steamer—if possible, outside the room you're working in. Fill the boiler with water, plug it in, and let the water come to a boil. Open the windows in the room to be stripped to keep condensation to a minimum. If you're using a garden sprayer, fill it with water and add wallpaper remover, mixing according to the manufacturer's directions. Pump the sprayer to pressurize it.

The steaming process is simple. Start at the bottom right corner of one wall and work up and toward the left, using your left hand to hold the steam plate flat against the wall and your right hand to scrape off the loosened paper with the paint scraper. Repeat to strip all four walls. Reverse this procedure if you're left-handed, starting at the bottom left corner and working up and toward the right. Use the small steam plate to get at tight spots.

If you're removing paper from the ceiling, set up a scaffold with two ladders and a sturdy plank. Wear safety goggles while you're working on or near the ceiling. Scrape the ceiling last, using the same corner-outward movement you used on the walls.

When all the paper has been stripped from walls and ceiling, wash with plain warm water to remove any remaining

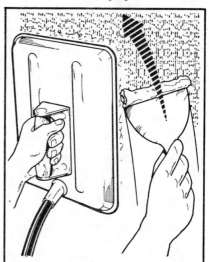

Working from a corner out, hold the steam plate flat on the wall, then scrape off loosened paper.

Use a garden sprayer to mist walls with wallpaper remover; scrape paper from the floor up.

glue. If there are stubborn patches of glue, use a strong household detergent instead of plain water. Finally, untape the dropcloths, bundle them up and throw the whole thing away, and replace switch cover plates.

The job is messier with a garden sprayer, but the technique is substantially the same. Wearing rubber gloves, wet down a section of wall from ceiling to floor, starting in a corner. Pump on the wallpaper-remover solution in a fine mist, using only enough solution to wet the paper; the wall should be wet but not streaming. Wait 5 minutes and repeat.

If the wallpaper is foil- or plastic-coated, sand it lightly with coarse sandpaper to score the surface, using enough pressure to break the foil or plastic seal but not enough to damage the plaster underneath. Spray with wallpaper remover as above.

About 5 to 10 minutes after the second spraying, test the wallpaper with a paint scraper; it should peel off easily, in large sections. Work from the bottom up and from the corner out, scraping carefully so you don't gouge the plaster underneath. Don't try to remove wallpaper from a ceiling with a garden sprayer. Finally, wash the walls, dispose of the mess, and replace switch cover plates.

Paper a Room

Like painting, hanging wallpaper is a skill that's easily acquired. What you may lack in expertise, you'll make up for in care. **Tools:** screwdriver, putty knife or paint scraper, sanding block, vacuum cleaner, wall-cleaning sponge, bucket and sponge, large paintbrush, measuring rule, pencil, hammer and nail, chalked plumb line, large table, large sharp scissors, large shallow water tray, bucket and mixing stick, stepladder, paperhangers' paste brush and smoothing brush, wallpaper seam roller, sharp utility knife and extra blades, steel straightedge. **Materials:** clean sheets, plastic dropcloths, masking tape, spackling compound, fine-grit sandpaper, strong household detergent, sizing, wallpaper or other wall covering, wallpaper paste, clean rags. Ask the wallpaper dealer what kind of sizing and wallpaper paste to buy. **Time:** about 1 day per room for patch-

ing, 1 day for sizing, and 1 day for papering.

Figure dimensions carefully when you buy wallpaper. A roll of wallpaper, whatever its width, holds about 36 square feet; of this, allowing for waste, you can use about 30 square feet. Double rolls—the way most paper is sold —are usually more economical, because they minimize waste. To figure the number of rolls of paper you need, calculate the square footage of the walls of the room to be papered and divide by 30. Subtract one roll for every two doors or windows, but always buy at least one roll extra. Make sure the edges are pretrimmed.

Before starting work, remove all furniture, rugs, drapes, and pictures from the room. If you can't move large pieces of furniture out, push them together in the middle of the room and cover them with clean sheets. Cover the entire floor, including the pushed-together furniture, with plastic dropcloths, and secure the edges with masking tape at the baseboards. Remove all switch and outlet cover plates.

Before you can paper, the walls of the room must be clean and smooth. Ideally, any old paper should be removed, but if it's sound and undamaged, you can paper over it. Fill cracks and holes in painted walls with spackling compound, smoothed on with a putty knife or paint scraper. Let the patches dry and sand them smooth with fine-grit sandpaper; repeat if necessary. Vacuum the room thoroughly and go over the walls with a wall-cleaning sponge to remove dirt and dust. If they're very dirty, wash them down with a strong household detergent.

Sizing is used for two reasons: it makes wallpaper paste stick better and it makes later wallpaper removal easier. Use the sizing recommended by your wallpaper dealer for use with your wallpaper and paste. Paint the walls with sizing, using a large brush instead of a roller; apply one or two coats, as recommended. Let dry completely.

With the walls patched and sized, you're ready to paper. Start at a corner

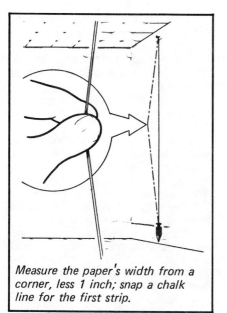

Measure the paper's width from a corner, less 1 inch; snap a chalk line for the first strip.

and work from left to right—or, if you're left-handed, from right to left. Along the top of the wall, measure a distance about 1 inch less than the width of the wallpaper. Set a nail and drop a chalked plumb line from this point, from ceiling to floor. Snap the line to mark your first wallpaper strip.

Cut strips to cover the entire wall before pasting them up. Measure the wall, baseboard to ceiling, to determine the length of paper you need. Add about 4 inches to this to allow for trimming and slippage. Cover your work table with a clean plastic dropcloth and unroll the paper on it. Measure off the length needed and cut the first strip; leave it on the table, face up.

The other strips of paper for the wall must be pattern-matched to the first one. Calculate the number of strips needed. Roll out a second strip of paper on the table, matching the pattern to the first strip; you may have to waste paper to match the strips.

Cut the second strip 4 inches longer than the measured wall height and move the first strip out of the way, leaving the second strip on the table. Repeat this matching and cutting, each time moving one strip farther along the

wall, until all the strips for one wall have been cut. Be sure to keep them in order. Cut short strips, still in order, as needed to work around doors and windows; make sure both overhead and underneath strips match the surrounding paper. Cut these strips too about 4 inches longer than measured.

If your wallpaper is prepasted, fill the water tray. Roll the first strip of paper loosely and set it in the water; let it soak for the recommended time before proceeding.

For unpasted papers, mix the paste, following the manufacturer's instructions. Lay the strip face down on the work table, with one end hanging over the table end.

Spread paste on the table end of the strip, smoothing it on with the paste brush, to cover about half the strip. Fold this pasted end over on itself, paste to paste, and slide the folded strip down the table so that the other end of the strip can be pasted. Spread paste on the other end of the strip and fold this end too back on itself, paste to paste, forming a folded-in U of paper. Keep the edges even, and don't crease the folds or the finished wall will also have creases in it.

Move the stepladder into the marked corner and stick the smoothing brush in your pocket, ready to use. To pick up the strip of pasted paper or moistened prepasted paper, slide your fingers under the edges of the folded-in strip, at the center of the U. Lift the paper care-

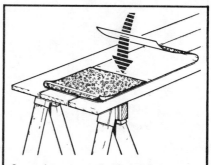

Spread paste on half the strip at a time; fold the ends over paste side in, all edges even.

fully, holding the top edge with your thumbs and forefingers. Catch the other end of the paper with your ring and little fingers if it starts to slide.

Climb the stepladder to start the paper at the ceiling. The long edge of the paper strip must line up *exactly* with the snapped chalk line on the wall. Leaving about 2 inches extra above the ceiling line, unfold the top half of the paper strip, lining up the right edge on the chalk line. Smooth the paper with your hand, working back from this edge toward the corner of the room. Fold the extra inch of paper at the far side of the strip around the corner and onto the other wall.

When the top part of the wallpaper strip is securely in place, carefully unfold the rest of the strip and smooth it onto the wall, making sure it lines up exactly with the snapped chalk line. Smooth the paper slowly and firmly with the smoothing brush to remove air bubbles and excess paste, working toward the edges of the strip. The paper should now be firmly in place; if it has slid a little, correct its position with a firm pressure on the brush. A strip that's badly out of place must be peeled off and repositioned.

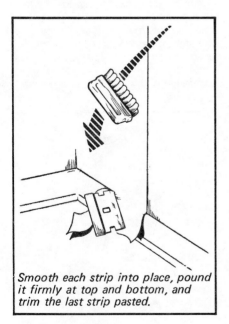

Smooth each strip into place, pound it firmly at top and bottom, and trim the last strip pasted.

To secure the wallpaper around the corner and along the ceiling and the baseboard, use the edge of the smoothing brush head-on, as a pounding tool. Strike the bristles against the edges and into the corner of the wall to push the paper firmly into place. Leave the edges untrimmed until the next strip of paper is hung.

Repeat this basic procedure all across the wall, making sure each new strip of paper is matched to the one before it. To place each strip correctly, match the pattern near the top edge, set the paper against the wall next to the previous strip, and slide it to butt exactly against the already pasted paper. Correct small mistakes in placement with the smoothing brush; peel off very badly set strips and reposition them. Smooth each strip with the brush as you go.

As each new strip is set into place and smoothed, pound its top and bottom edges into place. Then trim the excess from the top and bottom of the last strip, using a sharp utility knife and following the wall-ceiling joint carefully. Replace the knife blade as soon as it begins to get dull. Press each new seam carefully with a seam roller, and wipe the roller frequently with a clean cloth.

To work around a door, a window, or a similar interruption, set the precut short strip into place above the opening, handling it exactly like a full-length strip. Repeat, being careful to match the pattern, with strips under windows. Trim the edges and roll the seams as before.

Use the same technique to hang paper all around the room, matching and trimming as you go. Paper right over outlets and switches, then go back and cut out the excess paper. The switch plates will hide any ragged edges. If a strip of paper ends exactly in a corner, fold the next strip around to overlap it slightly. Cut closely along the overlapping edge with a sharp utility knife and a steel straightedge; fold back the top layer of paper, peel off the trimmed-off strip beneath it, and restick the new edge.

Finally, when papering and trimming are complete, pick up the dropcloths and replace switch and outlet cover plates. If you have paper left over, save one roll for patching and return the rest to the dealer.

Solve Wallpaper Problems

Keeping wallpaper in shape isn't as difficult as it might seem. **Tools:** paint pan, roller, and roller cover; bucket and sponge; artists' kneaded eraser, artists' small brush, seam roller, straight pin, sharp single-edge razor blade, colored felt-tip pens. **Materials:** prepared transparent wallpaper coating, liquid detergent, wallpaper paste, vinyl adhesive, wallpaper scraps. **Time:** 10 minutes for small repairs; several hours to apply protective coating.

Start protecting wallpaper when it's brand new. Save leftover wallpaper for patching; tape a piece or two on an inside closet wall to fade as the room does. Save leftover wallpaper paste in a small plastic squeeze bottle.

Most wallpapers can be covered, when new, with a clear protective wallpaper coating; ask your wallpaper dealer for information. Test the coating on a scrap before using it on the walls, then roll it on like paint. Wallpaper treated with this coating can be washed.

Sponge washable wallpaper with a mild detergent solution to remove dirt. On nonwashable papers, use an artists' kneaded eraser to clean the wall. You may have to clean the whole wall to eliminate the clean-spot effect.

Repaste loose seams with wallpaper paste; force paste under the edges from a squeeze bottle or apply it with an artists' small brush. Smooth the edge into place and press it down with a seam roller. Repaste overlaps and loose edges in vinyl wall coverings with vinyl adhesive.

To eliminate a blister in newly pasted wallpaper, puncture the blister with a sharp straight pin. Press the edges of

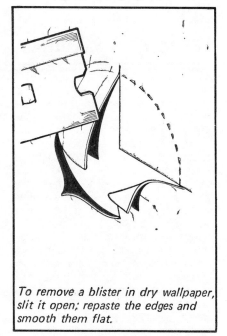

To remove a blister in dry wallpaper, slit it open; repaste the edges and smooth them flat.

the blister down toward the puncture to squeeze out excess paste. Wipe clean with a damp sponge and press with a seam roller. Remove a blister in completely dry wallpaper by cutting a cross in it with a sharp razor blade. Carefully bend the cut edges back, squeeze a little paste into the dried blister, and smooth the edges of the blister down flat. Remove excess paste with a damp sponge and press with a seam roller.

Use wallpaper scraps to patch torn or badly stained areas. Match a scrap exactly to the pattern in the damaged section. Tear out a patch from the scrap, slightly larger than the damaged spot. Tear the patch by hand in an irregular shape, feathering the back of the paper so that it doesn't have a sharply defined edge. Spread wallpaper paste on the back of the patch with your finger and set the patch into place, being careful to match the pattern and smoothing it from the center out. Remove excess paste with a damp sponge.

If the paper is badly worn and you have no scraps, touch up the colors carefully with felt-tip pens.

Make Wallpaper Cleaner

There's no need to buy special wallpaper cleaner. This inexpensive cleaning compound is strong enough for most stubborn stains, yet gentle enough for more delicate wallpaper. **Equipment:** measuring cup, large pot, stir stick, large mixing bowl, measuring spoons. **Ingredients:** water, salt, alum, kerosene, all-purpose flour. **Yield:** about 2½ to 3 pounds.

Pour 4 cups of water into a large pot and heat it to a boil. Add 1 pound of salt and 4 ounces of alum to the water, and stir until the solids dissolve. Transfer the solution to a large bowl and add 2 tablespoons of kerosene. Stirring constantly, sift in 2½ pounds (10 cups) of all-purpose flour; stir the mixture until it becomes doughy. Knead the dough by hand until it's free of lumps.

To use the compound, wipe the wall to remove dust. Rub the cleaner onto the wall, using single strokes in one direction; test an inconspicuous area before applying cleaner to the whole wall. Leave the cleaner on the wall for 10 to 12 hours; then remove it with a soft cloth.

Panel a Room

Paneling a room with plywood or hardboard sheets is a great way to finish a basement or cover badly damaged walls. On smooth, level interior walls, install the paneling directly over the old wall; otherwise, provide a sound base with a framework of 1 × 2 or 1 × 3 furring strips. Do not install paneling directly on an unfinished stud wall. The panels are hard to handle, so you'll need an assistant. **Tools:** measuring rule, long straight board, putty knife or paint scraper, sanding block, magnetic stud finder, pencil, chalked plumb line, hammer, staple gun, small paintbrush, two sawhorses, two long 2 × 4's; fine-toothed saber saw or circular saw, coping saw, and keyhole saw; safety goggles, scribing compass, level, tape, scissors, caulking gun, padded wood block, drill, miter box, fine-toothed backsaw for cutting molding, nail set. **Materials:** plastic dropcloths, spackling compound, coarse-grit sandpaper, 1 × 2 or 1 × 3 furring strips, shims, 8-penny common nails or steel masonry nails, heavy polyethylene sheet plastic, heavy-duty staples, paint to match panels, plywood or hardboard panels— the standard size is 4 × 8 feet, but if your ceilings are high, you can order 4 × 10 foot sheets — 2-penny or 4-penny finishing nails or colored nails provided by paneling manufacturer, panel adhesive, masking tape, prefinished ceiling and baseboard moldings, wood putty. **Time:** about 2 to 3 days.

Before buying wall paneling, calculate how many panels you'll need. Because the panels are a standard 4 × 8 feet—or, for high ceilings, 4 × 10—you need to figure only in terms of width. Measure the total diameter of the room in feet and divide by 4; subtract ½ panel for each door and ¼ panel for each window. The result is the number of panels you need. Ask the lumber dealer to calculate the amounts of furring strips, polyethylene sheet plastic, adhesive, and nails for you; buy a bundle of shims. Buy prefinished ceiling and baseboard molding by the foot, to match your paneling.

At least 48 hours before you start to work, move the panels into the room where they'll be installed. Lay several furring strips parallel on the floor and set the first panel flat on the strips; stack the rest of the panels the same way, with furring strips separating them. This is so they can adjust to the room's temperature and humidity.

Make sure the walls of the room to be paneled are smooth and level. Remove baseboards and molding from walls. With your assistant, hold a long straight board horizontally against each wall surface; slide it up and down over the wall to identify high spots and depressions. Spread plastic dropcloths to

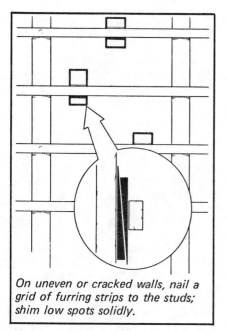

On uneven or cracked walls, nail a grid of furring strips to the studs; shim low spots solidly.

at every point where two wall panels will meet. Paint these verticals with any paint roughly the same color as the panels, so the furring strips won't show behind the finished wall.

Masonry walls must be specially treated. Attach furring strips horizontally with steel masonry nails: one strip at the floor, one at the ceiling, others at 16-inch intervals up the wall. Set vertical strips at the corners and at panel joints, shimming them out where necessary. Paint the joint-line strips and let dry. Then, before going any further, cover the walls with heavy polyethylene sheet plastic from floor to ceiling to protect the paneling from moisture. Staple the plastic carefully and evenly into place over the furring strips, making sure it's drawn smooth over the walls.

Finally, before you start to panel, remove switch and outlet cover plates. Pull the boxes out from the wall to match the thickness of the paneling, being careful not to disturb the wiring.

With the walls prepared, stand the paneling up around the room so you can see how it looks. Arrange it to balance full and partial panels and to match wood grains, and number the backs of the panels; start at a corner. Restack the panels in order, with the first panel up.

To cut the first panel, measure the distance from floor to ceiling at several points along the first 4-foot span. The panels must be nailed into place with a ¼-inch gap at both floor and ceiling, to allow for expansion of the wood. Mark the top of the panel to be trimmed, using the measured floor-to-ceiling distance and subtracting ½ inch for the gaps at top and bottom. Turn the panel face down over two sawhorses, with two long 2 × 4's under it to keep it from bending, and cut it to measure with a fine-toothed saber saw or circular saw. Wear safety goggles while you make the cut.

The first panel must be scribed so that it fits exactly into the corner. Stand the panel upright in the corner and wedge shims under it to raise it ¼ inch off the floor. Use a level to make sure

protect the floor. Fill low spots in the walls with spackling compound, smoothed on with a putty knife or paint scraper; sand high spots level with coarse-grit sandpaper.

If the wall is very uneven or badly cracked, you must nail 1 × 2 or 1 × 3 furring strips up to give the paneling a solid base. Use a magnetic stud finder to locate the studs across each wall; mark these points. Snap a chalked plumb line from each marked point to mark the nailing lines for the furring strips.

Nail furring strips horizontally across each wall with 8-penny common nails, nailing into the marked studs. Place one strip at the ceiling and one along the floor; space strips 16 inches apart, center to center, between ceiling and floor. Wedge shims behind the strips at any low spots, and drive a nail through both furring strip and shim into the wall.

When all horizontal furring strips have been nailed up, cut vertical pieces to fit between the horizontals. Set vertical strips from floor to ceiling in each corner, nailing them along the chalked stud lines. Nail vertical furring strips the same way, floor to ceiling, at wall studs

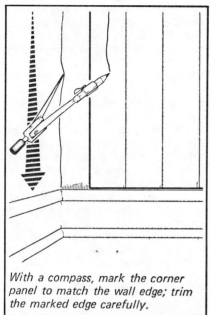

With a compass, mark the corner panel to match the wall edge; trim the marked edge carefully.

it's exactly vertical.

There will probably be an uneven gap between the panel edge and the corner. With your assistant holding the panel in place in the corner, set a scribing compass at the top of the panel, point in the corner and pencil on the panel. Hold the compass steady and draw it down the corner, pressing firmly enough to mark a fine pencil line down the panel. Trim the panel carefully along this line with the saber saw or a fine-toothed coping saw.

Install the panels with nails, adhesive, or a combination of the two, according to the manufacturer's recommendation. Heavy plywood panels should always be nailed up, and even lightweight panels should be nailed along the floor and the ceiling. The moldings used at floor and ceiling will cover these nails.

To install the panels with nails, use 2-penny finishing nails over furring strips, 4-penny finishing nails if you're setting the paneling right over the old wall; or use the colored nails provided by the paneling manufacturer. Set the first panel, with edge trimmed, carefully into place in the corner. Set the bottom

of the panel on shims again to maintain the ¼-inch gap at the floor, and make sure it's plumb.

Start nailing at the furring strip or on the stud line at the center of the corner edge. Drive a row of nails across the center of the panel at 12-inch intervals; use a nail set to sink the heads without damaging the paneling. Move up 16 inches to the next horizontal furring strip and repeat, working from the center of the panel up and out. Continue nailing up to the ceiling and then down to the floor, setting nails 12 inches apart along every horizontal furring strip, or on each marked stud line of a wall being covered directly. When the entire panel has been nailed down, drive nails every 6 inches around the edges, and remove the shims under the bottom edge.

Continue around the room, butting each new panel against the last one, measuring and trimming each panel as you go. Scribe each corner panel. To work around doors, windows, or outlets, use the protective paper sheets that come between the panels. Hold a sheet of paper against the wall, exactly where the panel will go, and have your assistant tape it firmly into place, top and bottom. Trace the outline of each obstruction with a pencil.

Untape the sheet and cut out the traced areas; lay the paper over the panel and trace the cutouts onto the panel. Cut out large openings with the saber saw or circular saw; drill small holes and use a coping saw or a keyhole saw to cut holes for switch plates.

To install the panels with adhesive, use the brand recommended by the panel manufacturer; apply the adhesive with a caulking gun. Start in the corner with the scribed and trimmed first panel. Run a solid bead of adhesive over all furring strips the panel will cover; if you're paneling over a solid wall, apply adhesive in a grid pattern. Set the panel into place in the corner, resting on shims to maintain the ¼-inch gap at the floor. With the panel exactly positioned, drive a row of nails at 12-inch intervals across the top of the panel.

At this point, reread the instructions

for the panel adhesive. Depending on the adhesive you're using, you may have to pull the panel away from the wall until the adhesive is tacky. If this is the case, pull the bottom of the panel out from the wall and prop it in place with a piece of scrap wood for the time specified by the manufacturer; then remove the prop and press the panel flat against the wall.

As soon as the panel is flat against the wall, set it permanently: using a padded wood block to protect the panel's surface, pound it firmly into place with a hammer. Go over the whole panel with the hammer and padded block. Finally, drive nails at 6-inch intervals all along the floor and ceiling edges of the panel, and remove the shims under the bottom edge.

When the first panel is pounded down and nailed into place, continue around the room, measuring and trimming as you go. Finish installing each panel before you go on to the next one.

To complete the newly paneled room, fill all nail holes with wood putty. Finally, install prefinished ceiling and baseboard molding. Miter corners with a miter box and a fine-toothed backsaw, and nail the molding into place.

Install Pegboard

Pegboard, a perforated hardboard, can be used to store almost anything—it holds hooks, jars, trays, brackets, clips, or racks, from sewing room to garage. Use ⅛-inch pegboard for light-duty jobs, ¼-inch for tools and other heavy items. It's a snap to install. **Tools:** measuring rule, magnetic stud finder, pencil, safety goggles; fine-toothed saber saw or circular saw, or fine-toothed crosscut saw; sanding block, coping saw, screwdriver or caulking gun, hammer, padded wood block, paintbrush. **Materials:** ⅛-inch or ¼-inch pegboard sheet, medium- and fine-grit sandpaper; 1½-inch screws, molly bolts, or toggle bolts, or hardboard adhesive; 4-penny common

nails, 1 × 2 or 1 × 3 furring strips or ½-inch rubber screw spacers, paint, hooks or other mounting fixtures as desired. **Time:** 1 to 2 hours.

Pegboard is sold in 4 × 8 sheets; cut it for wall storage areas or use whole sheets as room dividers. At least 48 hours before you install it, set it upright against a wall in the room where it will be used, so it will adjust to the room's temperature and humidity.

Before cutting the pegboard, measure the area to be covered. Using a magnetic stud finder, locate and mark the wall studs; in a garage or basement, simply measure the distance across studs. If possible, place the pegboard to extend across studs, with the edges of the board over the studs.

Wearing safety goggles, cut the sheet to the desired size, using a fine-toothed saber saw or circular saw; you can cut it with a crosscut saw, but the power saw is much easier. Cut the board face down with a power saw, face up with a crosscut saw. Mark and cut the board to avoid cutting through the holes.

Sand the edges of the board with medium-grit and then fine-grit sandpaper, being careful not to sand the face of the pegboard. If desired, round the corners of the pegboard carefully with a coping saw and then sand them.

To install pegboard over bare studs, set the board into place and fasten it with 1½-inch screws at the corners. Use screws every 12 inches on large boards. If the board won't have to hold much weight, it can be applied with hardboard adhesive instead of screws. Apply a solid bead of adhesive to the studs with a caulking gun, set the board firmly in place, and pound the adhesive joints with a hammer and a padded wood block.

To install pegboard on a finished wall, you must provide clearance behind the board for the hooks used in it. Nail 1 × 2 or 1 × 3 furring strips along the studs on the wall where the board will go; use 4-penny common nails. Set the pegboard into place on the furring strips and fasten it with 1½-inch screws at the corners.

If you don't want to use furring strips, provide hook clearance behind the board with ½-inch rubber spacers, available at hardware stores. Slip the spacers over the screw shanks and set the board into place; fasten the screws to the marked studs.

If you must set pegboard between studs, or if one end of the board falls between studs, use molly bolts instead of regular screws to fasten the board into place. For pegboard that will be used to hold tools or other heavy items, use toggle bolts.

Paint the pegboard as desired after installation; high-gloss enamel makes a nice accent. Apply paint sparingly, being careful not to clog the holes in the board, and let dry completely before inserting hooks.

Cover a Wall with Brick

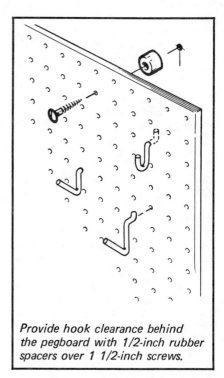

Provide hook clearance behind the pegboard with 1/2-inch rubber spacers over 1 1/2-inch screws.

Brick walls inside don't have to be plastic; the real thing is just as easy. Use bricks cast thin for interior use, and set them into place with adhesive. **Tools:** measuring rule, bucket and sponge; putty knife or paint scraper, sanding block, and wall-cleaning sponge, or large paintbrush and broad-bladed scraper; ⅜-inch dowel rod, line level, chalk, safety goggles, cold chisel and hammer, tile nippers, coarse file, notched trowel. **Materials:** graph paper, strong household detergent, plastic dropcloths; spackling compound and fine-grit sandpaper, or wallpaper remover and wall sizing; thin glue-on interior bricks, adhesive and adhesive solvent as recommended by the brick manufacturer, clean rags. **Time:** several hours for a small wall, after wall surface is prepared.

Before buying the bricks, plot the wall on a piece of graph paper. Draw the brick layout to be used and count the number of bricks needed, if any, to go around corners. Interior face brick is sold in packages to cover 5 square feet; to calculate the number of packages you need, compute the square footage to be covered and divide by 5. Buy an extra package of brick and a few extra corner bricks to allow for wastage. Ask the dealer how much adhesive and adhesive solvent to buy.

Prepare the wall before applying the bricks. If the wall is very dirty or greasy, wash it with a strong household detergent. Spread plastic dropcloths to protect the floor. Scrape painted surfaces and fill cracks and holes with spackling compound; let dry and sand smooth with fine-grit sandpaper. Remove all dust with a wall-cleaning sponge.

If the wall is papered, remove loose wallpaper; apply wallpaper remover with a large paintbrush, let it stand as directed by the manufacturer, and scrape carefully to remove all old paper. Go over the wall with clean water to remove all paste; let dry. Apply wall sizing to seal the wall, using one or two coats as directed by the manufacturer. Let dry completely.

Use a ⅜-inch dowel rod to measure

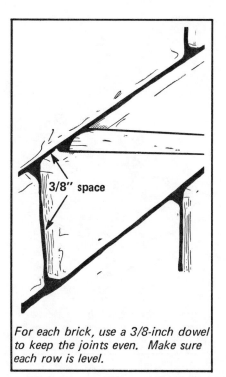

For each brick, use a 3/8-inch dowel to keep the joints even. Make sure each row is level.

set each brick, dab adhesive across the back of the brick and press it firmly against the wall; twist the brick slightly as you set it in place. Use the dowel rod to establish and maintain the ⅜-inch joint width between bricks.

Continue across and up the wall, setting one row of bricks at a time and spacing them a constant ⅜ inch apart. As each row is completed, check it with the line level to make sure the row is straight. If you must turn a corner, use special corner bricks.

When all the bricks have been set, fill in any gaps at the edges of the wall with adhesive. Finally, smooth joints where necessary, using the dowel rod, and clean adhesive from the brick face with a rag soaked in adhesive solvent. Throw dropcloths and solvent-soaked rags away.

Install Mirror or Cork Tiles

brick joints as you work. Use a line level to establish the bottom edge of the bricks along the floor; mark the line with chalk. Small gaps below the line can be filled in with brick adhesive. Set out two rows of bricks on the floor, ⅜ inch apart, so you can see how to place them on the wall. Arrange the bricks so that the bricks at the right end of each row will be the same size as those at the left end when they're cut to fit.

Wearing safety goggles, cut the end bricks to the correct size. Use a cold chisel and hammer to score both sides of each brick; then cover the brick with a rag and break it in two with a sharp hammer blow. Remove any pieces left along the broken edge with tile nippers; smooth the broken edge, if necessary, with a coarse file.

When the layout has been checked and end bricks cut, spread an even layer of adhesive on the wall with a notched trowel. Start at either corner, along the chalked line that marks the bottom row of bricks; cover only about 3 square feet of wall surface at a time. To

Cork tiles add warmth and make an instant bulletin board; mirror tiles make a small room bigger and are far less expensive than a plate-glass mirror. Both kinds of tile are easy to install. **Tools:** measuring rule, pencil, level, chalk line, scissors, chalk, yardstick; sharp utility knife or heavy-duty scissors, or glass cutter, safety goggles, and work gloves. **Materials:** graph paper; $3/_{22}$-inch-thick, distortion-free glass mirror tiles or cork squares; heavy-duty double-stick · wall-mount tape, newspaper. **Time:** about 2 hours for an 8 × 10-foot area.

Buy mirror or cork tiles precut in 1-foot squares. Before you buy the tiles, measure the wall or door to be covered and sketch it on graph paper. Plan the pattern you want to use—a simple block pattern is easiest, but you can also set the tiles in a diamond or other pattern. If you're tiling only part of a wall, you won't have to cut the tiles. If you're tiling the entire wall, plan your arrangement so that you have to cut as

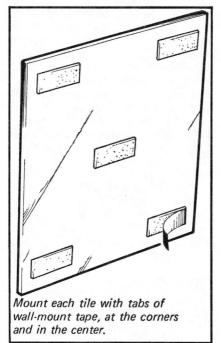

Mount each tile with tabs of wall-mount tape, at the corners and in the center.

Score mirror tiles with a glass cutter; snap back along the score to complete the break.

few tiles as possible at the edges of the wall.

Count the number of tiles you need; if you'll have to cut tiles, allow several extra for wastage. If the tiles don't come with mounting tape, buy heavy-duty double-stick wall-mount tape to put them up with.

Before tiling the wall, make sure it's clean and smooth. Remove any loose paint or wallpaper and smooth the wall surface as necessary.

Start setting tile at a bottom corner of the wall, or at the floor on one side of the area to be covered. Snap a chalk line down the wall at the corner and check it with a level to be sure it's plumb; adjust the line as necessary. If the corner is out of plumb, you're probably better off stopping the tiles short of the corner instead of cutting them to fit.

To install the first row of tiles, start with the bottom or corner tile. If the tiles already have mounting tape on the reverse side, peel off the backing paper as you place each tile. If the tiles don't include mounting tape, cut five 1½-inch pieces of heavy-duty double-stick

wall-mount tape. Apply a piece of tape to each corner of the tile, parallel with the tile edge, and set the last piece in the middle of the tile. Align the side of the tile on the chalk line and press it firmly but gently into place. Work up the chalk line to set each tile in the first row; work vertically and butt the bottom of each tile against the top of the last one. Place tiles the same way all across the area to be covered, butting the edge of each tile against the tile edge of the last row.

To cut cork tiles, measure and mark to the required width with chalk. Cut with a sharp utility knife and use a yardstick as a straightedge; if the tiles are thin, use a heavy-duty scissors. To cut mirror tiles, measure and mark to the required width. Spread newspaper to protect your work surface, and set the marked tiles face up on the paper. Wearing safety goggles, score each tile at the marked point with a glass cutter; hold the cutter vertically and cut along the yardstick as a straightedge. Wearing work gloves, turn the scored tile over and snap it sharply backward to break it at the scored line.

Finally, when all tiles have been cut and set, go back over the tiles to make sure they're solidly in place. Press each tile gently but firmly at the corners and in the middle to bond the wall-mount tape completely to the wall and to the tile surfaces.

Hang Heavy Objects

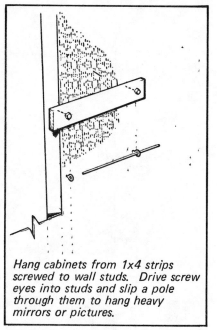

Hang cabinets from 1x4 strips screwed to wall studs. Drive screw eyes into studs and slip a pole through them to hang heavy mirrors or pictures.

There is no real mystery about hanging heavy objects, such as mirrors, cabinets, lights, or paintings. The trick is in selecting and installing the proper hanger hardware. **Tools:** hammer, sledgehammer, drill and drill set, masonry drill, star drill, wood or metal pole, wrench set, pliers, screwdrivers, level, measuring rule, chalk line, magnetic stud finder, putty knife, safety goggles. **Materials:** 1 × 4, contact cement, lag bolts, construction adhesive, screws; plastic, fiber, or lead anchors; concrete nails, hanger screws, molly bolts, toggle bolts, J-clips, L-clips, surface or screw plates, wire, decorative rope, or cord. **Time:** 5 minutes to 1 hour.

Use these hangers and hanging techniques to mount objects placing more than 10 pounds per square inch of shear or dead weight on the wall. Buy the necessary hardware at a hardware store or a home center.

Drywall or plaster. If possible, locate the wall studs or ceiling joists. Studs can usually be located with a magnetic stud finder. Most heavy objects can be hung on screws, screw hooks, lag screws, or annular-ring nails driven into the studs or joists. If you're hanging large cabinets, span the studs behind the cabinet with a length of 1 × 4, and fasten this strip to the studs with lag screws or heavy wood screws countersunk into the surface of the wood strip. Mount the cabinet to the strip.

If you can't locate the studs or joists —or if these framing members are inconveniently placed—use molly or toggle bolts designed for the thickness of the wall material. These fasteners fan or spring out behind the wall, gripping the wall when the screws are driven in. When using toggle bolts, remove the screw from the spring-loaded wings and run the screw through the object to be mounted; then reattach the wings to the screw and thread the wings through a predrilled hole in the wall. Once it's in the wall, you can't remove the bolt and reuse it; the bolt wings fall into the interior of the wall when it's unscrewed.

To mount heavy mirrors, use plastic L-clips or metal J-clips, fastened to the studs with screws or to the wall material with molly or toggle bolts. For extremely heavy paintings and mirrors, run screw eyes into the studs spanning the width of the object; make sure the eyes are aligned horizontally with each other. Slip a wood or metal pole through the screw eyes and hang the object with wire or decorative rope or cord attached to the pole.

If you don't want to drill a hole into the wall or ceiling, use a surface or screw

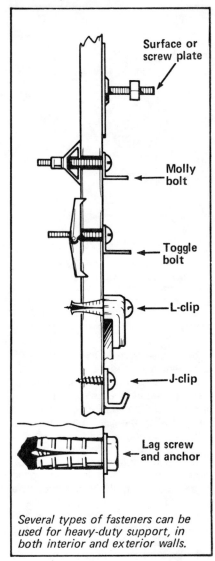

Several types of fasteners can be used for heavy-duty support, in both interior and exterior walls.

Surface or screw plate

Molly bolt

Toggle bolt

L-clip

J-clip

Lag screw and anchor

onto the lag or regular screw, and drive the screw into the anchor. *Caution: Wear safety goggles when drilling masonry.*

Hollow tile. Use a short toggle or molly bolt slipped through a hole drilled in the tile. To drill through hollow tile, use a variable-speed electric drill with a masonry bit; this protects the glaze. Run the drill slowly to prevent the drill from skipping over the tile.

Brick and concrete. Use lag screws, regular screws, and plastic, fiber, or lead anchors to set hangers into brick or concrete. Drilling anchor holes takes time; use an electric drill and a masonry bit, or, for more jagged holes, a star drill and a sledgehammer. *Caution: Wear safety goggles.*

Use masonry nails set in mortar joints for objects that put no more than 10 pounds per inch of shear weight on the nails. Don't use masonry nails for extremely heavy objects; the mortar joints will crumble.

Metal studs. Drill a hole through the wall and into the metal stud. Then use a self-tapping metal screw to hang the object.

Build a Wall Safe

A small wall safe in your home is a convenient way to protect valuables, and it's very easy to install. **Tools:** pencil, keyhole saw or saber saw, measuring rule, carpenters' square, hammer, caulking gun, magnetic stud finder, brace and bits, putty knife, butt chisel, adjustable wrench. **Materials:** wall safe, 2 × 4's, 16-penny common nails, ½ × 2-inch lag screws, spackling compound, construction adhesive, scrap drywall, sandpaper, finishing materials. **Time:** about 4 hours.

Because burglars like to hit and run, the odds are against a burglar's opening a wall safe or removing it from the wall. At least as important, a home wall safe is a protection against fire; many

plate that fastens to the wall with construction adhesive or contact cement. A metal rod protruding from the plate is threaded so a tap or nut can be used for support.

Concrete and cinder block. To hang heavy objects on a masonry wall, use lag screws or regular screws driven into plastic, fiber, or lead anchors. Drill a hole in the block where you want the hanger to be positioned. Insert an anchor into the hole, thread the hanger home safes are constructed to withstand temperatures up to 2000° F for 1 hour. Safes are available in a variety of styles and types. Buy the safe you need from a lock and safe company. Look in the telephone advertising pages for the listings.

The best location for a safe is in a wall that partitions off a closet area. The safe's depth may range from 6 to 10 inches or more; since it's installed between studs, back space is necessary to accommodate this depth. If wall space isn't available, the safe could be installed in a floor over a crawl space and covered with a trap door or throw rug. Choose a location out of the room's traffic pattern—under a shelf in the pantry, for example, or in a kitchen base cabinet.

To install the safe in a wall, choose a site and locate two parallel wall studs with a magnetic stud finder; most wall studs are 16 inches apart. Draw a vertical line identifying each wall stud; the safe will rest between these studs. Measure the length of the safe, and draw lines between the stud lines to mark the top, bottom, and sides of the safe.

With a brace and a ½-inch bit, drill holes in the wall at opposite corners of the outline, *inside* the lines and just touching them. Make sure the holes are inside the stud; once you've exposed the stud, it can serve as your vertical sawing guide. Saw out the hole for the safe with a keyhole saw or a saber saw. Trim any miscutting with a butt chisel. Remove the drywall over the studs where the flanges of the safe will be connected to the studs.

If there's a finished wall on the opposite side of the wall, remove the wall sheathing from the safe area on this side. Transfer the dimensions of the wall safe onto this opposite wall, drill starting holes, and cut along the lines as above; make sure the hole on the opposite side lines up perfectly with the original hole. Do *not* cut out drywall for the safe's flanges.

Measure and cut four 2 × 4's for headers to fit between the studs. Make double headers by nailing two 2 × 4's

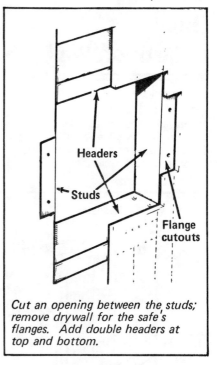

Cut an opening between the studs; remove drywall for the safe's flanges. Add double headers at top and bottom.

together with 16-penny common nails. Toenail these double headers to the wall studs, setting one just below and one just above where the safe will rest.

The safe is lag-screwed through the flanges to the studs. Position the safe in the hole, and have a helper hold it steady from the back while you pencil in the position of the lag screws on the studs. Remove the safe and drill pilot holes at the marked screw points with a ⅛-inch bit. Reinsert the safe, align it with the drilled holes, and have your helper hold it in place. Drive lag screws through the holes and into the studs with an adjustable wrench, and tighten them firmly.

When the safe is fastened into the wall, cover the flanges and the bolt heads with strips of scrap drywall; attach the drywall with construction adhesive. If necessary, cut tiny holes for the lag screw heads in the gypsum board. Fill all joints of the patches with spackling compound and let the wall dry. Then sand the surface smooth and finish the wall.

Build a Partition Wall

A non-load-bearing partition wall is the fastest, easiest, and least expensive way to divide a large room into several rooms or add closet space to almost any room. Build the partition wall on the floor and then set it into place. **Tools:** hammer, sledgehammer, saw, carpenters' square, measuring rule, level, putty knife, broad-bladed drywall knife, safety goggles. **Materials:** 2 × 4 or 2 × 3 pine stock, 16-penny common nails, coated or annular drywall nails, ⅜ × 4 × 8 drywall boards, drywall joint compound and joint tape, cedar shims, concrete nails (depending on flooring), medium-grit sandpaper. **Time:** about 6 hours, over 2 or 3 days.

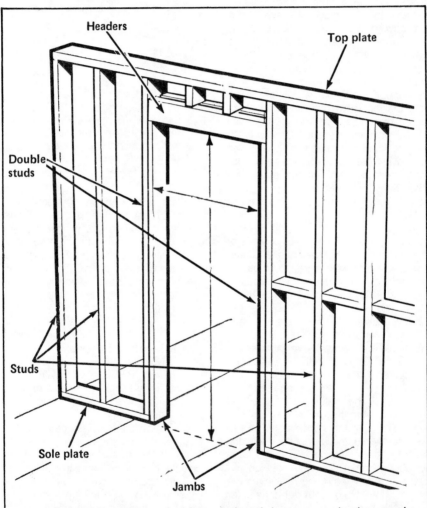

A partition wall is constructed with vertical studs between a sole plate, on the floor, and a top plate, along the ceiling. Double studs frame the door jambs; double headers are used at the top of the door.

132

If the ceiling above the proposed partition wall has exposed ceiling joists, the construction is easy. If the joists aren't readily accessible, you must remove part of the ceiling to provide access. At times, this means removing a few ceiling tiles, which can easily be resized and replaced; other ceiling constructions require more extensive work. Be sure you know what you're up against as far as the ceiling is concerned before building a partition wall.

Measure from the floor to the ceiling at several spots along the length of the proposed wall. Find the *shortest* distance from floor to ceiling, and work with that measurement; it's easier to shim or block gaps than to notch the top or the bottom (sole) plates of the wall to fit. The new wall will be sandwiched between the ceiling and the floor.

A wall frame is composed of two basic parts: the horizontal plates or boards that make up the top (top plate) and bottom (sole plate) of the wall; and the vertical studs, which stand between the top and sole plates.

Frame the wall with 2 × 4 or 2 × 3 pine stock; 2 × 4's are easier to work with. The studs are positioned between a 2 × 4 top and a 2 × 4 sole plate. Cut the studs to the floor/ceiling measurement, less 3 inches for the thickness of the plates.

Lay the pieces flat on the floor, and mark the position of the studs on the plates. Space the studs 16 inches apart, measuring from the center of one stud to the center of the other (on center). If you want a door in the wall, use double studs at the sides of the door opening (the jambs) and at the top of the door (the header). This gives the opening more strength. Make sure the marks on the top plate align with the marks on the sole plate.

Position the studs between the plates, following your marks. Nail straight through the faces of the plates into the studs—two nails at both the top and the sole plates. By nailing the studs through the faces of the plates, you eliminate toenailing (angled nailing), and avoid splits in the wood. This also adds strength to the wall, and floor-access nailing is easier.

Tip the wall frame up into position and plumb—vertically level—it. Nail the top plate to the ceiling joists and the bottom plate to the floor, using two 16-penny nails at each joist. If the floor is concrete, use concrete nails driven with a sledgehammer. Drive the nailheads flush with the surface of the sole plate and stop pounding; overpounding will cause the nails to loosen in the concrete. *Caution: Wear safety goggles when driving concrete nails.*

Fill any gaps between the top plate and the ceiling joists with cedar shims. Nailing the shims isn't necessary if they're wedged tight, but you may want to tack the shims into place.

When the frame of the wall is complete, nail drywall to the studs with coated or annular drywall nails; set the nails about 7 inches apart. Use two nails at each nailing point, to eliminate nail pops. Drive the nails flush with the drywall surface and then hammer them once more to sink the nails into the drywall. The dimple left by the hammer will be filled with joint compound.

Spread joint compound over the drywall joints with a putty knife; embed the joint tape in the compound with a broad-bladed drywall knife. Hold the knife at about a 45-degree angle across the tape, and lightly but firmly press the tape into the compound. Let the tape dry for at least 24 hours; then apply a fill coat of joint compound over the first layer, feathering it out. Let the compound dry for 2 days; then lightly sand the joints. If the humidity is high in the room, apply another coat of joint compound over the tape, let it dry, and sand the surfaces smooth.

If the wall will go around a corner, use metal outside corner strips to finish the drywall; set a strip over the corner, nail it into place, and tape the edges as above. For inside corners, crease the tape lengthwise to fit the corner; embed the tape in joint compound, and finish the corner as above.

When the wall is completely finished, apply a coat of primer. Finish the wall with two coats of paint; sand lightly between coats.

Floors and Stairs

Install Wall-to-Wall Carpeting

Installing carpeting takes preparation and care, but it doesn't take much special skill. Very large rooms require power stretchers, so leave those to the professionals—the rest of the house is yours. **Tools:** measuring rule, hammer, nail set, screwdriver, putty knife, vacuum cleaner, work gloves, tack hammer, ¼-inch-thick piece of scrap wood, small handsaw, heavy scissors, staple gun, paintbrush or fine-toothed notched trowel, utility knife with sharp heavy-duty blades; knee kicker, available on rental from most carpet dealers; block of scrap wood, plane. **Materials:** graph paper, flooring nails, wood putty, tackless carpet fastening strips, metal door edging strip for each doorway in room, latex or vinyl foam carpet padding, foam padding adhesive, heavy-duty staples, precut and preseamed carpeting. **Time:** 1 to 2 days, depending on preparation necessary.

Probably the most difficult part of installing carpeting is calculating exactly what to buy and how to place it. Carpeting is sold in 9-foot, 12-foot, and 15-foot widths; padding is sold in standard 4½-foot rolls. Before you buy, measure the room to be carpeted and draw a floor plan on graph paper—make sure your measurements are exact. Mark the exact position and width of all doors, windows, fireplaces, radiators, and other wall interruptions, and include the full depth of door frames. Take this floor plan with you to the carpet dealer.

Plan the layout of the carpeting and the padding carefully with the dealer to take advantage of the full width of the carpeting and to minimize seaming in heavy-traffic areas. Calculate the square yardage to be carpeted—length times width, divided by 9—and take the dealer's advice on the lengths of carpeting and padding you'll need.

It is possible to cut and seam the carpeting yourself, but this can be tricky. In a small room, no wider than the carpet roll, you won't have to make seams; otherwise, have the carpet dealer cut and seam the carpeting to fit the room.

The dealer should also determine the amount and type of tackless strip fastener you need. The fastener comes in 4-foot strips. The type depends on the thickness of your carpet and the floor you're covering; the strips have preset edge tacks and preset nails for installation over wood or concrete. Be sure to buy the right kind, and buy a strip or two extra to allow for mistakes. Have metal door edging strips cut to the exact measure of your doors.

Finally, rent a knee kicker from the carpet dealer. The kicker is used to stretch the edges of the carpet onto the fastening strips.

Before installing the carpeting, prepare the floor. Move all furniture out of the room and remove doors that open into the room. Pound in any loose nails and reset squeaky floorboards with flooring nails, using a nail set to drive the heads below the floor surface. Condensation can be a problem when resilient flooring is carpeted; if the floor is covered with resilient tile or sheet flooring, remove the old flooring and then prepare the subfloor.

To complete preparations for the carpet installation, remove floor register covers and, if you want it to cover the carpeting, quarter-round baseboard molding. Fill in any wide cracks in the floor with wood putty, smoothed over with a putty knife, and let the patches dry completely. Vacuum the room thoroughly before you start.

The first step is nailing down the fastening strips. Starting at a corner, nail strips along the edge of the floor, ¼ inch from the wall, with their teeth pointing toward the wall; use a tack hammer to drive the preset nails through the strips and into the floor. Wear work gloves to protect your hands. To make sure the strips are nailed evenly and to maintain the ¼-inch gap, slide a ¼-inch-thick piece of scrap wood, on edge, between the strip and the wall as you nail each fastener into place. Work around the room, sliding this guide board along the wall as you nail the fastener strips into place.

To work around corners, cut fastener strips to fit with a small handsaw. Nail strips in front of radiators unless there's enough clearance under them to admit the knee kicker with room to spare—there usually isn't. Set strips closely around open floor registers. Nail a metal door edging strip across the floor in each doorway, open rim pointing into the room and teeth pointing out. The rim should line up exactly under the edge of the door when both carpet and door are in place.

When all the fastener strips have been nailed into place, take the rolled-up carpeting and pull it into position in the room and unroll it, right over the bare floor. This is so you won't jerk the padding out of place later by pulling the carpeting across it. Roll the carpeting back from one side toward the center of the room, exposing the floor again.

Unroll a strip of foam padding along the edge of the floor across the bare side of the room from wall to wall, waffle-patterned side up. Cut the strip carefully with heavy scissors, leaving about 2 inches overlapping the fastening strips at each end. Pull the strip to position it over the bare end of the floor so that it overlaps the fastening strips on both ends and along the wall. Then staple it into place, using a staple gun to set staples diagonally every 6 inches or

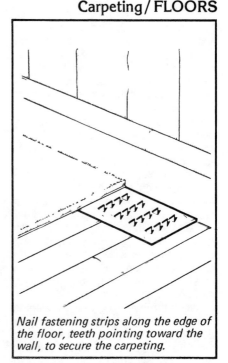

Nail fastening strips along the edge of the floor, teeth pointing toward the wall, to secure the carpeting.

so along all four edges of the padding.

Cover the rest of the room the same way, rolling the carpeting back so you can roll the padding into place. Butt the edges of the strips of padding and staple every 6 inches along every edge. Trim the padding as necessary to fit around obstacles, cutting as closely as possible around them.

On concrete floors, use carpet padding adhesive to anchor the foam padding. Position the padding as above and roll it back from one side, then spread adhesive on the exposed floor as directed, using a paintbrush or a fine-toothed notched trowel. Roll the padding out onto the adhesive, pressing and smoothing it into place. To complete the gluing, roll the padding back from the other wall, apply the adhesive, and unroll the padding. Repeat, butting the strips of padding, until the entire floor is padded. Fill in under radiators with small pieces of padding.

When all the padding has been set into position, trim off the edges overlapping the fastening strips. Use a utility knife with a sharp heavy-duty blade to

FLOORS / Carpeting

trim the excess padding; holding the knife at an angle toward you, cut the padding off exactly where it meets the inside edge of the fastening strips. The surface of the padding should be more or less level with the surface of the fastening strips.

Finally, unroll the carpeting over the padding and pull it carefully into position, overlapping the fastening strips all around the room. Slit the folded-up carpeting vertically where it goes around corners, being careful not to cut past the overlap into the main carpet, so that the edges lie flat against both corner walls. Make straight cuts and crosscuts to fit the carpeting around radiators and other obstructions; don't cut holes in the carpet to accommodate them. Trim carefully around open floor registers, leaving a slight overlap.

Attach the carpeting to the fastening strips with the knee kicker. Starting in a corner, set the head of the kicker flat on the carpet, about an inch from the wall and aimed slightly down and at an angle to the wall. Kneeling on the floor at the corner, hold the handle of the kicker with one hand and lean on the floor with the other. Put all your weight on the knee opposite the arm holding the kicker and move your other knee forward sharply to hit the cushioned end

Strike the knee kicker firmly to stretch the carpeting into place over the fastening strips.

of the kicker. The head of the kicker will stretch the carpeting under it to hook it onto the teeth of the fastening strip at the edge of the floor, leaving an untrimmed edge of carpeting still sticking up against the wall. Repeat the kicking process to fasten the carpeting on the opposite wall of the corner.

After kicking the first corner of the room into place, fasten the two adjacent corners the same way, leaving the diagonally opposite corner loose. Then work from your starting corner out along the two walls of the corner, holding the just-fastened carpeting in place with one hand and using the other to kick the next few inches of carpeting. Make sure the carpeting lies flat and doesn't shift as you work. Fasten the third side of the carpet, working toward the loose corner, and then fasten the fourth side.

Use a utility knife with a sharp heavy-duty blade to trim the edges of the carpeting, and replace the blade as soon as it begins to dull. Cut off the turned-up edge of carpeting evenly, leaving about ⅜ inch still sticking up above the tacked-down edge. Cut carefully, and snip off any ragged tufts of yarn.

To complete the installation, use a stiff putty knife to wedge the trimmed edge of the carpeting down into the ¼-inch gap between the walls and the fastening strips. Press the cut edge of the carpeting firmly into place all around the room. To finish the edge at doorways, trim the carpet edge carefully to fit under the curved rim of the door finishing strip. Push the raw carpet edge under the rim and use a hammer and a wood block to pound the rim firmly down over the carpet edge.

Finally, replace floor registers—you may have to trim the carpet edge back farther, but cut carefully. Replace quarter-round baseboard molding if you removed it earlier, and rehang the doors. If the new carpeting and padding are much thicker than the old floor covering, you'll probably have to plane the bottom edge of each door so it can open and close easily. Remove the door from its hinges and plane the bottom edge carefully, planing from both ends toward the center. Rehang the door. Move the furniture back into the room.

Carpet a Stairway

Stair carpeting takes a lot more abuse than room carpeting, and it often wears out much sooner. Replacing a worn stair runner or carpeting a bare stairway is no problem when you know the technique. **Tools:** pliers, vacuum cleaner, measuring tape or rule, chalk or pencil, work gloves, small handsaw, hammer, heavy scissors, $^3{}_4$-inch-thick piece of scrap wood, staple gun, utility knife with sharp heavy-duty blades, awl, tack hammer, stair wedging tool or broad-bladed chisel; knee kicker, available on rental from most carpet dealers. **Materials:** tackless carpet fastening strips, heavy rubber or felt stair carpet padding, paper, heavy-duty staples, carpet runner. **Time:** about 3 to 4 hours for a short straight stairway, longer for long or winding stairways.

First remove old carpeting from the stairs. Use pliers to pull up any carpet tacks left in the wood, being careful not to splinter it. Vacuum the stairway thoroughly.

Measure the stairs carefully for the new carpet. On straight stairs, stretch a measuring tape or rule around one entire stair, starting at the inside edge of the tread and moving over the outside of the tread and down along the riser below it to the top of the next tread. Add 1 inch and multiply by the number of steps, not counting the last riser to the top landing. Measure any landings and add these measurements to the tread figure; add 1 inch to be turned in at the ends. Divide the total by 36 to determine the number of yards of carpet runner you need. You'll need roughly the same length of padding; the exact length used will be less because the padding doesn't cover the stair risers completely.

To measure for carpeting on a winding stairway, first measure straight

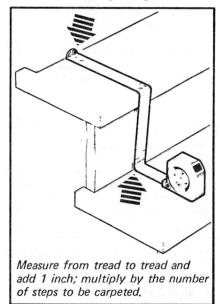

Measure from tread to tread and add 1 inch; multiply by the number of steps to be carpeted.

stairs and landings as above. Then measure each wedge-shaped or turning step at the widest point the carpet will cover, and add 1 inch. Measure each wedge-shaped step separately. To determine the number of yards of carpet runner and padding you need, add all the stair measurements together; add 1 inch for top and bottom edges and divide by 36.

Carpet runner is sold in standard 27-inch and 36-inch widths; buy the width that best fits your stairway. Don't try to use carpeting left over from a room installation—cut-to-fit carpet pieces have to be turned under at the edges all along the stairs, and that's tricky. Buy 6 inches or so more than you think you need, just to be safe.

Choose a high-quality heavy rubber or felt stair carpet padding; it doesn't pay to economize here. Ask the carpet dealer to figure the amount of padding and the number of tackless fastening strips you'll need—the strips will have to cover roughly twice the width of the stairway for each step.

Finally, rent a knee kicker from the carpet dealer. The kicker is used to stretch the carpeting tightly onto the fastening strips at each riser-tread intersection, producing a more stable runner than hand stretching techniques.

Begin the installation by nailing fastening strips at each riser-tread corner; wear work gloves. Measure the width of the stairway and subtract the part that will be covered by the carpet runner; divide by 2. This is the number of inches at each side of the stairs that won't be covered. Measure in this distance from one side of the stairway at the base of each riser and the inside of each tread; mark each of these points with chalk or pencil. Then measure in the same way from the other side of the stairs. Measure each stair across from mark to mark to make sure you've measured accurately; the carpet runner will be centered on these marks.

Cut the strips to the width of the runner with a small handsaw. On each stair, nail a strip centered on the riser, teeth pointing down, ¾ inch above the surface of the tread below it; use a ¾-inch-thick piece of scrap wood to hold the strip in place as you nail it. Nail another strip centered on the tread, teeth pointing in to the riser above it, ⅝ inch out from the riser. You'll end up with an open V of fastening strips at the

Nail fastening strips at each riser-tread corner; then staple a strip of padding to each tread.

back of each stair, straight or wedge-shaped, with one strip near the floor at the bottom of the lowest riser and one at the back of the top tread. Don't nail a strip onto the top riser.

After nailing the fastening strips, measure and mark the carpet padding. Measure the padding to the width of the carpet runner, less about ¼ inch so that it will be very slightly recessed under the carpet edge at each side. With a heavy scissors, cut a strip of padding to fit over each stair tread, long enough to wrap from the tread fastening strip around the tread and down about 2 or 3 inches onto the tread below it. Make a paper pattern to cut the padding for each wedge-shaped step; the padding must cover the tread, round the edge, and wrap over onto the riser below it.

Install the padding with staples. Center a trimmed piece of padding, waffle-patterned side up, on each tread, with its end butted against the fastening strip at the back of the tread. Staple the end of the padding to the tread, using a staple gun to set staples diagonally every 2 inches along the fastening strip. Stretch the other end of the padding out over the tread and down onto the riser below it; holding it evenly stretched, staple it into place. Use the paper pattern to cut padding for wedge-shaped stairs, and fasten the padding the same way.

Finally, unroll the carpet runner and drape it over the stairway, with the nap or pile leaning out and down from top to bottom. Winding stairways are treated as straight flights interrupted by wedge-shaped steps; lay the carpeting out over the bottom straight flight and up to the first wedge step. Pull the carpet runner into place from the bottom up, making sure that the nap or pile lies in the right direction (down) and that the carpet is positioned straight over the fastening strips and between the chalked centering marks on the stairs. Even a small skew at the bottom can magnify noticeably by the top of the stairway, so adjust the runner carefully.

Start fastening the carpeting at the bottom of the first riser. Position the end of the runner directly over the bottom fastening strip so that about ⅜ inch of carpet is turned up along the floor. Trim any uneven edges from the end of the runner with a sharp utility knife.

Push the point of an awl into the carpet at one side and use the awl to push the end of the carpet onto the fastening strip, leaving about ⅜ inch of loose carpet below the newly fastened edge. Smooth the carpet firmly into place along the strip, working across with the awl until the entire end has been fastened.

Finish the bottom of the runner by wedging the loose carpet end into the ¾-inch gap between the fastening strip and the floor. Use a tack hammer to drive the carpet end firmly into place along the floor at the bottom of the riser.

Stretch the carpeting up and over the stair with a knee kicker. Pull the carpet runner into place, making sure it's straight. Set the head of the kicker flat in the center of the tread, about an inch from the tread riser corner and aimed straight at the riser. Kneeling on the floor, hold the kicker with one hand; hold a stair wedging tool or a broad-bladed chisel ready in the other hand. Put all your weight on one knee and bring the other knee forward sharply to hit the cushioned end of the kicker; the head of the kicker will stretch the carpeting under it to hook it onto the teeth of the fastening strip on the tread. At the same time, as you work the kicker, push the carpet into place in the corner behind the tread fastening strip, using the wedging tool or broad-bladed chisel as a lever. Work from the center of the tread out to the sides, angling the kicker out toward the side you're fastening.

When the carpeting has been kicked and folded into the corner all along the step, wedge it permanently into place along the riser-tread joint, using a hammer to drive the wedging tool or chisel into the carpeted joint. Repeat the entire procedure to cover each succeeding stair, always working up from the last firmly fastened riser-tread joint.

To install the runner on winding stairs, work up to the last straight stair and wedge the carpet into the riser-tread joint. Stretch the carpet up onto

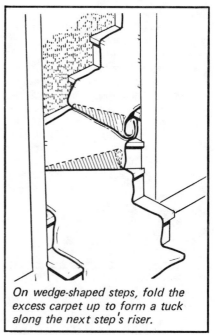

On wedge-shaped steps, fold the excess carpet up to form a tuck along the next step's riser.

the tread of the first wedge-shaped stair and angle it to reach the next step up, keeping the carpet pulled tight along the wide outside edge of the stair and letting it bulge over the riser where it was just wedged in.

Holding the carpet firmly in place at the correct angle, fold the bulging carpet firmly down over the riser, pulling it up at the inside edge of the stair to form a wedge-shaped tuck of carpeting behind the runner. The runner should appear to extend evenly up the stairs, with no part of the tucked-in carpeting visible from the front.

Fasten the tuck into place carefully. Fold the runner back from the tucked-under carpeting, bringing the loose carpet down but holding the tuck firmly in place. At the bottom of the tuck, as close to the riser-tread corner as possible, nail a second flat fastening strip straight across the folded carpeting, teeth pointing down. Then bring the runner back up over the fastened-down tuck, stretch it into position with the kicker onto the next tread fastening strip, wedge the riser-tread joint, and move on to the next stair. Repeat for each wedge-shaped stair.

At the top of the stairs, finish the end of the runner at the back of the last tread; don't extend the carpet up onto the last riser. Before you stretch the runner into place over the last riser, trim any excess carpeting evenly from the end of the runner, leaving about ⅜ inch of carpeting sticking up against the riser. Stretch the carpet into place with the knee kicker and wedge the cut end of the runner into the gap between the tread fastening strip and the last riser.

Repair Burns in Carpeting

With a little practice—and a lot of patience—most carpet burns can be successfully eliminated. **Tools:** small, sharp scissors (cuticle scissors are fine), sponge, tuft-setting tool, tweezers, hammer, ruler, chalk, sharp utility knife. **Materials:** liquid detergent, matching carpet scraps, tube of latex adhesive, carpet tape. **Time:** for surface burns, 15 minutes; for more serious burns, up to 2 hours.

Surface burns affect only the tips of the carpet pile. Carefully clip the charred tips with a small, sharp scissors, cutting only as much as necessary. Apply a small amount of detergent to the area with a damp sponge; rinse.

Retuft the carpet to mend deep burns, using a tuft-setting tool to insert carpet fibers one by one. Prepare the tufts by raveling the edge of a piece of scrap carpet, pulling out individual tufts or pieces of yarn. Each tuft should be twice the depth of the carpet pile. If you don't have carpet scraps, take fibers from a closet floor or other inconspicuous spot.

With a small, sharp scissors, cut away the charred carpet fibers down to the carpet backing. Pull out the stubs with tweezers. Squeeze a small amount of latex adhesive onto the carpet backing.

Fold a prepared carpet fiber in half,

making a V-shaped tuft. Place the tuft in the fork of the tuft-setter and drive it into the backing of the glued area, striking the tuft-setter lightly with a hammer. The newly set tuft will stay in place when you lift the tuft-setter. Repeat this procedure to fill in the entire burn area, setting one tuft at a time.

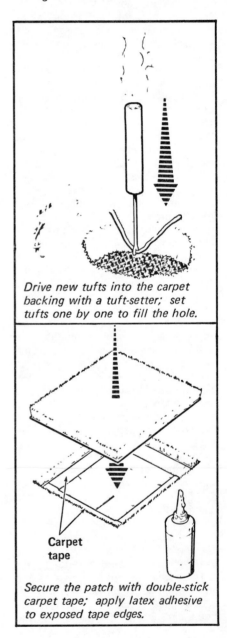

Drive new tufts into the carpet backing with a tuft-setter; set tufts one by one to fill the hole.

Carpet tape

Secure the patch with double-stick carpet tape; apply latex adhesive to exposed tape edges.

Set the tufts close together, working from one edge of the hole. Be sure to match any special tuft pattern used in the original carpet. If a tuft is too low, pull it up a bit with tweezers; if it's too high, tap it again with the hammer. Trim long tufts in the finished patch with a sharp scissors.

To repair more extensive burns, make a patch from scrap carpeting. Measure a square area slightly larger than the damaged spot. Find a piece of scrap carpeting that matches the tuft pattern in the damaged area, and turn it to match the direction of the damaged pile. Mark the back of this carpet scrap with chalk and cut a patch from it to the size measured around the burned spot. Place the scrap carpet patch over the damaged spot. Using the square patch as a template, cut the carpet underneath it with a sharp utility knife, cutting through the backing but not through the padding. Be sure to follow the lines of the patch exactly, or the patch won't fit.

Remove the cut-out section of damaged carpet and set the patch into the hole to be sure it fits. If necessary, trim the edges carefully with a sharp scissors.

Cut four pieces of double-stick carpet tape to fit each side of the newly cut hole. Stick the tape along the edges of the hole, setting each piece under the carpet edge so that half its width extends beyond the edge into the hole. Squeeze a small amount of adhesive onto the top (pile side) of the exposed tape, being careful not to get any on the carpet. Finally, insert the patch, setting it so that the tuft pattern in the patch matches the carpeting around it. Let the patched area dry for 5 hours before walking on it.

Spot-Clean Rugs and Carpets

Sooner or later even the most tenderly cared for rug gets spilled on, but it doesn't have to mean the beginning of the end. Keep the specifics on hand for fast treatment. **Tools:** clean sponges, spatula or dull knife, mixing cup and spoons. **Materials:** stain-removing carpet shampoo, white vinegar, ammonia, hydrogen peroxide, ice, dry cleaning fluid, clean cloths, alcohol-based dry cleaning fluid, mineral spirits. **Time:** about 10 minutes for most stains.

Remove stains immediately. Blot liquids thoroughly with a damp sponge, rinsing the sponge and blotting again to lift and remove as much of the spill as possible; scrape up solids with a spatula or a dull knife. Work from the edges of the stained area in, being careful not to spread the stain. Finally, treat the carpet gently—if sponging or light rubbing doesn't remove a stain, don't try to scrub it out. Call a professional cleaner.

Food, drink, and animal stains. These stains are best removed with water-based cleaners. Use dry cleaning fluid on these stains as a last resort, when all other methods fail.

Blot *coffee, tea, alcoholic* or *soft drinks,* and *fruit* stains to remove all liquid. Sponge gently with lukewarm water; sponge the stained area thoroughly with stain-removing carpet shampoo, diluted according to the manufacturer's instructions. Sponge again with clean water. If the stain persists, sponge the area with a mixture of 1 part white vinegar and 2 parts water. Let dry completely before walking on the cleaned area.

Remove *chocolate* stains the same way, blotting, sponging with carpet shampoo, and rinsing. Use a concentrated solution of carpet shampoo. If the stain persists, sponge the area with a mixture of 1 tablespoon ammonia and 1 cup of water. Let dry completely.

Blot *milk, ice cream,* and *gravy* stains and sponge with cold water; sponge the stained area thoroughly with a cool, strong solution of carpet shampoo. Repeat if necessary; rinse and blot dry. If the stain persists, sponge the area with a mixture of 1 tablespoon of ammonia and 1 cup of cold water; then sponge again with a mixture of 1 part white vinegar and 2 parts cold water. If a yellow stain remains, sponge a few drops of hydrogen peroxide into the stained area. Let dry completely.

Remove stains from *blood* or *egg* the same way. Blot, sponge with cold water, and work in a cool, concentrated solution of carpet shampoo; repeat if necessary and rinse. If the stain persists, sponge the area with first an ammonia solution and then a vinegar solution; apply hydrogen peroxide if necessary. Let dry completely.

Blot *urine* or *vomit* thoroughly. Sponge urine several times with lukewarm water; sponge vomit with cold water. Sponge thoroughly with a solution of vinegar, then of ammonia; then sponge again with vinegar solution. Clean the area if necessary with carpet shampoo; let dry completely.

Household stains. Most product stains are best removed with solvent cleaners; clean the area after removing the stain with carpet shampoo, if necessary. Before applying any type of solvent cleaner, test it on an inconspicuous area of the rug. If it bleaches the test spot, have stains professionally removed.

Remove *grease* or *oil* with dry cleaning fluid; apply the fluid with a clean cloth, rubbing gently and turning the cloth as you work so that a clean part of it is always against the stain. If necessary, clean the area as above with carpet shampoo. Let dry completely before walking on the cleaned area.

Harden *gum* or *wax* with an ice cube and then scrape it carefully out of the carpet with the edge of a spatula or a dull knife. Remove the residue with dry-cleaning fluid; let dry completely. Remove *crayon* marks with dry-cleaning fluid and let dry; clean the area as above with carpet shampoo and let dry completely.

Shoe polish and *furniture polish* marks are also waxy; remove them with dry cleaning fluid. If shoe polish stains persist, sponge them with ammonia and then vinegar solutions, as above. Clean the area thoroughly with carpet shampoo and let dry completely.

Remove *ballpoint ink* with an alcohol-based dry cleaning fluid and let dry. Blot *fluid ink* and sponge it with a concentrated solution of carpet shampoo, being careful not to spread the stain; don't ever rub ink stains. Continue to sponge the area, rinsing the sponge as necessary, until the ink is entirely removed; let dry completely. If the stain persists, have the rug professionally cleaned.

Paint is removed with the appropriate solvent. Sponge latex paint immediately with cool water, and shampoo as above; remove oil-base paint with mineral spirits and then shampoo. Let dry completely. *Lacquer* and *nail polish* are removable with lacquer thinner or nail polish remover, but these solvents can damage many carpets. Try to remove the stains with dry cleaning fluid; if that doesn't work, have the stains professionally removed.

Steam-Clean Wall-to-Wall Carpeting

Steam cleaning doesn't really involve using steam, and it really isn't difficult. Rent a special steam cleaner to do the job yourself. **Tools:** vacuum cleaner, sponge, portable steam carpet cleaner, small stiff brush. **Materials:** hot tap water; carpet prespotter, cleaner, defoamer, and deodorizer; newspaper, plastic wrap. **Time:** about 3 to 4 hours per room.

Steam cleaners work by a two-phase process. The cleaner shoots a jet of hot water and carpet cleaner into the carpet from a dispensing tank, lifting soil from the carpet fibers and holding it in suspension. It then immediately sucks the cleaning solution and the soil back into a receiving tank; this prevents overwetting and staining of the carpet. Rent the cleaner and buy prespotter, carpet cleaner, defoamer, and, if desired, deodorizer, at a grocery or housewares store. The cleaner will include detailed operating instructions; follow these instructions exactly.

Before cleaning the carpeting, move all the furniture out of the room. If this is impractical, clean half of the room and then the other half, but be sure the cleaned carpeting in the first half has completely dried before you move the furniture onto it. Vacuum the carpeting to remove surface dirt.

Start at one corner of the room, working in 3 × 3-foot squares along the wall and then working across the room. Don't clean yourself into a corner—work toward the door, not away from it. Before you clean the room, test-clean an inconspicuous area to make sure the cleaner won't damage the carpeting.

Following the instructions included with the cleaner, fill the machine's dispensing tank with hot tap water and add carpet cleaner and deodorizer as directed. Pour enough water into the receiving tank to cover the bottom of the tank, and add the defoamer. Finally, attach the dispensing hose and vacuum hose to the machine, as instructed.

Before cleaning the carpet, apply prespotter to badly soiled areas with a sponge, as directed. Prespot section by section as you go; apply the prespotter, let it stand for 5 to 10 minutes, and then steam-clean the prespotted section.

To operate the steam cleaner, move it to your starting point and apply light pressure on it; depress the release valve. Move the machine back and forth over a 3 × 3-foot area, working at a steady pace and pressure. Before ending each stroke, release the valve so the machine will suck up excess moisture.

With the valve released so the machine sucks in, vacuum the cleaned area thoroughly to dry the carpeting as much as possible; continue to vacuum until no more liquid enters the receiving tank. Be careful not to overwet the carpeting; don't release the cleaning solution into any area more than three times. Work across the room area by area until the entire carpet has been cleaned.

When the entire room is clean, turn the machine off and move it off the

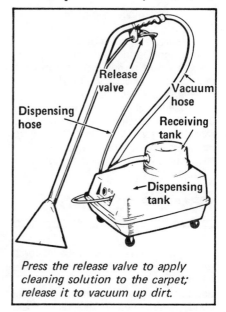

Press the release valve to apply cleaning solution to the carpet; release it to vacuum up dirt.

cleaned carpet. Spread newspaper on an uncarpeted floor to protect it and stand the machine on the paper; clean the machine thoroughly, using a small stiff brush if necessary and following the instructions provided. Let the machine dry before returning it.

Let the cleaned carpeting dry thoroughly before moving the furniture back into the room, at least 2 to 3 hours. To protect the carpeting, set a piece of plastic wrap under each furniture leg when you move the furniture back. Leave it in place for several days and then remove it.

Make Your Own Carpet Cleaner

You can save quite a bit of money by making your own carpet cleaner. It takes very little time to prepare. **Equipment:** measuring cup, mixing can, measuring spoons, stir stick. **Ingredients:** soda ash (sodium carbonate), fuller's earth, turpentine, liquid detergent. Buy fuller's earth and soda ash at a pharmacy. **Yield:** about 10 to 12 ounces.

Measure ½ cup of soda ash, ¼ cup of fuller's earth, and 1 tablespoon of turpentine into a mixing can and mix the ingredients thoroughly. *Caution: Turpentine is toxic and flammable.*

To use the cleaner, mix the preparation with just enough liquid detergent to make a stiff paste. Brush the mixture into the carpet and let it dry completely; then vacuum the carpet thoroughly.

Lay a Tile Floor

A new floor is a real face-lift for a room, and resilient floor tiles make the job easy. Vinyl tiles are the best; vinyl-asbestos is less expensive but still good. **Tools:** hammer, sanding block, chalk line, carpenters' square, soft lead pencil or grease pencil, steel straightedge, utility knife, heavy utility scissors; paintbrush, roller, or trowel for adhesive, as appropriate. **Materials:** nails, sandpaper, vinyl or vinyl-asbestos tile, tile adhesive, paper. **Time:** 1 to 2 days per room.

Before you buy, calculate how much tile and how much adhesive you'll need. Get a little extra of each, to allow for mistakes. Buy the adhesive recommended by the manufacturer of the tile you choose—not all types of adhesive work on all tiles. And unless the tile manufacturer specifically directs you to use troweling-consistency adhesive, buy the brush-on kind.

At least 24 hours ahead of time, set the boxes of new tile in the room where they will be used to bring them to the correct temperature and humidity. The temperature in the room must be at least 70° F, and it should be constant for a week after you tile the floor so that the newly applied tile can set properly.

Prepare the floor carefully. If it's a tile floor, and tiles are missing, either remove all the old tiles completely or fill in the missing tiles, setting them carefully in place with tile adhesive. If you add tiles to fill gaps in the old floor, wait until the new adhesive has cured completely before proceeding further.

The floor must be absolutely smooth before you can lay the new tile; any problem spots you ignore now will show on the new floor. Clean the floor thoroughly, remove all old wax, nail down loose boards or moldings, and drive in any protruding nails. Sand rough spots or high spots to level the floor.

Before laying out the tile, you must find the exact center of the room. To do this, ignore odd niches and corners and work with only the main rectangular space. If the room is L-shaped, divide it into rectangles and measure the two areas separately. Measure each wall to find its midpoint and set a nail at each midpoint. First across one way and then across the other, snap a chalk line to divide the floor in half and then in half the other way. Use a carpenters' square to make sure the chalk lines are exactly at right angles. The intersection of the two lines is the center of the room.

Starting from the center point of the room, set out a row of tiles, without adhesive, along the chalk line from the center of the room to the center of one

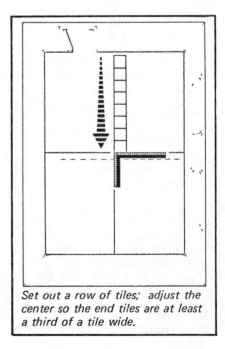

Set out a row of tiles; adjust the center so the end tiles are at least a third of a tile wide.

wall. Measure the distance from the last full tile to the wall. If it's less than a third of a tile wide, snap a new chalk line parallel to the old one and at right angles to the row of tiles, half a tile out past the old line. Move the line of tiles up to meet the new line and widen the gap at the wall.

Working from the first tile at the center of the room, set out a second row of tiles at right angles to the first and within the same quadrant of the floor, forming an L. If the gap at the wall is less than a third of a tile wide, snap a new chalk line in this direction too; then remove the nails used to snap the lines. Use these lines to establish the quadrants of the floor as you work.

Tile one quadrant of the floor at a time. Stick-on tiles don't require adhesive. For other tiles, spread adhesive over the entire quarter of the room, using a brush or roller for brush-on adhesive or a trowel for thick mastic. Follow the directions on the can, and wait the proper amount of time before setting the tiles in place. The adhesive should be tacky, not wet.

To minimize color variations, use tiles from all boxes alternately instead of emptying one box at a time. If the tiles have a grained pattern, lay them with the grain first one way, then the other, to produce a checkerboard effect.

Start setting tile at the center point of the room. Place a tile carefully in the intersection of the chalk lines, butting the edges against the lines and then setting the whole tile flat. Once the tile is down you can't move it, so be careful to position it correctly.

From this center tile, lay tiles alternately along the sides of the quadrant toward the walls, setting them firmly and carefully in place. Smooth each tile firmly toward the corners. Fill in the tiles in the middle as you go, working in an expanding wedge pattern toward the walls. Stop with the last full tile along each wall.

To fit the border tiles, place a loose tile exactly over the last full tile in each row. Set another tile on top of this one but butted against the wall, forming shallow steps up to the wall. With a soft

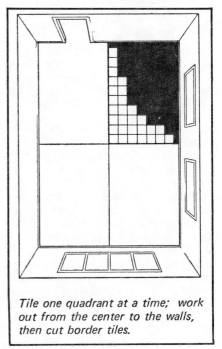

Tile one quadrant at a time; work out from the center to the walls, then cut border tiles.

lead pencil or grease pencil, trace the overlapping (inside) edge of the top tile onto the loose tile below it. Cut the loose tile on this line and set it into place to fill the gap next to the wall. Follow the same procedure to fit the border tiles along the other wall, marking the corner

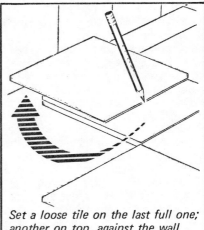

Set a loose tile on the last full one; another on top, against the wall. Mark and cut the middle tile.

tile once from each direction before you trim it.

Cut the border tiles with a steel straightedge and a utility knife—if the knife doesn't cut completely through the tile, bend the tile sharply back from the score to snap it. If you must fit tiles around pipes or irregular shapes, make a paper pattern and trace it onto the tiles. Cut curves and irregular shapes with utility scissors.

Lay tile the same way on the other three quadrants of the floor, being careful not to slide newly applied tiles or get adhesive on the tile surface. Be particularly careful to place the center tiles accurately, because any mistakes at the center of the room will be even more apparent at the edges.

Fill in odd corners after the main floor area is complete. To tile the second rectangle of an L-shaped room, work from the line where it meets the main rectangle, matching tiles from that point.

Don't walk on the completed floor until the full curing period of the adhesive has elapsed, and don't wash the new floor for at least a week.

Replace Vinyl Floor Tiles

Damaged vinyl tiles are easy to reglue or replace. **Tools:** electric iron or propane torch, putty knife or paint scraper, work gloves, hammer, chisel, grease pencil, notched trowel. **Materials:** aluminum foil, clean rag, floor tile mastic, scrap wood and weights to cover patch, dry ice, replacement tiles, sandpaper. **Time:** 20 minutes per tile.

Tiles that are loose or curled up at the corners can be reglued. Cover the loose tile with aluminum foil and spread a clean rag or small towel on the foil. Using moderate heat, press the edges of the loose tile with an iron to soften the old adhesive. Carefully lift the edges of the tile with a putty knife and scrape off the old mastic.

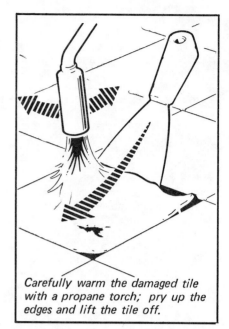

Carefully warm the damaged tile with a propane torch; pry up the edges and lift the tile off.

To reglue the tile, spread a thin layer of mastic on the cleaned area, scraping to remove any excess. Press the tile back into place, smoothing it from center to edges. Cover the entire tile with a piece of scrap wood and weight it with a can of paint or other heavy object. Leave the weight in place for the entire curing period of the new mastic, as recommended by the manufacturer.

Remove damaged or badly stained tiles entirely. Warm the damaged tile carefully with a propane torch, or press with an iron over a clean rag and aluminum foil. Being careful not to damage the surrounding tiles, pry up the edges of the damaged tile and lift it off. Let the mastic left under the tile harden and then scrape it off.

If heat doesn't loosen the tile, you can use cold. Wearing work gloves, cover the damaged tile with dry ice and allow it to stand for 5 to 10 minutes, then remove any remaining dry ice. The damaged tile should be cold and very brittle. Starting in the middle of the tile, use a hammer and chisel to split the tile and pry out the pieces. Work from the center to the edges, being careful not to chip the surrounding tiles. Scrape the floor under the tile to remove all old mastic.

Before gluing down the replacement tile, make sure it fits the opening exactly. If it binds at the edges or overlaps the surrounding tiles, smooth the edges carefully with sandpaper. Mark matching edges with a grease pencil to make sure you replace the tile correctly.

With a notched trowel, spread a thin layer of mastic in the opening for the new tile. Set one edge of the tile into place and lower it into the prepared opening. The new tile should be level with the rest of the floor. If it's too high, press firmly to squeeze out the excess mastic; if it's too low, lift the tile and apply more mastic before setting it into place again. Remove excess mastic and weight the new tile for the full curing time of the mastic.

Repair Vinyl Sheet Flooring

Scratches, holes, and worn spots in resilient sheet flooring are easy to repair. **Tools:** utility knife, shallow mixing pan, small stir stick, putty knife, steel straightedge, paint scraper, electric iron, notched trowel. **Materials:** scrap pieces of sheet flooring, clear nail polish, masking tape, grade 000 steel wool, package sealing tape, aluminum foil, clean rag, sandpaper, floor tile or sheet flooring adhesive, scrap wood and weights to cover patch. **Time:** about 1½ hours.

Make a patching compound to fill deep scratches and dents in resilient flooring. Bend a small piece of scrap flooring sharply, top surface out. Holding the bent piece of flooring over a shallow pan, scrape the bend with a utility knife to produce a fine powder. Scrape only as deep as the surface color; rebend the scrap flooring as you work to keep the scrapings a uniform color. Scrape enough powder to more than fill the hole or scratch.

Add a few drops of clear nail polish to the scrapings and mix to a thick paste. Use masking tape to cover the area around the scratch or hole to be filled. Apply vinyl paste to the scratch with a putty knife, smoothing the surface carefully. Let dry for about an hour and remove the tape around the patch. Using grade 000 steel wool, buff the patch to make it shiny.

Patch large holes and worn spots with scrap pieces of flooring. Choose a piece larger than the hole and set it over the bad spot. Line up the pattern of the patch exactly with the pattern on the floor; then, being careful not to move the patch, tape it firmly to the floor, all around the edges, with package sealing tape (not masking tape).

Using a sharp utility knife and a steel straightedge, cut a rectangular patch from the taped-down piece of flooring. The patch must be larger than the hole underneath it. If the floor has a pattern of bricks or other regular shapes, cut along joints or lines as much as possible.

The utility knife will not cut completely through the flooring at the first stroke. Keep the straightedge in place and cut

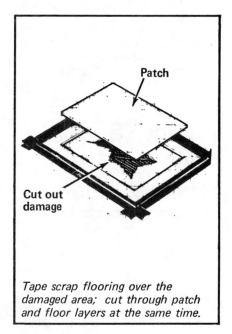

Tape scrap flooring over the damaged area; cut through patch and floor layers at the same time.

along the same score lines, being careful not to cut a ragged edge, until both the patch and the vinyl sheet beneath it are completely cut through. Untape the patch sheet and pop out the newly cut patch.

Cover the marked-off worn spot in the floor with aluminum foil, shiny side up, and spread a clean rag over the foil. Using an electric iron set at moderate heat, warm the floor to soften the adhesive under the bad spot. Remove the damaged patch with a putty knife—be sure the corners are cleanly cut. Let the adhesive left in the patch area harden for about an hour and then scrape it completely out.

Before you set the patch into place, make sure it fits the opening in the floor. Sand the edges of the patch slightly if necessary. Using a notched trowel, spread floor tile adhesive on the floor where the patch will go. Set the patch carefully into place in the opening, butting one edge against the surrounding flooring and then lowering the entire patch. Remove any excess adhesive.

Finally, seal the edges of the patch. Cover the edges with aluminum foil, spread a clean rag on the foil, and press with a hot iron. Press firmly, but don't hold the iron in one place for more than a few seconds. Remove the foil and cover the patch with a piece of scrap wood. Weight it with a can of paint or other heavy object for the entire curing period of the adhesive, and don't wash the floor for at least a week.

Remove Spots from Resilient Floors

Resilient floors are easy to maintain, but stubborn stains can be a problem. If spot-cleaning with all-purpose spray cleaner doesn't work, use stronger measures. **Tools:** plastic or dull metal spatula, plastic pot scrubber, rubber gloves, sponge mop and bucket. **Mate-**

rials: grade 000 steel wool, liquid floor wax, clean rags, liquid detergent, plastic bags, ice, kitchen cleanser, ammonia, hydrogen peroxide, rubbing alcohol, oxalic acid, white vinegar, paper towels, household cleaner—materials needed determined by type of stain. **Time:** a few minutes to several hours, depending on the spot.

The treatment depends on the stain. To remove *scuff marks, or paint or varnish,* dip grade 000 steel wool in liquid floor wax—for embossed vinyl, use a plastic pot scrubber instead of steel wool. Rub the spot gently, then wipe with a damp cloth. Paint and varnish spots can also be removed with steel wool and liquid detergent.

Tar, candle wax, and chewing gum must be hardened before they can be removed. Fill a plastic sandwich bag with ice and set it on the spot until the spot material is brittle. Remove the ice and scrape off the brittle spot material with a scraper. Remove any residue with dry kitchen cleanser and grade 000 steel wool or a plastic pot scrubber.

Use kitchen cleanser and grade 000 steel wool, or, for embossed vinyl floors, a plastic pot scrubber, to polish out *cigarette burns* and remove *shoe polish or nail polish.* Scrub gently, and stop as soon as the stain disappears.

Fresh *bloodstains* can usually be removed with cold water; to remove old stains, use a weak ammonia solution. Use straight hydrogen peroxide to remove *fruit and coffee* stains. Saturate a cloth with peroxide and set it on the stain for 10 minutes, then remove the cloth and wash the area. If there's still a stain, scrub it gently with cleanser and steel wool or a plastic scrubber.

Hydrogen peroxide is also good for removing *urine or mustard* stains. Saturate a cloth with peroxide and set it on the stain. Saturate a second cloth with ammonia and place it over the peroxide pad; leave both cloths in place for several hours. Remove the cloths and wash the area.

Use rubbing alcohol to remove *alcohol and ink* stains. Cover the stains for a few minutes with a cloth saturated with rubbing alcohol; then go over the spot area with a cloth moistened with ammonia.

Rust stains are harder to remove. Wearing rubber gloves, mix a weak solution of oxalic acid, available at paint and hardware stores. Pour a little of the solution onto the stain and scrub the spot gently with grade 000 steel wool or a plastic scrubber. Rinse with clear water.

If *drain cleaner* gets spilled or splashed on the floor, it must be neutralized immediately. Wear rubber gloves, and be careful—drain cleaners contain lye, which is a caustic. Flood the area with white vinegar. Mop up the mess with paper towels and dispose of the towels in a plastic bag; if the spill was a large one, repeat. Wash the floor.

The stain-removing process usually removes the floor wax as well as the stain. To bring the floor back into top condition, damp-mop or wash it with household cleaner, let it dry, and wax it.

Sand and Refinish Hardwood Floors

Refinishing wood floors is by no means an easy job, but it can be done. It demands more brute strength than special skill. **Tools:** *Hand tools*— screwdrivers, pliers, hammer, nail set, two sharp chisels, small wedges, soft lead pencil, adapter plugs, paint scraping tool, file; sanding block, vacuum cleaner, putty knife, paint roller and extension handle, mohair roller cover, roller pan, medium-size paintbrush. *Rental tools*—drum sander and disc sander with keys or wrenches for loading, with sandpaper for each machine in coarse, medium, and fine grits; floor polisher with fine steel wool pads. Ask the rental agent to show you how to load and operate the machines. *Protective gear*—work gloves, face mask, earplugs or ear muffs; safety goggles, if desired; rubber gloves. **Materials:** sheet plastic, masking tape, plastic bags, large plastic garbage bags,

sandpaper in coarse, medium, and fine grits; clean rags, penetrating sealer, fine-grade steel wool pads, tack cloths, polyurethane varnish (read sealer and varnish labels to determine amounts needed). **Time:** at least a week.

Sanding is best done before you move in. If you must refinish a floor in the house or apartment you're living in, move all furniture, rugs, drapes, and pictures out of the room. Remove floor register covers and cover all registers, both floor and wall, with plastic, taping the plastic all around the openings. Cover light fixtures with plastic bags. If there are built-in cabinets in the room, tape the doors shut and tape all around the doors. If possible, seal the room doors with plastic too.

Prepare the floor before you start to sand. Go over the floor carefully for metal carpet staples and protruding nails; remove the staples with pliers and drive the nails below the surface of the floor, using a nail set. Use chisels and small wedges to remove the quarter-round baseboard molding, starting at the door. Pry the sections out gently to avoid splitting the wood. Number the back of each section as you go, and make a chart of their placement, so that the molding can be replaced correctly, and set the quarter-round aside in another room.

Now you're ready to sand. Using the key or wrenches provided by the rental agent, load the drum sander with coarse-grit sandpaper. Plug the sander in—you'll probably need a three-prong adapter plug. Coil the cord and sling it over your arm to keep it out of the sander's path.

Begin sanding from a corner of the room, following the grain of the wood. Tilt the sanding drum up from the floor before turning the machine on; lower the drum gently and move slowly forward. Once the sander is turned on, don't stop or change pace or you'll leave low spots in the floor. When you reach the other side of the room, tilt the sanding drum up off the floor immediately. Pull the cord to the side and move back over the strip of floor you've just sanded, again moving slowly and

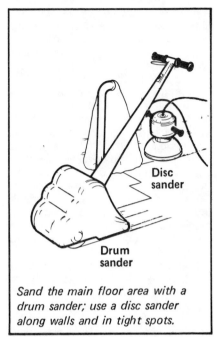

Disc
sander

Drum
sander

Sand the main floor area with a drum sander; use a disc sander along walls and in tight spots.

making an X over the entire floor.

After you've sanded the whole room, load the disc sander with coarse-grit paper and sand the edges of the room and any other spots you couldn't get at with the drum sander. Sand corners and other tight spots by hand. Where you must hand-sand, use a paint scraping tool to remove the worst of the old finish; clean and sharpen the blade with a file as you work. Go over the scraped area with sandpaper and a sanding block.

Follow the same procedure to sand the entire floor with the medium and fine sanding grits—first the main floor, then the edges, then the tight spots. Don't wait till the end to sand the edges or you'll leave a visible line where the edge meets the main floor. Make both second and third sandings with the grain of the wood, and also work with the grain for hand scraping and sanding.

When the entire floor has been sanded, clean the room thoroughly. Wearing thick socks so you don't mark the bare floor, vacuum to remove all sawdust, from walls and windowsills as well as from the floor. Change to clean clothes and socks and vacuum again. Save some of the dust from the final sanding to use as filler when you seal the floor.

The second major step is finishing the newly sanded floor. During the finishing process, be careful to wear clean clothes and thick socks. Any marks on the floor that get sealed in are there to stay.

First, go over the floor with a tack cloth. Then apply a penetrating sealer, available either clear or in typical wood stain colors. Wearing rubber gloves, wipe the sealer on with a clean rag; follow the grain of the wood and use long, even strokes. Remember not to paint yourself into a corner.

As soon as the sealer has soaked into the wood, 10 to 20 minutes after it's applied, the excess sealer must be removed. At this point you need a helper, because the area you started sealing must be mopped up immediately; you

steadily. Be sure to get complete instructions from the agent when you rent the sander; some types can be used only in a forward direction. If the machine you're using is one of these, tilt the drum off the floor before pulling the sander back over the newly sanded strip.

With the drum raised, move the sander a few inches into the room. Sand this strip of floor as you did the first. Repeat this procedure, always following the grain of the wood, until you've sanded the entire floor, and turn the sander off. Hold the drum tilted up off the floor until the machine has completely stopped. Empty the dust bag as necessary as you work, turning the sander off each time. Dump the sawdust into large plastic garbage bags and keep the bags closed; sawdust is both annoying and very flammable. Change the sanding belts as soon as they wear down; it's better to waste a little than to end up with an unevenly sanded floor.

If the floorboards are badly rippled, make your first sanding at a 45-degree angle to the grain of the wood. Sand again at right angles to the first sanding, can't finish the room first or the sealer will dry unevenly. As you apply the sealer, have your helper follow you across the room, working down the same strips you've just sealed and wiping up the excess sealer with clean rags. Dispose of soaked rags as you go; keep them separate from the bagged sawdust. Let the floor dry for at least 8 hours.

When the sealer has dried, fill any noticeable cracks and holes. Mix some of the fine sawdust you saved with a few drops of penetrating sealer, blending it to a smooth paste. Apply the paste to cracks with a putty knife, smoothing off the excess. Let the filler dry at least 8 hours and sand the patches smooth with fine-grit paper.

Load the rented floor polisher with a fine steel wool pad and go over the sealed floor, working with the grain of the wood. Replace the pad if it starts to look shredded. Finish edges and corners by hand with fine-grade steel wool pads. Vacuum thoroughly and go over the floor with a clean tack cloth.

Finally, apply the polyurethane finish. Read the directions on the can before you start, and don't stir unless this is specified. Use a paint roller with an extension handle, and a mohair roller cover; pour the finish into the roller pan gently to avoid forming bubbles. First paint the finish onto the edges and corners of the floor, then roll it onto the main floor area, working with the grain. Let the polyurethane dry completely, at least 8 hours.

Steel-wool the finished floor again, vacuum, and go over the floor with a tack cloth. Apply the second coat of finish across the grain of the wood.

Let the floor dry at least 24 hours; if you have the time, wait a few days. Then strip the masking tape, remove plastic bags and plastic sheets over registers, and replace the register covers. Nail the quarter-round molding back into place, replacing the sections in order as you removed them. Protect the floor with old blankets or clean dropcloths when you move furniture into the room. The finish will get tougher as it cures.

Mix Wood Floor Bleach

Streaked or discolored wood floors don't have to be a problem. After sanding, and before refinishing, treat the stained wood with this simple bleaching preparation. **Equipment:** bucket, stir stick, measuring cup, 6-quart pot. **Ingredients:** sodium metasilicate, sodium perborate, water. Buy these chemicals at a pharmacy. **Yield:** about 1½ gallons.

Mix 9 pounds of sodium metasilicate and 1 pound of sodium perborate in a bucket. Heat a gallon of water to boiling in a 6-quart pot; pour the boiling water into the mixture of salts and stir until the salts are dissolved. Let the bleaching solution cool.

Apply the bleaching solution generously to the floor with a mop, and let it stand for 1 hour or longer. Rinse the floor with water and dry. Refinish the wood as desired.

Make Your Own Wood Floor Cleaner

If your floors need a good cleaning, try this cleaner/conditioner; it restores the wood while it cleans. **Equipment:** measuring cup, quart jar with cover, measuring spoons, mixing spoon. **Ingredients:** mineral oil, vegetable oil, ammonia, turpentine. **Yield:** about 3 cups.

Pour 2 cups of mineral oil into a quart jar and add ½ cup of vegetable oil. Stir in 2 tablespoons of ammonia and 5 tablespoons of turpentine. Cover tightly.

To apply the floor cleaner, mix one part solution to 4 parts water. Apply with a sponge mop, rubbing thoroughly to remove dirt; wipe dry along the grain of the wood with a clean soft cloth. Do not rinse.

Replace Baseboard Molding

Cracked or chipped baseboard molding is ugly, but not irreparable. Replacing the damaged molding takes time, but it isn't difficult. **Tools:** measuring rule, putty knife, pry bar, wood wedges, hammer, pencil, miter box, backsaw, coping saw, magnetic stud finder, nail set, chisel, paintbrushes. **Materials:** replacement molding, replacement quarter-round or shoe molding, 2-penny finishing nails; coarse-, medium-, and fine-grit sandpaper; plastic wood, touchup paint or varnish. **Time:** 3 to 5 hours.

Measure the length of the molding to be replaced, and its height and thickness; take these measurements to the lumberyard when you buy the replacement molding. If you're replacing only one section of a long molding, remove the damaged section and bring it with you to be sure you get an exact match.

Molding is sold in pieces 3 to 20 feet long. The shorter pieces are less expensive, but harder to work with; buy pieces that can be installed with as few joints as possible. Choose the molding carefully so you don't get cracked or gouged pieces, and buy a few feet extra to allow for mistakes.

Remove the old molding carefully; if it isn't already broken, don't break it. Insert a putty knife between the quarter-round or shoe molding and the baseboard molding and pry gently to loosen the shoe molding, working along the entire length of the molding. When the shoe molding is loose, use a pry bar or a chisel to finish prying it off. Loosen the molding gradually, working along its entire length so that the entire piece of molding comes loose at the same rate;

leave the nails in the molding. When the quarter-round or shoe molding is completely loosened, remove it.

Pry the baseboard molding away from the wall, being careful not to damage either the molding or the wall. Work from one end of the molding to the other, loosening the molding gradually along its entire length. When you can pry the molding far enough out from the wall, insert wood wedges between the molding and the wall, wedging from one end to the other as you work, until the entire piece of molding is wedged. Pull the loosened molding carefully away from the wall, leaving the nails in it. Remove any nails left in the wall with a hammer.

Using the old baseboard molding as a pattern, measure and mark the new molding to size. Mark outside, mitered corners exactly on the new molding and cut the miters with a miter box and a backsaw; be careful to hold the molding steady while you cut it.

Inside corners must be joined in a coped joint, with one side of the molding overlapping and curving exactly around the other side. To make a coped joint, blunt-cut a piece of molding to fit tightly

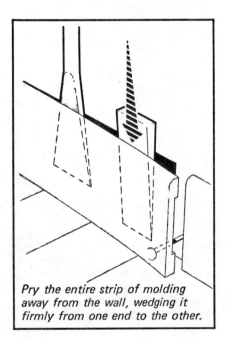

Pry the entire strip of molding away from the wall, wedging it firmly from one end to the other.

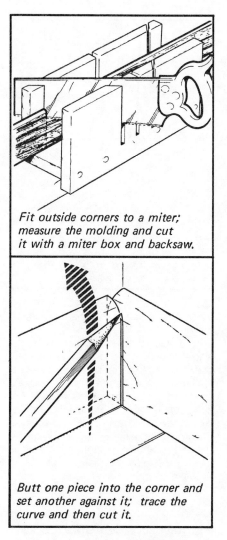

*Fit outside corners to a miter;
measure the molding and cut
it with a miter box and backsaw.*

*Butt one piece into the corner and
set another against it; trace the
curve and then cut it.*

into the corner along one wall. Hold the blunt-cut molding in place in the corner, or fasten it lightly with a 2-penny finishing nail driven partway in. Hold a second blunt-cut piece of baseboard—a scrap will do—along the other wall, butted against the corner-fitted piece. Trace the outline of the second piece of molding carefully onto the side of the fastened piece, keeping the pencil at a constant angle so the traced outline is exact.

Unfasten the corner-fitted molding and cut it slowly and carefully along the traced line with a coping saw, following

the outline on the molding exactly. To complete the coped joint, install a blunt-cut piece of molding along the wall you traced from; then set the traced and trimmed piece into place against it, jigsaw-puzzle fashion.

Attach the new molding to the wall at the wall studs; use a magnetic stud finder to locate the studs. If the old molding was properly installed, the nail holes left when you removed it will be at the studs. Set the new molding into place against the wall and join mitered or coped ends. Holding the molding firmly, nail it into place with two 2-penny finishing nails at each stud, one near the top of the molding and one near the bottom. Sink all nails with a nail set.

Measure and cut the new quarter-round or shoe molding, using the old shoe molding as a pattern. Mark and cut mitered and coped corners as above. Where quarter-round or shoe molding stops at a door frame, trim the exposed blunt end of the molding with a chisel to form a curve away from the door. Sand the chiseled edge to a smooth curve before nailing the molding into place.

Nail the shoe molding into place with 2-penny finishing nails driven through the molding into the floor; set nails about 12 inches apart. Sink all nails with a nail set. Fill all nail holes in both shoe molding and baseboard molding with plastic wood, and let dry.

To complete the job, paint or varnish the newly installed molding as desired.

Repair Damaged Parquet

Wood parquet is beautiful, but damaged blocks can be a problem. For invisible repairs, replace the damaged wood with matching parquet tile. **Tools:** drill or brace and bit, sharp chisel, hammer, needle-nosed pliers, putty knife, wire cutters, notched spreader or small mixing dish and stir stick, scrap wood block, weights. **Materials:**

matching prefinished parquet tile, medium-grit sandpaper, tile adhesive or epoxy cement, carpenters' glue, cloth, polish or wax. **Time:** about ½ hour per block.

To replace the damaged section of parquet, use a matching prefinished tile; if you can't get prefinished tile, finish the new tile to match before installing it. Use the whole tile or one piece of the unit, as required; replace as small an area as possible.

First, remove the damaged piece of wood. If the entire tile or unit is damaged, make a row of large holes across the block, against the grain, with a drill or a brace and bit. Drill completely through the damaged block, but not into the subfloor under it. Then, with a sharp chisel and a hammer, carefully split the block and pry up the pieces. Make sure you don't damage the surrounding pieces of wood.

Most parquet tile is held together with tongue-and-groove joints. At the grooved sides, carefully pull the pieces of the block out over the adjoining tongues. If the grooved sides stick, use the chisel to cut through only the top side of the groove; be careful not to damage the tongues of the abutting pieces. At the tongued sides of the tile, carefully pull out the tongue that held the damaged block to the next tile. If the tongue piece sticks, cut it off with the chisel and then carefully pry out the cut piece.

If only one piece of a parquet tile or unit is damaged, remove only that piece. With a sharp chisel and a hammer, very carefully split the damaged piece and pry out the splinters. If the pieces of the unit are held together by a wire spline, hold the damaged piece of wood with needle-nosed pliers; cut the spline with wire cutters to free the damaged piece.

After removing the damaged piece of wood, prepare the gap for the replacement piece. Scrape the subfloor to remove any remaining adhesive; make sure all parts of the old piece of wood have been removed. If you cut a wire spline to remove the old piece, trim the cut ends flush and tap them lightly with

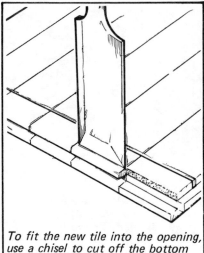

To fit the new tile into the opening, use a chisel to cut off the bottom edges of both grooved sides.

a hammer to flatten the sharp points of the wire.

To replace the damaged wood, use a whole matching tile or one piece of a matching unit. If you're using a whole tile, match the tongued and grooved edges to the surrounding tiles. With a sharp chisel and a hammer, carefully cut off the protruding bottom edges of the grooved sides; the new tile will fit on top of the abutting tongues instead of locking around them. Test the tile for fit to make sure you've cut enough.

If you're using one piece of a matching unit, carefully take the unit apart to remove the desired piece of wood; if necessary, cut the wire spline that holds the piece into the unit. Trim the cut ends of the spline flush, and tap them lightly with a hammer to flatten them. Test the piece of wood for fit in the gap. If the piece is too tight in the opening, sand the edges of the replacement piece lightly with medium-grit sandpaper. Be careful not to damage the finish on the wood.

To complete the repair, glue the new block of wood into position. If you're replacing a whole tile, use floor tile adhesive; apply the adhesive to the subfloor in the opening with a notched spreader. On the grooved sides of the tile, apply a thin coat of carpenters' glue to the bot-

Lay a Quarry Tile Entranceway

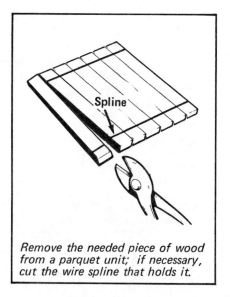

Remove the needed piece of wood from a parquet unit; if necessary, cut the wire spline that holds it.

A quarry tile floor is good-looking, practical, and durable in an entranceway, and it isn't hard to install. **Tools:** measuring rule, hammer, nail set, broom, utility knife with sharp heavy-duty blades, tile cutter, safety goggles, wheelbarrow or tub, shovel, masons' finishing trowel, work gloves, levels, small pointed trowel, scrap plywood, sponge, sponge mop. **Materials:** finishing strips or thresholds, as required; 15-pound roofing felt, ½-inch roofing nails, quarry tile, mortar mix, sheet plastic film. **Time:** 1 to 2 days.

The finished quarry tile floor will be a bit less than 1 inch thick, with a ½-inch mortar bed. Depending on the thickness of adjacent finished floors, you may need one or more transition pieces at doorways to adjust from one floor level to another. Special finishing strips are available for edging carpeting; a transition between uncarpeted floors and the tile floor can be made with a hardwood threshold. Some types of thresholds must be installed before tiling begins; check with your supplier and plan transitions before beginning the project.

To prepare the floor, remove all old finish flooring materials and baseboards, mopboards, or similar moldings. Make sure all nails in the subflooring are fully set. Sweep the subfloor clean. Install thresholds as required.

Cut strips of 15-pound roofing felt and lay them over the subfloor, with at least a 6-inch overlap at the seams. Wrap the felt up the walls for about 1 inch; at door openings, fold it up to make a pan. Nail the felt to the subfloor with ½-inch roofing nails, setting nails 3 to 4 inches apart along all seams and edges.

At a nearby flat working area, lay out all pieces, or at least large sections, of the quarry tile. Arrange the pieces as they will lie in the entranceway. If trim-

tom edge of the top groove. Carefully set the new tile into place, tongued sides first, to lock into the grooves of the abutting tiles; set the grooved sides firmly down over the abutting tongues.

When the tile is correctly positioned, set a block of scrap wood over it and tap it firmly down with a hammer to bond and level it. The edges of the new tile should be flush with the surface of the surrounding tiles. Quickly remove any excess adhesive with a damp cloth.

If you're replacing one strip or one piece of a unit, use epoxy cement to bond it into place. Mix the epoxy as directed by the manufacturer, and apply the epoxy to the back and to the edges of the replacement piece. Set the piece into place in the opening and tap it into place with a wood block and a hammer to bond and level it. Quickly remove any excess epoxy with a damp cloth.

To make sure the new piece of parquet bonds firmly, cover it with a piece of scrap wood and weight it for the entire curing time of the adhesive or epoxy, as directed by the manufacturer. Let the adhesive or epoxy dry completely before removing the weight. Finally, if the finish on the new piece of wood doesn't blend in with the surrounding floor, polish or wax the entire floor.

ming is necessary, rent a tile cutter, and cut the tiles as necessary before laying them—wear safety goggles for all trimming. Cut at least several rows of tiles before beginning the mortar work.

Following the manufacturer's instructions, mix a small amount of mortar in a wheelbarrow or tub—no more than you can use in about an hour. Make the mix fairly stiff in consistency, but still easily workable. At a corner of the entranceway, put two or three shovelfuls of mortar onto the roofing felt. Rough-level the mortar with the shovel blade, and then trowel it out with a mason's finishing trowel to a uniform thickness of ½ inch. Work the mortar with the trowel as little as possible.

One by one, set the tiles onto the mortar. Wear work gloves to protect your hands. As you work, rock each tile back and forth a few times to bed it firmly in the mortar, and to release any trapped air bubbles. Check frequently with a small level to see that no pieces are seriously tilted. Also check periodically with a long level to make sure the floor is plane.

After laying a section of tile, fill the joints between the tiles with fresh mortar, using a small pointed trowel. Smooth the mortar, but don't work it any more than you must. Scrape away excess mortar.

Let the mortar set and then tool the mortar joints. Test the mortar joints periodically, by pressing your thumb into the mortar. When it's hard enough so that you leave only a thumbprint, it's ready to tool—depending on the temperature and humidity, you may have to wait 2 hours or more. Be sure to allow yourself access to the first-laid portions of the floor without walking on newly laid tiles. If this isn't possible, set out a piece of scrap plywood to walk on; it will help distribute your weight.

Smooth and pack the mortar joints with a pointed trowel, using plenty of pressure. Joints are usually left flush with the tile surface, but you can indent them; the more they're indented, the harder it will be to clean the floor. As you work, wipe the tile clean with fresh water and a clean sponge. Continue until all joints have been tooled and the floor is clean.

Let the mortar cure for at least 3 days. To keep it from drying too fast, keep the entire surface of the floor thoroughly damp, even wet, during the curing period. Sponge-mop clean water onto the floor periodically and cover it tightly with sheet plastic film. At the end of the curing period, clean the floor with a sponge mop and cold water, and let the floor dry naturally.

Don't give the floor any treatment, other than cleaning with cold water, for at least 2—preferably 3—months after installation. Keep heavy traffic off the floor for 2 to 3 weeks; trim the roofing felt and replace baseboards or other trim immediately after the curing period. Finally, install thresholds as required.

Quarry tile floors are best left untreated, but if you prefer, apply a sealer or wax. Once you treat the floor, you must make reapplications regularly.

Install a Folding Attic Stairway

Climbing into an attic crawl space, or an unfinished attic, on a ladder can be risky and troublesome. A better way to gain access is with a folding stairway—buy the unit assembled; install it yourself. **Tools:** hammer, crosscut saw, measuring rule, carpenters' square, paintbrush. **Materials:** folding stairway to fit the rough opening into the attic, 16-penny common nails, lumber and boards for headers and braces (if needed), sandpaper; paint, stain, or varnish. **Time:** about 3 hours.

The rough opening for the access into most attics is 25 × 54 inches. This opening is set between the attic floor joists, and the joists have probably been framed at each end with a cross-header. A plywood panel usually covers the opening.

Folding stairways are designed to fit the access opening. Before buying a folding stairway, carefully measure the

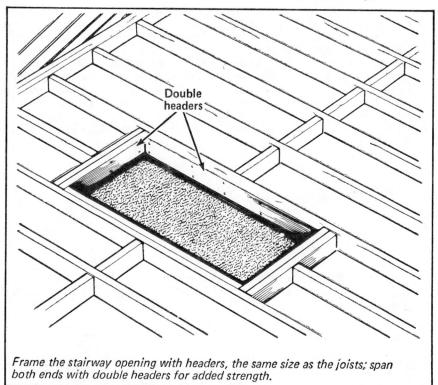

Frame the stairway opening with headers, the same size as the joists; span both ends with double headers for added strength.

width and length of the opening, from the faces of the joists and the headers. This measurement will be the rough opening of the access space. Some home center stores have several rough opening sizes of folding stairways.

Attic openings usually span the width of three joists. If the rough opening to your attic isn't large enough to accept a folding stairway, it probably spans only two joists. Enlarge the opening by cutting a section out of one joist to make a standard-size rough opening, plus the thickness of the headers. The cut-away joist will be the middle joist; headers will span across this joist, attached to the first and third joists.

Use double headers at both ends for added strength. The headers should be the same width and thickness as the in-joist framing; if the joists are 1½ inches thick, the four headers—doubled on each side—should total 6 inches of thickness. If the rough open-

ing size will be 54 inches in length, cut the joist to allow a 60-inch opening; the remainder will be filled with headers.

After cutting the joists, secure the headers to the joists with 16-penny common nails. Nail through the faces of the joists into the ends of the headers; tie the two headers together by nailing through the face of one header into the other. To complete the opening, saw down through the ceiling material.

With 1-inch-thick boards the same width as the joists, nail braces around the opening. This provides a frame around the opening for support. After bracing, the opening should be exactly the same size as the stairway. Any variations on these dimensions will be included in the stairway manufacturer's instructions.

To install the stairway, nail and/or screw it into position, as directed by the manufacturer. The steps are spring-loaded—you pull the steps downward with a rope, and the steps fold out and lock into place. A spring holds the steps up and the access panel closed when the stairs aren't in use.

Fasten the top of the stairway to one of the headers in the access opening. Use the screws and/or nails included with the kit, or follow the manufacturer's instructions for proper hardware. Work in the attic to make this connection; have a helper hold the folded-out steps while you fasten the unit to the header. Then slip the pull cord through the small opening in the access panel and knot it to complete the installation.

The access panel that faces the hallway or room below can be finished to match the room; apply paint, stain, or varnish as desired. Give the panel and trim two coats of finish, sanding the surface lightly between coats of finish. Let the finish dry completely.

Ceilings

Tile a Ceiling

An ugly or damaged ceiling is easy to redo with ceiling tile. If the old ceiling is smooth and level, just glue the tile into place; if it's uneven or badly damaged, install the tile over furring strips. Use acoustical tile to cut noise. **Tools:** stepladder, measuring rule, bucket and sponge, screwdriver, chalk line, carpenters' square, soft pencil, steel straightedge, utility knife with sharp heavy-duty blades, putty knife, magnetic stud finder, hammer, crosscut saw, staple gun, miter box. **Materials:** strong household detergent, 12 × 12-inch ceiling tiles, ceiling tile adhesive, 1 × 2 or 1 × 3 furring strips, 6-penny common nails, heavy-duty staples, 4-penny common nails, cove molding, 4-penny finishing nails. **Time:** 1 to 2 days.

Calculate the amount of ceiling tile you need by measuring the ceiling; its square footage is the number of tiles to buy. Buy a few extra to allow for cutting mistakes. If you're using adhesive, buy the type recommended by the tile manufacturer; read the label to figure how much you'll need. Measure around the room and buy molding to this measurement; get 2 or 3 feet extra.

If the old ceiling is smooth and level, you can put up the tile with adhesive. The ceiling must be clean—if it's greasy or very dirty, wash it with a strong household detergent and let it dry thoroughly before installing the tile. Remove ceiling light fixture covers; unscrew the plates that hold them in place, and let the fixtures hang loosely from the ceiling.

To establish a straight edge for the tile, measure across the ceiling along each wall and mark each center point.

Snap a chalk line on the ceiling from midpoint to midpoint, across the room one way and then the other. The point where the lines intersect is the center of the ceiling. Check the intersection of the lines with a carpenters' square to make sure it forms a 90-degree angle; if not, carefully snap a new chalk line to correct the angle.

Measure the ceiling carefully to determine the width of the tiles that will go around the edges; measure in feet and inches, across both chalked center lines. To calculate the width of border tiles, consider only the inches measured past the last full foot in each direction—5 inches, for example, from 17 feet 5 inches. Add 12 inches—the width of one full tile—and divide by 2. The result is the width of the border tiles at each end of each row of tile laid in that direction. If the inch measurement is 5, for example, border tiles in rows across the direction measured will be 8½ inches wide.

Calculate the width of border tiles along both directions. Start working in one corner of the room; from this corner, measure out the width of the border tiles in each direction. Mark these points on the ceiling. Snap a chalk line on the ceiling at a right angle through each of these points, making sure each of the two new lines is parallel to one of the chalk lines across the center of the ceiling. These new lines mark the rows of border tiles along the two walls that form the starting corner.

Set the corner tile first. Mark it to the measured size with a soft pencil; cut it, face up, with a sharp heavy-duty utility knife and a steel straightedge. Ceiling tiles are made to lock together, with two grooved edges and two tongued edges. The tongued edges of the starter tile must face toward the center of the room, so cut the grooved edges to trim the corner tile to size. The border tiles along the two starter walls will also be trimmed along the grooved edges; the tiles bordering the two far walls will be cut along the tongued edges.

Apply tile adhesive to the back of the trimmed corner tile with a putty knife,. dabbing adhesive in the center of the tile and about 1½ inches in from each corner. Place the tile into the corner, tongued edges out, and slide it into position exactly within the two chalked lines. Press it firmly into place.

Cut border tiles to work out from the corner tile along the two corner walls. Install two or three border tiles in one direction and then two or three in the other border row, always facing the two tongued edges of the tile out. As you work, slide the grooved edges of each tile over the exposed tongues of the last tiles to lock the tiles firmly together; press the tiles firmly against the ceiling.

Fill in between the border tiles with full-size tiles in an expanding wedge pattern, gradually extending the rows of border tiles and fanning tiles out to cover the entire ceiling. To work around light fixtures, hold the tile up to the ceiling before applying adhesive; carefully mark and cut off the area to be removed, then apply adhesive and slide the tile into place.

Continue to set tiles until you reach the far corner of the room. Before cutting border tiles for the two far walls, measure the gap left beyond the last full tile. Mark and cut border tiles along these walls one by one to make sure they fit the gap.

To install tile over an uneven or badly damaged ceiling, or over a papered ceiling, you must build a new base over the old ceiling. In this case, use furring strips nailed up across the ceiling. Use a magnetic stud finder to locate each ceiling joist in the room, and mark the joists on the ceiling all the way across the room. Nail 1 × 2 or 1 × 3 furring strips at right angles across the joists and along the edges of the ceiling with 6-penny common nails, 12 inches apart from center to center; use a carpenters' square to make sure the strips are even and properly angled. Cut the strips to fit, if necessary, with a crosscut saw.

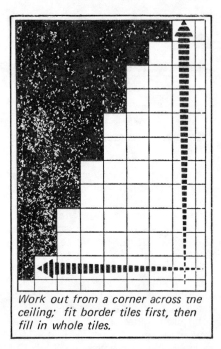

Work out from a corner across tne ceiling; fit border tiles first, then fill in whole tiles.

Measure and calculate border tile width as above. To mark the lines from the starting corner for the corner tile and the first two border rows, carefully snap a chalk line each way on the furring strips.

Cut the corner tile and set it into place, grooved side toward the center of the room and centered on the furring strips. Staple it to the furring strips with a staple gun, setting three staples along each exposed grooved edge. Nail the other two sides firmly into place with 4-penny common nails, as close to the walls as possible.

Continue across the room, setting border tiles and then filling in with full tiles, sliding new tiles in to lock over old ones as you go. Staple each new tile with three staples along each grooved edge. To fasten border tiles into place at the wall, drive three nails along each trimmed tongued edge, as close to the wall as possible. These nails will be covered by molding. Trim and set border tiles for the far walls one by one as you work.

Finish the job by nailing cove molding around the edges of the ceiling to cover

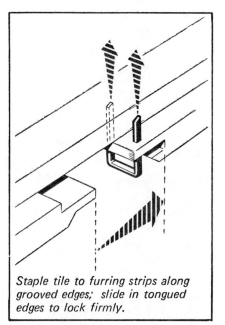

Staple tile to furring strips along grooved edges; slide in tongued edges to lock firmly.

exposed nailheads and hide any irregularities in the border tiles. Measure the molding carefully and cut it to measure; miter the edges with a miter box. Nail the molding into place with 4-penny finishing nails. Finally, replace ceiling light fixtures and fixture covers.

Paper a Ceiling

Papering a ceiling is tricky, but it's a great way to cover cracks that won't stay patched. Don't paper over major flaws, though; the ceiling must be firm and smooth. **Tools:** screwdriver, two stepladders and plank for scaffold, wall-cleaning sponge or bucket and sponge, putty knife or paint scraper, safety goggles, sanding block, vacuum cleaner, measuring rule, large paintbrush, pencil, chalk line, carpenters' square, long table, sharp scissors, paste bucket, paperhangers' paste brush and smoothing brush, sharp utility knife and extra blades, seam roller. **Materials:** plastic dropcloths, masking tape, strong household detergent,

spackling compound, fine-grit sandpaper, sizing as recommended by wallpaper dealer, wallpaper, wallpaper paste as recommended by dealer. **Time:** about 1 day per room for patching and sizing, 1 day for papering.

Choose paper with a slight texture to disguise ceiling flaws. The classic is white, but feel free to use colors and patterns. If the paper you like is prepasted, use wallpaper paste to put it on the ceiling—after soaking, most prepasted paper is too heavy to handle or to stick well to a ceiling. Make sure the paper is pretrimmed.

Figure the square footage of the ceiling and buy paper accordingly; most rolls of paper cover about 30 square feet. Buy at least one extra roll. Ask the dealer how much paste and sizing to buy.

Paper the ceiling before you do the walls. Before you start to paper, make sure the ceiling is clean. Move all furniture, rugs, drapes, and pictures out of the room; cover the floor with plastic dropcloths and secure them at the edges with masking tape. Wipe the ceiling with a wall-cleaning sponge. If it is very dirty or greasy, as in a kitchen, wash it with a strong household detergent and let it dry. Remove light fixture covers.

Prepare the ceiling by patching any cracks or holes; fill them with spackling compound, smoothed on with a putty knife or scraper. Let the compound dry and, wearing safety goggles, sand it smooth with fine-grit sandpaper; remove the plaster dust with a wall-cleaning sponge. Work from a scaffold made with a plank set across two stepladders. Vacuum the room.

Coat the ceiling with sizing, applying it evenly with a large brush. Apply one or two coats, as recommended by the manufacturer. Let dry completely.

Start papering at a corner, working across the width of the room rather than over its full length. Measure out from the corner of the ceiling to place the first strip of paper; mark a distance about 1 inch less than the width of the wallpaper. Set a chalk line from this point to a point exactly opposite on the

CEILINGS / Papering

other side of the ceiling; use a carpenters' square against the wall to make sure the line is straight. Snap the line against the ceiling to mark the edge of the first strip of paper.

Mix the paste as directed. Cover your work table with a clean plastic dropcloth and unroll a strip of wallpaper on it, face down. Measure the width of the ceiling across the chalk line and cut the strip of wallpaper about 4 inches longer than this, using a sharp scissors. If you're using a paper with a definite pattern, cut the strips for the entire ceiling at this point. Match the patterns exactly before cutting each strip; cut all strips about 4 inches longer than the measured width of the ceiling where they will be set into place. Unpatterned paper can be cut all at once or strip by strip, as you prefer.

Adjust the first strip on the table, still face down, so that one end lies flat and the other hangs over the table edge.

Brush paste evenly onto the strip of paper with the paperhangers' paste brush. Fold the pasted strip accordion-style, paste to paste, in folds about 18 inches long, lifting the paper at both edges and pulling it toward you to make each new fold. Be careful not to crease the paper at the folds, or the creases will show on the finished ceiling. Slide the piled-up paper to pull the dangling end of the strip up onto the table; paste this end and continue folding until the entire strip is folded together.

Position the stepladder scaffold under the chalk line so that your head clears the ceiling by about 6 inches. Start at the right corner if you're right-handed, the left corner if you're left-handed. Stick the smoothing brush in your pocket. Use a roll of paper to support the folded strip. Lift the roll of paper and the strip, being careful not to let the paper slip off the roll.

Lift the paper up to the ceiling with your left hand, top end toward the corner. With your right hand, set the top end of the paper carefully onto the ceiling, leaving about 2 inches extra at the top and the bottom end. The far edge of the paper will overlap onto the wall about 1 inch; press it into place with your fingers. Line up the edge of the

Fold the pasted strip accordion-style, paste to paste, in 18-inch folds; don't crease the edges.

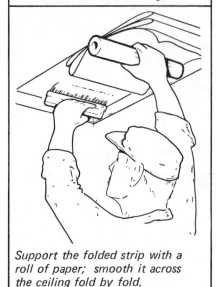

Support the folded strip with a roll of paper; smooth it across the ceiling fold by fold.

paper *exactly* with the chalk line on the ceiling. Correct a slight crookedness by gently sliding the paper into place; if it is very badly aligned, peel it off and re-apply it.

Unfold the paper gradually, smoothing it along the chalk line as you go and working toward the other side of the ceiling. Don't unfold more paper than you can smooth down easily. Once the paper is started, use the smoothing brush to help you set the rest of the strip, always keeping it exactly aligned on the chalk line.

When the entire strip has been applied to the ceiling, go back over it with the smoothing brush to remove air bubbles. Hold the brush with bristles edge-on to set the paper firmly into corners and along the wall joint, pounding firmly until the paper is well creased into place. Don't trim the overhanging edges yet; wait until the second strip is in place.

If you didn't cut all the strips before starting to paste, measure and cut the second strip and all succeeding strips the same way. Brush paste to the back of each strip, fold it accordion-style, and set it onto the ceiling, always starting at the right and working toward the left (or the reverse, if you're left-handed). Set each strip next to the last one and slide it gently into place to butt exactly against the last edge. Remove air bubbles with the smoothing brush and pound the wall edges into place.

As you finish setting each strip, go back to the one ahead of it and trim the overlapping edges with a sharp utility knife; change the blade as soon as it begins to dull. Match patterns carefully, if necessary. Seal the seams between strips as you work, pressing them firmly with a seam roller; wipe the roller often with a clean rag to remove any excess paste. Trim the last strip as necessary along the wall.

To work around light fixtures, measure carefully and mark the affected strips lightly on the right side before you apply the paste. If the fixture affects only the edge of a strip, cut a small slit in the paper and simply cover the fixture; trim the overlapping paper when you smooth the strip. If the fixture is more in the middle of the strip, cut a small X in the paper exactly at the center point of the fixture, no more than half the diameter of the fixture, and trim away the center points to leave a small hole. Paste the paper and set it into place, easing the precut hole carefully over the fixture. The paper will tear around the fixture as you push it into place; don't let it tear too far. Smooth the paper around the fixture with your fingers, being careful not to tear the edges. Trim excess paper after the strip has been smoothed into place.

To complete the job, remove any excess paste at the ceiling edges with a damp sponge. Replace light fixture covers and dispose of the dropcloths. Save unused wallpaper for repairs.

Install a Suspended Ceiling

Suspended ceilings cover a multitude of flaws, and they're easy to install. They work best where you don't mind losing ceiling height. **Tools:** stepladder, measuring rule, magnetic stud finder, pencil or chalk, chalk line, level, hammer, tin snips or hacksaw, carpenters' square, wire cutter, pliers, utility knife with sharp heavy-duty blades, steel straightedge. **Materials:** graph paper, components for suspended ceiling system (wall angles, main runner grid pieces, cross tee grid pieces, and ceiling panels), 6-penny common nails, string, heavy-duty screw eyes, 12-gauge hanger wire. **Time:** 1 to 2 days.

Suspended ceiling panels are sold in 2 × 2-foot and 2 × 4-foot sizes; choose the 2 × 2-foot size for use in smaller rooms. Measure the ceiling carefully and plot it on graph paper, marking the exact location of windows and doors in the room. Mark the direction of exposed ceiling joists. If the room has a finished ceiling, use a magnetic stud finder to locate the joists, and mark their direction on the diagram. Mark the joists on the ceiling itself, using a pencil or soft chalk to draw the joist lines all across the ceiling.

Take this diagram with you when you buy the materials for the ceiling. With the dealer, plan the layout for the ceiling

CEILINGS/Suspended Panels

panels, figuring full panels across the main ceiling and evenly trimmed partial panels at the edges. To calculate the width of the border panels in each direction, determine the width of the gap left after full panels are placed all across the dimension; divide by 2. The dealer should help you calculate how many panels you'll need, and should also tell you how many wall angle (in 10-foot lengths), main runner (in 12-foot lengths), and cross tee (in 4-foot or 2-foot lengths) grid sections and how much 12-gauge hanger wire to buy.

No preparation is necessary on the old ceiling. Begin work by marking the level the new ceiling will hang at; allow at least 4 inches clearance between the panels and the old ceiling. Snap a chalk line at this height across each wall, using a level to keep it straight. Make sure the lines meet exactly at the corners of the room.

Nail wall angle brackets along the chalk line all around the room, with the bottom leg of the L facing into the room and flush along the chalk line. Use 6-penny common nails to attach the brackets, setting them every 1½ to 2 feet. Cut the bracket to the required length with tin snips or a hacksaw.

The long panels of the ceiling grid are set parallel to the ceiling joists, so the main runner must be attached at right angles to the joists, every 4 feet across the ceiling. Hanger wire threaded through screw eyes in the joists suspends the main runners of the grid system.

To locate the points where the screw eyes should be driven in, consult your final ceiling layout diagram. Locate on the diagram the joints between the short sides of two long panels; if you're using 2 × 2-foot panels, count every joint at right angles to the joists. Mark these points along the angle bracket on each wall, measuring carefully according to the diagram. Stretch strings across the room from wall to wall at these marked points to show you where the main runners will hang.

Drive sturdy screw eyes into the joists directly above each string, placing one screw eye at the last joist on each side

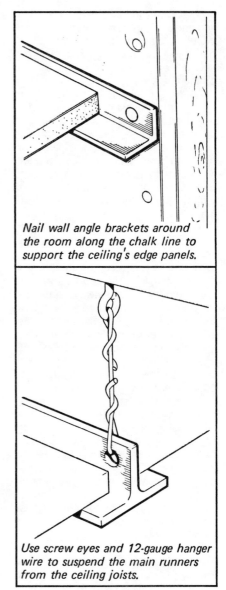

Nail wall angle brackets around the room along the chalk line to support the ceiling's edge panels.

Use screw eyes and 12-gauge hanger wire to suspend the main runners from the ceiling joists.

and one in every third joist across the ceiling. If you're covering a finished ceiling, drive the screw eyes at the marked joist lines; use long screw eyes to hold through the thickness of the ceiling.

Cut a length of hanger wire for each screw eye—long enough to fasten securely through the screw eye, extend down to the stretched runner string, and fasten the runner. Thread a wire through each screw eye and twist the end firmly around the dangling wire. Exactly at the point where the wire crosses the string beneath it, bend the wire sharply with pliers to a 90-degree angle.

When screw eyes have been driven into the joists and wires hung for all main runner sections of the ceiling grid, set the main runners into place. Cut main runner sections to the required length with tin snips or a hacksaw; if you must put two sections together to cover a long span, snap the pieces together with the preformed tabs.

Lift each long main runner and set one end into place on the wall angle bracket at one side of the T up; swing the other end up and position the runner exactly along the marker string and under the screw eyes in the joists. Thread the bent end of each hanging wire through a hole in the runner leg; bend the end of the wire up and secure it, twisting it firmly back over the hanging wire. Check each installed runner with a level to make sure it's straight, and adjust the length of the wire hangers if necessary. Repeat until all main runners have been installed.

Again working from your ceiling diagram, install the cross tee sections of the ceiling grid. These sections snap into place in slots in the main runner sections; since they're sold in 4-foot lengths, no cutting is necessary. Snap the sections into place every 2 feet along the main runners. If you're using 2 × 2-foot ceiling panels, use special 2-foot cross tees to divide each 2 × 4-foot panel in half; snap the sections together firmly.

Finally, when all main runners and cross tees are in place, install the ceiling panels. Tilt each panel to angle it through a grid opening, then carefully lower it until it rests on the bracket edges of the grid sections. Measure border panels carefully; cut them to size with a sharp-bladed utility knife, using a steel straightedge to guide the cut.

If you have to fit a panel around a post, carefully measure across the

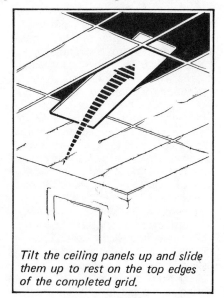

Tilt the ceiling panels up and slide them up to rest on the top edges of the completed grid.

opening to the post in both directions; sketch the opening and mark the post. Measure the diameter of the post. Mark the panel lightly where the post will go through it; cut the panel in two exactly through the center of the post, across the shorter dimension. Carve an opening for the post on the inside cut edge of each panel, forming two semicircular or rectangular cutouts. Cut only a little at a time; hold the cut sections up to the post frequently to fit them exactly. Set the two sections into place in the suspension grid; the cut will show hardly at all.

Install a Light in a Suspended Ceiling

The space between a suspended ceiling and what it's suspended from is more than adequate to accommodate fluorescent lighting. **Tools:** flashlight or trouble light, drill, screwdriver, wire strippers, pencil, saber saw or fine-toothed saw, handsaw. **Materials:** translucent acrylic plastic sheet, fluorescent fixtures, wirenuts; molly bolts, toggle bolts, masonry anchors, or screws. **Time:** 1 to 2 hours.

Caution: Before you start to work, flip the circuit breaker or remove the fuse that provides power to the fixture. If you don't know which circuit controls the fixture, turn off the main circuit breaker or remove the fuses to turn off all power to the house. If necessary, use a flashlight or a trouble light while you work.

If there's an old ceiling fixture above the suspended ceiling, it's easy to install a new fluorescent lighting fixture. Lift out several tiles in the center of the ceiling, and use a flashlight to locate old ceiling fixtures above the suspended ceiling. If the old fixtures are there—and they're where you want the new ones to be—you can begin installation. If the fixtures aren't where you want them—or if there's no fixture at all—have an electrician install the wiring. After the wiring is installed, you can do the rest.

First, choose a location for the lighting. Fluorescent tubes placed in the center of a room create a balanced effect, but you may want to position the light over an activity area, like a workshop or a cooking area. Exceptionally large rooms may require more than one large fluorescent tube; if so, place several small tubes to best illuminate the room.

Remove the old ceiling fixture from the line wires. The fixture is probably held to the ceiling with screws; the fixture's wires are probably attached to the line wires with wirenuts or crimped connectors.

Disassemble the new fluorescent fixture, if necessary, to expose its wires, one black and one white. With a helper holding the fixture, connect the fluorescent wires to the line wires; attach black wire to black, and white to white. Then reassemble the fixture, if necessary, and position it against the ceiling.

Most fluorescent fixtures come equipped with their own installation screws. Use these screws if you can drive them into ceiling joists or some other solid wood; otherwise, use molly or toggle bolts for drywall or plaster ceilings, or masonry anchors and screws for concrete ceilings. Drill pilot holes to size for bolts and anchors; drill

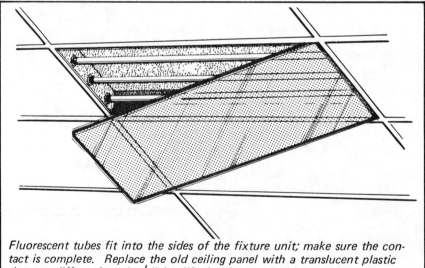

Fluorescent tubes fit into the sides of the fixture unit; make sure the contact is complete. Replace the old ceiling panel with a translucent plastic sheet to diffuse the tubes' light; lift the sheet and slide it up into the suspension grid.

pilot holes of slightly smaller diameter for wood screws. Then firmly screw or anchor the fixture to the ceiling, using the predrilled holes in the fixture to guide the screws.

Place the fluorescent tube into the contact slots on the sides, if it isn't already installed, and restore the power to the fixture. If the bulb doesn't light, make sure the wall switch is turned on. If it still doesn't work, there may be a problem in the ceiling wiring; call an electrician and have the circuit checked.

Once the light is working, install the plastic sheets where the tile used to be. Place the removed suspended tiles over the plastic sheet. Using the tiles as a template, trace the required size onto the sheet with a pencil. Cut the plastic to fit with a fine-toothed handsaw or a saber saw; ask the retailer for specifics concerning cutting.

Lift the plastic up into the suspended gridwork. If you're installing several small fixtures, use one plastic sheet for each fixture.

layout you want and count the beams you need; count both across-the-ceiling and along-the-edge beams. Measure the longest span to be covered. Buy beams long enough to cross this longest span, but don't worry about shorter spans—the beams are easily cut with a handsaw or serrated knife. Buy special corner beams for the edges where walls and ceiling meet.

Before installing beams, make sure the ceiling is sound and clean. If it's very dirty or greasy, wash it thoroughly with household detergent; rinse and let dry completely. Dull glossy paint with fine sandpaper where beams will be attached.

Install corner beams first; then set the middle beam and work out to the sides of the ceiling. To install each beam, carefully measure the span it will cross. Measure and mark the beam, using a carpenters' square to be sure the end is even. Cut it to measure with a small handsaw or a sharp serrated knife. Set the beam against the ceiling, exactly where you want it, and outline it lightly

Add Decorator Beams

It's easy to add rustic character to a room with artificial wood beams—the foam beams available now are good ones, and the skill required is minimal. **Tools:** stepladder, measuring rule, bucket and sponge, pencil, carpenters' square, small handsaw or sharp serrated knife, caulking gun. **Materials:** household detergent, fine-grit sandpaper, prefinished polyurethane foam beams and corner beams, cartridge-type ceiling tile mastic adhesive. **Time:** 1 to 3 hours.

Rigid polyurethane foam decorator beams are sold in sections up to 18 feet long, with a wide variety of wood finishes. Some beams are adhesive-backed; others require that you apply the adhesive.

Before buying beams, decide on the

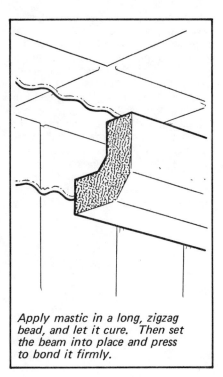

Apply mastic in a long, zigzag bead, and let it cure. Then set the beam into place and press to bond it firmly.

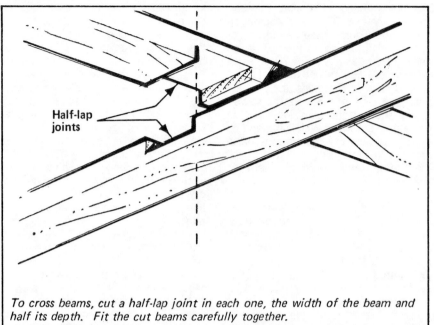

To cross beams, cut a half-lap joint in each one, the width of the beam and half its depth. Fit the cut beams carefully together.

on the ceiling with a pencil. Take the beam down.

If the beam is adhesive-backed, strip off the paper backing; set the beam carefully into place in its outline on the ceiling and press firmly. If the beam is not adhesive-backed, use a cartridge-type ceiling tile mastic adhesive to mount it. Apply a long zigzag bead of mastic to the back of the beam with a caulking gun; if the beam manufacturer specifies, also apply mastic to the ceiling or wall surface. Set the beam carefully into place against the ceiling, press it to spread the adhesive, and then remove it. Let the mastic on both beam and ceiling or wall cure, as directed by

the manufacturer. When the adhesive is tacky, set the beam into place and press it firmly against the ceiling.

To install crossed rows of beams, lay the beams out on a cleared floor exactly as you want them to be installed. At each point where two beams cross, mark each beam exactly to show the full width of the crossing beam. Cut a half-lap joint at each marked point, ½ inch narrower than the marked width, using a small handsaw or a sharp serrated knife to cut straight into the beam to half its depth. Fit the crossed beams together and shave off any excess. Install one row of beams completely; then install the entire cross row.

Windows

Unstick a Window

Double-hung windows are all too prone to sticking, but you can usually open them with muscle and common sense. **Tools:** stiff putty knife or paint scraper, hammer, chisel, 6-inch-long wood block, pry bar. **Materials:** medium-grit sandpaper, silicone spray lubricant. **Time:** ½ to 2 hours.

First check the window to make sure it's unlocked. Assuming the catch is open, the most common problem is that the window was painted shut, and the paint is holding the sash shut. Use a stiff putty knife or paint scraper to cut the paint sealing the groove between the window sash—the sliding part—and the frame. Push the blade of the knife straight into the groove. If it won't go in with mild pressure, tap it in lightly

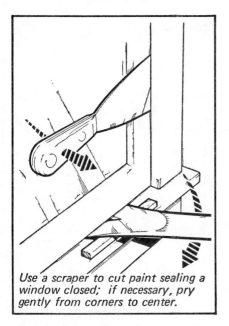

Use a scraper to cut paint sealing a window closed; if necessary, pry gently from corners to center.

with a hammer to break the paint all around the sash. If this was the only problem, the window should open.

If the window still doesn't open, the tracks the sash moves in may be blocked. Examine the tracks above the sash. If they're clogged with paint or dirt, clean them carefully with a chisel; don't dig into the wood, but remove lumps and bulges. Sand the inside of the tracks smooth with medium-grit sandpaper, then spray them with a silicone lubricant, and raise the window.

If the grooves are clean but the window still sticks, place a 6-inch-long wood block flat against the wood of the sash frame and tap it gently with a hammer to push the sash back from the window frame. Work all around the edges of the sash with the block and hammer, tapping very gently and evenly along the sash frame; then try to open the window. If it opens, clean, sand, and lubricate the tracks as above. If tapping on the sash doesn't work, tap the block sideways into the window frame, to push it the other way. Try the window again, and clean and lubricate as above if it opens.

As a last resort, use a pry bar. Work from the outside of the window if you can. Slip the flat end of the pry bar into the crack between the bottom of the window sash and the windowsill. Set the block of wood on the windowsill under the bar to improve leverage and protect the sill. Pry gently at the corners of the window, pushing the bar down to move the window up; pry first one corner, then the other, moving slowly back and forth toward the center of the sill. Work carefully, and don't force the window open. If it does open, clean, sand, and lubricate the tracks. If it doesn't, repeat the wood block procedure from the outside. Clean and lubricate as above.

If cutting, pounding, and prying don't

work, leave the window alone. The problem may be caused by excessive swelling from humidity, by extreme misalignment of the sash, or by uneven settling of the house. Don't make it worse; call a carpenter.

Replace Broken Glass

Replacing a windowpane is a job you can easily do yourself. **Tools:** heavy work gloves, chisel or scraper, hammer, propane torch or soldering iron (not essential), paintbrush, wire brush, tape measure or rule, glaziers' points, putty knife. **Materials:** linseed oil, glaziers' compound or putty (compound is better), new glass pane, paint. **Time:** 1/2 to 1 hour.

Wearing gloves, push the broken pieces of glass back and forth to loosen and remove them from the frame; if they don't come loose easily, knock the pieces out with a hammer. With a chisel or scraper, remove all old putty, bit by bit. Don't try to force long pieces out. Soften stubborn chunks with a propane torch or soldering iron, or paint the old putty with linseed oil, let the oil soak in, then scrape again.

If the window frame is wood, look for metal tabs (glaziers' points) as you work; in metal frames, look for spring clips. Remove them carefully and set aside. If points or clips are missing, get some when you buy the glass.

Wire-brush the frame to remove all traces of old putty. Coat the raw wood where the old putty was with linseed oil, all around the frame, and let the oil soak in completely.

Measure the inside of the frame carefully in both directions, subtracting 1/16 inch each way to allow for natural expansion and contraction and for any irregularities in glass or frame. If the lip of the frame is very wide, you can subtract as much as 1/8 inch from each dimension. Have the glass cut to measure at a hardware store or lumberyard.

With glass at hand, remove a large chunk of putty from the can. Roll the putty between your palms, shaping it into a narrow, roughly pencil-sized roll. Press the putty roll around the inside of the empty window frame, starting at a corner, where the glass will be pushed into place.

Working carefully, press the new pane of glass firmly against the rolled putty, pushing hard enough to force some of the putty out around the glass and remove any air bubbles. Insert the spring clips (metal frame) or glaziers' points (wood frame). Snap the clips back into their holes. Use the putty knife to insert glaziers' points into the wood frame, pushing in the sharp points every 6 inches or so around the frame.

Before going any further, look at other windowpanes nearby. The new putty should match the putty on these panes.

To apply putty to the outside of the new pane, make another putty roll. Press it firmly all around the new glass. Press hard enough so that there are no gaps.

Dip the putty knife in linseed oil and shake off the excess. Using long, even strokes, smooth the putty around the new pane. It should not be visible over the frame on the inside of the window. Use a razor blade or glass scraper to

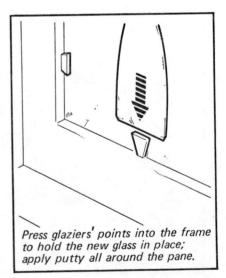

Press glaziers' points into the frame to hold the new glass in place; apply putty all around the pane.

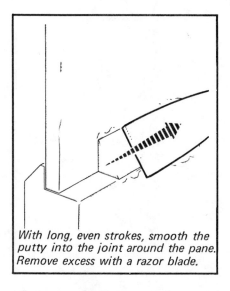

With long, even strokes, smooth the putty into the joint around the pane. Remove excess with a razor blade.

remove any excess putty, on both sides of the glass and frame.

Let the new putty cure for three days before painting it. If the surface of the putty is very rough, smooth it carefully with fine sandpaper. You don't have to repaint the whole window frame, but let the paint overlap a little onto both frame and glass, to make sure the putty is sealed at both edges. Use two coats, and let the paint dry thoroughly before cleaning the glass.

Replace a Broken Sash Cord

To make this repair a one-time-only effort, replace broken sash cords with chain. **Tools:** single-edge razor blade or sharp utility knife, putty knife, hammer, screwdriver, wire cutters, small weight, pliers. **Materials:** sash chain, medium-gauge wire, wood screws or nails. **Time:** ½ to 1 hour.

On the side with the broken cord, use a sharp razor blade or utility knife to cut the paint seal between the window frame and the inside stop molding that holds the sash in place. Being careful not to gouge either the stop or the

window frame, pry the stop strip away from the frame with a putty knife and remove it. The stop strip must be removed for access to either the top or the bottom sash; if you're replacing a cord in the upper sash, remove the lower sash and the parting strip—the piece of wood between the upper and lower sashes—first.

The sash cord is attached to the sash at a groove or indentation in the upper corner. Pull the side of the sash toward you out of the window frame, just far enough to expose this indentation Pull the knotted end of the cord out of the groove, or untie the knot. Remove the cord from the sash frame.

Lift the window carefully out of its track on the other side; you may need a helper to hold it in place. Untie the cord on that side and remove it from the sash frame, but do not release it—knot the end of the cord first, or it will slide into the wall. Remove the sash from the window frame and set it aside.

Sash cords operate on pulleys, visible at the sides of the window frame; the weight of the window sash is balanced by weights which hang inside

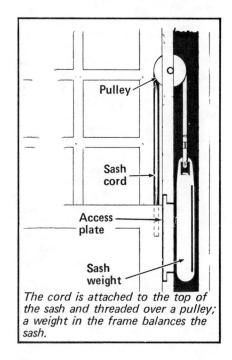

The cord is attached to the top of the sash and threaded over a pulley; a weight in the frame balances the sash.

the frame. To replace the sash cord, you must be able to get at these weights.

Some windows have access plates in the sides of the sash frame. Look carefully for these plates; they may have been painted over. If you can see only a vague outline, tap the track with a hammer until the edge of the plate is clear. Cut along the edge with a razor blade or utility knife, then remove the screws in the plate and lift it out. In very old houses, there usually are no access plates. In this case, you must remove the entire inside frame of the window. Use a putty knife to pry out the sides of the frame.

Remove the weight from the inside of the frame and untie the sash cord. Using the two pieces of the old cord, measure the length of sash chain needed to rehang the window. Cut the chain to the correct length, allowing several inches extra so it can be looped through the sash weight and fastened.

Attach a small weight to one end of the chain—anything small enough to feed through the pulley will do. Push the weighted end of the chain in over the pulley at the top of the window frame. Feed in the chain until it is visible in the access plate at the bottom of the frame, then remove the small weight.

Now attach the sash weight. Loop the chain through the weight and bind the end to the chain with sturdy wire, using pliers to pull it tight. The chain must be securely fastened or it will not hold. Replace the weight in the access hole and reel in any slack in the chain. Do not replace the access plate yet. Follow the same procedure to replace the sash cord on the other side with chain.

Set the window sash back into place at the edge of the window frame—you may need help again at this point. Attach the chain to one side of the sash, using wood screws or nails to hold it in place in the slot. Lift the window sash back into its track.

Attach the chain to the other side of the sash and raise the window (bottom sash) to its highest position, bracing it against the parting stop. Check the position of the sash weight; the bottom

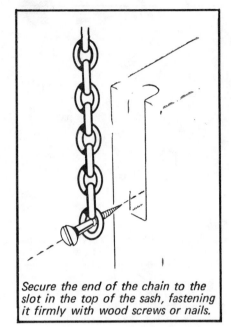

Secure the end of the chain to the slot in the top of the sash, fastening it firmly with wood screws or nails.

of the weight should be about 3 inches above the sill. If the weight is not in the right place, adjust the sash chain at both sides of the sash to correct its position.

Finally, when the weights on both sides of the sash are properly placed and the sash hangs evenly, replace the access plate or inside window frame. If the window is an upper sash, replace the parting strip, the lower sash, and the stop strip; if a lower sash, simply replace the stop strip.

Replace Sash Cords with Spring Lifts

Most windows in older homes are counterbalanced for opening and closing with cords, pulleys, and weights. In newer homes, the old cord/weight device has been replaced with spring lifts. Modernizing old windows with spring lifts is easy; so is repairing malfunctioning lifts. **Tools:** hammer, pry bar, jack plane, screwdriver, nail set, stiff-bladed putty knife, utility knife, butt chisel or brace and bit, wood or rubber mallet, 6-penny finishing nails, measuring rule, paintbrush. **Materials:** wood putty, new spring lifts, sandpaper; paint, stain, or varnish. **Time:** 1 to 3 hours per window.

With a putty knife, pry out the stop molding that holds the window sash in place in the window frame. To remove a paint seal between the stop and the window frame, cut carefully along the joint with a utility knife. Be careful not to damage the stop molding. Pull out the window sash, cutting the sash cord, if necessary, with a utility knife. Then remove the screws holding the pulley assembly in place, and remove the pulley assembly.

Buy a spring lift in a self-contained drum unit; this unit slips into the old

pulley hole. The unit must be secured below the surface of the frame. If necessary, enlarge the hole slightly to accommodate the unit; use a butt chisel, a brace and bit, and/or a utility knife to recess the unit's housing into the frame. Fasten the lift to the frame with the two screws provided, driving them through the predrilled holes into the frame.

Pull out the spring tape from the unit. If possible, fasten the free end of the tape to the side sash groove where the sash cord ran. Otherwise, install the tape flat against the sash frame. Use the flathead wood screw provided to fasten the tape to the sash. If the fit is too tight, use a jack plane to shave a thin layer of wood off the sash's edge; plane carefully, making sure the plane is square on the sash's edge.

Replace the window sash in the opening and renail the stop molding. Test the window. If it binds, remove the

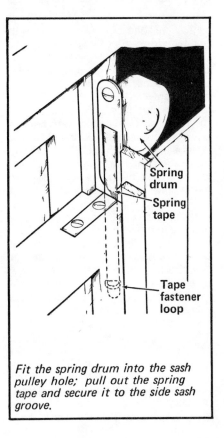

Fit the spring drum into the sash pulley hole; pull out the spring tape and secure it to the side sash groove.

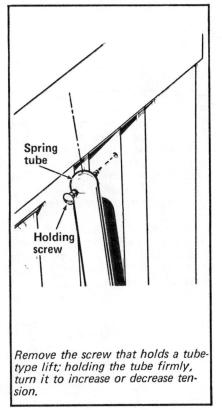

Remove the screw that holds a tube-type lift; holding the tube firmly, turn it to increase or decrease tension.

stop molding again. Remove the sash and carefully plane the edge of the window until it operates smoothly. Plane only as much as necessary to correct the window's operation.

If the window was built with spring lifts, they may be sealed in a small metal tube fitted along the window's channel. To repair the lift, push down the window to expose the tube and turn the screw at the top of the tube. Then pull the tube away from the window channel. As soon as the tube is away from the channel, grip the end of the screw; otherwise the tension on the spring inside the tube will be released.

If the window won't stay closed, turn the screw counterclockwise to release some of the tension; one or two turns is usually enough. If the window won't stay open, turn the screw clockwise to add tension to the spring. When the adjustment has been made, replace the spring in the window by reseating the holding screw.

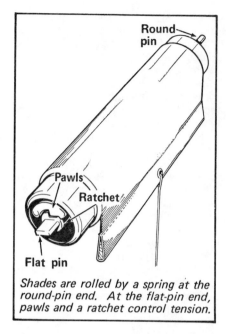

Shades are rolled by a spring at the round-pin end. At the flat-pin end, pawls and a ratchet control tension.

Fix a Broken Shade

Temperamental window shades are irritating and inconvenient—and also, fortunately, easy to fix. **Tools:** hammer, screwdriver, pliers, scissors, tweezers, staple gun. **Materials:** thin cardboard, sandpaper, plastic wood, silicone spray lubricant, clean soft rag, heavy-duty staples. **Time:** about 10 to 20 minutes.

Shades that bind at the edges or tend to fall down are probably all right; it's the brackets that need adjustment. If a shade hung outside the window frame binds, tap the brackets gently outward with a hammer. If it still sticks, take the shade down. On the end of the shade that has a round pin, remove the pin with pliers and pull the metal cap off the end of the shade roller. Sand the end of the wood roller to round it down; replace cap and pin and rehang the shade. In really bad cases, remove the shade; unscrew one bracket and move it out

slightly. Fill the old screw holes with plastic wood before replacing the bracket and rehanging the shade. A badly binding shade hung inside a window frame must be cut to fit; take it to a professional.

If the shade falls off its brackets, remove the shade; unscrew one bracket and move it in slightly. Fill the old screw holes with plastic wood before replacing the bracket and rehanging the shade. A loose shade hung inside a window frame must be removed and shimmed to hold it in place. Cut a piece of thin cardboard a little smaller than one bracket; remove the bracket. Set the shim against the back of the bracket and screw bracket and shim to the window frame, using the same screw holes. Rehang the shade. If it's still loose, repeat the shimming procedure with the other bracket.

Shades operate by spring tension. At one end of the shade roller is a flat pin; inside the roller at this end is a strong spring. Two pawls behind the pin are used to engage a ratchet when the shade is pulled, stopping the movement of the spring as soon as the pressure on the shade cord is released. Most shade problems are caused by problems in the roller spring or in the pawls and ratchet.

If the roller spring isn't broken, you can usually adjust its tension. A shade that doesn't stay up needs its roller spring tightened. Pull the shade down a few turns of the roller—if it's very loose, pull it down halfway. Holding the rolled-up shade firmly, lift the end of the roller with the flat pin out of its bracket. Roll the shade up tightly by hand, being careful to keep the edges even. Rehang the shade. If the shade still doesn't stay up, repeat the procedure.

A shade that's hard to pull down has the opposite problem. Lift the flat-pin end of the shade out of its bracket and unroll the shade a few turns; replace the pin in the bracket.

A shade that pulls down but doesn't stay down may need cleaning. Take the shade down and remove the metal cap from the flat-pin end of the roller. Using tweezers and a clean soft rag, clean the pawl and ratchet surfaces. Spray a little silicone lubricant into the assembly; replace the metal cap and rehang the shade.

A shade that rocks when it's raised or lowered probably has a bent pin. Take the shade down, examine the pins, and adjust the pins carefully with pliers; rehang the shade. When the shade rolls easily but at an angle, take it down, unroll it completely, and remove the staples that hold the fabric to the roller. Adjust the fabric so it's perfectly straight on the roller, staple it into place, reroll the shade, and set it back into the brackets. Adjust spring tension as necessary.

Renovate Venetian Blinds

Shabby tapes and frayed cords are standard problems with venetian blinds; fortunately, replacement tapes and cords are standard too. The job is painstaking, but not difficult. **Tools:** scissors, pliers, staple gun. **Materials:** replacement venetian blind cord and ladder tape, adhesive tape or transparent tape, heavy-duty staples, liquid detergent, clean bath towels, silicone spray lubricant. **Time:** about ½ to 1 hour to replace cords; about 2 to 3 hours to replace cords and tapes.

Replacing the lift cord in a venetian blind is a simple procedure; the blind doesn't even have to be taken down. If the blind has a wood frame, the ends of the ladder tapes are stapled over the knotted ends of the lift cord under the thick bottom slat; remove the staples that hold the tapes in place to reveal the knotted ends of the lift cord. If the frame is metal, the bottom slat is hollow. Remove the end caps and the metal clamps over the ladder tapes; the knotted ends of the lift cord are underneath the tapes.

Use either cotton or nylon venetian blind cord. Untie the knot on the side opposite the lift cord; hold the end of the cord so you don't lose it. Butt the end of the new cord to the unknotted end of the old lift cord and carefully join the two cords with lightweight adhesive tape or transparent tape. The joint should be as

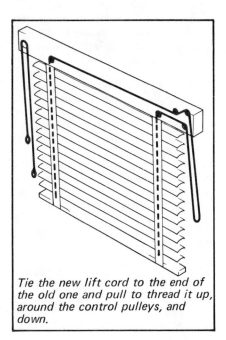

Tie the new lift cord to the end of the old one and pull to thread it up, around the control pulleys, and down.

strong as possible, but it must not be bulky, or this procedure won't work.

Carefully pull the side of the control cord that feeds from the top of the blind to gently pull the taped-together cords completely through the blind. The lift cord threads up through the slat of the blind on the starting side and through the control pulley at the top of the blind; then it threads down through the slats on the control cord side. As you pull gently on the old cord, the new cord, drawn by the old, will be correctly threaded through the slats of the blind. Leave a long loop of loose cord to form the new control cord.

When the new cord has been drawn completely through the blind, knot the starting end under the bottom rail and cut off the excess cord. Being careful to leave a loop of slack cord for the control cord, knot the finishing end of the new cord and cut off the excess. Both end knots must be secure or the blind will fall apart. Refasten the ladder tapes over the knotted ends of the new lift cord; replace the clamps over tapes in a metal blind, staple the tapes to the thick bottom slat in a wood blind.

To complete the job, remove the equalizer clip from the old cord and slide it onto the new control cord. Adjust the equalizer as necessary to keep the blind working smoothly.

Replace the tilt cord of the blind when you replace the lift cord; because the tilt cord doesn't control anything in the main blind, this is easy. Untie the knots that hold the tilt pulls and pull the cord to remove it from the blind. Thread one end of the replacement cord over the tilt cord pulley and push until it is rolled through the pulley and out. Holding the long end of the cord up to the pulley so that it doesn't exert any tilt control, pull the threaded-through end until it's positioned correctly. Slip the cord pulls over the ends of the new tilt cord and knot the ends of the cord to hold the pulls in place.

To replace shabby ladder tapes in a venetian blind, use replacement tapes made for the same width slats, and with the same number of ladders. Take the blind down and set it out on the floor,

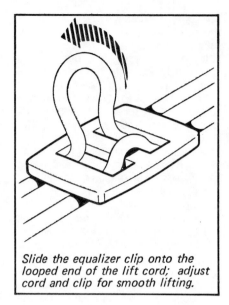

Slide the equalizer clip onto the looped end of the lift cord; adjust cord and clip for smooth lifting.

fully extended. If the frame is metal, remove the end caps and the metal clamps holding the ladder tapes to expose the knotted ends of the lift cord. If the frame is wood, remove the staples that hold the tapes.

Untie the knotted ends of the lift cord and pull the cord entirely out of the blind—because you must remove the cord entirely, this is a good time to replace it. Remove the equalizer clip from the cord and set it aside.

Slide the loose slats to one side through the tapes and out of the blind, stacking them carefully as you take them out. Clean the slats by soaking them in a mild solution of liquid detergent, then rinsing thoroughly—a bathtub is ideal for this. Set the slats carefully on dry bath towels to drain.

When the slats have been cleaned and set out to dry, remove the old ladder tapes from the blind assembly. Unclip the top of each tape at the tilt tube in the box at the top of the blind, the headbox; a U-shaped clip at each side of the tube holds the tapes in place. Attach the new tapes at the sides of the tube.

Set the clean, dry slats carefully into place between the new tapes of the blind, making sure they all face the right way. Then thread a new lift cord into the

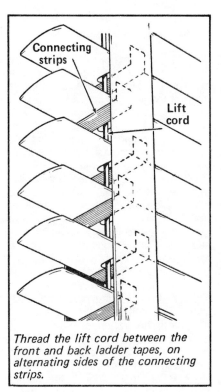

Thread the lift cord between the front and back ladder tapes, on alternating sides of the connecting strips.

lubrication to keep the pulleys operating smoothly. To lubricate the pulley mechanism, spray it lightly with a silicone spray lubricant.

Install Drapery Hardware

Technically, anything that holds up a drape is drapery hardware, but that definition covers a considerable range. Even the most complicated systems are easy to install. **Tools:** measuring rule, pencil, hammer, magnetic stud finder, drill, screwdriver. **Materials:** stationary or traverse rods; brads, ¾-inch or 1½-inch flathead screws, or molly or toggle bolts. **Time:** about 10 minutes for least complicated; about 1 hour for traverse rods.

The lightest drapery hardware is the small bracket that holds short, stationary rods for café curtains. To install this kind of bracket, hold the rod up across the window where you want it to be hung. Use the window frame as a guide to make sure the rod is straight; measure in on each side to make sure it's positioned evenly in the window frame. Hold a bracket up to each end of the rod and mark its position on each side of the frame. Nail the brackets up with brads and set the rod into place.

To install hardware for a stationary rod or a traverse rod over a window that has a casing, use the window casing as a guide. Mount the end brackets at the top outside corners of the window casing. Hold each bracket into place and mark the mounting holes on the window casing with a pencil. Drill a starter hole at each marked point and then mount the bracket on the predrilled holes with ¾-inch flathead screws, set firmly into the window casing.

Narrow windows need only end brackets, but any rod more than 48 inches long must be supported by a center bracket. Measure across the window to determine its center point. Position the center bracket at the center

blind—up the slats on one side, through the pulley system at the top of the blind, and down the slats on the other side. The ladder tapes are made with strips connecting the front tape and the back, first to one side of the tape's width and then to the other. Thread the new lift cord straight up the middle of the tapes, passing these connecting strips first on one side and then on the other. Leave a long loop of cord on the pulley side to form the new control cord.

When the entire lift cord has been threaded into place, knot the ends of the cord firmly under the bottom rail of the blind and cut off the excess. Fasten the new ladder tapes over the knotted ends of the new lift cord, replacing clamps on a metal blind or stapling the ends on a wood blind. Slip the equalizer clip into place on the lift cord and adjust it. To complete the job, replace the tilt cord with a new cord. Finally, rehang the blind.

Old blinds may occasionally need

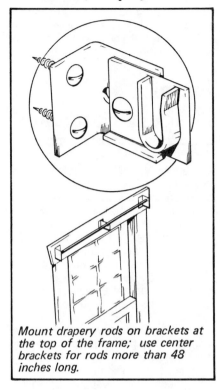

Mount drapery rods on brackets at the top of the frame; use center brackets for rods more than 48 inches long.

over studs in the wall. If a bracket is located over a stud, predrill the screw holes and mount the bracket with 1½-inch flathead screws, driven firmly through the wall and into the stud. If a bracket is not located over a stud, use molly or toggle bolts instead of flathead screws. Drill a hole through the wall where each bolt will be inserted; insert each bolt through the bracket and into the hole; then tighten the bolts to set the bracket firmly on the wall.

When the brackets are firmly mounted on the wall, set the rod into place. Slide stationary rods into their brackets; adjust them to the correct length by telescoping or extending the sections. Pull or push the rod at the ends and at each center support bracket to set it at the desired distance out from the window and the wall. Tighten the adjusting screw on each bracket to complete the installation; then hang the draperies.

Traverse rods must be adjusted for proper operation before they are mounted. Set the rod up on the mounting brackets to adjust it to the proper length; then set it face down on the floor, being careful not to change this length. Count the number of curtain hooks on your draperies and then count the number of plastic slides along the

point, at the top edge of the window casing; mark the screw mounting holes, predrill, and mount the bracket with ¾-inch screws. Position center support brackets at least every 48 inches across very long window spans, spaced evenly across the span.

To install hardware over a window that doesn't have a casing, measure and mark 4 inches up from the top of the window at each corner and out 6 to 18 inches at each side, depending on how much wall you want the drapes to cover. Position the top and outside edges of the brackets on these marked top and side points; position center brackets, if needed, with the top edge of each bracket on the 4-inch line above the window. Hold the brackets against the wall and mark the screw mounting holes.

Drapery rods mounted directly on a wall must be strongly supported. Use a magnetic stud finder to determine whether the brackets are placed directly

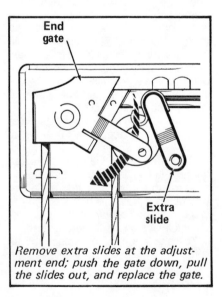

Remove extra slides at the adjustment end; push the gate down, pull the slides out, and replace the gate.

traverse rod. Remove extra slides from the rod at the side with the adjustment cords; push the end gate down and pull the slides out from the rod. Push the end gate back up to lock the rest of the slides in.

At the side of the rod with the adjustment cords, pull the outer cord as far as it will go and hold it there. This will bring the master slide on the side out to the end of the rod. Holding this cord firmly, push the second master slide out to the other end of the rod. The two master slides should now be positioned where the inside edges of the draperies will hang when they're pulled open.

The second master slide, the one you moved by hand, has two holes in it; through these two holes there is a short loop of cord, and just under the holes is a pointed lug sticking out from the slide. Hook the loop over the pointed lug. This locks the second master slide into operation with the first, so your drapes will open and close evenly.

With the master slides adjusted, set the traverse rod into place on the brackets. Adjust the brackets to the cor-

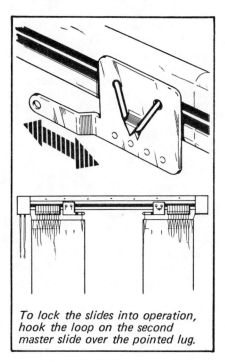

To lock the slides into operation, hook the loop on the second master slide over the pointed lug.

rect distance out from the wall and tighten the adjustment screw on each bracket. Finally, hang the draperies: hook each curtain hook through a plastic slide on the traverse rod, matching hook to slide along the rod.

Hang Interior Window Shutters

Interior window shutters, a favorite alternative to draperies, curtains, or venetian blinds, add practicality and style to any window. **Tools:** measuring rule, pencil; if required, power saw or handsaw; scrap pieces of 1 × 2, pencil, drill, screwdriver. **Materials:** shutters; shutter-hanging kit, including hinges, screws, knobs, and latches; if required, hanging strips; cardboard. **Time:** about 1 hour per window (4 shutter panels).

Ready-made shutters, ranging in height from 10 to 36 inches and in width from 6 to 18 inches, are stocked at most lumber and home building centers. Smaller or larger shutters can be ordered if necessary.

Decide how high you want the shutters to be. Carefully measure the width of the window's inside frame; if it's not at least half the width of a hinge, a hanging strip will be required. Hanging strips, sold where shutters are available, come with installation instructions. If you need hanging strips, subtract the width of the hanging strips from the overall width for the shutters. Allow $1/_{32}$ inch clearance between shutters, and 1/8 inch clearance between the bottom of the shutter and the windowsill. If one set of shutters is hung over another set, allow additional clearance at the top and bottom, and between the two sets.

Most windows require at least four shutters—two for each side. Very narrow windows—those less than 20 inches wide—need only two shutters. For example, if a window is 31 inches wide, you'll need four shutters. each 7¾ inches wide. Odd sizes are usually expensive; if the size you need is close to

179

the stock size, buy the next widest size—an 8-inch-wide shutter—and cut it down to size.

Lay the shutters on a flat surface just as they'll be hung, control rods facing up. Align the tops and bottoms of the shutters, and carefully measure them and the windows once more for proper clearance. If necessary, trim them to fit.

Place two pieces of scrap 1 × 2 parallel on a flat surface and lay the shutters, control rods down, on the 1 × 2 supports; align the shutters so that the tops and bottoms are even. Place the shutter hinges in position on the shutters, with the top hinge about 2 inches below the top block of the shutters and the bottom hinge just above the bottom shutter block. Make sure the hinge pins are straight and in line with the joint between the shutters. Make sure there's 1/32 inch clearance between the shutters to prevent binding; to maintain this clearance, insert a piece of cardboard above and below the points where hinges will be attached.

With the hinges in exact position, mark the locations for screw holes on the shutters. Drill pilot holes and drive the screws provided through the hinges into the shutters. Check the assembled shutters in the window opening to see if any further adjustments are necessary, and adjust the hinges as required.

Take the shutters down and lay them on a flat surface, control rods up. Attach

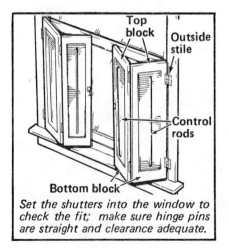

Set the shutters into the window to check the fit; make sure hinge pins are straight and clearance adequate.

the angle-type, loose-pin hinges to the outside shutter stiles, in line with the shutter hinges, with the angle part of the hanging hinges against the inside surface and edge of the stile. If desired, mortise the hanging hinge into the stile of the shutter; this gives you less space between the shutter and window frame, and makes a neater installation. Mark the locations for screw holes. Drill pilot holes and drive the screws through the hinges into the shutter stiles.

Carefully position the shutters on the window again, and mark the locations for screw holes on the window frame. Drill pilot holes in the frame and drive one screw through each hanging hinge into the window frame; then insert and tighten all remaining screws. Finally, attach shutter knobs and latches with the hardware provided.

Stain or paint the shutters as desired; remove the loose pins from the hanging hinges and lift the shutters down.

Mend a Screen

A screen with a hole in it is guaranteed to attract bugs, but the repair is an easy one. **Tools:** ice pick or toothpick, scissors or tin snips, needle, block of scrap wood. **Materials:** *for fiberglass screens*—nylon thread, patch of fiberglass screening; *for metal screens*—fine wire, patch of metal screening; *for either*—clear nail polish or household cement. **Time:** a few minutes to 1/2 hour.

Close tiny holes in fiberglass screens with a dab of clear nail polish or household cement. Use only a little cement, and blot any excess immediately. Sew clean cuts together carefully with nylon thread, using a zigzag stitch over the cut edges. Do not pull the thread too tight or the mend will pucker. Seal the join with clear nail polish.

For ragged cuts or large holes, cut away any damaged screening that remains in the hole. Cut a patch of fiberglass screening to size; it should

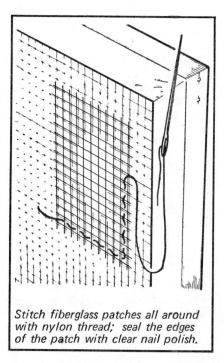

Stitch fiberglass patches all around with nylon thread; seal the edges of the patch with clear nail polish.

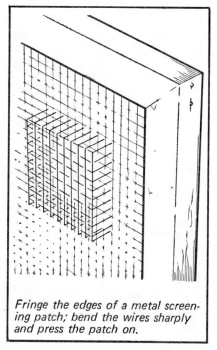

Fringe the edges of a metal screening patch; bend the wires sharply and press the patch on.

overlap the hole about ½ inch on all sides. Sew the patch carefully into place, using a firm but not tight running stitch. Seal the edges of the patch with clear nail polish.

To close a pinhole in a metal screen, use an ice pick or toothpick to push the bent wires back into place. If a small opening remains, close it with a dab of household cement or clear nail polish. Apply nail polish sparingly and let dry; repeat until the opening is filled. Sew long tears together with a needle threaded with fine wire. Seal the mend with clear nail polish.

To repair large holes, cut away any damaged wires that remain in the hole. Cut a square or rectangular piece of screening about 2 inches larger all around than the hole. Pull away the outside wires on all four edges to a depth of about ½ inch to make a fringe of wires on each side.

Bend the fringe wires on each side over a block of scrap wood, making a sharp, even right-angle bend all around the patch. Position the patch over the hole.

Press firmly and evenly on the patch to push the bent fringe wires through the mesh of the screen. The patch should lie flat and even against the screen. On the other side of the screen, bend the protruding fringe wires flat, folding them in toward the center of the patch. For a more secure patch, stitch around the edge of the patch with fine wire.

Replace Screening

Deal with rusty or badly torn screens at the source—take the frame apart and replace the screening. **Tools:** *for wood-framed screens*—stiff putty knife, pliers, chalk, sharp scissors or tin snips, C-clamps, scrap wood, bench or board and two sawhorses, staple gun, utility knife, hammer, nail set, small paintbrush; *for aluminum-framed screens*—screwdriver, sharp scissors or tin snips, scrap wood, putty knife, splining tool. **Materials:** replacement screening, heavy-duty staples or (aluminum frames) plastic splining, trim paint. **Time:** ½ to 1 hour per screen, plus ½ hour for repainting, if necessary.

Buy fine-mesh, rustproof screening—plastic or aluminum for wood frames, aluminum for aluminum frames. If you're replacing an aluminum screen, measure around the screen; buy a length of plastic screen splining, a few inches longer than measured, to replace the old metal spline.

Wood frames. To replace a wood-framed screen, set the screen on a flat work surface. Using a stiff putty knife, carefully pry off the molding that covers the screen edge, working out from the middle of the screen. Leave the brads in the molding as you remove it so that they can be used to reattach the molding when the new screen is in.

Remove the old screening from the frame, using pliers if necessary to loosen the staples or tacks that hold it in place. Pull out any remaining staples or tacks.

Lay the new screening over the empty frame and trace the frame's outline on the screening with chalk. Cut the screening to size with sharp scissors or tin snips, leaving 1½ inches excess all around the frame.

Lay the trimmed screening into position over the empty frame. Staple it along the top edge of the frame with a staple gun, setting staples at right angles to the edge of the frame every 2½ to 3 inches. If the replacement screening is plastic, turn the edge under 1 inch before stapling it into place.

Before you staple the other three sides of the screen, bow the frame; the technique is the same for plastic or aluminum screening. With the frame set the long way along a bench or on a board across two sawhorses, place a C-clamp on each long side at the center of the frame. Clamp the frame to the top of the bench or the board across the sawhorses, and tighten the clamps. Wedge a long block of scrap wood— 2 × 4 is ideal—between the screen and the bench top at each end of the frame, bowing it upward.

Pull the loose end of the new screening over the bowed frame, between the C-clamps. Stretch the screening evenly into place along the bottom edge of the frame and staple it firmly, setting staples every 2½ to 3 inches. Turn plastic screening under 1 inch before stapling.

When both the top and the bottom of the new screen are secure, loosen the C-clamps and remove the wood blocks. Stretch the screening into place along the two unfastened sides of the frame and staple them securely. Keep the screening stretched evenly across the frame. Trim excess screening, if necessary, with a sharp utility knife or tin snips.

Finally, replace the molding around the frame. Set it carefully into place over the new screening and drive the brads in to fasten it securely. Sink the brads with a nail set and cover them with wood putty. Repaint the entire frame.

Aluminum frames. To replace the screen in an aluminum frame, set it on a flat work surface. Using a screwdriver or a putty knife, pry up the metal spline that fastens the edges and peel it out of the groove. Remove the old screening.

Lay the new aluminum screening over the empty frame and trim it with sharp scissors or tin snips to just reach the outside edge of the frame. Set thin blocks of scrap wood under the screening to hold it level with the surface of the frame.

To install the screening, line up the edge of the screening with the outside edge of the splining groove in the frame, along one end and one side of the frame. Use a stiff putty knife or splining tool to bend the edges of the screening down into the groove; hold the screening in place as you work and make a sharp bend along the pushed-in edge with a block of scrap wood. Repeat the wedging procedure to secure the screening along the other two sides of the frame, pulling the screening firmly into place as you work.

When the screening is secured all the way around the frame, trim any excess with tin snips. Use a length of plastic splining to hold the screening in place. Starting at a corner, drive the splining

With a splining wheel, drive plastic splining to hold the new screening into the groove around the frame.

into the groove over the edges of the screening, using a splining wheel. Cut off excess splining as you round the frame to meet the starting corner.

Weatherstrip Windows

Drafty double-hung windows can dispose of heat almost as fast as your furnace can put it out. Solve the problem with weatherstripping. **Tools:** extension ladder, dusting brush, utility knife or scissors, measuring rule, hammer. **Materials:** adhesive-backed foam weatherstripping, or sponge or tubular vinyl weatherstripping and rustproof brads. **Time:** about 5 minutes per window with foam weatherstripping, about 20 minutes with vinyl.

Buy weatherstripping in bulk rolls, not window- or door-size kits. Adhesive-backed foam is the easiest type to install, but sponge or tubular vinyl lasts longer. If you use the vinyl type, be sure

to buy rustproof brads.

With the windows closed, apply weatherstripping on the exterior of each window, at every point where two separate surfaces meet. Set strips on each window as follows: bottom edge of bottom sash, bottom of top sash where it overlaps bottom sash, top edge of top sash, all side edges along parting stops. Place each strip of weatherstripping directly against the gap it should cover; butt the strips firmly at corners.

Use an extension ladder to reach high windows. Set the ladder firmly against the house, with the top sticking up above the edge of the roof; wear rubber-soled shoes, and move the ladder to work on each window. Dust each window frame with a brush to remove loose dirt before applying the weatherstripping.

To apply adhesive-backed foam weatherstripping, simply peel off the backing paper and stick the foam down. Start applying at a corner; unroll the

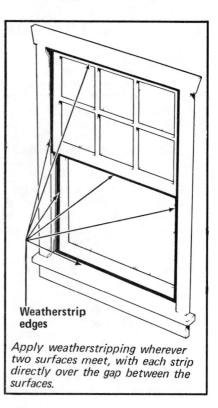

Weatherstrip edges

Apply weatherstripping wherever two surfaces meet, with each strip directly over the gap between the surfaces.

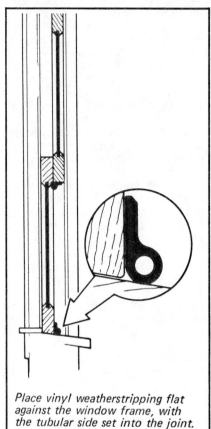

Place vinyl weatherstripping flat against the window frame, with the tubular side set into the joint.

weatherstripping and press it into place across the window as you go. Cut each strip to fit with a utility knife or scissors when you reach the end of the edge to be sealed.

Vinyl weatherstripping is roughly comma-shaped, with a hollow or sponge-filled tube and a flat edge. To apply this kind of weatherstripping, measure across the edge to be sealed and cut the vinyl to fit with a scissors or utility knife. Set the strip along the edge to be sealed, with the tubular side toward the gap and facing out and the flat side flat against the window frame; nail the strip into place with rustproof brads set through the prepunched holes. Cut all the strips needed for each high window before climbing the ladder.

Neither foam nor vinyl weatherstripping should be painted. If you paint the

window sash, remove the weatherstripping and then reapply it, or work around it. Leave the weatherstripping in place all year.

Build a Windowsill Shelf

A windowsill shelf is a handy place for plants or canisters, jars or any display items. **Tools:** pry bar, hammer, measuring rule, pencil, handsaw or power saw; if required, saber saw; plane, carpenters' square, nail set, paintbrush. **Materials:** 1 × 6, 1 × 8, 1 × 10, or 1 × 12 pine stock; carpenters' glue, 6-penny and 10-penny finishing nails, 1 × 4 pine stock, matching paint or stain. **Time:** about 2 hours.

The way you build your windowsill shelf depends on the window's construction. First, determine how to fit the shelf into the window's trimwork. Some, and possibly most, of the trimwork may have to be removed so you can cut it.

With a pry bar, pry off the apron below the windowsill. Remove the windowsill; you'll probably have to remove the side jamb trim and the side casing. Remove all trimwork carefully; make sure you don't damage it.

Measure and mark the sill so you can cut its inside edge—the edge facing the room—flush with the surface of the wall; cut the sill as marked and plane the cut edge smooth and square. Replace the sill.

To make the shelf, use 1 × 6, 1 × 8, 1 × 10, or 1 × 12 pine stock. The shelf can be as wide as 12 inches, and as long as the window is wide or longer, extending beyond the sides of the window. If the shelf extends beyond the sides, make it long enough to span a wall stud on either side; the shelf braces will be secured to these studs.

Leave the ends of the shelf square, or round or angle them as desired. Measure, mark, and cut the shelf to the length and configuration desired, using

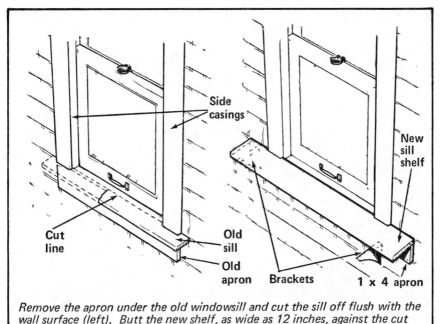

Side casings

New sill shelf

Cut line

Old sill

Old apron

Brackets

1 x 4 apron

Remove the apron under the old windowsill and cut the sill off flush with the wall surface (left). Butt the new shelf, as wide as 12 inches, against the cut edge (right); brace it with wood brackets and a 1 x 4 apron.

a saber saw to curve the edges as necessary. Set the edge of the shelf against the sill and the wall to check it for a tight fit. Plane and smooth the edge as necessary.

Measure the side pieces of the window frame to butt tightly against the top of the shelf, and trim them as necessary. Replace the side pieces and the side jambs in the window frame. Apply carpenters' glue to the bottom ends of the side pieces and to the edge of the shelf where it joins the sill and the window framework. Place the shelf into position and drive 6-penny finishing nails up through the shelf and into the ends of the side pieces to secure it. Countersink the nails with a nail set.

Next, install the shelf brackets. Attach the brackets solidly to the wall studs on both sides of the window and to the shelf, using 10-penny finishing nails. Countersink the nails.

Cut a piece of 1 × 4 pine stock for a new apron below the shelf. Fit the piece of 1 × 4 beneath the shelf to serve as additional support and to hide the exposed rough opening of the window.

Nail the 1 × 4 in place with 10-penny finishing nails. Countersink the nails.

Finally, finish the shelf and the new trimwork to match the window trim.

Build Plant Shelves in a Window

For a cheerful corner in any room, fill a window with your favorite plants. Build these sturdy shelves to fit. **Tools:** measuring rule, pencil, handsaw or power saw, carpenters' square, drill, screwdriver, hammer, paintbrush. **Materials:** 1 × 8, 1 × 6, and 1 × 2 pine stock; carpenters' glue, #8 flathead wood screws, 3-penny finishing nails, sandpaper, stain or paint, shelf brackets with screws, angle irons with screws. **Time:** about 2 to 4 hours, plus finishing time.

These shelves are designed to fit a

window 36 inches wide and 48 inches long. To fit other window sizes, alter measurements and materials to fit each window. Take measurements from the outside edge of the window frame, to keep the shelves a few inches from the windowpanes—direct contact with the glass can damage plants in very cold weather.

Cut two 49½-inch pieces of 1 × 8 pine stock for the sides of the shelf frame assembly; cut two 36-inch pieces of 1 × 8 for the top and bottom. Cut three 36-inch pieces of 1 × 6 pine for the shelves. To make shelf supports, cut six 5½-inch pieces of 1 × 2 pine. Use a carpenters' square to keep your cuts even.

Lay out the boards for the top, sides, and bottom of the frame on a flat working surface, on edge, with the top and bottom boards butted between the side boards. Apply a bead of carpenters' glue to the board edge at each joint, and join the frame pieces. For each joint, drill three pilot holes for three #8 flathead wood screws. Secure each corner of the frame assembly with three screws.

On the inside face of one side piece, mark the positions for three shelf supports. Measuring from the bottom of the frame, make marks 8 inches, 16 inches, and 32 inches from the bottom. Or, if desired, add shelves or vary measurements to suit your needs.

Place the shelf supports over the marks, with their ends flush with the edges of the sides. Drive three 3-penny finishing nails to secure each support. Measure and mark the locations for the shelf supports on the opposite side, and repeat the procedure for fastening them in position.

When the frame is assembled, stain or paint the frame and the shelves as desired. Let the stain or paint dry completely, as directed by the manufacturer.

To install the shelves, locate the wall studs at the sides and center of the window. Position a shelf bracket against each stud, ¾ inch below the window frame. Mark the locations for bracket screws on the wall. Drill pilot

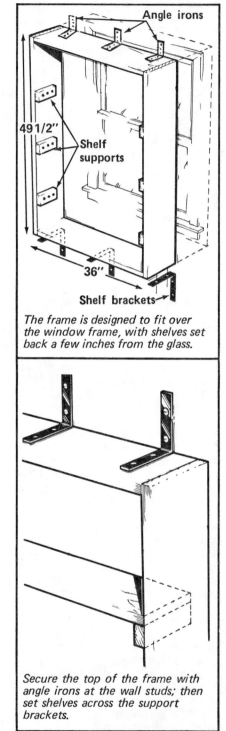

The frame is designed to fit over the window frame, with shelves set back a few inches from the glass.

Secure the top of the frame with angle irons at the wall studs; then set shelves across the support brackets.

holes for the screws, and fasten the brackets to the wall studs with the screws provided.

Set the shelf frame on the wall brackets, and mark the locations for bracket screws under the frame. Drill pilot holes into the frame, and fasten the frame to the brackets.

Position three angle irons—one at each corner and one between them—on top of the frame. Mark the locations for screw holes in the top of the frame and into the wall studs. Drill pilot holes for the screws, and fasten the angle irons to the frame and wall.

To complete the window-frame shelves, set a shelf on each pair of shelf supports.

Tighten Loose Leaded Glass

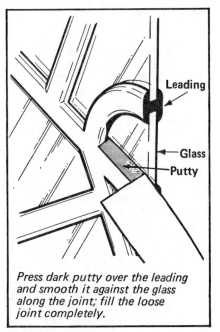

Press dark putty over the leading and smooth it against the glass along the joint; fill the loose joint completely.

Many old houses and apartments have one leaded glass window—usually in a first-floor stairwell or in a transom or side window near the front door. Over a period of years, the lead can stretch, causing the glass to loosen in the leading and the glass to rattle or leak. Repairing the damage is extremely simple. **Tools:** putty knife, toothbrush, soft cloth. **Materials:** linseed oil, linseed oil putty in a dark tone, glass cleaner. **Time:** about 15 minutes per pane.

Examine the leading around the glass—especially along the bottom of the panes and where the lead is exposed to the sunlight. Leading that appears to be pulled away from the glass has stretched. During inspection, press your fingers very gently against the individual panes of glass. All stretched leading and loose panes should be tightened.

For each pane, clean the joint between lead and glass with a toothbrush, removing all dirt, dust, and other debris. With a soft cloth, wipe linseed oil into the leading/glass joint. Although the materials will not absorb the linseed oil, the oil will make the repair easier.

Knead dark linseed oil putty, first forming a small ball and then making a thick string. Place the string of putty along the leading and press the putty into the leading/glass joint with your fingers; if necessary, use a stiff-bladed putty knife. Keep the putty knife at a 45-degree angle to the leading and wipe the putty into the joint until the joint is full.

Let the putty harden for 2 weeks or more. The surface of the putty will become glazed and hard to the touch. Then clean the oil off the glass with glass cleaner.

If the glass in the window is extremely loose, the window should be releaded or repaired by a professional.

Paint Windows and Doors

Painting flat surfaces is almost foolproof, but paneled doors and double-

WINDOWS / Painting

hung windows are trickier. Use this sequence to get professional results. **Tools:** dusting brush, small and medium-size paintbrushes, sash brush, stepladder, two large wedges, extension ladder. **Materials:** clean rags, newspaper, latex or oil-base interior or exterior trim paint, mineral spirits for oil-base paint, masking tape, coffee can. **Time:** about ½ to 1 hour per door or window.

Work when the weather is dry and warm. Plan to stay home while the paint dries so you don't have to close newly painted windows or doors.

Double-hung windows. Before painting a double-hung window, make sure both the top and the bottom sash move freely. Brush the window frame to remove loose dirt; if it's very dirty, wipe it clean with a damp rag and let it dry completely. Use a small brush or a special sash brush. If you're working inside, spread newspaper to protect the floor; use a stepladder as necessary. Outside, use an extension ladder to reach high windows. Set the ladder firmly against the house, with the top of the ladder sticking up above the edge of the roof; wear rubber-soled shoes. Pour a little paint into a coffee can instead of carrying the whole can of paint up the ladder. Move the ladder to work on each window.

Leave window hardware on so you can open and close the windows as you work. For easier cleanup, apply masking tape to the edges of each pane of glass. Clean up drips as you go.

Raise the lower sash and pull the upper sash down so you can reach the bottom of its frame. Paint the bottom rail of the upper sash, including the bottom edge, and as far as you can up the side rails and any windowpane channels. Then paint the bottom edge of the lower sash. Finally, paint the top of the inside of the window frame.

Lower both sash almost to the bottom of the window opening. On each side of the frame, paint first the outside channel and then the inside channel. Try not to get paint on the sash cord or chain.

Raise both sash almost to the top of the window opening. On each side of the frame, paint first the outside channel and then the inside channel. Then paint the bottom of the inside of the window frame.

Lower the lower sash almost to the bottom of the window frame. Paint any windowpane channels—horizontals first, then verticals. Then paint the sides and then the top rail of the upper sash.

Paint double-hung windows in the sequence shown, moving the top and bottom sash for access to all surfaces. Paint horizontal surfaces first, then verticals; sash channels first, then frames.

Finally, paint the lower sash—first any windowpane channels, then the sides, then the top rail, and finally the bottom rail. Leave both sash open about 1 inch so that the paint on the top and bottom edges can dry.

Let the paint dry completely, according to the manufacturer's instructions. Move both sash up and down occasionally during the drying period to prevent the paint from sealing them permanently in one position.

Paneled doors. To paint both sides of a paneled door, start on the side that opens away from the jamb and toward the wall—the inside of a heavy front door, the outside of a screen door. Close the door. Brush any loose dirt off the door; if it's dirty, wipe it clean with a damp rag and let it dry completely. Spread newspaper to protect the floor.

Starting at the top of the door, paint all inset panels, including any molding around them. Use a stepladder if necessary to reach the top. Brush paint on evenly along each surface; use just enough paint to flow smoothly. Then, again starting at the top of the door, paint the horizontal rails. Work carefully around the doorknob and lock to make a clean edge around the hardware; wipe up any drips immediately with a clean rag. Finish the first side of the door by painting the vertical stiles, from left to right across the door.

If you're painting both sides of the door, open the door carefully and wedge it firmly from each side to hold it wide open. Be careful not to mar the new paint on the other side. Paint the second side of the door in the same sequence. Finally, paint the top edge, the

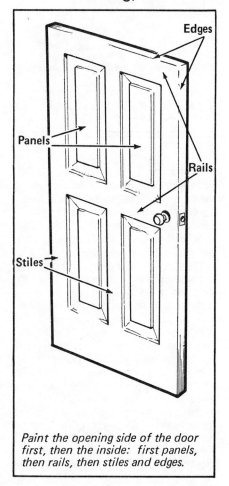

Paint the opening side of the door first, then the inside: first panels, then rails, then stiles and edges.

hinge edge, and then the doorknob or latch edge. Pick up the newspaper. Leave the door wedged open and let it dry completely, according to the paint manufacturer's instructions.

Doors

Unstick a Door

Doors stick for a variety of reasons—anything from loose screws to the settling of the house. In most cases it's easy to unstick them. **Tools:** screwdriver, large wedges, stepladder, scissors, block or jack plane, hammer, carpenters' square. **Materials:** flathead wood screws, wood toothpicks or hollow fiber plugs, carpenters' glue, ¼-inch-thick cardboard, shellac. **Time:** 10 minutes to 2 hours, depending on damage. An assistant may be needed.

First examine the hinges and tighten any loose screws. If a screw turns without tightening, either replace it with a longer screw, if possible, or fill in the screw hole to provide a snug fit. If you use a longer screw, make sure the head of the new screw is the same size as that of the original screw. To pad the hole, apply carpenters' glue to the outside of a hollow fiber plug and insert it into the hole; let it dry according to the manufacturer's instructions and then reinsert the screw. Or dip wood toothpicks into carpenters' glue and insert them into the hole in a funnel effect. Snap them off flush with the wood surface and let dry according to the manufacturer's instructions. Replace the screw; it should tighten securely.

If the screws that hold the hinge are tight, check the space between the door and the frame. If there's a gap between the door and the frame at the top on one side and at the bottom on the other, the door is tilted in the frame. To fix it, shim the hinge diagonally across from the binding edge of the latch side—the bottom hinge if the top swinging corner sticks, the top hinge if the bottom swinging corner sticks. Use a stepladder to reach the top hinge. If the door

has three hinges, shim the affected hinge and the middle hinge.

Open the door as wide as possible and set a wedge under it to keep it there. Remove the screws from the door frame that hold the hinge to be shimmed; leave the screws that attach the hinge to the door in place. Cut a ¼-inch-thick piece of cardboard to the same height and width as the hinge; cut slots in this shim to fit around the hinge screws. Set the slotted cardboard into the hinge mortise in the door frame, slotted side toward the door, and reposition the hinge over the cardboard. Screw the hinge firmly back into place, keeping the cardboard shim aligned behind it. Close the door to see if the gap is gone and the door unstuck. If not, cut a second shim and insert it under the hinge over the first shim.

If the door is hung evenly but has to be slammed shut, the wood has probably swollen. Examine the door to determine where it's binding. If the door is

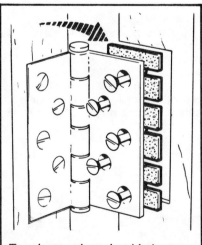

To release a door that binds at top or bottom, make a cardboard shim to raise the binding hinge.

too wide, plane the hinge side of the door; do *not* plane the doorknob side. If the door is too tall, plane the end that binds, either the top or the bottom. Plane carefully, removing a thin, even strip of wood all along the binding edge; be careful not to cut too much.

To plane the top of a door, open the door wide and wedge it open. Working from a stepladder, plane the top of the door carefully from the edges toward the center with a block plane; don't plane from the center toward the edges or the wood will split. After planing a small amount, try to close the door; if it still sticks, plane a little more and try again. When the edge is sufficiently planed, coat the raw edge of the door with shellac, thinned according to the manufacturer's instructions. Let dry at least 1 hour before closing the door.

To plane the bottom or the side of a door, take the door off its hinges. Remove the pin from the bottom hinge first, tapping it out with a screwdriver or a hammer; then remove the middle and top pins and lift the door out of the frame. Set the door on the floor with the hinged side up.

To plane the bottom edge, use a block plane to shave wood from the edge toward the center; then flip the

Plane the side of a door from center to edge; plane the top or bottom from edge to center.

door onto its hinged side and plane from the other edge toward the center. Coat the raw edge of the door with shellac and let it dry at least 1 hour; then rehang the door.

To plane the side of the door, remove the hinges. With a jack plane, shave wood from the center of the hinged side to the ends; plane only a little, and be sure to cut evenly. Fit the door into the door frame to test the fit; if necessary, plane again. Shellac the raw side of the door and let it dry at least 1 hour; then replace the hinges and rehang the door.

If neither hinge placement nor swollen wood is the problem, the door frame itself may be out of alignment; use a carpenters' square to check it. You may be able to unstick the door by adding shims or planing; if not, turn the job over to a professional carpenter.

Hang an Interior Door

Hanging a door is an exacting job, but not a tremendously difficult one—take your time and do it right. **Tools:** measuring rule, pencil, try square or carpenters' square, straightedge, power saw or handsaw, block or jack plane, wood wedges, hammer, sharp chisel, scissors, drill, small paintbrush, screwdriver. **Materials:** door with pre-drilled latch and lock holes, medium- and fine-grit sandpaper, two sturdy loose-pin door hinges, shellac, 1¾-inch flathead screws, thin cardboard, doorknob and latch assembly kit with installation screws. **Time:** about 4 to 5 hours.

Before buying a door, measure the inside of the door opening exactly, top to bottom and jamb to jamb—be sure to measure from the side jambs of the door frame, not from the stops. Allow ⅛ inch clearance at the top of the door and ¼ inch at the bottom; if the door will have to open or close over carpeting, allow ⅞ inch at the bottom. Subtract this

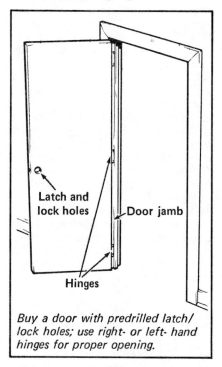

Latch and lock holes

Door jamb

Hinges

Buy a door with predrilled latch/ lock holes; use right- or left- hand hinges for proper opening.

clearance from the measured top-to-bottom height of the door opening. Allow ⅛ inch clearance at each side; subtract ¼ inch from the measured side-to-side width of the opening.

Decide exactly how you want the door to open—hinged at left or right, opening in or out. You'll need right-hand hinges to hang a door so it opens out from the right or in from the left; use left-hand hinges to hang a door so it opens out from the left or in from the right.

Various types of doors are available at lumberyards. Buy a door as close as possible to the size of the door opening; in most cases, this will be a standard size. Buy a door with predrilled latch and lock holes; if the latch edge must be beveled, make sure this is already done. Choose a doorknob and latch assembly kit and buy right-hand or left-hand hinges, as necessary.

Measure the new door exactly. If there are vertical side pieces or stiles jutting out at the top and bottom of the door, mark them to be trimmed flush

with the door edge; use a try square or carpenters' square and a straightedge. If the height or width of the door must be adjusted, measure and mark it carefully to the required size, allowing clearances as above. Cut excess length carefully with a power saw or a handsaw, being careful not to cut too close; plane the edges of the door gradually to the exact size required. If the latch edge of the door is beveled, plane the hinge side so you don't lose the bevel.

Make sure all the edges of the door are smooth and even. Sand cut or planed edges with medium- and then fine-grit sandpaper to eliminate rough spots; be careful not to damage the surface of the door.

At this point you'll need an assistant. Set the door into the door frame to make sure it fits properly; if it binds, plane and sand as necessary. Wedge the door on all four sides to hold it suspended in the opening with the proper clearance all around; drive wedges in with a hammer. Make sure the door is exactly positioned and clearances are exact all around—⅛ inch at top and sides, ¼ inch or ⅞ inch at the bottom.

With the door wedged firmly and exactly in position, measure and mark the position of the hinges. Set the top hinge in position 6 inches down from the top of the door, with the barrel of the hinge at the inside edge of the door; mark the top and bottom of the hinge with a pencil on the door and on the door frame. Repeat this procedure to measure and mark for the bottom hinge, 10 inches up from the bottom of the door. Take the door down.

Using a try square or a carpenters' square, extend the marks on the door frame to the side jambs where the hinges will be set. Remove the pins that hold the leaves of the hinges together. With your assistant holding the door firmly on edge, hinge side up, set the door half of each hinge carefully in place at the marked point on the door; outline the leaf with pencil on the edge of the door. Set the door frame half of each hinge at the marked point on the door frame, with the barrel of the hinge at the inside of the frame, and outline the leaf with pencil on the doorjamb.

Use a hammer and a sharp chisel to cut out the outlined areas so that the hinge leaves are set flush with the surrounding surface. To mortise each hinge opening, carefully score the wood just inside the pencil outline. With the chisel held parallel to the edge of the door or the jamb, make a series of small, closely spaced, slanted cuts down the length of the hinge opening, to the depth of the hinge leaf's thickness. Cut out the scored wood at the depth of the hinge leaf by turning the chisel at right angles to the door edge or jamb and tapping it under the scored wood.

Make sure each hinge leaf is exactly flush with the door or jamb surface; if you cut the mortise too deep, cut a shim from thin cardboard to bring the hinge leaf to the correct position. Make sure the mortises on the door edge line up exactly with the mortises on the jamb. If you aren't sure of your markings, set the door back into the frame and remeasure for alignment.

When all mortises have been cut, coat the raw edges of the door lightly with shellac, applied with a small brush. This is to keep the door from absorbing moisture and sticking. Let the shellac dry thoroughly, about 1 hour.

Set the hinges in place and mark the screw holes on the edge of the door and the doorjamb; be sure the hinges are in exactly the right position. Predrill the screw holes, being careful to drill straight; use 1¾-inch flathead screws, and predrill holes to a smaller diameter and length. With the hinges disassembled, screw them tightly into place, door leaves to the edge of the door and jamb leaves to the jamb.

Finally, set the door into the door opening and engage the two halves of each hinge, forming a solid, interlocked hinge barrel. Insert the hinge pins, first the top and then the bottom.

To complete the job, install the doorknob and latch assembly, following the manufacturer's instructions exactly. Carefully mark the location of the strike plate on the latch side of the doorjamb; outline the plate on the jamb and mortise it in as above. Predrill screw holes and screw the doorknob assembly and the strike plate securely into place.

Install a Folding Door

If you need a door where there just isn't room for it to open, put in a folding door—an accordion, which takes no more space than the depth of the door frame, or a bi-fold, which uses only half the space of a regular door. **Tools:** measuring rule, hacksaw, pencil, drill, screwdriver, hammer, sharp chisel, brace and expansion bit or hole saw attachment for drill, plumb bob, handsaw; adjustment wrench, as provided by door manufacturer. **Materials:** accordion or bi-fold door kit, with installation hardware; for bi-fold doors over carpeting, scrap wood block. **Time:** about 1 to 3 hours.

Accordion doors. Before buying a door, measure the inside of the door opening, top to bottom and side to side. Subtract ½ inch from the top-to-bottom measure to allow clearance for the door to operate. Buy a door to fit the measured size; you must allow at least ½ inch vertical clearance, but a little extra width is no problem.

Leave the door taped or tied in the folded position. Measure across the inside top of the door opening and then measure the metal track of the door. If necessary, cut the track to fit the opening with a hacksaw. Check the track's fit and adjust as necessary.

With the door folded together, slide the rollers at the top of the door into the metal track, as directed by the manufacturer. Holding the track with one hand, set the door in the opening so that its front folds align with the front edges of the doorjambs; if there is an old strike plate in the door frame, make sure the latch of the new door is on the same side. Mark the position of the track on the top of the doorframe and take the door down.

DOORS/Folding Doors

Remove the door from the track. Set the track into position across the top of the door opening, as marked; be sure the track is evenly placed. Mark the screw holes along the track and set it aside. Drill the marked screw holes across the top of the door opening as directed by the manufacturer.

With the door still folded together, slide the rollers into the metal track. Set the track in position in the door opening, aligned over the screw holes. Slide the door to one end of the track and attach the other end with the screws provided; then slide the door to the secured end and screw in the rest of the track.

Take off the tape or band around the door. On the hinge side of the door, the accordion door will have a long wood or metal strip; this strip must be attached to the doorjamb on that side. If nails are provided for installation, nail the strip firmly into place along the jamb, using the nail holes punched in the strip; be sure the edge of the door hangs straight in the door opening. If screws are provided for installation, mark the screw holes, predrill, and screw the strip into place. Follow any specific instructions

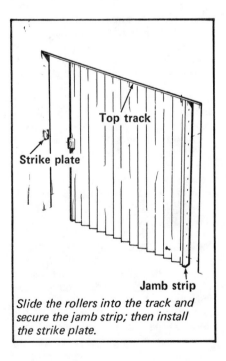

Top track

Strike plate

Jamb strip

Slide the rollers into the track and secure the jamb strip; then install the strike plate.

exactly for further connection.

Finally, install the strike plate for the new door. If there is an old strike plate in the door frame, remove it. Extend the accordion door so that the latch touches the doorjamb; mark the exact position of the latch on the jamb. Open the door. Set the new strike plate in position; if it replaces an old strike plate, mark the screw holes, drill, and screw the plate into place.

To install a strike plate where there is no old plate, set the plate in position and outline it on the doorjamb. Use a hammer and a sharp chisel to cut out the outlined area so that the plate is set flush with the jamb. With the chisel held parallel to the doorjamb, make a series of small, closely spaced cuts down the length of the outlined area, to the depth of the strike plate's thickness. Cut out the scored wood by turning the chisel at right angles to the cuts and tapping it under the cuts. At the point where the latch of the door will enter the strike plate, drill a hole as large and as deep as necessary to accommodate the latch; use a brace and an expansion bit or a drill with a hole saw attachment. Then mark and drill the screw holes and screw the strike plate into place.

Test the door for proper operation. If it binds or doesn't hang evenly, adjust it according to the manufacturer's instructions; use the special adjustment wrench provided with the door.

Bi-fold doors. Bi-fold doors are available with as few as two panels or as many as eight; two panels fit a standard door opening. Before buying a bi-fold door, measure the inside of the door opening. Subtract 1¼ inches for vertical clearance and ½ inch (or, for a four-panel door, ¾ inch) for horizontal clearance. Buy a door cut to fit this size opening; make sure the panels are already hinged together and the necessary pivots are included.

Install the door so that the face of the door aligns with the front edges of the doorjambs. Insert the top pivot bracket into the metal track that guides the door, as directed by the manufacturer. If you're installing a four-panel door, insert the second top pivot bracket into the other end of the track as directed.

Set the track in position across the inside top of the door opening, with the edge of the track flush with the edges of the doorjambs. Mark the screw holes along the track and set it aside; drill the screw holes as directed by the manufacturer and screw the track into place.

With the top pivot bracket at the corner of the opening where the door will fold together, drop a plumb bob from the center of the pivot bracket to the floor. Set the bottom pivot bracket on the floor at this point so that the holes in the two brackets line up exactly. Mark the screw holes for the bottom pivot bracket, drill, and screw the bracket into position on both the floor and the door frame. If you're installing a four-panel door, install the second bottom pivot bracket the same way, aligning it exactly under the top pivot bracket at the other side of the door frame.

If you're installing the door in a carpeted area, you must allow adequate clearance over the carpeting. Determine the position of the bottom pivot bracket or brackets as above, but don't attach them. Trace the outline of each bracket exactly on a block of scrap wood that is the same thickness as the carpeting. With a handsaw, cut the block of wood to the same size as the bracket. Set the block in place and screw the bottom pivot bracket into the block and the door frame.

To mount the door on the track, fold the panels together. The pivot panel has pivot pins at top and bottom to fit into the pivot brackets; the guide panel has a wheel that moves along the track. Set the bottom pivot pin into place in the bottom pivot bracket and tilt the folded-together door into the door frame. Slide the top pivot bracket over to the top of the tilted door and insert the top pivot pin into the bracket. Tilt the door slowly into position, sliding the top bracket back toward the pivot corner; insert the guide wheel in the track as soon as the angle of the door allows. Open the door to bring it firmly upright. If you're installing a four-panel door, repeat this procedure to install the second

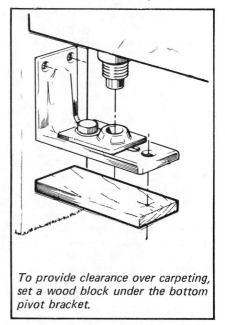

To provide clearance over carpeting, set a wood block under the bottom pivot bracket.

pair of panels on the other side of the door frame.

Test the door for proper operation. If it sticks or doesn't hang evenly, adjust it according to the manufacturer's instructions; use the special adjustment wrench provided with the door.

To complete the installation, attach the doorknobs provided on both sides of the hinge joint, as specified by the manufacturer. Mark and drill screw holes if necessary; then screw in the knobs with the screws provided. If you're installing a four-panel door, attach doorknobs to each set of panels; close the door and attach the aligner plates provided to hold the panels firmly together.

Fix a Broken Doorbell

A voiceless doorbell or chime is no use, but it's easily fixed. Once you locate the problem you're halfway there. **Tools:** screwdriver, 12-volt circuit tes-

DOORS/Broken Doorbells

ter, lamp socket, light bulb. **Materials:** masking tape, pencil, electrical tape; replacement doorbell button, bell or chime set, or transformer. **Time:** from 1 to 3 hours, depending on the problem.

Doorbells operate on very little current, about 10 to 18 volts; to fix most problems, it isn't necessary to turn the power off. You may feel a tingle if you touch a bare wire, but you won't get a serious shock.

The button that rings the bell or starts the chimes is often the source of the trouble. Unscrew the face plate over the button and remove it. Gently pull the button out as far as the wires allow and loosen the two terminal screws on the back of the button; disconnect the two wires and touch the ends of the wires together. If the doorbell rings, you've located the problem—you need a new button. Replace the old button with a new one, connecting the wires exactly as they were before. Replace the face plate over the button.

If the doorbell doesn't ring when you touch the bare terminal wires together, check the box that contains the bell or chimes inside the house. Remove the cover from the box, pulling it gently off the bell housing. At this point, to test the box, you'll need an assistant.

The box of a standard bell or buzzer has two wires connected to screw terminals. Loosen the terminal screws and disconnect the wires. Use a 12-volt circuit tester to check the wires; touch the two probes of the tester to the wires in the bell box and have your assistant push the doorbell button. If the bulb of the circuit tester lights, you need a new bell box.

Take the old bell box with you when you buy the bell box, and buy a box that requires the same voltage as the old one. It's safe to install the box without turning the power off. Following the manufacturer's specific instructions, connect the new box exactly the same way the old one was connected. Replace the cover over the box.

The box of a chime assembly is more complicated, but works on the same principle. It has three wires connected to three terminal screws—one for the front door chime, one for the back door bell or buzzer, and one for the transformer that supplies the power. Tag the wires with masking tape, marked 2, 1, and T for the front door, back door, and transformer terminals. Then loosen the terminal screws and disconnect all three wires.

To test the chime box, touch the 2 and T wires of the box to the probes of a 12-volt circuit tester, and have your assistant push the doorbell button. If the bulb of the circuit tester lights, the chime box must be replaced. Buy a new box that requires the same voltage as the old one and connect it exactly the way the old one was connected; follow the manufacturer's specific instructions.

If the bulb of the circuit tester doesn't light at the bell or chime box, check the transformer that supplies power to the system. The transformer is located on a junction box or panel near the main power source, usually at the main entrance panel or box.

Locate the transformer, and make sure that what you're working on is the transformer. The wires from the bell or chime box are connected to terminal screws on the outside of the transformer. *Caution: The wires inside the junction box that the transformer is mounted on are connected to the main power lines; do not touch them. Test only the terminal screws on the outside of the transformer.* Touch the outside terminal screws of the transformer with the two probes of the 12-volt circuit tester. If the bulb in the 12-volt circuit tester lights when you touch the outside terminal screws of the old transformer, the problem is not in the transformer, it's somewhere in the bell's wiring system. In this case, call an electrician. If the bulb doesn't light, the problem is in the transformer—either the transformer itself is defective or the power supply to the transformer is defective. The next step is to test the transformer.

Caution: The transformer is connected directly to the main power system. Before working on the transformer, trip the circuit breaker or remove the fuse that supplies power to the transformer. If there's no indication

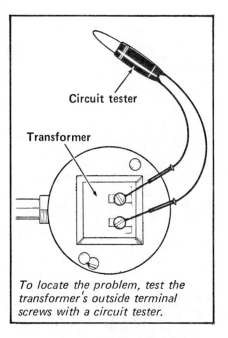

Circuit tester

Transformer

To locate the problem, test the transformer's outside terminal screws with a circuit tester.

stall the new transformer. Finally, connect the wires from the bell box to the outside terminal screws of the new transformer, and turn the power on.

Install Door Chimes

Putting in door chimes does call for some wire-stringing, but the wiring involved is minimal. **Tools:** measuring rule, screwdriver, pliers, magnetic stud finder, pencil, level, drill, staple gun, stepladder. **Materials:** door chime kit, including transformer, chimes, button, and insulated bell wire; additional wire as necessary, heavy-duty staples. **Time:** about 2 to 3 hours.

Before you buy door chimes, plan the way you'll run the wires from the door through the house to the main entrance panel or box. Measure the straight wall or floor distances and add about 20 percent; this is how much bell wire you'll need. Buy a door chime kit that comes complete with its own transformer, button, and bell wire; if the amount of wire in the kit isn't long enough for your wiring route, buy additional bell wire as long as your computed distance.

Start working with the transformer, the unit that supplies power to the door chimes from the main house power. The transformer is located on a junction box or panel near the main power source, usually at the main entrance panel or box. Locate the transformer of the old doorbell; it has two exposed terminal screws where the wires from the bell are connected to it.

Caution: The transformer is connected directly to the main power system. Before you touch it, trip the circuit breaker or remove the fuse that supplies power to the transformer. If there's no indication which circuit or fuse this is, turn off all the power for the entire building.

With the power off, remove the old transformer. Loosen the outside terminal screws and disconnect the wires to disconnect the old bell from the trans-

which circuit or fuse this is, turn off all the power for the entire building.

With the power off, disconnect the wires from the junction box or panel to the transformer. Use a lamp socket to test the circuit that supplies power to the transformer. Attach the wires from the junction box to the screw terminals under the lamp socket and screw a light bulb into the socket. If the screw terminals are exposed, cover them with a piece of electrical tape. Turn on the circuit breaker or replace the fuse that powers the transformer. If the bulb in the socket doesn't light, the circuit is not delivering power to the transformer. In this case, call an electrician.

If the bulb in the socket lights when you turn the power on, the transformer is defective, and must be replaced. *Caution: Before removing the transformer, trip the circuit breaker or remove the fuse that supplies power to the transformer, or turn off the power to the entire building.* Buy a replacement transformer of exactly the same electrical capacity; install it the way the old transformer was installed, following the manufacturer's instructions. *Caution: Be sure the power is off before you in-*

former. Disconnect the wires inside the junction box that connect it to the main house power; unscrew the wire connectors and pull the wires free. Loosen the nut that holds the old transformer to the junction box, using pliers if necessary, and remove the old transformer. Leave the power off; discard the old transformer.

Attach the new transformer to the junction box the way the old transformer was connected; tighten the mounting nut, twist the bare ends of the wires together, and then screw a wirenut over each joined pair of wires, following the manufacturer's specific instructions exactly. Turn the power on.

After installing the new transformer, mount the new chimes on the wall. Choose a location where the chimes will be audible throughout the house, and set them up high enough on the wall so that they're roughly at ear level. Mount the chime box over a wall stud; use a magnetic stud finder to locate the stud. Mark the box's position, and the necessary screw holes, using a level to make sure the chimes will hang plumb. Then drill the screw holes and attach the chime box to the wall with the screws provided, following the man-

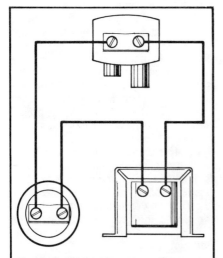

Route bell wire from transformer to chimes and chimes to push button; then connect the wires.

ufacturer's instructions.

After mounting the chimes, remove the push button for the old bell. Unscrew the face plate over the button and remove it; gently pull the bell out from the wall to expose the wires behind it. Loosen the two terminal screws on the back of the button and disconnect the wires. Lift the button out. Set the new button at hand, ready to be connected; discard the old button.

With transformer, chimes, and button in place, connect the wiring that powers the system. Doorbells operate on a very low-voltage current, so it isn't necessary to turn the power off except when you're working on the transformer. You may feel a tingle if you touch a bare wire, but you won't get a serious shock.

If the wiring of the old bell isn't defective, it could theoretically be used for the new system. Because chimes are usually mounted in a different location from that of the old bell, though, you'll probably have to remove the old wiring and install a new system. Disconnect the old bell box; remove the cover and disconnect the wires from the two terminal screws. Pull the old bell wire carefully out of the walls from the push-button opening and the bell box opening. If it doesn't come free easily, leave it in place; it won't hurt anything. Discard the old bell box.

Attach the transformer to the chimes and the chimes to the push button, following the manufacturer's wiring instructions. Start at the transformer, but don't connect the wires to the exposed terminals until all the bell wire is in place. Because of its low voltage, insulated bell wire can be laid directly along the wall at the ceiling or above the baseboard. Fasten the wire into place with a staple gun and heavy-duty staples, being careful to staple over and not through the wire. Use a stepladder to reach along-the-ceiling stretches.

Route wire from the transformer to the new chime box; connect it at the chime box according to the manufacturer's instructions. Then route wire from the chime box to the new push button and connect it as directed. Set the face plate over the button and screw it into place. Finally, connect the wires to the transformer, following the manufacturer's instructions exactly.

Install Doorknobs and Locksets

Two popular types of doorknobs, including the knobs and locking mechanism, are used in many homes—the tubular lockset and the cylindrical lock. Neither type is very difficult to install. **Tools:** grease pencil, electric drill with hole saw attachment or brace and expansion bit, round wood file, wood chisel, screwdriver, Phillips-head screwdriver. **Materials:** doorknob kit with hardware, sandpaper. **Time:** about 1 hour.

Wrap the template provided with the doorknob kit around the edge of the door, 3 feet up from the bottom of the door. With a grease pencil, mark the center of the latch bolt hole in the edge of the door. Depending on the length of the latch bolt, mark the center of the cylinder hole for the knobs on each side of the door.

Use an electric drill with a hole saw attachment or a brace and expansion bit to drill a hole of the size specified for the cylinder in the front of the door, as directed by the manufacturer. As soon as the saw or bit penetrates the wood, withdraw it and finish boring the hole from the other side of the door; this makes a smoother opening.

With a brace and the proper size bit, drill a hole into the edge of the door at the point marked for the latch bolt hole; this hole will intersect the bored cylinder hole. With a round wood file or sandpaper, smooth both openings.

Insert the latch bolt into its opening in the edge of the door and trace the plate outline onto the edge of the door. Make sure the beveled side of the bolt faces the strike plate as the door is closed. Remove the bolt and use a small wood chisel to carefully mortise the recess for the latch face plate; it should be flush with the edge of the door. With the chisel held parallel to the door, make a series of small, closely spaced cuts down the length of the outlined area, to the depth of the face plate's thickness. Cut out the scored wood by turning the chisel at right angles to the cuts and tapping it under the cuts. Reinsert the latch bolt and face plate, and secure it with the screws provided.

Push the latch bolt in and insert the

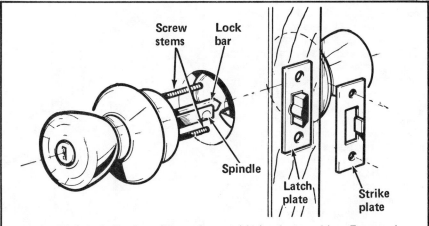

Screw stems Lock bar Spindle Latch plate Strike plate

With the latch bolt in place, insert the outside knob assembly. Engage the bolt's spindle or lip firmly with the doorknob assembly; insert the inside knob assembly, and secure both knobs to the door.

outside knob assembly. Tubular locks have a spindle that passes through the latch bolt; cylindrical units have lips that accept the end of the latch bolt mechanism. For either type, engage the latch bolt firmly with the doorknob assembly.

Insert the interior knob and align the screw stems and screw holes of both knob assemblies. Secure the doorknob assemblies with the screws provided, tightening them until the knob assemblies fit firmly against both sides of the door

Carefully close the door and mark the spot where the latch bolt touches the door jamb. Use a brace and the proper size bit to drill a ½-inch deep hole into the door jamb for the latch bolt. Center the strike plate over the hole in the jamb, and trace its outline onto the wood. With a small wood chisel, mortise the recess for the strike plate so that the plate lies flush with the door jamb. Insert the plate and secure it with the screws provided.

Trace the strike plate's outline onto the door jamb; mortise the jamb so the plate lies flush.

Install a Deadbolt Lock

A deadbolt lock provides both physical and mental security, and it isn't hard to install. **Tools:** scratch awl, brace and expansion bit or drill and hole saw attachment, wire cutters, pencil, hammer, sharp chisel, screwdriver. **Materials:** deadbolt cylinder lock, marking template, and installation screws; masking tape, short piece of dowel about the same diameter as the bolt of the lock, ½- or ⅝-inch brad. **Time:** about 1 to 2 hours.

Decide on a position for the lock, just above or just below the doorknob. To install the lock, use the paper marking template provided by the lock's manufacturer. Fold the template as marked and set it over the edge of the door, positioned so that the circles on the template are exactly where the lock will be installed. Tape the template into position with masking tape. Using a scratch awl, carefully punch through the

template bull's-eyes that mark the position of the lock on the face and on the edge of the door; press hard enough to mark the wood of the door under the template. Remove the template.

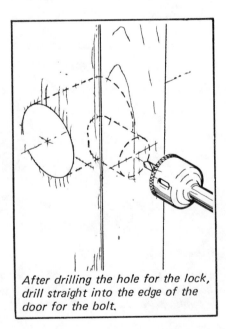

After drilling the hole for the lock, drill straight into the edge of the door for the bolt.

Using a brace with an expansion bit or a power drill with a hole saw attachment, drill straight into the face of the door at the marked center point to bore a hole to the size specified on the template. Drill only until the point of the drill penetrates the door completely; then remove the drill and complete drilling through the point of penetration from the other side of the door.

Drill another hole, to the diameter specified on the template, at the point marked on the edge of the door; drill straight into the door at right angles until you break through into the first hole. Remove the drill.

Before installing the lock, use the drilled lock and bolt holes to mark the point on the door frame where the bolt will enter the strike plate. Use a piece of doweling about the same diameter as the bolt, cut about 2½ or 3 inches long. Hammer a ½- or ⅝-inch brad about halfway in at the center point of one end of the dowel, and then cut off the head of the brad with wire cutters so that a sharp pin is left in the dowel end.

Slide the dowel into the drilled bolt hole in the door, pin side out, and close the door. Working through the drilled lock hole, press the dowel firmly through the bolt hole so that the pin is punched into the door frame outside the bolt hole; then remove the dowel and open the door. The pinhole in the door frame marks the bolt hole for the strike plate.

Insert the bolt assembly of the lock into the hole drilled in the edge of the door; push it in until the metal screw plate at the end of the bolt is flush with the edge of the door. Outline the metal plate against the door edge with a pencil and then remove the bolt and the plate.

The metal plate of the bolt must fit into the edge of the door so that it is flush with the surface of the wood. Use a sharp chisel and a hammer to mortise the marked plate area. Carefully score the wood just inside the pencil outline. With the chisel held parallel to the edge of the door, make a series of small, closely spaced, slanted cuts down the length of the plate area, to the depth of

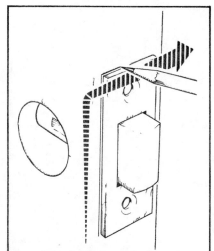

Insert the bolt assembly into the bolt hole and trace its outline onto the edge of the door.

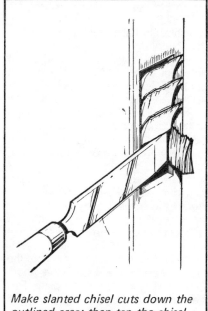

Make slanted chisel cuts down the outlined area; then tap the chisel under the scored wood.

the plate's thickness. Cut out the scored wood by turning the chisel at right angles to the edge of the door and tapping it under the scored wood. Fit the bolt and plate into the mortised area and correct the mortise as necessary so that

Insert the bolt assembly and the outside cylinder, engage the bolt, and insert the inside cylinder.

Burglar-Proof a Sliding Glass Door

The standard lock assembly on most sliding glass patio doors is laughably easy to pick, but if the door is secured with a bar it can't be opened even if the lock is released. A security bar is easy to custom-fit. **Tools:** measuring rule, fine-toothed hacksaw, small metal file, pencil. **Materials:** 4-foot length of ¾-inch aluminum tubing or thinwall electrical conduit, two crutch tips. **Time:** about ½ hour.

To fit the security bar to the door, close the door completely. Measure the distance across the fixed glass panel the door slides in front of, from the back edge of the door to the inside of the fixed panel's side jamb. With a fine-

the plate fits flat and straight into the edge of the door.

Mark the screw holes for the bolt plate with a pencil and remove the bolt and plate. Insert the outside lock cylinder from the outside of the door through the hole drilled in the door face, lining up the connecting stem so that it fits into the bolt assembly. Insert the inside cylinder from the inside of the door. Holding the parts of the lock in place, mark the screw holes on all sides of the door; then remove the pieces of the lock. Predrill the holes slightly smaller than the screws provided, reposition the parts of the lock in the predrilled holes, and screw the lock firmly into place.

Finally, drill a hole for the bolt at the pinhole mark on the door frame, where the bolt will enter the strike plate. Drill the same diameter opening as the bolt hole in the door, or follow the manufacturer's instructions for the strike plate hole. Hold the strike plate in place against the door frame and outline it with a pencil; mortise the plate area with a sharp chisel and a hammer. Set the strike plate into the mortise, mark the screw holes, predrill, and screw the plate firmly into place with the screws provided.

To fit the bar, measure across the fixed glass panel, from the jamb to the door's back edge.

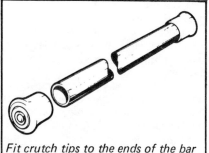

Fit crutch tips to the ends of the bar to hold it firmly in the bottom track of the door.

Tools: wedge or doorstop, scissors, utility knife or single-edge razor blade, measuring rule, scratch awl, fine-toothed hacksaw, pencil, drill, screwdriver. **Materials:** clean rags, adhesive-backed foam weatherstripping, plain or bottom door sweep with installation screws. **Time:** about ½ to 1 hour.

Seal the top and sides of the door with adhesive-backed foam weatherstripping; buy the weatherstripping in a bulk roll. Open the door wide, and wedge it or stop it to keep it open. Clean the inside of the door frame all around with a damp rag, wipe it dry, and let it dry completely.

With the door open, apply the foam weatherstripping around the inside of the door frame, on the narrow edge the door fits against when it closes. Start applying the foam at a corner. Peeling the paper backing off as you go, unroll and stick the weatherstripping evenly in place. Cut the foam at the end of each side with a scissors; butt the ends of the strips firmly in the corners. Seal the top edge of the frame and the two sides; do not seal the floor edge under the door.

toothed hacksaw, cut a 4-foot length of ¾-inch aluminum tubing or thinwall electrical conduit to 2 or 3 inches longer than the measured distance. Measure the cut piece of tubing accurately.

With a small metal file, smooth off the burrs on one end of the tubing. Fit a crutch tip firmly onto the end of the tubing and measure it again; the difference between the first measurement and the second is equal to the thickness of the crutch tip.

Measure and mark the piece of tubing from the open end to the outside surface of the crutch tip, to equal the distance across the fixed glass panel, from the back edge of the door frame to the inside jamb, minus the thickness of one crutch tip. Cut the tubing carefully with a hacksaw and file off the burrs on the cut end. Fit the second crutch tip firmly onto the cut end. To use the bar, set it in the bottom track of the door across the fixed glass panel, wedged snugly between the sliding door and the fixed door jamb.

Weatherstrip a Door

Folding a rug against the bottom of a door is inconvenient, and it keeps drafts out only when you remember to replace the rug. Install weatherstripping instead—it's a painless process.

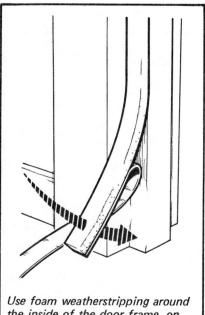

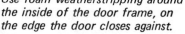

Use foam weatherstripping around the inside of the door frame, on the edge the door closes against.

DOORS / Constructing

On the doorknob edge of the door frame, cover the strike plate of the lock as you go; then cut away the foam over the plate with a utility knife or a single-edge razor blade. Cover the hinges on the hinge side of the door frame.

To close the opening under the door, between the door and the threshold, buy an aluminum and vinyl sweep to cover the bottom of the door. A plain sweep covers the outside edge of the door's bottom edge; many are flapped to fit tightly over the threshold. A bottom sweep fits over the bottom of the door in a U shape to seal the opening at the threshold. Either can be installed without removing the door from its hinges.

To install a plain door sweep, close the door. Measure the sweep to the width of the door and mark it with a scratch awl; cut it to size with a fine-toothed hacksaw. Set the sweep against the outside of the door so that it rests against the threshold; holding the sweep in place, open the door and adjust the sweep so that the door opens easily. Mark the screw holes in the sweep, and remove the sweep.

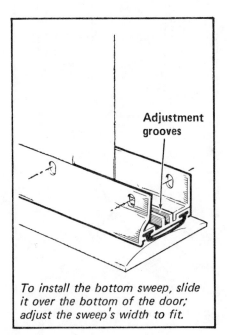

To install the bottom sweep, slide it over the bottom of the door; adjust the sweep's width to fit.

Use a drill to start the marked screw holes. Replace the sweep and screw it into place, using the screws included for installation with the sweep. Follow the manufacturer's specific instructions exactly.

To install a bottom sweep, close the door. Measure the sweep to the width of the door and mark it with a scratch awl; cut it to size with a fine-toothed hacksaw. Slide the sweep over the bottom of the door, covering the bottom edge completely; open the door. Remove the sweep, and adjust the removable side of the sweep, moving it into the appropriate groove on the base, to fit the thickness of the door exactly. Replace the sweep over the bottom edge of the door and close the door. Holding the sweep in place, adjust it so that the door opens easily. Mark the screw holes, predrill them, and attach the sweep to the door on both sides, using the installation screws provided. Follow the manufacturer's specific instructions exactly.

Construct a Simple Door

A batten door of the Z-brace style is very versatile and easy to make. **Tools:** measuring rule, pencil, carpenters' square, handsaw or power saw, pipe clamps, drill, countersink, screwdriver, plane, paintbrush. **Materials:** 1-inch tongue-and-groove boards, carpenters' glue, 1 × 4 stock, 1¼-inch #8 galvanized or brass flathead wood screws; hinges, latch assembly, and required hardware; stain or paint. **Time:** about 3 hours, plus drying time.

Measure the door opening and measure and mark a series of 1-inch tongue-and-groove boards to ⅛ inch shorter than the height of the door opening; use a carpenters' square to keep the ends even. Cut the boards carefully to the measured length with a handsaw or power saw. If necessary, trim the end board at one or both sides

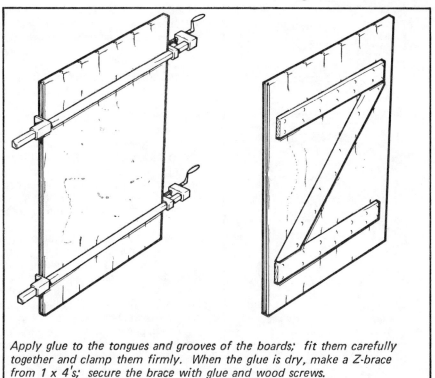

Apply glue to the tongues and grooves of the boards; fit them carefully together and clamp them firmly. When the glue is dry, make a Z-brace from 1 x 4's; secure the brace with glue and wood screws.

of the door so that when the boards are snugged together the door will be ⅛ inch narrower than the door opening. Cut off the tongue of the last board.

Apply a bead of carpenters' glue to both the tongue and the groove of each board. Working on a smooth, level work surface, fit all the boards together, aligning the ends carefully. Clamp the glued boards tightly together with pipe clamps and let the glue dry as recommended by the manufacturer.

To brace the door, cut three pieces of 1 × 4 stock, and arrange them on the door in a Z pattern. Cut the horizontal pieces to slightly less than the width of the door. Measure diagonally from top to bottom for the length of the long piece, and trim the ends at an angle to fit flush against the top and bottom arms of the Z-brace. Be sure to allow enough clearance between the door edge and the ends of the Z-brace arms so that the brace will clear the door jambs. Drill starter holes and secure the brace

members with carpenters' glue and 1¼-inch #8 galvanized or brass flathead wood screws. Countersink the screw holes so that the heads of the screws are flush with the surface of the brace.

Set the door into the opening and check for fit; plane or trim as necessary. Hang the door with substantial surface-mount hinges, and fit with a latch assembly—a colonial thumb latch works well on this kind of door. Stain or paint as desired.

Repair a Garage Door

Overhead garage doors, either swing-up or roll-up, are usually easy to repair when they bind or drag. **Tools:** adjustable wrench, screwdriver, rubber

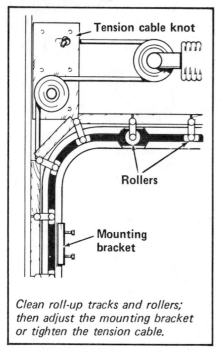

Tension cable knot

Rollers

Mounting bracket

Clean roll-up tracks and rollers; then adjust the mounting bracket or tighten the tension cable.

mallet or hammer and scrap wood block, level, measuring rule, large wedges, putty knife, paintbrush. **Materials:** rags, concentrated household cleaner, oil or silicone spray lubricant, garage door lubricant or powdered graphite, replacement hinges, hollow fiber plugs, carpenters' glue, plastic wood or wood putty, latex or oil-base exterior trim paint. **Time:** ½ hour to about 2 hours, depending on problem.

Garage doors work on metal tracks, and when a door doesn't work properly, the tracks are often at fault. Inspect the tracks bolted to the walls of the garage; using an adjustable wrench or a screwdriver, tighten the bolts or screws that hold the track mounting brackets to the walls. With the door closed, clean out hardened grease and dirt with concentrated household cleaner. Clean the rollers that run in the tracks. Lubricate the rollers with oil or silicone spray lubricant; lubricate the tracks with spray garage door lubricant or powdered graphite.

Finally, inspect the tracks for dents or flattened spots. With the door closed,

pound out any dents with a rubber mallet, or with a hammer and a block of scrap wood. If the tracks are badly distorted or damaged, they must be replaced; call a carpenter.

If the tracks are clean and in good condition but the door still binds, inspect them with a level. Check the horizontal tracks of a swing-up door; they should slant slightly down at the back of the garage. Check the vertical sections of roll-up door tracks to make sure they're plumb, and make sure the horizontal sections slant slightly down. Check both types of tracks to make sure both tracks are at the same height on the garage walls.

If the tracks are out of plumb or don't slant down evenly, close the garage door to clear the tracks. Using an adjustable wrench or a screwdriver, loosen the bolts or screws that hold the track mounting brackets to the wall; do *not* remove the bolts or screws. Tap the tracks into position with a rubber mallet, or with a hammer and a block of scrap wood. Check the tracks with a level to be sure they're plumb and then tighten the bracket mounting bolts or screws.

On roll-up garage doors, inspect the hinges that hold the sections of the door together, and tighten any loose screws. If the door sags to one side, wedge the sagging side up and examine the hinges. Remove any damaged hinges and replace them with new ones.

If the screw holes of a hinge are enlarged or the wood is cracked, remove the hinge. Use hollow fiber plugs to fill in enlarged screw holes—for each hole, coat a plug with carpenters' glue, insert it into the screw hole, and let dry according to the manufacturer's instructions. Then replace the hinge and tighten the screws. Fill screw holes in damaged wood with plastic wood or wood putty and let dry according to the manufacturer's instructions; then replace the hinge. If possible, move the hinge and set it into sound wood. Touch up patched areas with matching paint, and remove the wedges under the door.

If the door still doesn't operate properly after you've serviced the tracks and the hinges, examine the springs that operate it. *Caution: If the door has one torsion spring in the center, don't touch it; call a professional.* If the door has a spring on each side, open the door and adjust the spring tension. To adjust the tension on a swing-up door, move the spring hook one hole or notch tighter; to adjust the tension on a roll-up door, shorten the cable knotted through the spring plate near the door.

If the garage door mechanism is in good order but the door binds all around, inspect the door's paint. Wood doors can absorb considerable moisture through raw edges. If the door has swollen because of damaged paint, let it dry out thoroughly over several dry days. Then paint the door on both sides with latex or oil-base exterior trim paint; be careful to seal all edges completely.

Install a Garage Door Opener

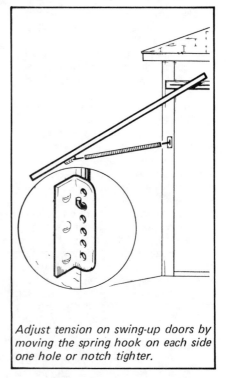

Adjust tension on swing-up doors by moving the spring hook on each side one hole or notch tighter.

Most automatic garage door openers are made for do-it-yourself installation. **Tools:** measuring rule, hacksaw, pencil, drill, screwdriver, adjustable wrench, magnetic stud finder, hammer. **Materials:** rags, concentrated household cleaner, oil or silicone spray lubricant, garage door lubricant or powdered graphite; automatic garage door opener kit, with necessary brackets, clamps, screws, and bolts; 3-foot piece of 2 × 4, 16- or 20-penny common nails, 1½-inch lag screws, batteries for transmitter units. **Time:** about 4 hours.

Before buying a door opener, measure the height and width of the door. Open and close the door and measure the clearance between door and ceiling at the highest point of the door's position; if it's less than 2 inches, an automatic door opener cannot be installed. Buy an opener made specifically for the size and type—swing-up or roll-up—of garage door you have. Choose a preassembled opener that can be plugged in at an existing outlet, and make sure it has an automatic reverse switch. Read the manufacturer's installation instructions carefully, and follow them exactly.

Before installing the garage door opener, make sure the door operates correctly. Clean the tracks to remove old grease and dirt; lubricate the rollers with oil or silicone spray lubricant, and the tracks with garage door lubricant or powdered graphite. If the door binds, repair it as necessary. Finally, remove the lock on the garage door or saw off the locking bar with a hacksaw.

The garage door opener works on a long track attached to the ceiling. To install the opener, measure across the top of the inside door frame and mark the center point. Attach the header bracket—including the automatic reverse switch—to the beam over the door, centered exactly on the marked point and at least 2 inches down from the ceiling. Mark the screw holes for the bracket and predrill them; set the bracket into place and fasten it with the screws included.

Next, attach the hanger straps—the door opener you're installing may have one set or more. If the ceiling has exposed beams, mount the straps directly to the side of a beam about three-quarters of the length of the opener track back from the door. Measure across the beam to position the straps exactly centered on the beam, directly aligned with the header bracket; attach the straps with 1½-inch lag screws and an adjustable wrench.

If the ceiling is finished, use a magnetic stud finder to locate the appropriate beam. Nail a 3-foot piece of 2 × 4 to the beam with 16- or 20-penny common nails; center the 2 × 4 on the beam. Attach the hanger straps for the door opener to the 2 × 4 with 1½-inch lag screws; position the straps exactly centered on the beam to align with the header bracket.

With preassembled openers, no further preparation is necessary. If your unit is not preassembled, attach the power unit firmly to the track, following the manufacturer's instructions exactly; attach the carrier and the hanger clamp to the track as directed.

You'll need an assistant to install the assembled track. Set the door end of the track into place in the header bracket over the garage door; bolt it into place but don't tighten the bolt. Then, with your assistant, lift the power unit end of the track and slide the hanger clamp into position over the hanger straps. Bolt the clamp and the straps firmly together with the hardware provided; then tighten the bolt that holds the track in place in the header bracket.

Next attach the connector arm that moves the door. Center the bracket plate at the top of the garage door, directly below the header bracket; mark screw holes, predrill, and attach the plate with the hardware provided. Set the end of the connector arm into place against the bracket, as directed by the manufacturer, and screw or bolt it into place. Attach the track end of the connector arm to the carrier in the track with the hardware provided; turn the

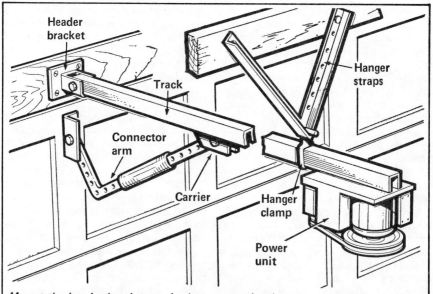

Mount the header bracket to the beam over the door; mount the hanger straps directly back from it. Attach the power unit to the track, bolt the track to the hanger straps, and attach the connector arm to the carrier.

unit by hand to slide the carrier out to the free end of the connector arm.

Finally, remove the power unit cover and connect the control wires to the terminals in the power unit; follow the manufacturer's instructions exactly to connect the wires. Install batteries in the hand transmitters; if the opener includes a garage light, screw in a light bulb. Replace the cover on the power unit and plug the opener in.

Check your installation by opening and closing the door several times; adjust it, as necessary, according to the manufacturer's instructions. Adjustments for proper fit in the door opening are made at the power unit; adjustments to the automatic reverse are made at the header bracket. Following the manufacturer's instructions, make sure the door closes and the automatic reverse functions properly.

Electricity

Replace a Ceiling Fixture

An old ceiling light fixture in a newly painted room can look awful, but there's no need to call an electrician. It's easy to replace the old incandescent fixture with a new one. **Tools:** flashlight or trouble light, stepladder, screwdriver, diagonal cutters, adjustable wrench, wire strippers. **Materials:** new ceiling fixture with mounting hardware, wirenuts. **Time:** about 15 minutes to ½ hour.

Caution: Before you start to work, flip the circuit breaker or remove the fuse that provides power to the fixture. If you don't know which circuit controls the fixture, turn off the main circuit breaker or remove the fuses to turn off all power to the house. If necessary, use a flashlight or a trouble light, plugged into another circuit, while you work.

Set up a stepladder for access to the ceiling fixture. Remove the fixture's globe and unscrew the light bulb or bulbs; then disassemble all mounting hardware. Generally, only screws secure a fixture to the ceiling electrical box; use a screwdriver to remove them. If the fixture is held by a nut, loosen it with a wrench. Mounting hardware may not always be obvious. If you don't see any screws or bolts, look for some decorative feature that may also serve as a fastener. It will probably unscrew counterclockwise by hand. Support the fixture with one hand so that it can't suddenly come loose and damage the wiring, and remove the mounting hardware.

Disconnect the fixture wires from the circuit wires behind the fixture's ceiling cover plate. If the wires are fused together with old insulating tape, cut the wires close to the tape joints. If the wires are joined with wirenuts, unscrew the wirenuts and disconnect the wires. Set the old fixture aside.

Examine the ends of the circuit wires—and *only* those wires—that you have just disconnected. If there is about ½ to ¾ inch of bare copper conductor on the end of each insulated wire, you're ready to connect the new fixture; if not, use wire strippers to remove about ½ to ¾ inch of insulation from the end of each wire.

Examine the new fixture. If the wires attached to it aren't ready to connect, with insulation already removed from the ends, remove ½ to ¾ inch of insulation from each fixture wire.

Now connect the fixture wires to the circuit wires. Twist the end of each circuit wire clockwise with the end of each fixture wire, white wire to white wire and black wire to black wire. Screw a wirenut tightly over each pair of twisted ends so that no bare copper conductor is visible.

NOTE: If the fixture has more than one socket, connect the black wire from each socket to the black circuit wire, and connect the white wire from each socket to the white circuit wire. If there are three or four socket wires joined to a circuit wire, use larger wirenuts to accommodate them.

When the wires are connected, mount the new fixtures, using the hardware provided. There are several ways to mount ceiling fixtures; usually the manufacturer provides instructions. Follow these instructions exactly to mount the fixture in one of the following ways.

Box with mounting tabs. Some simple fixtures have screws that are set into the mounting tabs on the sides of the ceiling electrical box. Attach this type of fixture by inserting the screws through the round part of the keyhole-shaped slots on the fixture and then rotating the fixture slightly so that the screws go into the narrow parts of the slots. Tighten the screws to secure the fixture to the ceiling.

Other fixtures have holes that are simply aligned with the holes in the box

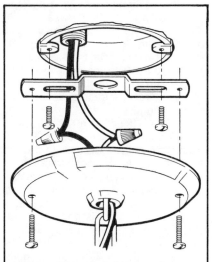

If the ceiling electrical box has mounting tabs, screw the fixture or the mounting strap to them.

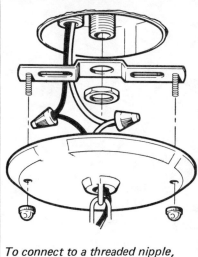

To connect to a threaded nipple, screw the mounting strap over the nipple and then screw on a cap nut.

mounting tabs. For this type, insert the mounting screws through the holes in the fixture and into the tabs, and tighten them to hold the fixture in place.

Box with mounting strap. Many fixtures use a mounting strap that's fastened across the electrical box by one screw to a center stud in the box or by a pair of screws to the box tabs. Other fixtures use a short piece of threaded pipe called a nipple; screw the nipple into the strap's center hole, set the fixture onto the nipple, and screw a cap nut onto the nipple under the fixture to hold the fixture in place.

Box with stud, nipple, and reducing nut. One type of fixture doesn't use a mounting strap. Instead, a nipple is connected to a box stud by means of a reducing nut—a nut that's threaded on one end to fit the stud, and on the other to fit a nipple. Screw the reducing nut into the box stud, set the fixture onto the nipple, and screw a cap nut onto the nipple under the fixture to hold the fixture to the ceiling.

Box with stud, nipple, and hickey. Some fixtures use a different device in place of the reducing nut. All

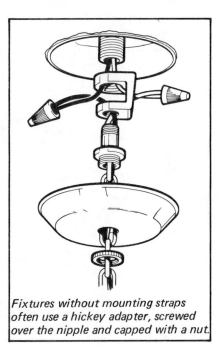

Fixtures without mounting straps often use a hickey adapter, screwed over the nipple and capped with a nut.

other parts may be the same, but the nipple is connected to the electrical box's stud by an adapter called a hickey. Mount the fixture with the hickey as above.

Final steps. No matter which type of ceiling fixture you're installing, fold the wires carefully back into the electrical box as you mount the fixture; make sure you don't catch the wires under the fixture as you tighten the mounting hardware.

Once the fixture is securely mounted on the ceiling, screw in the bulbs and install the globe or other covering for the bulbs. Finally, flip the circuit breaker or replace the fuse to turn the power back on.

Install Track Lights

For light exactly when and where you want it, and for striking light-and-shadow effects, add track lights to your electrical system; choose bold or subtle fittings to suit your design. **Tools:** screwdriver, ruler, pencil, drill. **Materials:** track assembly, desired fittings; screws, toggle bolts, or molly bolts; composition washers, wirenuts. **Time:** 10 to 30 minutes.

Caution: Before you start to work, flip the circuit breaker or remove the fuse that provides power to the old fixture. If you don't know which circuit controls the fixture, turn off the main circuit breaker or remove the fuses to turn off all power to the house.

Track lights consist of two basic parts: the track itself, which the lights plug into; and an adapter assembly that plugs into the track, connecting it to the house current. The adapter is either plugged directly into an outlet or wired to a ceiling junction box.

Choose a location for the track. If there's a ceiling fixture close to this location, buy a track assembly to connect to it. Otherwise, consider a track design that plugs into an outlet. The alternative is extending house wiring to the ceiling; this should be done by an electrician.

The plug-in track is easy to install. Position the track where you want it on the ceiling and mark with a pencil the position of the molly or toggle bolts; there will be predrilled holes in the track

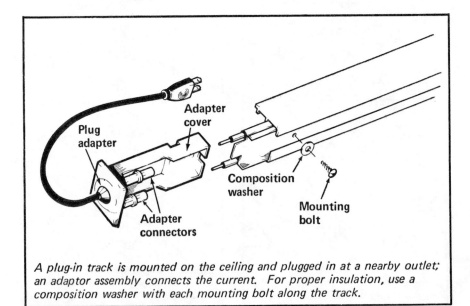

A plug-in track is mounted on the ceiling and plugged in at a nearby outlet; an adaptor assembly connects the current. For proper insulation, use a composition washer with each mounting bolt along the track.

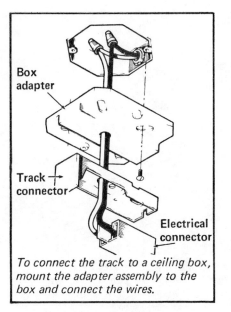

Tighten the bolts. Then insert the adapter into the terminal end of the track, pushing it in as directed by the manufacturer. Make sure the connection is tight.

Push the lights into their track terminals. Route the cord to an outlet and plug it in.

For a track light that connects to a ceiling junction box, the adapter assembly is in three pieces: a box adapter, a track connector, an electrical connector. The track itself is secured to the ceiling with clips. Installation is a matter of fitting these pieces together and connecting them to the junction box and the ceiling.

Remove the old fixture on the ceiling, exposing the wires from the junction box. Screw together the box adapter and the track connector with the screws provided. Thread the wires of the electrical connector through the center holes in the adapter/connector assembly. Connect the wires to the junction box wires with wirenuts, black wire to black and white to white. Position the adapter assembly on the junction box and screw it into the box's lip screw holes.

Measure the length of the track with a

Box adapter

Track connector

Electrical connector

To connect the track to a ceiling box, mount the adapter assembly to the box and connect the wires.

at these positions. Remove the track. Drill a pilot hole for the bolts and reposition the track, aligning its bolt holes with the drilled holes. Slip a composition (not metal) washer through each bolt and insert the bolts and washers through the track into the ceiling.

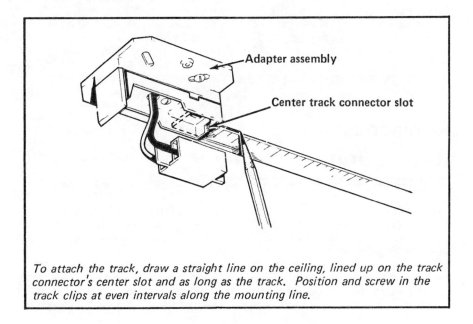

Adapter assembly

Center track connector slot

To attach the track, draw a straight line on the ceiling, lined up on the track connector's center slot and as long as the track. Position and screw in the track clips at even intervals along the mounting line.

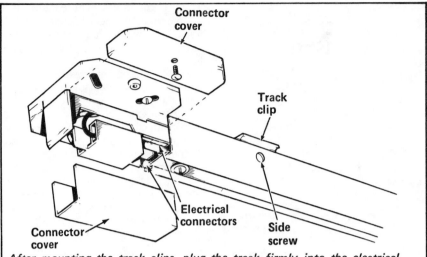

Connector
cover

Track
clip

Electrical
connectors

Side
screw

Connector
cover

After mounting the track clips, plug the track firmly into the electrical connectors and push it up into the clips. Tighten the side screws and set the connector cover into place; then plug in the light fittings.

ruler. Place the ruler on the ceiling, setting one edge of the ruler in line with the track connector's center slot. Draw a straight line from this point along the ceiling, as long as the track. Position and screw in the track clips at even intervals along this line; drill holes for the clips. Screw the ceiling screws in tightly; leave the side screws loose.

Plug the track securely into the electrical connector and push it up into the clips. Tighten the side screws to hold the track firmly. Then place the cover over the assembly, attach the lights to the track, and turn on the power.

Replace a Wall Switch

A malfunctioning wall switch can be a real problem, but it's simple to replace the switch yourself. **Tools:** screwdriver, flashlight, single-edge razor blade. **Materials:** new switch, of the same type as the old. **Time:** 15 to 20 minutes.

You must use the right type of switch. The most common type is the single-pole switch; it controls a light or a wall outlet that has no other switch control. If the light is controlled by two switches—at both the top and the bottom of a stairway, for instance—the switches used are the type called three-way switches. Be sure you get the right type. The instructions given here are for single-pole switches only.

Caution: Before starting to work, turn off the power to the switch: remove the fuse, or trip the circuit breaker, that controls the outlet. Use a flashlight if you need more light to work by.

With the power turned off, remove the cover plate. If it has been painted over, you can minimize damage to both wall and plate by cutting carefully around the edge of the plate with a single-edge razor blade. Remove the screws and lift the plate off.

The switch is attached to the switch box with two screws. Remove these screws and pull the switch carefully out from the box, just far enough so that you can get at the wires. Now examine the wiring.

If the switch is at the end of an electrical cable, it uses a switch loop; two wires are connected to the switch, one white and one black. If the switch is somewhere in the middle of a run of cable, you'll see two cables in the box, each with a white and a black wire. In this situation, a black wire from each cable is connected to two terminals on the switch, and the two white wires are connected to each other. Do not touch either these connected white wires or any bare or green ground wires that may be visible.

Now disconnect the old switch. Loosen the two terminal screws on the switch and disconnect the two wires connected to them. Discard the old switch.

Loosen the same two terminal screws on the new switch and set the switch into the box, holding it in place. To install the switch, connect each black wire to the proper terminal. To make the connections, set the loop at the end of each wire around the correct terminal screw, with the loop facing clockwise so that it can be screwed in neatly and tightly. Tighten the terminal screws.

Place the new switch into the switch

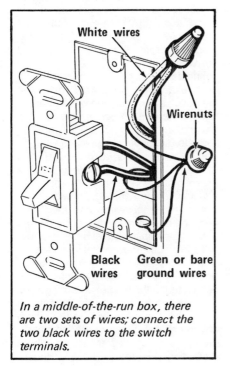

White wires

Wirenuts

Black wires   Green or bare ground wires

In a middle-of-the-run box, there are two sets of wires; connect the two black wires to the switch terminals.

box and secure it with its two mounting screws. Replace the switch's cover plate and secure it with its screws. Finally, restore power to the switch's circuit.

Install a Dimmer

It's as easy to install a dimmer switch for an incandescent light as it is to replace a faulty switch. **Tools:** single-edge razor blade, screwdriver, diagonal cutters. **Materials:** incandescent dimmer switch, of the same type (single-pole) as the old switch; wirenuts. Check the wattage of the bulbs the switch will control—full-range dimmers usually have a capacity of 600 watts, but two-way bright-dim controls can accommodate only 300 watts. Choose your new switch accordingly. **Time:** 15 to 20 minutes.

Caution: Before starting to work, turn off the power to the switch where you're installing the dimmer. If the cover plate is painted over, cut around the painted edges with a single-edge razor blade to keep the break clean. Remove the screws and lift off the plate.

Remove the screws that hold the switch in the switch box and pull the switch toward you out of the box to expose the two black wires. Disconnect the two wires connected to the terminal screws of the old switch. Remove the old switch.

Some dimmer switches have terminal screws like single-pole switches; to connect this type, connect each black wire to the proper terminal. Some switches have wire leads instead of terminal screws; to connect this type, use wirenuts.

Connect each wire lead to a black wire in the switch box. Hold the lead and the correct wire together, with exposed ends parallel, and push a wirenut over the stripped ends of the wires. Push the wires in firmly and twist the nut firmly clockwise. No bare wire should show outside the wirenut. If you can see exposed wire, remove the nut, snip the ends of the wires off with diagonal cutters, and reconnect the wires.

Finally, replace the switch in the switch box, being careful not to pinch the wires. Replace the screws that hold the switch in place. Replace the old cover plate or install a new one—some dimmer switches come with their own cover plates. Tighten the screws that hold the cover plate on and push the dimmer control knob down onto its shaft, following the directions on the package. Turn the power on.

To replace a three-way switch with a dimmer, use a switch called a single-pole, double-throw switch. Both switches will turn the light on and off, but only one switch of a pair can be controlled by a dimmer. Follow the same general procedure used for the single-pole switch, but be careful to connect the leads correctly according to the switch manufacturer's instructions. Be sure to turn the power off before you start to work.

Replace an Electrical Outlet

An outlet that doesn't work is more frustrating than no outlet at all, but it's easy to replace. **Tools:** screwdriver, single-edge razor blade, pencil, diagonal wire cutters. **Materials:** masking tape, new electrical outlet. **Time:** 15 to 20 minutes.

Caution: Before starting to work, turn off the power to the outlet; either remove the proper fuse or turn the circuit breaker off at the main entrance panel or box.

Replace the dead outlet with a new one of the same type, either ungrounded or grounded. Ungrounded outlets have slots for two-pronged plugs; grounded outlets also have holes to accept three-pronged plugs. Examine the old outlet and buy a new one of the same type to replace it.

To replace the outlet, remove the plate that covers it; unscrew the center

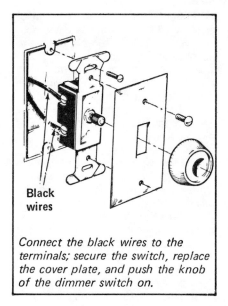

Black wires

Connect the black wires to the terminals; secure the switch, replace the cover plate, and push the knob of the dimmer switch on.

screw and lift the plate off. If the plate has been painted over, cut carefully around it with a single-edge razor blade before removing it.

Remove the two screws, one on each end, that hold the outlet in the electrical box. Carefully pull the outlet out of the box, as far as the wires inside will extend; don't force the wires out. Look at the wires carefully to see how they're connected; you must connect the new outlet exactly the same way. To remove the outlet, disconnect the wires from the terminal screws where they're attached. On an ungrounded outlet, there are two wires to disconnect, a black or red one and a white one; on a grounded (three-prong) outlet, there is also a green or bare wire. If you're not sure you can remember which wire goes where, mark the wires and their connections on the old outlet with masking tape labels. Lift the outlet out of the box.

To install the new outlet, connect the wires in the box to the terminal screws on the new outlet, exactly as they were connected to the old outlet. Connect the black or red wire to the dark screw on the outlet, the white wire to the silver-colored screw. For a grounded (three-prong) outlet, connect the green or bare grounding wire to the brass or green-

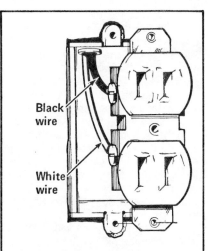

Black wire

White wire

An ungrounded outlet has two wires, one black or red and one white. Connect the wires to the outlet's terminal screws.

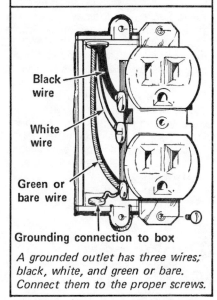

Black wire

White wire

Green or bare wire

Grounding connection to box

A grounded outlet has three wires; black, white, and green or bare. Connect them to the proper screws.

marked screw on the outlet and then to the electrical box. Connect each wire by looping it clockwise under the correct screw; tighten the screw firmly over the wire loop. If bare wire shows near the screw head, loosen the screw, disconnect the wire, and cut off the extra length with diagonal wire cutters; reconnect the wire.

Lamp Sockets / ELECTRICITY

After connecting the wires to the new outlet, set the outlet in place in the electrical box, folding the wires carefully in behind the outlet. Be careful not to pinch the wires behind the outlet. If the outlet is a grounding outlet and is set vertically in the wall, set it in with the holes for the third prongs toward the floor. Replace the two screws that hold the outlet in the box.

Finally, replace the outlet cover plate and the screw that holds it in place, and turn the power on.

Replace a Lamp Socket

Light sockets often don't last, but don't give up on a flickering lamp. Replacing the socket is both an inexpensive and easy job. **Tools:** small screwdriver, wire stripper, wire cutters. **Materials:** light socket assembly. **Time:** 20 minutes.

When a lamp flickers, check the bulb; if the bulb is tight, check the plug. If the plug is in good shape, you probably need a new socket, available in hardware and dime stores. Choose whatever color and kind of socket you want; three-way sockets fit in the same as regular ones.

Before working on the lamp, unplug it. *Caution: If you're working on a ceiling or built-in lamp with no plug, remove the fuse or trip the circuit breaker that controls it. It is essential that no electricity flow through the lamp.*

The replacement procedure consists of disconnecting the lamp's wiring from the old socket and connecting it to a new one. Remove the light bulb. The socket which holds the bulb is held in place with a plastic or metal shell covering that fits tightly into a brass cap at the bottom of the socket. Remove the socket shell by squeezing it at a spot marked *press* and pulling it up from the cap. Pull the cardboard lining out of the socket, leaving the socket attached to the wires and the cap beneath it.

217

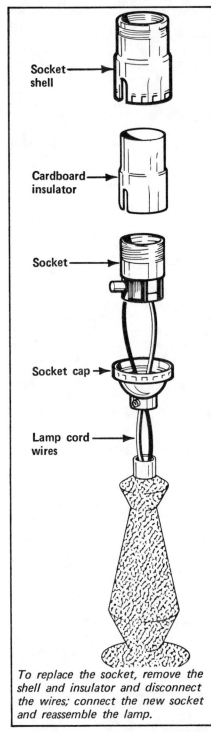

Socket shell

Cardboard insulator

Socket

Socket cap

Lamp cord wires

To replace the socket, remove the shell and insulator and disconnect the wires; connect the new socket and reassemble the lamp.

Disconnect the old socket from the wires of the lamp. The wires are connected to the lamp socket by two small screws under the socket; loosen the screws, pull the wires free, and examine the wires. There should be ¾ inch of bare wire exposed at the end of each wire. If the exposed wire is shorter than this or if the ends of the wire are ragged, strip the plastic coating off the wire with a wire stripper to expose ¾ inch of bare, sound wire, being careful not to cut into the wire. Cut off any ragged ends. Twist the bare end of each wire tightly clockwise, and curl each twisted end into a clockwise hook.

If you're installing a socket that's different from the old one, the socket cap must be replaced; take off the old cap and thread the new cap through the wires. If the new socket is the same type as the old, leave the old socket cap in place. Attach the two lamp wires to the two screws at the base of the new socket, looping the wires clockwise around the screws and then tightening the screws to hold the loops of wire firmly in place. Make sure the connection of wire to socket is good. Sometimes screws and wires are color-coordinated: black wire to brass screw, white wire to chrome screw. When the new socket is firmly connected to the lamp wires, slip the cardboard insulating sleeve and then the plastic or metal shell over the socket and snap the shell into the cap. Screw in a light bulb and plug the lamp in or turn the power back on.

Replace a Faulty Plug

The standard plug-pulling technique is to grab the cord and pull. You can put a temperamental lamp or appliance back into service by replacing the damaged plug. **Tools:** wire cutters, small screwdriver, utility knife. **Materials:** new electrical plug. **Time:** about ½ hour.

Electrical cords are made in three different ways. Lightweight cords are usually flat, with two wires side by side in a plastic casing. These are called zip cords. Heavier appliance cords use round wire. Heavy-duty cords have three wires, and require three-pronged plugs.

To replace a plug on zip cord, use a clamp-on plug; buy the kind that doesn't require either stripping or separation of the wires in the cord. Cut the old plug off and discard it. To connect the new plug, open the top clamp and push the cord into the plug case, then close the clamp. Pull firmly on the prongs of the clamp to draw them out of the plug case, and spread them firmly; this completes the contact inside the case. Press the prongs together again and push the parts of the plug firmly together.

To replace a plug on a heavier cord, use a standard two- or three-prong round plug. Cut the old plug off and discard it. Push the cut cord into the small opening of the new plug and pull it through to expose about 5 inches of cord. Working carefully, strip the outer insulation off the end of the cord with a utility knife, exposing the two (or three) inner wires for about 3 inches. The insulation on these inner wires must not be broken.

Being careful not to damage the interior wires, strip the insulation off the tips of the inner wires for about ½ inch. Twist the bare filaments of each wire, clockwise, to form a solid tongue of wire.

To complete the installation, tie an underwriters' knot with the inner wires of the cord, following the diagram here exactly. Pull the knot tight and draw the plug down the cord so that the knot is inside the plug case but the ends of the inner wires are exposed. Loosen the screws in the plug.

For either a two-prong or a three-prong plug, loop each inner wire around a prong of the plug. Twist the bare wire tip of each wire clockwise around a screw and tighten the screw. Each of the inner wires must be connected to a

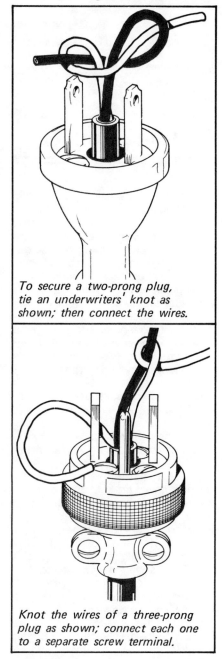

To secure a two-prong plug, tie an underwriters' knot as shown; then connect the wires.

Knot the wires of a three-prong plug as shown; connect each one to a separate screw terminal.

separate screw, as shown. Finally, replace the cardboard insulator over the prongs of the cord, and clamp the cord end of the plug if necessary.

219

Plumbing

Fix a Dripping Faucet

Leaky faucets waste water, burn up heating energy, and drive their owners to distraction. The repair is an easy one—this is a job you can and should do. **Tools:** towel or clean rag, screwdriver, utility knife, adjustable wrench, pliers, plumbers' seat wrench. **Materials:** penetrating oil, adhesive tape or electrical tape, replacement washer and brass washer screw or replacement diaphragm or replacement rubber seat ring; replacement valve seat; *for lever-type faucets*—manufacturer's cartridge assembly kit. **Time:** 1 to 2 hours.

Knob-controlled faucets. Knob-controlled faucets, either separate hot and cold knobs or a single control dial, operate by compression. Water in the supply pipes presses against a washer fitted against a U-shaped valve seat in the faucet; this pressure seals the washer against the seat and keeps the water from flowing into the faucet mouth. Turning the faucet on brings the washer up from the valve seat, releasing the water; turning it off fits the washer back into the seat. A drip is usually caused by a worn washer that allows leakage through the valve seat from the supply pipes. To eliminate the drip, replace the washer.

Turn off the water supply to the faucet. If there is a shutoff control under the sink, turn it off; otherwise, turn off the main water supply. Turn on the faucet and let the water in the pipes run out. Stop up the sink with a plug so you can't lose any parts down the drain. Place a towel or a clean rag under the faucet to protect the sink's finish.

Remove the screw from the top of the handle or knob; if there is a decorative cap on top of the screw, unsnap it or pry it off with a utility knife, or unscrew it. If the screw won't turn, apply a drop or two of penetrating oil to loosen it; then unscrew. Remove the faucet handle.

Once the handle is off, you'll see a tall stem anchored in the packing nut that fits over the body of the faucet. Wrap a piece of adhesive tape or electrical tape two or three times around the packing

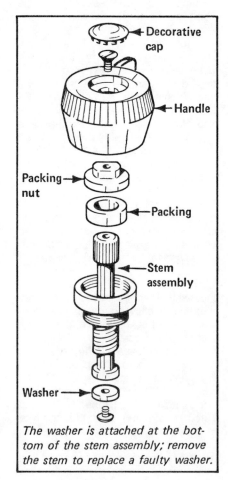

The washer is attached at the bottom of the stem assembly; remove the stem to replace a faulty washer.

nut and use an adjustable wrench to remove the nut. Then remove the stem; using pliers, twist it in the same direction the faucet turns on and lift it out. The washer is on the end of the faucet stem, held in place by a screw. Remove the screw, using penetrating oil if necessary, and remove the washer from the stem.

To replace the worn washer, use a new washer of exactly the same size and type. Take the old washer to the hardware store and buy an exact duplicate. Tell the hardware dealer whether the washer is for a hot- or a cold-water faucet. Also examine the screw that holds the washer to the stem; if it's damaged, buy an exact replacement when you buy the washer.

Set the new washer in place on the bottom of the stem, exactly as the old one was set. If the washer is beveled on one side, set it beveled side down into the faucet. Insert the washer screw and tighten it firmly. Set the stem back into the faucet, turning it in the same direction the water turns off. Replace the packing nut and the faucet knob or handle, insert the screw that holds it in place, and tighten the screw firmly. If necessary, replace the decorative cap over the screw. Turn the water supply on.

If something other than a washer is at the end of the faucet stem, it must be replaced exactly. Some faucets use diaphragms instead of washers; pry the diaphragm off from the bottom of the stem with a screwdriver and install the new one. Other types of faucets use rubber seat rings; hold the stem with pliers while unscrewing the center piece that holds the ring in place, then replace the ring. If a compression-type faucet has some other alien-looking device instead of a washer, either call a plumber or contact the manufacturer to get the address of a local supply store—check the phone book. Many manufacturers sell repair kits for their faucets; follow the manufacturer's instructions exactly.

If the faucet still drips after the washer has been replaced, replace the valve seat. Shut off the water supply. Remove the handle and the packing nut

and twist out the stem. Use a plumbers' seat wrench to remove the valve seat; insert the wrench into the U of the valve seat and turn it counterclockwise to unscrew the seat. Lift the seat out. Replace the valve seat with a new one exactly like it; take the old seat to the hardware store to be sure you get the right kind. Install the new seat by screwing it in with the seat wrench; turn the wrench clockwise to tighten the seat firmly. Twist the stem (and washer) into place and replace the packing nut and the handle. Turn on the water supply.

Lever-type faucets. Lever-type kitchen faucets operate with a cartridge assembly, not a seat-and-washer system. These faucets rarely drip; if a lever faucet does drip, the cartridge assembly must be replaced. Contact the faucet manufacturer to find a local supply store; buy the cartridge assembly kit made specifically for your faucet. To install the new assembly, follow the manufacturer's instructions exactly.

Fix a Leaky Pipe

The best thing to do when a pipe leaks is to replace the leaky section, but that's a big job. If the leak isn't catastrophic and the pipe is otherwise sound, you can often make the repair more simply. **Tools:** adjustable wrench, utility scissors, screwdriver, putty knife. **Materials:** pipe mending cement stick, rags; leak repair kit or rubber inner tube, scrap wood strips, and C-clamp or hose clamp; waterproof pipe-mending tape, plumbing epoxy paste, self-tapping plug. **Time:** about 20 minutes.

To stop tiny leaks, it's easiest to use a pipe mending cement stick, a special compound similar in form to a glue stick. This compound can stop a leak even when water is still running through the pipe, but it works best if the water supply is turned off. Turn off the water at the shutoff valve for the pipe or at the main water shutoff; drain the pipe by opening the faucet *below* the leaking section. Dry the pipe with a rag, rub the

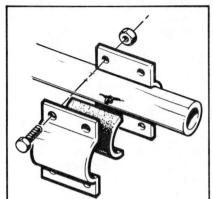

To use a leak repair kit, cover the leak with the rubber pad and bolt the plates firmly over the pipe.

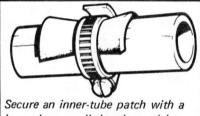

Secure an inner-tube patch with a hose clamp; pull the clamp tight and tighten the holding screw firmly.

cement stick over the leaky spot, close the open faucet, and turn the water on again.

To fix a minor leak in an otherwise sound pipe, use a leak repair kit or a piece of rubber cut from an inner tube. Leak repair kits usually include a heavy rubber pad to cover the leak and a pair of curved metal plates that bolt over the pad and around the pipe; just set the pad and the plates in place and bolt the plates firmly together with an adjustable wrench. To use an inner-tube patch, cut the patch at least 2 inches longer than the bad spot, and wide enough to wrap about halfway around the pipe. Center the patch over the leak and set a strip of scrap wood over it along the pipe; set another strip on the other side of the pipe. Secure the strips of wood and the patch with a C-clamp, or use a hose clamp; pull the clamp tight around the pipe and tighten the screw to hold it in place.

You can make a quick temporary repair to a leaky pipe with waterproof pipe-mending tape. Turn off the water supply and drain the water in the pipe by opening the faucet *below* the leak. Dry the pipe thoroughly. Wrap the tape firmly around the leaky section, at least 3 inches beyond the leak on each side; overlap it at least half the width of the tape as you wrap. Close the open faucet and turn the water supply on; repair the pipe permanently as soon as possible.

Leaks in pipe joints are more difficult to repair. One solution is sealing the joint with plumbing epoxy paste. Turn off the water supply and drain the water in the pipe by opening the faucet *below* the leaking joint. Then dry the joint thoroughly. Apply the epoxy with a putty knife according to the manufacturer's instructions, being careful not to leave any gaps; cover the entire joint. Let the epoxy dry completely, according to the manufacturer's instructions; then close the faucet and turn on the water supply.

If the leak is in a large pipe or a tank, use a self-tapping plug, a specially made pipe plug that screws directly into the hole in the pipe. Although they're available in different sizes, plugs aren't recommended for small-diameter pipes because they restrict the flow of water. Simply screw the plug firmly into the hole in the pipe or tank.

Clear a Clogged Drain

Sluggish or completely stopped, clogged drains are no fun—but you don't need a plumber to fix them. **Tools:** rubber gloves, rubber plunger, drain-and-trap auger, bucket, screwdriver, pliers or adjustable wrench, small stiff bottle brush. **Materials:** chemical drain cleaner, rags, petroleum jelly, liquid detergent or strong household detergent. **Time:** about ½ to 1½ hours, depending on the problem.

Deal with slow-running drains before

they quit entirely. Use a commercial chemical drain cleaner to improve drainage; follow the manufacturer's instructions exactly. *Caution: Most chemical drain cleaners are caustics. Handle them carefully, wear rubber gloves, and wash your hands and the gloves at another sink after using a chemical drain cleaner.*

When a drain clogs completely, don't use a chemical drain cleaner—if it doesn't work, caustics trapped in the pipes can be dangerous. In most cases, a rubber plunger can effectively remove the clog.

Use a plunger with a head or cap big enough to cover the blocked drain opening completely. Remove the strainer or stopper from the drain and add enough water to the sink or tub to cover the head of the plunger; if the sink or tub is full, dip out excess water so that only the head of the plunger will be covered. Block overflow outlets completely with wet rags. If any other drain is connected to the same line as the blocked drain—in a double kitchen sink, for instance, or where two laundry tubs drain into one pipe—block the connected drain completely with wet rags.

Coat the bottom edge of the plunger's cup generously with petroleum jelly and set the plunger in the sink or tub, sliding it into place to cover the blocked drain completely. Pump the plunger quickly up and down 10 or 12 times, pushing firmly to build up a strong pressure; then jerk the plunger quickly away from the drain. If the clog has been removed, the water will drain out of the sink or tub. If nothing happens, repeat the plunging procedure; plunge at least twice more before resorting to more drastic means.

If repeated plunging doesn't remove a clog, use a drain-and-trap auger—otherwise known as a plumbers' snake—to break up the obstruction. Dip any water out of the sink or tub and remove the strainer or stopper from the drain. Insert the end of the auger into the drain. To feed the auger wire in, tighten the thumbscrew that locks the wire in place. Turn the handle of the auger clockwise on the wire and push to force

the wire into the drain; then loosen the thumbscrew and slide the auger handle back up the wire. Repeat, tightening the thumbscrew, turning the handle clockwise, and pushing, to work the auger into the pipe.

Work the auger steadily into the pipe. If you hit a hard obstruction, the wire is probably hitting a bend in the pipe; move the auger handle right up to the drain opening and tighten the thumbscrew. Work the auger slowly into the pipe, twisting the handle to twist the wire inside the pipe, until the wire slides around the bend.

If you hit a soft obstruction, the wire has probably reached the clog in the drainpipe. Work the auger slowly into the obstruction, twisting the handle to twist the wire against the clog in the pipe. Work at the clog until you feel it break up; then twist the auger a few more times and pull the wire back, turning the handle counterclockwise to reel the wire in. Remove the auger from the drain. Flush the drain with a bucket of very hot water mixed with liquid detergent or strong household detergent.

If you can't remove an obstruction in a bathtub drain by using an auger inserted into the drain, remove the screws securing the overflow plate above the drain, and take the plate off. Insert the auger into the overflow outlet

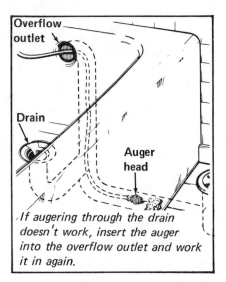

If augering through the drain doesn't work, insert the auger into the overflow outlet and work it in again.

and work it down through the overflow pipe and into the drainpipe; flush with very hot soapy water poured down the drain. If the auger still doesn't work, call a plumber.

If you can't remove an obstruction in a sink drain by using an auger inserted into the drain, tackle the clog through the U-shaped trap under the sink. Set a bucket under the trap. If there's a clean-out plug at the low point of the trap, remove the plug with pliers or an adjustable wrench. The water in the sink and the trap will run into the bucket.

Insert the auger into the clean-out opening, first up the branch of the trap toward the sink and then up the other branch toward the drainpipe. If you don't hit an obstruction in the trap, work the auger as far as you can into the drainpipe; in most cases you'll be able to clear the pipe. Pull the auger wire back and remove the auger; coat the threads of the clean-out plug with petroleum jelly and replace the plug. Flush the trap and drainpipe with very hot, soapy water.

If the sink trap doesn't have a clean-out plug, remove the entire trap. Set a bucket under the trap. Holding the trap with one hand, unscrew the slip nuts at the ends of the trap section, using pliers

or an adjustable wrench. Slide the nuts out of the way on the connecting pipes and carefully lift the trap out; empty it into the bucket. Check the trap for obstructions and clear it, if necessary, with the auger; then scrub it clean with hot soapy water and a small stiff bottle brush.

If the obstruction isn't in the trap, insert the auger into the drainpipe and work it into the pipe as far as you can. If you hit an obstruction, feed and twist the auger to break it up and then pull the auger wire in; remove the auger from the drainpipe.

Finally, replace the trap. Coat the threads of the trap and the pipes with petroleum jelly and reposition the trap, being careful to replace washers and slip nuts exactly as they were before. Tighten the slip nuts that hold the trap in place. If the obstruction was in the drainpipe, flush the pipe with very hot soapy water.

If you can't eliminate a sink clog at the trap, the obstruction may be in the main drainpipe, and may even be outside the house. Call a plumber to eliminate the clog.

Troubleshoot a Toilet Tank

If the water in your toilet runs constantly or you have to jiggle the handle every time it's flushed to keep it from running, it's time to work on the tank. **Tools:** utility knife, screwdriver. **Materials:** steel wool or emery paper, replacement tank ball, replacement split and bottom washers for ballcock assembly. **Time:** ½ to 1 hour.

Before you can fix it, you have to know how the toilet works. Take off the tank lid and set it out of the way. Look into the open tank and flush the toilet. A float ball, resting on a rod on top of the water in the tank, will sink as the water runs out; a tank ball on the bottom of the tank, shaped something like the cup of a plunger, will be raised while the water

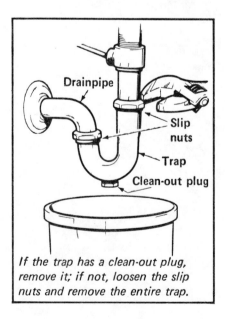

Drainpipe

Slip nuts

Trap

Clean-out plug

If the trap has a clean-out plug, remove it; if not, loosen the slip nuts and remove the entire trap.

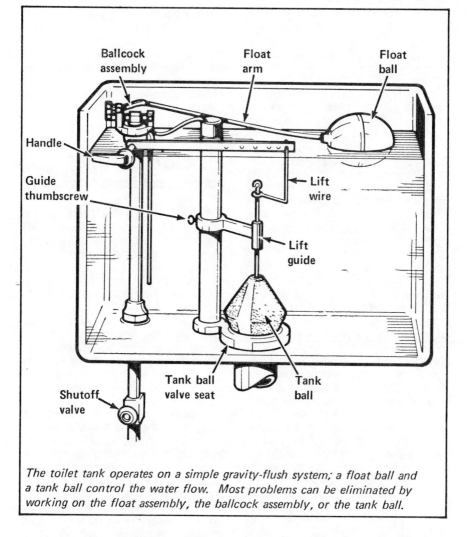

The toilet tank operates on a simple gravity-flush system; a float ball and a tank ball control the water flow. Most problems can be eliminated by working on the float assembly, the ballcock assembly, or the tank ball.

runs out and then it will drop back into place. Chances are one of these two balls is causing excess water flow.

Lift the float arm that holds the float ball. If the water stops running, the problem is in the float arm. Remove the float ball from the arm by twisting it counterclockwise; shake out any water that has collected in the ball and replace it on the float arm. If there was no water in the ball, bend the float arm down slightly, angling it into the tank, to lower the shutoff position of the ball. Bend the arm very gently, and be careful not to disturb its connection with the ballcock assembly at the other end. Replace the tank lid.

If the water still runs when you lift the float ball, the problem is probably in the tank ball at the bottom of the tank. Shut off the water supply to the toilet by turning the shutoff valve, usually under the tank, firmly clockwise. Flush the toilet to empty the tank. Unscrew the tank ball from the connecting arm, turning counterclockwise. If the ball is worn or damaged, replace it with a new one of the same type. Inspect the lip of the opening the tank ball fits into; if there are mineral deposits on it, remove them with steel wool or emery cloth, or scrape them off with a utility knife. Make sure the tank ball is firmly and properly positioned; then replace the tank lid and turn the water on.

If the water won't shut off until you jiggle the handle, the problem is probably in the guide that directs the tank ball into the valve seat below it. Turn off the water supply and flush the toilet. Holding the guide, loosen the thumbscrew that keeps it in position. Rotate the guide around the tank ball's lift wire until the ball is exactly centered over the valve seat; test its position by dropping the ball manually through the guide until it falls directly onto the valve seat. Tighten the thumbscrew, replace the tank lid, and turn the water on.

If you've bent the lift arm, replaced the tank ball, and adjusted the guide, and the toilet still runs, the problem is in the ballcock assembly. Turn off the water at the shutoff and flush the toilet. Examine the valve plunger in the ballcock assembly; it's usually held in place by two thumbscrews or two pins. Loosen the thumbscrews or disconnect the pins. Lift the valve plunger and locate the two washers on it: a split washer around a groove near the bottom and a flat washer attached to the bottom of the plunger with a screw. Remove the split washer by prying it out with a screwdriver; remove the bottom

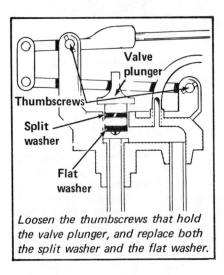

Loosen the thumbscrews that hold the valve plunger, and replace both the split washer and the flat washer.

washer by removing the screw that holds it in place. Replace both washers with identical ones; take the old ones to the hardware store and buy exact replacements. Install the washers and replace the valve plunger, tightening the two thumbscrews or reinserting the two pins. Replace the tank lid and turn the water on.

Unclog a Toilet

Few things are worse than a clogged toilet, but unclogging it usually isn't hard. In most cases you need the plumbers' friend, not the plumber. **Tools:** rubber gloves, bucket, tapered-lip toilet plunger, wire hanger, closet auger. **Materials:** none. **Time:** about 15 minutes to 1 hour.

To clear the toilet, use a tapered-lip toilet plunger. There must be just enough water in the bowl to cover the head of the plunger. If the toilet is empty, add water from a bucket; if the bowl is full, dip out excess water, wearing rubber gloves.

Wearing rubber gloves, set the plunger into place in the toilet, with its tapered lip in the outflow opening. Pump the plunger quickly up and down 10 or 12 times, pushing firmly to build up a strong pressure, then jerk it quickly out of the drain opening. If the clog has been pulled back into the bowl, the water will drain out of the bowl. Break up any obstructing material with a straightened-out wire hanger.

Test the toilet by pouring in water from a bucket; don't flush the toilet until you're sure it's draining properly. If it still doesn't drain, repeat the plunging procedure; plunge at least twice more before resorting to more drastic means.

If repeated plunging doesn't unclog the toilet, use a closet auger to remove the obstruction. Wearing rubber gloves, dip out excess water from the bowl. Insert the wire tip of the auger into the toilet outflow opening, being careful not to nick the ceramic with the auger's metal casing. Crank the auger handle

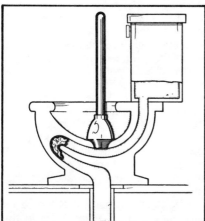

Set the tapered lip of the plunger into the outflow opening; pump firmly up and down to dislodge the clog.

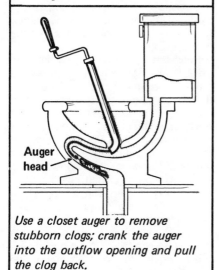

Auger head

Use a closet auger to remove stubborn clogs; crank the auger into the outflow opening and pull the clog back.

steadily clockwise to feed it into the outflow opening.

When you hit an obstruction, the auger wire has reached the clog. Crank the auger handle slowly to force the wire into the obstruction; every few turns, reverse and crank the auger counterclockwise a turn or so. When you've worked completely through the clog, crank the auger slowly in to pull the obstruction back into the toilet bowl; reverse and crank forward every few

turns so that the auger wire maintains its grip on the obstruction. Pull the auger out of the toilet outflow and remove the obstructing material; dispose of it immediately.

Test the toilet by pouring in water from a bucket; don't flush the toilet until you're sure the clog has been removed. If the toilet still doesn't drain completely, use the auger again to remove any remaining obstruction. Repeat several times, if necessary.

If repeated augering doesn't unclog the toilet, it will have to be removed from the floor. In this case, call a plumber.

Rod a Clogged Sewer Pipe

The plumbing waste system of a house is connected to the sewer or septic system by a large sewer pipe under the house. When the main house drain clogs, water from the sewer pipe backs up into the house. Eliminate the problem by removing the clog. **Tools:** bucket, pipe wrench, small sledgehammer, cold chisel, drain-and-trap auger, 50-foot garden hose with nozzle, rented power rooter. **Materials:** newspaper, rags. **Time:** about 1 to 2 hours.

The main drain is usually connected to the sewer pipe by a large black cast-iron pipe with a Y-shaped fitting, capped with a round clean-out plug. Look for this Y junction in the basement or crawl space, near the bottom of the soil stack or where the main drain leaves the house. The connection is at a low point because the drainage system works on gravity, not pressure.

Set a bucket under the clean-out plug. Spread a thick layer of newspaper on the floor, and have plenty of rags ready to sop up any water that pours out of the pipe.

With a pipe wrench, slowly unscrew the clean-out plug, turning it counterclockwise. If the plug is rusted tight, tap the edge of the plug *lightly* with a

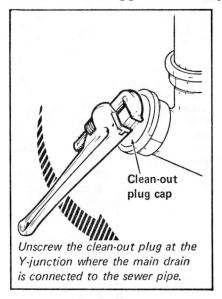

Unscrew the clean-out plug at the Y-junction where the main drain is connected to the sewer pipe.

small sledgehammer; then try the wrench again. If this doesn't work, carefully break away the rust with a cold chisel inserted in the joint between the bottom of the cap and the top of the pipe. Run the chisel around the cap, tapping the chisel lightly with the sledgehammer; do *not* hit it hard. If you can't unscrew the clean-out plug, don't try to force it; you could break off the square iron nipple that tightens the cap. Call a plumber to clear the pipe.

If a lot of debris comes out past the plug threads as you unscrew the clean-out, the blockage may not be in

With the water on full force, push a garden hose slowly into the sewer pipe to break up the clog.

the sewer pipe, but above it. Retighten the plug; then go back along the drain-pipe from the Y connection to the first clean-out plug you find. Set a bucket under the plug and spread newspaper under it; loosen the plug with a pipe wrench. If no debris comes out after the plug is unscrewed, the blockage is between this plug and the Y connection. To clear the drain at this point, use a drain-and-trap auger to break up the obstruction. If there's lots of debris at this point, move back along the line to the next clean-out plug and rod from there.

If no debris comes out of the sewer pipe clean-out, the trouble is in the sewer pipe. With a bucket under the plug and newspaper on the floor, remove the clean-out plug at the Y junction. Hook up a garden hose and turn the nozzle on the hose to its full-stream position. Insert the nozzle of the garden hose into the sewer pipe and turn on the water full pressure.

Push the hose slowly down into the sewer pipe, pushing and pulling it farther in as the water from the hose flushes away the debris in the pipe. If the water continues to back up, turn off the hose and remove it. If the stream of water doesn't back up, keep working the hose into the pipe; thread the entire length of the hose into the pipe before you stop working. Then pull the hose out, wiping it clean with a rag as you pull. Replace the clean-out plug and tighten it securely.

To make sure the drainage system is clear, flush the toilets in the house several times and turn on the water at one or more sink faucets. Let the water run to fill the sewer pipe with water; if the pipe is cleared, the water will flow freely out into the main sewer.

If you can't clear the sewer pipe with the garden hose, the line may be blocked by tree roots and debris; in this case, rent an electric rooter to clear the pipe. The rooter, an electric auger, has a cutting head with sharp, flexible blades to cut out obstructing roots and debris. Get operating instructions from the rental agent.

Insert the head of the rooter into the

clean-out plug at the Y junction or the clean-out plug closest to the blockage. Plug the rooter in and turn it on, following the rental agent's instructions. Feed the rooter cable slowly into the blocked sewer line; you should be able to feel it strain when the cutting head reaches the blockage. Work the rooter slowly through the blockage, pull it back, and work it through the cleared pipe again. Slowly pull the rooter out, wiping it clean as you pull.

Flush the cleared pipe with the garden hose, as above, and replace the clean-out plug. Flush the toilets and turn on the faucets to test the pipe; repeat the power rooting if necessary.

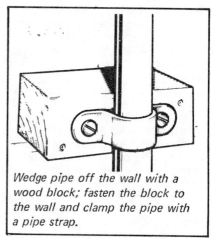

Wedge pipe off the wall with a wood block; fasten the block to the wall and clamp the pipe with a pipe strap.

Silence Noisy Water Pipes

Banging water pipes can be a major annoyance. Sometimes they can't be stopped without a major overhaul, but usually the problem is easily remedied. **Tools:** drill, hammer, screwdriver. **Materials:** rubber padding (garden hose, foam rubber, or sponge), sturdy wire, scrap wood block, long masonry nails, pipe strap and installation screws, pipe insulating tape. **Time:** about ½ to 1 hour.

If you hear a banging or knocking sound when you turn on a water faucet, most likely a pipe is striking something. Turn on the water and try to track down the source of the noise. If the pipe is exposed, check to see if it can move within its fasteners, such as a U-clamp or a pipe strap. If it's loose, wedge a piece of rubber padding between the pipe and the strap—a piece of old garden hose, foam rubber, or sponge—to stop the movement and the noise. If the pipe is behind a wall and can't be easily reached, pad the points where the pipe enters and leaves the wall. If two parallel pipes are striking against each other, wedge a piece of rubber padding between them and secure it with sturdy wire.

Sometimes a length of rigid pipe along a masonry wall vibrates and strikes the wall. To prevent this, wedge a block of scrap wood behind the pipe about midway along its length. Drill two pilot holes into the block on each side of the pipe and drive long masonry nails through the block and into the wall. Finally, fasten the pipe to the block with a pipe strap, screwing the strap firmly into the wood. *Caution: If you fasten a pipe with a strap, don't restrict it so that the pipe is prevented from expanding or contracting naturally with temperature changes.*

If you hear a knocking sound only when you turn off a hot water faucet, your water heater may be set too high. Turn down the temperature setting to see if that stops the noise.

Banging or knocking can also be caused by pipes that are too small in diameter, either because the original plumbing was badly done or because mineral deposits and scale have accumulated inside the pipes. To stop this kind of racket, new pipes are needed—an expensive solution. As a less satisfactory but cheaper alternative, wrap the pipes with pipe insulating tape to reduce the noise.

If a pipe bangs when you turn off a water faucet quickly, the problem may be water hammer, caused by fast-moving water coming to a sudden stop when there's nothing to cushion the flow. Air chambers or shock absorbers in the plumbing system usually prevent water hammer. If your system has such devices, the chambers may be waterlogged; you'll have to refill them with air.

The air chamber is a capped length of pipe above the faucet. Turn off the water to the pipe and open the faucet on the pipe to let the water drain out. When all of the water has drained out of the pipe, the chamber will be refilled with air. Turn off the faucet and turn the water supply back on.

If your plumbing system doesn't have air chambers, you'll need a plumber to eliminate water hammer. Have air chambers or shock absorbers installed, or reduce pressure to the pipe by having a pressure-reducing valve installed where the water supply line enters the building.

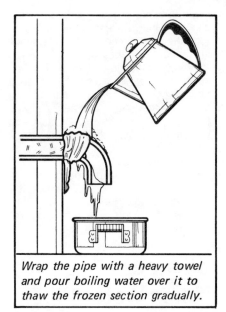

Wrap the pipe with a heavy towel and pour boiling water over it to thaw the frozen section gradually.

Thaw Frozen Pipes

Frozen pipes are a great inconvenience; worse, they can cause serious damage if they burst. If you're confronted with a frozen pipe, take immediate steps to thaw it. **Tools:** bucket, teakettle or coffeepot, and oven mitt; or propane torch with flame-spreader nozzle; or heating pad, hair dryer, or heat lamp and extension cord. **Materials:** heavy towel, sturdy cord, and boiling water, or aluminum foil. **Time:** ½ hour to several hours, depending on extent of blockage.

Before you work on a frozen pipe, open the faucet closest to the frozen section so the steam and meltwater produced during the thawing process can escape. Start thawing the pipe at the faucet and work your way back along the blockage; if you start at the blockage and work out, the pipe may burst.

The classic method of thawing a frozen pipe is to pour hot water over it. Wrap a heavy towel around the frozen

section of pipe and tie it in place with sturdy cord; the towel will hold the heat against the pipe. Set a bucket under the wrapped section. Heat water to boiling in a teakettle or coffeepot. Wearing an oven mitt to protect your hand, pour the hot water over the wrapped pipe. *Caution: Pour carefully so you don't scald*

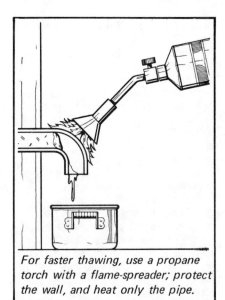

For faster thawing, use a propane torch with a flame-spreader; protect the wall, and heat only the pipe.

yourself. Repeat, emptying the bucket as necessary, until the frozen section of pipe is completely thawed and running freely. Turn the faucet off.

A risky but much faster heat source is a propane torch with a flame-spreader nozzle. Use a torch when the frozen pipe runs along a masonry wall, or there's a few inches clearance between the pipe and the wall. Move the torch back and forth along the pipe, keeping the flame concentrated only on the pipe; unless the wall is masonry, hold a double sheet of aluminum foil, shiny side out, between the pipe and the wall as you work. Heat the pipe until it's completely thawed and running freely; then turn the faucet off.

Caution: *Never leave the flame of the torch in one spot very long; keep it moving along the pipe. If you let the water in the pipe come to a boil, it may explode. If the pipe has soldered joints, be careful not to melt the joints; go over them very lightly. Use aluminum foil to protect the wall.*

Alternative heat sources for thawing frozen pipes are a heating pad, a hair dryer, or a heat lamp. Open the faucet and apply heat to the frozen pipe as above, working from the faucet back toward the frozen section. Be careful not to overheat the pipe; don't leave any heat source unattended. Heat the pipe until it's completely thawed and running freely; then turn the faucet off.

Install a Shutoff Valve

A plumbing fixture that doesn't have shutoff valves is inconvenient when you have to change a washer, and it can be a real pain when you have to cope with an emergency. Install the shutoffs yourself—the procedure is similar for any fixture. **Tools:** basin wrench, fine-toothed hacksaw, two pipe wrenches, adjustable wrench. **Materials:** *Fittings depend on the type of pipes in the system. For a lavatory with galvanized*

steel pipes—plumbers' thread-sealing tape or pipe joint compound, two angled shutoff valves, two lengths of flexible copper tubing with bayonet-head and compression-ring connectors. **Time:** about 1 hour.

To install shutoff valves for a lavatory with galvanized steel pipes, turn off the water at the main water shutoff for the house. The water supply pipe at each faucet is connected under the faucet with a coupling nut; loosen these coupling nuts with a basin wrench. Try to free the tops of the tailpieces—the sections of pipe just below the faucets—by carefully pulling them downward and to one side. If this doesn't work, cut a small section out of each pipe with a fine-toothed hacksaw, just above the elbow fitting fastened to the pipes that come out of the wall. After cutting, remove the pipe sections above the cuts.

The pipes that come out of the wall are called stub-outs. Grip the elbow fitting at the end of one stub-out with a pipe wrench and grip the stub-out itself with another pipe wrench to keep it from turning. Then unscrew the fitting from the stub-out. Repeat the procedure to unscrew the fitting from the other stub-out.

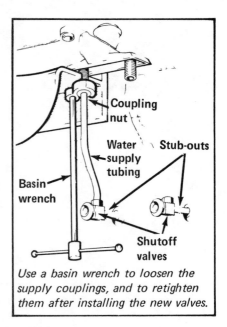

Use a basin wrench to loosen the supply couplings, and to retighten them after installing the new valves.

PLUMBING / Shutoff Valves

When the stub-outs are free, apply pipe joint compound to the threads of each stub-out with the brush provided by the manufacturer, or wrap plumbers' thread-sealing tape over the threads; cover the threads completely. Then screw an angled shutoff valve onto one of the stub-outs. Gripping the stub-out with a pipe wrench to keep it from turning, tighten the valve on the stub-out with an adjustable wrench. Repeat the procedure to connect the other valve to the other stub-out.

Use flexible tubing of suitable length, with a bayonet-head connector on one end and a compression-ring connector on the other, to connect the valves to the faucets. To install each piece of tubing, connect the end of the tubing with the compression ring to the shutoff valve, tightening it with an adjustable wrench. Connect the other end—the end with the bayonet head—to the faucet stem, tightening it with the basin wrench. Repeat the procedure for the other faucet.

Turn the water on at the main shutoff to restore the water supply. Finally, turn

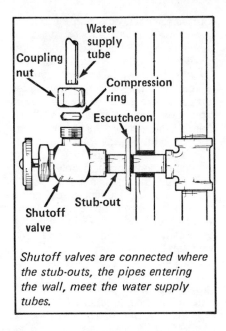

Shutoff valves are connected where the stub-outs, the pipes entering the wall, meet the water supply tubes.

both lavatory faucets on full force. Check all connections for leaks, and tighten them if necessary.

Finishing Touches

Make Decorator Shades

For a quick, clean designer look, re-place draperies with these instant-excitement shades, in any fabric you choose. Buy new shades or use the old rollers. **Tools:** tape measure, sharp scissors, large work surface, blanket and sheets, steam iron and press cloth, straight pins, pencil, yardstick, carpenters' square or triangle, sewing machine, needle, staple gun. **Materials:** shade laminating cloth, fabric, fusible web and contrasting fabric if desired, shade roller, thread, wood slat, pull cord or ring, heavy-duty staples, fringe or other trim if desired. **Time:** about 2 hours.

If you're using the old shade roller, take the shade down, and carefully re-move the slat from the shade and the shade from the roller. Make sure the roller works properly. If you're buying a new shade roller for the window, mea-sure the window exactly and buy a roller cut to fit. Buy a wood slat 1 inch shorter than the roller, and a shade ring or pull cord.

For the shade itself, buy a piece of shade laminating cloth—available where window shades are sold and at some fabric stores—at least 2 inches wider than the shade roller and 15 inches longer than the window. Use any fabric you like, cut to exactly the same size, to cover the laminating cloth; very heavy fabrics don't work well because they interfere with the operation of the shade. If you're using a plain fabric, you can also add appliqué figures or a fringe or other trim.

Choose a flat work space large enough to accommodate the entire size of the shade laminating cloth. Spread a heavy folded blanket over it and cover the blanket with a folded sheet, to pro-tect the surface; you'll use this prepared area as an ironing board. If the fabric is wrinkled, press it as necessary. Cut it to the exact size of the laminating cloth, or a little larger—make sure you place the pattern with the length of the cloth, so the design will fall properly on the finished shade.

If you're using a plain fabric and you want to add appliqués to the shade, back the desired appliqué fabric with fusible web and pin the layers together. Cut out the shapes you want, being careful to match the fabric and the fusi-

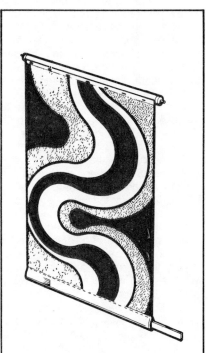

After laminating and trimming the shade, hem it and staple it to the roller; slide a slat into the hem.

233

ble web exactly; then remove the pins. Place the cutouts over the fusible web pieces on the fabric, as desired; baste them in place with the tip of a hot iron. Cover each cutout with a damp press cloth and fuse it in place with steam, following the manufacturer's instructions. Let the fabric cool completely.

Lay the laminating cloth on the prepared surface, adhesive side up. Spread the fabric on top of it, right side up, with the raw edges of the fabric and the laminating cloth lined up. With a hot iron, baste the two layers together by touching the tip of the iron to them at several places. Recheck the alignment of the layers, and adjust the fabric as necessary. Then, following any instructions provided with the laminating cloth, fuse the layers together with a steam iron, starting at the middle and working out to the edges. Smooth wrinkles and air bubbles out to the edges so that the layers are evenly and completely bonded. Make sure fusing is complete over the entire shade. Let the shade dry on your work surface until it's thoroughly cool and dry.

When the laminated shade is completely dry, measure the shade roller. On the shade, mark a trimming line on each side so that the shade width is ½ inch less than roller width. Use a yardstick to extend the marks the length of the shade, making sure the lines are perfectly straight and the width is maintained; check them with a carpenters' square or a triangle. Cut off the marked edges with a sharp scissors. Check the straightness of the top and bottom edges, and trim them if necessary so that they're exactly square.

Turn the bottom of the shade under 1½ inches, crease the laminated fabric to hold the hem, and stitch it across with a sewing machine. Insert a wood slat into the hem, 1 inch shorter than the roller. Close the ends of the hem with hand stitches. Attach the pull cord or ring to the center of the hem.

Fasten the top of the shade to the roller with a staple gun and heavy-duty staples. Make sure the roller is at a true right angle to the sides of the shade, or the shade won't roll up properly. If de-

sired, add a fringe or other trim over the slat. Roll the shade carefully and hang it up.

Revamp an Ugly Radiator

In buildings with steam heat, radiators are standard fixtures, and they're usually ugly. Fortunately, the cure is simple: paint. **Tools:** bucket and sponge, medium and small paintbrushes, wire brush, radiator brush, whisk broom, dustpan, vacuum cleaner. **Materials:** plastic dropcloth, strong household detergent, oil-base interior gloss or semigloss enamel, mineral spirits, rags, masking tape, cloth mending tape. **Time:** about 2 to 3 hours per radiator.

Sometimes radiators are disguised with perforated metal covers, massive boxes with solid tray tops. If they're in good shape, these covers can be easily painted with oil-base interior enamel—use semigloss to match the wall paint, semigloss or gloss for accent colors.

Turn off the radiator at the shutoff knob on the side, and spread a plastic dropcloth to protect the floor. Wash the radiator cover with a strong household detergent; rinse thoroughly and wipe with a clean rag. Let dry completely. Paint the cover carefully with a medium-size brush, stroking the paint evenly in one direction to avoid brush marks. If the air vent or steam valve is visible outside the cover, do *not* paint it. Leave the radiator turned off.

Let the cover dry completely, as recommended by the manufacturer, and apply a second coat of paint, brushing it on carefully to cover thin spots and lap marks. Let dry thoroughly before turning the radiator on. Clean up with mineral spirits and rags.

If there is no radiator cover, or if you don't like the cover, paint the radiator itself. Remove the cover, if any, by lifting it up and over the radiator. Turn the

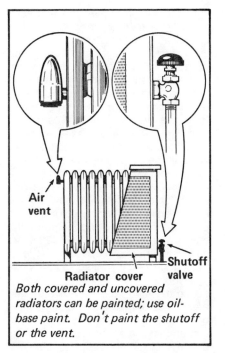

Radiator cover

Air vent

Shutoff valve

Both covered and uncovered radiators can be painted; use oil-base paint. Don't paint the shutoff or the vent.

Apply oil-base interior enamel to the radiator coils carefully, brushing evenly up and down along the coils. Use a small brush to reach tight spots. If you're painting the coils different colors, use masking tape to make a clean edge for each color, and work on one color at a time.

Let the paint dry as recommended by the manufacturer and apply a second coat of paint, brushing it on carefully to cover flaws in the first coat. Let dry thoroughly before turning the radiator on. Clean up with mineral spirits and rags.

If radiator pipes are exposed, paint them when you paint the radiator, using wall-color paint to make them less obvious or accent colors to match the radiator. If the pipes are covered with insulation, don't remove the insulation. Wrap the pipes firmly with cloth—not plastic—mending tape, in a color to blend or contrast with the walls.

radiator off and let it cool completely before you start to work on it.

Spread a plastic dropcloth to protect the floor. Remove loose or scaling paint from the radiator with a wire brush, scouring firmly to produce as even a surface as possible on all surfaces you can get at. Be careful not to hit the air vent, if the radiator has one. Brush the radiator coils periodically with a soft radiator brush to remove scaled-off paint chips, and wire-brush until no further debris is removed. Sweep up the debris and then vacuum the radiator and the area around it thoroughly, using the brush attachment to remove as much dust as possible.

Paint the radiator any color you like, from wall color to intense bright. Black paint is ideal for heat distribution. If you like, paint each coil of the radiator a different color, in shades of one color or in a spectrum. Semigloss enamel will tend to hide surface chips and flaws; gloss enamel will make chips more noticeable. Don't use aluminum paint or latex paint, and don't paint the air vent or steam valve.

Decorate a Floor with Paint

Even the ugliest of wood floors, if it's reasonably level, can be redeemed with paint. The effort involved is minimal, the results surprisingly good. **Tools:** measuring rule, screwdriver, bucket and sponge, scrub brush, putty knife, hammer, nail set, sanding block, rented floor polisher with steel wool pads, vacuum cleaner, soft pencil, chalk line, single-edge razor blades, paintbrushes for colors (size and number depend on design of floor), large paintbrushes for varnish. **Materials:** graph paper, household cleaner, clean rags, fine-grit sandpaper, plastic wood, grade 000 steel wool, tack cloths, light cardboard, masking tape, oil-base interior gloss or semigloss enamel, polyurethane varnish. **Time:** varies with design of floor; for a simple pattern, about 1 week, including drying time.

Measure the room and plan your floor design carefully. Make a floor plan of the room on graph paper, indicating doors, windows, and all floor obstructions, and draw your floor design on it in color. The easiest floor to paint is a plain one, all one color, but the possibilities are endless; stripes (in rainbow or earth colors), checkerboard or crossword patterns, borders on a plain ground, painted-on fool-the-eye rugs or tile patterns, supergraphics, art nouveau borders, or anything else you can think of. The only limitation is how much time you want to spend.

Buy paint after you decide on a pattern, and buy only as much as you'll need; use oil-base interior gloss or semigloss enamel. If you need special brushes, buy them when you buy the paint. Buy enough polyurethane varnish, preferably in a gloss finish, to give the floor three coats; read the label to figure coverage.

Before you paint, remove the furniture and prepare the floor. Remove any floor registers. Wash the floor thoroughly with a strong solution of household cleaner, using a scrub brush if necessary to remove all old wax. Scrape off any paint or putty spots with a putty knife as you wash the floor. Rinse the floor carefully to remove all traces of soap; wipe with a clean rag and let dry completely.

Examine the floor and correct any irregularities. Use a nail set to drive protruding nailheads into the floor; sand any rough spots with fine-grit sandpaper. Fill cracks and nail holes with plastic wood, smoothing it in with the putty knife, and let the patches dry thoroughly. Finally, to make sure the new paint will adhere to the old finish, go over the floor with a rented floor polisher loaded with steel wool pads. Scour the edges of the floor lightly by hand with grade 000 steel wool.

Vacuum the floor thoroughly to remove dust and bits of steel wool; close doors and windows to keep dust out. Wipe the floor down with a tack cloth for a final cleaning.

Transfer your design carefully to the prepared floor, using a soft pencil to mark light outlines. Wear clean, soft socks so you don't mar the floor. Measure carefully from the walls and snap chalk lines to mark long edges. For complicated patterns, mark a grid on the floor to correspond to your graph paper diagram. Transfer the pattern from the graph paper diagram to the floor, square by square; correct mistakes freehand. For simple repeat patterns, cut stencils from light cardboard with single-edge razor blades and trace the stencil design lightly onto the floor.

Paint one color at a time or one area of the room at a time, depending on the complexity of your pattern. Use one brush for each color. If the floor will have a solid background color under a pattern or border stripes, paint the background color first and let it dry completely before proceeding, at least 24 hours. Wear clean, soft socks while you work.

Use masking tape to separate large areas of color and to define stripes and borders. In general, paint large areas first and let them dry; then paint small patterns and detailed edgings. Let each color dry before applying another color

Before painting stripes or borders, define the edges with masking tape. Paint large areas first, then details.

directly next to it. When the entire design has been painted on the floor, let the floor dry for 24 hours; leave the door closed to keep dust out.

Seal the newly painted floor with polyurethane varnish. Wearing clean, soft socks, go over the floor lightly with a clean tack cloth. Apply varnish along the grain of the floorboards, brushing it on slowly to prevent air bubbles. Let the varnish dry for 12 hours and apply another coat, again brushing slowly along the grain of the floorboards to prevent air bubbles; let dry 12 hours. Apply a third coat of varnish and let dry at least 24 hours. Replace floor registers.

Let the floor dry for 2 or 3 days before moving furniture into the room; polyurethane hardens with time.

Paint a Supergraphic or Mural

Transform a plain room with a strong supergraphic; create your own indoor view with a full-wall mural. Either is easy to do with this simple grid system. **Tools:** pencil, measuring rule or tape measure, bucket and sponge, straightedge, paintbrushes. **Materials:** graph paper, household detergent, string, metal washers or small weights, masking tape, latex enamel paints. **Time:** 1 to 2 days or more, plus drying time.

Choose any design you like for your graphic or mural—arrows, arches, a rainbow, animals, trees, whatever. Draw the design accurately on a sheet of graph paper (four squares per inch is easiest to enlarge on a wall), or draw a grid (four squares per inch) directly onto the picture or print you want to duplicate.

Gauge the grid according to the size of the graphic or mural. For example, if your graph-paper design is 4 inches wide and 3 inches high, and you want it to be 8 feet wide on the wall, it will also be 6 feet high. The 4×3-inch pattern will have horizontal rows of 16 squares, and vertical rows of 12 squares. For 8 linear feet to contain 16 horizontal squares, each foot will have two squares, and each square must be 6 inches on a side. Determine the vertical measurement the same way. For both dimensions, the size of each square is determined by your graph-paper drawing and the size of the wall.

Before transferring your design to the wall, prepare the wall surface. Wash it thoroughly with a household detergent to remove dirt, dust, and grease. Let the wall dry completely.

Determine exactly where on the wall you want the mural to be. Starting at the upper left-hand corner, make the guidelines for the horizontal squares on the wall. Tape one end of a piece of string at the upper left-hand corner, letting it hang. Tie a metal washer or other weight to the bottom of the string. When the line hangs plumb, tape the bottom end of the string. Measure 6 inches to the right of the string, at top and bottom, and tape the second vertical string the same way. Repeat to place 17 strings, each 6 inches apart, forming 16 vertical divisions.

To complete the squares, measure an even distance down from the ceiling to the upper left and upper right vertical lines of the grid to determine the top of the mural. Stretch and tape a horizontal string between these two points; tape this string at several points to keep it from sagging.

Once the top horizontal string has been placed accurately, measure down 6 inches on both ends to position the next line. Repeat to place 13 horizontal strings, forming 12 rows of squares.

With all grid lines taped to the wall, transfer your design to the wall. Use a pencil to lightly copy your pattern—square by square—onto the wall. When the entire design has been transferred, carefully remove the tape and the strings; peel the tape off carefully so you don't damage the wall. Then final-draw the design, rounding curves evenly and adding any missing parts.

Paint the graphic or mural with latex

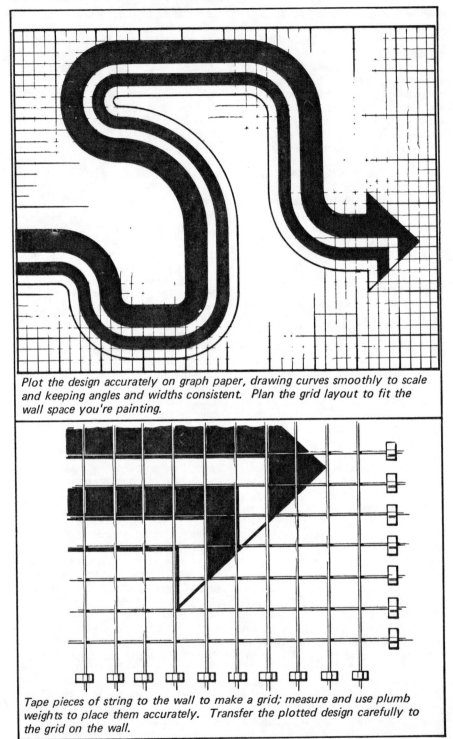

Plot the design accurately on graph paper, drawing curves smoothly to scale and keeping angles and widths consistent. Plan the grid layout to fit the wall space you're painting.

Tape pieces of string to the wall to make a grid; measure and use plumb weights to place them accurately. Transfer the plotted design carefully to the grid on the wall.

enamel paint, one color at a time. If the design has a background color, paint the background first. Let the paint dry for 24 hours before painting over the background color. Work color by color; wash your paintbrushes thoroughly between colors. Paint all solid areas first; then mix colors for highlighting or shading.

When the entire design is complete, let it dry thoroughly, for at least 24 hours. If desired, you can outline key areas in black; use a very fine brush to make hairline outlines. Be careful not to overdo this outlining.

Let the completed mural dry thoroughly before replacing furniture or drapes that touch it. Clean the wall surface very carefully, if necessary.

Make a Canvas Log Carrier

Hauling firewood is no chore with this easy-to-make log carrier. **Tools:** steam iron; sewing machine, hand stitcher, or heavy-duty needle and thimble; measuring tape, chalk or pencil, straight pins, sharp sewing scissors. **Materials:** 20-inch-long piece of 36-inch-wide canvas, with woven selvage edges; heavy-duty thread, two 18-inch pieces of ¾-inch wood dowel. **Time:** 1 to 2 hours.

Press the canvas with a steam iron to remove any wrinkles. Fold each long raw edge in ½ inch and press to crease it down; fold each edge in again ½ inch, to cover the raw edge, and press again. Stitch these hems firmly, using a sewing machine, a hand stitcher, or a heavy needle and a thimble; use heavy-duty thread. Backstitch or knot the thread at each hem end to keep the thread from pulling loose.

Spread the hemmed strip of canvas flat. On one narrow handle end, measure in 6 inches from each side; mark these points with chalk or a pencil. Draw a 6-inch-wide, 6-inch-deep U shape from marked point to marked

point, its open end on the outside end of the canvas.

Fold the strip of canvas together across its width, handle ends together and chalked U on the outside. Match the edges carefully and pin the two thicknesses of canvas together all along the handle end. With the handle edges pinned together, cut out the marked-off U shape through both thicknesses of canvas, being careful to keep the edges even. Unpin the edges and unfold the carrier.

Reinforce the raw edges of the U-shaped handle openings to keep them from raveling. If you're using a sewing machine, stitch all around the raw edge on each end of the carrier with a tight zigzag stitch, guiding the canvas so that the raw edge is bound in by the stitching. Backstitch at each end of each row.

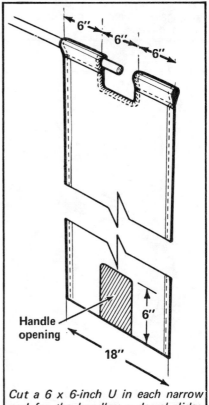

Cut a 6 x 6-inch U in each narrow end for the handles; a dowel slides through the hems for easy carrying.

Straight-stitch around the edge of the zigzag binding to outline and reinforce each handle opening; backstitch to reinforce the ends.

If you're using a hand stitcher or sewing the carrier by hand, overcast the raw edges tightly and evenly; make small, close stitches with heavy-duty thread over the cut edge and back through it. Overcast the entire raw edge of each cutout handle opening; stitch and knot the ends of the thread securely. Finally, stitch straight around the overcast binding to outline and reinforce each handle. Knot the ends of the thread securely.

When the raw handle edges have been securely bound, turn and sew the strips of canvas on each side of each U-shaped handle opening, forming the handle ends of the log carrier. Fold the canvas in ½ inch to the wrong side and press it firmly to crease it into place. Fold again, turning the ends in a full 1 inch, and press.

Stitch the turned-in ends firmly into place. If you're using a machine, stitch twice along each turned-in edge, and reinforce the seam with heavy backstitching at the ends of each seam. Each handle end of the carrier should be reinforced at four places—the two outside points where the handle meets the long edges of the carrier, and the two inside points where the legs of the cut-out U-shapes are folded under.

If you're using a hand stitcher or working by hand, stitch the turned-in ends as securely as you can; they'll have to support the weight of the logs carried. Stitch at least twice along each turned-in edge, and reinforce the four stress points on each handle end with heavy over-and-over tacking. Knot the thread securely.

To complete the log carrier, slide an 18-inch piece of ¾-inch-thick dowel through the reinforced handle tubes at each end of the carrier. If desired, stitch the outside ends of the canvas tubes together to hold the dowels permanently in place.

The carrier holds several large logs; the handle openings are bound and reinforced at stress points.

Make Decorator Pillows

A variety of pillows on sofa, chairs, floor, or bed makes a room both comfortable and relaxing, and pillows can also provide lively spots of color, texture, and pattern. It's easy to make your own. **Tools:** tape measure, tailors' chalk or pencil, scissors, straight pins, sewing machine, zipper foot, sewing needle, steam iron and ironing board. **Materials:** fabric, thread, pillow form, piping or cording, zipper; if desired, string and tassel. **Time:** 1 to 2 hours.

Pillow forms come in numerous sizes and shapes, and generally fall into two categories: tailored, with squared corners and boxy shapes, or casual—softer-looking, often made with softer materials. The easiest pillow covers to make are the casual type, for the square pillow form sometimes described as a knife-edge shape.

For the simplest knife-edge pillow, measure and mark two pieces of fabric to the size of the pillow form, plus a ⅝-inch seam allowance all around. Pin the two pieces together, right sides together, and straight-stitch all around the edge on a sewing machine; leave an opening large enough to insert the pillow form. Backstitch to reinforce the ends. Press the seams open, clip the corners, and turn the cover right side out. Insert the pillow form and hand-stitch the opening closed.

For a tailored look, add piping or covered cording around the edges of the pillow; buy ready-made piping or cording to match or contrast with the cover fabric.

Starting in the middle of one side, and working on the right side, pin the piping or cording all around the edges of the pillow top. Place the cording with its tape or seam allowance toward the edge of the fabric and the finished cording toward the center, with the stitching line ⅝ inch from the edge of the fabric. Clip into the seam allowance of the cording at the corners so it will lie flat.

Using a sewing machine with a zipper foot, stitch the cording into place along the stitching line, all around the pillow top. Be careful not to stretch it. Where the ends of the cording meet, open up the cording for about 1 inch. Trim the end of the cord to butt into the other end of the cord, where the piping starts; trim the fabric cover to overlap the other end of the cording about ½ inch. Fold the trimmed fabric edge under ¼ inch and fold the free end of the cording around the starting end, so that the cords butt together and the folded edge covers the joint. Stitch across both ends and about 1 inch beyond the joint; then backstitch to secure the piping.

To put the pillow together, pin the top and bottom pieces together, right sides together and cording in between. Using the zipper foot, stitch the two pieces together, following the line of stitching that holds the cording in place; leave an opening large enough to insert the pillow form. Backstitch to secure the ends of the seam. Remove the pins, press

the seams open, trim the corners, and turn the cover right side out; insert the pillow form and hand-stitch the opening closed.

To make a cover easier to remove for washing or cleaning, insert a zipper in one side seam. Use a zipper about 3 inches shorter than the side of the pillow—if the finished pillow will be 15 inches square, for example, use a 12-inch zipper. After attaching cording to the pillow top as above, mark a space on one edge of the pillow top, the length of the row of zipper teeth. Stitch the two ends of the seam, backstitching at the markings for added strength; leave the marked-off area open.

Set the sewing machine to the longest stitch length and machine-baste the open section of the seam where the zipper will go. Spread the two fabric pieces apart and press the seam open. On the wrong side, lay the closed zipper face down against the basted section of the seam, laying the zipper teeth slightly away from the side that's

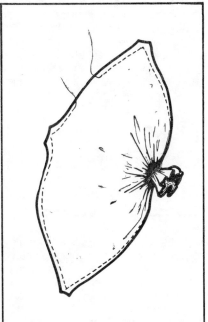

For a harem pillow, tie the corners inside the cover; turn it right side out and add corner tassels.

corded. Pin it into place.

Using the zipper foot, stitch across one end of the zipper tapes, along the tape on the side away from the cording —stay close enough to the teeth to catch the edge of the seam beneath the zipper—and across the other end of the tapes. Then fold the fabric on the side with the cording away from the zipper. Sew the other tape of the zipper to the seam allowance *only* of the pillow top and cording, stitching close to the teeth of the zipper. Remove the pins and the basting threads holding the seam closed. Place the cover pieces together, right sides together, and pin them. Stitch them together around the other three sides, as above. Press the seams open and trim the corners. Turn the pillow cover right side out, open the zipper, and insert the pillow form; zip the opening closed.

To make a harem pillow, make a knife-edge pillow without cording; use a zipper 5 inches shorter than the side of the pillow. On the inside of the cover, tie the corners firmly with string to form 2-inch ears; then turn the cover right side out and insert a soft pillow form. For extra plumpness, use a form a little large than the cover. If desired, attach tassels to the corners of the cover; sew the cord of a tassel into the seam at each corner before you tie the corners.

Make Café Curtains and Valances

These curtains and valances make a quick and easy redecorating project. **Tools:** tape measure, scissors, straight pins, sewing machine, steam iron and ironing board. **Materials:** café rods, single curtain rods, fabric, thread; if desired, café hooks or drapery pleater tape and hooks; if desired, scalloped or tabbed trim. **Time:** 2 to 3 hours per window.

Fabric. For each window, you'll need one café rod and one single curtain rod. Put the rods up before measuring for the curtains.

To determine the amount of fabric you'll need, measure the width of the café rod. Multiply by 2 or 3, depending on how full you want the curtains to be, and add 4 inches to allow for a double 1-inch hem on each side. If the fabric isn't wide enough to cover the window in one piece, you'll have to join equal lengths of fabric to make wide panels. The width of these seams depends on the pattern of the fabric; for plain fabric, add 1 inch seam allowance for each panel seam. Count the number of panels you'll need, and calculate the required length.

To determine the length of the material needed, measure the distance from the top of the café rod to the windowsill or apron, or to 1 inch from the floor— wherever you want the curtains to stop. Add 6 inches to this distance for a 3-inch double hem at the bottom of the curtain, and another 3 inches for the top hem. Multiply this total length by the number of panels you need and divide by 36; the total is the required yardage for the curtain.

For the valance across each window, use the same number of fabric panels required for the window. For a 12-inch valance, each panel must be 21 inches long—12 inches for the valance, 3 inches for the top hem, and 6 inches for a double 3-inch bottom hem. Multiply the number of panels you need by 21 inches and divide by 36; the total is the required yardage for the valance.

For the total yardage required, add the curtain and valance totals. If you're using a plain fabric, buy this amount of material. If you're using a print, you'll have to allow for extra fabric to match the pattern repeat—the larger the repeat, the more fabric you'll need. If you have trouble figuring yardage for a print, ask for help when you buy the fabric.

Assembly. Before cutting the curtains, square off the end of the fabric. Spread the fabric out on your work surface. Close to one end of the fabric, make a small cut into the selvage, and grasp one crosswise thread. Gently pull the thread to draw it right out of the fabric, across the entire fabric width. This will make a line across the fabric where the thread was; cut carefully along the line and discard the crooked end.

Clip the selvages of the fabric at 1-inch intervals to prevent puckering. Measure from the squared corner along the selvage edge to the required panel length, and carefully cut across the fabric. Repeat to cut each panel, adjusting for matching patterns as necessary.

If you have to join lengths of fabric to make a wide panel, place the two pieces of fabric together, right sides together and patterns matched. Pin one long side together. Straight-stitch the pinned edges together on a sewing machine, stitching ½ inch from the raw edge or as required to match the pattern properly; backstitch to reinforce each end. Remove the pins and press the seam open with a steam iron. Re-

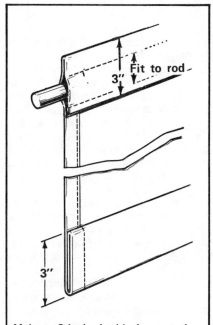

Make a 3-inch double hem at the bottom of the curtain. At the top, make a single 3-inch hem; stitch it across to make the rod pocket.

peat to add more panels, if necessary.

When the curtain is assembled to its full width, hem the sides. On each side, fold the fabric in 1 inch and press it flat; fold it in again 1 inch, press it, and pin it into place. Then machine-stitch it close to the inside edge; backstitch at each end of the hem. Remove the pins. Hem the bottom edge of the curtain the same way for a double 3-inch hem—turn the fabric up 3 inches, press, and turn it up again 3 inches; press, pin, and stitch close to the edge of the hem.

At the top of the curtain, fold the fabric down 3 inches and press it; then unfold it. Turn the raw edge under ¼ inch and press it; then fold the 3-inch hem down again and pin it into place. Stitch the hem close to the edge, backstitching to reinforce each end.

The curtain is hung by sliding the rod through a pocket in the top hem. To place the rod pocket, measure the depth of the café rod and add ½ inch. At one side hem, measure up this distance from the bottom of the top hem. At this point, pin across the curtain for a few inches, parallel to the hem. Slide the rod into the pocket formed by the pins; it should slide easily. If the pocket is too tight or too loose, move the pins down or up until you have a good fit. Then remove the rod. Stitch the pocket all across the top hem at the marked point, backstitching at both ends.

To make the valance, cut the required number of 21-inch-long panels. Join the panels side to side with a ½-inch seam at each join, the same way the curtain panels were joined. Hem the short ends with 1-inch double hems, as above; hem the bottom edge with a 3-inch double hem, and the top edge with a 3-inch single hem, as above. Stitch the rod pocket as above.

To hang the curtains and valance, slide the rods through the pockets in the top hems. Mount the rods and adjust the panels' fullness.

Variations. Once you've mastered the basics of making curtains, you can work for other effects. If you want the curtains to hang with café rings, finish the top edge of the curtains with a double 1-inch hem; sew or clip on café rings as desired. If you prefer pleated draperies, stitch drapery pleater tape across the top of each curtain; use pleater hooks to make even folds. For a special effect, add scalloped or tabbed trim across each top hem.

Make Daybed and Bolster Covers

A covered daybed serves many useful purposes as seating and as guest sleeping space, and is an economical approach to furnishing a first home or apartment. Make the cover with any fabric you like. **Tools:** tape measure, scissors, straight pins, sewing machine and zipper foot, tailors' chalk or pencil, straightedge, steam iron and ironing board, safety pin or bodkin. **Materials:** 44- or 45-inch fabric, ready-made piping or covered cording, thread, bolster form, plain cording. **Time:** about 2 to 4 hours.

Fabric. Since you may want to move the daybed from time to time, make a cover that conceals all four sides of the bed. Use 44- or 45-inch-wide fabric. You'll also need 6 yards of ready-made piping or covered cording, in a matching or contrasting color, and 2 yards of plain cording for the bolster. Buy a bolster form as long as the bed is wide.

To determine the amount of material you'll need, measure the length and width of the top of the daybed; add them together and multiply by 2. Add ½ yard (18 inches). Divide the total inches by 36 to obtain the yardage needed for the daybed. For the bolster cover, you'll need ¾ yard of 44- or 45-inch fabric for a bolster up to 36 inches long and not more than 8 inches in diameter. For a larger bolster, add more fabric; ask for help when you buy the material.

For example, for a daybed 76 inches long and 30 inches wide, the total yardage needed for the daybed cover is 230 inches, or 6⅜ yards—76 + 30 = 106; 106 × 2 = 212; 212 + 18 = 230 inches, or 6⅜ yards. Allowing ¾ yard for the bolster cover, the total yardage needed for both covers is 7⅛ yards of 44- or 45-inch fabric.

The daybed cover. To make the top of the cover, measure and cut a piece of material 1½ inches longer and 1½ inches wider than the top of the daybed. Starting at the middle of one short end, and working on the right side, pin matching or contrasting piping or covered cording all around the edges of the top piece. Place the piping with its tape or seam allowance toward the edge of the piece of fabric and the finished piping toward the center, with the stitching line ¾ inch from the edge of the fabric.

Using a sewing machine with a zipper foot, stitch the piping into place along the stitching line, all around the fabric. Be careful not to stretch the piping; ease it and clip the seam allowance so it will go around corners. At the other end of the piece of fabric, where the ends of the piping meet, open up the piping for about 1 inch. Trim the end of the cord to butt into the other end of the cord, where the piping starts; trim the fabric cover to overlap the other end of the piping about ½ inch. Fold the trimmed fabric edge under ¼ inch and fold the free end of the piping around the starting end, so that the cords butt together and the folded edge covers the joint. Pin the ends in place. Stitch across both ends and about 1 inch beyond the joint; then backstitch to hold the piping firmly.

To make the sides of the daybed cover, measure and cut a length of fabric equal to the length of the bed plus 3 inches. Divide it lengthwise into two strips, each one as wide as the distance from the floor to the top of the bed, plus 3 inches. Mark the line with tailors' chalk or a pencil and a straightedge, and carefully cut the pieces apart.

On one long side of each strip of material, turn the fabric under 1 inch and press it into place. Turn it under again 1 inch, press, and pin it in place. Turn it under again 1 inch, press, and

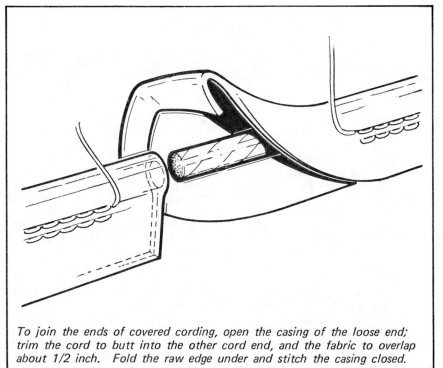

To join the ends of covered cording, open the casing of the loose end; trim the cord to butt into the other cord end, and the fabric to overlap about 1/2 inch. Fold the raw edge under and stitch the casing closed.

pin it in place. Machine-stitch the hem close to the folded-under edge; remove the pins as you stitch.

On both short sides of each strip, turn the fabric under ½ inch and press; turn it under again ½ inch, press, and pin. Machine-stitch each hem close to the folded-under edge; remove the pins as you stitch.

To assemble the cover, pin one long strip to one long side of the cover top, right sides together and raw edges matched, with the piping in between and the hemmed ends of the side panel matching the points where the piping tape turns the corners. Using the zipper foot, stitch the two pieces together, following the line of stitching that holds the piping in place. Backstitch at each end of the seam to hold it firmly in place. Repeat to attach the other side of the cover to the top.

To make the ends of the cover, measure and cut a length of fabric equal to the width of the daybed plus 3 inches. Cut it lengthwise into two strips, the same width as the long side panels were cut. Hem the bottoms and ends of the two end pieces the same way you hemmed the side pieces. Attach the end pieces to the ends of the daybed top the same way you attached the long sides; leave the corners open.

Finally, turn all the seam allowances toward the center of the cover and press them firmly with a steam iron. Topstitch around the top of the cover through all layers, ⅛ inch from the seams.

The bolster cover. The bolster cover is made from a single piece of material. Measure the length and the diameter of the bolster form; add them together and add 2 inches. This is the width the fabric should be cut. To find the proper length, measure the circumference of the bolster form and add 2 inches. For example, for a bolster form 30 inches long, 8 inches in diameter, and 25 inches around, a piece of material 40 × 27 inches is needed—30

+ 8 + 2 inches, and 25 + 2 inches.

Measure and cut the piece of fabric for the bolster. Fold the piece in half lengthwise, right sides together, and pin the edges together. Stitch the pinned edges together ¾ inch from the edge to form a tube. Press the seam open.

Make a 1-inch hem around each end of the tube, folding the edges under ½ inch and then ½ inch again. With sharp scissors, cut a few stitches in the seam on the inside of the hem. Cut a piece of plain cording 3 inches longer than the circumference of the bolster piece; tie one end of the cording to a safety pin or a bodkin. Insert the threaded cord into the opening in the hem, and push it completely through the hem and out again. Repeat at the other end of the tube. Turn the tube right side out.

Insert the bolster form into the tube. Draw the cords up tight and tie them. Tie a knot in the cord close to each end to prevent raveling. Tuck the extra cord inside the bolster cover so you'll be able to open the tied ends to remove the bolster when the cover needs washing or cleaning.

Make a Bedspread and Dust Ruffle

For the guest room, for the kids' room, or anywhere you want a special effect, a made-to-match bedspread and dust ruffle are a quick and easy answer. **Tools:** tape measure, pencil or fabric marker, scissors, straight pins, sewing machine, steam iron and ironing board. **Materials:** fabric, thread, old sheet or preshrunk muslin for top panel of dust ruffle; covered cording, woven trim, or fringe, as desired. **Time:** 1½ to 2½ hours for the bedspread, 2 to 3 hours for the dust ruffle.

Fabric. To make a bedspread for a twin bed, you'll need 5⅔ yards of fabric 36 to 45 inches wide; for a full-size spread, you'll need 5⅔ yards of 44- or 45-inch fabric. For a king-size spread,

buy 8⅞ yards of 44- or 45-inch-fabric, or 5⅞ yards of 54- to 60-inch-wide fabric. If the fabric is very light, you may want to add a lining. An old sheet is ideal for this; if you must buy material, buy inexpensive muslin. Preshrink it before you use it.

To make the dust ruffle, you'll need a panel of fabric the same size as the top of the box spring, plus ¾ inch all around —39 × 75¾ inches for a twin bed, 54 × 75¾ inches for a full-size bed, or 76 × 80¾ inches for a king-size bed. This panel will be concealed between the mattress and the box spring; use an old sheet, or use preshrunk inexpensive muslin. For the ruffle itself, you'll need 4⅛ yards of 44- or 45-inch fabric for a twin bed, 4⅔ yards for a full-size bed, or 5⅔ yards for a king-size bed.

The bedspread. This spread is designed to be tucked in at both sides and the foot, and folded over the pillows at the head. The finished size of a twin-size spread is 66 × 100 inches; of a full-size spread, 80 × 100 inches; of a king-size spread, 102 × 105 inches. Each spread is made up of a top panel and two side panels, varied in width to fit the width of the bed.

Before cutting out the pieces of the bedspread, square off the end of the fabric. Spread the fabric out on your work surface. Make a small cut into the selvage near one end, and grasp one crosswise thread. Pull this crosswise thread gently to draw it right out of the fabric, all across the width of the fabric. This will leave a line in the fabric where the thread was. Carefully cut along the pulled-thread line, and discard the crooked end.

To cut the pieces for the spread, measure down from the pulled-thread line across the fabric and mark the required length; cut each piece carefully, making sure you cut straight across the fabric. For a twin spread, cut the top piece 32 × 102 inches, and two side pieces each 18 × 102 inches. For a full-size spread, cut one piece 44 × 102 inches, and two pieces each 19 × 102 inches. For a king-size spread, cut one piece 44 × 110 inches and two pieces each 30 × 110 inches, if you have 44- or 45-inch wide fabric; for 54- to 60-inch-wide fabric, cut one piece 54 × 110 inches and two pieces each 27 × 110 inches.

When the panels are cut, assemble the spread. Place a narrow side panel over the center panel, right sides together and matched along one long edge. Pin the pieces together along the matched edge. On a sewing machine, straightstitch the pieces together along the pinned edge, ½ inch from the edge, backstitching to secure the ends. Remove the pins and press the seam open. Repeat, pinning and stitching, to attach the other side panel to the other side of the top panel.

When the spread is assembled, make a double ½-inch hem around all four sides; hem first the short sides and then the long ones. On each side of the spread, turn the raw edge under ½ inch and press it into place; turn it under again ½ inch and press again. Pin the hem into place and straight-stitch it near the inside edge, backstitching to secure the ends of the hem. Remove the pins.

Vary the bedspread as you like to suit the room and the fabric. To add decorative interest, insert covered cording in the seams, as for a daybed cover; or cover the seams with woven trim. To reinforce a very light fabric, add a lining cut from an old sheet or preshrunk muslin, in panels the same size as the spread panels. Lay out the spread and lining pieces together, wrong sides together, and treat them as one layer of fabric; assemble the spread as above.

If you prefer, make a coverlet instead of a tuck-in spread, to hang loosely over the dust ruffle. For a twin bed, cut the top piece 32 × 102 inches, and the two side pieces each 15 × 102 inches, for a finished size of 60 × 100 inches. For a full-size bed, cut the top piece 44 × 102 inches, and the two side pieces each 16 × 102 inches, for a finished size of 75 × 100 inches. For a king-size spread with a finished size of 97 × 105 inches, cut the top piece 44 × 110 inches and the two side pieces each 27 × 110 inches from 44- or 45-inch-wide fabric; or the top piece 54 × 110

inches and two side pieces each 24 × 110 inches from 54- to 60-inch-wide fabric. Make the spread exactly as above; if desired, round off the two bottom corners. Add fringe all around the edge, if you like.

The dust ruffle. The dust ruffle consists of a long strip and a panel over the box spring, as specified above. To make the panel, cut an old sheet to fit, or cut lengths of preshrunk muslin and seam them together to the proper width. Across one narrow end of the panel, turn the raw edge under ¾ inch and press it; turn it under again ¾ inch, press, and pin it into place. Stitch the hem along the inside edge, backstitching to secure the ends; then remove the pins.

Before cutting the ruffle, square the end of the fabric, if necessary, as above; draw out a thread and cut along the pulled-thread line. Then measure and cut the ruffle fabric into panels the width of the fabric and 16½ inches long, or the distance from the top of the box spring to the floor, plus 2½ inches — if this distance is more than 14 inches, you'll need wider panels, and more fabric. For a twin bed, you'll have nine panels 16½ inches long and 44 or 45 inches wide; for a full-size bed, ten panels; for a king-size bed, twelve panels.

To make the ruffle, sew the panels together end to end. Place two panels together, right sides together, and match the 16½-inch selvage edges on one end. Pin the matched edges and stitch them together ⅝ inch from the edge. Remove the pins.

Open the double panel and place another panel on top of one of the two attached panels, right sides together. Pin the 16½-inch edges together along the free end of the attached panel, and stitch them ⅝ inch from the edge, as above; remove the pins and unfold the panels. Continue this process, adding long panels accordion-style, until all the panels are stitched together end to end. Press all the seams open.

Make a double ¾-inch hem on each narrow end and on one long side of the strip. For each hem, turn the raw edge under ¾ inch and press it; turn it under ¾ inch again, press, pin, and stitch the hem. Remove the pins.

At the unhemmed top of the dust ruffle, gather the long edge of the strip. Loosen the upper thread tension on the sewing machine and lengthen the stitch length to make the thread easier to gather. With the ruffle right side up, make two parallel rows of stitching along the top edge, one row ⅝ inch from the edge and the other ¼ inch above it. Break the gathering threads and start again at each end-to-end seam along the ruffle; for each section, pull the bobbin thread with one hand and slide the fabric with the other to form and adjust the gathers.

When the ruffle is put together and gathered, measure the distance around two sides and one end of the box spring. Divide this number by the number of panels in the dust ruffle: 9 for a twin bed, 10 for a full-size bed, or 12 for a king-size bed. This figure is the distance between seams on the completed dust ruffle, gathered on the bed.

The assembled dust ruffle is attached to the plain sheet or muslin top panel on three sides; the hemmed end of the panel is left unattached, because the dust ruffle doesn't extend around the head of the bed. Starting at the hemmed end of one long side of the panel, make marks all around the panel's raw edges at the calculated seam interval. Pin the gathered ruffle to the three raw edges of the panel, right sides together, matching the seams in the ruffle to the marks on the panel. If the ruffle doesn't fit exactly, pull in or let out the gathering threads.

Reset the upper thread tension and the stitch length and stitch the ruffle to the top panel all along the pinned edges; work with the gathered fabric up so you can keep tucks and pleats from forming. Backstitch to secure the ends of the seam. Remove the pins. All along the dust ruffle, snip off the long ends of the gathering threads.

Press the seam away from the ruffle. To finish the dust ruffle, topstitch along

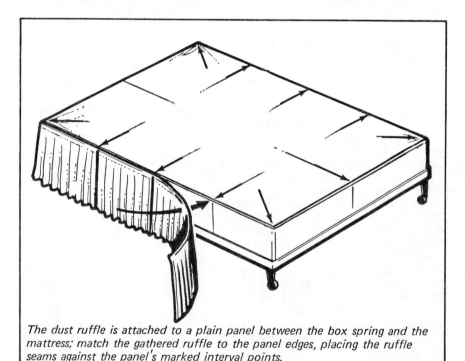

The dust ruffle is attached to a plain panel between the box spring and the mattress; match the gathered ruffle to the panel edges, placing the ruffle seams against the panel's marked interval points.

the seamed edges of the top panel, ⅛ inch from the seam, stitching through the pressed-up edges of the ruffle seam. The seam will be ⅝ inch in from the edge of the box spring, so it won't show. If you made a coverlet instead of a tuck-in spread, and added fringe to the edge of the coverlet, use fringe on the edge of the dust ruffle too.

To put the dust ruffle on the bed, slide the mattress off and position the panel on the bed, plain end at the head of the bed. Then replace the mattress and put the bedspread on.

Make Pillowcases from Worn Sheets

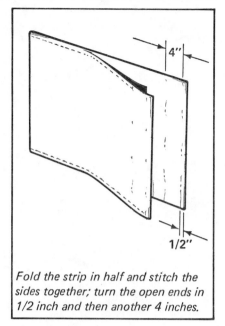

Fold the strip in half and stitch the sides together; turn the open ends in 1/2 inch and then another 4 inches.

Salvaged pillowcases can be a real moneysaver when you have a whole family's beds to provide for. **Tools:** scissors, steam iron and ironing board, tape measure, sewing machine, straight pins. **Materials:** old sheets of any size, flat or fitted; thread. **Time:** about 1 hour.

Look each sheet over carefully, holding it up to the light to see where the most worn spots are. Worn spots are usually in the center of the sheet; the sides may be in much better condition. Cut the corner seams of fitted sheets so they'll lie flat. If a sheet is badly wrinkled, press it with a steam iron.

To use a flat sheet in good condition along the sides, make a small cut across the selvage just above the bottom hem, and tear the hem off. Measure along the selvage edge 68 inches for standard-size pillowcases, or 88 inches for king-size. Make another cut across the selvage at that point and tear off the top of the sheet.

On the sheet, measure from a corner 21 inches along the torn edge toward the center. Cut down into the sheet an inch or so, then tear the fabric the rest of the way to the other end. Repeat on the other side. You now have two pieces, one from each side of the sheet,

each measuring 68 × 21 inches for standard-size cases, or 88 × 21 inches for king-size.

To use a fitted sheet, make the first crosswise tear at a point just below the fitted corner of the sheet. Then cut and tear as above.

Fold each piece in half crosswise, right sides together. Sew the sides together with a ½-inch seam down each side; use the straight stitch of a sewing machine.

To finish each pillowcase, turn down the raw edge around the open end of the case ½ inch all around; press it flat. Turn the folded edge down another 4 inches and press. Pin the hem into place. Machine-stitch around the entire opening ⅛ inch from the turned edge, overlapping the stitching for 1 inch at the end. Turn the case right side out and press it.

If the sheet is badly worn, there may not be enough good fabric along the sides to cut the pillowcases in one piece. In this case, cut two pieces for each case, 21 × 35 inches for standard-size or 21 × 45 inches for king-size cases. Use whatever parts of the sheet are still good. Assemble each

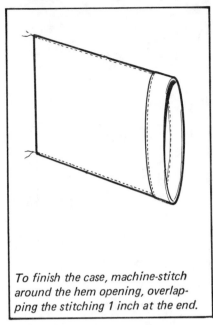

To finish the case, machine-stitch around the hem opening, overlapping the stitching 1 inch at the end.

pillowcase with a ½-inch seam around the two long sides and across one end, and make a 4-inch hem around the open end.

If the wide-hemmed end of a flat sheet is in good condition, you may be able to cut pillowcases from that end of the sheet and use the old hem. Cut a piece of 40 × 30 inches for a standard-size pillowcase, with the existing hem extending along a 40-inch side; or cut a 40 × 40-inch piece for a king-size case. Fold the piece in half, right sides together, with the hem at one end; sew across the other end and up the open side. Turn the seam allowance at the hem to one side or the other, tuck the raw edges under, and stitch the tucked edges down across the width of the hem.

Make a Tablecloth and Napkins

Table linens add elegance to even simple meals, but matched tablecloth-

and-napkin sets are expensive. You can custom-make your own sets with very little effort, for a fraction of the ready-mades' price. **Tools:** scissors, tape measure, straight pins, sewing machine, steam iron and ironing board. **Materials:** washable polyester/cotton fabric, thread; if desired, fringe. **Time:** 1 to 3 hours.

Fabric. Choose woven polyester/cotton fabric for easy care and washability; prints are good because they don't show stains. Make the tablecloth at least 12 inches wider than the table, to overhang each end at least 6 inches; make napkins 12 inches square. *For a 48-inch-square cloth* and four napkins (for a 30- or 36-inch table), buy 1¾ yards of woven 48-inch-wide fabric; the fabric must be a full 48 inches wide. *For a 60-inch-square cloth* and five napkins, buy 2⅛ yards of woven 60-inch-wide fabric. *For wider tables,* seam two equal widths of material together to the required width, at least 12 inches wider than the table. *For rectangular tables,* add length as required to make the cloth at least 12 inches longer than the table.

If desired, buy fringe to trim the edges of the cloth. Buy extra fabric as required for additional 12-inch-square napkins. The specifications given below are for a 48-inch-square cloth and four napkins; modify instructions as necessary to fit your requirements.

Assembly. Before cutting the tablecloth, square off the end of the fabric. Spread the fabric out on your work surface. Carefully trim off a 1/4-inch-wide strip along each selvage edge. Then make a small cut close to one end of the fabric into one cut selvage edge, and grasp one crosswise thread. Gently pull the thread to draw it right out of the fabric, across the entire fabric width. This will make a line across the fabric where the thread was; cut carefully along the pulled-thread line and discard the crooked end.

Measure 48 inches from the squared corner along the cut selvage edge; make another small cut in the edge at

structions, assemble the wiring post. The kit includes several rubber stoppers, of various sizes; find the stopper that best fits the top opening of your container. Thread the nipple of the wiring post or rod into the center of the stopper, and tighten it securely. Screw the brass washer and locknut onto the base end of the rod; screw the lamp socket onto the other end.

Insert the assembled wiring post into the weighted container, socket end up, and push the stopper firmly into place. This completes the wiring of the lamp.

To hold the lampshade, add a lamp harp, a screw-on wire attachment. Attach the harp to the socket base as directed by the manufacturer. Use any lampshade you like; remove the locknut at the top of the harp, set the shade into place, and replace the locknut. Finally, screw a light bulb into the socket and plug the lamp in.

If you're using a wicker basket and a long threaded rod to wire the lamp, start by drilling a hole in the bottom of the basket for the rod and the cord. If necessary, drill another hole in the bas-ket's cover, for the top of the rod to pass through. Drill the holes large enough to accommodate the rod itself on the bottom, and the rod's brass sheath on the top.

To assemble the components, thread the plug end of the cord through the rod and pull it through. Secure the socket at the top of the rod with the locking screws provided. Slip the brass sheath over the rod to butt into the socket at the top.

Tie a loose knot in the cord near the base of the rod, to reduce the stress on the cord. Then set the rod into place in the basket and pull the cord out through the opening in the bottom of the basket. To secure the rod at the lamp bottom, apply a bead of silicone adhesive to it at the bottom of the basket. Set the basket's cover over the rod and secure the rod into the opening with silicone adhesive.

To complete the lamp, weight the base as above; use a weighting material that won't sift out of the basket. Then clip the plug to the end of the cord, as directed by the manufacturer. Add a lamp harp, a shade, and a bulb, as above.

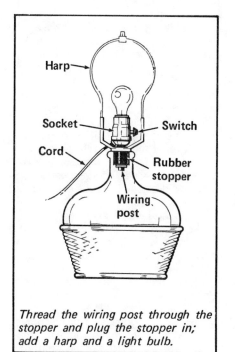

Thread the wiring post through the stopper and plug the stopper in; add a harp and a light bulb.

Make a Stovepipe Lamp

For a bold accent to a well-designed room, make this sleek, well-designed reading lamp—the candy cane is sections of stovepipe; all you add is wiring. **Tools:** measuring rule, pencil, handsaw or saber saw, fine-toothed flat file, power drill, caulking gun, scissors, screwdriver, wire cutters, wire stripper. **Materials:** 6-inch straight and elbow stovepipe sections, scrap ¾-inch plywood, construction adhesive, bricks or lead weights, heavy felt, white glue, porcelain lamp socket with screws, newspaper, masking tape, matte black or matte white spray paint for metal, lightweight lamp cord, lamp turn switch, quick-clamp plug, spray metal primer and high-gloss spray enamel; 40-, 75-, or 100-watt light bulb. **Time:** about 2 to 4 hours.

To make a stovepipe lamp, you can assemble pieces of pipe in any shape you like. This candy-cane-shaped lamp is 6 inches in diameter and 54 inches high, designed for reading or bedside use—paint it shiny red or any color you like. For a 54-inch-high candy cane, you'll need two 24-inch sections of straight pipe and two 90-degree elbow sections. Buy spray metal primer and a high-gloss spray enamel to finish the lamp; use matte black or white to finish the inside, depending on how bright you want the light to be. You'll also need 12 feet of lightweight lamp cord, a lamp turn switch, and a porcelain lamp socket.

To make the lamp base and the bulb base, cut two discs of scrap ¾-inch plywood, exactly the same diameter as the stovepipe. Measure the exact diameter of the uncrimped end of one straight section, and the crimped end of one elbow section. Set these sections on a piece of plywood and draw around them; adjust to the measured diameter.

Carefully cut out the two discs with a handsaw or a saber saw. Cut exactly on the traced lines; the discs must fit firmly inside the pieces of stovepipe. Smooth the edges of the discs with a fine-toothed flat file to get a snug fit inside the stovepipe sections.

To make the lamp base, use an electric drill to drill a hole about 12 inches up from the uncrimped end of the straight bottom pipe, to accommodate the lamp switch; drill the hole just large enough to accept the shank of your switch. On the other side of the pipe section, about 1¼ inches up from the uncrimped bottom of the piece of pipe, drill another hole just large enough to accommodate the lamp cord.

With a caulking gun, apply a bead of construction adhesive all around the cut edge of the plywood base disc. Carefully set the disc into the uncrimped end of the pipe, and adjust it from both ends of the pipe so that it's firmly wedged into the pipe, level and flush with the bottom pipe edge. To finish the outside of the

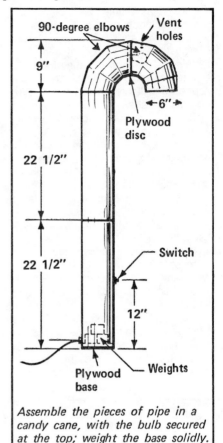

Assemble the pieces of pipe in a candy cane, with the bulb secured at the top; weight the base solidly.

lamp base, trace the section of stovepipe onto a piece of heavy felt, and cut a circle of felt to back the plywood disc. Apply the felt to the outside face of the disc with white glue, and smooth the felt to make a level base. Let the glue and the construction adhesive dry completely, as directed by the manufacturer.

When the base is dry, weight it with bricks or lead weights—use about 5 pounds of weights to keep the lamp stable. Attach the weights to the plywood base inside the pipe with construction adhesive; make sure you don't block the switch hole or the cord hole.

To make the top of the lamp, cut a narrow slice off one side of the other plywood disc, to leave room for the wires to enter the body of the lamp. Attach a porcelain lamp socket to the center of the disc, screwing it firmly in. Then apply a bead of construction adhesive to the cut edge of the disc, except for the sliced-off edge, and set the disc into the crimped end of one elbow section of pipe, socket side out. Make sure the disc is firmly anchored and set straight into the end of the pipe; the bulb will project straight out from the socket into the second elbow section, as illustrated.

Let the construction adhesive dry, as directed by the manufacturer. When the adhesive is dry, paint the inside of the lamp's bulb end. For a focused bedside light, use matte black spray paint; for more diffused light, use matte white. Set the second elbow section into place over the crimped end of the first one, so that the socket assembly is roughly in the middle of the two curved pieces of pipe, with the bulb socket facing out. Adjust the pieces of pipe to the angle desired, and push them firmly together.

Spread newspaper to protect your work area, and cover the socket opening in the elbow assembly with masking tape. Spray the inside of the assembled curved section with matte black or matte white paint, as desired. Cover the plywood disc and the entire inside surface of the pipe. Let the paint dry completely, as directed by the manufacturer; if necessary, spray again for complete coverage and let the paint dry.

When the paint is completely dry on the elbow sections, remove the masking tape from the socket. Screw a light bulb into the socket and note where the bulb lies inside the curved stovepipe sections; then remove it. Across the top of the stovepipe, above the light bulb location, drill three ⅜-inch holes to dissipate the heat of the bulb.

To assemble the lamp, thread the end of a 12-foot piece of lightweight lamp cord through the cord hole drilled in the bottom straight section, just above the plywood base. Leaving about 8 to 9 feet of cord outside the pipe, tie a loose knot in the cord to anchor it against the drilled hole. The remaining 3 to 4 feet of cord, inside the lamp, will be used to wire the lamp.

Bring the wire up the base piece of stovepipe and across to the drilled switch hole. At the point where the cord passes the switch hole, carefully separate the two insulated wires of the cord for a few inches. Cut one of these wires, and use a wire stripper to remove about ½ inch of insulation from the two cut ends; do *not* cut both wires. Connect the cut ends to the two screw terminals on the lamp switch. Insert the switch into the hole in the stovepipe and secure it with the lock ring provided.

When the switch has been wired in, complete the assembly of the lamp. Set the other straight piece of pipe onto the base piece, uncrimped end down, and push it firmly to join the two pieces securely. Pull the loose end of the wire up through the pipe.

Carefully separate the two insulated wires of the cord for about 6 inches at the loose end. Set the assembled curve of the candy cane onto the straight lamp base, pulling the separated ends of the cord up past the plywood disc through the cut-out area. With a wire stripper, remove about ½ inch of insu-

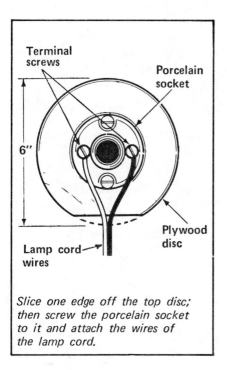

Terminal screws

Porcelain socket

6"

Plywood disc

Lamp cord wires

Slice one edge off the top disc; then screw the porcelain socket to it and attach the wires of the lamp cord.

lation from each wire, and connect the stripped ends to the screw terminals of the porcelain socket.

Firmly push the curved part of the lamp onto the straight part, so that the light opening and the switch are on the same side. To complete the lamp assembly, attach a quick-clamp plug to the free end of the lamp cord, as directed by the manufacturer.

Finish the lamp with spray metal primer and then high-gloss spray enamel. Before painting, cover your work surface with newspaper; cover the lamp cord and the switch with masking tape and newspaper. Cover the bulb opening with masking tape, and put a piece of tape over the vent holes on the inside of the top piece of pipe. Apply a light coat of primer and let it dry completely. Apply two or three coats of high-gloss spray enamel, following the manufacturer's instructions, to obtain a smooth finish. Let the paint dry completely; then carefully remove all tape and paper, and screw in a 40-, 75-, or 100-watt light bulb.

Cover a Lamp Shade

Renovate a shabby lamp shade or revitalize a dull one with this shirred slipcover—use any lightweight fabric you like. **Tools:** tape measure, sharp scissors, straight pins, sewing machine, steam iron and ironing board, safety pin or bodkin. **Materials:** plain lamp shade (no ruffles or pleats), lightweight fabric, thread, medium-weight round elastic cord. **Time:** ½ to 1 hour.

To cover the shade, choose lightweight fabric that will fall easily into soft folds. Buy 1 yard of 44- or 45-inch fabric; if the shade is more than 15 inches high, add another 2 inches of fabric for each additional inch of height. Buy 3 yards of medium-weight round elastic. If the lamp shade has fringe or other trim, remove it carefully, without damaging the shade.

Measure the height of the shade and add 3 inches. Cut two strips of material to that measurement across the width of the fabric—for example, if the shade is 12 inches high, cut two 15-inch strips across the width of the fabric. Place the strips of fabric with the right sides together at the selvage, pin the selvage ends together, and sew the pinned ends together on a sewing machine; leave a ½-inch seam allowance. Remove the pins and open the seamed pieces to form one long strip of fabric.

Measure around the bottom of the lamp shade, and multiply this circumference by 1½ to find the length needed for the strip of fabric. If the shade measures 50 inches around the bottom, for example, you'll need a strip about 75 inches long to cover it. This is a minimum fullness; if your fabric is quite soft or thin, it's all right to use more. Measure and trim the long strip to the required length, cutting from both ends of the fabric to keep the seam evenly centered.

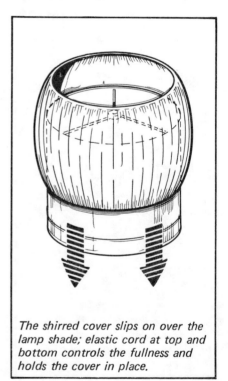

The shirred cover slips on over the lamp shade; elastic cord at top and bottom controls the fullness and holds the cover in place.

When the strip is trimmed to the proper size, fold it in half at the seam, right sides together, and stitch the two loose ends together with a ½-inch seam. Turn under ½ inch of fabric along each long raw edge of the piece and press it down; turn each folded edge under again ½ inch and press. Pin the hems in place and stitch them all around, leaving a 1-inch opening in each long hem. Backstitch at the beginning and the end of each hem.

Cut a piece of round elastic to the same length as the bottom circumference of the shade. Tie one end of it to a bodkin or a large safety pin and insert it into one of the hems through the 1-inch opening in the hem. Pull the elastic by the bodkin or pin all the way around inside the hem and out again, gathering the fabric onto the elastic as you go. Tie the two ends of the elastic in a square knot and let it slip inside the hem. Cut another piece of elastic the circumference of the top of the shade; insert it in the other hem of the fabric and tie the ends together the same way.

To use the cover, remove the lamp shade from the lamp. Slip the cover over the lamp shade and adjust the gathered fabric evenly all around. If the cover isn't snug enough, retie the elastic to make it tighter.

Build a Window Box

Window boxes are a cheerful addition to any room, both indoors and out. This sturdy, simple box is ideal for the garden of your choice. **Tools:** measuring rule, pencil, carpenters' square, handsaw or power saw, small mixing dish and stick, power drill with $^{11}/_{64}$-inch, ½-inch, and carbide-tipped bits, screwdriver, hammer, safety goggles. **Materials:** 1 × 2 and 1 × 8, 1 × 10, or 1 × 12 redwood or cedar stock; resorcinol glue, #8 × 1¼-inch brass or stainless steel flathead wood screws, 6-penny brass or stainless steel finish-ing nails, heavy-duty shelf brackets; #8 × 2-inch brass or stainless steel flathead screws, or 2-inch lag screws with lead masonry anchors. **Time:** about 1 to 1½ hours.

Build your window box to the full inside width of the window; use 1 × 8, 1 × 10, or 1 × 12 redwood or cedar boards for the box width and depth desired. The finished window box will be as wide and as deep as the boards you use.

To make the box, measure across the inside of the window frame. If you work from this measurement, the finished box will be about 1½ inches wider than the window on each side; adjust this width if desired to make the box narrower or wider. Using a carpenters' square to keep the ends straight, measure and mark three boards to the desired length of the box; cut them with a handsaw or a power saw. For each of the two side pieces, measure and cut a piece of board as long as the width of the stock, plus 1½ inches.

Put the pieces together with simple butt joints, with the front and back of the box butted over the bottom and all board edges flush. Set the side pieces directly over the open ends of the box, with the grain of the side pieces running the same way as the grain of the front and back, so that the pattern of the wood wraps around the box.

Fasten the box together with resorcinol glue and #8 × 1¼-inch brass or stainless steel flathead wood screws; attach the front and back boards to the bottom board and then secure the side pieces. For each joint, drill $^{11}/_{64}$-inch holes through the face of the board being attached—the front and back boards and the side pieces, but not the bottom board. Drill holes at each end of the board and about every 4 inches all along the joint line, set back about ⅜ inch from the edge of the board. Set the board into place, mark the screw holes on the board edge it's being fastened to, and drill starter holes into the board edge at the marked points.

Mix resorcinol glue as directed by the manufacturer. Apply glue to the edge of the board being fastened to and set the

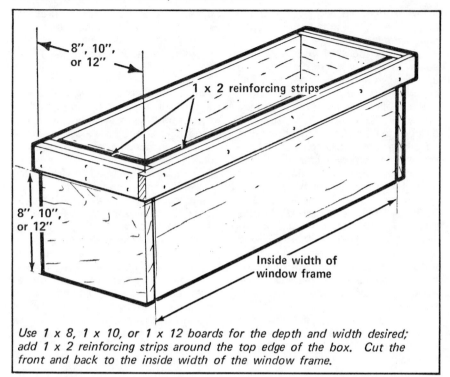

Use 1 x 8, 1 x 10, or 1 x 12 boards for the depth and width desired; add 1 x 2 reinforcing strips around the top edge of the box. Cut the front and back to the inside width of the window frame.

facing board into place against the glued edge, with all board edges flush. Secure the joint with #8 × 1¼-inch brass or stainless steel flathead wood screws through the predrilled holes and into the edge board.

For a stronger box, add a reinforcing strip across the front and around the sides; butt the front strip over the cut ends of the two side strips. Measure and cut strips of 1 × 2 redwood or cedar for this reinforcing band. Attach first the side strips and then the front strip, with the top edge of the 1 × 2's flush with the top of the box. To secure each strip, apply resorcinol glue to one face of the 1 × 2; position it on the box and nail it firmly into place with 6-penny brass or stainless steel nails set every 4 inches.

If you plan to use the box for plants that demand a lot of water, make weep holes in the bottom of the box to prevent waterlogging. Drill a series of ½-inch holes every 4 inches along the center of the bottom board. Cover the bottom of

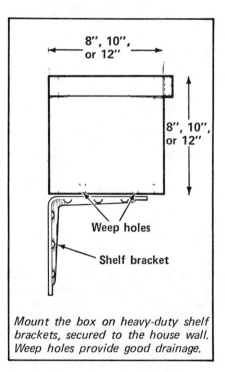

Mount the box on heavy-duty shelf brackets, secured to the house wall. Weep holes provide good drainage.

the box with gravel before filling it with soil.

Use heavy-duty shelf brackets to hang the box. Position the brackets to rest against wall studs under the window—straight down from the window edges and usually at the center of the window; for wide windows, at 16- or 24-inch intervals between the framing studs. Use two brackets for a short window box, three or more for a box 4 feet or longer.

Turn the completed window box upside down and attach the mounting brackets to the bottom with #8 × 1¼-inch brass or stainless steel screws; the vertical bracket legs should lie flush with the back of the box. Prop the box in place and secure the vertical bracket legs to the studs of the house wall with #8 × 2-inch brass or stainless steel flathead screws. To fasten the box to a brick or concrete block wall, use 2-inch lag screws driven into lead masonry anchors. Wearing safety goggles, drill holes for the anchors with a power drill and a carbide-tipped masonry bit; insert the anchors and then drive the screws in flush with the wall surface.

Fireproof a Christmas Tree

Evergreens, with their essential pine oils and turpentine, are highly flammable, and when they dry out they're downright explosive. The chemicals in this solution are used to fight forest fires; they're just as effective inside. **Equipment:** gallon container or bucket, measuring cup, measuring spoons. **Ingredients:** water, alum, boric acid, borax. **Yield:** 1 gallon.

Fill a gallon container half full with lukewarm water, or measure ½ gallon of warm water into a clean bucket. Add 1 cup of alum, 4 ounces of boric acid, and 2 tablespoons of borax. Stir well to dissolve and add warm water to fill the gallon container, or add ½ gallon of warm water to the bucket.

Spray the tree and other decorative greens thoroughly with this solution before you set them up. If you have any solution left over, pour it into the water in the tree stand.

Energy-Savers

Caulk Your House

To keep the elements out and the heat or cool in, make sure your house is well caulked. This job requires only caulk and patience. **Tools:** large paintbrush, utility knife, putty knife, single-edge razor blade and glass scraper, caulking gun, old wire hanger or stiff wire, stepladder or extension ladder. **Materials:** acrylic latex, butyl rubber, silicone, or roofing caulk in bulk tubes; solvent for butyl rubber or roofing caulk, concentrated household spray cleaner, paper towels. **Time:** varies with amount of work necessary; to caulk an entire house, plan to spend several hours a day over several weekends.

Good caulking is most important everywhere two outside surfaces meet, to seal out water, air, dirt, and bugs. Inspect your house yearly for damage and recaulk as necessary. Buy caulk in bulk tubes; read the label to estimate coverage, and buy one or two tubes extra. Deep open joints require more caulk than the usual allowance. For most applications, use acrylic latex or silicone caulk; silicone is expensive, but very durable and very easy to work with. To seal masonry-metal joints, use butyl rubber caulk; buy a solvent for cleanup. Use special roofing caulk as needed.

If possible, work in mild, dry weather; caulk doesn't adhere well in cold weather, and it gets runny in very hot weather. Caulk obvious places first—around doors and windows, along the joint at the intersection of house wall and foundation wall, around unit air conditioners. Work methodically around the house, examining each area and caulking as necessary.

After you've hit the high spots, go back and really look at the house, area by area. Caulk areas where steps or porches meet the house, where pipes or vents penetrate walls, and where sheets of siding meet. On the roof, caulk all around the chimney, along flashing, and along seams between shingles and flashing. Any joint that looks open should be sealed with caulk.

Caulking technique is simple. Clean loose dirt and debris from the joint with a large paintbrush; if the joint surfaces are really dirty, clean them with concentrated spray cleaner and paper towels. Let the joint dry completely before you caulk—the caulk won't bond to wet surfaces. Use a stepladder or an extension ladder to reach joints above your head.

Remove old caulking, peeling it out of the joint. Cut out stubborn strips of caulk carefully with a sharp utility knife, being careful not to damage the joint surfaces; pry out the old caulk with a putty knife. If you're caulking around glass, use a single-edge razor blade in a glass scraper to remove all old caulk, and clean the glass thoroughly. Dust the joint again to remove any cutout bits of old caulk.

Pull out the plunger of the caulking gun and set a tube of caulk into place, inserting the nozzle of the tube through the opening in the end of the gun. Cut the nozzle at an angle with a sharp utility knife, following the marks on the nozzle, to a diameter about the same as the width of the joints to be filled; the bead of caulk must be large enough to overlap both sides of the joints. Once you cut the nozzle you can make it larger but not smaller, so cut it to fit the narrowest joints first.

Push a piece of bent coat hanger or stiff wire down through the nozzle to break the seal where the nozzle meets the tube. Remove the wire. Start the caulk flowing by pulling the gun's trigger and pushing the plunger in against the

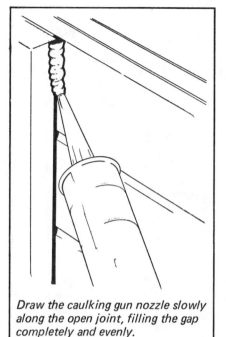

Draw the caulking gun nozzle slowly along the open joint, filling the gap completely and evenly.

tube, turning the L-bend so that it points up and the notches on the plunger engage. Quickly turn the gun to hold the tube of caulk nozzle up, and start to work.

To fill a joint with caulk, hold the caulking gun at a 45-degree angle, toward the direction you're caulking in. Start at a corner, if possible. Press the handle of the caulking gun firmly; after a few seconds, caulk will begin to flow from the open nozzle. Don't try to hurry it. The plunger of the gun moves one notch—one click—at a time. You can't control the flow of the caulk; you can only adapt your application to make the best use of it.

Draw the nozzle of the gun steadily along the open joint, being careful to keep the bead of caulk uniform. Move the gun as slowly as necessary to fill the joint completely, without gaps; don't stop moving the gun until you reach the edge of the joint, or the caulk will blob. At the end of the joint, twist the nozzle up and out of the joint and hold the gun nozzle up to minimize the flow of caulk—some wastage is inevitable as

the caulk released by the last click flows forward. To stop the flow of caulk, turn the plunger handle to disengage it and pull the plunger out from the tube.

As you work, use paper towels to mop up waste caulk and to clean your hands. Use a solvent to clean up after you use butyl rubber or roofing caulk; remove fresh acrylic latex caulk with soap and water. Let silicone caulk dry on your hands—5 or 10 minutes—and remove it by peeling or rubbing it off.

Install a Clock Thermostat

Recent studies have shown that programs to set back thermostats manually don't usually lower heating bills, because they're inconsistent. The same studies have revealed that setting the thermostat back automatically can result in considerable savings—as much as 16 percent in milder climates; the percentage is less in areas of severe winters, but the dollar savings are more. Installing an automatic thermostat is very simple. **Tools:** small screwdrivers. **Materials:** clock thermostat. **Time:** 15 to 30 minutes.

Before starting to work, turn off the power to the heating system; throw the circuit breakers or remove the fuse that controls the system. *Caution: You must turn off the power to the heating system. If you aren't sure which breaker or switch controls the system, turn off the power for the whole house.*

Pop off or unscrew the existing thermostat's front cover, and remove the mounting screws that are exposed. Pull the thermostat and its wires gently away from the mounting plate, junction box, or wall, and disconnect the wires from the screw terminals. If there's a mounting plate under the thermostat body, remove that too. Following the instructions that come with the clock thermostat, reconnect the wires to the proper terminals of the new unit; loop the wires clockwise around the terminal screws and tighten the screws firmly.

Remount the thermostat on the wall, either directly or with its base or mounting plate, as required. Then flip on the circuit breaker or screw in the fuse to restore power to the heating system.

Following the new thermostat's directions, set the timer mechanism to the hours you want the setback period to begin and end. Set the unit's clock to the correct time. The setback period should begin about ½ hour before you usually go to bed, and it should end ½ hour before you get up; if you can stretch this period out, you'll save even more. The usual temperature setback is 10° F, but increasing this to 15° will save you more. If you're away from home during the day, you may want to set the thermostat to maintain a low temperature during that time, provide more heat just before you get home, and drop the temperature again just before bedtime.

Insulate Your Water Heater

The U.S. Department of Energy has determined that an additional 1½ inches of blanket-type insulation wrapped around a water heater can save anywhere from $5 to $20 a year in operating costs. Water heater insulation kits, including all necessary material and instructions, can be used on either gas or electric heaters; they're designed for easy installation. You can also insulate an electric water heater with standard blanket insulation—do *not* use this method to insulate a gas water heater. The thicker the insulation you use—1½-inch, 4-inch, or even 6-inch—the more heat you'll save. **Tools:** measuring tape, face mask, safety goggles, work gloves, heavy utility scissors. **Materials:** length of blanket-type roll insulation, duct tape. **Time:** ½ to 2 hours.

To calculate the length of insulation

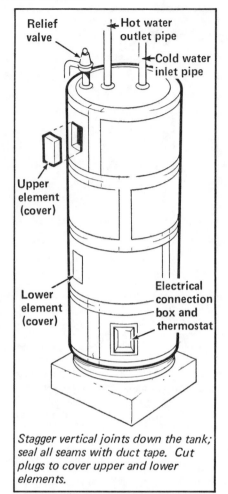

Stagger vertical joints down the tank; seal all seams with duct tape. Cut plugs to cover upper and lower elements.

needed, measure the circumference and the height of the water heater. You'll need pieces of insulation cut long enough to wrap around the water heater, and as many pieces as it takes to cover the heater from top to bottom, plus enough to cover the top—get a couple of extra feet to allow for mistakes. Buy either foil-backed or paper-backed blanket insulation, either 16 inches or 24 inches wide. Buy insulation at least 1½ inches thick; 4 inches or even 6 inches is better. Suppliers sell blanket insulation only by the full roll, but you may be able to buy whatever length you need from a building or insulating contractor.

Wear a face mask, safety goggles, and work gloves. Cut the insulation with a heavy utility scissors into pieces that will just wrap around the tank and butt together. Starting at the bottom of the tank, wrap a piece of insulation around the water heater, foil or paper out, and fasten the ends together with short strips of duct tape. Wrap another piece around the tank directly above the first, and continue up the tank until the tank sides are completely covered; be sure the ends of each piece are butted together evenly. Fold the top edge of the top piece of insulation over the top of the tank, but *do not* cover the relief valve.

Fit the insulation carefully around all pipes. Cut plugs out of the insulation where it covers the small access doors over the heater elements and thermostat, but leave the plugs in place; they can easily be removed and replaced for service work. *Do not* cover electrical control boxes. Take care not to wrap the insulation too tightly; the more the batting is compressed, the less insulating value it has.

After all pieces of insulation have been temporarily taped in place, adjust them as necessary to fit them evenly around the water heater. Apply strips of duct tape along all joints and seams to seal them completely. Finally, reset the thermostat. If you have a dishwasher, set the dial to 140° F; otherwise, set it for 110° to 120° F.

Stop Heat Loss with Insulating Shutters

One of the greatest sources of heat loss in most houses is through the windows, but insulating shutters and insulating glass can minimize the loss. It's easy to make insulating shutters, custom-fitted to your windows. **Tools:** measuring rule, carpenters' square, handsaw or power saw, pencil, ham-mer, utility knife; C-clamps or woodworking clamps, or miter box, backsaw, and miter clamps; paintbrush, drill, screwdriver. **Materials:** 1 × 2 pine stock, carpenters' glue, 4-penny finishing nails; 5/8-inch brads; 1/4-inch plywood, hardwood veneer plywood, or tempered hardboard for panel covers; 3/4-inch polyfoam insulation board, decorative molding and plywood veneer edging tape, paint or stain, foam weatherstripping, fixed-pin or loose-pin hinges, 1-inch wood screws, barrel bolts or catches. **Time:** for 1 shutter, about 2 to 3 hours.

The basic design of these insulating shutters can be adapted to fit any interior and exterior style. Choose your materials accordingly. Measure the exact dimensions of the inside of the window opening, from side to side and from sill to top. Subtract 1/16 inch from top, bottom, and sides to allow clearance for the finished shutter. Check the window opening for squareness with a carpenters' square; if it is out of square, build the shutter frame correspondingly out of square to make the shutter slightly oversized, and trim it to fit.

Make a rectangular frame for the shutter, like a picture frame, of 1 × 2 pine stock; use a carpenters' square to keep the corners true and join the pieces at the corners with simple butt joints or miter joints. Apply carpenters' glue to joints, clamp them, and then nail them with 4-penny finishing nails; be careful not to split the wood. If you use butt joints, clamp the frame with C-clamps or woodworking clamps; let the glue dry before proceeding, following the manufacturer's instructions. Then nail the joints. Cut mitered corners with a miter box and a backsaw; apply glue, clamp the corners with miter clamps, let dry, and nail the joints firmly.

Cut back and front panels—of 1/4-inch plywood, decorative hardwood veneer plywood, or 1/4-inch tempered hardboard—to cover the frame exactly, with the edges flush all around. Attach one panel to the frame with carpenters' glue and nail it into place with 5/8-inch brads. Carefully cut a piece of rigid 3/4-inch polyfoam insulation board to fit tightly inside the frame, and push it into place. Then glue and nail the second cover panel to the frame.

If desired, attach decorative molding to either or both faces of the shutter with carpenters' glue or brads; cover the edges with wide plywood veneer edging tape. Be sure to allow for the thickness of the edging when you build the frame. Finish the shutter with paint or stain.

Many windows are large enough to warrant a pair of shutters. To make sure the insulating seal is tight, modify the meeting edge of each shutter of the pair; cut an inside rabbet on one shutter and a matching outside rabbet on the other. Glue a strip of thin foam weatherstripping to the outside rabbet lip of one shutter.

To install insulating shutters permanently, mount them on fixed-pin hinges; use butt hinges that can be surface-mounted or decorative full-surface hinges. There are many varieties; check with your hardware supplier. Set the shutter in place and hold it there. Position the hinges and mark the screw holes on both the shutter and the window frame; take the shutter down. Drill screw holes and then screw the hinges

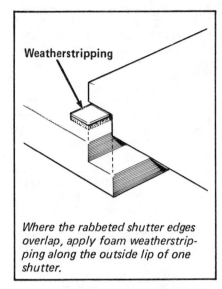

Where the rabbeted shutter edges overlap, apply foam weatherstripping along the outside lip of one shutter.

into place with 1-inch wood screws.

If you want to take the shutters down during warm weather, mount them with loose-pin hinges; remove the pins to take the shutters down as desired.

To complete the installation, fit the shutters with barrel bolts or catches on the inside to hold them firmly in place against the window stop when they are closed. Apply foam weatherstripping around the inside edge of the shutter for a tight seal, if desired.

Insulate an Attic

An uninsulated attic is a tremendous heat drain during the winter. An unfinished attic is also, fortunately, the easiest of rooms to insulate. **Tools:** measuring rule, work gloves, safety goggles, breathing mask, hard hat, trouble light, planks or scrap plywood, 3-foot piece of 2 × 4 for cutting insulation, sharp serrated knife or heavy-duty scissors. **Materials:** paper-backed fiberglass blanket or batt insulation—ask the insulation dealer for the best R-value for your area. **Time:** about 3 to 5

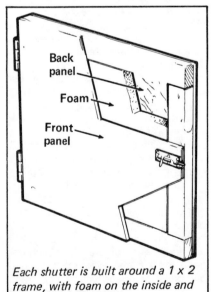

Each shutter is built around a 1 x 2 frame, with foam on the inside and plywood face panels.

hours, depending on size of attic.

Unfinished attics have exposed floor joists, usually 16 or 24 inches apart. Before buying insulation, measure the distance between joists in your attic; buy insulation in rolls cut to fit that width. If the attic space is very irregular, you may prefer to buy batt insulation; this is precut in 4-foot-long pieces and may be easier to handle. To calculate the number of feet of insulation you'll need, count the joist spaces across the room and multiply by the length of the attic. Buy paper-backed insulation, not foil-backed.

Wear heavy work clothes to handle fiberglass. *Caution: Fiberglass dust is very irritating. Wear work gloves, safety goggles, and a breathing mask.* If you have one, wear a hard hat while working in restricted areas.

Prepare your work space carefully. The exposed joists of the floor are the beams of the ceiling below; the surface exposed between the joists is the ceiling itself. *Caution: Do not step between the joists; if you put your weight on the exposed surface you'll break through the ceiling below.* Set wide planks or pieces of scrap plywood over the joists to work from; move them, leap-frog fashion, as you work. Rig

a trouble light to provide lighting.

Start installing insulation at the eaves on one side of the attic. Unroll blanket insulation or set batts into the exposed space between two joists, paper side down. *Caution: The paper side of the insulation must always be down, toward the heated part of the house, so that it acts as a vapor barrier. If the insulation is laid paper side up, it will absorb moisture and will not function properly.* Press the insulation firmly into the space between the joists; butt batts or pieces of blanket insulation firmly together.

Cut the insulation to fit with a large, sharp serrated knife or a heavy-duty scissors. Set the part to be cut on your working platform and press a 3-foot piece of 2 × 4 across it at the cutting point; saw through the compressed fiberglass with the knife or cut it across with the scissors. Cut the insulation as necessary to fit it around the chimney, pipes, or other obstructions. Do not cover vents, exhaust fan motors, light fixtures, or any heat-generating equipment, and do not move electrical wiring.

Work across the attic until all joist spaces have been covered. Finally, cover the door or trap door to the attic with insulation, paper side in.

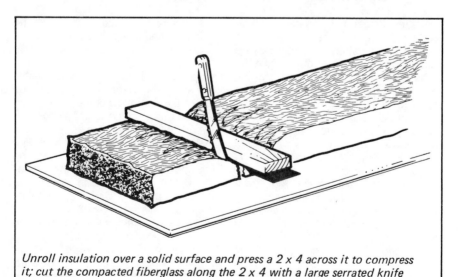

Unroll insulation over a solid surface and press a 2 x 4 across it to compress it; cut the compacted fiberglass along the 2 x 4 with a large serrated knife or a heavy-duty utility scissors.

Insulate a Crawl Space

A floor over an uninsulated crawl space is cold in winter; it absorbs moisture from the ground below it, and the room sometimes smells musty. Insulate and seal the crawl space to eliminate all three problems. **Tools:** measuring rule, work gloves, safety goggles, breathing mask, trouble light, sharp serrated knife or heavy utility scissors, small handsaw, hammer, utility knife. **Materials:** 3½-inch-thick, R11-rated foil- or paper-backed fiberglass blanket insulation; ½ × 1½-inch parting stop stock, 8- or 10-penny common nails, cylindrical pipe insulation, ¼-inch-thick insulating tape, 6 mil polyethylene sheet plastic, 2 × 4's to hold insulation in place. **Time:** about 4 hours, depending on size of space.

Before buying insulation, measure the distance around the crawl space in inches. Insulation is available in 15- and 23-inch widths; divide the distance around the space by 15 or 23 to determine the number of strips of insulation you'll need. Measure the height of the crawl space walls; each strip must be cut 2 feet longer than this height. Multiply the number of strips required by the length of the strips to calculate the amount of insulation to buy. Polyethylene sheet plastic is available in 3-, 4-, and 6-foot widths; calculate the square footage of the crawl space and buy enough plastic to cover this area, plus a generous allowance for overlap.

Wear heavy work clothes for this job. *Caution: Fiberglass dust is very irritating. Wear work gloves, safety goggles, and a breathing mask.* Rig a trouble light in the crawl space before you start to work. If the crawl space is very confined, cut insulation and plastic to fit before bringing it into the space.

Cut strips of insulation to the height of the crawl space walls, plus 2 feet, and as many strips as are needed to cover the walls all around the space. To cut

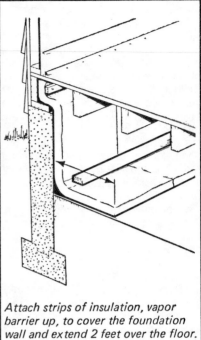

Attach strips of insulation, vapor barrier up, to cover the foundation wall and extend 2 feet over the floor.

the insulation, press a piece of 2 × 4 across it at the cutting point; saw through the compressed fiberglass with a sharp serrated knife or cut it with a heavy utility scissors. Cut pieces of ½ × 1½-inch parting stop to roughly the width of the insulation, to anchor the strips of fiberglass to the wall.

Starting at the corner near the door to the space, install strips of insulation to cover the walls. Set each strip against the wall, foil or paper side out, with the top of the strip against the wood band joist at the top of the wall. Place a strip of parting stop on the insulation, directly over and parallel to the band joist, and nail it firmly through the insulation and into the joist, compressing the insulation until it is firmly held in place along the top of the strip. Use 8- or 10-penny common nails, set every 3 to 4 inches; make sure they are driven firmly into the band joist. Butt the strips firmly side to side. *Caution: The foil or paper side of the insulation must always be out, toward the center of the crawl space, so that it acts as a vapor barrier. If the insulation is installed with the foil or paper against the wall, it will absorb moisture and not function properly.*

Crawl space vents should be kept closed in winter, open in summer. If your crawl space has vents, cut plugs of insulation to cover them in winter; do not cover them completely. If there are pipes in the crawl space, cover them with cylindrical pipe insulation, being careful not to leave any gaps. Tape the joints with ¼-inch-thick insulating tape.

When the walls of the crawl space are completely covered, cut strips of 6 mil polyethylene to the length of the crawl space. Starting at the far side of the space, spread a sheet of plastic along one wall, lifting the folded-in ends of the fiberglass strips to slide the plastic under it. Butt the edge of the plastic against the wall of the crawl space and adjust the fiberglass as necessary to form a smooth curve down the wall and onto the plastic-covered floor.

Spread successive sheets of plastic to cover the entire floor of the crawl space; overlap each sheet at least 6 inches over the preceding one. Lift the fiberglass strips all along the walls to smooth the plastic into place on the ground under it. As you spread plastic and smooth the insulation back into place, set 2 × 4's along the walls on top of the folded-in strips of insulation to hold them firmly in place. Place the plastic and weight the insulation as you work across the space, and step on the plastic as little as possible.

Finally, when the entire crawl space has been insulated and sealed, cut a piece of insulation to cover the door to the space. Nail it into place on the inside of the door, foil or paper side out.

Insulate Your Water Pipes

You can reduce energy costs by insulating accessible hot-water pipes in your home, including those that supply

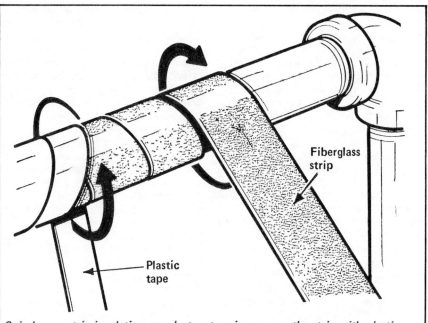

Spiral-wrap strip insulation over hot-water pipes; cover the strip with plastic tape wrapped the other way.

Fiberglass strip

Plastic tape

hot water to a heating system. At the same time, insulate cold-water pipes to prevent condensation sweating. **Tools:** utility knife. **Materials:** pipe insulation, duct tape. **Time:** several hours, depending on the amount of pipe to be insulated.

On hot-water systems, you must insulate as much of the system as possible, and preferably all of it. On cold-water pipes, only the portion where condensation occurs need be insulated. Apply any insulation carefully, with no cracks or gaps; seal all joints with duct tape. Wherever possible, insulate fittings and valve bodies too.

Strip or tape pipe insulation. This type of insulation, used only for hot-water pipes, is a narrow fiberglass strip that is spiral-wrapped around the pipe. The ends are secured with duct tape.

To insulate each pipe, tape one end of the insulation strip to the pipe with duct tape; wrap the strip around the pipe. The edges of the insulation strip should butt or overlap slightly. Wrap firmly but don't stretch the insulation—pulling it too tight reduces its effectiveness; wrapping it too loosely permits excessive heat loss. Secure the strip with duct tape at the end of the pipe.

To protect the fiberglass from dirt, moisture, and damage, cover the insulation with nonsticking plastic tape spiral-wrapped in the opposite direction. Secure the ends of the plastic tape with self-sticking tape.

Rigid pipe insulation. Rigid pipe insulation can be used for both hot-water and cold-water pipes. It comes in standard-size lengths, in sizes to fit different pipe diameters. Some kinds are made in two halves; clamp the halves over the pipe, secure them with a band or tape, and seal them. Some insulation of this type is made in one piece; slit it lengthwise with a knife and then slip it over the pipe. Trim the insulation as necessary or cut it to fit around fittings or valves with a utility knife.

Similar styles of insulation are made in semirigid and flexible forms of various materials. All are simple to install.

Insulate Your Electrical Boxes

If you live in cold-weather country, it pays to insulate your house thoroughly. One place cold air often gets through is the electrical boxes in exterior house walls. To stop drafts and reduce heat loss, insulate the wall switch and receptacle boxes. **Tools:** screwdriver, caulking gun, putty knife, scissors, pen. **Materials:** acrylic caulk, ¼-inch flexible polyfoam or foam rubber sheathing. **Time:** about 5 minutes per box.

To insulate the electrical boxes, don't use ordinary fiberglass insulation. Buy ¼-inch flexible polyfoam or foam rubber sheathing. Before starting to work, locate all exterior-wall switch boxes and electrical boxes so you can work efficiently from box to box. Don't bother with boxes in inside partition walls. *Caution: You must turn off the power to the boxes before you insulate them. Turn the circuit breaker off or remove the fuse that controls the main power for the house; don't try to figure out which circuits go to which boxes.* Remember that this shuts off power to the refrigerator and freezer. If the insulation job will take longer than an hour or two, work in several sessions so that the refrigeration units won't be turned off long enough to let food spoil.

With the power off, start to work. At each box, remove the screw that holds the cover plate and set the cover plate aside. Fill in the crack between the box and the wall with acrylic caulk; put in a good thick bead. Scrape away any excess with a putty knife.

With scissors, cut a rectangle of insulating foam just a bit bigger than the electrical box, but small enough to fit inside the cover plate. Using the cover as a pattern, trace the outline of the opening for the switch or the receptacles. Cut just inside the traced lines to make openings just enough undersized to fit snugly. Lay the foam over the switch or receptacle, properly aligned,

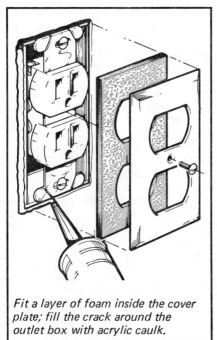

Fit a layer of foam inside the cover plate; fill the crack around the outlet box with acrylic caulk.

and set the cover plate on top. Force the screws through the foam and into the electrical box or receptacle frame, and screw the cover firmly into place.

Work around the exterior walls, box by box. After you've finished with all the boxes, or have completed a work session, flip the main circuit breaker or replace the main fuse to turn the power back on.

Cover an Air Conditioner

If you own a window or wall-mounted air conditioner, you can extend its life and lower your heating bills by covering it during the winter. For an easy-to-build, efficient cover, use rigid foam insulation board. **Tools:** measuring rule, felt-tip pen, carpenters' square, straightedge, utility knife with sharp heavy-duty blade, drill, pliers. **Materials:** ¾-inch rigid foam insulation

boards, contact cement, 1 or 1½-inch foam weatherstripping, 2-inch screw eyes, door springs; 2-inch eye bolts, washers, and locknuts. **Time:** about 2 hours.

To build the air conditioner cover, use ¾-inch rigid foam insulation board, sold in packages of six 2 × 4-foot panels. Put the cover together with contact cement—ask the insulation dealer to recommend a compatible cement, or test the cement on a scrap of insulation board before you start. If the cement is not compatible, it will melt or soften the foam.

Carefully measure the outside dimensions of the air conditioner. If the air conditioner is irregular in shape or has protruding parts, measure to these maximum dimensions. Also measure from the wall to the back of the unit; use the longest measured distance, to make sure the cover is deep enough to accommodate the unit. Cut top, bottom, and side panels to fit these dimensions.

To make the top and bottom of the cover, measure and mark two rigid foam panels to the measured depth and width of the air conditioner, plus 2 inches each way. Use a carpenters' square and a straightedge to keep your marking accurate. If the 2 × 4-foot foam panels aren't big enough, glue two panels edge to edge before marking the top and bottom panels. Apply contact cement to one long edge of each panel; let the cement dry as the manufacturer directs, and then butt the glued edges carefully together. Measure and mark the top and bottom as above.

Cut the marked panels with a utility knife with a sharp heavy-duty blade; use a straightedge to keep your cuts straight. Mark each piece as you cut it, to simplify assembly.

Measure, mark, and cut the two side panels for the cover, to the measured height and depth of the air conditioner plus 2 inches each way. Finally, measure and cut two 3-inch-square pieces to reinforce the cover's mounting bolts, and four 3-inch-wide strips—two the width of the top and bottom panels, two the height of the side panels—to reinforce its open side.

When the top and side pieces are cut, put them together to make an open box. Butt the panels firmly together, with the cut ends of the side panels covered by the top and bottom panels of the box. Keep all joints exactly square. Apply a layer of contact cement to the top edge of one side piece and to the edge of the butting side of the top panel; let the cement dry as directed by the manufacturer. Carefully set the two cemented pieces together, butting the edge of the side panel perpendicular against the bottom of the top panel. Repeat with the remaining panels, to cement all four sides of the cover squarely together.

To make the back panel of the cover, set the open box on a sheet of insulation board, with one open end down. Carefully trace around the box. Cut the back panel of the cover exactly as traced. Cement the back panel onto the open box with contact cement, butting the face of the panel over the end of the open box.

To reinforce the open end of the box, use the 3-inch-wide rigid foam strips cut to the cover's length and height. Cement a reinforcing strip onto each outside face of the box's open end, with the outside edge of the strip flush with the outside edge of the box. The combined width of the panel's covers and the reinforcing strips will form a lip on the open end of the box, where the cover will butt against the house wall.

Set the cover into place over the air conditioner and check its fit against the wall. Trim the foam as necessary to fit the siding and to match irregularities in the wall; carefully shave the lip of the box with a sharp utility knife. When the box is trimmed to fit tightly against the house, apply 1- or 1½-inch-wide foam weatherstripping all around the lip of the box, on the face that butts against the house. Join the strips firmly at the corners to minimize heat loss.

Replace the cover over the air conditioner, and press it firmly against the wall. Holding the cover in place, mark a point on each side of the box to fasten it

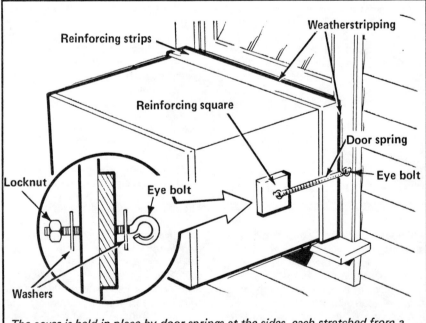

The cover is held in place by door springs at the sides, each stretched from a reinforced point on the side panel to an eye bolt in the house wall. Foam weatherstripping around the cover's lip seals out drafts and moisture.

to the wall, about 1 inch out from the cover and centered on its height. At each marked point, drill a hole and drive a 2-inch screw eye into the wall. The cover will be attached by springs at these side points; no other fastening is necessary.

Set the cover over the air conditioner again, and press it firmly against the wall. Attach a door spring to the screw eye on one side of the cover and stretch it straight out along the side of the cover, pulling it about 1 inch past its relaxed position. On the side of the cover, carefully mark the end position of the stretched spring. Repeat to mark the other side of the cover. The stretched springs will hold the cover firmly in place over the air conditioner.

On each side of the cover, cement a 3-inch square of rigid foam to the cover, centered over the marked spring point.

To complete the assembly of the cover, attach a 2-inch eye bolt at the marked spring point on each side. On each side, drill a hole through the reinforced spring point, centered on the 3-inch reinforcing block. Thread a washer onto the eye bolt and insert the bolt through the drilled opening, from the outside in. On the inside of the cover, secure the bolt with another washer and a locknut. Tighten the nut firmly, but don't crush the foam panels.

To install the cover, set the assembled cover over the air conditioner. On each side of the cover, attach a door spring to the screw hook in the wall and stretch it out along the side of the box; hook the end of the spring to the eye bolt through the cover. The tension of the springs will hold the cover flush against the wall, sealing out moisture and preventing heat loss.

Structural Work

Paint a House

Don't be afraid to paint your own house—it's a big job, but with good preparation and common sense, you can do it well. **Tools:** measuring rule, extension ladder or scaffolding, putty knife, hammer, nail set, wire brush, paint scraper, sanding block, bucket, sponge, scrub brush, garden hose, caulking gun, screwdriver; large, medium, and small paintbrushes; coat hanger, stir sticks; *for masonry houses*—paint pan, roller, and masonry roller cover. **Materials:** wood putty, medium-grit sandpaper, shellac, mild detergent, mildew remover, plastic dropcloths, putty; acrylic latex, silicone, or butyl rubber caulk; latex or oil-base exterior primer, exterior paint, exterior trim paint, and exterior porch and floor paint; rust-preventing metal primer, metal paint, masking tape, mineral spirits and fume or mildew repellent for use with oil-base paint, rags. **Time:** varies depending on size of house; allow at least several dry days.

The first consideration in outside painting is the weather. Work in late spring or early fall; both direct hot sun and below-40° F weather can ruin the job. Don't paint if rain is forecast in the next few days. Don't paint within 24 hours after a heavy rain, and don't paint early in the morning before dew evaporates.

First figure the amount of paint you'll need. Measure the distance around the foundation of the house; determine the average height of the surfaces to be painted and add 2. Multiply these two figures to obtain square footage and divide by 500 to calculate the number of gallons of paint you'll need. Estimate the square footage of trim areas. Allow for two coats of paint if the old paint is in bad condition, and ask the paint dealer to check your calculations.

In most cases, latex paint is the best type to buy. It cleans up easily and dries quickly, reducing the chance of damage to newly covered surfaces. But oil-base paint is preferable when wood in poor condition must be covered, and if you live where industrial fumes, smog, or mildew is a problem. If you use oil-base paint, add fume or mildew repellent as necessary. Make sure you buy the correct paint for wood or masonry.

Use a solid extension ladder, set firmly against the house; the top of the ladder should stick up above the edge of the roof. Work carefully, and move the ladder frequently as you work. If your house is very high, rent a scaffolding rig, and use it carefully.

Prepare the house carefully. Repair or replace any damaged siding. Clean and repair gutters and downspouts as necessary. Remove chipped and cracked putty and peel off damaged caulk. Reset loose nails with a nail set and seal all bare nailheads with a rust-preventing metal primer.

Wire-brush the siding to remove blistered or cracked paint; scrape it smooth with a putty knife or paint scraper, and sand any rough or uneven areas. Fill nail holes with wood putty. If the siding has any bare knotholes, seal them with a dab of shellac.

The house must be clean or the new paint won't stick. Use a large paintbrush to brush away webs and light dirt; hose down dirty siding. If the siding is very dirty, wash it with a mild detergent solution, rinse thoroughly, and let dry. Scrub thoroughly with a commercial mildew remover to clean mildewed areas; rinse well and let dry.

When the house is clean and prepared, spread plastic dropcloths to protect shrubs around the foundation. Apply primer to all bare or almost bare wood areas and let dry as the manufacturer directs. Reputty windows as necessary, and apply caulking compound wherever needed.

Plan your painting carefully. Paint the house surface by surface, and don't stop in the middle of a surface; you must complete an entire wall or section at a time or the break will show. Work from the top of the house down, painting only the siding. Cover the edge of the roof with dropcloths if you have to work near it, and wipe up drips as you go. Stir the paint well before starting and then every ½ hour or so as you work.

Apply the paint carefully. For masonry, use a brush or a roller with a long-nap masonry cover; roll paint on in long, even strokes. For wood or other siding, use a brush about as wide as one clapboard. Hang the can of paint from a rung of the ladder with a coat

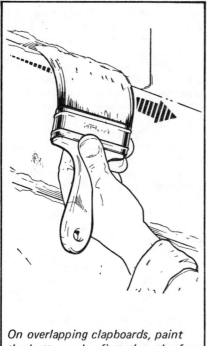

On overlapping clapboards, paint the bottom edge first, then the face; work on several boards at a time.

hanger bent into an S; flow paint on horizontally along the boards. On overlapping clapboards, paint under the narrow overlapping edge first and then the board face; work several laps and several faces at a time.

Let the paint dry completely, as specified by the manufacturer. If the old paint was in good condition or you're using oil-base paint, one coat is probably sufficient; with latex paint or over badly deteriorated paint, you may need two. Apply a second coat of paint if old bare spots show through, if the grain of the wood shows on wood siding, or if the completely dry paint is blotchy.

When the siding is completely painted and dry, paint the trim, using latex or oil-base exterior trim paint; let dry and apply a second coat as needed. Be careful not to drip trim paint on the siding, and clean up carefully as you work. Use porch and floor paint on porches and stairways; if you must have access by a stairway, paint alternate steps, let dry, and then fill in. Protect window glass with masking tape for a clean edge, and pad the top of the ladder with clean rags so you don't damage the new paint. Let the trim dry completely, according to the manufacturer's instructions, before removing the masking tape and cleaning the windows.

Prepare, prime, and paint metal trim and railings. Use rust-preventing metal primer to prevent bleeding through the new paint.

Finally, gather all dropcloths, tools, ladders, and scaffolding; clean brushes and paint pans. If you used oil-base paint, clean up with mineral spirits and dispose of cleanup rags immediately.

Paint Masonry

Painting masonry—concrete, concrete block, brick, stucco—is a demanding job, but not a difficult one. If you don't try to shortcut, you'll do at least as well as the professionals. **Tools:** sledgehammer, cold chisel, small sharp trowel, stiff wire brush, bucket and scrub brush, garden hose or sprayer, rubber gloves, safety goggles, large paintbrush or masonry paintbrush, vacuum cleaner, paint pan, paint roller with extension handle and long-nap masonry roller cover, stir sticks, paint scraper. **Materials:** liquid concrete bonding agent, cement mortar mix, strong household detergent, prepared concrete degreaser, muriatic acid, masonry filler-sealer; latex, portland cement, rubber-based or epoxy masonry paint; steel wool, masonry paint remover. **Time:** 1 day to 1 week, depending on preparation necessary.

Choose masonry paint carefully. In most cases, latex paint works well; it's easy to work with and to clean up. portland cement paint can't be applied over other paint, and it must be kept moist while it cures, but it waterproofs damp walls and wears well. Use rubber-based paint on cinder block or slag; in areas that take a lot of abuse, use epoxy paint. Apply a masonry filler-sealer to very coarse-textured surfaces. Check with the paint dealer if you aren't sure what type to buy.

Before painting any masonry surface, make sure it's in good shape. Fill all cracks and holes—clean and undercut joints, apply concrete bonding agent if necessary, fill with cement mortar, and let cure. Then prepare the surface for painting.

Unpainted surfaces. New masonry should not be painted for at least 6 months. To prepare masonry that's never been painted, scrub it with a stiff wire brush to remove dirt and debris; then scrub it down with a strong household detergent solution and rinse thoroughly, using a garden hose or sprayer. If the surface is very greasy, use a prepared concrete degreaser instead of detergent. Let the surface dry.

Very smooth concrete surfaces must be etched before they're painted. Open all windows for ventilation. Wearing rubber gloves and safety goggles, mix 1 part muriatic acid to 4 parts water. Apply to the surface with a scrub brush and let stand 4 hours; flush thoroughly

with cold water and let dry. *Caution: Muriatic acid is a strong corrosive. Wear rubber gloves and safety goggles, provide adequate ventilation, and do not inhale fumes; keep children and pets away from the area. Follow the manufacturer's instructions exactly. Wear old clothes, and wash your hands and your tools immediately.*

Efflorescence, the white bloom that sometimes appears on masonry, must be removed before the surface is painted. Wearing rubber gloves and safety goggles, mix 1 part muriatic acid to 4 parts water. Scrub the surface thoroughly with the acid, let stand 4 hours, flush thoroughly, and let dry.

Coat very coarse-textured surfaces with masonry filler-sealer before painting. Apply the sealer with a large brush or masonry brush; make sure it's compatible with the paint you're using. Let the sealer dry thoroughly, according to the manufacturer's instructions.

Finally, before painting, vacuum floor surfaces. Many paints must be applied to damp surfaces; check the instructions on the can. If pre-wetting is specified, use the fine spray of a garden hose or sprayer to moisten the surface evenly. Apply paint with a long-handled roller and a long-nap masonry roller cover; on very rough surfaces, use a masonry paintbrush. Let dry as directed; if you're using portland cement paint, mist the surface periodically during curing. Apply a second coat of paint, if necessary, as directed by the manufacturer; let dry completely.

Painted surfaces. Masonry that has been painted before is either very easy or very hard to prepare, depending on its condition. If the old paint is in good condition—no chalking, no chipping—scrub the surface with a strong detergent solution; rinse thoroughly and let dry. Dull any glossy spots with steel wool. Do not use portland cement paint unless the old finish is portland cement paint. Vacuum floor surfaces.

Apply paint with a long-handled roller. If you're using latex paint, apply two coats of paint. Thin each gallon of paint with 1 pint of water for the first coat; let dry and apply an unthinned second coat. Dampen the walls before painting as directed by the manufacturer.

If the old paint is chalking, scrub the surface with a strong detergent solution; rinse and let dry. Vacuum floor surfaces. Apply masonry filler-sealer before painting; paint as above.

A painted surface that's chipping or flaking must be stripped before it can be repainted. Scrub the surface with a stiff wire brush to remove as much paint as possible. Then, wearing rubber gloves, apply masonry paint remover. Following the manufacturer's instructions, let the paint remover work and scrape the old finish off. It may take several applications; you must remove all the old paint. Flush the surface thoroughly and let dry; then rinse and apply masonry filler-sealer. Paint as above.

Remove Mildew

Inside, mildew stains walls and bathroom tiles; outside, it disfigures and damages painted surfaces. Remove it quickly, and take steps to prevent it from coming back. **Tools:** cotton swab, rubber gloves, bucket and scrub brush, plastic squeeze bottle, toothbrush, garden hose. **Materials:** chlorine bleach, ammonia, household detergent, mildew eradicator, clean rags. **Time:** about ½ to 1 hour, depending on extent of problem.

Mildew is usually obvious inside, but may be hard to catch outside. Apply chlorine bleach to questionable areas with a cotton swab; if the stain disappears, it's mildew.

Wearing rubber gloves, scrub interior walls with a strong solution of chlorine bleach and hot water; for badly mildewed tile, apply straight bleach to grouted joints with a plastic squeeze bottle. Scrub grout joints with a toothbrush until stains disappear. Rinse very thoroughly with warm water, making sure all bleach is removed; then wipe the walls down with straight ammonia to kill all mildew spores. Rinse with clean water. *Caution: Be sure to remove all bleach entirely before applying ammonia; the two chemicals together form a very dangerous gas.*

Remove mildew from exterior walls with a solution of 1 quart chlorine bleach, ⅔ cup mildew eradicator, ⅓ cup household detergent, and 3 quarts warm water. Scrub the mildewed area thoroughly with a scrub brush and rinse it thoroughly with a garden hose.

To prevent mildew from forming again, trim trees or bushes that touch the wall. If the mildewed area is near gutters or downspouts, inspect them and correct any problems. When the house is painted, use latex paint, or add mildew inhibitor to oil-base paint.

Make Your Own Mildew-Proofer

If mildew is a problem around your home, use this excellent preventive to protect wood and fabrics in damp areas. **Equipment:** measuring cup, quart jar with cover, stir stick. **Ingredients:** copper naphthenate (banana oil), zinc bromide, amyl acetate, water. Buy these chemicals at a pharmacy. **Yield:** 1½ pints undiluted; 16 gallons diluted.

Measure 2 cups of copper naphthenate and ¾ cup of zinc bromide into a 1-quart jar. Stir the chemicals together; as you mix them, slowly add ¼ cup of amyl acetate to the mixture. Mix the compound thoroughly, cover it tightly, and store it in a safe place. *Caution: Copper naphthenate and amyl acetate are poisonous; wash measuring and mixing equipment thoroughly before using again. The compound is flammable; don't store or use near heat or flame.*

To use the mildew-proofer, pour ¼ cup of compound into a 1-gallon container of water and mix thoroughly. Brush or spray the compound onto the surface to be protected. Let treated objects air-dry before storing them.

Replace Damaged Siding

You don't have to rip off the whole side of your house to replace a damaged or rotted length of clapboard or shingle siding. **Tools:** hammer, butt chisel, hacksaw or backsaw, measuring rule, square, block plane, paintbrush, caulking gun, putty knife, drill. **Materials:** 16-penny common nails, aluminum nails, scrap wood or shingles for wedges, electrical tape, paint, acrylic latex caulk. **Time:** about 4 hours.

Make wedges from scrap lumber or use cedar shingles as wedges. To replace a damaged clapboard, drive the wedges up under the damaged siding to pull the siding away from the underlapped siding and the sheathing. Locate and remove all nails; if you can't remove them with a hammer, cut the nails with a hacksaw. Then drive wedges under the course of siding that overlaps the damaged siding, and remove all nails.

With a backsaw or a hacksaw—or the blade removed from a hacksaw and wrapped at one end with electrical tape for a handle—make two cuts through the siding, one on each side of the damaged area; this brackets the damage. Make a complete cut through the siding on each side. You may have to move the wedges around while cutting.

If the bracket cuts were successfully made—and the nails removed—the length of damaged siding should slide down and out with a little tugging. Otherwise, use a butt chisel to complete the bracket cuts. If the siding still won't pull out, hack at the damaged siding with the chisel, removing it in pieces. Don't hack at the siding until the bracket cuts have been made

Measure, mark, and cut the new siding to fit, and test-place the new piece in the void left by the old piece. The clapboard should underlap the top piece slightly and overlap the bottom piece. Plane the edges for a tight fit after you've made the initial cuts. When you're satisfied with the fit, prime the new siding piece with a coat of paint— both sides and the edges—and prime the cut edges of the old siding. Let the paint dry completely.

When the paint is completely dry, insert the new, primed siding into the gap and nail it with 16-penny nails to the siding above and below it. Then caulk the cracks with acrylic latex caulk;

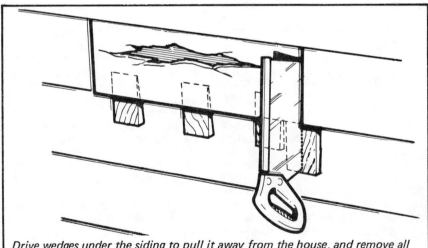

Drive wedges under the siding to pull it away from the house, and remove all nails. Bracket the damage with cuts at each side.

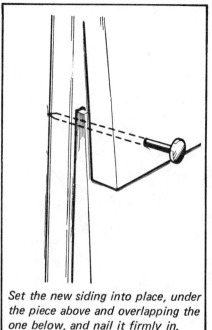

Set the new siding into place, under the piece above and overlapping the one below, and nail it firmly in.

If the clapboards or shingles are cracked or split, you may be able to repair them instead of replacing them. Tap the break together with a hammer and nail in aluminum nails 1 inch apart, through each side of the split. Then caulk the crack and paint the caulk to match the siding.

If rot is a problem on the siding, you'll have to stop the source of the rot—probably gutters and/or downspouts in poor condition. Moisture penetrating the siding from inside the house can also cause siding rot. Vent inside moisture with a fan or aluminum siding vents, or by installing insulation with a moisture vapor barrier facing *inside* the house.

Replace Damaged Porch Flooring

You don't have to replace or recover an entire porch floor if only a few flooring strips are damaged or rotted. An invisible patch is the quick answer. **Tools:** hammer, pry bar, carpenters' square, measuring rule, butt chisel, putty knife, keyhole saw or saber saw, brace and bit, crosscut saw, nail set, pencil, paintbrush, stones or bricks. **Materials:** short pieces of 2 × 4, new tongue-and-groove flooring boards, 16-penny finishing nails, wood preservative, water putty, porch and floor enamel, medium-grit sandpaper, sheet plastic film. **Time:** about 2 hours.

First, locate the joists under the flooring; nails will be aligned on the floor at the joists. With a carpenters' square, draw a square or rectangle around the damaged area, working from the inside of one joist to the inside of another. If the damage extends over a joist, draw the lines from the inside of the joists to the right and left of it.

With a brace and a ¾-inch bit, bore holes at the opposite corners of the guidelines, *inside* the lines, with one edge of the bored hole touching the line on each side of the line where the corners meet. Insert a keyhole saw or a

smooth the caulk with a putty knife or your finger. Let the caulk dry; then paint the new siding.

To replace damaged shingle siding, use similar wedging techniques. Drive the wedges under the course of shingles above the damaged area. Use a hacksaw blade to cut the siding nails if the nails can't be removed with a hammer. Wedge out and cut the nails on the shingles below the damaged shingles, if necessary. The damaged shingles can then be easily removed.

Instead of using new shingles, it's a good idea to replace damaged shingles with shingles from an inconspicuous part of the house. This way, the shingles for the patch will be weathered properly to match the shingles surrounding the patch. Repair the inconspicuous area with the new shingles.

Once the damaged shingles have been removed, insert the new shingles and nail them into position; use aluminum nails for this job. If the nail holes are not predrilled in the shingles, drill pilot holes with a small bit to prevent splitting and to make nailing easier.

279

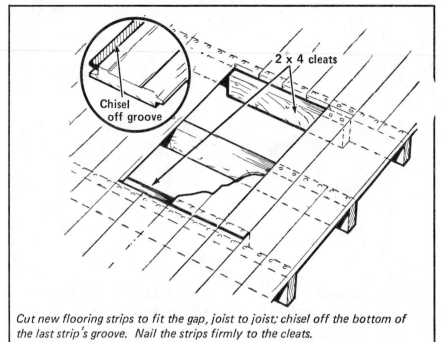

Cut new flooring strips to fit the gap, joist to joist; chisel off the bottom of the last strip's groove. Nail the strips firmly to the cleats.

saber saw into the holes and saw along the lines to cut out the marked section of flooring. Keep the cuts as square as you can; new flooring material must fit snugly into this space.

Pry out the damaged flooring. The flooring is probably tongue-and-groove boards, so work carefully with the pry bar. Make sure you don't split the grooves of the good strips of board next to the damaged flooring.

Carefully measure and cut new tongue-and-groove flooring strips to fit the gap in the floor. You'll have to remove the top groove piece of one tongue-and-groove strip to get a tight fit. Remove the groove with a butt chisel, being careful not to split the flooring. Once the chisel gets started along the wood, the groove will probably split off cleanly. Sand the surface lightly.

Measure and cut 2 × 4 cleats to fit along the inside of the floor joists on both sides of the patch. Give the cleats and the floor boards two coats of wood preservative on all surfaces—ends, edges, and faces. Let the preservative dry; then nail the cleats inside the joists,

flush with the tops of the joists. Make sure the cleats are flush before you drive the nails full-length into the cleats.

Insert the new flooring into the gap, board by board, with each end propped on its respective cleat. Nail the ends of the flooring to the 2 × 4 cleats with 16-penny finishing nails. Use two or three nails, spaced evenly, at the end of each piece of flooring. When the nailing has been completed, countersink the nails with a nail set and fill the holes and cracks with water putty.

Let the putty dry completely. When the putty is hard, lightly sand the patch with medium-grit sandpaper. Then prime the new wood with a coat of porch and floor enamel. When the primer is dry, paint the entire porch.

Porch floor damage is usually caused by moisture. To deter rot, cover the ground under the porch with sheet plastic. Lap the joints of the plastic about 6 inches up the sides of the porch frame, and weight it with stones or bricks to keep it in place. Finally, give the wood under the porch—flooring and joists—a coat of wood preservative.

Fix a Sagging Support Beam

Structural problems—cracks in foundation and interior walls, leaks, problems with doors and windows—can be caused by sagging floor joists. If you can get at the support beams under your house, and if your local building code permits, you can remedy the problem yourself. **Tools:** jackscrew—rent one if you don't want to buy—saw, hammer, measuring rule, level, chisel and sledgehammer, safety goggles, trowel. **Materials:** 4×8 and several 4×6 timbers, nails, adjustable jack posts, concrete mix for new post footings. **Time:** about 1 hour to set jackscrew; a few minutes a day during jacking-up; 1 to 2 days to pour 2 footings; about 1 hour to set jack posts.

Examine the joists in the area of the sag to locate the low point and determine the extent of the sag. Set a 4×8 timber flat on the floor at the low point to support the jackscrew. Measure both ways across the sag, including several sound beams in both directions. Cut a 4×6 to this measure and nail it flat across the sag, driving nails through the 4×6 into every joist.

Set the jackscrew at its lowest setting and place it on the 4×8 on the floor under the sag. It must be solidly footed and vertical. At the low point of the sag, measure from the 4×6 nailed across the beams to the top of the jackscrew. Cut a 4×6 to this measure, being careful to keep the cut even and level. Slide the 4×6 into place between the jackscrew and the 4×6, upright, forming a new post. Use a level to be sure this upright is plumb.

Slowly turn the handle of the jackscrew to raise the 4×6 post. Stop as soon as you feel resistance, or you'll cause serious structural damage.

The jacking-up process must be very gradual. After the initial placement of the upright, wait 24 hours; then turn the handle of the jackscrew one quarter-turn, no more. Repeat this quarter-turn adjustment every 24 hours—no more often, and no more than the quarter-turn. Each time you make an adjustment, check the beams with a level.

The sagging beams will eventually reach a level position. At this point, place an adjustable jack post at each end of each beam to keep the joists level. Jack posts are available at building supply stores; they work the same way the jackscrew does. Set the posts in place and mark the position of each post on the floor; then remove the posts.

Before setting the jack posts into place permanently, prepare a footing for each one. To do this, remove a two-foot-square section of the old floor, centered on the marked position for each post. Use a chisel and a heavy sledgehammer to break up the concrete; wear safety goggles while you work. Remove the old concrete to a depth of at least a foot. Remove all debris, clean the hole thoroughly, and spray the area with water to provide a firm base for the new concrete. Mix

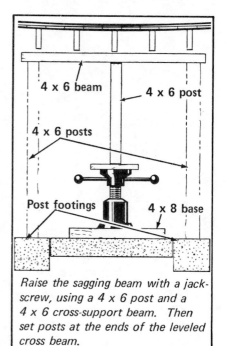

Raise the sagging beam with a jackscrew, using a 4 x 6 post and a 4 x 6 cross-support beam. Then set posts at the ends of the leveled cross beam.

prepared concrete mix according to the directions on the package, pour the footing, and level it with the existing floor.

Let the new footings cure as directed on the concrete mix package. When the new concrete has cured, set the jack posts carefully and plumb, and remove the jackscrew.

Repair Loose Mortar Joints

Loose or crumbling brick mortar joints can be very expensive to have fixed, but the repair work—called tuck-pointing—can be done by anyone with a strong arm. Because loose or crumbling mortar lets moisture through, it can result in damage to interior walls as well as hastening deterioration of sound mortar. For both reasons, tuckpoint as soon as weather permits when you notice damaged mortar joints. **Tools:** cold chisel, heavy hammer, safety goggles, garden hose, small sharp trowel, jointer or small piece of metal pipe, stiff brush (scrub brush). **Materials:** mortar mix (available in sacks; all you do is add water), mortar coloring, corrugated cardboard to use in matching color. Mix and coloring are available in hardware stores. **Time:** ½ day for small area; more for more serious damage.

Wearing safety goggles, use the cold chisel and hammer to clean out the old mortar, cutting at least ½ inch down into crumbling joints. You must remove all loose mortar so that you have a sound base for the new fill. Clean out the vertical joints first, then the horizontal ones.

Still wearing safety goggles, flush the newly cut joints with the garden hose, using a fairly strong water pressure to make sure all loose mortar and dust are removed.

Once the mortar joints are cut and flushed, mix the new mortar. Following the directions on the sack, mix a small amount of mortar, and smear it on a piece of cardboard. The mortar will dry very rapidly on the cardboard, letting you see what color it will dry to in the wall. If the new mortar is a different color from the old, add coloring, experimenting with test batches on the cardboard until you have a good match. Then mix the amount of mortar you need.

Before applying the new mortar to the wall, wet the cleaned joints again, using a heavy mist so that the brick is wet but not streaming. Using a small, sharp trowel, fill the cleaned-out joints with mortar, working first on the verticals and then on the horizontals. Pack the mortar in tightly, making sure there are no gaps or air holes.

Finish each joint as you fill it; don't fill all the joints first and then go back. If the old joints are V-shaped, use the point of the trowel to finish the new mortar. Holding it at a steady 45-degree angle, draw the trowel firmly along each joint as soon as it is filled. Shake the excess mortar off the trowel before you begin to fill the next joint. If the old mortar joints are U-shaped, use a mortar jointer or a piece of small-diameter metal pipe bent to give you a

Cut out the crumbling mortar, at least 1/2 inch deep, to provide a sound base for the new mortar joints.

Replace a Brick

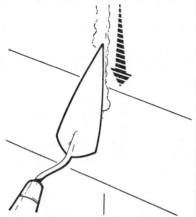

Fill the cleaned-out joints with mortar, packing it in tightly; fill first verticals, then horizontals.

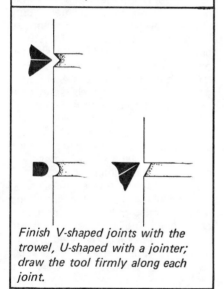

Finish V-shaped joints with the trowel, U-shaped with a jointer; draw the tool firmly along each joint.

A loose or broken brick in a wall or chimney looks bad, and it can lead to further damage. But the repair is an easy one. **Tools:** safety goggles, cold chisel, sledgehammer, bucket, wide brick chisel, wire brush, garden hose, mixing bucket and stir stick, sharp trowel, mortar jointer or thin metal rod, stiff scrub brush. **Materials:** mortar mix, mortar coloring, corrugated cardboard scrap, replacement brick. **Time:** 1 to 2 hours.

Wearing safety goggles, use a cold chisel and a sledgehammer to remove the mortar around a loose brick, working carefully to avoid damaging the loose brick or surrounding bricks. Lift the loosened brick out from the wall or chimney and set it in a bucket of water to soak.

If a loose brick cannot be easily removed, or if the brick is broken, break it up to remove it. Wearing safety goggles, chop out the damaged brick with a wide brick chisel and a sledgehammer, being careful not to damage surrounding bricks. Fill a bucket with water and set the replacement brick in it to soak.

Still wearing safety goggles, remove all remaining mortar from the hole where the brick was removed; use the sledgehammer and cold chisel to remove large chunks of old mortar and then wire-brush the cavity to remove any debris still adhering to the bricks. Flush the cavity thoroughly with the garden hose.

Mix a small batch of mortar according to the directions on the package. To see what color the mortar will be when it dries, spread a little mortar on a scrap piece of corrugated cardboard; as the cardboard absorbs water from the mortar, the mortar's color will lighten. Add mortar coloring as necessary, experimenting with mortar applied to the cardboard until the new mortar matches the old. Mix enough mortar to secure the brick, and add coloring in the proportion used in the test batch.

Before replacing the brick in the wall,

good grip. The technique is the same; draw the jointer or pipe firmly along the joint to leave a smooth concave surface.

To prevent the mortar from drying too quickly, wet the new joints down a few times a day for two or three days, using the fine spray of the garden hose. When the wall is completely dry, clean any excess mortar from the bricks with a dry, stiff brush.

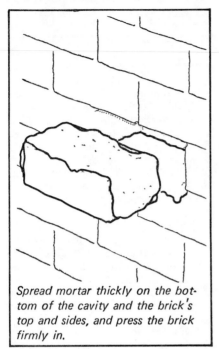

Spread mortar thickly on the bottom of the cavity and the brick's top and sides, and press the brick firmly in.

spray the cavity again with the garden hose to dampen it; the cavity should be wet but not streaming. Spread a thick bed of mortar on the bottom surface of the cavity, smoothing it roughly level.

Remove the replacement brick—salvaged or new—from the bucket of water and shake it to remove excess water. Apply mortar generously to the top and ends of the brick; don't mortar the back. Set the brick carefully into place in the prepared hole, pressing it in firmly. It should align with the bricks on each side of it; adjust it to match, applying more mortar as necessary. Make sure the face of the new brick is flush with the surface of the wall.

When the new brick is firmly in place, force mortar into the top and side joints of the brick to fill them completely. Smooth the mortar all around the new brick, making sure there are no gaps. Scrape excess mortar from the wall with the side of the trowel. Then, using the trowel, a brick jointer, or a thin metal rod bent to form a handle, tool the new mortar joints to match the joints in the rest of the wall.

To keep the new mortar from drying too quickly, spray it lightly with the garden hose several times a day for 2 or 3 days. When the mortar has set completely, use a stiff scrub brush to remove any excess mortar from the face of the wall.

Mend Crumbling Concrete Steps

Old houses and even middle-aged ones often have front or back steps that are crumbling along the edges. It takes time to recast the damaged steps, but it isn't difficult. **Tools:** safety goggles, cold chisel, sledgehammer, whisk broom, garden hose, hammer, sturdy wheelbarrow, shovel, stiff paintbrush, trowel, wood concrete float. **Materials:** boards as long and wide as the steps to be mended, bricks, boards for sides of form, short pieces of 2 × 4, 4-penny common nails, ready-mix sand concrete mix, liquid concrete bonding agent, plastic dropcloth. **Time:** about 1 day; if several steps must be recast, plan on spending more time. In addition, a few minutes several times each day during the curing period.

Prepare the edge of each damaged step by chiseling out the crumbling edge. Wearing safety goggles, use a cold chisel and a sledgehammer to deepen and widen the open edge down to solid concrete. Angle the chisel to cut straight back into the riser of the step and to cut sharply back and down into the tread, forming an acute open V along the edge of the step. Clean out the undercut edge with a whisk broom and flush it thoroughly with a garden hose.

Build a form around the step to be recast. Use a board as long and as wide as the front edge of the step is wide and high; set the board across the riser and stack several bricks against it at each end to hold it firmly in place. If possible, the top edge of the form should be level with the sound surface of the step.

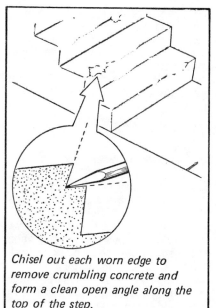

Chisel out each worn edge to remove crumbling concrete and form a clean open angle along the top of the step.

air spaces; pack the concrete firmly into the undercut edge. Level the surface roughly with the trowel to meet the surface of the old concrete.

Smooth the newly poured concrete with a wood float, being careful to hold the float level on the old surface and the new edge. Let the newly poured edge harden for about 45 minutes and then smooth the surface again with the wood float to match the texture of the old concrete. If you want a smoother finish on the recast step, wait until the film of water left on the concrete after the last float-smoothing has been absorbed, then smooth the edge of the step carefully with a clean trowel.

Let the concrete set until the film of surface water left by the final smoothing has been absorbed. Cover the steps with a plastic dropcloth, weighted above and below the mended steps and at the sides. Let the patched edges cure for a week before walking on them. Several times each day during the curing period, lift off the plastic and spray the recast steps lightly with the fine spray of

To close in the ends of the steps, set a board across each side of the chiseled-out step, flush against the concrete and level with the step surface at the top edge. Nail a piece of 2 × 4 across each board along the top of the step and wedge another piece of 2 × 4 under this brace to hold the forms solidly in place.

Prepare ready-mix sand concrete mix according to the directions on the package; pour the dry mix into a sturdy wheelbarrow, add water, and mix it thoroughly with a shovel. When the concrete mix is ready to use, mist the chiseled-out step with the garden hose to dampen the concrete. Working quickly, apply liquid concrete bonding agent to the undercut edge with a stiff paintbrush according to the manufacturer's instructions. Spread the bonding agent evenly into the undercut edge, being careful to cover the entire inside surface. Clean the paintbrush immediately with water.

Fill the boarded-in step edge cavity with concrete, using a trowel or the shovel to spread it along the edge. Slice through the new concrete with the sharp end of the trowel to remove any

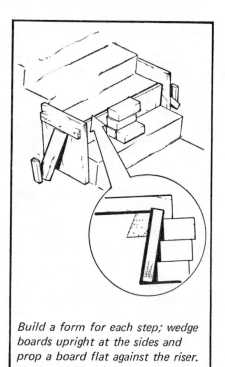

Build a form for each step; wedge boards upright at the sides and prop a board flat against the riser.

a garden hose, then replace the plastic. To keep the new edges from being damaged, leave the forms in place until the concrete has completely cured.

Mend Cracks in Brick or Concrete Block

Unless there's a serious structural problem, wide top-to-bottom cracks in brick or concrete block walls are easy to fill. Work through the broken bricks instead of trying to replace them. **Tools:** safety goggles, cold chisel, sledgehammer, brick chisel, wire brush, garden hose, mixing bucket and stir stick, small sharp trowel, wide board to cover crack, 2 × 4 prop, large funnel, rubber tubing to fit over funnel end, mortar jointer or thin metal rod, paintbrush. **Materials:** mortar mix, Portland cement, hydrated lime, sand, scrap corrugated cardboard, mortar coloring, duct tape, exterior paint or cement paint, solvent for paint. **Time:** about 3 to 4 hours for cleaning and initial filling; additional time depending on extent of damage.

Wearing safety goggles, clean all crumbling brick and mortar from the crack with a cold chisel and sledgehammer. Where the crack runs through a brick or a concrete block, use a brick chisel, angled into the crack, to widen and undercut the break. Enlarge the crack to a consistent width and clean the inside of the crack to its full depth, or as far in as you can reach. Wire-brush the crack, inside and out, to remove debris; flush it thoroughly with a garden hose.

Cracks that affect only a single layer of brick can be filled with mortar. Mix a small amount of mortar according to the directions on the package. Spread a little mortar on a scrap of corrugated cardboard; it will dry quickly. Add mortar coloring to the mortar as necessary to match the old mortar, experimenting

with the cardboard as you add coloring. When the test batch matches the old mortar, mix enough mortar to fill the crack and add coloring in the tested proportion.

Spray the crack thoroughly with the garden hose. Fill the crack with mortar, using a small sharp trowel to force the mortar in to the full depth of the crack. Treat the crack as one long joint, filling cleaned-out joints and the gaps in broken bricks or block evenly all along the crack.

When the crack is solidly packed with mortar, finish the surface with a jointer and the trowel. Match the old joints where the crack follows a joint; trowel the mortar to match the surface where the mended surface is block or brick. Let the crack cure thoroughly, at least 1 week; spray the patched area lightly with the garden hose several times a day during the curing period.

When the crack is very wide and deep, fill it with a thin grout mixture. Wearing safety goggles, chisel out, wire-brush, and flush the crack to clean it thoroughly. Mix a small amount of filler, using 1 part Portland cement, 1 part hydrated lime, and 6 parts sand; mix the dry materials and add water slowly to form a thin, easily pourable grout. Add mortar coloring, testing the mixture on a scrap of corrugated cardboard, to match the color of the old mortar; then mix a bucketful of grout in the same proportions.

Working quickly, spray the inside of the crack lightly to dampen it. Mask the lower third of the crack with duct tape set flat over the opening. Set a wide board flat against the wall to hold the tape in place, and wedge it firmly upright with a 2 × 4.

Use a wide-mouthed funnel and a length of rubber tubing to fill the crack; you'll need a helper for this. Push one end of the tubing over the narrow end of the funnel and set the open end into the crack. Hold the end of the tubing at least halfway into the crack and as near the bottom as you can reach over the board wedged against the wall. Pour grout slowly into the funnel to fill the bottom of the crack, and remove the

Mask the crack with tape and prop a board across it; pour grout through a tube to fill the crack gradually.

thoroughly, at least a week after the final application of grout. Spray the patched area lightly with the garden hose several times a day during the curing period.

Finish either mortar-filled or grout-filled cracks by painting the patch to match the surrounding wall. For a painted wall, touch up the newly filled and cured crack with the same exterior paint used on the wall. To hide the crack in a brick wall, use cement paint the same color as the bricks. Thin the paint and apply it carefully to the crack where it passes through bricks; repeat as necessary until the color is correct.

Clean Your Chimney

Professional chimney sweeps are coming back in style. They're fun to watch, but you can easily do the job yourself. **Tools:** extension ladder, work gloves, flashlight, hand mirror, whisk broom, dustpan, vacuum cleaner. **Materials:** scrap plywood or heavy plastic sheet, wide masking tape, burlap bag, newspaper, two bricks, heavy rope, 2-foot length of tire chain, plastic garbage bag. **Time:** about 1 hour, plus 15 minutes for cleaning after dust settles.

Clean the chimney at least once a year; soot caked in the flue can be a real fire hazard. Close the damper in the chimney. Set a piece of scrap plywood across the fireplace opening, flush against the wall, or tape a sheet of heavy plastic over the opening with masking tape. Seal the edges of either plywood or plastic with masking tape all around.

If the flue is straight, use a burlap bag to clean it. Fill the bag—potato sack size—with wadded newspaper, and weight it with two bricks. Tie a piece of heavy rope to the bag, long enough to reach all the way down the chimney. If the flue is curved, use 2 feet of a tire chain or other heavy chain instead of the burlap bag. Tie the chain to a piece

tubing from the crack. Rinse the funnel, the tubing, and the bucket thoroughly.

Let the partially filled crack set for about 1 day; then remove the board and the duct tape from the crack. Use a mortar jointer—or thin metal rod bent to form a handle—and a trowel to finish the crack, matching both joint and brick or block textures. Then fill the crack further.

Mix a bucketful of grout in the same proportions as before. Working quickly, spray the crack lightly with a garden hose. Mask the crack with duct tape and wedge the board into place against the wall. Using the wide-mouthed funnel, pour the grout into the crack. Let it dry for 1 day and remove the mask; finish the grout to match joints and brick or block.

Repeat the filling and finishing process daily, section by section, until the entire crack has been filled. Be sure to mix and color the grout in the same proportion each time. Let the grout cure

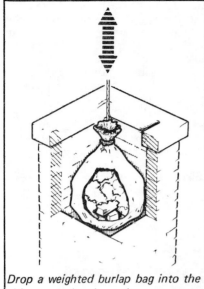

Drop a weighted burlap bag into the chimney to break up the soot; scrape up and down the sides of the flue.

bage bag open directly under the damper and open the damper, letting the soot fall directly into the bag. Shine a flashlight up the chimney and use a hand-mirror to make sure the chimney is clean. Wearing work gloves, reach up the flue through the damper and brush off the smoke shelf next to the damper. Finally, vacuum both the smoke shelf and the fireplace.

Make Your Own Chimney Cleaner

Cleaning a chimney is a dirty job from the outside, but you can prevent the buildup of soot and creosote while you use your wood-burning fireplace. **Equipment:** newspaper, measuring cup. **Ingredients:** zinc oxide powder, coarse table salt. Buy zinc oxide powder at a pharmacy. **Yield:** 2 cups.

Mix 1 cup of zinc oxide powder with 1 cup of coarse table salt on a double sheet of newspaper. To use, sprinkle the mixture on a hot fire. *Caution: Don't bend low over the fire; keep your head turned away while you pour the mixture on.* Use once or twice a year.

Fix a Leaky Roof

The hardest part of fixing a leak is finding it; once that's done, the job is easy. **Tools:** flashlight, chalk, stiff wire, extension ladder, propane torch, putty knife, pry bar, tin snips, utility knife with sharp heavy-duty blades, hammer, small trowel, measuring rule, sharp wood chisel, fine-toothed handsaw, hacksaw, nail set. **Materials:** troweling-consistency asphalt roofing compound, replacement shingles, sheet copper or sheet aluminum, 6-penny galvanized roofing nails, 15-pound roofing felt, liquid asphalt, roofing compound, large stiff brush or broom, mineral spirits, rags. **Time:** once you find

of heavy rope, long enough to reach all the way down the chimney. This can also be used to clean straight flues, if necessary.

Use an extension ladder to reach the roof, bracing it firmly against the house. The top of the ladder should stick up beyond the edge of the roof. Wear old clothes, rubber-soled shoes, and work gloves.

Climb up to the chimney, keeping one hand on the ladder as you climb. If you're using a weighted bag, drop it into the chimney and pull it up, keeping a firm grip on the end of the rope. Repeat five or six times, constantly scraping the sides of the flue with the weighted bag to break up the soot. If the chimney is large, repeat this process at each corner of the chimney to clean the flue thoroughly. Use the same procedure with the tire chain, slapping at the sides of the flue to break up soot and moving around the chimney.

Wait 2 hours to let the dust settle; then remove the plywood or plastic cover from the fireplace opening. Clean the soot from the fireplace with a whisk broom and dustpan. Hold a plastic garthe leak, about 10 to 15 minutes per shingle; about 1 to 2 hours per patch in a flat roof; about 1 to 2 hours to coat a flat roof.

You can't fix it while it's wet, but try to locate the leak while it's raining. If the leaky roof is above an unfinished attic or crawl space, climb into the attic. Shine a flashlight along all the beams in the general area of the leak to see where the water comes in; watch for the shine of the water in the light. In daylight, examine the roof for wet spots and discolored patches. Water coming in through a pitched roof usually runs down the beams before dripping through into the rooms below, so trace every wet spot or stream of water back to its source.

When you've located the leak, mark it. On the inside, draw a circle around the bad spot with chalk. If you can, force a stiff wire up through the roof deck until you feel it push through to the outside. The wire will flag the leak when you do the repair work.

If the attic is finished, you can only make an educated guess as to where

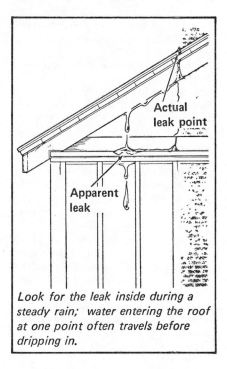

Actual leak point

Apparent leak

Look for the leak inside during a steady rain; water entering the roof at one point often travels before dripping in.

the leak is. Draw a rough plan of the roof above the leaky area, and mark chimneys, dormers, vent pipes, ridges, valleys, and flashing on the sketch. These are all potential trouble spots; any such situation anywhere near the leak inside might be the source of the problem outside.

When the rain has stopped and the roof has dried out completely, assemble your tools and set up an extension ladder to give you access to the roof. Make sure the ladder is firmly braced against the house; the top of the ladder should stick up above the edge of the roof. Wear old clothes and rubber-soled shoes.

Asbestos shingle roofs. In the leak area, look for missing or torn shingles, curled-up shingles, or—around the chimney or some other interruption—breaks in flashing joints or gaps in joints finished with roofing compound. If you can't find any evidence of damage, call a professional. The roof is no place to fool around.

To refasten a curled-back shingle, gently straighten the edges of the shingle. This is easy in hot weather; in cold weather you may have to soften the shingle first. To soften a brittle shingle, carefully place the diffused flame of a propane torch over the curled edges. Apply only enough heat to soften the shingle, not enough to ignite it. Apply roofing compound generously to the bottom of the loose shingle with a putty knife and press the shingle firmly into place.

To replace a torn or rotten shingle, carefully remove it from the roof. Lift the edges of the shingles that overlap the damaged one and carefully pry out the nails that hold the damaged one in place; use a pry bar. Slide the old shingle out from the surrounding ones and scrape out any roofing compound left in the opening.

If possible, replace damaged or missing shingles with matching shingles, saved from the original installation. If you don't have any of the original shingles and can't get shingles that match, use nonmatching shingles or cut shingle-size patches from sheet copper or aluminum. They won't look as good, but they'll do the job.

Round the back corners of the replacement shingle slightly with a sharp utility knife or, for sheet metal, tin snips. Slide the shingle into place, its front edge aligned with the other shingles in the row, its back edge under the overlapping shingles in the next row up. If you're using a sheet metal patch, apply roofing compound to the back of the patch before sliding it into place.

Nail the new shingle into place under the overlapping edges of the shingles above it. Gently lift the overlapping corners. Drive a roofing nail through each top corner of the new shingle and cover each nailhead with a dab of roofing compound. Smooth the lifted edges of the overlapping shingle into place.

Follow the same procedure to replace rows of shingles. To replace ridge shingles, use the same technique, but before nailing the new shingle into place, coat the back of the shingle with roofing compound. Nail the corners into place and cover the nailheads with roofing compound.

Examine flashings, valleys, and coated vent pipes for damage. If the metal flashing around a chimney or

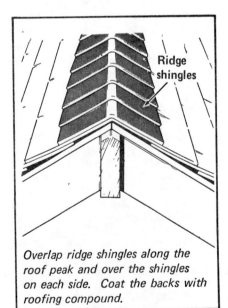

Overlap ridge shingles along the roof peak and over the shingles on each side. Coat the backs with roofing compound.

dormer is pulling loose from the mortar that holds it, it must be replaced; otherwise, apply roofing compound to questionable areas with a putty knife or small trowel. Cover any exposed nails with roofing compound. Clean up with mineral spirits and rags, and dispose of all waste materials immediately.

Flat roofs. Damage to flat roofs is usually easy to see. Look for blisters of roofing felt that have cracked. Cut the blister open with a sharp utility knife, being careful to cut only the blistered layer of felt. Lift the sliced edges back from the middle of the blistered spot. If there's water inside, press the surrounding area to force it out to the top; then use a propane torch, very carefully, to dry the inside of the blister. If the day is dry and sunny, let the blister dry naturally.

Apply roofing compound to the bottom edges of the loose flaps and press them down firmly. Nail the cut edges down with roofing nails and coat the entire blister with roofing compound. Cut a patch of 15-pound roofing felt to cover the blister area. Set it into place and nail it down with roofing nails, driving nails every ½ inch around the edges of the patch. Coat the entire patch with roofing compound, making sure nailheads are well covered.

To repair a hole in a flat roof, measure and mark an even patch around the hole. Cut out the damaged area carefully with a sharp utility knife, keeping the edges of the cut even. If the hole is a deep one, work through one layer of roofing felt at a time, cutting out and removing each layer that is visibly damaged. Remove all damaged layers, but don't cut deeper than you have to. Let the cutout area dry thoroughly, or, if necessary, dry it very carefully with a propane torch.

Cut a patch of 15-pound roofing felt to replace each damaged layer of felt you've removed. Cut patches carefully to fit the hole. Apply roofing compound to the bottom of the hole and set a roofing-felt patch into the hole; coat the top of the patch with roofing compound. Repeat to replace each cutout layer of roofing felt.

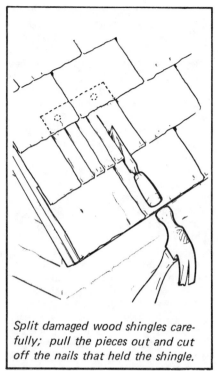

Split damaged wood shingles carefully; pull the pieces out and cut off the nails that held the shingle.

Coat the top patch layer with roofing compound, extending the compound 2 inches past the patch on all sides. To seal the repair, cut another patch 4 inches longer and wider than the filled-in hole. Set this patch carefully onto the surface of the roof over the patch and nail it into place, driving roofing nails every ½ inch around its edges. Finally, coat the heads of the nails with roofing compound.

Examine joints and flashings for damage and apply roofing compound to questionable areas. Cover any exposed nails with roofing compound. If the entire flat roof surface is badly worn, and you can see many worn spots or fine cracks, coat the entire flat roof with liquid roofing compound. Spread the compound with a large stiff brush or a broom—you'll have to throw away the brush, so don't use a good one. Clean up with mineral spirits and rags, and dispose of all waste materials immediately.

Wood shake or shingle roofs.

Replace split shingles or shakes with new ones of the same type; replace ridge shingles with specially mitered shingles. To remove the damaged shingle, split it carefully with a sharp wood chisel and a hammer, holding the chisel up into the shingle at the slant of the roof and being careful not to damage the surrounding shingles. Pull the broken pieces of the old shingle out of the roof.

Measure the opening to be filled and cut a new shingle ⅜ inch narrower with a fine-toothed handsaw. Before setting the shingle into place, cut off the nails that held the old shingle. Slide the blade of a hacksaw carefully under the overlapping shingles and saw off the nailheads, cutting as far down the nail shaft as you can.

Slide the new shingle into place, under the overlapping shingles and over the sawed-off nailheads. Nail it into position with two roofing nails, one on each edge of the shingle that's covered by the overlapping shingles above it. Set the heads of the nails with a nail set and cover them with roofing compound. Replace each damaged shingle the same way.

Install a Roof Ventilator

If your attic is already insulated, or if you plan to insulate it, consider installing a roof-mounted ventilator. The ventilator—either electric or wind-powered—helps remove excessive moisture in an attic. If your home is air-conditioned, it can also lower cooling costs, as much as 25 percent. **Tools:** keyhole saw or saber saw, 20-penny nail, hammer, measuring rule, screwdriver, brace and bit, chalk line, stick chalk; wide, flat pry bar; caulking gun, putty knife. **Materials:** ventilating fan, roofing nails, cartridge-type roofing compound, double-faced utility tape. **Time:** about 4 hours per unit.

Roof ventilators come packaged with

all the necessary mounting components; the cost is minimal and installation isn't difficult. To determine the proper capacity of the fan, multiply the square footage of the attic by 0.7. If the shingles on the roof are dark, add 15 percent. Bring this figure with you when purchasing the ventilator; if the attic is large, you may need two units.

Plan to mount the ventilator inconspicuously on the back of the roof. Make sure it's far enough down from the ridge of the roof to keep it hidden from the front of the house. Measure on the outside of the roof from the ridge to this spot.

Inside the attic, transfer this measurement from the ridge, drawing a line at the premeasured point. Measure from center to center, rafter to rafter, to find the rafter's center. Mark the center point. Most rafters are 16 inches on center; the mark would then be at 8 inches. At this point, drive a 20-penny nail through the sheathing and out the shingles so that the point of the nail sticks out above the roof's outside surface. This is the most critical part of the job; the measurement must be exact to cut the vent hole between the rafters. Double-check your measurements.

Out on the roof, locate the nail point. Use this nail as a compass point to outline the vent's circular hole. Tie a chalk line measuring half the diameter of the circle to the nail; the specific diameter will be included with the kit. Tie a piece of stick chalk to the end of the line and carefully draw a circle on the shingles.

Drill a hole through the roofing and sheathing with a brace and a ¾-inch bit, *inside* the scribed circle, so that one edge of the drill bit just touches the line. Insert a keyhole saw or a saber saw through this pilot hole and carefully saw out the circle. If possible, save the shingles for patching.

Place the roof vent over the opening and draw around the edges of its flashing with chalk. Remove the vent. With a wide, flat pry bar, carefully lift the shingles within this area. Place the vent over the hole again to test for proper fit; make sure the fan fits over the hole and the shingles have been cut back far enough. Then remove the vent and tape around the edges of the vent with one layer of double-faced utility tape.

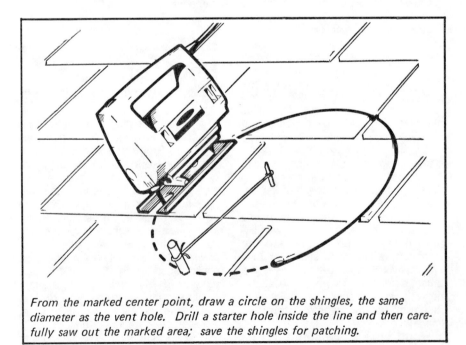

From the marked center point, draw a circle on the shingles, the same diameter as the vent hole. Drill a starter hole inside the line and then carefully saw out the marked area; save the shingles for patching.

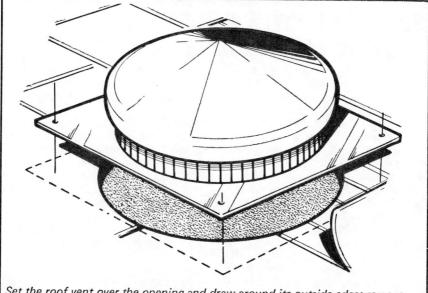

Set the roof vent over the opening and draw around its outside edge; remove all shingles inside the marked area. Fasten the vent over the prepared opening with double-faced utility tape, nail it down, and seal it.

Position the vent over the hole and the stripped-shingle area and stick the taped vent to the sheathing of the roof. Tap the flashing down with a hammer to seal the vent to the roof.

With roofing nails spaced 2 inches apart, nail the vent flashing to the roof sheathing. Then fill the joint between the flashing and the roof with cartridge-type roofing compound. Replace and renail the shingles around the vent, and seal the shingles and the heads of the nails with roofing compound. If necessary, use the extra shingles from the cutout circle for patching. Nail the patches into place or cement them down with roofing compound.

If the vent is wind-driven, the job is complete. If the vent is electrically powered, make the simple electrical connection to the attic's wiring, as instructed by the manufacturer. A diagram for this hookup is included with the vent fan, along with the proper accessories and materials. *Caution: Before you connect the fan, flip the circuit breaker or remove the fuse that supplies power to the circuit.*

Repair
Roof Valleys
and Flashing

The metal flashings around chimneys and dormers and the metal valleys where one roof pitch meets another are often the places roof problems start. Major leaks call for professional attention, but you can make some repairs yourself. **Tools:** extension ladder, trowel, safety goggles, cold chisel, sledgehammer, wire brush, paintbrush, mixing bucket and stir stick, small sharp trowel, caulking gun, screwdriver, tin snips. **Materials:** troweling-consistency asphalt roofing compound, cement mortar mix, roof caulk, 6-penny galvanized roofing nails, mineral spirits, rags, sheet copper or sheet aluminum to match existing flashings. Do not use a metal different from existing flashings; this can cause corrosion. **Time:** depends on extent of repairs necessary; about 2 to 3 hours to inspect joints and fill small gaps.

Set up an extension ladder to give you access to the roof. Brace the ladder firmly; the top of the ladder should stick up above the edge of the roof. Wear old clothes and rubber-soled shoes.

Inspect flashing and valley joints every spring. If the roofing compound along a joint looks worn or you can see thin spots or gaps, apply roofing compound generously along the entire joint with a trowel. Make sure the compound covers both edges of the joined surfaces completely.

Chimney flashing is installed in two sections, the base and the cap. The cap flashing is embedded in the mortar joints between bricks. If the mortar holding it in place is beginning to crumble or the cap flashing has pulled loose from the masonry, remove the lip of the flashing completely from the mortar joint. Do *not* pull the flashing away from the chimney; leave it in place except for the loose edge.

Wearing safety goggles, remove the

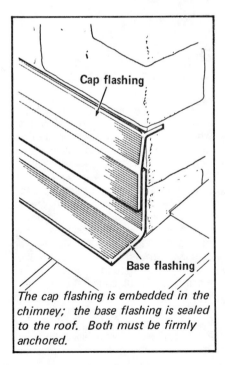

The cap flashing is embedded in the chimney; the base flashing is sealed to the roof. Both must be firmly anchored.

old mortar from the flashing joint; use a cold chisel and a sledgehammer to clean the joint completely. Be careful not to dislodge the chimney flashing any further. Wire-brush the chiseled-out joint to remove any remaining debris.

Mix cement mortar mix as directed. Dampen the cleaned joint with a wet paintbrush and fill the joint firmly with mortar, using a small sharp trowel; be careful not to leave any gaps. When the entire joint is filled, reset the lip of the flashing into the fresh mortar, pressing only hard enough to set it into place. If you press too hard, the flashing may spring back, pulling the new mortar out with it.

Let the newly mortared joint dry completely, according to the mortar manufacturer's directions. Then caulk all around the top of the cap flashing with roof caulk where the lip of the flashing meets the mortar joint.

Inspect vent pipes and apply roofing compound as necessary. If the protective collar at the base of the pipe is loose, knock it back against the pipe with the shaft of a screwdriver. Caulk around the collar with roof caulk.

Valley flashings, used where two roof pitches meet, are either open or closed. An open flashing is left uncovered; the metal shows all along the valley. A closed flashing is covered with shingles. You'll be able to see damage to open valleys; you'll also be able to repair them. Damaged closed valleys are indicated by leaks inside, directly under the valleys; they usually require professional attention.

Small holes in open valleys are easy to patch. Wire-brush the damaged area to remove dirt and debris. Using tin snips, cut a patch from sheet copper or aluminum—be sure it's the same metal the valley is—about 4 inches longer than the damaged area in each direction. Coat the entire area generously with roofing compound and press the patch into place, bending it to conform to the valley's shape. Cover the edges of the patch with roofing compound.

If you can't see any damage along an open valley but it has leaked, check to see whether the shingles along the

Replace Vent Pipe Flashing

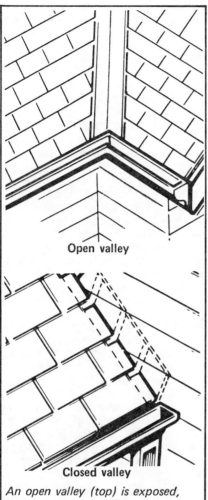

Open valley

Closed valley

An open valley (top) is exposed, with no shingles over it; patch holes with sheet metal and resecure loose edge shingles. A closed valley (bottom) is covered with shingles; have it repaired by a professional roofer.

Replacing leaky flashing around a vent pipe or an appliance chimney is a simple project, whether the pipe is on a pitched roof or a flat one. **Tools:** extension ladder, measuring rule, pry bar, work gloves, scrap wood block, claw hammer, utility knife with sharp heavy-duty blades, chalk, paint scraper or trowel. **Materials:** troweling-consistency asphalt roofing compound, replacement vent pipe or appliance chimney flashing of the same diameter and type as the old flashing, 6-penny galvanized roofing nails, mineral spirits, rags; for a flat roof, 15-pound roofing felt. **Time:** about 2 to 3 hours.

Buy a replacement flashing exactly like the old one. Set up an extension ladder to give you access to the roof. Brace the ladder firmly against the house; the top of the ladder should stick up above the edge of the roof. Wear old clothes and rubber-soled shoes.

Vents on pitched roofs. The flashing around a pitched-roof vent pipe is a single flat sheet, with a protective collar that fits around the pipe. This sheet of flashing is covered with shingles on the up-roof side, but left exposed on the down-roof side. To remove the old flashing, gently lift off the shingles over it with a pry bar. Be careful not to break the shingles; you'll have to replace them over the new flashing. Set the shingles aside.

Wearing work gloves, insert the blade of a pry bar under the edge of the old flashing; wedge a block of scrap wood under the pry bar so you don't damage the roof. Lever the old flashing up and lift it off over the vent pipe, being careful not to knock the pipe out of place. Pull out any nails left around the pipe with a claw hammer, and seal the holes with roofing compound.

Wearing work gloves, set the new

valley are loose. If the shingles are loose, set them back into place with roofing compound, applied generously; work from the bottom up. If the shingles were still firmly secured, the flashing may be too narrow; call a professional.

Clean the tools with mineral spirits and rags; dispose of all waste materials immediately.

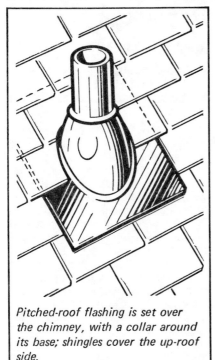

Pitched-roof flashing is set over the chimney, with a collar around its base; shingles cover the up-roof side.

Vents on flat roofs. The flashing over a flat-roof vent pipe covers the entire pipe, with a cylindrical pipe casing and a flat base sheet. The base is set into the roof itself, and is completely covered.

To remove the old flashing, brush any gravel on the roof away from the vent pipe to clear an area at least 4 feet across. Cut a slit through the roof just outside one edge of the flashing, using a utility knife with a sharp heavy-duty blade. Wearing work gloves, insert the blade of a pry bar into the slit and under the edge of the old flashing; wedge a block of scrap wood under the pry bar to improve leverage and protect the roof. Work along the cut edge of the flashing with the pry bar to separate the flashing from the roof beneath it; cut around the remaining three sides of the flashing to loosen it entirely. Be careful not to knock the pipe out of place as you pry up the old flashing.

Carefully lift the old flashing over the vent pipe, leaving an evenly cut hole in the layers of the roof. Before installing the new flashing, you must fill this hole with layers of roofing felt and compound until it's flush with the surface of the roof. Cut several pieces of 15-pound roofing felt to the exact shape of the hole, using the cutout old flashing as a pattern. Mark the pipe location on the roofing felt with chalk, and cut a hole in each patch to fit around the vent pipe.

Coat the bottom of the hole thickly with roofing compound and set a patch over the vent pipe and into the hole, pressing it firmly into place. Cover the patch generously with roofing compound. Repeat, alternating layers of roofing felt and compound, to fill the hole completely. Coat the last patch layer generously with roofing compound, applying it around the base of the vent pipe to seal it completely.

Wearing work gloves, set the new flashing in place over the vent pipe, with the cylindrical casing over the pipe and the base aligned the same way the old one was. Nail down the corners of the flashing with 6-penny galvanized roofing nails; cover the nailheads with roofing compound. Bend the top edge of the

flashing in place over the vent pipe, aligned the same way the old one was. Nail down the corners of the flashing with 6-penny galvanized roofing nails and cover the nailheads with roofing compound; apply the compound with a paint scraper or a trowel. Seal the edge of the protective collar around the vent pipe with roofing compound.

Finally, replace the shingles over the top of the new vent pipe flashing, covering the up-roof side the way the old flashing was covered. Nail each shingle firmly into place with four roofing nails and cover the nailheads with roofing compound; work from the bottom row up. When you reach the row directly below the shingles that have *not* been pried off, slide the top edge of each shingle under the overlapping bottom edge of the shingle above it; lift the shingle above to nail the loose shingles into place.

Clean your tools with mineral spirits and rags. Dispose of waste materials immediately.

Install Gutters and Downspouts

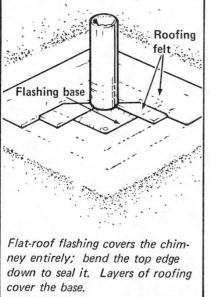

Flashing base

Roofing felt

Flat-roof flashing covers the chimney entirely; bend the top edge down to seal it. Layers of roofing cover the base.

casing cylinder down over the edge of the vent pipe to seal the flashing.

Cover the new flashing with two more patches of roofing felt. Cut one patch 6 inches longer and wider than the flashing's base plate; cut the second patch 12 inches longer and wider. Cut a center hole in each for the vent pipe.

Cover the base of the flashing generously with roofing compound, spreading compound 3 inches beyond the flashing all around. Set the smaller patch over the vent pipe and press it into place. Cover the patch generously with roofing compound, spreading compound 6 inches beyond the patch all around; be careful not to leave any gaps around the base of the vent pipe. Set the larger patch over the vent pipe and press it into place.

Secure the patch over the vent pipe with roofing nails; drive nails every ½ inch around the edges of the patch. Cover the nailheads with roofing compound. Finally, spread the gravel back over the patched area.

Clean your tools with mineral spirits and rags. Dispose of waste materials immediately.

Good stormwater drainage is essential, but a good gutter and downspout system can be expensive. Cut the cost of the improvement by installing the system yourself. **Tools:** two extension ladders or tall stepladders, measuring rule, hammer, pry bar, pliers, chalk line, level, fine-toothed hacksaw, fine-toothed file, short piece of 2 × 4, caulking gun, electric drill, putty knife. **Materials:** gutter components (gutter and downspout sections, slip connectors, end caps, inside and outside corners, drop outlets, elbows, shoe elbows; sleeve-and-spike supports, fascia brackets, or strap hangers; downspout clincher straps, stainless steel leaf strainers), acrylic latex or silicone caulk, 6-penny galvanized roofing nails, masonry nails, troweling-consistency asphalt roofing compound, mineral spirits, rags, masonry splash blocks. **Time:** about 1 to 2 days.

Calculate your gutter requirements carefully. Many hardware and building supply dealers have free gutter components checklists; ask your dealer for this checklist. Make a detailed sketch of your roof and gutter layout and work from the sketch to figure the exact number of each component you'll need.

In general, most gutters and downspouts are sold in 10-foot sections; these sections are put together with slip connectors and hung with sleeve-and-spike supports (the easiest), fascia brackets, or strap hangers. Special components are used to seal the open ends of the gutters, to turn inside and outside corners, and to make curves in downspouts. Downspouts are secured with clincher straps, attached to the gutter at drop outlets, and fitted with stainless steel leaf strainers. Supports or hangers should be used every 2½ feet along the gutter, with supports at both sides of corners; plan for one downspout for each 35 feet of gutter,

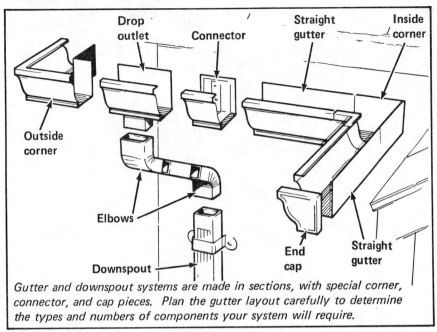

Drop outlet · Connector · Straight gutter · Inside corner · Outside corner · Elbows · Downspout · End cap · Straight gutter

Gutter and downspout systems are made in sections, with special corner, connector, and cap pieces. Plan the gutter layout carefully to determine the types and numbers of components your system will require.

with downspouts at each end of very long gutter runs.

Buy prefinished gutter components made of enameled steel, aluminum, or vinyl. Aluminum is easier to handle than steel, but it dents easily. Some new vinyl gutter systems just snap together, with no caulking necessary; these may be the easiest to work with.

Don't remove old gutters until you're ready to install the new ones, and work in dry weather. You'll need help both to remove old gutters and to install new ones; the 10-foot sections are awkward. Use extension ladders or tall stepladders to provide roof access; brace the ladders firmly and move them as you work. Wear old clothes and rubber-soled shoes.

Remove old gutters carefully, using a hammer to pull nails holding strap hangers, or a pry bar to loosen sleeve-and-spike supports or fascia brackets. Pry the gutters loose very gently, being careful not to damage roofing, fascia boards, or siding. Remove any remaining nails with pliers. Stack the old gutters out of the way for disposal.

Before installing the new gutters, lay

them out on the ground the way they'll be assembled. Then, using a level to make sure you're accurate, snap a chalk line across the top of the fascia along the first run of gutter, where the

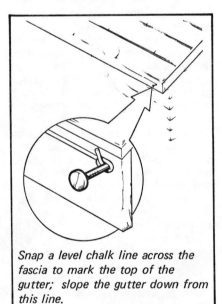

Snap a level chalk line across the fascia to mark the top of the gutter; slope the gutter down from this line.

top of the gutter should be. This line is exactly level, but the gutters must slope about ⅝ inch down for each 10 feet of gutter. To establish the proper slope for each run of gutter, measure down from the chalk line at the downspout end. Snap a new chalk line along this slope to mark the top edge of the new gutter.

On runs of gutter longer than 35 feet, set a downspout at each end and slope the gutter down toward each end from the middle. Measure to mark the midpoint of the run, measure down from the chalk line the correct distance at each downspout, and snap a new line from the midpoint of the gutter down toward each downspout. Generally, a fall of 1 inch on each side of a long run is sufficient; on very long runs, allow a fall of 1 inch for each 16 feet of gutter.

Assemble each run of gutter before you install it. Cut sections of gutter to measure with a fine-toothed hacksaw, inverting the gutter over a piece of 2 × 4 to support it. Smooth the cut edges with a fine-toothed file. Join the sections with slip connectors; unless you're using snap-together vinyl gutters, caulk the sides of each connector and the ends of the gutter sections. Fold connector edges over the gutter lip with pliers. Put in end caps the same way, caulking around the edges of each cap and pressing it firmly into place.

Sleeve-and-spike supports are installed through holes drilled through the gutter at the lip and at the back. If you're using these supports, drill holes every 2½ feet along the gutter for them, using a piece of 2 × 4 inside the gutter to support it. Drill holes for a support at each side of each corner. If you're using fascia brackets to support the gutters, nail them into place along the fascia with 6-penny galvanized roofing nails, making sure the brackets line up exactly along the chalk line that marks the gutter edge.

Lift the first section of gutter into place. While your helper holds the other end of the gutter, fasten the end or dead-end corner of the gutter to the house. If you're using sleeve-and-spike supports, insert each support through the predrilled holes in the gutter, front to

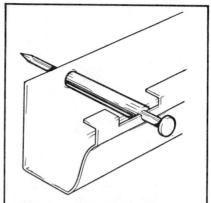

The sleeve-and-spike support is nailed to the fascia to hold the gutter.

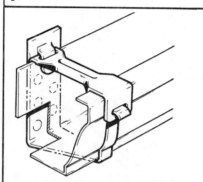

The fascia bracket is attached to the fascia; an arm clamps over the gutter.

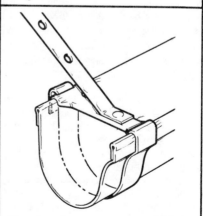

The strap hanger wraps around the gutter; the end is nailed to the roof.

299

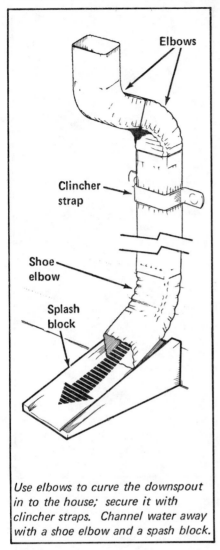

Elbows

Clincher strap

Shoe elbow

Splash block

Use elbows to curve the downspout in to the house; secure it with clincher straps. Channel water away with a shoe elbow and a spash block.

working from your starting run around the house. Be sure to caulk corner pieces and slip connectors where two runs meet.

Install downspouts after all the gutters are in place. Use elbows to curve each downspout in so that it rests flush against the house; push the elbow over the drop outlet and the downspout over the elbow. Secure each downspout to the wall of the house with at least two clincher straps, nailed directly to the wall—use roofing nails in wood; use masonry nails in stone, brick, or concrete block. Push a shoe elbow onto the bottom of each downspout to channel water away from the house.

If you used strap hangers, go back around the edge of the roof, lift the shingles above the hangers, and cover the exposed nailheads with roofing compound, applied with a putty knife. Press the shingles back into place. Clean the putty knife with mineral spirits and a rag, and dispose of the rag immediately.

To complete the installation, insert a stainless steel leaf strainer into the top opening of each downspout, pushing it in firmly just far enough to set it into place. Set a masonry splash block under each downspout to prevent erosion.

Maintain and Repair Gutters and Downspouts

back, and hammer the spike through the sleeve and into the fascia board. If you're using fascia brackets, clamp the holding arm of each bracket over the gutter. If you're using strap hangers, wrap the strap around the gutter and clamp it into place. To attach the strap, lift the shingle at the edge of the roof and nail the end of the strap firmly to the roof with a roofing nail.

Work along the gutter toward your helper to secure it all along its length. Install each run of gutter the same way,

Clean gutters regularly to keep them working properly; repair damaged sections at the same time. **Tools:** extension ladder, work gloves, plastic scoop, garden hose, plumbers' or electricians' snake, wire brush, tin snips, putty knife, pliers, hammer, electric drill, pop rivet tool. **Materials:** copper or stainless steel leaf strainer for each downspout, mineral spirits, rags, scrap wire screening, troweling-consistency asphalt roofing compound, sheet copper or sheet aluminum, 6-penny galvanized roofing nails; sleeve-and-spike supports, fascia brackets, or strap hangers; duct tape or pop rivets. **Time:** about 1 to 2 hours to clean gutters; in addition, time for repairs, depending on extent of damage.

Clean gutters at least twice a year, in late spring and late fall; more frequent cleaning is advisable if you live in a wooded area. Set an extension ladder against the house, bracing it firmly so that the top of the ladder sticks up above the edge of the roof. Wear old clothes and rubber-soled shoes.

Wearing work gloves, clean leaves and debris from the gutters with a plastic scoop. Move the ladder frequently; don't try to reach too far along the gutter from any one position. Flush any remaining debris from the gutter with a garden hose.

If downspouts are clogged, use a plumbers' snake or electricians' snake to break up the obstruction; flush the spout with a garden hose. To prevent clogs from forming, insert a wire leaf strainer into each downspout, just far enough to set it firmly into place. Use copper leaf strainers for copper gutters, stainless steel for other types.

You'll probably be tempted to buy plastic or wire mesh leaf guard to set over the length of the gutter—don't do it. Screening-type leaf guards don't eliminate the need for regular gutter cleaning, but they often discourage it.

Let the gutters dry and then patch holes and rust spots. Wire-brush the damaged area to remove loose rust and paint; clean the wire-brushed area thoroughly with a rag and mineral spirits.

To repair minor damage, apply roofing compound to the damaged area with a putty knife. To repair larger holes, cut a patch of wire screening about 2 inches longer each way than the hole or crack. Apply roofing compound generously to the damaged area; press the screening patch into the compound and coat it with another generous layer of roofing compound. Let dry; if necessary, apply more roofing compound to completely seal the patch.

Patch extensively damaged sections

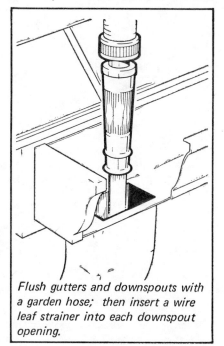

Flush gutters and downspouts with a garden hose; then insert a wire leaf strainer into each downspout opening.

with sheet metal—copper for copper gutters, aluminum for other types. Cut a patch of sheet metal with tin snips, roughly large enough to line the inside of the gutter completely over the damaged area and fold back over the outside lip of the gutter, at least 1 inch longer than the hole each way. Set the rough-cut patch into the gutter and bend it to fit exactly over the damaged area; remove it and trim the edges as necessary.

Coat the inside of the gutter generously with roofing compound where the patch will cover it. Press the patch into place over the roofing compound, smoothing it tightly into the corners of the gutter. Bend the outside edge of the patch with pliers to clamp it over the lip of the gutter. Coat the patch generously with roofing compound, making sure all edges inside the gutter are covered. Clean tools with mineral spirits and rags; dispose of waste materials immediately.

Where the gutter sags, it isn't being adequately supported. Reset gutter hangers at sagging spots: adjust or re-

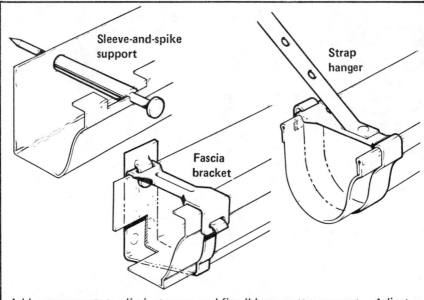

Add new supports to eliminate sags, and fix all loose gutter supports. Adjust or renail sleeve-and-spike supports; renail fascia brackets or strap hangers. Cover strap hanger nailheads with roofing compound.

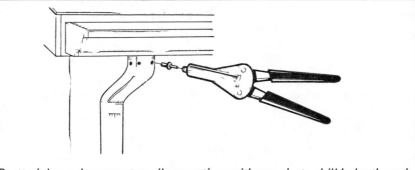

Reattach loose downspout or elbow sections with pop rivets; drill holes through both sections and then fasten them together with a pop rivet tool.

nail sleeve-and-spike supports; renail loose fascia brackets or strap hangers with 6-penny galvanized roofing nails. Cover strap hanger nailheads with roofing compound. If necessary, add new hangers to correct sag, spacing hangers about 2½ feet apart. Use either sleeve-and-spike or strap hangers; cover strap hanger nailheads with roofing compound.

Reattach any loose sections of downspout or elbow. For a temporary repair, use duct tape, but replace the tape as soon as possible with pop rivets. Pop rivets, put in with a special pop rivet tool, can be used directly on a hanging downspout or elbow. Hold the loose section in place and drill through both loose and attached sections at each side and at the front, using an electric drill with the bit specified by the pop rivet manufacturer. To insert each rivet, place a rivet in the pop rivet tool. Hold the drilled section of downspout in place, insert the tip of the rivet through the hole drilled on one side of the downspout sections, and squeeze the handles of the tool to set the rivet. Repeat for each fastening around the loose section.

De-Ice Roofs and Gutters

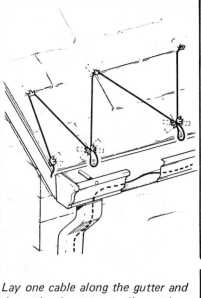

Lay one cable along the gutter and down the downspout; clip another in zigzags along the edge of the roof.

In extreme snowfall conditions, shoveling the roof is sometimes recommended, but this is both difficult and dangerous. In most cases, you can prevent the buildup of ice dams by installing electrical roof and gutter heating cables. Your electric bill will go up, but your house won't leak. **Tools:** measuring rule, extension ladder. **Materials:** roof and gutter heating cables with installation clips, epoxy cement, outdoor appliance extension cords. **Time:** 2 to 3 hours, depending on span of roof and gutter.

When deep snow covers a roof for several weeks, it often forms ice dams around the edges of the roof. Meltwater is trapped on the roof, and can back up under the shingles to leak through to the inside of the house. The problem is aggravated when gutters fill with snow and then freeze; meltwater is forced from the gutters up under the eaves. In either case, the damage that results can be considerable.

Install heating cables in fall when the weather is still fairly warm, and work when both roof and gutters are dry. Measure straight along the gutter and down the downspout to determine the length of gutter cable needed; calculate the cable required for the roof according to the cable manufacturer's directions.

Use an extension ladder, firmly braced against the house, to reach both roof and gutters. The top of the ladder should stick up above the edge of the roof. Wear old clothes and rubber-soled shoes.

Lay one cable into the gutter, starting with the plug-in end close to the outlet where the cables will be plugged in. Stretch the cable all along the gutter and drop the far end into the downspout at the end of the gutter. The cable should reach all the way to the bottom of the downspout.

Following the manufacturer's instructions, lay a second cable in a zigzag along the edge of the roof. Attach the cable with the clips supplied with it. On asphalt shingle roofs, set the clips under the shingles; on wood shingle roofs, use epoxy cement to place the clips. At the bottom of each zigzag, loop the cable slightly into the gutter, but do *not* let the roof and gutter cables touch or cross at any point.

Plug the cables into any convenient outlet, using outdoor appliance extension cords as needed. If you plug the cables in to an indoor outlet, be sure the window or door where they enter the house is weathertight over the extension cords; also be careful not to pinch the wires. Turn the cables on when snow falls and leave them on as needed to keep the roof and gutters clear.

Install a Soffit Vent

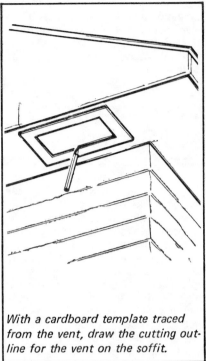

Heat buildup during the summer can send attic temperatures soaring. You can reduce the burden on your air conditioning system and keep your house more comfortable by adding or enlarging soffit vents. **Tools:** saber saw or keyhole saw, brace and bit, hammer, measuring rule, carpenters' square, chalk line, pencil, screwdriver, scissors, caulking gun; *for round vents*—electric drill with hole saw attachment, or brace and expansion bit. **Materials:** aluminum soffit vents, 16-penny nails, cardboard, caulking compound. **Time:** about ½ hour for each vent.

Soffit vents let the air circulate from under the soffit—the roof overhang—through the attic, and out the vents at the gable ends of the house; gable vents can be covered from inside the attic to block air flow during the winter. Besides lowering attic heat loads, soffit vents help eliminate moisture condensation in an attic. If you're adding insulation to your attic, soffit vents are recommended to keep heat and moisture levels within a normal range. The vents are also recommended when you add an attic fan or roof ventilator to your home.

Allow 1 square foot of vent opening for every 300 square feet of attic floor space. The vents—along the soffit of the roof—should be equally spaced, according to the square-foot figure. For an average-sized home, four soffit vents are usually required along each roof overhang.

With a measuring rule and pencil, mark the position of the vents on the surface of the soffit outside the house. Snap a chalk line along the soffit to keep the vents in alignment. Look for nails that fasten the soffit material to the overhang framing, and stay at least 2 inches away from the nails when making the necessary cuts.

Using a new vent as a pattern, trace the outline of the vent on a piece of thin

With a cardboard template traced from the vent, draw the cutting outline for the vent on the soffit.

cardboard. Then draw a second line ¾ inch inside the traced outline. Cut out the cardboard along this inside line. This template will provide cutting guidelines for the vent.

Trace around the cardboard template at each marked vent location. Drill a hole through the soffit (usually plywood) at opposite corners of the traced lines, *inside* the lines. Then, with a saber saw or a keyhole saw, cut through the holes and along the lines. If you use round vents, measure and mark the vent locations; drill the vent holes with an electric drill with a hole saw attachment or with a brace and an expansion bit.

If you're enlarging old vents, remove the old vents, place the template over the old cutouts, and trace around the template. Cut the enlarged openings without drilling holes for the saw blade.

Cut or enlarge just one hole at a time. Then set the new vent into position. The vent is usually held by screws driven through holes in the vent frame and into the soffit. Make pilot holes for the screws with a 16-penny nail, hammering in the nail to the depth of the screw and then removing it. Align the holes in the vent with the pilot holes in the soffit and drive in the screws.

The wide frames of soffit vents give you plenty of margin for cutting errors. If you miscut the hole badly and the soffit frame will not hide the error, fill the crack with caulking compound.

Stop Foundation Water Damage

Leaks and large cracks inside a house often mean problems in its foundation. Serious faults and extreme moisture problems demand professional attention, but you can keep damage to a minimum by taking steps to prevent uneven settling and cracking. **Tools:** small sharp trowel, hammer, cold chisel, wire brush, caulking gun. **Materials:** asphalt roofing compound, concrete mortar mix, caulking compound. **Time:** 1 to 2 hours.

The most important factor in foundation maintenance is control of water—above all, water should be kept away from the house. Examine the ground around the foundation; it should slope away from the house. If water collects around the foundation, regrade to eliminate such ponding. There must also be drainage channels away from the house, natural runoff routes. Watch the water flow during a heavy rain, and if these runoff routes have been blocked, open them.

Clean gutters and downspouts regularly to keep them flowing freely. Make sure downspout runoff is routed away from the house, with concrete splash blocks or long drain sleeves. Mend any holes in the gutter with asphalt roofing compound, applied with a small trowel.

Vegetation around the house should be planned to avoid problems. Do not plant bushes and trees right at the foundation. Make sure flowerbeds slope away from the foundation, and don't use edgings that could trap water near the house. Water plants evenly all around the house so that there are no areas of extreme wetness or dryness.

Repair cracks in the foundation as soon as possible. If there is severe damage or if cracks form and widen in spite of your water control measures, call a professional.

Deal with small problems yourself. Undercut small cracks with a hammer and chisel; remove loose mortar with a wire brush. Mix mortar as directed and fill the cracks, using a small sharp trowel and being careful not to leave any gaps. Caulk around windows and doors, and if the foundation is a different material from the rest of the house, also caulk along the joint where the foundation meets the main house walls.

Stop Leaks in Basement Walls

Water in the basement could be coming in through a weak foundation seam or through a crack in the foundation wall. Seepage all along a wall where it meets the floor can be stopped by an epoxy seal along the joint; cracks can be filled, inside and out. **Tools:** hammer, cold chisel, wire brush, small sharp trowel, spoon, stiff brush, spray bottle, rubber gloves. **Materials:** two-part epoxy mortar mix, mortar mix, or hydraulic cement mix, as appropriate; masonry waterproofing compound or paint. **Time:** 3 hours.

To stop seepage along a floor-wall joint, use a chisel and hammer to undercut the joint. Clean all loose material from the joint with a wire brush. Mix the two parts of the epoxy compound as directed and fill the cleaned floor-wall joint, applying the epoxy firmly and smoothly with a small sharp trowel. Use the back of an old spoon to smooth the joint. Apply epoxy only when the floor is dry, and let it cure at least 24 hours.

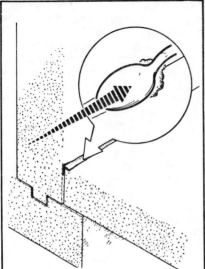

Fill floor-wall joints with epoxy mortar mix to prevent seepage; smooth the joints with the back of a spoon.

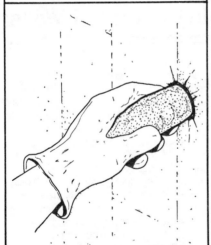

Plug open leaks with hydraulic cement; force a long plug of cement into the hole, then trowel the patch smooth.

Before filling cracks in a foundation wall, examine the outside surface of the wall. You must tuckpoint or repair cracks outside before doing inside work. Large cracks that extend well below ground level should be professionally repaired and waterproofed.

Fill small cracks as soon as outside repairs have been made. Widen and undercut the crack to a depth of 1 to 2 inches and remove all loose material with a wire brush. Mix mortar as directed. Wet the crack thoroughly; then force mortar into the undercut opening, making sure there are no gaps. Smooth the mortar level with the wall. To prevent the new mortar from drying too quickly, use a spray bottle to moisten the area several times a day for 2 or 3 days.

Open leaks and cracks that are always wet must be filled with hydraulic cement, which hardens even in flowing water. Undercut the crack or hole and remove loose material with a wire brush. Mix the cement as directed. If the problem is a crack, fill the crack from the top, gradually reducing the leaking area to a hole at the bottom of the wall. To stop a leak from a hole, form hydraulic cement into a long plug, the same diameter as the hole; wear rubber gloves. Just as the cement begins to harden, force this plug into the hole in the wall and hold it in place until it is firmly set. Trowel the patch smooth.

To eliminate dampness, paint the walls of the basement with a masonry waterproofing compound or special paint. Wire-brush the walls to remove dust and loose material. Some waterproofing compounds must be mixed, and require that the walls be wet; follow the manufacturer's instructions. Apply the compound or paint with a stiff brush. If necessary, use two coats.

Build a Dry Well

A leaking, wet, or moist basement/crawl space can be the result of several problems, including poor drainage away from the foundation of the house. You can eliminate a lot of this water by hooking the house's rain-carrying system to dry wells. **Tools:** shovel and long-handled shovel, pick, ¾-inch metal drill, drill, measuring rule, hacksaw or saber saw with metal-cutting blade, level, putty knife. **Materials:** 55-gallon steel drums, sheet plastic film; broken rocks, stone, or concrete blocks; 3-inch plastic pipe, plastic pipe downspout connectors, oakum, troweling-consistency roofing compound. **Time:** about 2 days for each dry well.

Position dry wells at the center of the wall on two or four sides of the house, or build one at each corner. If the water (rain/snow) in your area is severe, four dry wells may be necessary, but one or two are usually adequate. Use a 55-gallon steel drum for each dry well.

Measure the length and width of the 55-gallon steel drums and add 20 inches to both the length and the width. Dig the dry well holes to these measurements, 8 to 10 feet from the foundation of the house. Check with the utilities before digging to locate underground cable or pipes; plan your dry wells around these cables or pipes. To protect the lawn, lay a sheet of plastic film on the ground next to the hole site and pile the earth on the plastic.

After the holes for the wells are complete, dig a 1-foot-wide trench connecting the wells to the downspouts of the gutter systems. The trenches should be 30 inches deep at the well holes, sloping up slightly but consistently to the level of the earth next to the downspout openings. Connect one dry well to each downspout.

Drill a series of holes in the sides of each steel drum with a ¾-inch metal drill. Cut a large hole for a piece of 3-inch plastic drainage pipe, with a hacksaw or with a metal-cutting blade in a saber saw. Position this hole 6 inches down from the top of the drum.

Set and level the drums into the holes and fill them with stones, rocks, or broken concrete block. Don't pack the drums; just lay the fill in loosely. Place one end of a 3-inch plastic pipe into each drum's large hole and seal this joint with oakum and troweling-consistency roofing compound. Set the lids onto the drums and fill the holes with dirt.

Run the plastic pipe through the trenches back to the ends of the downspouts, and connect the pipes to the downspouts with plastic pipe downspout connectors. Use drainage pipe without slits or holes in it; this type of pipe slips together without adhesives. When the pipe is in position and hooked up, cover it with dirt.

A dry well is only one part of a drainage system. Make sure the gutters and

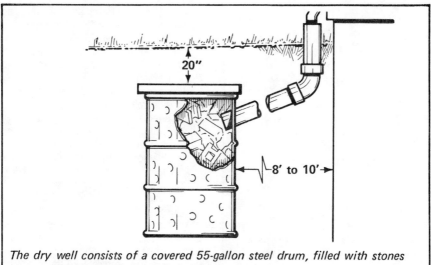

The dry well consists of a covered 55-gallon steel drum, filled with stones or concrete blocks; drainage holes disperse stormwater.

downspouts are in good repair. The ground should slope away from the foundation for water drainage; keep the level of the soil about 6 inches below the bottom course of siding. In the basement, insulate water pipes and vent washers and dryers. Make sure the foundation walls are in good repair.

Control Termites

If termites are a problem in your area, inspect your house twice a year for signs of damage, and take steps to prevent it. Don't buy a house without inspecting it thoroughly. **Tools:** ice pick or awl. **Materials:** none. **Time:** about 1 hour.

In termite areas, good construction is the best control: metal termite shields between foundations and timbers, chemically treated lumber, and adequate clearance between wood and soil. Check all around the house to make sure the soil doesn't touch wood at any point—steps, crawl spaces, trellises, planters. There should be at least 6 inches clearance between soil and siding, at least 18 inches between soil and structural (crawl space or porch) timbers.

Termites live in warm, moist conditions, and they live on cellulose—wood, paper, glue, cloth, live trees. Remove all debris from the vicinity of the house, and clean out crawl spaces and the spaces under porches. Make sure ventilation and stormwater drainage are adequate, and patch all cracks in the foundation wall immediately.

Look for signs of termites in the spring, when they swarm. Inspect the basement and the area around the foundation for pellets (dark, sand-size particles) and shed wings, and look for the insects themselves. Termites look similar to flying ants, but their antennae are blunt and they don't have narrow waists.

Inspect the foundation for tunnels of mud built from the soil up to the wood of timbers or siding. Test exposed wood with an ice pick or an awl—if you can push easily ½ inch or more into a timber, the wood is probably damaged.

If you see termites or signs of damage, you need professional help. Termites are controlled by the application of highly toxic chemicals around and under the foundation of the house; you shouldn't attempt this job yourself. Termite damage isn't immediate, but don't wait more than a few months to call an exterminator.

Hire a termite specialist or any reputable exterminator, but make sure you get a reliable firm. The U.S. Department of Agriculture warns you *not* to hire an exterminator who quotes a price on material used rather than on the total job, who claims to have a secret formula, who has no listed phone number, who shows up uninvited and claims to see termite damage in trees or houses, or who also wants to trim trees and do general repairs. Before you hire an exterminator, call the local Better Business Bureau to make sure there are no complaints filed against him.

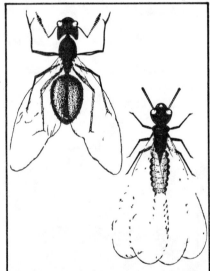

Flying ants (left), common in many areas, have angled, pointed antennae and narrow waists; termites (right) have blunt antennae and thick bodies.

Get Rid of Mice, Rats, Squirrels, and Bats

During the winter, rats, mice, and other gnawers often move inside, and without firm and immediate steps to remove them, they'll stay. Get them out and keep them out with a methodical campaign. **Tools:** mouse or rat traps, work gloves, paint scraper or putty knife, screwdriver, hammer, tin snips, caulking gun, cleaning tools, live traps. **Materials:** bait and fish oil, containers to dispose of rats or mice, rat or mouse poison, steel wool, spackling compound, baseboard molding or 1 × 2 pine, 2-penny or 4-penny common or finishing nails, steel roof flashing or sheet steel, heavy wire screening, caulking compound, cleaning supplies, mothballs or flakes. **Time:** about 1 hour to set traps or spread poison; 1 day to 1 week to seal house and complete extermination.

If you've seen only a few mice or rats, trap them. Bait mouse traps with peanut butter, bacon, or cheese; bait rat traps with peanut butter, strong cheese, or raw or cooked meat or fish. Rats detect human scent easily, so wash your hands before baiting the traps, and sprinkle a little fish oil on the bait to cover any scent you may have left. Wearing work gloves, set the traps where you know the mice or rats hide. Dispose of trapped rodents immediately in a sealed container; wear work gloves and wash your hands thoroughly after handling them.

For a more severe rat or mouse problem, use poison. Buy a poison that drives the rodents out of the house in search of water—a dead rat or mouse inside a wall will smell. Read the manufacturer's instructions and warnings carefully, and wear work gloves to handle the poison. Spread poison where the rodents hide, but not where children or pets can get at it. Wash your hands thoroughly. If one poison proves ineffective, try a different brand, with different active ingredients.

Keep rodents out by sealing every opening they could use as an entrance; they need less than $1\!/\!4$ inch to get in. Put poison into deep cracks or holes, stuff them with steel wool pushed in with a screwdriver, and close them with spackling compound. Cover large openings with strips of molding or 1 × 2's nailed firmly in place. Close large baseboard holes with pieces of steel roof flashing or sheet steel, cut to fit with tin snips; then nail new molding over the patch. Use heavy wire screening to cover vents, chimneys, and other spaces that let air through; fasten the screening completely around. Stuff cracks around pipes with steel wool and then caulk. Repair all damaged areas properly and thoroughly.

Finally, discourage rats and mice by removing the main attraction—food. Clean thoroughly, store all food in airtight containers, and dispose of garbage promptly. Even a candy wrapper can draw rats or mice.

Chipmunks, gophers, and squirrels, unlike rats and mice, are probably feeding outside, using your home as a nest—but they can do a lot of damage. Drive freely nesting animals out with plenty of mothballs or flakes—several pounds—spread all around the space; trap squirrels in live traps baited with peanut butter, nuts, or oatmeal. Release the animals outside, but be careful not to let them bite you. Seal all openings the animals could be using to get in.

Bats in the attic are another unpleasant problem. If there aren't too many, drive them out with plenty of mothballs or crystals spread in the attic and around the eaves; use several pounds. If there are a lot of bats, call a professional exterminator. Repair the roof immediately and seal all vent openings with heavy wire screening.

Caution: If you're bitten by any of these animals, call a doctor immediately. If possible, catch the animal that bit you, alive or dead; save it for rabies analysis.

Large Appliances

Replace a Refrigerator Gasket

A damaged, worn, or aged refrigerator or freezer gasket can impair the appliance's efficiency, shorten its life, and increase your operating costs. In most cases it's easy to replace the faulty gasket. **Tools:** screwdriver, nut driver, or socket wrench; putty knife. **Materials:** liquid detergent, soft cloth, mineral spirits, replacement gasket, gasket cement. **Time:** about 1 hour.

To check for a leaky door gasket, close the door on a piece of paper, and pull the paper out. If there's a definite resistance when you pull the paper out, the gasket is all right. If the paper falls out, or if it's easy to pull out, the gasket isn't providing a tight seal, and should be replaced. Buy a replacement gasket made for your refrigerator or freezer.

Before you replace the gasket, remove very perishable items from the refrigerator and store them elsewhere. Turn the refrigerator off.

On most refrigerators, the gasket is held to the door by a retaining strip, usually attached with screws. On some older refrigerators, the gasket is held by the edge of the door panel itself, and the panel is fastened with spring-steel pressure clips, bolts, or screws. To change the gasket, work on one side of the door at a time to release the old gasket, clean the door as necessary, and place and secure the new gasket.

Replace the gasket at the top of the door first; then work around the other three sides. To release the old gasket, lift the inner flap of the gasket where it lies along the inside surface of the door, and remove the fasteners from the retaining strip or the door panel. Remove screws or bolts with a screwdriver, a nut driver, or a socket wrench; remove clips by gently prying and twisting them off their studs. *Caution: Be careful not to pry spring-steel clips too hard, or the clips may suddenly fly off.*

When all the fasteners have been removed from the top of the door gasket, pull the retaining strip back or separate the top of the door panel from the door. If necessary, separate the retaining strip or the panel with the blade of a putty knife; be careful not to damage the door or mar its finish. Peel the old gasket away from the door and clean the gasket area thoroughly with warm water and liquid detergent. If you can't get the door surface clean with detergent, saturate a soft cloth with mineral spirits and carefully wipe any gummy residue off the door.

Set the new gasket into place along the top of the door, smoothing it evenly as directed by the manufacturer so that it lies the same way the old one did. If specified by the manufacturer, apply

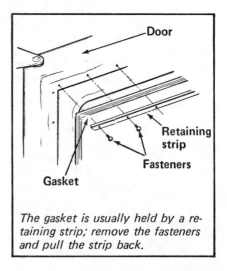

The gasket is usually held by a retaining strip; remove the fasteners and pull the strip back.

gasket cement to the back of the new gasket before installing it.

When the gasket is in place across the top of the door, make sure it lies flat, with all edges or flanges properly positioned and no part of the gasket curled under or misaligned. Repeat along the remaining three sides of the door. Then replace the retaining strip or door panel over the new gasket.

Remove excess gasket cement with mineral spirits; then turn the refrigerator back on.

Repair a Refrigerator

The sealed components in refrigerators or refrigerator/freezers must be professionally repaired, but you can make simple repairs and test the refrigerator before you call for help. **Tools:** voltage meter, small socket wrench, screwdriver, electrical tape, needle-nosed pliers, vacuum cleaner, level. **Materials:** replacement parts as required, cloths. **Time:** 15 minutes or more, depending on the problem.

Although refrigerators all work on the same basic principle, they don't conform to a specific design; use these repair procedures as guidelines, not absolute standards. If the parts of the refrigerator are held together with screws or plugs (friction-fit), you'll probably be able to make the repair. If the parts are held together with rivets or welds, call a professional repairman.

Replace worn or damaged parts with new parts made specifically for the refrigerator. Buy the parts from an appliance repair dealer or an appliance parts store, or order them directly from the manufacturer. Use a voltage meter to help identify refrigerator problems. *Caution: You must test the refrigerator when it's plugged in; be very careful. Follow the meter manufacturer's instructions. If you make any repairs, make sure the refrigerator is unplugged.*

The refrigerator compressor is a complicated component with one important function: it circulates coolant through the refrigerator. If the compressor fails, call a professional repairman. Many troubles that appear to be compressor-related, however, are caused by other factors, and are easy to fix.

If the refrigerator isn't receiving power—the inside light doesn't go on—check the cord connection, fuse box, or circuit breaker. Correct any defects in the power source or the connection.

If the compressor doesn't run, the problem may be in the defrost timer. Pull the refrigerator out and unscrew the back (or front) housing panel at the bottom of the refrigerator that covers the compressor parts. The defrost timer is usually a sealed component, bolted on somewhere in the compressor area.

Unplug the refrigerator. Remove the wires running from the defrost timer to the compressor; they should just pull off. Then plug in the refrigerator to test it. Working very carefully, place one leg of the voltage meter on one terminal of the defrost timer and the other leg on the other terminal. If the meter doesn't register power (check the instructions for proper reading), the defrost timer could be malfunctioning. Replace it with a new timer made for the refrigerator.

To replace the defrost timer, unplug the refrigerator. Remove the large bolt and the screws that hold the timer in place, and remove the timer. Set the new timer into position, secure it, and connect the wires to the proper terminals.

If the meter does register a reading, but the compressor doesn't run, look for defects in the wiring of the defrost timer. If you discover a bad wire, replace it with a new wire of the same type. Unscrew or unplug the wire from the necessary terminals, and connect the new one the same way.

Refrigerator malfunction is often caused by a faulty thermostat control. This component is usually inside the refrigerator; the visible control knobs can be turned to regulate the refrigerator/ freezer temperature. The control can be

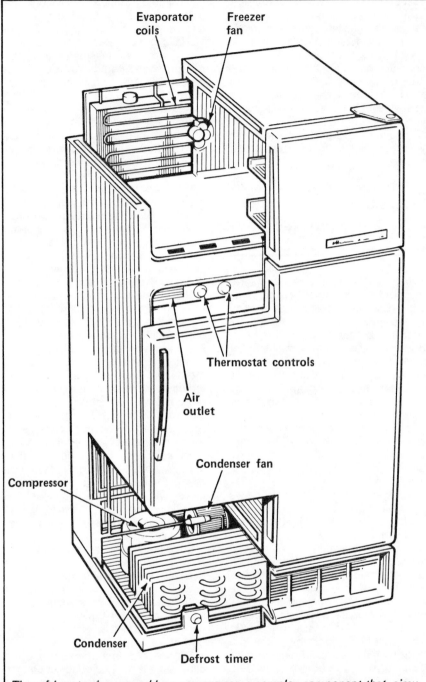

Evaporator coils

Freezer fan

Thermostat controls

Air outlet

Condenser fan

Compressor

Condenser

Defrost timer

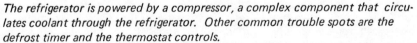

The refrigerator is powered by a compressor, a complex component that circulates coolant through the refrigerator. Other common trouble spots are the defrost timer and the thermostat controls.

tested in several ways, depending on the problem.

If the compressor runs all the time, turn the control knob to the *off* position. If the compressor still runs, unplug the refrigerator; then pull off the control knob and remove the screws that hold the thermostat in place. Pull out the thermostat and remove either the red or the blue wire from its terminal. Plug in the refrigerator. If the compressor doesn't run, replace the control with a new one made for the refrigerator. Many control knobs are screwed into position; unscrew the old knob and screw on the new one. If the compressor runs after the wire is removed, there's probably a short circuit somewhere in the wiring; call a professional repairman.

If the refrigerator runs but the box doesn't cool, unplug the refrigerator. Then, with a screwdriver, remove the thermostat. Disconnect both wires from the thermostat and tape the ends of the wires together with electrical tape. Plug in the refrigerator. If the refrigerator starts and runs normally, replace the thermostat with a new one.

If the freezer compartment is normal but the refrigerator box is warm, set the dials that control both compartments to mid-range. Pull off the control knobs. Then unscrew the temperature control housing—usually a plastic covering. You'll see an air duct near the controls. Replace the knob on the freezer thermostat and turn the knob to *off*. Open the refrigerator door, and look closely at the air duct; if it doesn't open wider in about 10 minutes, replace the control as above.

Inadequate cooling may also be caused by a defective fan, a blocked fan, or broken or bent fan blades. Examine the fan blades in the compressor area; if possible, free them. Try to align bent blades with a pliers. If this doesn't work, call a professional repairman.

Cooling problems are often caused by dirt. To keep your refrigerator working well, vacuum the coils regularly. Make sure the refrigerator has adequate air space behind it—a minimum of 2 inches.

If the refrigerator sounds noisy, it may be out of level. To level it, turn the level adjustment screws at the bottom of the refrigerator. Make sure the doors close tightly.

Replace a Range Heating Element

Replacing a top heating element in an electric range is a snap; so is changing an oven element. **Tools:** flashlight, screwdriver. **Materials:** new range element; if necessary, fuse. **Time:** about 15 minutes.

Before you start to work, make sure the range is receiving power. Check the outlet and the fuse box or circuit breaker. Some electric ranges have a separate fuse, generally located in the oven area. Use a flashlight and search the sides, top, and bottom of the oven for a fuse. You may not find one, but if you do—and if it's damaged—replace it with a new one of the same type.

Caution: Before starting to work, turn off the power to the range; flip the circuit breaker or remove the fuse that supplies power to the range. If you aren't sure which circuit controls the range, flip the main circuit breaker or remove the main fuse that supplies power to the entire house. Ranges often have fuses or breakers separate from the main power panel; double-check to make sure you turned off the power to the range.

The top heating element on most ranges is connected to a terminal block in the side of the element well. The connection is either held by two screws or push-fit into the terminal block—like a toaster or iron cord connection. To remove a screw-type element, remove the screws holding the wires; to remove a push-type element, just pull it out.

To test the element, remove a working element from its terminal block and connect it to the malfunctioning element terminal. Don't let the test element

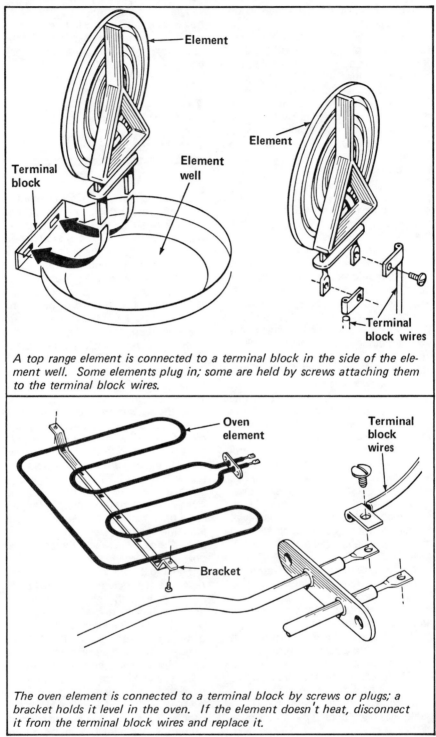

A top range element is connected to a terminal block in the side of the element well. Some elements plug in; some are held by screws attaching them to the terminal block wires.

The oven element is connected to a terminal block by screws or plugs; a bracket holds it level in the oven. If the element doesn't heat, disconnect it from the terminal block wires and replace it.

overlap the edges of the element well— keep the element inside the well, even if it doesn't fit perfectly. Turn on the power. If the working element heats, the malfunctioning element is bad; replace it with a new element made for the range. If the working element doesn't heat, the terminal block wiring may be faulty; call a professional repairman to test and repair it.

Oven elements are also connected to the power source with screws or plugs in a terminal block. If the oven element doesn't work, first check to see if the range is receiving power. If so, reset the automatic timer on the range to manual operation. If the element still doesn't heat, turn off the power to the range. Remove the screws or plugs that connect the element to the power, and remove the bracket that holds the element level in the oven. The bracket is also fastened to the range housing with screws. Have the element tested at an appliance store. If the element is faulty, don't have it repaired; replace it with a new one made for the range.

Service a Range Hood

To keep your range hood working properly, clean it regularly. If it does malfunction, it's easy to fix. **Tools:** screwdriver, pliers. **Materials:** soft cloths, sponge, liquid detergent, replacement parts as required. **Time:** about 1 hour.

A range hood is basically a horizontal exhaust fan with a filter under it; the advanced models have two-speed fan motors and two-level hood lights. The big difference between hoods concerns removal of heat from the range area: ducted models expel the air; ductless models recirculate it. Both types are subject to the same malfunctions.

Grease from the range quickly surrounds the inner parts of the range hood, blocking filters, damaging wires, and creating odors. The hood filter should be cleaned every week. Both ducted and ductless filters are held by clamps on the sides, making removal easy. Unclamp the filter and thoroughly wash it with water and liquid detergent. This cleaning protects the inner parts of the hood and may prevent fires.

Clean the motor assembly in the hood once or twice a year. Remove the filter, and then remove the clamp or bracket that holds the motor assembly in place. This clamp or bracket may be held by screws; otherwise, it can simply be unclamped. The motor is plugged into an outlet; pull out the plug and remove the assembly. Clean it with water and liquid detergent.

Ducted hoods have a blower connected to the motor. The blower comes out with the motor. Clean the blower and the motor with water and liquid detergent. Ductless hoods have charcoal pellets in an odor filter. Remove the old pellets and clean the motor; then replace the pellets with new ones of the same type.

While the motor/exhaust assembly is out of the hood, check the electrical cord that supplies power to the motor; grease can cause the cord's insulation to rot. If the cord has deteriorated, you may be able to replace it by unscrewing a plate on the motor housing, or unscrewing the motor housing itself. The cord is connected to screw terminals inside the housing. Unscrew the wire from the terminals and replace the wire with a new one made for the hood. Bring the old wire with you when you buy the replacement.

If the fan or the light isn't working, the switch should probably be replaced. Fan and light switches on range hoods are subject to malfunction because of heat and grease. The switch is held to the hood housing with screws, or with screw-type decorative washers that slip over the hub of the switch and protrude through the hood housing. If you suspect a faulty switch, replace it. It isn't worth trying to repair it.

Caution: Before starting to work, turn off the power to the switch. Flip the circuit breaker or remove the fuse that supplies power to the hood. If you're

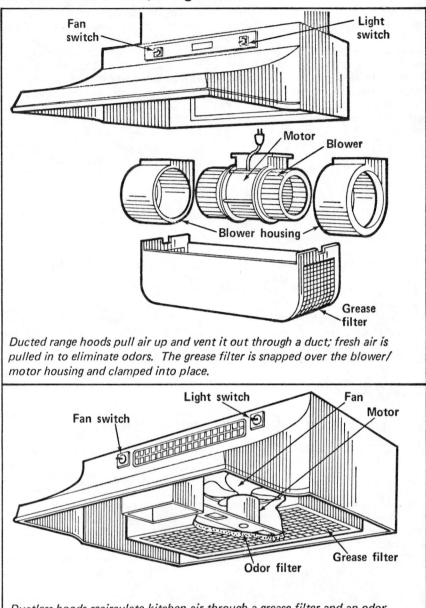

Ducted range hoods pull air up and vent it out through a duct; fresh air is pulled in to eliminate odors. The grease filter is snapped over the blower/motor housing and clamped into place.

Ductless hoods recirculate kitchen air through a grease filter and an odor filter; charcoal pellets in the odor filter absorb stale smells. Both filters should be cleaned regularly.

not sure which circuit controls the hood, flip the main circuit breaker or remove the main fuse that controls the power for the entire house.

Remove the switch by unscrewing or prying off the screw housing and then unscrewing the switch. The switch has lead wires screwed to terminals on the motor or the light; remove the lead wires. Replace the switch with a new one made for the range hood. Attach the lead wires first; then set the switch into the housing and screw it into place. Replace any decorative housing, either pushing it back on or screwing it on. Then turn the power back on.

Repair a Dishwasher

A timer, with its complicated mechanical/electrical components, sounds hard to change, but it isn't— with the right unit, you can repair the dishwasher very quickly. **Tools:** screwdriver,

Phillips-head screwdriver, plumbers' snake or wire coat hanger, adjustable wrench, needle-nosed pliers. **Materials:** replacement timer. **Time:** about 1 hour.

Although dishwashers all work on the same basic principle, they don't conform to a specific design; use these repair procedures as guidelines, not absolute standards. If the parts of the dishwasher are held together with screws or plugs (friction-fit), you'll probably be able to make the repair. If the parts are held together with rivets or welds, call a professional repairman; don't try to fix the dishwasher yourself.

Replace a worn-out timer with a new timer made specifically for the dishwasher. Buy the timer from an appli-

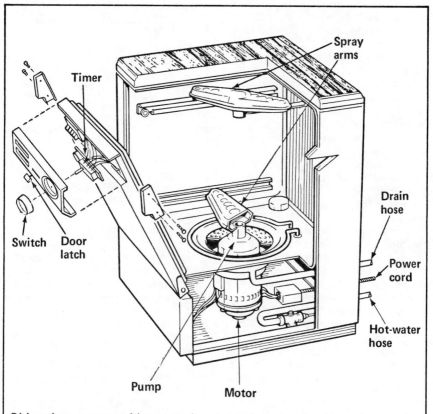

Dishwashers operate with a central motor and pump assembly, using rotating spray arms to distribute water. The timer, inside the door panel, is the key component; the door latch activates the timer.

ance repair dealer or an appliance parts store, or order it directly from the manufacturer.

Caution: Before you make any repairs to the dishwasher, make sure the dishwasher is unplugged.

The timer is the key component of the dishwasher; when it goes bad, the dishwasher won't work. Before working on the timer, make sure the dishwasher is receiving power; check the fuse or circuit breaker that controls it for damage or malfunction. Also make sure the dishwasher door is tightly latched; the door latch activates the timer controls.

To replace the timer, remove the front control panel of the dishwasher. The timer is directly behind the dishwasher's main control knob. Most dishwasher knobs and levers are friction-fit; pull them off. Some models may have a setscrew at the base of each knob; loosen the setscrew and pull the knob off the shaft.

The panel is held to the dishwasher housing with screws, usually threaded through pieces of metal molding or trim. You may have to remove only the side panels on the control panel, or you may have to remove the entire door panel to get at the timer control. Remove panels as necessary for access.

A dishwasher timer is connected to several wires, which operate the various cycles of the dishwasher. Have a helper hold the new timer next to the old one. Disconnect the wires of the old timer and connect the wires of the new timer one by one, to make sure you get the right wires on the right terminals. The wires are friction-fit; pull off the old wires and push on the new ones. Then remove the old timer and secure the new timer to the dishwasher. Finally, replace the access panels.

If the dishwasher doesn't drain properly, it probably has a clogged or kinked drain hose. To remove clogs from a drain hose, disconnect the hose from the drain pipe, and push a plumbers' snake or a wire coat hanger through the hose. Reconnect the dishwasher to the drainage system.

Poor drainage can also be caused by jammed or broken impellers. The im-

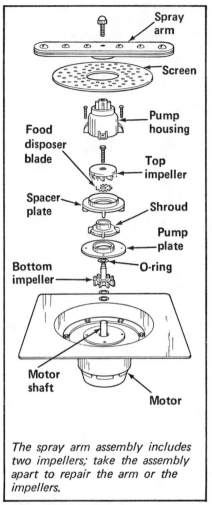

The spray arm assembly includes two impellers; take the assembly apart to repair the arm or the impellers.

pellers are part of the spray arm assembly; one impeller is under the pump housing, and the other is the bottom part of the assembly. Remove the screw or bolt at the top of the spray arm; the remaining parts should lift off. Check the impellers. If one or both are broken, replace them with new impellers made for the dishwasher. If an impeller is jammed, remove the jam and reassemble the parts.

If the dishwasher doesn't get the dishes clean, the problem may be a clogged or non-rotating spray arm. Remove the nut at the top of the spray arm with an adjustable wrench, and clean out the debris. If the spray arm is broken, remove the broken arm and replace it with a new one made for the dishwasher. Dirty dishes can also be the result of low water temperature; adjust the dishwasher heat control; set your water heater at 140° to 160° F.

Fix a Dishwasher Door

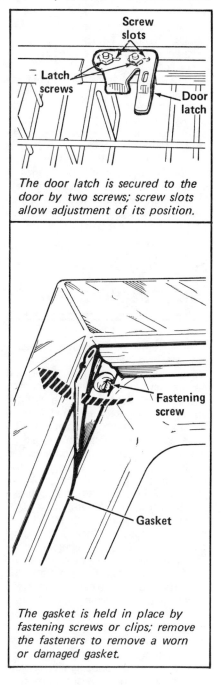

The door latch is secured to the door by two screws; screw slots allow adjustment of its position.

On many dishwashers, the latch activates the timer, which, in turn, switches on the motor and other working parts. If the latch isn't completely locked, the dishwasher won't start. It's easy to repair or replace the latch and the door gasket. **Tools:** screwdriver, Phillips-head screwdriver, needle-nosed pliers. **Materials:** replacement latch; if required, replacement gasket. **Time:** about 45 minutes.

The dishwasher door latch is usually held by two screws. These screws may be readily accessible from the top edge—or the side—of the door, or you may have to remove the door panel to remove the screws and the latch. The door panel's screws are located along the edge of the door or along the inner panel of the door near the door gasket, or both; you may have to remove several screws. Then lift out the door panel to expose the door latch and its screws.

The door latch may have slipped out of position, even if it seems to be locked. Move the latch slightly by loosening the screws and sliding the latch with your fingers or with pliers; the screw slots are specially enlarged for this purpose. If the latch still doesn't work, replace it with a new latch of the same type: remove the latch screws, lift out the damaged latch, and install the new one in the same position.

Reassemble the door panel, if necessary. Test the latch in the door. If it doesn't work, disassemble the panel, unscrew the latch, and readjust it. Repeat as necessary until the latch fits properly.

The gasket is held in place by fastening screws or clips; remove the fasteners to remove a worn or damaged gasket.

If the dishwasher leaks, the latch may be too tight or too loose. A tight latch compresses the door gasket against the rim of the dishwasher housing; a loose latch lets the gasket gap around the rim of the dishwasher housing. To correct the problem, tighten or loosen the screws that hold the latch in position.

If the dishwasher still leaks, the gasket may be defective. Check the gasket; it should feel spongy. If it's hard, or if it's torn or damaged, remove the gasket and replace it with a new one made specifically for the dishwasher. Do *not* buy a "universal" fit-all gasket. The gasket is held to the door by a series of screws and/or clips; remove these fasteners and lift out the old gasket. Install the new gasket, and replace the screws or clips to secure it firmly.

Service a Washing Machine

Washing machines present a special problem in repair diagnosis—a timer, for example, helps operate valves and motors that fill, empty, and spin the tub, and control water temperature. Special equipment is necessary to determine the exact problem, but with a little know-how, you may be able to fix the machine yourself. **Tools:** screwdriver, Phillips-head screwdriver, needle-nosed pliers, pliers, hammer. **Materials:** replacement parts as required, cloths. **Time:** 1 to 2 hours.

Although washing machines all work on the same basic principle, they don't conform to a specific design; use these repair procedures as guidelines, not absolute standards. If the parts of the washing machine are held together with screws or plugs (friction-fit), you'll probably be able to make the repair. If the parts are held together with rivets or welds, call a professional repairman.

Replace worn or damaged parts with new parts made specifically for your washing machine. Buy the parts from an appliance repair dealer or an appliance parts store, or order them directly from the manufacturer.

Caution: Before you start to work, *unplug the washer.*

Two common washing machine malfunctions are a tub that won't fill with water and a machine that won't work at all. The water problem is usually concerned with the mixing valves and solenoid; the failure of the entire machine usually involves the timer.

If the washer won't fill, make sure the water supply valves are open, and straighten any kinks in the washer's hoses. If these are in working order, turn the timer dial a couple of notches, push down hard on the control button, and push the reset button on the control panel. If this doesn't fill the tub, remove the hoses from the inlet ports on the washing machine; they're probably screwed onto the ports. With needle-nosed pliers, remove the screen from inside each port (or the hose), being careful not to damage the screens. Thoroughly wash any sediment off the screens, and replace the screens and the hose.

If the machine still won't fill, remove the hoses and unscrew the back panel of the washer. Examine the mixing valve for dirt. Even a little dirt in the valve holes can cause a valve malfunction.

To clean the valve, disassemble the screws holding the valve assembly in place. Unscrew the various parts of the valve, being careful to note the order of assembly. Wash the valve parts in clean water; then reassemble and replace the valves. If this doesn't solve the problem, replace the valve and the solenoid with new ones made for the machine; these are sold as assemblies. Screw the new parts into place.

If the water temperature is uneven, the mixing valves are probably leaking. Run the washer through several cycles to clear the valves. If this doesn't correct the water temperature, clean the valves or replace them, as above. Before opening the machine, make sure that the water supply lines are working properly and that the screen isn't clogged.

If the washer isn't working at all, the timer may be the problem; this part controls several washer components.

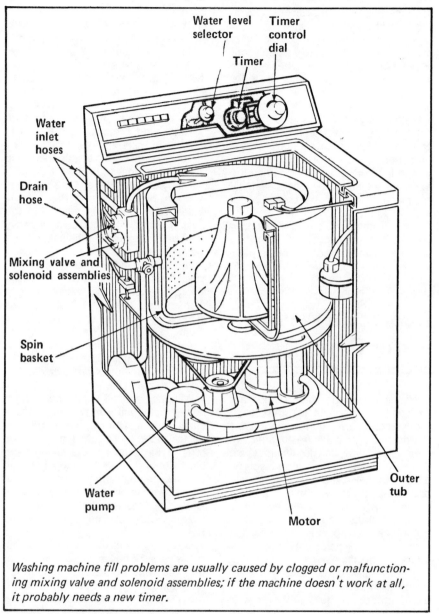

Water level selector

Timer control dial

Timer

Water inlet hoses

Drain hose

Mixing valve and solenoid assemblies

Spin basket

Outer tub

Water pump

Motor

Washing machine fill problems are usually caused by clogged or malfunctioning mixing valve and solenoid assemblies; if the machine doesn't work at all, it probably needs a new timer.

Before you replace the timer, be sure that the machine is receiving power, the door is tightly closed, and the clothes in the tub are evenly distributed and balanced. Also push the reset button.

Expose the timer by removing the control knobs and the panel that covers the controls. The control knobs are usually friction-fit; just pull them off. You may have to remove tiny setscrews at the base of the control knobs to get the knobs off the shafts. The panel is usually held by screws.

Examine the wires that connect the timer to other parts of the machine. If the wires are loose or disconnected, push them tightly into position. They fit into their terminals like plugs.

Most timers are single components; to replace a timer, unscrew and disconnect the old one and install the new one in reverse order. Use a timer made for your washing machine. Be careful to place the wires on the proper terminals. The best way to do this is to have a helper hold the new timer next to the old one as you work. Disconnect the old wires one at a time, placing each new wire in the correct terminals. Once the wires are set, screw the timer assembly into place. Reposition the control panel and the control knobs.

If the machine still doesn't work after you replace the timer, call a professional repairman. Most appliance parts dealers will let you return the salable timer.

Replace a Washer Water Pump

Washing machine water pumps are especially susceptible to breakdown; the symptoms are loud rumbling inside the machine or a failure to drain. In most cases, you can fix the machine yourself. **Tools:** long-bladed screwdriver, hammer, pliers, wire coat hanger, socket wrench. **Materials:** replacement water pump, heavy blanket, penetrating oil. **Time:** about 2 hours.

Although water pumps all work on the same basic principle, they don't conform to a specific design; use these repair procedures as guidelines, not absolute standards. If the parts of the water pump are held together with screws or plugs (friction-fit), you'll probably be able to make the repair. If the parts are held together with rivets or welds, call a professional repairman; don't try to fix the pump yourself.

Replace a worn or damaged pump with a new pump made specifically for your washer. Buy the parts from an appliance repair dealer or an appliance parts store, or order them directly from the manufacturer.

Caution: Before starting to work, make sure the washer is unplugged.

Before disassembling the machine, remove the water supply hoses from the back of the washer; they're usually screwed on. Extract the filter screens from the valve ports in the washer—or from the hoses themselves—with needle-nosed pliers; be careful not to damage the screens. Wash the screens thoroughly and then replace them and reattach the hoses.

If dirty screens weren't the problem, work on the water pump. Bail out any water in the machine's tub. Tip the washer over on its front, using a heavy blanket to protect the finish and the metal housing.

The back of the washer is held on by machine screws. Remove the screws along the edges of the metal panel and then remove the panel. If the screws are rusted tight and you can't remove them easily, apply several drops of penetrating oil to each screw; wait ½ hour and try again. Use a long-bladed screwdriver for stubborn screws. Remove the panel.

With the panel off, locate the pump, a heavy metal unit with two large hoses clamped to it. The two hoses are connected to the pump with spring or strap clips. If the clips are the spring type, pinch the ends of the clips together with pliers to release them; then slide the clips down the hose. If the clips are the strap type, unscrew the metal collar to loosen the clamp. Then disconnect the hoses.

Before working on the water pump, make sure the hoses are not crimped or blocked; this could cause poor tub drainage. Straighten out any kinks, and run a straightened-out wire coat hanger through each hose to check for blocks. If the trouble isn't in the hoses, work on the water pump.

First remove the old pump from the washer. Loosen the drive belt by sliding the washer motor out of position. Loosen the bolt that holds the drive belt taut and move the washer motor on the bracket to loosen the belt. Move the motor out of the way and unbolt the

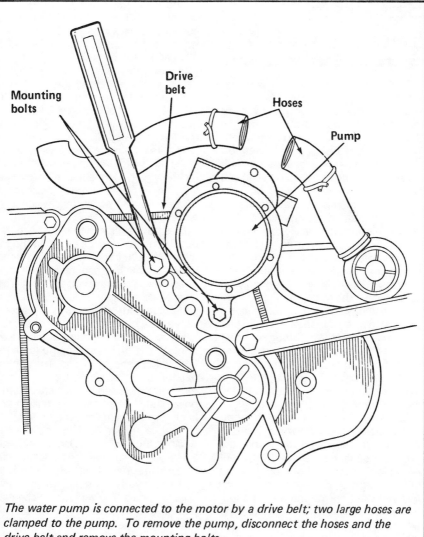

Mounting bolts

Drive belt

Hoses

Pump

The water pump is connected to the motor by a drive belt; two large hoses are clamped to the pump. To remove the pump, disconnect the hoses and the drive belt and remove the mounting bolts.

pump; it's usually held by two or three hex-head bolts located along the side of the pump housing. Use a socket wrench to loosen the bolts. As you loosen the last mounting bolt, support the pump with your free hand. Then lift the pump out of the washer housing.

Set the new pump into the washer, in the same position as the old pump. Bolt the new pump loosely to the housing, and then reattach the drive belt. Make sure the projecting pump lever is prop-erly engaged; you'll see how it fits as you bolt the pump into place. Attach the hoses to the water inlet and outlet and make sure the clamps are seated tight; then tighten the mounting bolts.

With a hammer handle, pry the motor back into position so the drive belt is taut. It should have about ½ inch de-flection when you push down on it with your hand. Tighten the bolt on the motor bracket when the belt is tightened prop-erly. Then stand the washer back up.

Service an Electric Dryer

Clothes dryers are complicated machines that may need professional service, but three common problems—a malfunctioning door switch, timer, or thermostat—are easily remedied. **Tools:** screwdriver, needle-nosed pliers. **Materials:** replacement parts as required, matches, cloths. **Time:** 1 to 2 hours.

Although electric clothes dryers all work on the same basic principle, they don't conform to a specific design; use these repair procedures as guidelines, not absolute standards. If the parts of the dryer are held together with screws or plugs (friction-fit), you'll probably be able to make the repair. If the parts are held together with rivets or welds, call a professional repairman.

Replace worn or damaged parts with new parts made for your electric dryer. Buy the parts from an appliance repair dealer or an appliance parts store, or order them directly from the manufacturer.

Caution: Before you start to work, make sure the dryer is unplugged.

Appliance repairmen claim that the two most common electric dryer problems are a blown fuse or tripped circuit breaker and a broken door switch. Many electric dryers operate on separate power circuits; to make sure the dryer is receiving power, check the main panel and also look for another fuse panel. Check the big plug in the power outlet for looseness, and punch the reset button on the dryer.

If the dryer still doesn't operate, check the door switch. The switch is located near the top of the drum and is exposed when you open the door. When the door closes, it pushes against this switch to activate the machine. If the dryer has a light inside the drum and the light doesn't work, and if the bulb isn't burned out and the dryer is receiving power, the switch is probably malfunctioning.

Check the switch to make sure it's not jammed with lint or other debris; make sure the connections are being made when the door shuts. If the switch looks all right but still doesn't work, replace it with a new switch made for the dryer.

The switch is held to the dryer with setscrews. Remove these screws. If, after removing the setscrews, you can't get at the lead wires, unscrew the top of the dryer and lift it off. Then unscrew the lead wires from the terminals and replace the switch with a new one made for the dryer. Connect the lead wires first; then replace the top of the dryer, if necessary, and screw the switch into place on the dryer.

If a new switch doesn't solve the problem, the dryer's timer may be faulty. A malfunctioning timer may keep the dryer from operating at all, or it may affect one aspect, such as the heat. The timer, located in the control panel, is a self-contained component; replace it with a new one made for the dryer.

For access to the timer, remove the control panel. Remove the screws around the panel's molding. The control panel knobs are usually friction-fit; pull them off. Or loosen the setscrew at the base of each knob and then pull off the knob. Lift the panel cover off.

Have a helper hold the new timer against the old one. Disconnect the wires of the old timer and connect the wires of the new timer one by one, to make sure you get the right wires on the right terminals. The wires are friction-fit; pull off the old wires and push on the new ones. Then remove the old timer and secure the new timer to the dryer with the setscrews that held the old timer.

If the drum revolves, but doesn't get hot—or if it heats too slowly—check the operating thermostats near the exhaust duct. To get at the thermostats, you'll probably have to remove the back of the dryer. Remove the machine screws that hold the back panel, and lift the panel off.

First, try tapping the housing of the thermostats *lightly* with the handle of a screwdriver. This tapping may jar the contacts loose. If this doesn't work, re-

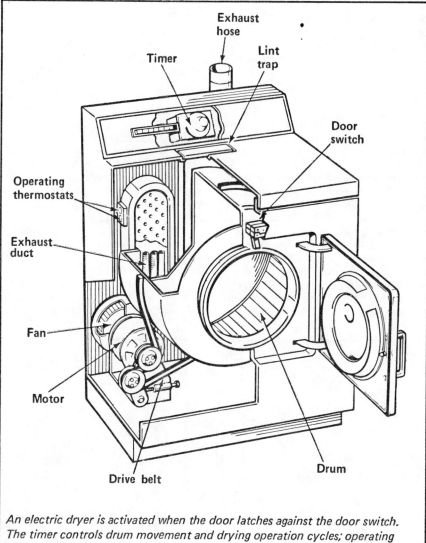

An electric dryer is activated when the door latches against the door switch. The timer controls drum movement and drying operation cycles; operating thermostats regulate the heat.

move the screws that hold the thermo-stats in place, and lift out the thermo-stats with pliers. You may have to twist the thermostats a little to get them out. Hold each thermostat for just a *second* over a burning match. If you hear a pop or click, the points are free. If you can't free the points, replace the thermostats with new ones made for the dryer; in-stall them exactly as the old ones were removed.

Install a Dryer Vent

Venting a dryer sounds like skilled labor, but there is an easy way to do it. Run the vent through a window and eliminate cutting through the house wall. **Tools:** putty knife, work gloves, pliers, measuring rule, grease pencil, tin snips, power drill, screwdriver, caulking gun. **Materials:** rags, glaziers' points, sheet aluminum, dryer vent kit with mounting hardware, glazing compound, acrylic latex or silicone caulk. **Time:** about 2 hours.

Position the dryer close to a window and choose a pane of glass as close as possible to the height of the dryer exhaust. Plan the vent to run through this pane, with as short a run as possible and no sharp bends or sags. Buy a dryer vent kit with a hose just long enough to provide the necessary ducting—the flexible plastic type is adequate for most situations.

To install the vent, remove the pane of glass near the dryer exhaust. Carefully chip out the putty around the pane with a putty knife, setting the blade of the knife flat against the glass and tapping the handle gently to loosen the old putty. In an aluminum-frame window, remove the spring clips that hold the glass in place, and set them aside. Wearing work gloves, carefully lift the glass out of the frame. In a wood-frame window, use the blade of the putty knife to remove the glaziers' points around the glass, and set them aside. If points are not already used every few inches around the pane, you'll have to buy additional glaziers' points to install the vent. Wearing work gloves, carefully remove the glass from the frame.

If you can't remove the glass from the window, break the pane. Cover the pane of glass completely with a heavy layer of rags; if possible, cover both sides. Wearing work gloves, strike the glass sharply with the butt of the putty knife handle to break it. Remove the broken glass carefully from the frame, using pliers if necessary to pry stubborn pieces loose; then clean the frame thoroughly to remove old putty.

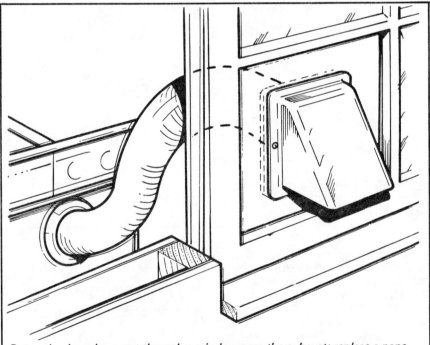

Route the dryer hose out through a window near the exhaust; replace a pane of glass with sheet aluminum, and mount the vent hood firmly through the metal pane. Seal all open edges.

Measure the glass pane exactly, or measure the inside of the empty window pane. Measure a piece of sheet aluminum to the exact size of the pane being replaced, mark it with a grease pencil, and cut the sheet with tin snips. Set the mounting ring of the vent hose on the piece of sheet aluminum, centered on the sheet, and carefully trace around it. Drive one blade of the tin snips through the aluminum in the center of the traced area and cut out the venting hole.

Following the instructions included with the kit, insert the tailpiece of the vent hood through the hole in the sheet aluminum. Secure one end of the dryer hose to the vent hood tailpiece with the clamp provided, so that the sheet of aluminum is between the hood and the hose. If a mounting plate is included for the inside of the vent, thread the plate over the hose and attach it to the piece of sheet aluminum as directed. Drill holes as directed to attach the hood assembly to the sheet aluminum, and fasten it to the sheet through the drilled holes with the sheet metal screws provided in the kit.

Supporting the mounted hose so the sheet aluminum doesn't bend, set the piece of aluminum into the window opening, with the hose inside and the vent hood out. You'll need an assistant to hold the vent and the sheet aluminum in the window opening while you complete the installation.

With the sheet aluminum firmly in the window opening, replace the spring clips that held the glass (aluminum frame) or drive glaziers' points every few inches around the window (wood frame), with the same technique used for replacing glass. Roll glaziers' compound between your palms to a pencil-diameter rope and press the compound firmly around the edges of the sheet aluminum pane, starting at a corner and working around the window frame to seal the whole piece of sheet aluminum to the frame like a pane of glass. Remove excess putty with a putty knife held at a 45-degree angle to the window surface.

To seal the vent completely, apply a bead of acrylic latex or silicone caulk all around the duct mounting plate, both inside and out. Complete the installation by sliding the free end of the dryer hose over the exhaust outlet of the dryer; secure it with the clamp provided. Let putty and caulk dry overnight before using the dryer.

Maintain Your Air Conditioner

Keep your air conditioner in top operating condition for maximum efficiency and economy. **Tools:** vacuum cleaner, garden hose or spray bottle, screwdriver, wrench, pencil, fin comb. **Materials:** replacement filter, coil cleaner, machine oil. **Time:** 15 minutes to 1½ hours, depending on the unit and its condition.

Central systems and room

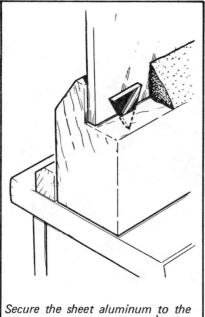

Secure the sheet aluminum to the window frame with glaziers' points or spring clips; seal it with glaziers' compound.

units. The most common air conditioner problem is a dirty filter. To keep your room or central unit working well, change or clean the filter at least once a month during the summer. If your air conditioner has a filter that can be cleaned, vacuum the filter regularly. Replace the filter when it starts to get ragged.

Use the fabric attachment of a vacuum cleaner to remove dust and dirt deposits from the bottom of the unit—around the filter retainer, on grillework, and anywhere else you see dirt accumulations. Then turn the air conditioner off. *Caution: Before working on the air conditioner, turn off the power. Unplug a room unit; flip the circuit breaker or remove the fuse that controls a central system. If you aren't sure which breaker or fuse controls the system, turn off the main power to the house.*

Clean the condenser and evaporator coils with a commercial coil cleaner,

available at refrigeration supply stores; follow the manufacturer's instructions. Spray the cleaner onto the coils and let it work for several minutes; flush the coils with a hose or a spray bottle. If the coils are still dirty, spray them again with coil cleaner and flush clean. Let the coils air-dry.

Examine the unit to see if it must be lubricated. If there are oil cups on the motor or elsewhere, put just a few drops of high-grade machine oil into each. Don't oil the unit if you don't see oil cups. After oiling a room unit, plug it back in; leave a central system off.

In the house itself, check all cold air outlets and room units for proper air flow. Adjust them to direct the air flow upward, toward the ceiling. Floor registers generally let cold air flow out across the floor, and air from these registers often doesn't mix properly with the warmer air higher up. If you can, arrange some sort of deflector at each floor register to force the cool air up-

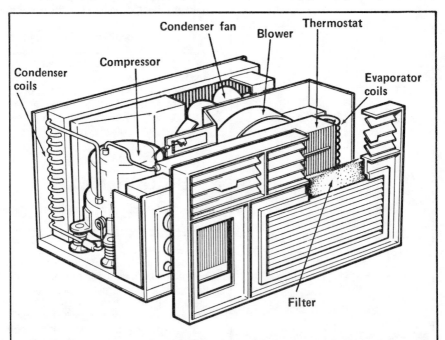

Room units are self-contained, with both the condenser and the evaporator coils inside the unit. Clean the coils with commercial coil cleaner; vacuum or change the filter regularly.

ward during the summer; remove the deflectors during the winter. Be sure draperies and other furnishings don't interfere with the air flow, and close off rooms or cold air outlets in areas where air conditioning is not needed.

Central air conditioning systems. Check the blower fan belt for proper tension. Push down on the belt halfway between the pulley; if the belt moves down more than ¾ inch, it's too loose; tighten the adjustment bolt with a wrench until the belt moves down about ½ inch when you test it. *Caution: Do not overtighten the belt; this can ruin both the belt and the bearings.*

Some units have adjustable pulleys. If your unit is this type, make sure the belt is set in the pulley grooves that operate the blower at the highest speed. Leave it this way during the cooling season. If necessary, set the belt back to a lower speed during the winter.

Bent evaporator coil fins result in lost efficiency and air flow. If a few fins are bent, straighten them with a pencil tip or a sliver of wood so that they're all in perfect alignment; do not use a metallic object to do this. If large areas of fins are bent, buy a special fin comb to straighten them. Finally, after servicing is complete, restore the power to the system; turn on the circuit breaker or replace the fuse that controls the circuit.

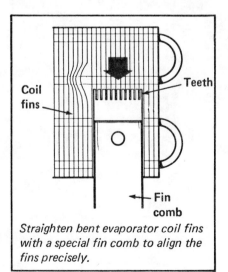

Straighten bent evaporator coil fins with a special fin comb to align the fins precisely.

If you have an outdoor condenser coil, try to provide shade for it—shade on the coil improves operating efficiency by as much as 2 to 3 percent. Keep shrubbery, plants, or other objects used for the purpose several feet away from the coil.

Clean a Water Heater

Get the highest efficiency from your gas hot water heater by keeping it clean and properly adjusted—a once-a-year tune-up will give you significant cost savings. **Tools:** screwdriver, pen, small wire brush, vacuum cleaner or shop vacuum, piece of thin wire, bucket. **Materials:** newspaper, masking tape, string, matches. **Time:** about 2 hours.

Before starting to clean the hot water heater, turn off the gas at the unit's shut-off valve, near the gas line's point of entry to the tank. *Caution: If your heater is electric or oil-fired, don't try to clean it yourself; have it professionally serviced.* Let the water heater cool completely.

When the water heater is cool, spread newspaper to protect the floor around it; then disassemble the heater's chimney to provide access to the inside of the tank. The chimney consists of sections slid together and held by friction, with the crimped end of one section fitted inside the plain end of the next; usually no fasteners are used. If the sections are held together with sheet metal screws, remove the screws section by section as you work.

Starting at the top of the chimney where it turns to run horizontally, carefully remove the sections, one by one. Label each section with a numbered strip of masking tape as you remove it; place the tape at a consistent point around the section so the chimney will be easy to reassemble. Set each section on the newspaper, and clean the inside of each section thoroughly with a small wire brush and a vacuum cleaner

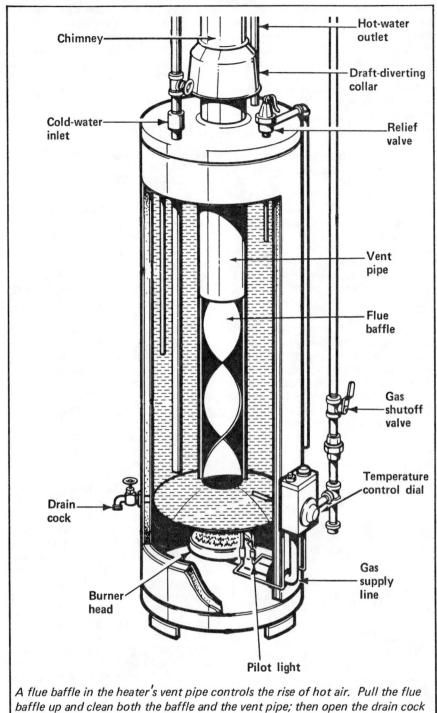

Chimney

Hot-water outlet

Draft-diverting collar

Cold-water inlet

Relief valve

Vent pipe

Flue baffle

Gas shutoff valve

Temperature control dial

Drain cock

Gas supply line

Burner head

Pilot light

A flue baffle in the heater's vent pipe controls the rise of hot air. Pull the flue baffle up and clean both the baffle and the vent pipe; then open the drain cock to drain sediment from the tank.

or shop vacuum. At the base of the chimney, remove the draft-diverting collar around the chimney.

Open the inspection door at the bottom of the water heater and spread several layers of newspaper over the burner head. As you clean the heater, soot will fall through it onto this newspaper. Work from the top of the water heater down.

At the top of the water heater, look into the vent pipe opening exposed by the removal of the chimney. Inside the vent pipe in the tank is the flue baffle, a twisted metal strip that slows hot air rising through the pipe to transfer as much heat as possible to the water in the tank. To keep the flue baffle working properly, remove all accumulated soot from it—if there's enough room overhead, pull the baffle straight out to clean it; if there isn't, rattle it up and down to dislodge caked-on dirt. Wire-brush and vacuum all reachable baffle surfaces.

If you can pull the flue baffle out to clean it, remove it entirely, and clean the vent pipe the baffle hangs in. Crumple newspaper into a ball the same diameter as the pipe; tie a long piece of sturdy string to it. Drop one end of the string into the vent pipe, retrieve it at the bottom of the water heater, and pull the ball of newspaper through the pipe to scour the sides of the pipe clean. Repeat until the vent pipe is clean.

At the bottom of the water heater, carefully remove the protective newspaper and the dislodged soot from the burner head. Remove dirt from the burner assembly with a vacuum cleaner or a shop vacuum. Examine the burner to make sure all orifices are clear; if any opening is clogged by dirt or corrosion, reopen it with the tip of a piece of thin wire. Vacuum thoroughly to remove all debris; then replace the flue baffle.

Set a bucket under the drain cock near the bottom of the water heater. Carefully open the drain cock to let a few gallons of water and sediment drain from the bottom of the water heater. When the water runs clear from the drain cock, close the valve and check for leaks. If the drain cock drips, reopen it to remove any debris from the valve and then close the valve again. Repeat this cleaning step monthly.

Reassemble the water heater carefully. Make sure the flue baffle is properly positioned, and replace the draft-diverting collar over the chimney opening. Working in reverse order, reassemble the chimney sections, pushing each section firmly into place as it joins the next one. Replace any sheet metal screws section by section as you work. Be careful to make the final joint secure, and make sure the entire chimney assembly is firm and stable.

When the chimney is firmly reassembled, turn on the gas to the unit and relight the water heater's pilot light, following the manufacturer's specific instructions. Turn the unit on and look at the burner head; there should be an even flame over the entire burner.

Turn the temperature dial down until the burner goes out, and then turn it up again to make sure the pilot light works. If the pilot is too low, it will go out; turn the adjustment screw on the unit's gas valve to raise it. If the pilot is too high, it will waste gas. Turn the adjustment screw the other way until the flame is less than 1 inch high, just touching the thermocouple near the burner.

Finally, set the water temperature control dial. In most cases, set the dial to 140° F. If you have a dishwasher, you may have to set the water heater higher; follow the dishwasher manufacturer's instructions.

Small Appliances

Repair an Appliance Cord

When an appliance doesn't work right, the first place to check is the cord. This is the major cause of malfunction; fortunately, it's very easy to fix. **Tools:** continuity tester, screwdriver, wire cutters, utility knife or wire stripper, crimping tool. **Materials:** replacement appliance plug or cord and plug, crimping nut. **Time:** about 20 minutes.

First make sure the problem is in the cord. It may be obvious: frayed, broken, or severed wires. If it isn't so obvious, test the cord with a continuity tester, an inexpensive device sold at hardware and electrical supply stores.

Remove the cord from the appliance; either pull the plug at the appliance end of the cord or unscrew part of the appliance to get the cord off. Remember how you take the cord off—you'll have to put it back the same way.

The continuity tester is a probe with a light that indicates a complete circuit; a wire on the other end of the probe has an alligator clip. To test the disconnected cord, fasten the alligator clip onto one prong of the plug and place the probe on one of the two wires or in one of the two holes at the appliance end of the cord. If the probe lights up, move the probe to the other wire. If it still lights, clip the alligator clip onto the other prong of the plug and test the two wires or holes again with the probe. If everything lights, the problem isn't in the cord. If the probe doesn't light up at any point, the problem is in the cord or in the plug.

To determine whether the cord or the plug is bad, snip off the plug with wire cutters. Retest the wires at both ends of the cord with the continuity tester. If the probe lights at all points now, the cord is not damaged; the plug must be replaced. Install a new plug.

If the probe does not light at some point of the testing, the cord must be replaced. Take the damaged cord with you when you buy the new cord; the replacement cord must be the same type. If possible, buy a cord with a plug attached and, preferably, the proper connection to fit into the appliance. Replace the cord in the appliance the same way you removed the old one, either inserting it into the appliance or screwing it in. If the old cord had a crimp connection, connect the new cord with a crimping connector, a small shell of metal that fits over the

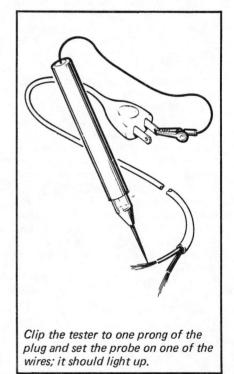

Clip the tester to one prong of the plug and set the probe on one of the wires; it should light up.

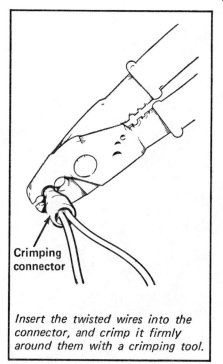

Crimping connector

Insert the twisted wires into the connector, and crimp it firmly around them with a crimping tool.

pliers, artists' brush, fine emery board, vacuum cleaner. **Materials:** replacement parts as required, silicone lubricant or heat-resistant oil, soft cloths. **Time:** about 2 hours.

Although toasters all work on the same basic principle, they don't conform to a specific design; use these repair procedures as guidelines, not absolute standards. If the parts of the toaster are held together with screws or plugs (friction-fit), you'll probably be able to make the repair. If the parts are held together with rivets or welds—and many toasters are—take the toaster to a professional repairman; don't try to fix it yourself. If the toaster needs extensive repairs, replacing it may be your best bet.

Replace worn or damaged parts with new parts made specifically for the toaster. Buy the parts from an appliance repair dealer or an appliance parts store, or order them directly from the manufacturer.

Caution: Before starting to work, make sure the toaster is unplugged.

Clean the toaster frequently with the blower of a vacuum cleaner or a small artists' brush. Crumbs and other food debris can cause the toaster to malfunction, and removing this debris sometimes eliminates the malfunction.

If the cleaning doesn't solve the problem, take the toaster apart. Remove the screws on the bottom of the toaster housing to expose the components. If the toaster doesn't have a one-piece housing, remove the side panels by slipping the panels up and off the toaster frame. The lever controls are usually friction-fit; pull them off with pliers.

If the toaster doesn't heat, make sure the power cord running into the toaster is properly connected to the terminals inside the toaster housing. Also check the heating element contact points; these points must touch for the elements to heat. If the points are out of alignment, push them back into position with needle-nosed pliers; or, if the bimetallic strip is exposed, turn the adjustment screw near the strip. To test alignment, push the control lever down,

wires. Using a utility knife or a wire stripper, remove about ¾ inch of insulation from the appliance end of the wire. Remove about ½ inch of insulation from the two inner wires and twist the bare wires firmly together clockwise. Insert the twisted-together wires into the wide end of the crimping nut. If the inner wires are exposed near the nut, remove the nut and cut the exposed wire to remove the excess; twist and insert into the nut. Crimp the nut firmly around the cord with a crimping tool, and plug the cord in.

Repair a Toaster

Jelly, bread crumbs, raisins, and melted butter can gum up important components of a toaster; if the bread toasts on only one side, an element may be burned out. Don't pitch the toaster; in most cases, you can repair it yourself. **Tools:** screwdriver, Phillips-head screwdriver, pliers, needle-nosed

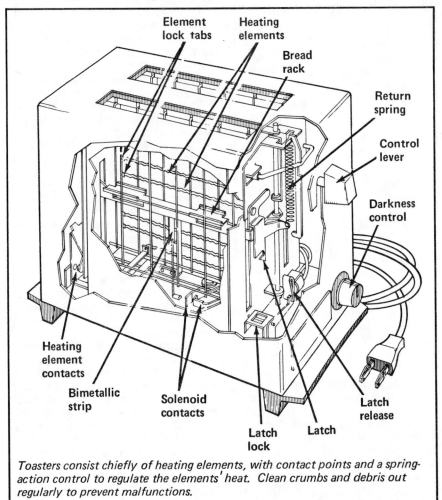

Toasters consist chiefly of heating elements, with contact points and a spring-action control to regulate the elements' heat. Clean crumbs and debris out regularly to prevent malfunctions.

the contact points should touch. Also check the solenoid contacts; clean them with a fine emery board or an artists' brush.

The no-heat problem can also be caused by a bad heating element. Unscrew the small metal strip holding the elements in place. If lock tabs are used to hold the individual elements in position, bend these tabs straight with needle-nosed pliers, and then slide the element off the tabs. Replace the element with a new one made for the toaster.

If the toast doesn't pop up out of the toaster, examine the return spring close to the lever. If the spring has slipped out of its holes on the top or bottom, reconnect it. If the spring is badly stretched or broken, replace it with a new spring; fit the spring into the top and bottom holes where the old one was.

Pop-up problems can also be caused by dirty or out-of-alignment solenoid contacts. Clean the contacts where they touch with a fine emery board; if they've moved out of position, reposition them with needle-nosed pliers. If this doesn't work, and you can unscrew or unplug the solenoid, replace it with a new solenoid made for the toaster.

Make sure that the trip lever and/or

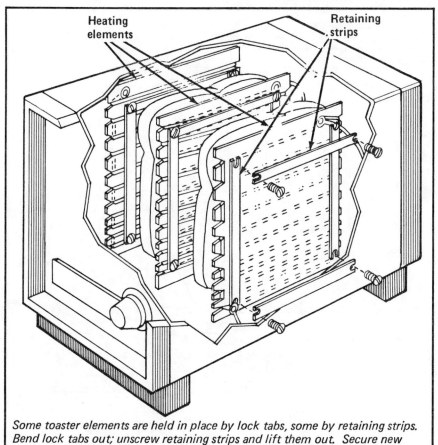

Heating elements

Retaining strips

Some toaster elements are held in place by lock tabs, some by retaining strips. Bend lock tabs out; unscrew retaining strips and lift them out. Secure new elements the same way.

latch is operating smoothly. If it sticks, lubricate the lever or latch with silicone lubricant or heat-resistant oil; fill any oil holes with the lubricant or apply it at all joints.

Repair a Percolator

A percolator that doesn't perk is a major morning catastrophe. The problem is usually a burned-out thermostat or a bad brewing element—and either one is easy to fix. **Tools:** screwdriver, Phillips-head screwdriver, small rattail

file, needle-nosed pliers or thin wrench, fine emery board, socket wrench extender or locking pliers, grease pencil. **Materials:** replacement thermostat and element. **Time:** about 1 hour.

Although electric percolators all work on the same basic principle, they don't conform to a specific design; use these repair procedures as guidelines, not absolute standards. If the parts of the percolator are held together with screws or plugs (friction-fit), you'll probably be able to make the repair. If the parts are held together with rivets or welds, take the percolator to a professional appliance repairman; don't try to fix it yourself. If the percolator needs extensive repairs, replacing it may be your best bet.

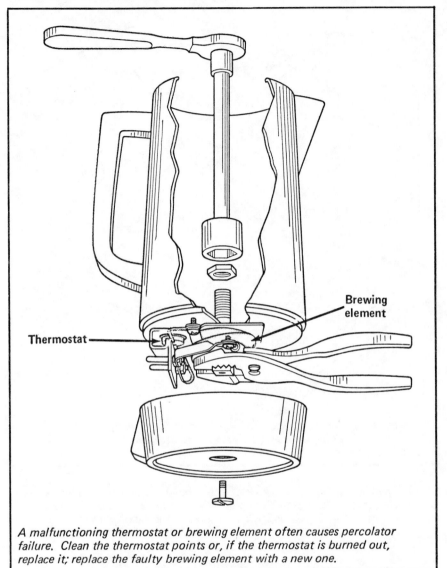

Thermostat

Brewing element

A malfunctioning thermostat or brewing element often causes percolator failure. Clean the thermostat points or, if the thermostat is burned out, replace it; replace the faulty brewing element with a new one.

Replace worn or damaged parts with new parts made specifically for the percolator. Buy the parts from an appliance repair dealer or an appliance parts store, or order them directly from the manufacturer.

Caution: Before you start to work, make sure the percolator is unplugged.

Before working on the thermostat, make sure the percolator is receiving power. Check the power cord, the outlet, and the fuse or circuit breaker that controls the outlet for damage or malfunction.

If the percolator is receiving power, unplug it and unscrew its base; the base is held by several screws driven up through the bottom of the pot. The working parts of the pot are probably attached to the bottom of the pot, or they may be contained in a base unit. The position of the parts doesn't affect the repair procedure.

The thermostat may have an aluminum covering; pry it off with the tip of a screwdriver or unscrew it. Under the cover is a simple thermostat—a flat metal band—with two contact points, spread open when the points are in an *off* position. File the points lightly with a fine emery board. If there are any heat shields around the thermostat, remove them to file the points; then replace them in their original positions. Make sure the heat shields are in the right place; if they aren't, the pot won't heat. Reassemble the pot and fill it with water; then plug it in and turn it on. If the water heats, the thermostat now works properly; if it doesn't, replace the thermostat assembly with a new one made for the percolator.

The thermostat assembly is held in place by one or two screws and/or tabs. Unplug the pot, unscrew its base, and remove the thermostat covering. Remove the thermostat's fasteners and remove the old thermostat. Place the new thermostat into position, secure it, and reassemble the pot. Many thermostats can be replaced with "universal" fit-all thermostats. If you can use this universal part, enlarge the mounting holes with a rattail file, if necessary. You may have to bend the metal bracket slightly to fit.

A malfunctioning brewing element can also cause trouble. Don't try to fix the brewing element; replace it with a new one made for the percolator. Do *not* use a "universal" element; it may not work properly.

To remove the element, remove the base from the pot. Hold the new element against the old one and mark the position it will fit into with a grease pencil. With a socket wrench extender or locking pliers, hold the nut inside the pot at the bottom of the element. Then, with pliers, remove the bolt at the bottom of the element at the base. This will release the element; remove it.

Install the new element the same way you removed the old one—in reverse—making sure the element is in the same position as the old one. Then reassemble the pot.

Fix an Electric Can Opener

Electric can openers are composed of many parts that get dull, get dirty, or break. Most of these parts can be easily and economically repaired. **Tools:** screwdriver, Phillips-head screwdriver, whetstone, needle-nosed pliers, pliers, fine emery board. **Materials:** replacement parts as required, soap and water, silicone lubricant or heat-resistant oil, clean cloths. **Time:** about 1 hour.

Although electric can openers all work on the same basic principle, they don't conform to a specific design; use these repair procedures as guidelines, not absolute standards. If the parts of the can opener are held together with screws or plugs (friction-fit), you'll probably be able to make the repair. If the parts are held together with rivets or welds, take the can opener to a professional appliance repairman; don't try to fix it yourself. If the motor dies, replace the can opener; a new motor costs as much as a new opener.

Replace worn or damaged parts with new parts made specifically for your can opener. Buy the parts from an appliance repair dealer or an appliance parts store, or order them directly from the manufacturer.

Caution: Before you make any repairs, make sure the can opener is unplugged.

The cutter wheel which opens the cans, and the drive wheel, which turns them, are the parts most susceptible to damage. Both are easy to repair or replace without opening the housing.

Remove the drive wheel and the cutter wheel by removing the appropriate screws. One screw is usually driven through the center of the cutter wheel. If a can being opened doesn't revolve around the cutter, replace the drive wheel with a new wheel made for the can opener. Note the way the damaged wheel came off, and position the new wheel exactly the same way.

SMALL APPLIANCES/Can Openers

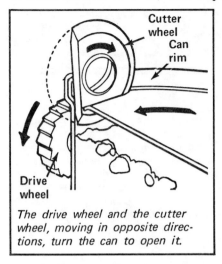

The drive wheel and the cutter wheel, moving in opposite directions, turn the can to open it.

If a can being opened revolves but isn't opened properly, sharpen the cutter wheel on a whetstone. Press the cutter on the whetstone with your thumb and rotate the cutter slowly, being careful to hone the wheel evenly around its cutting edge. If the cutting edge is nicked, or the wheel has been honed a few times, replace the cutter with a new one made for the can opener.

If the motor doesn't run, or runs all the time, open the can opener's housing to work on the switch; the housing should open after you remove a few screws. The two metal contacts under the switch button should touch when the button is pressed and separate when the button is released. If they don't touch when the button is pressed, bend the contacts toward each other with needle-nosed pliers. If they don't separate when the button is released, bend them apart slightly, but not so much that they don't touch when the button is pressed. Clean the contact points with a fine emery board to remove grease and debris.

If the opener growls, skips, or slides, the gear wheels inside it may be worn, especially the idler gear. Open the housing by removing the appropriate screws; then remove the screws that hold the motor in place. Pull off the spur gear and use needle-nosed pliers to remove the drive wheel. Pull out the idler gear.

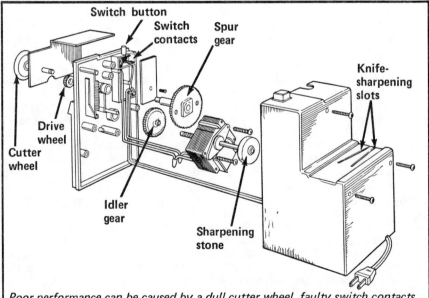

Poor performance can be caused by a dull cutter wheel, faulty switch contacts, or worn gears; a knife sharpener may need a new sharpening stone. Disassemble the opener as shown to repair it.

Replace worn gears with new gears made for the can opener. If the gears are not worn, clean them and lubricate them sparingly with silicone lubricant or heat-resistant oil. Lubricate the gears once a year.

If the can opener has a knife sharpener that doesn't work properly, replace the sharpening stone. Remove the old stone; remove the opener housing and then remove the tiny bolt that holds the stone to the drive shaft. Replace the stone with a new one made for the can opener, and replace the housing.

Repair an Electric Skillet

An electric skillet, like all heating appliances, relies on two primary components: an element and a thermostat. Thermostats are the most easily damaged in a skillet—and the easiest to repair. **Tools:** screwdriver, continuity tester, emery board, small socket wrench. **Materials:** soft cloths, replacement parts as required. **Time:** 1 to 2 hours.

Although skillets all work on the same basic principle, they don't conform to a specific design; use these repair procedures as guidelines, not absolute standards. If the parts of the skillet are held together with screws or plugs (friction-fit), you'll probably be able to make the repair. If the parts are held together with rivets or welds, take the skillet to a professional appliance repairman; don't try to fix it yourself. If the skillet needs extensive repairs, replacing it may be your best bet.

Replace worn or damaged parts with new parts made for your skillet. Buy the parts from an appliance repair dealer or an appliance parts store, or order them directly from the manufacturer.

Caution: Before you start to work, make sure the skillet is unplugged.

The skillet's heating element is usually sealed in the bottom of the skillet where it can't be removed; if the element goes bad, you'll have to replace the skillet. The element's exposed terminals, however, can usually be repaired or replaced, and thermostats can almost always be repaired.

If the skillet doesn't heat adequately, doesn't heat at all, or turns on and off frequently, first check the terminal pins protruding from the skillet base. Detach the thermostat/handle assembly from the skillet base and examine the terminal pins. If the terminals are loose,

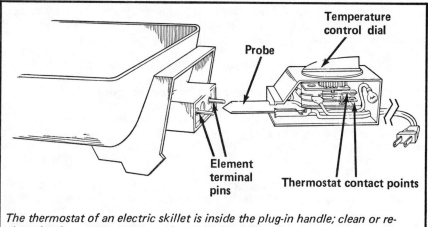

Temperature control dial

Probe

Element terminal pins

Thermostat contact points

The thermostat of an electric skillet is inside the plug-in handle; clean or replace the thermostat contact points. At the skillet, tighten loose element terminal pins, or replace damaged ones.

tighten the screws that attach them to the skillet. If the terminals look burned or pitted, replace them with new terminals. Remove the little screw nuts that hold the terminals in place, insert new terminals made for the skillet, and tighten down the screw nuts.

If the skillet still won't heat, test the heating element. Detach the thermostat/handle assembly from the skillet base. Use a continuity tester set at lowest resistance; touch the probes of the tester to each terminal pin. Follow the tester's instructions for proper reading. If no continuity is detected, the element is bad, and the skillet can't be repaired. If the continuity is good, the thermostat is probably malfunctioning; this can usually be repaired.

To repair the thermostat, remove the screws that hold the handle/thermostat together in a clamshell configuration; or remove the plate on top of the handle to expose the working parts inside the handle. Remove any aluminum foil covering that conceals the parts.

Near the base of the probe that goes into the skillet are the thermostat contact points. These points touch when heating and separate when the proper temperature is attained, or when the heat is turned off. Rub them gently with a fine emery board and a soft clean cloth.

If the skillet is overheating, the contact points may be fused together. Open them with the tip of a screwdriver and then smooth them down with an emery board. But be careful; the points are very delicate.

If you damage the points, or if they're already badly damaged, replace them, if possible. Use replacement points made for the skillet. The points may be held in place with screws or spring clips. Remove the old points, insert the new ones, and secure the points with the screws or clips.

If the emery board and new points don't solve the problem—or if you can't remove the points—replace the entire thermostat/handle assembly with a new one made for the skillet. The new handle will slip on and off the element's terminals the same way the old one did.

Repair a Waffle Maker

A waffle maker that doesn't work is a discouraging sight, but it's usually easy to fix. **Tools:** screwdriver, pliers, cotton swab or wooden match. **Materials:** replacement parts as required, electrical flux powder, cloths. **Time:** about 1 hour.

Although waffle makers all work on the same basic principle, they don't conform to a specific design; use these repair procedures as guidelines, not absolute standards. If the parts of the waffle maker are held together with screws or plugs (friction-fit), you'll probably be able to make the repair. If the parts are held together with rivets or welds, take the waffle maker to a professional appliance repairman; don't try to fix it yourself. If the waffle maker needs extensive repairs, replacing it may be your best bet.

Replace worn or damaged parts with new parts made specifically for the waffle maker. Buy the parts from an appliance repair dealer or an appliance parts store, or order them directly from the manufacturer.

Caution: Before you make any repairs, make sure the waffle maker is unplugged.

To determine the cause of the problem, remove the top and bottom grill plates. These plates are held in position by several retaining clips around the end of the waffle maker housing. Unbend the clips with a screwdriver or a pliers and remove the plates. The top grill usually has a heating element which is connected to power terminals. The bottom grill usually contains the power cord connections, control and thermostat components, and a second heating element.

If the waffle maker won't heat, the problem is probably the thermostat. Before you work on the thermostat, sight-check the heating elements for any breaks in the tiny element wires, and make sure the power cord termi-

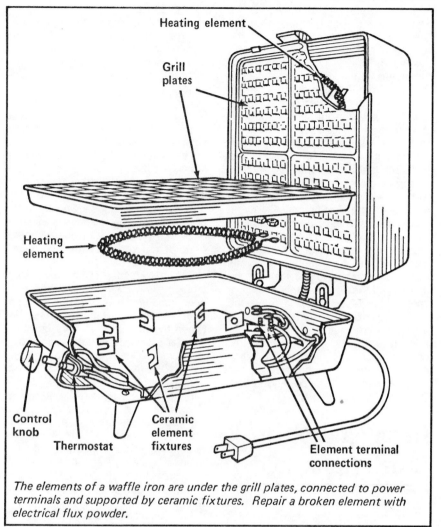

The elements of a waffle iron are under the grill plates, connected to power terminals and supported by ceramic fixtures. Repair a broken element with electrical flux powder.

nals are tightly connected and clean.

If the wire element is broken, you can usually repair it with electrical flux powder. Have a helper hold the element wires together. Make sure the element wires are clean, and overlap them about ¼ inch for the flux repair. Apply flux to the element with a cotton swab or wooden matchstick. Have your helper let go of the element wires, and plug in the waffle maker; the heat of the element will weld the flux-coated wires together. Don't twist the wires together; they're too brittle. Don't splice the break

with new wire; elements use a special heat-resistant wire.

If the element is badly damaged, replace it with a new one made for the waffle maker. The element is held and elevated in the housing by ceramic fixtures. Raise the element off these fixtures and unscrew the element at the power connection point. Position the new element the same way the old one was, and secure it in the housing.

If the power cord is frayed or damaged, disconnect the cord at the terminals inside the bottom element housing.

The terminals are usually held by screws or small screw tabs. Replace the cord with a new cord made for the appliance.

If the waffle maker is receiving power, if the terminals are clean and connected, and if the elements aren't broken, the thermostat is malfunctioning. To get at the thermostat, remove the control knob. Remove the setscrew that holds it to the shaft of the thermostat; or, if it's friction-fit on the shaft, pull it off. The thermostat itself may be held by screws driven into the housing of the waffle maker; remove the screws to disconnect the thermostat. Or, if the thermostat is connected to a bracket clipped to the housing, gently pry out the clip and thermostat with a screwdriver or pliers. Note the way it comes off, so you'll be able to install a new one correctly. If the thermostat is riveted or spot-welded to the housing, have the waffle maker repaired by a professional appliance repairman.

Replace the thermostat with a new one made for the waffle maker. Position it the way the old thermostat was set, screw or clip it into place, and secure the control knob.

Repair Motors in Small Appliances

If an appliance won't run at all, if it sparks, or if it runs erratically, there's a good chance that the motor needs repair—and an equally good chance that you can fix it. **Tools:** screwdriver, needle-nosed pliers. **Materials:** carbon brushes, heat-resistant oil, brush springs, coil. **Time:** about ½ hour.

Before starting to work, make sure the plug, the switch, and the individual gears are in good shape. Work on the motor only after you've eliminated these as the trouble spots. *Caution: Before you start to work, make sure the appliance is unplugged.*

Universal motors are standard in appliances that require reliable stop-and-go power, such as blenders or electric knives. The motors operate on both batteries and alternating current. Appliances that don't require such power—hair dryers and can openers, for example—use synchronous-type motors.

To get at the universal motor, open up the appliance's housing—usually a clamshell configuration held together by screws or clamps. The motor will have a fan at one end and a cylindrical shaft at the other. If there are oil ports in the motor's housing or in the bearings at the shaft's end, lubricate them lightly with a heat-resistant oil. Check the fan blades; if a blade looks bent, move it back into position with needle-nosed pliers. If you see a reset button on the motor, push it.

The major cause of universal-motor problems is worn carbon brushes. Carbon brushes rub against the commutator—a small, rotating cylinder between the armature and the fan; they transfer electricity to the rotating parts of the motor. The brushes are soft and subject to wear; sparking is a sign of damaged brushes.

If the motor is encased in an overall decorative housing, unscrew the housing to get at the brush assembly. The brushes are secured with two fairly large screws flush-mounted into the motor's housing. Remove the screws and turn the motor over, shaking it gently. The brushes can then be easily removed.

In order, disassemble the screws, the brush holders, the small springs, and the carbon brushes. The ends of the brushes are concave to fit the round commutator. After removing the old brushes, insert new carbon brushes into the brush channels and reassemble the appliance: brushes, springs, brush holders, and screws. If the springs look damaged, replace them. There may be some sparking at first after you install new brushes; this is normal.

Buy brushes and springs made specifically for the motor; look for the model information (numbers, make) stamped on a metal plate fastened to the motor,

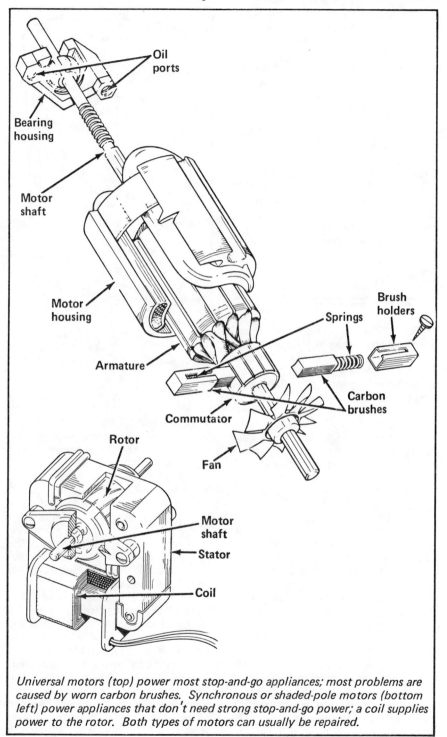

Oil ports

Bearing housing

Motor shaft

Motor housing

Armature

Commutator

Rotor

Fan

Springs

Brush holders

Carbon brushes

Motor shaft

Stator

Coil

Universal motors (top) power most stop-and-go appliances; most problems are caused by worn carbon brushes. Synchronous or shaded-pole motors (bottom left) power appliances that don't need strong stop-and-go power; a coil supplies power to the rotor. Both types of motors can usually be repaired.

or embossed in the metal housing of the motor. If this information isn't available, disassemble the brush assembly and take the old brushes and springs to the store to make sure you get the right kind.

Synchronous, or shaded-pole, motors operate on alternating current. Oversimplified, a synchronous motor turns when electricity is fed into a rotor. This motor's usual problem is a faulty coil. To replace the coil, unscrew the frame. Then open the halves of the frame, remove the coil, and insert a new coil of the same make and model number. If the frame is riveted together, replace the appliance; replacing the coil isn't worth the work involved.

Repair a Blender

Blender blades take a lot of abuse, and most blender problems occur in the 3-inch shaft that makes up the chopper assembly. Fortunately, it's easy and inexpensive to repair the assembly. **Tools:** screwdriver, Phillips-head screwdriver, adjustable wrench, small socket wrench with socket extender, needle-nosed pliers, slip-joint pliers, large nails. **Materials:** replacement parts as required, cloths. **Time:** about 1 hour.

Although blenders all work on the same basic principle, they don't conform to a specific design; use these repair procedures as guidelines, not absolute standards. If the parts of the blender are held together with screws or plugs (friction-fit), you'll probably be able to make the repair. If the parts are held together with rivets or solder, take the blender to a professional repairman; don't try to fix it yourself. If the blender needs extensive repairs, replacing it may be your best bet.

Replace worn or damaged parts with new parts made specifically for your blender. Buy the parts from an appliance repair dealer or an appliance parts store, or order them directly from the manufacturer.

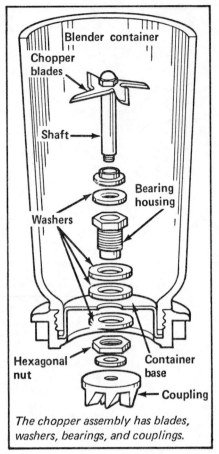

The chopper assembly has blades, washers, bearings, and couplings.

Caution: *Before you start to work, make sure the blender is unplugged.*

To determine the cause of the problem, remove the glass blender container and examine the chopping assembly. This assembly consists of the chopper blades, the bearings, the couplings, and the washers; take it apart to expose all components.

Remove the screws that hold the base of the blender, and remove the base to expose the fan blades at the end of the motor. To remove the chopper assembly, keep the chopper wheel from turning by holding the lower bearing plate of the motor, and then remove the screw or nut at the top of the chopper wheel. On some blenders, you can block the motor's fan blades by sticking a large nail up through the air ports in the base; then remove the screw or nut.

After removing the top screw or nut, lift the entire assembly out of the base, exposing all components. Disassemble the components, turning the pieces clockwise or counterclockwise as necessary to disconnect the shaft connections. If the parts don't seem to fit, try reversing the screwing direction. Lay the parts out in order as you disassemble the blender, and make a diagram as you work so you'll be able to reassemble them properly.

The chopper wheel and the bearings of the blender take a lot of wear and tear. Examine these parts carefully. If they look damaged, replace them with new parts made for the blender.

If the container leaks, but isn't cracked or broken, the trouble is probably a composition (not metal) washer at the base of the container. If the washer is eroded or split, replace it with a new one, made for the blender.

If the blender is noisy, the problem is probably in the gear-like couplings. The top coupling is the bottom part of the shaft assembly; the bottom coupling may still be attached to the base after the shaft assembly is removed. If the bottom coupling looks worn, remove it. You may be able to unscrew it, or you may have to hold a center screw in place while you turn the bottom coupling with your hand. Replace worn parts with new ones made for the blender. Screw them or attach them the same way they came off.

Blender motors seldom cause trouble, but they do get dirty. When you disassemble the blender to replace a part, remove the motor from its housing, removing the retaining screws as necessary. Wipe the motor parts clean with a soft cloth.

If the blender is used frequently, the motor's carbon brushes may be worn; if the mixer sparks, replace the carbon brushes with new ones made for the blender. Follow the procedure outlined in "Repair Motors in Small Appliances." If the blender's cord is frayed, remove the terminal screws at the terminal connection block, and replace the cord with a new one of the same type.

Fix an Electric Knife

An electric knife consists of two serrated blades moving back and forth at high speed; the blades are driven by a motor, and the motor is geared to move the blades parallel to each other. Repairing an electric knife is usually easy. **Tools:** screwdriver, pencil, small socket wrench. **Materials:** soft cloths, No. 10 nondetergent motor oil and friction-proofing oil (STP), replacement parts as required. **Time:** about 1 hour.

Although electric knives all work on the same basic principle, they don't conform to a specific design; use these repair procedures as guidelines, not absolute standards. If the parts of the knife are held together with screws or plugs (friction-fit), you'll probably be able to make the repair. If the parts are held together with rivets or welds, take the knife to a professional appliance repairman; don't try to fix it yourself. If the knife needs extensive repairs, replacing it may be your best bet.

Replace worn or damaged parts with new parts made specifically for the electric knife. Buy the parts from an appliance repair dealer or an appliance parts store, or order them directly from the manufacturer.

Cautions: Before you make any repairs, unplug the electric knife.

If the knife is a cordless one, make sure the batteries are working properly before you open the knife. Replace old batteries with new ones recommended by the knife's manufacturer. Knife batteries are usually nickel-cadmium cells, not the flashlight-type dry cells.

The clamshell housing of an electric knife is usually held together by screws or small bolts. For cleaning and repairs, first remove the blades and then unscrew and open the housing. A metal bracket fits over a worm wheel gear and drive assembly. To expose worn or dirty parts, unscrew this bracket and remove the bracket and the retaining plate.

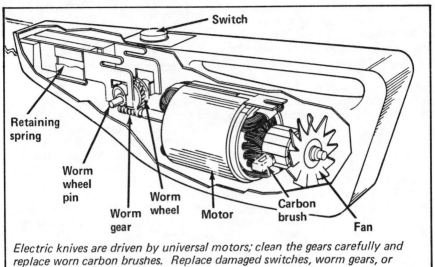

Switch

Retaining spring

Worm wheel pin

Worm gear

Worm wheel

Motor

Carbon brush

Fan

Electric knives are driven by universal motors; clean the gears carefully and replace worn carbon brushes. Replace damaged switches, worm gears, or retaining springs; lubricate moving parts.

If the motor or the gears bind, clean the working parts carefully and thoroughly with a soft cloth; a cloth stretched over a pencil point makes a good tool. Mix a small amount of No. 10 nondetergent motor oil and friction-proofing oil (STP) in equal parts, and lightly coat the working parts with this mixture.

If the motor doesn't run or won't turn off, the problem may be the switch. Unscrew the switch from the housing and disconnect the lead wires, which are attached with screws or slip-fit connectors. Replace the switch with a new one made for the knife. Connect the lead wires first, and then screw the switch into the housing. If the switch isn't held by screws, take the knife to a professional appliance repairman.

If the blades won't work but the motor runs, chances are the worm gear, the worm wheels, or the retaining spring is damaged. If the teeth on the worm gear are damaged or worn, replace the gear with a new one made for the knife. The worm gear fits onto a drive shaft and is either held by a setscrew or friction-fit. Also look for a cracked pin at the hub of the worm wheel. If the pin is cracked or broken, replace the wheel. Do *not* try to mend it with a metal patch filler.

The retaining spring for the blades is located in the assembly near the front of the knife. If this assembly is held together with screws, disassemble it. If the retaining spring is broken, replace it with a new one made for the knife. If the spring assembly is riveted together, replace the entire assembly; do *not* try to repair it.

If the motor doesn't run, sparks, or runs slowly, the motor's carbon brushes may be damaged or worn. Replace them with new carbon brushes made for the knife; follow the procedure outlined in "Repair Motors in Small Appliances."

Motor overheating—you can smell it and sometimes feel it on the knife housing—is usually caused by dirt. Disassemble the housing. Check the carbon brushes for wear and, if necessary, replace them. Clean and lubricate the gears, and reassemble the knife.

Fix a Mixer

When a mixer won't mix, it's probably clogged with debris; other common problems are worn gears and brushes.

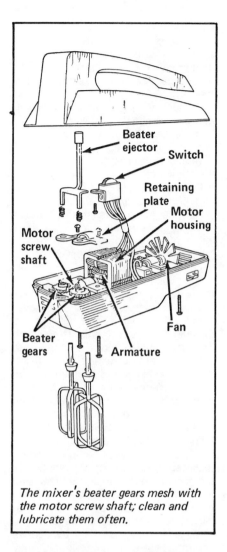

The mixer's beater gears mesh with the motor screw shaft; clean and lubricate them often.

All are easy to remedy. **Tools:** screwdriver, needle-nosed pliers. **Materials:** soft cloths, heat-resistant oil, replacement parts as required. **Time:** about 1 hour.

Although hand and upright mixers all work on the same basic principle, they don't conform to a specific design; use these repair procedures as guidelines, not absolute standards. If the mixer's parts are held together with screws or plugs (friction-fit), you'll probably be able to make the repair. If the parts are held together with rivets or welds, take the mixer to a professional appliance repairman; don't try to fix it yourself. If the mixer needs extensive repairs, replacing it may be your best bet.

Replace worn or damaged parts with new parts made specifically for your mixer. Buy the parts from an appliance repair dealer or an appliance parts store, or order them directly from the manufacturer.

Caution: Before you start to work, make sure the mixer is unplugged.

Hand and upright mixers are similar in construction. Both types generally have a plastic housing fastened together with screws. To open the housing, remove the screws; the housing splits apart in a clamshell configuration. Some mixers have a control cap on the end of the mixer. By unscrewing this cap—or prying it off with a screwdriver—you can get into the working parts of the mixer.

Most mixers have oil ports at the top of the motor assembly. Lubricate these ports with heat-resistant oil every 2 to 3 months, depending on how much you use the mixer. Clean any food debris from the motor with a clean cloth. Do *not* use abrasive paper.

If the beaters don't rotate, but the motor runs, check for broken or worn gears. The gears are located just above where the beaters fit into the housing; a small metal retaining plate above the gears holds them in position. Loosen the screws that hold the plate and remove the plate. Pull out the gears for inspection.

If the gears are worn or broken, replace them with new gears made for the mixer. Do *not* buy "universal" gears. Place the new gears into position exactly where the old gears were. When the gears are in position, turn the motor shaft by hand. If the gears don't mesh, reposition the gears and turn the motor shaft again. Repeat until the gears run smoothly on the screw shaft. Clean the gears frequently and lubricate them with heat-resistant oil.

Mixer attachments, such as coffee grinders, operate off gears similar to the beater gears. If trouble occurs with the attachments, check these gears for wear or breakage. The gears are located in the attachment itself; you'll probably have to unscrew a cover plate to get at them. If the gears are worn or broken, replace them with new gears made for the attachment. Clean and lubricate the gears frequently.

If the motor won't run at all, the problem is probably in the switch or the motor; if the motor runs all the time, the problem is in the switch. Before working on these parts, make sure the appliance is getting power from the circuit, and examine the cord. If the cord or the plug is damaged, replace the cord with a new one of the same type.

To replace the switch, remove the screws that attach the switch to the housing and disconnect the lead wires. Replace the switch with a new one made for the mixer. Reconnect the lead wires first; then screw the switch into the housing. If the switch is riveted to the housing, have it replaced by a professional appliance repairman.

If the motor still doesn't run, or if it runs erratically, makes noise, smells, or sparks, the motor's carbon brushes are probably worn. Replace them with new carbon brushes made for the mixer. Follow the procedure outlined in "Repair Motors in Small Appliances."

Repair a Vacuum Cleaner

The major complaint about vacuum cleaners is no suction; the major cause of the problem is air blockage. Although some repairs demand professional service, you can take care of most problems yourself. **Tools:** wire coat hanger, needle-nosed pliers, coarse-toothed comb, nail, screwdriver, sharp knife or wire stripper. **Materials:** silicone lubricant, replacement parts as required. **Time:** about 1 hour.

Although vacuum cleaners all work on the same basic principle, they don't conform to a specific design; use these repair procedures as guidelines, not absolute standards. If the parts of the vacuum are held together with screws or plugs (friction-fit), you'll probably be able to make the repair. If the parts are held together with rivets or welds, take the vacuum to a professional repairman.

Replace worn or damaged parts with new parts made specifically for the vacuum cleaner. Buy the parts from an appliance repair dealer or an appliance parts store, or order them directly from the manufacturer.

Caution: *Before you start to work, unplug the vacuum cleaner.*

All vacuum cleaners suck air through a sweeper assembly, past a fan, and into a dust bag. When this passageway becomes blocked, the suction of the vacuum cleaner is reduced.

If the vacuum cleaner has a hose and the hose becomes blocked—there's no suction when you hold your hand over the nozzle—connect the hose to the exhaust port instead of the intake port. The air pushed through the hose by the exhaust should clear the hose. If the hose is still blocked, straighten out two wire coat hangers, twist them together with pliers, and carefully push them through the hose to remove the obstruction. Work slowly; be very careful not to damage the hose.

If hose blockage is not the problem, make sure the dust bag is empty and the gasket around the dust bag housing is tightly sealed. Sometimes a leaky gasket can cause poor suction; a hissing noise may indicate this problem. The gasket may be held by screws and/or clips on a metal plate, or it may be slip-fit around the edge of the dust bag housing. Replace a faulty gasket with a new one made for the vacuum cleaner.

Also look for suction trouble where the hose hooks onto the tank and where the metal tubes of the handle slip together. If these parts are bent, pinch them back together with pliers to tighten the connection. If they're badly worn, replace them with new ones made for the vacuum. The metal connection at the tank is usually screwed on; the connections on the hose itself are pushed together.

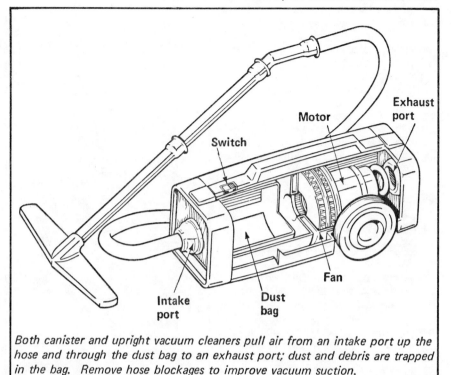

Both canister and upright vacuum cleaners pull air from an intake port up the hose and through the dust bag to an exhaust port; dust and debris are trapped in the bag. Remove hose blockages to improve vacuum suction.

Upright vacuums can malfunction when the beater brushes become clogged, blocking the air passage. Remove the plate on the bottom of the vacuum; the plate is either screwed on or held by spring clips. Remove the drive belt that surrounds the brush and lift out the brush; if necessary, flip the lock clamp at the side of the brush. Wash the brush and fluff it with a coarse-toothed comb to restore its original effectiveness.

Examine the drive belt before replacing the brush. Stretched or worn belts can cause dirt-pickup problems. If necessary, replace the belt with a new one made for the vacuum; note the way the old belt comes off, and position the new one the same way.

If the brush or the belt is not the problem, straighten a wire coat hanger and probe the passageways between the beater brush and the fan and between the fan and the dust bag connection. Sometimes just removing the dust bag and starting the appliance will clear the passageway.

If the vacuum doesn't run at all, check the plug. If the plug is loose or damaged, replace it with a new one of the same type.

Most plugs are permanently attached to the power cord. To replace a plug, sever the cord behind the damaged plug. Strip off the cord's insulation with a sharp knife or a wire stripper to expose the wires. Strip off the insulation on the wires for about ½ inch, and connect the bare wires to the new plug's terminals. Wrap the bare wires clockwise around the screw terminals, so that the wires will tighten on the terminals as you tighten the screws.

Switches seldom need to be replaced, but if the plug isn't defective, the problem may be in the switch. Replace the switch with a new one made for the vacuum. Remove the screws that hold the switch assembly in place, and remove the switch. Disconnect the switch's lead wires from the inside terminals; loosen the terminal screws, or pull off friction-fit wires. Put the new switch into place. Connect the lead wires first; then screw the switch housing into the vacuum cleaner.

If the vacuum cleaner still doesn't work, check the motor's carbon brushes. If the brushes are worn, replace them with new ones made for the vacuum. Follow the procedure outlined in "Repair Motors in Small Appliances."

Repair a Steam Iron

The most common steam iron problem, and the easiest to remedy, is mineral deposits clogging the soleplate's ports. More serious problems result from accidental drops; unless the iron is badly damaged, the repair is easy. **Tools:** shallow pan, screwdriver, Phillips-head screwdriver, needle-nosed pliers, pliers, fine emery board, nail, cotton swabs. **Materials:** replacement parts as needed, commercial iron cleaner, fine steel wool, soft cloths, white vinegar. **Time:** 1 to 2 hours.

Although steam irons all work on the same basic principle, they don't conform to a specific design; use these repair procedures as guidelines, not absolute standards. If the parts of the iron are held together with screws or plugs (friction-fit), you'll probably be able to make the repair. If the parts are held together with rivets or welds, take the iron to a professional appliance repairman; don't try to fix it yourself. If the iron needs extensive repairs, replacing it may be your best bet.

Replace worn or damaged parts with new parts made specifically for the iron. Buy the parts from an appliance repair dealer or an appliance parts store, or order them directly from the manufacturer.

Caution: *Before you start to work, make sure the iron is unplugged.*

If the ports in the soleplate of the iron

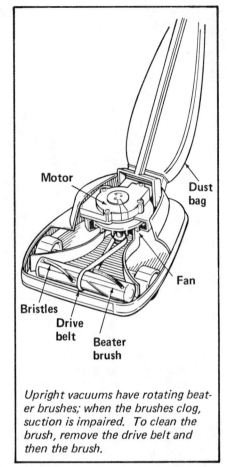

Upright vacuums have rotating beater brushes; when the brushes clog, suction is impaired. To clean the brush, remove the drive belt and then the brush.

are caked with white mineral deposits, use a commercial iron cleaner or run white vinegar through the iron. Let the cleaner or vinegar heat and make steam; hold the iron up flat so that it steams, to flush the ports thoroughly. The cleaner or vinegar will remove all mineral salts. Or set the cold iron flat in a pan of white vinegar for 8 to 10 hours to dissolve the deposits. To keep deposits from forming, use distilled water in the iron.

If the bottom or soleplate of the iron is encrusted with starch, as well as minerals, remove the deposits with fine steel wool dipped in white vinegar; rub the bottom of the iron gently. Carefully clean out the ports with a nail and a cotton swab. Do *not* use steel wool if

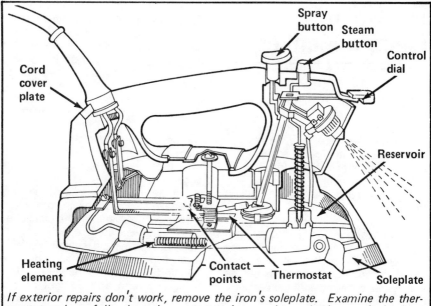

Spray button
Steam button
Control dial
Cord cover plate
Reservoir
Heating element
Contact points
Thermostat
Soleplate

If exterior repairs don't work, remove the iron's soleplate. Examine the thermostat and carefully clean the contact points; replace a broken or faulty heating element with a new one.

the iron's soleplate has a nonstick plastic coating; you can't replace or repair damaged plastic coatings.

If the iron doesn't heat, examine the cord's entry into the iron. If the cord is obviously frayed or broken, replace the cord with a new one of the same type; bring the old cord with you when you buy the new one. Some cords simply plug in. If the cord runs down into the iron, unscrew the cover plate over the cord's connection and tighten the terminals with a screwdriver and/or a pliers. If the cord is frayed under the cover plate, disconnect the terminals, remove the cord, and replace it with a new one of the same type. Make sure the terminals on the new cord match the terminals on the old cord.

If a new cord doesn't solve the problem, you'll have to open the iron. Each iron is put together differently, and there's no guarantee that once it's open you'll be able to replace damaged parts. If you can't isolate the problem or damage is extensive, take the iron to a professional appliance repairman, or replace it.

To remove the soleplate, remove any screws on the bottom of the plate. Examine the handle, the cover plate, and other parts for other soleplate screws, and remove them as necessary. Detach the soleplate from the body of the iron to expose the inside. Make a sketch of the iron as you work so you'll be able to reassemble it properly.

Inside the iron, just inside the soleplate, is a thermostat with two contact points. If these contact points are dirty, the iron won't heat or will heat erratically. Clean the points carefully with a fine emery board. If the iron still doesn't heat, the heating element may be faulty. The heating element is usually next to the thermostat. Remove the element, if possible, by removing the screws that hold it; replace it with a new element of the same type. Make sure the connections are clean and tight.

Finally, replace the soleplate of the iron and replace all screws to secure it; tighten them firmly and carefully. If you replaced the element, the new element may smoke the first time you use the iron; this is normal.

Repair an Electric Blanket

A malfunctioning thermostat or a sticky contact point in the control box can make an electric blanket turn cold fast. With care, you may be able to warm it up again. **Tools:** screwdriver, fine emery board. **Materials:** none. **Time:** about ½ hour.

Although electric blankets all work on the same basic principle, they don't conform to a specific design; use these repair procedures as guidelines, not absolute standards. If the parts of the blanket are held together with screws or plugs (friction-fit), you'll probably be able to make the repair. If the parts are held together with rivets or welds, take the blanket to a professional repairman; don't try to fix it yourself. If the blanket needs extensive repairs, replacing it may be your best bet.

Caution: Before starting to work, make sure the blanket is unplugged.

The thermostats in an electric blanket are activated by room temperature; the blanket may not operate in a room that's too warm. If that isn't the problem, make sure the blanket is receiving power before attempting repairs. Check the outlet and the main fuse box or circuit breaker.

If power isn't the problem, and the room is cool enough, work on the thermostats. An electric blanket usually has a series of tiny thermostats spaced within the blanket itself. Most blankets also have a separate control box—also a thermostat—that turns the blanket on and off and sets the temperature.

First, examine the control box. Remove two or four screws to open the housing. Inside the housing are a bimetallic strip and contact points. Clean the points by lightly stroking a fine emery board across the metal where they touch.

Reassemble the housing and test the blanket. If it still doesn't work, locate the

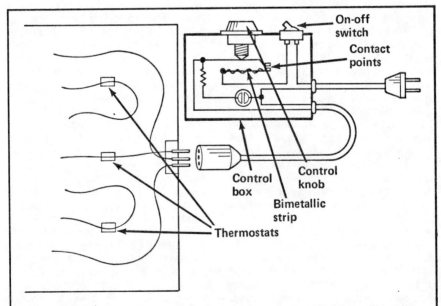

In the blanket's control box, clean the contact points at the bimetallic strip. In the blanket itself, locate the thermostats and tap them lightly to free the contact points inside them.

thermostats within the blanket; you should be able to feel them through the cloth. When you find a thermostat, lightly tap it with the handle of a screwdriver—sometimes the contact points in blanket thermostats stick shut, and a gentle rap with a screwdriver handle will jar them loose. Tap each thermostat a few times. Then plug in the blanket and test it for heat.

If none of these procedures works, take the blanket to a professional repair outlet, or return it to the manufacturer for repair. Do *not* open the blanket, repair or replace thermostats, or splice connecting wires.

Clean, Oil and Lubricate a Sewing Machine

Many sewing machine problems are due to lint, bits of thread, and a lack of periodic general maintenance; the sewing debris that accumulates in the machine can build up to the trouble point within just a few projects. Put together a small maintenance kit and give your sewing machine regular cleaning and lubrication. **Tools:** pencil, small and medium screwdrivers, toothbrush, long-bristled brush, toothpicks, tweezers, vacuum cleaner with crack-cleaning attachment, sharp hobby knife. **Materials:** masking tape, soft cloth, concentrated household cleaner, extra-fine-grit cloth-backed sandpaper, fine-grit emery cloth, sewing machine oil with pinpoint oiler, dental floss, sewing machine gear lubricant. **Time:** about 1 hour.

Unplug and remove the hand-removable lead cords of the machine and inspect them for cracks or breaks; repair or replace any defective cord. Remove all hand-removable parts of the sewing machine: needle, presser foot, thread, bobbin, bobbin case (if removable), needle plate, etc. As you remove each part, tag the part and its lo-cation with masking tape; number all parts and their locations.

Use a screwdriver to remove the upper, side, and bottom access covers to expose the machine's works. Each screw can be a different size, so number them all. Remove the needle plate; most are attached with screws, but some are hand-removable. Don't tighten or loosen any other setscrews or adjusting screws within the machine's works, unless the screws are obviously ready to fall out.

With all removable parts set aside, delint the works of the sewing machine. With a toothbrush, a long-bristled brush, toothpicks, and tweezers, remove all lint, threads, and debris you can find. Use a vacuum cleaner with a crack-cleaning attachment to pick up the debris; if your vacuum has a blower, turn the blower on the cleaned sewing machine. Search for buildups of thread winds, and cut out any tangled threads with a sharp hobby knife. With a soft cloth and concentrated household cleaner, wipe off any obvious grime.

After cleaning and delinting the main section of the sewing machine, brush and clean the components removed earlier. Most of the chrome parts are thread-handling parts. Inspect them for burrs, sharp nicks caused by needle strikes; these nicks can cause threads to fray or break. Smooth any burrs you find on the thread-handling parts with extra-fine-grit cloth-backed sandpaper, and then with fine-grit emery cloth. Be careful not to get sanding debris into the cleaned sewing machine; work away from the spread-out parts. When all burrs have been sanded smooth, lubricate the machine; use sewing machine oil with a pinpoint oiler and special sewing machine gear lubricant. Do *not* oil the gears.

Oil all metal-to-metal moving parts at the point where they make contact; to locate the points of contact, rock, rotate, and swivel the handwheel back and forth and watch the parts move. Many levers and shafts have an oil hole at the points of contact; place a drop of oil in each oil hole. Don't over-oil—one drop of oil at each contact point is all that's

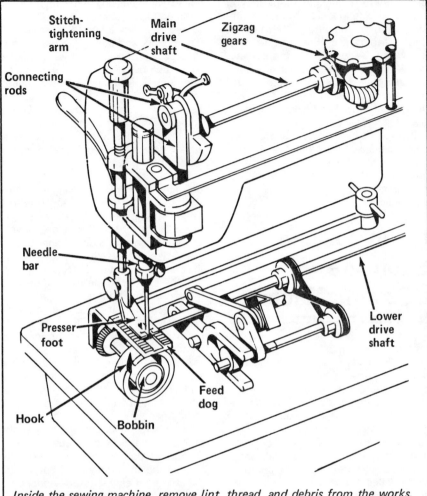

Inside the sewing machine, remove lint, thread, and debris from the works. Cut out tangled threads and smooth burrs; then oil all metal-to-metal parts at the contact points, and lubricate all gears.

needed. ***Caution:*** *Do not oil the motor; oil on the commutator can cause motor damage.* Don't oil the tension discs, but run the edge of a soft cloth in between them or use a piece of dental floss to remove lint. Lubricate toothed gears with sewing machine gear lubricant; smear the gel on with your fingers.

Finally, replace the pieces of the sewing machine in reverse order from the way you removed them. Remove the masking tape tags as you replace each part.

Balance Sewing Machine Tensions

Many sewing machine stitch problems are caused by poorly adjusted thread tensions, or by simple problems that affect the tension mechanisms.

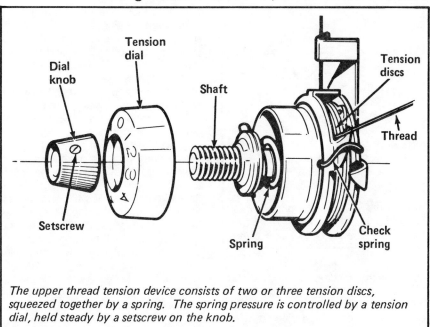

The upper thread tension device consists of two or three tension discs, squeezed together by a spring. The spring pressure is controlled by a tension dial, held steady by a setscrew on the knob.

Here's how to solve or adjust most sewing machine tension problems. **Tools:** dental floss, toothpick, screwdriver, new medium-size sewing machine needle. **Materials:** thread, white paper, medium-weight cotton material. **Time:** 5 minutes to ½ hour.

Before you make any adjustments to the machine, make a sequence of tension checks to see where the problem is. This requires a working knowledge of how tensions function. The thread tension mechanisms are two separate devices that apply pressure to the upper spool thread supply and to the lower bobbin thread supply. The upper tension device consists of two or three tension discs squeezed together by a coiled spring; the spring pressure is controlled by a numbered or calibrated dial. On most sewing machines, the lower tension device is a flat metal spring clip squeezed by a setscrew; this controls the pressure on the bobbin thread. Other machines have an arm that presses against the bobbin to apply the needed pressure, via a setscrew on the bobbin case. On any machine, the upper and lower pressure must be

equal to make a good lock stitch.

Start your sequence of tension checks with the threading of the machine. Be sure the machine is properly threaded, as specified in your owner's manual; many tension problems are due to a misthreaded machine. The thread must pass between the upper discs, not in front of or behind them. The tension dial should usually be set on *4* or *5*, or *normal*; however, *3* or *6* can also be within a proper range, depending on the material's thickness.

Next check the upper tension discs. Raise the presser foot lifter; this releases the coiled spring's pressure and lets the discs separate. Look between the discs. If any lint or threads have accumulated between the discs, use a piece of dental floss or a toothpick to remove the debris.

Check the lower tension device for lint, loose threads, or burrs—little nicks on the thread-handling parts. Remove debris and smooth burrs as necessary. If the area is visually clear of lint and debris, a piece of hidden lint could be caught behind the bobbin case spring clip. Sometimes it's possible to remove

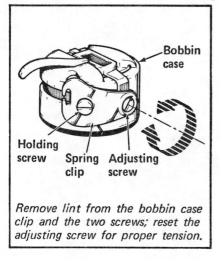

Remove lint from the bobbin case clip and the two screws; reset the adjusting screw for proper tension.

this lint with a piece of dental floss, but to be sure all debris is removed from the bobbin case clip, remove the bobbin case. Set the case on a piece of white paper, and look for one or two screws that hold the clip in place.

One of these screws is the holding screw; the other is the adjusting screw —if there's only one screw, it's an adjusting screw. NOTE: If your machine is a self-winding, top drop-in bobbin type, then the only screw is an adjusting screw; it should *not* be disassembled.

If the problem is the bobbin case, remove the screws and the spring clip, making sure you keep track of which screw goes where. Remove any debris within the clip or case. Replace the clip and replace the two screws, returning them to the same holes they came from. The holding screw should be snug, but the adjusting screw must be set and adjusted with the bobbin and thread in place as in normal sewing operation. Pull the bobbin thread and tighten or loosen the adjusting screw to achieve a thread tension between tight and loose. Then replace the bobbin case.

Check the upper thread pressure by threading the machine to the tension discs; stop threading there. Lower the pressure foot lifter and pull the thread through the discs. If the thread is very tight, turn the dial to a slightly lower set-

ting; if it's much too loose, turn the dial to a higher setting. Once an average pressure is obtained, complete the threading of the machine and test-sew a seam.

Place a new medium-size needle in the needle clamp. Sew your test seam on folded medium-weight cotton material; use standard thread. Examine the stitch after 6 to 8 inches of stitching.

If the top thread of the stitching lies flat on the top of the material and the bottom thread is loose, turn the upper thread tension dial to a higher setting. If the bottom thread lies flat and the top thread lies loose, the upper thread may be too loose or the lower thread too tight; adjust the thread tensions and sew again. Repeat by sewing, examining the stitches, and adjusting the tension controls as necessary, until the top and bottom lines of stitching are evenly interlocked and balanced.

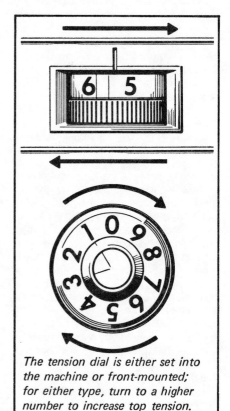

The tension dial is either set into the machine or front-mounted; for either type, turn to a higher number to increase top tension.

Remove Sewing Machine Burrs

Threads break, fray, and snag because of burrs, little nicks or sharp spots or rough edges on sewing machine parts. Burrs can be created by needle strikes, pin scrapes, or other metal-to-part blows; they're usually easy to remove. **Tools:** screwdriver, magnifying glass. **Materials:** extra-fine-grit cloth-backed sandpaper, fine-grit emery cloth. **Time:** 10 to 45 minutes.

The most common burrs are located on the needle plate of the sewing machine. These burrs, often on the needle plate hole, are easy to see. Needle plate burrs can sometimes be removed with the needle plate in place, but in most cases you'll have to take the plate off the machine. Remove the screws that hold the plate and take the plate off. If your machine has a magnet-type needle plate, pull it up to remove it; if it has a lever-type plate, move the lever to the off position. If possible, work away from the machine to keep sanding debris out of it.

If the burr marks are very numerous and deep, buy a new plate; however, most burrs can be removed with extra-fine-grit cloth-backed sandpaper and fine-grit emery cloth. Tear a thin strip from a piece of sandpaper and thread the strip through the needle hole; move it up and down with a pull-and-tug motion to rub the sandpaper around the edges of the needle plate hole. Repeat with a thin strip of emery cloth to polish the sanded edges of the needle plate hole. Sand the surface of the needle plate smooth with a larger piece of sandpaper, and polish with emery cloth. To remove very small burrs, use only emery cloth.

Burrs on the bobbin or the bobbin case also fray thread and cause stitch problems; they're easy to find. Inspect

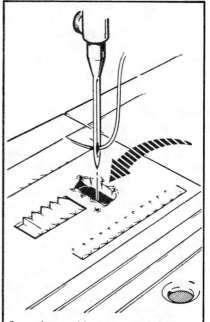

Scratches and burrs around the edges of the needle plate hole can snag thread and fabric; remove them by fine-sanding.

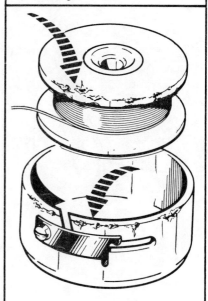

Inspect bobbin and bobbin case edges for burrs and rough spots; sand any burrs smooth.

the outer edge of the bobbin; sand any burrs smooth or replace the bobbin. Some metal bobbins have a manufacturing ridge where the inner hole connects with the outer part of the bobbin; this ridge can snag threads like a burr. Smooth the ridge as above or replace the bobbin. Inspect the bobbin case, whether built-in or the type you set into the machine; sand any burrs smooth.

Hook burrs are the most difficult to find and remove. The best way to find the hook is to remove the needle plate, bobbin, and bobbin case (if removable). Turn the handwheel with the needle in place and watch the needle go down. The moment the needle begins to come up, a sharp object will pass by the back side of the needle; this is the hook. If the hook on your machine is removable, a set of latches will hold a keeper in place to house the hook; remove the needle plate and extract the hook. If the hook is not hand-removable, turn the handwheel to fully expose the point of the hook. Sand any burrs on the hook with a thin strip of sandpaper, using a mag-

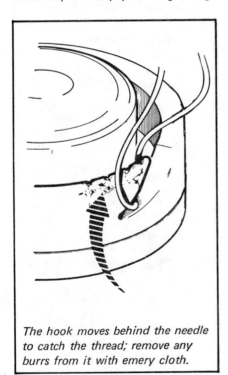

The hook moves behind the needle to catch the thread; remove any burrs from it with emery cloth.

nifying glass if necessary; polish the hook smooth with a strip of emery cloth.

You may find burrs on other parts of the sewing machine; if they're in a place where they might snag threads, sand and polish them smooth. To prevent snags on a notched spool of thread, load the thread onto the machine with the notch placed away from the direction the thread unwinds.

Clear a Jammed Sewing Machine

A sewing machine can jam so tight it won't move. Bad mechanical binds are a job for a repairman, but most jams are easy to clear. **Tools:** tweezers, screwdriver, toothpicks, toothbrush or long-bristled brush, sharp hobby knife. **Materials:** sewing machine oil with pinhole oiler, sewing machine gear lubricant. **Time:** 5 to 45 minutes.

Sewing machine jams are usually caused by debris inside the machine; a tiny piece of thread or lint can lodge in the stitching mechanism and lock it. To release this kind of jam, move the handwheel back and forth with a rocking motion—if necessary, rock it vigorously. If the thread jam in the lower mechanism breaks free, inspect the lower mechanism for any loose debris, and remove it with tweezers.

If the rocking method doesn't work, remove the bobbin and bobbin case (if removable), the needle, and the thread, and take the needle plate off, removing the screws that hold it and then lifting the plate out. Some built-in bobbin cases have a small black spring clip that holds them in place. Move the spring keeper over to free this type of bobbin case. The keeper type of bobbin case has a groove around the outer side of the case; inspect the groove for threads or matted lint and remove them with a toothpick. Place a drop of sewing machine oil in the bobbin case groove and brush out any extra lint threads from the lower mechanisms, using a

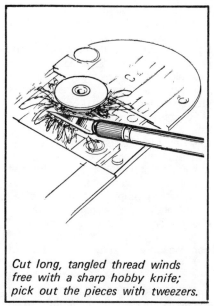

Cut long, tangled thread winds free with a sharp hobby knife; pick out the pieces with tweezers.

toothbrush or a long-bristled brush. Then replace the bobbin case.

A jam can also be caused by debris caught in the hook, the sharp piece of metal that moves up to catch the thread from the needle. To eliminate a hook jam, remove the hook, if it is hand-removable. Take the needle plate and move the set of latches that hold the keeper housing the hook; extract the hook. If your machine doesn't have a removable hook, work around the lower mechanisms. Remove any threads or lint, and replace the hook. A machine that is jammed can also have a mechanical bind that will require a qualified repairman to correct; however, even these binds can be minor.

Gear-driven machines can often be jammed by debris caught between the teeth of the gears. Use a screwdriver to remove the upper, side, and bottom access covers of the machine, and locate the gears. With a toothbrush or a long-bristled brush, clean off the gears and inspect them for jammed debris; remove threads and lint with tweezers. If any of the gears is missing one or more teeth, call a repairman; the problem is more than a simple jam. While you have the access covers off, oil all metal-to-

metal moving parts with sewing machine oil in a pinhole oiler, and lubricate the gears with sewing machine gear lubricant. Then replace the access covers.

Small threads and lint are the most usual problems, but you may encounter other obstructions. If the kids have used the sewing machine as a slot machine, there may be pencils, coins, or paper clips in the works; remove them carefully. If the machine is obviously damaged, call a repairman. Long pieces of thread sometimes get wound around parts, levers, and shafts and cause a jam; cut thread winds free with a sharp hobby knife and pick them out with tweezers.

If the machine is clear of debris but it still doesn't move, the problem may be as simple as a lack of oil in critical oil points. Even if you oil frequently, you may have missed one or more oil points, and that extra drag in the sewing machine's works can cause it to seize up. Oil each metal-to-metal oil point and each marked oil hole. Rock the handwheel until movement begins; stay with it until the machine moves freely.

Replace or Adjust a Sewing Machine Belt

The motor of a sewing machine is connected to the handwheel by one of three methods: gears, a friction pressure wheel, or, most commonly, a belt system. A slipping belt can cut off the power to the handwheel, but the problem is easy to solve. **Tools:** screwdrivers, small wrench. **Materials:** aluminum foil, replacement pulley shim, replacement belt. **Time:** 5 to 45 minutes.

First, determine whether the belt needs to be replaced or adjusted or whether the machine needs maintenance or repair. Take a look at your sewing machine; the motor is either internal or external. If your machine has an external motor, the belt system is easily accessible. If it has an internal motor, remove the access panel that covers the belt system; check your owner's manual and follow the diagram.

Belt systems are engineered to suit the manufacturer's design, but all systems use the same fundamental components: motor, pulley, handwheel, belt, and motor adjustment bracket. The motor's shaft extends about 1 to 1½ inches from the side of the motor; the pulley is connected to the shaft by a setscrew or a pressure shim fitting. The pulley is round and larger than the shaft, and has a large groove around it for the belt to fit into. The belt extends around this small pulley and over the handwheel, a large pulley; when the motor turns, so does the belt and so does the handwheel.

The handwheel is connected to the levers and additional shafts that make the sewing machine work, and when the belt slips the connection to the machine is sporadic or is cut off entirely. When this happens, inspect the system carefully to identify the problem—sometimes what the machine needs is maintenance, or thorough cleaning, oiling, and lubrication. A stiff or frozen machine will cause the belt to slip even if it's in good condition.

Check the pulley on the motor shaft to see whether it has a setscrew or a shim. If it has a setscrew, make sure the screw is tight; if the screw is tight and the belt still slips, the machine must be professionally serviced. If the pulley has a shim, a small metal sleeve around the shaft under the pulley, the problem is probably insufficient pressure on the pulley. Take the shim out, bend it to open it slightly, and replace it; or reinforce it with a small piece of aluminum foil to increase the pressure of the pulley on the shaft and keep it from slipping. If the shim is broken or worn thin, replace it with a new one; take the old shim to a sewing machine service center and buy the same type.

Check the clutch, the small knob on the side of the handwheel, to make sure it's turned to the sewing position and

not the bobbin-winding position. Then check the belt. If the belt has stretched slightly but is in good shape, it can be tightened; if it's frayed, cracked, broken, or peeling, it must be replaced. Bring your old belt to a sewing machine service center and get a replacement belt sized for your machine.

To tighten the belt or install a new one, use a small wrench to loosen the bolt or bolts holding the bracket that connects the motor to the machine. Move the motor down to tighten the belt until it's just snug on the pulleys—don't overtighten it or the motor will run slow. Some internal motor machines use an offset eccentric washer to apply pressure on the belt. To tighten this kind of belt, loosen the center lock screw and turn the eccentric washer with the blade of a screwdriver inserted through a slot next to the center screw. Some external motor machines use a rubber stretch belt; simply stretch the belt over the motor and handwheel pulleys.

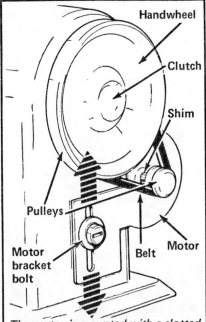

The motor is mounted with a slotted motor bracket; to adjust belt tension, loosen the bracket bolt and move the motor.

Yard and Patio

Plant a Lawn

The type of lawn you plant depends on where you live, but although there are many species of grass, the basic procedure is always the same. **Tools:** lawn spreader, rented tiller, garden hose, rake, lawn roller, lawn mower. **Materials:** lime or gypsum, peat moss, grass seed, fertilizer, chemical weed killer. **Time:** 2 days to prepare and plant; regular watering and mowing.

The most important factor in a new lawn is the grass seed. The type of seed you should buy depends on the type of soil, the climate, and the available sunlight; ask a neighbor with a healthy lawn for advice, and consult your lawn and garden supply dealer. Don't buy cheap annual seed; it's no bargain. Buy a good-quality perennial seed mix specifically recommended for the light conditions in your yard—full sun, partial shade, or shady mix. Buy fertilizer for the lawn as recommended in the instructions on the grass seed package.

Before you can plant a lawn, you must prepare the soil. The acidity of the soil is important; call your county agricultural agency and arrange for a soil test—it's usually free. Some seed stores also make soil tests, at a small fee. Adjust the pH of the soil, if necessary, by adding lime or gypsum—lime if it's too acid, gypsum if it's too alkaline. Spread the lime or gypsum with a lawn spreader, as recommended by the soil tester.

The soil must have the proper texture, neither too sandy nor too thick and clayey. In most areas, it's a good idea to add peat moss to the soil to improve its texture. Spread a layer of moss 3 or 4 inches thick on the entire area to be planted. If the fertilizer you're using should be applied after the grass is planted, as specified by the manufacturer, you're ready to till the soil. If it should be applied before the grass is planted, spread the fertilizer over the lawn area with the lawn spreader, at the setting recommended by the manufacturer. Then till the soil.

Rent a power tiller to till the soil. After adding lime or gypsum, spreading peat moss, and fertilizing as necessary, break up the soil to the consistency of small lumps with the tiller, following the rental agent's instructions to operate it. Till the soil until the entire lawn area is evenly broken up and the soil and peat moss are evenly mixed. Rake the area to slope the earth evenly and gradually away from the house; then wet the tilled soil thoroughly with the fine spray of a garden hose. If water collects in low spots, rake again to correct the slope. Return the rented tiller, and wait 24 hours before proceeding.

Use a lawn spreader to spread the grass seed over the prepared soil; set the spreader according to the instructions on the grass seed package. Roll the spreader slowly and carefully back and forth over the lawn area, making sure you don't leave any unplanted strips. Rake the seeded soil lightly and then roll the area with a lawn roller, rolling only once, to press the seeds into the soil. Be careful not to leave deep footprints or wheel marks in the newly seeded lawn.

If the fertilizer you're using should be applied after the grass is planted, spread it carefully over the raked and rolled lawn area, using the lawn spreader at the setting recommended by the manufacturer. Finally, water the lawn thoroughly with the fine spray of a garden hose, wetting the seeded area well Be careful not to disturb the soil.

The seeds will germinate in several weeks, as specified on the package. During the germination period, water the lawn two or three times a day with the fine spray of the hose, keeping the soil damp at all times. When the grass is about 2 inches high, mow it to thicken the new growth. Mow once a week until the grass is as thick as it should be.

There is no foolproof way to keep people and animals off the lawn, or to keep birds from eating the seed, but do your best. Keep weeds out by pulling them up; don't use chemical weed killer on the grass until it's survived a winter.

To fill in bare spots on an existing lawn, work during the fall. Rake the lawn to expose bare spots; if it's weedy, spread a chemical weed killer, as directed by the manufacturer. Wait until the weeds die and rake the lawn again to remove the dead weeds.

Mow the lawn, cutting it short. If the dirt in the bare spots is fairly loose, loosen the top 1 inch of soil with a rake; if the soil is hard, loosen the soil to a depth of 6 inches.

Sow grass seed by hand in small areas, to the thickness recommended on the package; spread fertilizer over the spots and rake the seeds in lightly. Press them into the earth with your hands. Thoroughly dampen the soil with the fine spray of a garden hose; water as necessary, two or three times a day, until the seed germinates. Water and mow as above after germination.

Lay Sod

For an instantly beautiful lawn, lay sod in a bare-dirt yard. **Tools:** measuring rule, rented tiller, lawn spreader, rake, garden hose, lawn sprinkler, work gloves, sharp knife or lawn edger, lawn roller. **Materials:** lawn and garden gypsum, 18-24-6 starter fertilizer, mulch as specified by the sod dealer, sod to cover the desired area, 27-3-3 fertilizer. **Time:** about 2 days for a 50 × 50-foot area.

Sod is sold by the square yard, in rolled 1½ × 6-foot strips. To determine how much sod you'll need, multiply the length of the area you want to cover by its width; divide by 9. If your yard is an irregular shape, figure square yardages for each main area and add the area figures. Allow a strip or two extra for patching odd-shaped areas.

Order top-grade instant turf from a nursery or a lawn and garden center; buy 18-24-6 starter fertilizer and 27-3-3 fertilizer, and, if the sod dealer in your area specifically recommends it, a sodding mulch. In most areas no mulch is necessary. Before placing your sod order, figure your times carefully; make sure you'll have time to prepare the soil before the sod is delivered. Arrange for delivery just before you're ready to lay the sod.

Prepare the soil carefully. Use a rented tiller to break up the soil to marble-size chunks; work over the entire area to be sodded, being careful not to leave the edges untilled. Remove large stones. Spread lawn and garden gypsum over the tilled soil with a lawn spreader to loosen it, using the spreader setting recommended by the manufacturer.

Rake the tilled soil thoroughly to mix in the gypsum and to slope the soil evenly and gradually away from the house, leaving no low spots. Water the tilled and graded soil with a garden hose or a sprinkler to see if water collects in low spots in the prepared area; if there are any low spots, rake again as necessary to eliminate them. Wait 24 hours before proceeding further.

Before laying the sod, apply 18-24-6 fertilizer to the prepared soil with a lawn spreader, using the spreader setting recommended by the manufacturer. If the sod dealer particularly recommended a mulch because of demanding soil or climate conditions in your area or because the specific turf type requires it, spread the mulch evenly over the prepared area. At this point you're ready for the sod to be delivered.

Sod is delivered in rolled strips, grass side in. Have it unloaded as close to the prepared area as possible, but not onto it; the less you have to handle it the better. Wear work gloves to handle the sod, and carry each rolled strip carefully into place before unrolling it—you'll probably need an assistant.

Start laying sod along one straight edge of the yard, rolling each strip out into position and butting the ends of the strips firmly together. Work as accurately as possible; you won't be able to adjust the rolled-out strips much. Make sure all joints are firmly fitted together; if they aren't tightly fitted the grass will wither all around the edges of the strips. Set succeeding rows of strips with staggered joints, as if you were laying brick; be sure to keep the joints tight. Cut the sod as necessary with a sharp knife or lawn edger, slicing cleanly through both grass and root mat. To work around obstructions—trees, bushes, flowerbeds, fence posts— unroll the sod right up to the edge of the obstruction and cut it to fit. Patch in odd-shaped areas with smaller pieces of sod as necessary, but cut the patches in as few pieces as possible,

and keep the joints tight.

When the sod is completely laid over the yard, roll it with a lawn roller to press the roots of the sod into the prepared soil; check the seams and adjust as necessary. Water the sod with a lawn sprinkler to soak it thoroughly.

Sprinkle the new sod daily to moisten it; do *not* soak it. Check the sod every week or so to make sure the roots are taking hold; don't cut the grass for several weeks, until the new root system is firmly established. If the sod doesn't seem to take hold or turns yellow at the edges, call the sod dealer for advice.

Finally, 6 to 8 weeks after the sod is laid, apply a 27-3-3 fertilizer to the sodded area with a lawn spreader, using the spreader setting recommended by the fertilizer manufacturer. Water the lawn as directed.

Prune a Tree

Tree pruning is done for several reasons: to remove deadwood before it's blown down, to cut back branches too near a house, or to prevent lopsided growth. Whatever the reason for pruning, the job isn't difficult. **Tools:** work gloves; hand pruner, lopper or long-handled pruner, and pole pruner; pruning saw and pole saw, stepladder or extension ladder, paintbrush. **Materials:** tree dressing. **Time:** about 1 to 2 hours per tree for extensive pruning; 10 minutes to ½ hour for routine maintenance.

Prune trees in spring when leaf growth makes deadwood easy to identify; work as early in the year as possible. If a tree is damaged by wind or lightning, trim the shattered wood and treat the damage immediately. Prune only as absolutely necessary when trees are bare.

Wear work gloves to protect your hands, and handle pruning tools carefully. Use a hand pruner for small branches, a lopper or long-handled pruner for larger ones, a pole pruner for high branches. To cut thicker limbs, use

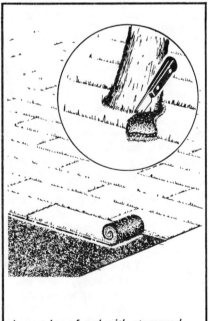

Lay strips of sod with staggered joints, butted tightly; trim closely around trees, shrubs, and posts.

a pruning saw or a pole pruner. If possible, work from the ground; use a stepladder or a firmly braced extension ladder only if it's absolutely necessary. Wear rubber-soled shoes to work on a ladder, and be very careful with your pruning tools.

Except when you're removing dead or diseased wood, restraint is the key to good pruning. Cut only as much wood as you must, and always cut to preserve the general shape of the tree. Do *not* try to thin a tree by cutting a main limb, or prune a tree into a different shape. Step back and look at the tree frequently as you work; the newly cut branches should be hard to see. Encourage growth in one direction by cutting back minor branches growing the other way, but don't cut large branches unless you have to.

Cut branches carefully to encourage healthy growth. Cut back to live wood, but don't overcut. Choose a healthy bud on the outside of the branch; cut carefully ¼ inch above the bud, at a slight angle compatible with the angle of the

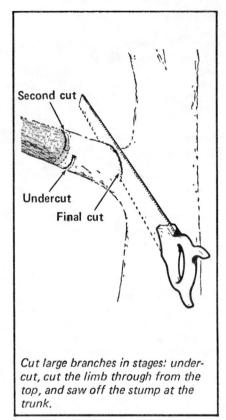

Cut large branches in stages: undercut, cut the limb through from the top, and saw off the stump at the trunk.

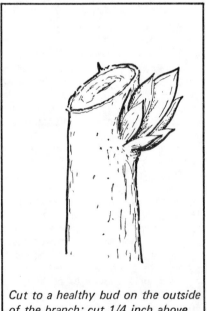

Cut to a healthy bud on the outside of the branch; cut 1/4 inch above the bud, at an angle compatible with it.

bud. If a large branch must be removed, cut back to a live branch or to the main trunk of the tree so that no stub is left; work in stages to avoid damaging the tree. Make an undercut with the pruning saw about 5 inches out from the trunk or the healthy branch, no more than halfway through the wood. About 1 inch out from the undercut, cut again from the top to remove the dead limb. Finally, saw off the stump at the trunk or the healthy branch.

Caution: Be very careful with large limbs; make sure no one is in the way of the falling wood. Don't let pruned branches fall into the tree itself or onto a house or other building below it.

Because newly cut wood is vulnerable to insects and decay, seal saw cuts with a commercial tree dressing to protect them. Apply the dressing generously with a paintbrush, as directed by the manufacturer.

Plant Shrubs

Many landscaping problems can be solved with a few carefully placed shrubs. Low, spreading bushes— Japanese evergreens, junipers, forsythia, bridal wreath, and burning bush—make a distinctive screen; taller shrubs—lilac, honeysuckle, buckthorn —grow into attractive and effective barriers. Follow these planting guidelines to add beauty and privacy to your yard. **Tools:** shovel, knife, garden hose. **Materials:** shrubs, plastic sheet, peat moss. **Time:** 1 to 2 hours.

Space the shrubs as recommended by the nursery or garden center dealer, to accommodate growth patterns and to achieve the desired effect. Vertical-growing bushes planted to create privacy should be spaced about 4 feet apart; strictly decorative plants should be placed to best show their beauty. Space low-growing spreaders as recommended to hide foundation walls.

The success of any shrub depends a great deal on the way it's planted—as one old proverb says, $1 plant deserves $5 hole. If possible, plant shrubs in cool weather. Work in the evening or on an overcast day so newly planted shrubs won't dry out, and prepare the planting area carefully. Follow any specific instructions provided by the nursery or garden center dealer.

For each shrub, dig a hole as deep as the plant's root system (no deeper), and at least three times the width of the root ball. The base of the bush should never be placed below ground level, but you must allow plenty of extra space to provide stability and encourage rapid root development. Protect grass around the planting area with a sheet of plastic.

Mix the dug-out soil with peat moss—2 parts peat moss to 1 part soil. Peat moss is necessary to prevent the soil from compacting, allow expansion of the roots, and retain ground moisture; don't skimp on it.

Before planting each shrub, carefully remove the covering from the roots.

Remove and discard the plastic containers young plants are sold in; at least partially remove the burlap coverings used for older shrubs. Cut and remove any ropes, especially those tied around the base of the stem, so they don't cut into the growing area. Poke a few holes in the burlap with a knife, being careful not to damage the root ball; any remaining burlap will give way to new roots.

Soak the prepared hole thoroughly before planting each shrub; use the gentle spray of a garden hose. Don't use so much water that it pools in the hole; the soil should be wet but not muddy. To plant each shrub, hold it by the stem and position it in the prepared hole. Holding the plant upright, fill the hole with the peat-moss/soil mixture; pour the moss/soil filler evenly around the roots to fill the hole firmly but gently. Fill the hole around the roots to almost ground level and firm the soil. Leave a slightly saucer-shaped depression around the plant stem to retain water.

After the plant is in place and the soil is firmed, water the shrub thoroughly with the gentle spray of a garden hose;

Plant the shrub in a hole as deep as its root system and three times as wide; leave a depression around the stem.

let the water run until the planting area and the filled-in soil are completely moistened. Water young bushes at least once a day until they're firmly established—evergreens in particular require a good deal of water for several months if they are to survive the transplanting and grow. Extra watering may be necessary in periods of extreme heat.

Mix Japanese Beetle Spray

If your yard or garden is plagued by Japanese beetles, mix this effective spray. It doesn't damage trees or shrubs. **Equipment:** measuring cup, gallon container, measuring spoons, stir stick. **Ingredients:** calcium hydroxide powder, alum, water. Buy calcium hydroxide at a feed and grain store or a chemical supply house. **Yield:** 1 gallon.

Measure ½ cup of calcium hydroxide powder into a gallon container; add 1 tablespoon of alum. Fill the container with water and mix thoroughly.

To use the mixture, pour it into a garden sprayer and liberally spray affected trees and shrubs.

Build a Pyramid Garden

A pyramid garden is ideal for small yards—plant a wide variety of vegetables in a deceptively small space; you'll be surprised at its yield. **Tools:** shovel, tinsnips, pop rivet tool or screwdriver, drill, work gloves, rake, mallet, measuring rule. **Materials:** plastic or metal lawn-and-garden edging strip, pop rivets or sheet metal screws, ample supply of good garden soil, stakes, short section of heavy-duty garden hose and small circular-pattern sprinkler. **Time:** about 3 to 4 hours.

To lay the garden out, bend a strip of lawn-and-garden edging into a 5- or 6-foot-diameter circle where you want the garden. If one strip isn't long enough to run the full perimeter of the circle, splice on another piece of appropriate length with a pop rivet tool; drill holes for the rivets and then insert them with the riveter. Or drill holes and secure the pieces together with sheet metal screws.

Carefully remove the sod within the circle with a shovel; lay the sod somewhere else in the yard, if desired. Then thoroughly spade and break up the soil within the circle, removing all grass roots and other vegetation. Wearing work gloves, press the edging about 4 inches into the ground, with about the same amount above the surface. Fill the circle to the top of the edging with good garden soil and level the soil with a rake.

Embed a smaller ring of edging strip

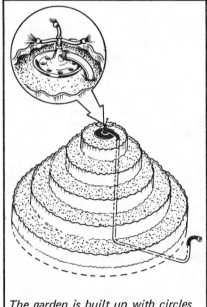

The garden is built up with circles of edging; each layer is filled with soil. A sprinkler at the top provides water.

inside the first, about 1 to 1½ feet less in diameter than the garden's base circle. If necessary, drive wood stakes into the soil to keep the edging strips vertical and in place; use a mallet to drive the stakes. Attach the strips to the stakes with sheet metal screws, if desired. Fill the top ring with soil and level it. Repeat, adding smaller rings and filling them with soil, to make as many planting layers as you want. Eventually the soil will settle a bit, and you may have to add some.

As you build the pyramid garden, you may want to build in a simple watering system. Route a short section of heavy-duty garden hose with one end protruding from the top of the garden and the coupling end sticking out from under the bottom edging ring; let the coupling end extend out about 1 foot for easy accessibility. Attach a small, circular-pattern sprinkler to the hose at the top of the garden.

Install a Sprinkling System

You can reduce your summertime lawn chores considerably by installing a lawn sprinkling system. **Tools:** water flow gauge, sod cutter, shovel, utility knife, screwdrivers, adjustable wrench, level. **Materials:** flexible polyethylene water supply pipe, pop-up sprinkler heads, and fittings; saddle-tee fitting, shutoff valve and antisiphon assembly, stakes. **Time:** about 1 day for a simple system with two sprinkler heads.

First, locate a dealer who sells lawn sprinkling equipment, and ask him to design a system for your lawn. Dealers usually do this free of charge, provided you buy your system components from them. The dealer will lend you a water flow gauge to determine the water flow rate of your plumbing system, and should also make sure that the proposed sprinkling system complies with the local plumbing code. Buy flexible polyethylene water supply pipe, pop-up

sprinkler heads, fittings, and a shutoff valve and antisiphon assembly, as specified by the dealer.

When you have all the parts of the sprinkling system, uncoil the flexible plastic pipe and leave it in the sun for 1 to 2 hours. As it warms, it will soften and become easier to work with.

When you're ready to work, determine the exact locations of the sprinkler heads on the lawn, as indicated on the dealer's plan. Dig V-shaped trenches about 6 inches deep from the house's outside sillcock to the location of the sprinkler heads, and between the heads. Remove the sod carefully with a sod cutter, so you can replace it later; store in a shady area while you work.

Place the plastic pipe in the trenches, making connections where necessary. Cut the plastic pipe with a utility knife; make connections by joining sections of pipe with slip-in fittings and securing the joints with stainless-steel band clamps. Use branch-tee fittings wherever the

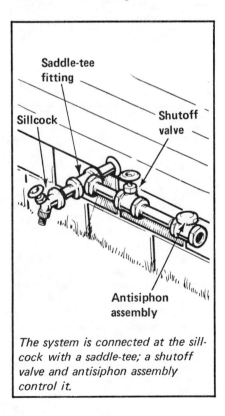

The system is connected at the sillcock with a saddle-tee; a shutoff valve and antisiphon assembly control it.

system branches off from the main pipeline, and connect the last sprinkler head to the pipe with a 90-degree elbow fitting.

Shut off the house's main water supply. Tap a shutoff valve and antisiphon assembly into the sillcock, the outside faucet. Use a saddle-tee fitting to make the connection. The antisiphon will prevent water from the lawn system from entering the house's system. Then connect the plastic pipe to the shutoff valve.

Prop up the sprinkler heads with stakes to check their operation. Turn on the main water supply and test the system briefly. If all connections are watertight and the heads work properly, fill the trenches with soil to bury the pipelines. The pipe should be pitched toward the house at about ¼ inch per foot; check the pipe with a level as you work.

Finally, carefully replace the sod. Make sure the sprinkler heads are level with the ground; they'll pop up when the system is turned on. Water the lawn thoroughly to keep the cutout sod green.

Fix a Leaky Hose

A leaky garden hose that's in good condition otherwise is easy to repair. Use a hose repair kit, available at hardware stores and lawn and garden centers. **Tools:** sharp knife or single-edge razor blade, hammer, screwdriver, pan of hot water. **Materials:** garden hose repair kit, hose washer. **Time:** about 20 minutes.

Choose a repair kit sized to fit the diameter of your hose, ½ inch or ⅝ inch; buy a crimp or hose clamp kit for a rubber hose or a screw insert kit for a plastic hose. If you aren't sure what size and type your hose is, cut off a short section of hose at the leak and bring it with you to the store.

If the leak is at the coupling of the hose, examine the coupling before cutting the hose. Open the coupling and

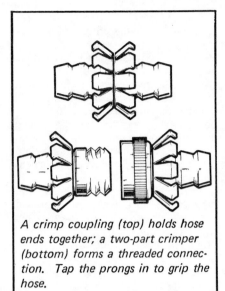

A crimp coupling (top) holds hose ends together; a two-part crimper (bottom) forms a threaded connection. Tap the prongs in to grip the hose.

remove the washer; if the washer is cracked or deteriorated, replace it with a new hose washer and retighten the coupling. If the washer was causing the leak, the new washer will stop it.

If the leak is in the hose itself, use a sharp knife or a single-edge razor blade to cut the hose apart at the leak. Cut straight into the hose to produce two blunt, square ends of hose; if necessary, trim the cut ends to square them. Cut out and discard any damaged length of hose. To mend the hose, join the cut ends with a new coupling from the repair kit.

Rubber hoses. To attach a crimp-type coupling on a rubber hose, insert the cut ends of the hose into the coupling, with the gripper teeth toward the main hose on each side and the cut end of each piece of hose in firm contact at the center with the center rim of the fitting. Tap the gripper prongs lightly with a hammer all around the hose to bend them into place; pound hard enough to give the coupling a firm grip but not hard enough to drive the prongs through the hose.

Some repair kits have crimp couplings for each cut end of the hose, with a threaded connection to join the two pieces. Install these couplings the same way, inserting each cut end into its coupling with the gripper prongs toward the main hose and the cut end of the hose set firmly into the coupling. Tap the gripper prongs in with a hammer and screw the pieces of hose together at the new couplings.

Hose clamp menders work on the same principle, but the mending connection is held in place by a hose clamp instead of gripper prongs. Insert the cut ends of the hose into the mender coupling and pull the clamps tight to join the hose firmly; secure the clamps with a screwdriver.

Plastic hoses. To join the cut ends of a plastic hose, use a screw insert coupling. Carefully heat one cut end of the hose in a pan of hot water, just enough to make the plastic flexible; do *not* boil the hose. Push the threaded insert into the softened end of the hose and tighten the insert a few turns. Set the coupling over the end of the hose and seat the hose against the inside of the fitting. Use the tool provided with the repair kit to tighten the bushing of the coupling until it's flush with the cut end of the hose inside the fitting.

Repeat the procedure to attach a coupling to the other cut end of the hose, softening the hose, installing the threaded insert and the coupling, and tightening the bushing. Screw the pieces together at the new couplings.

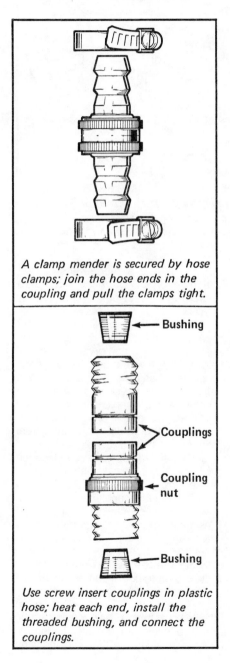

A clamp mender is secured by hose clamps; join the hose ends in the coupling and pull the clamps tight.

Use screw insert couplings in plastic hose; heat each end, install the threaded bushing, and connect the couplings.

Tune Up a Hand Mower

Hand lawn mowers are very dependable machines, but they do need some attention—blades get dull, and parts gunk up, need lubrication, or wear out. The exterior finish can deteriorate, too, leaving bare metal exposed to the elements. You can remedy all this with a simple tuneup. **Tools:** pencil, wrenches, pliers, screwdrivers, putty knife or old kitchen knife, dishpan, toothbrush or mechanics' parts-cleaning brush, stiff wire brush, fine-toothed flat file, vise, whetstone. **Materials:** penetrating oil, mineral spirits, newspaper, rags, rust-removing gel or naval jelly, replacement parts as necessary, household oil, fine-grit valve-grinding compound, masking tape, spray rustproofing metal

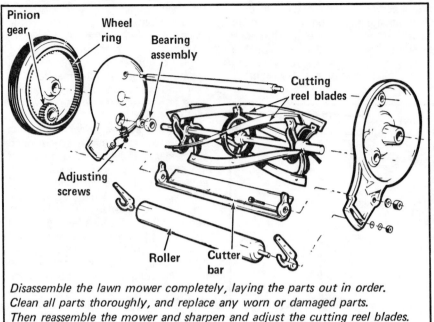

Pinion gear

Wheel ring

Bearing assembly

Cutting reel blades

Adjusting screws

Roller

Cutter bar

Disassemble the lawn mower completely, laying the parts out in order. Clean all parts thoroughly, and replace any worn or damaged parts. Then reassemble the mower and sharpen and adjust the cutting reel blades.

primer and enamel paint. **Time:** 3 to 6 hours, not including repainting.

The first step is to disassemble the mower—not as complicated a job as it sounds, because hand mowers are really pretty simple. If you have an illustrated owner's manual, use the illustration to work from; if you don't have an illustration, make notes and sketches as you take the machine apart so you'll be able to reassemble it properly. Work in an open garage or in a well-ventilated area.

Disassemble the lawn mower with wrenches, pliers, or screwdrivers, as required. Lay out the parts in order as you disassemble the mower on a workbench or garage floor; be careful not to mix them up or lose anything. If any parts are badly gummed up or rusted together, apply penetrating oil liberally and wait a few minutes; then try to free the part. Repeat if necessary to free all frozen parts.

Scrape caked mud, grass, and grease from all parts with a putty knife or an old kitchen knife. Then pour mineral spirits into an old dishpan and finish cleaning the parts in the pan with a toothbrush or a mechanics' parts-cleaning brush. *Caution: Don't use gasoline or lacquer thinner as a solvent, and be sure to work outside or in a well-ventilated area.* Remove rust deposits with rust-removing gel or naval jelly, rinse clean, and dry; or scrub rust off with a stiff wire brush. Set the parts out in order on clean newspaper to dry. After cleaning, check all parts for damage or wear, and replace them with new parts as necessary. Pay particular attention to the wheel and cutting reel bearings; if these are loose or wobbly, replace them. If you have to replace the bearings, take an old one with you to make sure you get the right size. Depending on the popularity and age of your mower, you may not be able to find designated replacement parts from the manufacturer; if this is the case, the ball bearings or bronze bushings can usually be matched up at mower repair shops or automotive supply outlets.

Reassemble the mower, using new fasteners where needed—don't forget the lockwashers. Oil all moving parts. Be sure to lubricate the ball bearings or bronze bushings, if they are the type that need lubrication, and the wheel ring gears and pinion gears.

With a fine flat file, dress the edges of the cutting reel blades, eliminating nicks and gouges and striving for a plane and properly angled cutting surface. Secure the cutter bar in a vise and sharpen and true the top edge only of the cutting edge. Then stroke the edge with a whetstone for final sharpening.

Turn the mower upside down, and adjust the cutter bar so that it just makes contact with the reel blades. With your fingertip, wipe a layer of fine-grit valve-grinding compound along the inside edge of the cutter bar, where the reel blades make contact. Rotate the reel backwards by hand so that each blade passes the bar a dozen times or so. This will lap the blades to the bar for a true cutting action. If necessary, readjust the bar slightly and repeat the procedure, until each blade properly and cleanly meets the bar edge. When you're satisfied, wipe the compound off the blades and bar.

If the machine needs repainting, mask the areas that shouldn't be painted, such as bearing surfaces, with masking tape and newspaper. Wipe a light film of oil onto the edges of the cutting reel and cutter bar. Treat bare metal with a rustproofing metal primer and then spray on two or three thin coats of enamel or special metal paint; let dry completely between coats, as directed by the manufacturer. When the paint is completely dry, remove the masking tape and newspaper and wipe the cutting reel and cutter edges clean.

Sharpen a Power Mower

Keep your rotary power lawn mower in condition year after year with proper maintenance. Most important, sharpen and balance the blade for efficient mowing. **Tools:** grounding clip, work gloves, scrap wood block, open-end or adjustable wrench, screwdriver, ham-

mer, vise, medium-rough flat file, fine-toothed flat file. **Materials:** replacement blade stiffener, if necessary. **Time:** about ½ to 1 hour.

Sharpen and balance the blade on your power mower at least twice a year—more frequently if you use the mower extensively. Wear work gloves to handle the blade.

Before removing the blade, disconnect the spark plug wire to prevent the engine from starting accidentally. Pull the wire clear of the plug and attach it to another part of the mower with a special grounding clip, or remove the wire entirely so that there's no chance that it will reconnect. Tilt the mower on its side, with the oil-fill hole higher than the crankcase so that the oil won't run out.

Wearing work gloves, grasp the blade firmly; wedge it with a block of scrap wood to keep it from turning. With an open-end or adjustable wrench or a screwdriver, remove the bolts or screws that hold the blade in place. Tap stubborn or rusted bolts lightly with a hammer to loosen them. Lift out the blade.

Directly under the blade is a reinforcing bracket called the blade stiffener; check this part for cracks or dents. If the stiffener is damaged, replace it with a new one made for your mower; buy the stiffener at a hardware store or where you bought the mower, or order it directly from the manufacturer. Don't use a homemade substitute; it could ruin the mower's engine.

After checking the stiffener, examine the mower blade for damage. Clamp the blade in a vise. Remove nicks from the cutting edges with a medium-rough flat file; stroke the blade firmly in one direction only, toward the edge of the blade and along the angle of the cutting edge. Remove nicks from both cutting edges. Don't try to remove deep notches; they don't affect the blade's performance.

After removing nicks, sharpen the cutting edges with a fine-toothed flat file. Work along the cutting edge, stroking out toward the edge and maintaining the existing bevel of the cutting edge. Make sure you don't leave burrs or rough edges on the blade.

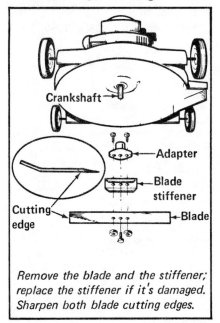

Crankshaft

Adapter

Blade stiffener

Cutting edge

Blade

Remove the blade and the stiffener; replace the stiffener if it's damaged. Sharpen both blade cutting edges.

Before putting the blade back on the mower, check to see if it's balanced. Stick the blade of a screwdriver through the center hole of the blade; the blade should balance evenly on the screwdriver. If one end of the blade is heavier than the other, carefully file the blunt end of the blade; don't file the newly sharpened cutting edge or the lift. Check the balance again and adjust it as necessary; then turn the blade over and balance the other side.

Finally, put the stiffener and the sharpened blade back on the mower, replacing all parts exactly as they were; the lifts of the blade should point up toward the top of the mower. Secure the blade firmly with its fastening bolts or screws. Turn the mower upright and reconnect the spark plug.

Anchor a Utility Building

The number one problem with small backyard metal and wooden storage buildings is wind. A strong wind can tip the building and bend it out of square or, worse, blow it over. The best solution is small auger-type anchors. **Tools:** hammer, level, piece of pipe or long screwdriver, shovel, screwdriver. **Materials:** anchoring kit, bricks and/or concrete blocks. **Time:** about 1 hour.

Any small utility building must be level on the ground. If the building is not level, add or remove dirt from around its perimeter. Use bricks for shims, if necessary; or, if the ground has considerable slope and digging is not practical, use concrete blocks.

Auger-type anchors are twisted into the ground; to hold the building, heavy cable is attached to the anchors and run up through or over the building's roof. If the wind conditions in your area are moderate, the ends of the building are all that need anchoring. If the wind is heavy, use six or even eight anchors.

Install the anchors first. Set the anchors parallel to each other on opposite sides of the building; you can align them on each side of the building with the ribs or panels in the siding. Turn the anchors into the ground, using a piece of pipe or a large screwdriver inserted into the eye of the anchor.

Drive each anchor into the ground, keeping 3 inches of the anchor shaft, as well as the screw eye, above the ground. The anchors must be set a *minimum* of 18 inches into the earth. If rocks or tree roots are in the way—and you can't get down to the 18-inch minimum—remove the anchor and reposition it.

Thread one end of the anchor cable through the screw eye on top of an anchor. Attach the packaged cable clamp to the cable, securing the cable to the anchor. Tighten the fasteners in the cable clamp firmly to keep the wire from slipping.

Run the wire cable up under the roof panel at a rib or panel joint in the siding, or run it over the roof of the building. To run the wire under the roof, simply thread it up under the roof panel, across the roof beams inside the building, and out the other side of the building under the roof panel. The under-the-roof method of anchoring hides the wire

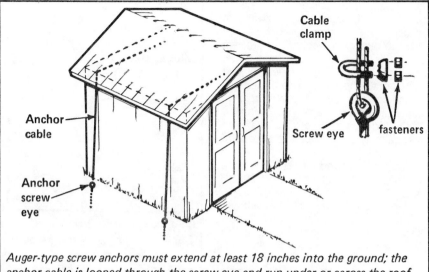

Anchor
cable

Cable
clamp

Screw eye   fasteners

Anchor
screw
eye

Auger-type screw anchors must extend at least 18 inches into the ground; the anchor cable is looped through the screw eye and run under or across the roof. Clamp each anchor cable firmly with the cable clamp provided.

cable from view; if appearance isn't a consideration, simply run the cables over the roof of the structure.

Then—whether the cable runs through or over the roof—attach the other end of the cable to the parallel anchor on the opposite side. Pull the cable taut, but don't overtighten it; over-tightening can cause damage to the metal edges of the structure. Attach the clamp when the cable is taut.

Each spring, after the ground has thawed, check the cables for tautness. If the cables are loose, tighten them by turning the anchors clockwise in the ground. If the cables are too tight, loosen them by turning the anchors counterclockwise. If this is impossible, loosen the clamps, pull the cables taut (or loosen them), and reclamp the wire.

Maintain Your Swimming Pool

To keep your swimming pool clean, clear, and healthy, give it regular atten-tion and care. **Tools:** test kit; pool vac-uum head, hose, and pole; pole brush. **Materials:** chlorine, muriatic acid, baking soda; diatomite, if necessary. **Time:** about ½ hour per week during season.

Caution: Although pool-cleaning chemicals are safe when handled properly, they can be dangerous if mixed. Always read labels carefully. When treating your pool with two sepa-rate chemicals, wait 1 hour between treatments. Keep chemicals from con-tact with your skin, and wash up thor-oughly after working.

A pool's water is kept clean by chemicals and filters. Test the water frequently for chemical composition, and keep the filters clean and function-ing. Remove debris weekly with a pool vacuum head, hose, and pole.

Buy a two-part test kit to monitor the composition of the most important chemical functions: chlorine content and pH level. A four-part test kit, al-though not essential, provides more information than just the pH factor; it specifies the acid demand and the total alkalinity.

A test kit has vials set in color-coded calibrated scales. A two-part test kit has two vials, one for chlorine and one for pH. These kits come equipped with test solutions that, when added to the water, react to the water's chemicals. To test the water, fill the vials with pool water and add the specified amount of test solution to the vials. The water will change color; match the water color to the colors beside the vial. Following the calibrated scale, determine the type and quantity of chemicals to be added to the pool.

The most important test concerns chlorine, which can also affect the pH level. The chemical chlorine kills algae and bacteria. Suntan oil, perspiration, urine, dust, and rain introduce new bacteria into the pool, lowering the chlorine level; sunlight lowers the level by transforming the chlorine into a gas, freeing it from the water. Maintain a chlorine residual of no lower than 0.6; check this level every day.

Chlorine is available in many forms: tablets, granular, liquid, or concentrate. All are equally effective. Following the manufacturer's instructions, add chlorine as necessary to maintain the proper level.

Chlorine becomes ineffective when it's transformed into a gas or when it's neutralized by nitrogen. The chlorine that's neutralized by nitrogen remains in the pool and eventually builds up to irritating levels. Signs of too much nitrogen-neutralized chlorine are a strong chlorine smell and swimmers' eyes getting red and burning. When this happens, you'll have to release the neutralized chlorine from the nitrogen through a process known as super-chlorination.

Superchlorination means, simply, adding a large amount of chlorine to the water—enough to raise the chlorine level to five times the normal level. During heavy swimming seasons, after a rain or dust storm, or in very hot weather, superchlorinate every other week. *Caution: Superchlorinate overnight; don't allow swimming in the pool until the chlorine level falls to the normal level.*

The pH factor concerns the acid/alkaline balance. If this balance is off,

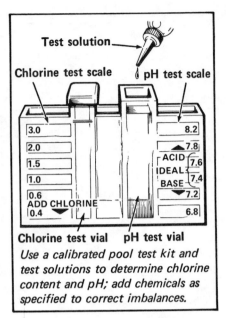

Use a calibrated pool test kit and test solutions to determine chlorine content and pH; add chemicals as specified to correct imbalances.

the chlorine loses its effectiveness, water becomes cloudy, scale forms on metal, and the filter becomes less effective. The desirable pH range is from 7.4 to 7.6, as indicated on the pH scale in the test kit.

To compensate for overalkalinity, add muriatic acid; to correct overacidity, add baking soda. Use your test kit to calibrate the amount of acid or base to be added. Never add more than 3¼ fluid ounces of muriatic acid per hour; never add more than 4 ounces of baking soda per hour. If you're adjusting both chlorine and pH levels, wait 1 hour between treatments.

Filtration is an especially important part of water care. Many experts suggest running the pump constantly to ensure adequate filtration; the pump is capable of full-time operation, but electrical costs may necessitate a shorter running time. Most pumps have a timer to automatically turn them off. Run the pump long enough to keep the water crystal clear; the drain at the bottom of the pool must always be visible.

Most pumps have bucket-like drain strainers. Clean the pump's strainer once a week. Turn off the filtration system, remove the lid on top of the pump, and remove the strainer. Empty the strainer and replace it; then fill it with water and secure the lid. If the pump system has air-relief valves, open the valves before turning on the pump. Turn on the pump, and watch these valves. When water begins spilling out of them, close the valves.

Different filters are cleaned in different ways. Most older filters should be backwashed from time to time, usually every 3 weeks during the season, to remove dirt. Follow the manufacturer's instructions for specific techniques. Some pumps require the addition of diatomite when the filter is cleaned; follow the manufacturer's instructions. Newer cartridge-type filters have elements that must be hosed down every week; follow the manufacturer's instructions for hosing techniques.

To keep the filter from malfunctioning, remove foliage and other debris from the water daily with a pole brush.

Revamp Lawn Furniture

Keep lawn furniture in good shape with seasonal maintenance; salvage worn or damaged furniture with new component parts. **Tools:** bucket and sponge, garden hose, screwdriver, slip-joint pliers, small paintbrush, electric drill, tape measure, scissors, pop rivet tool. **Materials:** liquid detergent, towels; rust remover or replacement brass, aluminum, or galvanized screws or rivets, as necessary; paste wax, aluminum polish or fine steel wool, moisture-displacing spray lubricant, fine-grit sandpaper, redwood sealer; replacement canvas covers or vinyl webbing or tubing kits, and installation sheet metal screws and washers, pop rivets, or spring clips. **Time:** about ½ to 1 hour per chair for regular maintenance; about 1 hour to replace vinyl webbing or tubing.

Maintenance. Before you start to use your lawn furniture each year, clean it thoroughly with warm water and liquid detergent, working outside. Rinse the cleaned furniture with a garden hose and dry it with clean towels, or, in hot weather, let it dry in the sun.

Inspect each piece of furniture. Tighten any loose screws; tighten loose bolts with slip-joint pliers. If screws or pop rivets have rusted, clean them with rust remover or replace them with brass, aluminum, or galvanized screws or rivets of the same size and type. Protect the cleaned or new fasteners with paste wax. Remove corrosion from aluminum with aluminum polish or fine steel wool, and apply paste wax as directed to protect the cleaned aluminum. Spray all hinges and joints with a moisture-displacing spray lubricant.

Coat redwood furniture every year with redwood sealer. Clean the furniture as above and let dry completely. Carefully sand out any stains with fine-grit sandpaper and wipe the wood clean. Brush on redwood sealer with the grain of the wood; let dry completely, according to the manufacturer's instructions.

Canvas covers. Replace worn canvas sling covers with new ones of the same type; lift the old cover off and slide the new one into place on the metal frame. Replace director's chair covers with new ones—unscrew the hinges or clamps that hold the seat cover on, slide out the dowels, remove the old cover, and slide the new one into place; replace the dowels and retighten the screws or clamps. Remove the back cover by lifting it over the chair back; then slide the new cover into place. For a canvas cover held to a metal chair frame with lacing, buy a replacement cover of the same type and size as the old one; remove the old cover and lace the new one into place the same way.

Vinyl webbing. To reweb a lawn chair, buy a 73-foot vinyl reweb kit, available in hardware or garden stores; to reweb a chaise longue, buy two 73-foot kits. To fasten the new webbing to the chair or chaise, use the screws or spring clips that hold the old webbing; replace damaged or missing fasteners with new ones of the same type. If the old webbing is fastened with pop rivets, replace the rivets with short sheet metal screws and washers slightly larger than the rivets, or with new pop rivets of the same size. Read the instructions on the reweb kit, and be sure to buy fasteners if they aren't included in the kit.

First remove the old webbing, keeping lengthwise and crosswise strips separate. If it's fastened to the chair frame by screws, remove the screws and washers and set them aside; use the same screws to hold the new webbing. If the old webbing is fastened by spring clips, examine the clips to see how they work; you'll have to replace them the same way. Remove the clips and set them aside. When you install the new webbing, replace damaged or missing screws or clips with new ones of the same type and size.

If the old webbing is held to the metal chair frame with rivets, remove the rivets with an electric drill, drilling them out with as small a bit as possible. In this case, fasten the new webbing with short sheet metal screws, slightly larger than the rivets, or install new pop rivets of the same size. For more secure fastening, set a washer under each screw or rivet head.

Start working at the back of the chair seat, with the strips running from side to side across the seat. Using the old webbing as a pattern, measure and cut strips of webbing to the correct length. If the old webbing is badly stretched or damaged, measure the seat frame from side to side and add 6 to 8 inches to allow for folding under at each side.

Fold the end of the first strip of webbing to make a pointed end, turning in first one corner and then folding the other over it to form a small triangle. Make a small hole in the center of the folded triangle with the point of the scissors and insert a screw or rivet through it, from right side to folded side. Set the end of the strip of webbing into place over the metal frame, with the strip wrapped over the outside of the tube and the screw or rivet aligned over the old screw or rivet hole; fasten it firmly into place. If you're using spring clips,

just clip the end of the strip into place the way the old webbing was clipped on.

Stretch the strip of webbing across the chair frame and fold the end under as above. Pull the webbing firmly over the outside of the tube and under to cover the screw hole, and mark the location of the hole on the strip with the point of the scissors; if necessary, trim any excess webbing. Make a small hole with the scissors, insert a screw or rivet, stretch the strip firmly into place, and fasten the screw or rivet. Repeat to stretch and fasten all crosswise strips in the chair seat; then follow the same procedure to attach all crosswise strips across the seat back, bottom to top.

When all crosswise strips have been attached on the chair seat and back, weave in the long strips that run from the top of the chair back to the outside edge of the seat. Measure and cut the strips as above. Starting at one side,

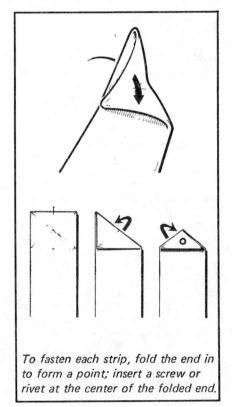

To fasten each strip, fold the end in to form a point; insert a screw or rivet at the center of the folded end.

Vinyl tubing. To retube a lawn chair, buy a 73-foot vinyl tubing kit; to retube a chaise longue, buy two kits. Remove the old tubing, cutting it if necessary—you won't need it to measure from. Work from either the top or the bottom of the chair, looping the tubing across the frame from one end of the chair to the other.

Tie the end of the new tubing to the side of the chair frame at your starting point, following any specific fastening instructions given by the manufacturer. Wrap the tubing around the empty frame, looping it over and around one side of the frame and then behind and around the other side, making successive figure-eight loops. Stretch the tubing firmly into place as you work and keep successive loops close together. Continue wrapping, without cutting the tubing, to cover the entire chair. Tie the loose end firmly at the side of the chair and cut off the excess.

Stretch strips of webbing across the chair back and seat; then weave long strips down from the top of the frame. Pass each long strip behind the hinge rod between the chair back and the seat.

fold the end of a long strip as above and fasten it securely to the top of the chair back. Weave the strip over and under the crosswise strips on the chair back; when you come to the hinge rod separating the back from the seat, pass the strip *behind* the rod at the back of the chair, and then keep weaving. Attach the strip at the outside edge of the seat as above, pulling it as tight as you can and then securing it with a screw or rivet.

Repeat this procedure to stretch and fasten all long strips across the chair back and seat, alternating your weaving pattern to produce a basketweave effect. The long strips must always be placed behind the hinge rod. Instead of weaving alternate strips over the rod, skip a crosswise strip in your weaving so you can place the long strip behind the rod where it belongs. Continue weaving to reweb the entire chair.

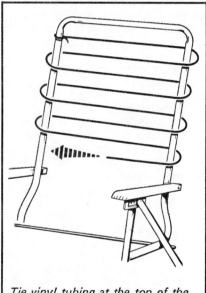

Tie vinyl tubing at the top of the frame. Wrap the tubing around the frame, looping it in tight figure-eights from one side to the other. Keep the tubing firmly stretched, and push the loops close together.

377

Paint Metal Lawn Furniture

With preparation and the right paint, you can give metal railings, grilles, and lawn furniture a very professional finish. **Tools:** bucket and sponge, stiff wire brush or power drill with wire brush attachment, safety goggles, small paintbrushes, toothbrush, garden hose or sponge, rubber gloves, painters' mitt. **Materials:** mineral spirits, clean rags; copper, brass, bronze, or aluminum cleaner; household detergent, fine steel wool, medium- and fine-grit sandpaper, naval jelly or rust remover, metal filler, plastic dropcloth, masking tape, newspaper, rust-preventing metal primer, aerosol spray or brush-on oil-base or rust-preventing metal paint. **Time:** about 4 hours for a simple lawn chair.

Choose your paint carefully. Most paints can be applied to metal, but latex paint can cause rust to form on steel or iron. Buy a rust-preventing metal primer and an oil-base or special rust-preventing metal paint, in aerosol cans or to be brushed on. Check the labels on the cans to make sure primer and paint are compatible.

To prepare new or unpainted metal, clean it thoroughly with mineral spirits to remove any dirt, grease, or wax. Make sure ventilation is adequate, and don't smoke. Clean copper, brass, bronze, or aluminum with a commercial cleaner, following the manufacturer's instructions; wipe dry with a clean rag. Don't paint galvanized steel until it has weathered for at least six months.

To prepare painted metal in good condition, clean it thoroughly with household detergent and wipe it dry. Roughen the surface slightly with fine steel wool or fine-grit sandpaper; remove dust with a clean rag.

To prepare painted metal that's rusting or flaking, clean it with household detergent and wipe it dry. Remove small rust spots with fine steel wool or with medium- and then fine-grit sandpaper; sand the entire surface lightly and wipe it down to remove dust. For more serious rusting or to remove flaking paint, scrub the surface with a stiff wire brush; or, wearing safety goggles, use a power drill with a wire brush attachment. Smooth the chipped areas with fine steel wool or sandpaper and sand the entire surface.

Clean badly rusted steel or wrought iron with naval jelly or rust remover. Work outside on a paved surface, if possible; if you must work inside, protect the floor with a plastic dropcloth and make sure ventilation is adequate.

Apply naval jelly or rust remover with a paintbrush and let it work, according to the manufacturer's instructions. Wearing rubber gloves and safety goggles, wire-brush the surface thoroughly to remove all rust and old paint; clean hard-to-reach spots with a toothbrush. Rinse thoroughly with a garden hose or wipe clean with a wet sponge; wipe dry with clean rags. If necessary, fill deep pits or dents with metal filler, available in hardware stores; let dry at least 8 hours and sand smooth.

Unpainted or newly stripped metal must be primed; check the label on the paint can and follow the manufacturer's instructions. Apply primer carefully to bare spots or unpainted metal. Don't prime painted metal in good condition. Let dry according to the manufacturer's instructions.

Apply quick-drying spray paint outside, if possible; work in an area protected from wind. Apply long-drying paint inside, if possible, to minimize dust or debris on the finished surface. Spread newspaper to protect your working area, and carefully cover surfaces that shouldn't be painted with newspaper and masking tape.

Apply three thin coats of spray paint, working carefully to apply paint evenly on all surfaces. Let the paint dry between coats as specified by the manufacturer; let dry at least 24 hours before using. To paint railings or grilles, use a good-quality small paintbrush. Brush paint evenly along the primed surface, using enough paint to flow smoothly but not enough to drip. Work on a small area at a time, and feather out brush marks as you go. To paint vertical metal surfaces, such as pipes or radiators, use a painters' mitt—an applicator glove.

Make a Recycled Tire Planter

A retired tire can end its days as a handsome container for vegetables or flowers; use a tire on a wheel to grow a complete salad in a container. **Tools:** chalk, sharp heavy-duty utility knife or pocketknife. **Materials:** old tire on wheel cylinder, scrap piece of sheet metal, stones or pieces of broken flowerpot, enriched potting soil. **Time:** 1 to 2 hours.

For a plant container on a stand, make this planter with an old tire mounted on a wheel. It's big enough to hold a standard tomato plant, with lettuce and radishes around the edges.

Use an old tire mounted on a wheel to make the planter. Mark X's and O's around the top of the tire, and cut between them in zigzags. Turn the tire inside out to form a container.

To make the planter, mark an *O* with chalk about every 4 inches around the outer edge of the tire. On the inner edge, mark an *X* halfway between each two *O*'s. Draw lines between the *O*'s and the *X*'s, forming a star-shaped pattern on the top of the tire. Then cut along the chalked lines of the star, all around the tire, with a sharp heavy-duty utility knife or a pocketknife.

Turn the tire over. Punch down the inside wheel cylinder to form the planter's stand. Fold the cut flaps on the bottom of the tire up, to turn the tire inside out and form a star-shaped planting container on a stand. Cover the hole over the wheel cylinder with a piece of sheet metal.

Line the bottom of the planter with stones or pieces of broken flowerpot; fill the planter with enriched potting soil. Water thoroughly, and plant whatever you like.

Build a Deck

A backyard deck can transform your yard to an outdoor resort. Build this simple deck in a weekend—its framework rests flat on the ground; its surface is about one step up. **Tools:** measuring rule, stakes, carpenters' square, shovel, wheelbarrow, utility knife, power drill with ½-inch wood-boring speed bit and bit extension, heavy sledgehammer, hammer, pencil, power saw, level, 16-penny nail or yardstick, straightedge. **Materials:** string, sand or fine gravel, 6 mil polyethylene sheet film, 4 × 4 ground-contact pressure-treated beams, long spikes, scrap exterior plywood, 2- to 3-foot lengths of ½-inch concrete reinforcing bar; treated wood shims; 1 × 4, 2 × 4, or 2 × 6 redwood or cedar decking stock; 10-penny aluminum or stainless steel annular nails. **Time:** about 2 days to 1 week, depending on the size of the deck.

Plan your deck carefully for a flat site; figure it so you can use standard lengths of lumber—12 × 12 feet is a good size for a small backyard deck. Buy 4 × 4 ground-contact pressure-treated lumber for beams; do *not* use untreated lumber. Buy 1 × 4, 2 × 4, or 2 × 6 redwood or cedar decking stock; these woods resist rot and insects and can be left untreated. Don't use decking boards wider than 6 inches; they tend to cup.

Lay out the deck with stakes and string on a flat site; measure carefully and use a carpenters' square to make sure the laid-out deck is square. Within the outlined area, remove the sod and all plants and root systems, and dig out the topsoil to a depth of at least 2 to 4 inches. Fill the excavated area with sand or fine gravel, and stamp the fill down to level and compact it. To prevent weed growth, cover the filled deck area with strips of 6 mil polyethylene sheet film, overlapping the strips about 2 feet.

Frame the deck in with 4 × 4 beams, laid flat all around the perimeter of the deck area and butted tightly together at the corners and at any end-to-end joints. Set beams inside the perimeter frame to support the decking. Place the beams 16 inches apart, center to center, if you're using 1 × 4 decking; place beams 42 to 48 inches apart if you're using 2 × 4 or 2 × 6 decking.

Secure the corners of the 4 × 4 frame and fasten the interior beams to the frame with long spikes. Drive the spikes through the beam side, not the butted-up beam end; set two spikes diagonally at each fastening point. Predrill the spike holes with a power drill, using a bit of the same diameter as the spikes and a bit extension. Drive the spikes in with a sledgehammer. Where two beams butt end to end, splice them together with a scrap of exterior plywood, firmly nailed across the joint on the side of the beams. Cut beams as necessary with a power saw.

For additional stability, anchor the deck frame with 2- to 3-foot lengths of ½-inch concrete reinforcing bar, commonly called rebar. At convenient points around the frame, about 4 feet apart, drill a ½-inch hole centered on the beam width and completely through

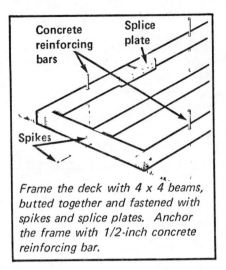

Frame the deck with 4 x 4 beams, butted together and fastened with spikes and splice plates. Anchor the frame with 1/2-inch concrete reinforcing bar.

the beam; use a power drill with a ½-inch wood-boring speed bit and a bit extension. Drive a length of rebar through each drilled hole and into the ground below it; keep pounding until the top of the rebar is flush with the beam surface.

As you work, check the frame frequently with a carpenters' square to make sure it's square; adjust the beams as necessary. Use a level to make sure the tops of the beams are properly aligned. If necessary, adjust the level of the beams with treated wood shims, or relevel the sand or gravel base under the frame. Remove the perimeter stakes and string as you set each perimeter beam into place.

When the frame of the deck is complete, lay the decking. Lay the decking stock flat across the beams, with the edge of the first board overhanging the beam 1 inch and the end of each plank sticking out several inches past the outside of the frame. Use a simple straight-across pattern; diagonal decking is harder to put down and results in more waste. Space the decking planks evenly, about 3/16 inch apart; use a 16-penny nail or a yardstick set on edge as a guide. If the decking boards aren't long enough to cover the frame in one span, measure and cut them so that the decking joints are centered over a 4 × 4 beam.

Build a Mortarless Patio

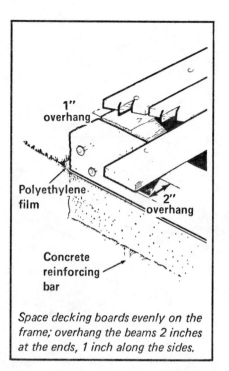

1" overhang

Polyethylene film

2" overhang

Concrete reinforcing bar

Space decking boards evenly on the frame; overhang the beams 2 inches at the ends, 1 inch along the sides.

This job requires strength and imagination, but almost no skill. The results are beautiful. **Tools:** mallet, measuring rule, shovel, level, long 2 × 4, garden rake, garden hose, lawn roller, work gloves, sturdy wheelbarrow for hauling, sledgehammer, push broom. **Materials:** stakes, string, sand, heavy sheet polyethylene, grade SW (severe weathering) brick. **Time:** varies with size of patio, but considerable digging and preparation involved; about 1 day to set brick when preparations have been completed.

Lay out the patio area, driving stakes and joining them with string to define the perimeter of the brick. Make a rough sketch of your brick layout. Measure the staked-out area carefully and take its dimensions and the sketch with you when you buy brick.

Go to a construction materials outlet and ask the dealer to calculate the amount of brick you'll need. Buy either new or used brick; it must be grade SW (severe weathering) or it will fall apart. The brick must be set on a 2-inch-thick bed of sand; ask the dealer to calculate the amount of sand you'll need, too. Buy heavy polyethylene sheeting at the same time, following the dealer's advice on quantity. Do *not* arrange for immediate delivery—tell the dealer you'll call when you're ready for delivery. You'll need plenty of time to do the groundwork.

Dig out the entire patio area, inside the stakes, to a depth of about 4¼ inches—you'll have to dispose of the dirt away from the patio area. The dug-out area must be smooth and fairly level, but the whole area should slope slightly away from the house, at a slope of about ¼ inch per foot—a difference of 3 inches across a 12-foot patio. Check the slope with a level on strings staked from edge to edge of the area; use a long 2 × 4 set on edge to keep

Nail the decking boards into place as you set them down. If you're using 1 × 4 or 2 × 4 decking, drill two nail holes through the end of each board and into the beam under it; drive two 10-penny aluminum or stainless steel annular nails through the drilled holes to secure the board. If you're using 2 × 6 decking, drill three holes through each board end, and secure the board with three nails. Check the decking for proper alignment as you nail it down, and maintain an even ³⁄₁₆-inch spacing between boards.

When all the decking boards are laid down, trim the edges of the boards evenly as necessary. The long edges of the first and last boards should overhang the perimeter beams by about 1 inch; the board ends should overhang the beams about 2 inches. Mark the boards across with a pencil and straightedge, using a carpenters' square to make sure the marked edge is even; then trim away uneven boards with a power saw.

For the easiest maintenance, don't finish the deck; let the wood weather.

the bottom of the dug-out area even.

Dig a roughly 2½-inch-wide trench, 1½ inches deeper than the excavated bed, all around the perimeter of the patio. Bricks will be set on end all along this trench to form the border of the patio.

When all the digging is done, and slopes and levels have been checked and confirmed, call the construction materials dealer and make arrangements for delivery of your sand, polyethylene sheeting, and brick. Arrange the delivery for early morning of the day you'll actually start work—no earlier.

Lay a 2-inch-thick bed of sand over the entire patio area, raking it evenly with a garden rake. Spread a 2-inch-thick layer of sand in the border trench around the patio, but don't fill the trench completely; you must be able to stand the border bricks on end in the trench. As you spread the sand, moisten it with the fine spray of a garden hose; do not wet it so much that it gets sloppy.

Roll the sand with a lawn roller to level it and tamp it down firmly; tamp the sand in the border trenches with the edge of a 2 × 4. Work carefully, spreading, misting, and leveling the sand and then rolling it, until there is a dense, even, 2-inch-thick bed of sand over the entire patio area.

When the sand bed is ready, cover it with a layer of heavy polyethylene sheeting to stop weed growth. Lay strips of polyethylene smoothly across the packed-down sand, overlapping them slightly; run the edges of the plastic down into the perimeter trench.

Wearing work gloves, lay the brick; start from a corner of the patio near the house, and work outward toward the edges in an expanding wedge pattern. To form the border of the patio, stand bricks upright in the perimeter trench, wider side along the trench. The border bricks should be level with the patio surface. Lay bricks flat for the surface of the patio, in any pattern you like; a simple parquet style is easiest. Leave about ⅛ to ¼ inch space between bricks.

Work from the starting corner out to

Lay the bricks on a 2-inch bed of sand; set border bricks on end, their tops level with the patio surface. Fill the joints firmly with sand, sweeping it into the joints.

cover the entire patio area. As you work, correct any unevenness by tamping in more sand or smoothing away excess sand. Tamp each row of brick as you complete it, using a 2 × 4 and a sledgehammer to settle the bricks firmly into place. Lay the border bricks on the far sides after the entire patio surface has been covered.

To finish the job, spread sand over the newly bricked patio and sweep it into the brick joints with a push broom. Fill the joints completely with sand. Spray the patio with the fine spray of a garden hose to dampen and compact the sand; let the surface of the brick dry. Spread another layer of sand over the patio and sweep again to fill the brick joints thoroughly; spray the patio again. Repeat if necessary to fill the brick joints completely.

Pour a Patio

A patio is one of the most valuable and satisfying home improvements you can make, but building it is a big—and expensive—job. For a simple solution to both problems, here's a sensible alternative: a concrete patio you can pour yourself, section by section. **Tools:** measuring rule, stakes, sledgehammer, shovel, wheelbarrow, rake, hammer, power saw or handsaw, carpenters' square, level, garden hose, portable cement mixer (3-cubic-foot capacity), 6-foot 2 × 4 for striking off, wood float, steel trowel, push broom, weights. **Materials:** string, gravel; 2 × 4 and 1 × 3 pressure-treated ground-contact lumber, or 2 × 4 and 1 × 3 cedar or redwood stock; 2-inch-wide masking tape; 8-penny galvanized common nails; premixed gravel-mix concrete mix, or Portland cement, sand, and coarse aggregate; plastic sheet film. **Time:** varies with size; at least 2 days for a 9-foot-square area.

Choose the patio site carefully. Plan the patio for an area that's level and well drained, and slopes slightly away from the house. Take sun, shade, and wind into consideration.

The patio is constructed as a grid of 3-foot-square concrete units, framed by wood. Make a sketch of the yard area and plan the patio in 3-foot-square units; it can be as few or as many units as you like. When you've decided on a design, outline the patio area on the construction site with stakes and string, to give you an idea of how it looks and to mark the site. Measure accurately; be careful to keep the corners of your staking square.

When you've finalized the size and shape of the patio, excavate the entire marked-off area to a depth of about 7 inches—3 inches for a gravel base and 4 inches for the concrete itself. Keep the sides of the patio excavation vertical, and keep the bottom as level as possible. Then fill the entire dug-out patio area with a 3-inch-thick layer of gravel, and rake the gravel level.

To frame the patio, build a grid of 2 × 4 pressure-treated ground-contact lumber on the excavated site. You must use treated wood or the frame will rot in the finished patio; of, if you prefer, build the grid of 2 × 4 cedar or redwood stock.

Build the outside frame for the patio first, butting the 2 × 4's together at the corners; then place dividers to form the 3 × 3-foot grid, first one way and then the other. Make sure all top edges are flush; they'll be a part of the finished patio. Nail the 2 × 4's together with 8-penny galvanized common nails; check the joints with a carpenters' square as you work to be sure all joints are strong. Use at least two nails through the 2 × 4 face at each joint.

To hold the frame in place, drive 12-inch stakes all around the frame; set a stake at each corner and at each grid joint all around the frame. Cut the stakes from 1 × 3 pressure-treated ground-contact lumber, or from 1 × 3 cedar or redwood. Drive each stake carefully to hold the frame at a vertical; pound the end of the stake below the top edge of the 2 × 4 frame.

When the frame is completely assembled, check its pitch. The patio should slope evenly away from the house, about ¼ inch for every 12 feet. Adjust the pitch as necessary, raking the gravel in the excavated area to the required slope. Fill low spots under unsupported frame members, and remove gravel as necessary to level high spots; rake to level the entire patio area to a smooth, evenly sloping pitch.

When the patio area is firmly framed in, you're ready to pour the concrete. Because the patio will probably—unless you live in a very warm area—be exposed to freezing and thawing, you must use machine-mixed concrete; hand-mixed concrete is not as strong. The easiest way to work is to rent a portable cement mixer with a 3-cubic-foot capacity—one mixer load will mix just enough concrete to fill one grid unit of the patio, 4 inches thick. Depending on the size of the patio, you can schedule the pouring to suit yourself and to make best use of the mixer; pour one 3-foot-square section at a time, as few or as many as you like.

To mix the concrete, it's easiest to use sacks of premixed gravel-mix concrete—4½ sacks of concrete mix make up one mixer load, or one 3-foot-square unit of the patio. If you have the storage space, and the patio is a big one, it's cheaper to mix your own concrete; use a mixture of one sack of Portland cement, 2½ cubic feet of sand, and 3½ cubic feet of coarse aggregate to each 5 gallons of water. Get operating instructions for the portable cement mixer from the rental agent. You'll also need a wood float to smooth the surface of the concrete.

Work section by section to pour the patio. About 1 hour before you mix the cement, soak the gravel base with the fine spray of a garden hose, to keep the concrete from drying too quickly. Protect the top edges of the wood frame around each unit with 2-inch-wide masking tape.

Load the cement mixer and add water as directed, using about half of the ingredients for one mixer load. Start the mixer, add the remaining ingredients, and mix the concrete for the full time specified by the rental agent—at least 3 minutes. Then, working quickly, empty the prepared concrete out of the drum—if possible, directly into the prepared frame; otherwise, into a wheelbarrow.

Spread the concrete into the corners of the unit with a shovel, jabbing the shovel through the concrete to eliminate air holes. Smooth the top surface of the unit as evenly as you can; it should be slightly overfilled, and about 4 inches thick.

With a helper, level the surface of the newly poured concrete. Use a 6-foot piece of 2 × 4 to strike off the unit; with each person on one side of the square, set the 2 × 4 on edge across the frame and pull it in a zigzag across the wet concrete. This sawing-across process removes excess concrete and levels the surface of the unit.

As soon as the concrete is leveled, smooth the surface with a wood float.

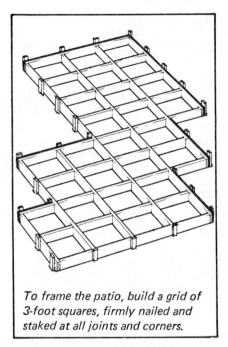

To frame the patio, build a grid of 3-foot squares, firmly nailed and staked at all joints and corners.

Push and pull the float across the wet concrete to smooth the surface thoroughly and to bring a sheen of water to the top.

When the surface of the unit is smooth and evenly water-sheened, stop working and let the concrete stand. Wait until the water sheen disappears from the surface—as little as 10 to 20 minutes in hot, windy weather, as long as 4 to 5 hours in cool weather.

As soon as the sheen disappears, trowel the concrete smooth with a steel trowel; press firmly, and work evenly over the entire surface. For a nonslip finish on the concrete, lightly pull a damp push broom across the troweled surface.

After finishing the surface of the unit, cover it with plastic sheet film and weight the plastic down. Let the concrete cure for at least 1 week. During the curing period, wet the concrete once or twice a day with the fine spray of a garden hose; replace the plastic after soaking the concrete.

Depending on how you schedule the pouring, pour individual units of the patio to allow for easy access. For a large patio, you may find it easier to work in alternate squares. Let each unit cure completely before walking on it; wait 1 week more before putting furniture on the new concrete. Remove the protective masking tape after the curing period.

Build a Picnic Table and Benches

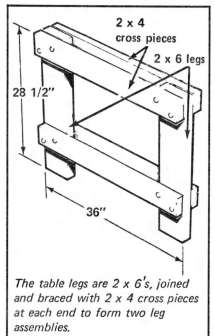

The table legs are 2 x 6's, joined and braced with 2 x 4 cross pieces at each end to form two leg assemblies.

You can build a sturdy and good-looking picnic table for about half the cost of ready-made—a project well worth your time, in savings and enjoyment. **Tools:** measuring rule, pencil, carpenters' square, handsaw or power saw, C-clamps; power drill with ⅜-, ⁷⁄₃₂-, ⁷⁄₆₄-, and ¼-inch bits; adjustable wrench, hammer, large screwdriver, block plane, belt sander or sanding block. **Materials:** 2 × 6 and 2 × 4 redwood stock; ⅜ × 5½-inch (for table) or ¼ × 5½-inch (for benches) carriage bolts, flat washers, and locknuts; scrap board, 10-penny common nails, masking tape, 5½-inch #12 × 3 flathead brass wood screws, coarse-, medium-, and fine-grit sanding belts or sandpaper. **Time:** about 4 to 6 hours for the table; about 2 hours per bench.

The table. Make the picnic table with redwood 2 × 6 and 2 × 4 stock, cut to a standard size. For the leg assemblies at each end of the table, measure and mark two 2 × 6's to a length of 28½ inches, using a carpenters' square to make sure the ends are even. Cut the 2 × 6's as marked with a handsaw or a power saw. Measure and mark four 2 × 4's to a length of 36 inches; cut them as marked. Repeat to cut two 2 × 6's and four 2 × 4's for the other leg assembly.

To put each leg assembly together, lay two 2 × 4's flat on a flat work surface, parallel to each other and about 15 inches apart. Over these cross pieces, at right angles and placed to lie flush with the 2 × 4 ends, set two 2 × 6's for the two legs at that end of the table, forming a square-topped A shape. Set two more 2 × 4's across the 2 × 6 legs, exactly over the first pair of 2 × 4's, to sandwich the legs between two sets of braces. Using a carpenters' square, adjust and square up the assembly carefully, and clamp it firmly together with C-clamps.

At each joint, drill a diagonal pair of ⅜-inch holes through all three boards. Insert a ⅜ × 5½-inch carriage bolt through each hole, place a washer and a locknut on each bolt, and tighten the bolts with an adjustable wrench. Remove the C-clamps.

Repeat the procedure to build the second leg assembly, making sure the bottom cross braces are positioned at exactly the same height as the bottom braces on the first set of legs.

Next, install a 2 × 6 stretcher between the two leg assemblies. Measure, mark, and cut a piece of 2 × 6 to a length of 68 inches. At each end of the board, mark the lengthwise centerline of the board's width. On each leg assembly, mark the center point of each outside bottom 2 × 4 cross piece.

Prop a leg assembly upright, and position one end of the 2 × 6 over the lower cross pieces, with the end of the 2 × 6 flush with the outside face of the cross piece. Align the centering marks and clamp the assembly together firmly. At each end of the stretcher, drill two ⅜-inch holes through the stretcher and through each of the two cross pieces so that there are four holes in each end of the stretcher. Insert a ⅜ × 5½-inch carriage bolt through each hole to hold the stretcher to the 2 × 4; place a washer and a locknut on the end of each bolt. Tighten the bolts with an adjustable wrench and remove the clamps. Maneuver the second leg assembly into position at the opposite end of the stretcher, and attach the stretcher the same way to the bottom cross pieces.

Square up the leg assemblies and align them properly with one another; to keep them in position temporarily, nail a piece of scrap board across each side with 10-penny common nails, close to the top of the leg assemblies. Leave the nails sticking out a little so they'll be easy to remove.

To make the tabletop, cut seven pieces of 2 × 6 to a length of 72 inches. Set the 2 × 6's across the leg assemblies, overhanging the legs by 2 inches at each end of the table, with the ends of the boards exactly flush on both ends. On each end of each board, mark the points where the board lies over the centerlines of the two top cross pieces, so you'll know where to drill holes for the assembly screws. Then remove the 2 × 6's for individual attachment.

Set the first 2 × 6 across the leg assemblies, overhanging the legs at each end about 2 inches and with its long edge extending about ½ inch past the outside of the leg assembly. Align the board carefully, straight across the leg assemblies, and clamp it into place or hold it firmly. At each marked line where the end of the board lies above a cross piece, drill two ⁷/₆₄-inch holes through the plank into the cross pieces below it, to a depth of about 2½ inches; wrap

a scrap of masking tape around the drill bit to mark the proper depth point. Change to a ⁷/₃₂-inch bit and redrill the holes to a depth of 1½ inches. Each end of the plank should have four holes in it, two through each cross piece. To secure the 2 × 6 in place, drive a 5½-inch #12 × 3 flathead brass wood screw into each of the eight predrilled holes, setting the screws until the heads are just flush with the surface.

To complete the table, set the remaining six planks across the leg assemblies and adjust them for uniform spacing between planks, with the ends exactly flush and the last board overhanging the leg assembly about ½ inch. Drill and screw down each plank successively.

If desired, use a block plane to slightly bevel all the exposed corners and edges of the table; slightly round all exposed edges with a belt sander and coarse-, medium-, and fine-grit belts. Retighten all the bolts a bit. Sand off any rough spots with a belt sander,

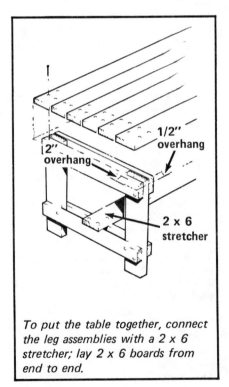

To put the table together, connect the leg assemblies with a 2 x 6 stretcher; lay 2 x 6 boards from end to end.

using first a coarse-grit belt and then medium- and fine-grit belts; or sand by hand with a block. Leave the table unfinished to weather naturally.

The benches. For each bench, measure and cut four pieces of 2 × 4 to a length of 17½ inches, to make the bench legs. For the cross braces, measure and cut eight pieces of 2 × 4 to a length of 10½ inches. Use a carpenters' square to make sure your cuts are even. Put the leg assemblies together the same way the picnic table is assembled; clamp the parts together, drill the holes through the legs and the braces, and bolt the braces to the legs. Use ¼ × 5½-inch carriage bolts, flat washers, and locknuts; tighten the nuts with an adjustable wrench. Then remove the clamps.

Measure and cut a piece of 2 × 4 to a 48-inch length for the bench stretcher. Mark the center of the board's width at each end, and mark the center point of the outside bottom cross piece on each leg assembly. Prop the 2 × 4 stretcher flat across the lower cross pieces of the leg assemblies, with the stretcher ends flush with the outside faces of the cross pieces, and clamp it in place. Drill two ¼-inch holes through the stretcher and each of the two cross pieces at each end, so that each end of the stretcher has four holes in it. Bolt the stretcher into place with ¼ × 5½-inch carriage bolts, flat washers, and locknuts; tighten the bolts with an adjustable wrench and then remove the clamps.

Straighten, square, and align the leg assemblies, and nail a scrap piece of wood between them if necessary to hold them in position. Measure and cut two 2 × 6's to a 72-inch length; set them across the leg assemblies and align them, with a ½-inch gap between the two boards. Clamp the boards to the leg assemblies.

At each end of each 2 × 6, drill four $7/_{64}$-inch holes to a depth of about 3 inches, through the 2 × 6 and down into the upper cross pieces of the leg assemblies. Redrill the holes to a depth of 1½ inches with a $7/_{32}$-inch drill. Drive a 5½-inch #12 × 3 flathead brass wood screw into each predrilled hole to

secure the bench-top planks; set the screws so the heads are just flush with the surface.

Finally, if desired, bevel the exposed edges of the bench slightly with a block plane, as above. Round all exposed edges slightly with a belt sander, using successively finer-grit sanding belts; or sand by hand with a block. Leave the benches unfinished.

Build a Patio Bench

This patio bench is just right for comfortable outdoor seating. The redwood is solid and maintenance-free; the bench can be disassembled for winter storage. **Tools:** measuring rule, pencil, carpenters' square, handsaw or power saw, 30/60-degree triangle or protractor, C-clamps, power drill with ⅜-inch bit and bit extension, adjustable wrench, hammer, nail set, block plane, belt sander or sanding block. **Materials:** 4 × 4 and 2 × 4 redwood stock; ⅜ × 7-inch and ⅜ × 5-inch carriage bolts, flat washers, and locknuts; 6-penny and 16-penny brass or galvanized finishing nails; coarse-, medium-, and fine-grit sanding belts or sandpaper. **Time:** about 4 hours.

Buy redwood stock and fastening hardware as specified above. To make the legs of the bench, measure and mark four pieces of 4 × 4 redwood to a length of 12½ inches; use a carpenters' square to keep the ends even. Cut the legs as measured with a handsaw or a power saw. Measure, mark, and cut eight 2 × 4's for the leg cross braces. With a 30/60-degree triangle or a protractor, mark the ends of the braces to slant outward at a 30-degree angle, with the slanted edge on each end 30 degrees off-vertical at the top edge to form a trapezoid. Carefully cut the ends of the braces at the marked slant; keep the cuts as uniform as possible.

To assemble the legs, set a pair of braces on edge on a flat surface, long

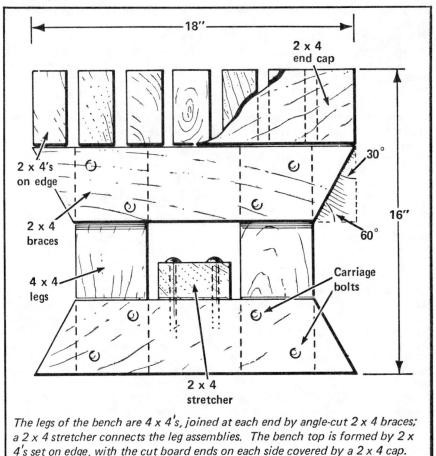

2 x 4 end cap

18"

2 x 4's on edge

2 x 4 braces

4 x 4 legs

Carriage bolts

30°

16"

60°

2 x 4 stretcher

The legs of the bench are 4 x 4's, joined at each end by angle-cut 2 x 4 braces; a 2 x 4 stretcher connects the leg assemblies. The bench top is formed by 2 x 4's set on edge, with the cut board ends on each side covered by a 2 x 4 cap.

sides down. Set a 4 × 4 leg piece between the braces at each end, with the outside face of the 4 × 4 flush with the top corner of the slanted brace; the bottom corner of the brace should extend beyond the leg. Clamp the assembly together with C-clamps.

Drill a diagonal pair of ⅜-inch holes through each leg and brace joint, completely through the braces and the leg; use a power drill with a bit extension. Insert a ⅜ × 7-inch carriage bolt through each hole, outside to in, and thread a washer and a locknut onto each bolt; tighten the nuts with an adjustable wrench and remove the clamps. When all the bottom bolts are in place, turn the assembly upside down and repeat the procedure to fasten a

second set of cross braces at the top of the legs, with the ends of the braces slanting in from the top toward the center of each leg. Assemble the second pair of legs the same way.

To brace the bench the long way, measure, mark, and cut a 2 × 4 to a length of 47 inches. In each end of this stretcher, drill a diagonal pair of ⅜-inch holes, centered ¾ inch back from the end and 1 inch in from the sides. Set the leg assemblies opposite one another, in position to support the bench top. Lay the stretcher across the bottom leg braces, centered between the legs, its ends resting on the inside bottom leg braces.

Carefully adjust the position of the leg assemblies and mark holes in the top

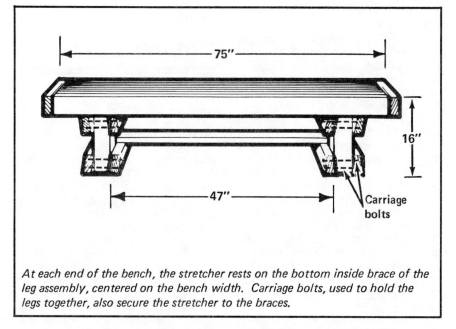

At each end of the bench, the stretcher rests on the bottom inside brace of the leg assembly, centered on the bench width. Carriage bolts, used to hold the legs together, also secure the stretcher to the braces.

edges of the inside braces to correspond to the holes in the stretcher; drill ⅜-inch holes completely through the inside bottom braces at the marked points. Set the stretcher into place across the braces and insert a ⅜ × 5-inch carriage bolt into each drilled hole, through the face of the stretcher and completely through the brace below it. Thread a flat washer and a locknut onto

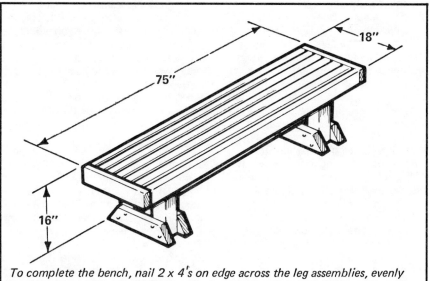

To complete the bench, nail 2 x 4's on edge across the leg assemblies, evenly spaced, the outside boards flush with the corners of the top braces. Close the ends of the bench with 2 x 4 caps over the edge-set 2 x 4's.

each bolt and tighten the bolts with an adjustable wrench.

To make the bench top, measure and cut seven 2 × 4's to a length of 6 feet, and mark each one 6 inches in from each end. Set one 2 × 4 on edge across the two leg assemblies, with its outside face flush with the top corner of the brace's slanted edge on each end of the bench. Adjust the 2 × 4 lengthwise so that each end extends 6 inches past the leg assemblies; use the marks you made to get it into the correct position. Nail the 2 × 4 on edge to the leg assemblies with four 6-penny brass or galvanized finishing nails to secure it to the cross braces; toenail the 2 × 4 to the brace with two nails on one side and then two on the other. Hold the 2 × 4 firmly as you nail it down so that its long edge stays flush with the ends of the cross braces. Set the heads of the nails below the surface with a nail set.

Set the other six 2 × 4's into position across the top braces, on edge, with the long outside face of the last board flush with the top corners of the braces. Adjust the 2 × 4's to space them evenly across the top of the bench, with about 1 inch between boards. Position each successive board, nail it into place, and set the nail heads. Work across the bench to secure all seven 2 × 4's to the bench frame.

Finally, cap the bench ends. Measure the exact distance across the ends of the bench top, and measure and cut two pieces of 2 × 4 to this length; use a carpenters' square to keep the cuts even. Place the flat side of one 2 × 4 cap piece flat against the cut boards at one end of the bench top, with all surfaces flush. Using 16-penny brass or galvanized finishing nails, drive two nails through the face of the cap piece into the end of each bench-top 2 × 4; set the nail heads. Follow the procedure to cap the other end of the bench.

If desired, bevel the exposed edges of the bench slightly with a block plane. Round all exposed edges slightly with a belt sander and coarse-, medium-, and then fine-grit sanding belts; or sand by hand with a block. Leave the bench unfinished to weather naturally.

Build an Umbrella Table

For sunny-day gatherings all summer, build this sturdy, four-person redwood umbrella table. **Tools:** measuring rule, pencil, carpenters' square, handsaw or power saw, electric drill with hole saw attachment, screwdriver, wood chisel, fine-toothed flat file; if desired, paintbrush. **Materials:** 1 × 4 clear grade redwood and 2 × 4 construction heart-grade redwood stock; 2-inch, 1½-inch, and 2½-inch #8 flathead brass wood screws; sandpaper; if desired, redwood oil or stain; patio umbrella with 1½-inch shaft. **Time:** about 4 to 6 hours.

To build the table, use 1 × 4 clear-grade redwood and 2 × 4 construction heart-grade redwood. First, construct the tabletop frame. Cut two 44-inch pieces of 1 × 4 redwood. Drill two $^{11}/_{64}$-inch holes in each end of each piece, ⅜ inch back from the ends and 1 inch in from the edges. Cut two 42½-inch pieces of 1 × 4.

Stand the four frame pieces on edge in a rectangle, with the shorter pieces butted between the longer ones and the corner joints aligned. Fasten the pieces together with two 2-inch #8 flathead brass wood screws at each joint, driven through the drilled holes. Because redwood is soft, it usually isn't necessary to drill pilot holes or countersink screws; set the screw heads flush with the wood surface.

To make the table legs, cut four 26¾-inch pieces of 2 × 4. Drill five $^{11}/_{64}$-inch holes through the tabletop frame at each corner, as illustrated in the assembly diagram. Position a 2 × 4 leg at each inside corner of the tabletop frame. Secure each leg with three 1½-inch #8 flathead brass wood screws driven through the holes and into the face of the leg, and two 2-inch #8 flathead brass wood screws driven through the holes and into the edges of the 1 × 4's.

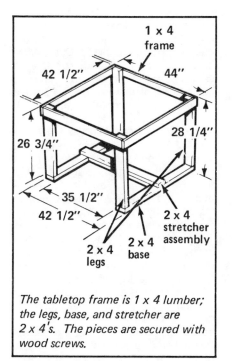

The tabletop frame is 1 x 4 lumber; the legs, base, and stretcher are 2 x 4's. The pieces are secured with wood screws.

approximately 1⅛ inches. Do *not* bore all the way through the wood. Break splinters out of the hole with a small wood chisel.

In the 42½-inch piece of the stretcher assembly, drill a series of $^{11}/_{64}$-inch holes, as illustrated in the assembly diagram. Set the 42½-inch piece on top of the 35½-inch piece, with the long edges flush and the large center holes perfectly aligned. Fasten the pieces together with 2½-inch #8 flathead brass wood screws driven through the series of $^{11}/_{64}$-inch holes.

With the table right side up, mark the midpoint—halfway between the legs—of the base pieces. Place the stretcher assembly between the two base pieces, centered on the marks; the shorter piece fits between the base pieces. Fasten the stretcher assembly to the base pieces with two 2½-inch #8 flathead brass wood screws driven through the drilled holes at each end.

Mark the centerline of the table frame

Cut two 42½-inch pieces of 2 × 4 for the table base. Drill two $^{11}/_{64}$-inch holes in each end of each base piece, spaced ¾ inch in from the end and 1 inch in from the edges. Turn the table upside down, and lay the two base pieces across the two pairs of legs. Align the joints, and secure the base pieces with two 2½-inch #8 flathead brass wood screws driven through the holes at each joint.

Cut one 42½-inch piece and one 35½-inch piece of 2 × 4 for the stretcher assembly. Find the centerpoint of each of these pieces; draw a line across the 2 × 4 face at the halfway point, then measure to find the middle of the line. With an electric drill and a hole saw attachment, bore a 1⅝-inch hole through the 42½-inch piece, centered on the centerpoint. Drill just until the bit in the hole saw penetrates to the back of the 2 × 4; then turn the 2 × 4 over and complete the hole from the opposite side to prevent splintering the wood.

Bore a 1⅝-inch hole in the 35½-inch piece of 2 × 4, but only to a depth of

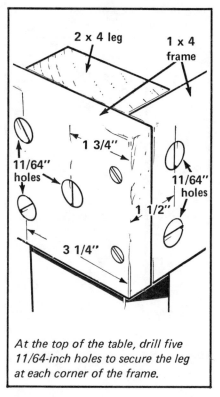

At the top of the table, drill five 11/64-inch holes to secure the leg at each corner of the frame.

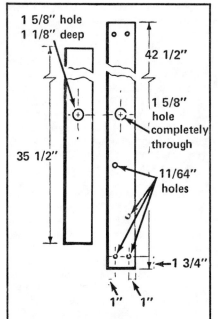

Bore a 1 5/8-inch hole in the short stretcher piece, and another through the long piece. Drill 11/64-inch holes as shown.

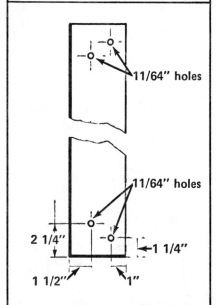

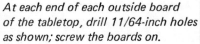

At each end of each outside board of the tabletop, drill 11/64-inch holes as shown; screw the boards on.

on two opposite sides of the frame's top edge by measuring in 22 inches from each end of a side piece. Cut a 46¼-inch piece of 1 × 4 redwood for the center board of the tabletop. Find the centerpoint of this piece, and bore a 1⅝-inch hole completely through it, centered on the center point. At each end of the piece, drill two ¹¹/₆₄-inch holes, 1¼ inches back from the end and 1 inch in from the sides. Position the piece at the center of the tabletop frame, centering it on the centerline marks, and adjust it so that it overhangs the frame by 1⅛ inches on each end. Secure the board to the frame with two 1¼-inch #8 flathead brass wood screws at each end, driven through the drilled holes and into the frame edges.

To complete the table, cut 12 more 46¼-inch pieces of 1 × 4 redwood. For the ten inside boards of the tabletop, drill two holes in each end of each board, as above. For the two boards that will lie at the outside on each side of the table, drill screw holes the same way on the inside edge, but space the holes toward the outside edge 1½ inches in and 2¼ inches back from the ends.

Starting at the center board, set each interior 1 × 4 into position successively, aligned with the center board and spaced ¹/₁₆ inch apart. Secure each board with 1¼-inch #8 flathead brass wood screws, driven through the drilled holes. Finish the top of the table with the two specially drilled outside pieces, laid with their odd holes to the outside. The ¹/₁₆-inch spacing specified is based on a uniform board width of 3½ inches. If your boards are slightly wider or narrower, reposition them to maintain even spacing across the tabletop.

To complete the table, round the upper edges and corners of all tabletop boards and smooth off the cut ends and any rough spots, using a fine-toothed flat file and sandpaper. If desired, apply redwood oil or stain to preserve the redwood's color. To use the table, slide the shaft of your patio umbrella down through the hole in the center of the tabletop and into the hole in the stretcher assembly.

Walks, Drives, Walls, and Fences

Make a Mailbox

A sturdy, good-looking rural mailbox is easy to make from plywood or scrap cedar or redwood siding. **Tools:** measuring rule, pencil, carpenters' square, straightedge, handsaw or power saw, fine-toothed flat file, hammer, tin snips, electric drill, pop rivet tool, scratch awl, screwdriver, paintbrush. **Materials:** ⅝-inch exterior plywood, or smooth cedar or redwood siding; sandpaper, carpenters' glue, 3-penny aluminum nails, small doorknob or door pull with magnetic catch, butt hinges and screws ½ inch longer than screws provided, 1-inch brads, heavy-gauge scrap sheet metal, ⅛ × ½-inch aluminum or galvanized steel strap, pop rivets, 1-inch #8 roundhead galvanized or plated wood screws and #8 flat washer, 1-inch L-shaped screw hook, paint or stain and red paint, 1½-inch #10 lag screws with washers. **Time:** about 2 to 3 hours, plus finishing time.

To make the mailbox, use ⅝-inch exterior plywood, or smooth cedar or redwood siding. A homemade rural mailbox must be approved by your local postmaster, so submit plans and a list of materials before you make the box. According to U.S. Postal Service regulations, a custom-built box must conform generally to the same requirements as approved manufactured boxes relative to flag, size, strength, and quality of construction. There are three standard approved sizes: 19 inches long, 6½ inches wide, and 8½ inches high; 21 inches long, 8 inches wide, and 10½ inches high; and 23½ inches long, 11½ inches wide, and 13½ inches high. Plan your mailbox to roughly conform to one of these sizes, or to be between the largest and smallest standard sizes.

The box can be painted any color you like, but the Postal Service prefers that the box and its supports be white. If a box number is required, it should be painted or affixed in a contrasting color in characters not less than 1 inch high on the side of the box facing the mail carrier. If there are several boxes in a group, the number of each box should be on its door. Placing your name on the box is optional. Posts or other supports for the box must be neat and strong; locks are not necessary, although they can be used.

To make the box, cut the six main pieces from ⅝-inch exterior plywood or

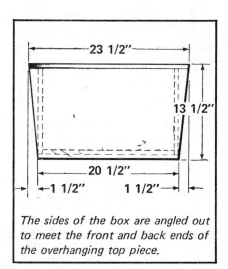

The sides of the box are angled out to meet the front and back ends of the overhanging top piece.

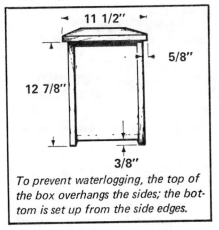

To prevent waterlogging, the top of the box overhangs the sides; the bottom is set up from the side edges.

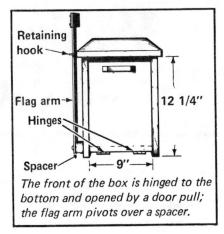

The front of the box is hinged to the bottom and opened by a door pull; the flag arm pivots over a spacer.

siding: for the top, a piece 23½ × 11½ inches; for the bottom, a piece 19¼ × 9 inches; for the sides, two pieces each 23⁵⁄₁₆ inches long at the top and 20½ inches long at the bottom, with each end cut to equal meeting angles; for the back, a piece 12⅞ × 9 inches; and for the door, a piece 12³⁄₁₆ × 8⅞ inches. Trim and smooth the edges of all pieces.

Apply carpenters' glue to one end of the 19¼ × 9-inch bottom piece and set the 12⅞ × 9-inch back piece against it so that the bottom edge of the back extends ⅝ inch below the bottom surface of the bottom. Fasten the back to the bottom with three 3-penny aluminum nails.

Lay the assembly on its side. Apply a bead of carpenters' glue along the uppermost edge, and set one of the side pieces into place. One lower corner of the side should meet the lower corner of the back; the top edge should be flush with the top edge of the back, and the bottom edge should overlap the bottom by ⅝ inch. Secure the side piece with three 3-penny aluminum nails driven into the back piece, and five 3-penny nails into the bottom piece. Then turn the box over and fasten the other side the same way.

With a fine-toothed flat file, bevel each end of the top piece to a slight angle. Apply a bead of glue along the top edges of the sides and back, and set the top into position with the corners

and bevels flush. Nail the top into place with six 3-penny aluminum nails spaced along each side, and two more spaced across the back.

To hold the box closed, use a small knob or a door pull with a magnetic catch. Center the knob or door pull about 2 inches down from the top edge of the front piece, and fasten it with the hardware provided.

Secure two butt hinges to the bottom edge of the door; instead of using the screws provided with the hinges, substitute others of the same diameter but ½ inch longer than the originals. Set the mailbox upside down—on its top—and set the door into position. Fold the free hinge leaves out flat on the bottom of the box, and adjust the door until there's ¹⁄₁₆ inch clearance at its top edge and along each side. Secure the hinges to the bottom of the box with the screws provided. If further fitting is needed, carefully shave the door edges with a file until the door operates without binding or scraping.

Mount the magnetic catch body centered on the underside of the top piece, with its face 2⅛ inches back from the front edge of the top. Mount the catch plate centered on the inside of the door, flush with the top edge. Then move the catch body forward slightly until the door plate makes positive contact with the catch and the door is vertical. Tighten the catch body mounting screws.

Cut a 1-inch square of plywood. Apply glue to one side and center the plywood square on the side at a point 1 inch above the bottom of the box and 4 inches back from the lower front corner. Secure the plywood square with two 1-inch brads.

To make the flag, cut a 1½ × 2½-inch piece of heavy-gauge scrap sheet metal. Along one 1½-inch side, drill two ⅛-inch holes, ¼ inch in from the edge and ⅜ inch from the top and bottom.

Cut a 17-inch piece of ⅛ × ½-inch aluminum or galvanized steel strap. At one end, drill two ⅛-inch holes to match those drilled in the flag, with the top edge of the flag flush with the end of the strap and the side of the flag flush with the side of the strap. At the other end of the strap, drill a 5/32-inch hole, centered ½ inch back from the end and on the longitudinal centerline of the strap. Fasten the flag to the strap with two ⅛-inch pop rivets.

Mark the center of the 1-inch-square plywood spacer block on the side of the box. Punch a small starter hole with a scratch awl, and drive a 1-inch #8 roundhead galvanized or plated wood screw partway in. Remove the screw, position the hole in the end of the flag arm over the hole in the plywood, and drive the screw tight, using a #8 flat

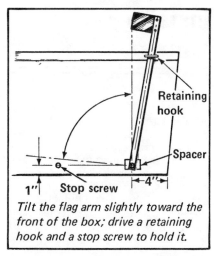

Tilt the flag arm slightly toward the front of the box; drive a retaining hook and a stop screw to hold it.

washer between the flag arm and the plywood block. Then back the screw off just enough so that the flag arm moves freely.

Lower the flag arm. Near the flag, 1 inch up from the bottom of the box, drive a 1-inch #8 roundhead galvanized or plated wood screw partway into the side of the box. This stop screw will keep the flag arm from falling past the bottom of the box.

Raise the flag until it's tilted slightly forward — about 10 degrees past the vertical position — and mark the point where the arm crosses the edge of the top. Drive a 1-inch L-shaped screw hook into the edge of the top at this point. Screw the hook in far enough so that the flag arm can be pushed between the hook and the edge of the top; this holds the flag in place when it's raised.

Unless the mailbox is made of cedar or redwood, apply a finish. Remove all hardware, and sand the entire box smooth. Apply whatever finish you like, but paint the flag bright red; leave the arm unfinished. After the finish is completely dry, add the box number and/or your name, if required or desired.

Replace the hardware. Mount the box solidly on a post or other support, using two 1½-inch #10 lag screws, with washers, driven down through the bottom of the box.

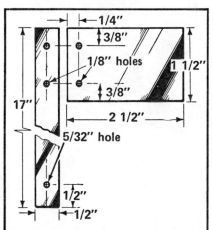

Cut the flag from heavy-gauge sheet metal; use aluminum or steel strap for the arm. Fasten them with pop rivets.

Install a Lamppost

For illumination and decorative effect, install a lamppost at your front walk or drive. **Tools:** shovel, pliers, pipe wrench, screwdriver, brace and bit, garden hose, paintbrush. **Materials:** lamppost kit, premixed concrete mix, gravel or flat rocks, underground cable/conduit (check the electrical codes in your area), sheet plastic film, short piece of 1 × 3, two pieces of 2 × 4 × 8, wood preservative, wirenuts. **Time:** 1 day.

Caution: Follow the electrical codes for your area when installing a lamppost. The lamppost retailer will probably know code restrictions; if not, check with the city electrical department. Although connections to house power are fairly simple and instructions for this are usually included with the kit, don't try to make the connection if you don't know how; install the lamp and have it connected by an electrician.

Buy an exterior lamppost assembly in kit form, with all necessary parts included. Lampposts are available in a wide variety of styles to fit into the architectural and landscaping plan of your home.

To install the lamppost, dig a trench for the power lines, from the power source to the lamp itself. To protect the lawn, spread sheet plastic on the grass next to the trench and pile the dirt on this plastic. Dig the trench 18 inches deep—check the electrical codes—and just wide enough to hold the cable/conduit. Set the cable/conduit into the trench; do *not* connect it.

If the cable/conduit must go under a walk or driveway, use a garden hose to make a pathway under the concrete. Dig a hole at the edge of the walk or

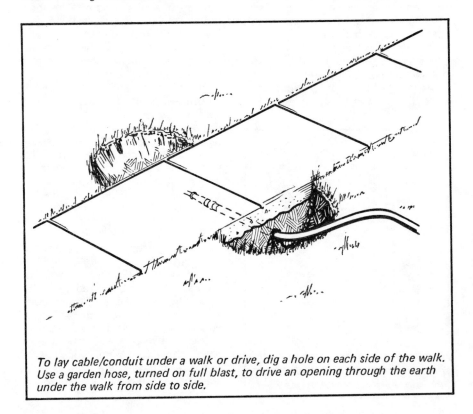

To lay cable/conduit under a walk or drive, dig a hole on each side of the walk. Use a garden hose, turned on full blast, to drive an opening through the earth under the walk from side to side.

driveway, 6 inches below the slab's bottom. Dig another hole to the same depth on the opposite side of the slab. Then insert a garden hose, with the nozzle turned on full blast, under the slab, and turn the water on. The hose will act as a water ram as you push and pull it through the earth. When the hose appears in the opposite hole, turn off the water; then fasten the cable/conduit to the hose and pull out the hose with the cable/conduit attached. Set the cable/conduit into the trench; do *not* connect it.

Dig the hole for the lamppost—about a third of its length, or according to the manufacturer's instructions. Cover the bottom of the hole with gravel or with a layer or two of flat rocks, for drainage.

If the lamppost is wood, give it at least two coats of clear, paintable wood preservative before setting it into the hole, even if the post has been pressure-treated with preservative. The extra ef-

fort and slight cost will add from 5 to 10 years to the life of the post. Let the preservative dry completely.

Connect the electrical wiring to the lamppost after the preservative is dry, and before setting the post into the hole. Follow the manufacturer's instructions for connecting the wiring to the lamppost.

With the wiring connected, set the lamppost into the hole. The lamppost should be set in concrete; you'll need a helper to hold the post while you pour the footing.

With your helper holding the post, pour a third of a sack of concrete mix into the hole. Add water to the mix, following the manufacturer's instructions. Stir and tamp the mix with a short piece of 1 × 3. Add another third of a sack of concrete, and repeat the mixing procedure. At this point, plumb (vertically level) the post. Then fill the hole with concrete mix and water and stir. Crown

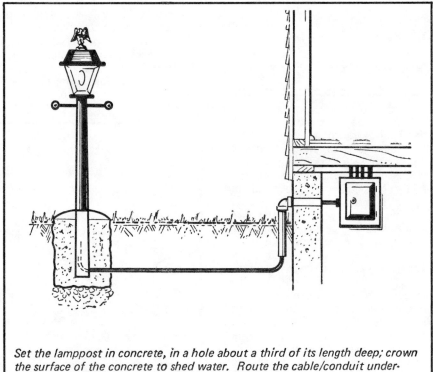

Set the lamppost in concrete, in a hole about a third of its length deep; crown the surface of the concrete to shed water. Route the cable/conduit underground from the lamppost to the power source.

the top of the concrete with the back of a spade to slope the concrete away from the post; the crowned concrete sheds water like a roof.

Brace the post with 2 × 4's until the concrete sets—about 2 hours. Keep the concrete damp for a week to help it cure properly.

To complete the job, fill the cable/conduit trench with dirt and connect the lamp to the power source.

If you're replacing an old lamppost with a new one—or if there's an available outside junction box—the connection is easy. *Caution: Flip the circuit breaker or remove the fuse that controls the outdoor junction box.* Remove the cover to the junction box and connect the box's wires to the lamp's wires, following the lamppost manufacturer's instructions. Use wirenuts to make the connection.

If there is no available outdoor junction box, have an electrician install the proper wiring.

Make Your Own Pavers

Concrete pavers are both expensive and hard to transport. If you have the time to make them, you can cut costs and eliminate transportation problems by casting your own. **Tools:** measuring rule, pencil, carpenters' square, handsaw or power saw, hammer, wire cutters, paintbrush, wheelbarrow, shovel, scrap piece of 2 × 4; finishing trowel, broom, or rake; garden hose. **Materials:** 1 × 2, 1 × 4, or 2 × 4 lumber for frames; 6-penny or 8-penny common nails, 6 mil sheet polyethylene film, lengths of ⅜-inch concrete reinforcing bar sized to the desired pavers, mechanics' wire, motor oil, sand-type premixed concrete mix, weights. **Time:** about 15 minutes to 1 hour to make a mold; about ½ to 1 hour for pouring pavers.

Make molds for your pavers in what-ever shape you like; a square or rectangle is easiest. Small pavers, up to about 1 square foot, should be about 1½ to 2 inches thick; use 1 × 2 lumber for the frames. Large pavers should be correspondingly heavier, about 2½ to 3 inches thick; use 1 × 4 or 2 × 4 lumber for the frames. Make up several individual forms or one or two fairly sizable multiple molds to turn out several pavers at once. Don't make multiple molds too big, though, or you'll have trouble releasing the pavers from the molds.

To make each mold, measure and mark the framing lumber to the desired dimensions; cut it to size with a handsaw or a power saw. Join the cut framing members with simple butt joints and nail them firmly together with 6-penny or 8-penny common nails. Make sure the forms are tight at the corners so the concrete doesn't spread out of the desired shape.

Spread a sheet of 6 mil polyethylene film on a smooth, fairly level surface, such as a sheet of plywood, the garage floor, or a driveway; set the forms out on the plastic. Choose a shady spot for pouring and curing the concrete. If you're making large pavers, make a reinforcing grid for each mold out of ⅜-inch concrete reinforcing bar; have the supplier cut the bar in pieces a little

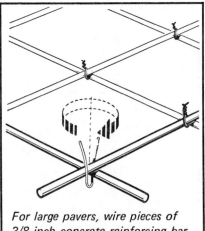

For large pavers, wire pieces of 3/8-inch concrete reinforcing bar together to make a grid for each mold.

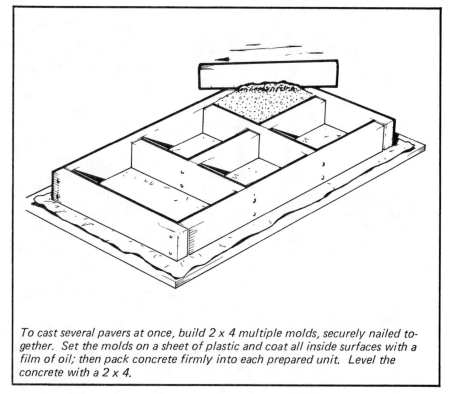

To cast several pavers at once, build 2 x 4 multiple molds, securely nailed together. Set the molds on a sheet of plastic and coat all inside surfaces with a film of oil; then pack concrete firmly into each prepared unit. Level the concrete with a 2 x 4.

shorter than the mold. Wire the bars together with mechanics' wire to form an open grid with 2-inch squares and reinforced joints; set the grid at hand near the mold. Paint the inside faces of each mold, wood and plastic, with a thin film of motor oil.

Mix a bath of premixed sand-type concrete mix in a wheelbarrow; use a shovel to mix the concrete thoroughly. Use only enough water to make the mix quite stiff, just loose enough so that you can handle it. Shovel the concrete into the prepared molds, packing it down firmly to eliminate air holes. If you're making large pavers, fill each mold only halfway; then bed the reinforcing grid into the half-filled mold and pour more concrete to fill the mold. Use a piece of scrap 2 × 4 to level the filled molds; pull the board across each mold in a zigzag pattern to produce a relatively smooth surface. Make the top of each mold as level as possible.

Let the concrete cure about 2 hours,

until the water film on the surface begins to disappear. Test the surface by pressing it with your thumb; when you can make only a slight indentation, the concrete is ready to be finished. Finish the surface of each paver with a finishing trowel to a dense, very smooth surface; use plenty of pressure. Or, if desired, texture the surface with a broom or a rake, or make patterns by pressing forms into the concrete.

When the pavers are completely finished, spray them lightly with a garden hose and cover them with a sheet of 6 mil polyethylene film, weighted in place. Let the concrete cure for at least 3 days; during the curing period, remove the plastic once or twice a day and spray the pavers lightly with a garden hose. When the pavers are completely cured, release them from the forms by tapping gently on the concrete and slipping the forms off. Be careful not to chip the pavers as you unmold them.

Cast a Flagstone Walk in Place

One of the easiest ways to make an attractive and long-lasting walkway in your yard is to pour the pavers where you want them. **Tools:** stakes, mallet, pencil, scissors, sod cutter or masons' trowel, shovel, wheelbarrow, garden hose, short piece of 2 × 4, masons' finishing trowel. **Materials:** string, lightweight cardboard, sand-type pre-mixed concrete mix, sheet plastic film, weights. **Time:** about 20 to 30 minutes per stone, plus a few minutes a day during the curing period.

Before you start, plan the walkway's design. Make a sketch of the way you want it to look, with random or evenly shaped stones. The sketch doesn't have to be exact, but use it as a rough guide while you work.

Lay out the line of the walkway with stakes and string; drive the stakes with a mallet. Then make a cardboard template for each flagstone shape, the same size you want it to be. The flagstones can be random shapes, but you must design them so they will interweave on the pathway, with enough straight sides to make even perimeter lines. All the shapes can be entirely different, but a pattern that repeats itself every 4 or 5 feet will make the job go faster.

Lay out the cardboard templates within the walkway outline, and arrange them to follow your design. Leave at least 1 inch between stones. Carefully cut around each template with a sod cutter or a masons' trowel to remove the corresponding chunk of sod beneath it. Lift out the sod pieces and deepen the holes, forming vertical sides about 2 inches deep. Scrape the bottoms of the holes flat.

With a shovel, prepare sand-type premixed concrete mix in a wheelbarrow as directed by the manufacturer, using enough water to make it fairly stiff but still loose enough to be readily workable. Lightly mist the bottoms of the holes with a garden hose—the dirt should be reasonably wet, but not puddled or muddy. Shovel the prepared concrete into the holes, packing it firmly. Carefully level the top of each poured stone with a piece of 2 × 4 held on edge; pull the board in a zigzag across the top of the concrete. Make the flagstone tops as level as possible.

This leveling will leave the flagstone tops fairly rough. If you want a smoother finish, wait about 2 hours, until the water film on the concrete surface begins to disappear. Test the surface by pressing it with your thumb; when you can make only a slight indentation, the concrete is ready for finishing. Pack and smooth the flagstone surfaces with a masons' finishing trowel, using plenty of downward pressure; remove all excess concrete. Then spray the flagstones lightly with a garden hose.

Cover the entire walkway with a strip of sheet plastic film, weighted in place, so it doesn't dry out too fast; let the con-

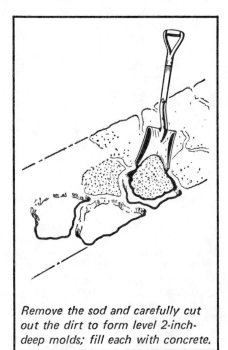

Remove the sod and carefully cut out the dirt to form level 2-inch-deep molds; fill each with concrete.

crete cure for about 3 days. During the curing period, remove the plastic once or twice a day and spray the flagstones lightly with a garden hose; replace the plastic.

Dry-Lay a Brick Walkway

A brick walkway gives a country-estate look to the towniest of houses, and it isn't hard to make. Set the brick without mortar, on a bed of sand. **Tools:** measuring rule, stakes, mallet, sod cutter or sharp knife, shovel, pencil, handsaw or power saw, rake, garden hose, short piece of 4 × 4, 3- to 4-foot piece of 2 × 4, scrap plywood, wheelbarrow, push broom. **Materials:** grade SW (severe weathering) brick, string, 1 × 4 redwood stock, sand, portland cement. **Time:** about 1 hour per square yard of brick laid.

To figure the amount of brick you'll need, lay out a course of bricks to the width of the walk. Use a simple parquet layout, with pairs of bricks set at right angles to each other. Count the bricks across and measure the width and the total length of the walk; give these measurements to the building supply dealer. Buy grade SW (severe weathering) brick.

To lay out the walk, set a course of bricks in place with the joint spacing you want; measure across and add 1½ inches. Drive stakes just outside the measured width to mark the edges of the walk. Lay out the path of the walkway with stakes and string, keeping the width constant and the stakes just outside the walk's edges. Keep the walk as straight as possible; change direction, if necessary, with right-angle turns. Change elevation in gentle, gradual slopes.

Using the string as a guideline, cut and remove the sod from the marked-out walk area; use a sod cutter or a sharp knife. Dig out the soil in the walk

area to a depth of 4 inches, and rough-level the bottom of the trench.

Use 1 × 4 redwood boards to edge the walk and prevent the bricks from creeping. Measure and mark some of the redwood into 1¾-inch-wide, 18-inch-long stakes; cut them with a handsaw or a power saw. Set 1 × 4's on edge along the sides of the trench, butted firmly end to end. To hold the edging strips in place, drive redwood stakes outside the strips, with the flat face of the stake parallel to the walk and flush with the cut edge of the sod, just below the top of the 1 × 4. Cut 1 × 4's to fit as necessary.

Fill the redwood-edged trench with a 2-inch layer of sand, so that the bricks will lie flush with the top of the edging strips. Pack the sand in firmly. As you work, rough-level the sand with a rake, spray it lightly with a garden hose, and tamp it with the end of a short piece of 4 × 4. Level the sand bed with a 3- to 4-foot piece of 2 × 4; hold the board edgewise and scrape it across the sand to provide a firm, flat surface. Thorough tamping and leveling are important to the appearance of the finished walk, so don't skimp.

Set the bricks into place on the leveled sand; bed each brick firmly, but try not to disturb the lie of the sand in the process. When several bricks are in place, settle them firmly with a piece of scrap plywood. Set the plywood over the bricks and stamp on it; make sure the plywood is level, and stamp straight down. If this final setting dislodges or misaligns a brick, pry it up and add or remove sand to relevel it; replace the brick and resettle it.

Fill the brick joints with a dry mixture of 1 part portland cement and 3 parts sand. Pour the dry filler over the bricks and sweep it into the joints with a push broom; brush the excess away, but keep the joints filled right to the top. Spray the walk lightly but thoroughly with a garden hose to moisten the filler completely; wait 15 minutes and spray again. Repeat the spraying at least once more to wet the sand-cement mixture thoroughly; let it dry before walking on the bricks.

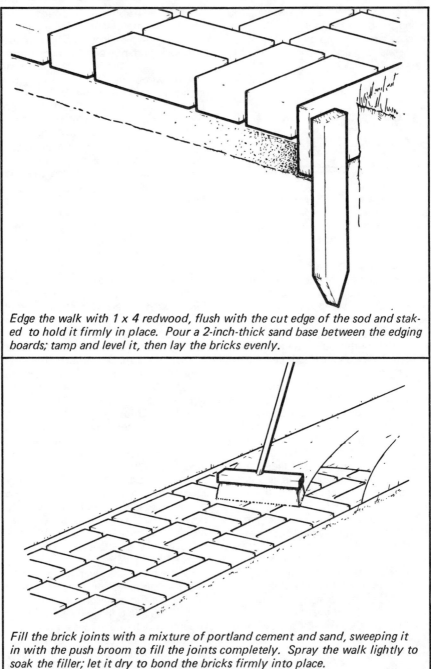

Edge the walk with 1 x 4 redwood, flush with the cut edge of the sod and staked to hold it firmly in place. Pour a 2-inch-thick sand base between the edging boards; tamp and level it, then lay the bricks evenly.

Fill the brick joints with a mixture of portland cement and sand, sweeping it in with the push broom to fill the joints completely. Spray the walk lightly to soak the filler; let it dry to bond the bricks firmly into place.

Weather and frost heaving may move the bricks. To repair the damage, lift out the affected bricks and add or remove sand as necessary; refill the joints with sand-cement mix and spray the newly filled joints to reset them.

Level a Walk

Normal settling, moisture, freezing, and thawing can cause sections of a concrete walkway to heave or sink, making the walk uneven and hard to walk on. In most cases, you can level the walk without replacing the slab. **Tools:** pry bar, shovel, sledgehammer, brick chisel, several pieces of 2 × 4, level, garden hose, broom. **Materials:** packaged sand/gravel mix, sand. **Time:** ½ hour or more, depending on condition of walk.

For sunken or heaved walks made of brick, paving brick, patio block, or flagstone, the leveling job is easy. Lift the affected paving units with a pry bar; remove the dirt or sand in the joints of the units with the pry bar's tip and dig out the units with the pry bar's edge. After one unit has been removed, hand-lift the others out of the problem area.

If the paving units are sunken, add packaged sand/gravel mix to the base to elevate them. Tamp the mix lightly with the end of a 2 × 4; then return the pavers to the base and level them. You may have to add—or remove—sand/gravel mix until the units are level with the surrounding surface. Then fill the joints with sand. Lightly sprinkle the area with water, and fill the joints again with sand. Repeat until the joints are well filled with sand.

If the walk has heaved, remove the units as above. Remove some of the dirt or sand base underneath them. Tamp the sand or dirt base with a 2 × 4 and reset the units; level them with the surrounding units. Then add sand to the joints as above.

Leveling concrete walks is more involved. First, make sure the section is large enough and intact enough to lift. If the walk is badly broken, you may have to remove the damaged concrete and replace it with new concrete.

To lift a large section, dig a hole along the side of the walk. For prying purposes, dig the hole at least 3 to 4 inches below the concrete's bottom surface.

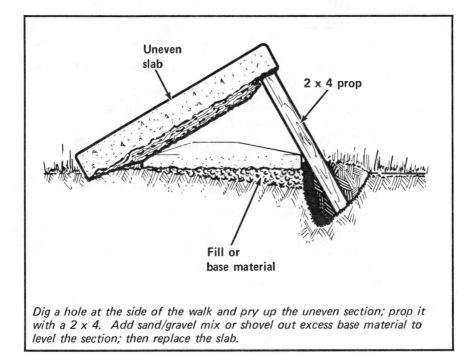

Dig a hole at the side of the walk and pry up the uneven section; prop it with a 2 x 4. Add sand/gravel mix or shovel out excess base material to level the section; then replace the slab.

Dig some earth out from under the slab, making a pocket. Stick the end of a 2 × 4 into this pocket and pry up on the slab. You may have to enlarge the pocket and add a brick or wood prop under the 2 × 4 for more leverage.

Once the slab has been lifted, prop it up with a piece of scrap wood; you'll need a helper for this. Prop the slab high enough to fully expose the base underneath. Then add sand/gravel mix to the base, if the walk is sunken; shovel away some of the base material, if the walk has heaved.

For a sunken slab, add a little more of the sand/gravel mix than you think is necessary to level the walk's top surface; the weight of the walk, plus moisture, will drop the level of the walk about ½ to 1 inch over a period of time. For a heaved walk, level the walk exactly to match the adjoining concrete; it won't sink over time. Finally, remove the props and replace the slab.

Veneer
an Old Walk

Broken and uneven walkways are both unsightly and dangerous, but replacing them can cost plenty. For a fast and easy solution, veneer the walk with flagstone. **Tools:** brick chisel, sledgehammer, pry bar, broom, trowel, wheelbarrow or tub and stir stick, pry bar, level, shovel, hoe, garden hose, broom, safety goggles, grease pencil. **Materials:** premixed cement mortar mix, short piece of scrap 1 × 4, flagstone, burlap, sheet plastic film. **Time:** about 1 hour per square yard of veneer.

Flagstone is available in various sizes; the shapes are irregular and the thickness varies. Buy stones of uniform or random size, to fit over the walkway like a jigsaw puzzle.

Remove the worst sections of the walk with a sledgehammer and a pry bar. Don't remove parts of the walk that are only slightly raised, sunken, or

broken. Remove any loose heavy debris and sweep the walk clean.

Set the flagstones on the pavement to determine proper fit, working in 3-foot-square sections. Cut them to fit as necessary by scoring them with a brick chisel and breaking them with a sledgehammer. *Caution: Wear safety goggles to protect your eyes.* Place each stone on a solid surface to score it; then elevate the stone with a piece of 1 × 4 and strike the chisel lightly along the score line to break the stone.

Vary the joints between the stones from about ¼ inch up to about ¾ inch; wide and narrow joints will enhance the design of the new walk surface. As you finish laying out and trimming each 3-foot-square section, number each stone with a grease pencil for position. Remove the stones and set them aside, in order.

Mix cement mortar with water to a fairly thin consistency. Shovel the mortar onto the walk section, and level it with a shovel. Then set the flagstones into the mortar base, following the marked numbers to keep them in order. Tap each flagstone to true level with the handle of a trowel, and check your work with a level. Repeat for each 3-foot-square section until the walk is completely covered.

Let the completed walk cure for 1 or 2 days. Then mix cement mortar to a thin, soupy consistency. Pour and trowel this mixture into the flagstone joints, smoothing the joints with the trowel's point. When the mortar is fairly dry—about ½ hour, depending on the temperature—wipe the joints with damp burlap to finish the mortar. Remove excess mortar from the surface of the flagstones with burlap. Don't worry about a mortar glaze on the flagstones' surface; this glaze is easy to flush off with water when the job is complete.

Let the mortar cure for 1 week. During the curing period, cover the walk with sheet plastic; several times a day, soak the walk with the fine spray of a garden hose.

In time, hairline cracks may appear in the mortar joints. These cracks are the result of normal settling. Mix mortar to a

Spread a base of mortar on the walk and level it. Set the flagstones into the mortar base, fitting them into position section by section. Let the base cure; then fill the joints with mortar and finish them.

thin, soupy consistency to fill the cracks; fill cracks as you spot them to prevent water from damaging the flagstone veneer.

Patch Cracks in Concrete

A cracked driveway or patio can break up fast if you let it go, but even wide cracks are easy to mend. **Tools:** safety goggles, cold chisel, sledge-hammer, stiff broom, garden hose, sponge, sturdy wheelbarrow, shovel, stiff paintbrush, trowel, short piece of 2 × 4. **Materials:** sand, ready-mix sand concrete mix, liquid concrete bonding agent. **Time:** about ½ to 1 day, plus a few minutes several times each day during the curing period.

Cracks must be undercut before they can be filled. Wearing safety goggles, use a cold chisel and a sledgehammer to enlarge the crack; angle the chisel into the sides of the crack so that the bottom of the opening is wider than the top. Remove large chunks of concrete and then sweep along the crack with a stiff broom to remove any remaining debris. Flush the crack thoroughly with a garden hose; remove standing water with a sponge.

If the crack goes all the way through the slab, pour a layer of sand along it, not filling the crack but bringing the level of the opening flush with the bottom edges of the cracked slab sections. Spray the sand with a garden hose to dampen it thoroughly.

Mix sand concrete mix according to the directions on the bag; pour the dry mix into a sturdy wheelbarrow, add water, and mix thoroughly with a shovel. When the sand mix is ready to

Fill Potholes in Concrete

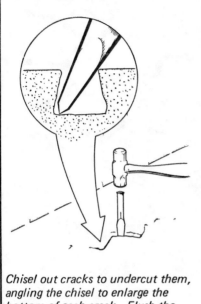

Chisel out cracks to undercut them, angling the chisel to enlarge the bottom of each crack. Flush the cleaned cracks thoroughly.

Potholes in the streets are bad enough; potholes in your driveway are worse. You can't do much about the public roads, but you can fix your own. **Tools:** safety goggles, cold chisel, sledgehammer, stiff broom, garden hose, sponge, sturdy wheelbarrow, shovel, stiff paintbrush, trowel, 2 × 4 long enough to extend completely over patch area, wood cement float, push broom. **Materials:** ready-mix concrete mix (sand mix for small holes, gravel mix for large or deep holes), liquid concrete bonding agent, plastic dropcloth, weights. **Time:** about 1 day for a good-sized hole, plus a few minutes several times each day during the curing period.

Remove all loose pieces of concrete from the hole. Wearing safety goggles, use a cold chisel and a sledgehammer to chop out the crumbling concrete; cut down to sound concrete, roughening the interior surface of the hole. Angle the chisel to undercut the edges of the hole, so that the hole is wider across the bottom than it is across the top. Remove large chunks of broken concrete and sweep out the hole with a stiff broom; flush it thoroughly with a garden hose. Remove standing water with a sponge.

Mix ready-mix concrete according to the manufacturer's instructions; use sand mix for small holes, gravel mix for large or deep ones. Pour the dry mix into a sturdy wheelbarrow and add water; mix the concrete thoroughly with a shovel.

When the concrete is ready to use, quickly pour liquid concrete bonding agent into the hole. Following the manufacturer's instructions and working quickly, spread the bonding agent evenly over the entire inside surface of the hole with a stiff paintbrush; be sure to coat the undercut corners completely. Clean the paintbrush im-

use, quickly pour liquid concrete bonding agent along the crack, spreading it with a stiff paintbrush according to the manufacturer's directions. Cover the entire inside surface of the crack. Clean the paintbrush immediately with water.

Fill the prepared crack with sand mix before the bonding agent dries. Shovel or trowel the concrete into the crack. Force concrete into the undercut opening with a trowel, pressing firmly to fill the crack completely and smoothing the concrete along the crack. Let the concrete set for about 45 minutes.

When the new concrete has begun to harden, smooth the surface of the patched crack level with the surrounding concrete. Set a short piece of 2 × 4 on edge across the crack. Starting at one end of the crack, pull the 2 × 4 in zigzags along the surface of the new concrete.

Let the patched crack cure for about a week before walking on it. During the curing period, spray the crack several times a day with the fine spray of the garden hose to keep it from drying out too quickly.

mediately with water.

Fill the prepared hole before the bonding agent dries. Shovel concrete into the hole and trowel it into place, pressing firmly to pack the opening completely full. Mound the surface of the patch slightly above the level of the surrounding concrete and then tamp it firmly down with the back of the shovel; add more concrete and tamp again, if necessary, to pack the hole densely.

To level the patch, set a 2 × 4 on edge across the filled hole. You'll need a helper at this point if the patch is a large one. Starting at one end of the filled hole, draw the 2 × 4 in zigzags over the new concrete, pushing and pulling alternately with your helper, one person at each end of the 2 × 4. The smoothed-over patch will have a film of water on its surface.

Let the concrete set for about 45 minutes to 1 hour. When the surface of the concrete is no longer filmed with water, smooth the patch again with a wood cement float. Continue smooth-

ing, using long, even sweeps with the float, until the surface of the patch is filmed with water again.

If desired, finish the surface of the patch with a push broom. Let the patch set after the second float-smoothing until the film of surface water disappears. Then, starting on the old concrete beyond the patch, move the head of the push broom steadily over the filled-in hole and onto the old concrete again.

Let the concrete set until the film of surface water left by the final smoothing has been absorbed. Cover the patch area with a plastic dropcloth, weighted at the edges if necessary to hold it in place. Be careful not to set the weights on the new concrete. Let the patch cure for about a week before walking on it. Several times each day during the curing period, remove the plastic and spray the patched area with the fine spray of a garden hose; recover the patch and re-weight the plastic sheet to hold it in place.

Patch Broken Blacktop

Patching a blacktop driveway is one of the easiest of outdoor repairs. Work in summer; the patching mix gets stiff in cold weather. **Tools:** trowel, stiff broom, shovel, 3- to 4-foot piece of 4 × 4, stiff push broom. **Materials:** gravel, blacktop patching mixture, sand, liquid blacktop sealer, mineral spirits, rags. **Time:** about 1 to 2 hours for most repairs; about 1½ to 2 hours to apply sealer.

Work on a warm, dry day. Remove loose blacktop from a crumbled area with a trowel, digging in firmly to cut down to solid asphalt. Chop down to sound blacktop all around and inside the hole. Remove large chunks of debris from the hole and sweep it out thoroughly with a stiff broom. Keep the chopped-out hole dry.

Fill deep holes partially with gravel,

Fill the hole and pull a 2 x 4 back and forth across the patch to level it; then smooth it with a wood float to finish the surface.

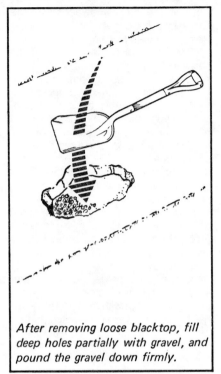

After removing loose blacktop, fill deep holes partially with gravel, and pound the gravel down firmly.

Liquid blacktop sealer both mends and protects asphalt drives. Work in warm weather, and make sure the blacktop is entirely dry.

To fill a narrow crack, pour sand along the crack to partially fill it. Pour blacktop sealer over the sand to fill and seal the crack; add more sealer if necessary as the sand absorbs the sealer. To fill larger cracks, mix blacktop sealer with sand to a mortarlike consistency. Fill the crack with this sand-sealer mix, using a trowel to force it into the full depth of the crack; trowel the surface smooth.

Coat a deteriorating or newly patched driveway with liquid blacktop sealer to protect it from further damage. Apply the sealer to the drive like paint; working on one section at a time, pour out a pool of sealer and spread it evenly on the blacktop with a stiff push broom. Throw the head of the push broom away after using it; clean up with mineral spirits and rags.

shoveling it in to 3 or 4 inches below the surface of the driveway. Pound the gravel in firmly with the back of the shovel.

Pour blacktop patching mixture directly from the bag into the cleaned-out hole, filling it to just below the surface. Spread the loose patching mixture evenly and tamp it firmly into the hole with a 3- or 4-foot piece of 4 × 4, using the square end of the 4 × 4 to flatten the patch. Add more patching mixture, mounding it about ½ inch higher than the surface of the drive, and tamp the patch down again to level it flush with the drive.

Drive over the newly filled patch several times, running the car's tires directly over the patch. If the patch sinks under the weight of the car, add more patching mixture, tamp it in, and test again until the patch is solid and level. Unless you're going to seal the driveway, sprinkle the patch with sand to keep the fresh asphalt from being tracked around.

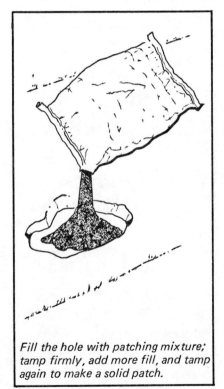

Fill the hole with patching mixture; tamp firmly, add more fill, and tamp again to make a solid patch.

Build a Railroad-Tie Retaining Wall

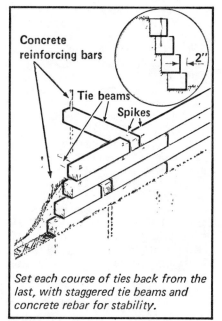

Set each course of ties back from the last, with staggered tie beams and concrete rebar for stability.

Retaining walls are useful and attractive when your landscaping involves two or more grade levels. There are easier ways to make a railroad-tie retaining wall, but this setback method is the most effective—it takes a little extra effort, but you won't have to do it all over again in a couple of years. **Tools:** shovel, power drill with ½-inch wood-boring speed bit and bit extension, heavy sledgehammer, garden hose, measuring rule, bow saw or chain saw. **Materials:** railroad ties, nails, string, 2- to 3-foot lengths of ½-inch concrete reinforcing bar, long spikes. **Time:** at least 1 day for a wall 8 to 10 feet long and 4 feet high.

A set-back retaining wall is built stair-step fashion, with each successive course of ties set back from the leading edge of the course below by about 2 inches, or a third of the width of the tie. The first step in building the wall is to plan the way the wall will lie on the bank, and to carve away the amount of soil necessary where the wall will be built. Shovel out the soil as required on the low side of the grade, and rough-level the undisturbed soil where the first row of ties will lie. If you want to sink the first row of ties into the ground, cut a channel 2 or 3 inches deep for the base ties. Lay out the first row of ties along the ground, butted tightly together end to end; do this by eye or stretch a string between nails driven into the ties.

In the middle and at each end of each tie, drill a ½-inch hole, centered on the tie width, completely through the tie; use a power drill with a ½-inch wood-boring speed bit and a bit extension. Drive a length of ½-inch reinforcing bar, commonly called rebar, through each hole and into the ground; use rebar 2 or 3 feet long, depending on the width of the ties. Drive the rebar with a heavy

sledgehammer; keep pounding until the top of the rebar is flush with the tie surface. This holds the base row in place. Shovel dirt and rocks in against the back of the line of ties on the high side of the grade, tamping it firmly up to the level of the ties. Dampen the soil with a garden hose to aid in compaction, but don't let it get muddy.

Line up the next row of ties on top of the first ones, set back about 2 inches from the outside face of the first row. Use ties cut to a length different from those in the first row, so the joints of the rows of ties are staggered like brick joints. If all your ties are the same length, cut a tie in half with a bow saw or chain saw and use the cut halves as end ties to stagger the joints. Stagger each successive row of ties so that no two rows have corresponding joints.

At the end of every third or fourth tie, depending on their length, insert a tie beam, a railroad tie lying at right angles to the wall, with its outward end flush with the face of the row of ties. Calculate the tie beam's length and cut it so that at least a foot at the far end of the beam extends out past the wall and rests against undisturbed soil.

Secure the second row of ties to the base row with spikes long enough to go completely through one tie and two-thirds of the way through the tie beneath it. With the second row of ties in place, drill a hole at each end of each tie, completely through the tie and slightly into the tie below it. Use a drill bit of the same diameter as the spikes, and a bit extension. Drive the spikes in with a sledgehammer, securing the second course of ties to the first. Fasten the exposed end of the tie beam with two spikes set diagonally into the end; don't place the spikes side by side. At the banking end of each tie beam, drill a ½-inch hole through the beam, and drive a length of rebar through the beam and into the ground to pin the beam into place. Shovel more fill dirt in behind the second row, and tamp the earth down hard.

Lay out and fasten the third row of ties the same way, but without tie beams. Use tie beams in the fourth course of ties and in every other course as you work; stagger the tie beams so that no tie beam lies above a tie beam in a lower course.

Continue setting course ties and tie beams, setting each row back 2 inches from the row below it, until you reach the full height of the wall; pack the dirt in firmly behind the retaining wall as you go. The last course of the wall should reach just above the finished high grade level at the back of the wall.

Build a Mortarless Stone Wall

If you have a handy source of fieldstone, you can build an attractive and economical mortarless stone wall—it's very demanding work, but you can do the job a little at a time. **Tools:** shovel, measuring rule, crowbar, wheelbarrow, heavy leather gloves, heavy work boots, garden hose, heavy sledgehammer or hand sledge and brick chisel, safety goggles. **Materials:** fieldstone. **Time:** at least 6 hours to build 3 or 4 linear feet of a 4-foot-high wall.

Before you start building, prepare a foundation for the wall. If the ground is relatively level, lay out the line of the wall and dig a trench about 1½ feet wide and 1 foot deep. Make the bottom fairly level and clean. On uneven terrain, change elevations in the trench bottom stair-step fashion, not in slopes.

Pile your fieldstones near the wall site so you'll be able to choose stones as you work. Use a crowbar to lift the edges and a wheelbarrow for heavy hauling; wear heavy leather gloves and heavy work boots.

Set the first course of stones, on the bottom of the trench, as a double row. Use the worst stones here—those with awkward shapes, or poor faces. Bed each stone firmly into the earth, fitting the stones carefully together side by side with the flattest faces upward. Don't use stones with very smooth or rounded faces in the wall; they don't provide enough surface friction for good bonding. Pack dirt in around the stones and tamp firmly; spray them lightly with a garden hose to pack the earth, but don't turn it into mud.

If you need another course of stones to reach approximate grade level, lay them down. Fit these stones together, twisting and turning and nesting them as tightly as possible so they cling to one another. This is a trial-and-error process, and it will take some time for you to get the feel of it and recognize which stones will fit where. Again, pack dirt into all the cracks and crannies between the stones, but don't depend on the dirt to support the rocks. Spray the packed stones lightly with the garden hose.

Pick out some of your better stones, and start laying the above-grade courses. At least every 3 or 4 feet, set one stone in each course extending through the wall from front to back, solidly nested. This helps tie the wall together. Wherever possible, make the stones slant slightly inward toward the

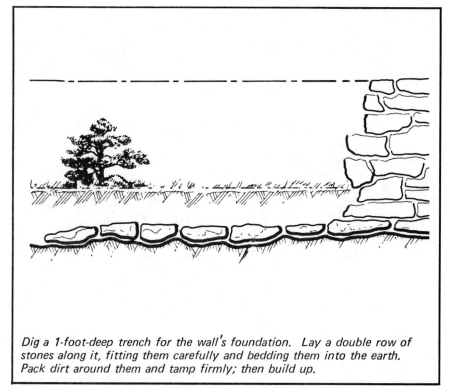

Dig a 1-foot-deep trench for the wall's foundation. Lay a double row of stones along it, fitting them carefully and bedding them into the earth. Pack dirt around them and tamp firmly; then build up.

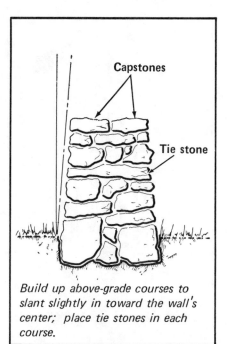

Capstones

Tie stone

Build up above-grade courses to slant slightly in toward the wall's center; place tie stones in each course.

centerline of the wall, so they push against one another; stones tilted toward the outside faces of the wall have a tendency to slide out. You can shim and fill small gaps by chinking them with small stones, but do this as little as possible. Try to do most filling-in work on the inside face of the wall.

If you have to break large stones or trim away knobs and protrusions, use a heavy sledgehammer or a hand sledge and brick chisel to fit the stones. Wear safety goggles and heavy leather gloves for all stone-breaking.

Continue laying courses of stone until the wall reaches a height of about 4 feet. Build the sides of the wall in a vertical line on each face; they can slant slightly inward on either or both faces, but they should never slant outward. Set aside the best and flattest stones as you work to use as capstones for the top course of the wall. Fit this last course together carefully to make the top of the wall as flat as you can.

Build a Board-and-Board Fence

For privacy without total enclosure, a board-and-board fence is the answer. **Tools:** stakes, sledgehammer, posthole digger, shovel, posthole bar or scrap piece of 2 × 4, level, measuring rule, handsaw or power saw, hammer. **Materials:** string, gravel; 4 × 4 and 1 × 4 or 1 × 6 pressure-treated, ground-contact lumber, or cedar or redwood; 10-penny and 8-penny galvanized common nails. **Time:** about 1 day per 20-foot fence section.

For the best results, use pressure-treated, ground-contact lumber to build the fence; or, if you prefer, use cedar or redwood. With these woods, no finishing is required; the fence can be left to weather naturally. If you must, you can use untreated wood for fence boards and top rails, and for bottom rails that are at least 4 inches above grade level. You'll need 4 × 4 lumber for fence posts and 1 × 4 or 1 × 6 fence boards, 4 to 6 feet long.

Lay out the approximate fence line—make sure you're not on your neighbor's property—and then establish the exact location of the first end or corner post. Dig a posthole of a diameter just large enough to accommodate a 4 × 4 post, and at least 18 inches deep. For a fence that's 5 or 6 feet high, dig a 24-inch-deep posthole.

Pour about 3 inches of gravel into the bottom of the hole and set the end of a post into the hole. Holding the post upright, add another 6 inches of gravel and then shovel a 4-inch layer of soil into the hole. Compact the soil with the butt end of a posthole bar or a scrap piece of 2 × 4. Continue filling and tamping in 4-inch layers of soil, checking the post with a level as you work to make sure it's straight.

After setting the first post, determine the exact location for the opposite end or corner post. Set this post the same way you set the first one.

To set the intermediate posts, measure the height of each end post above grade level to make sure both are the same height. Drive a nail partway into the face of each post, facing the direction of the fence line, just above ground level. Tie a piece of string to one nail, stretch it to the other post, and secure it to the other nail. Using the string as a guide, drive stakes to locate the intermediate postholes—posts are usually spaced either 8 or 10 feet apart, and are 4 to 6 feet high. Then remove the string and nails.

Drive a nail into the top center of each end post, and stretch a piece of string between them, securing it to the nails. Dig each intermediate posthole, as above; use the twine as a guide for height, and check the posts on the twine with a level to make sure their tops are even. If necessary, make height adjustments by varying the depth of the gravel in each posthole.

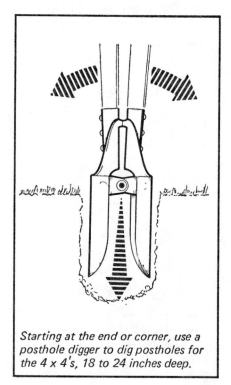

Starting at the end or corner, use a posthole digger to dig postholes for the 4 x 4's, 18 to 24 inches deep.

Cut 2 × 4 rails to fit flat along the tops of the posts. The rails can extend from post to post, or a rail can span two sections. Measure and cut each rail individually, to allow for slight variations in fence-post spacing. Butt the ends of the rails firmly together. Then, beginning at one end of the fence line, nail the rails into place, using two 10-penny galvanized common nails at each end.

Measure and cut a 2 × 4 bottom rail to fit snugly between each pair of posts. Position the rails flat between the posts, anywhere from slightly above grade level to 12 inches up. Toenail the bottom rails into place with one 10-penny common nail driven through the fence post and into the end of the rail on each side. Use a level to keep the rails even.

When the rails are in place, measure and cut the fence boards. The boards should be of uniform length, as long as the distance from the bottom of the bottom rail to the top of the top rail, as measured at one of the posts. Use 1 × 4 or 1 × 6 fence boards, as desired. Starting at one end, nail the boards to one side of the rails, with a space equal to a single board width between each; use a board as a spacer as you work. Secure each board to the rails with two 8-penny galvanized common nails at the top and two at the bottom. Nail the tops first, flush with the top of the top rail; then nail the bottoms, pulling or pushing the bottom rail into alignment as you work.

When the boards are nailed all along

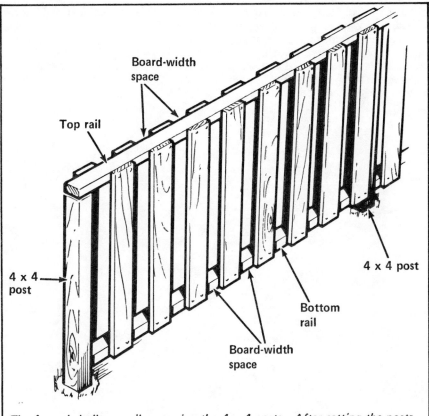

Board-width space

Top rail

4 x 4 post

4 x 4 post

Bottom rail

Board-width space

The fence is built on rails spanning the 4 x 4 posts. After setting the posts, nail the top and bottom rails into place; then nail fence boards on alternate sides of the rails, with a board's width between them.

one side of the fence, nail alternate fence boards to the other side of the rails, positioning the boards to cover the spaces left by the boards on the opposite side of the fence. Keep the top and bottom of each board flush with the top and bottom rails.

To complete the fence, repeat to build each line of fence, setting posts, adding rails, and then securing fence boards as above.

Replace a Broken Fence Picket

Replacing an unsightly broken fence picket is a snap. **Tools:** measuring rule, pencil, handsaw or power saw, carpenters' square; coping, saber, or keyhole saw; hammer, paintbrush. **Materials:** replacement board the same width as the fence pickets, 8-penny galvanized nails; exterior primer and paint, or stain. **Time:** about 30 to 40 minutes, plus drying time.

Measure one of the unbroken pickets to get the correct width and length; use a board the same width as the pickets or cut down a wider one. Measure and mark the board and cut it to the correct size, using a handsaw or a power saw; use a carpenters' square to make sure your cuts are straight.

Set the cut board against an unbroken picket and trace the picket top onto the new board. Cut the picket top to match the others; for a curved top use a coping, saber, or keyhole saw. If the fence is painted, give the new picket a coat of top-quality exterior primer; leave the picket bare if it is to be stained.

Remove the broken picket by hammering and prying it away from the fence rails. Pull out any nails left in the fence rails, set the picket against the fence rail, align it properly, and nail it firmly into place with 8-penny galvanized nails. Give the new picket a coat of paint or stain to match the rest of the fence.

Car

Clean and Regap Spark Plugs

As a general rule, spark plugs should be cleaned or replaced and regapped about once every six months or 6,000 miles for older cars, about once every nine months or 9,000 miles for late-model cars. It's a time-consuming job, but it requires no special mechanical skill. **Tools:** spark plug ratchet wrench, extension, and spark plug socket; safety goggles, wire brush, ignition point file, round-wire spark plug gapping gauge. **Materials:** spark plugs, clean rags, solvent or lacquer thinner, short piece of heater hose. **Time:** about 1 hour.

Don't try to work while the engine is hot. Before you start, mark the spark plug wires or cables with tape so you'll be able to replace them correctly. For each plug, hold the cable by the cap shield or boot; twist slightly and pull out gently. Do *not* jerk the cables.

Next, loosen the spark plugs. Use a ratchet wrench with a spark plug socket. Turn each plug counterclockwise, making only one or two full turns; do not remove the plugs yet. Turn the ignition switch for a few seconds to crank the engine, to remove any loose dirt from the plugs.

With the socket wrench, take the spark plugs out one at a time. Set them down in order as you take them out; they must be replaced in the same order after they're cleaned and regapped.

Now examine the plugs. In general, if a spark plug's ground electrode is intact, the plug can probably be cleaned and reused. If the electrode is badly worn or corroded, the plug should be replaced. Some common plug conditions include:

Plug in good condition. Insulator tip grayish-brown or tan; little or no wear on electrodes. Plug can be gapped and reused.

Carbon fouling. Electrodes and insulator tip covered with soft soot. This means plug temperature is too low; possible causes include a plug in the wrong heat range, too rich air-fuel mix, sticking choke, clogged air filter, retarded engine timing, weak ignition, or stop-and-go driving. If only one plug is affected, plug cable could be worn or damaged. Clean and gap plug; make sure it is in the proper heat range.

Oil fouling. Oil on electrodes, insulator tip, and shell. This means oil is leaking into the combustion chamber; the cause could be worn piston rings or engine valve guides, defective PCV valve, or old engine. Clean and gap plug. Problem can be solved temporarily by use of plugs in slightly hotter range.

Splash fouling. Spots of oil or dirt on electrodes, insulator tip, and shell, caused by loosening of built-up deposits; tune-up is overdue. Clean and gap plug.

Ash fouling. Heavy tan or white ash deposits on electrodes and insulator tip, caused by incomplete fuel or oil combustion. Clean and gap plug; change brand of gas used. If problem persists, change type of oil used; change oil filter.

Insulator glazing. Hard, dark glaze on insulator tip. Combustion deposits are melting on insulator instead of burning off; this can be caused by hard, fast acceleration, or by a plug in the wrong heat range. Replace with new plug and regap. If problem persists, replace with plug in slightly colder range.

Detonation (knocking, pinging). Insulator tip cracked or broken. This indicates explosions in the combustion chamber, rather than steady burning, and resultant mechanical shock. Possible causes include improper ignition timing, gas of too low octane, too lean air-fuel mix, or damage to center plug electrode. Replace with new plug and regap. Determine cause of problem and correct.

Pre-ignition. Tip of ground electrode missing; hard, dark deposits on insulator tip and stub of ground electrode. Fuel charge is igniting prior to timed spark; possible causes include combustion chamber deposits, hot spots in combustion chamber, piston scuffing (can result from poor lubrication or improper clearance of engine parts), detonation, cross-firing between plugs, or plug in too hot a range. Replace with new plug and regap; determine cause of problem and correct.

Overheating. Both electrodes corroded, insulator tip white and clean, and possibly cracked or blistered. This means plug temperature is too high; plug is probably in too hot a range. Causes could also include too lean air-fuel mix, over-advanced engine timing, or sticking heat riser valve. Replace with new plug and regap; determine cause of problem and correct. If necessary, replace with colder plug.

Worn-out plug. Insulator tip brownish-gray, electrodes worn and rounded. Heat range is correct, but proper gapping is not possible. Replace with new plug and regap.

Examine each plug and decide whether to clean and regap it or replace it. If the plugs are near the end of their life, it's better to install new ones.

To clean usable plugs, wipe off oil and grease with a clean rag, using a small amount of solvent if necessary. Dry thoroughly with a clean rag. Wearing safety goggles, wire-brush threads and electrodes to remove any deposits. With ignition point file, file the inside flat surface of the ground electrode until it is shiny; file the center electrode until it is clean and flat.

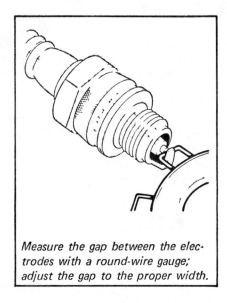

Measure the gap between the electrodes with a round-wire gauge; adjust the gap to the proper width.

Now regap the plugs—new spark plugs must also be regapped, as well as old ones. Make sure you're using the proper plugs; many electronic ignition systems require wide-gap plugs. Don't try to use narrow-gap plugs if wide-gap plugs are specified in your owner's manual, or wide-gap plugs if narrow-gap are specified.

Use a round-wire spark plug gapping gauge to measure the gap between the electrodes of each plug. Your owner's manual or service manual should list the correct gap width. Use the bending tool on the gauge to adjust the gap to the proper width.

Finally, install the spark plugs. With a clean rag, wipe the plug sockets in the engine to remove any loose dirt. Screw in each plug, tightening by hand; if you can't get it started, use a short piece of heater hose over the end of the plug as a handle. With the ratchet wrench, tighten each plug another ¼ to ½ turn. Tapered plugs have no gaskets; if your car uses these plugs, tighten only about ¼ turn.

Reconnect the spark plug cables, making sure you keep them in the correct order. To do this, push the boot of each cable firmly over the top of the corresponding plug. Remove all tape markers.

Test Your Battery

Testing your car's battery periodically is a good way to keep it from going dead when you least expect it. **Tools:** battery hydrometer. **Materials:** plain water, rag, toothpicks. **Time:** about 10 to 15 minutes.

Raise the hood of the car and remove the battery's vent caps. Check the fluid level. If it's too low, add plain water, run the car for at least 15 minutes, and allow it to cool for about the same period before you begin to test it.

If the level of battery fluid is correct, insert the hydrometer into each cell. Squeeze the hydrometer's bulb and release it to suck enough fluid to obtain

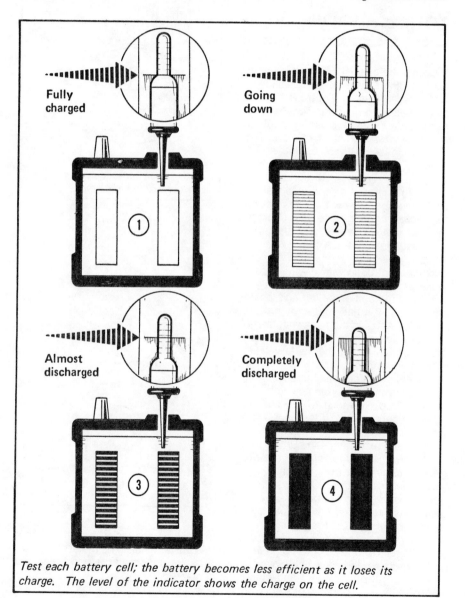

Fully charged

Going down

Almost discharged

Completely discharged

Test each battery cell; the battery becomes less efficient as it loses its charge. The level of the indicator shows the charge on the cell.

a reading. Compare the reading for each cell with the illustration to determine the state of your battery.

Before replacing the vent caps, clean them with a rag; clean the vent holes with toothpicks. Then replace the caps and close the hood.

Clean Your Battery

One of the easiest jobs to keep your car's starting system in top condition is cleaning your battery. **Tools:** wrench or pliers, battery terminal puller, battery-terminal-and-clamp cleaning tool or steel wool, wire brush. **Materials:** old clothes, masking tape, baking soda, water, pint container, clean rags, petroleum jelly. **Time:** about ½ hour.

Caution: Don't smoke or expose the battery to open flame; batteries emit a flammable and explosive gas. Change into old clothes before you start this task. Batteries contain a corrosive acid, so don't let it touch your skin. If it does, wash it off at once with plenty of cool water.

Raise the hood of the car and locate the battery. If it has vent caps on top, cover the holes in the caps with masking tape to prevent cleaning solution from contaminating the battery fluid. This step isn't necessary for maintenance-free batteries without caps.

Remove the cable clamps from the battery. Use a wrench to loosen nut-and-bolt connections; if the cables are connected by spring-type clamps with prongs, squeeze them with pliers to free them. *Remove the clamp on the ground cable first,* using a battery terminal puller. **Caution:** *On most cars, this is the negative (−) cable. On cars with positive-ground electrical systems, however, it is the positive (+) cable. If your car has a positive-ground system, remove the positive cable first.*

Now remove the other cable clamp.

Use a battery-terminal-and-clamp cleaning tool, a wire brush or steel wool

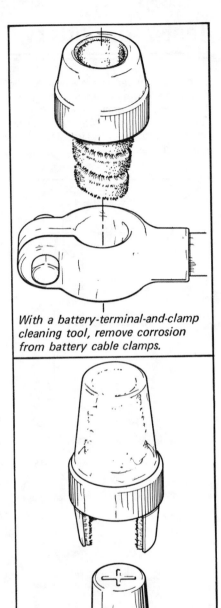

With a battery-terminal-and-clamp cleaning tool, remove corrosion from battery cable clamps.

Strip corrosion from the terminals with the cleaning tool, rubbing until the metal is shiny.

to clean any corrosion from the clamps and the terminals. The metal parts must be shiny to provide a good electrical contact.

Mix ½ cup of baking soda in a pint of

water. Pour the soda solution over the top of the battery and wait until it stops fizzing and foaming. Scrub the top of the battery with a stiff wire brush to remove dirt, grease, and corrosion; rinse the battery thoroughly with water and dry it with a rag.

Replace the cable clamps at the proper terminals, securing the *ungrounded* cable first—the opposite of the way you disconnected the cables—and then the grounded cable, the one connected to the car's frame or engine. Finally, remove the masking tape from the battery vent caps and coat the ends of the cables and the clamps with petroleum jelly to protect them from corrosion.

Charge Your Battery

Whenever your car's battery needs recharging, give it a slow charge. Although this takes 12 hours or more, there's less chance of damaging the battery than with a quick charge, and the battery will hold the charge longer. **Tools:** battery charger, pliers or wrench, battery .terminal puller. **Materials:** steel wool, petroleum jelly, rag. **Time:** charging time varies, depending on state of battery; about 10 minutes setup time.

Maintenance-free battery. If your car is equipped with a maintenance-free battery, check the state of the battery's charge by looking at its test indicator. If there is a green dot, the battery is charged. If the indicator is light or bright, replace the battery; don't attempt to charge it. If, however, the indicator is dark, the battery should be charged until a green dot appears in the indicator.

Conventional battery. Before charging a conventional battery, remove the vent caps from the battery and check to see that the battery fluid is at the correct level. If the level is low,

add plain water, but don't overfill the battery.

Charging the battery. If you plan to charge the battery while it's in the car, disconnect the negative (−) cable first, then the positive (+) cable. NOTE: On cars with positive-ground electrical systems, disconnect the positive cable first. Use pliers to remove spring-type cable clamps; use a wrench for clamps with nuts. If necessary, use a battery terminal puller to pull the clamps off the terminals.

Before connecting the charger, clean the battery terminals with steel wool. Then clamp the positive cable of the battery charger to the positive battery terminal, then the negative cable of the charger to the negative terminal of the battery.

Plug the battery charger in and turn it on. Set the charger for the voltage of your battery; usually this is 12 volts. If the charger is adjustable, set it to charge at a 5- to 15-amp rate.

If the charger doesn't have an automatic cutoff feature, you'll have to check progress hourly with a hydrometer that has a thermometer. For a maintenance-free battery, check the test indicator. **Caution:** *Don't allow the temperature to exceed 125° F. If the fluid in the battery cells bubbles actively, lower the rate of charge at once.*

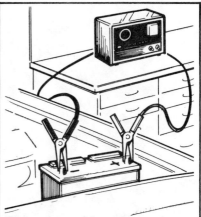

Clamp the positive cable to the positive terminal, the negative cable to the negative terminal.

After the battery has been fully charged, turn off the charger and disconnect the cables—positive cables first, then negative. Reconnect the battery cables—positive cable first. On a conventional battery, replace the vent cap. Tighten the battery cable clamps securely and coat the connections with petroleum jelly.

Adjust Tire Air Pressure

Improper tire inflation is one of the main causes of excessive tire wear, so it pays to check your car's tires regularly. **Tools:** tire pressure gauge. **Materials:** compressed air. **Time:** about 10 to 15 minutes.

Before checking tire pressure, you'll have to know the recommended pressure for your car's tires; it varies according to the size of car you own, the load it normally carries, the type of tires, and whether you have front- or rear-wheel drive. This information is listed in your owner's manual, and perhaps also on a sticker inside the glove compartment.

Check the tire pressure when the tires are cool. If you check a properly inflated tire after extended driving, it will indicate an overinflated condition because it's hot, but when the tire cools, the pressure will return to normal.

Remove the cap on the tire's air valve; it unscrews counterclockwise. Place the end of your tire pressure gauge on the valve and press down to obtain a pressure reading in pounds per square inch (psi) on the gauge's indicator. If the pressure is correct, replace the tire air valve cap.

If the tire pressure is too high, depress the pin in the center of the valve and release some air; recheck the pressure with the gauge. Repeat, letting out a little air at a time, until the pressure is correct.

If the tire is underinflated, place the end of the compressed air supply hose over the tire's air valve and press down. If the nozzle of the hose is equipped with a lever, squeeze it to release air into the tire; hoses without a lever supply air when you press the end of the nozzle down on the tire's air valve.

If the air supply hose has an indicator that shows the amount of air pressure in your tires, use it only as a general guide; such gauges are often inaccurate. Check the pressure with your own pressure gauge. Add air until you reach the proper tire pressure.

When the gauge shows the proper inflation for the tire, replace the air valve cap, screwing it on clockwise. Repeat the procedure for each tire.

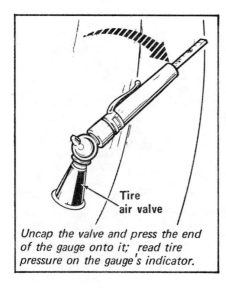

Tire air valve

Uncap the valve and press the end of the gauge onto it; read tire pressure on the gauge's indicator.

Check the Motor Oil

Oil is the lifeblood of your car's engine. Check the motor oil frequently, perhaps every time you fill the gas tank. **Tools:** oil filler spout or can opener and funnel. **Materials:** motor oil, rag. **Time:** about 5 minutes.

Park the car on a level site. Before checking the level of the motor oil, shut the engine off and wait about 3 minutes so the oil can drain into the oil pan.

Raise the hood and locate the dipstick; it should be on one side of the engine. Remove the dipstick and wipe the end with a clean rag. Replace the dipstick completely, and then remove it again.

Check the marks on the end. If the level reaches the *full* mark or is close to it, replace the dipstick and close the hood.

If, however, the level is at or below the mark that indicates you should add 1 quart, replace the dipstick and locate the motor oil filler cap. This cap is usually located on the engine valve cover. Generally, the cap twists off, but on some cars it may pull out. Remove the cap.

Buy a quart of oil of a type recommended in your owner's manual; open the can and pour its contents through a filler spout or a funnel into the oil filler opening. When the can is empty, remove it, replace the cap, and close the hood.

Check Automatic Transmission Fluid

You can avoid many costly troubles with your car's automatic transmission if you check the fluid level and condition periodically. **Tools:** funnel. **Materials:** automatic transmission fluid, rag. **Time:** about 10 minutes.

Start the car and let it run for about 15 minutes so that it reaches normal operating temperature. Park the car on a level site, but don't turn off the engine; leave it running. Engage the parking brake and put the car in park or neutral.

Raise the hood and locate the transmission dipstick; it's similar to the one used for checking the motor oil. Usually it's near the firewall (the rear of the engine) on the passenger side of the car. *Caution: Be careful working in the en-*

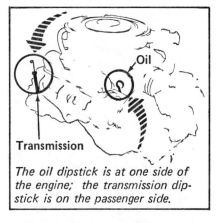

The oil dipstick is at one side of the engine; the transmission dipstick is on the passenger side.

gine compartment. Avoid moving components and touching hot parts of the engine.

Remove the dipstick and wipe the end with a clean rag. Replace the dipstick completely, then remove it again.

Look at the fluid on the dipstick. Normal automatic transmission fluid is red or green. If it's yellowish-brown or brown, it should be changed—a job for a mechanic. If the fluid is dark brown and has a strong burnt odor, your transmission is damaged—you need professional transmission service.

Check the fluid level on the end of the dipstick; it should be somewhere between the *low* (or *add*) and *full* marks. If the level is below the *low* mark, insert a funnel into the dipstick housing. Add transmission fluid of the type recommended in your owner's manual to bring the fluid level up between the two marks. Be careful not to add too much; excess fluid can damage the transmission.

Replace the dipstick, close the hood, and turn off the engine.

Check Your Coolant

The coolant in your car's cooling system—a mixture of water and antifreeze—helps keep the engine from overheating in hot weather and from freezing in cold weather. Year-round, inhibitors in the coolant help prevent the system from clogging due to rust and corrosion. Check your coolant periodically to keep the cooling system working well. **Tools:** antifreeze tester, pliers, gallon container. **Materials:** water, antifreeze, rags. **Time:** about 15 to 30 minutes.

If the car has been standing for a long time and the engine is cold, start the car and run the engine for about 15 minutes to allow it to reach normal operating temperature. Don't shut the engine off; it must be running to obtain an accurate reading. If the engine is too warm, shut off the engine, raise the hood, and wait about 20 minutes; then start the car again.

Carefully begin to remove the radiator's pressure cap. *Caution: The coolant is hot and under pressure; follow these precautions. Place heavy rags over the cap for protection and turn the cap very slowly counterclockwise. Be prepared to get out of the way in case hot coolant sprays out.* Some caps have a lever, which is flipped up to relieve pressure; others are turned one notch to lower the pressure and then pushed down and turned further to remove them. Be careful with either type.

With the radiator cap off, examine the level of the coolant in the radiator by looking down the filler opening. The level should be about 1 to 1½ inches below the neck of the filler, or as marked on the radiator tank; check your owner's manual for exact specifications. If the coolant is clean and clear, go ahead; otherwise, if the coolant is rusty or dirty, it should be replaced—follow the procedure outlined in "Flush Your Cooling System."

The antifreeze tester is a specially scaled hydrometer. Squeeze the bulb, insert the tester into the radiator, and release the pressure on the bulb to draw in a sample of coolant. Examine the scale on the tester and compare it with the floating indicator or with the number of floating balls. Most testers have a chart that tells you, from the sample, how much antifreeze protec-

tion you have in the radiator.

If the tester reading shows that you have protection down to --20° F, your coolant should be sufficient for most regions. But if you live in an extremely cold region, you may want to get the system down to −34° F. To do this, shut off the engine; carefully open the radiator drain petcock with pliers and drain 2 quarts of coolant into a container. *Caution: The coolant is hot; don't scald yourself!* Then close the petcock and add 2 quarts of pure antifreeze.

If the tester reading is between +10° F and −19° F, you'll have to drain as much as 4 quarts of coolant and replace it with pure antifreeze. If the reading is +11° F or higher, your best course is to drain the entire cooling system and refill it with a half-and-half mixture of water and antifreeze. Your owner's manual will indicate how much coolant your car's cooling system holds.

If your cooling system is protected to the proper degree, but the level of the coolant is low, add a 50/50 mixture of water and antifreeze to the radiator. Adding plain water would dilute the coolant and reduce the system's degree of protection.

Draw coolant into the hydrometer; compare the floating balls or indicator with the tester's chart.

NOTE: Late-model cars usually have a coolant recovery, or reserve, tank system that is connected to the radiator. It indicates the level of coolant in the system—with the engine cold or warm—by means of a transparent plastic reservoir. If you have such a system, you can add the mixture to this tank.

After checking the coolant, and adding additional water and antifreeze if necessary, replace the radiator pressure cap properly. Start the engine to mix the coolant and, finally, check to be sure that the level is correct.

Make Your Own Antifreeze

If you've bought a gallon or two of antifreeze recently, you know it's not cheap. Mix your own for an inexpensive and just as effective alternative. **Equipment:** measuring cup, funnel, gallon container with cap. **Ingredients:** glycerin, denatured alcohol, water. Buy the ingredients at a pharmacy. **Yield:** 1 gallon.

Measure 2 cups of glycerin and 4 cups of denatured alcohol into a 1-gallon container. Fill the container with water, cap it tightly, and shake well.

Mix the antifreeze with the proper amount of water for the degree of coolant system protection desired.

Flush Your Cooling System

Many cars overheat because their owners ignore the inexpensive maintenance needed by the cooling system. Check your owner's manual and drain, flush, and replenish the cooling system when your car requires it. **Tools:** large pan, pliers, utility knife, screwdriver, garden hose. **Materials:** flushing tee kit, antifreeze, rags. **Time:** about 1 hour.

The easiest way to flush the cooling system is to install a flushing tee in a heater hose. Flushing tee kits cost only a few dollars and take only about 10 minutes to install. Once you've installed the tee, flushing the cooling system becomes a very easy and fast procedure.

Caution: Don't attempt this job if the engine is warm. Allow the car to cool completely, because you'll have to completely drain the radiator coolant.

When the car's engine is cool, raise the hood, place a large pan under the radiator's drain petcock, and remove the radiator cap. Using pliers, open the radiator petcock at the bottom of the radiator. Let the coolant drain completely. After the coolant has been drained, close and tighten the petcock, but leave the radiator cap off.

Locate the heater hoses between the engine and the firewall. There are two of these hoses. One runs to the water pump, the other one—this is the one you're looking for—runs from the firewall to the engine block.

Near the firewall, use a sharp knife to cut the heater hose going to the engine block. At this point in the hose, insert the flushing tee from the kit. Secure the flushing tee in the hose with two clamps provided with the kit. The kit will also contain a cap to seal off the flushing tee fitting when you aren't using it, but leave the cap off for now.

Insert the splash pipe that came with the kit into the radiator filler opening; angle the pipe so that the flow of water will be directed to the front and away from the engine. Attach a garden hose to the flushing tee in the heater hose, and turn on the water full force. The coolant in the engine will be forced back through the system, up through the radiator, and out the splash pipe. Run the water until the flow out of the radiator is clean and colorless, indicating that the system is clean.

Turn off the water and disconnect the garden hose from the flushing tee, but don't close the flushing tee. Pour the correct amount of pure antifreeze—

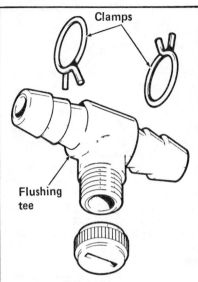

The flushing tee, with cap and clamps, is installed in the heater hose that runs to the engine block.

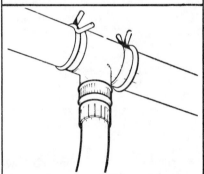

Insert the arms of the tee into the ends of the heater hose, clamp them, and attach a garden hose.

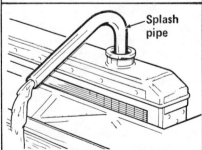

Insert the splash pipe into the radiator opening, angled away from the engine, and turn on the water.

according to your owner's manual—into your car's cooling system through the radiator opening; the antifreeze will displace the water in the system, which will flow out through the flushing tee. When you've added the proper amount of pure antifreeze for the degree of protection you require, close the flushing tee with its cap.

Finally, replace the radiator cap, close the hood, and start the car to mix the coolant in the cooling system.

Check Power Steering Fluid

If your car is equipped with power steering, the fluid level in the power steering pump should be checked often, at regular intervals. It only takes a minute or two and can be quickly done whenever you raise the hood. **Tools:** wrench, tire iron. **Materials:** power steering fluid, rag. **Time:** less than 5 minutes, once car is at normal operating temperature.

To check the power steering fluid level, start the car and run it for about 15 minutes or so, until it reaches normal operating temperature. Straighten the wheels and turn the engine off. Raise the hood and locate the power steering pump. Wipe the cap of the pump's filler to prevent any dirt from getting into the reservoir, then remove the cap.

Most power steering units have a dipstick built into the filler cap; check to see if the fluid level is up to the *full* mark. If the level is low, pour in more power steering fluid, of the type recommended in your owner's manual, until the dipstick registers at the *full* level.

If your car's power steering unit doesn't have a dipstick, check level of fluid in the reservoir; it should be about 1 inch below the filler opening. In either type of unit, if the fluid level is very low, the power steering system should be

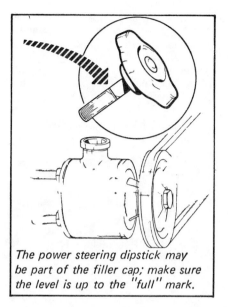

The power steering dipstick may be part of the filler cap; make sure the level is up to the "full" mark.

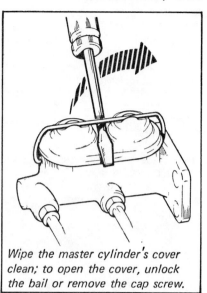

Wipe the master cylinder's cover clean; to open the cover, unlock the bail or remove the cap screw.

checked professionally for leaks.

When you check the fluid, take a look at hose connections between the pump and the steering box to make sure they're in good condition; have the hoses replaced if they're damaged. Also depress the drive belt on the pump's pulley—for correct tension, the belt should depress about ½ inch. Adjust the tension, if necessary, by loosening the bolt on the power steering unit's support bracket and apply pressure between the power steering unit and the engine with your car's tire iron; then tighten the bolt and check the tension again.

Check Your Brake Fluid

Your car's master cylinder is the main reservoir for the brake system's hydraulic fluid. Check the fluid level periodically; loss of fluid could indicate a leak in the brake system. **Tools:** screwdriver. **Materials:** clean rag, hydraulic brake fluid. **Time:** about 10 to 15 minutes.

With the engine off and the parking brake engaged, raise the hood. Locate the master cylinder; it's in the engine compartment on the side of the driver's seat. The master cylinder is connected to the brake pedal by a rod.

Wipe the master cylinder's cover with a clean rag. Using a screwdriver, open the cover; it's secured either by a bail-type locking device or by a cap screw.

Check the level of fluid in the reservoir; it should be within ¼ inch of the top. If the fluid level is low, add hydraulic blake fluid to within ¼ inch of the

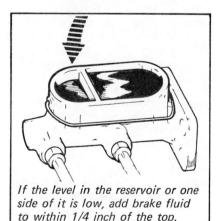

If the level in the reservoir or one side of it is low, add brake fluid to within 1/4 inch of the top.

top. Then replace the cover, secure it, and close the hood.

Now get into the car. If you have power brakes, apply and release the brake pedal five or six times to exhaust the vacuum pressure in the system. If you have manual brakes, this step is not necessary.

Pump the brake pedal several times and then keep a steady pressure on the pedal with your foot for about 30 seconds. If the pedal recedes under this steady pressure something is wrong with the master cylinder. If this is the case, have a qualified mechanic check your brake system.

Finally, if you added brake fluid to the master cylinder, recheck it in a few days; a small fluid loss is normal.

Rotate Your Tires

The four tires of a car usually wear unevenly. To level out any unevenness that may develop and thus extend their life, rotate them—change their position on the car's wheels—periodically. Follow the recommendations for tire rotation in the owner's manual for your car. **Tools:** screwdriver and socket wrench or jack handle, four wheel chocks, jack, four safety jack stands. **Materials:** none. **Time:** about 1 hour.

NOTE: This procedure uses four safety jack stands to support the car while you rotate the tires. If you don't have jack stands, you will have to use the procedure outlined in "Change a Tire," which will nearly double the time required for this task.

Park your car on a level site and put it in park. Remove all the wheel covers, using a screwdriver or the pointed end of a jack handle to pry them off.

Using the lug wrench end of the jack handle or a socket wrench, loosen the lug nuts on all four wheels about one turn. Most nuts loosen counterclockwise, but some cars have nuts that loosen clockwise. Such lug nuts may have the letter L on them to indicate a left-hand thread.

Wedge a wheel chock under the front and the rear of each rear wheel. Set the jack into position at the front of the car and jack up the car until the front wheels are off the ground. Carefully place two safety jack stands under the axle housing at the front of the car to support it. Remove the jack.

Set the jack into position at the rear of the car and jack up the rear until the wheels are off the ground. Carefully place two jack stands under the rear axle housing to support the car. Remove the jack.

Now remove the lug nuts from all four wheels and lift the tires off the car. Be sure to keep track of which tires went where. Reposition the tires according to the type of tires you have. NOTE: Stowaway or space-saver tires should never be included in a rotation plan; they are designed for emergency use only.

Radial or bias-belted tires. If you're rotating all four tires, move them from front to back and from back to front on the *same* side of the car. If you're using a spare tire as part of the rotation, move the spare to the right rear wheel, the right rear tire to the right front wheel, the right front tire to the spare's position, the left rear tire to the left front wheel, and the left front tire to the left rear wheel.

NOTE: If you have a car with front-wheel drive and radial tires, some tire makers recommend that you don't rotate the tires at all. These manufacturers claim that the rear radial tires will probably last the life of the car if they're not rotated.

Conventional (bias) tires. If you're rotating all four tires, move the right rear tire to the left front wheel, the left front tire to the left rear wheel, the left rear tire to the right front wheel, and the right front tire to the right rear wheel. If a spare tire is part of the rotation, move the spare to the left front wheel, the left front tire to the left rear wheel, the left rear tire to the right front wheel, the right front tire to the right rear wheel, and the right rear tire to the spare's position.

Remount all the wheels in their new

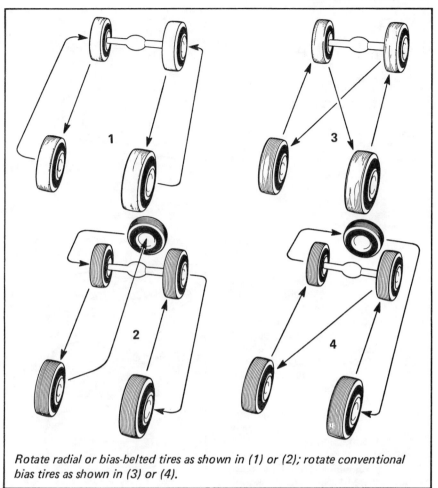

Rotate radial or bias-belted tires as shown in (1) or (2); rotate conventional bias tires as shown in (3) or (4).

positions; turn each so that its bolt holes line up with the lug bolts on the wheel mounting and set the wheel into place. Screw the lug nuts on, but only tighten them by hand. Begin with the nut at the top, tighten the nut directly opposite, and continue around the tire, tightening opposing pairs of nuts. Check to see that each wheel and lug nut has been seated properly, and make any necessary adjustments.

Raise the rear of the car with the jack and remove the two rear jack stands. Lower the rear of the car to the ground.

Wedge a wheel chock under the front and the rear of each rear wheel. Raise the front of the car with the jack and remove the two front jack stands. Lower the front of the car to the ground.

Now tighten the lug nuts on each wheel completely, using the lug or socket wrench. Start with the nut at the top and then the one directly opposite; tighten the other nuts the same way, in opposing pairs, until all lug nuts have been wrench-tightened. Finally, replace the wheel covers and remove the chocks.

After rotating the tires, check and adjust the air pressure in each one, following the procedure outlined in "Adjust Tire Air Pressure." You may also have to have your wheels rebalanced after rotating the tires, especially if they were originally balanced while on the car.

Change Your Air Filter Element

Change your car's air filter element when it's dirty, to keep the engine running efficiently and on less gasoline. Your owner's manual will tell you how often this maintenance job should be performed. **Tools:** wrench. **Materials:** clean rags, petroleum-based solvent, replacement paper or polyurethane air filter element of the same type as the old one, motor oil. **Time:** about 10 to 30 minutes.

Paper air filter element. On cars with a paper air filter element, raise the hood and remove the filter housing cover. This cover is usually secured by a wing nut. It may, however, be held by a hex nut; if so, use a wrench to loosen it. Lift the cover and remove it. There may be a gasket under the cover; if so, remove this too. Then lift out the filter element inside.

Examine the interior of the filter housing. If it's dirty, wipe the inside with a clean rag dipped in petroleum-based solvent. *Caution: Don't use gasoline!*

Set the replacement filter element into position and replace the gasket, if any, and the filter housing cover. Make sure the cover is seated properly and secure it with the wing nut or hex nut.

Polyurethane air filter element. Some newer cars use filters made of polyurethane stretched around a metal support screen. Unless the filter element is damaged, it can be washed—not replaced.

Raise the hood and remove the air filter housing cover as above. Remove the polyurethane filter element from its screen. If the filter element is damaged, replace it with a new one of the same type. If it can be reused, wash it in a petroleum-based solvent. Squeeze the excess solvent out of the element and dip the element in clean motor oil. Squeeze excess oil out of the element.

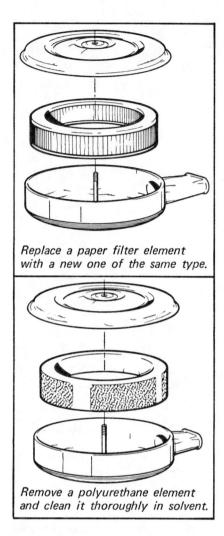

Replace a paper filter element with a new one of the same type.

Remove a polyurethane element and clean it thoroughly in solvent.

Stretch the element over its screen, replace the assembly in the filter housing, and resecure the cover, making sure it's seated properly.

Other types of elements. Some older models use a wire mesh filter that is soaked in a bath of motor oil in the filter housing. On such cars, the entire housing must be removed. It is lifted out much like other air filters.

Empty the dirty oil out of the housing and clean the housing with a petroleum-based solvent. Replace the wire mesh, reinstall the housing, and fill the housing with fresh motor oil. Finally, resecure the filter housing cover.

Change Your Oil and Oil Filter

You can save quite a bit of money and extend the life of your car's engine by changing its oil and oil filter, at the recommended intervals or when necessary. **Tools:** jack and two jack stands or two ramps and wheel chocks, oil drain pan, oil filter wrench. **Materials:** replacement oil filter, motor oil, rags. **Time:** about 30 to 45 minutes.

Start the car and run the engine for about 15 minutes to allow it to reach normal operating temperature. Raise the front end of the car. **Caution:** *Don't work under the car while it's raised with a bumper jack. Use a jack only to put the front of the car on a pair of jack stands; or use a pair of auto ramps, and block the rear wheels.*

Position the oil drain pan under the oil drain plug; it's located under the engine.

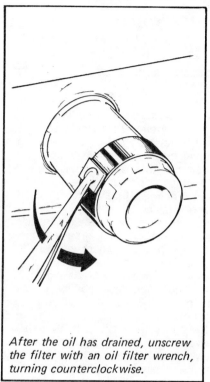

After the oil has drained, unscrew the filter with an oil filter wrench, turning counterclockwise.

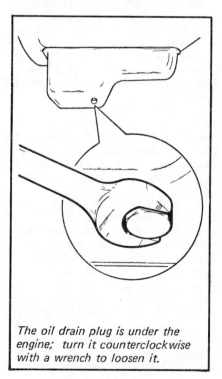

The oil drain plug is under the engine; turn it counterclockwise with a wrench to loosen it.

Using a wrench, loosen—don't remove yet—the drain plug; it turns counterclockwise. Move out of the way so hot oil won't splash or drip on you, and carefully remove the plug. After all the oil has drained into the pan, replace the plug and tighten it securely.

Using an oil filter wrench, unscrew the filter counterclockwise. If the filter is removed from underneath the car, position the drain pan to catch any oil. Rub a little fresh motor oil on the oil filter gasket on top of the replacement filter. Screw the filter on, but only hand-tighten it—don't use the wrench.

Lower the car. Remove the oil filler cap on the engine. Refill the engine with the correct amount and type of motor oil specified in your owner's manual; because you've changed the filter, add an extra quart. Replace the oil filler cap.

Start the car and look for leaks at the drain plug and the oil filter. Stop the engine, wait about 5 minutes, and final-check the oil level on the dipstick.

Lubricate the Chassis

You can save money and prolong your car's life by lubricating the chassis yourself. **Tools:** wheel chocks, screw or hydraulic jack, safety jack stands, cartridge-type grease gun, trouble light, wrench. **Materials:** molybdenum disulphide-type chassis grease, paper towels or rags, grease fittings. **Time:** about 1 hour.

Before beginning to lube the chassis, determine how many grease fittings your car has and where they are located. This can be done by consulting the service manual for your car or by checking a lubrication chart for your car at a friendly service station. NOTE: Older models have numerous fittings on steering linkage, front suspension, and drive train; newer models have only a few fittings. Late-model cars have a number of plugs capping grease points. These points don't need lubrication until your car has traveled a certain number of miles; at that point, the plugs are replaced with standard grease fittings and the fittings are lubricated as usual.

If your car has automatic transmission, put it in "Park"; a manual transmission should be placed in first gear. Engage the emergency brake and block the back of the rear wheels with chocks. Jack the car's front end up and rest the vehicle solidly on safety jack stands. To determine how to jack it up, note the location of the coil spring. If it's above the control arm, lift from below the frame. If it's between the two control arms, jack from under the lower control arm. *Caution: Make sure the car is safely supported by the jack stands before sliding under the car!*

Slide under the vehicle with your grease gun, trouble light, and paper towels or rags. Locate each grease fitting, wipe it clean, engage the grease gun on the fitting, and pump in the molybdenum disulphide grease. Do *not* wipe residual grease off the fitting.

Grease fitting

Grease gun

At each fitting, engage the grease gun and pump grease in; stop pumping when the fitting is full.

If grease squirts out around the tip of the gun, it may not be properly engaged. Remove it from the fitting, wipe the fitting clean, and try again. If the problem persists, the fitting may be blocked. Unscrew it with a small wrench and replace it with a new fitting of the same type.

Be sure to pump grease into ball joints and steering linkage until the joints are full. NOTE: On Ford and American Motors cars, stop pumping grease when the boot around the joint begins to swell; on Chrysler and General Motors cars, stop pumping when grease begins to ooze from bleed holes at the bottom of the joint.

Some universal joints are sealed and cannot be greased. For those that have fittings, leave the front of the car supported by jack stands, jack up the rear of the car, and use two more safety jack stands to support the car solidly. Then release the emergency brake and put the transmission in "Neutral." Rotate the drive shaft by hand to spot the fittings, and pump in grease until it begins to exude from the joint. Lower the car.

Lube Latches and Other Moving Parts

Like most car owners, you probably change the engine oil and lubricate the chassis regularly. Extend your preventive maintenance with regular spring-and-fall lubrication of hinges, latches, and other moving parts. **Tools:** none. **Materials:** white lithium grease or nonstaining stick-type lubricant, powdered graphite or silicone spray lubricant, clean rags. **Time:** about ½ hour.

Open the hood of the car and wipe the hood-latching mechanism clean. Apply white lithium grease or a stick-type lubricant to the latch and the hood-release mechanism. Do the same for the hood hinges and close the hood. Repeat the procedure for the trunk latch and hinges.

At each door, clean the latch, the strike plate, and the hinges. Apply white lithium grease or a stick-type lubricant to these parts. Open and close the doors several times to work the grease in.

Lubricate each door lock and the trunk lock with powdered graphite or a silicone spray lubricant formulated for this purpose. Wipe any excess lubricant from around the locks.

If your car's gas cap has a hinged cover, apply a little white lithium grease or stick-type lubricant to the hinges. Open and close the cover several times to work the grease in.

Apply silicone spray lubricant to weatherstripping around door frames, the luggage compartment, and to rubber moldings around windshield, rear window, and side windows to keep the rubber from cracking.

Inside the car, clean the tracks of adjustable seats and seats with backs that fold forward. Apply white lithium grease to the tracks; this is especially important for power seats. Also lubricate any seat hinges.

For windshield visor hinges, use a nonstaining stick-type lubricant. Use a light application of the same lubricant for push-pull control knobs on the dashboard. Wipe the knobs clean first; then apply the grease and work the lubricant in by moving the knob in and out a few times.

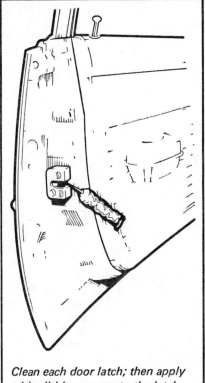

Clean each door latch; then apply white lithium grease to the latch mechanism.

Clean Your Engine

When you wash your car, do you ever think about cleaning the engine? It should be cleaned whenever it gets grimy, because dirt and grease increase the hazard of an under-hood fire, and a clean engine runs cooler and better. **Tools:** wrench, screwdriver or pliers, old paintbrush, garden hose,

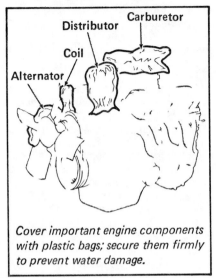

Distributor
Carburetor
Coil
Alternator

Cover important engine components with plastic bags; secure them firmly to prevent water damage.

putty knife. **Materials:** old clothes, golf tees, engine degreaser, plastic bags; transparent tape, rubber bands, or string; clean rags. **Time:** about 2 hours.

Wearing old clothes start the car. Run the engine for about 15 minutes to get it up to normal operating temperature. Turn the engine off, raise the hood of the car, and remove the air filter housing. This housing cover can usually be removed by unscrewing a wing nut on top of the housing; otherwise, use a wrench to loosen the nut.

Examine the filter housing's air intake to locate any connections. Loosen hose clamps with a screwdriver or pliers and pull off any hoses; note the location of all connections so you can reconnect the hoses properly later. If you remove any vacuum hoses, plug the open end with a golf tee to prevent dirt from entering. When all hoses have been disconnected, lift the filter housing off the carburetor.

Cover all engine components that may be affected by water with plastic bags. Be especially careful to cover the distributor and the carburetor—now fully exposed with the air filter housing removed. Other components to cover include the coil, the alternator, and the oil filter. Secure the plastic bags to the covered components with transparent tape, rubber bands, or string.

Caution: Don't smoke; some degreasers are extremely flammable. It's also a good idea to mask paintwork areas—the fenders and cowl—around the engine compartment to protect them from degreaser, because it may damage the paint finish.

Carefully following the manufacturer's instructions, coat the entire engine with degreaser. Use an old paintbrush to coat hard-to-reach areas. Let the degreaser stand for the time directed and then hose the engine clean with a garden hose. Apply degreaser again if necessary to clean extremely grimy areas; scrape stubborn spots clean with a putty knife.

When all dirt has been removed from the engine, flush it with the garden hose. Remove the plastic bags covering engine components and replace the air filter housing, being careful to reconnect all hoses correctly.

Finally, remove the masking material from around the engine compartment and close the hood. Start the engine. If you have trouble starting it, raise the hood and wipe the ignition wiring, the ignition coil, and the distributor dry with a clean rag.

Inspect Your Brakes

Unless your car has had a very recent brake overhaul, a brake inspection should be a part of every major tune-up. **Tools:** wheel chocks, lug wrench, jack, safety jack stands, screwdriver, slip-joint pliers, diagonal cutters, adjustable wrench, soft-bristled brush, torque wrench, mallet. **Materials:** clean cloths, cotter pins. **Time:** about 2 hours.

Front drum brakes. Park the car on a level surface and engage the parking brake. Remove the wheel covers and loosen the lug nuts on both front wheels with a lug wrench. Place wheel chocks behind each rear wheel, jack up the front of the car, and place a

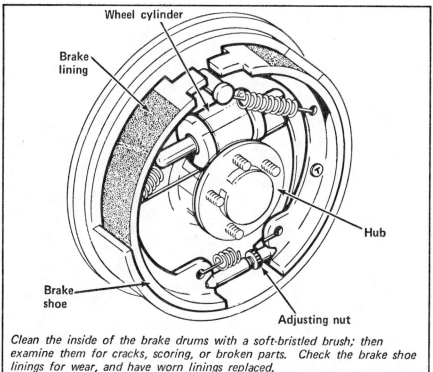

Wheel cylinder

Brake lining

Hub

Brake shoe

Adjusting nut

Clean the inside of the brake drums with a soft-bristled brush; then examine them for cracks, scoring, or broken parts. Check the brake shoe linings for wear, and have worn linings replaced.

pair of safety jack stands under the frame.

Remove the lug nuts and hub dust cover from one wheel; you can take off the cover by prying it off with a screwdriver, or by gripping it with slip-joint pliers and wiggling it free.

Use diagonal cutters to cut the cotter pin from the axle spindle, and discard the pin.

Slide the nut lock off the axle spindle, and use a large adjustable wrench to remove the adjusting nut. NOTE: Some cars use a castle nut. Slide the washer off the axle spindle.

Wiggle the brake drum; the outer wheel bearing will move outward so you can remove it. Place the bearing on a clean cloth

Grasp the brake drum firmly, rotating it slightly forward as you remove it. The brake assembly is now exposed.

Use a soft-bristled brush to remove the dust from the brake assembly and interior of the brake drum. **Caution:**

Don't breathe this dust. Also remove any accumulations of grease and dirt.

Examine the drum's friction surfaces for signs of cracks and scoring; the surface should be smooth. If they are worn in some way, they should be resurfaced by a professional machine shop.

Examine the wheel cylinder on the brake assembly for any broken parts.

Finally, examine the brake shoe lining. If the lining is riveted, see if any rivet heads are worn—level with the lining surface. If the linings are bonded, they should be at least $1/16$-inch thick. If the linings are worn, have a qualified mechanic replace them.

Replace the drum on the axle spindle; you may have to rotate it slightly. Replace the wheel bearing; the drum may have to be wiggled to seat the bearing correctly. Slip the washer over the axle spindle, and replace the adjusting nut, tightening it to 7½ foot-pounds with a torque wrench.

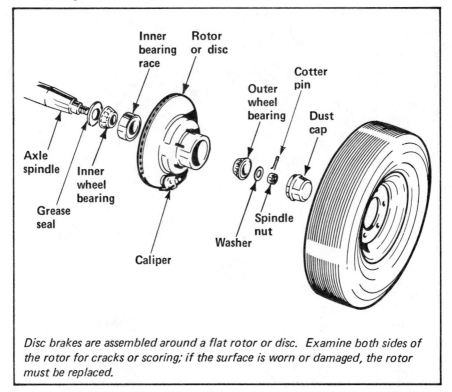

Disc brakes are assembled around a flat rotor or disc. Examine both sides of the rotor for cracks or scoring; if the surface is worn or damaged, the rotor must be replaced.

Back up the adjusting nut no more than $1/6$ turn to align the openings for the cotter pin. Insert a new cotter pin and bend the ends to secure the nut.

Slide the nut lock onto the axle spindle, and replace the dust cap, tapping it on with a mallet. Replace the wheel and lug nuts; only tighten the nuts by hand.

Repeat the procedure to examine the drum brake on the other side of the car.

After the brakes on both wheels have been examined, jack the car up, remove the jack stands, and lower the car. Tighten the lug nuts, replace the wheel covers, and remove the wheel chocks.

Front disc brakes. Follow the procedure outlined for examining "front drum brakes" until the wheels have been removed. NOTE: It's not necessary to remove the dust cap or other components.

Examine the surface on each side of the rotor for signs of cracks or scoring. NOTE: On some rotors, there's a groove

machined on the friction surface; otherwise the surface should be smooth. If a surface is worn in some way, it should be resurfaced by a professional machine shop.

Examine the brake pads on both sides of the rotor from the front of the car; they should be at least $1/16$ inch thick. Turn the front wheel and examine the pads on both sides from the rear to see that they, too, are at least $1/16$ inch thick. If there are differences between the front and rear of the pads, see a professional mechanic; the caliper may need realignment.

Repeat the procedure to examine the disc brake on the other side of the car.

After both disc brakes have been examined, replace the wheels, following the procedure outlined in "front drum brakes."

Rear drum brakes. Park the car on a level surface, and engage the parking brake. Remove the wheel covers and loosen the lug nuts on both rear wheels

Jump-Start a Car

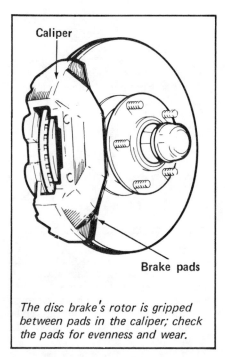

Caliper

Brake pads

The disc brake's rotor is gripped between pads in the caliper; check the pads for evenness and wear.

with a lug wrench. Place wheel chocks in front of the front wheels, jack up the rear of the car, and place safety jack stands under the frame.

Remove the lug nuts from one wheel and remove the wheel.

Grasp the brake drum firmly, rotating it slightly forward, and pull the drum free of the studs. NOTE: One stud may have a spring steel clip; if so, pry it off with a screwdriver before attempting to remove the drum. Remember to replace it later.

Clean and examine the brake assembly, following the same procedure as for the front drum brakes.

Replace the drum; you may have to rotate it slightly forward as you place it over the studs. Replace the wheel and lug nuts; only tighten the nuts by hand.

Repeat the procedure to examine the drum brake on the other side of the car.

After the drum brakes on both rear wheels have been examined, jack the car up, remove the jack stands, and lower the car. Tighten the lug nuts, replace the wheel covers, and remove the wheel chocks.

If your car has a run-down battery, don't pay for a professional service call. You can get going fast with a set of jumper cables and the help of a neighbor's car. **Tools:** hydrometer, jumper cables. **Materials:** plain or distilled water. **Time:** about 10 to 20 minutes.

Caution: To prevent serious injury to yourself and damage to your car, follow this procedure exactly, provided your car has a negative-ground electrical system. Some older cars and imported models use a positive-ground system, and a different procedure must be used to start these cars. To lessen the risk of a short circuit, take off rings and other metal jewelry. Don't let battery fluid—a corrosive acid—touch your eyes, skin, or clothes or the car's paintwork. Never expose the battery to open flame or electric sparks; batteries emit a flammable and explosive gas.

Before you start, make sure that your car's battery and the booster battery in the other car are the same voltage; both should have the same number of cells. Both cars must also use negative-ground systems.

Line up the cars nose to nose, but be careful that they don't touch. Raise the hoods of both cars and remove the battery vent caps from both batteries to check their fluid levels. If the level is low in either battery, add water, using a hydrometer. Replace the caps. *Caution: If the fluid in the run-down battery is frozen, don't try to boost the battery; this could damage it or even cause an explosion.*

If your battery is a maintenance-free battery—without vent caps—check its test indicator to determine whether it can be jump-started. If it can, go ahead; otherwise, you'll have to replace the battery following the procedure outlined in "Replace a Battery."

Turn off all electric motors and accessories in both cars. Turn off all lights except those needed to protect the car

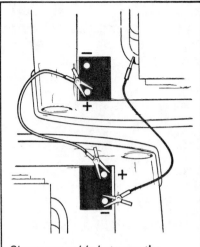

Clamp one cable between the batteries, positive to positive; clamp the other from the booster battery's negative terminal to a metal ground.

or to illuminate the working area. Turn off the ignition, apply the parking brake, and put the automatic transmission in park (put a manual transmission in neutral) in both cars.

Clamp the end of one jumper cable to the positive (+) terminal on the rundown battery. Clamp the other end of this cable to the positive (+) terminal of the booster battery. Usually, the positive terminal has a red cable connected to it and the negative terminal has a black cable.

Clamp one end of the other cable to the grounded negative (−) terminal of the booster battery. Then, to reduce the chance of an explosion due to sparks, clamp the other end of this cable to a solid, stationary metal part on the engine. If possible, make this connection at least 18 inches away from the battery; never connect the cable to a fan or any other moving part. Check the cables to make sure they won't be in the path of a fan blade, a belt, or any other moving component.

Start the car with the booster battery, and run the engine at a moderate speed; then start the car with the rundown battery. Once the jump-started

car is running, disconnect the jumper cables in the reverse order. First disconnect the negative cable from the engine; then remove the other end of this cable from the negative terminal of the booster battery. Remove the positive cable from the terminal of the discharged battery, and, finally, from the booster battery. Close the hood of the car.

Replace Wiper Blades

It's literally a snap to change your car's windshield wiper blades. Change rubber wipers twice a year—in spring and fall—or whenever they're worn or damaged. **Tools:** none. **Materials:** pair of rubber wiper refills. **Time:** about 5 to 15 minutes.

Remove the old wipers by releasing the locking device that holds the rubber blades on the blade frame. One type has a red or black plastic button or pin about a third of the way up the frame;

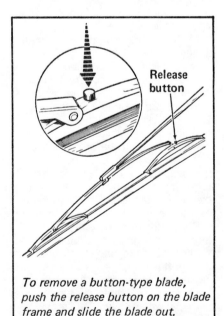

Release button

To remove a button-type blade, push the release button on the blade frame and slide the blade out.

blades use a simple locking mechanism at one end of the blade. The mechanism flexes downward out of the groove the retaining clips on the frame fit into, allowing the blade to be released and slid out of the frame.

Slide the replacement rubber wiper blades onto the wiper frame, reversing the procedure you used to remove the old blades. Be sure to engage all retaining clips on the wiper frame as you slide the rubber refill into place. Check to see that the locking device has been engaged and that the new wiper will not slide off; if you don't install the wipers properly, the frame clips could permanently scratch your car's windshield. Adjust the new blades as necessary.

Replace a Headlight

Replacing a burned-out bulb is usually an easy task, and headlights are no exception. Headlights are important to the safe operation of your car, so replace a burned-out one immediately. **Tools:** Phillips-head screwdriver. **Materials:** replacement headlight. **Time:** about 10 to 15 minutes.

Car headlights are set behind decorative trim rings or moldings, which are usually held in place by one to four Phillips-head screws. Remove the screws and lift off the trim ring over the burned-out headlight. On a few cars, a grille section, also held by Phillips-head screws, may have to be removed; loosen the screws and lift the grille section off.

After removing the molding, examine the visible screws around the headlight. The two larger ones are for adjusting the headlight's beam; don't touch these. Usually, there are three other, smaller screws that hold an inner retaining ring. This ring holds the sealed-beam headlight in place. You may not have to completely remove these screws to remove the headlight—experiment as you work. Loosen or remove the three

Some blades are held by metal tabs; squeeze the tabs together and slide the blade out.

Locking mechanism

To release a polycarbonate blade, flex the locking mechanism out of the retaining clip groove.

push the button down and slide the rubber blade out of the frame clips. Another type has two small metal tabs at one end of the blade; squeeze the tabs together and slide the blade out of the frame clips. New polycarbonate wiper

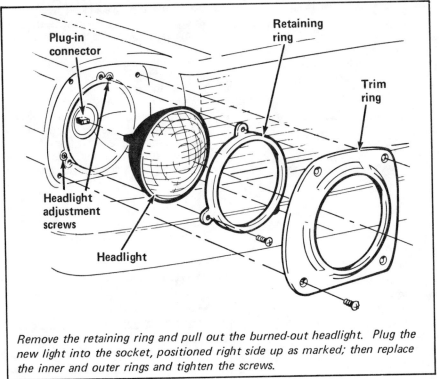

Remove the retaining ring and pull out the burned-out headlight. Plug the new light into the socket, positioned right side up as marked; then replace the inner and outer rings and tighten the screws.

Labels in figure:
- Plug-in connector
- Retaining ring
- Trim ring
- Headlight adjustment screws
- Headlight

screws and remove the retaining ring.

Pull the headlight out and disconnect the electrical plug behind the headlight; it unplugs like any appliance. Plug in the new headlight, making sure you set it into place right side up. The correct position is usually indicated by the word *top* or an arrow on the light. Finally, replace the headlight's retaining ring and tighten the screws; then replace the trim ring or molding (and the grille section, if necessary) and tighten these screws.

Change a Tire

Flat tires aren't as frequent as they used to be, but everyone who drives should know how to change a tire. It's a simple project, but there are some important safety rules to follow. **Tools:** wheel chocks or rocks, auto bumper jack. **Materials:** spare tire, emergency warning devices (flares, blinkers, etc.). **Time:** about 15 to 20 minutes.

Caution: Before attempting to change a tire after a flat, drive the car to a level site as far from the road as possible. Turn on the car's hazard-warning flashers, turn off the engine, and raise the hood. Place emergency warning devices well behind the car to warn oncoming traffic of the road hazard. Place a wheel chock or rock under the front and rear of the tire diagonally opposite the flat.

Remove the spare tire, bumper jack, and jack handle from your trunk. Assemble the jack and place it under the frame—or in the jack slot at the bumper—at the corner of the car with the flat, following the jacking instructions in the owner's manual for your car or posted somewhere in your trunk by the manufacturer. Jack up the car only high enough to exert some pressure on the jack, but not high enough to raise the flat tire off the ground.

Remove the wheel cover from the flat tire; this is usually done by wedging the pointed end of the jack handle under an edge of the wheel cover and prying it off. With the lug wrench end of the jack handle, loosen—don't remove—the lug nuts about one full turn. Most nuts loosen counterclockwise, but some cars have nuts that loosen clockwise. Such nuts may have the letter *L* on them to indicate a left-hand thread. Set the wheel cover aside, dished side up.

Jack the car up until the flat tire is off the ground. Remove the loosened lug nuts from the wheel and place them in the wheel cover so they don't get lost. Carefully lift the flat tire off and set it out of the way behind the car—don't let it roll away from the car.

Take the spare tire out of the trunk or tire housing. Turn it so that its bolt holes line up with the lug bolts on the wheel mounting and ease the wheel carefully into place.

Screw the lug nuts on, but only tighten them by hand. Begin with the nut at the top, then tighten the one directly opposite; tighten opposing pairs of nuts, until all nuts have been fastened. Check to see that the wheel and

lug nuts have been seated properly.

Lower the car, remove the jack, and tighten the nuts completely with the lug wrench. Start with the nut at the top and then the one directly opposite; tighten the other nuts the same way, in opposing pairs.

Remove the wheel chocks or rocks under the tire. Replace the wheel cover, tapping it into place, and store the bumper jack, flat tire, and emergency warning devices in the car. Close the hood and shut off the hazard-warning flashers. Don't forget to get the flat tire repaired as soon as possible.

Replace a Blown Fuse

If several lights on your car suddenly go out or if some other electrically powered component—such as the heater fan—stops working, one of the first things to check is the fuse block. Age, vibration, a momentary overload, or a more serious electrical problem can cause a fuse to blow; it's simple to replace. **Tools:** flashlight, fuse-puller. **Materials:** replacement fuse. **Time:** about 5 minutes.

Locate the fuse block in your car; check your owner's manual if you don't know where to find it. The manual also lists the fuse type and sizes you need. The fuse block is usually labeled, with each fuse's circuit and electrical rating printed on it. The block is usually under the dashboard near the steering column or on the inside firewall above the pedals; it may also be in the glove compartment or under the hood near the firewall. You may need a flashlight to find it.

Look for a blown fuse. If all the fuses are intact, the problem is elsewhere. If a fuse has burned out, remove it with a fuse-puller. Don't use a screwdriver or some other tool; it could break the fuse.

Snap a new fuse into place; if your car uses ATO-type fuses with two prongs, plug the fuse in. *Caution: Use*

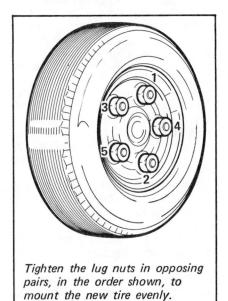

Tighten the lug nuts in opposing pairs, in the order shown, to mount the new tire evenly.

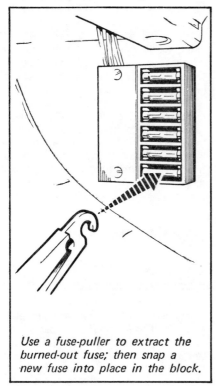

Use a fuse-puller to extract the burned-out fuse; then snap a new fuse into place in the block.

a fuse with the electrical rating specified in your owner's manual, and never substitute aluminum foil or other metal in place of a fuse; this can cause wiring to burn and start a fire.

With the new fuse in place, the circuit it protects should operate. If the replacement fuse also burns out, consult a qualified mechanic.

Replace Taillights and Other Bulbs

Taillights, turn signals, brake lights, backup lights, parking lights, side marker lights, courtesy lights, license plate lights, instrument lights, and dome lights are among the dozens of bulbs on your car that can burn out without

warning. These bulbs are all easy to replace, but some—especially instrument lights—can be very difficult to get to; you may have to remove part of the dashboard or ventilation ductwork to reach them. If you don't feel confident about doing this, take your car to a service station. **Tools:** Phillips-head screwdriver, heavy gloves or thick cloth, bulb base gripper, drill. **Materials:** replacement bulb; fine-grit sandpaper, emery cloth, or steel wool. **Time:** varies, depending on bulb location.

Before replacing a bulb, check your owner's manual for information about procedure. The manual lists the types and sizes of bulbs used in your car; be sure to buy the right bulb.

Replacement procedure depends on the bulb, but the technique for replacing a taillight, brake light, or turn signal is typical. Begin by examining the light. The plastic lens cover may be held by two or more Phillips-head screws. Remove the screws and cover to reach the bulb. On some cars, access to a taillight is gained through the car's rear compartment. In this case, remove the bulb's socket—the housing the bulb fits into—by twisting it counterclockwise a quarter- or half-turn.

Taillights, brake lights, and turn signals are bayonet-type bulbs. This kind of bulb has two knobs on its base. Grasp the bulb, push it inward slightly, and give it a quarter-turn counterclockwise. *Caution: If the bulb is difficult to remove, don't force it; it could break in your hand.* To protect yourself, wear heavy gloves or use a thick cloth to turn the bulb. If you still can't loosen the bulb, use a special bulb base gripper; grip the base of the stubborn bulb, turn it gently but firmly, and lift the bulb out.

Examine the bulb's socket. If there are signs of corrosion, clean the socket with fine-grit sandpaper, emery cloth, or steel wool.

Align the knobs on the base of the new bulb with the socket, and install the bulb by pushing it in and twisting it clockwise a quarter-turn. Finally, if water tends to collect behind the light's lens, drill a small hole in the lower part

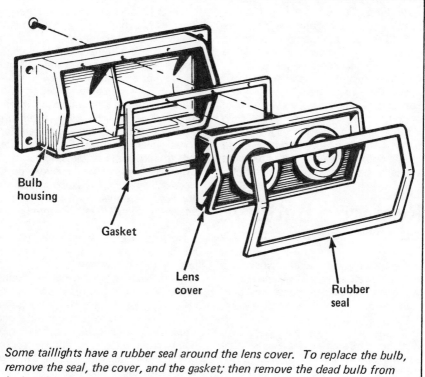

Bulb housing

Gasket

Lens cover

Rubber seal

Some taillights have a rubber seal around the lens cover. To replace the bulb, remove the seal, the cover, and the gasket; then remove the dead bulb from its housing and insert the new one.

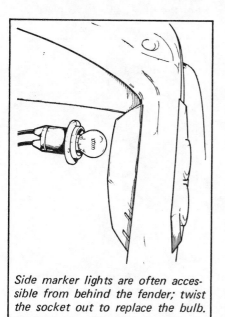

Side marker lights are often accessible from behind the fender; twist the socket out to replace the bulb.

of the plastic lens cover to allow water to drain out.

If you removed the socket from its housing to reach the bulb, replace it by inserting it in the housing and turning the socket clockwise. If you removed the lens cover, replace it. Be careful not to overtighten the retaining screws; this could crack the plastic lens.

Side marker lights are very similar to taillights. On some cars, the lens cover may be held by Phillips-head screws; remove the cover to reach the bulb. On other cars, you can reach the bulb's socket from behind the fender; turn the socket counterclockwise to remove it from its housing. Remove the old bulb and install the new one. Replace the lens cover, or resecure the socket with a clockwise twist.

On some interior lights, including many dome lights, screws may not secure the plastic lens cover; most likely, the cover is held in place by one or more tabs. To remove this type of cover, squeeze it gently at opposite ends to release the tabs, or depress a tab with a screwdriver, or use some similar method. Some dome lights use a bayonet-type bulb, similar to those used in taillights; others use cartridge-type bulbs, which snap in and out of retaining clips. Replace the old bulb with the type specified in your owner's manual. To avoid blowing a fuse, close the car doors and make sure the dome light is off before you replace the bulb.

Replace a Battery

The battery is the heart of your car's electrical system. When the time comes to replace it, you can make the transplant easily. **Tools:** wrench, pliers, battery terminal puller, battery-terminal-and-clamp cleaning tool or steel wool, wire brush. **Materials:** penetrating oil, baking soda, water, pint container, clean rags, replacement battery, petroleum jelly. **Time:** about 30 to 45 minutes.

Raise the hood of the car. Apply pen-etrating oil to the hold-down bolts on the frame or bracket securing the battery in the car. Using a wrench, loosen and remove the bolts.

Remove the battery cable clamps. Use a wrench to loosen nut-and-bolt connections; if the cables are connected by spring-type clamps with prongs, squeeze them with pliers to free them. *Remove the clamp on the ground cable first,* using a battery terminal puller. **Caution:** *On most cars, the ground cable is the negative (−) cable. On cars with positive-ground electrical systems, however, it is the positive (+) cable. If your car has a positive-ground system, remove the positive cable first.*

Now remove the other cable clamp, and lift the old battery from the car. Before installing the new battery, clean any corrosion from the cable clamps using a battery-terminal-and-clamp cleaning tool, a wire brush, or steel wool. Mix ½ cup of baking soda and water in a pint container. Pour the solution over the battery hold-down bracket or frame and wait until it stops foaming; wire-brush the frame clean. Rinse the frame with clean water and dry it with a clean rag.

Set the new battery into place and

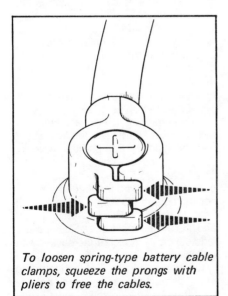

To loosen spring-type battery cable clamps, squeeze the prongs with pliers to free the cables.

Remove the clamp on the battery's ground cable first, using a battery terminal puller.

secure it with the hold-down bolts. Connect the battery cables to the proper terminals, securing the *ungrounded* cable first—the opposite of the way you disconnected the cables—and then the grounded cable, the one connected to the car's frame or engine. Finally, coat the ends of the cables and the clamps with petroleum jelly to protect them from corrosion.

Replace an Antenna

If your car has a broken radio antenna, you can replace it yourself. **Tools:** wrenches, screwdrivers, pliers, screw or hydraulic jack, safety jack stands, lug wrench. **Materials:** replacement radio antenna and cable with mounting hardware. **Time:** about 1 hour.

Behind the dashboard, locate the antenna cable where it connects to the radio. Disconnect the antenna lead; this is done by unscrewing a knurled ring at the connector and pulling it straight out of the radio or by simply pulling the cable connector straight out.

To disconnect the other end of the antenna cable and remove the damaged antenna, you'll have to determine how the antenna is attached. Most standard AM and AM/FM aerials are secured with one large retaining nut. Some cars, however, have a side-cowl-mounted antenna that has two retaining nuts on a pair of mounting posts, or mounting posts fastened by Phillips-head screws and retaining nuts. NOTE: Unless the antenna is mounted near the luggage compartment, you'll probably have to remove something to reach the base of the antenna. Although some aerial bases are located up under a corner of the dashboard or behind an interior kick panel, most are located under a front fender. If the antenna is mounted on a front fender, you'll have to gain access up through the fender well. Most fender wells have

splash shields, and you'll have to remove the splash shield to reach the antenna mount.

Place wheel chocks behind the rear wheels. Remove the wheel cover, or hubcap, on the wheel closest to the antenna and loosen the lug nuts with a lug wrench. Jack the front of the car up and support it solidly with a pair of safety jack stands. Remove the lug nuts and the wheel.

Reach up into the fender well and unbolt the splash shield with a wrench.

Use a wrench or pliers—whichever is necessary—to loosen the antenna retaining nut under the fender. Unscrew the nut and remove the antenna and old cable from the car; the nut and lock washer will slide along the cable as you withdraw it—set them aside if this hardware is not provided with the replacement antenna.

Connect the new antenna cable to the antenna mounting hole in the fender. From under the fender, slip the lock washer and nut onto the cable. Set the new antenna into the mounting hole and adjust it so it is at the proper angle. Screw the retaining nut on the base of the antenna mount under the fender and secure it tightly.

Replace the wheel and screw on the lug nuts. Remove the safety jack stands and jack the car down. Tighten the lug nuts with the lug wrench, replace the wheel cover, and remove the wheel chocks.

Route the new antenna cable back to the radio, following the route of the old cable. At the radio, connect the new cable.

Replace the Fan Belt

One of the most important drive belts in a car's engine is the one that powers the cooling system's fan and water pump and drives the alternator. Give it a quick inspection every time you raise the hood of the car, and change or adjust the belt promptly. **Tools:** socket wrench, pry bar. **Materials:** replacement fan belt. **Time:** about 20 to 30 minutes.

Caution: Shut off the engine before proceeding.

Raise the hood and locate the fan belt. Check to see if it's soaked with oil, cracked, brittle, glazed, frayed, torn, or otherwise damaged. If so, it should be replaced. Most wear occurs under the belt, so twist it to check underneath.

If the belt is in good condition, check its tension. Press down on the belt with your finger or thumb; it shouldn't deflect more than ¾ inch. If it gives more than this, it's too loose; if it doesn't give at least ½ inch, it's too tight. Loosen the adjustment bolt the slotted metal arm swings on and apply pressure to adjust the belt tension—pull out to tighten the belt, in to loosen it. Check the tension again; the belt should deflect between ½ and ¾ inch. Then tighten the adjustment bolt again.

If the belt is damaged, you must replace it. Examine the engine to see if any other drive belts will be in the way of removing the fan belt. If so, loosen their adjustment bolts or the bolts securing the components they drive. Start with the belt nearest the radiator. Use a socket wrench to loosen bolts and move the component toward the fan so you can remove the belt. As you work, examine these other belts too, and replace them if necessary; be sure to buy the proper replacements.

Using the wrench, loosen the alternator's bolt at its base. You may have to loosen another alternator adjustment bolt as well. Move the alternator toward the fan and remove the fan belt.

Set the new fan belt into position and replace the other belts, beginning with the belt closest to the engine and working back toward the radiator. Don't try to force a belt on with a screwdriver or other tool; this will weaken or otherwise damage the belt.

After you've replaced all belts, insert a pry bar between the engine and the alternator to apply tension on the belts. While keeping the fan belt taut, tighten the alternator adjustment bolts and any other bolts you loosened. There should be no more than ¾ inch deflection in the belt.

Finally, check to see that all belts are seated properly; adjust them as necessary. Then start the engine and, standing safely out of the way, observe the operation of the belts. If a belt squeals, it is either very loose or very tight; adjust it as necessary to the proper deflection.

Check the belt again in a few weeks for proper tension; new belts may stretch slightly. Adjust the belt as necessary.

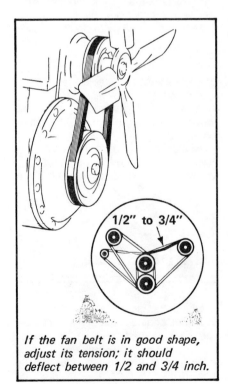

If the fan belt is in good shape, adjust its tension; it should deflect between 1/2 and 3/4 inch.

Replace Radiator Hoses

Your car has an upper and a lower radiator hose; both should be checked periodically. Replace the hoses when they are obviously swollen, cracked, or otherwise damaged, or if they feel soft

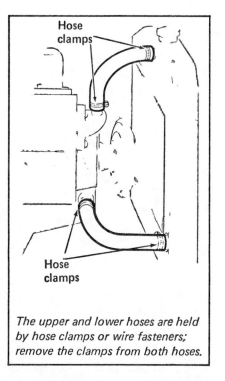

Hose clamps

Hose clamps

The upper and lower hoses are held by hose clamps or wire fasteners; remove the clamps from both hoses.

and spongy when squeezed. Generally, if one hose must be replaced, chances are the other hose should be changed, too. **Tools:** pliers, screwdriver, utility knife, rags, large pan, brush. **Materials:** replacement radiator hoses, gasket sealer, four hose clamps, sandpaper. **Time:** about 1 to 1½ hours.

Caution: Don't attempt this job if the engine is warm. Allow the car to cool completely, because you'll have to drain the radiator coolant.

Raise the hood of the car and place a large pan under the radiator's drain petcock; remove the radiator cap. Using pliers, open the petcock located at the bottom of the radiator. After the coolant has been drained, close the petcock. NOTE: Some older cars don't have a drain petcock on the radiator. If your car is one of these, either siphon off the coolant or drain it by removing the lower radiator hose.

Loosen the clamps securing the upper and lower radiator hoses. On some cars, the hoses are held by heavy wire fasteners; use pliers to loosen

these. On others, worm-drive clamps hold the hoses; use a screwdriver to loosen the screw on this type of fastener. Remove or slide the clamps back on the hoses, and remove the hoses. If this is difficult, you may have to cut the hoses with a sharp utility knife and pry them off.

If the old clamps are not made of wire and are not corroded, you can reuse them; otherwise, replace the clamps. They come in different sizes; be sure to get the correct size.

Obtain the exact replacement hoses for your model of car—if necessary, take the old hoses to your auto supply store. Buy preformed hoses. If these are not available, you can use flexible hoses, provided they are the correct size and length.

Before attaching the new hoses, clean each of the connection points for the hoses with sandpaper to remove any old sealant. Slide a hose clamp over each end of each hose. Brush gasket sealer around the hose connection points on the car.

Finally, slide the ends of the hoses onto their fittings. Each clamp should be about 1 inch from the end of the hose. Tighten each clamp.

Refill the radiator with coolant, replace the radiator cap, and start the engine. Let it run for about 15 minutes to reach normal operating temperature, then carefully check the hoses and connections for leaks. Retighten the clamps, if necessary.

Replace Your Thermostat

The thermostat regulates your car's cooling system, preventing coolant from reaching the radiator when the engine is cold and opening so the coolant can circulate through the system when the engine is warm. A stuck thermostat can cause the engine to overheat or prevent your car's heater from generating sufficient heat, but it's easy to replace.

CAR/Thermostat

Tools: metal or plastic container, pliers or screwdriver, wrench, scrap wood block, hammer, putty knife. **Materials:** clean rags, thermostat and gasket, gasket sealer, antifreeze. **Time:** about ½ hour.

Caution: Don't do this job unless the engine and the coolant are cold.

Remove the radiator pressure cap. Place a metal or plastic container under the radiator's drain petcock and open the petcock with a pair of pliers. Drain enough coolant from the radiator so that its level is below that of the upper radiator hose; then close the petcock. Set the drained coolant aside so you can replace it later.

Locate the thermostat housing. Usually it's on the top front of the engine at one end of the upper radiator hose. Loosen the clamp on the end of the hose closest to the housing, using pliers or a screwdriver as required. Slide the clamp back along the hose out of the way and disconnect the hose from its fitting on the thermostat housing.

Use a wrench to remove the two cap screws that secure the thermostat housing; remove the housing. If the housing is difficult to remove, place a block of scrap wood against it and tap the block gently with a hammer to dislodge the housing.

Lift the thermostat out and stuff a clean rag into the recessed opening to prevent dirt from falling into it. With a putty knife, scrape the old gasket material and sealer from the mounting surface around the opening. Remove the rag from the opening. Seat the new thermostat in the opening. The thermostat will have some indication stamped on it, such as *Front* or *Up,* telling you which way it should be installed; this part of the device must face the radiator. Also, the spring part of the thermostat should face down into the engine or away from the radiator.

Apply gasket sealer to the new gasket with the applicator brush, or spray it on. Place the gasket on the mounting surface over the thermostat. Replace the thermostat housing and tighten the two cap screws. *Caution: Don't overtighten the cap screws.*

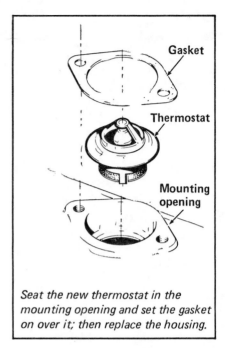

Seat the new thermostat in the mounting opening and set the gasket on over it; then replace the housing.

Place the end of the upper radiator hose onto the thermostat housing's fitting, slide the hose clamp back into position, and tighten the clamp. Pour the coolant you drained back into the radiator and replace the radiator cap.

Start the engine and run it for about 15 minutes so that it reaches normal operating temperature. Examine the thermostat housing and the area around the upper radiator hose. If there's a leak, stop the engine and try to tighten the hose clamp or the housing cap screws to stop the leak; tighten the housing cap screws very slightly.

After stopping any leaks, shut off the engine. Place rags over the radiator cap, and carefully turn the cap to release the pressure in the cooling system. *Caution: Be ready to move out of the way fast to avoid being injured by hot coolant.* The release of pressure will eliminate any air pockets in the system. Check the level of coolant in the radiator; it should come to within about 1 inch of the top. If the coolant is low, add a 50/50 mixture of water and antifreeze to the radiator and replace the radiator cap.

Install Ignition Cables

If your ignition or spark plug cables are obviously damaged—the wires are oil-soaked, cracked, or abraded; the rubber boots are hard or brittle—it's time to replace them. If your ignition system has been in use for more than 30,000 miles, it's a good idea to replace the cables the next time the engine is tuned; they may appear to be in good condition, but they do wear out. **Tools:** screwdriver or pliers, wrench. **Materials:** replacement set of ignition cables, golf tees, masking tape, rag, silicone spray. **Time:** about ½ hour.

Caution: Before you begin, make sure your replacement ignition cables are designed for your car. Let the engine cool completely if the car has been running—you'll be working near the exhaust manifold, which could burn you if it's hot.

Raise the hood of the car. If there are any vacuum hoses connected to the air filter over the carburetor, disconnect them. Plug the open end of any vacuum hose with a golf tee to keep dirt out.

To make it easier to reach the cables, remove the air filter. Remove the wing nut or hex nut securing the filter's cover and lift off the cover; then, lift off the filter housing.

Locate the ignition cable that is farthest from the distributor—on V-engines, start on either side. Carefully remove the rubber boot from this spark plug, using a twisting motion to loosen the boot. Trace the cable back to the distributor, and remove that end of the cable from the distributor the same way.

NOTE: If the cables run through separators or other devices to keep them in place, make a simple sketch showing the placement of each wire. If you still feel uncertain, tag each cable with masking tape and number the cables so you can replace them correctly.

Compare the ignition cable you've just removed with the cables in the re-

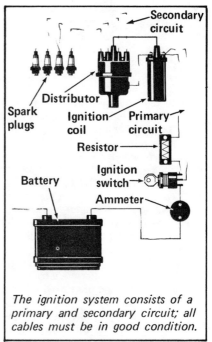

The ignition system consists of a primary and secondary circuit; all cables must be in good condition.

placement set and find its match; make sure both are the same length. Discard the old cable.

Attach one end of the new cable to the distributor, pushing the rubber boot and connector down firmly as far as it's supposed to go to obtain a good connection. Route the cable in the same manner as the one you removed, and attach the other end to the terminal stud of the spark plug, making sure you have a good connection. Repeat this procedure with each ignition cable, one at a time, until all the cables have been replaced.

Finally, locate the ignition coil—usually a black, cylindrical unit located near the distributor. You can easily find the ignition coil by following the heavy ignition cable from the center of the distributor cap; it leads to the coil. Remove the cable connected to the top of the coil's tower the same way you removed the cables at each spark plug; also remove the other end of the cable at the distributor. Install the high-tension cable supplied with the set of ignition cables, connecting the cable carefully at the ig-

447

nition coil and at the distributor. Be sure that you have good connections at both ends of the high-tension cable.

Replace the air filter on the carburetor. Remove the golf tee from any disconnected vacuum hose and reconnect it.

High Energy Ignition systems. If your car has a High Energy Ignition (HEI) system, the installation procedure is slightly different. The ignition cables for an HEI system are larger in diameter. There is no high-tension cable at the coil; it's part of the distributor assembly. And the cables are connected to the distributor in a different way.

To install cables for an HEI system, lift off the retaining ring from the distributor cap; move the latch clips out and lift the ring upward. Then disconnect the distributor cap end of a spark plug ignition cable from the ring by pressing down with your thumb. Remove the other end of the ignition cable from the spark plug, twisting the rubber boot carefully to loosen it.

Match each new cable against the old one for length. To install the new ignition cable in the retaining ring, spray the distributor cap end of the cable with a

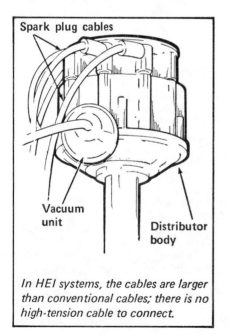

Spark plug cables

Vacuum unit

Distributor body

In HEI systems, the cables are larger than conventional cables; there is no high-tension cable to connect.

silicone spray lubricant and press it into the retaining ring. When all cables have been installed, replace the ring on the distributor and close the latch clips.

Replace Shock Absorbers

If your car bounces excessively when you come to a stop or when you drive over a bump, you probably have one or more defective shock absorbers. **Tools:** wheel chocks, jack, safety jack stands, socket wrenches, box-end wrenches, hammer, punch, adjustable wrench. **Materials:** shock absorbers. **Time:** about ½ to ¾ hour per pair.

NOTE: Shock absorbers should be replaced in pairs—two front or two rear, or all of them—never singly.

Rear shocks. Place wheel chocks in front of the front wheels, jack up the rear of the car, and place a pair of safety jack stands under the rear axle housing. NOTE: Some cars, generally small ones, have top-rear shock mounts that can be reached without jacking the car up; the fasteners for these mounts should be removed before jacking up the car. The car, however, will have to be raised to reach the bottom mounts.

Use a socket or box-end wrench to remove the fasteners from the top of a shock absorber. Where necessary, use a hammer and punch to drift out the bolt. If the replacement shock absorber doesn't include installation instructions, carefully note the order in which washers and retainers are removed from the old shock.

Use a socket or box-end wrench to remove the fastener from the bottom of the shock. NOTE: On some cars, it is necessary to remove the lower retaining plate from the rear axle housing to reach the mount. Use a socket wrench to remove the plate, if necessary.

Remove the shock absorber.

Install the new shock absorber by attaching the fasteners at the top mount

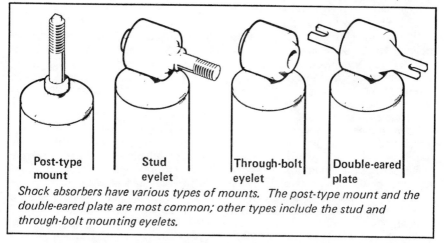

| Post-type mount | Stud eyelet | Through-bolt eyelet | Double-eared plate |

Shock absorbers have various types of mounts. The post-type mount and the double-eared plate are most common; other types include the stud and through-bolt mounting eyelets.

first. Then, push up or pull down slowly on the shock to align the bottom mount with the hole or plate on the rear axle housing. Install the bottom fasteners.

Repeat the procedure for removing the old shock and installing the new one on the other side of the car.

After both rear shocks have been installed, jack up the car, remove the safety jack stands, and lower the car. Remove the wheel chocks.

Front shocks. Raise the hood of the car and locate the top shock absorber mount. NOTE: On some cars, the mount may be hidden by a flexible shield over the front fender well.

Apply a box-end wrench to the top fastener of the shock absorber and a

small adjustable wrench to the projection on the tip of the mounting post; this will keep the actuating rod from turning as you remove the fastener. Remove the fastener.

Place wheel chocks in back of the rear wheels, jack up the front of the car, and place safety jack stands under the car frame.

Use a socket or box-end wrench to

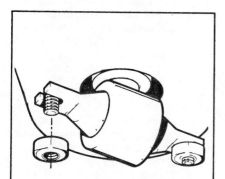

Front shocks are often secured at the bottom with a double-eared plate; remove the bolts.

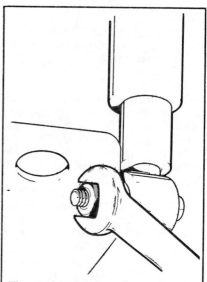

The stud eyelet is an integral part of the shock absorber; use a wrench to remove the bolt.

remove the fasteners from the bottom mount of the shock absorber.

Remove the shock absorber from the bottom. NOTE: Sometimes, the shock will have to be removed from the top. If this is the case, you will have to remove three cap-screw fasteners from the top mounting plate before the shock can be withdrawn.

Fully extend the new shock absorber, and install it by first attaching the bottom fasteners.

Repeat the procedure for the shock absorber on the other side of the car.

Jack up the front end of the car, remove the safety jack stands, and lower the car.

Attach the top fasteners of both shock absorbers. Close the hood and remove the wheel chocks.

Time the Engine

Ignition timing is the relationship of the instant of fuel ignition in the cylinders to the position of the pistons. Pistons and valves can be damaged if the timing is advanced too much. Power is lost and fuel consumption is increased if it's retarded too much. **Tools:** dwell-tachometer, timing light, offset distributor wrench. **Materials:** rag, white chalk, tape, stick, golf tee. **Time:** about 1 hour.

The car's engine should be at normal operating temperature to accurately time the engine. If the engine is cold, start it and let it run for about 15 minutes to reach normal operating temperature. Raise the hood and connect a dwell-tachometer to the ignition coil and a ground, following the directions that come with the test instrument. *Caution: Take care to avoid coming in contact with the fan and other moving components.*

Check to see that the engine is running at the proper idle speed; you can find this specification on a tune-up decal in the engine compartment or in the service manual for your car. Compare the specification with the dwell-tachometer reading. If it's too high or too low, you can adjust it by turning the idle adjusting screw located on the carburetor. Usually, turning the screw clockwise will increase the idle; turning it counterclockwise will lower the idle. Turn the screw very slowly and watch the dwell-tachometer as you make the adjustment.

If the idle speed is too high and you lower it to the proper speed, the engine should then run smoothly. However, if it runs roughly, something is probably wrong with the fuel or electrical system, and you should seek the help of a professional mechanic.

If the engine runs smoothly at the specified idle speed, you can proceed to time it. Stop the engine and disconnect the dwell-tachometer. Connect the timing light to the battery and the engine's No. 1 spark plug, following the directions that come with this test instrument. Locate the timing mark on the engine's crankshaft pulley, the engine vibration damper, or flywheel. You may have to "jog" the engine with the starter a few times to get it into view. NOTE: On some models you may only be able to see it by looking from under the car. Use a rag to clean the timing mark and the index pointer, which you'll find on the timing gear cover or the bell housing. If the mark and pointer don't stand out clearly, use white chalk to make them visible. NOTE: The timing mark and pointer are not always easy to reach. You may have to tape the chalk onto a length of stick to reach these parts.

Start the engine. Unless the tune-up decal under the hood or your service manual states otherwise, pull the vacuum hose off the vacuum advance unit. Plug the end of this hose tightly with a golf tee.

With the engine idling, aim the timing light at the timing mark and pointer. If the timing is correct, the rotating timing mark will appear to be stationary, directly opposite the index pointer. If the timing is incorrect, loosen the distributor's hold-down clamp bolt under the distributor with a wrench; it is easier and sometimes necessary to use a special offset distributor wrench to loosen this

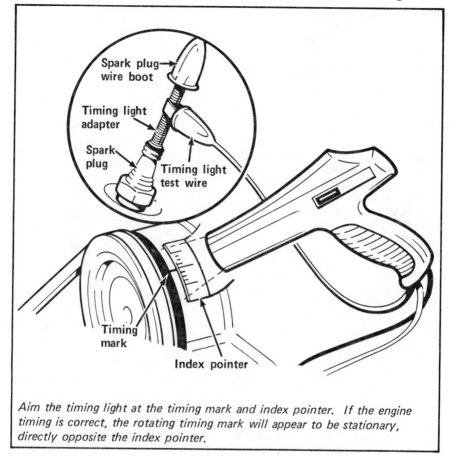

Spark plug wire boot

Timing light adapter

Spark plug

Timing light test wire

Timing mark

Index pointer

Aim the timing light at the timing mark and index pointer. If the engine timing is correct, the rotating timing mark will appear to be stationary, directly opposite the index pointer.

bolt. Loosen the bolt just enough so you can turn the distributor with your hand. Aim the timing light at the mark and pointer and slowly turn the distributor by hand. NOTE: Depending on the position of engine components, you may need an assistant for this. Turn the distributor in one direction slowly. If the mark and pointer begin to get farther apart, turn the distributor in the opposite direction. If the mark and pointer begin to come closer together, you're turning in the correct direction; keep turning until the mark and pointer are aligned according to specification.

Tighten the distributor hold-down clamp bolt securely, and recheck the timing with the timing light to make sure that it didn't change. If it has shifted, repeat the procedure until the mark and pointer are aligned.

Now you must check the vacuum advance unit for proper operation. Have an assistant sit behind the steering wheel. Remove the golf tee plugging the vacuum hose. Have the assistant gradually depress the accelerator pedal, speeding up the engine slowly. At the same time, aim the timing light at the mark and pointer, and pop the vacuum hose on and off the vacuum advance unit several times. The timing mark should shift position rapidly. If it is steady or moves very slightly, the vacuum advance unit is probably leaking and needs to be replaced.

If the vacuum advance unit is operating properly, replace the hose on the unit and stop the engine. Disconnect the timing light and close the hood.

Make Radiator Sealant

It may not be necessary to have your car's leaking radiator repaired or replaced, especially if the leaks are minor. Before you go to all that expense, try this simple preparation. **Equipment:** small container, measuring cup. **Ingredients:** whites of 2 eggs, asbestos powder, water. Buy asbestos powder at a paint or hardware store. **Yield:** one treatment.

When your car's engine is cold, raise the hood and remove the radiator cap. Separate the whites of 2 eggs into a small container and pour the whites into the radiator's filler opening. Add 1 ounce of powdered asbestos to the radiator. *Caution: Don't breathe in any asbestos powder; it is a hazardous substance.*

Check the level of coolant in the radiator. If it's low, add enough water to bring it to the proper level. Replace the radiator cap.

Start the car and run the engine for about 15 minutes until it reaches normal operating temperature. Turn the engine off and check for leaks.

Make Radiator Rust Remover

Flush your car's cooling system with this solution; it's formulated to remove rust, scale, and other accumulated particles from the radiator to keep the system in top operating condition. **Equipment:** measuring cup, gallon container with cap, rubber gloves. **Ingredients:** oxalic acid, sodium bisulphite, water. Buy these chemicals at a pharmacy. **Yield:** 1 gallon.

Measure 4 ounces of oxalic acid and 4 ounces of sodium bisulphite into a gallon container. Add water to fill the container. Cap the container tightly and shake until the chemicals are dissolved. *Caution: Sodium bisulphite is a caustic poison; avoid contact with skin. Wear rubber gloves. Oxalic acid is poisonous if taken internally.*

To use this preparation, drain the car's cooling system. Add the gallon of rust remover to the radiator. Start and operate the engine for about 15 to 30 minutes. Stop the engine, drain the solution from the cooling system, and back-flush the system with water until it runs out clean. Refill the cooling system with a 50/50 mixture of antifreeze and water.

Repack Trailer Wheel Bearings

Trailer wheel bearings should be repacked with grease at the beginning of every trailering season, or twice a year if the trailer is used extensively. **Tools:** screw or hydraulic jack, safety jack stands, pliers, diagonal cutters, large slip-joint pliers, screwdriver, parts-cleaning brush, parts-cleaning pan, brass drift or wooden block, hammer, mechanics' wrenches, soft-bristled brush, torque wrench, lug wrench. **Materials:** wheel bearings, grease seal, clean rags, petroleum-based solvent, automotive or marine grease, cotter pins. **Time:** less than 1 hour per wheel.

Remove the wheel covers. Jack up one side of the trailer, and place a safety jack stand under the frame. Lower the trailer until the frame rests solidly on the jack stand.

Pry off the dust cap with a screwdriver or remove it by wiggling it off with large slip-joint pliers. Remove the cotter pin placed through the spindle and spindle nut by cutting it off with diagonal cutters. Use a wrench to turn the spindle nut off. Wiggle the wheel; the washer and outer wheel bearing will pop loose. Remove and set them aside.

Pull the wheel-and-drum assembly straight out, and take it off the spindle.

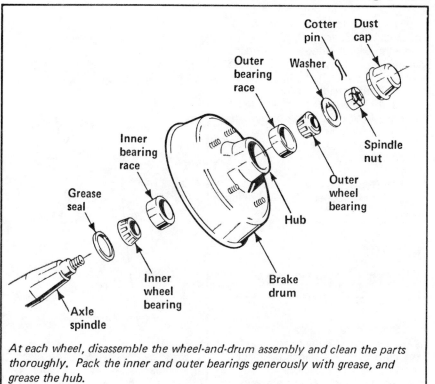

Cotter pin   Dust cap

Outer bearing race   Washer

Inner bearing race

Spindle nut

Grease seal

Outer wheel bearing

Hub

Axle spindle

Inner wheel bearing

Brake drum

At each wheel, disassemble the wheel-and-drum assembly and clean the parts thoroughly. Pack the inner and outer bearings generously with grease, and grease the hub.

Set the assembly on the ground hub-face-up. With a hammer and brass drift or wood block, drive the inner bearing out by tapping on the outer race. The grease seal and bearing should come free after a few solid taps. Set the bearing aside. *Caution: Be careful not to damage the bearing or race.*

Discard the grease seal, and remember which is the *inner* bearing and which is the *outer* bearing.

Thoroughly wash the bearings in a pan with a petroleum-based solvent and a parts-cleaning brush, but handle them by the race only.

Inspect the bearings. If the race is bent; if the rollers show burned or bluish marks, scratches, chips, or scores; or if the bearing sounds gritty or raspy, or binds when you spin it slowly, replace the bearing.

Use a soft-bristled brush to clean off any loose dust from the backing plate and the inside of the brake drum. Clean

off any accumulations of grease and grime. Also clean the spindle and the inside of the hub thoroughly with solvent.

Set the wheel hub-face-down on blocks, and wipe a film of wheel-bearing grease over the entire inside surface. NOTE: If you are working on a boat trailer, use grease specifically formulated for this purpose. Pack the inner wheel bearing generously with grease, working it into all crevices with your fingers.

Set the bearing into its cup, and carefully tap a new grease seal into place with a hammer and brass drift or a block of wood. Take care to keep the seal properly aligned; work slowly so the seal seats perfectly. Place the hub and wheel assembly back over the spindle.

Pack the outer wheel bearing generously with grease, and slip it over the spindle and into its cup. Replace the spindle washer and spindle nut. Snug the nut with a torque wrench to the manufacturer's specification.

Spin the wheel. If the wheel doesn't spin freely, back the spindle nut off no more than ½ turn. Line up the holes on the spindle and spindle nut for the cotter pin, insert a new cotter pin, and bend the ends of the pin apart. Replace the dust cap on the hub.

Jack up the frame, remove the safety jack stand, and lower the trailer to the ground. Check to see that the lug nuts are tight. Replace the wheel cover.

Repeat the procedure for the other wheel.

Repair Minor Scratches

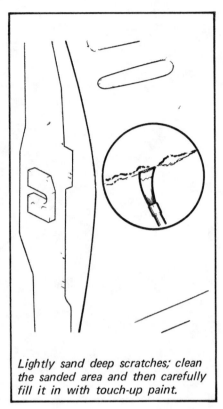

Lightly sand deep scratches; clean the sanded area and then carefully fill it in with touch-up paint.

Scratches on a car's paint finish are the easiest type of body damage to fix. Take care of these minor blemishes after washing your car. **Tools:** sponge, small artists' brush. **Materials:** clean soft cloths, rubbing compound, extra-fine-grit wet-or-dry sandpaper, mineral spirits, tack cloth, touch-up paint, cream polish. **Time:** varies, depending on the damage; about 15 minutes to 1 hour, plus painting time.

Shallow scratches. Examine the scratch. Run your fingernail across it; if your nail doesn't catch, the scratch can be removed very simply.

Fold a clean soft cloth into a pad and dampen it with a little water. Add a small amount of rubbing compound to the pad. Using just the tip of one finger, gently rub back and forth along the scratch with the compound until the scratch vanishes. *Caution: Rubbing compound is an abrasive that can remove paint and primer. Check your progress often and stop as soon as the scratch disappears.* Wax the car after removing the scratch.

Deep scratches. Examine the scratch. Run your fingernail across it; if your nail catches, you'll have to refinish the damaged area.

First, sponge the scratch with plenty of cold water. Carefully and lightly sand along the scratch with extra-fine-grit wet-or-dry sandpaper. Squeeze more water onto the scratch as you sand.

After wet-sanding the scratch, wipe the area dry with a soft cloth. Clean the scratch area with mineral spirits and then wipe the scratch with a clean tack cloth. With a small artists' brush, apply touch-up paint that matches the car's finish to the scratch *only*; don't let the paint go beyond the edges of the scratch. Let the paint dry for ½ hour.

If the touched-up scratch is still visible as a depression, apply a second coat of touch-up paint to level it; let the paint dry for ½ hour. If the touched-up scratch is higher than the surrounding paint, use a little rubbing compound on a slightly damp cloth to even it out.

Finally, apply cream polish to the repair to help protect the new paint. Then wax the car.

Repair a Minor Dent

Repairing a minor dent can be easy if the metal isn't creased; all you need is confidence and care. **Tools:** screwdriver, basketball, bicycle pump and needle valve, scrap wood block, hammer, electric drill, locking-jaw pliers; auto body repair tool kit, including blunt-faced hammer and mushroom dolly; sanding disc attachment for drill. **Materials:** sheet metal screw, medium-grit sanding disc. **Time:** depends on the damage; about ½ hour to pop out a shallow dent or pound out a small area.

Before starting to work, examine the dent and decide whether you can fix it and whether you have enough confidence to do a good job. If the sheet metal has a sharp crease—even if the dent is small—special body repair tools will be required to fix it; take the car to a professional.

If the dent is in a relatively flat area, such as the middle of a door, however, you may be able to remove it in one of several ways. If the dent is a shallow, round depression, remove part of the inside door panel so that you can squeeze a deflated basketball connected to a bicycle pump into the door, directly behind the dent. Then, using the bicycle pump, carefully inflate the basketball. Sometimes the dent will pop out, restoring the door to its original shape.

As an alternative for large bulging dents, remove the door panel completely and strike the center of the dent sharply with the heel of your hand once or twice. Or place a block of wood against the dent and strike it with a hammer.

If these methods don't work, drill a small hole into the center of the dent from the outside and twist a sheet metal

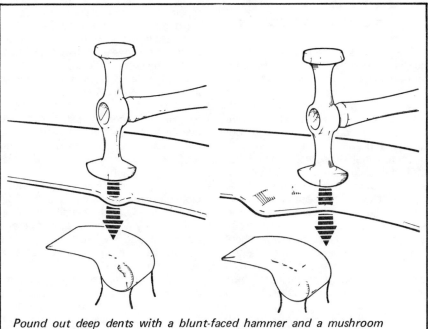

Pound out deep dents with a blunt-faced hammer and a mushroom dolly, set against the inside of the dented panel. Pound directly over the middle of small dents; work in from the edges of large ones.

screw about half or three-quarters of the way into the hole. Grip the head of the screw with locking-jaw pliers and yank. Remove the sheet metal screw.

If these methods don't work, buy an auto body repair tool kit; you'll need special body repair tools. The tool kit should include a blunt-faced hammer and a mushroom dolly, a heavy piece of metal used to contour the dent out.

Remove the inside door panel. Set the curve of the mushroom dolly against the inside of the dent and hammer the outside surface with the blunt-faced hammer until the approximate original contour of the sheet metal is restored. Then sand the repaired area down to bare metal, using an electric drill with a sanding disc attachment and a medium-grit sanding disc. To remove imperfections in the metal, use body filler and spot putty as you would to fix rust spots and holes.

Fix Rust Spots and Holes

Rust begins as a tiny spot, but it quickly progresses to a hole. Be alert for rust spots, and repair them as soon as they appear. **Tools:** electric drill with sanding disc and rotary wire brush attachments, or sanding block and wire brush; safety goggles, plastic spreader (included in auto body repair kit), ball-peen hammer, scissors, sharp knife. **Materials:** coarse- and medium-grit sanding discs or sandpaper, white vinegar, clean cloths; auto body repair kit, or auto body filler and hardener; spot putty, mineral spirits, tack cloth, scrap fiberglass screening. **Time:** about ½ to 3 hours, depending on damage.

Rust spots. Sand a rust spot on the car body down to the bare sheet metal to remove all traces of rust. If possible, use an electric drill with a sanding disc attachment and a coarse-grit sanding disc. *Caution: Wear safety goggles while sanding.* If you don't have a drill, use a sanding block and coarse-grit sandpaper.

Pour some distilled white vinegar onto a clean cloth and rub the sanded area thoroughly; then use the electric drill fitted with a rotary wire brush to remove any remaining traces of rust. *Caution: Wear safety goggles while using the rotary brush.* If you don't have a drill, use a stiff, fine-textured wire brush.

After sanding, examine the area for any indentations in the metal. If the surface isn't smooth, mix auto body filler and hardener according to the manufacturer's instructions. Apply the filler to the sanded area with a plastic spreader to fill indentations; use a little more than necessary, so you can sand the excess off. Let the filler harden thoroughly, according to the manufacturer's instructions.

Sand the repair carefully by hand with fine-grit sandpaper until it blends in smoothly with the surrounding area. For an even smoother final finish, apply a thin layer of spot putty over the repair with a plastic spreader. Let the putty dry completely, as directed, and sand the repair again with fine-grit sandpaper.

Pour a little mineral spirits onto a clean cloth and wipe the repaired area clean; then wipe it with a tack cloth. Prime and paint as desired.

Rust holes. Sand the damaged area for a few inches around the rust hole down to the bare sheet metal to remove all traces of rust. If possible, use an electric drill with a sanding disc attachment and a coarse-grit sanding disc; wear safety goggles while sanding. Or sand by hand.

Pour some white vinegar onto a clean cloth and rub the sanded area thoroughly. Then use the electric drill fitted with a rotary wire brush to remove any remaining traces of rust; wear safety goggles while using the rotary brush. Or wire-brush by hand.

Beat the edges of the rust hole inward at a 45-degree angle with a ball-peen hammer; then cut a piece of fiberglass screening slightly larger than the hole. Mix body filler and hardener according to the manufacturer's instructions and apply a ridge of filler

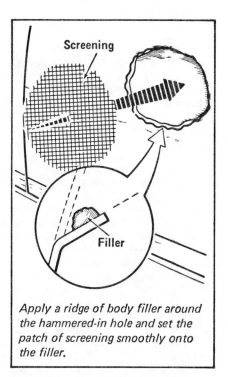

Screening

Filler

Apply a ridge of body filler around the hammered-in hole and set the patch of screening smoothly onto the filler.

with the plastic spreader; let it dry thoroughly. Sand the patch again with a medium-grit sanding disc or medium-grit paper.

For a smoother finish, apply a thin layer of spot putty over the repair with a plastic spreader; let the spot putty dry completely, according to the manufacturer's instructions. Sand the repair carefully by hand with medium-grit sandpaper, feathering the edges to blend the patch in with the surrounding sheet metal. Pour a little mineral spirits onto a clean cloth and wipe the repair clean; then wipe it with a tack cloth. Prime and paint as desired.

Replace Weatherstripping

Weatherstripping that has hardened, cracked, or broken loose can cause wind noises and allow water to seep into your car. It's easy to repair or replace the damaged weatherstripping. **Tools:** single-edge razor blade and scraper holder. **Materials:** weatherstripping adhesive, automotive weatherstripping, petroleum-based solvent, rags. **Time:** varies with the amount of weatherstripping to be replaced or repaired, about ½ hour for one door.

Examine loose weatherstripping around the car's trunk or doors. If it is not hard, chipped, cracked, or otherwise damaged, glue it into place with weatherstripping adhesive, being careful not to get glue on the surrounding surfaces. If the weatherstripping is damaged, peel it off carefully. Scrape off any glue left by the old weatherstripping, using a single-edge razor blade in a scraper holder. Clean the area with a rag dampened with a petroleum-based solvent, and wipe it dry with a clean rag.

Using the old weatherstripping to measure by, cut a length of new weatherstripping slightly longer than the length of material you are replacing; it

about ¼ inch high to the hammered-in area, completely around the hole. Set the fiberglass screening over the hole and press its edges down through the ridge of filler, stretching the fiberglass smoothly and tightly over the hole. Smooth the filler away from the hole with a plastic spreader, blending the hole in with the surrounding area. Let the filler harden thoroughly according to the instructions.

Mix another batch of body filler and hardener. Apply it to the fiberglass screening with the plastic spreader and smooth the filler over the repair. Let the filler partially harden. At this point, use a knife to shape the repair to the proper contour, if necessary. Let the filler harden thoroughly.

Sand the repair smooth, using the electric drill with a coarse-grit sanding disc or coarse-grit sandpaper. Feather the edges of the patch so that it blends in with the surrounding sheet metal.

If there are still imperfections in the repaired area, mix more body filler and hardener and smooth it over the repair

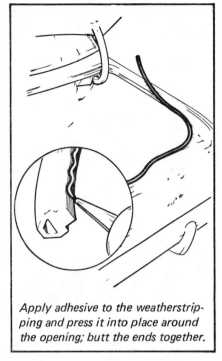

Apply adhesive to the weatherstripping and press it into place around the opening; butt the ends together.

should be done any time body parts are replaced. Generally, if a car is more than three months old or has been driven more than 3,000 miles, rustproofing isn't a good idea. It's hard, messy work, but by using a rustproofing kit, available in auto supply stores, you'll end up spending about 80 percent less for the job. **Tools:** wire brush, vacuum cleaner, electric drill and drill bits, auto jack, four jack stands, safety goggles. **Materials:** auto rustproofing kit, kerosene or mineral solvent, rags. **Time:** about 4 to 5 hours.

Rustproof your car on a dry day with low humidity. Your kit will include detailed instructions, but in general, it's important to remember two things: don't rustproof areas subject to heat (engine, transmission, drive shaft, radiator core, manifold, differential, exhaust), and stay away from rubber (seals, gaskets, tubes). Wear old clothes—you'll need two sets—and be prepared to throw them away when you've finished the job.

Your car must be clean, inside and out. Have the engine and engine compartment professionally steam cleaned, and wash the outside thoroughly yourself; vacuum the interior. Using a wire brush, remove loose rust from the body of the car. Pay attention to inconspicuous or hidden areas—inside the trunk, for instance—as well as to main panel areas. Consult your service manual to locate the car's drain holes, and clear them.

can be trimmed later. Apply adhesive to the back of the weatherstripping and press it into place, starting at one end and working carefully around the opening. When you reach the other end, trim the excess weatherstripping carefully with a razor blade.

Before closing the door or trunk, let the adhesive dry thoroughly, according to the manufacturer's instructions.

To prolong the life of your car's weatherstripping, treat it with a good preservative at least once a year, following the manufacturer's directions for application.

Rustproof Your Car

Rustproofing can add years to the life of your car. A new car should be rustproofed as soon as possible before you drive it, and touch-up rustproofing

Rustproofing includes injecting the protective compound into hollow body parts. Following the instructions in the kit, drill access holes in doors, door jambs, quarter panels, and anywhere else specified. If your car has power windows, be careful not to drill into electrical connections.

Jack the car up and set it solidly on jack stands. *Caution: Make sure the car is properly supported by safety jack stands before getting under the vehicle.* Wearing safety goggles, wire-brush the bottom of the car to remove loose rust, being careful to avoid areas where heat builds up. Following the instructions in the kit, coat the underbody.

Remove the jack stands and jack the car down.

At this point, you'll probably be pretty tarry. To avoid getting more rustproofing compound on the car than you have to, clean your hands and change to your second set of old clothes.

Rustproof all upper body sections specified in the instructions—under the hood, inside the trunk, wheel cover panels, mounting brackets, firewall,

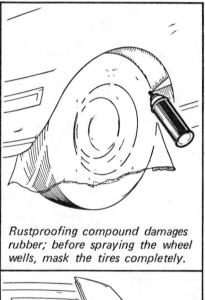

Rustproofing compound damages rubber; before spraying the wheel wells, mask the tires completely.

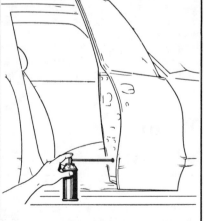

Using the extension tube, inject compound through the access holes into hollow body parts.

battery mount, and anywhere else appropriate. Remember to stay away from rubber; mask the tires before spraying the wheel wells.

Remove all removable exterior trim. Rustproof both trim and all mounting holes and clips, and replace the trim.

Now install the extension tube on the rustproofing applicator. Following instructions carefully, inject the rustproofing compound into hollow body parts through the access holes drilled at the beginning of the job. Your kit will also include sealer grommets to keep rustproofing compound from seeping out of hollow parts, and moisture and dirt from getting in. Install the grommets carefully. Remove excess compound from your car and yourself with kerosene or mineral solvent.

Install a Hood or Trunk Light

For a very small expense, you can have the convenience of instant illumination whenever you open your car's hood or trunk. **Tools:** electric drill with bit, pliers, wrench, Phillips-head screwdriver, diagonal cutters, wire stripper. **Materials:** automatic hood or trunk light kit, electrical tape, wire connectors. **Time:** ½ to 1 hour.

Hood light. Raise the hood and select an underhood mounting location on a cross brace or subpanel of the hood. It should be a spot where it will be easy to mount the light, and where the light will illuminate the engine compartment best. Do *not* choose a location on the hood panel itself.

Mark the spot, and drill mounting screw hole(s) of an appropriate size for the mounting hardware provided with the light kit. *Caution: Apply a slight, but steady pressure to the drill, but be careful that the drill bit doesn't suddenly break through and damage the hood panel.*

Fasten the light into place with the hardware supplied, as directed by the

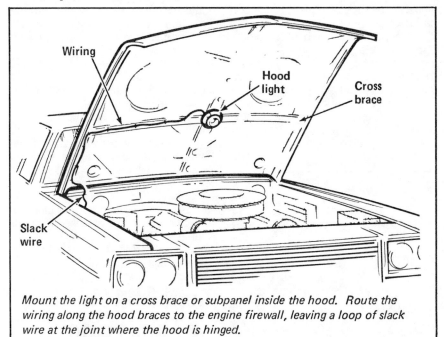

Mount the light on a cross brace or subpanel inside the hood. Route the wiring along the hood braces to the engine firewall, leaving a loop of slack wire at the joint where the hood is hinged.

manufacturer. Make sure the light is level when the hood is closed. The light is equipped with an integral mercury-operated switch, which turns the light on when the hood is opened and off when it is closed. If it isn't level, it will stay on all the time and run your battery down.

Route the wiring from the light along the hood braces and down to the engine firewall, leaving some slack at the hood closure joint. Make sure the wires will not touch the engine or catch on anything when the hood is closed. Use electrical tape to secure the wires to other wires on the firewall. Then run the wires through the firewall with other existing wires.

Under the instrument panel, locate wires for accessories that always are energized; interior light wires and wires supplying power to a dashboard clock are some good choices. You can splice the two wires from the light to the two from, for example, the clock by stripping and joining positive (+) wire to positive wire and negative (−) wire to negative wire. Cover the joints with electrical tape. NOTE: You also can use a special 2-wire connector that doesn't require stripping the existing wires; these connectors are available in automotive supply stores. Test the light.

Trunk light. To install a trunk light, use the same mounting procedure as outlined for the hood light. The only difference in the installation is that you must run the trunk light's wires into the passenger compartment and under the carpeting and interior floor molding to the connection point under the instrument panel.

Mount Splash Guards

Fender splash guards deflect mud and gravel away from the body of your car to protect its finish and to keep it clean. **Tools:** scratch awl, hammer, electric drill with bit, screwdriver or small wrench. **Materials:** rags, set of splash guards with mounting hardware. **Time:** about 1 hour.

NOTE: Try to buy splash guards that are specifically designed for your car—they'll be easier to mount. If you buy a "universal" style, you'll have to trim the guards to fit. Splash guards are made of rubber, vinyl, stainless steel, and combinations of these materials.

Most splash guards are attached with sheet-metal screws or machine screws and nuts to the lip of a fender's trailing edge. Clean this area of each fender before installing the splash guards.

Position a splash guard on the trailing edge of a fender for the best possible fit and contour alignment. Using the splash guard as a template, mark the position of each screw hole on the fender lip with a scratch awl Set the guard aside and make a hole-starting indentation in the fender lip with the awl and hammer at each marked point. Drill a hole at each of the points.

Fasten the splash guard to the fender lip with the hardware supplied.

Repeat this procedure for the other three fender splash guards.

Install Body Molding

Molding not only dresses up the appearance of a car, it also offers protection from dents and scratches. Adhesive-backed body molding is easy to apply. **Tools:** level, pencil, utility knife. **Materials:** petroleum-based solvent, clean cloths, masking tape, adhesive-backed molding. **Time:** about 1 hour.

Use a petroleum-based solvent to clean both sides of the car along the area where the molding is to be applied. Dry the finish thoroughly and make sure that it is free of dust, wax, and road film.

Plan the precise position of the molding. NOTE: For best protection, apply the molding along the point of maximum car width.

Apply a strip of masking tape along one side of the car just above where you plan to place the molding; the tape will guide you in applying the molding.

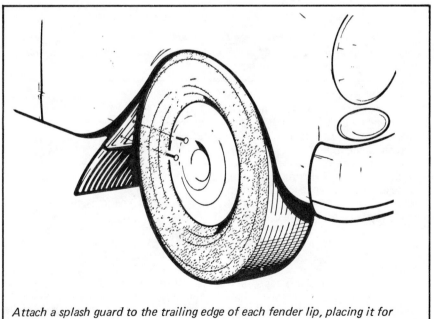

Attach a splash guard to the trailing edge of each fender lip, placing it for optimum fit and alignment.

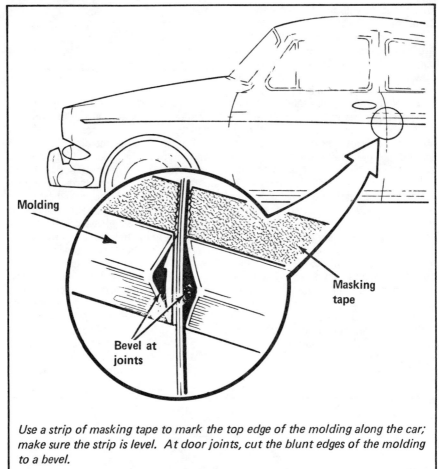

Use a strip of masking tape to mark the top edge of the molding along the car; make sure the strip is level. At door joints, cut the blunt edges of the molding to a bevel.

NOTE: You can check to see if the tape is horizontal by using a level. If it's not, simply lift up the tape strip and realign it.

Beginning on one side of the car, measure and mark each section of molding. Trim it to fit with a utility knife, and make sure that a section butting up to a door joint is trimmed properly; it should be beveled if trimmed close to the joint.

Begin applying the sections of molding; peel off the protective backing on a section, align its top edge with the bottom edge of the masking tape, and press the molding firmly into position.

Repeat the procedure for molding on the other side of the car.

Finally, remove the masking tape.

Install a Vacuum Gauge

A vacuum gauge is a useful aftermarket accessory that lets you monitor the performance of your car's engine and helps you increase fuel efficiency. **Tools:** electric drill with bits, screwdriver, utility knife, wrench, wire stripper. **Materials:** vacuum gauge kit, rubber grommet, electrical tape, quick-clamp wire connector. **Time:** about 1 hour.

Mount the vacuum gauge in a convenient location where it will be visible to the driver. If the gauge is a self-mounting type, peel the paper off the adhesive-coated pad on the rear or base of the device, and press it firmly against the mounting surface on the dashboard. If the gauge is mounted on a bracket, drill screw holes, using the bracket as a template. *Caution: Make sure the drill bit does not damage anything behind the mounting location.*

Mount the bracket with the screws provided, and secure the device in the bracket.

Route the vacuum hose that comes with the gauge through an opening in the firewall into the engine compartment. NOTE: If you must drill a hole for this hose, make it large enough to insert a rubber grommet to protect the hose from chafing.

Connect one end of the vacuum hose to the gauge, according to the manufacturer's instructions.

Raise the hood and locate a vacuum hose at the intake manifold or carburetor on the engine; instructions with the kit should provide a diagram to help you locate such a hose. Using a utility knife, cut this vacuum hose and insert the T-fitting provided in the kit.

Attach the end of the gauge's vacuum hose to the T-fitting. Tape the gauge's vacuum hose to other hoses or supports in the engine compartment to keep it from coming in contact with engine components. Close the hood.

NOTE: Illuminated vacuum gauges generally have two wires to connect—a red, positive (+) wire and a black, negative (−) ground wire. Connect the ground wire to any nearby bare metal under the dashboard. You can do this by loosening a screw or bolt and scraping any paint from around the fastener to ensure contact with bare metal. Using a wire stripper, strip about ½ inch of insulation from the end of the ground wire, twist the strands of wire together, and form them into a loop. Secure the wire loop under the screw or bolt head and tighten the fastener.

Connect the red, positive (+) wire to a positive "hot" wire for the instrument panel lights. This can be done by using a quick-clamp wire connector available in automotive supply stores. The clamp connector enables you to splice the two wires together without having to strip any insulation.

Install a Coolant Recovery System

A surprisingly easy way to improve your car's cooling system is to install an inexpensive coolant recovery tank—if your car doesn't already have one. Such a system prevents coolant loss—if the coolant boils over, it will flow into the tank, not the road—and also helps keep your car running cooler by eliminating air in the cooling system. **Tools:** screwdriver, electric drill and bit, utility knife. **Materials:** coolant recovery tank kit, sheet metal screws, plastic or wire ties, rag. **Time:** about ½ hour.

Caution: Since you'll be working with the cooling system, don't tackle this job when the engine is warm; allow the engine—and coolant—to cool before beginning.

When the engine is cool, raise the hood and remove the radiator cap. Also remove the tubing from the radiator's overflow tube.

The coolant recovery tank kit includes a roll of flexible coolant transfer tubing. Attach one end of this roll of tubing to the radiator's overflow tube. Route the tubing to a suitable location for the recovery tank inside the engine compartment, making sure that both tubing and tank will be safe from moving engine parts and will not interfere with operation or maintenance of the car. Once you've located a suitable spot, secure the recovery tank to the car, following the manufacturer's instructions. Usually, you'll have to drill a few holes for sheet metal screws. The screws may be provided with the kit.

Use a utility knife to cut off excess coolant transfer tubing; then attach the other end of the tubing to the recovery tank's inlet-outlet tube. If necessary,

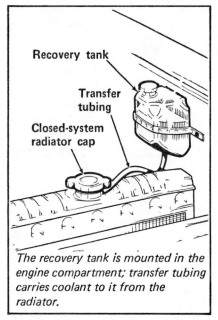

Recovery tank

Transfer tubing

Closed-system radiator cap

The recovery tank is mounted in the engine compartment; transfer tubing carries coolant to it from the radiator.

use plastic or wire ties to fasten the coolant transfer tubing so that it remains in place. Be careful not to pinch or damage the tubing with the ties. Finally, install the new closed-system radiator cap on the radiator.

Start the engine and run the car for about 15 minutes to reach normal operating temperature. Then observe the coolant level in the recovery tank. If the level is below the *warm* mark, add a 50/50 mixture of water and antifreeze through the recovery tank's filler opening until the correct level is reached.

Check the coolant level again in a few days, both when the engine is cool and when it's warm.

Install a Rear-Window Defroster

Of all the rear-window defrosters available for cars, the electric-grid is the simplest type to install. It consists of a sheet of self-adhering plastic with a grid or heating wire in it. **Tools:** Phillips-head screwdriver, electric drill and bit, wire stripper, terminal connectors, terminal crimping tool. **Materials:** glass cleaner, vinegar, paper towels, electric-grid defroster kit, electrical tape. **Time:** about 1 hour.

Clean the inside of the rear-window glass *thoroughly;* if you use glass cleaner, wash the glass again with vinegar and rinse it with clear water. Dry it completely.

Peel off the protective paper backing sheet from the grid, align the grid carefully on the inside of the rear window, and press it into place, following the manufacturer's instructions. NOTE: It is best to smooth the grid from the center outward to remove any trapped bubbles of air.

Run the positive (+) "hot" wire from the grid under the rear-window trimwork, behind and under the rear seat, and under doorsill trim to the driver's side of the instrument panel. Avoid routing the wire under carpeting or floor mats.

Find a convenient location for the defroster's on/off switch on the front or bottom portion of the instrument panel. Drill a hole in the panel for the switch or drill screw holes for the switch bracket in the bottom portion of the panel.

Connect the "hot" wire from the defroster to one terminal of the switch, and connect another length of wire to the other switch terminal. Mount the switch in the panel or bracket with the hardware provided.

Connect the remaining free wire end from the switch to a terminal on the ignition switch or to an accessory terminal at the fuse block under the instrument panel. However, make sure the connection is to a power source that is energized only when the ignition switch is on. Use an appropriate connector, as directed by the manufacturer.

Run the negative (−) ground wire from the grid to a convenient, nearby section of bare metal on the car's chassis, and secure it firmly with an existing metal screw or bolt. If the metal under the screw or bolt head is painted, scrape off the paint to achieve a good ground.

NOTE: Some electric-grid defroster kits include an indicator light to show when the device is on. Unless this light is an integral part of the defroster's switch, wire the indicator light into the circuit, according to the manufacturer's instructions.

Install
Stereo Speakers

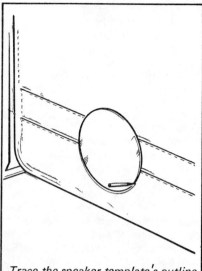

Trace the speaker template's outline onto the door panel; then cut away the outlined vinyl or fabric.

Door- or rear-deck-mounted stereo speakers are accessories any car owner can install. **Tools:** screwdrivers, Phillips-head screwdriver, felt-tip pen, utility knife, electric drill, saber saw, wire stripper. **Materials:** stereo speaker kit with wiring, connectors, and mounting hardware; rubber grommets, electrical tape, duct tape. **Time:** about 2 to 3 hours, depending on whether sheet-metal cutting is required.

First, decide where to place the speakers; two common locations are the rear window deck and the front-door trim panels. Before finally deciding on a location, check the sheet metal behind the rear deck and the door panels. There may already be cutouts in the metal for speaker installation; these can save you considerable time and trouble.

Door-panel installation. Roll down the door window completely. Pry up the corner of one of the front-door trim panels from its retaining clips so you can check inside for a precut speaker opening. Also check to make sure speaker installation won't interfere with the window mechanism.

Once you've determined the exact location for the speaker, place the template provided with the speaker kit against the door trim panel, and outline the speaker area with a felt-tip pen. Use a sharp utility knife to cut away the outlined vinyl or fabric on the panel; follow your outline carefully.

With an electric drill, bore a hole

Drill a starter hole inside the marked edge; then carefully cut out the speaker area with a saber saw.

through the inside of the panel, inside the edge of the outline, large enough to accommodate a saber saw blade. *Caution: Be careful not to drill through the door or damage any components in the door.* Insert the blade of a saber saw and cut out the speaker opening; if the panel is sheet metal, use a metal-

CAR/Stereo Speakers

cutting blade in the saw.

Using the template or the speaker as a guide, drill the mounting holes for the speaker's retaining clips. Attach the clips.

Route the ends of the speaker wires behind the door panel and out the speaker opening. If necessary, attach connectors to the stripped ends of the wires, and attach the connectors to the speaker's terminals, following the manufacturer's instructions exactly.

Drill a small hole through the edge of the door in a suitable place, large enough to accommodate the speaker wires and a rubber grommet. Directly opposite this hole, drill another hole of the same size through the door frame on the car body. Thread the speaker wires through a rubber grommet and insert the wires and the grommet into the hole in the door edge. Repeat to thread the wires through another rubber grommet into the hole in the door frame.

Attach the waterproof covering to the rear of the speaker. If the speaker doesn't come with a protective covering, make one with duct tape. Then mount the speaker in its retaining clips in the door panel, and screw or snap the speaker cover into place. Repeat to install the other door speaker.

With both speakers installed, remove the excess slack in the speaker wires, and route the wires from both speakers to the location of the car radio. With the radio turned off, connect the speaker wires to the radio, as directed by the manufacturer. There are many different ways to connect speakers to a radio. Some radios have extension wires with connectors spliced to the stripped ends of the speaker wires—negative wires to negative wires, and positive wires to positive wires. Some speakers have a short negative wire that is connected to the metal of the car frame near the speaker's location; only the positive wire is routed to the car radio. Some speaker kits have special connectors on the ends of the speaker wires; these mate with connectors on or at the radio. Follow the manufacturer's specific instructions for your speakers.

Rear-deck speakers. Many cars have precut openings in the rear window deck for speaker installation. Basically, installation in this location is very similar to that for door panel installation; wires from rear-deck speakers are routed behind the rear seats, along the floor and door sill trim, and behind side kick panels to the radio. Protective coverings are not required for the speakers.

Health/ Personal Care

Make Your Own Internal Remedies:

Cough Syrup

This lemon-and-honey syrup is a real soother for minor coughs. **Equipment:** saucepan, sharp knife, strainer, funnel, 8-ounce bottle with cap, measuring spoons. **Ingredients:** lemon, water, glycerin, honey. **Yield:** 1 cup.

Put a whole lemon in a saucepan with enough water to cover the lemon, bring it to a boil, and simmer it for 10 minutes. Remove the lemon and cut it in half. Squeeze the juice and pulp from each half through a strainer and funnel into an 8-ounce bottle; add 2 tablespoons of glycerine. Fill the bottle with honey, cap it tightly, and shake well.

Take 1 tablespoon of the syrup as required; shake well before pouring.

Sore Throat Gargle

The first sign of an impending cold may be a dry, scratchy throat. You can do as well as the drug companies with this simple solution. **Equipment:** drinking glass, teaspoon, toothpick. **Ingredients:** salt, aspirin tablets, water, red food coloring. The red food coloring lets you know the liquid in the glass is not just water. **Yield:** enough for one use.

Place ½ teaspoon of salt into the glass; fill the glass half full with hot water and stir until the salt dissolves. Place two aspirin tablets in a teaspoon, add a few drops of hot water, and break up the tablets with a toothpick. When the tablets have broken down into a paste, add the paste to the salt solution in the glass. Add 4 or 5 drops of red food coloring, fill the glass almost full with hot water, and stir.

Gargle small portions of this solution; rinse your mouth lightly with plain cold water. *Caution: If pain persists after several days, consult your doctor.*

Laryngitis Treatment

If you're dependent on your voice— for teaching, singing, acting, or speaking—you know how annoying laryngitis can be. Most medical treatments are touch and go, but you can get some relief with this classic remedy. **Equipment:** 3-quart saucepan, measuring cup, mixing spoon. **Ingredients:** water, bran flakes or all-bran cereal, honey. **Yield:** about 2 quarts.

Heat 2 quarts of water to a boil in a saucepan and add 1 cup of bran flakes or all-bran cereal; sweeten as desired with honey. Both bran and honey soothe and protect irritated tissues.

Drink hot throughout the day; you should feel an improvement within 24 hours. *Caution: In persistent or severe cases of laryngitis or hoarseness, consult a doctor.*

Sore Throat Soother

After the first sneeze, colds and flu manifest themselves through sore throats and all the other well-known symptoms. Nothing really cures a cold, but this mixture can make your throat feel better. **Equipment:** measuring spoons, measuring cup, small saucepan, pint jar with cover, funnel, coffee filter, mixing spoon. **Ingredients:** aniseed, water, honey, brandy or cherry liqueur. **Yield:** about 1¼ cups.

Measure 2 tablespoons of aniseed into a small saucepan and add 1 cup of water. Bring to a boil over medium heat and simmer for 15 to 20 minutes; cool. Pour into a clean pint jar through a funnel lined with a clean coffee filter. Add ¼ cup of honey and 1 tablespoon of brandy or cherry liqueur; stir to mix well.

Take 1 tablespoon of this mixture every 3 hours.

Sleeping Potion

While not necessarily serious, insomnia can be decidedly annoying. For a mild sleeping potion without drugs, try this effective preparation. **Equipment:** cup, measuring spoons, mixing spoon. **Ingredients:** tincture of valerian, vinegar, honey, gin or vodka, milk. Buy tincture of valerian at a pharmacy. **Yield:** about ½ cup, enough for 1 serving.

Measure 1 tablespoon of tincture of valerian into a cup; add 1½ teaspoons of vinegar, 3 tablespoons of honey, and 2 tablespoons of gin or vodka. Stir, add 2 tablespoons of hot milk, and stir again.

Drink the mixture warm or hot about ½ hour before going to bed. If you're still awake in an hour, repeat the dose. Do not take more than two portions in an evening.

Digestive Aid

This simple digestive compound is pleasanter than the commercial remedies, and it's far less expensive. **Equipment:** measuring cup, small saucepan, measuring spoons, small bottle with cover, funnel, coffee filter. **Ingredients:** water, aniseed, honey. **Yield:** about 1 cup.

Measure 1 cup of water into a small saucepan and heat it to boiling; add 1 teaspoon of aniseed and 1 teaspoon of honey. Simmer the mixture for 10 minutes, remove from heat, and let it cool. Strain the mixture into a small bottle through a funnel lined with a clean coffee filter. Cover tightly.

Take 1 to 2 tablespoons of the mixture about ½ hour after eating, as needed.

Make Your Own External Remedies:

Sunburn Soothers

You can relieve much of the sting of sunburn with these simple mixtures.

QUICK-RELIEF CREAM. Use this ointment to soothe mild sunburn. **Equipment:** small mixing bowl, measuring spoons, cup, mixing spoon. **Ingredients:** baking soda, witch hazel, water, peppermint extract. Buy witch hazel at a pharmacy. **Yield:** enough for one application.

Measure 4 tablespoons of baking soda into a mixing bowl; measure 2 tablespoons of water and 1 tablespoon of witch hazel into a cup. Add just enough water/witch-hazel mixture to the baking soda to moisten it, and stir it to a smooth paste. Add the remaining liquid slowly, stirring to keep the mixture smooth. Finally, add 5 drops of peppermint extract and mix again.

Remove the dressing from the bowl and apply it gently to the sunburned area. For easier spreading, add more liquid.

COOLING COMPRESSES. For more serious sunburn, don't rub in cream or lotion; use compresses to avoid further damage to your skin. **Equipment:** mixing bowl, mixing spoon, measuring cup, measuring spoons, small saucepan. **Ingredients:** cake camphor, rubbing alcohol, limewater, water, boric acid, vinegar, perfume. Buy camphor, limewater, and boric acid at a pharmacy. **Yield:** enough for one application.

Place a cake of camphor into a mixing bowl. Pour a few drops of rubbing alcohol onto the cake and crush it into powder with a mixing spoon. Add ¼ cup (4 tablespoons) of limewater to the alcohol-and-camphor mixture, and stir well.

Measure 2 tablespoons of water into a small saucepan, and bring the water to a boil. Add 2 tablespoons of boric acid to the boiling water and stir to dissolve; then remove the solution from the heat and pour it into the alcohol-camphor mixture. Add 6 tablespoons of white vinegar and stir well. If desired, add a few drops of perfume.

Let the mixture cool completely. To apply the solution, saturate clean soft cloths with the liquid and apply the wet compresses to sunburned areas. Keep the compresses moist.

Diaper Rash Ointment

Cope with diaper rash with this effective, inexpensive ointment. **Equipment:** measuring spoons, mixing bowl, mixing spoon, small jar with cover. **Ingredients:** aquaphor ointment, aluminum acetate solution (Burrow's solution), zinc oxide paste. Buy the ingredients at a pharmacy. **Yield:** about 2½ ounces.

Measure 2 tablespoons of aquaphor ointment into a mixing bowl; add 1 tablespoon of aluminum acetate solution (Burrow's solution) and mix the ingredients thoroughly to dissolve the aluminum acetate. Add 1 ounce of zinc oxide paste and mix again. Transfer the ointment to a small jar and cover it tightly.

Apply the ointment liberally after each diaper change. If the rash is worse after 2 days of treatment, consult your pediatrician.

Athlete's Foot Powder

Athlete's foot is the classic locker-room/camp complaint—itching, burning, stinging feet, and no joke. Get rid of it with this simple powder. **Equipment:** large mixing bowl, measuring cup, mixing spoon, shaker container. **Ingredients:** boric acid, talcum powder, sodium thiosulfate. Buy sodium thiosulfate at a pharmacy. **Yield:** about 1¾ cups.

Measure 1 cup of boric acid into a large mixing bowl and add ½ cup of talcum powder and ¼ cup of sodium thiosulfate; stir to mix thoroughly. Pour into a clean shaker container.

Sprinkle the athlete's foot powder on your feet and between your toes twice a day, morning and evening. Be aware that the symptoms don't go away overnight; treatment usually runs from about 2 weeks to a month. *Caution: In very severe or persistent cases of athlete's foot, consult a doctor.*

Liniment

Liniments provide two-way relief for sore muscles; they act to draw blood into the affected area under the skin, and they are applied by rubbing, which

469

produces heat through friction. This liniment is a good one to have on hand. **Equipment:** measuring cup, measuring spoons, mixing spoon, small mixing bowl, small bottle with cover, funnel, coffee filter. **Ingredients:** rubbing alcohol, camphor, synthetic oil of wintergreen (methyl salicylate), tincture of green soap, water. Buy the ingredients at a pharmacy. **Yield:** 1 cup.

To make the liniment, measure 1 cup plus 2 tablespoons of rubbing alcohol into a small mixing bowl. Break the camphor up into small pieces and add approximately 1 teaspoon of these chunks to the alcohol; then add ½ teaspoon of synthetic oil of wintergreen. When the camphor has dissolved, add 3 tablespoons tincture of green soap and stir until the mixture is clear. Add enough water to measure 8 ounces and mix; set the mixture aside for 24 hours in a cool place. Then pour the liniment into a small bottle through a funnel lined with a coffee filter, and cover it tightly.

Rub in the liniment to relieve muscle aches; do not apply to bruised or broken skin.

Poison Ivy Lotion

Use this effective, fast-acting lotion to relieve the itching and rash caused by contact with poison ivy or other poisonous plants. **Equipment:** measuring cup, two small saucepans, measuring spoons, funnel, pint bottle with cap. **Ingredients:** water, alum, white vinegar. **Yield:** 1 pint.

Measure ½ cup of water into a saucepan and add 4 tablespoons of alum; heat the water until the alum dissolves. Heat ½ cup of white vinegar in another saucepan and pour the warm alum solution into the vinegar; a white precipitate should appear. Remove the mixture from the heat and let it stand until all of the precipitate settles to the bottom of the saucepan.

Carefully decant the solution into a pint bottle and discard the white precipitate. Cap the bottle tightly.

Apply the lotion as soon as possible for relief within 24 hours. Before using it, wash the affected area thoroughly and wipe it with rubbing alcohol. Then pour the lotion onto a soft clean cloth to make a wet compress; apply the compress to the skin for about 10 minutes. Let the lotion dry on the skin. Apply in the morning, at bedtime, and once during the day. For severe allergic reactions, consult a doctor.

Prickly Heat Lotion

Prickly heat, a condition endemic among small children during the summer, doesn't have to spoil their fun. Relieve the itching and burning of the rash with this soothing formula. **Equipment:** measuring spoons, mixing bowl, mixing spoon, measuring cup, funnel, pint bottle with cap. **Ingredients:** zinc oxide powder, baking soda, glycerin, rubbing alcohol, witch hazel, rose water. Buy the ingredients at a pharmacy. **Yield:** 1 pint.

Measure 1 tablespoon of zinc oxide powder and 2 teaspoons of baking soda into a mixing bowl; add 1 tablespoon of glycerin and stir to a smooth paste. Add ½ cup of rubbing alcohol and ½ cup of witch hazel and stir well. Pour the mixture into a 1-pint bottle and fill the bottle with rose water; cap the bottle and shake it well.

Apply the lotion to affected areas as often as needed.

Analgesic Balm

Analgesic balm is an ointment that contains medicinal ingredients—besides feeling good when you rub it on, it works directly to relieve the pain of sprains, stiffness, and aches. **Equip-**

ment: double boiler, mixing spoon, measuring spoons. **Ingredients:** anhydrous lanolin, beeswax, synthetic oil of wintergreen (methyl salicylate), water. Buy lanolin, beeswax, and synthetic oil of wintergreen at a pharmacy. **Yield:** enough for one application.

Place 3 tablespoons of anhydrous lanolin into the top of a double boiler and set it over low heat. When the lanolin melts, add about ⅓ ounce (10 grams) of beeswax—about 2 teaspoons when the wax has melted. Remove the double boiler from the heat. When the beeswax is completely melted, stir the mixture to blend the lanolin and wax, and add 1 tablespoon of synthetic oil of wintergreen (methyl salicylate). Finally, stir in 1 tablespoon of water. Stir continually until the mixture is the consistency of thick jelly.

Rub gently into the skin to relieve muscle pain. Do not apply to broken skin.

Nosebleed Remedy

Nosebleeds are messy and scary for children to deal with; they're no treat for anyone. Stop them fast with this simple remedy. **Equipment:** measuring spoons, small saucepan, mixing spoon, measuring cup, small bottle with cap, funnel, coffee filter. **Ingredients:** alum, water, vinegar. **Yield:** about 3 ounces.

Measure 2 tablespoons of alum and 2 tablespoons of water into a small saucepan; heat over medium heat, stirring occasionally, to dissolve the alum. Add ¼ cup of vinegar and stir the mixture again; remove from the heat. Strain the mixture into a small bottle through a funnel lined with a coffee filter. Cap the bottle.

To use the mixture, soak a small piece of absorbent cotton with the solution. Press out excess liquid. With the patient lying on his back, place the wet cotton into the affected nostril. Remove the cotton after 5 to 10 minutes.

Quick Quantity Rubdown

This rubbing compound is a great one for athletic families—it's inexpensive enough to make and use in quantity, to soothe everybody's aches. **Equipment:** measuring cup, gallon container with cover, funnel, measuring spoons. **Ingredients:** synthetic oil of wintergreen (methyl salicylate), rubbing alcohol, witch hazel, water, after-shave lotion or cologne. Buy synthetic oil of wintergreen at a pharmacy.

Pour ¼ cup of synthetic oil of wintergreen—methyl salicylate—into a clean gallon container, using a funnel as necessary. Add 3 pints of rubbing alcohol, cover the container and shake well. Remove the lid and add 2 pints of witch hazel and enough water to completely fill the container. If the odor of wintergreen is too strong, add 1 teaspoon of your favorite after-shave lotion or cologne.

Shake the rubbing compound well each time you use it; rub it into aching muscles as needed. Do not apply to bruised or broken skin.

Mustard Plaster

The good old-fashioned mustard plaster is still remembered as an effective treatment for the chest congestion of colds; it can also be used on the back to relieve muscle aches. **Equipment:** measuring spoons, mixing bowl, mixing spoon, muslin or cheesecloth. **Ingredients:** dry mustard, flour, water. **Yield:** enough for one application.

Measure 2 tablespoons of dry mustard and 2 tablespoons of flour into a mixing bowl; add enough warm water to make a thick but spreadable paste. Mix thoroughly to remove lumps.

Spread the paste on a piece of muslin or double layer of cheesecloth large enough to cover the chest area; cover the paste with another piece of muslin or cheesecloth. Spread a thin layer of petroleum jelly on the chest area, to ease the removal of the plaster, and place the prepared plaster on the chest and spread a towel over it to hold it down. *Caution: Do not spread the mustard mixture directly on the skin. Do not use the plaster on small children or on patients with sensitive skin.*

Lift the plaster periodically to look at the skin; when the skin turns pink, remove the plaster. Two or three applications a day should break up the congestion; if congestion persists, consult your doctor.

Cut Your Own Hair

Once you learn how, you'll wonder why you ever hesitated to cut your own hair. **Tools:** razor comb, two mirrors, barbers' comb, sharp haircut scissors, large hair clips. **Materials:** newspaper, towel. **Time:** ½ to 1 hour.

If you have very short hair, you can trim it with a razor comb, a simple device that's used just like a comb. Comb the razor comb through your hair, working evenly over your head and following the manufacturer's instructions; you'll end up with a short, cropped, tidy hairdo.

Most of us prefer to leave a little more hair on our heads, and cutting longer hair takes a little more care. Before you start, spread newspaper on the floor to catch the clippings. Drape a towel around your shoulders to keep cut hair off your clothes.

Set up two mirrors so that you can see both the front and the back of your head while you cut. Since you must depend on the mirror for cutting the back of your hair, you'll achieve the best results by relying on the mirror when you cut the front of your hair as well; don't make any cuts unless you're actually looking in the mirror. Don't just snip blindly!

Use a special barbers' comb and a sharp haircut scissors; they'll give you much better results than an ordinary comb and scissors. Use the same hand to hold the comb and the scissors, as needed, so that you'll always be measuring the amount of hair to cut with the same fingers of your other hand; always hold your hair with one hand and hold either the comb or the scissors with the other. Cut your hair so that it will fall away from you when you cut, and not back down on your head. Cut your hair when it's freshly washed and still damp.

Short hair. If your hair is shoulder-length or longer and you want it short, wet it thoroughly, comb it out, and rough-cut it so that it hangs above your shoulders; it will be easier to work with this way. Comb the wet hair straight back and off your face. Lift a small amount of hair at the front and center of your head straight up with the comb and hold it taut with the fingers of your other hand. Holding the stretched hair firmly, put down the comb, pick up the scissors, and cut off the desired amount.

Cut the next portion of hair directly behind the newly cut portion and work back toward the crown of your head; continue this process until all the hair on the top of your head is cut. Use the cut-off hair as a guide to keep your cutting even from portion to portion.

Next cut the hair on the sides of your head. Follow the same procedure to comb, stretch, and cut, working from top to bottom and from front to back. Hold the comb at an angle that conforms to the side of your head, and cut at that angle as you work. Continue cutting all the way around your head to the back, using the mirrors as your guide. Work from one side of your head around to the back and then from the other side around to the back. Do *not* work from one side all the way around to the other. Make sure the hair is cut to the same length at each side of your face.

On the back of your head, cut the top

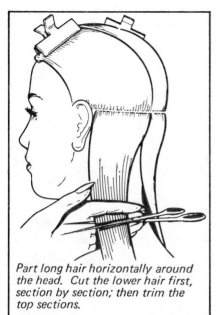

Part long hair horizontally around the head. Cut the lower hair first, section by section; then trim the top sections.

sure to trim the sides evenly. Then un-clip the top hair at each side and trim it the same way, working on one side at a time. If you want your hair to turn under, cut the top hair on each side about ½ inch longer than the bottom hair. Finally, comb out your hair and make sure it's even at the sides and across the back; adjust as necessary.

Fold the newspaper together and discard it.

Cut Your Family's Hair

You can save a lot of money with home haircuts, and you can keep your family happy by doing the job right—with a minimum of equipment, patience, and planning, it's easy to give both men's and women's cuts. **Tools:** mirror and hand mirror, razor comb, barbers' comb, sharp haircut scissors, large hair clips. **Materials:** newspaper, towel, nail polish to mark comb or scissors. **Time:** ½ to 1 hour.

Work in front of a mirror, so both you and your subject can see what you're doing. Give your subject a hand mirror for back views; this will prevent a lot of fidgeting. Spread newspaper on the floor to catch the clippings, and drape a towel around the subject's shoulders. The hair should be freshly washed and still damp.

Use a razor comb to trim very short hair, using it just like a comb. Comb through your subject's hair with the razor comb, working evenly over the head and following the manufacturer's instructions. For all other haircuts, use a special barbers' comb and a sharp hair-cut scissors; they'll give you much bet-ter results than an ordinary comb and scissors. Use the same hand to hold the comb and the scissors, as needed; hold the hair to be cut with your other hand. If you want a cutting guide to measure the hair you're trimming, mark your scissors or comb with nail polish in inch and ½-inch gradations.

part of your hair and then the lower part; check the mirror constantly to be sure you're cutting evenly. Finally, comb your freshly cut hair straight back and use the two mirrors to cut along the bottom of your hair in back. Cut it straight across the bottom or feather the edge, as desired. If you want your hair to turn under a little at the back, hold the scissors at an angle as you cut so that the hair on the outside is slightly longer than the hair on the inside.

Fold the newspaper together and discard it.

Long hair. If your hair is long and you want to keep it that way, you'll only need to trim it. Part your wet hair in the center and comb it straight down all around. Part your hair vertically from the nape of your neck and pull it to the front on each side. Part each hank of hair horizontally to divide it into an upper and a lower half, and part each large section of hair again vertically to divide it in two. Clip the upper hair on each side at the top of your head with a large hair clip.

Trim the lower hair on each side. Comb the hair straight forward and cut off the desired amount, front to back. Be

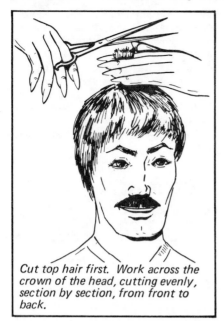

Cut top hair first. Work across the crown of the head, cutting evenly, section by section, from front to back.

then match the front of the second side to it; do *not* work from one side all the way around the head. Make sure the hair is the same length at both sides.

When all the side hair is trimmed, cut the back hair. Comb all the hair straight back and cut it straight across the bottom, or feather the edge, as desired. If you have trouble cutting a straight line, use the comb as a cutting guide. To make the hair turn under a little, hold the scissors at an angle as you cut so that the hair on the outside is slightly longer than the hair on the inside.

Fold the newspaper together and discard it.

Long hair. Most people who have long hair and want to keep it long just need an occasional trim. Part the wet hair in the center and down the center at the back; part it again horizontally to divide it into upper and lower portions. Part each large section of hair again vertically to divide it in two. Clip the upper hair up at the top of the head with large hair clips.

Trim the lower hair on each side; comb it straight forward and cut off the desired amount, from the front all around to the back. Be sure to trim the sides evenly; if you want the hair to fall in an oval shape at the back, angle the cut line down toward the back. The sharper you make the cutting angle, the more pronounced the curve from front to back will be.

Short hair. If the hair is shoulder-length or longer and you're going to cut it short, wet it thoroughly, comb it out, and rough-cut it so that it hangs above the shoulders; it will be easier to work with this way. Comb the wet hair straight back from your subject's face. Lift a small section of hair at the front and center of the head with the comb and hold the hair stretched taut with the fingers of your other hand. Holding the stretched hair firmly, put down the comb, pick up the scissors, and cut off the desired amount of hair.

Cut the next portion of hair directly behind the newly cut portion and work back to the crown of the head; work back and across until the hair on the top of the head has been trimmed. Use a newly cut section of hair as a guide to keep your cutting even as you work, or measure with the marked comb or scissors.

To cut the side hair, hold the comb so that it angles with the natural line of the side of the head. Follow the same procedure to comb, stretch, and cut, being careful to angle your cutting properly; work from top to bottom and front to back. Work on one side of the head and

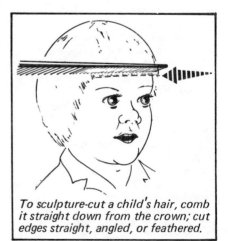

To sculpture-cut a child's hair, comb it straight down from the crown; cut edges straight, angled, or feathered.

When all the lower hair is trimmed, unclip the top hair at each side and trim the same way, working on one side at a time, front to back. If you want the hair to turn under, cut the top hair about ½ inch longer than the bottom hair. Finally, comb out the hair and make sure it's even at the sides and across the back; adjust as necessary.

Fold the newspaper together and discard it.

Children's hair. Cut children's hair the same way you'd cut an adult's hair; simple styles are best. You can have fun sculpting little boys' and girls' hairdos by combing the trimmed hair straight down from the crown of the head all around; cut the edges all around as desired, with straight, feathered, or angled cuts.

Make Your Own Hair Care Products:

Bronze Henna Shampoo

Henna, a centuries-old favorite, won't damage your hair the way dye or bleach can. To give a bronze or reddish cast to dark hair, try this gentle henna shampoo. **Equipment:** measuring cup, saucepan, measuring spoons, mixing spoon, pint container with cap, funnel, coffee filter, sharp knife. **Ingredients:** water, powdered henna, borax, liquid laundry bluing, castile soap. **Yield:** about ½ pint.

Pour 1 cup of water into a small saucepan and bring it to a boil. Remove it from the heat and add 1 teaspoon of powdered henna, ¼ teaspoon of borax, and ¼ teaspoon of liquid laundry bluing. Stir the mixture and strain it into a pint container through a funnel lined with a clean coffee filter. Pour the mixture back into the saucepan.

Cut a small, hand-size cake of castile soap into quarters with a sharp knife. Cut one quarter of the soap into shavings, and add the shavings to the mixture. Heat the mixture over a low flame until the soap dissolves and strain it again into the pint container. Cover it tightly.

Protein Shampoo

Mix this high-protein shampoo fresh whenever you need it—it does the job at least as well as store-boughts. **Equipment:** small mixing bowl, electric mixer or egg beater, measuring cup, measuring spoons, mixing spoon. **Ingredients:** egg white, water, gelatin, ammonia, cologne, rubbing alcohol. **Yield:** enough for one shampoo.

In a small mixing bowl, beat the white of an egg until frothy with an electric mixer or egg beater. Soften 1 packet of gelatin in ¼ cup of warm water and add the mixture to the egg white; mix well. Add 3 tablespoons of ammonia and mix thoroughly; add a few drops of your favorite cologne to mask the ammonia. Finally, add ¼ cup of rubbing alcohol and mix thoroughly.

Shampoo the mixture thoroughly into your hair; only one application is necessary. Rinse your hair thoroughly and apply a standard conditioning rinse as directed.

Cream Shampoo

For a natural, gentle, effective shampoo, mix this simple cream formula. **Equipment:** measuring cup, saucepan, mixing spoons, quart jar with cover. **Ingredients:** water, soap flakes, glycerin, borax, perfume. **Yield:** about 1 quart.

Measure 2 cups of water into a saucepan and heat it. Add 1 cup of soap flakes to the hot water and stir to dissolve. Remove the pan from the heat and add 1½ cups of glycerin and ¾ cup of borax; if desired, add a few drops of your favorite perfume. Stir the mixture thoroughly. Pour it into a quart jar and cover it; let it cool completely before using.

Dandruff Treatment

Troubled by dandruff? This dandruff treatment should work wonders. **Equipment:** measuring cup, small saucepan, measuring spoons, mixing spoon, small jar with cover. **Ingredients:** mineral oil, anhydrous lanolin, tincture of iodine. Buy lanolin at a pharmacy. **Yield:** about 6 ounces.

Measure ½ cup of mineral oil into a small saucepan and warm it over a low flame. Empty a 1-ounce tube of anhydrous lanolin into the warm oil and add 2 teaspoons tincture of iodine; stir to blend thoroughly and remove from the heat. Pour the warm mixture into a small jar and cover it tightly.

Massage the lotion into the scalp daily.

Liquid Hair Bleach

This gentle liquid hair bleach is easy to mix and use. **Equipment:** measuring cup, small saucepan, eyedropper, mixing spoon, bowl. **Ingredients:** vegetable oil, hydrogen peroxide (3 percent solution), ammonia. **Yield:** enough for one application.

Measure ¼ cup of vegetable oil into a small saucepan, and heat it gently over low heat until it's warm. Remove from the heat. Add ¼ cup of 3 percent solution hydrogen peroxide and 20 drops of ammonia; stir to blend. Pour the bleach into a bowl.

To use the bleach, swab the mixture into the hair with absorbent cotton. Leave it on the hair for about 20 minutes; rinse thoroughly and shampoo.

Give Yourself a Permanent

With all the home permanents on the market, you don't have to go to a professional hair stylist—curls, waves, or body, all the styling you need is right on the shelf. **Tools:** comb, sharp scissors, mirror, hand mirror, hair clips, rollers or curling rods (included with permanent kit), clock or timer. **Materials:** towels, home permanent kit, hair conditioner (often included with kit). **Time:** about 2 hours.

Choose a permanent carefully to make sure you get one that's right for your hair; look for the gentlest one you can find for the effect you want. Buy a one-step permanent, with waving and neutralizing all in one step, so all you have to do is mix the solution and apply it to your hair.

Before you start, read the directions for your permanent carefully. Follow the manufacturer's instructions for your hair type and condition—oily, hard-to-curl hair requires the maximum time, bleached hair the minimum. Do not use a permanent if your hair is damaged or if you've had a permanent recently.

Wash your hair, comb it out, and clip any split ends. Work in front of a mirror, and use a hand mirror so you can see the back of your head. Part your hair in the middle, across the top of your head and all the way down the back. Make a horizontal part around your head over your ears, dividing your hair into four sections. Clip each section together with a hair clip. On each side of your head, divide each of these main sections of hair again into sections as wide as the rollers or curling rods included in your permanent kit; make at least three top and two bottom sections on each side. Secure each section with a clip.

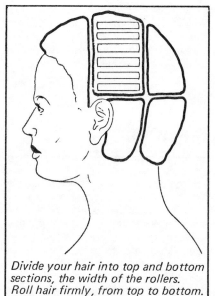

Divide your hair into top and bottom sections, the width of the rollers. Roll hair firmly, from top to bottom.

Now roll strands of damp, clean hair around the rollers or curling rods included with the permanent kit; work from top to bottom, section by section, from one side of your head around to the other. Use the end papers included with the permanent kit to keep each strand of hair neatly together; roll each strand firmly but not tightly under to the scalp and secure it. If your permanent includes rollers of different sizes, use them as recommended by the manufacturer on different parts of your head. Check the back of your head as you work with the hand mirror to make sure no loose strands have escaped from the rollers.

When all your hair is rolled on the curling rods, mix the permanent solution in the applicator bottle, as directed by the manufacturer. Mixing instructions vary by type of permanent and by brand, so follow directions carefully. Let the solution stand for the time specified—usually 15 to 35 minutes, depending on hair type. Time each step of mixing and standing exactly with a clock or timer.

When the solution is ready, apply it carefully to your hair with the applicator bottle provided, squeezing the solution gently on to saturate the hair on each curling rod completely. Drape a towel around your shoulders to protect your clothes. Wait the proper amount of time as specified by the manufacturer for your hair type—no more and no less. Setting time is usually about 20 to 35 minutes. Then, with the rollers still in your hair, rinse your hair thoroughly for at least 2 full minutes.

Gently remove the rollers from your hair, unrolling each strand of hair carefully. Then apply a conditioner to your hair; a tube of conditioner is often included in the permanent kit. Leave the conditioner in your hair for at least 1 minute, or as directed by the manufacturer; then rinse your hair thoroughly.

Set newly permed hair as usual, but don't use any sort of blow dryer, hood dryer, or curling iron; let your hair dry naturally. Don't wash your hair for at least 3 days after it's permed, and don't use a blow dryer or other dryer or curling iron until your hair feels normal again. If your hair is bleached, don't use any type of heat on your hair.

Make Your Own Hair Care Products:

Hair Dressing

To keep unruly hair in place, try this lightly scented conditioning dressing. **Equipment:** double boiler, measuring spoons, small saucepan, measuring cup, mixing spoon, small jar with cover. **Ingredients:** beeswax, castor oil, anhydrous lanolin, vegetable oil, oil of bergamot. Buy beeswax, lanolin, and oil of bergamot at a pharmacy. **Yield:** about ¾ cup.

In the top of a double boiler, slowly melt ½ ounce of beeswax, about 1 tablespoon. In a small saucepan, heat ¼ cup of castor oil, ¼ cup of anhydrous lanolin, and 1 tablespoon of vegetable oil; stir to blend the oils. Add the melted beeswax to the oils and stir well; then add 2 teaspoons of oil of bergamot and stir again. Pour the mixture into a clean jar and let cool.

To use the dressing, place a small dab on one palm and rub your palms together to spread it; run your hands through your hair to distribute the dressing evenly. Use only a little; more than a dab will make your hair greasy.

Hair Setting Lotions

If you're dissatisfied with commercial setting lotions, try these simple mixtures—no gimmicks, just the basics.

SCENTED SETTING CREAM. **Equipment:** measuring cup, mixing bowl, mixing spoon, measuring spoons, small jar with cover. **Ingredients:** powdered karaya gum, rubbing alcohol, perfume or cologne, borax. Buy karaya gum at a pharmacy. **Yield:** enough for one application.

Measure ½ cup of powdered karaya gum into a mixing bowl. Add just enough rubbing alcohol to give the mixture the consistency of thick, heavy syrup; mix well until the mixture is free of lumps. Add 1 or 2 drops of perfume or cologne and mix thoroughly.

To mix enough lotion for future use, double the ingredients and add 2 teaspoons of borax as a preservative. Spoon the mixture into a small jar and cover it tightly.

Use the cream as you would a commercial preparation.

QUANTITY WAVING LOTION. **Equipment:** measuring cup, mixing bowl, measuring spoons, mixing spoon, pint jar with cover. **Ingredients:** rose water, tragacanth gum, glycerin. Buy the ingredients at a pharmacy. **Yield:** 1 pint.

Measure 2 cups of rose water into a mixing bowl and add 2 tablespoons of tragacanth gum and 2 tablespoons of glycerin. Mix the ingredients thoroughly. Pour the lotion into a pint jar and cover it tightly.

Use the lotion as you would a commercial preparation.

Give Yourself a Facial

Everyone knows clean skin is healthy skin, but there's more to a glowing complexion than soap. For the best results, follow a regular skin care regimen to clean, moisturize, and deep-cleanse your skin. **Tools:** clean facial sponge or washcloth, large pot, heatproof pad, bath towels. **Materials:** unscented, undyed soap; washable cleansing cream or lotion, hand and body lotion, astringent, moisturizer, facial soap with scrubbing grains, drying lotion, clay or gel face mask. **Time:** regular care, a few minutes a day; about ½ hour several times a week.

Cleaning. Wash your face in the morning and evening with warm water and the proper cleanser for your skin type; use a clean facial sponge or washcloth. Stroke lather or cleansing cream onto your face in gentle upward circles, working up and out over your cheekbones and up toward your temples. Rinse thoroughly with warm water and then rinse again with cool water; blot your face dry with a clean towel. If you wash your face during the day between these cleansings, don't use soap; just rinse your face with cool water and blot it dry.

For normal skin, use unscented, undyed soap or a washable cleansing cream or lotion. After washing, apply an astringent to the oily areas at nose, chin, and forehead; apply a moisturizer to dry, taut areas. During the day, use an astringent before applying makeup; at night, apply hand and body lotion or a moisturizer, using circular upward strokes. Do not use astringent at night or moisturizer during the day.

For dry skin, use a washable cleans-

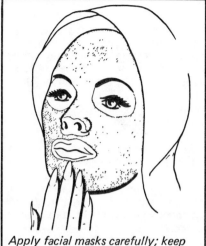

Apply facial masks carefully; keep both clay and gel types away from your eyes, mouth and hair.

ing cream or lotion; do not use soap. Don't cleanse your face with cold cream; it doesn't get skin completely clean. Apply a mild astringent after washing your face in the morning, and follow with a moisturizer; also use a moisturizer at night. In cold weather, protect your face with a rich moisturizer. Make sure your skin is completely dry before you go outside.

For oily skin, use a facial soap with scrubbing grains; don't use harsh hand-scrubbing soap. Work up a good lather with the soap, and gently scrub oily areas at nose, chin, and forehead—don't be too rough or you'll leave your skin raw. Rinse thoroughly to remove all trace of the scrubbing grains. After washing, apply an astringent and then a drying lotion to your entire face.

Steam facials. For smoother, softer skin, restore moisture to your face with a steam facial. This treatment is good for all types of skin; it's especially beneficial for dry skin. Heat a large pot of water to a full boil and remove it from the heat. Carefully set the full pot on a heatproof pad on a steady table or countertop.

Drape a bath towel over your head and shoulders in a deep hood to hold steam against your face; close your eyes, and bend down with your face over the steaming pot for 5 to 10 minutes. *Caution: Go only as close to the steam as you're comfortable. Be careful not to scald yourself.* Remove the towel, splash your face with warm water and then cool water, blot dry, and apply astringent and/or moisturizer as appropriate for your skin type.

Facial masks. For deep cleansing, use a facial mask—once or twice a week for normal or dry skin, at least three times a week for oily skin. Be careful not to get the mask preparation in your eyes or on your hair. To absorb dirt and excess oil, use a clay-type mask; apply the mask, let it dry as directed and wash it off. The clay tightens as it dries, stimulating circulation as it absorbs impurities. To restore moisture to your skin while cleansing it, use a gel-type mask; apply the mask, let it dry as directed, and peel or rinse it off. After removing the mask, splash your face with warm water and then cool water; blot dry.

Make Your Own Facial Care Products:

Natural Facial Masks

To restore moisture and deep-cleanse your face, use a facial mask regularly. These home-blended masks are designed for the three common skin types.

NORMAL-SKIN MASK. **Equipment:** small bowl, wire whisk, measuring spoons. **Ingredients:** egg, honey, brewers' yeast or cider vinegar. **Yield:** enough for one application.

Beat an egg in a small bowl, using a

wire whisk to blend yolk and white thoroughly. Add 1 teaspoon of honey and ¼ teaspoon of brewers' yeast—or, if you don't have brewers' yeast, 1 tablespoon of cider vinegar. Whisk again to blend. Apply the mask to your face, being careful not to get it in your eyes or on your hair. Let it dry for about 20 minutes, and then rinse it off thoroughly with warm water. Splash your face with cool water and blot it dry.

DRY-SKIN MASK. **Equipment:** paring knife, blender, measuring spoons. **Ingredients:** banana, honey. **Yield:** enough for one application.

Wash a banana thoroughly. Slice the banana and half of its peel into the container of a blender; add 1 tablespoon of honey and blend to a liquid. Apply the mask to your face, being careful not to get it in your eyes or on your hair. Let it dry for about 20 minutes, and then rinse it off thoroughly with warm water. Splash your face with cool water and blot it dry.

OILY-SKIN MASK. **Equipment:** paring knife, blender, measuring spoons. **Ingredients:** cucumber, yogurt. **Yield:** enough for one application.

Wash a cucumber thoroughly. If the cucumber skin is waxed, remove it; if possible, however, leave the cucumber unpeeled. Slice the cucumber into the container of a blender; add 1 tablespoon of plain unsweetened yogurt and blend to a liquid. Apply the mask to your face, being careful not to get it in your eyes or on your hair. Let it dry for about 20 minutes, and then rinse it off thoroughly with warm water. Splash your face with cool water and blot it dry.

Clay Facial Mask

To absorb dirt, oil, and impurities from your skin, mix this soothing clay. **Equipment:** measuring spoons, double boiler, mixing spoon, measuring cup. **Ingredients:** beeswax, anhydrous lanolin, borax, rose water or water, ful-

ler's earth. Buy the ingredients at a pharmacy. **Yield:** enough for one application.

Measure ¼ ounce of beeswax—about 1½ teaspoons—into the top of a double boiler; add 2 ounces (4 tablespoons) of anhydrous lanolin. Stir to blend. Measure ½ cup of rose water or plain water; add 1 tablespoon of borax and stir to dissolve. Slowly pour the borax-water mixture into the melted wax and lanolin, stirring constantly until the water is completely absorbed. Remove the mixture from the heat.

Add ½ pound of fuller's earth to the blended wax and water, stirring to a smooth paste. Let the mixture cool before using it.

Apply the facial pack liberally to your skin, being careful not to get it in your eyes or on your hair. Let it dry completely, about ½ hour, and rinse with warm water to remove all traces of the clay. Finally, splash your face with cool water and blot it dry.

Skin Softener

Many beauty experts recommend cucumbers as an effective skin softener and nourisher. This softener is especially good for oily skin. **Equipment:** sharp knife, blender, spatula, saucepan, measuring cup, mixing spoon, two quart jars with covers, funnel, coffee filter. **Ingredients:** fresh cucumbers, rubbing alcohol, benzoic acid. Buy benzoic acid at a pharmacy. **Yield:** about 2½ to 3 cups.

Thinly peel 2 or 3 large cucumbers and cut them into small pieces; place in a blender and puree to a fine pulp. Turn the pulp into a saucepan and heat to boiling; let cool. Stir in 1 pint of rubbing alcohol and ¼ cup of benzoic acid; this keeps the cucumber juice from spoiling. Stir to mix thoroughly.

Pour the mixture into a quart jar and cover it tightly; refrigerate it for 2 weeks. Strain it into a clean jar through a funnel lined with a coffee filter; cover tightly. Apply to skin as desired.

Lip Cream

If you spend a lot of time outside, you've probably suffered from dry, chapped lips due to cold, sun, or wind. This simple cream both soothes and heals. **Equipment:** measuring spoons, double boiler, mixing spoon, small jar with cover. **Ingredients:** beeswax, castor oil, anhydrous lanolin, spirits of camphor. Buy the ingredients at a pharmacy. **Yield:** about 2½ ounces.

Melt 1 ounce—about 2 tablespoons—of beeswax in a double boiler; add 2 tablespoons of castor oil and 1 tablespoon of anhydrous lanolin, and stir thoroughly. Remove from heat and let the mixture cool. When cool, add 1 teaspoon of spirits of camphor and mix thoroughly. Spoon the mixture into a small jar and cover it tightly.

Apply the cream to the lips as needed.

Skin Whiteners

Honest-to-goodness freckles are a permanent fixture, but discolorations and dark spots are easy to remove.

Lemon-Vinegar skin whitener. Equipment: sharp knife, blender, measuring cup, two quart jars with covers, funnel, coffee filter. **Ingredients:** lemons, wine vinegar, rubbing alcohol, water, perfume. **Yield:** about 1½ pints.

Cut 2 or 3 lemons into small pieces. Liquefy the pieces of lemon in a blender. Add a pint of inexpensive wine vinegar, ½ cup of rubbing alcohol, and ½ cup of water, and blend for a few seconds.

Pour the mixture into a quart jar and cover; refrigerate it for 3 days. Add a few drops of your favorite perfume until the mixture smells good to you. Strain the mixture into another quart jar through a funnel lined with a clean coffee filter, and cover it tightly.

To use the skin whitener, spread it

between two pieces of muslin. Set this poultice on your skin for as long as convenient, preferably overnight.

Natural Face Bleach. Equipment: measuring cup, mixing bowl, mixing spoon, measuring spoons, pint jar with cover. **Ingredients:** colloidal oatmeal, hydrogen peroxide (3 percent solution), lemon juice, tincture of benzoin. **Yield:** about 1½ cups.

Measure ¼ cup of colloidal oatmeal into a mixing bowl. Add ½ cup of 3 percent solution hydrogen peroxide and stir well; be sure the peroxide is fresh and at full strength. Add ½ cup of lemon juice and ¼ teaspoon of tincture of benzoin to the mixture. Stir to blend the ingredients thoroughly. Pour the mixture into a pint jar and cover it tightly.

Apply the bleach weekly; let it dry before rinsing.

Get Rid of Wrinkles

Wrinkles are a result of aging, and most of us would like to get rid of them, but a surgical face-lift is pretty drastic. Short of surgery, there are some other ways to help eliminate and hide wrinkles. **Tools:** mirror, scissors, needle. **Materials:** sun-blocking cream or lotion, moisturizer, albumin or collagen protein cream, lotion, or facial mask, or egg whites, or hormone cream; isometric beauty band, or gauze or adhesive tape, thin elastic tape, thread, and cosmetic adhesive. **Time:** 5 minutes to ½ hour.

Prevention. Wrinkles are caused by loss of flexibility in the collagen fibers, the mesh-like cells that give skin its form and shape. As we age, the collagen fibers lose their ability to withstand normal facial motions; at the same time, we lose facial fat. The result is wrinkles.

If you work to eliminate wrinkles before they form, you have a good chance of staving them off. Don't drink alcohol in excessive amounts; it robs your body of moisture. Don't smoke. Avoid excessive sun, and protect your face with sun-blocking creams and lotions. Restore moisture to your skin by splashing your face with cool water, giving yourself a facial, drinking lots of water and juice, and using plenty of moisturizers.

Exercise. If you already have wrinkles, you can take steps to hide and eliminate wrinkles. Exercise at least once a day to firm your skin and muscles; thoroughly moisturize your face and neck before you exercise.

To correct a droopy chin, a weak jaw, or a wrinkled neck, place the tip of your tongue on the roof of your mouth as far back as it will go; your chin, jaw, throat, and neck will tighten automatically. Repeat several times.

To firm your chin, neck, and throat, stretch your chin up high and thrust it forward, hard; at the same time, pull your head back as far as you can. Repeat this forward and backward motion several times. For a firming exercise you can do anywhere, turn your head to the left, touch your chin to your shoulder, turn your head back to center, and repeat the process to the right. Repeat several times.

To help eliminate a double chin, point your chin toward the ceiling. With your mouth closed, stick out your lower jaw as far as possible until you can feel the tendons in your neck stretch. Hold this position for a slow count of 10; repeat three times. This exercise also smooths out neck wrinkles and strengthens a weak jaw.

Face creams and masks. Many products claim to remove wrinkles, and many of them actually work for some people. Albumin or collagen protein creams or lotions contain collagen, the albuminoid substance that gives skin its shape. Creams and lotions that contain collagen act to fatten up and reshape cells that have lost elasticity. They can and do help smooth wrinkles, but they do not cause a drastic improvement. For a less expensive treatment, apply fresh egg white to your face; because it's rich in albumin, it will contract the skin and temporarily improve disfiguring

lines. Let the egg white dry for about 20 minutes, rinse it off with warm water, and then splash your face with cool water. Facial masks—commercial or homemade—that contain collagen or albumin are also effective; these include egg-based or milk masks and many other natural masks. Use the masks regularly, as directed.

Hormone creams contain estrogen, progesterone, or steroids. These creams are very controversial, but many claim fantastic results. If you want to try a hormone cream, use it as directed for a month or two—don't expect overnight results. If you see no results, stop using the cream. If you do see an improvement after a month or two, stop using the cream for two or three months to see what happens. After this time, if you want to use it again, go ahead; follow the manufacturer's instructions.

Instant face-lift. At least two products available provide an instant face-lift. One is an isometric beauty band to lift and smooth sagging facial skin; this is a handy version of a standard theatrical makeup trick, and can be purchased from most cosmetic supply houses. The second is called an instant face-lift; buy it at any shop that sells theatrical makeup, or make your own.

The instant face-lift consists of two bands over your head, to lift the skin of

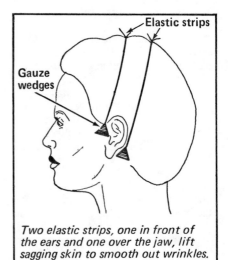

Two elastic strips, one in front of the ears and one over the jaw, lift sagging skin to smooth out wrinkles.

your cheeks, chin, and jaw. These two bands are the ear lift and the chin lift.

To make the ear lift, cut two 1-inch-long triangles of gauze. Sew one end of an 8-inch piece of thin elastic tape to one corner of each piece. Using a cosmetic adhesive, glue a piece of gauze close to your hairline and directly in front of one ear with the elastic strip aimed at the top of your head; repeat to attach the other piece of gauze in front of your other ear. Pull the elastic strips up and tie them tightly together at the back of your head.

To make the chin lift, cut triangles of gauze and sew elastic strips to them as above. Attach one triangle just below and behind each earlobe. Pull the strips up, tighten them, and tie them.

Cut off excess elastic. Arrange your hair to cover both the gauze wedges and the strips of elastic.

For the best results with an instant face-lift, you must use a cosmetic adhesive—ask a theatrical makeup supplier or a cosmetologist. Or try cutting the triangles out of adhesive tape instead of gauze. Practice as necessary to achieve the results you want.

Make Your Own Skin Care Products:

Wrinkle Cream

Wrinkle creams are expensive, and the more elegant, the higher the price. This recipe is a little unusual, but it works. **Equipment:** small dish, measuring spoons, measuring cup, mixing spoon, double boiler, electric mixer, clean jar with cover. **Ingredients:** alum, orange flower water, gelatin, glycerin, anhydrous lanolin, spirits of camphor, tincture of benzoin. Buy the ingredients at a pharmacy. **Yield:** about 1½ cups.

In a small dish, dissolve ¼ teaspoon of alum in 2 teaspoons of orange flower water; add 1 teaspoon of gelatin and soak until the gelatin is softened. Add ¼ cup of glycerin and pour into the top of a double boiler; heat over low heat until the gelatin is completely dissolved. Add 8 ounces of lanolin to the mixture and stir it together slowly. Add ¼ teaspoon of spirits of camphor and ¼ teaspoon of tincture of benzoin; stir to blend.

Remove from heat. Beat the warm mixture with an electric mixer at medium speed until the cream is cool and fluffy. Spoon into a clean jar and cover tightly.

Apply to the skin at night; massage the cream in well for 5 to 10 minutes.

Facial Hair Bleach

This effective cream hair bleach is both inexpensive and easy to prepare. **Equipment:** measuring spoons, mixing bowl, mixing spoon. **Ingredients:** hydrogen peroxide (3 percent solution), ammonia, white henna. **Yield:** enough for one application.

Measure 2 tablespoons of 3 percent solution hydrogen peroxide into a mixing bowl; make sure the peroxide is fresh and at full strength. Add 10 drops of ammonia and stir in enough white henna to produce a smooth paste, not too thick or too runny.

Apply the bleach to the hair and leave it on for about 15 minutes, or until the desired shade is achieved. Rinse off the bleach thoroughly. Complete the treatment by washing thoroughly.

Skin Food Cream

If you want to replenish your skin's beneficial oils and supply it with nutrients, there's no need to buy expensive cosmetics. This gentle cream is as rich as they come. **Equipment:**

measuring spoons, double boiler, mixing spoon, measuring cup, mixing bowl, wire whisk or egg beater, small jar with cover. **Ingredients:** beeswax, coconut oil, anhydrous lanolin, almond oil or heavy mineral oil, tincture of benzoin, orange flower water. Buy the ingredients at a pharmacy. **Yield:** about 5½ ounces.

Melt ½ ounce—about 1 tablespoon—of beeswax in a double boiler; add 2 tablespoons of coconut oil and 1 ounce (2 tablespoons) of anhydrous lanolin, and stir to blend thoroughly. Stir in 2 ounces (¼ cup) of almond oil or heavy mineral oil, 2 or 3 drops of tincture of benzoin, and 1 ounce (2 tablespoons) of orange flower water. *Caution: Almond oil vapors are toxic.*

Pour the mixture into a mixing bowl and beat it with a wire whisk or an egg beater until it's creamy. Spoon the cream into a small jar and cover it tightly.

To use, rub the cream into the skin and massage vigorously.

Tissue-Toning Cream

Tissue-toning creams add moisture to dry skin and improve its texture. This cream preparation is easy and inexpensive to make. **Equipment:** double boiler, measuring cup, measuring spoons, two small saucepans, mixing spoon, pint jar with cover. **Ingredients:** beeswax, anhydrous lanolin, almond oil or heavy mineral oil, witch hazel, rose water, borax. You can buy these ingredients at a pharmacy. **Yield:** about 10 ounces.

Melt 1 ounce of beeswax—about 2 tablespoons—in the top of a double boiler; add ¼ cup (2 ounces) of anhydrous lanolin. Warm 5 ounces of almond oil or heavy mineral oil in a small saucepan and add it to the lanolin-and-wax mixture; stir to blend. *Caution: Almond oil vapors are toxic.* In another small pan, heat 2 tablespoons of witch hazel and 2 tablespoons of rose water; dissolve a pinch of borax in this solution. Add to the lanolin-and-wax mixture and mix thoroughly. Pour the mixture into a pint jar and cover it tightly.

Apply the cream sparingly and rub it into your skin gently.

Give Yourself a Manicure/Pedicure

All you need is patience to give yourself professional-looking manicures and pedicures. **Tools:** straight-edged nail clipper or manicure scissors, fine gem-dust nail file or fine emery board, small bowl, cuticle trimmer, callus-removing stone. **Materials:** lanolin-based nail polish remover, sterile cotton balls, liquid detergent, cuticle remover, cotton swabs, hand lotion or cream, tissues; nail base coat, polish, and top coat. **Time:** 1 to 1½ hours.

Manicures. Remove any old nail polish with a lanolin-based nail polish remover; use sterile cotton balls to get all the old polish off your nails. If your nails are very long, cut them down to manageable size with a straight-edged nail clipper or nail scissors.

Shape your nails to a semi-oval with a fine gem-dust nail file or emery board. Using as few strokes as possible, file the sides of each nail straight and at an inward angle to your fingertip; do *not* file into the sensitive nail bed. Then file the top of the nail straight across. Round off the top of each nail as desired, and make sure all filed edges are smooth.

Soften your cuticles by soaking your fingertips in a dish of warm water for 5 minutes; add a few drops of liquid detergent to the water. Dry your hands and apply a cuticle remover to each nail. Following the manufacturer's instructions, let the cuticle remover work; then, with a cotton swab, gently remove loose cuticles. Use a cuticle trimmer to finish the job. Work carefully, and don't gouge at your cuticles—it's better to remove too little cuticle than too much.

Apply polish to each nail in three even strokes, first down the center and then along the sides.

After filing your nails and removing loose cuticles, apply hand lotion or cream generously to your hands. Wipe your palms clean with a tissue and remove any lotion from your nails with cotton balls soaked in the detergent solution.

Apply a base coat to your nails. Make three even strokes to coat each nail from the nail base to the tip: first down the center of the nail, then along the sides. Be careful to keep the polish from seeping into the edge of the nail bed. Let the base coat dry completely, at least 5 minutes; never apply another coat of polish to a coat that isn't dry yet.

When the base coat is completely dry, apply the first coat of polish in a thin layer, making three even strokes to cover each nail. Let the polish dry for at least 5 minutes; then apply a second thin coat of polish. Let the polish dry completely. If you're doing your nails at night, wait until the next morning to apply the second coat of polish.

After applying a base coat and two coats of polish, apply a top coat sealer to protect the polish. Let the top coat dry completely, and try not to do any messy work until the top coat has completely hardened. To protect your manicure, take care of your nails. Wear gloves when doing household chores.

Pedicures. To give yourself a pedicure, follow the same steps as for a manicure; however, you may not want to worry so much over the cuticles. Be very gentle when you're working with cuticles. Clip toenails straight across, not shaped in a semi-oval. Smooth rough areas with a callus-removing stone, and apply lotion generously to keep your feet soft and smooth.

Apply polish as above, using a base coat, two coats of polish, and a protective top coat. Don't skimp on polish. To keep your toes separated while you work, wedge cotton balls between them. Make sure each coat of polish is dry before you apply the next one.

Pedicures usually last longer than manicures because toes do less work than fingers, and are often protected by shoes, hose, and socks. If you're as careful in polishing your toenails as you are with your fingernails, your pedicure should last about twice as long as your manicure.

Make Your Own Hand and Nail Care Products:

Fingernail Hardener

Nails, like hair, often need conditioning. Use this simple nail hardener recipe to keep your nails from splitting or cracking. **Equipment:** measuring cup, measuring spoons, mixing spoon, small jar with cover. **Ingredients:** water, witch hazel, glycerin, green food coloring, alum. **Yield:** about ½ cup.

To ¼ cup of water in a measuring cup, add ¼ cup of witch hazel, 2 tablespoons of glycerin, and a drop of green food coloring—the coloring is just for identification. Add 2 teaspoons of alum and stir to mix well. Pour into a small jar and cover tightly.

Apply the solution nightly for several nights; dip your nails into the solution and let them dry. Repeat as necessary until your nails are hard, as desired. If you wear nail polish, remove the polish and don't reapply it until your nails have hardened as desired.

Heavy-Duty Hand Lotion

For winter-cracked hands, try this lotion. Glycerin and rose water are a classic combination, and this version has the added benefit of witch hazel. **Equipment:** mixing bowl, measuring cup, measuring spoons, mixing spoon, small jar with cover. **Ingredients:** glycerin, bay rum, witch hazel, rose water. Buy the ingredients at a pharmacy. **Yield:** about ½ cup.

Measure ¼ cup of glycerin into a mixing bowl. Add 2 tablespoons of bay rum, 2 tablespoons of witch hazel, and 2 tablespoons of rose water; stir the mixture thoroughly. Pour into a small jar and cover tightly.

Shake the lotion thoroughly before using.

Nail Bleach

Blotchy or mottled fingernails aren't pretty, but they're easily dealt with. Mix this fragrant lotion to correct the problem. **Equipment:** measuring spoons, measuring cup, funnel, 8-ounce bottle with cap. **Ingredients:** glycerin, hydrogen peroxide (3 percent solution), orange flower water. Buy glycerin and orange flower water at a pharmacy. **Yield:** 8 ounces.

Measure 2 tablespoons of glycerin and 5 ounces—⅝ cup—of 3 percent solution hydrogen peroxide into an 8-ounce bottle; fill the bottle with orange flower water. Cap the bottle and shake it well.

To use the bleach, soak your nails in this mixture for about 15 minutes. Repeat as needed.

Nail Softener

If your nails are too tough to cut or shape, try this effective softener. **Equipment:** double boiler, measuring spoons, mixing spoon, small jar with cover. **Ingredients:** hydrous lanolin (containing water), soap flakes, glycerin, vegetable oil, perfume or cologne. Buy lanolin at a pharmacy. **Yield:** about 3 ounces.

Empty a 2-ounce tube of hydrous lanolin into the top of a double boiler and melt the lanolin over low heat. Add 1 tablespoon of soap flakes, 2 teaspoons of glycerin, and 1 teaspoon of vegetable oil; stir well. If desired, add a few drops of your favorite perfume or cologne.

Remove the mixture from the heat and stir to dissolve the soap flakes. Pour the mixture into a small jar and cover it tightly.

Apply the softener to the nails daily, until the nails are as soft as desired.

Nail Whitener

There's no need to go out and buy expensive nail whiteners; it's easy to make your own: **Equipment:** double boiler, measuring spoons, mixing spoon, small jar with cover. **Ingredients:** hydrous lanolin (containing water), zinc oxide powder, talcum powder, almond oil or heavy mineral oil, glycerin. Buy the ingredients at a pharmacy. **Yield:** about 4½ ounces.

Empty a 2-ounce tube of hydrous lanolin into the top of a double boiler and melt the lanolin over low heat. Add 2 tablespoons of zinc oxide powder and 2 tablespoons of talcum powder and stir the mixture to form a smooth, creamy paste. Then add ¼ teaspoon of glycerin and 1 tablespoon of almond oil or heavy mineral oil, mixing them thoroughly into the paste. *Caution: Almond oil vapors are toxic.* Transfer the paste to a small jar and cover it tightly.

To use the whitener, apply the paste under the nails with an orange stick.

Make Your Own Personal Care Products:

Dusting Powder

Dusting powder is expensive, but there's no need to buy it—mix your own, in whatever fragrance you like. **Equipment:** measuring cup, mixing bowl, mixing spoon, shaker container. **Ingredients:** baking soda, talcum powder, borax, perfume. **Yield:** about 1½ cups.

Measure ½ cup of baking soda, ½ cup of talcum powder, and ½ cup of borax into a mixing bowl; mix well. Add a few drops of your favorite perfume and mix thoroughly to distribute the perfume. Pour the powder into a clean shaker container.

Powder Deodorant

There are two types of preparations sold as deodorants—those that reduce the flow of perspiration, and those that eliminate the odor. This inexpensive powder does both. **Equipment:** measuring cup, mixing bowl, mixing spoon, measuring spoons, shaker container. **Ingredients:** baking soda, boric acid, zinc oxide powder, talcum powder, perfume as desired. Buy zinc oxide powder at a pharmacy. **Yield:** about ¾ cup.

Combine ¼ cup of baking soda and

¼ cup of boric acid; then add 2 tablespoons of zinc oxide powder and 2 tablespoons of talcum powder. Mix well. If desired, add a few drops of perfume and mix thoroughly. Pour the thoroughly mixed powder into an empty shaker container and tighten the lid.

Toothpaste

Tired of the taste of your toothpaste? This peppermint-flavored version is both easily made and economical. **Equipment:** measuring cup, mixing bowl, mixing spoon, small jar with cover. **Ingredients:** precipitated chalk, soap flakes, glycerin, liquid saccharin, peppermint extract. Buy chalk and glycerin at a pharmacy. **Yield:** about 4 ounces.

Measure ¼ cup of precipitated chalk and ¼ cup of soap flakes into a mixing bowl. Add enough glycerin to form a thick paste. Add a few drops of liquid saccharin and a few drops of peppermint extract; stir to blend well. Blend the ingredients thoroughly to a smooth paste. Transfer the paste to a small jar and cover tightly.

Healing Skin Balm

This simple balm is ideal for chapped hands or windburned skin. **Equipment:** measuring cup, double boiler, measuring spoons, mixing spoon, small jar with cover. **Ingredients:** water, powdered laundry starch, glycerin, bay rum, cologne. **Yield:** about ½ cup.

Measure ¼ cup of cold water into the top of a double boiler; add 2 tablespoons of powdered laundry starch and ¼ cup of glycerin and mix well. Heat over low heat, stirring continually, until slightly thickened; be careful not to let the mixture lump. Let cool slightly; then add 2 teaspoons of bay rum and 3 to 4 drops of your favorite cologne. Pour the mixture into a small jar and cover it tightly. Apply as needed.

Electric Pre-Shave Lotion

Why pay a high price for electric pre-shave when you can make your own? This simple lotion does the job as well as any store-bought. **Equipment:** measuring cup, measuring spoons, funnel, pint bottle with cap. **Ingredients:** rubbing alcohol, glycerin, water, cologne. **Yield:** 1 pint.

Measure 1 cup of rubbing alcohol and 2 tablespoons of glycerin into a pint bottle; fill the bottle with water. If desired, add a few drops of your favorite cologne. Cap the bottle tightly and shake the mixture well.

Apply the lotion to your beard before shaving with an electric razor.

After-Shave Lotion

There's an amazing array of after-shaves available, and most of them are expensive. This one, besides being cheap and easy to make, is an excellent preparation for closing the pores. **Equipment:** large mixing bowl, measuring spoons, mixing spoon, measuring cup, gallon jar with lid, funnel, coffee filter. **Ingredients:** boric acid, glycerin, rubbing alcohol, witch hazel, water, cologne as desired. **Yield:** 1 gallon.

Measure 1 tablespoonful of boric acid into a large mixing bowl and add ½ cup of glycerin; mix thoroughly, being careful to get all the lumps out. Stirring constantly, add 1 pint of rubbing alcohol

and 1 pint of witch hazel. Let stand 1 hour.

Pour the mixture into a clean gallon jar through a funnel lined with a clean coffee filter; add water to the jar to fill it completely. If desired, add a few drops of your favorite cologne.

Foot Bath

Mix this foot bath to relieve tired, aching feet in short order. **Equipment:** measuring cup, mixing bowl, mixing spoon, 2-pound coffee can or large jar with cover. **Ingredients:** alum, borax, Epsom salts, colloidal oatmeal. Buy the ingredients at a pharmacy. **Yield:** about 1½ to 2 pounds.

Measure ¼ cup of alum, ½ cup of borax, and 1 cup of Epsom salts into a mixing bowl; mix the ingredients thoroughly. Add 1 cup of colloidal oatmeal and mix well again. Pour the mixture into a clean, 2-pound coffee can or a large jar, and cover it tightly.

To use the preparation, stir ½ tablespoon of this mixture into a basin of warm water.

Mechanics' Soap

If you do your own car repairs, you know how hard it is to remove grease and oil from your arms and hands. Use this slightly abrasive soap to get rid of the stains. **Equipment:** measuring cup, mixing bowl, measuring spoons, stir stick, pint container with cover. **Ingredients:** soap flakes, borax, soda ash (sodium carbonate), powdered pumice stone. Buy soda ash and powdered pumice at a pharmacy. **Yield:** about 12 ounces.

Measure 1¼ cups of soap flakes and ⅛ cup of borax into a mixing bowl; add 1 tablespoon of powdered pumice and stir together well. Pour the mixture into a pint container and cover. Use mechanics' soap with water.

Protective Skin Ointment

To protect your hands from chemicals or irritating substances when you can't wear rubber gloves, use this protective ointment. **Equipment:** measuring spoons, double boiler, mixing bowl, mixing spoon, wide-mouth jar with cover. **Ingredients:** anhydrous lanolin, beeswax, soap flakes, water, ammonia. Buy lanolin and beeswax at a pharmacy. **Yield:** about 4 ounces.

Measure 2 tablespoons of anhydrous lanolin and 1 ounce of beeswax—about 2 tablespoons—into the top of a double boiler; melt them together over low heat. Measure 2 tablespoons of soap flakes and 2 tablespoons of hot water into a mixing bowl and stir to dissolve the soap. Add the melted lanolin-wax mixture to the soap solution and stir to blend; add ¾ teaspoon of ammonia and mix thoroughly. The mixture should have the consistency of honey. Transfer the ointment to a wide-mouth jar and cover it tightly.

To use the ointment, wash your hands with soap and water. With the soap still on your hands, rub a generous amount of ointment over your hands until the ointment is completely absorbed and your hands are dry. Remove it with soap and warm water.

Food and Drink

Grow Eatables in Pots

Vegetables, fruits, and herbs need light, warmth, water, and soil; but they don't insist on traditional planting. If you can satisfy their requirements, they'll flourish in containers on your patio, roof, or balcony. **Tools:** hose or watering can; trowel, gardening fork, or hand cultivator; artists' brush. **Materials:** containers, soil or potting mix, seeds, seedlings or plants, fertilizer, water. **Time:** 2 hours or more for planting, depending on garden size; regular care, a few minutes a day.

First, study your site. Check the wind velocity and direction; on high roofs or balconies you may have to water twice as much as on a patio because of the wind. Check the light; most eatables need 5 to 6 hours of direct sunlight a day. Plan your planting so the taller plants don't shade the shorter ones. Take surrounding buildings into account—they may cut, reflect, or deflect sun and wind.

The size of the space will determine how large and how many containers you can have. In general, use containers that are large enough not to dry out too fast and heavy enough not to blow over in the wind. If you want to use the containers for several years, they should be of material that won't rot or rust—wash buckets, flue tiles, plastic containers, tires, barrel halves, and redwood or cedar planters are all good. One-season containers are easy to improvise from old drawers, wood crates, peach baskets, or boxes. Make sure drainage is adequate in all containers.

Start with well-established seedlings or plants, if possible; or, if you have space and time, start plants from seed. Choose small varieties of plants, developed especially for confined areas. The plants listed below grow well in container gardens; follow the cultivation and watering instructions provided by the seed distributor. Water, fertilize, and cultivate plants as directed.

Beans: Plant bush beans in a large pot or box. Plant pole beans to grow onto a balcony railing.

Cabbage: Small, early varieties are best. Grow single cabbages in 8-inch pots.

Corn: Small varieties grow successfully in washtubs.

Cucumbers: Cucumbers can be grown as hanging plants or trained to grow upwards from a pot, tub, or tire planter. Choose a bush or small-space variety.

Lettuce: Lettuce needs lower temperatures, and does well in partial shade; it performs well in any container. Grow leaf lettuce or butterhead lettuce as single plants in 4-inch pots.

Green onions: Plant onion sets in any container; you can plan on harvesting 8 to 10 green onions from an 8-inch flower pot.

Green peppers: Grow individual plants in any large pot or container—1 cubic foot of soil is adequate.

Root crops: Beets, carrots, and turnips can be grown in any container at least 8 to 10 inches deep; radishes can be grown in 4 inches of soil. Be sure to keep the soil moist. Choose the shorter, more compact varieties of root crops.

Squash: Bush-type summer squash, such as zucchini and pattypan, grow well in washtubs, tire planters, or any medium or large container. Vining-type winter squashes can be trained to grow along a railing, but you may have to make slings to support the vegetables.

Tomatoes: Dwarf tomatoes can be grown in 1 cubic foot of soil; standard tomatoes need 2 to 3 cubic feet of soil. Small-fruited tomatoes do well in hanging baskets, or staked along with other vegetables in a planter. Plant tomatoes where they'll get full sun.

Strawberries: Strawberries in containers don't fruit as heavily as ground-planted ones, but you'll still harvest a few. Plant them in a strawberry jar, a large planter, or a hanging basket.

Herbs: Most herbs do excellently in containers of any size. Some herbs, such as mint, should be contained to keep them from growing rampant.

NOTE: If your garden is up too high, you may not have any insects, and you'll have to pollinate by hand. Use a clean, fat artists' brush to transfer pollen from blossom to blossom; consult a gardening manual for precise instructions.

Grow Lettuce Under Lights

For fresh lettuce year-round, grow leaf or butterhead lettuce inside, under fluorescent lights. Plant your lettuce garden in the basement, the attic, or anywhere the temperature stays between 65° and 70° F during the day, and drops about 10 degrees at night.

FOR LIGHTING. **Tools:** drill. **Materials:** heavy eye bolts or screw hooks, table, sash or other chain, 4-foot fluorescent light fixture for 4 to 8 tubes, cool-white 40-watt fluorescent tubes. **Time:** about ½ to 1 hour.

FOR PLANTING. **Tools:** mister or watering can, hand cultivator, kitchen shears. **Materials:** extra-large plastic dishpans to hold plant containers, 6- to 8-inch pots or 6- to 8-inch-deep plastic dishpans, enriched potting soil, water, lettuce seeds, fertilizer. **Time:** about ½ hour to plant; regular care, a few minutes a day.

To set up your lettuce garden, drill starter holes and fasten heavy eye bolts or screw hooks to the ceiling joists above your planting area. Suspend a 4- to 8-tube fluorescent light fixture from the hooks, using sash or other light chain. Set a planting table directly under the light fixture and adjust the fixture's chains so that it hangs evenly about 12 inches above the table; make sure you'll be able to readjust it as necessary. Install cool-white 40-watt fluorescent tubes in the fixture, as directed.

Use 6- to 8-inch pots or 6- to 8-inch-deep plastic dishpans as potting containers; punch drainage holes in the bottom of the dishpans. Fill pots or dishpans with enriched potting soil and water with a mister or a watering can until the soil is completely wet; let the soil drain thoroughly. Plant lettuce seeds in the prepared containers as directed on the seed packet. Set the lettuce containers into extra-large plastic dishpans on the table under the light fixture, and adjust the fixture's hanging chains as necessary so that the fluorescent tubes are 4 to 6 inches above the planted seeds. Turn the fixture on.

Water, cultivate, and fertilize the lettuce as directed on the seed packet. Water from the bottom to keep the soil consistently moist, but don't let the pots stand in water all the time. Leave the lights on 24 hours a day; as the lettuce grows, readjust the hanging chains to keep the fluorescent tubes 4 to 6 inches above the plants.

When the lettuce starts to get full, harvest it from the outside; cut leaves carefully with a kitchen shears. This encourages the plants to produce more leaves.

Grow an Asparagus Patch

Unlike most other vegetables, asparagus is a perennial; with a little care and patience, it will supply you with years of abundant harvests. **Tools:**

shovel, rake, hoe, garden hose. **Materials:** one- or two-year-old asparagus roots, pasteurized rotted manure, 5-10-5 fertilizer. **Time:** after soil preparation, about ½ hour for planting.

Asparagus can be grown anywhere in the United States except in Florida and along the Gulf Coast, and it continues to produce for 20 years or more. Choose a variety of asparagus recommended for the growing conditions in your area, or ask for advice from a seed and bulb dealer. Although asparagus can be grown from seeds, you can shorten the growing period and get a faster yield by buying one- or two-year-old roots.

The secret of a healthy asparagus patch is in the soil preparation and planting. After all danger of frost has passed—check with the seed and bulb dealer to be sure—dig a 12-inch-deep trench for the asparagus; place the trench as recommended for adequate sun. Line the trench with pasteurized rotted manure to a depth of 4 inches, raking it evenly. Set one- or two-year-old asparagus roots into the prepared trench, about 2 feet apart, and cover them with 2 inches of topsoil. As the summer progresses, add additional topsoil gradually until the trench is filled in and the new stems are covered. Water the newly set roots thoroughly.

To control weeds and aid in cultivation, hoe the soil weekly. Water the asparagus only when the topsoil is dry and compact. Twice during the growing season, sprinkle a handful of 5-10-5 fertilizer around each plant to encourage growth.

Asparagus matures very slowly. It should be allowed to grow for three years before the stalks are harvested—two years after planting for one-year-old roots, one year for two-year-old roots. After the plants are mature, harvest the stalks when they reach a height of 8 inches and the buds are still tightly compressed. Gently bend the stems until they break; cutting is not recommended as it can injure other stems before they have a chance to emerge.

Asparagus is through producing for the season when the stalks grow no larger than ½ inch in diameter. At that time, give the plants an additional feeding of 5-10-5 fertilizer to nourish them during dormancy and prepare them for the next season.

Grow Sprouts

Sprouts of all kinds are a nutritional bargain. All they need is water, a jar, and a few days in a dark, warm spot. **Equipment:** measuring cup, 1-quart wide-mouth jar, cheesecloth or nylon net, rubber band. **Ingredients:** mung beans, soybeans, alfalfa seeds, pumpkin seeds, lentils, barley, wheat, or rye; warm water. **Yield:** about 2 cups.

Wash and pick over ¼ cup of mung beans, soybeans, alfalfa seeds, pumpkin seeds, lentils, barley, wheat, or rye; discard any imperfect beans or seeds. *Caution: Do not use any seeds intended for outdoor planting; they may have been treated with poisonous chemicals.* Put the beans or seeds into a 1-quart wide-mouth jar and pour in 2 cups of warm water. Fasten a double layer of cheesecloth or nylon net over the mouth of the jar with a rubber band.

Soak the beans or seeds for 8 to 12 hours; pour the water out through the cheesecloth. Fill the jar with warm water, not removing the cheesecloth, and drain it again. Place the jar in a dark spot with a temperature between 70° and 80° F. Rinse with warm water twice a day until the sprouts are as large as desired. Use the sprouts as snacks or in salads, Oriental dishes, or sandwiches.

Mung beans sprout in 4 to 5 days; soybeans in 5 to 6 days; alfalfa seeds in 6 to 7 days; pumpkin seeds in 4 to 5 days; lentils in 4 to 5 days; barley, wheat, and rye in 2 to 3 days. Sprouts grown in the dark are whitish. For green sprouts, bring the jar into the light for the last couple of days.

Make Your Own:

Yogurt

With a cup of commercial yogurt priced higher than a quart of milk in some areas, you can figure on making your own yogurt at about a third of the cost of commercial yogurt. You don't even need a yogurt maker. **Equipment:** measuring cup; 2-quart glass or enamel pan, or glass bowl; spoon, dairy or food thermometer that registers as low as 100° F; 1- or 2-quart wide-mouth vacuum bottle, or heating pad and insulating gear. **Ingredients:** low-fat or skim milk, instant dry milk powder; plain, unsweetened yogurt (with no gelatin added). **Yield:** about 1 quart.

To eliminate bacteria that can spoil yogurt, wash all equipment in very hot, soapy water. Rinse thoroughly, first with hot water and then with boiling water. Fill a 1- or 2-quart wide-mouth vacuum bottle with hot water and let it stand as you make the yogurt.

Measure 1 quart of low-fat or skim milk and 1 cup of instant dry milk powder into a 2-quart pan and stir to blend; or, for even less expensive yogurt, mix instant dry milk powder as directed to make 1 quart, and add another ⅓ cup instant dry milk powder. Set the thermometer in the pan and heat the milk over low heat to about 180° F; do not let it boil. Remove from heat and let the milk mixture cool to 115° F. Stir in ¼ cup plain, unsweetened yogurt and mix until well blended.

Empty the hot water out of the vacuum bottle and pour in the milk mixture. Cap the bottle tightly. Let the yogurt stand for 3 to 4 hours; then test a spoonful, recapping the bottle quickly. If you like mild yogurt, 3½ hours may be enough incubation; for a tarter taste, incubate longer—about 8 hours for thick, tangy yogurt. Test every ½ hour. When the yogurt reaches the taste and consistency you like, place the cap on loosely and refrigerate the vacuum bottle. The yogurt will continue to thicken as it chills. When cool, transfer the yogurt to another container.

If you don't have a vacuum bottle handy, pour the yogurt into clean, hot jars or other containers with lids; incubate it by one of the following methods:

• If you have a gas oven with a pilot light, before mixing the yogurt, set the oven for 275° F. When the yogurt is ready to be incubated, pour it into a glass bowl. Set the bowl in the oven and turn the oven off; let stand about 8 hours.

• Wrap a heating pad around a 1-quart jar of yogurt and fasten it in place with string or rubber bands. Set the pad on low.

• Line a cardboard box with newspaper or old blankets; put a heating pad in the bottom and place containers of yogurt on it. Cover with more newspaper or blankets. Set the pad on low.

• Place a heating pad in the bottom of a foam picnic cooler; place yogurt containers on the pad and cover the picnic cooler. Turn the pad on low.

• Fill a large pan with 1 or 2 inches of hot water and set it in a warm place. Put the yogurt containers in the pan and place a thermometer in the water; check the temperature frequently. When the temperature of the water falls below 100° F, add more hot water.

Granola

Commercial granola is expensive, and it's usually very sweet. This delicious mixture has no sugar, but a little honey—and a far superior taste. **Equipment:** measuring cup, large mixing bowl, saucepan, mixing spoon, measuring spoons, cookie sheets, spatula, large jars or cans with airtight covers. **Ingredients:** rolled oats, whole-wheat cereal (any type of cold wheat cereal), shredded coconut, wheat germ, chopped almonds or other nuts, raisins or minced dried fruit, sesame seeds, chopped toasted soy-

493

beans, vegetable oil, honey, vanilla. **Yield:** about 2 quarts.

In a large mixing bowl, combine 2½ cups rolled oats, 1½ cups whole-wheat cereal (any type of cold wheat cereal), 1½ cups of shredded coconut, 1 cup of wheat germ, 1 cup of chopped almonds or other nuts, 1 cup of raisins or minced dried fruit, and ½ cup of sesame seeds. If desired, add 1 cup of chopped toasted soybeans. Any of these ingredients can be varied, as desired. Toss the dry ingredients to mix them thoroughly. Set aside.

In a small saucepan, heat ½ cup of vegetable oil, ½ cup of honey, and 2 teaspoons of vanilla, stirring to blend. Heat just until warm and well mixed; then remove from heat and cool slightly.

Pour the warm honey mixture over the grain mixture and toss to coat all the dry ingredients evenly. Spread the granola on cookie sheets and toast it at 350° F for about 20 minutes; as it bakes, turn the granola often with a spatula, moving the mixture at the edges to the center for even browning. Watch carefully during the last few minutes so the grains don't overbrown.

Remove the cookie sheets from the oven and let the granola cool completely. Pour the cooled cereal into large jars or cans and cover it tightly; store at room temperature.

Peanut Butter

Buy raw peanuts or peanuts in the shell and you'll save money making your own naturally fresh peanut butter. **Equipment:** cookie sheet; blender, food processor, or peanut butter maker; measuring cup, measuring spoons, rubber spatula, quart jar with cover. **Ingredients:** shelled raw peanuts, vegetable oil, salt. **Yield:** about 2¾ cups.

Use 1 pound of either raw or roasted peanuts. To roast peanuts, spread 1 pound of shelled raw peanuts—with or without skins—on a cookie sheet. Bake at 300° F for about 15 minutes, or until lightly browned. Let cool completely.

Grind the peanuts in a blender, a food processor, or a special peanut butter grinder. Place 1 cup of roasted or raw peanuts in the container. For smoother peanut butter, add 2 tablespoons of vegetable oil and blend or process until the peanut butter is the desired consistency. You may have to stop the blender or processor and push the peanuts to the blades.

Remove the peanut butter from the blender or processor with a rubber spatula and put it into a quart jar. Repeat the blending process with the remaining peanuts and 2 tablespoons more vegetable oil, blending about 1 cup of peanuts at a time. Stir in ¼ teaspoon salt, if desired. Cover the peanut butter tightly and refrigerate it; chilling firms the peanut butter and prevents the oil from separating.

Mayonnaise

Grocery-store mayonnaise not only is expensive; it just isn't as good as homemade. Try this quick blender variety—you'll never go back. **Equipment:** electric blender or mixer, mixing bowl, measuring spoons, wire whisk, measuring cup, quart jar with cover, spatula. **Ingredients:** eggs, salt, honey or prepared mustard; lemon juice, or cider or wine vinegar; olive oil or peanut oil. **Yield:** about 2 cups.

Break 2 eggs into an electric blender container or a mixing bowl and add 1 teaspoon of salt, 1 tablespoon of honey or prepared mustard if desired, and 1 to 6 tablespoons of lemon juice or cider or wine vinegar, to taste. Blend to mix thoroughly or beat with a mixer at medium speed, or beat by hand with a wire whisk until the mixture is well blended.

Add 1½ cups of olive oil or peanut oil, pouring in a little at a time and blending or beating thoroughly after each addition. Be careful not to add too much oil at once; if you do, the mayonnaise will separate. If desired, add more salt, lemon juice, or vinegar; for a milder taste, add a few drops of cold water. Blend or mix thoroughly.

Turn the mayonnaise into a quart jar with a spatula and cover it tightly; keep it refrigerated.

Herbed mayonnaise. For a spicier mayonnaise and a good salad dressing, add herbs to the basic recipe; add one or more herbs just before you blend in the oil, and mix thoroughly after each addition. Add ¼ to ½ teaspoon of one or more of these herbs, to taste: basil, rosemary, dry mustard, paprika, celery salt, white pepper, parsley, sage, or cumin.

Frozen Yogurt Sherbet

Freeze this piquant sherbet in small paper cups or ice-cream-on-a-stick containers; use fruit in season or splurge on a midwinter treat. **Equipment:** sharp knife, measuring cup, mixing bowl, mixing spoon; electric mixer, blender, or food processor; shallow pan or tray. **Ingredients:** plain yogurt; apricots, peaches, plums, or berries; apricot, strawberry, pineapple, grape, or cherry preserves; or ripe avocado. **Yield:** 1 to 2 pints, depending on fruit added.

For 1 pint of plain yogurt, use 1 cup of chopped apricots, peaches, plums, or berries—cooked or uncooked, whichever you prefer. Or, if you don't have fresh fruit on hand, use ¾ cup of apricot, strawberry, pineapple, grape, or cherry preserves. For an exotic dessert, use 1 ripe avocado, peeled, seeded, and mashed.

Chop desired fruit to measure 1 cup, or crush berries, or peel, seed, and mash avocado. Mix 1 pint of plain yogurt with fruit, preserves, or avocado, by hand or with an electric mixer, or whirl briefly in a blender or food processor. Turn the mixture into a shallow pan or tray and freeze it until it's just frosty; or freeze until solid, about 4 hours. Cut the sherbet into cubes, and

pile the cubes into sherbet glasses. For fluffier sherbet, freeze the yogurt partially; whirl the semi-frozen mixture in a blender or food processor or beat it thoroughly. Refreeze until solid.

Yogurt Cream Cheese

Your homemade, fresh yogurt is easy to turn into a tangy cream cheese for dips or spreads—for a real treat, try it with fresh strawberries. **Equipment:** colander or strainer, cheesecloth, bowl or pan, spatula, pint container with cover. **Ingredients:** freshly made plain yogurt. **Yield:** about 2 cups.

Line a colander or large strainer with several layers of cheesecloth and put it in the sink. As soon as your yogurt has finished incubating, and before you refrigerate it, pour 1 quart of yogurt into the cheesecloth-lined colander.

Gather the corners of the cheesecloth and tie them together to form a bag. Hang the bag to drain—hang it from the faucet to drain into the sink, or from a cupboard door handle to drain into a bowl or pan underneath. Let the yogurt drain at least 8 hours.

With a spatula, turn the drained cheese out of the cheesecloth bag into a pint container; cover tightly. Chill before using.

Fruit Leathers

The name doesn't sound too appetizing at all, but anyone who's ever tasted these chewy treats knows fruit leathers are delicious. Tuck the sheets of dried puree into lunchboxes, backpacks, tackleboxes, or bike bags. **Equipment:** paring knife, large pot with cover, mixing spoon, strainer or colander, cheesecloth, large mixing bowl, food mill or food processor, measuring spoons, standard-size cookie sheets, spatula, low-temperature oven or de-hydrator, oven thermometer, wire racks, sifter or small strainer, wax paper, storage container. **Ingredients:** apricots, peaches, or prune plums; pineapple or other fruit juice, honey, almond extract, cornstarch. **Yield:** about 1 quart—2 cookie sheets.

Wash, halve and pit about 3 pounds of apricots, peaches, or prune plums, cutting out any bad spots. You should have about 1 gallon of fruit. Measure the fruit and 1½ cups of pineapple or other fruit juice into a large pot. Cover and heat slowly over low heat until the fruit is tender; watch carefully and stir occasionally to prevent sticking.

Pour the cooked fruit into a strainer or colander lined with cheesecloth, set over a large mixing bowl. Drain the fruit well, stirring gently to help it drain. When as much juice as possible has drained, transfer the fruit to a food mill or a food processor; save the juice for other uses. Press the fruit through the food mill into a large bowl, or process it to puree. Discard the fruit skins or stir them into the pulp to be part of the leather, as desired. Add honey, 1 tablespoon at a time, and taste until the mixture is as sweet as you like. If desired, stir in 1 tablespoon of almond extract. The pureed fruit should be the consistency of apple butter or thicker; if it's too thin, cook and stir it over low heat until thick.

Lightly butter two standard-size cookie sheets, or an equivalent number of others. Spread the puree on the greased cookie sheets, about ¼ inch thick. Dry the puree at no higher than 120° F until the leather is stiff enough to lift off the cookie sheets with a spatula, about 12 hours; check the oven temperature or dehydrator temperature periodically to be sure it doesn't go too high.

When the leather is firm enough to lift off the sheets, carefully slide it onto wire racks and let the sheets cool and dry completely. To store the leather, use a sifter or a small strainer to sift a light coating of cornstarch over it. Set a sheet of wax paper over the leather, flip it carefully, and sift cornstarch over the other side. Roll each piece of leather between two sheets of wax paper. Store the rolls of fruit leather in a tightly covered container or a sealed plastic bag; keep them in a cool dry place or refrigerate them.

To eat the leather, cut it into strips or tear off bite-size pieces.

Cherry Heering Cheddar Spread

This elegant cheese spread makes a terrific gift—if, that is, you can bear to give it away. Pack it in a crock, a mug, or in any container you like. **Equipment:** shredder, measuring cup, blender or food processor, sharp knife, rubber spatula, 2-cup container. **Ingredients:** cheddar cheese, milk, Cherry Heering liqueur, chopped ripe olives. **Yield:** about 2 cups.

Shred ½ to ¾ pound of cheddar cheese and put 1 cup of the cheese into a blender or a food processor. Add ¾ cup milk and ⅓ cup Cherry Heering liqueur; blend or process until smooth. Add the remaining cheese and blend until smooth. Add ½ cup of chopped ripe olives. If you're using a blender, remove the jar and stir in the olives; if you're using a food processor, add the olives and process very briefly. Turn the spread into a 2-cup crock or other container and cover it tightly. Chill thoroughly; store in the refrigerator.

Port Wine Spread

For a rich and elegant snack, mix this classic favorite; serve it with walnuts, crackers, and more port. **Equipment:** shredder, measuring cup, blender or food processor, mixing bowl, rubber spatula or fork, 2-cup crock or serving container. **Ingredients:** sharp cheddar cheese, milk, port wine. **Yield:** about 2 cups.

Shred ½ to ¾ pound of sharp cheddar cheese and put 1 cup of the cheese into a blender or food processor; add ¾ cup of milk and blend or process until smooth. Add the remaining cheese and blend again until smooth. Turn the creamed cheese into a mixing bowl and add ½ cup of port wine; stir with a fork or rubber spatula just enough to swirl the wine through the cheese. Turn the spread into a crock or other container and cover it tightly. Chill thoroughly; store in the refrigerator.

Herb Vinegars

Put a little vim in your vinegar by infusing it with your favorite herb. Herb vinegars make salad dressings sparkle and add zest to any recipe; they're excellent gifts, too. **Equipment:** measuring cup, 1-quart wide-mouth jar with lid, cheesecloth, funnel; 1-pint jar or small decorative jars, bottles, or cruets. **Ingredients:** herb leaves, such as basil, chervil, dill, fennel, marjoram, mint, parsley, sage, savory, tarragon, or thyme, or dried herb; whole herb sprigs, white cider vinegar or white or red wine vinegar. The milder the vinegar, the more pronounced the herb flavor. **Yield:** 1 pint.

Slightly crush herb leaves—basil, chervil, dill, fennel, marjoram, mint, parsley, sage, savory, tarragon, or thyme—to make ¾ cup. Pour the leaves into a 1-quart wide-mouth jar and add 2 cups of white cider vinegar or white or red wine vinegar. Cover the jar tightly and shake it a little to moisten all the leaves. Let it stand in a cool, dark place for 5 days to steep. Strain the vinegar through cheesecloth into a pint jar; discard the herb leaves. If desired, pour the vinegar into smaller containers. As a decorative touch, add a whole sprig of the herb to the container. Cover the vinegar tightly and refrigerate it.

Experiment with these ideas:

Hot pepper vinegar. Drop 4 or 5 small, fresh hot peppers into a pint bottle and fill it with vinegar. Let it steep for 3 or 4 days, then remove the peppers. Sprinkle a few drops of this vinegar on spinach, greens, or other vegetables. The peppers are hot enough to season several refills of vinegar.

Garlic vinegar. Drop 3 or 4 peeled garlic cloves into 1 pint of red wine vinegar and let them steep for a week. Add more garlic cloves for a stronger flavor.

Potpourri vinegars. Mix herbs of your choice, or herbs and garlic, for vinegars with a special zing.

Long-keeping vinegars. For herb vinegars that can be stored on the shelf, boil the vinegar after you've strained it and pour it into sterilized, hot canning jars. Screw the lids on tightly and store the jars in a cool, dark place for up to 3 months. Refrigerate after opening.

Bake Your Own:
Soft Pretzels

Let the kids help make these pretzels—they'll especially enjoy rolling and twisting the dough. **Equipment:** measuring cup, two large mixing bowls, mixing spoon, measuring spoons, electric mixer or long-handled wooden spoon, large cutting board or counter, sharp knife, cookie sheets, spatula, wire racks. **Ingredients:** whole-wheat flour, all-purpose flour, active dry yeast, salt, water, vegetable oil, honey, coarse kitchen salt.

Measure 2 cups of whole-wheat flour and 2 cups of all-purpose flour into a large bowl, and stir the flours together. In another large bowl, combine 1½ cups of the flour mixture with 1 full package of active dry yeast and 1 teaspoon of salt. Add 1⅓ cups of hot tap water, 3 tablespoons of vegetable oil, and 1 tablespoon of honey and beat until smooth, using an electric mixer or a long-handled wooden spoon. Stir in enough flour to make a moderately stiff dough.

Turn the dough out onto a lightly floured cutting board or counter and knead it until smooth, about 5 minutes. With a sharp knife, cut the dough into 12 pieces.

Roll each piece of dough into a rope about 15 inches long. Sprinkle coarse kitchen salt generously on your work surface and roll each rope in salt. To tie each pretzel hold the ends, loop them to the center, twist, and gently press the ends into place.

Place the salted, twisted pretzels on lightly greased cookie sheets, widely spaced. Bake at 425° F for 20 minutes, or until lightly browned. Remove from the sheets immediately with a spatula; eat hot or cool.

Pocket Bread

Pita, the Middle Eastern version of the tortilla, forms a pocket inside as it bakes; hence its name, and its popularity. Cut pita in half and fill the pocket with any sandwich filling you like. **Equipment:** measuring cup, large mixing bowl, mixing spoon, measuring spoons, saucepan, electric mixer or long-handled wooden spoon, large cutting board or counter, plastic wrap, sharp knife, cookie sheets, spatula, wire racks. **Ingredients:** whole-wheat or all-purpose flour, active dry yeast, water, vegetable oil, sugar, salt. **Yield:** 16 small pocket loaves.

Measure 2 cups of whole-wheat or all-purpose flour into a large mixing bowl; add 2 packages of active dry yeast and stir together. Measure 2 cups of water, ¼ cup of vegetable oil, 1 tablespoon of sugar, and 2 teaspoons of salt into a saucepan. Heat over low heat, stirring to blend, just until warm (110° to 120° F). Add the warm liquid to the flour-yeast mixture and beat until smooth, using an electric mixer or a long-handled wooden spoon. Add 1 more cup of whole-wheat or all-purpose flour and beat again; add 2 to 3 cups more flour and stir to make a moderately soft dough.

Turn the dough out onto a lightly floured cutting board or counter and knead it until smooth and satiny, about 10 minutes. Cover the dough with an inverted bowl or plastic wrap and let it rest for 30 minutes.

With a sharp knife, cut the dough into 16 equal portions. Shape each portion into a ball. Flatten each ball into a circle 5 inches in diameter, and place the circles of dough onto greased cookie sheets. Let them rise, uncovered, in a warm place until puffy, about 30 to 45 minutes. Bake at 400° F, on the bottom rack of the oven, for about 10 minutes or until very lightly browned. Remove from the cookie sheets immediately; cool on wire racks. Store in plastic bags.

Oatmeal Batter Bread

This no-knead yeast bread is delicious served warm with cream cheese and apple butter. **Equipment:** measuring cups, large mixing bowl, mixing spoon, measuring spoons, saucepan, electric mixer or long-handled wooden spoon, clean towel or plastic wrap, two 1½-quart round casserole dishes or soufflé dishes, pastry brush, wire racks. **Ingredients:** whole-wheat or all-purpose flour, active dry yeast, molasses or honey, butter, water, salt, baking soda, small-curd cream-style cottage cheese, eggs, rolled oats, sugar. **Yield:** 2 round loaves.

Measure 1½ cups of whole-wheat or all-purpose flour into a large mixing bowl; add 2 packages of active dry yeast and stir together. Measure ⅓ cup of molasses or honey, 3 tablespoons of butter, ¼ cup of water, 2 teaspoons of salt, and ½ teaspoon of baking soda into a saucepan; stir to blend. Add 1 pound (2 cups) of small-curd cream-style cottage cheese, and stir well. Heat over low heat just until warm (110° to 120° F), stirring to blend.

Add the cottage cheese mixture to the flour-yeast mixture and beat until smooth, using an electric mixer or a long-handled wooden spoon. Add 2 eggs and beat until blended. Add 1 more cup of the whole-wheat or all-purpose flour and beat again to blend thoroughly. Stir in 1 cup of rolled oats and the remaining 1 cup of whole-wheat or all-purpose flour; mix well.

Cover the mixing bowl with a clean towel or plastic wrap and let the dough rise in a warm place until doubled, about 1 hour. Stir the batter down with a wooden spoon and beat it briefly. Turn the batter into two greased 1½-quart round casserole dishes or soufflé dishes. Brush the tops of the loaves with melted butter and let the bread rise, uncovered, in a warm place until nearly doubled, about 45 minutes.

Bake the loaves at 350° F for 35 minutes. Let the loaves cool in the baking dishes for 10 minutes; then turn them out onto wire racks, and let them cool completely. Before serving, brush the tops of the loaves with more melted butter and sprinkle them lightly with sugar. Store in plastic bags at room temperature or in the refrigerator, or freeze.

Basic Wheat Bread

Use whole-wheat flour or combine it with all-purpose flour in this easy, basic bread recipe. **Equipment:** measuring cups, large mixing bowl, mixing spoon, measuring spoons, saucepan; electric mixer with dough hooks, food processor, or long-handled wooden spoon; large cutting board or counter, clean towel, sharp knife, two 8½ × 4½-inch loaf pans, pastry brush, aluminum foil, wire racks. **Ingredients:** whole-wheat or all-purpose flour, as desired; active dry yeast, milk, water, sugar, vegetable oil, salt. **Yield:** 2 loaves.

To make this basic bread, use whole-wheat and all-purpose flour in any combination you like. Bread made entirely from whole-wheat flour rises more slowly and turns out denser than a loaf made with all-purpose flour, but whole-wheat is much more nutritious.

Measure 2 cups of whole-wheat or all-purpose flour into a large mixing bowl and add 2 packages of active dry yeast; stir together. Measure 1 cup of milk, 1 cup of water, 2 tablespoons of sugar, 2 tablespoons of vegetable oil, and 1 tablespoon of salt into a saucepan; heat over low heat only until warm (110° to 120° F), stirring to blend. Add the liquid ingredients to the flour-yeast mixture and beat until smooth. Add 1 cup more of the flour and beat again.

Using an electric mixer with dough hooks, a food processor, or a long-handled wooden spoon, stir in 2½ to 3½ cups more flour to make a moderately stiff dough. Turn the dough out onto a lightly floured cutting board or counter, and knead it for 8 to 10 minutes; the dough should be smooth and satiny. Gently press two fingers into the dough. When it springs back, leaving only slight indentations, you've kneaded enough.

Shape the dough into a ball. Grease a large mixing bowl and set the dough into it; cover the bowl with a clean towel and let the dough rise in a warm place until doubled. Whole-wheat dough takes 1 to 1½ hours to rise; all-purpose dough rises somewhat faster. Gently press your fingers into the dough; if the indentations remain, the dough has risen enough.

Punch the dough down and turn it out onto a lightly floured surface. Cut the dough in half with a sharp knife and shape the halves into balls; cover the balls with clean towels and let them rest for 10 minutes.

To shape each loaf, flatten a ball of dough into a rectangle 9 inches wide; fold the rectangle in half lengthwise. Press the edges firmly to seal them, roll the loaf to round it out, and put the loaf into a well-greased 8½ × 4½-inch loaf pan, seam side down.

Brush the tops of the loaves with vegetable oil. Let them rise in a warm place until doubled, about 1 hour. Bake at 400° F for 30 to 35 minutes. If the tops of the loaves start to get too brown before the baking time is up, cover them lightly with aluminum foil.

Check for doneness by tipping a loaf out of the pan and tapping the bottom; the loaf should sound hollow. Remove the loaves from the pan immediately, and brush the tops of the loaves with oil if you want a soft crust. Cool on a wire rack. Store in plastic bags, at room temperature or in the refrigerator, or freeze.

Polish Pickle Rye

This extraordinary rye bread will improve your whole repertoire ' of sandwiches—especially sandwiches with pickles. The hearty round loaves look as good as they taste. **Equipment:** measuring cups, two large mixing bowls, mixing spoon, small saucepan, measuring spoons, heatproof cup; electric mixer with dough hooks, food processor, or long-handled wooden spoon; large cutting board or counter, plastic wrap, sharp knife, two 1-quart round casserole dishes or soufflé dishes, pastry brush, aluminum foil, wire racks. **Ingredients:** whole-wheat flour, rye flour, active dry yeast, water, dill seeds, juice from jar of Polish-style pickles, buttermilk, sugar, vegetable oil, salt, caraway seeds, egg. **Yield:** 2 round loaves.

Measure 4 cups of whole-wheat flour and 2 cups of rye flour into a large mixing bowl, and stir together. Measure 2 cups of the blended flour into another large bowl or the large bowl of an electric mixer; stir in 2 packages of active dry yeast. Heat ½ cup of water to boiling in a small saucepan. Measure 2 teaspoons of dill seeds into a heatproof cup and pour the boiling water over them; let stand for 10 minutes. In the same saucepan, mix ½ cup of water, ½ cup of the juice from a jar of Polish-style pickles, and ½ cup of buttermilk; add 2 tablespoons of sugar, 2 tablespoons of vegetable oil, and 2 teaspoons of salt.

Heat over low heat only until warm (110° to 120° F). Stir in the dill-seed/water mixture and add 2 teaspoons of caraway seeds.

Add the pickle-juice/seed mixture to the flour-yeast mixture and beat until smooth. Using an electric mixer with dough hooks, a food processor, or a long-handled wooden spoon, add the remaining 4 cups of wheat and rye flours to make a soft dough.

Turn the dough out onto a lightly floured cutting board or counter and knead it gently until smooth, about 5 to 8 minutes. Cover the dough with an inverted bowl or plastic wrap and let it rest for 40 minutes. Cut the dough in half with a sharp knife and shape the halves into balls, tucking the edges under and pinching to hold them in place.

Set each ball into a greased 1-quart round casserole dish or soufflé dish. With a sharp knife, cut three shallow slits in the top of each ball of dough. For a soft crust, brush the tops of the loaves with oil; for a firm, shiny crust, brush with a beaten egg. Let the loaves rise, uncovered, in a warm place until doubled, about 40 minutes.

Bake the loaves at 350° F for 50 to 55 minutes; cover the tops of the loaves with aluminum foil during the last 10 minutes to prevent overbrowning. Remove the loaves from the casserole dishes immediately; cool them on wire racks. Store in plastic bags at room temperature or in the refrigerator, or freeze.

Three-Grain Bread

This solid, nourishing bread has the rich texture and all the satisfying flavor of the real old-time variety. **Equipment:** measuring cups, teakettle, large mixing bowl, mixing spoon, measuring spoons; electric mixer with dough hooks, food processor, or long-handled wooden spoon; large cutting board or counter, clean towels, sharp knife, three

9⅝ × 5½-inch loaf pans, wire racks. **Ingredients:** water, cornmeal, whole-wheat-biscuit cereal, rolled oats, active dry yeast, honey, salt, whole-wheat flour, all-purpose flour. **Yield:** 3 large loaves.

Measure 1 quart of water into a teakettle and bring it to a boil. In a large mixing bowl, stir together 1 cup of cornmeal, 1 cup of crumbled whole-wheat-biscuit cereal, and 1 cup of rolled oats; pour the 1 quart of boiling water over the grain mixture, stir, and let the mixture cool.

Dissolve 2 packages of active dry yeast in 1 cup of warm water. When the cornmeal mixture is just warm, add the yeast mixture to it. Stir in ½ cup of honey, 1 cup of warm water, and 2 teaspoons of salt; blend thoroughly. Stir in 2 cups of whole-wheat flour, 1 cup at a time.

Using an electric mixer with dough hooks, a food processor, or a long-handled wooden spoon, add 6 to 8 cups of all-purpose flour. When the dough gets too thick for the spoon, mix with your hands. Add only enough flour to make a soft, sticky dough.

Turn the dough out onto a large, well-floured cutting board or counter, and knead it for 5 minutes. The dough will be sticky. Grease a large mixing bowl and set the dough into it; cover the bowl with a clean towel and let the dough rise in a warm place until doubled, 1 hour or more.

Punch the dough down and turn it out onto a well-floured board. Cut it into three portions with a sharp knife; shape the portions into three loaves and put each portion into a well-greased 9⅝ × 5½-inch loaf pan. Cover the loaves with clean towels and let rise in a warm place until doubled, 1 hour or more.

Bake at 350° F for at least 65 minutes, until the loaves are evenly browned. Check for doneness by tipping a loaf out of the pan and tapping the bottom; the loaf should sound hollow. Remove the loaves from the pans immediately; cool them on wire racks. Store in plastic bags, at room temperature or in the refrigerator, or freeze.

Pour Your Own:

Apple Cider

Nothing tastes better than natural apple cider, especially if it's homemade. You can make cider year-round with this simple technique. **Equipment:** sharp knife, measuring cup, blender; large, freestanding strainer; large pan, cheesecloth, spoon, large bowl or teakettle for weight, quart jar with cover. **Ingredients:** red delicious, jonathan, or other eating apples; water. **Yield:** 3 cups.

Chop red delicious, jonathan, or other eating apples to measure 2 cups, and place in a blender; add 1 cup of water. Blend thoroughly until the mixture is evenly pulpy.

Set a large, freestanding strainer into a large pan. Line the strainer with cheesecloth, letting the cloth overlap the edges enough so that it can be folded back over the top of the strainer. Pour the pulped apple mixture into the strainer and fold the ends of the cloth

Drain the pulp into a pan through a cheesecloth-lined strainer; press the juice out with a full bowl or teakettle.

501

over it to wrap the pulp firmly in the strainer.

Fill a large bowl or a teakettle with water to weight the pulp. Set the weight on the wrapped pulp and press it into the strainer until the cider stops flowing into the pan; then remove the strainer. Discard the pulp or add it to the compost pile.

Pour the cider into a quart jar. Cover the jar tightly and refrigerate it; serve chilled or hot.

Ginger Beer/ Ginger Soda

Back when summer evenings were made for porch-sitting, ginger beer and ginger soda were favorite drinks. It's easy to recapture their satisfying, zesty-sweet taste.

GINGER BEER. **Equipment:** sharp knife, large pot, large soup kettle with cover, measuring cup, mixing spoon, funnel, cheesecloth, wire whisk, measuring spoons, three gallon jugs with covers. **Ingredients:** ginger root, water, light raw sugar, lemon juice, honey, egg, lemon extract. **Yield:** 3 gallons.

Thinly slice 3 ounces of ginger root and bruise the slices with the back of the knife. Set the sliced ginger into a large pot and add 3 quarts of water; bring to a boil and simmer for 30 minutes. Remove from heat.

Measure 2½ pounds (5 cups) of light raw sugar into a large soup kettle and add ¼ cup of lemon juice and ¼ cup of honey; add 8½ quarts of cold water and stir to dissolve. Strain the ginger extract into the syrup mixture through a funnel lined with cheesecloth, and stir to mix the ingredients well. Let the mixture cool completely.

When the ginger mixture is cool, add 1 well-beaten egg and 1 teaspoon of lemon extract; blend well with a wire whisk. Cover the kettle and let the mixture stand for 3 to 4 days, until the liquid

has cleared and any impurities have settled.

Carefully pour the ginger beer into three clean gallon jugs; cover the jugs tightly. Chill well before serving.

GINGER SODA. Make this sweeter, more carbonated drink for children. **Equipment:** sharp knife, large soup kettle with cover, measuring cup, measuring spoons, mixing spoon, funnel, cheesecloth, two gallon jugs with covers. **Ingredients:** ginger root, light raw sugar, lemon juice, cream of tartar, yeast, water. **Yield:** 2 gallons.

Thinly slice 2 ounces of ginger root, and bruise the slices with the back of the knife. Set the sliced ginger into a large soup kettle and add 2 pounds (4 cups) of light raw sugar, ¼ cup of lemon juice, 1 tablespoon cream of tartar, 1 cup of yeast, and 2 gallons of water. Stir well. Let the mixture stand in a warm place for 24 hours.

Pour the ginger soda through a funnel lined with cheesecloth into two clean gallon jugs; cover the jugs tightly and let them stand overnight. Chill well before serving.

Dandelion Wine

Before spraying your yard to get rid of the annual yellow nuisance, put the dandelions to good use—you'll enjoy the crisp, dry, unique taste of dandelion wine. **Equipment:** measuring cup, large pan, two gallon glass jugs, funnel, cheesecloth, fermentation lock, 3-foot piece of ⅜-inch plastic tubing, 4 fifth bottles with screw caps. **Ingredients:** water, dandelion petals, sugar, lemon juice, all-purpose wine yeast, aluminum foil. **Yield:** 4 fifths of wine.

Pick dandelions in early spring, as soon as they open—early morning is the best time to work. Use only dandelions from areas you know haven't been treated with weed killer; stay away from roadside areas where plants absorb lead from car exhaust. Use only the petals of fresh, newly picked blossoms.

Heat 2 quarts of water to boiling in a large pan and add 2 quarts of fresh dandelion petals; return to a boil and simmer for 30 minutes. Remove from heat. Pour 1½ pounds (3 cups) of sugar into a 1-gallon glass jug and add ¼ cup of fresh lemon juice. Pour the hot dandelion extract into the jug through a funnel lined with cheesecloth, and shake the jug to dissolve the sugar mixture.

Add ⅕ packet—a heaping ¼ teaspoon—of all-purpose wine yeast and enough cool water to almost fill the jug, and shake again. Cap the jug with a fermentation lock and fill the lock with water; set the capped jug in a warm, dark spot for about 3 weeks. After 3 weeks, pour the wine into a clean glass jug, leaving the sediment behind. Cap the jug with a water-filled fermentation lock and let it ferment for about 5 weeks more. The wine will stop working at an alcohol content of 14 percent.

When the wine has stopped working, carefully siphon it into a clean gallon glass jug, using a 3-foot piece of ⅜-inch plastic tubing. Leave the sediment in the bottom of the first jug. Cover the top of the filled jug with a piece of aluminum foil—don't cap it tightly. Let the wine rest for about 2 weeks, until any additional sediment has settled and the liquid has cleared. To bottle the wine, siphon it into 4 clean fifth bottles, filling the bottles to about 2 inches from the top. Cover the bottles tightly and age the wine for 3 to 6 months in a cool dark place. The distinctive flavor and bouquet of the wine make the wait worthwhile.

Quick-Mix Liqueurs

Now there's an easy way to make your own liqueurs. What price elegance? **Equipment:** quart saucepan, measuring spoons and cup, spoon, empty screw-top liter or half-gallon liquor bottle. **Ingredients:** for Coin-

treau-type liqueur—sugar, water, fifth or quart of vodka; for B&B-type cordial—brandy; for either—commercial fruit extract. **Yield:** 1 fifth or quart of liqueur.

The fruit extract is the secret of a good liqueur, and you can't make this yourself. One reliable source is a French firm, Noirot; Noirot extracts are used in these recipes. Some wine-making stores carry Noirot products, but if you can't find them locally, write to Semplex of USA, 4805 Lyndale Avenue North, Minneapolis, Minnesota 55430.

Cointreau, that sweet and unforgettable orange liqueur, can be approximated with a base of vodka. First, make a sugar syrup, stirring together 1 cup sugar and 1 cup water in a saucepan. Bring just to a boil and let cool slightly. Into a clean liquor bottle, pour the syrup (you should have 1 cup) and a full bottle of Noirot Orange Triple Dry Extract. Add the fifth or quart of vodka —remember that a quart contains nearly seven ounces more than a fifth, so liqueur mixed with a full quart of spirits will taste more strongly alcoholic. Cap the bottle and shake it to mix thoroughly. Let it cool before drinking.

B&B is another all-time favorite. You can come pretty close to the real thing, at nowhere near its price, with a fifth or a quart of brandy, a full bottle of Noirot Reverendine Extract, and half a bottle of Noirot French Yellow Brandy Extract. Just pour the extracts into a clean liquor bottle, add the brandy, and mix thoroughly.

Rich Coffee Liqueur

The real thing is expensive, but you can make this coffee liqueur for far less than the premium price. The taste is rich; you needn't be to enjoy it. **Equipment:** two ½-gallon or gallon bottles with covers, measuring cup, funnel, coffee filter. **Ingredients:** rich instant coffee, vanilla bean, sugar, water, inexpensive vodka. **Yield:** about 1½ quarts.

Measure ¼ cup of rich instant coffee into a clean ½-gallon or gallon bottle, using a funnel if necessary. Split a vanilla bean down the center and drop it into the bottle; add 4 cups of sugar and 2 cups of water and shake well to mix. Add 1 fifth bottle of inexpensive vodka—don't invest in good vodka; it won't taste any better in the liqueur. Cover the bottle tightly and store it in a cool dark place for 4 to 6 weeks. Shake the bottle at least once a week during this period. Strain the liqueur into a clean bottle through a funnel lined with a coffee filter, and cover it tightly.

Old-Fashioned Fruit Bounces

Bounces are old-time fruit liqueurs made by steeping fresh fruit in spirits; enjoy them as after-dinner treats or use them as spirited dessert sauces. **Equipment:** wide-mouth ½-gallon jar with tight-fitting lid, wooden spoon, measuring cup, strainer, large bowl, funnel, decanter or liqueur bottle. **Ingredients:** ripe cherries, raspberries, or damson plums; sugar; vodka, gin, brandy, or scotch. **Yield:** about 2 quarts.

To make bounce, use ripe, perfect fruit; don't use bruised fruit or pieces of fruit. Wash the fruit thoroughly, drain it well, and remove any stems.

Place 1 quart of washed and drained fruit into a wide-mouth ½ gallon jar; as you fill the jar, break the skins of the fruit gently with the back of a wooden spoon. When the jar is filled with fruit, pour 2 cups of sugar over the fruit; then add 1 fifth or quart of vodka, gin, brandy, or scotch, as desired. Do not stir.

Cover the jar tightly and set it in a cool dark place for about 2 months. Shake the jar a few times each month to redistribute the sugar and juices.

After 2 months, strain the liqueur off the fruit into a bowl, and funnel or pour the liqueur into a decanter or a liqueur bottle. Discard the fruit.

Cherry bounce. Use ripe, red, tart cherries, unpitted, and the spirit of your choice.
Raspberry bounce. Use red or black raspberries, and the spirit of your choice.
Damson plum bounce. Use whole, unpitted damson plums, and the spirit of your choice.

Dry Your Own:

Fruits

Dried fruit, like most nourishing food, is expensive—but it needn't be. Take advantage of seasonal sales to dry your own apples, apricots, peaches, plums, and more. **Equipment:** measuring spoons, measuring cup, mixing spoon, stainless steel paring knife, pastry brush, large pot, large strainer, large bowl, cookie sheets, low-temperature oven, oven thermometer that reads as low as 100° F, spatula, airtight containers. **Ingredients:** fresh, blemish-free fruit (apples, pears, apricots, peaches, plums, prune plums, nectarines, or bananas); crystalline or powdered ascorbic acid, water, lemon juice. **Time:** 12 to 24 hours, depending on the fruit.

To prevent discoloration, most fruits must be brushed with a solution of ascorbic acid before drying—buy either the crystalline or the powdered form. Some fruits must be blanched briefly to prevent enzyme action. Use a deep pot, a strainer to dip in it, and a large bowl filled with cold water to stop the blanching action. Use only fresh, blemish-free fruit.

Dry fruits with a steady oven temperature of about 100° to 120° F; check the temperature periodically with an oven thermometer that registers as low as 100° F. If the oven temperature goes above 120° F, turn the oven off or open the oven door for a while. For even drying, turn trays of fruit occasionally and rotate their positions in the oven.

Dry fruits completely, as detailed below—usually from 12 to 24 hours. Let them cool thoroughly. Store dried fruits in airtight containers, and keep them in a cool, dry, dark place.

Apples or pears. Choose tart cooking apples or slightly underripe pears. Combine 2½ teaspoons of crystalline or powdered ascorbic acid with 1 cup cold water; stir to dissolve. Pare and core the fruit and cut it into ¼-inch slices or rings. As you cut the fruit, use a pastry brush to coat each piece with the ascorbic acid mixture; coat all sides.

Spread the sliced fruit in a single layer on cookie sheets. Dry at no higher than 120° F until the fruit is leathery and pliable—around 12 hours. Check the oven temperature and rearrange the trays from time to time; stir the fruit to move outside pieces to the center.

Let the fruit cool completely; then pack it into airtight containers. Store for up to 8 months.

Apricots. Choose fully ripe but not mushy apricots. Wash and drain the fruit. Combine 1½ teaspoons of crystalline or powdered ascorbic acid with 1 cup of cold water; stir to dissolve. Cut each apricot in half and remove the pit; as you work, paint each apricot half with the ascorbic acid mixture.

Spread the apricot halves in a single layer on cookie sheets, pit side up. Dry at no higher than 120° F until the apricots are leathery and pliable—around 18 hours. Check the oven temperature and rearrange the trays from time to time; stir the apricots to move outside pieces to the center.

Let the fruit cool completely; then pack it into airtight containers. Store for up to 8 months.

Peaches. Select perfect, fully ripe but not soft peaches. Blanch peaches by placing them in a large strainer; lower them into a large pot of boiling water just long enough to loosen their skins, and then dip them into a large bowl of cold water immediately. Drain well. Combine 1½ teaspoons of crystalline or powdered ascorbic acid with 1 cup of cold water; stir to dissolve. Peel, halve, and pit the peaches; leave them in halves or slice, as desired. As you work, coat each piece with the ascorbic acid mixture.

Arrange the peaches in a single layer on cookie sheets—cut side up, if halves. Dry at no higher than 120° F until the peaches are leathery and pliable—around 12 hours for slices, up to 24 hours for large halves. Check the oven temperature and rearrange the trays from time to time; stir the peaches to move outside pieces to the center.

Let the peaches cool completely; then pack them into airtight containers. Store for up to 8 months.

Plums and prune plums. Choose ripe, perfect fruit. Wash and drain the plums. Blanch in boiling water for 45 seconds, just enough to split the skins, and then dip them into a bowl of cold water. Drain well. Halve and pit the plums—no ascorbic acid is needed. Arrange the halves in a single layer on cookie sheets, pit side up. Dry at no higher than 120° F until the plums are firm, leathery, and pliable—around 12 hours. Check the oven temperature and rearrange the trays from time to time; stir the plums to move outside pieces to the center.

Let the plums cool completely; then pack them into airtight containers. Store for up to 8 months.

Nectarines. Choose ripe but not soft fruit. Wash and drain the nectarines. Combine 1½ teaspoons of crystalline or powdered ascorbic acid with 1 cup of cold water; stir to dissolve. Halve the nectarines and remove pits; then slice the nectarines into ¼-inch pieces. As you work, coat each piece with the ascorbic acid mixture.

Arrange the sliced nectarines in a single layer on cookie sheets. Dry at no higher than 120° F until leathery and pliable—around 12 hours. Check the oven temperature and rearrange the trays from time to time; stir the slices to move outside pieces to the center.

Let the nectarines cool completely; then pack them into airtight containers.

Store for up to 8 months.

Bananas. Select barely ripe bananas with no brown spots. Slice the bananas into ¼-inch slices; as you work, paint each slice with bottled lemon juice.

Arrange the slices in a single layer on cookie sheets. Dry at no higher than 120° F until the slices are almost brittle. Some people like banana chips very crisp; others like them chewy—dry for 8 to 10 hours for chewy chips, 10 to 14 hours for crisp ones.

Let the banana chips cool completely; then pack them into airtight containers. Store for up to 8 months. Eat as a snack; don't try to reconstitute.

Vegetables

Carrots, celery, mushrooms, onions, peppers, and squash are all easy to dry, and very handy for sauces, soups, and stews. **Equipment:** paring knife, vegetable peeler, chopping board and knife, shredder, deep pot with cover, steamer, cookie sheets, low-temperature oven, oven thermometer that registers as low as 100° F, spatula, airtight containers. **Ingredients:** fresh, blemish-free vegetables (carrots, celery, mushrooms, onions, red or green sweet peppers, or summer squash). **Time:** about 12 hours.

Before drying, most vegetables must be steamed briefly to stop enzyme action. Use a deep pot with a cover, and a steamer. Use only fresh, blemish-free vegetables.

Dry vegetables with a steady oven temperature of about 100° to 120° F; check the temperature periodically with an oven thermometer that registers as low as 100° F. If the oven temperature goes above 120° F, turn the oven off or open the oven door for a while. For even drying, turn trays of vegetables occasionally and rotate their positions in the oven.

Dry vegetables completely, as detailed below—usually about 12 hours. Let them cool thoroughly. Store them in airtight containers, and keep them in a cool, dry, dark place. Use dry or reconstitute as usual.

Carrots. Choose crisp, young, tender carrots. Wash them well, peel them, and cut off the tops and ends. Slice them into ⅛-inch slices or shred them. Steam sliced carrots in a steamer for 4 minutes; steam shreds for 2 minutes. Drain well.

Arrange carrot slices in a single layer on cookie sheets; arrange shreds no more than ½ inch deep on cookie sheets. Dry at no higher than 120° F until very tough and leathery—around 12 hours for slices, 8 hours for shreds. Check the oven temperature and rearrange the trays from time to time; stir the carrots to move outside pieces to the center.

Let the dried carrots cool completely; then pack them into airtight containers. Store for up to 10 months.

Celery. Use tender stalks with leaves. Wash stalks and leaves well; shake them dry. Trim the root ends. Remove leaves and separate them so they will lie flat; slice the stalks no thicker than ⅛ inch. Steam stalks and leaves for 2 minutes and drain well.

Spread celery slices and leaves in a single layer on cookie sheets. Dry at no higher than 120° F until brittle—around 12 hours for slices, 6 to 8 hours for leaves. Check the oven temperature and rearrange the trays from time to time; stir the celery to move outside pieces to the center.

Let the dried celery cool completely; then pack it into airtight containers. Store for up to 10 months.

Mushrooms. Choose fresh, even-sized mushrooms with tightly closed heads. Wash the mushrooms very gently. Cut off any stems that are tough or woody; trim off the ends of all other stems. Leave small mushrooms whole; slice large ones. Steam the mushrooms for 2 minutes and drain well.

Arrange the mushrooms in a single layer on cookie sheets. Dry at no higher than 120° F until leathery and hard—around 12 hours. Thin slices may be brittle. Check the temperature and rearrange the trays from time to time; stir

Herbs

the mushrooms to move outside pieces to the center.

Let the mushrooms cool completely; then pack them into airtight containers. Store for up to 10 months.

Onions. Select large, flavorful, perfect onions. Onions can be dried directly; they don't have to be steamed. Cut off the stems and bottoms and remove the skins. Slice the onions ⅛ inch thick or chop them fine. Separate slices into rings.

Arrange the onion pieces or rings in a single layer on cookie sheets. Dry at no higher than 120° F until the onion is very crisp and brittle—around 12 hours. Check the oven temperature and rearrange the trays from time to time; stir the onions to move outside pieces to the center.

Let the onions cool completely; then pack them into airtight containers. Store for up to 10 months.

Sweet green or red peppers. Choose ripe, tender red or green sweet peppers. Peppers can be dried directly; they don't have to be steamed. Cut out the stems and seeds and chop the peppers into ¼-inch pieces.

Arrange the chopped peppers in a single layer on cookie sheets. Dry at no higher than 120° F until the peppers are brittle—around 12 hours. Check the oven temperature and rearrange the trays from time to time; stir the peppers to move outside pieces to the center.

Let the peppers cool completely; then pack them into airtight containers. Store for up to 10 months.

Summer squash. Use young, tender zucchini, pattypan, or crookneck squash. Wash the squash, cut off the ends, and slice the squash ¼ inch thick. Steam it for about 3 minutes and drain well.

Arrange the squash in a single layer on cookie sheets. Dry at no higher than 120° F until brittle—around 12 hours. Check the oven temperature and rearrange the trays from time to time; stir the peppers to move outside pieces to the center.

Let the squash cool completely; then pack it into airtight containers. Store for up to 10 months.

Drying your own herbs yields year-round pleasure for a fraction of what store-bought dried herbs cost. Harvest the leaves just before the plants bloom, when the essential oils are most concentrated. **Equipment:** paper towels, cookie sheet, low-temperature oven and oven thermometer, glass storage jars with airtight lids, paper bag, string. **Ingredients:** basil, dill, chervil, chives, marjoram, parsley, tarragon, oregano, thyme, savory, celery leaves, or whatever herb your garden produces in abundance. **Yield:** ½ to ¾ cup of crumbled herb for each 1 cup of fresh leaves.

Pick individual healthy leaves or sprigs from the top two-thirds of the plant; for chives, use garden scissors to cut sprigs from the edges of the plant. Wash the herb quickly with cold water; pat dry with paper towels. Spread the leaves evenly in a single layer on a cookie sheet. Using an oven thermometer to check temperature, dry in the oven at no higher than 120° F until the herb is brittle and crumbles when pinched, about 1 hour.

When the leaves are completely dry, remove them from the oven. Crumble and pour into airtight glass storage jars, or store whole. Flavors and colors change in sunlight and heat; store in a cool, dark, dry place. If you notice moisture inside the container, quickly remove the herb and return it to the oven for further drying.

Drying without an oven. Hang small bunches of herbs, stems up, in a shady, dry spot and let them dry until they crumble when pinched. Store in airtight glass jars.

Drying seeds. Dill, caraway, anise, fennel, cumin, and coriander perform the seed-drying process automatically; all you have to do is gather the seeds before the wind scatters them. Pick the pods or flower heads when they're almost dry and spread them on a cookie sheet to dry completely at room temperature; then shake the heads to loosen the seeds. Or pick the entire plant and hang it upside down inside a large paper bag. Punch a few holes around the top of the bag for air circulation and hang it up; the seeds drop into the bag as they dry. Store seeds in airtight glass jars in a cool, dark, dry place; use them whole or finely ground.

Make a Box Dehydrator

Cut the flaps off a carton and line it with foil; thread a trouble light in through one corner. Set a shallow pan firmly over the box, all sides sealed; as the pan absorbs heat, food spread in it will dehydrate.

For drying small batches of fruit or vegetables, a box dehydrator is easier and more economical than most ovens. Make one dehydrator or several; both cost and labor are minimal. **Tools:** utility knife or scissors. **Materials:** aluminum jelly roll pan or cookie sheet, cardboard carton, newspaper, spray can of quick-drying matte black paint, heavy-duty aluminum foil; 60-watt trouble light or light bulb with socket, cord, and plug; screening or cheesecloth cover for food. **Time:** about 15 minutes.

To make the dehydrator, use an aluminum jelly roll pan or a cookie sheet and a cardboard carton the same length and width of the pan—the rim of the pan should rest on the side of the box when you put the pan on top of the box. Spread newspaper to protect the floor and spray the bottom of the pan with quick-drying matte black paint. Let the paint dry completely, as directed by the manufacturer.

Cut the top or the top flaps off the cardboard carton. Cut a small hole in one bottom corner of the carton, just big enough for an electric cord to go through. Line the box completely with heavy-duty aluminum foil, shiny side up. Thread the end of a 60-watt trouble light or light bulb and socket through the opening in the corner of the box, with the light bulb in the center of the box. Prop the bulb up at a slight angle on a crumpled piece of aluminum foil, and patch the corner hole closed with a scrap of foil.

To use the dehydrator, prepare fruits or vegetables as directed for drying. Spread the prepared food in a single layer on the jelly roll pan, and set the pan over the light in the cardboard carton; cover the food with a screening or cheesecloth cover to keep it clean. Turn on the trouble light or light bulb, and let the food dry until it tests done.

Make Your Own Beef Jerky

Jerky, a favorite snack and take-along food, doesn't have to be expensive. You can oven-dry or smoke lean beef to make a jerky much better than store-bought. **Equipment:** sharp knife, cutting board, large bowl or pan, measuring cup, measuring spoons, mixing spoon, plastic wrap; smoker and green hardwood or hardwood chips, or low-temperature oven, oven thermometer that reads as low as 100° F, and cookie sheets. **Ingredients:** lean round steak or flank steak; seasoned salt and pepper, or vegetable oil, soy sauce, vinegar, sugar, sherry or lemon juice, onion powder. **Time:** 18 to 24 hours.

Use lean round steak or flank steak to make jerky; trim it carefully to remove all fat. Season the meat mildly if you're making jerky for a camping trip. For snacking or appetizer jerky, marinate the meat before drying it. To make 1 pound of jerky, buy 3 to 5 pounds of meat cut 1½ inches thick.

To prepare the jerky, set the meat in the freezer until it's partly frozen; then slice it very thin with a sharp knife. If you're using flank steak, slice across the grain.

For mildly seasoned jerky, sprinkle the meat with seasoned salt and pepper and go on with the drying process. For stronger flavor, make a marinade. In a large bowl or pan, combine 1 cup of vegetable oil, ⅓ cup of soy sauce, 3 tablespoons of vinegar, 2 tablespoons of sugar, 2 tablespoons of sherry or lemon juice, and 1 teaspoon of onion powder; stir together to blend. Set the meat into the marinade and toss it gently to coat all surfaces; cover the bowl or pan with plastic wrap and refrigerate. Marinate the meat for 4 to 10 hours, depending on how spicy you want the jerky; turn the meat in the marinade once or twice.

Dry the seasoned or marinated meat in a smoker or a low-temperature oven. Preheat the smoker to 90° F, or preheat the oven to 110° to 120° F. Check oven temperature periodically with an oven thermometer that registers as low as 100° F; if the oven goes over 120° F, turn it off or open the oven door for a while.

If you marinated the meat, remove it from the marinade and drain it well. Arrange the seasoned or marinated strips of meat on a well-oiled rack in the smoker; or on a well-oiled oven rack or cookie sheets for oven drying. Leave space between the pieces for air circulation. Smoke or oven-dry the strips of meat until the jerky is dry and brittle, about 18 to 24 hours.

Let the jerky cool completely. Store it in airtight containers or sealed plastic bags.

Build a Refrigerator Smoker

If you have the space and the wood, you can turn an old refrigerator into a smoker for meats and seafood. Check the dump, an appliance dealer, or a repair shop for a refrigerator that's beyond repair. **Tools:** screwdriver, pliers, hammer, grease pencil, hacksaw or heavy-duty metal cutter, shovel, oven thermometer, matches. **Materials:** old refrigerator with two shelves, sturdy chain and lock, aluminum foil or duct tape, 10 to 12 feet of clay pipe or stovepipe and one elbow piece, butterfly draft or vent, cement blocks, large garbage can lid or heavy piece of sheet metal; green, not dry, hardwood fuel (hickory, oak, beech, elm, maple, or apple); hickory or other hardwood chips. **Time:** about 4 hours, plus fire-building and smoking time.

Choose your refrigerator carefully. Make sure the door will close; make sure the refrigerator has two shelves. Look for a refrigerator that has as little plastic inside as possible. Before making the smoker, buy a heavy chain and lock; lock the refrigerator securely so that children cannot shut themselves inside. To build the smoker, you'll also need cement blocks, a butterfly draft or vent, 10 to 12 feet of clay pipe or stovepipe and one elbow piece, and a large garbage can lid or a piece of heavy sheet metal to cover the fire pit.

First, prepare the refrigerator. Remove the compressor, ice cube compartment, any plastic parts, and any removable parts except the shelves from inside the refrigerator. Block off any ducts or openings, except those in the bottom, with aluminum foil or duct tape. If there isn't a hole in the bottom of the refrigerator, mark and cut a hole the same diameter as the elbow pipe; use a hacksaw or a heavy-duty metal cutter to cut the hole. Mark and cut another hole

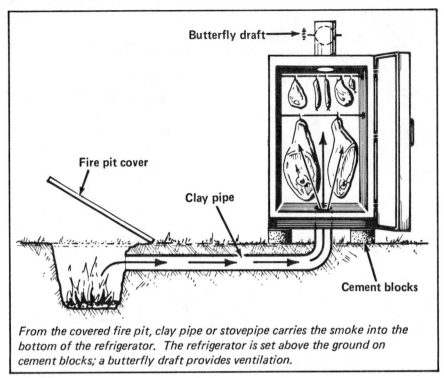

Butterfly draft

Fire pit cover

Clay pipe

Cement blocks

From the covered fire pit, clay pipe or stovepipe carries the smoke into the bottom of the refrigerator. The refrigerator is set above the ground on cement blocks; a butterfly draft provides ventilation.

in the top of the refrigerator or on one side near the top, to hold the butterfly draft or vent. Install the draft or vent in the cutout hole, following the manufacturer's instructions.

About 10 to 12 feet from where you'll set the refrigerator, dig a fire pit about 2 feet deep. If possible, set the refrigerator on a slight hill and dig the pit downhill from it, on the side of the refrigerator that's sheltered from the prevailing wind. Dig a trench 6 inches deep and 6 inches wide from the fire pit to where the center of the refrigerator will be, and line the trench with sections of clay pipe or stovepipe; fit the sections together carefully. Cover the pipe with dirt, but leave the refrigerator end of the trench open.

At the open end of the trench, set cement blocks to hold the refrigerator firmly and evenly over the end of the trench. Set the refrigerator into place on the blocks. Fit the elbow piece of clay pipe or stovepipe into place in the hole in the refrigerator's bottom, with the tail

of the pipe extending into the end of the trench. Fill in the rest of the trench with dirt.

To use the smoker, you'll need green, not dry, hardwood fuel—hickory, oak, beech, elm, maple, or apple. Build a fire in the fire pit near the smoker, using dry wood for kindling—do *not* start the fire with paper. For more smoke, soak hickory or other hardwood chips in water for ½ hour; then add them to the fire.

Cover the fire pit with a large garbage can lid or a piece of heavy sheet metal, and adjust the cover so that smoke flows slowly into and through the smoker, and the fire is very low—if the fire is allowed to get high, the insulation in the refrigerator could ignite. Place an oven thermometer on a rack in the smoker, and close the refrigerator door.

Check the smoker's temperature periodically. Make sure the smoke flows slowly and the fire stays low. When the smoker reaches the temperature specified in the recipe you're using, set the food onto the smoker's racks.

Check the smoker regularly, adding fuel, adjusting the cover, and adding more soaked chips as needed to maintain the required temperature and smoke. Check the food for doneness with a meat thermometer or as the recipe directs. When the food is done, remove it; put the fire out by closing the smoker vent and the fire pit cover, or with water. Chain and lock the refrigerator securely when not in use.

Smoke Your Own:

Turkey

A smoked turkey's crisp ebony skin and tender, tasty meat make a superb centerpiece for a special-occasion buffet. Serve the turkey cold, with oven-cooked stuffing. **Equipment:** large, deep dishpan, or container big enough to hold turkey; cover for container, large pan, measuring cup, mixing spoon, weight, paper towels, wire rack, wire or cheesecloth screen cover, meat thermometer, small bowl, pastry brush, smoker or covered barbecue with well-oiled rack, green hardwood or hardwood chips as required. **Ingredients:** whole dressed turkey (not stuffed), rock salt, water, honey, sherry. **Time:** 8 hours to soak and 1 hour to dry; about 2 hours per pound for smoking.

Note the weight of the turkey; it must smoke for about 2 hours per pound, so plan accordingly. If you're using a covered barbecue, follow the manufacturer's cooking instructions; barbecue temperatures are higher, so cooking time will be much less. Set the turkey in a large, deep dishpan or other container. In a large pan, mix 1 pound (2 cups) of rock salt with 1 gallon of water, and stir to dissolve. Pour the salt solution over the turkey. If the brine doesn't cover the turkey, mix more salt solution in the same proportions and add it to the pan to cover the turkey entirely. Cover the container and place a weight on the cover to hold the turkey under the brine. Refrigerate or set in a cold place for at least 8 hours, or overnight.

When the soaking time has elapsed, lift the turkey out of the brine and gently press out the liquid. Pat the turkey dry inside and out with paper towels. Set the turkey on a wire rack in a cool, well-ventilated place and let it air-dry for about 1 hour—if necessary, protect it from insects with a wire or cheesecloth screen cover.

Preheat the smoker to 90° F. If you're using a covered barbecue, follow the manufacturer's instructions for preheating and adding hardwood chips.

Insert a meat thermometer into the turkey's thigh, with the tip of the thermometer in the center of the flesh, away from the bone. Set the turkey on a well-oiled rack in the smoker. Do *not* stuff the turkey; if you want stuffing, prepare it separately. Smoke at 90° F, with dense smoke, for 1 hour per pound of the turkey's weight. Gradually increase the temperature to 200° to 225° F, and smoke for 1 hour per pound longer, or until the meat thermometer reads 185° F.

During the last few hours of cooking, baste the turkey. Combine 1/3 cup honey and 1/4 cup of sherry in a small bowl; brush the honey-sherry mixture onto the turkey every 1/2 hour or so.

Chill the turkey before serving.

Fish Fillets

Smoke your own catch or the grocery store special for a savory, inexpensive delicacy. **Equipment:** large bowl or pan, measuring cup, mixing spoon, measuring spoons, plastic wrap, small weight, paper towels, wire rack, fork, smoker or covered barbecue with well-oiled racks, green hardwood or hardwood chips as required. **Ingredients:** fillets of firm, white-fleshed fish, water, salt, sugar, spices as desired (white or black pepper, onion or garlic powder, tarragon, dill, ginger or mace, grated lemon peel, hot pepper sauce, dried red pepper flakes, bay leaf, lemon slices). **Time:** about 1½ to 2½ hours, plus marinating time.

Both freshwater and saltwater fish smoke well, so use whatever fish you like—bass, catfish, chub, perch, salmon, trout, or whitefish; cod, flounder, halibut, herring, mackerel, mullet, pollack, pompano, or snapper. Marinate the fish for 2 to 3 hours for a mild salt-spice flavor; for more pronounced spiciness, marinate them from 6 to 10 hours.

In a large bowl or pan, combine 1 quart of water, ½ cup of salt, and ½ cup of sugar; stir to dissolve the salt and sugar completely. Add ¼ to ½ teaspoon of white or black pepper, onion or garlic powder, tarragon, dill, ginger or mace, grated lemon peel, hot pepper sauce, or dried red pepper flakes—use one or two spices as desired. Or add a bay leaf or lemon slices, as desired.

Use 4 to 5 fillets, about 1 pound each, of any firm, white-fleshed fish. Set the fish fillets into the pan of marinade and cover the pan with plastic wrap; weight the wrap to hold the fish under the surface of the marinade. Marinate, in the refrigerator, from 2 to 10 hours as desired.

Remove the fish from the marinade and rinse the fillets thoroughly with cold water; pat them dry with paper towels. Arrange the fillets on a wire rack and let them air-dry for ½ to 1 hour.

Preheat the smoker to 90° F. If you're using a covered barbecue, follow the manufacturer's instructions for preheating and adding hardwood chips.

Arrange the fish on well-oiled racks in the smoker, skin side down, with space between the pieces for smoke to circulate. Start smoking at 90° F. After 15 minutes gradually increase the temperature to between 135° and 140° F. Smoke until the fish is golden brown and flakes when prodded with a fork, about 1 to 2 hours. If you're using a covered barbecue, follow the manufacturer's cooking instructions; because barbecue temperatures are higher, smoking time will be less.

Serve the fish hot or chilled; if desired, wrap tightly and freeze.

Ribs or Pork Chops

Tender smoked ribs or pork chops are an affordable delicacy when you do the smoking yourself. Use a smoker or a covered barbecue grill to cook them. **Equipment:** pastry brush, smoker or covered barbecue with well-oiled racks, green hardwood or hardwood chips as required. **Ingredients:** pork chops trimmed of fat, or spareribs or back ribs; seasoned salt, barbecue sauce. **Time:** about 3 hours; varies with thickness of meat.

Preheat the smoker to between 80° and 85° F. If you're using a covered barbecue, follow the manufacturer's instructions for preheating and adding hardwood chips.

Rub the ribs or pork chops with seasoned salt. Arrange them on a well-oiled rack in the smoker or barbecue. Smoke at 80° to 85° F for 1½ to 2 hours. If you're using a covered barbecue, follow any cooking instructions provided by the manufacturer; barbecue temperatures are much higher than smoker temperatures, and cooking time may be shorter than with a special smoker.

Gradually increase the smoker temperature to 250° F and smoke for 30 to 45 minutes longer, or until meat is well done; it will fall from the bones when done. Baste the ribs and chops with barbecue sauce for the last 15 minutes of cooking, if desired; serve with additional sauce.

Beef, Lamb, or Pork Roast

Choose top-quality roasts for smoking—it's a wonderful change from oven-roasting. **Equipment:** meat thermometer, smoker or covered barbecue with well-oiled racks, green hardwood or hardwood chips as required. **Time:** depends on the size of the roast; a 3½-pound boneless rolled beef roast will take about 4 hours for medium-done. Use a meat thermometer to check the meat's internal temperature; pork must reach 170° F.

Preheat the smoker to 225° F. If you're using a covered barbecue, follow the manufacturer's instructions for preheating and adding hardwood chips.

Rub the roast with seasoned salt and insert a meat thermometer into it so that the tip of the thermometer is in the center of the thickest part of the meat, away from fat and bone. Set the roast on a well-oiled rack in the smoker or barbecue. Smoke to the desired done-ness; most smoked meats are best medium or well done. Pork must reach an internal temperature of 170° F. If you're using a covered barbecue, the cooking time will be shorter than in a special smoker because barbecue temperatures are higher. Follow the manufacturer's directions if you use a covered barbecue.

Oysters

Succulent smoked oysters are a real delicacy—buy them in season, and provide the gourmet touch with your smoker. **Equipment:** plastic bucket or pan, measuring cup, mixing spoon, sharp knife, colander or paper towels, shallow pan, smoker or covered barbecue with well-oiled racks, green hardwood or hardwood chips as required. **Ingredients:** water, rock salt, oysters, vegetable oil. **Time:** about ½ hour.

Preheat the smoker to 180° F. If you're using a covered barbecue, follow the manufacturer's instructions for preheating and adding hardwood chips.

In a plastic bucket or pan, mix 1 gallon of water and 2½ cups of rock salt, and stir to dissolve the salt. Clean, shuck, and wash as many oysters as desired and place them in the salt water; let stand 5 minutes and then drain the oysters thoroughly in a colander or on paper towels. Place the oysters in a shallow pan and pour just enough oil over them to coat them lightly.

Arrange the oysters one by one on a well-oiled rack in the smoker, with space between them for air circulation. Use a wire cake rack if the spaces in the smoker's rack are too wide.

Smoke at 180° F for 15 minutes; turn and smoke 15 minutes longer. If you're using a covered barbecue, follow any cooking instructions provided by the manufacturer. Eat smoked oysters hot or refrigerate them for a day or two, or freeze them in airtight containers for up to 2 months.

Smoke-Flavored Salt

For instant smoke flavor whenever you want it, smoke salt while you're smoking other foods. **Equipment:** shallow pan, smoker or covered barbecue, jar with cover. **Ingredients:** table salt. **Time:** 3 to 4 hours.

Spread the desired quantity of table salt in a shallow pan. Put the pan on a rack in the smoker while you're smoking other foods at 85° to 90° F. Smoke for 3 to 4 hours, or until the salt is golden. Store in a covered jar.

Freeze Your Own:

Unsweetened Fruit

Take advantage of summer sales and pick-your-own crops to put up a winter's worth of desserts. Some fruits can be frozen as is—freeze small fruits whole; cater to no-sugar diets by packing berries and other appropriate fruit without sweetening. **Equipment:** large strainer, paper towels, cookie sheets or shallow trays, freezer bags or rigid freezer containers, fork, sharp knife, spatula, freezer marker. **Ingredients:** whole fresh, ripe small fruits (blackberries, blueberries, cranberries, currants, gooseberries, grapes, figs, plums, prune plums, raspberries, or strawberries); or rhubarb; or avocados or ripe bananas and crystalline ascorbic acid. **Yield:** in most cases, equal volumes; in one 24-hour period, you can freeze 2 to 3 pounds of fruit per cubic foot of freezer capacity.

Tray freezing. Tray freezing is the simplest method for freezing small, whole fruits and delicate berries—fresh berries, grapes, figs, or plums. Wash the fruit in cold running water and drain it well; pat it gently dry with paper towels; if necessary, remove stems and hulls. If desired, halve and pit figs or plums. Spread the fruit in a single layer on cookie sheets or shallow trays; leave space around each piece of fruit. Set the sheets or trays into a freezer that maintains a temperature of 0° F, and freeze the fruit solid—about 1 to 3 hours.

When the fruit is frozen solid, remove it from the freezer. Working quickly, transfer the fruit to freezer bags or rigid freezer containers. Seal the containers carefully and label them by name and date; return the fruit to the freezer. To use the fruit, pour out the amount desired, and return the rest to the freezer.

Whole-pack freezing. If you don't have room to freeze delicate berries or small fruits on trays, pack the fruit into containers before freezing it. The same fruits are suitable for this treatment. Wash and drain the fruit, pat it dry, and stem, hull, or halve it as appropriate. Pack it into freezer bags or rigid freezer containers; leave ½ inch of space at the top of pint containers, 1 inch in quart containers. Seal the containers carefully, label, and freeze.

Sliced, crushed, or pureed fruit. If you prefer, slice or crush berries or small fruits for use as toppings or fillings. Wash and drain the fruit, slice it,

and then pack it into containers; sliced rhubarb freezes well with no sweetening. Or crush berries or other fruit with a fork as you pack it into rigid containers; leave ½ inch of space at the top of pint containers, 1 inch in quarts. Mashed banana and mashed or pureed avocado can also be frozen without sweetening; dissolve crystalline ascorbic acid as directed and mix in ½ teaspoon of acid per 1 to 2 cups of mashed banana, or ⅛ teaspoon per 4 cups of avocado puree. Seal the containers carefully, label, and freeze.

Sweetened Fruit

Berries and other small fruits can be frozen unsweetened, but most fruits should be packed with sugar or syrup. Buy fruits now in bulk—for quick, easy preserving, freeze extra fruit for later use. **Equipment:** large strainer, sharp knife, huller or pitter, measuring cup, large bowls, measuring spoons, large spoon, wide-mouthed rigid freezer containers, wax paper, damp cloth, freezer marker. **Ingredients:** fresh, ripe fruit; sugar, crystalline ascorbic acid, water, salt. **Yield:** as listed below; in one 24-hour period, you can freeze 2 to 3 pounds of fruit per cubic foot of freezer space.

Freezing in sugar. Sugar packing is the best freezing method for juicy fruits, fruits that don't darken, and fruits you plan to use for cooking. Wash the fruit in cold running water, and drain it well. Remove stems or hulls, pit, peel, or core, as appropriate; if desired, slice or halve. Some fruits must be sprinkled with a solution of crystalline ascorbic acid and water; some, such as apples, should be kept from darkening in a salt water solution. Follow the instructions below for each fruit.

To pack the fruit, measure the prepared fruit into a large bowl and sprinkle it with the required sugar. Mix gently until the sugar dissolves and the fruit gets juicy. Spoon the fruit and the juice into wide-mouthed rigid freezer containers; fill each pint container to within ½ inch of the top, each quart container to within 1 inch.

Crumple a small piece of wax paper and set it on top of the fruit to hold the fruit down in the juice. Wipe the rims of the containers with a damp cloth, and carefully seal each container. Label each container by fruit, pack, and date. Freeze in a freezer that maintains a temperature of 0° F.

Apples: 1½ pounds yields 1 pint; 1 bushel—48 pounds—yields 32 to 40 pints. Peel, core, and slice into a solution of 2 tablespoons salt to 1 gallon of cold water. Drain immediately. Use ½ to 1 cup sugar per quart of sliced apples.

Apricots: 4/5 pound yields 1 pint; 1 crate—22 pounds—yields 28 to 33 pints. If desired, peel; halve and pit. Sprinkle prepared apricots with a solution of ¼ teaspoon ascorbic acid and ¼ cup cold water per quart of fruit. Use ⅓ to ⅔ cup sugar per quart of halved apricots.

Berries (firm blackberries, boysenberries, gooseberries, huckleberries, loganberries, youngberries): 1½ pints yields 1 pint; 1 crate—24 quarts—yields 32 to 36 pints. Use ¾ cup sugar per quart of berries.

Cherries: 1½ pounds yields 1 pint; 1 bushel—56 pounds—yields 36 to 44 pints. Stem and chill thoroughly; pit. Use ¾ to 1 cup sugar per quart of pitted cherries.

Peaches, nectarines: 1 to 1½ pounds yields 1 pint; 1 lug—20 pounds—yields 13 to 20 pints. Peel, halve, and pit peaches; halve and pit nectarines; if desired, slice. Sprinkle prepared fruit with a solution of ¼ teaspoon ascorbic acid and ¼ cup cold water per quart of fruit. Use ½ to ⅔ cup sugar per quart of prepared fruit.

Raspberries: 1 pint yields 1 pint; 1 crate—24 pounds—yields 24 pints. Use ¾ cup sugar per quart of berries.

Strawberries: ⅔ quart yields 1 pint; 1 crate—24 quarts—yields 38 pints. Hull; if desired, slice. Use ¾ cup sugar per quart of sliced berries.

Freezing in syrup. Syrup packing is the best freezing method for fruits that discolor and for fruits you plan to serve as desserts or salads. Before preparing the fruit, mix sugar and water, as specified below for each fruit; stir to dissolve the sugar and chill the syrup well. You'll need ½ to ⅔ cup of syrup per pint of prepared fruit.

Wash the fruit and drain it well. Remove stems or hulls, pit, peel, or core, as appropriate; if desired, slice or halve. Some fruits must be frozen with syrup mixed with crystalline ascorbic acid. Follow the instructions below for each.

To pack the fruit, mix and chill the required syrup; add ascorbic acid as required and stir to dissolve. Pour ½ cup of syrup into each freezer container. Pack fruit directly into containers as you prepare it; fill each pint container to within ½ inch of the top, each quart container to within 1 inch. Add more syrup to each container to just cover the fruit.

Crumple a small piece of wax paper and set it on top of the fruit to hold the fruit down in the syrup. Wipe the rims of the containers with a damp cloth, and carefully seal each container. Label each container by fruit, pack, and date. Freeze in a freezer that maintains a temperature of 0° F.

Apples: 1½ pounds yields 1 pint; 1 bushel—48 pounds—yields 32 to 40 pints. Use a syrup of 3 cups sugar and 4 cups water to pack 8 to 11 pints; add ½ teaspoon ascorbic acid per quart of syrup. Peel, core, and slice.

Apricots: 4/5 pound yields 1 pint; 1 crate—22 pounds—yields 28 to 33 pints. Use a syrup of 3 cups sugar and 4 cups water to pack 8 to 11 pints; add ¾ teaspoon ascorbic acid per quart of syrup. If desired, peel; halve and pit

Berries (blackberries, boysenberries, gooseberries, huckleberries, loganberries, youngberries): 1½ pints yields 1 pint; 1 crate—24 quarts—yields 32 to 36 pints. Use a syrup of 3 to 4¾ cups sugar and 4 cups water to pack 8 to 11 pints.

Cherries: 1½ pounds yields 1 pint; 1 bushel—56 pounds—yields 36 to 44

pints. Use a syrup of 7 to 8¾ cups sugar and 4 cups water to pack 12 to 16 pints of sour cherries; use a syrup of 3 cups sugar and 4 cups water to pack 8 to 11 pints of sweet cherries. For sour cherries, add ½ teaspoon ascorbic acid per quart of syrup. Stem and chill thoroughly; pit.

Grapefruit, oranges: 1 pint segments yields 1 pint. Use a syrup of 3 cups sugar and 4 cups water to pack 8 to 11 pints; add ½ teaspoon ascorbic acid per quart of syrup. Peel, segment, and remove membrane and seeds; if desired, cut up.

Melon (cantaloupe, crenshaw, honeydew, Persian, watermelon): 1 to 1½ pounds yields 1 pint; 1 dozen cantaloupes—28 pounds—yields 22 pints. Use a syrup of 2 cups sugar and 4 cups water to pack 6 to 10 pints. Halve, seed, and peel; cut into chunks, balls, or slices.

Peaches, nectarines: 1 to 1½ pounds yields 1 pint; 1 lug—20 pounds—yields 13 to 20 pints. Use a syrup of 3 cups sugar and 4 cups water to pack 8 to 11 pints; add ¾ teaspoon ascorbic acid per quart of syrup. Peel, halve, and pit peaches; halve and pit nectarines; if desired, slice.

Plums, prune plums: 1 to 1½ pounds yields 1 pint; 1 crate—20 pounds—yields 13 to 20 pints. Use a syrup of 3 cups sugar and 4 cups water to pack 8 to 11 pints; add ½ teaspoon ascorbic acid per quart of syrup. Halve and pit; if desired, cut into chunks.

Raspberries: 1 pint yields 1 pint; 1 crate—24 pounds—yields 24 pints. Use a syrup of 3 cups sugar and 4 cups water to pack 8 to 11 pints.

Strawberries: ⅔ quart yields 1 pint; 1 crate—24 quarts—yields 38 pints. Use a syrup of 4¾ cups sugar and 4 cups water to pack 10 to 14 pints. Hull; if desired, slice.

Fresh Herbs

An herb garden is a good-tasting moneysaver all summer. It's easy to extend both taste and savings—freeze herbs in packets to use in cooking. **Equipment:** kitchen shears, large strainer or salad basket, paper towels; small plastic bags or plastic wrap, freezer tape, stiff cardboard, staples, freezer marker. **Ingredients:** fresh herbs. **Yield:** equal volumes.

Pick or cut fresh, perfect sprays of any herb you have lots of—basil, chervil, chives, dill, fennel, marjoram, mint, oregano, parsley, rosemary, sage, tarragon, or thyme. Wash well in a large strainer or a salad basket under cold running water; drain thoroughly and pat gently dry with paper towels.

Cut or separate the sprays into convenient recipe-size amounts—they won't make good garnishes, so plan to use them only for cooking. Pack recipe-size amounts of sprays into small plastic bags, or make small packets from plastic wrap. Seal the bags or packets carefully with freezer tape.

For the easiest storage, staple bags or packets of herbs to a piece of stiff cardboard; arrange the packets in overlapping rows and staple along one edge. Label by herb and date; freeze in a freezer that maintains a temperature of 0° F. To use, snip frozen herbs directly into cooking food.

Vegetables

For economical eating all year, grow your own vegetables; or buy them by the bushel at pick-your-own farms or already-picked farmstands. Freeze extra vegetables for later use. **Equipment:** large pot with cover and perforated insert or wire basket, large strainer, vegetable brush, sharp knife, cutting board, vegetable peeler, plastic dishpan, sauté pan, large spoon, measuring cup, measuring spoons; wide-mouthed rigid freezer containers, freezer bags, or boilable pouches and bag sealer; cookie sheets or shallow trays, damp cloth, freezer marker. **Ingredients:** fresh, ripe vegetables; salt, water, ice. **Yield:** as listed below; in one

24-hour period, you can freeze 2 to 3 pounds of vegetables per cubic foot of freezer capacity.

Use young, fresh vegetables; if possible, chill them until you're ready to work. Slightly undermature vegetables are better than vegetables that are past their prime.

Vegetables must be heated before they're packed to stop enzyme action; if you don't preheat them, they'll decay. Use a large covered pot with a perforated insert or wire basket to blanch the vegetables. To keep them from overcooking, cool them immediately in a plastic dishpan filled with ice water—you'll need about 1 pound of ice per pound of prepared vegetables. No packing liquid is needed; vegetables are packed dry.

To prepare the vegetables for packing, wash them thoroughly under cold running water; use a vegetable brush to remove dirt from thick-skinned vegetables. Don't soak vegetables. Sort by size and handle like sizes together to ensure even heating and cooling. Peel, trim, and cut or slice, or shell, as appropriate; follow the instructions below for each vegetable.

Take the insert or basket out of the blancher and fill it with water; use at least 1 gallon of water per pound—4 cups—of vegetables blanched at once. Cover the pot and bring the water to a boil over high heat. Fill a clean plastic dishpan with cold water and ice—you'll need about 1 pound of ice per pound of prepared vegetables. Set out your freezer containers.

When the water in the blancher comes to a full rolling boil, put the prepared vegetables into the blancher insert or wire basket and lower the basket into the boiling water; keep the heat high. Cover the pot and begin timing immediately; heat for the time specified for each vegetable, as detailed below. If you live more than 5,000 feet above sea level, add 1 minute to the time specified.

When the full blanching time has elapsed, immediately uncover the pot. Lift the basket out of the strainer and let it drain for a few seconds; then quickly immerse the hot basket in the dishpan of ice water to stop the cooking. Keep the vegetables in the ice water for about the same time as blanching time, or until they're well chilled. Then lift the basket out of the ice water and drain the vegetables thoroughly.

Quickly pack the blanched, drained vegetables into freezer containers; use wide-mouthed rigid containers, freezer bags, or boilable pouches. Pack vegetables gently but firmly into the containers; leave ½ inch of space for expansion at the top of each container. Wipe the rims of rigid containers with a damp cloth, and carefully seal each container. Press air out of freezer bags and seal tightly, leaving ½ inch of space for expansion; seal boilable pouches as directed with a bag sealer. Label each container by vegetable and date; freeze the packed vegetables in a freezer that maintains a temperature of 0° F. Cook in a little boiling water, as indicated below.

If you prefer, spread delicate vegetables in a single layer on cookie sheets or shallow trays; leave space around each piece of vegetable. Set the sheets or trays into a freezer that maintains a temperature of 0° F, and freeze the vegetables solid — about 1 to 3 hours. When the vegetables are frozen solid, remove them from the freezer. Working quickly, transfer the vegetables to freezer containers and seal the containers. Label them by name and date and return the vegetables to the freezer. Cook in a little boiling water, as indicated below.

Asparagus: 1 to 1½ pounds yields 1 pint; 1 crate—24 pounds—yields 15 to 22 pints. Sort by size; remove scales and cut off tough ends; leave stalks whole or cut into 1- or 2-inch pieces. Blanch small stalks 1 to 2 minutes, medium stalks 2 to 3 minutes, large stalks 3 to 4 minutes. Cook 5 to 10 minutes.

Green beans, wax beans: ⅔ to 1 pound yields 1 pint; 1 bushel—30 pounds—yields 30 to 45 pints. Snap off ends and sort by size; leave whole, break into pieces, or slice. Blanch 2 to 3

517

minutes. Cook 12 to 18 minutes for whole beans, 5 to 10 minutes for sliced.

Beets: 1¼ to 1½ pounds (without tops) yields 1 pint; 1 bushel—52 pounds—yields 35 to 42 pints. Use beets no larger than 3 inches in diameter; cut off tops, leaving ½ inch of stem. Cook in boiling water 25 to 30 minutes; cool; peel and slice or cube as desired. Cook just until beets are heated through.

Broccoli: 1 pound yields 1 pint; 1 crate—25 pounds—yields 24 pints. If broccoli has insects in it, soak for ½ hour in solution of ¼ cup salt and 1 gallon water. Rinse in fresh water. Cut off tough ends and leaves; cut stalks to fit containers, splitting stalks so heads are 1 to 1½ inches across. Blanch 3 minutes. Cook 5 to 8 minutes.

Brussels sprouts: 1 pound yields 1 pint; 4 quarts yields 6 pints. Sort by size. Blanch small sprouts 3 minutes, medium sprouts 4 minutes. Cook 4 to 9 minutes.

Carrots: 1¼ to 1½ pounds (without tops) yields 1 pint; 1 bushel—50 pounds—yields 32 to 40 pints. Cut off tops; scrub or peel, as desired. Leave small carrots whole; slice or chunk larger carrots. Blanch small, whole carrots 5 minutes; blanch sliced or chunked carrots 2 minutes. Cook 5 to 10 minutes.

Cauliflower: 1⅓ pounds yields 1 pint; 2 medium heads yield 3 pints. If heads have insects in them, soak for ½ hour in solution of ¼ cup salt and 1 gallon water. Rinse in fresh water. Break and cut into 1-inch flowerets. Blanch 3 to 4 minutes in water mixed with ¼ cup salt per gallon of water. Cook 5 to 8 minutes.

Corn: 2 to 2½ pounds on the cob yields 1 pint; 1 bushel—35 pounds—yields 14 to 17 pints. Use fresh sweet corn; if corn is older, prepare it cream-style. Husk ears, remove cornsilk, and trim ends. For whole-kernel corn, blanch ears 4 minutes and cool; cut kernels from cobs at two-thirds the depth of the kernel; cook 3 to 5 minutes. For creamed corn, blanch ears 4 minutes and cool; cut kernels from cobs at the center of the kernel and scrape

cobs; cook 3 to 5 minutes. For corn on the cob, sort ears by size. Blanch small ears 5 minutes, medium ears 8 minutes, large ears 10 minutes. Cook 3 to 4 minutes.

Greens (beet greens, chard, collards, kale, spinach, turnip greens): 1 to 1½ pounds yields 1 pint; one 12-pound bushel yields 8 to 12 pints; one 18-pound bushel yields 12 to 18 pints. Remove tough stems and damaged leaves; leave whole or tear into pieces as desired. Blanch 2 minutes; use 2 gallons of boiling water per pound of greens. Cook 8 to 10 minutes.

Mushrooms: 1 to 2 pounds yields 1 pint. Sort by size; use only fresh mushrooms. Slice or quarter large mushrooms, as desired. Do not blanch—sauté in butter until almost done; cool immediately. Cook just until heated through.

Peas: 2 to 2½ pounds yields 1 pint; 1 bushel—30 pounds—yields 12 to 15 pints. Shell peas; snip off ends of edible-pod peas and remove strings. Blanch 1½ to 2 minutes. Cook 5 to 10 minutes.

Peppers (sweet): ⅔ pound (3 peppers) yields 1 pint. Halve, cut out stems, and remove seeds. Slice, chop, or cut into rings, as desired. For use in salads, do not blanch; pack raw. For use in cooking, blanch 2 to 3 minutes. Cook 5 minutes.

Summer squash: 1 to 1¼ pounds yields 1 pint; 1 bushel—40 pounds—yields 32 to 40 pints. Cut off ends but do not peel. Slice ½ inch thick; halve or quarter large slices for uniform size. Blanch 3 minutes. Cook 10 minutes.

Winter squash: 3 pounds yields 2 pints. Cut into pieces and scoop out seeds. Steam or cook in boiling water until soft, about 15 to 20 minutes; scrape pulp from rind and mash or puree. Cook 10 to 12 minutes.

Tomatoes: 1 bushel—55 pounds—yields 30 to 40 pints. For whole tomatoes, cut out stems and wrap whole in plastic wrap or small bags; freeze raw. Hold under hot water for a few seconds to loosen skin; peel and add to cooked dishes. For stewed tomatoes, blanch for 30 seconds to 1 minute to loosen skins; peel and core; cut into chunks and simmer 10 to 20 minutes or until tender. Cook just until heated through.

How to Can and Preserve Safely

Canning turns a bumper crop or bargain into year-long good eating. To assure safe and successful results, follow these important basics.

• Work in a clean kitchen with clean equipment and clean hands. If you use a wood cutting board, sterilize it with liquid bleach, wash and rinse it well, and let it dry before using.

• Organize all equipment and ingredients before starting a canning session; allow plenty of time.

• Wash fruits and vegetables thoroughly under running water, and drain well. Do not soak fruits or vegetables.

• Process fruits in a boiling water bath canner for the correct amount of time for each fruit, as detailed in individual recipes. Process vegetables in a pressure canner for the correct amount of time given for each vegetable. Carefully read the instructions that come with your canner; you risk food poisoning with incorrect processing. Don't use one type of canner if the other type is specified.

• Use only standard canning jars and lids for canned fruits and vegetables; use canning jars or pint or half-pint glasses for jelly and jam. Jars and glasses must be free of nicks and cracks; run your finger around the top of each jar or glass to make sure it's flawless. Use only new, undamaged lids and screw rings.

• Protect your hands when working with hot foods, jars, and canners. Use hot pads, long-handled tongs, or a jar lifter.

• Prepare glasses or jars and lids carefully. Wash them in hot, soapy water and rinse thoroughly. To sterilize jelly glasses, set them in a large kettle

filled with cold water; heat kettle and jars to a boil over low heat, and simmer until you're ready to use them. Keep canning jars and lids hot in a large kettle filled with hot water. Drain glasses or jars immediately before filling, and set them on a folded towel or a wire rack.

• Avoid any sudden changes in temperature when working with hot jars. Putting a hot jar on a cold counter or in a cold draft could break it. Set out folded towels or wire racks to put the hot jars on.

• Seal canning jars immediately after filling. For each jar, dip a lid into hot water and set it firmly into place on the jar; tighten the screw band over it. Invert sealed jelly or jam jars for ½ hour; then turn them right side up again. Seal open jelly glasses immediately with a ⅛-inch-thick layer of melted paraffin; melt paraffin carefully in a double boiler over low heat. Use only new paraffin.

• Let canned food cool undisturbed for at least 12 hours before storing it.

• Once the jars are completely cool, check to make sure they've sealed completely. On jars with lids, the lid should be slightly depressed. Press on the lid; if it springs back up, it hasn't sealed. Repack unsealed food in clean, hot jars and reprocess the jars. If a paraffin seal is imperfect, refrigerate the jelly or jam and use it immediately.

• Before using home-canned foods, check them carefully for signs of spoilage—bulging or unsealed lids, spurting liquid, slime, mold or off odor. Dispose of spoiled food where no humans or animals can get at it.

Preserve Your Own:

Apple Jelly

After apple picking, spice up your kitchen with a batch of apple jelly. Its fresh smell and taste make it a traditional favorite. **Equipment:** paring knife, large pot with cover, measuring cup, long-handled spoon, masher, jelly bag or cheesecloth, strainer or colander, bowls, ten 8-ounce glasses or canning jars with lids, large kettle, towels or wire racks, double boiler, paraffin, ladle, wide-mouthed funnel. **Ingredients:** ripe, tart, juicy apples or crabapples; powdered pectin, sugar, cinnamon sticks or small geranium leaves. **Yield:** 10 cups.

Use 5 pounds of ripe, tart, juicy apples. Wash the apples and remove the stem and blossom ends, but don't pare or core them. Cut the apples into small chunks and place the chunks in a large pot; add 5 cups of water, cover, and heat to boiling. Reduce heat and simmer for 10 minutes; then crush the soft apple chunks with a masher and simmer for 5 minutes more.

To extract the juice, use a jelly bag or several layers of cheesecloth lining a strainer or colander; set the strainer over a large bowl to catch the juice. Pour the soft apples into the jelly bag. For crystal-clear jelly, let the apples drain for several hours or overnight, until you have 7 cups of juice. For quicker results and less chance of contamination, pour off what juice you can and then, with a spoonful or two of pulp at a time, press the pulp into the strainer to force the juice out. You'll need 7 cups of juice.

When you're ready to make the jelly, wash and rinse ten 8-ounce glasses or canning jars and lids, and heat them in a large kettle of water to sterilize them. Set out folded towels or wire racks to put the hot glasses on. If you're using jelly glasses, carefully melt paraffin in a double boiler over low heat. Drain and set out the prepared glasses or jars.

Measure 9 cups (4 pounds) of sugar into a bowl, and set it aside. Measure 7 cups of apple juice into a large pot and add 1 box of powdered pectin; stir to dissolve. Bring the juice to a full rolling boil over high heat, stirring occasionally; add the measured sugar and stir again. Return to a full rolling boil, stirring constantly, until you can't stir the boiling down, and then boil hard for 1 full minute. Remove the pot from the heat and skim off the foam.

Quickly pour the jelly into the prepared glasses or jars, using a ladle and a wide-mouthed funnel. If you're using glasses, fill each glass to within ½ inch of the top; then carefully pour a ⅛-inch layer of melted paraffin into the glass to seal it. If you're using canning jars, fill each jar to within ⅛ inch of the top; set the lid on, tighten the screw band over it, and invert the jar onto a folded towel or wire rack.

Let the glasses or jars cool undisturbed for at least 12 hours. If you're using canning jars, turn the jars right side up after the jelly has cooled for ½ hour. Store the jelly in a cool, dark, dry place.

Crabapple jelly. Use 5 pounds of ripe, juicy crabapples; extract the juice and make the jelly as above.

Spiced apple jelly. For a touch of cinnamon flavor, put a cinnamon stick into each prepared jar before filling the jars with jelly. Or, for a subtler tang, put a clean, perfect geranium leaf into each filled jar; wash the leaves and pat them dry before adding them.

Frozen Grape Juice Jelly

Every kid loves grape jelly, and it usually goes fast. Use frozen concentrated grape juice for a real sandwich treat. **Equipment:** four 8-ounce glasses or canning jars with lids, large kettle, towels or wire racks, double boiler, paraffin, measuring cup, bowl, large pot, long-handled spoon, ladle, wide-mouthed funnel. **Ingredients:** frozen concentrated grape juice, sugar, powdered pectin, water. **Yield:** 4 cups.

Wash and rinse four 8-ounce glasses or canning jars with lids, and heat them in a large kettle of water to sterilize them. Set out folded towels or wire racks to put the hot glasses on. If you're using jelly glasses, carefully melt paraffin in a double boiler over low heat. Drain and set out the glasses or jars.

Measure 3¾ cups of sugar into a bowl and set it aside. Pour one 6-ounce can of thawed frozen concentrated grape juice into a large pot and add 1 box of powdered pectin; stir to mix well. Add 2 cups of water and stir to mix. Bring the juice almost to a boil over high heat and add the measured sugar. Stirring constantly, bring to a full rolling boil that you can't stir down, and boil hard for 1 full minute. Remove the pot from the heat and skim off the foam with a spoon.

Quickly pour the jelly into the prepared glasses or jars, using a ladle and a wide-mouthed funnel. If you're using glasses, fill each glass to within ½ inch of the top; carefully pour a ⅛-inch layer of paraffin into the glass to seal it. If you're using canning jars, fill each jar to within ⅛ inch of the top; set the lid on, tighten the screw band over it, and invert the jar onto a folded towel or wire rack.

Let the glasses or jars cool undisturbed for at least 12 hours. If you're using canning jars, turn the jars right side up after the jelly has cooled for ½ hour. Store the jelly in a cool, dark, dry place.

Frozen orange juice jelly. Use one 12-ounce can of thawed frozen concentrated orange juice, 2½ cups of water, 4½ cups of sugar, and 1 box of powdered pectin; make the jelly as above. Yields 6 cups of jelly.

Wine Jelly

Use sherry, burgundy, sauterne, or port to make this elegant jelly; serve it with meat, poultry, or fish. **Equipment:** five 8-ounce glasses or canning jars with lids, large kettle, towels or wire racks, double boiler, paraffin, measuring cup, bowl, large pot, long-handled spoon, ladle, wide-mouthed funnel. **Ingredients:** sugar, powdered pectin, water; sherry, burgundy, sauterne, or port. **Yield:** 4½ cups.

Wash and rinse five 8-ounce glasses or canning jars with lids, and heat them in a large kettle of water to sterilize them. Set out folded towels or wire racks to put the hot glasses on. If you're using jelly glasses, carefully melt paraffin in a double boiler over low heat. Drain and set out the glasses or jars.

Measure 4½ cups of sugar into a bowl and set it aside. In a large pot, mix 1 box of powdered pectin and ¾ cup of water; stir to dissolve. Bring to a full rolling boil over high heat, until you can't stir the boiling down, and boil hard for 1 full minute, stirring constantly. Quickly add 3 cups of sherry, burgundy, sauterne, or port, and the measured sugar, and stir to dissolve over medium heat for about 5 minutes. Remove the pot from the heat and skim off the foam with a spoon.

Quickly pour the jelly into the prepared glasses or jars, using a ladle and a wide-mouthed funnel. If you're using glasses, fill each glass to within ½ inch of the top; carefully pour a ⅛-inch layer of melted paraffin into the glass to seal it. If you're using canning jars, fill each jar to within ⅛ inch of the top; set the lid on, tighten the screw band over it, and invert the jar onto a folded towel or wire rack.

Let the glasses or jars cool undisturbed for at least 12 hours. If you're using canning jars, turn the jars right side up after the jelly has cooled for ½ hour. Store the jelly in a cool, dark, dry place.

Real Mint Jelly

This fresh-tasting jelly, delicious with lamb, bears little resemblance to the grocery-store variety. Add a sprig of mint to each jar to dress it up. **Equipment:** six 8-ounce glasses or canning jars with lids, large kettle, towels or wire racks, double boiler, paraffin, kitchen shears, measuring cup, large pot with cover, masher, strainer, bowl, measuring spoons, long-handled spoon, ladle, wide-mouthed funnel. **Ingredients:** fresh mint leaves, canned or frozen apple juice, lemon juice; green food coloring, if desired; liquid pectin. **Yield:** 5 to 6 cups.

Wash and rinse six 8-ounce glasses or canning jars with lids, and heat them in a large kettle of water to sterilize them. Set out folded towels or wire racks to put the hot glasses on. If you're using jelly glasses, carefully melt paraffin in a double boiler over low heat. Drain and set out the glasses or jars.

Wash fresh mint under cold running water and remove stems with a kitchen shears. Shake the leaves to drain them. Measure 2 cups of mint leaves, packed tight, into a large pot and crush them in the pot with a masher. Add 2½ cups of canned or frozen prepared apple juice. Heat the mint-juice mixture to boiling over medium heat; then remove it from the heat, cover, and let steep for 10 minutes.

After 10 minutes, pour the juice through a strainer into a bowl; discard the mint leaves. Add 2 tablespoons of lemon juice to the mint-apple juice in the bowl; if desired, add a drop or two of green food coloring. Stir to blend and return the juice to the pan.

Add 3 cups of sugar to the juice and heat, stirring constantly, to a full rolling boil. Add ½ bottle of liquid pectin and stir well. Return to a full rolling boil, stirring constantly, until you can't stir the boiling down, and then boil hard for 1 full minute. Remove the pot from the heat and skim off the foam with a spoon.

Quickly pour the jelly into the prepared glasses or jars, using a ladle and a wide-mouthed funnel. For a special touch, add a perfect sprig of mint to each filled glass; wash the sprigs and pat them dry before using them. If you're using glasses, fill each glass to within ½ inch of the top; carefully pour a ⅛-inch layer of melted paraffin into the glass to seal it. If you're using canning jars, fill each jar to within ⅛ inch of the top; set the lid on, tighten the screw band over it, and invert the jar onto a folded towel or wire rack.

Let the glasses or jars cool undisturbed for at least 12 hours. If you're using canning jars, turn the jars right side up after the jelly has cooled for ½ hour. Store the jelly in a cool, dark, dry place.

Peach Jam

Rich, sunny peach jam improves any breakfast. Make it all-peach or add pears, in whatever proportion you like. **Equipment:** seven 8-ounce glasses or canning jars with lids, large kettle, towels or wire racks, double boiler, paraffin, measuring cup, bowl, paring knife, sharp knife or food grinder, cutting board, measuring spoons, large pot, long-handled spoon, ladle. **Ingredients:** fresh, ripe peaches; if desired, ripe pears; lemon juice, sugar, water; if desired, nutmeg and cinnamon or ginger; powdered pectin. **Yield:** 7 cups.

Wash and rinse seven 8-ounce glasses or canning jars with lids, and heat them in a large kettle of water to sterilize them. Set out folded towels or wire racks to put the hot glasses on. If you're using glasses, carefully melt paraffin in a double boiler over low heat.

Use 3 pounds of fresh, ripe peaches; or if desired, use one-third or one-half fresh, ripe pears. To prepare the fruit, wash it and peel it carefully—to make peaches easy to peel, dip them into boiling water for about 30 seconds; then dip into cold water, drain, and slip off the skin. Remove pits from peaches and cores from pears, and chop the fruit fine or grind it in a food grinder.

Drain and set out the glasses or jars. Measure 5½ cups of sugar into a bowl, and set it aside. Measure the prepared fruit into a large pot, to make 4 cups; if necessary, add water to make 4 cups. Add 2 tablespoons of lemon juice and stir to mix well. If you want a spicy jam, add ½ teaspoon of nutmeg and ½ teaspoon of cinnamon or ginger. Add 1 box of powdered pectin and stir to mix well.

Stirring constantly, bring the fruit to a full rolling boil over high heat and add the measured sugar. Return to a full rolling boil, stirring constantly, until you can't stir the boiling down, and then boil hard for 1 full minute. Remove the pot from the heat and skim off the foam with a spoon. Let the jam cool for 5 minutes; skim off the foam and stir occasionally.

Quickly ladle the jam into the prepared glasses or jars. If you're using glasses, fill each glass to within ½ inch of the top; carefully pour a ⅛-inch layer of paraffin into the glass to seal it. If you're using canning jars, fill each jar to within ⅛ inch of the top; set the lid on, tighten the screw band over it, and invert the jar onto a folded towel or wire rack.

Let the glasses or jars cool undisturbed for at least 12 hours. If you're using canning jars, turn the jars right side up after the jam has cooled for ½ hour. Store the jam in a cool, dark, dry place.

Any Berry Jam

Use whatever fruit the summer offers to make this rich old-time jam—blackberries, boysenberries, dewberries, loganberries, raspberries, or youngberries. Make blueberry jam with its own proportions. **Equipment:** nine 8-ounce glasses or canning jars with lids, large kettle, towels or wire racks, double boiler, paraffin, bowls, long-handled spoon, sieve, measuring cup, large pot, ladle. **Ingredients:** fresh, ripe berries (blackberries, boysenberries, dewberries, loganberries, raspberries, or youngberries, or blueberries); water, sugar, powdered pectin, lemon juice. **Yield:** 8 to 9 cups.

Wash and rinse nine 8-ounce glasses or canning jars with lids, and heat them in a large kettle of water to sterilize them. Set out folded towels or wire racks to put the hot glasses on. If you're using glasses, carefully melt paraffin in a double boiler over low heat. Drain and set out the glasses or jars.

Rinse and drain 2 quarts of fresh, ripe berries. In a large bowl, thoroughly crush the berries with the back of a spoon, one layer at a time. If the berries have large seeds, press half the pulp through a sieve, if desired, and discard the sieved seeds. Measure 7 cups (3 pounds) of sugar into another bowl, and set it aside.

Measure the crushed berries into a large pot, to make 5 cups; if necessary, add water to make 5 cups. Add 1 box of powdered pectin and stir to mix well.

Stirring constantly, bring to a full rolling boil over high heat and add the measured sugar. Return to a full rolling boil, stirring constantly, until you can't stir the boiling down, and then boil hard for 1 full minute. Remove the pot from the heat and skim off the foam with a spoon. Let the jam cool for 5 minutes; skim off the foam and stir occasionally.

Quickly ladle the jam into the prepared glasses or jars. If you're using glasses, fill each glass to within ½ inch of the top; carefully pour a ⅛-inch layer of paraffin into the glass to seal it. If you're using canning jars, fill each jar to within ⅛ inch of the top; set the lid on, tighten the screw band over it, and invert the jar onto a folded towel or wire rack.

Let the glasses or jars cool undisturbed for at least 12 hours. If you're using canning jars, turn the jars right side up after the jam has cooled for ½ hour. Store the jam in a cool, dark, dry place.

Blueberry jam. Use 1½ quarts of ripe blueberries, 4 cups of sugar, and 1 box of powdered pectin; add 2 tablespoons of lemon juice to the crushed berries after measuring.

Favorite Combination Jams

Everybody loves strawberry—but for a real treat, combine it with rhubarb or pineapple. Either makes a very special jam. **Equipment:** seven 8-ounce glasses or canning jars with lids, large kettle, towels or wire racks, double boiler, paraffin, bowls, long-handled spoon, measuring cup, sharp knife, cutting board, food grinder, large pot, ladle. **Ingredients:** ripe strawberries; fresh, red-stalked rhubarb or fully ripe pineapple; sugar, water, powdered pectin. **Yield:** 6 to 7 cups.

Wash and rinse seven 8-ounce glasses or canning jars with lids, and heat them in a large kettle of water to sterilize them. Set out folded towels or wire racks to put the hot glasses on. If you're using glasses, carefully melt paraffin in a double boiler over low heat.

Strawberry-rhubarb jam. Wash, drain, and hull 1 quart of ripe strawberries. In a large bowl, thoroughly crush the berries with the back of a spoon, one layer at a time. Set the crushed berries aside. Wash 1 pound of fresh, red-stalked rhubarb and shake it dry. Slice the stalks thin or chop them fine; don't peel them. Combine the crushed berries and the rhubarb and stir to mix thoroughly.

Drain and set out the glasses or jars. Measure 5½ cups of sugar into a bowl, and set it aside. Measure the prepared fruit into a large pot, to measure 4 cups; if necessary, add water to make 4 cups. Add 1 box of powdered pectin and stir to mix thoroughly.

Stirring constantly, bring the fruit to a full rolling boil over high heat and add the measured sugar. Return to a full rolling boil, stirring constantly, until you can't stir the boiling down, and then boil hard for 1 full minute. Remove the pot from the heat and skim off the foam with a spoon. Let the jam cool for 5 minutes; skim off the foam and stir occasionally.

Quickly ladle the jam into the prepared glasses or jars. If you're using glasses, fill each glass to within ½ inch of the top; carefully pour a ⅛-inch layer of paraffin into the glass to seal it. If you're using canning jars, fill each jar to within ⅛ inch of the top; set the lid on, tighten the screw band over it, and invert the jar onto a folded towel or wire rack.

Let the glasses or jars cool undisturbed for at least 12 hours. If you're using canning jars, turn the jars right side up after the jam has cooled for ½ hour. Store the jam in a cool, dark, dry place.

Strawberry-pineapple jam. Wash, drain, and hull 1 quart of ripe strawberries. In a large bowl, thoroughly crush the berries with the back of a spoon, one layer at a time. Set the crushed berries aside. Pare a fully ripe, medium-size pineapple; it should be golden and fragrant. Slice the pineapple, cut out the eyes, and chop it fine or grind it in a food grinder. Combine the crushed berries and the pineapple and stir to mix thoroughly.

Drain and set out the glasses or jars. Measure 4½ cups of sugar into a bowl, and set it aside. Measure the prepared fruit into a large pot, to measure 3½ cups; if necessary, add water to make 3½ cups. Add 1 box of powdered pectin and stir to mix thoroughly.

Stirring constantly, bring the fruit to a full rolling boil over high heat and add the measured sugar. Return to a full rolling boil, stirring constantly, until you can't stir the boiling down, and then boil hard for 1 full minute. Remove the pot from the heat and skim off the foam with a spoon. Let the jam cool for 5 minutes; skim off the foam and stir occasionally.

Quickly ladle the jam into the prepared glasses or jars. Seal, cool, and store as above.

Frozen Strawberry Jam

Even in winter, homemade strawberry jam is easy to come by. Instead of fresh berries, use the quick-thawing frozen kind. **Equipment:** five 8-ounce glasses or canning jars with lids, large kettle, towels or wire racks, double boiler, paraffin, bowls, long-handled spoon, measuring cup, large pot, measuring spoons, ladle. **Ingredients:** quick-thawing frozen sweetened strawberries, sugar, water, powdered pectin. **Yield:** 4 to 5 cups.

In a large bowl, thaw three 10-ounce packages of quick-thawing frozen sweetened strawberries, as directed on the package. While the berries thaw, wash and rinse five 8-ounce glasses or canning jars with lids, and heat them in a large kettle of water to sterilize them. Set out folded towels or wire racks to put the hot glasses on. If you're using glasses, carefully melt paraffin in a double boiler over low heat. Drain and set out the glasses or jars.

When the fruit is completely thawed, thoroughly crush the berries with the back of a spoon, one layer at a time. Measure 3 cups of sugar into a bowl, and set it aside.

Measure the crushed strawberries into a large pot, to make 3 cups; if necessary, add water to make 3 cups. Add 2 tablespoons more water and stir. Add ½ box—about 2½ table-spoons—of powdered pectin, and stir to mix well.

Stirring constantly, bring the fruit to a full rolling boil over high heat and add the measured sugar. Return to a full rolling boil, stirring constantly, until you can't stir the boiling down, and then boil hard for 1 full minute. Remove the pot from the heat and skim off the foam with a spoon. Let the jam cool for 5 minutes; skim off the foam and stir occasionally.

Quickly ladle the jam into the prepared glasses or jars. If you're using glasses, fill each glass to within ½ inch of the top; carefully pour a ⅛-inch layer of paraffin into the glass to seal it. If you're using canning jars, fill each jar to within ⅛ inch of the top; set the lid on, tighten the screw band over it, and invert the jar onto a folded towel or wire rack.

Let the glasses or jars cool undisturbed for at least 12 hours. If you're using canning jars, turn the jars right side up after the jam has cooled for ½ hour. Store the jam in a cool, dark, dry place.

Sweet Cherry Freezer Jam

Eliminate the hot-stove work—for a fast, easy treat, turn the summer's sweet cherries into rich, no-cook jam. **Equipment:** six 8-ounce glass or plastic containers with airtight covers, large kettle or teakettle, cherry pitter, food grinder, measuring cup, large bowl, measuring spoons, long-handled spoon, saucepan, ladle. **Ingredients:** sweet cherries, lemon juice, water, sugar, powdered pectin. **Yield:** 5½ cups.

Wash and rinse six 8-ounce glass or plastic containers with airtight covers. Heat glass containers and lids in a large kettle of water to sterilize them; pour boiling water from a teakettle onto plastic containers to scald them. Drain and set out the containers.

Wash and drain 1 quart of sweet cherries; remove the stems. Pit the cherries and grind them in a food grinder. Measure the cherries into a large bowl, to make 2 cups; if necessary, add water to make 2 cups. Add 2 tablespoons of lemon juice and stir to mix thoroughly.

Add 4¼ cups of sugar to the cherries, and stir to mix thoroughly. Let the fruit stand for 10 minutes. In a saucepan, add ¾ cup of water to 1 box of powdered pectin and stir to dissolve.

Stirring constantly, bring the pectin solution to a full rolling boil over high heat, until you can't stir the boiling down, and then boil hard for 1 full minute. Remove the boiling pectin solution from the heat and stir it into the prepared fruit; stir constantly for a full 3 minutes to blend fruit and pectin completely and prevent excessive crystal formation.

After 3 minutes' stirring, quickly ladle the jam into the prepared containers; leave ½ inch space at the top for expansion during freezing. Cover the containers tightly and let them set at room temperature for 24 hours. Store the jam in the freezer until you're ready to use it; keep open containers in the refrigerator.

Apple Butter

Apple butter's long, slow cooking and spicy taste and fragrance make it a wonderful cold-day project. Serve it warm or chilled, in any weather. **Equipment:** sharp knife, large heavy pot with cover, large bowl, measuring cup, long-handled wooden spoon, sieve or food mill, measuring spoons, grater, eight 8-ounce glasses or canning jars with lids, large kettle, towels or wire racks, double boiler, paraffin, ladle. **Ingredients:** tart cooking apples, cider or apple juice, sugar, cinnamon, clove; if desired, lemon. **Yield:** 6 to 8 cups.

Plan a full day to make apple butter. Thoroughly wash 4 pounds of tart cooking apples. Cut out the stem and blossom ends and cut the apples into chunks, but don't peel or core them. Put the cut-up apples into a large, heavy pot and add 2 cups of cider or apple juice. Cover the pot and cook over very low heat, stirring occasionally, for about 1 hour, until the apples are soft. Remove the pot from the heat and press the apples through a sieve or a food mill into a large bowl; do not drain off the juice.

Measure the pulped apples and return the pulp to the heavy pot. For each 1 cup of apple pulp, add ½ cup of sugar to the pot; also add 2 teaspoons of cinnamon and ½ teaspoon of clove, or more to taste. If desired, grate the rind of a lemon and squeeze the juice; add the lemon rind and juice to the apple pulp. Stir to mix thoroughly.

Cover the pot and cook the pulp over low heat, stirring occasionally, until the sugar dissolves. Remove the cover and cook over very low heat to thicken and darken the apple butter; stir occasionally with a wooden spoon to prevent scorching. Cook the apple butter for 3 to 5 hours, until it's very thick and smooth; it should be a rich brown color. To test the apple butter for doneness, spoon a little onto a cold plate; when the butter is thick and smooth, it's ready. Stir more often during the last hour of cooking.

When the apple butter is ready, prepare the glasses or jars. Wash and rinse eight 8-ounce glasses or canning jars with lids, and heat them in a large kettle of water to sterilize them. Set out folded towels or wire racks to put the hot glasses on. If you're using glasses, carefully melt paraffin in a double boiler over low heat. Drain and set out the glasses or jars.

Remove the thickened apple butter from the heat and ladle it quickly into the prepared glasses or jars. If you're using glasses, fill each glass to within ½ inch of the top; carefully pour a ⅛-inch layer of paraffin into the glass to seal it. If you're using canning jars, fill each jar to within ⅛ inch of the top; set the lid on, tighten the screw band over it, and invert the jar onto a folded towel or wire rack.

Let the glasses or jars cool undisturbed for at least 12 hours. If you're using canning jars, turn the jars right side up after the apple butter has cooled for ½ hour. Store the apple butter in a cool, dark, dry place.

How to Use a Water Bath Canner

To process fruit, sauces, and pickles, use a water bath canner—a large covered pot with a rack to hold jars. The water bath canner heats the prepared canning jars to 212° F to kill the bacteria that cause spoilage. Several manufacturers make water bath canners; most are aluminum. Look for a 20- to 21-quart-capacity pot with a lid and a rack. **Equipment:** standard pint or quart canning jars with lids, large kettle, towels or wire racks, water bath canner, teakettle, rubber spatula, long-handled tongs or jar lifters. **Ingredients for processing:** prepared fruit, sauce, or pickles. **Time:** varies by recipe; allow at least 2 hours for even a few jars.

Wash and rinse pint or quart canning jars; keep them hot in a large kettle of hot water. Prepare the lids as the manufacturer directs. Set out folded towels or wire racks to put the hot jars on.

Set the water bath canner on the range and pour water into it to fill it 4 to 4½ inches deep; start heating the water. At the same time, put water on to boil in a teakettle.

Following the precise instructions for the recipe you're using, prepare the fruit, sauces, or pickles. Prepare the packing liquid as directed in the recipe. Drain and set out the jars.

Fill the prepared jars to within ½ inch of the top, as directed in the recipe; if directed, add liquid to fill each jar to within ½ inch of the top. Run a rubber spatula down the side of each jar to release air bubbles; if necessary, add more liquid to fill the jar to within ½ inch of the top. To seal each jar, wipe the top and the threads with a damp cloth; set the lid on and tighten the screw band over it, as directed by the canning jar manufacturer.

Lower the prepared jars into the water bath canner, using long-handled tongs or a jar lifter. Arrange the jars on the rack so that they aren't touching each other or the sides of the pot. Add more boiling water to cover the jars with at least 1 inch of water; pour the water down the side of the canner, not onto the jars. Cover the canner and return the water to a boil. When the water boils, begin timing for processing.

Process the jars for the full time specified in the recipe, for pint or quart canning jars. During processing, add more water as necessary to keep the jars covered by at least 1 inch of water; adjust the heat so that the water boils gently but steadily. Keep the canner covered.

When the full processing time has elapsed, turn the heat off under the canner. Carefully lift the jars out of the canner with long-handled tongs or a jar lifter, and set them on folded towels or

Jars rest on a rack inside the canner; they must be covered by at least 1 inch of water during processing.

wire racks to cool. Let the jars cool undisturbed for at least 12 hours.

When the jars are cool, check the seal—if the center of the lid can be pushed down and springs back up, the jar is not sealed. Repack and reprocess it, or use it immediately. Repack and reprocess any jar that has leaked, or use it immediately. Store the cooled jars in a cool, dark, dry place.

High-altitude canning. If you live more than 1,000 feet above sea level, you must increase processing time. For processing times of 20 minutes or less, add 1 minute to the processing time for each 1,000 feet of elevation. For processing times of more than 20 minutes, add 2 minutes for each 1,000 feet of elevation.

Can Fruit Without Sugar

You can pack fruit in water, other fruit juice, or its own juice. Here's how to extract juice from fruit for canning. **Equipment:** large bowls, long-handled spoon; sharp knife, blender, or food processor; cutting board, large pan, large strainer or colander, cheesecloth. **Ingredients:** ripe fruit of your choice, water. **Yield:** varies with fruit; about 1 cup per pound.

To extract juice for canning fruit, wash ripe fruit thoroughly under cold running water, and drain it well. Put berries into a large bowl and crush them thoroughly with the back of a spoon, one layer at a time. Remove any pits and stems from other fruit and chop it with a sharp knife, a blender, or a food processor.

Put the crushed or chopped fruit into a large pan and add just enough water to keep it from sticking. Cook over low heat, stirring often, until the fruit is soft, about 1 hour.

Line a large strainer or a colander with several layers of cheesecloth, and set it over a large bowl to catch the juice. Pour the soft fruit into the prepared strainer. For crystal-clear juice, let the fruit drain naturally—from 2 to 3 hours to overnight, depending on the fruit. For faster results and less chance of contamination, pour off what juice you can and then, with a spoonful or two of fruit at a time, press the fruit into the strainer to force the juice out. Discard the pulp.

Use the juice to replace syrup in canning recipes; you'll need 1 to 1½ cups of juice for each quart jar of fruit.

Can Your Own:

Apples

Put by the pick of the apple crop in a light syrup—canned apples are delicious chilled and served with cream or ice cream. **Equipment:** standard pint or quart canning jars with lids, large kettle, towels or wire racks, measuring cup, large bowl, measuring spoons, sharp knife, water bath canner, teakettle, large pot, long-handled spoon, wide-mouthed funnel, ladle. **Ingredients:** crisp, firm apples; water, salt, vinegar, sugar or juice; cinnamon sticks. **Yield:** 2½ to 3 pounds yields 1 quart; 1 bushel—48 pounds—yields 11 to 20 quarts.

Wash and rinse pint or quart canning jars; keep them hot in a large kettle of hot water. Set out folded towels or wire racks to put the hot jars on.

Measure cold water into a large bowl. For each gallon of water, add 2 tablespoons of salt and 2 tablespoons of vinegar; stir to mix well. Wash, peel, and core crisp, firm apples in the quantity desired—2½ to 3 pounds of apples yields 1 quart of canned apples. As you work, cut the apples in quarters or slices and put them into the salt-vinegar solution to keep them from darkening.

Fill a water bath canner 4 to 4½ inches deep and start heating the water. Put water onto boil in a teakettle. You'll need 1 to 1½ cups of syrup or juice for each quart of apples. To make 5 cups of syrup, combine 2 cups of sugar and 4 cups of water in a large pot; heat to a boil and simmer for 5 minutes; skim off foam with a spoon and keep the syrup hot. If you're using juice, heat the juice to a boil in a large pot and lower the heat to keep it at a simmer.

Drain the apples, rinse them quickly in cold water, and drain again. Add the apples to the boiling syrup or juice and bring them to a boil; then boil it gently for 5 minutes. Drain and set out the jars.

Using a wide-mouthed funnel and a ladle, quickly pack the apples into the hot jars; fill each jar to within ½ inch of the top. Bring the remaining syrup or juice to a boil and pour it over the packed apples to within ½ inch of the top. If desired, add a cinnamon stick to each jar. Carefully seal each jar.

Process the apples in the water bath canner for 15 minutes for pint jars, 20 minutes for quarts. After processing, carefully lift the jars out of the canner and set them on folded towels or wire racks. Let them cool undisturbed for at least 12 hours. Store the apples in a cool, dark, dry place.

528

Peach or Pear Halves

Peaches and pears look as good as they taste when you arrange them in overlapping layers—pack them separately or combine them for a sunny silver-and-gold treat. **Equipment:** standard pint or quart canning jars with lids, large kettle, towels or wire racks, measuring cup, large bowls, measuring spoons, sharp knife, water bath canner, teakettle, large pan, bowl, large strainer, long-handled spoon, ladle. **Ingredients:** firm, ripe peaches or pears; water, salt, vinegar, sugar or juice. **Yield:** 2 to 3 pounds yields 1 quart; 1 lug—22 pounds—yields 8 to 12 quarts.

Wash and rinse pint or quart canning jars; keep them hot in a large kettle of hot water. Set out folded towels or wire racks to put the hot jars on.

Measure cold water into a large bowl. For each gallon of water, add 2 tablespoons of salt and 2 tablespoons of vinegar; stir to mix well. Carefully wash firm, ripe peaches or pears in the quantity desired—2 to 3 pounds yields 1 quart of canned fruit. Do not use bruised or overripe fruit. Drain well. Dip peaches into boiling water for about 30 seconds to loosen their skins; then dip into a bowl of cold water, drain, and slip off the skin. Halve and pit the skinned peaches. Peel pears carefully, halve them, and remove the cores. As you work, put the prepared fruit into the cold salt-vinegar solution to keep it from darkening.

Fill a water bath canner 4 to 4½ inches deep and start heating the water. Put water on to boil in a teakettle.

You'll need 1 to 1½ cups of syrup or juice for each quart of peaches or pears. To make 5 cups of syrup, combine 2 cups of sugar and 4 cups of water in a large pan; heat to a boil and simmer for 5 minutes; skim off foam with a spoon and keep the syrup hot. If you're using juice, heat the juice to a boil in a large pan and lower the heat to keep it at a simmer. Drain and set out the jars.

Drain the peaches or pears, rinse them quickly in cold water, and drain again. Pack the halved fruit into the hot jars in overlapping layers, pit side down; fill each jar to within ½ inch of the top. Ladle in boiling syrup or juice to fill each jar to within ½ inch of the top. Carefully seal each jar.

Process the peaches or pears in the water bath canner for 25 minutes for pint jars, ½ hour for quarts. After processing, carefully lift the jars out of the canner and set them on folded towels or wire racks. Let them cool undisturbed for at least 12 hours. Store the peaches or pears in a cool, dark, dry place.

Cherries

For pie or for eating, cherries are a treat any time. Can sweet or sour cherries in season; enjoy them all year. **Equipment:** standard pint or quart canning jars with lids, large kettle, towels or wire racks, water bath canner, teakettle, large strainer or colander, cherry pitter, measuring cup, large pan, long-handled spoon, funnel, ladle. **Ingredients:** fresh, ripe cherries; sugar, water; if desired, juice. **Yield:** about 2½ to 3 pounds yields 1 quart; 1 lug—22 pounds—yields 12 to 14 quarts.

Wash and rinse pint or quart canning jars; keep them hot in a large kettle of hot water. Set out folded towels or wire racks to put hot jars on. Fill a water bath canner 4 to 4½ inches deep and start heating the water. Put water on to boil in a teakettle.

Wash the desired quantity of ripe cherries under cold running water in a large strainer or colander—2½ to 3 pounds yields 1 quart. Stem and pit the cherries, and discard any imperfect ones.

You'll need 1 to 1½ cups of syrup or juice for each quart of cherries. For sweet cherries, combine 3 cups of sugar and 4 cups of water in a large pan, to make 5½ cups of syrup; heat to a boil and simmer for 5 minutes; skim off foam with a spoon and keep the syrup hot. For sour cherries, combine 4¾ cups of sugar and 4 cups of water, to make 6½ cups of syrup. If you're using juice, heat the juice to a boil and lower the heat to keep it at a simmer.

Drain and set out the jars. Quickly pack the cherries into the hot jars, shaking them down to make sure the jars are firmly packed. Fill each jar to within ½ inch of the top. Ladle in boiling syrup or juice to fill each jar to within ½ inch of the top. Carefully seal each jar.

Process the cherries in the water bath canner for 20 minutes for pint jars, 25 minutes for quarts. After processing, carefully lift the jars out of the canner and set them on folded towels or wire racks. Let them cool undisturbed for at least 12 hours. Store the cherries in a cool, dark, dry place.

Berries

Strawberries are the only berries that don't can well—if you can't eat them all, use them for jam. Other berries pack beautifully for pies and desserts all year. **Equipment:** standard pint or quart canning jars with lids, large kettle, towels or wire racks, water bath canner, teakettle, large strainer or colander, large pot with cover, measuring cup, long-handled spoon, wide-mouthed funnel, ladle. **Ingredients:** ripe berries, sugar, water; if desired, juice. **Yield:** 1 to 2 quart boxes yields 1 quart; 1 24-quart crate yields 12 to 18 quarts.

Wash and rinse pint or quart canning jars; keep them hot in a large kettle of hot water. Set out folded towels or wire racks to put the hot jars on. Fill a water bath canner 4 to 4½ inches deep and start heating the water. Put water on to boil in a teakettle.

Firm berries. Wash the desired quantity of firm berries under cold running water in a large strainer or colander—1 or 2 quart boxes yields 1 quart of canned berries. Pick them over and remove any stems. Drain well.

Measure the drained berries into a large pot. For each quart of berries, add ¼ to ½ cup of sugar, to taste. Stir very gently to distribute the sugar. Drain and set out the jars.

Cover the pot and bring the berries just to a boil over medium heat; shake the pot to keep the berries from sticking. Quickly pack the berries and juice into the hot jars, using a wide-mouthed funnel and a ladle; shake the jars to be sure the berries are firmly packed. Fill each jar to within ½ inch of the top. If you run out of juice, add boiling water to fill each jar to within ½ inch of the top. Carefully seal each jar. Process the berries in the water bath canner for 10 minutes for pint jars, 15 minutes for quarts. After processing, carefully lift the jars out of the canner and set them on folded towels or wire racks. Let them cool undisturbed for at least 12 hours. Store the berries in a cool, dark, dry place.

Delicate berries. Dip the desired quantity of raspberries or other delicate berries, in a large strainer or colander, into a bowl of cold water; pick them over and remove any stems. Drain well.

You'll need 1 to 1½ cups of syrup or juice for each quart of berries. To make 5 cups of syrup, combine 2 cups of sugar and 4 cups of water in a pot; heat to a boil and simmer for 5 minutes; skim off foam with a spoon and keep the syrup hot. If you're using juice, heat the juice to a boil and lower the heat to keep it at a simmer.

Carefully pour the drained berries into the hot jars, shaking them down to make sure the jars are firmly packed. Fill each jar to within ½ inch of the top. Quickly ladle boiling syrup into each jar to fill it to within ½ inch of the top. Carefully seal each jar. Process, cool, and store as above.

Apricot Halves

Have your canner ready when apricots make their brief appearance—

you'll enjoy their sunny color and rich flavor all winter. **Equipment:** standard pint or quart canning jars with lids, large kettle, towels or wire racks, measuring cup, large bowl, measuring spoons, sharp knife, water bath canner, teakettle, large pot, long-handled spoon, wide-mouthed funnel, ladle. **Ingredients:** ripe, firm apricots; water, salt, vinegar, sugar or juice. **Yield:** 2 to 2½ pounds yields 1 quart; 1 lug or box—22 pounds—yields 7 to 11 quarts.

Wash and rinse pint or quart canning jars; keep them hot in a large kettle of hot water. Set out folded towels or wire racks to put the hot jars on.

Measure cold water into a large bowl. For each gallon of water, add 2 tablespoons of salt and 2 tablespoons of vinegar; stir to mix well. Carefully wash ripe, firm apricots in the quantity desired—2 to 2½ pounds yields 1 quart of canned apricots. Do not use bruised or overripe fruit. Drain well. Halve and pit the apricots; as you work, put them into the salt-vinegar solution to keep them from darkening.

Fill a water bath canner 4 to 4½ inches deep and start heating the water. Put water on to boil in a teakettle.

You'll need 1 to 1½ cups of syrup or juice for each quart of apricots. To make 5 cups of syrup, combine 2 cups of sugar and 4 cups of water in a large pot; heat to a boil and simmer for 5 minutes; skim off foam with a spoon and keep the syrup hot. If you're using juice, heat the juice to a boil in a large pot and lower the heat to keep it at a simmer. Drain and set out the jars.

Drain the apricots, rinse them quickly in cold water, and drain again. Add the apricots to the boiling syrup or juice and cook until they're heated through, about 2 minutes. Using a wide-mouthed funnel and a ladle, quickly pack the apricots and syrup or juice into the hot jars; pack each jar firmly, and fill it to within ½ inch of the top. Bring the remaining syrup or juice to a boil and pour it over the packed apricots to within ½ inch of the top. Carefully seal each jar.

Process the apricots in the water bath canner for 25 minutes for pint jars, ½ hour for quarts. After processing, carefully lift the jars out of the canner and set them on folded towels or wire racks. Let them cool undisturbed for at least 12 hours. Store the apricots in a cool, dark, dry place.

Whole Plums

Whole plums are a treat eaten plain or used as a pie filling. Use prune plums, greengages, or other very meaty plums; the juicier varieties tend to fall apart. **Equipment:** standard pint or quart canning jars with lids, large kettle, towels or wire racks, sharp-tined fork, water bath canner, teakettle, measuring cup, large pot, long-handled spoon, funnel, ladle. **Ingredients:** firm, ripe plums; sugar, water; if desired, juice. **Yield:** 1½ to 2½ pounds yields 1 quart; 1 lug—24 pounds—yields 12 quarts.

Wash and rinse pint or quart canning jars; keep them hot in a large kettle of hot water. Set out folded towels or wire racks to put the hot jars on.

Carefully wash firm, ripe plums in the quantity desired—1½ to 2½ pounds yields 1 quart of canned plums. Do not used bruised or very soft fruit. Drain the plums well. With a sharp-tined fork, prick the skin of each plum to prevent bursting.

Fill a water bath canner 4 to 4½ inches deep and start heating the water. Put water on to boil in a teakettle.

You'll need 1 to 1½ cups of syrup or juice for each quart of plums. To make 5½ cups of syrup, combine 3 cups of sugar and 4 cups of water in a large pot; heat to a boil and simmer for 5 minutes; skim off foam with a spoon and keep the syrup hot. If you're using juice, heat the juice to a boil in a large pot and lower the heat to keep it at a simmer. Drain and set out the jars.

Add the prepared plums to the boiling syrup or juice and cook until they're heated through, about 2 minutes. Using a wide-mouthed funnel and a ladle, quickly pack the plums and syrup or juice into the hot jars; pack each jar firmly, and fill it to within ½ inch of the top. Bring the remaining syrup or juice to a boil and pour it over the packed plums to within ½ inch of the top. Carefully seal each jar.

Process the plums in the water bath canner for 20 minutes for pint jars, 25 minutes for quarts. After processing, carefully lift the jars out of the canner and set them on folded towels or wire racks. Let them cool undisturbed for at least 12 hours. Store the plums in a cool, dark, dry place.

East India Relish

Here's the perfect relish for pot roast, lamb, or chicken—it adds zest to any dinner, and it makes a perfect gift. **Equipment:** sharp knife, cutting board, large pot, bowl, large strainer, grater, six standard pint canning jars with lids, large kettle, towels or wire racks, water bath canner, teakettle, measuring cup, measuring spoons, long-handled spoon, wide-mouthed funnel, ladle. **Ingredients:** onions, green tomatoes, zucchini, carrots, light corn syrup, white vinegar, salt, coriander, ginger, red pepper, cumin. **Yield:** about 6 pints.

Peel and chop 8 medium onions and put them into a large pot. Wash 8 medium green tomatoes and peel them; dip them into boiling water for 20 to 30 seconds, dip them into a bowl of cold water, and slip off the skins. Cut out the stem ends and chop the tomatoes, and add them to the pot. Wash 2 pounds of zucchini, cut off the stems, and chop it; wash 1 pound of carrots and shred them. Add the zucchini and carrots to the pot.

Wash and rinse six pint canning jars; keep them hot in a large kettle of hot water. Set out folded towels or wire racks to put the hot jars on. Fill a water bath canner 4 to 4½ inches deep and start heating the water. Put water on to boil in a teakettle.

To the chopped vegetables in the pot, add 2 cups of light corn syrup, 2 cups of

white vinegar, 2 teaspoons of salt, 1 tablespoon of coriander, 2 teaspoons of ginger, 1 teaspoon of crushed red pepper, and ½ teaspoon of cumin. Stir to mix all ingredients thoroughly. Heat the relish to a boil over medium heat, stirring occasionally; lower the heat and simmer for 5 minutes. Drain and set out the jars.

Quickly pack the relish into the hot jars, using a wide-mouthed funnel and a ladle. Fill each jar firmly to within ¼ inch of the top. Carefully seal each jar.

Process the relish in the water bath canner for 10 minutes. After processing, carefully lift the jars out of the canner and set them on folded towels or wire racks. Let them cool undisturbed for at least 12 hours. Store the relish in a cool, dark, dry place.

Homemade Chili Sauce

This spicy, rich sauce will make your family sit up and take notice—add it to other recipes or serve it cold as a condiment. **Equipment:** bowl, large strainer, sharp knife, cutting board, large pot, pan with cover, steamer, measuring cup, long-handled spoon, eight pint canning jars with lids, large kettle, towels or wire racks, water bath canner, teakettle, measuring spoons, wide-mouthed funnel, ladle. **Ingredients:** ripe tomatoes, green peppers, onions, celery, brown sugar, cider vinegar, cinnamon, clove, nutmeg. **Yield:** 6 to 8 pints.

Wash and drain 4 pounds of ripe tomatoes, and peel them. Dip each tomato into boiling water for 20 to 30 seconds, dip it into a bowl of cold water, and then slip the skin off. Cut out the stem ends and chop the tomatoes; remove any green seeds. Put the chopped tomatoes into a large pot. Wash 2 large green peppers and steam them for about 5 minutes in a steamer; remove the stems and seeds and chop them. Peel and chop 8 medium-size onions; wash and chop 2 stalks of celery, about 1 cup. Add the chopped peppers, onions, and celery to the tomatoes in the pot.

Cover the pot and bring it to a boil over medium heat. Lower the heat and simmer for 1 hour, stirring occasionally.

When the tomato-onion mixture has simmered for 1 hour, add 1½ cups of firmly packed brown sugar, 1½ cups of cider vinegar, 1½ teaspoons of cinnamon, ½ teaspoon of clove, and ½ teaspoon of nutmeg. Stir to mix all ingredients thoroughly. Return the sauce to a boil and simmer it for ½ hour longer, stirring occasionally.

Wash and rinse eight pint canning jars; keep them hot in a large kettle of hot water. Set out folded towels or wire racks to put the hot jars on. Fill a water bath canner 4 to 4½ inches deep and start heating the water. Put water on to boil in a teakettle.

Drain and set out the jars. Quickly pack the chili sauce into the prepared jars, using a wide-mouthed funnel and a ladle. Pack each jar firmly to within ⅛ inch of the top. Carefully seal each jar.

Process the chili sauce in the water bath canner for 5 minutes. After processing, carefully lift the jars out of the canner and set them on folded towels or wire racks. Let them cool undisturbed for at least 12 hours. Store the chili sauce in a cool, dark, dry place.

Crispy Zucchini Slices

Zucchini is one crop that produces like mad toward fall. Put up the extra and give yourself a treat with these tangy, crisp pickle slices. **Equipment:** sharp knife, cutting board, large bowl, measuring cup, seven standard pint canning jars with lids, large kettle, towels or wire racks, water bath canner, teakettle, large pot, measuring spoons, long-handled spoon, large strainer or colander, wide-mouthed funnel, ladle. **Ingredients:** fresh small or medium-sized zucchini, onions, garlic cloves, pickling salt, ice cubes, sugar, white vinegar, mustard seed, pickling spice, celery seed, turmeric. **Yield:** about 7 pints.

Carefully wash 6 pounds of fresh, small or medium-size zucchini under cold running water, and drain well. Cut off the ends of the zucchini and slice them about ⅛ inch thick; don't peel them. Put the sliced zucchini into a large bowl. Peel and chop 1 pound of small or medium-size onions and slice them ⅛ inch thick; add them to the zucchini and toss lightly to mix. Peel 2 large garlic cloves and stick each on a wood toothpick; add them to the zucchini and onions.

Sprinkle ⅓ cup of pickling salt onto the sliced vegetables, and toss them to distribute the salt evenly. Empty two trays of ice cubes onto the top of the bowl, and set the vegetables aside for 3 hours.

Wash and rinse seven pint canning jars; keep them hot in a large kettle of hot water. Set out folded towels or wire racks to set the hot jars on. Fill a water bath canner 4 to 4½ inches deep and start heating the water. Put water on to boil in a teakettle.

In a large pot, combine 4 cups of sugar and 3 cups of white vinegar; add 1½ tablespoons of mustard seed, 1½ teaspoons of pickling spice, 1 teaspoon of celery seed, and ½ teaspoon of turmeric. Stir to mix thoroughly. Bring the mixture to a boil over medium heat, stirring constantly to dissolve the sugar; then simmer for 5 minutes. Drain and set out the jars.

Drain the zucchini and onions well in a large strainer or a colander, and pick out the garlic cloves. Rinse the vegetables thoroughly under cold running water and drain them well. Add the drained vegetables to the boiling sauce and cook over medium heat just until the mixture starts to boil.

Quickly pack the hot vegetables and sauce into the hot jars, using a wide-mouthed funnel and a ladle. Fill each jar firmly to within ½ inch of the top; add more sauce as necessary to cover the pickles and fill each jar to within ½ inch of the top. Carefully seal each jar.

Process the pickles in the water bath canner for 5 minutes. After processing, carefully lift the jars out of the canner and set them on folded towels or wire racks. Let them cool undisturbed for at least 12 hours. Store the pickles in a cool, dark, dry place.

Dill-Pickled Beans

As a salad or a relish or even the garnish in martinis, dill-pickled beans are an unusual treat. **Equipment:** seven standard pint canning jars with lids, large kettle, towels or wire racks, water bath canner, teakettle, sharp knife, cutting board, measuring spoons, large pan, measuring cup, long-handled spoon, funnel, ladle. **Ingredients:** fresh green beans, dill seed, whole peppercorns, water, cider vinegar, pickling salt. **Yield:** 6 to 7 pints.

Wash and rinse seven pint canning jars with lids; keep them hot in a large kettle of hot water. Set out folded towels or wire racks to put the hot jars on. Fill a water bath canner 4 to 4½ inches deep and start heating the water. Put water on to boil in a teakettle.

Rinse and drain 4 pounds of fresh, uniform-sized green beans. Cut off the ends and trim the beans to a uniform length so they'll stand upright in the jars; or cut them into 2-inch pieces. Drain and set out the jars.

Pack the trimmed beans into the hot jars, standing upright; fill each jar firmly. The beans should come to within ½ inch of the jar tops; trim off any beans that stick up higher than this. To each jar, add ½ teaspoon of dill seed and 3 whole peppercorns.

In a large pan, combine 3 cups of water and 3 cups of cider vinegar; add ⅓ cup of pickling salt. Bring to a boil over high heat, stirring to dissolve the salt. Remove the pan from the heat and pour the boiling liquid into the jars of beans, to cover the beans and fill each jar to within ½ inch of the top. Carefully seal each jar.

Process the beans in the water bath canner for 10 minutes. After processing, carefully lift the jars out of the canner and set them on folded towels or wire racks. Let them cool undisturbed for at least 12 hours. Store the pickled beans in a cool, dry, dark place.

Pickled Pumpkin

Flavored with ginger and orange juice, these pumpkin pickles are tangy and delicious—an unusual gift that won't be forgotten. Save the pumpkin seeds for roasting. **Equipment:** sharp knife, cutting board, large pot with cover, measuring cup, measuring spoons, long-handled spoon, eight standard pint canning jars with lids, large kettle, towels or wire racks, water bath canner, teakettle, wide-mouthed funnel, ladle. **Ingredients:** whole fresh pumpkin, sugar, cider vinegar, water, cinnamon sticks, fresh ginger root, whole allspice, whole cloves, frozen concentrated orange juice. **Yield:** about 8 pints.

Wash a ripe 5- to 6-pound pumpkin. Cut the pumpkin into 1-inch chunks; discard the stem and the fibrous insides and save the seeds to roast. Pare the peel from the chunks.

In a large pot, combine 4 cups of sugar, 1 quart of cider vinegar, and 3 cups of water. Add 2 cinnamon sticks, broken into pieces, and 2½-inch chunks of fresh ginger root; also add 1 tablespoon of whole allspice and 1½ teaspoons of whole cloves. Stir thoroughly to mix all ingredients.

Bring to a boil over high heat, stirring constantly until the sugar dissolves. Stir in one 6-ounce can of thawed frozen concentrated orange juice and add the pumpkin chunks. Stir to coat the chunks evenly and bring the mixture to a boil; partially cover the pot and lower the heat to a simmer. Simmer, stirring occasionally, until the pumpkin is just tender, about ½ hour.

Meanwhile, wash and rinse eight pint canning jars with lids; keep them hot in a large kettle of hot water. Set out folded towels or wire racks to put the hot jars on. Fill a water bath canner 4 to 4½ inches deep and start heating the water. Put water on to boil in a teakettle.

When the pumpkin is just tender, drain and set out the jars. Quickly pack the pumpkin into the hot jars, using a wide-mouthed funnel and a ladle. Pack each jar firmly to within ⅛ inch of the top. Carefully seal each jar.

Process the pumpkin in the water bath canner for 5 minutes. After processing, carefully lift the jars out of the canner and set them on folded towels or wire racks. Let them cool undisturbed for at least 12 hours. Store the pumpkin pickles in a cool, dark, dry place.

Dill Pickles

With a 2-gallon crock and a little patience, you can make real old-time dill pickles. **Equipment:** 2-gallon crock, large pot, measuring cup, measuring spoons, long-handled spoon, plate, weight, eight standard quart canning jars with lids, large kettle, towels or wire racks, water bath canner, teakettle, ladle. **Ingredients:** small cucumbers, fresh dill, water, cider vinegar, pickling salt, pickling spice. **Yield:** about 8 quarts.

Thoroughly wash about 50 to 60 small cucumbers—about 8 to 10 pounds. Drain them thoroughly. Put 2 sprigs of fresh dill into the bottom of a clean 2-gallon crock, and pack the drained cucumbers into the crock, to within about 3 inches of the top. Add 2 more sprigs of fresh dill.

In a large pot, combine 1 quart of water and 1 quart of cider vinegar; add ¾ cup of pickling salt and 6 tablespoons—⅜ cup—of pickling spice. Heat to a boil over medium heat, stirring to dissolve the salt. Pour the hot brine over the cucumbers to fill the crock to within about 2 inches of the top; if necessary, add water to fill the crock.

Cover the crock with a plate that just fits inside it; weight the plate lightly to hold the cucumbers under the brine. Let the cucumbers stand at room temperature for 2 to 3 weeks—check them after 2 weeks to see if they're completely pickled.

When the pickles are ready, pack them into quart jars. Wash and rinse eight quart canning jars; keep them hot in a large kettle of hot water. Set out folded towels or wire racks to put the hot jars on. Fill a water bath canner 4 to 4½ inches deep and start heating the water. Put water on to boil in a teakettle.

Drain and set out the jars. Quickly pack the pickled cucumbers into the hot jars, touching them as little as possible. Fill each jar firmly, leaving about ¼ inch space at the top. Quickly pour the brine from the crock into a large pot and heat it to a boil; skim off any foam with a spoon. Pour the hot brine over the packed cucumbers to fill each jar to within ¼ inch of the top. Carefully seal each jar.

Process the pickles in the water bath canner for 15 minutes. After processing, carefully lift the jars out of the canner and set them on folded towels or wire racks. Let them cool undisturbed for at least 12 hours. Store the pickles in a cool, dark, dry place; chill before serving.

How to Use a Pressure Canner

All canned vegetables must be heated to 240° F to kill bacteria—especially the kind that causes botulism poisoning. To process vegetables, use a pressure canner—a large, tightly sealed pot that's heated to create pressurized steam. Never use a water bath canner to process vegetables; you risk botulism poisoning if you don't use a pressure canner.

Several manufacturers make pressure canners. They range in capacity from 8 to 22 quarts. Look for a heavy pressurized covered pot with a pressure gauge, a sealing gasket and lock, and a rack to hold jars.

Equipment: standard pint or quart canning jars with lids, large kettle, towels or wire racks, pressure canner, teakettle, rubber spatula, long-handled tongs or jar lifters. **Ingredients for processing:** prepared vegetables. **Time:** varies by recipe; allow at least 2 hours for even a few jars.

Before using the pressure canner, carefully read the manufacturer's instructions. Study the canner and the instructions to familiarize yourself with canning technique. Look at the cover; examine the dial or pressure control and the vents. Check to make sure the gasket and locking mechanism work. Don't use the canner until you're sure you know how to use it correctly.

Some canners have dial-type pressure gauges; some have weighted gauges. Before each canning season, and also during the season if you use the canner often, make sure the gauge works properly. Clean a weighted gauge thoroughly; have a dial gauge checked by the manufacturer, the dealer, or the closest state or county agricultural extension office. If the gauge doesn't work properly, have it replaced.

If you own a pressure cooker, you can use it to process pint jars. The pressure cooker must have an accurate gauge and a tight seal; if it can't maintain a steady 10-pound pressure, don't use it. Have the gauge checked as above.

During the canning season, handle the pressure gauge carefully. Never rest the cover on a dial gauge; never turn the cover upside down over a full pan when the gauge is attached. Clean the petcock and vent openings frequently. Use only standard canning jars and lids; only jars tempered for canning can stand up to the pressurized-steam process.

When you're ready to use the pressure canner, wash and rinse pint or quart canning jars; keep them hot in a large kettle of hot water. Prepare the lids as the manufacturer directs. Set out folded towels or wire racks to put the hot jars on. Put water on to boil in a teakettle.

Following the precise instructions for the recipe you're using, prepare the vegetables. Prepare packing liquid as directed in the recipe. Drain and set out the jars.

Fill the prepared jars to within ½ inch of the top, as directed in the recipe; if directed, add liquid to fill each jar to within ½ inch of the top. Run a rubber spatula down the side of each jar to release air bubbles; if necessary, add more liquid to fill the jar to within ½ inch of the top. To seal each jar, wipe the top and the threads with a damp cloth; set the lid on and tighten the screw band over it, as directed by the manufacturer.

Set the pressure canner on the range, set the rack into place, and pour boiling water into the canner to fill it 2 to 3 inches deep. Lower the prepared jars into the canner, using long-handled tongs or a jar lifter. Arrange the jars on the rack so that they aren't touching each other or the sides of the pot. If you're processing two layers of jars, use another rack between the layers, and stagger the second layer of jars over the first one.

Cover the canner and put the pressure gauge on, as directed by the manufacturer; seal and lock the cover securely. Following the manufacturer's instructions, heat the canner until steam flows steadily out of the vent. Let the steam continue to flow for at least 10 minutes, as directed by the manufacturer, to remove all air from the canner. Then close the petcock or put on the weighted pressure gauge, as directed.

Keep heating the canner to raise the pressure. Processing pressure is usually 10 pounds. When the pressure in the canner reaches 10 pounds, begin timing for processing.

Process the jars for the full time specified in the recipe, for pint or quart canning jars. During processing, adjust the heat under the canner as necessary to keep the pressure constant.

When the full processing time has

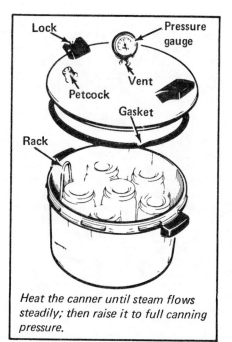

Heat the canner until steam flows steadily; then raise it to full canning pressure.

Labels: Lock, Pressure gauge, Vent, Petcock, Gasket, Rack

it, or use it immediately. Repack and re-process any jar that has leaked, or use it immediately. Store the cooled jars in a cool, dry, dark place.

High-altitude canning. If you live more than 1,000 feet above sea level, you must increase processing pressure. If your canner has a weighted gauge, have it adjusted for altitude by the manufacturer; or process jars at 15 pounds instead of 10. If your canner has a dial gauge, add 1 pound of pressure for each 2,000 feet of elevation.

Pressure-Can Your Own:

Tomato Chunks

Grocery-store tomatoes are hardly even worthy of the name. Enjoy salads with flavor even in winter; can your own home-grown tomatoes. **Equipment:** standard pint or quart canning jars with lids, large kettle, towels or wire racks, teakettle, pressure canner, large pan, bowl, large strainer, sharp knife, cutting board, large spoon, measuring spoons. **Ingredients:** firm, ripe, juicy tomatoes; salt. **Yield:** 2½ to 3½ pounds yields 1 quart.

Wash and rinse pint or quart canning jars; keep them hot in a large kettle of hot water. Set out folded towels or wire racks to put the hot jars on. Put water on to boil in a teakettle, and set out a pressure canner.

Wash firm, ripe, juicy tomatoes in the quantity desired—2½ to 3½ pounds yields 1 quart. Boil water in a large pan and dip the tomatoes into the boiling water for about 30 seconds; then dip them into a bowl of cold water and slip the skins off. Cut out the stem end of each tomato and cut out any blemishes; cut the tomatoes into quarters. Drain and set out the jars.

Working quickly, pack the tomatoes into the hot jars. Press the tomatoes

elapsed, remove the canner from the heat and let the canner stand until the pressure is reduced to zero. A canner with a weighted gauge may take up to 45 minutes to cool. Do *not* pour water over the canner or otherwise try to speed the cooling; the pressure must come down slowly. Nudge the control on a weighted-gauge canner with a pencil; when no steam escapes, the pressure is down. A dial gauge reads *zero* when the pressure is down.

When the pressure is completely reduced, remove the jars from the canner. If you have a weighted-gauge canner, remove the weight control. Unlock the canner's cover. Open the canner carefully, lifting the cover away from you so that the steam will escape on the far side. Carefully lift the jars out of the canner with long-handled tongs or a jar lifter, and set them on folded towels or wire racks to cool. Let the jars cool undisturbed for at least 12 hours.

When the jars are cool, check the seal—if the center of the lid can be pushed down and springs back up, the jar is not sealed. Repack and reprocess gently down with the back of a spoon to press out the juice and eliminate air spaces. Add ½ teaspoon of salt to each pint jar, or 1 teaspoon of salt to each quart jar. Fill each jar to within ½ inch of the top; don't add water or any other liquid. Carefully seal each jar.

Fill and heat the pressure canner as directed. Process the tomatoes at 10 pounds of pressure for 10 minutes. After processing, carefully lift the jars out of the canner and set them on folded towels or wire racks. Let them cool undisturbed for at least 12 hours. Store the tomatoes in a cool, dark, dry place.

Tomato Puree

Home-canned tomato puree is the perfect solution to an inundation of tomatoes—and the perfect source of supply for the winter's spaghetti sauce. **Equipment:** sharp knife, cutting board, large pot with cover, long-handled spoon, sieve or food mill, large bowl, standard pint or quart canning jars with lids, large kettle, towels or wire racks, teakettle, pressure canner, wide-mouthed funnel, ladle. **Ingredients:** fresh, ripe tomatoes. **Yield:** varies widely, depending on tomatoes and thickness of puree.

Wash fresh, ripe, juicy tomatoes; drain them well. Cut out the stem ends and remove any underripe or bad spots, but don't peel the tomatoes. Cut the tomatoes into chunks and put them into a large pot.

Cover the pot and cook the tomatoes over medium heat, stirring occasionally, until the tomatoes are very soft. Remove the pot from the heat. Press the soft tomatoes through a sieve or a food mill into a large bowl, and discard the sieved-out skins. Return the tomatoes to the pot and bring the puree to a boil over medium heat; then lower the heat. Simmer, stirring occasionally, for ½ to 1 hour over very low heat, until the puree is as thick as desired.

When the puree has thickened as desired, wash and rinse pint or quart canning jars; keep them hot in a large kettle of hot water. Set out folded towels or wire racks to put the hot jars on. Put water on to boil in a teakettle, and set out a pressure canner. Then drain and set out the jars.

Quickly fill the hot jars with puree, using a wide-mouthed funnel and a ladle. Fill each jar to within ½ inch of the top. Carefully seal each jar.

Fill and heat the pressure canner as directed. Process the puree at 10 pounds of pressure for 15 minutes. After processing, carefully lift the jars out of the canner and set them on folded towels or wire racks. Let them cool undisturbed for at least 12 hours. Store the puree in a cool, dark, dry place.

Asparagus

For an elegant midwinter salad, serve home-grown, home-canned asparagus, chilled and lightly dressed in vinegar and oil. **Equipment:** standard pint or quart canning jars with lids, large kettle, towels or wire racks, teakettle, pressure canner, sharp knife, cutting board, measuring spoons. **Ingredients:** fresh, uniform-sized asparagus spears; salt; water. **Yield:** 2½ to 4½ pounds yields 1 quart; 1 bushel—45 pounds—yields about 11 quarts.

Wash and rinse pint or quart canning jars; keep them hot in a large kettle of hot water. Set out folded towels or wire racks to put the hot jars on. Put water on to boil in a teakettle, and set out a pressure canner.

Wash and drain fresh, uniform-sized asparagus in the quantity desired—2½ to 4½ pounds yields 1 quart. Trim off the scales and the tough ends and wash the spears again; drain well. Cut the spears into uniform 1-inch pieces.

Drain and set out the jars. Pack the asparagus firmly into the hot jars, pressing them in but not crushing them; fill each jar to within ½ inch of the top. Add ½ teaspoon of salt to each pint jar, or 1 teaspoon of salt to each quart jar. Pour boiling water into each jar to fill it to within ½ inch of the top. Carefully seal each jar.

Fill and heat the pressure canner as directed. Process the asparagus at 10 pounds of pressure for 25 minutes for pint jars, ½ hour for quarts. After processing, carefully lift the jars out of the canner and set them on folded towels or wire racks. Let them cool undisturbed for at least 12 hours. Store the asparagus in a cool, dark, dry place.

Summer Squash

Summer squash—zucchini, pale green pattypan, crookneck, or yellow squash—can be an overwhelming producer. After the salads and pickles, can the surplus for all-winter eating. **Equipment:** standard pint or quart canning jars with lids, large kettle, towels or wire racks, teakettle, pressure canner, sharp knife, cutting board, measuring spoons. **Ingredients:** young, tender, thin-skinned squash (zucchini, pattypan, crookneck, or yellow); salt, water. **Yield:** 2 to 4 pounds yields 1 quart; 1 bushel—40 pounds—yields 10 to 20 quarts.

Wash and rinse pint or quart canning jars; keep them hot in a large kettle of hot water. Set out folded towels or wire racks to put the hot jars on. Put water on to boil in a teakettle, and set out a pressure canner.

Thoroughly wash young, tender, thin-skinned squash, in the quantity desired—2 to 4 pounds yields 1 quart. Drain well. Trim off the ends of the squashes, but don't peel them. Slice the squash ½ inch thick, and cut large slices into halves or quarters so that the pieces are uniformly sized.

Drain and set out the jars. Pack the squash firmly into the hot jars, pressing the slices down to eliminate air spaces. Fill each jar to within 1 inch of the top; the squash will expand during processing. Add ½ teaspoon of salt to each pint jar, or 1 teaspoon of salt to each quart jar. Pour boiling water into each

jar to fill it to within ½ inch of the top. Carefully seal each jar.

Fill and heat the pressure canner as directed. Process the squash at 10 pounds of pressure for 25 minutes for pint jars, ½ hour for quarts. After processing, carefully lift the jars out of the canner and set them on folded towels or wire racks. Let them cool undisturbed for at least 12 hours. Store the squash in a cool, dark, dry place.

Creamed Corn

Home-grown corn packed in its own cream is a real treat—a far cry from the bland commercial variety. **Equipment:** standard pint canning jars with lids, large kettle, towels or wire racks, teakettle, pressure canner, sharp knife, cutting board, bowls, large spoon, measuring spoons, wide-mouthed funnel, ladle. **Ingredients:** freshly picked sweet corn, salt, water. **Yield:** 3 to 6 pounds yields 2 pints; 1 bushel—35 pounds—yields 15 to 20 pints.

Wash and rinse pint canning jars; do *not* use quart jars. Keep them hot in a large kettle of hot water. Set out folded towels or wire racks to put the hot jars on. Put water on to boil in a teakettle, and set out a pressure canner.

Husk freshly picked sweet corn in the quantity desired—3 to 6 pounds, on the cob, yields 2 pints. Remove all cornsilk from the ears, and wash the ears well; drain thoroughly. Work quickly, to keep the corn at the peak of its flavor.

With a sharp knife, cut down each ear of corn to cut the kernels off; cut at about the center of the kernels, so half the kernel is still on the cob. Then, as you finish cutting each ear, set it over a bowl and scrape down the cob with the knife to extract the juice, or cream, from the cut kernels. Thoroughly mix the cut kernels and the cream; discard the scraped cobs.

Drain and set out the jars. Using a wide-mouthed funnel and a ladle, pack corn and cream firmly into the hot jars; do not press down or shake the jars. Fill each jar to within 1½ inches of the top; the corn will expand during processing. Add ½ teaspoon of salt to each jar. Pour boiling water into each jar to fill it to within ½ inch of the top. Carefully seal each jar.

Fill and heat the pressure canner as directed. Process the corn at 10 pounds of pressure for 1 hour and 35 minutes—don't underprocess. After processing, carefully lift the jars out of the canner and set them on folded towels or wire racks. Let them cool undisturbed for at least 12 hours. Store the creamed corn in a cool, dark, dry place.

Green or Wax Beans

Even a small garden can produce a big crop of beans. Can green beans or wax beans when they're young and easy to snap. **Equipment:** standard pint or quart canning jars with lids, large kettle, towels or wire racks, teakettle, pressure canner, sharp knife, cutting board, measuring spoons. **Ingredients:** fresh, young green beans or wax beans; salt, water. **Yield:** 1½ to 2½ pounds yields 1 quart; 1 bushel—30 pounds—yields 15 to 20 quarts.

Wash and rinse pint or quart canning jars; keep them hot in a large kettle of hot water. Set out folded towels or wire racks to put the hot jars on. Put water on to boil in a teakettle, and set out a pressure canner.

Wash and drain fresh, tender green beans or wax beans in the quantity desired—1½ to 2½ pounds yields 1 quart. The beans should snap easily. Trim off the ends and cut the beans into uniform 1-inch pieces.

Drain and set out the jars. Pack the beans firmly into the hot jars, pressing them in to eliminate air spaces; fill each jar to within ½ inch of the top. Add ½ teaspoon of salt to each pint jar, or 1 teaspoon of salt to each quart jar. Pour boiling water into each jar to fill it to within ½ inch of the top. Carefully seal each jar.

Fill and heat the pressure canner as directed. Process the beans at 10 pounds of pressure for 20 minutes for pint jars, 25 minutes for quarts. After processing, carefully lift the jars out of the canner and set them on folded towels or wire racks. Let them cool undisturbed for at least 12 hours. Store the beans in a cool, dark, dry place.

Clothes

Alter Clothes to Fit

Off-the-rack clothes seldom fit perfectly, but with a little practice, you can usually eliminate the alterations fee. **Tools:** scissors, tape measure, steam iron and ironing board, sleeve board, pressing cloth, sponge, mirror, straight pins, yardstick or skirt marker, sewing needles, sewing machine, pinking shears, seam ripper, pencil. **Materials:** white vinegar; ribbon, lace, or bias seam binding, or wide bias seam tape; thread, fabric as necessary, paper. **Time:** 1 hour or more, depending on alteration needed.

Rehemming. The most common problem with new clothes is the hem—too short, too long, or uneven. Remove the old hem and press out the crease with a steam iron. If you're lengthening the garment and the old crease shows, sponge the crease with white vinegar and press it with a damp pressing cloth. Then put the garment on.

For the best results, work with a helper to mark the new hem. Stand in front of a mirror, in good light. Have your helper mark the new hem with straight pins at the desired point; keep pins close together. To make sure all pins are placed correctly, measure from the floor up with a yardstick or a skirt marker. Stand straight and turn slowly as your helper marks the new hem.

Take the garment off and set it on an ironing board, wrong side out. Turn the fabric up at the marked hemline and press it firmly to crease the new hem; remove the pins as you go. If you're hemming sleeves or pants legs, use a sleeve board as necessary to press the hem. Make sure the hem is plainly creased all around the garment.

Leaving the hem turned up, adjust the hem allowance as necessary to make an even hem, about the same width as the old one. For most garments, 1 to 2 inches is a good width for hems—use 1-inch hems for sleeves or pants legs, 2-inch hems for skirts or jackets. Measure up from the crease into the hem allowance and trim the hem to the correct width all around.

Before stitching the hem into place, you must finish the edge of the fabric if it is raw. For fabrics that don't ravel much, straight-stitch along the edge of the hem on a sewing machine, ¼ inch from the edge; pink the edge with a pinking shears. For lightweight woven fabrics, turn the raw edge under ¼ inch and straight-stitch it. For fabrics that ravel easily, straight-stitch along the edge of the hem, ¼ inch from the edge; overcast the edge by hand or with a zigzag machine stitch. For loosely woven fabrics or where you want to avoid bulk, finish the raw hem edge with seam binding; use ribbon or lace binding for straight hems, bias binding for curved or flared hems. Overlap the binding half its width over the raw edge; straight-stitch it into place.

If you're letting the old hem down and there's less than 1 inch of hem allowance for the new hem, finish the raw edge with a facing of wide bias seam tape. Lay the tape along the evenly trimmed edge of the hem allowance, right sides together and outside edges flush. Straight-stitch the tape into place ¼ inch from the edge; be careful not to stretch the tape. Then turn the tape up so the raw edges are underneath it, and press the seam open.

If the hem has a considerable curve or flare, pull in excess fullness before finishing the raw edge, to make sure the new hem will lie flat. Adjust the sewing machine to loosen upper thread tension and increase stitch length. On the right side of the hem allowance, straight-stitch along the hem edge, ⅜ inch from the raw edge. Then, with the right side of the hem allowance up, pull the bobbin thread with one hand and gather the fabric to the required fullness with the other. Check the gathered hem for proper fit before stitching it.

When the hem is properly trimmed and finished, stitch it into place. Stitch by hand, using matching thread. For most garments, use the hemming stitch; working from right to left, take a stitch in the hem edge and then catch one or two threads in the garment. For a strong hem in children's clothes or knits, use the catchstitch; work from left to right, catching one or two threads in the hem edge and then in the garment. For turned and stitched hems in lightweight woven fabrics, use the slipstitch; working from right to left, stitch along the hem fold, catching a thread of the garment periodically. Fasten the ends of the hem securely with small knots.

Refitting. Almost all other alterations are made to deal with clothes that are either too tight or too loose. Unless the size is drastically wrong, this is usually fairly easy to accomplish.

Letting out: If there is sufficient seam allowance, you can often solve the problem of tightness by opening the seams and restitching them closer to the raw edges. Sometimes it may be feasible to insert panels of extra fabric to provide additional width or length.

Where the garment is cut to fit closely, tightness is difficult to correct, because there's no extra fabric. If a sleeve is too tight around the shoulder and upper arm, it usually isn't possible to loosen it. The best solution for a shirt or dress may be to remove the sleeve altogether and finish the armhole with a facing.

To remove a sleeve, use a seam ripper to carefully remove all the seams that join the sleeve to the garment body. Open the side seam of the garment to the waist. Open the garment flat. Using the garment's sleeve opening as a

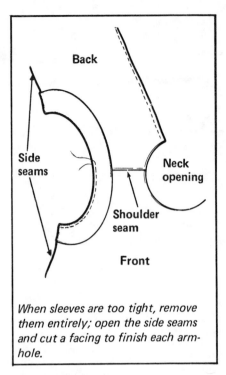

When sleeves are too tight, remove them entirely; open the side seams and cut a facing to finish each armhole.

pattern, trace the curve of the opening onto facing material; cut a piece of fabric 2 inches wide to follow the entire curve. Use a fabric of the same weight as the garment, in a matching or coordinating color; if the garment had long sleeves, cut the new facing from the sleeve material.

Finish the outside edge of the curved facing by turning the edge under ¼ inch; straight-stitch along the turned edge on the sewing machine. Place the facing over the outside (right side) of the opened armhole, right sides together, to match the curve exactly, and pin it into place. Straight-stitch the facing to the armhole opening, leaving a ⅝-inch seam allowance.

After stitching the facing onto the armhole, clip into the seam allowance every 1 to 2 inches around the armhole, cutting close to, but not into, the seam. Restitch the side seam of the garment, following the old seam line exactly. Turn the facing to the inside of the garment, press it down, and pin it into place. Sew the facing to the inside of the garment by hand, using a hemming stitch; be careful to catch only one thread of the garment fabric.

Taking in: Making clothes tighter is easier than letting them out. To get a really good fit, remove the stitching from the seam involved; try the garment on and have a helper pin or baste the seams in the correct position. Cut off excess fabric, if necessary; then restitch the seams as marked, curving them very gradually into the line of the old seams. Don't just take in all existing seams—if the garment fits unevenly, a poorly made alteration will not correct the problem. Remove all seams affected, try on, and pin or baste; restitch seams in the new position and adjust as necessary.

To take in a shirt or the bodice of a dress, you may have to remove the sleeves and adjust the side seams. In this case, to prevent changing the shape of the sleeves, open the side seam to the waist and make a paper pattern of the armhole, as above; mark the sleeves as you remove them so you'll be able to replace them correctly. After adjusting the garment's seams, use the pattern to cut the armhole to its old shape, as necessary. Then restitch the side seams and replace the sleeves.

Custom-Fit Pants

Taking in or letting out a pair of pants can make all the difference in the fit, and you don't need a tailor to do the job. Use this technique on men's pants and some women's pants. **Tools:** seam ripper, scissors, fabric marker or pencil, straight pins, needle, sewing machine. **Materials:** pants, thread. **Time:** ½ to 1 hour.

Men's pants—and sometimes women's—are designed to be adjusted at the center back seam, and can be taken in or let out 1 inch or more without affecting the fit elsewhere. Have the wearer try the pants on to see how much adjustment is needed, and esti-mate the work you'll have to do.

If there's a belt loop at the top of the center back seam, carefully remove it with a seam ripper. With the seam ripper, remove the stitching from the waistband facing for 2 or 3 inches on each side of the seam. Then remove the stitching from the seam, being careful not to damage the fabric. Open the seam with the seam ripper, almost down to the crotch.

On the inside of the pants, mark a line on each side of the pants where you estimate the new seam should be, either farther into the pieces of fabric or closer to their cut edges. Mark the lines with a fabric marker or a pencil. Starting at the top of the seam, draw a smooth, gradual curve on each piece of fabric, tapering gradually to blend into the old seam line at the bottom. Don't curve the new seam sharply or the new seam won't fit properly.

Pin the seam together along the new seam lines and then baste it together and remove the pins. Have the wearer try the pants on again to make sure the pants fit correctly. If the seat of the pants is baggy, open the inseams of the pants legs, from the crotch down 10 or 12 inches. Make a new seam line along each inseam to narrow the back of the leg slightly; taper the new seam line into the old one. Pin, baste, and have the wearer try the pants on; readjust as necessary until you get a good fit.

If you opened the inseams of the pants legs, stitch the new inseams, tapering the new seam line into the old one on each leg. Stitch the new seam line at the back of each leg to the old seam line at the front of the leg. Trim away excess fabric.

When no further adjustments are necessary, stitch the crotch seam with a sewing machine. In the seat area, stretch the seam a little as you sew; or, if your machine has a stretch stitch, use it in this area. Make a second row of machine stitching ⅛ inch closer to the cut edges of the seam, to reinforce it. Backstitch at the beginning and the end of each line of stitching. If you're taking the pants in, trim excess fabric after stitching.

Finally, adjust the waistband to match the new back seam. Open the back seam on the waistband and either let out the fabric or take in the same amount you took in from the back pants seam. Stitch the new waistband seam closed. Turn the waistband down and smooth it back over the back of the pants and the adjusted seam; stitch it into place the way it was stitched before. If you removed the back belt loop, replace the loop; sew it on the same way it was attached before.

Put In a Hem

Putting in a hem is no problem with fusible web, a lightweight iron-in mending and interfacing material. **Tools:** steam iron, pressing cloth or handkerchief, scissors, straight pins. **Materials:** fusible web (available in precut strips in sewing stores or sewing departments), in the width desired. **Time:** about 1 hour.

Before you start, make sure the fabric can stand up to the heat needed to set the fusible web. Set the iron to the temperature specified on the fusible web package. Turn the garment inside out and fold a seam edge out flat from the body of the garment so that the iron will touch only the seam allowance, not the garment itself. Using a pressing cloth or clean handkerchief, press as directed on the package. If the fabric puckers, the new hem cannot be put in with fusible web; otherwise, go ahead.

Rip out the old hem, cutting the thread at short intervals and being careful not to pull the threads of the fabric. Remove the bits of cut thread left from the old hem. Turn the fabric up to the proper length, keeping the hem width even, and pin the hem into place with straight pins. Press, using steam, to remove the old hem crease and keep the new hem evenly turned up and in place. Remove the straight pins. If you're letting the old hem down, you may have to dampen the old hem fold with white vinegar to remove the

crease, since this part of the fabric will now be visible on the right side of the garment.

Trim any excess fabric, leaving a hem about 1 to 2 inches wide for skirts or jackets, about ½ to 1 inch for sleeves or pants. Press the hem again all around, making sure it is smooth and even.

Cut a length of fusible web strip as long as the hem measures around the garment. Place the web between the hem and the garment fabric, sliding it under the turned-in edge.

Following the directions on the package, fuse the web in place, pressing firmly with the steam iron to melt the web's adhesive and bond it completely to both fabric surfaces. Use a pressing cloth between the garment and the iron, and do *not* touch the web directly with the iron. If you do get glue from the web on the sole plate of the iron, it can be removed after the iron cools completely, with a dry plastic dish scrubber.

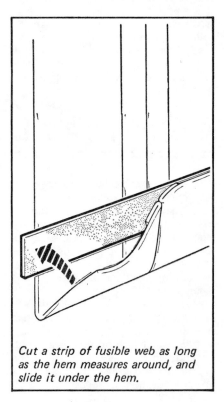

Cut a strip of fusible web as long as the hem measures around, and slide it under the hem.

Make Fashion Scarves

The right scarf can dress an outfit up or down, emphasize color, add texture contrast, pull a look together or make a whole new look. Good scarves can be prohibitively expensive, but it couldn't be easier to make your own. **Tools:** measuring tape, seam ripper, steam iron and ironing board, straightedge, pencil or fabric marker, sharp scissors, fine straight pins, sewing machine, needle. **Materials:** fabric, thread, fringe or trim as desired. **Time:** ½ to 2 hours.

Fabric for scarves should have just enough body and resilience to tie well and drape gracefully; natural fabrics are more comfortable than synthetics. Silk, the obvious choice, can be expensive, but a search through the remnant table may turn up just the right thing. Lightweight cottons are perfect scarves to wear with jeans and cotton shirts. For a square scarf, buy a piece of fabric at least 13 inches square, and preferably 18 inches or larger. For an oblong scarf, you'll need a piece of fabric at least 9 × 36 inches. A ½-yard piece of 36-inch-wide fabric will make two 18-inch-square or two 9 × 36-inch oblong scarves.

Because a scarf requires so little material, you may be able to salvage fabric from old clothes. Take a good look at your wardrobe, or investigate thrift shops. An old silk dress or blouse, or a chiffon or satin evening gown, may provide enough material for several scarves. Rip seams carefully to free the fabric, and make sure it's clean and pressed.

To make the scarf, spread the fabric wrong side up on a flat work surface. With a straightedge and a pencil or fabric marker, outline the scarf on the back of the fabric, about ½ inch larger on each side than you want the finished scarf to be.

With a sewing machine or, if necessary, by hand, make a line of straight stitching all around on the outline marked on the fabric. Use a new needle of the correct size for the fabric; consult your sewing machine instruction book to determine needle size and type.

Cut the scarf out about 1/16 inch outside the line of stitching. Roll the stitched edges under twice to form a narrow hem; pin the hem in place with fine straight pins, or, if desired, baste it in place.

For the most professional-looking edge, stitch the rolled hem by hand, using a careful hemstitch to catch the rolled-under hem to the scarf. Don't pull the thread too tight or the hem will pucker. Be careful to fold the corners flat. If you don't mind whether the hem shows, stitch hems on heavier fabrics by machine; be careful not to pucker the corners.

An alternative edge finish, especially for heavier fabrics, is machine zigzag stitching. For a zigzag-finished scarf, outline the scarf to its desired finished size, not ½ inch larger. Make a line of straight stitching around the marked outline. Cut the scarf out about 1/16 inch outside the stitching.

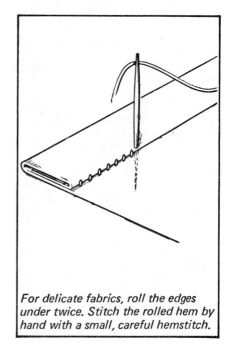

For delicate fabrics, roll the edges under twice. Stitch the rolled hem by hand with a small, careful hemstitch.

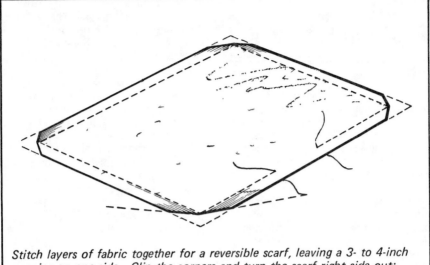

Stitch layers of fabric together for a reversible scarf, leaving a 3- to 4-inch opening on one side. Clip the corners and turn the scarf right side out; blindstitch the opening.

Set the machine to make a close-set zigzag stitch (about ⅛ inch wide or less) and zigzag around the edge over the line of straight stitching. Start and end along a side or end, not at a corner. Before you stitch the scarf, experiment with a scrap piece of fabric to see if it has a tendency to stretch or pucker. Be sure to use the proper size and type of needle.

Two-layer scarves. If the fabric is very lightweight or if you want a warm scarf, make the scarf from two layers of fabric. Use two pieces of the same fabric, or join complementary or contrasting pieces to make a reversible scarf; back lacy fabric with a solid-color sheer, or tweed with silk. Measure, mark, and cut the two pieces of fabric ½ inch larger than desired on all sides. Place the two pieces on a flat surface, right sides together, and pin them to hold them in place.

Sew a ½-inch seam all around the pinned edges, leaving a 3- to 4-inch opening on one side. Clip the corners; then turn the scarf right side out and press the seams flat. Blindstitch the opening and clip any remaining threads. If desired, add fringe or other trim.

Maintain Your Clothes

Good clothes are an investment, and a big one—give them regular care for the maximum return. **Tools:** vacuum cleaner, washing machine and dryer, window screen or flat surface, steam iron, clothes brush, sewing tools. **Materials:** selection of hangers, garment bags, and storage boxes; shelf paper, soap or sachet, moth spray, tissue paper, mending supplies, accessory items as desired, laundry detergent, mild fabric detergent, fabric softener, towels. **Time:** regular care, about 1 hour weekly; additional time as required for mending and storing.

Closets and drawers. Overcrowding and careless handling are hard on clothes; assess your closet and drawer space and make the most of it. Make sure you have adequate and suitable hangers for all your clothes; use padded hangers or smooth wood or plastic hangers instead of wire ones. Hang jackets and coats on hangers curved to fit their shoulders. To conserve space, use multiple hangers for pants, blouses or shirts, and skirts; use special tie, belt, stole, and suit hangers as required. Buy a few hangers at a time until you have a properly equipped closet.

Store fine knits, scarves, and delicate fabrics in drawers, folded flat; store sweaters folded flat in a chest or in drawers or sweater boxes. Keep shoes clean and polished, and store them in a shoe bag or chest. Line the drawers with clean shelf paper and add a bar of soap or a sachet for a fresh scent. Once a year, remove everything from every drawer and closet and vacuum thoroughly; reline the drawers with clean paper. Spray closets and drawers with moth spray, if necessary, before replacing the clothes.

Cleaning. Read the manufacturers' care labels in your clothes and follow their instructions; wash clothes or have them professionally dry cleaned as required. Machine washing and drying is adequate for most clothes, but it's worth the extra time to wash delicate clothes by hand. Use a mild fabric detergent, and follow the manufacturer's instructions; squeeze suds gently through the fabric, without wringing or twisting. Blot or roll in a clean towel and hang on a plastic hanger to dry. In half an hour, smooth the material out and shake out as many wrinkles as possible. Fabric softener in the final rinse, for both hand and machine washing, also helps eliminate wrinkles.

Dry sweaters and soft, stretchy knits flat. Blot the wet garment with a towel; then spread it flat on a clean towel to dry. For the quickest drying, use a clean window screen; set the screen across a tub, cover it with a towel, and spread the wet garment on it. If you don't have a screen, use any flat surface—a table, a chest-type freezer, whatever. Cover a wood table with a plastic tablecloth to protect it.

Mending, storing, and updating. It's easy to ignore small problems until everything you own needs mending.

The only real solution is discipline. Take out each item that needs mending—a gap under the sleeve, a loose hem, a missing button—*and mend it,* or have it mended. Discard anything that's too worn or damaged to be salvageable; either add it to your rag supply or give it to a charitable old-clothes organization.

When the seasons change, go through your clothes and decide what to do with each garment. If you haven't worn something for a whole season, decide whether it's worth rehabilitating or whether it's ready to move on to a new owner before it's completely out of style; don't forget donations to charities are tax-deductible. Mend anything that needs mending, and wash or clean everything—dirt becomes increasingly hard to remove, and attracts moths and silverfish. If you expect to change the length of a light-colored garment, clip out the hem stitching and brush any dirt out of the fold before it's washed or cleaned. Even with dry cleaning, a dull, slightly dirty line tends to form at the bottom edge of the hem.

As you go through your clothes, assess them for up-to-date styling. It's often possible to revive a garment with new buttons, a new belt, suede patches, binding, or one good accent accessory. Keep a list of what you need, and buy on sale if you can.

Store clothes carefully, on hangers and in garment bags; to prevent creasing, stuff the shoulders and sleeves with tissue paper. Store soft fabrics flat; use long underbed chests or sweater boxes. Don't store clothes in a hot attic; dryness ages fabrics. Don't store them anywhere dampness is a problem. The care you give your clothes will pay off in years of wear.

Make Your Own Sachets

Aromatic sachets are charming, old-fashioned, and expensive. Use this simple substitute to give your drawers and closets any scent you like. **Equipment:** measuring cup, mixing bowl, measuring spoons, mixing spoon, funnel, small vials. **Ingredients:** plaster of paris, water, cologne or toilet water. **Yield:** enough for several sachets.

Measure ¼ cup plaster of paris into a mixing bowl. Add 1 to 2 tablespoons of water, and stir to a creamy consistency. Pour the mixture into small vials, filling each vial half full. Let the plaster of paris harden overnight.

When the plaster has hardened, fill each vial with your favorite cologne or toilet water; let the vials stand until the liquid is absorbed by the plaster. Set the vials, uncovered, in drawers and closets as desired. When the scent fades, recharge the vials with more cologne or toilet water.

Rejuvenate Worn Clothes

Stains and tears in clothes don't have to mean the end of their utility as school or work clothes—cover the damage with embroidery, pockets, or appliqués for clothes that look and feel like new. **Tools:** sewing scissors, embroidery needle, sewing needles and/or sewing machine, steam iron and ironing board, straight pins, pencil, seam ripper, patterns as needed. **Materials:** embroidery thread, matching or contrasting thread; embroidered ribbon, tape, or braid; iron-on patches, embroidered appliqué motifs, matching or coordinating fabrics, paper, suede-cloth. **Time:** 15 minutes to 2 hours, depending on effect desired.

For small tears and not-too-bad stains, the simplest solution is embroidery—a flower, a sun, a star, or any bright design will cover the damage. An equally simple coverup is an edging of embroidered ribbon or tape; you can use braid or ribbon to face a torn pocket, reinforce a raveled-out seam, or disguise a stained hem. For more extensive damage, use appliqués or pockets for patches that are not just fill-ins but imaginative decorating tools.

Before you can decorate to hide the damage, make the necessary structural repairs. If the fabric is torn, stitch back and forth across the tear on a sewing machine or with a running stitch by hand, to hold the torn edges together. Steam-press the mended spot so that it lies flat.

Appliqués. Sewing stores, department store notions departments, and even grocery stores sell iron-on patches and small embroidered appliqué motifs. The iron-ons are a good fast answer for children's play clothes—cut the patch to the shape you want and press it on as directed. For a more finished look on school or work clothes, use individual appliqués; arrange several appliqués to create a new design instead of using one or two for an obvious spot coverup.

Position the embroidered appliqués as desired and pin them into place. Because the edges are prefinished, you can stitch the appliqués on with a straight or a zigzag machine stitch or a backstitch by hand; make firm, close stitches with matching or contrasting thread. If you have a zigzag sewing machine, use the basic stitch set at about two-thirds of its widest width and 20 stitches to the inch or more for an extra-smooth finish. Stitch all around the edge of each appliqué motif.

If you have fabric scraps on hand, you can make your own appliqués. Stars, geometric shapes, and flowers are easy to draw, or look for other simple designs. Make a paper pattern of the design and draw around it lightly on the surface of the fabric; allow a ¼-inch seam allowance beyond the line. Turn the seam allowance under and press it down all around the appliqué, clipping curves and corners as necessary so that the entire pattern lies flat.

Pin the appliqué into place over the damaged spot or stain; baste it in place if desired. Stitch the appliqué all around with a close machine zigzag stitch, as above, or work a fine, close buttonhole stitch by hand.

Pockets, patches, and edging.
Patch pockets in a contrasting fabric add a bright touch and cover a damaged spot or stain at the same time—gingham on denim, solid color on print, or whatever appeals. If you need a pocket to cover a spot on one side of a garment, make it a very bold color or size; or, for a more formal effect, add a matching pocket to the other side to balance the design.

Use a pocket pattern from any commercial pattern for a similar garment, or copy a pocket from another garment. Cut the pockets, hem the top edges, and press the edges under all around. If you're using two pockets, measure carefully to place them evenly on the garment. Pin and baste them into place; use the pattern directions if you've never made a pocket before. Edge-stitch around the pockets with a straight machine stitch or hand backstitch.

A good jacket or sweater lasts for years, but the elbows always go first. You can spruce up a jacket with worn elbows or cuffs, or cover a cigarette burn at the hip, with ¼ yard of suede-cloth—it's worth paying for the better-quality suede-cloth. If the jacket originally had patch pockets, remove them carefully with a seam ripper. Use the old pockets as a pattern and cut new suede-cloth pockets to the finished size; leave a hem allowance for the top of the pocket only. If you're adding patch pockets to a plain hipline or over welted pockets, refer to a pattern of a similar design. Like real suede, suede-cloth needs no seam allowance on the edges, but you should hem the top edge of the pockets.

To make elbow patches, cut rectangles of suede-cloth 5 inches by 6 inches, and round off or right-angle the corners as desired. On each sleeve, carefully undo the stitching to detach the sleeve lining at the lower edge of the cuff. Slip one hand between the sleeve and the lining, pull the lining up out of the way, and pin the patch into place on the sleeve, attaching it only to the outer fabric. Make sure you don't catch the lining. With a backstitch or a buttonhole stitch, sew around the patch,

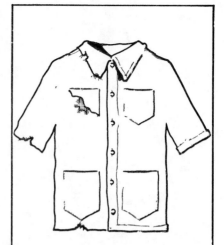

Cover worn edges and hems with tape or ribbon edging; cover extensive damage with patch pockets or appliqués.

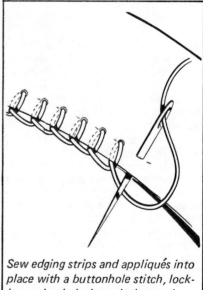

Sew edging strips and appliqués into place with a buttonhole stitch, locking each stitch through the one before it.

securing it only to the outer fabric. When the patch is securely attached, replace the lining and hand-stitch it back around the inside of the sleeve.

To refinish the worn edge of a jacket

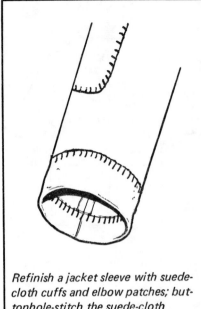

Refinish a jacket sleeve with suede-cloth cuffs and elbow patches; buttonhole-stitch the suede-cloth around the edges.

Fix a Broken Zipper

A garment with a broken zipper is unwearable—new or old, shabby or not. Instead of abandoning it, repair the zipper, or replace it with a new one. **Tools:** needle, sewing scissors, needle-nosed pliers, seam ripper, straight pins, sewing machine. **Materials:** thread, small safety pin or paper clip, old zipper of similar size; replacement zipper, if required. **Time:** 5 to 15 minutes for repair; ½ to 1 hour for replacement.

Before you decide to replace a zipper, examine it carefully to see if you can repair it. If a tooth is missing in the upper two-thirds of the zipper's tracks, the zipper should be replaced. If a tooth

sleeve, measure the distance around the cuff and cut a strip of suede-cloth about 2 inches wide and slightly longer than the measured distance. Turn the sleeve inside out and pin one edge of the strip to the turned-up sleeve hem, ¾ inch up from the bottom of the sleeve, starting and finishing at the underarm seam. The remaining width of the strip should be hanging down over the edge of the sleeve. Turn the ends of the strip to the outside of the sleeve and stitch a seam that matches the sleeve seam line to hold the ends of the strip together, making a suede-cloth ring around the inside of the sleeve.

Attach the pinned edge of the strip to the inside hem of the sleeve with a backstitch or a buttonhole stitch. Turn the sleeve right side out and fold the other edge of the strip up over the worn edge onto the outside of the sleeve; attach it with the same stitch used on the other edge. If the sleeve hem is very shallow, you may find it easier to release the lining first and pull it back out of the way, then restitch it over the sewn-in cuff edging.

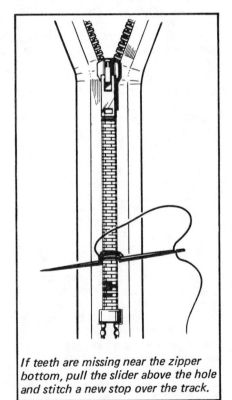

If teeth are missing near the zipper bottom, pull the slider above the hole and stitch a new stop over the track.

is missing near the bottom of one of the tracks, zip up the zipper so that the slider is above the damage. Thread a needle and make several stitches around both rows of teeth, just above the missing tooth, to make a new stop for the slider. Stitch over the new stop several times to make sure it's firm.

If the problem is a missing pull tab, check to see whether the slider has a hole where the pull tab was attached. If so, slip a tiny safety pin or paper clip through the hole to serve as a substitute. If there is no hole, try to salvage a clamp-on pull tab from an old zipper of a similar size; put the tab onto the slider with a needle-nosed pliers.

If the slider is off the track on a metal zipper, carefully rip out the stitching around the lower ends of the zipper tapes. Pry off the metal stop at the bottom of the zipper, being careful not to tear the tapes. Remove the zipper foot entirely.

Guide the track tapes into the grooves of the slider, inserting them into the top and pushing them through the slider to the bottom; use a pin if necessary to work the track tapes through. Pull the tapes carefully so that the slider is evenly seated on the tracks.

When both tapes have been threaded through the slider, carefully pull the slider up until the locked track teeth appear at the bottom. Make sure the slider is evenly seated on the tracks, or the zipper won't close evenly at the top. Sew a new stop at the bottom of the tracks with needle and thread, and repair the stitching that holds the zipper in the garment.

If the zipper is beyond repair, replace it with a new one of the same length. Buy a zipper in a matching color, and be sure it's the right weight and kind for the garment.

With a seam ripper, carefully remove the stitching holding the old zipper in place. As you work, note how the old zipper was put in, and in what order the various lines of stitching were made; pants zippers especially may be put in with several lines of stitching. If a waistband is involved, remove no more stitching than necessary to free the upper ends of the zipper. Remove the old zipper and pull out all loose thread ends.

Following the directions on the zipper package, pin the new zipper into place and stitch it the same way the old zipper was stitched; use a sewing machine with a zipper foot. Make the final topstitching on the outside of the garment, by hand or by machine.

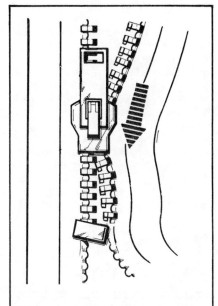

When a metal zipper separates, pry off the stop and remove the slider; then guide the tracks in and stitch a new stop.

Mend Rips and Tears

Often a towel, a sheet, or a garment can be saved from discard by a skillful mending job, and usually the job requires only a few minutes' work. **Tools:** steam iron and ironing board, sharp scissors, sewing needles in a variety of sizes, sewing machine, tailors' chalk or pencil, sponge. **Materials:** iron-on mending tape, thread in appropriate colors, patching materials, heavy brown paper, tissue paper. **Time:** 15 minutes or more, depending on damage.

The mending technique you use should depend on whether it matters how much the mend shows, and whether the piece is worth spending much time on. For mending denim pants, children's play clothes, everyday sheets, and so on, the easiest and most effective method is making the repair with iron-on mending tape, or with the sewing machine's straight or zigzag stitch.

Most tears are either straight or L-shaped, because they tend to follow the grain of the fabric. If the fabric is medium-weight or slightly heavier, use mending tape. Cut a piece of tape about 1 inch wider and 1 inch longer than the tear, and round off the corners.

Lay the piece to be mended on an ironing board so that the torn portion faces up, wrong side up. If it's hard to lay out the item so that the edges of the tear stay together, make a large temporary patch of either fabric or heavy brown paper, and baste it lightly to the side of the fabric *opposite* the side where the mending tape will be attached. Be sure the basting threads are far enough from the tear so they won't be caught by the mending tape.

Lay the mending tape, adhesive side down, over the tear. Position it carefully; then use tailors' chalk or a pencil to mark around it at several points. Take it off temporarily and preheat the torn area by ironing it briefly.

Replace the mending tape over the tear inside your markings. Iron it down according to the directions on the mending tape package; make sure the tape is completely bonded to the fabric. Let the patch cool completely before moving the mended item. If you used a basted fabric or paper holding patch, remove it when the item is completely cool.

Sometimes the edges of a tear can't be brought together neatly because some of the fabric is missing or is so badly damaged it has to be cut away. When this happens, use iron-on or fabric patches, or hide the damage with decorative appliqués or patch pockets. Zigzag machine stitching is ideal for either patching or appliqué.

When a lightweight fabric needs mending—a torn curtain, for example —iron-on tape is sometimes too stiff or heavy. For such light fabrics, hand or machine stitching makes a more flexible mend.

To repair a straight or L-shaped tear by machine, set the machine for a straight stitch, with about 10 to 12 stitches to the inch. Lay the piece under the presser foot so that the tear runs crosswise in front of you and the left-hand end of it is ½ inch to the right of the presser foot. Put the needle and the presser foot down on the fabric and sew in a zigzag pattern back and forth across the tear, switching the machine from forward to reverse and back again, pull the fabric gently with your left hand to keep it moving slowly from right to left under the presser foot. The mended tear should be held together by even zigzag rows of straight stitching, making a very strong but usually conspicuous mend.

Where the mend can't be obvious, hand stitching can be made much less visible. Use a fine sewing needle (size 8 or 9) and fine thread; make tiny stitches back and forth across the tear. If the tear is very long or the fabric difficult to hold, you may need to keep the edges in place while you work by basting the fabric to a piece of white tissue paper. Work back-and-forth rows of stitching through both fabric and tissue; sponge the tissue lightly to soften it, if necessary. Then carefully tear the paper away and remove the basting thread.

Remove Paint Stains

Removing dried paint from your clothes is a tough job, but it can be done. This mixture can handle all but the worst stains. **Equipment:** measuring cup, glass or stainless steel bowl, stir stick. **Ingredients:** ammonia, turpentine. **Yield:** enough for one garment.

Measure ½ cup of ammonia and ¼ cup of turpentine into a glass or stainless steel bowl; mix thoroughly. Soak the paint-stained garment in the mixture for at least 20 minutes; for stubborn stains, soak as long as necessary. After soaking, wash the garment thoroughly with soap and water; launder as usual.

Remove Mildew Stains

To remove unsightly mildew stains from canvas tents, vinyl boat cushions, bathroom tile grout, and other mildew-prone surfaces, use this simple formula. **Equipment:** measuring spoons, measuring cup, pint bottle with cap. **Ingredients:** ammonia, hydrogen peroxide, distilled water. **Yield:** about 1 cup.

Mix 1 teaspoon of ammonia, ¼ cup of fresh hydrogen peroxide, and ¾ cup of distilled water in a pint bottle. Cap the bottle tightly and shake it to mix the contents.

To use, soak the mildew stain with the mixture for about 15 minutes, and rinse with water. *Caution: Hydrogen peroxide may bleach some materials, test a small area for colorfastness before using.*

Mend a Raveling Sweater

Hand-knit sweaters and most sweaters made to look hand-knit can be mended quite smoothly when they've been badly frayed or snagged. Many good sweaters are even sold with a bobbin of yarn attached. Test for needle sizes by slipping needles into the existing stitches—the body is usually knitted

on a needle that is a size or two larger than the cuffs. **Tools:** yarn needle, straight knitting needles sized for the sweater cuffs or body, sharp scissors, crochet hook sized for the yarn. **Materials:** matching yarn of the same color, weight, and type as that used for the sweater (acrylic, wool, etc.). **Time:** 1 to 2 hours.

When one thread in a sweater is snagged and broken, a horizontal tear opens between two rows of stitches. The tear can be rewoven in a stitch that looks almost like the original. Work with the right side of the sweater toward you, from the right end of the tear. With the point of a yarn needle, pick the two loose ends of broken yarn out far enough back to give you a length that can be tied to a new piece of yarn. Cut a piece of matching yarn about 1 foot long and tie one end of it to the loose end of the old yarn at the right end of the tear. Tie a small knot on the wrong side of the sweater, leaving 1½ inches of yarn on the end to be woven in on the wrong side after the repair is made. Thread the end of the new piece of yarn into the yarn needle.

Starting from the knot, bring the needle up through the first loop or stitch on the bottom edge of the tear, from the wrong side to the right side. Carry the needle across the opening and up through the opposite stitch on the top edge of the tear, from right side to wrong side. Bring the needle from the wrong side to the right side through the next stitch on the top of the tear, then down across to the first stitch on the bottom edge of the tear, from right side to wrong side, so there's one up and one down strand in each loop. Continue, forming a row of loops like the knitted stitches between the two rows of stitches that form the edges of the tear. After the last stitch at the left of the tear is woven, tie the end of the mending yarn to the loose end of the sweater yarn, on the wrong side of the sweater. With a crochet hook, weave the loose ends into stitches on the wrong side of the sweater.

If the neckband or the cuffs are frayed or torn—sometimes caused by

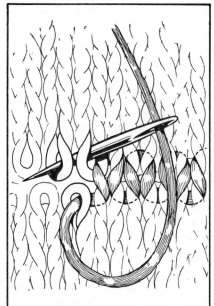

To mend a horizontal ravel, weave the edges together; loop the yarn through each knitted stitch.

the ribbing doesn't break again; rebind carefully. The band will probably be two or three rows shorter than it originally was.

If the old yarn is too badly damaged to use, or if matching yarn of the same color, weight, and type (acrylic, wool, etc.) is readily available, reknit the cuff or neckband with new yarn, following the procedure above.

Lengthen or Shorten Sweater Sleeves

The cuffs of hand-knit sweaters and most sweaters made to look like hand-knits can be raveled and reknitted to the proper length. Test for needle sizes by slipping needles into the existing stitches—the body is usually knitted on a needle that is a size or two larger than the cuffs. **Tools:** sharp scissors, straight knitting needles sized for the sweater cuffs and body, yarn needle, steam iron and ironing board, pressing cloth. **Materials:** matching or coordinating yarn for lengthening, of the same weight and type as that used for the sweater (acrylic, wool, etc.). **Time:** about 2 to 3 hours.

With a sharp scissors, clip the stitching that holds the sleeve's underarm seam together, from the bottom of the cuff well up into the sleeve. Be careful not to cut into the knitting. Smooth the cuff out to lie flat. Clip the yarn in the bind-off or cast-on row at the lower edge of the cuff and pull the end of the yarn to ravel the cuff, rolling the yarn into a ball as you go.

To shorten the sleeve, ravel the desired length into the sleeve above the cuff—ravel 1 inch into the sleeve for every 1 inch you want to shorten it. With the raveled edge upward and the right side of the sleeve toward you, pull the yarn to ravel it exactly to the right-hand end of the last row. With a straight knitting needle sized for the sweater cuffs,

binding off too tightly—clip the stitching that holds the cuff or band seam, from the outside edge well past the cuff or band. Be careful not to cut into the knitting. Smooth the ribbed part flat and clip the yarn in the bind-off or cast-on row at its edge; pull the edge of the yarn to ravel the ribbing. Ravel the entire ribbed band, rolling the yarn as you go; tie broken ends of yarn together as you go.

With the raveled edge and the right side of the ribbing toward you, pull the yarn to ravel it exactly to the right-hand end of the last row. With a straight knitting needle sized for the sweater cuffs, pick up the loose stitches from the left end, slipping the point of the needle into the right side of each stitch so that all stitches lie evenly in the same direction.

Reknit the cuff or neckband with the raveled yarn, using the same ribbing pattern as the old cuff or band; when you come to a place where the broken ends of yarn were tied together, bring the knot to the wrong side of the sweater as you reknit. Leave enough yarn to bind off loosely so the edge of

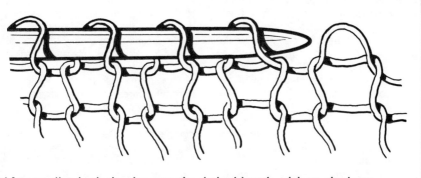

After raveling back the sleeve to the desired length, pick up the loose stitches from left to right; make sure the stitches lie evenly on the needle. Reknit the cuffs with the raveled-back yarn, in the original ribbing pattern, and bind them off.

pick up the loose stitches from the left end. Slip the point of the needle into the right side of each stitch so that all stitches lie evenly in the same direction on the needle, and no stitches are twisted.

Use the raveled yarn to reknit the cuff in the original ribbing pattern. When the cuff is the same length that it was at first, bind it off in a ribbing pattern. Resew the underarm seam, using the leftover raveled yarn and a yarn needle. After reknitting with raveled yarn, steam the area with a steam iron and a pressing cloth to blend the reknitted part into the rest of the sweater.

Lengthening poses more of a problem unless you knitted the sweater yourself and you still have leftover yarn. If not, try to get the same weight and type of yarn (acrylic, wool, etc.) in a matching or nicely coordinating or contrasting color. Clip the sleeve seam and ravel the cuff from the bottom as above. At the end of the cuff, pick up the sleeve stitches on a straight knitting needle sized for the sweater body, and reknit the sleeve as long as you want it with the yarn raveled from the cuff. Use the new yarn for the ribbed cuff so that if the match isn't exact, it won't be as obvious.

If you're using yarn that's a coordinating or contrasting color, make it work for you decoratively. Ravel the

sleeve back a little further than necessary and knit several bands or horizontal stripes of the new color; or knit in any decorative pattern you like. You may want to lengthen the body of the sweater the same way; if you do this, knit in matching stripes on the body. Bind the new cuff off in a ribbing pattern and resew the underarm seam; press with a steam iron and a pressing cloth.

Rehabilitate Thrift-Store Clothes

It's always fun to get a bargain, whether it's a designer suit from a rummage sale or something from the "final marked down" rack. Make it live up to its name with a little basic rehabilitation. **Tools:** sharp scissors, sewing needle, seam ripper, steam iron and ironing board, straight pins, sewing machine. **Materials:** thread, buttons, seam binding, bias tape, grosgrain ribbon; accessory belt, scarf or collar; trimmings as desired. **Time:** 15 minutes to a few hours, depending on project.

The first step is to make the garment fit properly. Shorten or lengthen hems to fit; take in or let out the waist; make any repairs necessary. Use a basic sewing book for specific instructions.

If long sleeves are too short or the cuffs are damaged, convert them to short sleeves, either the roll-up type or plain short hemmed sleeves. Cut the sleeves off just above the cuff opening, hem them narrowly, and roll them up if desired. Wear shortened-sleeve garments layered over a shirt or over a light sweater if the fabric is more suited to cool weather.

Major surgery usually isn't worthwhile, especially on tailored pants or jackets. But it may be worth your time to remake the skirt of a very good suit. Skirts usually get harder wear than jackets; if the skirt fabric looks more worn or shabby than the jacket, take a good look at the wrong side—many woolens are completely reversible. If the fabric is reversible. pick out all the seams and darts with a seam ripper and steam-press the fabric, especially along the seams and hems. Remake the skirt inside out, with the less worn side of the fabric showing; fit it exactly to your size.

If the waistband of a good skirt is very worn or it's too small to let out to fit, take the band off completely, and adjust the darts or gathers that control the waist size. Make a new band of a double layer of 1-inch-wide grosgrain ribbon. Slip the skirt fabric between the layers of the ribbon to form a new waistband.

Even clothes that don't need altering can usually use some help. The usual problem with bargain clothes is the buttons or the belt—they're missing, they've worn out or changed color, or they were a bad choice originally. Buttons can rarely be matched; if even one is missing, cut them all off and replace them. Take the garment with you when you buy new buttons so you can see the finished effect. If the belt is lost or worn out, you'll probably have to get a coordinating or contrasting one rather than a perfect match. Make it work with another accessory of the same color—a scarf, a pin, whatever you like. Take the garment with you when you shop.

If a collar is wilted-looking or a neckline unbecoming, add a scarf, a white or neutral embroidered or lace collar, a ruffle; or cut the collar off. Bind the neckline with grosgrain ribbon, seam binding, bias tape, or any trim you like, or use the old collar as a pattern to cut a new one, with any fabric or trim you like.

The trimmings and decorations on bargain clothes may not suit your taste. Look at them carefully in a good light to see whether they can be removed completely without leaving a mark. If a braid or edge trimming doesn't seem up to the quality of the rest of the garment, examine it well to see if it can be removed; if so, remove it carefully and replace it with a better braid or edging, or one in a color more to your liking. Sew the new trimmings on by hand.

Reuse Old Clothes Creatively

Old clothes, like old friends, grow more comfortable with age; don't consign them to the ragbag too hastily. With a little imagination, you can rejuvenate even the most elderly members of your wardrobe. **Tools:** scissors, steam iron and ironing board, seam ripper, tape measure, straight pins, sewing needle, sewing machine, tailors' chalk or pencil, patterns. **Materials:** thread; trim, buttons, fasteners, or fabric, as required. **Time:** ½ hour to several hours, depending on changes made.

The cutoff. After the simple painting—or gardening—clothes syndrome, the easiest form of reuse is the cutoff. This includes, of course, making shorts from pants, or shortening sleeves, but it can be carried further. If the sleeves of a shirt or dress are too tight, or it's too tight across the back, remove the sleeves; bind the armholes or make a facing for them. If a shirtwaist dress is too tight in the hips, cut it off to make a shirt. Use a seam ripper to open the seams, and leave a slit at each side;

tack the top of each slit for added strength. For a cutoff in reverse, use a very full long skirt or a long full-skirted dress to make a sundress. Remove the skirt from the waistband or dress, and add a bodice band and strips; if desired, sash in the fullness with a ribbon or other belt.

The disguise. A classic form of reuse is simply transference. One of the best candidates for disguise is a large white or pastel shirt. To turn an old shirt into a peasant-type coverup, just add trim—stitch embroidered braid, ribbon, or rickrack in rows down each side of the front placket, around the sleeves near the elbow, or across the shoulder and all down the sleeves. Measure to see how much trim you'll need; pin it into place and stitch it on by hand or machine, turning all raw ends under.

Another aspect of the disguise is literally that. Decorate old clothes to hide worn spots and stains; cover holes with pockets or appliqués. To cover an old hemline on a coat and give it a little new excitement, add a band of fake fur at the collar, around the hem, and over each cuff; wear the coat with a fake fur boa. Follow the principle of disguise for any garment that's still structurally sound.

The alteration. If a jacket or shirt is too tight, you can often solve the problem with new fasteners. Cut off the buttons and hand-whip the buttonholes together. To replace them, buy matching or contrasting braid frogs; make sure they're suitable for the jacket. Pin the frogs into place over the closed buttonholes and the marks left by the buttons; blindstitch them all around by hand.

A variant on rehemming is the flounce. The flounce is obviously limited in application, but to lengthen a too-short summer skirt, it can be very effective. Take flounce material from another skirt, or even from old curtains or a dust ruffle. With lightweight flounce material, you can make flounced sleeves for a sleeveless blouse—worth a try if you're an experienced sewer.

The remake. If you've completely had it with a piece of clothing, try turning it into something else. At the conservative end of the scale, it's easy to make a skirt from a pair of jeans. If you have cutoff parts of other jeans, you can simply open the inseams of the jeans to the front zipper; restitch the loose material into a skirt, adding a long triangle of fabric if necessary to widen the front and back.

Or cut off the legs of a pair of very wide-legged jeans, and wear the tops as shorts; fray the edges or bind them with braid or other trim. Use the flaring pants legs to make a four-gore skirt. Rip out the hem and inseams, but leave the outer seams to become the hip seams of the skirt. Make a center front and a center back seam, joining the legs to form one tube.

Try the skirt on to fit the waist; tie a string around your waist, over the skirt, and pull the fullness in. When the skirt hangs properly, mark the string line with straight pins or tailors' chalk. Run a gathering thread on this line, and trim off the excess fabric to leave a ½-inch seam allowance. Install a 7- to 9-inch zipper from the top of the back seam, following the zipper manufacturer's instructions; use an embroidered ribbon, a strip of bandana print, or a piece of another old pair of jeans to make a waistband. Rehem the skirt.

If you have a very outdated dress, with a fitted bodice, long full sleeves, and a full skirt, you can remake it into a loose-fitting shirt. Carefully take the dress apart along the seams, keeping the sleeves and collar intact. Press out the skirt and use a favorite blouse or shirt pattern to cut a new body front and back from the old skirt. If the dress didn't have pockets or a collar, you can use the old bodice material to cut them. Put the shirt together with the new front and back, and rehem it.

A remake that takes almost no effort is the towel-and-washcloth one. Use small towels to make children's beach coverups. Sew the ends of two same-sized towels together for the outer one-third of the towel's width; the stitched ends become a shoulder seam.

Make loops from bias binding and sew on buttons to fasten the opposite shoulder; place them along the outer one-third of the towel's width. Sew 1-inch bias binding across the wrong side of each towel, at the waistline, to form casings, and thread a ribbon or a cable cord—at least twice the width of one towel—through the casings to make a belt.

Use leftover or mismatched towels or washcloths wherever an absorbent fabric is needed. To make a baby bib, pin and stitch double-fold bias tape around the edge of an old washcloth; turn the binding to the other side and stitch the binding closed. Cut two 12-inch lengths of bias tape and stitch each closed on the open side; attach one piece to each side of the neck opening to fasten the bib. For a handy beach pillow, make a pillow cover of two large washcloths or two small towels.

Salvage. At the end of the recycling line, you can often use total-loss clothes for other purposes. If you cut off straight-legged jeans, make stuff sacks from the leg sections. Leave all the seams intact; cut the sections into 12-inch pieces. For each stuff sack, turn a section inside out. With right sides together, stitch twice across one open edge to close the bag. Work two vertical buttonholes, ¾ inch long, on opposite sides of the bag, 1½ inches down from the raw edge. Fold the raw edge under ¼ to ½ inch and press; fold it under again 1 inch, press, and pin the hem into place. Stitch the hem close to the inside edge. To close the bag, cut two pieces of cable cord about 8 to 10 inches longer than the circumference of the bag; thread them into the hem casing through the buttonholes to make handles. Knot the ends of the cords together.

One strictly salvage project is rescuing parts of old clothes. Good buttons are the obvious thing to look for; you can often find worthwhile buttons on junk-store throwaways. Tatted or crocheted edgings often outlast the linens they were used on—remove them carefully, wash them with a mild bleach,

and use them to decorate blouses, children's clothes, or new linens. Save still-good motifs from worn-out crocheted bedspreads or tablecloths; use them as appliqués around a skirt hem, on a shawl, or on new linens.

Finally, there's the ultimate salvage operation. If the fabric of a full-cut garment is in good condition but the garment itself is hopeless, carefully take it apart. Clean or wash the fabric, press it, and cut a whole new garment from it; use any new pattern you like. Or, if you're short on material, cut a scarf or a shawl from the biggest piece of fabric; use the rest of the fabric for patchwork or a braided rug.

Slim a Wide Tie

Old super-wide ties are decidedly outdated, but they can be saved. To give an old tie new style, remodel it to the standard width. **Tools:** scissors, seam ripper, sewing needle, tailors' chalk or pencil, straightedge, steam iron and ironing board. **Materials:** thread. **Time:** about 1 hour.

The standard width for neckties is currently 3½ inches at the wide end; to

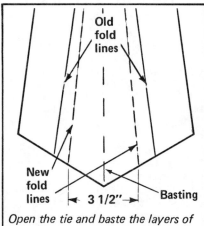

Open the tie and baste the layers of fabric together. Then measure the desired width and baste to mark the new fold lines.

be in style, a tie shouldn't vary from this standard more than ½ inch either way. To narrow a super-wide tie, recut it to the standard width.

First remove the label on the back of the tie. Carefully open the seam at the wide end of the tie to about half the length of the tie. Spread the tie open on a flat surface.

Inside the tie, a piece of lining is attached to each end; the wide end is lined for about 6 to 8 inches and the short end for about 4 inches. Inside the lining is a separate interlining that runs almost the entire length of the tie. All three layers of the tie must be adjusted.

Thread a needle with a contrasting thread and make large basting stitches down the center of the tie to hold the interlining in place temporarily. Turn the tie over. On the outside of the wide end of the tie, measure the width you want the tie to be. Mark this width on each side of the tie with a short length of basting thread; stitch only through the tie fabric, not into the lining.

Turn the wide end of the tie inside out, so that the lining and the end of the tie form a bag with the side seams on the outside. Lay the tie out flat again, with the interlining up and the inside-out lining underneath. With a long straight-edge and tailors' chalk or a pencil, mark a straight line along the length of the tie from each basted edge line, to mark the new width of the tie. Taper the line on each side of the tie to run from the basted edge line at the end to blend into the original fold line toward the middle of the tie. Most of this line will fall on the interlining.

Carefully cut the interlining along the marked lines to remove excess width; do *not* cut the tie fabric. Turn the end of the tie right side out, so that the lining is on the inside again.

To narrow the tie fabric, fold the long edges of the tie carefully over the narrowed interlining; fold from the basted mark on each side all along the edge of the interlining to the center of the tie. Be careful not to stretch the bias edges of the fabric. Press the edges carefully to crease the tie into its new width.

With the sides of the tie fabric folded over each other, mark both sides of the lining where the fabric sides meet at the middle of the tie. From these points, mark lines upward on the lining along the tie, about ⅛ inch out from the center of the tie, to indicate where the lining will be sewn to the narrowed tie fabric. Unfold the tie and hand-stitch the lining directly to the tie fabric along the marked lines, for the entire 6- to 8-inch length of the lining.

Lay the tie out flat. With a long straightedge, draw a line on each side of the tie fabric to mark the new edge, from ⅜ inch outside the new lining-fabric seam to meet the old fabric edge at the center of the tie. Carefully cut off the excess tie fabric along the marked lines.

To finish the tie, fold the sides over each other along the new edge creases. Leave the edge of the bottom side raw. On the overlapping side, turn the raw edge under about ½ inch, folding both fabric and lining from the end of the tie to the center. Taper the fold to match the old fold at the center of the tie. Carefully press the folded edge flat;

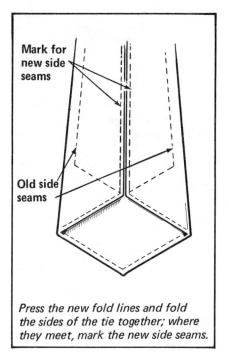

Mark for new side seams

Old side seams

Press the new fold lines and fold the sides of the tie together; where they meet, mark the new side seams.

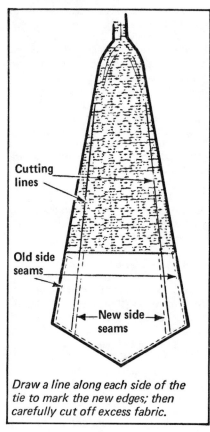

Cutting lines

Old side seams

New side seams

Draw a line along each side of the tie to mark the new edges; then carefully cut off excess fabric.

make sure you don't stretch the raw edge of the fabric.

Finally, fold the tie together again, with the pressed-under side folded over the raw edge of the other side. Blind-stitch the sides of the tie together along the middle of the tie, using fairly loose stitches; be careful not to stitch through to the front of the tie. Remove the basting threads and replace the label.

Make a Caftan

Most garment-making requires a commercial pattern, but it's easy to make a simple caftan. **Tools:** scissors, straight pins, tape measure, tailors' chalk or pencil, straightedge, dinner plate, sewing machine, steam iron and ironing board, sewing needle. **Materials:** fabric, thread, double-fold bias tape, trim or braid as desired. **Time:** 2 to 3 hours.

Fabric. For a caftan that will fit most sizes, buy 4⅛ yards of 36- to 45-inch-wide fabric. This pattern is wide enough for a 40-inch bust or chest measurement and long enough for a fairly tall person. A ½-inch seam allowance is used; hem lengths vary according to your height.

For a very small or very tall person, cut the pattern shorter or narrower. Cut each of the four main panels to measure one-fourth the required bust or chest measurement, plus 1 inch seam allowance and 1 inch fabric ease. For a 36-inch bust, for example, each panel should be 11 inches wide at the bust area.

Pattern. Before laying out the caftan, square off the ends of the fabric. Spread the fabric out on your work surface. Close to one end of the fabric, make a small cut into the selvage, and grasp one crosswise thread. Gently pull the thread to draw it right out of the fabric, across the entire fabric width. This will make a line across the fabric where the thread was; cut carefully along the line and discard the crooked end. Repeat to square the other end of the fabric.

Mark the pattern as illustrated in the cutting diagram. Fold the squared fabric in half crosswise, right sides together and selvages matching. Pin the selvage edges together every 12 inches. Measure 5 feet (60 inches) along the selvage from the cut ends of the fabric, and make a mark on the selvage with tailors' chalk or a pencil. With a straightedge, draw a line straight across the fabric, at right angles to the selvage, to 12 inches from the other selvage edge. This is the bottom edge of the caftan's back panels.

At the cut ends of the folded fabric, measure and mark 30 inches along the raw edge; from this point, measure and mark a line 12 inches into the fabric, parallel to the selvage. This is the edge

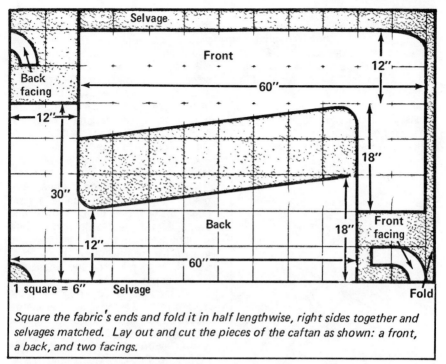

Square the fabric's ends and fold it in half lengthwise, right sides together and selvages matched. Lay out and cut the pieces of the caftan as shown: a front, a back, and two facings.

of the sleeve. Continue measuring and marking as illustrated in the cutting diagram, making an 18-inch-long sleeve and a 12-inch-wide chest or bust area. Where the side and the sleeve meet at the underarm, trace the curve of a dinner plate to mark the armhole, about 3 inches out from the intersection of the straight lines.

Measure and mark the front panel layers the same way, using the measurements provided in the cutting diagram. To mark the caftan's neck, mark curves on both back and front pieces. On the back panels, measure down 1 inch and over 3⅜ inches from the neck corner; draw an inward curve inside this area. On the front panels, measure down 6 inches and over 3 inches from the neck corner; draw a smooth outward curve from point to point.

After marking the pieces, pin the two layers of fabric together every 8 to 12 inches inside the cutting lines, all around the front and back pieces. Cut the fabric carefully along the lines and remove the pins; label the pieces or set

them where you'll remember which is which.

The neck of the caftan can be bound with double-fold bias tape or faced. If you want to face the neck, mark a facing piece for each of the four main pieces. For both front and back panels, trace the neck edge curve onto an unused part of the fabric, as illustrated. Measure and mark out 2½ inches from the curve, along its entire length; square the ends of the pieces to follow the weave of the fabric. Pin and cut out the facings as above.

Assembly. Place the two front panels together, right sides together, with all edges matching. Pin them together along the selvage edges, at the center front of the caftan. On a sewing machine, straight-stitch the two pieces together along the pinned side, ½ inch from the edge, from the neck opening to the bottom end; backstitch to reinforce the ends of the seam. Remove the pins and press the seam open with a steam iron. Repeat to join the two back panels along the selvage edge; remove the pins and press the seam open.

Place the front of the caftan on top of the back, right sides together. Pin the top sleeve edges together, matching the neck openings and the ends of the sleeves. Straight-stitch along the pinned edge ½ inch from the edge, backstitching at each end. Remove the pins and press the seam open.

If you're using facings to finish the

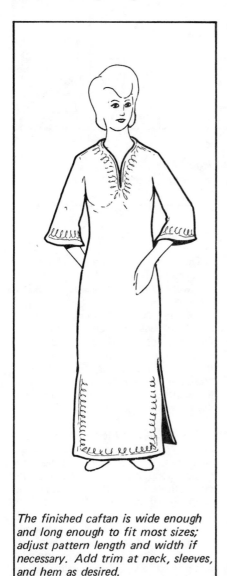

The finished caftan is wide enough and long enough to fit most sizes; adjust pattern length and width if necessary. Add trim at neck, sleeves, and hem as desired.

neck opening, assemble and attach them next. Pin the two front facing pieces together, right sides together, and stitch the center front seam, leaving a ½-inch seam allowance and back-stitching at the ends. Repeat to join the two back facing pieces at the center back seam. Then place the front and back pieces together, right sides together, with the squared ends matching. Pin the ends together, stitch them, and remove the pins; then press all the facing seams flat.

To finish the raw edge of the assembled facing, turn the outside curved edge of the facing under ½ inch and press it into place. Pin it and then straight-stitch or zigzag-stitch around the entire perimeter of the facing; backstitch to reinforce the ends. Remove the pins.

To attach the facing, open the caftan from the sewn-together neck and sleeve edge. Place the neck facing over the neck of the caftan, right sides together, with all seams and edges matching. Pin the facing into place, making sure it's properly matched. Straight-stitch the facing to the caftan all around the neck opening, ½ inch from the edge; backstitch to reinforce the end.

Remove the pins and clip the curved edge close to, but not into, the line of stitching. Turn the facing to the inside of the caftan and press the neck opening flat along the facing seam. If desired, topstitch around the neck opening to hold the facing down, ⅛ inch from the edge.

Turn the front and back sections of the caftan together, right sides together. Pin the front and back together all along the bottom of the sleeves and the sides, matching all edges. Straight-stitch the pinned edges ½ inch from the raw edge; backstitch to reinforce each end.

For a closed caftan, stitch the sides all the way to the bottom hem. To make side slits, leave the side seams open from the bottom to the knee, or as high as desired. After stitching the side seams, turn under the raw edges of the seam allowance along the sides of each slit, and hem them all along the slit.

If you didn't use a neck facing, finish the raw neck opening with double-fold bias tape. Pin the bias tape to the neck edge, right sides together, and straight-stitch it near the edge all around; be careful not to stretch the tape. Fold the front corner to miter it neatly; overlap the ends about ½ inch. Remove the pins, fold the tape over to the inside of the caftan, and pin it into place. Stitch the tape down with a hand blindstitch or straight-stitch it all around; backstitch to secure the ends.

Finally, try on the caftan to determine sleeve and hem lengths; if possible, work with a helper. Mark the hems at the desired length with pins and take the caftan off. Turn each hem up and press it to crease the hemline; turn it up again, press, and pin it into place. Stitch each hem by hand with a hemming or catchstitch. Add trim as desired.

Tie On a Skirt

If you're a junk-shop addict or simply a saver, you probably have a collection of old ties, out of style but too good to throw away. Use them up and make something from nothing by turning them into a skirt. **Tools:** tape measure, scissors, seam ripper, steam iron and ironing board, straight pins, sewing machine, sewing needle. **Materials:** old ties, thread, 7- to 9-inch skirt zipper, 2-inch-wide grosgrain ribbon, waistband hook and eye. **Time:** 2 to 3 hours.

The number of ties you'll need depends on how full you want the skirt to be. One tie will provide 5 or 6 inches of width at hip level; allow for the desired fullness and figure accordingly. Decide how long you want the skirt to be from waist to hem and add 3 inches; this measurement is the length the ties should be.

To prepare the ties, measure each tie to the required length, from the center point of the wide end toward the narrow end. Cut off the excess length at the narrow end. For each tie, remove the label and open the back seam with a seam ripper; then remove the interlining. After opening the ties, have them cleaned or wash them, as required, to remove the marks of the fold lines.

After opening and cleaning the ties, press each tie to remove the fold lines; use a steam iron on the wrong side of the tie. Open the seams attaching the lining to the tie fabric, from the cutoff end of the tie to the outer corner of the wide end. Do not open the pointed wide end of the tie; leave all three corners stitched.

Place one tie over another, right sides together and long edges matching on one side, so that the outside corners of their pointed ends are exactly matched. The bottom of the skirt will be formed by the pointed ends of the ties, in a large zigzag all around. Pin the matched edges of the ties and straight-stitch them together on a sewing machine, ⅜ inch from the edge; backstitch to secure the ends. Remove the pins. Don't worry if the linings aren't the same length; they'll be trimmed later.

Unfold the ties and place another tie over one of the sewn-together ties, right sides together and pointed ends matching. Match the long free edge of the attached tie to one edge of the other one, pin the edges together, and stitch the seam ⅜ inch from the edge. Continue, adding ties accordion-style, until the panel of sewn-together ties is as wide as the finished skirt should be. Press all the seams open.

Try the skirt on, wrapping it around your waist. Adjust the seams as necessary from hip to waist so that the skirt fits smoothly; you may have to take each seam in a little at the top of the skirt. Restitch the seams. To join the sides of the panel, insert a 7- to 9-inch skirt zipper in the final seam, following the instructions on the zipper package.

Make a waistband for the skirt from 2-inch-wide grosgrain ribbon, in a color to complement or pull the ties together. Measure and cut a piece of grosgrain 4 inches longer than your waist measurement. Pin the ribbon around the inside of the raw waist, with 2 inches overlapping at each side of the zipper,

Make a Baby Kimono

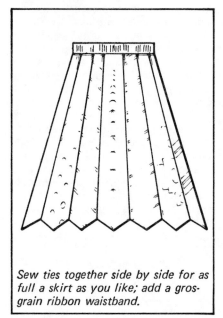

Sew ties together side by side for as full a skirt as you like; add a grosgrain ribbon waistband.

Comfort, washability, and easy off-and-on are musts for baby clothes, and the ready-mades don't have a corner on the market. This kimono fills the bill, and you can make it either short or long. **Tools:** tape measure, pencil or fabric marker, scissors, sewing needle, straight pins, 4-inch dish or saucer, sewing machine, steam iron and ironing board; if desired, crochet hook, and/or embroidery needle. **Materials:** soft cotton fabric such as outing flannel, thread, ¼-inch twill tape; double-fold bias tape or, if desired, soft yarn; if desired, embroidery thread. **Time:** about 1 hour for a basic kimono; additional time for crochet edging or embroidery.

Fabric. To make three short kimonos, buy 1 yard of 36-inch-wide fabric—soft cotton is best. To make two long kimonos, buy 1¹/₆ yards of 36-inch-wide fabric. You'll also need 6 inches of ¼-inch twill tape for each kimono, and matching or coordinating double-fold bias tape—7 yards for a short kimono, 9 yards for a long one.

Pattern. Lay out the kimonos as illustrated in the cutting diagrams. For a short kimono, measure and cut a piece of fabric 12 inches wide and 26 inches long; measure and cut two sleeve pieces 5 inches wide and 7 inches long. For a long kimono, flare the front and back sides of the body piece. Cut the center of the body piece to a 12-inch width, as above, for 6 inches on each side of the shoulder line at the center of the piece; then cut at an angle to flare the body piece to about an 18-inch width at the bottom. Cut the kimono to the length desired; to cut two long kimonos from 1¹/₆ yards of fabric, use an 18-inch shoulder-to-hem length.

Assembly. Construction is exactly the same for a short kimono or a long

so that a scant half the width of the ribbon is on the skirt and the other half sticks up above the raw edge.

Stitch the ribbon to the skirt, close to the edge of the grosgrain; backstitch to secure the ends. At each lapped zipper end of the ribbon, turn the end under ½ inch and then under ½ inch again. Stitch the folded ends down with the rest of the ribbon. Remove the pins.

Turn the unattached edge of the ribbon down over the outside of the skirt, forming a 1-inch-wide waistband and sandwiching the raw waist between the two layers of ribbon. Pin the ribbon into place. Stitch the waistband on the outside of the skirt, close to the edge of the ribbon. At each folded end, turn the skirt and stitch the open end closed. Backstitch to secure the ends. Sew the sides of a waistband hook and eye to the ends of the waistband to fasten the skirt closed.

To finish the inside of the skirt, trim the joined lining pieces so that they're all even. At the raw lining edge, turn the lining under ½ inch and topstitch or blindstitch it by hand. Tack the lining into place at the seams to finish the corners of the zigzag hem.

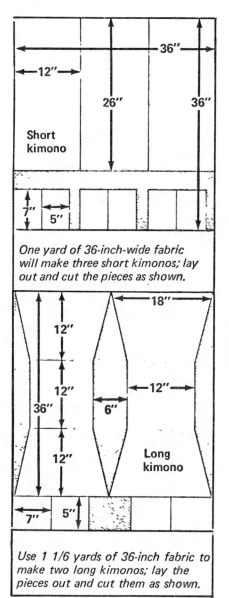

One yard of 36-inch-wide fabric will make three short kimonos; lay out and cut the pieces as shown.

Use 1 1/6 yards of 36-inch fabric to make two long kimonos; lay the pieces out and cut them as shown.

centered on the width of the piece of fabric, with about one-third of its width on one side of the line, and two-thirds on the other. Trace around the dish with a pencil or a fabric marker. This is the neck opening, and the side on which it's cut lower is the front of the kimono.

Carefully cut out the marked circle. Leave the remaining basting in place. Fold the body piece in half lengthwise and cut along the front fold to the neck opening.

On one of the 5 × 7-inch sleeve pieces, find the center of a 7-inch side and mark it with a pin. Lay the sleeve piece on the body piece, right sides together, with the edges matched and the center marking of the sleeve lined up with the basted shoulder marking on the body piece. On a sewing machine, straight-stitch the sleeve to the body, ½ inch from the raw edges; backstitch to secure the ends. Repeat to attach the second sleeve to the other side of the body. Press the seams toward the sleeve with a steam iron.

Fold the kimono crosswise, right sides together, with the sleeves pulled out away from the body and the basted shoulder line on the fold. Match and pin the underarm and sleeve edges; straight-stitch pinned edges ½ inch from the edge on each side of the kimono. Remove the pins.

After the sleeves are closed, there will be a right-angle corner at each underarm. To reinforce these corners, cut two pieces of ¼-inch twill tape about 2 to 3 inches long. Pin a piece of twill tape over each underarm seam and stitch it down, following the original line of stitching; backstitch to reinforce the ends. With sharp scissors, clip into the corner of each sleeve, almost but not quite to the line of stitching. Do not cut the stitching or the twill tape.

Finish the raw edges of the sleeves and body with double-fold bias tape. Starting at a corner of the neck opening, pin the bias tape to the edge of the fabric, right sides together; work down one side of the front, around the corner, around the bottom, and up the other side. Fold the front corner to miter it neatly; or, if desired, round off the

one. Fold the large body piece in half crosswise. Thread a needle with contrasting thread and mark the location of the fold by making a straight line of basting across the width on the fold. Open the body out flat again; the basted line is the shoulder line of the kimono.

To mark the kimono's neck, use a 4-inch-diameter dish or saucer. Set the saucer on the basted shoulder line,

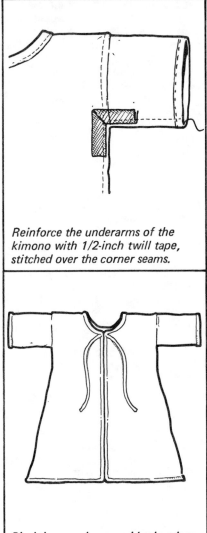

Reinforce the underarms of the kimono with 1/2-inch twill tape, stitched over the corner seams.

Bind the raw sleeve and body edges with double-fold bias tape; leave extra tape at the neck for ties.

the edge on each side to make ties; stitch down the open side of each tie to close it.

If you like to crochet, a crocheted edging of soft yarn is a good alternative to the bias binding. Make a row of single crochet around all raw edges; then add a second row of single crochet, with two chain stitches added between single crochets every three stitches. Or, if desired, finish the edges of the body with a rolled hem; bind the neck and make ties with bias tape. For a dress-up kimono, add embroidery as desired.

Resole Your Shoes

Get more mileage out of your shoes by resoling and reheeling them—with a little practice, you'll do as well as a shoemaker. **Tools:** utility knife, rasp or file, pliers, hammer, screwdriver, vise. **Materials:** composition half-soles and heels, flexible shoe-repair contact cement, panel nails. **Time:** about ½ hour.

Buy composition half-soles and heels from a shoemaker or at a variety store. New half-soles and heels are available in different sizes; make sure you buy soles or heels roughly the right size for the shoes to be repaired. The old soles on the shoes should be in fair shape, with no large holes or torn sides.

First, clean the soles of the shoes; remove mud, grease, and other debris. If you use water, let the soles dry thoroughly before repairing the shoes.

When the shoes are thoroughly dry, prepare the soles. If the old soles have pulled away from the insoles, cut off the old soles near the heels with a razor knife. The new half-soles will butt against the cut surface. With a file or a rasp, scuff the leather, rubber, or composition soles on the shoes. This provides a little tooth on the sole, ensuring a better bond.

Some shoe soles are self-adhering. If the new half-soles are not self-adhering, coat the old soles and half-

corner and ease the tape around the curve. Be careful not to stretch the tape. Straight-stitch the tape near the edge, all around the kimono; then remove the pins, fold the tape over to the inside of the kimono, and repin. Straight-stitch the tape near the edge all around.

To finish the neck opening, bind it with double-fold bias tape, as above. Extend the tape 6 to 8 inches beyond soles with flexible shoe-repair contact cement. Let the adhesive set as directed by the manufacturer until it has a dry-looking shine. Then carefully press each new half-sole onto the old sole, making full contact. Be sure to position the half-soles correctly; they can't be moved once adhesive contact has been made.

Put on the shoes and walk around in them for several minutes. This clamps the new half-soles to the old soles.

When the new soles are tightly cemented to the old ones, trim off any overlapping composition material around the soles with a utility knife. Follow the edge of the old soles to guide the knife. Then smooth the cut edges with a file or a rasp, being careful not to scuff the leather of the uppers.

To install new heels on the shoes, pry off the old heels with the tip of a screwdriver. Pull out any protruding nails with pliers. Apply flexible shoe-repair contact cement to the new heels and to the heel surface on the shoes; let it dry as directed and then carefully press the new heel into place. Secure the new heel with 3 to 5 panel nails. Put the heels of the shoes over a closed metal-working vise and drive in the nails with a hammer; space the nails around the perimeter of the heel, about ⅜ inch in. The vise will bend the nails if the nails stick up through the soles of the shoes. Trim and smooth the heels with a utility knife and a rasp or file.

Remove Stains from Leather and Suede

Leather and suede shoes, boots, clothes, and bags can take a lot of abuse, and pick up a lot of stains. In most cases, it's easy to clean them. **Tools:** clean soft cloths, sponge, fine emery board, suede brush, small mixing dish and spoon. **Materials:** liquid leather cleaner, dry-cleaning fluid, white

cream dressing, shoe polish as appropriate, white vinegar, saddle soap, white petroleum jelly, aerosol suede conditioner/cleaner, fuller's earth or cornstarch, aerosol foam wool upholstery cleaner. **Time:** about 5 to 30 minutes, plus drying time, depending on stain.

Smooth leather. Most spots can be removed with liquid leather cleaner; rub the cleaner in lightly with a clean soft cloth and let dry as directed by the manufacturer. To remove stubborn *grease* spots, apply commercial dry-cleaning fluid; test for color-fastness in an inconspicuous place before using. Clean white leather with a white cream dressing; apply the dressing with a soft cloth and wipe clean. Polish shoes as appropriate.

To remove *salt* stains from shoes and boots, apply a mixture of half white vinegar and half water. Rub the mixture in well and wipe clean with a clean, damp cloth. Saddle-soap boots and heavy shoes. Use a clean sponge to lather the soap; apply the foam to the leather and rub it in gently. Rinse the sponge, squeeze it out, and wipe the leather clean. Use only the foam of the saddle soap, and be careful not to soak the leather; squeeze the sponge almost dry. Let the leather dry completely, at least 12 hours, and then buff with a soft clean cloth; polish as appropriate.

To remove *mildew* stains, apply white petroleum jelly to the damaged leather and rub gently to remove the stain. Wipe clean and apply petroleum jelly again; let stand 24 hours and then buff with a clean soft cloth. Polish shoes as appropriate, and store shoes and luggage away from moisture.

Suede. Remove *rain* spots from suede by rubbing them gently with a fine emery board. Spray with aerosol suede conditioner/cleaner and, when dry, brush as directed with a suede brush to restore the nap of the suede. Remove spots with liquid leather cleaner; rub the cleaner in lightly with a clean soft cloth, let dry, and brush to restore the nap of the suede. If necessary, spray with aerosol suede conditioner/cleaner, let dry, and brush again.

To remove stubborn stains, mix fuller's earth or cornstarch to a paste with liquid leather cleaner. Apply paste to cover the stain completely and let dry about 8 hours; wipe off. Spray the cleaned area with suede conditioner/cleaner and brush to restore the nap of the suede.

Remove *salt* stains from suede shoes with a mixture of half white vinegar and half water; rub gently with a clean soft cloth to remove the stain. Spray with suede conditioner/cleaner, let dry, and brush to restore the nap of the suede.

To clean very dirty suede shoes and bags, use aerosol foam upholstery cleaner made specifically for wool upholstery. Spray the foam on and rub it in with a clean damp sponge; rinse and squeeze out the sponge as you work. Let dry at least 8 hours. Apply suede conditioner/cleaner as directed, let dry, and brush to restore the nap of the suede.

Mix Leather Waterproofer

Snow, rain, and mud are murder on leather shoes and boots. Waterproof smooth leather with this light penetrating oil. **Equipment:** double boiler, measuring cup, measuring spoons, mixing spoon, 8-ounce bottle with cover, funnel. **Ingredients:** paraffin, neat's-foot oil, mineral oil. **Yield:** about 7 ounces.

In the top of a double boiler, melt 4 ounces of paraffin, 5 tablespoons of neat's-foot oil, and 4½ teaspoons of mineral oil; stir well. Pour into a clean 8-ounce bottle and cover tightly.

To apply the waterproofer, rub it into shoes or boots with your hands or a clean cloth, working the compound well into the leather. Let dry completely before wearing. *Caution: Do not apply to suede; the oil will flatten and darken the suede. Use a commercial suede spray on this type of leather.*

Make a Pair of Sandals

Store-bought sandals get expensive, and they often don't make it through the season. With a little time and effort, you can make a pair of good-looking sandals that will stand up to everyday wear and tear better than any you could buy. **Tools:** tape measure, scissors, pencil, linoleum or carpet knife with new blades, rotary punch, rivet setter, hammer. **Materials:** for an average adult foot, 3-yard strip of ⅛ × ¾-inch vegetable-tanned russet cowhide, stiff cardboard, 12 × 20-inch piece of 8-ounce (¼-inch) sole leather, ¾-inch (inside width) buckles, fabric rivets, waterproof shoe repair adhesive, 9/16-inch shoemakers' tacks, wax shoe polish. **Time:** 4 to 6 hours.

Buy the materials for your sandals at a craft shop or a shoe repair shop. For the uppers, get a 3-yard strip of vegetable-tanned russet cowhide, ⅛ inch thick and ¾ inch wide. For the soles, buy a 12 × 20-inch piece of 8-ounce (¼-inch-thick) sole leather. No sewing is needed; use 9/16-inch shoemakers' hand tacks. To fasten the sandals, buy two buckles, with a ¾-inch inside width.

Make the sandals to fit your feet exactly. To determine the length of each sandal's strap, wrap a tape measure loosely around your foot the way you want the straps to go. Cut the straps to the desired length with a sharp scissors. Besides the long straps, cut a 3-inch buckle strap for each sandal, to secure the long strap at the ankle.

To measure for the soles, set a piece of stiff cardboard on the floor. Set one foot on the cardboard and put your full weight on it. Draw around the foot, keeping the pencil absolutely upright, to make a pattern. Cut around the pattern, staying a bit outside the traced lines and smoothing out the bumps; square off the toes or heel as desired. Mark the foot traced, right or left, on the top of the pattern. Repeat to trace the other foot.

For each sandal, wrap the leather strap around your foot the way you want the finished sandal to be. Set your wrapped foot on the pattern traced from it and mark the points where the edges of the straps meet the sole; also mark the edges of the buckle straps. Cut a slit in the cardboard sole pattern at each marked point where the strap wraps through the sole; each slit should be ¼ inch from the edge of the sole and ¾ inch long, parallel to the edge of the pattern.

To transfer the pattern to the sole leather, set the sole leather on a flat surface, grain side up. Set the patterns on the leather and draw around each pattern with a pencil. Trace two right soles and two left soles, so you have four traced soles. Don't waste any leather; you'll need more for the sandals' heels. On one right and one left sole, mark the location of the strap holes.

To cut the soles, use a linoleum or carpet knife with a new blade. Cut through the leather in stages. Make the first cut carefully to score the leather. Then set the leather over the edge of a table, cut side up, and bend the leather so that the cut opens a bit. Continue cutting to cut completely through the leather. Cut all four traced soles.

Cut the marked slits in the upper soles with a rotary punch and the linoleum or carpet knife; punch two holes at the edges of the straps and then cut out the slit between the holes. Cut slits for both the long straps and the buckle straps.

Attach the buckles to the buckle straps with a rivet—set the rivets with a rivet setter. For each buckle, make a punch hole for the buckle prong to pass through; slide the buckle onto the strap and fold the end over to see where the prong falls. Slip the other end of the buckle strap into its slit in the upper sole, and adjust it to the proper length. Apply waterproof shoe repair adhesive to the bottom of the sole and to the strap surface, as directed by the man-

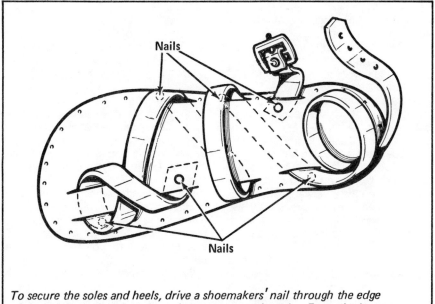

Nails

Nails

To secure the soles and heels, drive a shoemakers' nail through the edge of the sole at each point where the strap meets the sole. From the bottom, drive tacks all around the edge of each sandal, sole and heel.

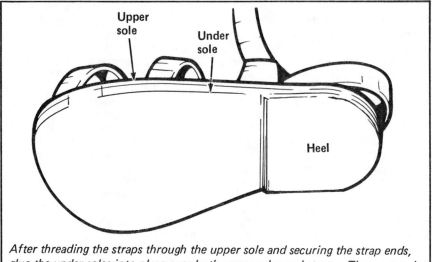

Upper sole

Under sole

Heel

After threading the straps through the upper sole and securing the strap ends, glue the under soles into place over both upper soles and straps. Then cut and glue the heels, aligning them exactly on the soles.

ufacturer. Let the adhesive cure as directed and then press the end of the buckle strap against the sole to hold it firmly in place.

For each sandal, thread the long strap through the starting slit and pull it almost all the way through. Secure the loose end to the bottom of the upper sole with waterproof shoe repair adhesive. Thread the strap through the cut-out slits and adjust the sandal on your foot for the proper fit.

With the sandal straps adjusted and the strap ends secured to the bottoms of the soles, attach the second cut-out sole to each sandal. Apply waterproof shoe repair adhesive to the bottom of the upper sole and to the facing side of the bottom sole. Don't apply adhesive to any point where straps are located, in order to keep the straps adjustable. Let the adhesive cure as directed by the manufacturer; then set the two soles together and press them firmly to bond them.

Cut a heel for each sandal from the remaining sole leather; trace the heel from the last 2½ inches of each cardboard pattern at the heel end. Attach the cut heel of each sandal with waterproof shoe repair adhesive,

aligning the edges of the heel exactly with the edges of the sole.

Secure the soles and heels with shoemakers' tacks. Set the sandals right side up on a hard surface, such as a concrete floor. On each sandal, hammer in a shoemakers' tack to secure the glued ends of the long strap and of the end of the buckle strap. Set a tack to hold the soles together, on the outside edge of the sole at each point where the strap meets the sole. Don't tack the strap itself or it won't slide for final adjustment. When these tacks are firmly hammered in, turn the sandal over and nail tacks all around the edge of the sandal at ½-inch intervals; stay away from the straps. The points of the nails will flatten out on the concrete floor.

Put the sandal on and tighten each section of the strap as desired from glued end to buckle end. With the rotary punch, punch holes in the end of the long strap so it can be secured to the buckle.

Give the sandals a coat of wax shoe polish before wearing them. Wax them often during the summer to keep them supple and prevent them from drying out.

Crafts and Hobbies

Pay Less for Craft and Hobby Supplies

A shop doesn't have to be a hobby shop for it to yield supplies for your favorite crafts and hobbies. Hardware stores, variety stores, and stationery stores are just some of the alternative sources for high-quality, low-priced supplies.

You can find your own supplies for any craft or hobby. For example, different thicknesses of dowels can be cut, sanded, and varnished to make fine knitting needles—or drilled, painted, and strung into necklaces and hangings. Nuts, bolts, moldings, and a host of other materials can be used to make toys, wall displays or hangings, dollhouse furniture, and more. Crochet and macrame enthusiasts will find ordinary household string goes a long way for making inexpensive and attractive projects. If decoupage and collage or dollhouse decorating is your specialty, don't limit yourself to the prints found in craft stores. Explore stationery shelves and second-hand bookstores; you can sometimes find an old illustrated book for just a few cents.

Of course, you don't have to go to any store at all; use the materials you have on hand. The money you save on yarn for rug-hooking, weaving, knitting, and crochet by cutting old clothes and curtains into strips will soon pay for a professional strip cutter. And don't limit your search for found materials to your own home. Carpenters and cabinetmakers are gold mines for wood discards usable for tole painting, collage, decoupage, or stitchery cover-ups. Or

how about other hobbyists? A weaver's "strums" from warping the loom are useful fill-in yarns for stitchery.

If you've ever bought a kit, you know that a lot of what you pay for is the labor that goes into cutting and measuring materials and the little papers and cartons that hold them. Many of these steps can easily be done by you. For instance, it takes very little time to cut yarn into lengths for rug hooking, but uncut yarn costs a lot less. Rubber bands, empty margarine tubs, and plastic bags from the supermarket hold supplies nicely and neatly. Instructions can be purchased separately or clipped from magazines. Use your ingenuity—and whatever supplies you can locate by it. The savings are worth the effort, and the effort can become almost as rewarding as the hobby itself.

Hook a Rug

To soften a floor or to spark an empty wall, a hand-hooked rug will give you years of beauty and utility. All you need is time for this uncomplicated craft. **Tools:** pencil, steam iron and ironing board, straightedge, felt-tip pens, weights, scissors, sewing needle, latchhook or rug hook, carpet needle, paintbrush. **Materials:** graph paper, rug backing canvas, thread, precut 6-ply wool or acrylic rug yarn, carpet thread, liquid latex, burlap or heavy cotton backing fabric. **Time:** varies, depending on size; for a small rug, at least several evenings.

Preparation. If you buy a rug-hooking kit, you'll get instructions, precut yarn, and an open-weave canvas backing with a printed design. If you want to design your own rug, draw the

CRAFTS / Hooked Rugs

design to scale on graph paper before you buy yarn and canvas. Pick a simple design; stripes or a bold geometric shape—a diamond, for instance—are easiest to work with. Mark the color you want on each square of your drawing.

Hooked rugs are made with special open-weave canvas, available from 12 to 48 inches wide. Buy good-quality rug backing canvas as wide as you want the rug to be, and about 6 inches longer. The canvas should have 3½, 4, or 5 meshes per inch; 5-mesh canvas makes the thickest rug. Buy precut 6-ply wool or acrylic rug yarn in standard 2½-inch lengths. One package of yarn covers from 3½ to 5½ square inches, depending on the canvas; read the instructions on the package. Buy a rug hook or latchhook to work with.

To finish the rug, you'll need liquid latex, which seals the loops of yarn to the canvas. For a more protective backing, use burlap or heavy cotton to cover the back of the rug completely.

Assembly. Rug backing canvas is printed with a grid on one side for laying out the pattern. Spread the canvas flat; if it's creased or buckled, press it flat with a steam iron. Working on the printed grid side, mark the outline of the rug on the canvas with a straightedge and felt-tip pen. On the selvage edges, leave 1 grid square outside the outline, to be turned under when the rug is finished. On the cut edges, leave at least 2 inches of canvas, to be turned under and hooked double-thickness.

Trim off the excess canvas on the cut edges to an even 2 inches. Turn the cut edges under on the marked line, creasing the canvas firmly along the edge; match the holes in the two layers exactly. Sew the two layers together by hand, keeping the holes lined up exactly.

Working from your graph-paper drawing, carefully transfer your design to the grid on the canvas; mark directly on the canvas with felt-tip pens. Use a different color pen for each color wool in the rug.

When the backing is prepared, start hooking the rug. Work on a large, flat surface, with the entire rug spread out in front of you; weight the rug to hold it evenly. Work from the lower left corner across from selvage to selvage, row by row, pulling the rug toward you as you go. Work in parallel rows to hook strands of yarn from mesh to mesh; change colors as necessary. Work all the way to the marked outline. Do *not* hook all one color and then the next; work straight across the canvas, following your graph-paper chart and the markings on the canvas. Hook a yarn loop into each mesh of each row of holes in the canvas.

To make the yarn loops of the rug, use the latchhook or rug hook to anchor loops of yarn around the meshes of the canvas. For each mesh, hold the latchhook in one hand and fold a piece of yarn in half with the other. Slip the loop of yarn over the hook of the latchhook, beyond the latch.

Holding the ends of the yarn loop, push the latchhook through the first mesh of the canvas at the left-hand corner of the first row, and up through

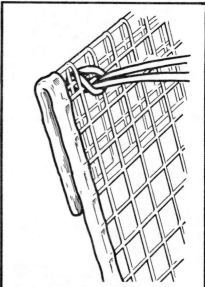

At the ends of the rug, hook through both the canvas and the folded-under edge, knotting the two layers together.

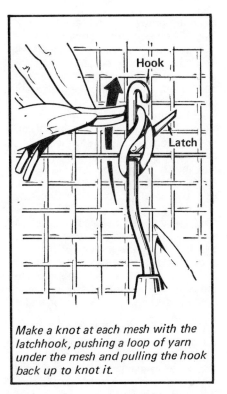

Make a knot at each mesh with the latchhook, pushing a loop of yarn under the mesh and pulling the hook back up to knot it.

the mesh just in front of it. Pull the ends of the looped yarn into the hook of the latchhook. Pull the latchhook back up through the loop and through the canvas, knotting the ends of the yarn through the loop. Pull the ends to tighten the knot, and go on to the next mesh. Repeat to hook across the entire rug, row by row, changing colors as necessary to work the desired pattern.

Finishing. When you've hooked across the entire rug, shake the rug to fluff the pile. If any pieces of yarn stick up above the pile, trim them to match. Fold the selvage edges of the rug under as close to the loops of yarn as you can, and crease the edges sharply. Stitch the turned-down selvage edges securely to the canvas back of the rug, using a carpet needle and carpet thread; fold the ends in at an angle to miter the corners.

Seal the back of the rug with liquid latex to bond the loops of yarn to the canvas; apply the latex evenly with a paintbrush, as directed by the manufacturer. Let the latex dry completely, as directed.

To reinforce the rug and keep the edges firm, back it with a piece of burlap or heavy cotton, about 1 inch larger all around than the finished rug. Turn the raw edge of the backing fabric under 1 inch all around, folding the corners to miter them neatly. Stitch the mitered corners together; then stitch the backing into place all around the back of the rug. Be careful not to catch strands of yarn, or you'll pull them through to the wrong side.

Braid a Rag Rug

An old-fashioned rag rug—especially a hand-braided one—adds warmth and charm to any room. For a real old-time look, use recycled fabrics for your rug. **Tools:** scissors, sewing needle, safety pins, flat needle or bodkin. **Materials:** scraps of heavy wool fabric, heavy buttonhole or rug thread. **Time:** a few days to several weeks, depending on the size of the rug.

Because of its durability and strength, heavy wool is the best material for rugs. Buy wool by the pound at fabric stores, or choose old fabrics that are the same weight—make sure they're clean and sturdy. A variety of colors makes the rug more interesting, so the strips don't have to match.

Tear the fabric scraps into 3-inch-wide strips. To start the rug, stitch the ends of fabric strips together diagonally to decrease bulk and strengthen the braid. Add strips, stitching as you go; the longer the strips, the more braiding you'll be able to do at one time. Roll the strips into a ball for ease of handling; if desired, hold the ball together with a safety pin. Make three balls of sewn-together strips.

Take the ends from the three fabric balls and pin them together with a safety pin. Put this end in a drawer and

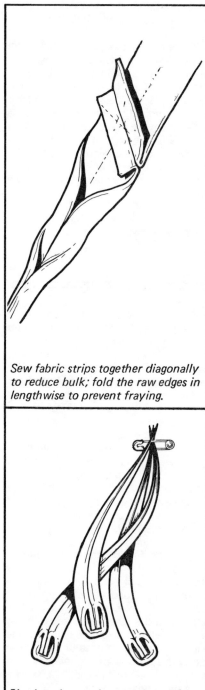

Sew fabric strips together diagonally to reduce bulk; fold the raw edges in lengthwise to prevent fraying.

Pin three long strips together and fold them into a firm, flat braid, turning the edges in toward the center.

close the drawer. Then braid the three strips together until the braid is about 2 feet long, tucking the lengthwise edges of each strip into the center as you work to prevent fraying. Metal clips can be purchased to turn the strips automatically as they're braided, but heavier wool may be too bulky for their use.

Form the braid carefully to keep it flat. With its edges tucked in to the center, grasp the right-hand strip and fold it over the center strip; be sure the tucked edges are kept to the top of the braid. Use your thumbs to tuck in the raw edges as you braid. The first strip is now the center strip. Take the left-hand strip and fold it over the center strip; this, in turn, is now the center strip. Be sure to keep the tension even. When the braid is about 2 feet long, remove the starting end from the drawer and brace it between your knees or under your foot.

Continue braiding until there is about 6 inches of material remaining on the shortest strip; the strips will most likely be uneven in length. Stitch on additional strips and continue braiding. Make sure the braid is flat and the tension even.

When the braid is about 20 feet long, start to make the rug itself. Secure the end of the braid with a safety pin to keep it from unbraiding. Unpin the strips at the beginning of the strip, and work the loose ends into the beginning of the braid. Blindstitch them into place.

An oval rug is easiest for a beginner. Decide on the overall size of the rug you want to braid—for example, a 4 × 6-foot rug. The difference between the length and width of the rug is the length of the center strip—for a 4 × 6-foot rug, 2 feet. Use this as a wrapping guide.

On a large flat surface, begin winding the braid. Using a flat needle or a bodkin and heavy buttonhole or rug thread, attach the thread to the braid and weave it in between the braids to hold them into their coiled position. Gently ease around curves to prevent the rug from puckering into a conical shape.

When about 3 feet of braid remain, add more strips and continue as before. When the rug is nearly the desired size, begin tapering the width of the strips to

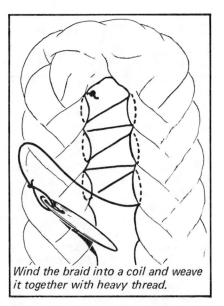
Wind the braid into a coil and weave it together with heavy thread.

narrow the braid; this prevents a blunt edge. To finish the rug, work the end of the braid into the curve, and secure it with blindstitches.

Weave a Place Mat

Hand-woven place mats add a distinctive touch to any table. **Tools:** scissors, hammer, small crochet hook. **Materials:** jute or rug yarn; old picture frame, picture stretcher, or 1 × 2 wood frame; small finishing nails, stiff cardboard. **Time:** 3 hours or more.

Weaving is based on the warp—the series of vertical parallel strands in the fabric—and the weft, the horizontal strands interlaced over the warp. To shape the place mat, you'll need a weaving frame—about 2 inches larger each way, inside diameter, than you want the finished mat to be.

To make the frame, use an inexpensive picture frame or stretcher, or a rough frame of 1 × 2 wood butted together at the corners. Use the long dimension of the frame as the warp dimension. On each warp side of the frame, drive small finishing nails along

the outside edge, spaced very close together and about halfway into the frame; align the nails from side to side as much as possible. The protruding nailheads will hold the warp yarn in place. Drive another nail into the top left side—the weft side—about 2 inches below the corner warp nail.

Start weaving by setting up a warp. Tie the end of your warp yarn onto the end nail at a top corner of the frame. Wrap the yarn evenly up and down the frame, looping it around each nail on each warp end. Wrap the yarn firmly, but don't stretch it; it should be just snug on the nails. When the warp is wrapped across the entire frame, tie the yarn onto the last nail at the final corner of the frame, and cut it off; leave a 1- to 2-inch tail.

When the warp is complete, weave in the weft yarn across the frame. To hold the weft yarn, cut a piece of stiff cardboard about 6 inches long and 1½ inches wide, and cut 1½-inch-deep curved notches into the narrow ends. Round off all corners so they don't catch on the warp yarn. Wind the weft yarn around the notches of this shuttle.

Leaving a 3- to 4-inch tail, tie the end of the weft yarn around the side nail near the top left corner of the warp. Weave the yarn through the warp strands across the frame, passing the shuttle over the first warp strand and under the second, over the third and under the fourth, and so on across the frame. At the end of the warp, turn the shuttle to weave back the other way.

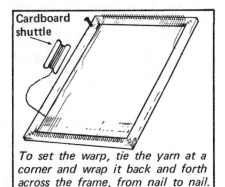
Cardboard shuttle

To set the warp, tie the yarn at a corner and wrap it back and forth across the frame, from nail to nail.

Alternate the second weft row by going over the warp threads you went under in the first row, in an over-one, under-one weave; this is called a tabby weave. Or weave a variation of the tabby by passing the weft yarn over two and under two warp strands. If you weave over-two, under-two, more of the warp material will show than in a standard tabby weave. In any weaving pattern, be careful not to pull the weft yarn too tight; this could pucker the finished place mat.

To keep your weaving firm and even, use a heddle cut from stiff cardboard. Cut a piece of cardboard 1 inch longer than the width of the place mat, and 1 inch wide. Weave it through the warp strands, keeping it about 2 inches below the woven-in weft strands at the top of the frame. With every other row of weaving, tilt the heddle up to separate the warp. Pass the shuttle quickly through the separated warp strands; you won't have to weave over and under each strand on these rows.

Continue to weave down the warp on the frame, using the heddle on every other row, until the place mat is complete. Stop weaving about 2 inches above the bottom of the frame, to leave 2 inches of free warp at both ends of the mat. Leave about 3 to 4 inches of weft yarn at the bottom corner and cut the weft.

To finish the mat, cut or untie the beginning and end of the warp, and cut the first weft strand from the top corner. Then very carefully lift the warp threads off the nails to detach the mat from the frame. Lay the mat on a flat work surface. Cut the looped warp strands and knot them together two at a time to secure the weft. Pull the knots uniformly firm across the mat, but don't pull them tight enough to pucker the edge. Trim the ends of the knotted warp threads carefully to make a uniform fringe.

At the starting and ending corners, use a small crochet hook to weave the loose tails of the weft yarn into the mat. Cut each weft end to 2 to 3 inches long and carefully weave it in; if the end sticks out, cut it off close to the back surface of the mat.

Experiment with Granny Squares

The granny square is the easiest of all crochet squares to make, and it's a wonderful way to use up odds and ends of yarn. **Tools:** crochet hook size J, scissors, yarn or tapestry needle. **Materials:** 4-ply knitting yarn. **Time:** once you're proficient, 15 to 20 minutes per 6-inch square.

The granny square consists entirely of repeated clusters of three double crochet stitches (3 dc), separated by spaces formed by two chainstitches (ch 2); each cluster of 3 dc fits into a space in the row before it. Corners are formed by putting two 3 dc clusters into a single ch 2 space, with a ch 2 between them. The only tricky part is getting from one row, or round, to the next.

To start, ch 4 and join the ends with a slipstitch (sl st) to form a ring. Then go on in four rounds to make an increasingly larger square.

Round 1: ch 3 (this represents the first dc of the cluster of three), 2 dc into the center of the ring, ch 2, *3 dc into the ring, ch 2; repeat from * twice more. Join the ends of the round by making a sl st into the third ch of the ch 3 at the beginning. Sl st across the next 2 dc. This brings you to the ch 2 space between 2 clusters of dc.

At this point, you can change colors if you want the square to be multicolored. Simply break off the first color and begin Round 2 with the new one, going back and tying the two yarns in a firm knot after the new color is worked in.

Round 2: ch 3, 2 dc into the ch 2 space, ch 2 3 dc into the same ch 2 space (this forms the first corner). *Ch 2, 3 dc into the next space, ch 2, 3 dc into the same space; repeat from * twice more. Ch 2. Join ends with sl st into third ch of ch 3 at the beginning of the round, sl st across next 2 dc.

Round 3: Follow Round 2 directions for making the first corner; then *ch 2, 3 dc into the next ch 2 space, ch 2, 3 dc into the next ch 2 space (corner), ch 2, 3 dc into the same space; repeat from * twice more. Ch 2, 3 dc into the next ch 2 space, ch 2. Join ends and sl st across the next 2 dc exactly as with Round 2.

Round 4: Follow Round 3 directions; increase by one 3 dc cluster on each of the four sides.

Four rounds will make a square about 6 inches in size. If you want smaller squares, use fewer rounds. If you want larger squares, use more rounds; follow the directions for Round 3 and increase each succeeding round by one 3 dc cluster on each of the four sides. For different effects, experiment with other yarns and hook sizes.

To join granny squares, you can either sew or crochet the edges together. To sew them, use a yarn or tapestry needle threaded with yarn. Lay the squares right sides together and sew loosely through the back loops of the outer rows of dc and ch stitch.

To crochet squares together, use the same weight yarn and hook you used to make the squares. Lay the squares back to back. Starting at a corner, either sl st or single crochet (sc) through the back loops of each pair of dc and ch stitch. Crocheting adds a little more texture and color interest than sewing; experiment to see which effect is better for each project.

To make a pillow, just keep adding rounds to a granny square until it's the size you want. Join two squares or back one square with fabric; insert a pillow.

For a purse, make two 10-inch granny squares and join them on three sides. Put in a fabric lining; cut the lining to 11 × 21 inches, fold it crosswise, and make a ½-inch seam on each side. Turn the top edges back ½ inch, insert the lining into the bag, and sew the top folded edge of the lining to the top edge of the bag. Attach a handle made of two layers of grosgrain ribbon with the edges stitched together.

You can make hats, shawls, ponchos, and a hundred other things from the humble granny square. Make the squares in small sizes and join them to form afghans, wall hangings, place mats, or tablecloths; use them singly, as patches or pockets; join them to form whole garments such as vests or sweaters. Use rows of small squares to add interest to any garment—apply a row of squares around a fabric skirt a few inches above the hem, or attach them around the bottom of a fabric vest. Keep experimenting—you won't run out of ideas.

Make Acrylic Desk Accessories

A letter rack and a pencil holder are essential for a well-equipped desk. These elegant, inexpensive acrylic accessories are surprisingly easy to make. **Tools:** ruler, pencil, triangle or carpenters' square, C-clamp, scrap wood block, fine-toothed hacksaw, craft knife, artists' brush. **Materials:** ⅛-inch-thick sheet acrylic; 2½-inch, 2-inch, and 1½-inch outside diameter acrylic tubing; masking tape, medium- and fine-grit wet-or-dry sandpaper, soft cloth, acrylic glue. **Time:** 2 to 3 hours.

Buy ⅛-inch-thick sheet acrylic from a plastics supplier—you'll only need about 1 square foot, but there's no leeway for waste at the edges; to allow for cutting errors, invest in a larger sheet. If possible, buy acrylic tubing cut to measure by the supplier: two 3-inch pieces of 2½-inch-diameter tubing, one 5-inch piece of 2-inch-diameter, and one 1¾-inch piece of 1½-inch diameter. Choose clear, smoked, or colored.

Lightly mark a grid of 1-inch squares on the protective paper covering the acrylic sheet; use a triangle or a carpenters' square to keep your lines even. Following the cutting diagram illustrated, mark off the rectangular pieces of acrylic sheet for the letter rack and the pencil holder base: one 5 × 4-inch piece, one 5½ × 4-inch, one 4½ × 4-inch, one 3½ × 4-inch, one 2½ × 4-inch, and one 6 × 6-inch piece. Leave the protective paper on the acrylic sheet, and don't press hard enough to mar the surface. If you bought a larger

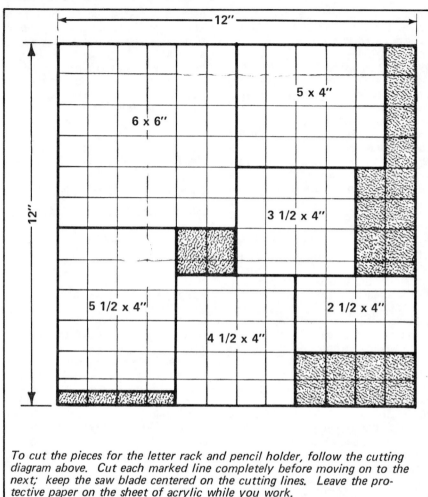

To cut the pieces for the letter rack and pencil holder, follow the cutting diagram above. Cut each marked line completely before moving on to the next; keep the saw blade centered on the cutting lines. Leave the protective paper on the sheet of acrylic while you work.

sheet of acrylic than 1 square foot, leave a little space between pieces to allow for cutting and sanding.

To cut the marked rectangles, leave the protective paper in place. Clamp the acrylic sheet to your work surface, paper side up, with a C-clamp; set a block of scrap wood between the sheet and the clamp to protect the plastic. Keep the cutting line close to the table edge for extra support.

With a fine-toothed hacksaw, carefully cut along each marked cutting line; work slowly so the acrylic doesn't splinter. If you have cutting leeway between pieces, cut each piece of acrylic

along the outside of the marked lines to allow for sanding the rough edges; leave the protective paper on. Don't stop cutting in the middle of a marked-off section; keep your cutting lines straight and even. Loosen and reclamp the sheet as necessary to cut all required pieces of acrylic.

If necessary, cut the acrylic tubing to measure. Acrylic tubing doesn't have a protective covering; to prevent damage, wrap the tubing with masking tape to cover the surface completely. Measure and mark four pieces of tubing, as detailed above. To cut each piece of tubing, set it into the corner of a wood chair, where the back and seat meet. Hold it firmly into this joint to prevent slipping, and cut it at a right angle with a fine-toothed hacksaw. Saw through the protective masking tape, being careful to keep the ends of the tubing square; check them with a triangle or a carpenters' square to make sure.

After cutting the acrylic, finish all cut edges to a smooth, even surface; do not remove the protective paper or tape. Spread a sheet of medium-grit wet-or-dry sandpaper on a flat work surface and pour a few drops of water into the center of the paper. Holding the sheet or tube of acrylic with its cut edge flat against the paper and its face perpendicular to the work surface, rub the cut edge on the wet sandpaper with circular strokes. Keep the piece of acrylic upright to keep the edge flat against the paper.

Sand the cut edge, adding a few drops of water as necessary, until it's as smooth as you can get it. Then sand again with fine-grit wet-or-dry sandpaper, using the same technique. Repeat to sand all cut edges, on both sheet pieces and tubes. Make sure the sanded edges are absolutely flat; this is especially important with the tubing. Dry the finished edges carefully with a soft cloth. When all the pieces of acrylic have been finished, assemble the desk accessories.

The letter rack. To make the letter rack, carefully mark the positions of the four uprights on the protective paper of the 5 × 4-inch base piece, as illustrated. Mark off a ⅛-inch-wide bar on each 4-inch end; 1½ inches in from the inside edge of each marked bar, mark another ⅛-inch-wide bar. These four evenly spaced ⅛-inch strips mark the base positions of the rack's upright dividers.

To expose the base area for each divider, carefully cut the protective paper along the marked line. Cut only through the paper; make sure you don't cut into the acrylic sheet. Peel off the cutout ⅛-inch-wide strips of paper that mark the divider positions.

Using an artists' brush, quickly coat one exposed edge strip on the base

piece with acrylic glue. Coat one 4-inch polished edge of the largest divider piece, 5½ × 4 inches, with glue, and set the divider on edge along the glued strip on the base; do not remove the protective paper. Make sure that the divider is perpendicular to the base, and that the sides of the divider are flush with the sides of the base. Hold the glued edges together for 1 minute to let the glue set.

Repeat, applying glue to the exposed base strip and to one 4-inch edge of the divider piece, to position successively smaller divider pieces along the exposed base strips: first 4½ × 4-inch, then 3½ × 4-inch, and finally 2½ × 4-inch. Hold each newly glued piece in place for 1 minute, and be careful not to knock other pieces out of place as you work.

Let the assembled letter rack dry completely, as directed by the glue manufacturer. When the glue is dry, peel the remaining protective paper off the dividers and the base.

The pencil holder. To make the pencil holder, carefully mark the positions of the four tubes, as illustrated. On

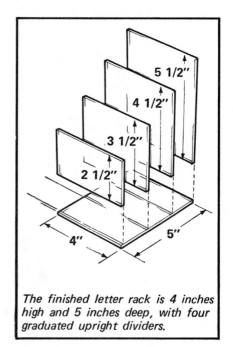

The finished letter rack is 4 inches high and 5 inches deep, with four graduated upright dividers.

the protective paper of the 6 × 6-inch acrylic sheet base piece, draw a line ½ inch in from each side; use a triangle or a carpenters' square to make sure your lines are even. Draw the outlines for the tubes by setting them into position and drawing around the inside and outside base edges; leave the protective masking tape on. Set the two 3-inch pieces of 2½-inch-diameter tubing into opposite corners of the base, flush against the ½-inch line on each side. Set the 5-inch piece of 2-inch-diameter tubing and the 1¾-inch piece of 1½-inch tubing into the remaining corners, flush against the ½-inch corner lines.

Remove the tubes from the base. With a sharp craft knife, carefully cut through the protective paper around the marked rings; make sure you don't cut into the acrylic base. Peel off the ring of cutout protective paper that marks the base of each acrylic tube. Attach the tubes to the exposed mounting circles on the base as above; do not remove the protective masking tape. Using an artists' brush, apply acrylic glue to both bonding surfaces; set each tube into place on its glued mounting circle and

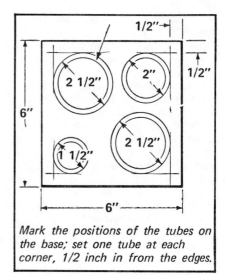

Mark the positions of the tubes on the base; set one tube at each corner, 1/2 inch in from the edges.

hold it firmly in place for 1 minute.

Let the assembled pencil holder dry completely, as directed by the glue manufacturer. When the glue is completely dry, peel off the protective paper from the base piece, and carefully remove the masking tape from the acrylic tubes.

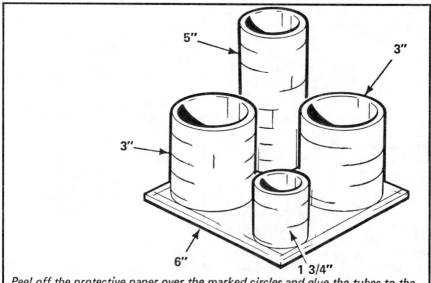

Peel off the protective paper over the marked circles and glue the tubes to the exposed rings on the base, as shown; leave the protective masking tape on the tubes.

Make a Terrarium

A terrarium is a great way to have plants even if you don't have time or a green thumb. The commercial variety costs quite a bit, but it's easy and inexpensive to make your own. **Tools:** scissors, small trowel, squirt bottle or plant mister. **Materials:** fishbowl, brandy snifter, or other glass container; plants, coarse gravel, activated charcoal, scrap plastic screening, foam rubber, rocks, potting soil, glass saucer or plate. **Time:** ½ to 1 hour.

To make a simple terrarium, choose a glass container—a fishbowl, a large brandy snifter, or any container you like. Buy tiny plants for the terrarium, get cuttings from a friend and root them, or use plants from the woods or your backyard. Small, low-growing plants work best; aloe vera, small wild flowers like yellow clover, meadow plants like lichen, and swamp and forest plants like ferns and mosses are all good choices. Choose plants that grow well in indirect sunlight or shade; if the terrarium must be in direct sunlight, the plants will grow toward the light and give your garden a lopsided look. If you take plants from the woods, take only a few plants from any one area. Be sure to get plenty of earth with each plant so that the roots will be intact.

Put the terrarium together with the standard potting materials. Cover the bottom of the fishbowl or snifter with a layer of coarse gravel; spread a thin layer of activated charcoal over the gravel. Set a piece of plastic screening over the charcoal to keep the soil from filtering down into the spaces between the pieces of gravel and charcoal.

Cut a thin strip of foam rubber about 1½ to 2 inches long and secure it in one of the holes in the plastic screening, so that about 1 inch or a little more sticks up. This piece of foam serves as a wick to redistribute water throughout the terrarium. Set a few flat rocks on top of the screen to hold it in place, and cover it with 2 to 3 inches of potting soil.

Poke holes in the soil and set your plants into place as desired—make sure the roots are well spread and supported. Water the terrarium lightly with a squirt bottle or a plant mister; water as usual thereafter. For a no-maintenance terrarium, cover the container with a glass saucer or plate or a piece of glass cut to fit; this closes the ecosystem so that the moisture inside continually recycles. Very little care or watering is

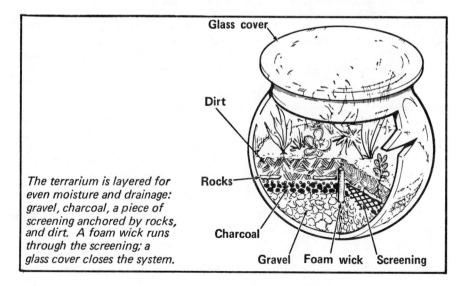

The terrarium is layered for even moisture and drainage: gravel, charcoal, a piece of screening anchored by rocks, and dirt. A foam wick runs through the screening; a glass cover closes the system.

581

needed from this point on—if the terrarium looks dry, add 1 to 2 tablespoons of water periodically. If the plants grow too high, snip them back; they'll bush out nicely.

Dry Flowers

To enjoy a flower garden all year, dry your favorite cut flowers for winter arranging. Choose sand-drying or air-drying for an easy, inexpensive, and very satisfying project.

SAND-DRYING. This method can be used to dry a wide variety of flowers. **Tools:** wire cutter, sharp knife, toothpicks, soft artists' brush, measuring cup. **Materials:** fresh cut flowers, deep open boxes, #20 or #24 florists' wire, white glue, wax paper, white sand, airtight containers. Buy sandbox or fine silica construction sand. **Time:** 1½ to 2 hours preparation; 1 to 3 weeks drying time; ½ hour after drying.

Choose flowers for drying carefully. Tulips, roses, peonies, dahlias, marigolds, snapdragons, daisy-type flowers, and flowering branches—lilac and similar shrubs—dry well. Do not use flowers that last only one day, such as day lilies or rose of sharon; do not use asters, azaleas, chrysanthemums, geraniums, petunias, phlox, pinks, poppies, or violets. Otherwise, experiment —you may have good luck.

Cut flowers at the peak of their show; any imperfections will be exaggerated by the drying. Pick flowers after dew has evaporated in the morning. Blossom, leaves, and stem should all be dry.

For the best results, work in dry, warm weather. Drying conditions determine the vividness of the dried flowers' color: rapid drying in a very warm dry place, with bright light, produces bright colors; slower drying in a less warm or dry area produces more muted shades. The best drying area is an attic during dry, hot weather; a service room with a dehumidifier set at 60 percent is also good. To speed the process, you can use a gas oven with a pilot light but no heat. Oven-drying usually takes from 4 days to 1 week; if you need to use the oven, remove the flowers and return them after the oven has cooled completely.

To prepare the flowers, reinforce the stems and the flower heads with florists' wire or white glue, as appropriate. For daisy-type flowers, flowering shrubs, and similar flowers, support the stems with #20 or #24 florists' wire. Cut 6-inch lengths of wire. For each flower, push a piece of florists' wire up through the stem and completely through the flower head; then bend the end of the wire into a hook over the flower head and carefully pull the wire down to secure the head to the stem.

For flowers that are dried face up, such as tulips or roses, cut off all but ¾ to 1 inch of the stem; insert florists' wire as above. For many-petaled flowers, secure the flower head with white glue instead of wire. Pour a little glue onto a piece of wax paper and dilute it with a few drops of water; mix it evenly with a toothpick. Apply a thin coat of glue at the base of each petal, working the glue into the base of the flower to attach each individual petal to the base. Work carefully to keep from damaging the petals. For double roses or similar flowers, apply glue in several rows on the inside base of the flower. Let the glue dry completely.

To dry the flowers, slowly cover them with white sand in deep drying containers. Dry *cup-shaped or rose-shaped flowers* face up—tulips, roses, peonies, dahlias, or marigolds. Fill one end of a deep drying container with sand, deep enough to hold the flowers in an upright position, and support the lower petals. With your hand or the base of a cup, make a slight depression in the sand. Bend the wire at the base of the flower and position the flower in the sand.

Fill a measuring cup or other spouted cup with sand, and slowly pour sand from the cup around the base of the flower; hold the flower steady as you work. Build up sand around the side of the flower so that the sand flows under and over the outer petals only. When the flower is firmly supported, place another flower in the container and start to build the sand up around it. Continue, adding flowers one by one, to fill the container. As you add flowers, the sand will even out in the box. Keep pouring sand, gently and gradually, around the flowers. The sand will flow into the center of each flower, supporting the natural shape of the flower head.

Be sure to pour the sand *slowly.* It takes some practice to pour the sand evenly enough to preserve the natural shape of the flower. If you pour too much sand over a petal, bending it out of its natural shape, stop pouring and carefully brush the sand away with your finger or a small artists' brush. Work as delicately as possible so you don't damage the petals. Cover each flower completely with sand.

Dry *daisy-type flowers* face down. Pour an even base of sand into the drying container, and make an indentation in the sand with your hand in the same shape as the flower. Steadying the flower with one hand, build up sand around the flower until it's completely covered.

Dry *snapdragons, lilac, and other elongated flowers and flowering branches* horizontally. Pour an even base of sand into the drying container. Lay the flowers on the sand, leaving enough space to pour sand around and between flowers and into individual flowers; position flowering branches face up. Carefully pour sand first on one side, then on the other. Lift the flower slightly with the end of a soft artists' brush so that the bottom petals aren't flattened by the pressure of the sand.

When all the flowers are covered with sand, carefully move the full drying containers to your drying area. Let the flowers dry undisturbed until they're completely dry—about 1 to 3 weeks, depending on the temperature and the humidity of the area. Then carefully move the drying containers to your work surface. Be careful not to jar them.

To prevent breakage, remove the sand very carefully. Tip a drying container slightly to let the sand *slowly* flow from one corner of the box. As each flower is released from the sand, catch it and lift it out carefully. Wait until each flower is completely uncovered; if you pull a flower before it's completely uncovered, you may lose some of the petals. Sand often sticks to glued areas, even though the glue was dry before you put the flower in the sand. Remove sand carefully from these areas, brushing it off lightly with a soft artists' brush.

Arrange the flowers as you would fresh flowers, or store them for later arranging. To protect the dried flowers from humidity, seal them carefully in airtight containers; use large cans, tins, or plastic boxes sealed with masking tape, or seal cardboard boxes inside airtight plastic bags. If you live in a humid climate and don't have air conditioning, store dried arrangements in tightly sealed plastic bags during the summer.

AIR-DRYING. Herbs, everlastings, and many ornamental grasses can be successfully air-dried. **Tools:** hammer. **Materials:** fresh cut flowers, herbs, or grasses; rubber bands, large nails or wire hangers. **Time:** ½ hour preparation; 1 to 3 weeks drying time.

Cut perfect plants with long stems. Drying conditions determine the vividness of the dried flowers' color, but most colors become muted as the flowers dry. Hang flowers to dry in a dark, dry area with good air circulation, such as an attic, an open closet, or a service room. Drive large nails across open beams to hang the flowers, or hang them on wire hangers.

To prepare the flowers or grasses, strip the leaves from the lower stems. Arrange the flowers in small bunches and fasten the end of each bunch together with a rubber band; do not use string. Open each bunch into a fan shape so that the flowers aren't crushed.

Keeping the flower heads down, hang the bunches from nails or on wire hangers in a dark, dry place. Let them dry for 1 to 3 weeks, until all moisture has evaporated from the flowers. Display or store as above.

Build
a Potting Table

A potting table is invaluable for working with flats and potted plants. Here's a basic design you can modify to suit your own space and working requirements. **Tools:** measuring rule, pencil, carpenters' square, handsaw or power saw, hammer, fine-toothed file, drill, keyhole or saber saw. **Materials:** 2 × 4 construction-grade pine stock, 1 × 4 stock, 6-penny and 8-penny common nails, ¾-inch grade C-D plywood, ⅛-inch tempered hardboard, ¾-inch finishing nails; large, heavy-duty plastic dishpan. **Time:** about 3 to 4 hours for a 4-foot table; 4 to 5 hours for larger sizes.

Plan the table to fit your work space;

choose a spot for it and decide on the size of the table and its component parts. The width of the table should be at least 2 feet, but if you want more room, you can make it 2½ or 3 feet wide. The bench length can be varied from 4 to 8 feet and, as with any workbench, you should tailor the height to whatever is most comfortable for you—as little as 30 inches for a relatively low table, as much as 36 inches if you're tall.

From the bench dimensions, work out the necessary quantities of lumber you'll need, as specified above. Buy a sheet of ⅛-inch tempered hardboard for a smooth, replaceable work surface; it isn't essential, but it's a nice finishing touch. Buy a large, heavy-duty plastic dishpan for mixing potting soil.

Measure, mark, and cut the four 2 × 4 legs to the desired height of the table, less the thickness of the top; use a carpenters' square to keep the cuts

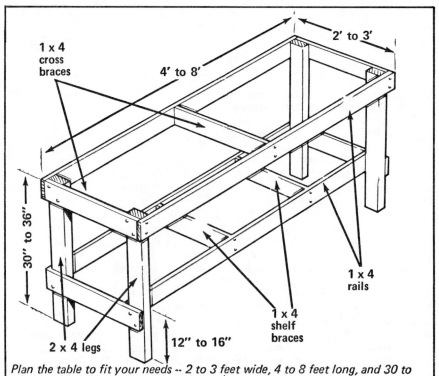

Plan the table to fit your needs -- 2 to 3 feet wide, 4 to 8 feet long, and 30 to 36 inches high. Build the frame of 1 x 4's, with 2 x 4 legs.

even. Cut the wood with a handsaw or a power saw. Measure, mark, and cut four 1 × 4 braces to the desired width of the table—24 inches or more. Lay out each pair of 2 × 4 legs flat on a level surface and nail the end braces across them with two 6-penny common nails at each end; place the top end brace flush with the tops of the legs, and the bottom brace with its top edge about 12 to 16 inches above the floor. You can vary this 12- to 16-inch brace height depending on what height you think is best for a storage shelf.

Measure, mark, and cut the two back rails and the top front rail to the desired table length, from 4 to 8 feet. Prop the leg assemblies up and connect them to each other with the three rails; nail the rails in place to both the legs and the end braces with two 8-penny nails at each joint, with the ends of the rails flush with the faces of the end braces. Measure, mark, and cut the lower front rail to fit inside the legs of the table—about 1½ inches shorter than

the other three rails. Nail the rail to the front legs and to the end braces, exactly aligned with the lower back rail, with two 8-penny nails at each end.

Cut a lower cross brace to fit across the table's width under the bottom shelf. One brace is adequate unless the table is more than 6 feet long, or if you'll set heavy loads, such as stacks of clay pots, on the shelf; for extra strength, use two cross braces. Measure, mark, and cut a 1 × 4 cross brace to fit tightly from the front bottom rail to the back. End-nail the cross brace to the bottom rails with two 8-penny common nails at each end. Cut another cross brace and nail it to brace the top rails; use two braces for a table more than 6 feet long.

Measure and cut the bench top to the desired size from ¾-inch grade C-D plywood, allowing for a lip of 1 to 2 inches at the front and, if desired, at the ends. Check to make sure the bench frame is square at all corners and position the bench top on the frame; nail it in place with 8-penny common nails

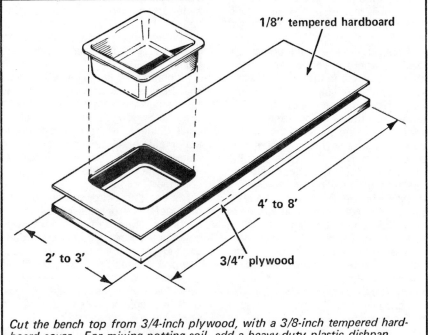

1/8" tempered hardboard

4' to 8'

3/4" plywood

2' to 3'

Cut the bench top from 3/4-inch plywood, with a 3/8-inch tempered hardboard cover. For mixing potting soil, add a heavy-duty plastic dishpan, set into the top with its rim resting on the hardboard cover.

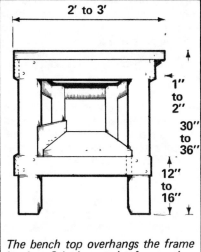

2' to 3'

1" to 2"

30" to 36"

12" to 16"

The bench top overhangs the frame by 1 to 2 inches at the front; the shelf is set back from the legs.

plywood shelf piece to fit in front of the backer, with its back edge butted against the backer and its front edge just behind the table legs. Nail the shelf into place with 8-penny common nails, setting nails from the back of the shelf into the bottom of the backer and from the front of the shelf to the front bottom rail. The shelf ends should be flush with the outside faces of the end braces, and the front edge of the shelf should be flush with the outside face of the rail.

Add paraphernalia to the bench as desired—an under-the-counter wire rack, for instance, makes good bulb storage. Leave the wood unfinished, or paint or stain it as desired.

Mix Potting Soil

spaced about 12 inches apart. Measure and cut the cover of ⅛-inch tempered hardboard, the same size as the plywood top. Position it exactly over the plywood top and nail it to the bench top with a few ¾-inch finishing nails. Round off the sharp edges of the hardboard with a fine-toothed file.

To set a dishpan into the bench top, position it wherever you want it; be sure the pan will clear the cross braces below. Carefully mark the outline of the body of the dishpan—*not* the lip or flange—on the tabletop; then drill a starter hole in the center of the marked area and use a keyhole or saber saw to cut the outlined section out of the bench top. Set the dishpan into the hole, with its lip resting on the tabletop. The fit should be snug, so that the dish-pan won't move around and the rim or flange has ample bearing surface on the bench top.

Measure and cut a shelf backer, the length of the bench, from plywood, or use a wide board the length of the bench. The backer should be about 8 to 12 inches wide. Nail the backer across the inside edges of the table legs, set flat across the bottom end and cross braces; use three or four 8-penny nails at each end. Measure and mark a

There are as many different blends of potting soil as there are plants to grow, but these basic mixtures are good ones for most plants. **Tools:** large baking pan, tablespoon, aluminum foil, oven. **Materials:** garden dirt or packaged potting soil; leaf mold, sphagnum moss, or peat moss; coarse sand, potting charcoal, steamed bone meal. **Time:** about 1 hour.

Plants require firm, rich, and porous soil. Firmness is provided by a clay substance, such as garden dirt or packaged potting soil. A rich supply of organic material is best supplied with leaf mold, peat moss, or shredded sphagnum moss. Use coarse sand—never fine sand—to ensure good drainage.

Mix one part dirt or potting soil, one part leaf mold or peat or sphagnum moss, and one part sand in a large baking pan. For cacti, mix three parts sand to one part dirt or potting soil and one part leaf mold or moss. For plants with very fine hair-like roots—such as begonias, coleus, and ferns—mix two parts leaf mold or moss to one part dirt or potting soil and one part sand.

Home-mixed soil must be sterilized to kill bacteria that can damage plants. Spread the soil evenly over the baking pan and cover it with aluminum foil, shiny side down. Preheat the oven to 200° F and bake the soil for ½ hour, stirring occasionally; replace the foil each time you stir. The soil will smell bad for a while after heating; mix a large batch so you don't have to endure the stench more often than necessary.

After sterilizing the soil, remove it from the oven and let it cool completely. To each potful of soil, add a small handful of potting charcoal at the bottom of the pot; mix 1 tablespoon of steamed bone meal into the soil and fill the pot.

Make Scented Candles

Candle-making, a craft born of necessity, has become a fascinating and enjoyable hobby. Start with scented candles; once you learn the basics, you can experiment to create an abundance of unusual candles. **Tools:** molds (empty quart milk carton, tin can, wide-mouthed glass, muffin tin, etc.), pastry brush, scissors, wood dowels, small hammer, stainless steel or enameled steel pitcher with open spout, large heavy pot, hot plate or stove, candy thermometer, measuring spoons, stir sticks, oven mitt. **Materials:** newspaper, masking tape, vegetable oil, candle wicking, small lead sinkers, candle wax, solid candle dye, oil-based scent or perfume. **Time:** about 1 to 2 hours for poured candles, more for dipped candles.

Buy candle wax, solid dye, and wicking at a hobby and craft shop; the wax is sold in 10- or 11-pound slabs. Don't use grocery-store paraffin; it smokes. Use any type of oil-based perfume.

Spread your work area with newspaper to protect it from hot wax. Before melting the wax, prepare the molds for the candles. The simplest mold is a clean, empty quart milk carton; rinse and dry the carton and wrap it with masking tape to reinforce it. If you pre-

fer a round shape, use a clean tin can, a wide-mouthed glass, or, for small candles, a muffin tin. Brush the inside of each can, glass, or muffin mold with vegetable oil to make it easier to unmold the candle.

Prepare the candle wicks carefully. Cut a piece of wicking about 3 inches longer than each mold is deep. For each candle, tie one end of the wick to a piece of wood dowel and set the dowel across the top of the prepared mold, suspending the wick in the center of the mold. Tape the free end of the wick to the bottom of the mold with a small piece of masking tape. For large candles, or where oil in the mold makes taping impractical, attach a small lead sinker to the free end of the wick so that the wick is held taut inside the mold.

If you plan to dip candles, prepare a place for them to hang while the dipped wax hardens. Use a piece of dowel long enough to hold several wicks; arrange a place to set the dowel so that the wicks will be able to hang freely. Cut a piece

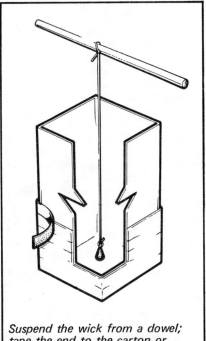

Suspend the wick from a dowel; tape the end to the carton or attach a lead sinker to hold it taut.

of wick about 40 inches long, but don't cut the individual wicks yet.

Break up the slabs of candle wax with a small hammer; you'll need about 2 pounds of wax for a milk-carton candle. Put the chunks of wax into a stainless steel or enameled steel pitcher with an open spout, and set the pitcher into a large heavy pot filled with water. An ordinary double boiler is usable, but the pitcher makes it much easier to handle and pour the hot wax.

Melt the wax slowly over low heat on a hot plate or a stove; add solid candle dye to get the color you want. Set a candy thermometer in the melting wax to make sure it doesn't overheat. *Caution: Wax is extremely flammable; do not melt it over direct heat or leave it unattended.* Check the candy thermometer frequently as the wax heats; when the liquid wax reaches 195° to 210° F, remove it from the heat. Add a scant ¼ to ½ teaspoon of any oil-based scent or perfume you like—½ teaspoon is ample for a 2- to 3-pound candle. Stir to blend the scent into the wax.

Poured candles. Let the melted, scented wax cool slightly and then pour it slowly and carefully over the suspended wicks and into the prepared molds; fill the molds as full as desired. *Caution: Wear an oven mitt to protect your hand; pour slowly to avoid spilling the wax.* Let the candles harden overnight in a cool place; don't handle the molds while they're hot. When the wax is completely hardened, peel off the cardboard milk carton or slip the candle out of its oiled mold. Cut the wick to free the candle from the dowel.

Dipped candles. To dip candles, dip a 40-inch piece of wicking into the melted wax and hang it straight up and down to dry. When the wax has hardened to form a straight, rigid 40-inch wick, cut the wick into pieces about 2 inches longer than you want the candles, or 2 inches longer than the depth of the melted wax. Tie the stiffened wicks to a long piece of wood dowel, spaced evenly; for easier dipping, attach a very small lead sinker to the free end of each wick.

Let the melted, scented wax cool

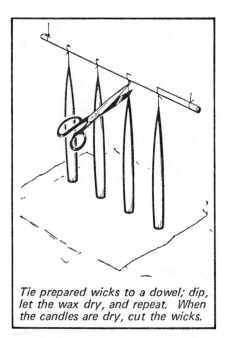

Tie prepared wicks to a dowel; dip, let the wax dry, and repeat. When the candles are dry, cut the wicks.

slightly and then carefully dip the prepared wicks into it, holding the dowel and submerging the tied wicks in the wax to the depth desired. If the wax doesn't stick to the wick, it's probably too hot; let it cool slightly and then try again. Set the dowel in its prepared drying spot and let the dipped wicks harden; then, being careful not to bend the wicks, dip them again. Repeat, dipping and hardening, until the candles are as thick as you want them.

While the finished candles are still warm, shape them, if desired, by rolling them on a smooth surface; cut the wicks at the dowel to release the candles. Spread the candles on a smooth surface to harden, or let them hang overnight from the dipping dowel.

Clean and Repair an Antique Quilt

Antique quilts make wonderful wall hangings, and many are still sturdy enough to be used as their makers intended. Clean and restore old quilts carefully before you use them. **Tools:** bathtub, fine sewing needle, sharp scissors, steam iron and ironing board, pressing cloth, fine straight pins. **Materials:** mild soap flakes or liquid detergent made especially for quilts, large white towels, cotton thread, lightweight fusible web interfacing; pieces of old fabric similar to those in quilt, new 100 percent cotton fabric, or sheer fabric (voile or silk organza) in a neutral beige shade. **Time:** about 2 hours to wash a quilt; about 4 hours to repair moderate damage.

Cotton quilts in relatively good condition—even very old ones—can be hand-washed. Some antique quilts are too fragile and too valuable to be cleaned and repaired by anyone except a professional textile restorer, and all silk and velvet quilts must be professionally cleaned. If you're not sure your quilt can withstand washing, get a professional opinion before working on it; ask a museum with a good textile collection for references. Clean the quilt or have it cleaned before repairing it.

Cleaning. To wash a cotton quilt in good enough condition to survive it, fill a bathtub with tepid water and add mild soap flakes or liquid detergent made especially for quilts, as directed by the manufacturer. Immerse the quilt and let it soak for about 10 minutes; then drain the water from the tub, pressing the quilt to remove excess water. Don't lift the wet quilt; the weight of the water could tear it.

Let the quilt drain for a few minutes and then fill the tub again with tepid water. Agitate the quilt gently to rinse it; let it soak for a few minutes and drain the tub again. Repeat, rinsing and gently agitating the quilt, until no soap or dirt shows in the rinse water. Drain the water out and press the quilt firmly but gently to remove as much water as possible; blot it with large towels to soak out more water, and let it drain for a few minutes more.

You'll need an assistant to remove the quilt from the tub. Spread white towels over the shower rod or another straight rod where you can hang the

quilt to dry. When the quilt is completely drained, lift it gently with your assistant, with your hands supporting as much of the wet quilt as possible. Lift the quilt over the rod and spread it carefully over the towels on the rod; make sure the quilt is smooth and its weight is evenly distributed. Let the quilt dry completely on the rod; as it dries, squeeze water out of the bottom edges with towels about once an hour. Do *not* machine-dry the quilt.

In warm weather, dry the quilt outside if you can to give it a fresh smell. Spread towels over the clothesline before you hang the quilt, and drape the quilt over the line without using clothespins. Don't dry the quilt in direct sunlight, and don't hang it outside on a very windy day; the wind will whip the quilt and could cause tears in the fabric.

Repairing. Check the quilt carefully for loose or frayed pieces of fabric. If the stitching holding a piece of fabric has broken but the fabric itself is undamaged, just turn the loose edge under and restitch it carefully with small slipstitches; use a fine sewing needle and cotton thread.

To mend small tears in the fabric itself, cut small pieces of lightweight fusible web interfacing. Slip a piece of fusible web into the quilt through the tear and smooth the fabric over the web. Cover the area with a damp pressing cloth and press with a steam iron to fuse the web to the torn fabric, following the instructions on the fusible web package; be careful not to scorch the quilt. The fused web will hold the fabric together in an almost invisible repair.

If the quilt fabric is badly tattered, cut new patches to replace the damaged ones. Old fabric usually matches best, but it can be hard to find; try secondhand stores or garage sales to find pieces of material similar to those in the quilt. If you can't find old fabric to match the quilt, buy 100 percent cotton fabric in solid colors or small prints. Wash the fabric and hang it in the sun so it fades as it dries.

To replace a damaged quilt piece, carefully snip the stitching around the old piece and remove it. Cut a new

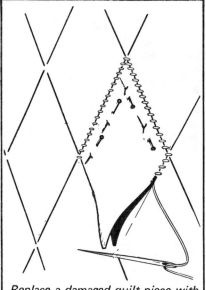

Replace a damaged quilt piece with new fabric; turn the edges under, pin it, and stitch into place.

piece from your patching fabric, using the old piece as a pattern and allowing ¼ inch seam allowance all around. Turn the seam allowance under so that the new piece is exactly the same shape as the old one, and press the piece of fabric carefully with a steam iron. Lay the new piece into place where the old one was, pin it carefully, and attach it to the surrounding pieces of material with small slip stitches. Use a fine sewing needle and cotton thread.

If a piece in the quilt is tattered and you can't get replacement fabric, the safest and least obvious method of preservation is to cover it with a sheer neutral fabric. Use voile or silk organza in a neutral beige shade for an unobtrusive covering. Leave the torn piece in place and cut a covering piece to the same size and shape, allowing about ⅛ inch seam allowance all around. Turn the seam allowance under, press the piece of fabric, and set it over the damaged piece; stitch it into place with

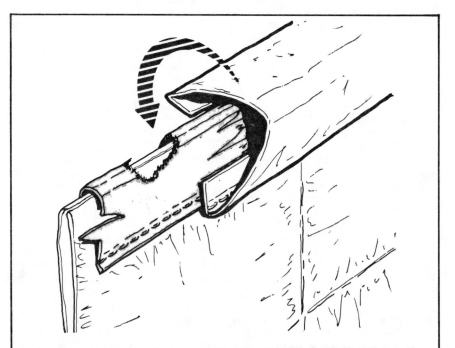

Cover a frayed binding with a bias strip of neutral fabric. Stitch the bias strip along one edge and fold the unstitched edge over to cover the old binding. Turn the raw edge under and stitch the binding into place on the other side.

small slip-stitches. Use a fine sewing needle and cotton thread.

Use the same technique to cover worn binding on the edges of the quilt. Cut the sheer fabric into strips on the bias, twice as wide as the original binding on one side plus ¼ inch seam allowance on each side. Piece and seam the strips to form one strip long enough to go all the way around the quilt; use a basic sewing book for detailed instructions on cutting and piecing bias strips.

When the bias strip is completely pieced and seamed, turn each long edge under ¼ inch; press the strip with a steam iron, being careful not to stretch the fabric. Set the strip over the original binding on the right side of the quilt, with its edge to the inside edge of the binding and its excess on top of the quilt. Stitch the strip into place along the old binding with small running stitches, knotting the ends carefully. Use a fine sharp sewing needle and cotton thread. To finish the binding, fold the unstitched edge of the protective binding over the edge of the quilt and stitch it into place over the binding on the back of the quilt.

Repair or Rebind a Book

Hardbound books can take a real beating over the years, and new bindings sometimes crack and come apart at the first reading. Keep your library in shape by repairing worn books; rebind the badly damaged ones to suit yourself. **Tools:** artists' brush, burnishing tool, books to use as weights, steam iron, pressing cloth or handkerchief, pencil, ruler, scissors, craft knife, pocketknife, small paintbrush, triangle or carpenters' square, drawing pen. Buy a burnishing tool at an art supply or craft store. **Materials:** wax paper, white glue, tissues, onionskin paper, bookbinders' glue, bond paper, light cardboard, brown paper, book cloth, wallpaper paste, heavy cardboard, drawing ink. Buy bookbinders' glue and book cloth at

a bookbinders' supply store. **Time:** 10 minutes to repair minor damage; about 2 to 3 hours to rebind a book.

Damaged pages. Repair torn pages with white glue. Set a piece of wax paper under the torn page and brush glue along the torn edges with an artists' brush. Carefully join the torn sections and press the edges of the tear together with the blunt end of a burnishing tool. Remove excess glue with a tissue. Set another piece of wax paper over the glued tear and weight the mended page with another book for about 8 hours.

Use a steam iron to smooth out crumpled or folded pages. Set the iron at the low steam setting. Smooth out the crumpled page, cover it with a pressing cloth or a clean handkerchief, and press firmly to steam the page flat. Be careful not to scorch the paper or melt the glue of the binding.

Refasten loose pages with hinges made of onionskin paper. For each loose page, measure and cut a strip of onionskin ½ inch wide and the length of the page. Crease the strip of onionskin in half lengthwise. Set a piece of wax paper over the page ahead of the loose one, and another piece over the page following it.

Brush a thin coat of white glue onto one outside surface of the onionskin hinge. Pulling the wax paper back just enough to expose the inside edge of the page, attach the glued half of the hinge to the page following the loose page, with the folded half flush against the spine and the ends even with the top and bottom of the page. With the blunt end of a burnishing tool, carefully smooth down the glued flap of onionskin and press it into the spine of the book.

Apply a thin coat of white glue to the outside of the other half of the onionskin hinge. Carefully attach the spine edge of the loose page to the glued hinge surface, keeping it as tight to the binding as possible. Press the hinged page firmly but carefully into place with a ruler; make sure all other page surfaces are protected with wax paper. Wipe off excess glue as necessary with a tissue and close the book. Weight the mended book with another book for about 8 hours.

Damaged spine. If one cover of the book has torn loose from the spine, you can probably reattach it. Carefully cut the cover free; if necessary, use a craft knife to cut the end paper so it doesn't tear. Remove the old glue from the exposed part of the spine and the spine backstrip, using a craft knife or a pocketknife to scrape the surfaces clean.

Apply a thin layer of bookbinders' glue to the cleaned spine surface and let it dry, as directed by the manufacturer. Apply a thin layer of bookbinders' glue to the backstrip and, with the book closed, press the backstrip smoothly down over the spine.

To reattach the cover to the book, make a hinge of bond paper. Measure and cut a strip of bond paper, 1 to 2 inches wide and as long as the end papers of the book. Crease the strip in half lengthwise.

Brush a thin coat of white glue onto one outside surface of the prepared hinge and attach the glued hinge to the last (or first) page of the book, with the folded edge flush against the spine and the ends flush with the book's top and bottom. Apply glue to the other outside half of the book and attach the second half of the hinge to the loose cover to secure it to the spine. Fit the folded edge of the hinge carefully into the curve of the spine, and press the hinge surfaces into place with a burnishing tool. Weight the book lightly and let it dry for about 8 hours.

If the backstrip of the book's binding is damaged and the spine has completely separated from it, carefully cut the end papers along the spine to free the cover from the book. Remove the cover entirely; cut the backstrip to separate it completely from the front and back covers. Make a new backstrip to replace the old one.

Cut a new backstrip from light cardboard; use the old strip as a pattern, or cut the strip to the length of the cover boards and the width of the book's spine. To strengthen the backstrip, cut a piece of brown paper

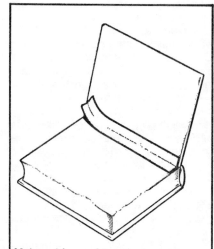

Make a hinge of bond paper to re-attach a cover; fit the folded edge smoothly into the curve of the spine.

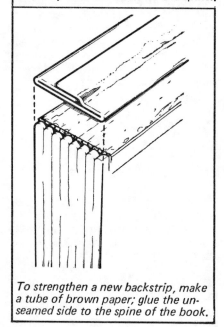

To strengthen a new backstrip, make a tube of brown paper; glue the unseamed side to the spine of the book.

the same length as the book's spine and twice its width plus ½ inch. Measure and mark the exact width of the spine on the brown paper strip, centered on its width, and fold the strip lengthwise at each marked point to make a tube exactly the width of the spine. Glue the overlapping edges of

Cut a piece of book cloth ½ inch longer than the book's cover and 2 inches wider than the spine. Working quickly, brush a thin layer of white glue or wallpaper paste onto the wrong side of the book cloth; coat it evenly and completely. Quickly center the new cardboard backstrip on the glued cloth and smooth it firmly down. Set the front and back covers of the book onto the edges of the strip, leaving a hairline opening between the backstrip and the covers so that the new cover will fold together easily; press the covers into place. Fold the top and bottom edges of the glued cloth over the new backstrip and the book's covers, and smooth them down firmly.

Position the inside of the book on the newly assembled cover, with the brown paper reinforcing tube centered on the new backstrip. To attach the book to the cover, make hinges from bond paper as above. Fit each hinge firmly into the curve of the book's spine. Let the new spine dry for at least 8 hours.

Damaged cover. If the corners of a book are frayed, work white glue into the layers of cardboard and cloth with an artists' brush. Press the corners firmly together, using a burnishing tool to smooth the glued cloth evenly over the corners. Protect inside page surfaces with a sheet of wax paper between the cover and the book; let the glue dry at least 8 hours.

If the cloth at the corners of the book is too worn to reglue but the cover boards themselves are solid, cover the corners with matching or contrasting book cloth. For each corner, cut a triangle of book cloth to the size desired, plus ¾ inch to fold over onto each side. Cut a ½-inch-deep curve into the outside corner of the triangle so the new corner can be smoothly folded and glued.

Working quickly, brush a thin coat of white glue or wallpaper paste over the entire triangle of book cloth. Smooth the glued triangle over the worn corner, fold the new curved corner in to fit the old corner exactly, and fold the sides of the triangle smoothly down over the cover. Glue the mitered corner securely.

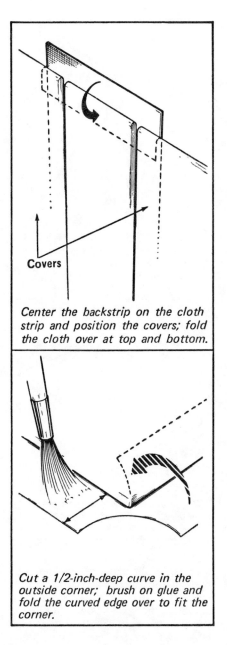

Center the backstrip on the cloth strip and position the covers; fold the cloth over at top and bottom.

Cut a 1/2-inch-deep curve in the outside corner; brush on glue and fold the curved edge over to fit the corner.

the paper tube to form a ½-inch lengthwise seam.

To reassemble the book, remove old glue from the book's spine with a craft knife or a pocketknife. Apply a thin coat of bookbinders' glue to the unseamed side of the brown paper tube and attach the tube firmly to the book's spine.

If desired, cut new end papers to cover the edges of the corner patches. Use bond paper, with the grain of the paper parallel to the book's spine—to determine the grain, dampen a scrap of the same paper; it will curl along the grain.

For both the front and the back cover, fold a sheet of bond paper in half, to fit into the bound edge and cover the old end papers completely. Cut the folded paper to the exact size of the old end papers. Apply a thin coat of white glue to one outside surface of the new end paper, coating it lightly and completely. Set the folded sheet carefully into place, fitting the folded edge into the curve of the book's spine and smoothing the glued outside surface evenly over the inside of the book's cover. Press the fitted edge of the new end paper firmly with a burnishing tool to secure it.

Rebinding. If the cover is badly damaged, rebind the book completely. Carefully remove the old cover from the book, using a craft knife if necessary to separate the end papers. Using the old boards as a pattern, cut new cover boards from heavy cardboard—use thick one-layer cardboard, not corrugated. Cut a new backstrip from light cardboard; use the old backstrip as a pattern or cut the strip to the length of the cover boards and the width of the book's spine. Clean the spine and attach a reinforcing paper tube as above.

Center the new cover boards and the backstrip on the wrong side of a piece of book cloth, large enough to overlap the new cover ¾ inch all around; leave a hairline space as above to make sure the new cover will fold together easily. Use a triangle or a carpenters' square to make sure the boards are squared on the book cloth. With a pencil and a straightedge, mark the exact position of all three pieces on the cloth; then remove the boards and set them at hand.

Brush a thin coat of wallpaper paste over the marked book cloth, covering the entire piece of cloth smoothly and evenly. Work quickly; the cloth will curl as you brush the paste on.

To assemble the cover, set the cover boards and the backstrip into place on

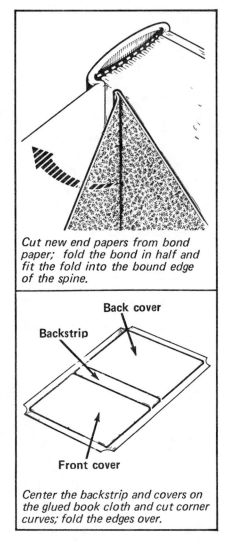

Cut new end papers from bond paper; fold the bond in half and fit the fold into the bound edge of the spine.

Back cover

Backstrip

Front cover

Center the backstrip and covers on the glued book cloth and cut corner curves; fold the edges over.

the glued cloth, exactly as marked, and press them firmly to the cloth. Quickly cut each corner as above in a shallow curve about ½ inch deep. Fold the edges of the cloth over the sides of the boards and the backstrip, and fold and glue the trimmed corners as above to form smoothly overlapped corners. Smooth all glued edges with a burnishing tool, and round the corners of the new cover slightly.

To attach the book to the new cover, glue the old end paper at each end of the book over the inside of the new cover, pressing the folded edge firmly into the curve of the spine and smoothing the paper over the edges of the cover cloth. Or, if desired, make new end papers for the book, as above.

Finally, set a sheet of wax paper inside each cover of the book, butted into the spine. Weight the book closed for about 2 minutes, using several other books. Remove the weights and open the front cover at a 90-degree angle; smooth the freshly glued end paper with a burnishing tool. Turn the book over and repeat to smooth the back end paper; then close the book and weight it firmly for at least 8 hours.

Label the newly bound book with a drawing pen; use black, colored, or gold ink as desired.

Load Your Own Film

If you use a 35 mm camera, you can save money by loading your own film, without a darkroom or any knowledge of photographic processing. **Tools:** daylight bulk film loader, reloadable 35 mm film cartridges, beer can opener, scissors. **Materials:** 50- or 100-foot roll of bulk film (color or black-and-white), narrow masking tape. **Time:** about 10 minutes.

Before opening the package of film, read the manufacturer's directions for your bulk film loader. The roll of film must be loaded into the bulk loader in total darkness or your film will be ruined. Work in a *completely* dark space—if you can't be sure of darkness any other way, put the film into the loader at night, and work in a closet with the door closed, in a room with the lights off and doors and windows closed. Follow the manufacturer's instructions exactly to load the roll of film.

After the film is loaded into the bulk loader, you can roll cartridges of film in daylight. To roll a cartridge of film, pry off the blank end of a plastic cartridge—the end that doesn't have a

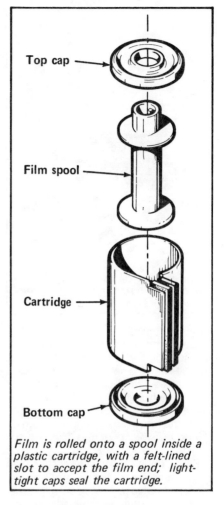

Top cap

Film spool

Cartridge

Bottom cap

Film is rolled onto a spool inside a plastic cartridge, with a felt-lined slot to accept the film end; light-tight caps seal the cartridge.

protruding spool shaft—with a beer can opener; be careful not to bend the cap. Remove the spool and set the cartridge body and top aside.

Wrap a 2-inch-long piece of narrow masking tape at right angles around the cartridge spool, with the ends of the tape left loose, sticky sides aligned and facing together but not attached. Make sure the tape is lined up straight on the spool. Then, holding the spool so that the take-up shaft is to the right, insert the loose end of film from the bulk loader between the ends of the tape around the spool. Press the ends of the tape together to seal the film between them.

595

Develop Black-and-White Film

Tape the end of the film to the spool and insert the spool into the cartridge; snap the end cap on.

Processing black-and-white cassette or roll film is a simple chore that doesn't even require a darkroom—you'll save money, you'll always know where your film is, and you'll probably end up with better negatives than the ones commercial labs turn out. **Tools:** black-and-white roll or cassette film, film changing bag, stainless steel developing tank and reel, bottle opener, scissors, measuring flasks, darkroom thermometer, large pan, film manufacturer's processing chart, watch with second hand, film clips. **Materials:** fine-grain developer, hypo (fix), hypo neutralizer, wetting agent, envelopes or glassine envelopes. Buy your supplies at a photo supply store. **Time:** about 1 hour.

The critical factor in developing film is getting the exposed film off the roll and into the developer. Because it's hard to achieve complete darkness outside a darkroom, invest in a changing bag, a light-tight mini-darkroom made specifically for loading and unloading film. Buy the best developing tank and reel you can afford—the stainless steel ones cost more than plastic, but they're worth it. You'll also need graduated photo processing flasks, film clips, and a darkroom thermometer—don't try to use another type of thermometer.

Ask the photo supply dealer what type of developer and hypo (fix) to buy; for most film types, a fine-grain developer is preferable. If possible, get a developer that's used once and discarded. To save your hot water supply, buy a hypo neutralizer; to prevent spots on the film, buy a wetting agent. Stick to well-known brand-name products.

The first processing trick to master is transferring the film from the cassette or roll onto the developing tank reel. Most modern cassettes and rolls are easy to

Insert the spool carefully into the plastic cartridge by working the film into the felt-lined slot in the body of the cartridge; follow the bulk loader manufacturer's instructions exactly. With the spool in place, snap the end cap firmly onto the cartridge; make certain it snaps into place or the film will be ruined.

Following the manufacturer's instructions, insert the cartridge into the bulk loader and close the door. Turn the loader's film drum to the load position, set the counter to zero, and crank 20 or 36 frames onto the cartridge, as desired. Crank five turns more for the film leader. Return the loader's film drum to the open position and open the door to expose the full cartridge. Cut the film close to the loader, remove the cartridge, and pull 6 inches of film out of the cartridge; trim this exposed film back to about 4 inches for the film leader.

Label each cartridge you load with the type of film, the number of exposures, and the date. Store the cartridge in a plastic container; for long-term storage, keep the container in the refrigerator.

Inside the changing bag, feed the film smoothly onto the developing reel; handle it carefully by the edges.

onto the reel, with no kinks or jam-ups. Finally, set the loaded reel into the developing tank and cover the tank securely. After you get the hang of it, practice the procedure with a film changing bag, as directed by the bag's manufacturer, until you're sure you can load the film successfully every time.

You don't need practice for the actual developing process. Using the changing bag to ensure total darkness, open the film cartridge, clip the end of the film, and load the film onto the reel. Place the loaded reel in the tank and cover the tank securely. From this point on you can work in full light.

Work at a source of running hot and cold water. Mix the developer in a graduated flask, as specified by the manufacturer; mix hypo (fix) in the other flask as instructed. With a darkroom thermometer, determine the temperature of the solutions. Optimum temperature for developer is 68° F, and higher or lower temperatures affect film development time. Adjust the temperature of the solutions as necessary by setting the flasks in a large pan of hot or cold water until the darkroom thermometer registers the proper temperature.

Using the film manufacturer's processing chart—this chart is included in the film package—determine the proper developer and hypo (fix) times for the roll of film. Follow the manufacturer's guidelines exactly; monitor times by a watch with a second hand, and check developer and hypo temperatures frequently.

Development time is usually 3 to 9 minutes, plus 10 seconds for tank filling. Pour the developer solution into the tank through the access hole at the top of the tank. Immediately put the cap on the tank and rap the bottom of the tank sharply two or three times on a counter or tabletop to release air bubbles. Then agitate the tank for about 30 seconds: tilt it slowly 180 degrees, turning it up and down three or four times. Keep your agitation steady and gentle; if you shake too hard the film will streak. Agitate for the first 30 seconds and stop; then agitate for 5 seconds every 30 seconds during the developing period,

open; just snap one end off with a bottle opener and remove the film. Roll film must also be cut to separate the light-proof paper from the film at the end of the roll. Before you try to develop film, determine how to open the cassette or roll and remove the film you're processing. Take apart an old, no-good cassette or roll and look at it closely; if you don't have any old film, sacrifice a new roll.

Practice in good light until you're familiar with the film-loading procedure. Snap the cassette open, or remove the end of the roll film cartridge with a bottle opener. Remove the spool of film carefully from the cartridge, holding it only at the edges and making sure it doesn't unroll. Then, still holding the rolled film, clip the end of the film off square with a scissors to remove the leader tongue of the roll.

Following the instructions provided with the developing tank, feed the cut end of the film smoothly into the loading slots of the developing reel; handle the film by the edges only, bending it very slightly to stiffen the strip. Keep pushing to feed the entire length of film smoothly

Quickly pour in the developer and cap the tank; rap the tank sharply and then agitate it as specified.

as specified in the manufacturer's processing chart.

About 5 seconds before the end of the developing period, start pouring the developer back into the graduated flask; pour slowly to fill out the developing time. Immediately fill the tank with fresh tepid water, swirl the water around, and empty the tank; refill, swirl again, and empty. Then pour the prepared hypo (fix) into the tank and monitor the time recommended for fixing the film. Agitate the tank the same way you did with the developer: continuously for the first 30 seconds, and then for 5 seconds every 30 seconds. At the end of the fixing period, empty the hypo from the tank into the flask, remove the tank cover, and set the tank under running water at 65° to 70° F. Developed and fixed film must be thoroughly washed to stop the action of the processing chemicals. With warm water, this takes 20 to 30 minutes—an expensive proposition for a home water heater. To speed the process, mix hypo neutralizer, if necessary, as directed. When the film has been rinsed for a few min-

utes, empty the tank and fill it with the prepared neutralizer. Let the film stand and then rewash as directed by the neutralizer manufacturer.

Finally, when the developed film has been thoroughly washed, refill it with a wetting agent, as directed by the manufacturer. Swirl this wetting agent in the tank for about 30 seconds or less and then empty the wetting agent back into its container; you can use it again.

Remove the film reel from the developing tank. Working carefully and handling the wet film only by its edges, attach a film clip firmly to the end of the film. Without touching the wet emulsion or letting it touch anything else, carefully remove it from the reel, holding one end up and unrolling the reel with the other hand. Attach a film clip to the bottom of the film to weight it. Hang the wet strip of film to dry at room temperature in a dust-free and draftless spot, like a closet or large cabinet. Don't touch it until it has dried *completely*. Then cut the film into strips of a few frames; store the strips in clean white envelopes or special glassine envelopes for film.

Make a Contact Print Frame

As every photography buff knows, the cost of film processing can be staggering. To minimize expensive printing mistakes, make this 8 × 10 contact print frame to screen your negs. **Tools:** ruler, scissors, pencil. **Materials:** 8 × 10-inch piece of plywood or particle board, 8 × 10-inch piece of single-strength glass, 3-inch gaffers' tape or duct tape. **Time:** about 1 hour.

Use an 8 × 10-inch piece of plywood or particle board to make the frame—be sure it's solid and unwarped. Use an 8 × 10-inch piece of single-strength glass to hold the negatives in place, and 3-inch gaffers' tape or duct tape to put the pieces of the frame together.

To make the frame, cut a 10-inch piece of gaffers' tape or duct tape, and cut it in half lengthwise to make two 10 × 1½-inch strips. On one long edge of one strip, make six pairs of parallel cuts, with each pair of cuts about 1⅜ inches apart and each cut about ½ inch deep, to hold six 35mm negative strips of six frames each. Space the pairs of cuts evenly along the 10-inch length of the tape. Fold the clipped section of tape between each pair of cuts under, so it sticks to the back of the strip and forms a notch. Attach the tape along one 10-inch side of the glass, notched side in, ¾ inch from the edge of the glass.

Cut the remaining 10 × 1½-inch piece of tape in half lengthwise to make two 10 × ¾-inch strips. Fold each strip over one long edge of the glass to cover the cut edge. Cut another piece of tape 8 inches long and cut it into ¾-inch-wide strips; fold two of these strips over the unprotected short edges of the glass.

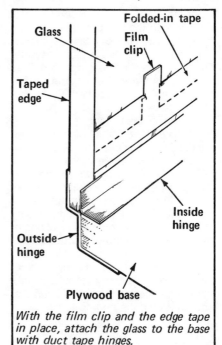

With the film clip and the edge tape in place, attach the glass to the base with duct tape hinges.

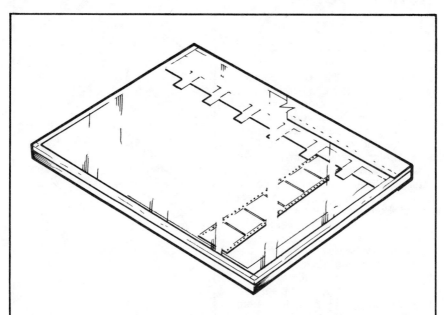

To use the completed frame, set it wood side up; slide the negative strips into the notched film clip along the hinge. In the darkroom, lay a sheet of photo paper over the strips, emulsion side down, and close the frame. Expose the entire frame, glass side up.

Set the glass on the piece of wood, the side with the notched tape against the wood. Cut a piece of tape 10 inches long and fold it over the glass and the wood, hinge fashion, to join them on the long side where the notched-tape negative holder is attached. Open the hinged glass top and press a 10 × ¾-inch piece of tape along the inside of the hinge connecting the glass with the wood, along the spine of the hinge. Trim any excess tape at the corners.

To use the frame, open it, wood side up. Set the negative strips into the notches formed by the folded-back tape along the hinge side. In the darkroom, or in total darkness, set a sheet of photo printing paper on top of the negatives, emulsion side down; then fold the wood down over the top. Turn the entire frame over and expose it for a contact sheet; sandwiched between the glass and the wood backing, the negatives can't slip or curl.

Fold an empty mount along the crease at the top. Place a single frame into the recess in the mount and align the film carefully; you may have to trim off some of the film on the edges. Place the trimmed frame in the mount, fold the mount closed, and hold it in place.

With the transparency properly positioned in the mount, press firmly along one edge of the mount with a hot iron. Don't twist the iron, and be careful not to touch the film with the iron. After a few seconds move the iron to another side of the mount and repeat, continuing around the mount until all sides are completely sealed. Don't touch the film or cover it with the hot iron, and watch your fingers—the slide will stay hot for a while.

After the slide has cooled, inspect the finished mount for any gaps along the edges. Reseal as necessary with the hot iron.

Mount Your Own Slides

Color slides are the least expensive form of 35 mm color photography, and you can save even more money by mounting your slides yourself. Just have your processed film returned unmounted, and mount only the best shots. **Tools:** desk lamp or slide viewing tray, sharp scissors, electric iron. **Materials:** lightweight, lint-free cotton gloves; white paper, 35 mm heat-seal mounts. Both gloves and mounts are available at photo supply stores. **Time:** 5 minutes per slide.

Wearing lint-free cotton gloves, unwrap the unmounted slides. Set the strips of film on a piece of white paper held over a desk lamp, or set them on a slide viewing tray. Examine them closely and choose the slides to be mounted. Cut away unwanted frames. Cut the film to be mounted into individual frames and set the frames singly on a sheet of white paper.

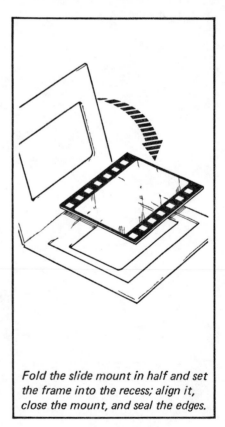

Fold the slide mount in half and set the frame into the recess; align it, close the mount, and seal the edges.

Display Your Collectibles

Save at Auctions, Flea Markets, and Garage Sales

Displaying your collectibles where you can see them and show them off to best advantage will maximize your pleasure in them. Some items need to be kept under glass; others gain decorative value when backed by reflecting mirrors or fabrics. Small collectibles become more important when grouped together.

There are lots of display cases made especially for particular types of collectibles, such as spoon racks. But often a little ingenuity will go a long way toward creating a more distinctive display—and for a lot less money. Stones, shells, and other natural objects look great mounted on pieces of weathered wood picked up at beaches, near rivers or lakes, or in open fields. If you don't want to glue things down, pile them into inexpensive glass jars like the old-fashioned penny candy displays. Or look around for some deep picture-box frames, and glue or nail in a few strips of wood as shelves. Frames with the glass intact are great for items that need protection against dust. A big, deep frame with a glass top makes a handsome coffee-table/display-case combination. An old tray is another good alternative; add a piece of glass cut to fit the tray.

Many small objects lend themselves to this kind of functional rethinking. For example, salt shakers make good hatpin or stickpin holders; glass paperweights serve as unique and protective cases for bits of lace and embroidery.

Display paper items like stamps in inexpensive frames, made more interesting and relevant with randomly cut and pasted valueless stamps. "Throwaway" stamps can also be used to decorate old boxes and small tabletops, or the covers of stamp albums. Glue the stamps on patchwork-fashion, or cut and paste them into abstract or realistic figures. Use your imagination—the possibilities are endless.

Even at auctions, flea markets, and garage sales, many of yesterday's giveaways are fetching hefty prices. But whatever the cost, from giveaway to splurge, second-hand buys are both less expensive and more distinctive than any store-bought counterparts. Watch the classified ads for real estate auctions, custom house and post office auctions, and auctions of office furniture and equipment. Don't go to auctions that move from place to place.

Some who buy at these ever more popular marketplaces not only save but make money by reselling. Successful buying or selling depends on a little luck and a lot of perseverance and know-how. With these basic tips, you can buy, sell, haggle, and bargain-spot with the best of them.

How to buy. For good buying, it's the early bird who gets the worm. For auction-goers, this means arriving in time for the sale preview, an absolute must for intelligent bidding; buy a catalog, and register if you plan to bid. When the auction starts, listen to the bidding and familiarize yourself with its terms and price increments. Bid only up to your maximum price.

Smart flea-market buyers arrive on the scene while the sellers are still setting up; or many a good buy has been made at dusk, with only a flashlight to zero in on the treasure. For garage sales it sometimes pays to call a day ahead.

The early-bird watchword is less important if your interests and needs focus around the less sought-after type of merchandise. In this case, it may pay to wait until the end of the sale, when prices are often lowered to clear out the leftovers and when auctioneers incline to the quick knock—rapping the gavel to indicate a sale without pausing to allow another bid.

Weather and publicity are also important factors. You can get fantastic buys no matter what time you come, provided it rains. If the sale hasn't been advertised well, so much the better. Well-advertised sales in good weather tend to offer fewer bargains.

Whenever and whatever you buy, know the rules of the game. *Let the buyer beware* rules the auction and flea market trade: what you buy is what you get; there are no refunds and no returns. With this in mind, inspect everything closely. Look for hidden cracks beneath dust; turn chairs upside down; bring a jeweller's loupe or magnifying glass; use a magnet to spot metal repairs and a tape measure to check how objects will fit into a space in your home. Make sure what you're getting is something you want; don't buy something if you don't like it or can't afford it.

What you buy is also what you carry home. Take shopping bags for small purchases; come back as soon as possible for large things bought at an auction. If you buy something as you start making the rounds of a flea market and want to pick it up later, be sure to write down its exact location.

How to sell. The imperatives guiding you as a buyer are obviously going to shift if you turn seller. The unreserved auction, where everything is sold regardless of how low the bid, is fine for the buyer. The reserved auction, where a minimum or reserve price is fixed, protects the seller. By the same token, the better advertised a sale, the bigger and more affluent the crowds, and the nicer the weather, the better your likelihood of realizing a fair return.

The best market outlet depends on what you have to sell, your time, and your personal inclinations. Valuable items are likely to fetch the best prices at well-established auction houses— but this is not a hard and fast rule.

If you don't have enough to sell to warrant your own flea market table or garage sale, there are several options. You can sell or consign what you have

to a flea market dealer, or you can get together with a group of neighbors for a multi-family garage sale.

The crucial question, no matter what you sell, is pricing. A good gauge of the prevailing supply and demand is making a survey of how much similar merchandise is available and what it's fetching. As a rule of thumb, several general pricing guidelines have worked for others. Utilitarian used clothing and furnishings should be marked one-seventh to one-tenth the price of comparable new items in stores; impractical, low-demand, and upholstered items should be tagged as real bargains. The highest price tags belong on the things falling into the antiques-collectibles realm. If you suspect you've got some real treasures, it may pay for you to call in an appraiser. If you have just one or two good pieces you might request sealed bids—interested buyers leave their names, addresses, phone numbers, and offering prices in sealed envelopes.

How to haggle. The thing about bargaining is that many people are either too timid or too outrageous. If you're one of the timid, take heart from the realization that many dealers won't appreciate your easy acquiescence to the first price asked. Such unquestioning assent tends to leave the dealer forever wondering if you got the best of the deal. On the other hand, if you use the ploy of pretended disinterest, the dealer is likely to see through your pose and raise the price, convinced by your attitude that you know something he or she doesn't. In general, it's best to bargain privately, when you and the seller are out of earshot of others. Don't act as if you hate something, but don't show off about how you're going to use your purchase—show your interest, but hide your passion. If you're buying costly items, a cash discount is a legitimate bargaining point. Take a cue from the pros who buy by the box and sell by the piece: if things are scattered around a booth, point them out and ask the price for the whole lot. Finally, at auction previews, watch the pros, and listen to their questions. Write down the price you want to pay, and stick to it.

How to spot a bargain. To recognize a bargain you've got to know the merchandise. There's a book written on practically any period, style, and merchandise category, and several trips to the local library to read and study will pay many dividends. So will visits to shops, galleries, and auctions where the best examples of things you like can be examined. Only when you've developed a feel and understanding of what a treasure is can you recognize it in the midst of an otherwise undistinguished assortment of goods.

Be aware too that the treasures the seller doesn't recognize as such tend to be tucked under tables, behind screens, or inside boxes. Don't overlook these corners and crannies. At garage sales, don't assume that everything that's available to you is on display. Ask if someone has this or that. It doesn't cost anything, and it may yield something great.

Finally, while good buys are as near as the next-door garage sale, remember that what's valuable where you live is often ordinary elsewhere. The farther from home you look, the likelier you are to spot bargains for yourself. Professional dealers who regularly shop where it's cheap and sell where it's dear call this float-buying; you can profit too.

Playthings

Make Your Own Play Dough

What child doesn't enjoy modeling? This smooth-textured, easy-to-shape dough is far superior to the expensive brand-name variety. It's simple enough to let the kids help with the "cooking." **Equipment:** large mixing bowl, fork, measuring cup, measuring spoons, 2-quart saucepan, locking plastic bag or air-tight container. **Ingredients:** flour, salad oil, alum, water, salt, food coloring as desired. **Yield:** 3 cups.

In a large mixing bowl, combine 2 cups of flour, 2 tablespoons of salad oil, and 2 tablespoons of alum; stir with a fork to moisten the dry ingredients evenly. Set aside. Measure 2 cups of water into a 2-quart saucepan; add ½ cup salt and food coloring as desired. Heat to a boil and simmer, stirring occasionally, until the salt dissolves.

Add the hot water solution to the flour mixture in the bowl and stir to blend thoroughly. Let cool slightly; then knead the dough until it's soft and pliable. Store dough between uses in a locking plastic bag or an air-tight container.

Make Your Own Poster Paints

You can create a bright spectrum of poster paints unmatched by the store-bought variety, and for half the cost. The main ingredient is powder paint, sold in hobby shops and the art supply sections of department stores. **Equipment:** small saucepan, measuring cup, mixing spoon, small jars with covers, measuring spoons. **Ingredients:** water, flour, powder paint, clear liquid detergent, liquid laundry starch. **Yield:** 4 small jars of poster paint.

Buy a variety of powder paints so you can mix several colors. The three primary colors—red, yellow, blue—and white are good basics; go on from there to mix whatever colors you like.

In a small saucepan, slowly add 1 cup water to ¼ cup flour, stirring constantly. Cook over medium heat, stirring constantly, until the paste begins to thicken. Remove from heat and cool.

Use a small jar with a cover for each color desired. Measure ¼ cup paste into each jar and add 2 tablespoons of water. Add 3 tablespoons of any color of powder paint, and mix well. If the mixture seems too dry, add water, ½ teaspoon at a time; stir well after each addition. For a glossy finish, add ½ teaspoon of clear liquid detergent to each jar; for an opaque finish, add ½ teaspoon of liquid laundry starch.

Cover the jars tightly; stir before each use.

Quick detergent paints. For instant poster paints, mix 2 teaspoons of powder paint with 1 tablespoon of clear liquid detergent for each color desired. Stir well.

Make a Piñata

A piñata, the classic children's-party attention-getter, is still unmatched for inexpensive entertainment. Whether you want an ark or a space ship, an elephant or a pumpkin, it's easy to make your own. **Tools:** scissors, measuring cup, bowls, mixing spoon, saucepan, serrated knife, artists' brushes, ice pick. **Materials:** large and small balloons, newspaper, flour, water, cardboard tubes from toilet paper or paper towels, transparent tape or masking tape, white glue, poster paint or colored tissue paper; construction paper, crepe paper, yarn, or pipe cleaners, as desired; sturdy string; hard candy and small toys, as desired. **Time:** about 2 to 4 hours, plus 2 to 3 days drying time.

Use a large balloon to build the piñata on, roughly the same shape you want the piñata to be. Use a round balloon for a round fruit or vegetable or a funny head; use a long balloon for a plane or ship. Make sure you get a balloon large enough to hold candy for the whole party; a diameter of 12 inches is usually adequate. To make a head, if you need one, get a 6½-inch balloon. Just in case, get at least one extra balloon in each size.

The piñata is built up of papier-mâché strips smoothed over the balloon. Before you blow up the balloon, cut or tear

newspaper into 1¼-inch-wide strips. Prepare more strips than you think you'll need; the balloon must be covered with several layers of paper. Spread newspaper on your work surface to protect it.

When you have enough newspaper strips, make a flour and water paste for the papier-mâché. Mix ¼ cup of flour and 1 cup of cold water, pressing out all lumps; set it aside. Measure 5 cups of water into a saucepan and bring the water to a boil. Add a spoonful of boiling water to the flour-and-water paste, and stir to mix well; then, stirring constantly, slowly pour the paste mixture into the boiling water. Lower the heat and simmer for 2 to 3 minutes, stirring occasionally. Let the mixture cool.

When the paste mixture is cool, blow up the balloon and close the opening firmly. If you have a bowl larger than the balloon, set the balloon into it to contain the mess.

To make a piñata with arms and legs,

The piñata is built up of papier-mâché strips spread over a balloon base. Saturate the strips thoroughly and smooth them evenly over and around the balloon, overlapping them about 1 inch. Leave the tied end uncovered.

use cardboard tubes from rolls of toilet paper or paper towels. Cut the tubes to the desired length and tape them into place on the balloon with transparent tape or masking tape. Make sure they're anchored firmly.

To make a head for the piñata, if desired, use a small balloon, about 6½ inches in diameter. Blow up the balloon and close the opening firmly. Set the small balloon into a separate bowl, and build it separately from the body. To make the head for a long-headed animal with an open mouth, such as a horse or a dog, use a toilet paper tube as a base for the papier-mâché, as described below. Add a cardboard tube to the body balloon for a neck, if desired.

When the base of the piñata is prepared, apply the papier-mâché. Working with one strip of paper at a time, soak precut strips of newspaper in the cooled paste and smooth them onto the balloon body. Soak each strip of newspaper liberally; the paper must be thoroughly wet. Wipe off excess paste with your fingers, and smooth the wet strip onto the balloon for the piñata's body.

Repeat, soaking strips of paper and smoothing them on, to cover the entire balloon with a two-thickness layer of overlapping newspaper strips; crisscross the strips around the balloon, overlapping them about 1 inch. Leave the tied end of the balloon uncovered. If the piñata has arms and legs, cover the tubes with strips long enough to run the entire length of the tube and overlap onto the balloon; build up the tubes to the desired shape. If the ends of the strips start to come up, apply more paste and smooth them down again.

When the entire body balloon is covered with newspaper strips, cover the head balloon. Use the same technique, soaking strips of paper and smoothing them on, to cover the entire balloon with two overlapping thicknesses of paper.

To make the head for a long-headed animal, flatten a toilet paper tube to an oval. Crumple strips of newspaper and soak them liberally in the paste; attach them to the tube with long uncrumpled strips to build up the top of the head. Add more crumpled newspaper, attached with long strips, to build the head to the desired shape; leave one end of the flattened tube open for the mouth. To complete the head, dip your fingers into the paste and apply a light coating of paste to the built-up head, smoothing the strips as you go.

Let the piñata body and head dry completely. For a stronger piñata, let the body and head dry for several hours, until the papier-mâché is stiff. Then apply another double thickness of paste-soaked strips, smoothing strips over the balloons as above; mix more paste as necessary. Let the completed piñata body and head dry for 2 to 3 days, to make sure the papier-mâché is brittle.

When the piñata is completely dry, put it together and decorate it. At the open end of each hardened balloon, pop the balloon and pull it out through the hole. With a sharp-pointed serrated knife, carefully cut a small hole—about 2 inches in diameter—in the piñata body, to attach the head; if you made a neck, this isn't necessary. Cut a corresponding hole in the head where it should join the body or neck. Don't assemble the piñata yet; you'll need the hole left by the balloon, or the head or neck opening, to fill the piñata.

Decorate the piñata—and, if required, the head—with poster paint, or cover it with layers of colored tissue paper. Add construction-paper ears or wings, crepe paper streamers, or yarn or pipe cleaner tails, whiskers, or hair—use your imagination. If the piñata head has an open mouth, paint the inside of the mouth black; if it doesn't, paint on a smile or a big-toothed grin. Let the paint dry.

Before filling the piñata, carefully punch a small hole on each side of its top; use an ice pick, and be careful not to crush the papier-mâché. Thread a long piece of sturdy string through the holes to hang the piñata. Then fill the piñata—and, if it's hollow, the head—with hard or wrapped candy and small toys. Attach the head to the body with white glue; set it firmly into place, using glue liberally. Let the assembled piñata dry completely.

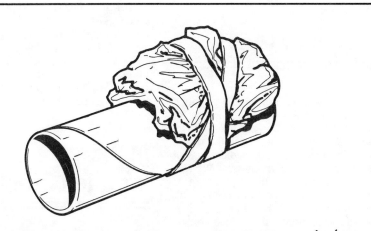

For a long-headed animal, build up the head with crumpled papier-mâché strips on a cardboard tube. Attach the crumpled strips to the tube with long strips, smoothing them around and over the built-up head.

At party time, hang the piñata from a tree limb or rafter—keep it low enough to be reached. Blindfold each child in turn, and give him or her a light bat or a stick; turn him around three times and then send him toward the piñata. Only one child will break the piñata, but they'll all get the prizes.

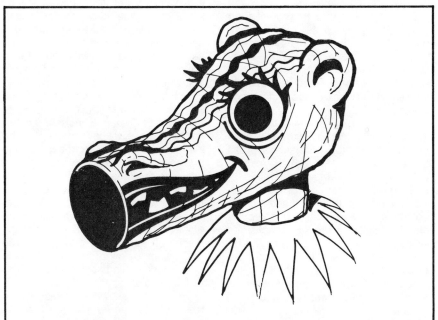

Paint the completed head with poster paint; add construction-paper eyelashes or any yarn, crepe paper, pipe cleaner, or other decorations. Paint the inside of the mouth black. When the paint is dry, attach the head.

Make a Jigsaw Puzzle

Jigsaw puzzles are almost as much fun for adults to make as they are for kids to play with. Choose your subject and cut the pieces to match the user's skill. **Tools:** sharp craft knife, fretsaw or power jigsaw, fine-toothed flat file. **Materials:** picture (cartoon, photograph, magazine picture, or other illustration), ⅛-inch or ¼-inch hardboard or plywood, newspaper, spray white shellac or polyurethane varnish. **Time:** about ½ to 1 hour for a simple puzzle.

Any picture you like can be turned into a jigsaw puzzle—a cartoon, a photograph, a magazine picture, or any illustration. Use a piece of ⅛-inch or ¼-inch hardboard or plywood to back the picture. Trim the picture and cut the backing hardboard or plywood to the desired size, so that the picture and the backing are the same size.

Spread newspaper to protect your work surface. Place the hardboard or plywood face up on the newspapers, and the picture face down. With a spray can of white shellac or polyurethane varnish, apply a thin coat of shellac or varnish to the back of the picture and the front of the board.

Let the varnish get slightly tacky. Then, working quickly, carefully align the picture on the board, and press the two together. Smooth the picture onto the board, removing all air bubbles. Spray another coat of white shellac or varnish onto the bonded picture. Let the shellac or varnish dry completely, following the manufacturer's instructions.

The maximum size of the puzzle depends on the capacity, or throat, of the saw you use to cut it; use a fretsaw for simple puzzles, a power jigsaw for more complicated ones. Use the thinnest saw blade, with the greatest number of teeth per inch, you can find; the finer the blade, the smoother the edges on the puzzle pieces.

Cut the puzzle into interlocking pieces, keeping in mind the ability of its intended user. To make large puzzles easier to handle, cut them into quarters before cutting the puzzle pieces. After cutting, check the pieces for rough edges; file any rough edges smooth with a fine-toothed flat file.

Make Wooden Blocks

Wood building blocks are an all-time favorite toy, and there usually aren't quite enough to go around. With just a little effort, you can make a set of blocks for every kid in the house. **Tools:** measuring rule, pencil, carpenters' square; saber saw, or miter box and backsaw, and coping saw; vise, compass; if desired, drill, small paintbrush. **Materials:** 1 × 2 clear pine stock, 1-inch wood dowel; if desired, 1 × 3 or 2 × 2 clear pine stock, and/or ⅜-inch wood dowel; medium- and fine-grit sandpaper; if desired, nontoxic, child-safe gloss paint. **Time:** about 3 to 4 hours; if desired, additional time for painting.

To make blocks for a small child, use 1 × 2 clear pine stock. The actual size of 1 × 2 is ¾ × 1½ inches, so the finished blocks will be ¾ inch thick, and either ¾ inch or 1½ inches wide. Use pieces of 1-inch wood dowel to cut short and long columns.

If you want larger blocks, cut them from 1 × 3 clear pine stock, for an actual width of 2½ inches. Or, for square alphabet-type blocks, cut 1½-inch-long pieces of clear 2 × 2 pine stock. The dimensions below are for 1 × 2 stock; modify your cutting as desired for larger or thicker blocks.

To make the blocks, measure and mark the desired length on a piece of wood; use a carpenters' square to make sure the ends are square. Mark and cut one block at a time. Clamp the piece of wood in a vise and cut each block with a saber saw; or use a miter box and a backsaw to keep the ends even. After cutting all desired blocks from the 1 × 2, cut them in half as required; then cut special shapes and pieces of dowel for columns. For a 58-piece block set, cut 1 × 2 and dowel pieces as detailed below.

Measure and cut 14 pieces of 1 × 2 3½ inches long, to make 1½ × 3½-inch blocks. Measure and cut four pieces 3½ inches long, to be cut in half. Set them aside.

Measure and cut 14 pieces of 1 × 2 1½ inches long, to make 1½-inch-square blocks. Measure and cut four pieces 1½ inches long, to be cut in half. Set them aside.

Mark four 3½-inch-long pieces in half the long way, and carefully cut them in half to make eight ¾ × 3½-inch blocks. Mark four 1½-inch pieces in half along the grain of the wood, and carefully cut them in half to make eight ¾ × 1½-inch blocks. At this point, you should have a total of 28 full-width blocks and 16 half-width blocks.

Next, make special shapes. Measure and cut two 3½-inch-long pieces of 1 × 2, to make four triangles from two 1½ × 3½-inch blocks. On each block, draw a diagonal line between two opposite corners; carefully cut along the line to make two 3½-inch-high triangles.

Measure and cut two 3½-inch-long pieces of 1 × 2 to make arches. For each arch, use a compass to draw a 1-inch-radius semicircle at the center of one long edge, to form a 1-inch-high arch on one long side. Clamp the block firmly and then carefully cut the arch with a saber saw or a coping saw.

After cutting the triangles and arches, cut pieces of 1-inch wood dowel to make columns. Measure and cut four pieces 3½ inches long and four pieces 1½ inches long. Besides the 44 plain blocks, you should now have 14 special shapes, for a total of 58 blocks.

If desired, add connector pieces of

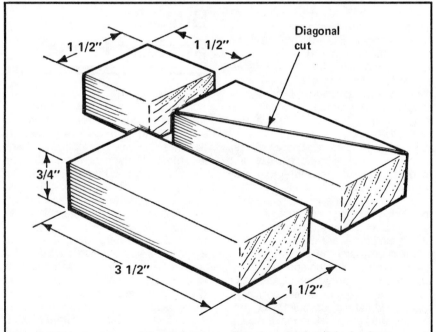

Cut 1 1/2-inch pieces of 1 x 2 for square blocks, and 3 1/2-inch pieces for long blocks; cut some in half along the grain to make narrow blocks. For triangles, cut 3 1/2-inch blocks in half diagonally.

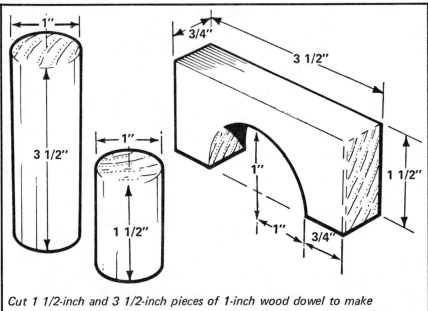

Cut 1 1/2-inch and 3 1/2-inch pieces of 1-inch wood dowel to make columns. For arches, use long blocks: draw a 1-inch-radius semicircle on the edge of the block, clamp the block firmly, and cut out the marked arch.

⅜-inch or smaller wood dowel to make a fit-together construction set. For connectors of various lengths, cut 10 to 15 dowels each, 2 inches, 4 inches, 6 inches, and 8 inches long. On the faces and around the edges of the blocks, about ½ inch apart, drill ⅜-inch holes about ¼ to ⅜ inch deep. Don't drill more than two holes along the side of a 1½-inch-wide block.

To finish the blocks, sand all edges, all corners, and all surfaces; use first medium-grit and then fine-grit sandpaper. The blocks must be very smooth; they may end up in a child's mouth. Make sure you remove all rough spots and all splinters. Remove all dust before the blocks are used.

If desired, paint the blocks—a solid color, different colors on opposite sides, or, for square blocks, with pictures and letters of the alphabet. Use only nontoxic, child-safe gloss paint; the container should clearly state that the paint is a dry-film, baby-safe type. Apply the paint and let it dry completely before the blocks are used, as directed by the manufacturer.

Build a Rocking Horse

Toddlers love to rock, and this wooden rocking horse is as much fun to use as it is to build. Give your imagination free rein when you build this fantasy friend. **Tools:** measuring rule, pencil, ruler, straightedge, scissors, saber saw, weights or clamps, wood file, drill, countersink, screwdriver, brace and bit, compass, paintbrushes, hammer. **Materials:** brown paper, ¾-inch grade A-B plywood, carpenters' glue, 2 × 4 and 2 × 6 pine stock, 2-inch #12 flathead wood screws, 1½-inch #10 flathead wood screws, 1-inch wood dowel, wood filler; primer and nontoxic, child-safe gloss paints; leather strips and scraps, 1-inch and ½-inch studs. **Time:** about 2 days.

On a large sheet of brown paper, at least 48 inches square, use a pencil, ruler, and straightedge to mark off a

24 × 24-square grid of 2-inch squares. Using the cutting diagram illustrated, transfer the pattern for the rocking horse pieces onto your grid, and cut them out. For the seat and legs, trace only half of the pattern; then fold the traced piece over and cut it double-thickness, to ensure that the two halves of each piece will be symmetrical.

Use the paper patterns to trace each piece onto ¾-inch grade A-B plywood. Use a saber saw to cut out the three pieces of the head and body, the two leg pieces, and the seat.

Stack the three head/body pieces to check them for fit; minor differences can be smoothed later. Apply carpenters' glue liberally between the three pieces, and weight or clamp the pieces together. Let the clamped pieces dry overnight.

To assemble the horse, cut a 2¼ × 5-inch slot in each of the leg pieces to lock the legs onto the body. Cut two 9-inch-long body braces from 2 × 4 pine stock. Use a wood file to round one long edge of each brace.

Temporarily align the legs on the head/body pieces with a body brace between them; the top rounded edge of

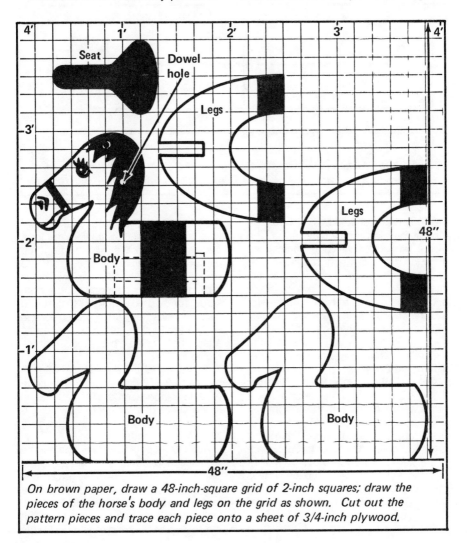

On brown paper, draw a 48-inch-square grid of 2-inch squares; draw the pieces of the horse's body and legs on the grid as shown. Cut out the pattern pieces and trace each piece onto a sheet of 3/4-inch plywood.

611

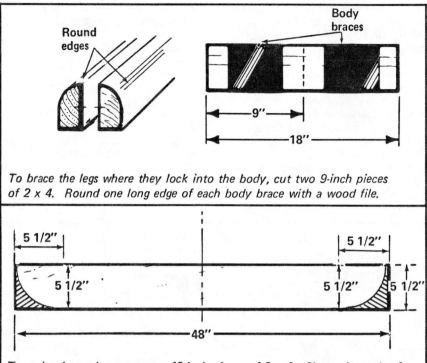

To brace the legs where they lock into the body, cut two 9-inch pieces of 2 x 4. Round one long edge of each body brace with a wood file.

To make the rockers, cut two 48-inch pieces of 2 x 6. Shape the ends of the pieces to a smooth curve, so that the assembled horse will rock evenly.

the body brace should be even with the tops of the legs. Apply glue to the side of the brace that will butt against the body of the rocking horse. Drill and countersink three holes—two 1½ inches from each end of the body brace and one centered between them—for two 2-inch #12 flathead wood screws. Drive the screws through the brace to secure it to the horse's body. Repeat to secure the other body brace to the other side of the body.

Cut two 16-inch-long leg braces from 2 x 4 stock. Apply glue to one 2 x 4 brace where it butts with the bottom of a leg piece; the bottom edges of the brace and the leg must be flush. Drill and countersink two holes through each of the leg braces for two 2-inch #12 flathead wood screws. Drive the screws through the brace to secure it to the leg piece. Repeat to secure the other leg and leg brace.

Apply glue to the edges of the slot on

the front leg piece and to the point where the leg will butt against the front end of a body brace; slip the front leg piece, brace facing to the rear, into place. Drill and countersink two holes through the front leg piece on both sides for two 1½-inch #10 flathead wood screws, and drive the screws to secure the legs to the brace. Repeat to attach the rear legs; place the leg brace facing forward.

To make the rockers, cut two 48-inch pieces of 2 × 6 pine stock. Use a compass to shape each end of each piece to the curve of a 5½-inch-diameter circle, so that the rockers curve up to a point at each end.

Align and center a rocker against the leg pieces on one side of the horse. Apply glue to the ends of the leg braces and the bottom part of the edges of the legs, and fasten the rocker to the legs. Drill and countersink two holes through the rocker at each point where it butts against the leg braces, for two 2-inch #12 flathead wood screws. Drive the screws through the rocker and into the leg braces.

Align the second rocker so that it matches the first one. Glue the rocker into place and secure it with wood screws, as above.

Use a brace and bit to bore a $^{31}/_{32}$-inch hole into the head, as indicated on the cutting diagram, for the handle. Cut a 10 inch-length of 1-inch dowel, and hammer the dowel into the hole until an equal length is on both sides.

Apply glue to the top edge of the back of the rocking horse, and set the seat into place. Drill and countersink two holes through the seat near each end for two 2-inch #12 flathead wood screws. Drive the screws through the seat and into the back to secure the seat.

To finish the horse, fill all countersunk screw holes and any imperfections with wood filler. Use a wood file to round all rough or sharp edges, including the exposed ends of the dowel through the head. Sand the entire rocking horse smooth.

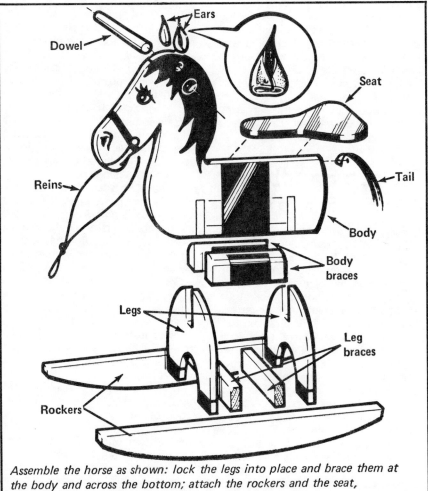

Assemble the horse as shown: lock the legs into place and brace them at the body and across the bottom; attach the rockers and the seat, slide the dowel through the drilled dowel hole, and add reins and tail.

Apply a coat of primer to the entire horse and let it dry, as directed by the manufacturer. Apply two coats of paint to the horse; use nontoxic child-safe gloss paint, specified as dry-film, baby-safe. Let the paint dry thoroughly between coats. Paint the body and the details whatever colors you like—use your imagination to paint the horse's mane, saddle, cinch, eyes, nose, and nose rein.

When the paint is completely dry, cut two 30-inch strips of leather for the reins. Attach one strip to each side of the head with 1-inch-diameter studs. Tie the other ends of the strips together and rest them on the handles.

Cut random lengths of leather for the tail. To attach each strip, pin one end of the strip through a ½-inch stud and hammer the stud into the rear of the horse. To make the ears, cut two equal triangles from a 6-inch square of leather. For each ear, fold two corners of a triangle over so they overlap slightly, and secure the ear to one side of the head with a ½-inch stud.

Make a Sandbox

For a favorite all-summer-long toy, build this sturdy, well-put-together covered sandbox. **Tools:** measuring rule, pencil, carpenters' square, straightedge, power saw, hammer, drill, screwdriver, plane, sanding block, finetoothed flat file, paintbrush. **Materials:** ¾-inch grade A-B or B-B exterior plywood, 2 × 4 and 1 × 2 pine stock, 6-penny common nails, 1½-inch #8 flathead galvanized or brass wood screws; six utility strap hinges and four utility handles with machine screws, washers, and nuts; sandpaper, primer and latex or oil-base exterior trim paint or porch and floor enamel. **Time:** about 5 to 6 hours, plus finishing time.

To make the sandbox, use ¾-inch grade A-B or B-B exterior plywood. Be sure to make allowances for the width of saw cuts between pieces, and remember that plywood sheets may not measure exactly 4 × 8 feet.

Measure, mark, and cut a bottom panel for the sandbox, 44½ inches square. Cut two pieces of 2 × 4 pine stock, 46 inches long, for skids under the sandbox; angle-cut all four ends of the 2 × 4's to about 25 degrees.

Lay the 2 × 4's parallel on a flat surface, and place the bottom panel of the sandbox on top of them, with two sides of the panel parallel with the skids. Adjust the skids so that they lie 12 inches in from each side of the bottom; set the skid ends equidistant with the edges of the bottom panel. Tack the skids into place temporarily with two 6-penny common nails driven only partway in.

Turn the bottom panel over. Drill a series of $^{11}/_{64}$-inch holes, about 12 inches apart, through the plywood bottom panel, for screws to secure the skids. Drill *only* through the plywood bottom panel; do *not* drill into the skids. Attach the skids to the bottom panel with 1½-inch #8 flathead galvanized or brass wood screws, driven through the bottom panel and into the skids. Set the screw heads flush with the surface of the wood. Turn the assembly over and remove the 6-penny nails.

To make the sides of the box, cut two 12 × 46-inch plywood pieces and two 11¼ × 44½-inch plywood pieces. At the upper corners of the 12 × 46-inch pieces, cut notches 8 inches long and ¾ inch deep, to accommodate the sandbox's seat boards.

Set the two 11¼ by 44½-inch pieces at opposite ends of the bottom panel; make sure the ends are flush with the open edges of the panel and the bottom edge is flush with the underside of the panel. Tack each end piece into place temporarily with two 6-penny nails driven only partway in.

Drill a series of $^{11}/_{64}$-inch holes, about 8 inches apart, near the bottom edge of these end pieces. Drill *only* through the end pieces; do *not* drill into the bottom panel. Fasten the end pieces to the bottom panel with 1½-inch #8 flathead wood screws, driven through the faces of the end pieces into the bottom panel. Set the screw heads flush.

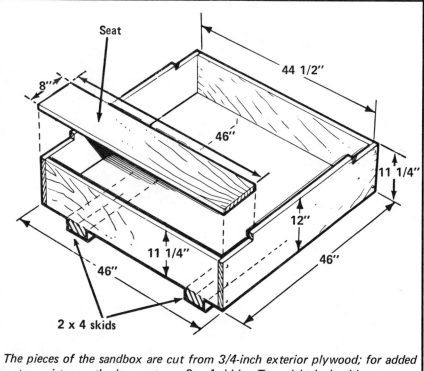

The pieces of the sandbox are cut from 3/4-inch exterior plywood; for added water resistance, the box rests on 2 x 4 skids. Two eight-inch-wide seats are set into the sides; the end panels are notched so that all top edges are flush.

Following the same procedure, attach the two 12 × 46-inch pieces to the other two edges of the bottom panel. Drill holes for three additional screws through the ends of these pieces; drive the screws into the ends of the 11¼ × 44½-inch pieces. Set the screw heads flush. Remove all temporary 6-penny nails.

To make the sandbox seats, cut two 8 × 46-inch pieces of plywood. Set the seats into the notches cut in the end pieces. Drill $^{11}/_{64}$-inch holes every 8 inches along each seat, through the seat *only*. Secure the seats with 1½-inch #8 flathead wood screws, driven through the faces of the seats into the ends of the sandbox. Set the screw heads flush.

For the sandbox cover, cut two 23 × 46-inch pieces of plywood. Attach three utility strap hinges to the outside edge of each piece. Using the hinges as templates, mark the locations for screw holes. Drill holes for the hinge screws through each cover piece. Secure the hinges with machine screws, washers, and nuts, with the screw heads to the inside of the sandbox and the nuts on the outside.

Mark the locations for screw holes for two utility handles near the inside edge of each cover piece. Drill holes for the handles' screws through each cover piece. Attach the handles, using machine screws, washers, and nuts.

Attach a strip of 1 × 2 pine stock to the meeting edge of one cover piece so that it will overlap the other piece when closed to seal out rainwater. Fasten the strip with 1½-inch #8 flathead wood screws.

To finish the sandbox, carefully round and bevel all corners and edges with a plane, a sanding block, or a fine-toothed flat file. Pay particular attention

615

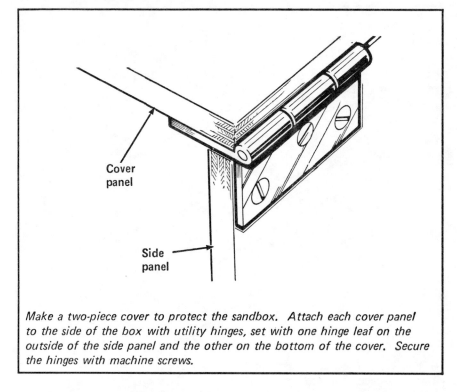

Make a two-piece cover to protect the sandbox. Attach each cover panel to the side of the box with utility hinges, set with one hinge leaf on the outside of the side panel and the other on the bottom of the cover. Secure the hinges with machine screws.

to the seat boards and the upper edges of the sides. Check for splinters or rough spots, and sand as necessary to smooth all surfaces. Finally, apply a coat of primer and at least two coats of exterior latex or oil-base trim paint or porch and floor enamel. Paint the inside, the outside, and the bottom of the sandbox. Let the paint dry completely between coats, as directed by the manufacturer.

Build a Child's Sled

This small sled is simple, sturdy, and very easy to build. Paint it a bright color and add decals or stencils for a toy worth handing down. **Tools:** measuring rule, pencil, carpenters' square, handsaw or power saw, compass, keyhole or saber saw, power drill with ¾-inch and ⅟₆₄-inch bits, small mixing dish and stir stick, screwdriver, C-clamps, jack or block plane, fine-toothed flat file, paintbrush. **Materials:** ¾-inch exterior grade plywood, 1 × 2 and 2 × 2 wood stock, resorcinol glue, #8 × 1½-inch flathead wood screws; coarse-, medium-, and fine-grit sandpaper; exterior primer and trim or porch and floor enamel, decals or stencils, sturdy towing rope. **Time:** about 3 to 4 hours, plus painting.

To make sure the sled is waterproof, choose your materials carefully. Use ¾-inch exterior-grade plywood and exterior trim or porch and floor enamel; use resorcinol resin glue to secure the joints.

To make the sled's runners, measure and mark two pieces of ¾-inch exterior-grade plywood 32 inches long and 6 inches wide; use a carpenters' square to keep the edges even. Cut the pieces out with a handsaw or a power saw. Use a compass to mark a 2-inch-radius arc in one corner of each piece, making an even curve for the front of the runner. Carefully cut off the corners outside the marked-off curves with a keyhole saw or a saber saw. Round the opposite corner of each piece slightly for the back of the runner.

In the square top corners of each runner, measure and mark notches for the sled's cross braces. Mark a notch 1½ inches deep and ¾ inch wide in each top corner, with the length of the notch along the side edge of the runner. Cut out the marked areas with a keyhole or saber saw. To make the braces, cut two 14-inch strips of 1 × 2 stock.

Assemble the runner-brace structure carefully. In each end of each brace, drill two $^{11}/_{64}$-inch holes, set back ⅜ inch from the end of the brace. Fit the cross braces into the cutout notches in the runners to connect the runners across the front face and across the back; the ends of the braces should fit flush with the outside faces of the runners. Mark the drilled screw holes on the ends of the runners and take the braces off. At the marked points, drill starter holes for the screws into the ends of the runners.

Mix resorcinol glue as directed by the manufacturer, and apply the glue to the cut edges of the notch at one end of each runner. Set a brace into the glued notches to connect the two runners, with the ends of the brace flush with the

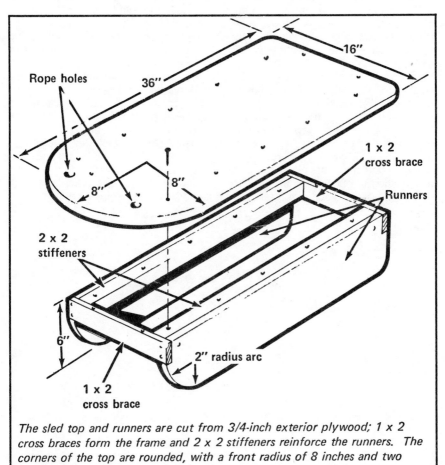

The sled top and runners are cut from 3/4-inch exterior plywood; 1 x 2 cross braces form the frame and 2 x 2 stiffeners reinforce the runners. The corners of the top are rounded, with a front radius of 8 inches and two rope holes.

outside faces of the runners, and secure it with two #8 × 1½-inch flathead wood screws through the predrilled holes at each end. Repeat to attach the brace at the other end of the runners.

Complete the runner assembly with lengthwise braces along the inside faces of the runners. Measure and cut two pieces of 2 × 2 stock to fit exactly between the front and back cross braces. At each end of each runner, where these side braces will butt against the cross braces, drill two $11/64$-inch holes through the runner, set back ⅜ inch from the face of the cross brace.

Apply resorcinol glue to one long side of each 2 × 2, and set the 2 × 2's carefully into place along the inside faces of the runners, with the top edges of the braces flush with the tops of the runners. Clamp the 2 × 2's firmly in place with C-clamps, and secure them to the runner frame with two #8 × 1½-inch flathead wood screws at each end, driven through the predrilled holes in the runner and into the ends of the clamped 2 × 2's.

To make the top of the sled, measure and cut a piece of plywood 16 inches wide and 36 inches long. Use a compass to mark a 2-inch-radius arc in each corner at one end of the piece, to make the rounded front corners; or mark the entire front of the piece with an 8-inch-radius arc. Cut off the corners outside the marked curves with a keyhole saw or a saber saw. Round the two back corners slightly.

Set the top piece on the sled frame and align it carefully. On the surface of the top, mark the longitudinal centerlines of the two side braces and the longitudinal centerlines of the two cross braces. Remove the top and drill a series of $11/64$-inch holes through the marked lines, centered on the lines and about 6 inches apart. Apply resorcinol glue to the top edges of the runner frame, set the sled top firmly into place, and secure it with #8 × 1½-inch flathead wood screws through the predrilled holes and into the runner frame. Drill two ¾-inch holes through the sled top near the front for the towing rope.

To complete the sled, plane or file all sharp corners and edges smooth, using a jack or block plane or a fine-toothed flat file. Sand the runners and any rough spots as necessary with successively finer grits of sandpaper.

To complete the sled, prime it and apply two coats of exterior trim or porch and floor enamel; let the paint dry completely between coats, as directed by the manufacturer. Decorate the sled with decals or stencils, and attach a sturdy towing rope with knots through the drilled holes in the sled top.

Sports

Build a Ski Rack

Ski equipment isn't cheap, but there's one special item you can make yourself. Use a cartop carrier to build this simple ski rack. **Tools:** stiff wire brush, electric drill, measuring rule, hacksaw, pliers or adjustable wrench, scissors. **Materials:** cartop carrier, steel wool, 4-foot piece of ½-inch thinwall electrical conduit, large galvanized washers, 6-inch eyebolts with locknuts, rustproofing spray paint, newspaper, elastic shock cord. **Time:** about 3 hours, plus drying time.

Any cartop carrier in reasonably good condition can be converted into a ski rack. Inspect the carrier; if it's rusty, remove all rust with a stiff wire brush and then steel wool. Some carriers have

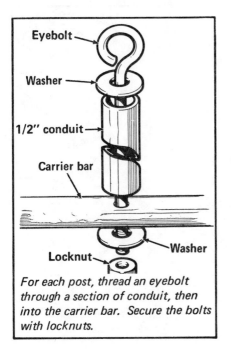

For each post, thread an eyebolt through a section of conduit, then into the carrier bar. Secure the bolts with locknuts.

holes drilled along each crosswise bar; some don't. If your carrier is solid, drill six evenly spaced holes along each crosswise bar, at least 6 inches apart. Use an electric drill to make the holes, and drill them just large enough to accept the eyebolts.

With a hacksaw, cut a 4-foot piece of ½-inch thinwall electrical conduit into 12 pieces each 4 inches long; keep your cuts even so the pieces will stand straight. These pieces of conduit are the posts of the ski rack.

When all the conduit posts are cut, assemble the carrier. Set a post at each of the six holes drilled in each crosswise bar, or at six evenly spaced points along racks with predrilled holes. For each post, set a large galvanized washer onto a 6-inch eyebolt; thread the bolt through a section of conduit so that the washer rests flat against the top of the conduit. Insert the end of the bolt through the hole in the crosswise bar and secure it on the other side of the bar with another washer and then a locknut; tighten the nut with pliers or an adjustable wrench. Repeat for each post on the rack.

When both crosswise bars are completely assembled and all the eyebolts are securely tightened, paint the rack with rustproofing spray paint. Spread newspaper under the rack to protect your work area, and apply two or three light coats of spray paint, as directed by the manufacturer; !et each coat dry completely. Turn the rack as you work to spray both the top and the bottom of the rack.

For each post, cut elastic shock cord to a length that will stretch from the eye of the bolt around a pair of skis, under the rack, and back to the eye to hold the skis firmly at the post. Allow enough extra length to secure the cord at each end, but stretch the cord firmly so that it has to stretch to accommodate the skis.

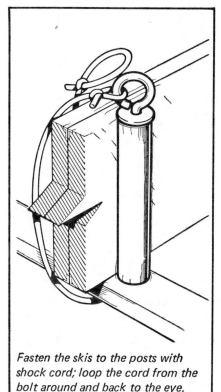

Fasten the skis to the posts with shock cord; loop the cord from the bolt around and back to the eye.

Knot one end of the length of cord and thread it through the eye of the bolt; tie a small loop in the other end of the cord so it can be slipped securely over the eyebolt. Make sure all knots are tight.

Mount the ski rack on your car the same way the cartop carrier was secured; set pairs of skis across the carrier from post to opposite post on the two crosswise bars. To use the carrier for other luggage in summer, remove the four center posts on each bar of the rack.

Repair Ski Poles

Spring, balance, and turning ability on the slope or trail all depend on ski poles. In cross-country skiing the poles are usually bamboo or lightweight aluminum; in downhill, they're heavy-gauge metal, fiberglass, solid wood, or some exotic composite material. You can repair and mend most types yourself. **Tools:** pliers, pocketknife, vise or hammer. **Materials:** replacement handles, baskets, straps, or tips, as required; fine-grit sandpaper, waterproof glue, lubricant (household oil, hand lotion, etc.), fiberglass tape. **Time:** about 10 minutes to ½ hour.

Handles.   Twist old or broken handles off the poles with pliers. Sand the ends of the poles lightly with fine-grit sandpaper to remove debris; wipe off the sanding residue. Apply a bead of waterproof glue around the top of the pole and the pole end of the new handle, and press-fit the handle onto the pole shaft.

Wrist straps.   Wrist straps are pushed through a slot in the pole handle and wedged into place at the short loop side with a small metal wedge. Remove the old strap with a pocketknife; discard the metal wedge that held it in the handle. To install the new strap, jam-fit it through the slot in the handle so that the loop of strap inserted through the slot

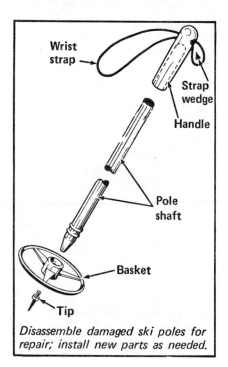

Disassemble damaged ski poles for repair; install new parts as needed.

just sticks out at the other side of the slot. Insert the metal wedge for the new strap into the small loop at this side and push it firmly in with the butt or side of the pocketknife; pull the loop of the wrist strap from the other side to tighten it.

Baskets. Baskets are snap-fit into a ring groove near the pole's base. Remove the old basket with pliers. Apply a lubricant to the inner ring of the replacement basket—household oil works fine, but any lubricant will do, even hand lotion. Press-fit the new basket into the ring groove.

Tips. Most ski pole tips are small, light metal pieces screwed into the pole's base; occasionally they work their way out and get lost. To replace a lost tip, simply apply a small drop of waterproof glue to the tip around the fastening screw. Screw the new tip into place with pliers.

Breaks and bends. Broken poles should be replaced, but you can repair them temporarily; wrap a broken pole

firmly with fiberglass tape and handle it gently. A more common problem is bends. You can usually rebend a pole by straightening it and clamping it in a vise; or roll the pole on a flat surface and straighten it with gentle, repeated hammer taps. Whichever method you use, work slowly and gently; ski poles are fairly fragile.

Sharpen Your Skis

Modern metal and fiberglass downhill skis will last a lifetime if given proper care. Major repairs are best left to the experts, but you can sharpen your ski edges yourself. **Tools:** large, medium-coarse flat file; work gloves. **Materials:** silicone spray lubricant. **Time:** 1 to 2 hours.

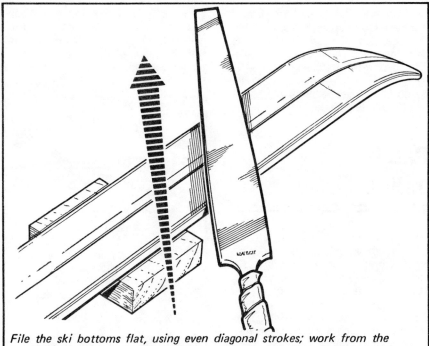

File the ski bottoms flat, using even diagonal strokes; work from the boot area toward the tip and then back. Treat only the center section of each ski; leave the tips and the tails unfiled.

Set the skis on a sturdy table or a pair of benches, bottoms up. Examine the metal edges of each ski carefully. Look for deep scars in the bottom of each ski that cut across the edge, and check the edge in these areas for loose or chipped metal. If you find a loose edge, have the ski professionally repaired; otherwise, go ahead.

Begin by flat-filing the ski bottoms, concentrating on the area under the boot and working toward the front of each ski. Keep the file flat against the ski bottom.

Use even diagonal strokes, working up and down each ski. File until the metal edges are shiny over the entire length of the ski, from 12 inches behind the boot area to the front. Do not file the tips or tails of the skis.

When both skis have been flat-filed, turn them on edge and carefully dress the edge sides with the file. Keep the file perpendicular to the bottom of the ski to produce a square edge. File only enough to make the ski edges shiny.

Run your finger carefully along the edges of each ski to feel for burrs. If there are rough spots, refile the entire ski edge; don't file just the bad spots. Use long, even strokes, again working up and down the ski edge. When all edge surfaces are smooth, coat the edges with a silicone spray lubricant to retard surface rusting.

Patch a Bike Tire

Everyone who's ever pedaled a bicycle has had a flat tire one time or another. Don't let flats put you out of commission—mend the tire yourself. **Tools:** adjustable wrench, chalk, two tire irons, bicycle pump, bucket, bicycle tire pressure gauge. **Materials:** rags, bicycle tire patch kit, talcum powder. **Time:** about ½ hour.

To give you access to the damaged tire, remove the wheel from the bike.

With an adjustable wrench, loosen the nuts that hold the wheel in place. For the rear tire of a single-, 3-, or 5-speed bike, remove the break band attached to the lower frame of the bike; unscrew the screw that holds the metal band and remove the band. Remove the wheel from the bike frame.

Carefully examine the wheel for nails, glass, or other sharp objects; pry out any sharp object wedged into the tread, and mark the damaged spot with chalk. Then remove the tire from the wheel. Pry the tire off by hand, if possible; press firmly with your thumbs to work the tire over the rim. If you can't remove the tire by hand, use bike tire irons. Don't try to use screwdrivers or any other sharp-bladed tool; you could damage your tires.

Starting at a spoke, insert the plain end of a tire iron carefully between the rim and the tire; make sure it's firmly held by the edge of the tire. Keeping that end of the tire iron in place, pull the slotted end down and behind the spoke, and hook the slot over the spoke to hold the tire iron firmly in place. Insert a second tire iron at the next spoke and repeat to pry more of the tire off the rim. Repeat, moving tire irons alternately around the rim, until you can work the

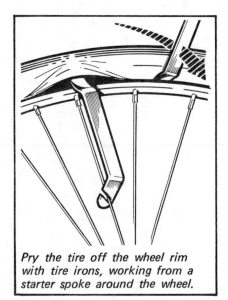

Pry the tire off the wheel rim with tire irons, working from a starter spoke around the wheel.

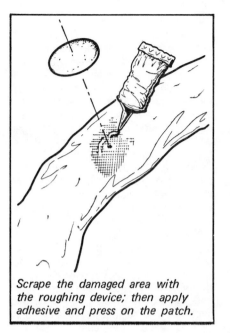

Scrape the damaged area with the roughing device; then apply adhesive and press on the patch.

tire off the rim by hand. Then carefully remove the tube from the tire, pushing the tube valve through the hole in the wheel rim and pulling the tube gently free of the wheel.

Use a bicycle pump to fill the tube until it's firm. Then, with a bucket of water, look for the leak in the tube. Hold a section of the inflated tube underwater and watch for air bubbles; turn the tube in the water until you locate the leak. Check the entire tube; there may be more than one leak. Remove the tube from the water, wipe it dry, and mark the bad spots with chalk.

Bike tire patch kits usually include a roughing device. With the roughing device or the top of the kit, scrape the damaged area of the tube to clean it and provide a rough surface for the patch to bond to. Apply a coat of adhesive to the scraped area of the tube, as directed by the instructions in the patch kit. Let the adhesive dry as directed.

Choose a patch of the appropriate size and peel off its protective backing; press it smoothly and carefully into place over the glued area. Press firmly to seal the patch in place, making sure the edges are entirely bonded. Let the

patch dry for 5 minutes and then sprinkle it with talcum powder so it won't adhere to the inside of the tire.

Check the tire once more, inside and out, to be sure nothing sharp is still wedged in it; remove anything stuck in the rubber. Press the uninflated tube into place inside the tire. Carefully insert the valve stem of the tube into the hole in the rim, and push the tire into place over the rim with your thumbs. When it gets too hard to replace the tire by hand, carefully insert the plain end of a tire iron under the tire and pry the tire into place around the rim. Work gently, being careful not to pinch the tube between the tire and the rim or the rim and the tire iron. Use the tire irons only when necessary.

Finally, with the tire in place, inflate it to the correct pressure with the bicycle pump, as marked on the side of the tire. Wait a few minutes to make sure the tire is holding air; then replace the wheel in the bike frame and tighten the nuts that hold it in place. If necessary, replace the break band.

Clean or Replace a Bicycle Chain

Exposed to dirt and constant stress, a bike chain takes a licking. Give it a checkup every season to keep it working smoothly. **Tools:** needle-nose pliers or chain rivet extractor, shallow pan, small stiff brush or toothbrush, chalk. **Materials:** kerosene, motor oil, rags, replacement master link or replacement ⅛-inch or ³/₃₂-inch bicycle chain. **Time:** about ½ to 1 hour, plus drying time.

Cleaning. Single-speed and 3-speed bikes use a ⅛-inch chain with a master link; 5-speeds and 10-speeds use a ³/₃₂-inch continuous chain. Both types should be cleaned regularly. Examine the way the chain is installed on the bicycle, and sketch it if you aren't sure you can remember it. You must replace the chain exactly the same way after you clean it.

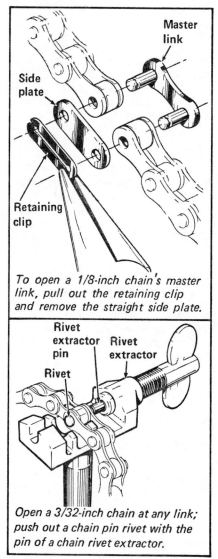

To open a 1/8-inch chain's master link, pull out the retaining clip and remove the straight side plate.

Open a 3/32-inch chain at any link; push out a chain pin rivet with the pin of a chain rivet extractor.

the center of the chain but leave it hanging from the far side. The chain will separate as the rivet is loosened.

Immerse the chain in kerosene in a shallow pan. Scrub it firmly with a small stiff brush or toothbrush to remove all dirt and old oil, and hang it to dry for about 1 hour. Immerse the cleaned chain in motor oil, remove it, and wipe off the excess oil with rags. Let the chain dry until it stops dripping.

To reinstall the chain, replace it around the rear sprocket and the front chainwheel, exactly as it was before you removed it. Reattach the master link to the loose ends of a ⅛-inch chain; replace the side plate and the retaining clip. Rejoin the ends of a ³/₃₂-inch chain with a chain rivet extractor; loosen the screw pin, align the pin over the loose rivet where the ends of the chain meet, and tighten the screw pin. Adjust the rivet carefully so that it's exactly flush with both sides of the chain.

Check the chain tension to be sure it's correct; the wrong tension can be dangerous. On a derailleur bike, chain tension is adjusted automatically; if you think the tension is wrong, take the bike in to a shop. Single-speed bikes and 3-speed bikes with gears in the hub can be manually adjusted.

Set a yardstick flat across the tops of the rear sprocket and the chainwheel. At the midpoint of the chain between the two sprockets, the top length of chain should sag about ½ inch below the bottom of the yardstick. Adjust the chain tension as necessary. Loosen the nuts on the rear wheel axle and move the wheel forward or back until the sag is correct; then tighten the axle nuts.

Damaged or broken chains. If a ⅛-inch chain comes apart at the master link, replace the master link with a new one. Adjust the chain to position it correctly, hook the new master link through the loose ends, and fasten the link. A chain that is damaged or breaks in the middle, or a damaged or broken ³/₃₂-inch chain, should be replaced. Remove the chain as above and take it with you to the bike shop; buy a new chain of the same type.

To fit a new chain to the bicycle, re-

Remove the chain from the bicycle. The master link of a ⅛-inch chain has straight side plates. To open the master link, pull out the retaining clip with a needle-nose pliers; then remove the side plate. Pull the link out of the chain to release the ends. To remove a ³/₃₂-inch chain, push out a chain pin rivet anywhere along the chain. Align a chain rivet extractor with its screw pin over a rivet; tighten the screw of the extractor just enough to push the rivet through

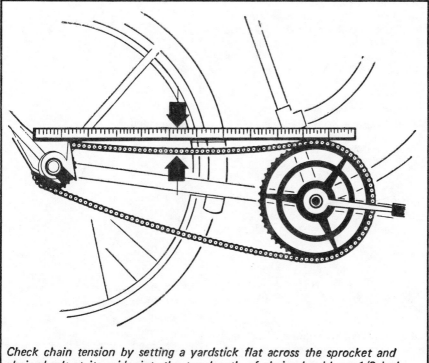

Check chain tension by setting a yardstick flat across the sprocket and chainwheel; at its midpoint, the top length of chain should sag 1/2 inch below the yardstick. Adjust the chain as necessary to this tension.

move links as necessary to adjust the chain to the proper length. If the old chain is in one piece, measure the new chain to this length and mark it with chalk. If you can't measure by the old chain, check chain length by stretching the chain into place around the rear sprocket and the front chainwheel, exactly as the old chain was installed, with the two ends meeting at the front chainwheel. Adjust the chain to the proper tension as above and slip the ends onto the sprockets of the wheel to mate them exactly; mark the exact link where the end link on one side meets the other side of the chain.

Remove any excess links from the end of the new chain with a chain rivet extractor. Replace the chain around the rear sprocket and the front chainwheel and join the ends with the master link or the chain rivet extractor. Be sure the connecting rivet is flush with both sides of the new chain.

Replace a Bicycle Spoke

A broken or bent wheel spoke can cause further problems with your bike, but replacing it is easy. **Tools:** adjustable wrench, two tire irons, wire cutter, bicycle spoke wrench, file, bicycle pump. **Materials:** replacement spoke. **Time:** about ½ hour.

Set the bicycle upside down and prop it firmly in place. Using an adjustable wrench, loosen the nuts that hold the wheel in place; remove the wheel. Let the air out of the tire. Remove the tire from the wheel by hand, if possible; or use tire irons to work the tire over the rim. Starting at a spoke, carefully insert the plain end of a tire iron between the rim and the tire. Holding that end in place, pull the slotted end down and behind the spoke, and hook the slot over the spoke. Insert a second tire iron at the next spoke; repeat, moving the irons alternately around the rim, until you can work the tire off by hand. Then remove both tire and tube.

Once the tire has been removed, you're ready to replace the damaged spoke. On most bikes, the heads of the nipples that hold the wheel spokes in place are covered by a large rubber band. Pull this band over the rim and remove it. If the broken spoke has fallen out of the wheel, examine the wheel to find the empty hole where the new spoke will go. If the old spoke is still in the wheel, cut it off at both ends with wire cutters. Remove any pieces of old spoke left in the wheel rim or the hub.

The new spoke must be exactly the same length and diameter as the old one. To make sure you get the right size, either take the whole wheel to the bike shop or remove a good spoke from the same side to measure by. Don't accept any differences in either length or diameter.

To make the repair, insert the head of the spoke, the end that doesn't have a nipple, into the empty hole in the hub. The spoke head should curve away from the hub. You may have to bend the spoke slightly to get it into place, but don't bend it sharply.

When the spoke is in place, insert the nipple through the hole in the wheel rim and thread it carefully onto the end of the spoke. Hand-tighten the nipple; don't use the spoke wrench yet.

Replace the wheel rim in the fork of the bicycle frame; tighten the wheel nuts. Spin the rim firmly with your hand. As it spins, sight directly down the wheel to see if the spin is even. The wheel will probably be warped away from the side where the new spoke was installed. Stop the wheel and tighten the new spoke a little with the spoke wrench, then respin the wheel and check the wheel alignment again.

Repeat, tightening the new spoke nipple, until the wheel spins freely and evenly. If the wobble persists after you've tightened the new spoke nipple

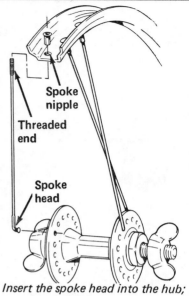

Insert the spoke head into the hub; insert the threaded end through the wheel rim and screw the spoke nipple on.

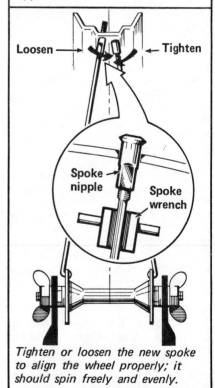

Tighten or loosen the new spoke to align the wheel properly; it should spin freely and evenly.

two or three full turns, loosen the spokes opposite the new spoke to correct the alignment.

After you've aligned the tire, check the new spoke to make sure it doesn't stick out through the rim end of the nipple. If necessary, file it flat. Finally, replace the rubber band over the spoke nipples, replace the tube and tire, and pump the tire full.

Tune Up Your Bicycle Brakes

The caliper brakes on 3-speed, 5-speed, and 10-speed bikes are easy to adjust when they don't perform properly. **Tools:** third hand, adjustable wrench, pliers. **Materials:** bicycle spray lubricant, replacement rubber brake pads or shoes. **Time:** about ½ hour.

Inadequate braking is often the result of a loose brake cable on one or both bike wheels. Place a third hand—a special tool available at bike shops—over the brake shoes; use it to draw the

brake shoes into contact with the wheel rim.

With an adjustable wrench, loosen the cable clamp nut that secures side-pull brakes or the cable anchor bolt that secures center-pull brakes. Grip the end of the cable with a pliers and pull the cable through the clamp or anchor until it's tight; holding the cable tight with one hand, tighten the cable clamp nut or cable anchor. Release the brake.

Test the brake by squeezing the brake lever; the brake should grip when the lever is depressed about ½ inch. If it doesn't, the cable could still be too loose; repeat the tightening procedure. Lift the bike so that its front wheel is off the ground, and spin the wheel. If the wheel binds, loosen the cable a bit.

Follow the same procedure to tighten the brake cable on the back wheel of the bike. Test the brake by squeezing the brake lever and spinning the wheel; adjust cable tension as necessary.

Finally, after you adjust the brake cable tension, check the brake levers on the handlebars. If they're stiff or squeaky, spray them with bicycle spray lubricant at the pivot points.

If the brake cables are tight, faulty braking can result from wear to the

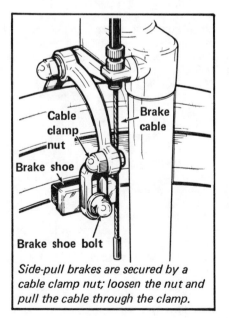

Side-pull brakes are secured by a cable clamp nut; loosen the nut and pull the cable through the clamp.

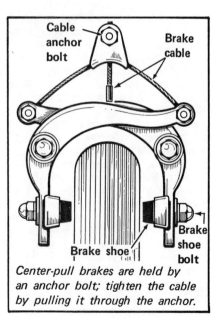

Center-pull brakes are held by an anchor bolt; tighten the cable by pulling it through the anchor.

brake shoes, the blocks of rubber that press against the wheel rims when the brake levers are squeezed. Examine the rubber brake shoes carefully. The rubber should be flexible; if a shoe is hardened or cracked, or if it's less than ½ inch thick above the metal mounting plate, it must be replaced. Buy four new brake shoes of the same type; take an old one with you to the bike shop to make sure you get the right type. Change all four old shoes.

To replace the brake shoes, use an adjustable wrench to remove the bolts that hold them into the slots in the U-shaped brake arms on each wheel. Take out the old brake shoes. Set the new shoes into place in the adjustment slots, aligned the same way the old ones were. The shoes must rub only the rim of the wheel when the brake is applied; be careful to position them correctly. Replace the bolts over the brake shoes and tighten them with a wrench.

Patch a Fiberglass Hull

A holed fiberglass sailboat or canoe looks bad, but unless the boat is structurally damaged, it's easy to repair. With patience, you can rebuild the hull as good as new. **Tools:** disc sander or electric drill with sanding disc, buffing attachment for sander or drill, scissors, mixing can and stir stick, paintbrushes, sanding block. **Materials:** medium-grit sanding discs, soft cloths, acetone, light cardboard, plastic wrap, masking tape; quart-size polyester resin fiberglass repair kit, or polyester resin and hardener, 10-ounce roving, and 7½-ounce fiberglass cloth; fine, very fine, and extra-fine wet-or-dry sandpaper; gel coat to match hull, fiberglass rubbing compound, car wax. **Time:** about 2 days, depending on size of hole.

To patch the hole, buy a quart-size polyester resin fiberglass repair kit at a marine store; from the boat's manufacturer, buy gel coat to match the color of your boat. If you can't find a repair kit buy 1 quart of polyester resin and hardener, and 2 square feet each of 10-ounce roving and 7½-ounce fiberglass cloth. Buy fiberglass rubbing compound to finish the repair.

To prepare a firm base for the patch, enlarge the hole. Grind down the edges of the hole to firm fiberglass with a disc sander or an electric drill with a sanding attachment, and a medium-grit sanding disc. When you've exposed sound fiberglass all around the hole, taper the ground hole out into the sound hull, so that the outside edge of the hole is at least 2 or 3 inches wider than the inside edge. This provides a firm bonding surface for the patching material.

When the hole is completely sanded, wipe the dust off with a soft cloth and then clean the damaged area with a cloth soaked in acetone. *Caution: Acetone is extremely flammable. Work in a well-ventilated area, and don't smoke; dispose of acetone-saturated cloths immediately in an outside vented container.*

To contour the patch to match the shape of the hull, cut a backing piece from light cardboard. Cut the cardboard at least 2 inches larger than the hole all around. Cover the piece of cardboard smoothly with plastic wrap, taped into place, so that the patch won't stick to it, and then set the backing into place on the inside of the hull; it should cover the hole completely. Carefully bend the cardboard to match the curve of the hull, and tape it firmly into place with masking tape. The curve of the cardboard must match the hull contour precisely or the patch will be weak.

When the hole is backed, prepare the patching material. The hole will be filled with pieces of 10-ounce roving to the thickness of the hull; the top layer is cut from 7½-ounce fiberglass cloth to match the hull surface.

Cut the first layer of roving to fit the inside diameter of the hole, at its smallest point. Cut successive layers slightly larger, to overlap the inside layers and feather out over the tapering edges of the hole. Stack the layers of roving in the hole as you cut them so you can see

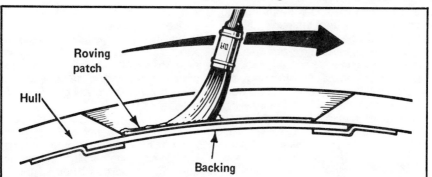

Brush the first patch of roving with resin and set it into the prepared hole against the cardboard backing; press it smoothly into place with the brush, stroking lightly from the center toward the edges.

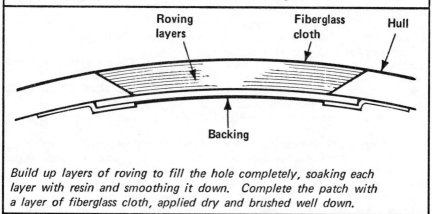

Build up layers of roving to fill the hole completely, soaking each layer with resin and smoothing it down. Complete the patch with a layer of fiberglass cloth, applied dry and brushed well down.

how many thicknesses to cut. When you have enough layers of roving to make the depression just level with the surrounding hull surface, cut a piece of fiberglass cloth to complete the patch, overlapping well onto the sound hull surface.

Lay the pieces of roving and fiberglass out in order on a clean surface near the boat. Then, with your patching material at hand, mix polyester resin and hardener in a can as directed by the manufacturer. Mix only as much resin as you can apply in less than ½ hour; it hardens quickly. Make sure the temperature in your work area is at least 60° F.

Set the first patch of roving—the smallest one—on a clean piece of cardboard near the boat. Working quickly, apply catalyzed resin to the roving with a small paintbrush; brush the resin well into the roving to soak it thoroughly. The roving should be completely wet through, but not dripping. Pick up the piece of wet roving and set it into the prepared hole in the hull, centered in the bottom of the depression. Press it smoothly into place with the brush, dabbing it from the center toward the edges.

Set the next smallest patch of roving on the cardboard and apply catalyzed resin to it as above; soak it thoroughly. Position the saturated roving over the first layer in the hole, and smooth it into place with the brush. Repeat, applying resin and smoothing each roving layer into place, to build up a smoothly graduated patch of new material in the hole, tapering with the edges of the hole to match the contour of the hull.

When all the layers of roving have been applied, close the patch with the prepared piece of fiberglass cloth. Instead of soaking the cloth with resin, set it directly over the patch, dry, and work it down into the resin-soaked roving with the paintbrush. If necessary, add a small amount of additional resin to saturate the edges of the fiberglass cloth, but be sparing; too much resin will weaken the patch. Use only enough resin to thoroughly wet and darken all the roving and cloth.

Let the completed patch dry for at least 8 hours, as specified by the resin manufacturer. When the patch is completely dry, remove the cardboard backing from the inside of the hull; the patch should follow the contour of the hull exactly. Remove any irregularities in the patch surface, and correct contour as necessary, with a disc sander or an electric drill with a sanding attachment, and a medium-grit sanding disc; do *not* oversand, but smooth the area to match the hull contour exactly. Then smooth the sanded surface by hand with a sanding block and fine-grit wet-or-dry sandpaper, using long back-and-forth strokes over the patch.

When the patch is smooth and matches the hull contour, clean the area with acetone to remove all dust. Finish the patch with gel coat, to match the color of the hull. Mix the gel coat as directed by the manufacturer. Brush a thin layer of gel coat onto the patch area, to cover the patch completely and evenly. Then, working quickly, carefully smooth a large piece of plastic wrap directly over the wet gel coat, smoothing out all air bubbles and wrinkles, to cover the patch completely. If necessary, use overlapping strips of plastic to cover the patch completely. You must cover the gel coat with plastic or it won't dry smooth.

Let the gel coat dry for at least 8 hours, as directed by the manufacturer. When the gel coat is completely dry, peel off the plastic wrap; the patch surface should be very smooth. Carefully hand-sand the patch area with fine-grit

wet-or-dry sandpaper to remove any excess gel coat and contour the patch to match the hull exactly. Smooth the sanded patch carefully and remove any scratches with very fine and then extra-fine wet-or-dry sandpaper; use enough water to prevent scratching the gel coat.

Finally, clean the rebuilt hull area thoroughly with a wet cloth. To polish the patch, apply fiberglass rubbing compound to the sanded gel coat and buff the surface as directed by the manufacturer; use the buffing attachment of the disc sander or electric drill. After buffing the patch, apply a protective coat of car wax to the hull surface.

Make Boat Line Protectors

The synthetic line used for anchor and mooring lines is extremely strong, but it can break at chafe points if you don't protect it. Extend its life with garden hose chafe guards. **Tools:** sharp knife, candle and matches. **Materials:** section of old garden hose, lightweight nylon line. **Time:** about 20 minutes.

Cut the section of hose into 1-foot pieces. If you want a longer chafe guard to protect the anchor line from the bowsprit, cut it as long as desired.

To make each line protector, carefully slit a piece of hose along one side by setting the blade of a sharp knife inside the hose and pulling it out and along the hose. Cut a small hole about ½ inch from each end of the hose section, opposite the slit side.

To make safety lines for each chafe guard, cut lightweight nylon line into 1-foot pieces. Light a candle and carefully sear the ends of each piece of line; keep the line in the candle flame just long enough to melt the nylon fibers together. Blow the candle out. Loop the seared line in half and pass the looped end through the hole in one end of the hose; thread the other ends of the line through the loop and pull the knot tight.

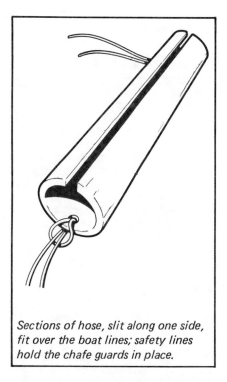

Sections of hose, slit along one side, fit over the boat lines; safety lines hold the chafe guards in place.

Repeat to place a line at the other end of the chafe guard.

Repeat this procedure to make as many chafe guards as you need, to protect dock lines, anchor lines, painters for the tender, and the mooring line attached to the mooring buoy. Cut extra sections of hose but don't slit them; slip them over the ends of the line to protect it from tar-covered pilings, rough concrete walls, or anywhere else your line needs temporary protection.

Make Custom Dry Cockpit Cushions

Few things are more annoying than sitting on an unexpectedly soggy cushion, and boat cockpit cushions are particular offenders. Solve the problem permanently with waterproof, ventilated built-ins. **Tools:** measuring rule or tape, power saw or handsaw, carpenters' square, hammer, electric drill or brace and bit, paintbrush, sharp utility knife, sharp scissors, staple gun. **Materials:** $\frac{1}{2} \times \frac{3}{4}$-inch parting stop stock, $\frac{5}{8}$-inch brads, $\frac{3}{8}$-inch exterior-grade plywood, high-gloss polyurethane varnish, 4-inch-thick heavy-duty closed-cell foam, waterproof fabric or vinyl, copper-clad heavy-duty staples. **Time:** about 4 hours per cushion, plus drying time.

Choose the materials for your cushions carefully; everything you use must be waterproof and noncorroding. Be sure to buy closed-cell foam—the open-cell kind absorbs water.

For each cushion you're replacing, measure the old cushion carefully. Plan the frame of the cushion to be 1 inch smaller than the cushion each way, and measure and cut a piece of $\frac{3}{8}$-inch exterior plywood exactly to that size; use a carpenters' square to make sure your cuts are straight.

Cut four pieces of $\frac{1}{2} \times \frac{3}{4}$-inch parting stop stock to form the sides of the frame, with two pieces the same length as the sides of the plywood square and two pieces cut short enough to butt between the other pieces at the corners of the boat cushion frame. Nail the strips of parting stop into place on the sides of the plywood to form a shallow tray; use $\frac{5}{8}$-inch brads to attach the strips to each other at the corners and to the plywood backing of the frame.

When the frame of the cushion is assembled, drill four to eight $\frac{1}{4}$- to $\frac{1}{2}$-inch ventilation holes in the plywood base, depending on the size of the frame. Use an electric drill or a brace and bit. Varnish the completed frame thoroughly with high-gloss polyurethane varnish, covering the wood generously to prevent it from delaminating. Varnish the plywood base on the edges and both sides, being careful to cover the insides of the drilled ventilation holes; varnish all exposed surfaces of the parting stop frame. Let the frame dry completely, as directed by the manufacturer, and apply a second generous coat of varnish; let dry again.

For each cushion, measure and cut 4-inch-thick heavy-duty closed-cell

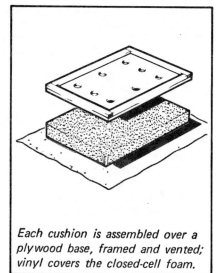

Each cushion is assembled over a plywood base, framed and vented; vinyl covers the closed-cell foam.

Tune an Outboard Motor

At least once a year, to extend its life and ensure its reliability, give your outboard motor a tune-up. Follow these general maintenance steps; consult your owner's manual for specific instructions. **Tools:** owner's manual, screwdriver, Phillips-head screwdriver, adjustable wrench, pliers, hammer, coffee can or other container. **Materials:** soft cloths, lower-unit lubricant, replacement nuts and bolts as required, waterproof marine grease, replacement spark plugs, replacement fuel filter element, car wax, fresh fuel and oil. Buy lubricant, bolts, filters, and marine grease at a marine store. **Time:** about 3 hours.

Whatever brand or size outboard you have, use the maintenance schedule outlined in your owner's manual. Follow any specific recommendations and use any special applicable procedures. Use only specified lubricants and replacement parts; if you use different ones you'll void your warranty.

Start your preseason checkout with a visual inspection. With the motor off, remove the cowling to expose the power head. Starting at the propeller, at the bottom of the lower unit, examine the motor for signs of leaking lubricants; look around the propeller and below the fill screws on the side of the gear housing. A little oil is normal, but if there's a dark oil stain running down from the propeller, there could be a leak in the seals behind the propeller. This should be repaired by a qualified outboard mechanic.

A bad propeller wastes fuel and increases wear to the lower unit; examine the propeller carefully. Look for small cracks in the blades near the hub, for large nicks in the blade tips; check to see whether the blades are bent or misaligned. If you find any of these conditions, take the propeller to a propeller specialist or to the dealer; don't

foam exactly to size with a sharp utility knife. The foam should be 1 inch larger than the plywood frame each way. Using the foam as a pattern, cut a piece of waterproof fabric or vinyl about 7 inches longer than the foam all around, so that it can be folded over the foam toward the middle of the cushion and stapled into place. Make sure to leave enough fabric to cover the sides of the frame on all sides.

Spread the fabric on the floor and center the foam on it; then set the plywood base of the cushion on top of the foam, frame side up and flat side to the foam. Starting at one corner, fold the fabric up over the foam and the frame. Turn the cut edge under and staple the fabric into place on the plywood inside the parting stop frame, using a staple gun and copper-clad heavy-duty staples. Pleat the corners of the fabric in to miter them neatly as you work. Repeat to fasten the opposite side of the fabric, pulling it firm but not flattening the foam; then staple the other two sides.

Follow the same procedure for each cushion you're replacing, being careful to make the new cushions exactly the same size as the old. To install the cushions, just set them in place in the cockpit.

try to repair the damage yourself.

If your owner's manual recommends periodic lubricant changes for your motor's lower unit, remove the unit's top and bottom fill plugs and let the lubricant drain into a coffee can or other container. Replace the lubricant with the type recommended for your motor. Insert the lubricant applicator's nozzle into the bottom fill hole and squirt the lubricant into the gear case. When the lubricant starts to come out the top fill hole, replace the top plug; then remove the applicator nozzle and replace the

bottom plug. Remove excess lubricant with a soft cloth.

Inspect the lower unit, working upward, for loose or missing nuts or bolts; consult the drawings and follow the precise instructions provided in your owner's manual. Tighten loose screws, nuts, and bolts; replace missing hardware with the exact type recommended for use in your motor.

At the transom clamp bracket, lubricate the grease fittings, as directed in your owner's manual. Lubricate the swivel bracket—the bearing the motor

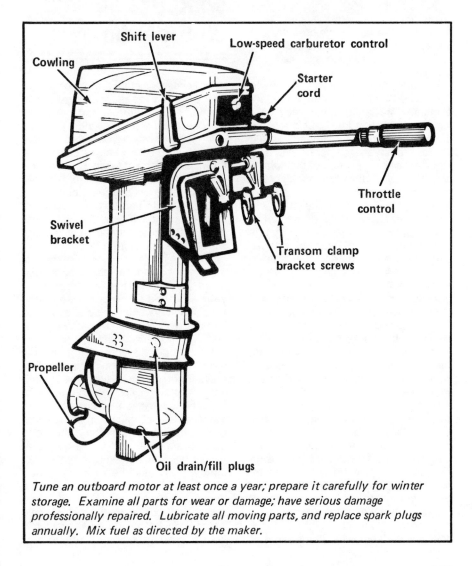

Shift lever

Low-speed carburetor control

Cowling

Starter cord

Throttle control

Swivel bracket

Transom clamp bracket screws

Propeller

Oil drain/fill plugs

Tune an outboard motor at least once a year; prepare it carefully for winter storage. Examine all parts for wear or damage; have serious damage professionally repaired. Lubricate all moving parts, and replace spark plugs annually. Mix fuel as directed by the maker.

turns on—with the waterproof marine grease recommended for your motor; then lubricate the transom clamp screw threads with the same grease.

Work the throttle control on the engine; twist the hand throttle or move the control lever the throttle control cable is attached to. As you work the throttle control, watch the motor to identify moving parts inside the power head. Lubricate all moving parts with the waterproof marine grease recommended for your motor. Move the forward-reverse shift lever and watch for movement inside the motor; lubricate all pivot points. Then gently pull the starter cord and watch the starter pinion gear that engages the flywheel at the top of the motor; lubricate the gear and the bearing inside.

After lubricating moving parts inside the power head, disconnect the spark plug wires. Be careful to note their location exactly so you'll be able to replace them correctly. Using an adjustable wrench, remove each spark plug and replace it with a new one of the correct type for your motor; first hand-tighten and then wrench-tighten each plug. Be careful not to overtighten the plugs; excessive pressure could damage the aluminum cylinder head.

At least once a year, to ensure smooth running, replace the motor's fuel filter; use a new filter of the type recommended for your motor. The fuel filter is usually located inside the motor's cover at the engine end of the fuel pump, or incorporated into the fuel pump; check your owner's manual and follow the manufacturer's instructions. Clean out any accumulated water and sediment, and replace the filter element with a new one of the correct type.

Replace the cowling on the engine. To protect the finish and prevent corrosion, apply a coat of car wax to the cowling, as directed by the manufacturer. Then mix fuel for the motor, using the proportions of fresh fuel and oil specified in your owner's manual. Mount the motor, in water for testing.

Finally, with the motor mounted, start the engine. Immediately check for a flow of water somewhere at the rear of the engine; this indicates that the water pump is functioning properly. Let the engine warm up for at least 2 minutes and then adjust the low-speed carburetor jet, turning the fuel-mix knob on the front of the motor until the motor idles smoothly. Put the motor into gear and go for a short ride; then idle down and readjust. If your motor has an idle adjustment, turn the control until the engine idles smoothly and doesn't die when you shift into gear.

Winterize an Outboard Motor

To keep your outboard motor in top shape from year to year, prepare it carefully for winter storage. **Tools:** owner's manual, freshwater flushing unit, garden hose, screwdriver, adjustable wrench, coffee can or other container, tarp, piece of scrap wood. **Materials:** fuel conditioner, rust-preventive oil, lower-unit lubricant, soft cloths, replacement nuts and bolts as required, touch-up paint, car wax. Buy lubricant, oil, and fuel conditioner at a marine store. **Time:** about 2 hours.

Whatever brand or size outboard motor you have, follow the specific recommendations and instructions given in your owner's manual. Use only specified lubricants and replacement parts; if you use different ones you'll void your warranty.

If you operate your motor in salt water, it must be thoroughly flushed to prevent corrosion. To flush the motor, use a freshwater flushing unit made to fit your motor. Attach the unit's fitting to the motor's cooling system as directed by the manufacturer; attach the coupling at the other end of the unit to a garden hose. Run the motor for several minutes at less than half throttle, exactly as directed, to remove all salt from the motor.

Whether you operate the motor in salt water or in fresh, you must protect it from corrosion. The last time you use the motor before storing it, add to the fuel tank 1 ounce of fuel conditioner for each gallon of fuel in the tank. Operate the motor for about 5 minutes to make sure the fuel conditioner has reached the carburetor. Then disconnect the fuel line or turn off the fuel, and squirt a liberal amount of rust-preventive oil into the air intake of the carburetor; use the type of oil recommended by your motor's manufacturer. The engine should sputter, smoke, and die. If it doesn't, squirt in more oil; then shut the motor off and shift it into neutral gear. Dismount the motor and let it cool.

With the motor disconnected, drain the fuel from the carburetor. Remove the cowling and disconnect the spark plug wires; be careful to note their location exactly so you'll be able to replace them correctly. Using an adjustable wrench, remove the spark plugs. Inject about 1 ounce of rust-preventive oil into each cylinder, and slowly crank the flywheel on the top of the motor to spread the oil over the entire cylinder surface. Then replace and hand-tighten the spark plugs; leave the ignition wires disconnected.

If your owner's manual recommends periodic lubricant changes for your motor's lower unit, remove the unit's top and bottom fill plugs and let the lubricant drain into a coffee can or other container. Replace the lubricant with the type recommended for your motor. Insert the lubricant applicator's nozzle into the bottom fill hole and squirt the lubricant into the gear case. When the lubricant starts to come out the top fill hole, replace the top plug; then remove the applicator nozzle and replace the bottom plug. Remove excess lubricant with a soft cloth.

Inspect the lower unit for loose or missing nuts or bolts; consult the drawings and follow the precise instructions provided in your owner's manual. Tighten loose screws, nuts, and bolts; replace missing hardware with the exact type recommended for use in your motor.

After lubricating and inspecting the motor, soak a soft cloth in rust-preventive oil and squeeze it out. Rub

the cloth over all exposed parts of the motor to coat them with oil and prevent corrosion. Then replace the cowling.

Inspect the cowling for chipped or peeling paint; touch up bad spots with matching paint. Use a touch-up kit made for your motor, or any good enamel; follow the manufacturer's instructions for application and drying. When the motor is completely dry, apply a coat of car wax to the cowling, as directed by the manufacturer. For further protection, rub the cowling with an oil-soaked cloth to coat it lightly with oil.

Store the motor in a dry, dust-free place; cover it with a tarp to protect it from dirt. If the motor has a battery, remove the battery and store it separately; set it off the floor on a piece of scrap wood. Make sure the case is clean and the water in the cell is at the correct level.

During the winter, work the throttle control every few weeks to keep the moving parts from corroding; twist the hand throttle or move the control lever the throttle control cable is attached to. Gently pull the starter cord to engage the gears. If the motor has a battery, check the water level in the cell and add water as necessary to maintain the charge.

Build a Boat Cover Frame

Enclosed boat storage is expensive, but an unprotected boat ages quickly. Store your boat in your own yard with this lightweight, easily disassembled cover frame. **Tools:** pencil, slip-joint pliers, rented conduit bender, scratch awl or grease pencil, hacksaw, screwdriver, staple gun, measuring rule, scissors or sharp utility knife. **Materials:** 3½-inch octagonal electrical boxes, ½-inch or ¾-inch thinwall setscrew connectors, ½-inch or ¾-inch thinwall electrical conduit, scrap wood blocks, scrap pieces of carpeting, heavy-duty staples, heavy plastic tarp, duct tape, sturdy cord. **Time:** about 6 to 8 hours.

To calculate the materials you'll need, figure from the length of your boat. Divide the length of the boat by 3 and add 1; this is the number of 3 ½-inch octagonal electrical boxes you'll need. Thinwall electrical conduit is sold in 10-foot sections; buy ½-inch conduit for small boats and ¾-inch conduit for wide boats. You'll need sections for the support legs of the cover frame, for the ridgepole, and for snow support posts. Divide the length of the boat by 3 and multiply by 2; this is the number of sections needed for the support legs. Divide the length of the boat by 3; this is the number of ridge sections you'll need. Add 3 to 6 sections for snow support posts at the ridge-leg intersections, depending on how much snow falls in your area. Rent a thinwall conduit bender to simplify the frame assembly; get instructions from the rental agent.

To cover the boat, buy a heavy plastic tarp, at least 5 feet longer than the boat and at least 3 times as wide. Check at outdoor stores or industrial supply houses for the best buy. If possible, choose an opaque black tarp, to speed melting of piled-up snow.

Before you start work, plan the assembly of the cover frame, and sketch your plan so you can refer to it as you work. Space arched cover support legs over the boat at each end of the boat and every 3 feet along its length; connect the supports with a ridgepole. Brace the framework firmly with three to six support posts holding the top of the frame above the boat's deck.

Prepare the electrical boxes by removing the knockout plugs on the sides of the boxes; strike them sharply with the handle of a slip-joint pliers and then twist the tabs off with the jaws of the pliers. Insert a thinwall setscrew connector into each side opening of each junction box and tighten the locknuts firmly with the pliers.

Construct the support legs of the frame first. Insert a section of conduit into the conduit bender and align it with the edge of the bender; then make a 135-degree bend in the pipe—45 degrees out from a right angle—as directed by the rental agent. Repeat to bend each support leg section of conduit. Insert two sections of conduit at the bent ends into the openings on opposite sides of an electrical box, making an angular tent shape; don't tighten the setscrews yet. You'll need an assistant at this point to determine the desired height of the legs.

Hold the assembled but not secured support over the boat, straddling the boat at a center support point so that the angled-out legs touch the edges of the boat. Adjust the support to the desired height over the boat and have your assistant mark the deck intersection point with a scratch awl or grease pencil. Cut the conduit legs at these points with a hacksaw; then reinsert the legs into the electrical boxes and firmly tighten the setscrews to hold them in place.

Repeat this procedure to place and cut each support leg, setting legs at the ends of the boat and every 3 feet along its length. The supports at the center of

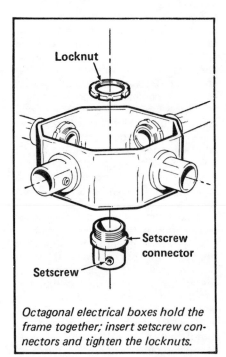

Octagonal electrical boxes hold the frame together; insert setscrew connectors and tighten the locknuts.

the boat will be higher than the supports at bow and stern, forming a pitched cover to shed snow and rain. Set each pair of support legs in order as you work so that you'll be able to assemble the frame in sequence.

When all the support legs have been bent and cut, cut 3-foot sections of conduit to form a connecting ridgepole from support leg to support leg. Assemble the conduit frame by connecting the support sections with 3-foot ridge sections; tighten the setscrews holding the connecting sections in place. At this point the frame will be a long tent-shaped skeleton that covers the length and width of the boat exactly.

Set the assembled frame onto the boat. To protect the boat, insert a block of scrap wood under each conduit leg. Pad the top corners of the frame and cover the electrical boxes with pieces of scrap carpeting, wrapped around and stapled together with a staple gun and heavy-duty staples.

To complete the framework, add three to six snow support posts, depending on the snow load in your area and the deck or cockpit you're working over. At each support point, where the

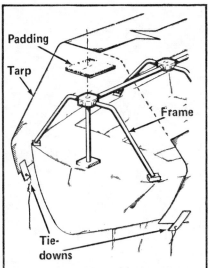

Padding
Tarp
Frame
Tie-
downs

The completed frame is braced on the deck; tape tie-down tabs hold the plastic cover to the boat trailer.

support legs and the ridge sections are connected at the sides of an electrical box, measure the distance from the bottom of the box to the deck or cockpit directly below it. Cut a section of conduit to the measured distance and connect it to the bottom opening of the box with a setscrew connector, forming an upright brace inside the framework. Set a block of scrap wood under the brace to protect the deck.

With the completed frame in place over the boat, spread a heavy plastic tarp over the frame to cover it entirely. The tarp must extend at least 1 foot past the deck all around; if the boat is any color but white, cover the entire hull, if possible, to prevent fading.

To secure the tarp over the framework, attach a tab of duct tape every 2 to 3 feet around the boat. For each tab, cut a piece of duct tape about 1 foot long. Stick 4 inches of one end of the tape to the outside of the plastic tarp and fold the tape over on itself to stick 4 inches at the other end to the inside, with a double 2-inch-long tab of tape sticking out beyond the edge of the plastic. Cut a small hole in each tab with a scissors or a utility knife.

Attach the tarp to the boat trailer with sturdy cord, cut as needed and looped securely through the duct tape tabs. Be careful to fasten the cover down securely, with no loose or flapping edges; strong wind could damage a poorly secured tarp. Disassemble and reassemble the cover frame as needed each season.

Repair a Damaged Tent

A small tear in a tent can worsen quickly, but it's easy to repair even on the trail. Carry mending materials with you to keep your tent secure. **Tools:** small scissors, sewing awl, straight pins, grommet setter. **Materials:** *for nylon tents*—ripstop nylon repair tape, seam sealer made for nylon; *for canvas* *tents*—taffeta repair tape, seam sealer made for canvas; *for both*—waxed thread, scrap nylon screening, grommets. **Time:** 10 minutes to 1 hour, depending on the damage.

Most rips, tears, and leaks occur because a tent has been pitched too rigidly; find ways to set up your tent so that it can flex in high wind conditions. Use shock cords wherever possible. Check your campsite for dangerous limbs, projecting roots, and sharp rocks that could cause damage; if you must pitch your tent on a hazardous site, pad sharp rocks and clear away debris before pitching it.

Rips and tears. To mend small tears, cover the damaged area with cloth repair tape—ripstop nylon for nylon tents, taffeta for canvas tents. Apply a liberal patch to both sides of the tear, smoothing the edges of the tape carefully to prevent snags and leaks. Coat the edges of the patch with seam sealer, on both sides of the tent. Be sure you're using the right sealer; canvas sealer could damage a nylon tent.

Large tears must be sewn closed or patched with repair tape. If the tear is in a part of the tent where extra pressure doesn't matter, turn the top edge of the tear under about ¼ inch and stitch the turned fabric over the outside of the bottom torn edge, using a sewing awl and strong waxed thread, forming a new seam. Plan your sewing to account for water runoff; turn the edges of the patch to create a shingle effect to shed water, not a shelf to hold it. Make your stitches short and close together; double seams are strongest. To ensure a watertight seal, apply a bead of seam sealer to the bottom edges of the overlap or patch, on the outside of the tent.

Patch holes or tears in tightly stretched areas of the tent with strips of repair tape cut at least 1½ inches longer and wider than the damage; if necessary, overlap strips in a shingle pattern to cover the damage completely. Tape both sides of the damaged area, and seal all edges of the tape with seam sealer, inside and out. If the patch isn't sturdy enough, replace it when you get home with a patch of tent fabric.

Cut the patch about 3 inches larger than the damaged area all around. Set it over the damaged area on the outside of the tent and pin it in place. Turn the edges of the patch under 1 inch and repin it. Topstitch around the entire patch ¹⁄₁₆ to ⅛ inch from the edge. Topstitch again ⅛ to ¼ inch in from the first row of stitching and remove the pins. On the inside of the tent, trim the damaged area into a square or rectangle, trimming as close to the damage as possible. Clip the corners in diagonally 1 inch. Turn the cut edges under 1 inch,

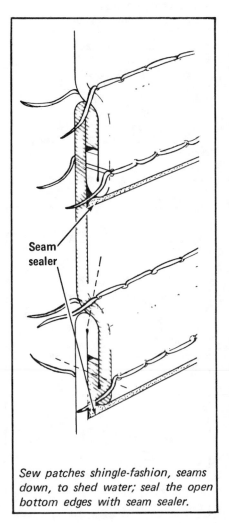

Sew patches shingle-fashion, seams down, to shed water; seal the open bottom edges with seam sealer.

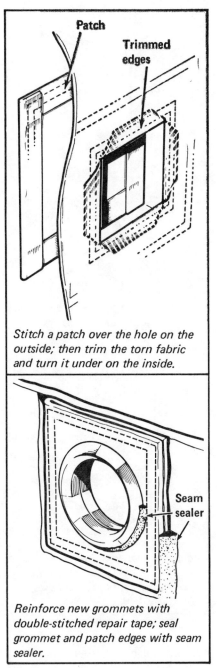

Stitch a patch over the hole on the outside; then trim the torn fabric and turn it under on the inside.

Reinforce new grommets with double-stitched repair tape; seal grommet and patch edges with seam sealer.

pin them into place, and topstitch close to the edge around the entire hole. Topstitch again ⅛ to ¼ inch from the first row of stitching, and remove the pins. If desired, make additional topstitching in a quilting fashion to strengthen the patch. Finally, apply a bead of seam sealer to the perimeter of the patch on the outside of the tent.

Reattach torn ties, flaps, windows, and zippers the same way, forming overlapping shingles and applying seam sealer to the finished mend. Patch torn screens with a patch slightly larger than the tear or hole, stitching all around the edges with the awl.

Grommets. Tears around grommets require the removal of the old grommet and replacement of the damaged material. Cut the grommet out with a small scissors, being careful to remove as little fabric as possible. Reinforce the grommet area with repair tape; stick the tape to one side of the fabric and fold it over on itself to produce a double-strength patch over the grommet hole. Stitch the patch into place with a double seam. Set in a new grommet with a grommet setter and seal its edges with seam sealer. Seal the edges of the stitched-in patch with seam sealer on the outside surface of the tent.

Leaks. To stop a leak in the rain fly or upper surface of your tent, apply seam sealer when the fabric has dried out. Leaks in the floor are probably the result of tears. Locate and repair the tear; be certain that the ragged part of your seam is on the inside surface of your tent. Seal this seam. To protect the patch, cover it with repair tape. To prevent any further damage to a waterproof floor, use a plastic dropcloth under your tent.

Make Canvas Waterproofer

Canvas tents, tarps, and outdoor furniture all benefit from waterproofing. This formula really works. **Equipment:** quart jar with cover, measuring cup, mixing spoon. **Ingredients:** soybean oil, turpentine. **Yield:** 1 quart.

Measure 2½ cups of soybean oil into a quart jar and add 1½ cups of turpentine; stir to mix well. Cover tightly; shake well before using.

To apply the waterproofing, paint the mixture onto the canvas with a small paintbrush; let dry completely. Apply a second coat for thorough waterproofing; let dry completely before storing or using the treated item.

Make a Tarp

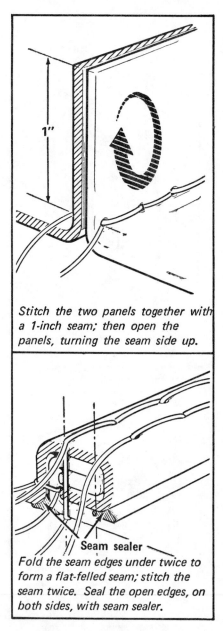

Stitch the two panels together with a 1-inch seam; then open the panels, turning the seam side up.

Fold the seam edges under twice to form a flat-felled seam; stitch the seam twice. Seal the open edges, on both sides, with seam sealer.

Anyone who camps or has kids who build backyard forts has good use for a big tarp. This inexpensive, easy-to-build version has a myriad of uses; its finished size is roughly 10 feet square. **Tools:** tape measure, sharp sewing scissors, candle, sewing machine, straight pins, chalk, grommet setter. **Materials:** 7 yards of 60-inch-wide coated nylon, matches, seam sealer for nylon, cloth adhesive tape, eight grommets, all-purpose thread. **Time:** 4 to 6 hours.

Cut the material into two 3½-yard sections. In a well-ventilated room, singe and seal all cut edges of both pieces of material. Light a candle. Hold the fabric with one cut edge stretched between your hands, and carefully pass the stretched edge of the fabric near the candle flame so that the fibers at the cut edge melt and fuse together. This prevents the finished tarp from raveling. Sear the cut edges of both pieces of material, working slowly and carefully around the panels. Blow the candle out.

Place one piece of material directly over the other, coated sides together. Pin together along the seam line. Sew the two pieces of material together lengthwise along one 3½-yard edge, using a sewing machine set to make close stitches; leave a 1-inch seam allowance. Remove the pins along the seam. Open the sewn-together panels to form one large sheet with a seam down the middle, seam side up.

Holding the two seam allowances together, fold them under lengthwise and then fold them again in the same direction to produce a flat-felled seam of five thicknesses. Pin the seam and stitch it in two parallel rows down the tarp, once close to the fold and again close to the original seam. This flat-felled seam is the inside of the tarp. Remove the pins along the seam.

Turn the edges of the tarp under 1 inch and then under again 1 inch to make a 1-inch hem on the inside; pin the hem in place and then stitch it all around close to the folded-under edge. Backstitch at the beginning and end and tie off the thread ends. Remove the pins. For added strength, topstitch close to the edge around the entire tarp. This is all the sewing you'll have to do.

To complete the tarp, set grommets around its edges within the 1-inch hem. Mark grommet points with chalk in each corner, midway on both of the long sides (parallel to the center seam), and just next to the points where the center seam hits the shorter sides; if desired, place more grommets along the sides of the tarp. Reinforce each marked grommet point with a piece of cloth adhesive tape. On the inside, set a grommet at each reinforced point with a grommet setter.

Finally, apply seam sealer for nylon along the open joints of the center seam, sealing the entire length of both the inner and outer surfaces. Let the sealer dry completely, as directed by the manufacturer, before using the tarp.

Resole Hiking Boots

Replacing the soles on hiking or work boots is a challenging and money-saving home project. **Tools:** small screwdriver or nail puller, sharp knife, sewing awl, work gloves, hammer, scrap wood boards, sturdy cord or clamps, small wood blocks. **Materials:** rags, acetone, replacement rubber insoles, heavy-duty waxed thread, coarse sandpaper, replacement Vibram soles; flexible, waterproof shoe-repair adhesive; replacement heel fasteners. Buy Vibram soles of the correct size from a recreational outfitter; buy flexible shoe-repair adhesive and heel fasteners at a shoe repair shop. **Time:** about 1 to 2 hours.

Before you can replace the old soles,

you must remove them. Normally, boot-soles are either sewn or glued. If they're sewn, there will be threads visible around the upper edge of the sole. Examine the soles for attaching screws or nails in the heel; remove any fasteners

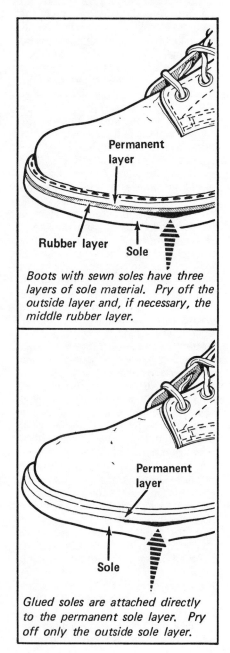

Boots with sewn soles have three layers of sole material. Pry off the outside layer and, if necessary, the middle rubber layer.

Glued soles are attached directly to the permanent sole layer. Pry off only the outside sole layer.

with a screwdriver or a nail puller, and save them to attach the new soles.

After removing the heel fasteners, separate the old soles from the rest of the boot. If the boots are sewn, you'll find three layers of material: the old sole, a middle rubber layer, and a permanently attached leather layer. To separate the old soles from your boots, insert the blade of a sharp knife between the sole and the middle rubber layer; carefully work it around the boot until the sole is free. If the boots are glued, there will be only two layers, the old sole and a permanent layer. Separate these in the same manner.

Once you've removed the old soles, clean the middle rubber layer with acetone until all excess glue and debris are gone. On sewn shoes, check the sewing for breaks, and check the rubber layer for tears. If this rubber layer is torn, it must be replaced too. Remove the damaged rubber layer the same way you removed the sole, inserting the blade of a sharp knife between the rubber layer and the permanently attached leather layer. Mend breaks in the stitching or attach a new middle layer with a sewing awl and heavy-duty waxed thread, making stitches all around the new insole.

After you're satisfied with the soundness and cleanliness of this surface, use coarse sandpaper to roughen both the inside surface and the bonding surface of the new Vibram soles. Wear work gloves, and wipe off any sanding debris thoroughly. Be careful not to touch either the insole or the sole—body oils repel most adhesives.

Apply flexible shoe-repair adhesive evenly to both surfaces; be especially liberal around the edges. Follow the manufacturer's instructions exactly; join the soles immediately or let the adhesive get tacky before bonding as specified. Align the new sole over the prepared boot surface and press it into place, starting at the toe and working down toward the heel; curl the new sole into place and stretch it toward the heel as you go.

Finally, set the boot on a flat surface, sole up, and pound the entire sole

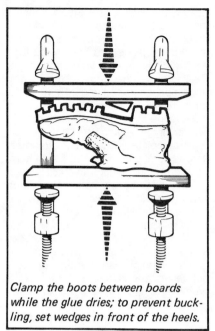

Clamp the boots between boards while the glue dries; to prevent buckling, set wedges in front of the heels.

vigorously with a hammer. To assure a good bond, tie or clamp each boot between two flat boards for 24 hours; place a small wedge under the sole just forward of the heel.

When the new soles are dry, trim off excess sole material with a sharp knife, working slowly and deliberately around each boot to assure a professional finish. Finally, if the new Vibram soles have predrilled holes for heel fasteners, set new heel fasteners into the holes and pound them firmly in.

Make Insect Repellent

Don't let flying insects like mosquitoes ruin your outdoor fun. Prepare yourself for summer with this fragrant insect repellent. **Equipment:** measuring spoon, funnel, pint bottle with cap. **Ingredients:** citronella oil, sandalwood oil, patchouli oil, rubbing alcohol. Buy the oils in a craft shop that sells candle-making materials. **Yield:** 1 pint.

Measure 4 tablespoons of citronella oil, 2 teaspoons of sandalwood oil, and 1 teaspoon of patchouli oil into a pint bottle; fill the bottle with rubbing alcohol. Cap the bottle and shake well.

Apply the repellent as often as needed.

Regrip a Golf Club

Composition golf club grips become worn and damaged after years of heat (clubs left in a car trunk) and water (playing golf in the rain). You can buy new grips at most golf supply centers. Installing the grips on your clubs is a simple job. **Tools:** sharp craft knife, vise. **Materials:** fine steel wool, double-faced adhesive tape, new grips, mineral spirits, mild detergent, golf club resin. **Time:** about ½ hour per club.

Preformed golf grips eliminate the process of stretching and winding grips to fit the handle of a golf club. There are several styles and colors available.

With a sharp craft knife, split the old grip lengthwise down the handle of the club. Then peel off the old grip. The old grip will probably be stuck to adhesive tape; peel off the tape to expose the bare metal shaft. The shaft may have a wooden pin stuck in the top of the handle. Do not remove this pin; it may be used to properly weight the club. Remove any adhesive residue from the shaft with fine steel wool and mineral spirits.

Carefully spiral-wrap double-faced tape around the shaft, from the top of the shaft to within about ⅛ inch of the end of the new grip. Make sure the edges of the tape are slightly separated —not overlapped. If you want to build up the grip, add one or two more layers of tape to the first layer. When the grip is the proper size, the tips of your fingers should just touch the palm of your hand. If there's a gap here, the grip is

too large; if your fingers overlap into the palm of your hand, the grip is too small. Your fingers should just comfortably touch the palm of your hand.

Lock the shaft in a vise, padding the jaws of the vise so the jaws don't damage the metal. Then coat the tape with mineral spirits to make it slick. Slide the new grip over the tape, being careful not to rip the tape or the grip. If the tape catches and holds the grip, reslick the tape with more mineral spirits. Grasp the grip by the open end and pull it down over the shaft. On most grips, the top of the grip has a straight line or design embossed in the material. Work the grip around the club so that the line is centered on top of the shaft. Finally, after installing the grip, squeeze the grip with your hand several times so the tape adheres to the inside surface of the grip.

Store your clubs in a cool, dry area. Wash the grips occasionally with mild detergent and water; rinse and dry them thoroughly. After playing golf in wet weather, be sure to dry the grips—and other parts of the clubs — before you

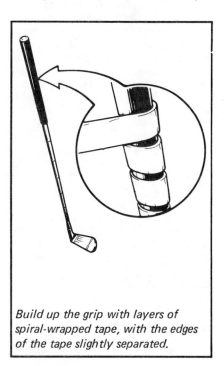

Build up the grip with layers of spiral-wrapped tape, with the edges of the tape slightly separated.

store the clubs. You can often restore the "tacky" touch to grips by covering them with special golf club resin, sold at many golf outlets.

If the grips on your golf clubs have a special "flat side" or raised ridge for hand position, you may want a professional to change the grips to meet your individual swing/grip specifications.

Refinish a Golf Club

Most golfers would rather fight than switch a set of good woods—even though the wood's finish looks like the bottom of a boxcar. If you and your woods fit this description, the answer is a refinishing job. **Tools:** small Phillips-head screwdriver, shallow pan, small natural-bristle brush, artists' brush. **Materials:** paint and varnish remover, fine steel wool, masking tape, wiping stain, aerosol spray varnish or lacquer, soft cloth, hard wax, black or white metal paint, toothpicks, waterproof glue, epoxy filler. **Time:** about 2 hours per wood, over a 2- or 3-day period.

Wash the club thoroughly; remove all the dirt in the cross slots of the sole plate's screws. Use a screwdriver small enough to fit easily into the slots; too big a screwdriver could damage the soft brass screws.

Unscrew and remove the sole plate and soak it in a pan of paint remover for 1 hour. While the sole plate is soaking, work on the woods. After the plate has soaked for 1 hour, polish it with fine steel wool, and set it aside.

Protect the string windings and plastic insert plates of the woods with masking tape. Carefully coat the wooden head of the club with paint remover, using a clean natural-bristle brush. Let the remover work for 10 minutes, and then wipe it away with fine steel wool. This treatment should take off the old finish; if not, repeat.

Lightly buff the wood with fine steel wool. If you want the wood stained, apply a coat of wiping stain with a clean natural-bristle brush, and then wipe it off with a soft cloth. Bring the old woods with you when you buy stain that has to match; the degree of darkness depends on how many coats you apply and how long you leave each coat on before wiping it off. Follow the manufacturer's instructions for appropriate darkness.

When you've achieved the stain color you want, let the woods dry for 1 to 2 days. Then, very gently, buff the wood with fine steel wool. Clean the wood with a soft cloth and then spray it with clear varnish or lacquer from a spray can; use a dull or high-gloss finish, as desired. Let the finish dry completely.

When the varnish or lacquer has dried, very lightly buff the finish with fine steel wool and wipe the surface with a clean soft cloth. Then spray the wood again.

If you want a solid enamel finish on the wood, substitute dull or gloss enamel for the stain.

Let the finish dry for 2 full days. Then rub the wood with several coats of hard wax and buff it until it's smooth and shiny.

To restore the sole plate, carefully fill in the recessed lettering on the plate with black or white metal enamel, using an artists' brush. Wipe off excess enamel as you work. Let the enamel dry completely. When the enamel is dry, coat the sole plate with one or two applications of clear varnish or lacquer. Let the finish dry completely; then screw the sole plate back onto the wood.

If the screws are stripped and won't tighten, fill the holes with toothpicks and waterproof glue. Break up the toothpicks, fill the screw holes, and add a few drops of glue. Trim the toothpicks flush with the bottom of the wood. Work the screws halfway into the glued toothpicks and let the glue dry; then drive in the screws.

Use an epoxy filler to fill holes and dings in the wood. Do *not* use wood filler or steel wool; the weight of this material could change the swing weight of the club. Buy the epoxy filler at a golf supply store.

Maintain Roller Skates and Skateboards

Skates or skateboards, the most important parts are the wheels. To keep them moving at top speed, service the bearings whenever the wheels start to bind. **Tools:** two small adjustable wrenches, pliers, screwdriver. **Materials:** household oil, bicycle grease, replacement ball bearings, rags. **Time:** about 15 minutes to ½ hour.

When skateboard or roller skate wheels drag or bind, the problem is usually in the wheel bearings. Spin the wheel that's binding and look at the space between the axle and the edge of the wheel, behind the wheel nut. If you don't see small steel bearings in this space, the wheel bearings are sealed; have them adjusted or replaced by the skate dealer. If you see small ball bearings around the wheel, the wheel is constructed with open bearings, eight balls on each side of each wheel. You can lubricate and adjust these bearings yourself.

To service ball-type bearings, lubricate them periodically. Spin the wheel that's binding. If the bearings are noisy, they should be lubricated with oil. Apply household oil sparingly to each side of each wheel, every other time you skate. Don't over-oil; excess oil attracts dirt.

If the bearings are quiet, they should be lubricated with grease. With a small adjustable wrench, remove the wheel nut from the axle. Unscrew the cone over the bearings and remove it. Take the wheel off the axle.

The bearings are held into the bearing races by bicycle grease. To lubricate them, apply a coat of bicycle grease to the balls and the race; remove excess grease from the wheel with a rag. Lubricate the bearings and the race on each side of the wheel, and then replace the wheel on the axle. Replace the cone over the bearings and hand-tighten it;

then replace the wheel nut.

After greasing the bearings, adjust the cone and the wheel nut to the proper tightness. Hold the cone with a small adjustable wrench to keep it from turning. With another wrench, tighten the wheel nut. Tighten the nut only until the wheel spins freely but doesn't wobble; the wheel should not bind. It's better to leave the wheel a little loose than to overtighten it.

Each wheel should have 16 ball bearings, eight on each side of the wheel. If bearings are missing, replace the complete set of bearings with new bearings; buy the replacements at a roller rink or a skate shop. Even if only a few bearings are missing, buy a complete set of new bearings for all wheels; don't mix new and worn balls.

To replace the ball bearings, remove the wheel nut from the axle; unscrew the cone and remove it. Take the wheel off the axle. On each side of the wheel, remove the remaining old bearings from the bearing race, and clean old grease from the race with a rag. Coat the race with a thin layer of bicycle grease and set eight steel ball bearings into the race; the grease will hold the bearings in place.

After replacing the bearings on both sides of the wheel, replace the wheel on the axle. Replace the cone and the wheel nut, and adjust the wheel as above so that it spins freely.

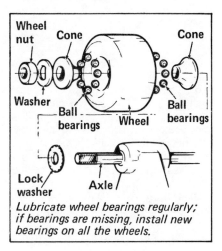

Lubricate wheel bearings regularly; if bearings are missing, install new bearings on all the wheels.

Professional Services

Sell Your Own Home

Selling your home "by owner" can save you the high percentage commission real estate agents charge—currently, about 8 percent of the value of your house or condominium. You'll need to hire the services of two professionals, an appraiser and a lawyer.

Appraisal. Before you can sell your house or condominium, you must know its fair market value. Hire a professional appraiser to assess the house; ask the bank that holds your mortgage, or your local bank, to recommend a good appraiser. When you have the professional's detailed appraisal, call three local real estate firms and inform them of your intent to sell; ask them if they would give you an idea of the value of your property. Don't ever tell an agent that you already have an appraisal; simply say that you're considering selling your home "by owner" and that you're getting several opinions of its value.

Asking price. Compare the various estimates of the value of your house and decide on an asking price; add at least $800 or $900 so you can come down on it. This way you can get the price you want while the buyer feels that he's getting a good deal. Once you've set the price, call your lawyer and secure his professional services in selling your home.

Cleanup/fix-up. Before you advertise your home for sale, straighten it up—a clean, tidy home is a well-cared-for home, and sells much faster than a sloppy house. Paint shabby rooms; sweep out the basement; wash the windows and replace cracked panes of glass. Fix leaky faucets, take care of doors or windows that stick, and clean out all closets, pantries, and cabinets so that they look as spacious as possible. The better it looks, the better the price you'll get.

Data sheet. Prepare a data sheet that lists all the pertinent information on your house or condominium—lot size, taxes, assessments, room sizes, type of heat, cost of heat per month, sewer or septic system, carpeting, house style, location, schools and shopping, improvements, and so on. Get a sample property data sheet from a local real estate firm and work from that; just ask to see several of the firm's listings.

Advertising. For starters, put a sign up in front of your house: "For Sale: By Owner." Take out a classified ad that emphasizes location, convenience, and price. Keep the ad short, simple, and to the point. In big cities, the Sunday papers are excellent choices; so are the Monday morning editions. Local or neighborhood papers are also good prospects. Give your phone number and make appointments for viewing.

Open house. When people come to look at the house or condominium, or if you decide to hold an open house, put on some soft music, turn on all the lights no matter what time of day it is, put the dog and cat out, turn off the TV, send the kids to a neighbor's house, light a fire in the fireplace if there is one, and bake something that smells good. The homier the atmosphere, the more comfortable your lookers will be, and the more they'll want to make your house their own. Put up a sign at the end of the block to bring people to your open house.

The sale. After you've made the sale, you should have a prepared checklist to complete with the buyer. Include the buyer's name and current address, a brief description of the property, the purchase price agreed upon, the earnest money to be put up, mortgage information, items included in the purchase price (stove, refrigerator, carpeting, etc.), items *not* included, and attorney's name. Take this information to your lawyer and let him complete the transaction.

Move Without Movers

Planning a move any time is a major effort, but you can ease the financial burden by moving yourself. You can usually save as much as half the cost by eliminating the professionals.

Plan ahead. Never wait until the last minute to plan a move—make preparations at least a month in advance, and more if at all possible. Most important, be flexible. Allow time for emergencies; always build in an extra day or two as a fudge factor.

The vehicle. Most of us don't own a truck or van large enough to accommodate all of our belongings; truck and trailer rentals are the way to go. Comparison-shop by phone. Call *all* the truck and trailer rentals in your area; check on both weekly rates and daily rates. After you find the best deal, check on insurance for your household goods. Make all arrangements well in advance for picking up and returning the vehicle. Protect yourself in advance against last-minute policy changes; insist on a written agreement stating the terms of the arrangement exactly. If a rental outfit doesn't want to give you a written agreement, do business with someone else.

Boxes, pads, papers, tape. As soon as you're sure you're going to move, start to collect boxes and newspapers. Bookstores, department stores, office supply places, hardware stores, liquor stores, and grocery stores are all excellent sources for cartons and boxes. Select *all sizes:* small to medium, sturdy boxes for books; large, roomy boxes for kitchenware and bedding; heavy, durable cartons for breakables; and so on. You'll need cushioning for appliances and furniture—old bedding or carpet pads work well. Use pillows, mattresses, foam pads, and any other soft furnishings to cushion other pieces. Most truck rentals have packing materials available; if you need more pads, rent them along with the vehicle.

For packing dishes and other breakables, crumpled newspaper is an excellent cushioning material. Save all the old papers you can; you'll never have too much. Stock up with rolls and rolls of masking tape or reinforced package tape—don't get the kind you have to moisten. Have lots of cord and twine on hand, and mark your boxes clearly according to room. Color-coding is a good way to do this—blue for kitchen, green for bedroom, and so on.

Helpers. If you're lucky, you can call on several strong-bodied, willing friends to help you pack the truck; however, if none are available, hire two or three workers beforehand. Many areas have youth employment offices or school placement agencies; check with these organizations and with community unemployment offices, local schools, or community centers. But, again, never wait until the last minute; make arrangements well in advance. Also arrange for friends to meet you at the other end of the move. If you're moving locally, this is no problem. If you're moving long-distance, work through the realtor or rental office you bought or rented your new home from. Make sure definite arrangements are completed before you move.

Moving. Have everything packed, labeled, and ready to go before your actual moving day. Arrange furniture and boxes in reverse order of what you'll want first—what goes into the truck first will come off it last. Make sure everything is labeled plainly so your helpers know exactly what goes where and what goes next. One person should stay inside the house or apartment and supervise the move. Unpack in reverse, putting furniture and boxes into the appropriate rooms as you work. Return the truck as quickly as possible, and be sure to get a signed receipt.

Earn Academic Credit at Home

The benefits of a good education are undeniable, but the costs—both in time and in money—can be astronomical. One way to beat these costs is correspondence courses, offered for high school and university credit by many major colleges and universities throughout the United States and Canada. Take advantage of these courses to earn academic credit in your own home—toward a high school diploma or a college degree, for occupational advancement, or for your own personal development and enjoyment. Fees vary from one institution to another, but the standard cost ranges from $7 to $30 per credit hour on the university level.

Getting information. First of all, write for the names of institutions that offer correspondence courses. In the United States, write to the National University Extension Association, Correspondence Study Division, 1 Dupont Circle, Suite 360, Washington, DC 20036; for information on Canadian schools, write to the Director, Division of Part-Time Studies, Mackintosh-Corry Hall, Queens University, Kingston, Ontario, Canada K7L 2N6. Include in your letter what type of course you're interested in taking or the field of study you want to pursue, if you have something particular in mind.

Once you have a list of institutions that offer correspondence courses, choose schools you're most interested in and write to them for further information. Ask for their correspondence bulletin and an application form.

Applying your courses. A large variety of courses are offered through the mail—accounting, agriculture, art, dramatics, marketing, engineering, languages, law, literature, radio and TV, technical writing, creative writing, and on and on. If your goal is a diploma or degree and you'd like to use your correspondence courses toward that goal at an institution near you, be sure to check with that specific school to see if it will approve your correspondence courses. Do this *before* enrolling in any correspondence study.

Working on the course. When you do enroll in a correspondence course, you'll receive a packet of material. This usually contains the textbook, a workbook or lab manual, a guide on how to study correspondence courses in general, other explanatory material, and a study guide for the specific course you're enrolled in. It may take you about a week to complete each lesson; the length of the course varies from school to school and discipline to discipline. Usually, however, there's a time limit of 2 years to complete each course to receive credit—more than ample time.

Clean and Repair Jewelry

With a few inexpensive tools and a little know-how, you can clean your jewelry and make repairs as well as the professionals. **Tools:** measuring spoons, bowl, measuring cup, soft brush, needle-nosed pliers, tweezers, needle, craft knife or pocket knife, beading needle, darning needle. **Materials:** liquid detergent, ammonia, soft cloths, epoxy compound or superglue, stiff paper, masking tape, replacement spring clasp, replacement beads, beading cord or nylon thread, white glue. **Time:** 10 minutes to 1 hour, depending on repairs needed.

Cleaning. Measure 1 tablespoon of liquid detergent into a bowl and add 2 cups of hot water; add 2 or 3 drops of ammonia. *Caution: Do not use ammonia for pearls, amber, opals, or other porous jewels.* Set the jewelry into the detergent solution and clean it carefully with a soft brush. Rinse with hot water. If the piece of jewelry has stones, drain the detergent solution through a cloth to catch any stones that may have come loose. Dry and polish the jewelry with a soft, lint-free cloth.

Resetting a stone. Use epoxy compound or superglue to reset loose stones. Handle these compounds carefully, and follow the manufacturer's instructions exactly.

To fix a loose stone in a pronged mount, as in a ring setting, use needle-nosed pliers to bend the prongs out slightly, releasing the stone. Work gently, being careful not to mark the prongs or the stone. Apply a drop of epoxy or superglue to the base of the stone and carefully set it into place, using tweezers if necessary. Gently bend one prong into place, and then bend the prong directly opposite it. Repeat, bending opposite prongs, to secure the stone. Let the epoxy or glue dry completely, as directed. If one or more prongs are broken, take the ring to a jeweler.

To replace a stone in a pegged mount, as in an earring, squeeze a little epoxy or superglue onto a piece of stiff paper. With a needle, apply epoxy or superglue to the peg and to the mounting hole in the stone. Press the peg and the stone carefully together and let dry completely.

Repairing a clasp or a link. The most common jewelry clasps are the fold-over, the V-spring, and the round spring clasp. To tighten a fold-over clasp, open the clasp and hold it firmly. With a needle-nosed pliers, gently bend the folding arm of the clasp into a curve to fold over the bottom part. Bend in the flange at the end of the arm until the top of the clasp engages the bottom with a firm click.

The V-spring clasp slides into a sheath. A loose clasp is usually caused by a misshapen spring, but sometimes the sheath is also damaged. To reshape the V-spring, wrap the blade of a craft knife or the small blade of a pocket knife

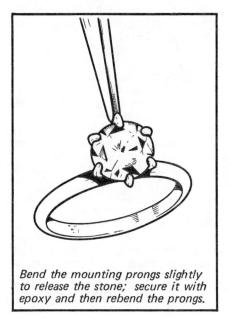

Bend the mounting prongs slightly to release the stone; secure it with epoxy and then rebend the prongs.

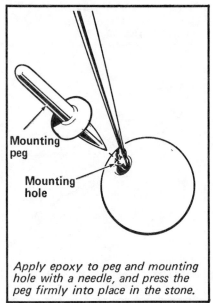

Mounting peg

Mounting hole

Apply epoxy to peg and mounting hole with a needle, and press the peg firmly into place in the stone.

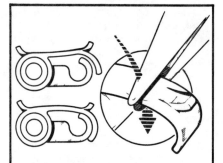

Reshape a fold-over clasp with needle-nosed pliers so that the top locks firmly over the bottom.

To reshape the sheath of a V-spring clasp, bend it carefully until it accepts the spring clasp.

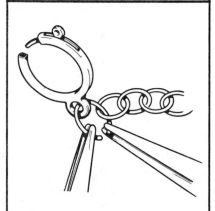

Pry open the link that holds a spring clasp; remove the old clasp and put in a new one.

with masking tape. Insert the wrapped knife blade between the leaves of the V-spring and twist it gently to widen the V. The spring should engage the sheath with a firm click. To reshape the sheath of a V-spring clasp, carefully bend the misshapen sheath with a needle-nosed pliers until the sheath accepts the clasp.

A broken spring clasp—the round clasp opened by a thumbnail—should be replaced; buy a replacement clasp at a hobby store. With a needle-nosed pliers, gently pry open the link that holds the clasp; slide the broken clasp off the link and slip a new clasp into place. Close the link with the pliers to secure the new clasp.

To repair a misshapen link, straighten it with a needle-nosed pliers. If the link is broken, either remove it entirely or replace it with a new link of the same type; buy new links at a hobby store. Bend the links as little as possible to avoid weakening them.

Restringing a necklace. If only a few beads are missing, restring the necklace without them. If several beads are missing, buy matching or complementary beads at a hobby or craft store. Use beading cord or nylon thread to restring the necklace.

Fold a sheet of stiff paper into an M-shape to make a trough for the beads; fold the ends up to keep the beads from falling out. Set the beads in order in the trough. Cut the beading cord 12 inches longer than the finished necklace, and make a knot at least 1½ inches from the end of the cord. The tied-off end will be used for attaching the clasp. If the cord is stiff enough, thread the beads without a needle; if it isn't, thread the unknotted end of the cord through a beading needle.

If the beads are very small, just slip them one by one onto the beading needle and slide them onto the knotted cord. For larger beads, tie a knot after each bead. To tie the knot, make a loose loop in the thread. Insert a finger in the loop and gently guide the loop down the thread toward the bead; be careful not to let the loop tighten before it reaches the bead. When the loop is almost to the bead, slip your finger out

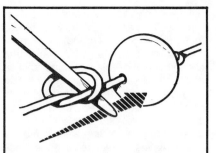

Tie knots to hold large beads in place; use a darning needle to push the knot firmly against the bead.

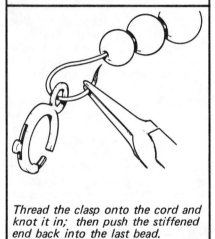

Thread the clasp onto the cord and knot it in; then push the stiffened end back into the last bead.

hole in the last bead until only the knot shows. Secure the knot with a drop of epoxy or superglue, and let it dry as directed. Repeat this process to attach the other side of the clasp to the other end of the necklace.

Split Wood

More and more people are supplementing gas, oil, and electric heat with heat from wood-burning fireplaces and stoves; a whole new generation is finding out what it means to make firewood. For the most efficient burning, and some very good exercise, split your own cordwood. **Tools:** hard hat or helmet with face protector, heavy work gloves, heavy shoes; hydraulic splitter or splitting device, or steel splitting wedges, ax, and heavy sledgehammer or 6- or 8-pound splitting maul. **Materials:** well-seasoned wood. **Time:** a few minutes per log.

Wood splits easiest if it's allowed to season over the winter and the following summer; usually well-seasoned wood already has cracks from freezing and thawing water. Though dry wood splits easier, unsplit logs take longer to dry, and some people prefer to split their wood before seasoning to be sure that it dries out enough to use the next year.

Splitting is about 90 percent technique, 5 percent luck, and 5 percent strength. Your choice of tools— hydraulic splitter, splitting device, wedges or splitting maul—will determine which techniques you use. Whatever your method, protect yourself from flying wood chips and splinters. Shield your face and head with a hard hat or helmet with a face protector; wear heavy work gloves and heavy shoes.

Machine power. Mechanical wood splitters can work well, but they have several disadvantages. The hydraulic splitter is usually gasoline-powered; to operate it, you press logs lengthwise against a permanently attached splitting wedge. This initially seems to be very

and insert a darning needle into the loop. Pull the thread tight, pushing the knot firmly against the bead, and remove the needle. Repeat, threading beads and knotting them into place one by one, to restring the entire necklace. Make sure each knot is tight against the adjacent bead before you tie the next knot.

When all the beads have been restrung, attach the clasp. Slip the knotted end of the thread through the link on the clasp. Knot the link tightly against the last knot in the string and clip off excess thread, leaving a length equal to the last bead plus the two knots. Dip the end of the cord into white glue and let it dry, to stiffen it. When the cord is dry, grasp the glued end with needle-nosed pliers; bend it back and push it into the

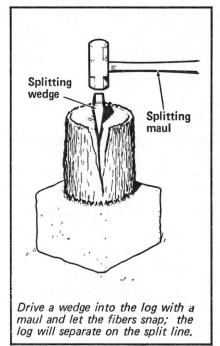

Splitting wedge

Splitting maul

Drive a wedge into the log with a maul and let the fibers snap; the log will separate on the split line.

fast, but the splitter has two problems. First, large logs, irregularities in the wood, or tough spots generally choke out the motor. Second, most splitters simply drop the split pieces on the ground on either side of the splitter. It isn't likely that this machine is worth the rental fee unless you have six or more full cords of wood to split.

Many catalogs now sell a variety of splitting tools that guillotine logs lengthwise by hitting them with a sledge. These splitters usually work well, but they're both slow and brittle, and they must be anchored securely. It's doubtful that such devices stand up well to heavy work loads.

Muscle power. The best splitting tools are the old-fashioned ones: steel splitting wedges and a heavy sledgehammer or a splitting maul—a type of wedging ax or heavy sledge. Choose a steel wedge that's sharply angled at one end but that fattens rapidly, or use a 6- or 8-pound maul with a similar shape; this design spreads the wood faster. Don't use an ax, especially a sharp one—the ax

head will only slice the wood, not split it.

To use either a splitting wedge or a maul, set each log on end, as perpendicular as possible, on a hardwood chopping block—the upended section of a log makes a good chopping block. If you're using a steel wedge, strike the end of the log with a blow from a dull ax across the main diameter. Remove the ax and place a splitting wedge into the slot it leaves. Strike the wedge once with a sledgehammer or a splitting maul, and stop; listen to the wood fibers of the wedged log giving way. With this stop-and-listen technique you won't waste your own energy; let the wedge do its work. Once the snapping stops, strike the wedge again. Continue, wedging and pausing, until the log separates along the split line. If you have problems working from one direction, remove the wedge, turn the log over, and work from the opposite side. A good wedge should split very large logs.

If you're using a splitting maul, strike the upended log across its main diameter with the maul. If the log doesn't split on the first blow, wait until its fibers stop snapping; then remove the maul and strike again. Repeat until the log separates completely.

Be very careful in removing either a wedge or a maul from a log; don't pinch off a finger while working your splitting tool back and forth in the log. Stack the split wood neatly as you work.

Tune Up a Typewriter

Electric typewriters need professional maintenance, but you can service a manual typewriter yourself. Give your typewriter the once-over whenever it smudges or sticks, to keep it working at top speed. **Tools:** stiff toothbrush, vacuum cleaner, nail file or sharp knife, large soft artists' brush. **Materials:** newspaper, household oil, soft cloth, platen cleaner or rubbing alcohol, contact cement, replacement ribbon. **Time:** about 1 hour.

When dirt works into the joints and bearings of a typewriter, it causes wear and sticking. More obviously, keys clogged with dirt and ink produce smudgy, hard-to-read type. To prevent or correct both problems, clean your typewriter periodically. Spread newspaper on your work surface to catch dirt and ink.

Start working on the machine's type bars. Remove dirt from the type bars with a stiff toothbrush, and pick up the loosened debris with the wand of a vacuum cleaner. Don't use pins or other sharp objects on the type bars; you could scratch them.

Clean between the arms that control the type bars with a nail file or a thin, sharp knife; brush the arms and the type bars with a large soft artists' brush. Clean under the type arms by depressing several keys at a time to raise the arms; use a soft artists' brush to wipe away dust and dirt. As you work, use the vacuum cleaner to remove all loose debris.

Turn the typewriter upside down. Clean all the parts you can reach with a soft artists' brush, carefully wiping away dirt and ink. Pick up loose dirt with the vacuum cleaner, and turn the typewriter right side up.

With the typewriter upright, release the margins so that the carriage can move to both ends of its track. Carefully clean the carriage and then the track from side to side with a soft brush; move the carriage as you work to expose the full width of the track. Pick up loose dirt with the vacuum cleaner.

When the typewriter is clean, lubricate it with household oil. Carefully apply a drop or two of oil to each end of the carriage track, and move the carriage back and forth to distribute the oil over the track. Depress the shift key and look for a screw near the carriage where the shift control pivots; lubricate the screw with a drop of oil. Press the space bar and watch the ribbon mechanism; give the linkage a drop of oil at each pivot point of the mechanism's moving parts. Lubricate the hinges on the small arms that hold the ribbon tight to the spools.

Turn the typewriter over. Under the typewriter, apply a drop of oil to each nut or linkage of moving parts. Move the spacer bar and watch for movement; apply a drop of oil to each joint in the small arm and wires that link the bar to the spacing mechanism. Depress a key and watch the movement of its linkage; apply a drop of oil at each pivot point. Repeat for all keys and moving parts. Apply oil very sparingly; too much oil attracts dirt.

Turn the typewriter right side up again. Clean the rubber platen roller with platen cleaner or rubbing alcohol.

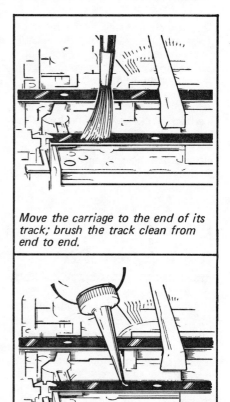

Move the carriage to the end of its track; brush the track clean from end to end.

Apply oil to the track and move the carriage back and forth to distribute the oil.

Pivot screw

Press the shift keys and locate the shift control pivot screws; apply a drop of oil to each screw.

Apply the cleaner with a soft cloth; rub it across the platen and rotate the roller to clean its entire surface. Apply platen cleaner or alcohol to the type bars, and wipe them dry with a soft cloth.

Finally, if any key tops are loose, replace them. Apply contact cement to the back of the key top and to the key base; let the cement dry as directed by the manufacturer and then carefully set the top back into place. Before using the typewriter, replace the ribbon with a new one of the same type.

Install a TV Antenna

Upgrade or install an outside antenna for a clear, sharp television picture. **Tools:** extension ladder, 50 feet of sturdy rope, hammer, screwdriver, adjustable wrench, pliers, wire cutters, wire stripper or sharp utility knife, drill, caulking gun, putty knife. **Materials:** television antenna for the correct reception range, including VHF, FM, and UHF elements; 5-foot antenna mast, steel chimney strap kit, 300-ohm lead-in wire, insulated stand-off brackets, coupler or signal splitters; roofing compound in cartridges, or troweling-consistency roofing compound; acrylic

latex or silicone caulk. **Time:** about 8 hours.

Choose an antenna carefully. TV antennas are available for four reception ranges: deep fringe, for up to 125 miles from the broadcast station; fringe, for 50 to 100 miles away; suburban, for 20 to 50 miles away; and urban, for less than 20 miles from the station. The largest antenna does not necessarily give you the best picture; follow the manufacturer's range recommendations and buy the size antenna you need.

Buy an antenna that comes with all installation hardware. You'll also need a 5-foot antenna mast, a steel chimney strap kit, a 300-ohm lead-in wire, and insulated stand-off brackets. Buy a coupler if you have more than one television or plan to hook up an FM receiver; buy a signal splitter if your television has separate VHF and UHF terminals. Make sure the antenna you choose has VHF, FM, and UHF elements.

Set up an extension ladder to give you access to the roof; brace it firmly against the house, with the end of the ladder sticking up above the edge of the roof. Before you start to work, set up a safety line; use a 50-foot length of sturdy rope. Tie the rope securely around the chimney, and stretch it across any open pitch you'll have to work on. Secure the ends of the rope to make fixed hand lines across the roof. Wear old clothes and rubber-soled shoes.

Caution: Don't work in very windy weather. Stay away from power lines. Do not carry or erect the antenna or the lead-in wire near high-tension lines or lines leading into the house.

The antenna is installed against the chimney, at the high point of the house. To hold it in place, use steel chimney straps with mounting brackets. Wrap the steel straps around the chimney, with the antenna mounting brackets on the side of the chimney that faces the broadcast station—usually toward the city. Securely tighten the bolts, pulling the straps tight against the chimney, with the two mounting brackets aligned.

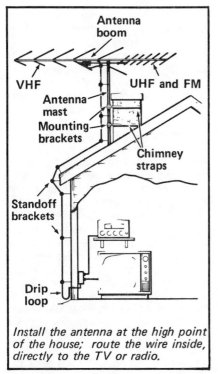

VHF

UHF and FM

Antenna boom

Antenna mast

Mounting brackets

Chimney straps

Standoff brackets

Drip loop

Install the antenna at the high point of the house; route the wire inside, directly to the TV or radio.

On the ground, assemble the antenna and mast, as instructed by the manufacturer. Unfold the VHF, FM, and UHF elements, as directed, and tighten the bolts that hold the antenna boom to the mast. Then fasten the lead-in wire to the antenna boom. Cut off the end of the wire and strip 1 inch of insulation off the end of the wire, using a wire stripper or a sharp utility knife. Separate the two inner wires for about 1 to 2 inches and connect the wires to the screw terminals on the antenna; at each terminal, loop the wire clockwise around the screw and tighten the screw.

Carefully carry the antenna assembly and the long antenna wire up to the roof. Set the antenna mast into the mounting brackets in the chimney straps, so that it's standing on the side of the chimney that faces the broadcast station. Tighten the brackets to hold the mast firmly in place, not touching the roof or the chimney.

Just above the roof, attach a 7½-inch insulated stand-off bracket to the an-

tenna mast. Install another bracket at the top of the mast, about 6 inches down from the boom, and place one or two more stand-off brackets midmast. The brackets will hold the lead-in wire in place, from its terminal connection on the antenna boom to the surface of the roof.

Starting at the antenna connection, twist the flat lead-in wire to make at least one turn per foot and thread it down through the top stand-off bracket. Thread the wire through the brackets on the mast and down to the roof, twisting the wire as you go to make at least one turn per foot.

When the wire is threaded through to the roof, plan the course of the antenna wire across the roof and into the house. The wire should run as directly as possible from the antenna to the television set; if you have more than one television, it should run to the basement or crawl space so you can route the wire up through the house. Don't run the wire along a gutter or down a downspout; don't route it in through a window or near a window air conditioner, a large metal object, or an electric motor.

Use 7½-inch-long insulated stand-off brackets to anchor the antenna wire to the house; drill a pilot hole and screw each bracket in perpendicular to the roof or wall surface. Set brackets about 3 to 4 feet apart along the entire run of the wire, to maintain a 7½-inch clearance from all roof and wall surfaces. Where the wire must cross a gutter, attach a stand-off bracket to the outside edge of the gutter to maintain a 7½-inch clearance all around the gutter.

When all the roof stand-off brackets are in place, seal the entry point of each bracket with roofing compound; use cartridge-form compound and a caulking gun, or apply troweling-consistency compound with a putty knife.

When the wire is in place all across the roof, route it into the house. Use stand-off brackets to maintain a 7½-inch clearance along the wall of the house to the entry point. At the entry point, drill an upward-slanting hole completely through the wall. Thread the antenna wire through the hole and into the house, leaving a loop of wire on the outside of the house for water to drip off. Seal the drilled opening with acrylic latex or silicone caulk, both inside and out.

Once the antenna wire is in the house, lead it as directly as possible to the television. If you have more than one television, or want to hook up an FM receiver to the antenna, attach a coupler to the antenna wire. Strip the end of the antenna lead-in wire and attach the wire to the antenna side of the coupler, as directed by the manufacturer; attach individual leads to each television. Most televisions will accept the 300-ohm lead-in wire. If your set has two antenna terminals, one for VHF and one for UHF, attach the antenna line to a splitter; attach the individual leads to the antenna terminals on the TV, as directed by the manufacturer.

Finally, to make sure you're getting the best reception, turn on the television and let it warm up. Arrange a way to communicate with a helper inside, and go back up on the roof. While your helper looks at the television, loosen the mounting brackets a little and rotate the antenna toward the broadcast station, a few degrees at a time, until you get the best picture. Have your helper turn the TV from channel to channel; you may have to compromise if channels are broadcast from different areas.

When antenna position is correct, securely tighten the bolts to lock the antenna in position. Remove the roof safety lines.

Groom Your Pets

Cats and dogs need more than love and affection; they also need regular grooming. Take care of them well to keep them healthy. **Tools:** soft hairbrush and comb or wire dog brush, small sharp scissors; nail scissors or clipper, or special pet nail clipper; tub or basin, tweezers, measuring spoons, measuring cup. **Materials:** baby or pet shampoo, flea repellent rinse, towels, salt, mineral oil, cotton swabs or absorbent cotton. **Time:** regular care, a few minutes a day; about 5 to 10 minutes to clip nails, or 1 to 2 hours to bathe a dog.

Grooming and cleanliness. A dog or cat's fur serves as its protection from weather and temperature changes; it should be shiny, clean, and free of tangles and snarls. Brush dogs and longhaired cats several times a week with a soft hairbrush; use a comb to get out loose hairs and untangle matted hair.

If you find large mats of fur as you brush your pet, cut the mats out with a small sharp scissors. Being very careful to keep the scissors away from the animal's body, push the blades of the scissors under the mat of fur and cut it in half; repeat to cut the mat again until you can comb out the clipped-out mat. If a large dog's fur is badly matted, and the dog is a breed that can be clipped, take it to a veterinarian and have it closely clipped and groomed.

Baths aren't necessary very often; frequent brushing will keep your pet clean and good-smelling. Don't try to bathe cats; if it's absolutely necessary, take the cat to a vet. Bathe dogs only when it's really necessary. If possible, work inside, with the dog in the bathtub or a large basin. If your dog is too big for the bathtub, work outside on a warm day, with the dog in a large tub.

Bathe the dog gently with warm water and baby shampoo or a nonirritating pet shampoo; work up a good lather with your fingers. Rinse thoroughly with warm water. If the dog is prone to fleas, or you live in an area that has a lot of pests, follow the shampoo with a flea repellent rinse; ask your vet to recommend a mild repellent, and follow the instructions carefully. Towel-dry the dog thoroughly, and keep it inside until its fur is completely dry.

Nail-clipping. Indoor pets usually don't wear their claws or nails down as quickly as outdoor pets. To eliminate the floor-clicking of indoor dogs and the furniture-shredding of cats, trim their nails regularly. Do *not* have cats declawed; their claws are their only natural defense.

Cut cats' claws about once every two weeks. Before doing this yourself, ask your vet for a demonstration. Inside each claw is a blood vessel; the claw must be clipped beyond the end of the blood vessel or it will bleed. Hold the cat firmly and gently grasp one front paw; press it to pop the claws out and spread them apart. Clip the sharp tip of each claw with a regular nail scissors or clipper—you don't need a special tool. Cut at an angle compatible with the curve of the claw, so that its general shape stays the same. Repeat to cut the claws on both front paws. It usually isn't necessary to cut cats' back claws; if you do, cut them first so you won't be clawed.

Cut dogs' nails when the floor-clicking gets noticeable; ask your vet for a demonstration before trying it yourself. Inside each nail is a blood vessel; you must clip the nail beyond the end of the blood vessel or it will bleed. Use a special pet nail clipper, available at pet shops or from your vet; work calmly and quickly to cut all the dog's nails, generally parallel to the floor. Some dogs have dewclaws; the dewclaw is on the inside of the leg just above the paw. Clip the dewclaws if necessary to keep them from irritating the skin.

Eyes and ears. Cats' eyes need little care. Gently wipe away any exudate at the nasal corners of the eyes. If a hair curls into the eye and irritates it, remove the hair gently with tweezers. Treat dogs' eyes the same way. Dogs with large, protruding eyes sometimes need an eye bath; mix ½ teaspoon salt to 1 cup warm water and bathe the dog's eyes gently. Don't ever let any animal stick its head out of a moving car.

Ear troubles affect both cats and dogs, and they're very painful—check your pet's ears weekly to make sure they're all right. Clean cats' ears as necessary with mineral oil; apply the oil carefully with a cotton swab and wipe the ears clean. Massage mineral oil gently into a dog's ears to loosen dirt and wax buildup, and wipe the ears clean with absorbent cotton. Work quickly and calmly, and speak reassuringly to your pet as you work.

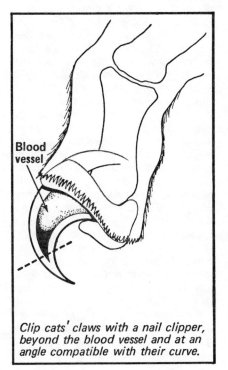

Clip cats' claws with a nail clipper, beyond the blood vessel and at an angle compatible with their curve.

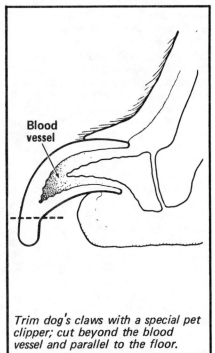

Trim dog's claws with a special pet clipper; cut beyond the blood vessel and parallel to the floor.

Care For Your Pets

Owning a cat or dog is both a pleasure and a responsibility; sometimes it can be downright expensive. Take your pets to a veterinarian for regular immunizations and medical treatment, but give them daily veterinary care at home. **Tools:** tweezers, measuring spoons, eyedropper. **Materials:** flea, tick, and lice tags; parasite medication as prescribed by a vet, commercial liquid antacid or antidiarrheal, mild soap, heavy towels. **Time:** regular care, a few minutes a day.

Prevention. To keep your dog or cat healthy, feed it a balanced diet of the appropriate pet food; ask your vet for brand-name recommendations. Don't overfeed your pet or give it sweets, and make sure it always has clean drinking water available. Give your pet as much exercise as possible; if you have a dog, walk it or let it run several times a day, and give it a good run at least two or three times a week.

Parasites. Pets are vulnerable to both interior and exterior parasites. Young animals sometimes develop worms; check the animal's stools regularly. If you see any indication of worms, get the animal to a vet; get a prescription for a worming medication and give it to your pet exactly as directed. Dogs should be protected against heartworm; ask your vet for the proper medication.

The most common parasites are fleas and ticks. Groom your pets and keep them clean. At least once a week, check them thoroughly for live-in guests; at the first sign of pests, hang a commercial flea and tick tag around your pet's neck. Remove ticks immediately with tweezers. Buy a tag specifically for a cat or a dog, and don't use flea collars; they could irritate your pet's neck. Thoroughly wash or discard infested bedding. If your pet is badly infested, take it to a vet for a professional pest-removing bath.

If your pet shakes its head or scratches at its ears frequently, it may have ear mites, a type of lice. Examine the ears thoroughly, and take the animal to a vet; ear mites cannot be removed by pest tags or baths. Get a prescription for ear mite medication and apply it exactly as directed by the vet, for the full time directed; keep a close check on the animal's ears and get back to the vet if the mites persist. If you have other pets, examine them too; ear mites are persistent and contagious.

Illness. If your pet is listless, has vomiting or diarrhea, or acts strangely for more than a day or so, call a vet and take the animal in for a checkup. Both cats and dogs get colds too, and vomiting or diarrhea can be caused by anything from spoiled food to gluttony or emotional upsets. Withhold food and give your pet a commercial liquid antacid or antidiarrheal—½ teaspoon every 2 hours for a cat or small dog, 1 teaspoon for a medium or large dog, and 2 teaspoons for a very large dog. After 12 hours, give the animal food and water. If the condition persists or gets worse, call a vet. *Caution: Never give your pet prescription medicine your doctor has given you, or any over-the-counter remedy except a liquid antacid or antidiarrheal. If you ever suspect your dog or cat has eaten poison, get it to a veterinarian immediately.*

Injuries. In most cases, there's nothing you can do for minor injuries. Approach a hurt animal carefully and slowly; speak in a gentle, reassuring voice. Check for bleeding immediately. If the area is very dirty, and your pet is used to baths, clean the injury gently with warm water and mild soap; otherwise, leave it alone. Never apply an antiseptic—your pet will probably lick it off, and antiseptics are often poisonous; moreover, if the medication stings, you could get bitten or clawed. Let the animal strictly alone, make sure it eats and sleeps well, and keep it in for a few days so the wound can heal.

If a cat or dog is seriously injured, get it to a veterinarian immediately, regardless of the hour. Wrap heavy towels around an injured cat so it can't claw you or the vet. Speak reassuringly, and handle the animal as gently as possible. When you bring your pet home, follow the vet's specific instructions for treatment and medication.

Give Your Dog a Haircut

To keep your dog clean and well groomed, brush and comb him regularly. When more than brushing is needed, use the same techniques the professionals do to trim, strip, or clip your dog's fur. **Tools:** soft brush or wire dog brush, comb, haircut scissors, stripping comb, dog clippers. **Materials:** none. **Time:** 10 minutes to ½ hour for trimming; 1 to 2 hours or more for stripping or clipping, depending on size of dog.

Trimming. Groom your dog regularly and thoroughly; use a soft brush for smooth fur, a wire dog brush for rough or shaggy breeds. Work burrs and mats of fur out with a comb. To remove stubborn mats or burrs, carefully insert a sharp haircut scissors under the knot and away from the dog's skin. Clip the mat in half, away from the dog's skin, and comb it out. Repeat the clipping process until you can easily brush or comb out the pieces of matted fur.

If your dog has long, shaggy fur, it may need an occasional trim. If the dog's eyes are completely covered by overhanging fur, carefully brush out the fur over the dog's face. Working very carefully, trim the fur back to expose the dog's eyes. Cut only long, overhanging fur; do *not* touch the fur around the dog's eyes. Work with slow movements to avoid alarming the dog, and talk to it reassuringly as you trim. Remove all trimmed-off fur to keep it out of the dog's eyes.

Some shaggy dogs have a long, straggly beard. It isn't necessary to cut this beard, but you can trim it period-ically to prevent the fur from soaking up water and picking up food. Working very carefully, cut the beard with a sharp haircut scissors to a length of about ½ inch. Work with slow movements to avoid alarming the dog.

If your dog chews at its paws frequently, check between the toes of each paw for matted or straggly hairs. In summer, matted fur between the dog's toes collects dirt; in winter it can collect ice. On each paw, carefully separate the toes and clip the long or matted hairs with a haircut scissors. Work very carefully; dogs usually don't like to have their paws touched, and your dog may pull away from you. Make sure you don't touch the skin on the toes or pull the hairs.

Stripping. Short-haired breeds should not be trimmed, but dogs with thick or long, glossy fur may sometimes need a haircut. If your dog is a show dog, have it professionally groomed; there are specific grooming techniques and requirements for each breed. For a non-show dog, use a stripping comb, available at pet shops, to trim its coat evenly and to remove dead hairs. Do *not* use clippers to trim dogs with smooth fur.

Stripping a dog's fur takes time and patience, for you and for the dog. To use the stripping comb, gather a small section of fur between the blade of the comb and your thumb; then press your thumb firmly against the blade and pull the hair down, in the direction of its growth. Do *not* pull the stripping comb upward.

Work over the dog's body section by section, as you would to brush the fur. Stripping cuts only a little of each hair; if necessary, strip again to trim the fur to the desired length. Do not use the stripper on the dog's face, head, ears, paws, or tail. After stripping, groom your dog thoroughly.

Clipping. Dogs with fuzzy coats instead of smooth fur are often clipped—poodles, Airedales, sheepdogs, and other shaggy breeds. If your dog isn't a show dog, you can give it a simple puppy cut or kennel cut, an all-one-length cut. The puppy cut doesn't look professional, but it serves as well as a professional cut to keep your dog neat and comfortable.

Use judgment in clipping your dog; the fur is there for good reason. Don't clip dogs to the skin; this exposes them to insects and weather. Don't clip your dog's fur very short during the winter. Buy a special dog-grooming clipper, available at pet shops.

The dog clipper includes various cutting head attachments, to cut the fur to various lengths. Read the manufacturer's instructions carefully, and use the clipper attachment recommended for your dog's breed. Do *not* use a clipper on short-haired dogs or dogs with long, smooth coats.

Following the manufacturer's operating instructions, work over your dog's body with the clippers; be very careful not to nick the skin. Start clipping along the dog's back; then clip down the legs, across the chest and neck, and over the stomach. Do *not* clip the dog's face or paws; these areas must be hand-trimmed with a haircut scissors.

After clipping the dog, carefully trim the fur on its face. Shape the hair on the crown of the dog's head and at the end of its tail as desired. Working very carefully, trim the dog's paws closely; trim matted or straggly fur from between the toes as above. Finally, brush the dog to make any long spots of fur stand up; trim as necessary.

Make Your Own Will

In some states, making your own will can be as simple as writing a letter and signing it. A will made in this way is called a holographic will. But holographic wills are valid in only half the states, and even these states differ in just what is accepted as legal. To make sure your will is valid according to the state you live in, draw it up according to specific guidelines, and follow your state's statutes for the execution and attestation of your will.

A will—whether simple or complex—is a typewritten or handwritten document in which you identify yourself, appoint a person to administer your estate, name the people who are to receive your possessions on your death, and appoint a guardian for your minor children, if any. You must sign this document according to your state's statutes. A simple will is usually made up of the following parts.

The *introduction* identifies the person making the will and states his or her place of residence.

The *appointment of fiduciaries* identifies and appoints the executor, executrix, guardian, or trustee. Many people cite their bank and trust company as an executor or co-executor, especially if they have a large estate.

The *disposition clauses* name those people who are to receive your possessions and properties on your death, and specifically designate what goes to each person.

The *execution and attestation* are the signing and witnessing of your will—check your state's statutes for the specific requirements where you live. Signing and witnessing is usually done before a lawyer, a notary public, or a clerk of court; in most states, three witnesses are sufficient. The procedure is simple: you tell the witnesses that the document is your last will and testament, you sign the original copy in their presence, and you ask them to attest to your will with their signatures; they each sign the original in your presence and each other's presence. Finally, the witnessing official signs the document.

Once you've made a will, keep the original in a safe place that's available to both you and your executor—a vault, a fireproof safe or box, or somewhere similar. Don't put the will in a safe deposit box; court orders are often required to open a box after the owner's death. Place at least two unsigned copies in different locations for purposes of information.

Small Claims Court: Represent Yourself

Small claims court is a quick, fair, inexpensive, and relatively simple system of justice available to everyone. If your problem is a civil matter with no criminal aspects to it, and if it involves the sum of $1,000 or less, you can take your case before a small claims court and represent yourself.

If your complaint is against a corporation, you have one advantage: corporations cannot sue in a small claims court, but they can be sued. Since a defendant corporation has to hire an attorney, many small claims suits never get to court—it's usually cheaper for the corporation to settle with you out of court and save attorneys' fees.

If you must go to court, find out exactly who you're suing—an independent businessman? A neighbor? A corporation? Then, with the help of a local court clerk, determine which court in your area has jurisdiction over the party you're suing. Once you have all the necessary information, go to the court and file your suit. The clerk of court will give you a simple form to complete and will help if you have any questions; there will be a small filing fee, usually less than $5. The court will then arrange to serve the defendant with a summons and a complaint, and you will be advised of the trial date—usually six weeks to two months later. This time period gives you the opportunity to prepare your case.

Make sure you have all the facts. If your complaint involves the purchase of faulty merchandise, you must have the receipt and date of purchase. Remember, the person suing carries the burden of proof.

When your trial date arrives, go to court and check the court calendar for the day to make certain your case is listed; if it isn't, tell the clerk immediately. If you're offered the choice between a court arbitrator or a judge, remember that while an arbitrator will try to work out a settlement between you and the defendant and the results are more immediate, arbitration does not always carry with it the opportunity to appeal if you aren't satisfied. Trial before a judge always allows this right.

If the case is tried before a judge, you and the defendant get an equal opportunity to present your stories; however, the defendant or his attorney may cross-examine you. Don't panic; answer questions honestly and simply; *do not argue!*

The defendant may choose to take the stand, but he doesn't have to. If he does, you may cross-examine him; if you do, keep your questions to the point. Finally, each side is allowed to deliver a closing statement—a summary of your positions. State your case firmly and positively, but not aggressively.

You may find out the judge's decision immediately; if the judge decides to think about the case, you'll hear the outcome within a week. If you win your case, the court will attempt to execute the verdict; or, in some states, you may have to obtain a *writ of execution* to turn over to a sheriff. Ask the court clerk what the correct procedure is in your state.

Useful Information

Basic Tools

After you've acquired the basic foundation of hammer and pliers, screwdrivers and wrenches, what are the essentials? For most jobs, you'll need measuring and marking tools, saws, and a drill; planes, files, and clamps are next in line. Add tools and accessories as your budget permits. Power tools do what hand tools do—faster and, usually, easier.

There is only one cast-in-concrete rule about tools: buy good ones. Quality tools are safer and easier to use, and they will last a lifetime if you take care of them. You can spot a quality tool by its machining: the metal parts are smooth and shiny and the tool is well balanced. Inexpensive tools are often painted to hide the defects or roughness of the metal parts, and the machining is crude. You can also tell quality by the price tag—you'll pay an average of 25 percent more for quality equipment. But cheap tools are no economy—you get what you pay for.

Measuring and Marking Tools

Measuring rule or tape measure. Flexible tape measures are available in lengths of up to 50 feet; 16 to 24 feet is usually adequate. Buy a tape at least 5/8 inch wide, so it will stay rigid when extended. Many rules have an automatic power return.

Folding rule. Folding rules are available in 4-, 6-, and 8-foot lengths; they're used for laying out carpentry projects where absolute accuracy is necessary. The rules fold down to 6 inches; care must be taken not to strain the metal joints at the folding points. Some rules have a metal insert in the first 6 inches. This insert is pulled out of the rule for use as a depth gauge or marking gauge, or for extremely critical measurements. It can also be used for measurements inside door or window frames or between parallel surfaces.

Carpenters' square. The standard sizes are 18 or 24 inches (body) by 12 or 18 inches (tongue), and the size is important for laying out projects on plywood and hardboard. Carpenters' squares are steel or aluminum; they have multiple scales for figuring board-foot requirements, brace (rafter) height, stairstep stringer angles, and rafter cuts.

Combination square. For small jobs, a combination square is easier to use than a carpenters' square because the combination square is smaller. The body of the square slides along a handle, and the blade can be fixed at any point with a thumbscrew. The handle of the square may incorporate a small bubble level or a scratch awl, which can be used for leveling and marking. This square can also be used as a depth gauge, a miter square, and, with the blade removed, as a straightedge and ruler.

Try square. This tool looks like

a small carpenters' square with a wood handle. The measurements go across the metal blade only (not the handle), and the square is generally used to test the squareness of edges in planing and sawing work. It can also be used to check right-angle layouts. The tongue has a maximum length of 12 inches; it is fairly wide, but it can be used as a straightedge, ruler, and depth gauge.

Level. Two- and three-bubble levels are standard for most leveling and plumbing (vertical level) projects. Some of the bubbles are in vials that can be moved for angle "leveling;" these vials can sometimes be replaced if they are damaged or broken. The edges of a level can be used as a straightedge. Laid flat against a vertical surface, the level can determine both horizontal and vertical levels—often needed when installing cabinets, hanging wallpaper, or hanging pictures. Level frames are either wood or lightweight metal such as aluminum; lengths range to 6 feet.

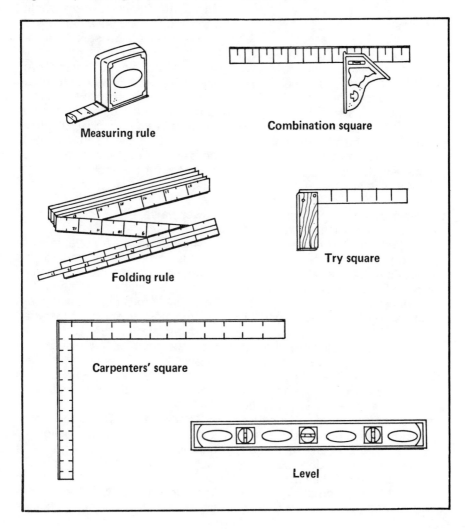

Measuring rule

Combination square

Folding rule

Try square

Carpenters' square

Level

Chalk line. Chalk lines are available in a metal canister or case, or in a ball like heavy twine. In the canister type, the line is chalked with powdered chalk poured into the canister. In the ball type, the chalk is hard chalk similar to that used for blackboards. To use a chalk line, stretch it taut along a surface and snap the line; the chalk leaves a blue line along the work for measuring and cutting. Chalk line is also used to suspend plumb bobs, for vertical lines, and to lay out walks, driveways, and foundations.

Handsaws

Crosscut saw. The crosscut, as its name implies, cuts across the grain of the wood. Crosscut saws have from 5 to 10 or more teeth per inch to produce a smooth cut in the wood. They are used for cutting plywood and hardboard panels, and sometimes to cut miters. They can be used for ripping, but are not as fast as the ripsaw.

Ripsaw. The ripsaw cuts along the grain of the wood, called ripping. Its teeth are spaced from 3 to 5 teeth per inch. The ripsaw's teeth are wider-set than those of the crosscut saw, so they slice through the wood like a chisel. The final cut of a ripsaw is fairly rough, and the wood usually has to be planed or sanded to its final measurement.

Backsaw. A backsaw has a reinforced back to stiffen the blade; its teeth are closely spaced—like those of a crosscut saw—so the cut is smooth. A backsaw is generally used for making miter cuts and for trimming molding. It is designed for use in a miter box; the reinforced back serves as a guide.

Keyhole saw. This saw has a 10- to 12-inch tapered blade; it's used to cut openings for pipes, electrical boxes, and almost any straight or curved internal cuts that are too large for an auger bit, drill, or hole saw. Quality keyhole saws have removable blades with a variety of tooth spacings, for various materials such as wood, plastic, metal, and hardboard. Similar to the keyhole saw is the compass saw, which has a blade 12 to 14 inches long. A compass saw is used like a keyhole saw, but the keyhole saw can make a tighter turn.

Coping saw. This saw looks like a C-clamp with a handle. The blades are thin, and replaceable; the blade is secured with two pins at the ends of the saw, and the handle turned to put the proper tension on the blade. A variety of blades is available, with both ripsaw and crosscut tooth spacing. Blades can be inserted into the frame to cut on the forward or backward stroke, depending on the sawing project; the pins can also be turned to set the blade at an angle for special cuts.

Power Saws

Circular saw. A portable electric tool, the circular saw is the power version of a crosscut and/or ripsaw. The guide on the saw can be adjusted to cut miters and pockets in almost any building material. Several blades are available: crosscut, rip, masonry, metal, and plastic. Accessories for the saw include a table, so the saw can be mounted to work as a small table saw.

Saber saw. The saber saw, sometimes also called a jigsaw, consists of a short—about 4 inches—blade, driven in an up-and-down reciprocating motion. This portable power tool is designed with a wide variety of blades

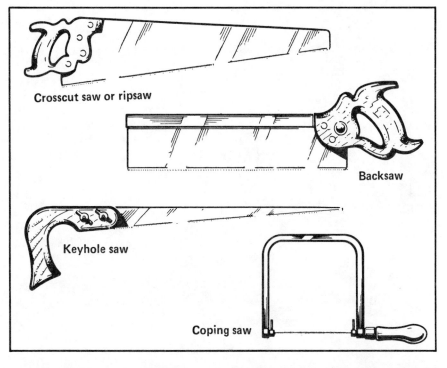

Crosscut saw or ripsaw

Backsaw

Keyhole saw

Coping saw

for a wide variety of materials, including wood, metal, plastic, masonry, ceramic, and high-pressure laminate. This is the power counterpart to the keyhole and the coping saw; it will make smooth fine-line or contour cuts either with or across the grain.

Drills and Drill Bits

Hand drill. The hand drill is like an egg beater; a drive handle moves bevel gears to turn a chuck in which a drill has been locked. This drill can't make large holes, but it can make small-diameter, shallow holes in wood and soft metals.

Push drill. The push drill requires only one hand to use; as you push down on the handle, the shank turns a chuck into which a small bit fits. This is a limited-capacity tool, but it's excellent for making pilot holes, and is handy for

setting hinges and similar jobs. The bits are usually stored in the handle of the drill; sizes are available up to ¼ inch.

Brace. The hand brace has a rotating offset handle that turns a chuck with a ratcheting mechanism; auger bits, countersinks, and screwdriver attachments are available, and the ratchet also lets you work in restricted areas. The large-capacity chuck handles bits that will cut holes up to 1½ inches in diameter. The brace is the counterpart of the electric drill, but a hand brace chuck is not designed for twist drills, unless the drills have a special shank for hand use.

Electric drill. Three sizes of chucks are available for power drills: ¼-, ½-, and ⅜-inch capacity. The two popular sizes are ¼ and ⅜ inch, since this range spans the ½-inch chuck. The ¼-inch chuck has a capacity of ¼-inch drills in

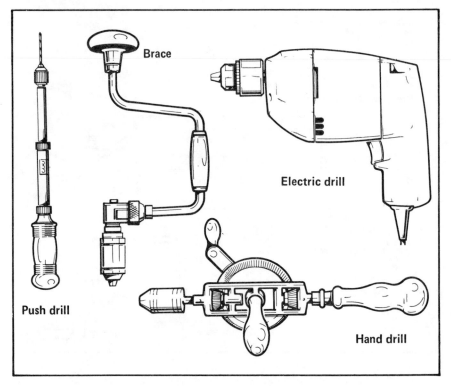

Brace

Electric drill

Push drill

Hand drill

metal and ½ inch in wood; it can handle only a limited range of drilling operations, but it is the least expensive type of electric drill. It should not be used for prolonged hard jobs. Accessories are available.

The ⅜-inch drill can make ⅜-inch holes in metal and ¾-inch holes in wood; a hole saw can also be used with this tool, to cut holes up to 3 inches in diameter. Many ⅜-inch drills have a hammer mode that permits drilling in concrete, along with a reversing feature handy for removing screws. A variable-speed drill is recommended; this type can be started slowly and then speeded up. A variety of attachments and accessories is available, including wire brushes, paint mixers, and even a circular saw attachment.

Drill bits. The most common drill bits include:

Bit	Drill Type	Use
Twist drill	Hand, power, drill press	Small-diameter holes in wood and metal
Spade bit	Power, drill press	Holes up to 1½ inches in wood
Auger bit	Hand	Holes up to 1½ inches in wood
Expansion bit	Hand	Holes up to 3 inches in wood
Fly cutter	Drill press	Holes up to 6 inches in wood; smaller holes in other materials
Hole saw	Power, drill press	Holes up to 3 inches

Planes

Jack plane. The jack plane removes excess wood and brings the surface of the wood to trueness and smoothness. The plane is 12 to 14 inches long. Depending on the job, it can also be used to true long edges for gluing.

Smoothing plane. This plane, slightly smaller than the jack plane, is used to bring wood to a final finish. The plane measures from 6 to 9 inches long.

Block plane. The block plane is small, designed to smooth and cut the end grain of wood. The plane has a low blade angle that permits smooth cutting, and only one hand is needed to use it. Although the block plane is a cabinetmaker's tool, it can be used to smooth almost any soft material, even aluminum. For large jobs, a smoothing or jack plane should be used, since both are longer and wider.

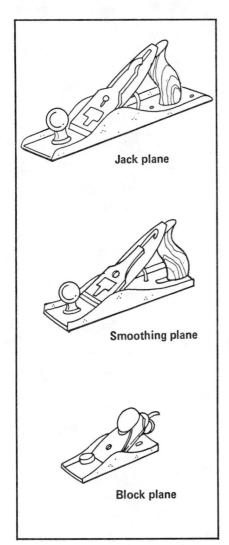

Jack plane

Smoothing plane

Block plane

Wood Files

A wood rasp, with a rasp and/or curved-tooth cut, is used to remove excess wood; the piece of wood is final-smoothed with a single- or double-cut file. As a starter set, buy an assortment of flat files—wood rasp, bastard, second-cut, and smooth files.

Clamps

Clamps are very inexpensive, and they're essential for many jobs. Start with several C-clamps and a set of bar clamps; if you plan to work on furniture, get strap clamps too.

C-clamps. These clamps are made from cast iron or aluminum, and have a C-shaped body; a screw with a metal pad applies the tension on the material being clamped. Since C-clamps can exert lots of pressure, buffer blocks of scrap wood or other materials should be inserted between the jaws of the clamps and the material being clamped. A wide range of sizes is available.

Screw clamps. These clamps have parallel wood jaws; they are the basic woodworking clamps. Tension is applied by hand with two threaded wood spindles; the clamps can be adjusted to angles by moving the spindles. Screw clamps are expensive.

Bar clamps. These clamps are made to fit on long metal rods or pieces of pipe; tension is applied by tightening a screw. Bar clamps are used for gluing boards together and on wide surfaces where the throats of C-clamps are too shallow to accept the work. Bar clamp fixtures and bars or pipe can be purchased separately.

Strap or web clamps. These clamps are simply webbing straps, usually nylon, with a sliding tension clamp. The clamp is used for four-way tensioning on odd-shaped or four-cornered pieces. Since the clamps are fabric, the pressure from the straps will not damage the material being clamped.

Spring clamps. These clamps look like large metal clothespins; they're used for clamping light jobs, such as veneers glued to core material. Spring clamps also come in handy as holding devices. They are very inexpensive.

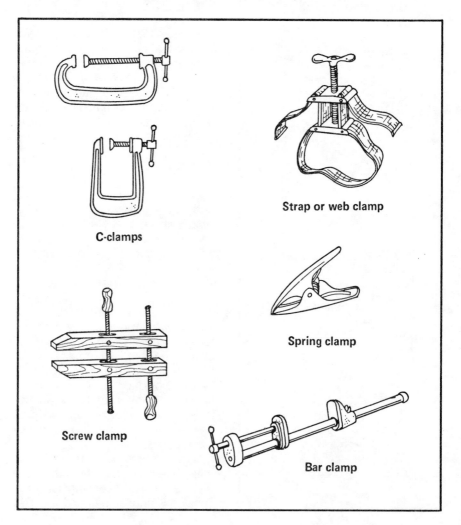

C-clamps

Strap or web clamp

Spring clamp

Screw clamp

Bar clamp

Adhesives

Multipurpose Adhesives

White glue (polyvinyl acetate). PVA glue is a white liquid, usually sold in plastic squeeze bottles; it's recommended for use on porous materials—wood, paper, cloth, porous pottery, and nonstructural wood-to-wood bonds. It is not water-resistant. Clamping is required for ½ to 1 hour, until the glue sets; curing time is 18 to 24 hours. School glue, a type of white glue, dries more slowly. PVA glue dries clear. It is inexpensive and nonflammable.

Epoxy. Epoxies are sold in tubes or in cans. They consist of two parts, resin and hardener, which must be thoroughly mixed just before use. They are very strong, very durable, and very water-resistant, and are recommended for use on metal, ceramics, some plastics, and rubber; they are not recommended for flexible surfaces. Clamping is required for about 2 hours for most epoxies. Drying time is about 12 hours; curing time is 1 to 2 days. Epoxy dries clear or amber. It is expensive.

Cyanoacrylate (instant) glue. Cyanoacrylates are similar to epoxy, but are one-part glues; they form a very strong bond. They are recommended for use on metal, ceramics, glass, some plastics, and rubber; they are not recommended for flexible surfaces. Apply very sparingly. Clamping is not required; curing time is 1 to 2 days. Cyanoacrylates dry clear. They deteriorate gradually when exposed to weather, and weaken in temperatures above 150° F. They are expensive.

Contact cement. A rubber-based liquid sold in bottles and cans, contact cement is recommended for bonding laminates, veneers, and other large areas, and for repairs. It can also be used on paper, leather, cloth, rubber, metal, glass, and some plastics; it dries flexible. It is not recommended for repairs where strength is necessary. Contact cement is applied to both surfaces and allowed to set; the surfaces are pressed together for an instant bond. No repositioning is possible once contact has been made; a sheet of paper can be used to prevent contact until positioning is correct. Clamping is not required; curing is complete on drying. Contact cement is usually very flammable; it is also fairly expensive.

Polyurethane glue. This high-strength glue is an amber paste, sold in tubes; it forms a very strong bond, similar to epoxy. Polyurethane glue is recommended for use on wood, metal, ceramics, glass, most plastics, and fiberglass; it dries flexible, and can also be used on leather, cloth, rubber, and vinyl. Clamping is required for about 2 hours; curing time is about 24 hours. Polyurethane glue dries translucent, and can be painted or stained; its shelf life is short, and it is expensive.

Silicone rubber adhesive or sealant. The silicone rubber glues and sealants are sold in tubes; they're similar to silicone rubber caulk. They form very strong, very durable, waterproof bonds, with excellent resistance to high and low temperatures. They're recommended for use on gutters and on building materials, including metal, glass, fiberglass, rubber, and wood; they can also be used on fabrics, some plastics, and ceramics. Clamping is usually not required; curing time is about 24 hours, but the adhesive skins over in less than 1 hour. They dry flexible, and are available in clear, black, and metal-colored forms. They are expensive.

Household cement. The various adhesives sold in tubes as household cement are fast-setting, low-strength glues. They are recommended for use on wood, ceramics, glass, paper, and some plastics; some dry flexible, and can be used on fabric, leather, and vinyl. Clamping is usually not required; setting time is 10 to 20 minutes, curing time up to 24 hours. Household cements are inexpensive.

Hot-melt adhesive. Hot-melt glues are sold in stick form and used with glue guns. A glue gun heats the adhesive above 200° F; for the best bond, the surfaces to be joined should also be preheated. Hot-melt adhesives are only moderately strong, and bonds will come apart if exposed to high temperatures; this type of glue is recommended for temporary bonds of wood, metal, paper, and some plastics and composition materials. Clamping is not required; setting time is 10 to 45 seconds, and curing time 24 hours. Hot-melt adhesives are medium-priced; a glue gun is necessary, but the gun can be reused.

Wood Glues

Yellow glue (aliphatic resin, carpenters' glue). Aliphatic resin glue is a yellow liquid, usually sold in plastic squeeze bottles, and often labeled as carpenters' glue. Bulk quantities are also available. Yellow glue is very similar to white glue, but is recommended specifically for general woodworking, and forms a slightly stronger bond. It is only slightly more water-resistant than white glue. Clamping is required for about ½ hour, until the glue sets; curing time is 12 to 18 hours. Yellow glue dries clear; it does not accept wood stains. It is usually inexpensive.

Plastic resin glue (urea formaldehyde). Plastic resin glues are sold in powder form, and mixed with water to the consistency of thick cream. They're recommended for laminating layers of wood and for gluing structural joints. Plastic resin glue is water-resistant but not waterproof, and is not recommended for use on outdoor furniture; it is resistant to paint and lacquer thinner. Clamping is required for up to 8 hours; curing time is 18 to 24 hours. Use plastic resin glue only at temperatures above 70° F. It is inexpensive.

Resorcinol glue. This two-part glue, consisting of a liquid and a powder, is sold in cans. It is waterproof, and forms strong and durable bonds; it is recommended for use on outdoor furniture, kitchen counters, structural bonding, and boats and sporting gear; it can also be used on concrete, cork, fabrics, leather, and some plastics. Resorcinol glue has excellent resistance to temperature extremes, chemicals, and fungus. Clamping is required; curing time is 8 to 24 hours, depending on humidity and temperature. It is fairly expensive.

Hide glue. Hide glue, the traditional woodworkers' glue, is available in either liquid or flake form; the flake form must be soaked for about 12 hours in water heated to 150° F, and applied hot. Hide glue forms a strong bond, but it is not moisture-resistant. Clamping is required; curing time is about 12 hours. Hide glue dries to a clear amber; it does not accept wood stains. It is inexpensive.

Casein glue. Casein glue is made from milk; it's sold in powder form and mixed with water to the consistency of thick cream. It forms strong bonds, and is recommended for laminating resinous or oily woods; it is moisture-resistant but is not recommended for outdoor use. Clamping is required for about 4 hours; curing time is about 12 hours. Casein glue must be stored tightly sealed. It is moderately priced.

Adhesives for Glass and Ceramics

China and glass cement. Many cements are sold for mending china and glass, usually in tubes. Acrylic latex-based cements have good resistance to water and heat; other types are not recommended. Clamping is usually required until the glue has set.

Silicone rubber adhesives. Only silicone adhesives made specifically for glass and china are recommended. They form very strong bonds, with excellent resistance to water and temperature extremes. Clamping is usually required until the adhesive has set.

Metal Adhesives and Fillers

Steel epoxy. Steel epoxy is a two-part compound sold in tubes, similar to regular epoxy. It forms a very strong, durable, heat- and water-resistant bond, and is recommended for patching gutters and gas tanks, sealing pipes, and filling rust holes. Drying time is about 12 hours; curing time is 1 to 2 days. Steel epoxy is expensive.

Steel putty. This metal putty consists of two putty-consistency parts, which are kneaded together before use. It forms a strong, water-resistant bond, and is recommended for patching and for sealing pipes that aren't under pressure; it can also be used for ceramic and masonry. Curing time is about ½ hour; when dry, it can be sanded or painted. Steel putty is expensive.

Plastic metal cement. Plastic metal is a one-part adhesive and filler; it is moisture-resistant but cannot withstand temperature extremes. It is recommended for use on metal, glass, concrete, and wood, where strength is not required. Curing time is about 4 hours; when dry, it can be sanded or painted. Plastic metal cement is moderately expensive.

Plastic Adhesives

Model cement. Model cements are usually sold in tubes as "model maker" glues. They form a strong bond on acrylics and polystyrenes, and can be used on most plastics; do not use them on plastic foam. Clamping is usually required until the cement has set, about 10 minutes; curing time is about 24 hours. Model cement dries clear, and is inexpensive.

Vinyl adhesive. Vinyl adhesives, sold in tubes, form a strong, waterproof bond on vinyl and on many plastics; do not use them on plastic foam. Clamping is usually not required. Vinyl adhesive dries flexible and clear; curing time is 10 to 20 minutes. Vinyl adhesive is inexpensive.

Acrylic solvent. Solvents are not adhesives as such; they act by melting the acrylic bonding surfaces to fuse them together at the joint. They are recommended for use on acrylics and polycarbonates. Clamping is required; the bonding surfaces are clamped or taped together and the solvent is injected into the joint with a syringe. Setting time is about 5 minutes; the joint dries clear, but may look slightly rough. Solvents are inexpensive.

Glues for Flexible Repairs

Plastic rubber (neoprene). Plastic rubber, a thick cream, seals and bonds rubber, leather, vinyl, and rubberized fabric; it can also be used on shoes, and on wood, metal, glass, and some plastic. Clamping is usually not required, but weighting in place is recommended; curing time is about 1 hour. Plastic rubber is medium-priced.

Shoe repair (nitrile-phenolic) adhesive. Nitrile-phenolics form a strong, durable bond on leather and canvas; they are recommended for heavy-duty mending jobs on shoes and boots, and can also be used on wood, metal, ceramic, and some plastics. The adhesive is applied to both surfaces and allowed to set, like contact cement; bonding is immediate and permanent when the two bonding surfaces make contact. Nitrile-phenolics are moderately expensive.

Latex fabric mender. Latex fabric menders are water-based, and can be used on all fabrics; they can also be used on leather and on some plastics. Fabric menders are recommended for low-strength repairs, but they can be washed and dried. No clamping or weighting is required; curing time is about 20 minutes. Fabric menders are inexpensive.

Construction and Building Adhesives

Construction adhesive. This heavy-duty adhesive is sold in cartridges and in bulk containers. It forms a strong, fast bond, and is recommended for use on wood, drywall, paneling, flooring, rigid foam, and masonry; it can also be used on uneven surfaces. Some support is required on vertical surfaces; curing time is about ½ hour. The adhesive dries medium-brown. Adhesives labeled for use on subfloors are of better quality. Construction adhesives are moderately priced.

Synthetic rubber adhesives. Synthetic rubber is a thick paste, sold in cans; it is waterproof, and is recommended for heavy-duty bonding of metal, glass, masonry, fixtures, and some plastics. It can be used for bonding over uneven surfaces, and to fill gaps or horizontal or vertical surfaces. Clamping is required, especially on vertical surfaces. Setting time is about 4 hours; curing time is about 2 days. Synthetic rubber is available in black or white, and can be sanded or painted when dry. It is moderately expensive.

Floor and wall covering adhesives. Floor covering adhesives are available for indoor and outdoor use; the outdoor types are water-resistant. Clamping is not required for floor and wall adhesives; setting time is about 25 minutes. These adhesives are medium-priced.

Fixture adhesive. This mastic-type adhesive is very similar to construction or synthetic rubber adhesives, but it is sold in small tubes. Fixture adhesives are water-resistant or waterproof, and setting time is about 20 minutes. They are fairly expensive.

Fasteners

NAILS

The easiest way to fasten two pieces of wood together is with nails, and nails are manufactured in a variety of shapes, sizes, and metals, to do almost any fastening job. Most commonly, nails are made of steel, but other types—aluminum, brass, nickel, bronze, copper, and stainless steel—are available for use where corrosion could occur. Nails are also manufactured with coatings—galvanized, blued or cemented—to prevent rusting and add holding power.

Nail size is designated by penny size, originally the price per hundred nails. Penny size, almost always referred to as "d," ranges from 2-penny, or 2d—1 inch long—to 60-penny, or 60d—6 inches long. Nails shorter than 1 inch are called brads; nails longer than 6 inches are called spikes.

The length of the nails is important: at least two-thirds of the nail should be driven into the base, or thicker, material. For example, a 1 × 3 nailed to a 4 × 4 beam should be fastened with an 8-penny, or 8d, nail. An 8d nail is 2½ inches long; ¾ inch of its length will go through the 1 × 3, and the remaining 1¾ inches will go into the beam.

Nails are usually sold by the pound; the smaller the nail, the more nails to the pound. You can buy "bulk" nails out of a nail keg; the nails are weighed and then priced by the retailer. Or you can buy packaged nails, sold in boxes ranging from 1 pound to 50 pounds.

There are several different types of nails: common, box, casing, and finishing nails; brads, spikes, and nails for special applications.

Common nails. Common nails are made from wire, cut to the proper length; they have thick heads, and can be driven into tough materials. They're used for most medium-to-heavy construction work. Common nails are available in sizes from 2d to 60d.

Box nails. Box nails are similar to common nails, but they are both lighter and smaller in diameter. Box nails are designed for light construction and household use.

Finishing nails and casing nails. Finishing nails are lighter than common nails, and have a small head. They're used primarily in building furniture. Casing nails are similar, but are heavier; they're used mostly for woodwork.

Brads. Nails less than 1 inch long are called brads; they're used to tack on trim and moldings. Brads are sold not by weight but in boxes, by size, from ³/₁₆ inch to 1 inch.

Spikes. Nails longer than 6 inches are called spikes; they're used for heavy construction, and are available in sizes from 6 to 12 inches. Spikes are sold individually.

Flooring nails. Both rectangular-cut and spiral flooring nails are available. Spiral nails are recommended for secure attachment of floorboards.

Roofing nails. Roofing nails, usually galvanized, have a much larger head than common nails, to prevent damage to asphalt shingles.

Annular-ring nails. These nails have sharp ridges all along the nail shaft; their holding power is much greater than that of regular nails. Nails made for drywall installation are often ringed.

Masonry nails. Three types of nails are designed specifically for use with concrete and concrete

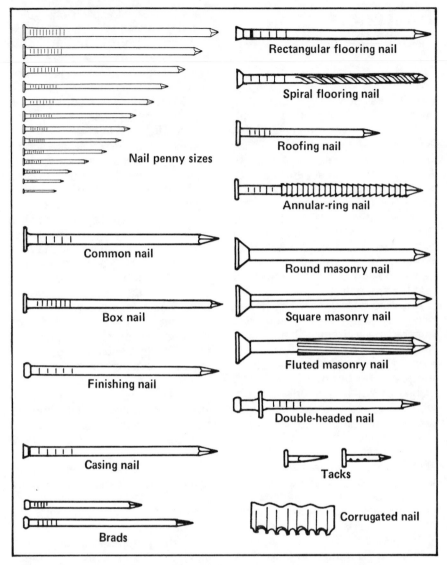

Nail penny sizes

Common nail

Box nail

Finishing nail

Casing nail

Brads

Rectangular flooring nail

Spiral flooring nail

Roofing nail

Annular-ring nail

Round masonry nail

Square masonry nail

Fluted masonry nail

Double-headed nail

Tacks

Corrugated nail

block: round, square, and fluted. Masonry nails should not be used where high strength is required. Fastening to brick, stone, or reinforced concrete should be made with screws or lag bolts.

Double-headed nails. These nails are used for temporary fastening jobs. The nail is driven in as far as the first head; the second head sticks out for easy removal.

Tacks and upholstery tacks. Tacks, made in both round and cut forms, are used to hold carpet or fabric to wood; upholstery tacks have decorative heads.

Corrugated nails. These fasteners, sometimes called wiggly nails, are used for light-duty joints where strength is not important. The fasteners are set at right angles to the joint.

SCREWS

Wood screws. Screws provide more strength and holding power than nails do; and, if the work will ever be disassembled, screws can be removed and reinserted without damage to it. For these reasons, screws should be used instead of nails for most woodworking.

Most commonly, screws are made of steel, but other metals are used—brass, nickel, bronze, and copper—for use where corrosion could occur. Like nails, screws are also made with coatings—zinc, chromium, or cadmium—to deter rust.

Screws are manufactured with four basic types of heads, and also with different types of slots. Flathead screws are always countersunk into the material being fastened, so that the screw head is flush with the surface. Oval-head screws are partially countersunk; about half the screw head lies above the surface. Roundhead screws are not countersunk; the entire screw head lies above the surface. Fillister-head screws are raised above the surface on a flat base, to keep the screwdriver from damaging the surface as the screw is tightened.

Most commonly, screws have plain slots, and are driven with regular slot screwdrivers. Phillips-head screws have crossed slots, and are driven with Phillips-head screwdrivers. Stopped-slot screws are less common; they're driven with a special screwdriver.

Screw size is measured in two dimensions: length, and diameter at the shank. Shank diameter is stated by gauge number, from 0 to 24. Length is measured in inches: in ⅛-inch increments from ¼ to 1 inch, in ¼-inch increments from 1 to 3 inches, and in ½-inch increments from 3 to 5 inches. All lengths are not available for all gauges, but special sizes can sometimes be ordered.

The length of screws is important: in most cases, at least half the length of the screw should extend into the base material. For example, if a piece of ¾-inch plywood is being fastened, the screws that hold it should be 1½ inches long.

To prevent the screws from splitting the materials being fastened, pilot holes must be made before the screws are driven. For small screws, pilot holes can be punched with a bradawl or ice pick, or even with a nail. For larger screws, drill pilot holes with a small drill or a combination drill/countersink.

Sheet-metal screws. Sheet-metal screws, used to fasten pieces of metal together, form threads in the metal as they are installed. There are several different types of machine screws. *Pointed pan-head screws* are coarse-threaded; they are available in gauges from 4 to 14 and lengths from ¼ inch to 2 inches. Pointed pan-heads are used in light sheet metal. *Blunt pan-head screws* are used for heavier sheet metal; they are available in gauges from 4 to 14 and lengths from ¼ inch to 2 inches. Both types of pan-head screws are available with either plain or Phillips-head slots.

Partial-tapping roundhead screws have finer threads; they can be used in soft or hard metals. They are available in diameters from $3/16$ inch to 1¼ inches. *Self-tapping roundhead screws* are used for heavy-duty work with thick sheet metal; they are available in diameters from gauge 2 to ¼ inch and in lengths from ⅛ inch to ¾ inch. Both types of roundhead screws are

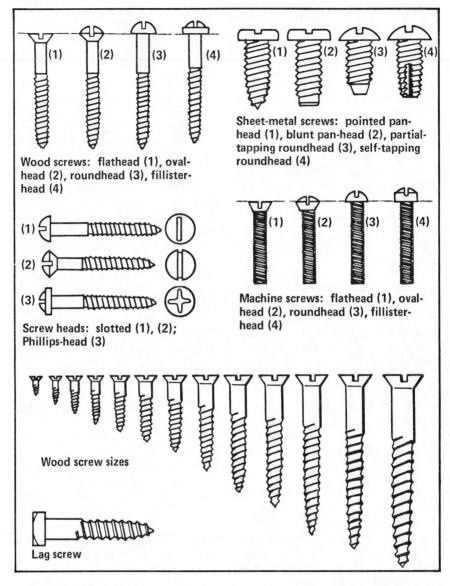

Wood screws: flathead (1), oval-head (2), roundhead (3), fillister-head (4)

Sheet-metal screws: pointed pan-head (1), blunt pan-head (2), partial-tapping roundhead (3), self-tapping roundhead (4)

Screw heads: slotted (1), (2); Phillips-head (3)

Machine screws: flathead (1), oval-head (2), roundhead (3), fillister-head (4)

Wood screw sizes

Lag screw

available with either plain or Phillips-head slots.

Nail-type sheet metal screws are pounded in, not screwed in; they have spiral thread-cutting shafts with pointed ends. The heads of these screws are not slotted. They are used for heavy-gauge sheet metal and for fastening other materials to metal.

Machine screws. Machine screws are blunt-ended screws used to fasten metal parts together; they are commonly made of steel or brass. Like other fasteners, they are also made with coatings—brass, copper, nickel, zinc, cadmium, and galvanized—to deter rust. Machine screws are manufactured with the four basic types of heads—flathead, oval-head, roundhead, and fillister-head—and with both plain and Phillips-head slots. They are available in gauges 2 to 12 and diameters from ¼ inch to ½ inch, and in lengths from ¼ inch to 3 inches.

Lag bolts. Lag bolts, while known as bolts, are actually heavy-duty screws. They are driven with a wrench, and used primarily for fastening to masonry. For light work, lead, plastic, or fiber plugs can be used to hold large screws. For larger jobs and more holding power, lead expansion anchors and lag bolts are used. The anchors are inserted into holes drilled in the masonry, and the lag bolts driven firmly into the anchors.

BOLTS

Bolts are used with nuts or locknuts, and sometimes with washers. The three basic types are carriage bolts, stove bolts, and machine bolts. Other types include the masonry bolt and anchor and the toggle and molly bolts, used to distribute weight when fastening to hollow walls.

Machine bolts are manufactured in two gauges, fine-threaded and coarse; carriage and stove bolts are coarse-threaded. Bolt size is measured by shank diameter and by threads per inch, expressed as diameter × threads—for example, as ¼ × 20. Carriage bolts are available up to 10 inches long, stove bolts up to 6 inches, and machine bolts up to 30 inches; larger sizes must usually be special-ordered.

Carriage bolts. Carriage bolts have a round head with a square collar; they are driven with a wrench. When the bolt is tightened, the collar fits into a prebored hole or twists into the wood, preventing the

bolt from turning. Carriage bolts are used in making furniture; they are coarse-threaded, and are available in diameters from ³/₁₆ to ¾ inch and lengths from ½ inch to 10 inches.

Stove bolts. Stove bolts are available in a wide range of sizes. They have a slotted head—flat, oval, or round, like screws—and are driven with a screwdriver or a wrench. Most stove bolts are completely threaded, but the larger ones may have a smooth shank near the bolt head. Stove bolts can be used for almost any fastening job; they are coarse-threaded, and are available in diameters from ⁵/₃₂ to ½ inch and lengths from ⅜ inch to 6 inches.

Machine bolts. Machine bolts have either a square head or a hexagonal head, and are fastened with square nuts or hex nuts; they are wrench-driven. Machine bolts are manufactured in very large sizes; the bolt diameter increases with length. They are either coarse- or fine-threaded, and are available in diameters from ¼ inch to 2 inches and lengths from ½ inch to 30 inches.

Masonry bolts and anchors. These bolts work on the same principle as the lag bolt or screw; a plastic sleeve expands inside a predrilled hole as the bolt is tightened. Various types and sizes are available.

Hollow-wall bolts. Toggle bolts and molly bolts are used for light-duty fastening to hollow walls. Toggle bolt wings are opened by a spring inside the wall; the bolts are available in diameters from ⅛ to ½ inch and lengths up to 8 inches. Molly bolts are inserted into an expansion jacket, which expands as the bolt is tightened; they are available for walls as thick as 1¾ inches.

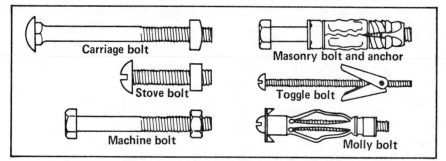

DRILLING FOR WOOD SCREWS

Gauge Number	Decimal Diameter	Fractional Diameter	Shank Hole Twist Bit	Shank Hole Drill Gauge	PILOT HOLE HARDWOOD Twist Bit s	Twist Bit p	Drill Gauge s	Drill Gauge p	SOFTWOOD Twist Bit s	Twist Bit p	Drill Gauge s	Drill Gauge p	Auger Bit Number	Threads Per Inch
0	.060	1/16−	1/16	52	1/32	—	70	—	1/64	—	75	—	—	32
1	.073	5/64−	5/64	47	1/32	—	66	—	1/32	—	71	—	—	28
2	.086	5/64+	3/32	42	3/64	1/32	56	70	1/32	1/64	65	75	3	26
3	.099	3/32+	7/64	37	1/16	1/32	54	66	3/64	1/32	58	71	4	24
4	.112	7/64+	7/64	32	1/16	3/64	52	56	3/64	1/32	55	65	4	22
5	.125	1/8−	1/8	30	5/64	1/16	49	54	1/16	3/64	53	58	4	20
6	.138	9/64−	9/64	27	5/64	1/16	47	52	1/16	3/64	52	55	5	18
7	.151	5/32−	5/32	22	3/32	5/64	44	49	1/16	3/64	51	53	5	16
8	.164	5/32+	11/64	18	3/32	5/64	40	47	5/64	1/16	48	52	6	15
9	.177	11/64+	3/16	14	7/64	3/32	37	44	5/64	1/16	45	51	6	14
10	.190	3/16+	3/16	10	7/64	3/32	33	40	3/32	5/64	43	48	6	13
11	.203	13/64−	13/64	4	1/8	7/64	31	37	3/32	5/64	40	45	7	12
12	.216	7/32−	7/32	2	1/8	7/64	30	33	7/64	3/32	38	43	7	11
14	.242	15/64+	1/4	D	9/64	1/8	25	31	7/64	3/32	32	40	8	10
16	.268	17/64+	17/64	I	5/32	1/8	18	30	9/64	7/64	29	38	9	9
18	.294	19/64−	19/64	N	3/16	9/64	13	25	9/64	7/64	26	32	10	8
20	.320	21/64−	21/64	P	13/64	5/32	4	18	11/64	9/64	19	29	11	8
24	.372	3/8	3/8	V	7/32	3/16	1	13	3/16	9/64	15	26	12	7

s = Slotted head   **p = Phillips-head**

Abrasives

SANDPAPER

Grit	Number	Grade	Papers Available[1]	Uses
Very coarse	30	2½	F,G,S	Rust removal on rough finished metal.
	36	2	F,G,S	
Coarse	40	1½	F,G,S	Rough sanding of wood; paint removal.
	50	1	F,G,S	
	60	½	F,G,A,S	
Medium	80	0(1/0)	F,G,A,S	General wood sanding; plaster smoothing; preliminary smoothing of previously painted surfaces.
	100	00(2/0)	F,G,A,S	
	120	3/0	F,G,A,S	
Fine	150	4/0	F,G,A,S,	Final sanding of bare wood or previously painted surfaces.
	180	5/0	F,G,A,S	
Very fine	220	6/0	F,G,A,S	Light sanding between finish coats; dry sanding.
	240	7/0	F,A,S	
	280	8/0	F,A,S	
Extra fine	320	9/0	F,A,S	High finish on lacquer, varnish, or shellac; wet sanding.
	360	—[2]	S	
	400	10/0	S	
Superfine	500	—[2]	S	High-satinized finishes; wet sanding.
	600	—[2]	S	

[1]F = flint; G = garnet; A = aluminum oxide; S = silicon carbide. Silicon carbide is used dry or wet, with water or oil.
[2]No grade designation.

STEEL WOOL

Grade	Number	Uses
Coarse	3	Paint and varnish removal; removing paint spots from resilient floors.
Medium coarse	2	Removing scratches from brass; removing paint spots from ceramic tile; rubbing floors between finish coats.
Medium	1	Rust removal; cleaning glazed tiles; removing marks from wood floors; with paint and varnish remover, removing finishes.
Medium fine	0	Brass finishing; cleaning tile; with paint and varnish remover, removing stubborn finishes.
Fine	00	With linseed oil, satinizing high-gloss finishes.
Extra fine	000	Removing paint spots or stains from wood; cleaning polished metals; rubbing between finish coats.
Superfine	0000	Final rubbing of finish; stain removal.

ABRASIVE CLOTHS

Type	Grades	Uses
Emery	Very coarse through fine	General light metal polishing; removing rust and corrosion from metal; wet or dry sanding.
Crocus	Very fine	High-gloss finishing for metals.
Aluminum oxide	Very coarse through fine	Power sanding belts.

ABRASIVE POWDERS

Type	Uses
Pumice	Rubbing between finish coats; final buffing; stain removal.
Rottenstone	Buffing between finish coats; final buffing; stain removal.
Rouge	Metal polishing.

Plywood Grades

Interior Grade	Face	Back	Inner Plies	Uses
A-A	A	A	D	Cabinet doors, built-ins, furniture where both sides show.
A-B	A	B	D	Alternate for A-A. Face is finish grade, back is solid and smooth.
A-D	A	D	D	Finish grade face for paneling, built-ins, backing.
B-D	B	D	D	Utility grade. One paintable side. For backing, cabinet sides, etc.
C-D	C	D	D	Sheathing and structural uses such as temporary enclosures, subfloor. Unsanded.
Underlayment	C-Plugged	D	C,D	For underlayment or combination subfloor-underlayment under tile, carpeting.

Exterior Grade	Face	Back	Inner Plies	Uses
A-A	A	A	C	Outdoors, where appearance of both sides is important.
A-B	A	B	C	Alternate for A-A, where appearance of one side is less important. Face is finish grade.
A-C	A	C	C	Soffits, fences, base for coatings.
B-C	B	C	C	For utility uses such as farm buildings, some kinds of fences, base for coatings.
C-C (Plugged)	C-Plugged	C	C	Excellent base for tile and linoleum, backing for wall coverings, high-performance coatings.
C-C	C	C	C	Unsanded, for backing and rough construction exposed to weather.

Index

INDEX

E

INDEX

INDEX

S

INDEX

T